Philosophy and Culture East and West

East

UNIVERSITY OF HAWAII PRESS / HONOLULU / 1968

Philosophy and Culture and West

EAST-WEST PHILOSOPHY IN PRACTICAL PERSPECTIVE

Charles A. Moore / Editor

MANUFACTURED IN THE UNITED STATES OF AMERICA
DESIGNED BY KENNETH KINGREY
FIRST PRINTING, 1962
SECOND PRINTING, 1968
LIBRARY OF CONGRESS CATALOG CARD NUMBER 61-17921

Preface

The title of this volume, *Philosophy and Culture—East and West,* reflects the purpose and the work of the conference which it reports, that is, the effort to achieve mutual understanding of the practical aspects of the lives of the peoples of Asia and the West by reference to their basic and underlying philosophies, in the sense that "culture is the manifestation of the human mind in human behavior."

This Preface deals exclusively with the text of the volume and not with the subject-matter or with the conference of which this is the official Report. The background of this volume, the conference itself, and its predecessors are dealt with in the Introduction.

This volume contains the proceedings of the Third East-West Philosophers' Conference, held at the University of Hawaii during the summer of 1959. It contains all the formal papers, in the order in which they were presented at the conference. It is divided into six major Sections, following the agenda of the conference.

Some of the discussion which took place at the conference meetings is included as "Questions" and "Answers" at the end of some of the papers—in those cases where the authors wished to include such discussion.

In an Appendix are included the five Public Lectures presented to general audiences during the period of the conference by representatives of the major traditions considered at the conference. (The style of these lectures, and the editing, are less formal and academic than in the case of the technical papers.)

One somewhat special feature should be explained, namely, the way in which Chinese, Japanese, and Korean characters are included—and the fact that they are available for those who are interested. Such characters are indicated in the body of the papers and in the footnotes by raised small letters which refer to characters that appear at the end of the respective chapters. The order of lettering follows the body of the chapter itself and then the footnotes in their numerical order. In the cases of Sanskrit, Pāli, and Arabic, the transliterated form of the original is provided, usually within parentheses, in the body of the papers and in the notes.

Editing complexities and difficulties inevitably abound in a volume of this particular kind, composed as it is of some forty papers (and five Public Lectures) by recognized authorities representing the differing major philosophical traditions of the world.

The editing of the material in this volume has had for its purpose accuracy, clarity, and completeness. An endeavor was made to provide clarity of exposition despite considerable variation in style and technical involvements on the part of the representatives of the several sometimes widely differing philosophical traditions and the technical languages used.

Appreciation is hereby expressed to the authors for their indulgence with what may have seemed over-zealous editing procedures and requirements, and for their fine co-operation in caring for the many detailed chores involved.

In the editing, although there was an attempt to achieve uniformity of style within the body of each paper and some large degree of uniformity among all the papers despite almost prohibitive complexity and variations, there was no attempt to impose rigid, mechanical, and mandatory rules for consistency of style. After all, the writers of these papers are outstanding experts, and each has a right to his special interpretation and style of presentation. In some cases, in fact, there is no necessarily correct form or style to require. Therefore, despite the apparent "rule" which demands uniformity and consistency in style, the editor in this case respected the differing preferences of the scholars involved wherever such preferences were expressed.

With this foreword, it may be advisable to list now some of the inconsistencies or non-uniformities which would be confusing—or even irritating—to readers were they not forewarned of such complexities. Among such items are the following:

(1) Common usage is occasionally followed rather than strictly accurate style, although this is rare (example: *brāhmin*).

(2) The order of Chinese, Japanese, and Korean names varies, somc following traditional style, others modern usage, according to the author's preference. For accuracy, please see the Index. (The use or non-use of diacritical marks in personal names is also complicated in this procedure.)

(3) Dates are not always provided for thinkers and periods—usually depending upon the author's preference; nor, for the same reason, do dates always agree.

(4) For the same reason, in some papers Greek script is used, in others the romanized form.

(5) The style of romanizing the "s" at the end of plurals of words in Asian languages has been used, although it is not technically correct.

(6) Usually, the "S" has been used in such words as Self or Soul to refer to the universal Self or the Absolute Self—or Soul—whereas the "s" has been used to refer to the individual self or soul, because this seems to provide greater clarity. (This "rule" is not adhered to absolutely in some of the papers because of authors' preferences.)

(7) The same word will occasionally appear with differing translations, sometimes because the word is used in different contexts and has different meanings, sometimes because the authors differ in their interpretations.

(8) Even the documentation does not follow an absolutely uniform style. For example, although documentation is usually found in the footnotes, sometimes, where many references are used, textual citations are included in the text in parentheses.

(9) Hyphenation and capitalization of complex Sanskrit (etc.) texts and compound expressions are not always consistent, but it is hoped that clarity is achieved.

(10) Seeming over-use of capitalization has been discouraged but has not been "prohibited," and will be found here and there in some of the papers.

(11) As a final word on the mechanics or details of editing, let it be noted, with apologies if necessary, that, in cases where rules do not supply all the answers, there have been some instances of detailed or "petty" editing (chiefly in hyphenation, punctuation, and capitalization) as a result of personal preference on the part of the editor. Such editing was always for the sake of what was deemed to be greater clarity and for the avoidance of possible confusion. Whenever an author expressed decided preferences, his style was followed.

A completely detailed Index for a volume of this kind would have been endless. Some compromise was necessary. An attempt was made to present a basically sound Index and one that is comprehensive in all important matters. An attempt was also made in the Index to provide more adequate form for terms, titles, and names in the Arabic field, although it was realized that it was unjustifiable to require absolute uniformity of style.

The numerous diacritical marks have presented a problem. Special attention is called to the sometimes faulty macrons, most frequently encountered in italicized Sanskrit words. All that can be done, if publication is not to be further delayed, is to offer apologies.

Thanks are due to certain individuals who have been of immense assistance in the extremely difficult task of editing this complicated volume.

Very special personal thanks are hereby extended to Mrs. Aldyth V. Morris, Editor of the University of Hawaii Press, who has labored with interest and dedication far beyond the call of duty and far beyond the hours that could have possibly been expected in order that the editing of this volume may be its very best. Personal thanks also go to Mr. Thomas Nickerson, Chairman of the University of Hawaii Press Committee, for his interest and support before and throughout the process of publication.

On the strictly scholarly side, very special appreciation goes to Dr. Wing-tsit Chan for his indispensable assistance in many ways, among these being the matter of providing and checking Chinese characters for all the papers in the Far Eastern field. In the same area, thanks are due to Dr. Kenneth K. Inada, particularly in connection with the papers on Buddhist philosophy and Japanese culture. Also to Dr. George T. Artola, Professor James J. Y. Liu, Dr. Bertha Mueller, and Professor Yukuo Uyehara, who served as language consultants.

Thanks are also due to Mr. S. Tsukiyama, who provided the calligraphy for the Chinese, Japanese, and Korean characters, an essential part of this particular type of volume. Also to Mrs. Barbara de Grazia for meticulous care during the proofreading stages, and to Mr. James Dickey for a final proofreading and checking of the entire volume.

Great appreciation is hereby expressed to the staff of the Reference Room of the Gregg M. Sinclair Library, University of Hawaii, for their constant help and infinite patience in checking doubtful items throughout the volume—namely, Miss Joyce M. Wright, Mr. Shiro Saito, and Mrs. Clarissa H. Halsted.

Special thanks are also due to Professor Kenneth Kingrey for the obviously fine aesthetic quality brought to this volume by the design and typography, for which he is entirely responsible. He has the deep appreciation of the editor—and, surely, the continuing thanks of all future readers of this volume. The drawings are the work of Mrs. Sueko M. Kimura.

Thanks are due also to those in the Administration of the Center for Cultural and Technical Interchange between East and West for a substantial grant toward the publication of this expensive volume. Additional funds for this purpose were taken from grants made by several Foundations and other organizations (cited in the Introduction) for the conduct and reporting of the Third East-West Philosophers' Conference.

Appreciation to those who were especially helpful in planning and conducting the conference itself is expressed in the Introduction.

CHARLES A. MOORE

Honolulu, Hawaii
October 9, 1961

Contents

Introduction

CHARLES A. MOORE — *East-West Philosophy in Practical Perspective* — 3

I. The Relation of Philosophical Theories to Practical Affairs

SIDNEY HOOK — *Philosophy and Human Conduct* — 15

G. P. CONGER — *Societal Structures and Processes* — 33

S. K. SAKSENA — *Relation of Philosophical Theories to the Practical Affairs of Men* — 50

HERBERT W. SCHNEIDER — *Western Philosophy and Practical Affairs* — 67

WING-TSIT CHAN — *Chinese Theory and Practice, with Special Reference to Humanism* — 81

SHOSON MIYAMOTO — *The Relation of Philosophical Theory to Practical Affairs in Japan* — 97

ROBERT ROSSOW, JR. — *Natural Man, Philosophy, and Behavior* — 117

II. Natural Science and Technology in Relation to Cultural Institutions and Social Practice

W. H. WERKMEISTER — *Scientism and the Problem of Man* — 135

STELLA KRAMRISCH — *Natural Science and Technology in Relation to Cultural Patterns and Social Practices in India* — 156

N. BAMMATE — *The Status of Science and Technique in Islamic Civilization* — 172

HIDEKI YUKAWA — *Modern Trend of Western Civilization and Cultural Peculiarities of Japan* — 188

HU SHIH — *The Scientific Spirit and Method in Chinese Philosophy* — 199

III. Religion and Spiritual Values

T'ANG CHÜN-I — *The Development of Ideas of Spiritual Value in Chinese Philosophy* — 225

HIDEO KISHIMOTO	*Some Japanese Cultural Traits and Religions*	245
S. RADHAKRISHNAN	*The Indian Approach to the Religious Problem*	255
P. T. RAJU	*Religion and Spiritual Values in Indian Thought*	263
M. M. SHARIF	*Islam and Spiritual Values*	293
W. T. STACE	*The Mystical Form of Western Spirituality*	302
CONSTANTIN REGAMEY	*The Meaning and Significance of Spirituality in Europe and in India*	316
VAN METER AMES	*Aesthetic Values in East and West*	342

IV. Ethics and Social Practice

VIRGIL C. ALDRICH	*Beyond Ethics?*	365
HERBERT W. SCHNEIDER	*American Traits and Principles*	384
F. J. VON RINTELEN	*Values as a Foundation for Encounter*	400
HSIEH YU-WEI	*Filial Piety and Chinese Society*	411
D. T. SUZUKI	*Basic Thoughts Underlying Eastern Ethical and Social Practice*	428
NIYAZI BERKES	*Ethics and Social Practice in Islam*	448
T. M. P. MAHADEVAN	*Indian Ethics and Social Practice*	476
SWAMI NIKHILANANDA	*The Realistic Aspect of Indian Spirituality*	494

V. Legal, Political, and Economic Philosophy

F. S. C. NORTHROP	*Comparative Philosophy and Science in the Light of Comparative Law*	521
GRAY L. DORSEY	*The Influence of Philosophy on Law and Politics in Western Civilization*	533
FRANK H. KNIGHT	*Philosophy and Social Institutions in the West*	549
D. M. DATTA	*Political, Legal, and Economic Thought in Indian Perspective*	569
PAUL MUS	*The Problematic of the Self—West and East, and the Maṇḍala Pattern*	594
JOHN C. H. WU	*Chinese Legal and Political Philosophy*	611
HAJIME NAKAMURA	*Basic Features of the Legal, Political, and Economic Thought of Japan*	631
PAUL K. RYU	*"Field Theory" in the Study of Cultures: Its Application to Korean Culture*	648

VI. *Conspectus of Practical Implications for World Understanding and Cooperation*

E. A. BURTT	*A Basic Problem in the Quest for Understanding between East and West*	673
CORNELIUS KRUSÉ	*Concluding Remarks*	692
CHARLES A. MOORE	*Retrospect and Prospects: Achievements and Unfinished Business*	699

Appendix

Public Lectures

N. BAMMATE	*The Islamic Cultural Tradition and the West*	721
D. T. SUZUKI	*Zen and Parapsychology*	732
S. RADHAKRISHNAN	*The Present Crisis of Faith*	754
HU SHIH	*John Dewey in China*	762
F. S. C. NORTHROP	*Comparative Philosophy and World Law*	770

Biographies and Index

Who's Who 781

Index 801

Philosophy and Culture East and West is published for and with financial assistance from the third East-West Philosophers' Conference and the Center for Technical and Cultural Interchange Between East and West. This book constitutes the third East-West Philosophers' Conference volume. It is the first in a series of East-West Center publications.

Introduction

CHARLES A. MOORE

East-West Philosophy in Practical Perspective

This volume constitutes the "official" Report or the "Proceedings Volume" of the Third East-West Philosophers' Conference, held at the University of Hawaii during the summer of 1959. This conference was the successor of previous conferences, held in 1939 and 1949, also at the University of Hawaii. All of these conferences have been conducted in Honolulu, under the sponsorship of the University of Hawaii—with the financial support of numerous Foundations—primarily because of two factors: first, the great interest which the University of Hawaii—and all of Hawaii—has had over the years in mutual understanding between the peoples of Asia and the peoples of the West, and, second, the fact that Hawaii, because of its cosmopolitan population, predominantly Asian but also thoroughly Westernized in education, institutions, etc., presents an ideal location between East and West where racial prejudice is relatively unknown and where both Easterner and Westerner may feel fully at home, neither an "outsider." Although a willingness was expressed by the University of Hawaii to hold the fourth conference—in 1964—elsewhere, it will be held in Honolulu, on the basis of the enthusiastic, unanimous vote of the members of the 1959 conference.

The over-all theme of these conferences has been expressed as follows: "On the premise that in the modern world provincialism in reflective thinking is inexcusable and dangerous, the University of Hawaii in 1939 and again in 1949 [and now also in 1959] conducted East-West Philosophers' Conferences in an effort to bring about a more comprehensive perspective in philosophy, to overcome provincial prejudice, and to encourage a greater mutual understanding of the peoples of Asia and the peoples of the West by a study of their respective philosophies." The two earlier conferences dealt chiefly with the basic technical philosophical theories, concepts, and methods of Asia and the West, respectively, and achieved a remarkable degree of open-mindedness, cordiality, and mutual understanding at that level—and led (directly or indirectly) to numerous other significant results, such as books, articles, conferences, courses, a journal (*Philosophy East and West*), travel to foreign countries for further study in the field, and exchange and visiting professorships.

"At these conferences, however, the practical, social significance and applications of the basic theories and methods discussed were not explicitly developed. In fact, one of the formal conclusions of the 1949 conference was that several important 'remaining questions'—especially and specifically in the field of 'ethics and social philosophy'—had to be resolved before the full value of the conferences could come to fruition."

The 1939 and 1949 conferences helped immeasurably in taking the subject of Asian philosophy out of the realm of the occult, in creating and fostering a significantly new climate in which work in this field can be carried on and respected, and in encouraging important research in the area, in promoting the comparative study of basic philosophical problems, and in bringing to work in this area a greater degree of scholarly thoroughness, depth, and responsibility than it had known before—but this was not enough. The practical significance of these achievements had not been thoroughly examined and, in view of today's troubled world, in which mutual understanding is mandatory, this was an inevitable and indispensable development of the work of the earlier conferences.

It was felt, therefore, that another conference was necessary to follow through on the work of the earlier conferences and to supplement the work of those conferences by concentrating exclusively upon the more practical aspects of East-West philosophy. For this reason, the specific sub-title of the 1959 conference was "East-West Philosophy in Practical Perspective."

This theme of the conference was further explained in the words "to consider the practical implications of comparative philosophy for cultural institutions as a basis for world understanding and co-operation."

To this end, the University of Hawaii sponsored the Third East-West Philosophers' Conference to consider particularly the problem of greater mutual understanding of East and West at the level of social philosophy—in such areas as law, economics and business, politics, international relations, ethics, aesthetics, and religion—by working out the practical applications and implications of the metaphysical, methodological, and ethical conclusions reached at the previous conferences. In each of these fields, and also as a problem of special consideration, a study was planned on the relations between philosophical convictions and practical ways and institutions in East and West, with special reference to today's world. The program called for the seeking of understanding on the basis of the fundamental ideas and ideals that underlie, motivate, and determine attitudes and actions in the various fields of practice—past and present.

The third conference was something of a departure from the comprehensive attitudes and purposes underlying the earlier conferences. While those conferences were devoted to mutual understanding, there were also the more or less strictly philosophical purpose of searching for new ideas and the effort to bring about "a more comprehensive perspective in philosophy." The conference reported in this volume, however, settled upon one purpose and one attitude, namely, the exclusive attempt to seek mutual understanding of the various cultures of Asia and the West in terms of or through an understanding of the basic philosophical attitudes, ideas, and methods which constitute the background or bases of social practice. This very question concerned the conference for one of its five weeks of concentrated consideration of specific problems. The assumption underlying this procedure was itself challenged and examined rather thoroughly and critically—one week of the conference was devoted exclusively to the question concerning the relation between philosophical theories and practical affairs or the significance of philosophical attitudes and theories for practice and culture generally. It was assumed at the conference, however, that understanding can be achieved only in terms of essentials, and these essentials were considered to be the basic philosophical systems and attitudes of the respective areas under consideration.

Negatively, the 1959 conference, in contrast to the earlier conferences, was not devoted to the attempt to reach a world philosophy or anything like a synthesis of the philosophies of East and West. It was not particularly devoted to a search for principles of agreement between the peoples of Asia and the peoples of the West. It was not devoted to, nor was it supposed to involve, mutual criticism of theories or practices explained by representatives of the various traditions. Furthermore, it was not specifically concerned, as were the earlier conferences, with what the East could learn from the West or what the West could learn from the East.

Of course, all of these possible goals of East-West philosophy were in the minds of many members throughout the conference, but the specific purpose of this particular conference was to attempt to understand each other, East and West, to let representatives explain in their own words their own cultures and their philosophical foundations. Of course, this was foreseen as an extremely difficult limitation of perspective, one that was certain to be extremely difficult to keep constantly in mind, but it was the avowed purpose of the conference—and was to be adhered to as fully as possible—because of the vital need in today's world for greater mutual understanding at the cultural level, in view of the overwhelming misunderstandings that currently exist between the peoples of Asia and those of the West.

The conference was devoted to the study of cultures rather than technical philosophy—except insofar as the latter provided the basic and perhaps exclusive means of understanding the practical aspects of the various cultures.

In view of the specific and exclusive goal of mutual understanding, most of the papers in this volume are fundamentally, if not exclusively, descriptive in nature. This is as it should be. The papers were not intended to present personal convictions or personal theories. They were intended, rather, as basic and substantial descriptions and explanations—for others—of the fundamental ideas and values of the several cultures. If one may be permitted an editorial comment in an introductory chapter like this, the writer would like to suggest that, in very large degree, the papers in this volume do decidedly live up to the purpose of the conference by explaining in a thoroughgoing yet sympathetic manner the basic aspects of the cultures of the peoples under study. These papers, all of which are written by personal representatives of the cultures in question, follow the only procedure which can possibly produce genuine understanding, namely, the description of those cultures by representatives of those cultures in the light of what the ideas, ideals, and practices of those cultures mean to the peoples in those specific cultures and why the peoples in those cultures accept these ideas, ideals, and practices as their fundamental ways of life.

As a whole, then, the conference represented in this volume was an experiment in "applied" philosophy, dealing mostly with the area of social thought and action, and attempting to reach genuine understanding—and to avoid superficial understanding or misunderstanding—by thinking in terms of fundamentals or essentials, namely, the basic philosophical attitudes and beliefs of the peoples concerned. The uniqueness of this conference lay in the attempt to search beneath the surface for the strictly philosophical bases upon which the cultures of the peoples of Asia and the peoples of the West are grounded—even though, even in advance and certainly during the course of the conference, it was realized that there are problems of great stature, as it were, in this undertaking. The unique significance of the conference lay, then, in the belief that real understanding can be achieved only through knowledge of the fundamental convictions of the peoples of Asia and the West, in the effort to explore the philosophical basis of East-West understanding comprehensively and intensively, and in the attempt to promote more comprehensive perspective in the field of social philosophy as distinct from the more technical areas of metaphysics and methodology considered in the earlier conferences.

In order to insure that the work of the conference would be as specifically and strictly as possible devoted to the over-all purpose of the conference, the work was divided into six major divisions or sections, as follows:

1. The Relation of Philosophical Theories to Practical Affairs
2. Natural Science and Technology in Relation to Cultural Institutions and Social Practice
3. Religion and Spiritual Values
4. Ethics and Social Practice
5. Legal, Political, and Economic Philosophy
6. Conspectus of Practical Implications for World Understanding and Co-operation

This volume is patterned in accordance with the program of this agenda, section by section.

It will be noticed in this program that, as indicated above, the very relation of philosophical theory to practical affairs was one of the major problems of the conference. Also, attention may be called especially to the second major topic, namely, the status of science and technology in the various cultures under consideration and the relation of such an attitude and method to cultural institutions and social practice. The inclusion of this seemingly extraneous problem was based upon the two facts, first, that lack of real understanding concerning the status and nature of scientific thought in the various cultures has long constituted a basis of misunderstanding and even of philosophical and cultural isolation, and, second, that recent studies have indicated quite conclusively that the scientific or non-scientific attitude has unquestionable, and possibly most fundamental, determinative influence upon the social practices of people in any culture.

The 1959 conference, like those of 1939 and 1949, was six weeks in duration. This unique plan provided the significantly long-time opportunity for personal give-and-take among the members, for constant association and companionship, and for a great number of informal meetings—all of which were decidedly to the good insofar as the work of the conference was concerned. These six weeks also provided the opportunity to devote a significant amount of time to a concentrated study of specific aspects of the over-all problem of the conference. One full week was devoted to each of the six topic-sections described above. Each of the topic-sections represented a basic aspect of any culture: they also represented five rather distinct areas of uncertainty and misunderstanding. The problem was to attack these specific areas one by one and in detail, as far as time permitted, and thus to avoid—whether this is wise or not is another question—confusing overlapping of problems which might becloud the issue and make specific understanding difficult of achievement.

The last week of the conference, item six in the above agenda, was devoted to recapitulation and a working out of the conclusions and generalizations which seemed to be the result of the five weeks of concentrated study in specific areas. The final three chapters in this volume attempt to bring into focus the achievements and the shortcomings of the conference as a whole. Despite the repetition, may the writer strongly emphasize the fact that the areas of philosophy and culture which constitute the first five topic-sections of the agenda, and which occupied the conference for the first five weeks of its meeting, have long constituted areas of basic misunderstanding—mutually—and consequently areas of significant and tragic neglect or criticism or both. For this reason, the explanatory chapters herein are of added significance, not only as explanations of the cultural attitudes and practices of the peoples concerned, but also as substantial answers to criticisms and as correctives for misunderstandings and misinterpretations.

In detail, the conference was attended by some one hundred philosophers from Asia and the West—specifically representing Australia, Burma, Canada, China, Europe, Hong Kong, India, Japan, Korea, the Near East, Pakistan, and the United States.

The conference was built primarily around the work of forty-two "Program Members." With few exceptions, all of these Members presented papers to the conference, and all engaged in as full discussion as time permitted. In addition, there were some sixty-odd "Non-Program Members" and "official" visitors, some of whom were invited, either to introduce them to the field of Oriental and East-West philosophy or to stimulate the development of their interest in this field. Others attended "on their own." Because of the attempt to provide concentrated discussion and study of the specific problems on which the Program Members had prepared papers, discussion was limited to Program Members—the Non-Program Members attending as Auditors.

As said above, the conference lasted for six weeks. Throughout this time, as far as possible, all conference members lived on or near the campus of the University and were in rather constant association with each other in living quarters, at meals, in the faculty club room, and on the campus.

The period of the conference coincided with the six-week session of the Summer School at the University. In conjunction with the conference, six specialized courses were offered by conference members in the summer session. These courses were: Introduction to Indian Philosophy, Introduction to Chinese Philosophy, Introduction to Buddhist Philosophy, East-West Comparative Ethics, East-West Comparative Legal and Political Philosophy, and East-West Comparative Philosophy of Religion.

In addition to these activities, the conference included five Public Lectures by conference members, namely, Dr. N. Bammate, UNESCO, "The Islamic Cultural Tradition and the West"; Dr. D. T. Suzuki, Otani University, Emeritus, "Zen and Parapsychology"; Dr. S. Radhakrishnan, Vice President of India, "The Present Crisis of Faith"; Dr. Hu Shih, President, Academia Sinica, "John Dewey in China"; and Dr. F. S. C. Northrop, Yale University, "Comparative Philosophy and World Law." These public lectures are included in this volume in the Appendix.

In the course of the conference, honorary degrees were conferred upon Dr. Hu Shih, Dr. S. Radhakrishnan, and Dr. D. T. Suzuki.

The Program Members of the conference were:

Virgil C. Aldrich, *Kenyon College*
Van Meter Ames, *University of Cincinnati*
N. Bammate, *UNESCO*
A. Niyazi Berkes, *McGill University*
E. A. Burtt, *Cornell University*
Wing-tsit Chan, *Dartmouth College*
G. P. Conger, *University of Minnesota*
D. M. Datta, *Santiniketan*
Gray L. Dorsey, *Washington University*
Sidney Hook, *New York University*
Hsieh Yu-wei, *National Cheng-chih University*
Hu Shih, *Academia Sinica*
Hideo Kishimoto, *University of Tokyo*
Frank H. Knight, *University of Chicago*
Stella Kramrisch, *University of Pennsylvania*

Cornelius Krusé, *Wesleyan University*
T. M. P. Mahadevan, *University of Madras*
Harold E. McCarthy, *University of Hawaii*
Shoson Miyamoto, *University of Tokyo*
Charles A. Moore, *University of Hawaii*
Paul Mus, *Collège de France* and *Yale University*
Winfield E. Nagley, *University of Hawaii*
Hajime Nakamura, *University of Tokyo*
Swami Nikhilananda, *Ramakrishna-Vivekananda Center*
F. S. C. Northrop, *Yale University*
S. Radhakrishnan, *Vice-President, Government of India*
P. T. Raju, *University of Rajputana*
Constantin Regamey, *University of Lausanne*
F. J. von Rintelen, *University of Mainz*
Robert Rossow, Jr., *Department of State*
Paul K. Ryu, *Seoul National University*
S. K. Saksena, *Saugar University*
Herbert W. Schneider, *Columbia University*
M. M. Sharif, *Islamia College*
Walter T. Stace, *Princeton University*
A. K. Stout, *University of Sydney*
D. T. Suzuki, *Otani University*
T'ang Chün-i, *New Asia College*
U Thittila, *University of Rangoon*
W. H. Werkmeister, *University of Southern California*
John C. H. Wu, *Seton Hall University*
Hideki Yukawa, by paper only, *Research Institute for Fundamental Physics, Kyoto University*

The Non-Program Members were:

Professor Paul H. Ackert, *Otterbein College*
Professor José A. Benardete, *Kansas State College*
Dr. Paul J. Braisted, *The Edward W. Hazen Foundation*
Professor Cecil C. Brett, *Indiana University*
Professor D. Mackenzie Brown, *University of California, Santa Barbara*
Professor Harry M. Buck, Jr., *Wellesley College*
Professor Jane Cauvel, *Agnes Scott College*
Professor M. N. Chatterjee, *Antioch College*
Professor George A. Clark, *Lafayette College*
Mr. Richard De Martino, Graduate Student, *Columbia University*
Dr. Richard A. Gard, *Asia Foundation*
Professor E. Boyd Graves, *Mary Washington College*
Professor Thomas F. Green, *Michigan State University*
Prof. Lewis E. Hahn, *Washington University*
Professor William H. Harris, *Southern Illinois University*
Mrs. Philoméne Harrison, Graduate Student, *Claremont College*
Professor Richard Hocking, *Emory University*
Visiting Professor S. G. Hulyalkar, *Yale University*

Mr. Kenneth Inada, Graduate Student, *University of Tokyo*
Mr. Charles Jones, Graduate Assistant, *University of Hawaii*
Professor Paul W. Kurtz, *Trinity College*
Professor Samuel E. Lindley, *Allegheny College*
Professor Morris J. Morgan, *South Dakota State College of Agriculture & Mechanic Arts*
Professor Arthur W. Munk, *Albion College*
Mr. Donald Munro, Graduate Student, *Columbia University*
Professor Gerald E. Myers, *Williams College*
Professor Niels Nielson, Jr., *The Rice Institute*
Professor Jennings J. Olson, *Weber College*
Dr. Troy Organ, *Ohio University*
Professor Yasumasa Oshima, *Tokyo Education University*
Mr. C. R. Pang, Graduate Student, *Banaras Hindu University*
Professor Herta Pauly, *Upsala College*
Professor Bernard Phillips, *University of Delaware*
Karl H. Potter, *University of Minnesota*
Mr. John Reissig, Graduate Student, *Northwestern University*
Professor (Captain) Herbert Y. Schandler, *U. S. Military Academy*
Professor Delton L. Scudder, *University of Florida*
Professor Clarence Shute, *University of Massachusetts*
Professor Jerry Stannard, *Pennsylvania State University*
Professor Wendell C. Stone, *Rollins College*
Professor Robert P. Sylvester, *Baldwin-Wallace College*
Miss Kiyoko Takagi, Graduate Student, *Harvard University*
Mr. Franklin Takei, Graduate Assistant, *University of Hawaii*
Professor Nguyen Dang Thuc, *University of Saigon*
Professor William S. Weedon, *University of Virginia*
Mr. Guy R. Welbon, Graduate Student, *Northwestern University*
Miss Beatrice Yamasaki, Instructor in Philosophy, *Bryn Mawr College*

The conference was supported by a significantly large number of Foundations and other organizations. Perhaps this belongs in the Preface, but the writer of this Introduction, who was also the Director of the conference, wishes at this time to express deep appreciation to all of these organizations and to the individuals who were instrumental in securing the grants which made the conference possible. The Foundations and organizations which supported the conference were:

American Council of Learned Societies
The Asia Foundation
The Juliette M. Atherton Trust
Carnegie Corporation of New York
Samuel N. and Mary Castle Foundation
The Council on Economic and Cultural Affairs, Inc.
The Danforth Foundation, Inc.
The Farfield Foundation, Inc.
Frear Eleemosynary Trust
The Edward W. Hazen Foundation

The Foundation for Idealistic Philosophy
The McInerny Foundation
UNESCO
The Watumull Foundation

The Steering Committee of the conference consisted of:

Edwin A. Burtt, *Cornell University*
Wing-tsit Chan, *Dartmouth College*
Abraham Kaplan, *University of California, Los Angeles*
Cornelius Krusé, *Wesleyan University*
Charles A. Moore, *University of Hawaii*
Filmer S. C. Northrop, *Yale University*

The planning and conduct of this conference would have been impossible without the genuine and enthusiastic support of many persons on the staff of the University of Hawaii. Wholehearted appreciation is hereby extended to President Laurence H. Snyder and all of his associates in the Administration of the University—particularly to Dr. Willard Wilson, Provost, who was directly concerned with the conference; to Dr. Bruce E. White, Dean of Faculties; to Dr. Shunzo Sakamaki, Dean of the Summer Session; to Mr. Thomas Nickerson, Director of the Office of Publications and Information, who supervised, and to Mr. Roger Dionne, who carried out, public relations activities in connection with the conference; to Mr. Joseph M. Skorpen, then University Treasurer, and his staff; to Mrs. Violet Borges and her staff in the Stenographic Pool; to Mrs. Elsie Boatman and her staff at the University Cafeteria; to Mr. Frank E. Hinton and his Maintenance Staff; and to many, many others. To all of these a special debt is owed for their indispensable help and support before and throughout the conference.

We are deeply appreciative, too, of the understanding and valuable cooperation of the Honolulu press and of representatives of national periodicals.

Mrs. Philomène Harrison, conference secretary, brought ability and boundless energy and also devotion and tact to her office, which amounted to that of Administrative Assistant. Every conference member would agree that her contribution was invaluable. Even this tribute is inadequate.

The work of this conference seemed to be completely in line with the "Major Project" of UNESCO, which consists of a long-time effort to achieve greater mutual understanding of the cultural values of the peoples of East and West. The only difference, although it may be a significant one, lies in the fact that the 1959 East-West Philosophers' Conference approached this all-important problem in the unique way described above, namely, that of seeking such mutual understanding of the cultural values of the peoples of East and West through a direct search for and understanding of these cultural values in terms of underlying philosophical beliefs, attitudes, and methods—in other words, by an attempt to get at the "mind" of each of the traditions under study so as to understand that "mind" in action. This may well be a most difficult, if not impossible, undertaking, both in essence and also in its comprehensive program and goal. However, difficult as the problem undoubtedly is, the attempt had to be made, the problem had to be attacked directly, even though only partial and perhaps indefinite results could be envisaged even by the most optimistic. But, results were achieved, many and important results, as the following chapters demonstrate and which the final three chapters herein attempt to summarize as specifically as was, in the nature of the case, possible.

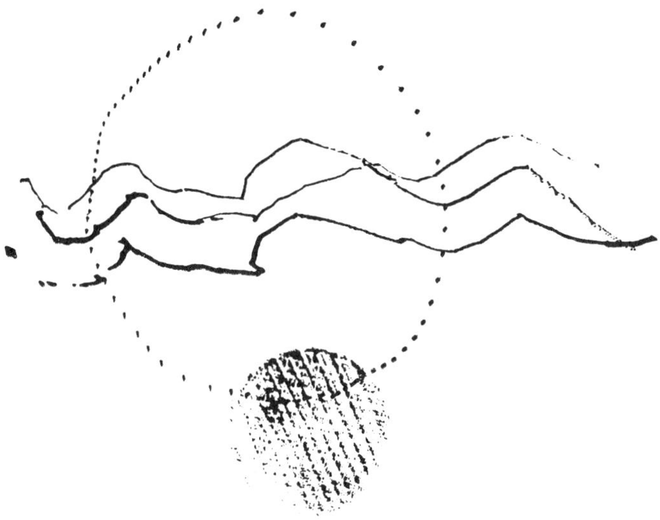

I. The Relation of Philosophical Theories to Practical Affairs

SIDNEY HOOK

Philosophy and Human Conduct

I.

That philosophy counts in human affairs is acknowledged by governments as well as by landladies. Few governments until recent times have been indifferent to the philosophic ideas professed by their citizens, and especially by the teachers of their citizens. And it is hardly fortuitous that all groups in possession of power have been biased in favor of philosophical ideas which celebrate eternity rather than those which glorify change. Even when power manifests itself most nakedly it often seeks to clothe itself in philosophic thought. Although such thought may rightly be characterized as a rationalization, it would be hazardous to dismiss rationalizations as inconsequential. Some people live and die by their rationalizations.

On a more mundane plane, few would deny the insight in G. K. Chesterton's remark that it is more important for a landlady to know her boarder's philosophy than the contents of his trunks. For the reference is obviously to the boarder's moral principles. But the insight becomes highly problematic when, instead of to moral principles, the reference is to the boarder's epistemology or metaphysics. The withers of most landladies would be completely unwrung at the news that their boarder had surrendered his belief in the *Ding-an-sich* for the view that a thing is a complex of sense-data.

This suggests the necessity of making a few preliminary distinctions in order to sharpen our question. If philosophical ideas play a role in determining social practice, this indicates that some ideas have relevance to conduct. But the fact that ideas and beliefs are efficacious in experience is not by itself evidence that philosophical ideas have the same role. For belief that scientific and technological ideas are implicit plans of action which have momentous bearing on the affairs of experience may be coupled with the view that philosophical ideas have no such bearing at all. For example, Bertrand Russell has maintained in a book in which he declares political theory to be one of the three dominant causes of political and social change that: "The belief that metaphysics has any bearing upon practical affairs is, to my mind, a proof of logical incapacity."[1] That in a subsequent writing Russell asserts that some philosophies are dangerous because of their influence on practice, that the epistemology of empiricism is more congenial to liberalism than to conservatism, and that "the only philosophy that affords a theoretical justification of democracy in its temper of mind is empiricism"[2] indicates some confusion on Russell's part. Nonetheless, in principle there is no inconsistency in holding the view that ideas count in practice but not philosophical ideas.

Since in this paper I shall contend that both (a) ideas in science and technology and (b) ideas in philosophy are important determiners of conduct, I begin with a brief consideration of the view that all ideas are epiphenomenal, that they are the effects of certain ultimate causes and are never themselves proximate causes of effects. If this position is valid, it follows that philosophical ideas are fanciful notions or vapors thrown up by the movements of things and social forces, comparable to the surface patterns of foam moved by the forces of the deep. If, on the other hand, the position is invalid, this does not by itself establish the validity of (b). It shows only that it may possibly be true.

1.

It requires considerable intellectual sophistication to deny causal influence to ideas in human affairs. For, aside from instinctive and habitual conduct, what we do is largely determined by what we believe, and even habitual conduct often presupposes that certain beliefs had been accepted as true in the past. The world we live in is an interpreted world. The evidence for this is so massive that no one but philosophers would doubt it. Ideas are sometimes stronger than the strongest natural impulses. We know that human beings have starved in the sight of nourishing food because they believed certain animals to be sacred or certain plants poisonous. Nor is it necessary for ideas to be true to have determining significance. Witches do not exist. But how many unfortunate creatures have been brought to a miserable end because of the belief in the existence of witches? To be sure, one may believe in witches and not burn them but put them to work on useful tasks. This testifies only to the influence of other ideas about witches. It still remains true that if we did not believe in witches thousands of innocent women would not have been tortured to death.

The view that ideas have no influence on human conduct is hardly intelligible in the light of the anticipated consequences of the enunciation of that view. But it may be instructive to examine some of the grounds offered for the belief in the inefficacity of ideas. The most important ground offered is that ideas are events either in a man's biography or in a culture and, like all

[1] Bertrand Russell, *Freedom versus Organization* (New York: W. W. Norton & Company, 1932), p. 196.
[2] Bertrand Russell, *Philosophy and Politics* (London: Cambridge University Press, 1947), p. 20.

events, have causes. But that ideas have causes is not incompatible with the proposition that ideas have consequences. If it were, then, since "the causes" of ideas are themselves caused by antecedent events, these "causes" would have to be denied efficacy. It would then be illegitimate to say that ideas were *their* consequences. In other words, once we recognize the operation of proximate causes, we can no longer call into question the efficacy of ideas which are themselves caused.

A second reason for questioning the practical import of ideas is that they and the behavior patterns which define them are not sufficient to explain their alleged effects. Multiple causes and multiple factors, limiting objective conditions, are invariably present. Historians of ideas often assert that "the time must be ripe," "possibilities must be open," "the stage must be set," "the situation must be prepared" before ideas can take hold. All this may be true, but this indicates only that ideas are not omnipotent and that they cannot explain everything about a situation. Men are creatures of interests, habits, passions, as well as thought. Unless it is argued that a resultant effect would have occurred anyway, independently of the presence or absence of ideas, causal imputation cannot be denied to ideas.

From two diametrically opposed, yet related, points of view the efficacy of ideas in history has been denied. The dialectical idealism of Hegel, as well as the dialectical materialism of Marxism, in their standard versions, renders ideas otiose for different reasons. In Hegel, the world is conceived of as embodied Reason, developing, to be sure, but developing out of time. The real is *already* rational. At most, human thinking recognizes the immanent necessities in things in order to proclaim them necessary, reasonable, and therefore good, rather than to transform or change them. "Reason is already in the world," says Hegel, just as God is in the world, and the progress of thought is the progress of recognition of the fact.

What is true for human ideas generically in Hegel is true for philosophical ideas specifically. In his famous lines in the Preface to his *Philosophy of Law*, he writes:

> The task of philosophy is to comprehend that which exists, for that which exists is Reason. As far as the individual is concerned, everyone is a son of his time; so, too, is philosophy an expression of its time in thought. It is just as foolish to suppose that any philosophy can transcend its contemporary world as to suppose that any individual can jump out of his time....
>
> Philosophy always comes too late to teach the world what it should be.... When it paints its gray upon gray, a form of life has already become old and with gray upon gray life cannot be rejuvenated but only understood. The owl of Minerva takes its flight only when the shades of twilight have fallen.[3]

In Marx, the mode of economic production takes the place of the Hegelian developing *Begriff*, or concrete universal, as the basic cause of historical change.

[3] *Grundlinien der Philosophie des Rechts*, Lasson Ausgabe (Leipzig: Verlag von Felix Meiner, 1921), pp. 15, 17.

Human beings are moved by ideas, but these ideas are epiphenomenal (or superstructural); they have neither autonomy nor independent force. Strictly speaking, there is no such thing for Marx as a history of ideas but only a history of modes of production whose needs create the interests which reflect themselves in the construction of morality, religion, and philosophy. In *Die deutsche Ideologie*, Marx and Engels write:

> In complete opposition to German philosophy which descends from heaven to earth, we here mount from the earth to heaven. We do not take our point of departure from what men say, imagine, conceive, nor from men as they are described, thought about, imagined or conceived in order to arrive at men in the living flesh. We start from real, active men. We present the development of their ideological reflexes and echoes as products of their real life-processes. Even the fantasies in the human brain are the necessary sublimates of the life-processes which are tied to material presuppositions of an empirical and verifiable character. Morality, religion, metaphysic, and other ideology and their corresponding forms of consciousness herewith lose their semblance of independence. They have no history, they have no development. Human beings in consequence of their material production and material intercourse transform their existence and therewith also their thinking and the products of their thinking. It is not consciousness which determines *life* but life which determines consciousness.[4]

Neither Hegel nor Marx consistently defends his position in denying causal efficacy to ideas. In Hegel, this is apparent in his denunciation of the mischievous effects of what he regards as mistaken ideas. When he turned against the ideas of the French Enlightenment, it was because he held it and its mode of thinking responsible for practices and events which threatened the security of the German States. Instead of leaving to God and the Absolute or *die Lust der Vernunft* the correction of the liberal ideas of Fries and his school, Hegel approved of police measures against them.

In Marx's case, although all other ideas merely sanctify the social status quo by interpreting it differently, his own ideas were offered as a means of revolutionizing it. Although he says "not criticism but revolution is the driving force of history and also of religion, philosophy, and all theory,"[5] his own criticisms and ideas are advanced as the *preface* to revolution as a means of rallying the masses to action. The failure of revolutions to develop where objective conditions are ripe for them is attributed to the influence of traditional ideas or to the absence of proper political organization, which in part depends upon correct ideas of organization.

Even aside from their inconsistencies, both Hegel and Marx fail to do justice to the so-called fact of "reflection" or "expression." Ideas and ideals may "reflect" or "express" social forces or conditions or national interests. But they may reflect or express in different ways. A philosophy which pleads for human

[4] *Marx-Engels Gesamtausgabe*, Erste Abteilung, Bd. 5, V. Adoratski, ed. (Moscow and Berlin: Marx-Engels Verlag, 1932), pp. 15–16.

[5] *Ibid.*, p. 27.

freedom and one which justifies caste or class discrimination may both be properly described as "reflecting" or "expressing" existing institutions, but this leaves unexplained their differential effects. Burke's philosophy is a reflection of the French Revolution; so are the writings of Robespierre, de Constant, St. Just, and de Maistre. No set of ideas merely reflects or expresses given conditions. To the extent that it is believed or commands influence, it *strengthens* or *weakens* conditions. And since social relations always show some fluidity, since some choices and alternatives are always open, the *mode* of expression or reflection becomes a contributory, if not always decisive or even weighty, factor, in determining the movement of affairs.

2.

It is not enough to vindicate the efficiency of ideas in social and practical affairs. The question is whether what is true of ideas in science, technology, and everyday intercourse is true of philosophical ideas. Those who grant that ideas are influential in human affairs but deny that philosophical ideas play the same role as other ideas do so on four generic grounds. They maintain (1) that philosophical ideas, insofar as they can be distinguished from others, are transcendental or non-empirical and therefore have no differential bearing or relevance on human behavior; (2) that there is no observable personal connection between the philosophy a man holds, his theory of reality, and, say, his social views or views on any practical matter; (3) that whatever other connection exists is demonstrably not one of necessary entailment, and, since it is logically possible to combine belief in any theory of reality with any practice, there is no problem; (4) and, finally, that if there are causal connections between philosophical ideas and practices either one may be the cause of the other or both may be caused by some other state of affairs.

Granted, then, that ideas, as John Dewey was fond of observing, are the most practical things in the world, can we say this or something similar to this about philosophical ideas? At first glance, it seems that we may say this only if philosophical ideas are cognitive and make knowledge claims and only if these knowledge claims are about empirical matters or have consequences, direct or indirect, for practice. But it is possible to challenge the cognitive character of all assertions in philosophy, and, independently of this, to challenge the relevance of philosophical assertions to life on the ground that even if they have cognitive validity they are compatible with all social sytems and human practices no matter how contrary the latter are to each other. The motto of the old *American Journal of Speculative Philosophy* used to read: "Philosophy can bake no bread, but she can procure for us God, freedom, and immortality." What philosophy so conceived can procure for us is no mean thing, but how does it bear in any specifiable way on human conduct? Suppose we believe that God exists and that everything happens by the will of God. What follows for practice? Nothing specific, because everything *after* the event can be construed as happening by Divine Will. Despite the village atheist: there is no inconsistency in praying "Thy Will Be Done" in a church whose steeple flaunts a lightning rod to divert a bolt from on high. To the pious, both the bolt and the ingenuity to divert it happen by the will of God. Similarly, human beings may differ over the justification and nature of various punishments, but acceptance or unacceptance of metaphysical freedom of the will is compatible with all positions taken. The belief in immortality is closer to an empirical proposition, although few of those who believe in immortality are clear about the nature of the self. Usually, what takes place is an extrapolation of the complex of feelings, hopes, fears, and desires of the existing self to another state independently of the material conditions upon which the existing self seems to depend. But, by itself, a belief in immortality does not involve commitment to a specific course of conduct unless it is associated with other beliefs of a factual nature like those in heaven or hell or moral beliefs in a path of salvation and a schedule of duties to be observed in this life. It is hard to see what specific practice the belief in immortality *per se* commits one to in life. But, where the belief in immortality takes the form of a belief in reincarnation (*saṁsāra*), where this belief is allied with the doctrine of *karma,* or a cosmic law of justice or retribution, and where it is assumed that the status in the hierarchy of future reincarnated beings is a function of piety toward and observance of caste duties in the present state of existence, then it may be argued with some plausibility that upon the acceptance of some propositions of philosophy—those of natural theology—an entire mode of social life depends, and not merely the baking of bread. At the very least, belief in some philosophical propositions, in some historical situations where traditions of otherworldliness are deep-rooted, would be necessary for social stability and the domination of one class over others. To be sure, it has been argued that these religious and philosophical beliefs arose at a time when it was necessary to consolidate existing social institutions. But, even without raising the question of causal priority, the fact that these beliefs had definite influence on the practical behavior of those nurtured on them seems incontestable. To the extent that reform movements such as Buddhism and Jainism in the East and Protestantism in the West break with dominant traditions many social practices associated with these traditions are repudiated.

The most important point I wish to make here, however, and which I shall develop later, is that if transcendental philosophical or religious beliefs are denied relevance to practical conduct because they are compatible with all varieties of empirical behavior this overlooks the possibility that the connection may not be theoretical or cognitive but attitudinal. That is to say, from the statements "Everything is mind," "All is feeling," "Reality is will," "Everything is vanity (or illusion)" nothing differential in the way of cognitive belief may be inferred and the *differences* between experiences may be surreptitiously acknowledged by adjectival distinction. Nevertheless, these assertions may express attitudes, commitments, evaluations which have a bearing upon conduct none the less effective for being vague, discontinuous, or episodic. As with so many other things, the influence of ideas on behavior is a matter of more or less, not an affair of either-or, all or none.

3.

The most common reason for denying that philosophical ideas and social practices are integrally related is that the philosophical ideas of individual thinkers and their social views and/or practices are often different from what we should expect if there were an organic connection between philosophy and practice. For example, empiricism and materialism are associated with liberalism and radicalism, but Hobbes was a royalist, Hume a Tory, and Santayana sympathetic to Fascism. On the other hand, idealism has been associated with conservatism, but T. H. Green was a liberal, and Felix Adler, like many others influenced by Kant, was a great exponent of social reform. The most outstanding rationalist and idealist in America, Brand Blanshard, is a freethinker and democratic socialist. One can find many other illustrations. The empiricist Francis Bacon was politically reactionary and the non-empirical rationalist Spinoza was a liberal in social and political affairs and an eloquent advocate of tolerance. The same absence of connection holds for outstanding individuals who were not professional philosophers. The radical William Blake professed to being a Berkeleian immaterialist, while that Tory's Tory, Samuel Johnson, scoffed and kicked when Berkeley's views were mentioned.

All these instances seem to me to establish conclusively that there is no personal psychological connection between personality or temperament, as expressed in social or political life, and philosophical belief. This does not deny that causal influences are at work in determining a man's beliefs about even the most recondite things as well as his daily behavior. But, unless there is specific empirical evidence to warrant it, we are not justified in assuming that the same set of causes determines both his personal philosophy and his personal practice, or that one is the cause of the other. Two men of the most diverse temperaments may subscribe to an identical set of theoretical propositions. Two men equally fanatical in temperament may be at each other's throats doctrinally. The same man may embrace at different times in his career contrary brands of fanaticism. Two men who subscribe to the same set of philosophical beliefs may differ in their political and social allegiance, whereas two men who differ in their philosophic beliefs, e.g., Dewey and Russell, may support the same social and political program.

But all this is beside the main point, which asserts, not that there is a general connection between the *personal* social and political commitments of philosophers and their philosophies, but that the *significant connection is to be found between social movements and philosophical doctrines.* Such connections are *historical,* not primarily psychological or personal. A doctrine or a theory may be put to social uses quite different from those the individual author of the doctrine or theory intended or approved of. Ideas and doctrines have historical effects rarely explicable in terms of personal intent. The rise of experimental science is undoubtedly part of the intellectual movement which contributed to the liberation of Western Europe from medievalism. But this was certainly not the intent of Catholic scientists such as Galileo and others. Bacon was personally a time-serving royalist and extreme conservative, but his doctrine that knowledge is power and his critique of the idols of the human mind inspired the French Encyclopedists and contributed to undermining social institutions and prejudices which were personally congenial to him.

Hobbes for our purposes may serve as an ideal case. Certainly, he was a conservative. But his views about the nature and grounds of sovereignty were flatly incompatible with the doctrine of divine rights. They had a chilling effect on the royalists whom he personally supported. It was as if they put the person of the king in the shadow of the gallows or execution block.[6] Hobbes's appeal to the principle of self-interest struck his fellow conservatives as seditious, and his belief, restated in many different ways, that "in sum all actions and habits are to be esteemed good or evil by their causes and usefulness in reference to the commonwealth" as a standing invitation to social criticism of all institutions including the absolute monarchy. For all of Hobbes's transparently sincere *personal* willingness to serve them, the conservative forces and movements of his time and subsequent times could not *use* his doctrines. On the other hand, it was the liberals in subsequent generations who developed his implicit utilitarianism, his anti-clericalism, his secular and scientific approach to political issues. Hobbes's doctrines are part of the same family tree as those of Bentham and the other leading figures of philosophical radicalism. And we shall see below why this is so.

4.

I have previously quoted Russell's remark, "The belief that metaphysics has any bearing upon practical affairs is, to my mind, a proof of logical incapacity." What Russell obviously means is the belief that metaphysics has any *logical* bearing upon practical affairs is a proof of logical incapacity. It is quite true that no metaphysical proposition (except where disguised value-judgments are involved) entails anything about practical affairs, since there seems to be nothing contradictory in holding the view that "Reality is X" and "Y should be done" or "Y should not be done." But there may be some connection, as we have seen, which is other than one of "entailment"; in ordinary discourse we speak of many different kinds of "necessary connection" where "necessary" is not a strictly logical relation. If we insist upon the presence of strict entailment relations before we relate thought to conduct, we will have to rule out the influence of all ideas—even scientific and technological ideas—upon human conduct. It is not logically contradictory to assert, "X is a poisonous substance" and "I should eat it." To insist on relations of logical entailment in assertions bearing on human conduct seems to me to betray a fundamental

[6] One critic says of the identification of the law of Nature with the counsels of self-interest, "Woe to all the Princes of the earth, if this doctrine be true or become popular; if the multitude believe this, the Prince . . . can never be safe from spears and barbed irons which their ambition and personal interest will provide." *Tenison, Creed of Mr. Hobbes Examined* (1670), p. 156, as quoted by Dewey in *Studies in the History of Ideas,* Vol. I, edited by the Department of Philosophy of Columbia University (New York: Columbia University Press, 1918), p. 91.

lack of common sense. It would lead not only to what C. D. Broad calls silly philosophy but to views that are plain silly. It is as if someone were to argue that, if *all* we knew about an individual whom we wanted to hire as a bodyguard was that he was a member of Murder, Inc., pledged to commit crimes, we would not be warranted in considering him unfit for his post because it would not be logically impossible for such an individual to be a secret member of the FBI.[7] It is not *logically* impossible for something to be both a pig and to fly. But if anyone gave this as a reason for mounting a pig to take off into the blue we would question his sanity.

From a strictly logical point of view there is no reason to infer that a belief that one possesses absolute and infallible truth or that one is the recipient of a uniquely revealed message necessitates a policy of intolerance toward those considered to be in error or lost in heresy. As important as the belief in absolute truth may be, the belief that freedom to err is part of the vocation of the free man, whose personality has an absolute value, is not incompatible with it, and some of us are familiar with individuals who hold both beliefs. A revelation that one has received a unique truth from on high may be compatible with another enjoining believers to permit others without persecuting them to find their own paths to salvation or damnation. Nonetheless, I think it would be generally admitted that the belief that one group, class, party, or church possesses absolute and infallible truth about things that matter is more likely to encourage patterns of intolerant conduct toward those who disagree with these alleged truths than the belief that no human being possesses absolute truth and that we are all fallible. Similarly, a belief that we are the exclusive custodians of a unique revelation from God is more likely to encourage patterns of fanaticism and religious intolerance than the belief that God's revelations are continuous and not restricted to any one individual or group.

If one believes that the world of sensuous experience is illusory, that time is unreal, that in some sense everything is one and that separation is the result of a finite perspective, it is still possible to be curious about the forms illusion takes, the apparent differences of things, and the qualities of experience which mislead us into thinking that time is both objective and important. But, by and large, any culture where such beliefs are widely held will be one in which science is not likely to develop, technology will be limited to gratification of needs necessary for life, inventiveness will not be encouraged and institutionalized. Why, indeed, should one immerse himself in disinterested study of the details of the Book of Nature if it is not considered to be a Book of Truth?

In all these illustrations, and they can be easily multiplied, there is a certain social connection between doctrine and practice which is less than logical, more than personal, and other than casual.

[7] Robert Hartman, "Group Membership and Class Membership," *Journal of Philosophy and Phenomenological Research,* XIII, No. 3 (March, 1953), 353.

5.

Our task is not yet done. Grant, for the moment, that there is some determinate connection between organic theories of society, which teach that the welfare and values of all groups, classes, and individuals are inherently harmonious, and the special interests and needs of a bureaucratic class to maintain existing power relations; between atomistic or individualistic theories of empiricism and movements of social reform, decentralization, and opposition to the constraints of tradition; between theories of renunciation, rejection of, and withdrawal from, the world and conditions of social chaos and disorder—this does not by itself establish where the causal primacy lies. The orthodox Marxist view assumes that there is a one-way dependence of philosophical views on political and socio-economic conditions and that if there is no clear line of causal connection between them then *both* can be shown to be consequences of an earlier set of social conditions.

I do not see how it can be established a priori which way the causal connection runs. Although orthodox Marxists claim that they are espousing merely a heuristic hypothesis, they have done very little to test it in a critical or scientific spirit. But the decisive point is this: even if it were the case that philosophical beliefs arose to meet a social situation or to further an interest, in some cases it is clear that they subsequently influenced social developments, so that one can legitimately assert that the history and practical life of a culture in important respects would be inexplicable without reference to them. This is apparent in the philosophy or social ethics of both Christianity and modern democracy.

There have been many attempts to enunciate the Christian "ethos," but it seems to me that the best warranted formulation is to be found in the work of the famous German scholar Ernst Troeltsch: "The lasting and eternal content of the Christian Ethos," he maintains, "recognizes differences in social position, power and capacity, as a condition which has been established by the inscrutable Will of God; and then transforms this condition by the inner upbuilding of personality and the development of the mutual sense of obligation into an ethical cosmos."[8] Whatever the social conditions were which gave rise to the Christian ethos, it is clear that this ethos played a powerful role in practical affairs in two ways. First, it tended to reconcile and gloss over conflicts of social interests, and by legitimizing existing power relations contributed to stabilizing society. Second, for those who accepted this ethos it made life supportable or endurable even if their status was that of the slave or serf. It generated a kind of spiritual buoyancy, a confidence and cosmic hope which prevented those on whom the hard and cruel chores of the world fell from being dragged down by their sufferings and weariness into apathy or despair[9] or from being goaded into a continuous state of resentment and pe-

[8] Ernst Troeltsch, *The Social Teaching of the Christian Churches*, Olive Wyon, trans. (London and New York: The Macmillan Company, 1932), p. 1005.

[9] Herbert Butterfield, *Christianity and History* (London: G. Bell and Sons, Ltd., 1949), pp. 175 ff.

riodic revolt. Whether early Christianity be conceived of as a this-worldly spiritual revolutionary movement or as an otherworldly compensatory revolutionary movement, it is noteworthy that the frequency and intensity of slave revolts decreased sharply with the Christianization of the Roman Empire.

That modern democratic theory and practice are born of the developing European capitalist economy is believed not only by Marxists but also by the school of Hayek and von Mises, who draw different political conclusions from this alleged causal dependency. But an unprejudiced analysis of the impact of the democratic faith upon the development of Western society establishes its independent influence upon social, political, and economic life. The affirmation and reaffirmation of the democratic faith, particularly as a consequence of two wars in which the slogans of democracy became common coin, played a powerful role in the extension of democratic practices in the United States. The United States Supreme Court's desegregation decision reversing previous decisions on racial questions is a weighty piece of evidence that principles of social philosophy can be effective. To be sure, conditions must be ripe before the principles become operative. But conditions may be ripe, and yet, without belief, they may never mature. Sometimes, what human beings believe is an index or a part of the ripeness of conditions. What is true of the appeal and impact of the democratic ideal in the United States is true of its spread as a slogan, a rallying cry, a set of abstract principles, in most regions of Asia and Africa.

Yet, for all the "reciprocal influence" of philosophical ideas and ideals on events and practices, this does not establish the view that all philosophical ideals have this function. That, broadly speaking, ethical ideals or propositions have an influence on behavior may be granted. But have ontological or epistemological ideas either a direct influence on behavior or a mediate influence through their influence on ethical ideals? The philosophy of dialectical materialism is a good test case. It is an open question whether the Russian October Revolution and the construction of the economy of socialism in one country are compatible with belief in the theory of historical materialism as Marx and Engels interpreted it. There can be hardly any doubt, however, that they followed from Lenin's interpretation of Marxism. And, with some modifications, I believe a plausible case can be made for the contention that the Bolshevik-Leninist political ideology or theory is still the most fruitful guide to Soviet practice. But, despite the official pronouncement that dialectical materialism is the logical basis of communism and the guide to the theory and practice of the Soviet regime, no one has succeeded in showing in a single instance the influence of the so-called laws of dialectic or the other general principles of dialectical materialism upon any *specific* Soviet practice. That is to say, despite official pronouncement to the contrary, the laws of dialectic provide no guide to any specific judgment or practice. It is true that sometimes the philosophy of dialectical materialism has been invoked to condemn some theory in astronomy, biology, chemistry, physics, or psychology. But in no case has any analysis shown that the laws of dialectic are incompatible with the proposition condemned. Indeed, in every case a more plausible explanation can be found why one proposition was approved and the other rejected by the Politbureau; for example: in Lysenko's case the hope that his theories would increase the wheat yield; in other instances, the desire to sustain the intellectual authority of Marx-Engels-Lenin's views on Nature and science because of the key place that their political doctrines held in the communist program. In other words, were the communists to abandon all belief in the laws of dialectic tomorrow, nothing of moment would be altered; no one could show why anything should be different except that scientists and other scholars and teachers profess allegiance to them. This obviously would not be the case if the communists abandoned their theory of the State, or their views of the class struggle or of the nature of capitalism.

II.

That the philosophical views of some groups are associated with, and do influence, their social practices is easier to establish for some periods of history than that there is *always* a determinate connection between philosophical theory and practice, in the sense that, once we know *in the abstract* what philosophy a group supports, we can predict what their social practices will be or on which side they will line up with respect to practical issues such as trade unionism, the relation between Church and State, birth control, or a world State. Here I believe that every assertion of universal connection is false, whether it be Hegelian or Marxian; and, if we take the historical approach, which both schools urge, to the connection between philosophy and culture, we can establish the absence of any universal connection. Many things in addition to philosophical belief may determine practical commitment, so that, even when the philosophical beliefs are the same, other factors such as national interest, religious traditions, and sectional ties may be the overriding considerations. This suggests the possibility that, although a philosophical belief may *tend* to influence conduct in a certain direction, it may be counteracted by the effect of other factors which determine action.

In line with this possibility, I should like to venture a hypothesis about the relation between philosophical views, when these are conceived in a certain way, and social practices. I understand by philosophical views, as distinct from purely scientific views, interpretations of existence from the standpoint of value. Values may not be rooted in interests, but whenever conflicts of value arise they involve or are related to interests—and, to the extent that the content of interests is social, to social interests. No plausible account of the history of Western culture (perhaps of Eastern cultures, too) can be written which does not recognize the enormous role of conflicting group and class interests in the struggle for political power and the distribution and control of economic wealth. It is obviously to the interest of those groups or classes which enjoy the dominating position in society, and who command the posts of strategic power, to attenuate, moderate, and, whenever possible, conceal conflicts of interest. Otherwise, society would be in a state of chronic civil war in which the very advantages of domination would be imperiled. The interest of any class or group in power is, in other words, to conceal conflict of interests, to develop and reinforce attitudes, habits, and beliefs which make the customary appear the natural, the reasonable, and the necessary. Every vested interest will shy away from an experimental or empirical approach which will test slogans and principles by performance, examine causes and consequences of social policies, and expose to the light the interests which are furthered or repressed by them.

Consequently, we should expect that those who are in positions of social authority and power would be predisposed to support views and attitudes which tend to rationalize the social status quo. Those who wish to reform or revolutionize the existing order will support views and attitudes which tend to reveal the roots of interest under the trees of accepted theory and bring to light the conflicting interests whose vitality and growth and satisfaction are frustrated by existing social institutions. They will adopt this outlook until they themselves come to power, when, if they develop vested interests of their own, they will tend to shift toward a modification of their doctrines. The first group, the "in-group," will be inclined to support a philosophical outlook which is organic, hierarchical, idealistic, which stresses that everything has its necessary place in the universe and therefore every man his necessary station in society with fixed duties. Or it will be sympathetic to philosophies that give great scope to revelation, intuition, authority, and tradition, providing that the necessity of some institution to interpret them is conceded. The second group, the "out-group," will tend to be empirical and experimental, materialistic or naturalistic, insisting upon reducing large and grandiose abstractions about social peace, harmony, and unity to denotative differences in practice.

This hypothesis in its general outline is not novel except possibly for the explicit reference to social interest. We have seen that Russell maintains that the empirical theory of knowledge, which he identifies with the scientific outlook, "is the intellectual counterpart of what is, in the practical sphere, the attitude of Liberalism,"[10] and that it is the "only philosophy that affords a theoretical justification of democracy," but he gives no convincing reason why this should be so. Our hypothesis would explain it.

The works of Dewey are studded with references to the social implications of philosophical positions. He is perhaps the most notable contemporary philosopher who has stressed the relation between philosophy and social action. His most pointed attempt to trace the specific relation between the philosophy of Kant—its dualism of "the world of sense and mechanism and the world of the supersensible and purpose"—and the culture of Imperial Germany must be regarded as a failure.[11] Nonetheless, he feels convinced that "one can say with considerable assurance that a hierarchically ordered and subordinated

[10] *Philosophy and Politics*, p. 22.
[11] John Dewey, *German Philosophy and Politics* (New York: Henry Holt & Co., 1915), p. 121.

State will feel an affinity for a philosophy of fixed categories while a flexible democratic society will, in its crude empiricism, exhibit loose ends."[12] The reason for this affinity is that an organic view tends to minimize the significance of specific conflicts of interests by showing that all interests are servants of one general interest which is both all-inclusive and harmonious.[13]

Even more emphatic in this connection is the memorable passage in John Stuart Mill's *Autobiography*:

> The notion that truths external to the mind may be known by intuition or consciousness, independently of observation or experiences, is, I am persuaded, in these times, the great intellectual support of false doctrines and bad institutions. By the aid of this theory, every inveterate belief and every intense feeling, of which the origin is not remembered, is entitled to dispense with the obligation of justifying itself by reason, and is erected into its own all sufficient voucher and justification. There never was such an instrument devised for consecrating all deep seated prejudices.[14]

If our hypothesis is tenable, there are certain things which we should be prepared to expect. It is unlikely that "the official philosophy" or the dominant philosophy in any culture riven by strong conflicts of interest will be experimental. To the extent that materialism allies itself with scientific method in social affairs, it is unlikely that materialism will ever be a regnant philosophy in such a culture. The Soviet Union is not an exception. The Marxist philosophy, which functioned essentially as a critical instrument to lay bare the political and social interests behind ideologies, and their connections with the mode of economic production, became transformed when it was elevated to the rank of official State philosophy of the Soviet Union, into a shamefaced variety of objective idealism. In that role it functions just as much as an ideology as any of the dominant philosophies in previous ages, preaching, for example, that "a unity of interest" existed between the workers and peasants during the very times when the peasants were being expropriated from their holdings. That is why, although in the physical sciences an empirical and experimental approach is accepted within certain limits, in the social sciences it is not tolerated.

We should further expect that close relations will exist between the dominant or official philosophy and the dominant or official religion of a period, although there will be differences in the *manner* in which the rationality or acceptability of traditional values is defended.

Our hypothesis will also explain why most specific metaphysical assertions are irrelevant to social practice. For, although assertions like "Reality is will or feeling or matter" may express personal judgments of value, in the sense that those who hold them thereby indicate their interest in, or preference

[12] *Ibid.*, p. 44.

[13] John Dewey, *Reconstruction in Philosophy* (enlarged ed., Boston: Beacon Press, Inc., 1948), p. 191.

[14] John Stuart Mill, *Autobiography*, J. J. Cross, ed. (first unaltered ed., New York: Columbia University Press, 1924), p. 158. Cf. also pp. 191–194.

for, some special feature of experience, it is difficult to show their bearing on existing social interests.

However, there are certain obvious difficulties with this hypothesis. The first is that sometimes a group struggling to further its interests against the existing power complex may invoke the ideal of the dominant philosophy and religion. Where this is the case one would expect the philosophy of the opposition to contain more empirical elements than the official creeds they oppose, to pay more attention to the facts of social experience. The history of religious movements illustrates a similar tendency. Although the religious dogmas are common, the interpretations vary. The social and political opposition tends to liberalize the theology. So the Cromwellians against the Crown and the Levellers against both. The Left Hegelians were more empirical than the Right Hegelians despite their common jargon. Nonetheless, this phenomenon—the use of the same philosophical tradition for different social purposes—weakens the force of the assertion of the relation between philosophical doctrine and social allegiance.

A more formidable objection to this hypothesis about the social bearing of philosophical doctrines is formulated by Professor Feuer,[15] who believes that psychoanalytical motivation is the key to the kind of view which flourishes. He calls attention to the fact that, whereas the revolutionists of the eighteenth century were *intuitionists* and *apriorists*, Burke, who opposed them, was a historical and empirical conservative. Although detailed studies are necessary to explore these connections, I venture the judgment that Burke in his *Reflections on the French Revolution* did not take an empirical approach to history but a fetishistic one. He is really an a priori traditionalist using the language of historical tradition. An appeal to history is an appeal to a succession of events which contain all sorts of changes, including revolutions—when they were justified and when they were not; but the upshot of Burke's *Reflections* was that revolutions were never justified in any circumstances.

The case of the revolutionary natural-law intuitionists of the eighteenth century is much more difficult. I am convinced, however, that in Locke, in the French materialists, and especially in Jefferson, "natural rights" are really synonymous with "moral rights" and that moral rights are justified by an implicit utilitarianism which, despite the historical fiction of the social contract, places chief emphasis upon present-day consequences. Taken literally, of course, this utilitarianism is incompatible with the belief that certain rights are absolute or "inalienable," since any right, if unlimited, may have disastrous consequences upon the community. Nonetheless, it is obvious that the language of inalienable rights was never taken literally. Otherwise, we could hardly explain the practices defended in their name. The easy assumption was that the rights of life, liberty, property, and happiness were always compatible with each other. When it was discovered that they were not always

[15] Lewis Feuer, "The Sociology of Philosophic Ideas," *The Pacific Sociological Review*, VIII (1958), 77.

compatible, they were in fact treated as "alienable." Historically, the right to private property was given precedence over the others. With the extension of the franchise and the growth in power of the masses, other rights conceived as necessary to human happiness and welfare were, on occasions, given legislative, if not, judicial priority. The right to property was more clearly grasped as only one among other human rights. The upshot of all this seems to me to be adequately expressed by Morris R. Cohen, who, after a life-long study of natural law and natural rights, concluded with the observation: "Ultimately, then, the essence of all doctrines of natural rights is the view that any established or proposed social order or institution must defend itself before the *bar of human welfare*."[16]

Several things should be noted about our hypothesis. Even if it is sustained, it does not justify sweeping statements about philosophical positions and social commitments. Certainly there is little evidence that most technical doctrines in philosophy, about which philosophers are professionally concerned, have any relevance to problems of social importance unless they are extrinsically coupled with differences in attitude or with differences in opinion about fact. Further, the relevance of philosophy to social practice is to be tested wherever policies involving values and value-formations are being formulated. In this connection, the study of philosophy of education and the habits of thought and action stressed in educational institutions are highly pertinent. Whatever else philosophy of education is, it concerns itself with the ends of education. The liberal and democratic outlook is associated with emphasis upon finding out, upon the right to challenge, and dissent, upon empirical inquiry guided by the authority of objective, scientific methods, and upon self-discipline. The conservative outlook stresses the acceptance of tradition, respect for authority, the security of results won rather than the adventure of doubt, and discipline imposed from without. An investigation of the values stressed in educational systems at different periods, and of the relation of these educational objectives to the philosophy embraced by those who exercised the decisive roles in fashioning and guiding the educational systems, would provide some empirical test of the hypothesis.

Finally, the hypothesis is not arbitrary in that there are plausible grounds for expecting a connection to be present. A community is liberal and/or democratic to the extent that all the interests present within it are represented, to the extent that they have an opportunity legally to oppose the majority decision when it goes against them, and to become the nucleus of a new majority. The assumption is that until men become angels there will be not only disagreements among them about how to implement their common interests but also objective differences of interests among them. The only alternatives to democratic society are the despotism of a minority, malevolent or benevolent, or anarchy, which is the reign of a thousand despots. The democrat assumes vis-à-vis the despot, especially the benevolent despot, that most

[16] M. R. Cohen, *Reason and Law* (Glencoe, Ill.: The Free Press, 1950), p. 190. Italics mine.

men in the open light of clash and criticism of interests are better judges of their own interests than anyone else. Vis-à-vis the anarchist, the democrat assumes that men have more significant interests in common than the interests which divide them, even if it be little more than a desire to live in peace with one another's conflicting interests. What is common to all forms of empiricism is the belief that truth is an affair of observational consequences. Although the hypothesis may turn out to be false, it is not unreasonable to assume that where men are willing to test their beliefs, not by their alleged presuppositions, but by their observable consequences, they will probably be more willing to compromise their demands, to negotiate differences, to take the standpoint of the other, to live together, to let live, and to help each other to live rather than to fight and die together.

This connection, I repeat, is only plausible. It has been challenged by several thinkers who, although they believe it true that empiricism in philosophy has practical consequences, maintain that the practical consequences, if logically drawn, would be, not liberalism or democracy, but totalitarianism. In each case, I believe the contention mistaken. Since, however, we are dealing with an empirical assertion in the history of ideas, the truth of the matter must be determined not primarily by argument but by patient historical inquiry. Even if it were true that the abstruse and recondite consequences of a philosophical position, if drawn, would require in the interests of consistency some modification of a practical attitude, this is not evidence of historical connection.[17] Even *simple* logical consequences are sometimes not drawn and the subtle complex consequences hardly ever. Men who make history, fortunately or unfortunately, are not mathematical logicians. Intelligence in human affairs requires something more than a passion for consistency. The springs of action are impulse and desire, ambition, hope, and fear. Intelligence, by exploring the meanings of belief, may govern, moderate, strengthen, or check the springs of action. Whoever, therefore, would trace the influence of large and general ideas on human behavior must find the paths of connection between human interest and human thought.

QUESTION: Suppose someone believes that "God is love." Doesn't this metaphysical or theological proposition have an influence on his practical behavior?

ANSWER: This is an illustration of what I call a disguised ethical statement —and I have admitted that general ethical statements under certain conditions may influence conduct. What I am denying is that from the proposition "God exists" one can derive the proposition that "God is love" or "God is justice." My contention is that human beings impute to God (or reality or the Absolute) moral attributes whose validity they regard as justified on the basis of considerations other than those which lead them to assertions about the existence of God or any metaphysical entities. The argument is not "God exists, there-

[17] This seems to me to bear upon the contentions of J. W. N. Watkins, "Epistemology and Politics," *Proceedings of the Aristotelian Society*, LVIII (1957–1958), 74–102.

fore he exhibits the power of love or justice," but "Love or Justice is the highest value, therefore God as the most perfect being exhibits it." It seems to me a quite plausible generalization to say that men build Gods in their own moral images and that the development of religion reflects the growth of a moral insight which is derived, not from any metaphysical statement, but from reflection upon the fruits of human action in daily experience.

Incidentally, I should point out that we must be careful not to assume too easily that the person who asserts "God is love" will therefore act in a loving way toward his neighbors. He must believe what he asserts. The difficulty is that we often cannot tell what a person really believes until we have observed his actions. We may sometimes conclude that a person believes that God is the principle of love even though he does not assert it and that he does not really believe it even when he asserts it.

GEORGE P. CONGER

Societal Structures and Processes

In order to land at once in the midst of the field, let us say that social philosophy must take account of both sociology and social psychology, must have bearing on both economics and politics, and need not hesitate to pass beyond a descriptive to a prescriptive or normative ethics.

Once landing in it, we find that the field is a maze of beaten tracks. No matter where one touches down, or what direction he takes, or at what point he hopes to arrive, he finds that some man or some group has been there and has taken that route or one very much like it. The only hope of reaching any new insight lies in one or another shift of emphasis.

To aid in getting our bearings, I propose that we use two quotations from the ancient world, where questions were simpler and answers somewhat more evident. Appropriately for this conference, one of the quotations comes from the West, the other from the East. In the Western wisdom there are some words which in time of controversy ought to be quoted more often than they are. They come from the opening sentences of Aristotle's *Nichomachean Ethics.*

> Our discussion will be adequate if it has as much clearness as the subject matter admits of, for precision is not to be sought for alike in all discussions. . . . It is the mark of an educated man to look for precision in each class of things just so far as the nature of the subject admits.[1]

Some of the context of this passage may raise questions, but the import is clear enough. Ethics is not an exact science, and, we may go on to say, social philosophy must often be content with generalities and approximations.

The quotation from the Eastern wisdom we shall meet presently.

[1] *Ethica Nichomachea,* 1094*b,* 11–25, in W. D. Ross, ed. and trans., *The Works of Aristotle Translated into English,* Vol. IX (Oxford: Clarendon Press, 1925), p. 3.

I.

If we are to get beyond a makeshift opportunism, we shall need to detect some general principles which in one way or another pervade the tangled mass of data. Pluralism and positivism may decry the use of general principles—that is, general principles other than their own—but we may leave those controversies to subside automatically, while we seek to detect and discuss a principle so often dichotomized that it looks like two principles, though an essential point of our argument will be that the two components are superficially disjoined and in reality should not be separated. The limitations of language and thought are such that, if we go into any detail, we have to consider first one and then the other, but such disjunction is only provisional and methodological. Any abstraction, in the root sense of the word, from *abstrahere,* is a "dragging away" of something from something else, and, in the concrete, again in the root sense of the word, from *concrescere,* all abstractions must "grow together."

The "two" principles are *structure* and *process.* Even if the distinctions between them are our own, they confront us everywhere. Every structure exhibits an ordering of parts, and the order and the parts change from time to time. We speak, perforce, of structures and processes, but the two abstractions are correlative. Never is there structure without some process; never is there process without some structure. To ask which comes first, either ontologically or logically, is to ask a fruitless question. It is about equally distorting to say that a primal structure gets going or to say that a primal process takes form; if there is any choice, the first way of speaking seems a little more realistic, but one need not insist. It would help if we could impose the yoke of a hyphen and speak of structure-process or process-structure, or, perhaps still more, if we could fuse the two words into one. But all such devices collapse, and we are thrown back on the specious but useful duality.

II.

Structure is everywhere obvious in physics, chemistry, astronomy, and biology. If it is not obvious, it can be detected in psychology. In sociology, however, it is either overlooked or underestimated. Some reasons for this stem from the reaction against the so-called organic or organismic theories of society which flourished at the turn of the century and were done to death by their friends who pushed the analogies too far. These theories were succeeded in favor by the psychological theories of society, according to which society is essentially the product of minds. This was agreeable to the still influential idealist philosophies and was encouraged by the rise of pragmatism, with its emphasis on changes, especially those wrought by human effort and control. The emphasis on change was reinforced both from the side of practice and from the side of theory; the turn of the century saw some marked political changes, and the old views that matter was static and inert began to give way to theories that matter was some form of energy.

The result has been that on the whole in the West process has been emphasized at the expense of structure. In this general trend, three of the beaten paths taken by various writers may be roughly distinguished. The distinctions, as Aristotle would have expected, are only rough; most of the writers have wandered from one of the paths to one or both of the others. First, we find that structure has been neglected or, where processes were recognized, subordinated. Second, where societal structure has been accorded more recognition, it has been interpreted in psychological terms. Third, where structure has been recognized, it has been obscured by abstractions. Without going back to the year 1, a few examples may be cited from the enormous literature of sociology.

In the 1920s, two well-known books were Ogburn's *Social Change*[2] and Sorokin's *Social Mobility*.[3] Neither man is to be criticized for not saying in one book everything that he had to say; it is the choice of title and angle of treatment, as well as the vogue of the two books, that is significant. Ogburn says next to nothing about structure; society is usually described in psychological terms, such as sociability, gregariousness, association, responses to stimuli, and consciousness. Sorokin, recognizing that there are simple and cumulative social groups, and providing almost countless illustrative details to support his thesis, is much closer to the facts of societal structure but misses some fundamental features of it in following a metaphor. He says that an investigation of social mobility presupposes a preliminary study of social stratification, which is manifested in the existence of upper and lower social layers. In these strata social mobility may be either "horizontal" or "vertical": he illustrates this in economics, politics, and occupational groups.[4]

Most of the authors whom we cite deal in one way or another with group theories in sociology, but with, as L. Wilson says, ambiguity of conceptualization and classification. Those writers, he goes on to say, who organize the subject-matter of sociology primarily in terms of social processes may be expected to give only an incidental topical treatment of groups, but the majority of the textbooks which do take up the group explicitly and in some detail show an uncertainty and inconsistency about where to place it within the schemes of topical organization. The net result in most instances is a hodgepodge of classifications and generalizations.[5] Just such a hodgepodge, we may add, marks the treatments of the closely related topic of societal structure.

Already in the 1920s, in a book not so well known as those of Ogburn and Sorokin, B. Warren Brown was outstanding for his emphasis on groups. He says that social life implies relationships of one sort or another between individuals, and those relationships inevitably fall into regular channels and forms. Whenever these forms are consistent enough to permit observation and classification, we note a social structure. The outstanding characteristic of social structure is the tendency of individuals to combine into groups; we cannot have

[2] W. F. Ogburn, *Social Change* (New York: B. W. Huebsch, 1927; Viking Press, 1950).

[3] P. A. Sorokin, *Social Mobility* (New York and London: Harper & Brothers, 1927).

[4] *Ibid.*, p. 11, and chapters following.

[5] L. Wilson, "The Sociology of Groups," in G. Gurvitch and W. E. Moore, eds., *Twentieth Century Sociology* (New York: Philosophical Library, 1945), p. 155.

social structure without groups. But when he comes to enumerate the factors which make group life possible, Brown lists contact, physical basis, homogeneity, and—fourth in the list—structure.[6]

On the threshold of the thirties came a small book by G. L. Coyle, oriented in the direction of social work, entitled *Social Process in Organized Groups.* As a group emerges within the community, certain of the relationships set up between its members tend to assume a more permanent character; structure consists of those relatively permanent forms of relationships by which the purpose of the group is to be attained. This illustrates the psychological interpretation of structure, which is said to assume its particular form in response to functional demands, though it in turn modifies function.[7] The psychological factor is also emphasied in E. Sapir's article, "Groups," in the *Encyclopedia of the Social Sciences,* which appeared in 1932. Any group is constituted by the fact that there is some interest which holds its members together.[8] In the same year E. E. Eubank, in his *The Concepts of Sociology,* noting that after the work of Herbert Spencer and L. F. Ward the "constructional aspect" of human society received smaller stress, goes on to say that, while attention to forms is of recent years being distinctly subordinated to attention to activities and processes, so long as society is centered about the associated life of mankind, it must in large measure be a study of the forms that association takes. He lists three concepts as of pivotal emphasis in sociology: first, structure, then society—i.e., humanity, and group—i.e., "lesser society."[9] Structure is emphasized here, but the whole treatment is in terms of concepts.

Going on in the thirties, E. S. Bogardus, like Brown, is outstanding for his emphasis on groups, but declares that, in the deepest sense, sociology is the study of the social processes of group life.[10] There is no index entry for "structure." D. Sanderson, in an article on "Group Description," in 1938, enumerates five major sets of characteristics for the description of a group. Structure is the fifth.[11]

A few years before the works last mentioned, the first edition of a well-known book by R. M. MacIver was already in the field, but in later revisions it can be traced beyond the thirties. The title at first was *Society, Its Structure and Changes.* In later titles the word "Structure" does not appear.[12] Throughout the editions, societal groups are recognized, especially in the distinction between communities and associations,[13] and there is emphasis on societal

[6] B. Warren Brown, *Social Groups* (Chicago: The Faithorn Company, 1926), pp. 3, 8.

[7] G. L. Coyle, *Social Process in Organized Groups,* Contemporary Society Series (New York: R. R. Smith, 1930), pp. 78, 94.

[8] E. Sapir, "Groups," in E. R. A. Seligman and Alvin Johnson, eds., *Encyclopedia of the Social Sciences,* Vol. VII (New York: The Macmillan Co., 1932), p. 179.

[9] E. E. Eubank, *The Concepts of Sociology* (Boston and New York: D. C. Heath and Company, 1932), pp. 121 f.

[10] E. S. Bogardus, *Sociology* (New York: The Macmillan Co., 1932), p. 15.

[11] D. Sanderson, "Group Description," *Social Forces,* XVI (1938), 309 ff; XVII (1938), 196 ff.

[12] R. M. MacIver, *Society, Its Structure and Changes* (New York: Ray Long and Richard R. Smith, 1931); *Society, A Textbook of Sociology* (New York: Farrar and Rinehart, 1937); and C. H. Page, *Society, An Introductory Analysis* (New York: Rinehart and Company, 1949). Hereafter referred to as MacIver, 1931, MacIver, 1937, and MacIver, 1949, respectively.

[13] MacIver, 1931, pp. 9 ff; MacIver, 1937, pp. 8 ff; MacIver, 1949, pp. 8 ff.

processes, especially as those processes are psychological. Typical of the first emphasis is the statement that society exists only as a time sequence, a changing equilibrium of present relationships. It is a process, not a product.[14] The latest revision adds that as soon as the process ceases the product disappears.[15] The second, the psychological, emphasis is illustrated by the statement that interests create social formations beyond and outside the range of individual associations.[16] In the first two books we find that "the social structure exists only as the creation of mentality; behind the differentiated form lies always the differentiating mind." At the corresponding place in the 1949 edition[17] this sentence has been omitted.

In 1937 came the first and in 1949 the second edition of Talcott Parsons' *The Structure of Social Action.* Neither edition affords much in the way of a structural theory of society; the later is especially psychological, not to say epistemological and phenomenalistic. Parsons' interest is in the development of a voluntaristic theory. He cites Znaniecki's four schemata in which the same facts about man in society may be stated. Social action, which is listed first, may be regarded as more elementary. Social groups—suggesting societal structures—are third in the list.[18]

In 1945, L. Wilson, in the volume cited above, contributed a detailed historical account of "The Sociography of Groups." In the same volume, Znaniecki contributed a chapter on "Social Organization and Institution." He says it is impossible to introduce logical order into the terminological chaos. Wilson reports Znaniecki as using four leading schemata—social actions, social relations, social persons, and social groups. His treatment, again, is markedly psychological; we must begin by finding out what societies are in the experience of their own members.[19]

The subordination of structure to process, specifically mental process, is still more evident in R. K. Merton's *Social Theory and Social Structure.* The first edition appeared in 1949, the second in 1957. His project is "functional analysis," functionalism being interpretation of data by establishing their consequences for larger structures in which they are implicated. While he admits that structure affects function, and function affects structure, in his paradigm for functional analysis, listing 11 factors or concepts which are relevant, the concepts of structural context or structural constraint are numbered 8, and in his provisional list of 26 group-properties the ecological structure of the group is numbered 23. He has much to say about reference groups and examines a few structural elements which are involved in reference-group behavior, conceived as social process, among them observability or visibility. A basic character of social structure is seen when a particular social status involves an array

[14] MacIver, 1931, p. 391; MacIver, 1937, p. 394.

[15] MacIver, 1949, p. 511.

[16] MacIver, 1937, p. 269.

[17] MacIver, 1931, p. 434; MacIver, 1937, p. 496; Cf. MacIver, 1949, p. 511.

[18] T. Parsons, *The Structure of Social Action* (Glencoe, Ill.: Free Press, 1949; New York: McGraw-Hill Company, 1957), pp. 30, 46, 753.

[19] F. Znaniecki, "Social Organization and Institution," in Gurvitch and Moore, eds., *op. cit.*, pp. 172, 182. Cf. Wilson, *ibid.*, p. 140.

of associated roles. Eventually "a patterned arrangement of role sets, status sets, and status sequences can be held to comprise the social structure."[20]

F. H. Allport, in his *Theories of Perception and the Concept of Structure,* published in 1955, also shows a decidedly psychological emphasis. He speaks of the "aggregation of individuals (that is, their behavior structure)" into collective or social aggregates. The terms "individual" and "group" are said not to refer to agents or even to entities, but to become merely rough signposts to help us locate and chart the precise structurings concerned.[21]

Mention should be made of a book in which certain societal structures are more clearly recognized than in most of the foregoing; it is as if a more philosophical outlook corrected some of the myopia of the sociologists. The book is Baker Brownell's *The Human Community,* which appeared in 1950. Function, he says, is an aspect of structure. A community, after all, is a number of men; it is "inalterably people." It is a structural concept which often may be exemplified in small groups, but is not limited to them. The community is corrupted by universals. Still, the interpretation is psychological; the community is said to be human behavior in which values emerge and take form because of the nature of value itself. And the effect of the book is almost lost because of the prejudice against urban life, and the despairing word that "the stench of decay is all about us."[22]

III.

Without attempting further to thresh around in the maze of conflicting theories, our suggestion is that we try, less psychologically, though necessarily somewhat abstractly, to think of societal structures first, and of societal processes as going on within them. This brings us to the second of our quotations from the wisdom of the ancients.

With all its archaic features and defects, no statement about societal structures is more perceptive than a famous passage in the Confucian *Great Learning.*

> The ancients who wished to manifest illustrious virtue throughout the world, first ordered well their own states. Wishing to order well their own states, they first regulated their own families. Wishing to regulate their own families, they first cultivated their own selves. Wishing to cultivate their own selves, they first rectified their own minds. Wishing to rectify their own minds, they first sought for absolute sincerity in their thoughts. Wishing for absolute sincerity in their thoughts, they first extended their knowledge. This extension of knowledge consists in the investigation of things. Things being investigated, only then did their thought become sincere. Their thought being sincere, only then did their mind become rectified. Their mind being rectified, only then

[20] R. K. Merton, *Social Theory and Social Structure* (Glencoe, Ill.: Free Press, 1949; 2d ed., 1957), pp. 47, 50 ff., 281 ff., 336, 369 f.

[21] F. H. Allport, *Theories of Perception and the Concept of Structure* (New York: John Wiley & Sons, Inc., 1955), pp. 662–664.

[22] B. Brownell, *The Human Community, Its Philosophy and Practice for a Time of Crisis* (New York: Harper & Brothers, 1950), pp. 13, 55, 197, 204, 223 ff., 227, 295.

did their selves become cultivated. Their selves being cultivated, only then did their families become regulated. Their families being regulated, only then did their states become rightly governed. Their states being rightly governed, only then could the world be at peace.[23]

The schema could be diagrammed structurally in a series of circles, not necessarily concentric. As a process, it is first centrifugal and then centripetal. Taken along with our first quotation, from Aristotle, the suggestion, in brief, is that without claiming utter precision we may fairly say that *society is zoned.* Of course, something of all this has appeared in the West,[24] but it is likely to be so overlaid with other considerations that it is lost to view.

When, spurred by the ancients, we come to look at society, whether Eastern or Western, some structural elements are not hard to discern. To detect them most clearly, however, it is well to think first of the situation as it was, let us say, in the sixteenth century, when the civilization of Asia and Europe was much more uniform and homogeneous than it came to be in more recent centuries, largely because of Western mechanizations. To get the picture in its broad outlines we may also disregard distinctions like that between *Gemeinschaft* and *Gesellschaft,*[25] and between communities and associations.

As of the sixteenth century and basically ever since, the structure of society appears in a series of successive zones which are successively larger groupings of individuals. As Brownell says, the community is unalterably people. The first grouping, everywhere acknowledged, is one form or another of the family. With or without clans and tribes, the next inclusive grouping is often regarded as the neighborhood. Then there is the small village or the larger town; then, successively, larger groupings, district, state, nation, alliance of nations, great regional cultures—in the sixteenth century, the Hindu-Muslim complex in India and Christendom in the West. And finally, though dimly apprehended in the sixteenth century and still sometimes hard to see, "above all nations, humanity."

Such, we maintain, is the basic configuration, the societal structure, which later changes have often modified. But this, so far, takes little account of the concomitant processes. To deal with these, we find, first, that the structures indicated are marked, respectively, by characteristic ethical interests. Speaking with high generality, let us say that these interests are, first, eugenic, with the word defined in a broad sense to include the bringing of children into the world and provision for their health and competence; second, economic, the securing of food and shelter, with various emoluments; third, political, the establishment and maintenance of various controls over these processes; and, fourth, what we shall call euthenic, the attempts to repair various deficiencies or malfunctionings. Speaking broadly, the last-named interests include the

[23] *Ta Hsüeh* (The *Great Learning*) (4–5). See Fung Yu-lan, *A Short History of Chinese Philosophy* (New York: The Macmillan Co., 1945), pp. 181 f.

[24] E.g., MacIver, 1937, p. 133.

[25] See F. Tönnies, *Gemeinschaft und Gesellschaft, Grundbegriffe der reinen Soziologie* (1887) (Berlin: Karl Curtius, 1912).

curing of disease, public education, charities, and corrections. Granting some lack of precision, these great ethical concerns can be correlated with societal structures.

Thus, the family is primarily the locus of eugenic interests and of the rules of intersexual morality. If not the single family, or the neighborhood, then the local community was once the locus of economic interests; even today, most of us live where we work or where someone on whom we depend works. The community, the district, the state, the nation are the loci of successively broadly based political procedures and controls. The political groupings, largely because of their ties with territory, are relatively easy to discern.

This, as we said, is fairly clear as regards the sixteenth century, but much has happened since. Populations have increased and spread, and are still increasing, if not spreading. Along with them, with increasing mechanization, the harnessing of steam and electricity, and the prospective harnessing of atomic power, the economic interests have spread altogether beyond their original zonal boundaries and have all but swamped families, communities, and nations by their insistence. Partly because of their insistence, it is still hard to specify the interest which has for its locus humanity. Economically and politically for this inclusive zone, all is confusion and dispute. Ethically and religiously, humanity is embryonic. The shadows are relieved by one ray of hope: culturally, aesthetically, scientifically, we have the beginnings of mutual regard and co-operation. Peruvian pottery, Bali dancers, Soviet violinists, touring orchestras, international art exhibits, and scores of congresses and conferences —including this one—bear witness to this trend.

IV.

Particularly by the aid of the notion of integration, it is easy to argue here for a process of evolution. We are tempted to picture an amalgamation of families into villages or tribes, of tribes into confederations, and of these becoming unified in larger and larger political units. There is, in fact, a good deal of evidence for such a process as Giddings describes,[26] but we can never get an adequate picture of the process until, granting that we retain the notion of evolution, we see that integration, as Herbert Spencer would say, is complemented by differentiation,[27] and that evolution is, as has been said, convergent.[28] Many authors have seen this; it is no great news, but it is of huge importance for societal structure.

The structural fact is that in the groups larger than the family or neighborhood or small village, secondary groups, subgroups, are differentiated and in their way penetrate the primary groups. Face-to-face grouping[29] is in that way perpetuated. Many communities and practically all States and nations are so

[26] F. H. Giddings, *Principles of Sociology* (New York: The Macmillan Co., 1902), pp. 73, 158 ff., 258.
[27] H. Spencer, *First Principles* (London: Williams and Norgate, 1862), chap. xv.
[28] W. F. Ogburn, *op. cit.*, 1927, pp. 87 f.
[29] C. H. Cooley, *Social Organization* (New York: Charles Scribner's Sons, 1927), p. 23.

large that they are unmanageable; we cannot deal adequately or directly with them, or, perhaps better said, they cannot deal adequately with themselves. In each case, some essential function must be delegated to one or another subgroup, which retains its face-to-face structure and function. Like other features of societal structure, this is often obscured, particularly by a widely used abstraction. Naturally, there has been a good deal of discussion of "social institutions." These are said to include, for example, marriage, property, war, slavery, primogeniture, priesthood, kingship, etc., and problems of society are discussed in such terms. When these are examined as they are actually found, each of them, except property, is seen to be or to involve a more or less simple grouping of individuals. Marriage is typically a grouping of two individuals; it is a union of two persons, which Simmel takes as the simplest societal group.[30] War and slavery are huge groupings which are to be deplored; kingship and priesthood are terms for groupings which are being tried in the balances. Property is not a grouping of individuals, at least as long as individuals are not lost in living merely for their possessions; property is an arrangement of materials, if not insubstantial roles, pertaining to one or another individual, group, or subgroup.

Structurally, as we seek to discern structure, it would seem that these subgroups of individuals are the true "institutions";[31] it is they who are "in-stituted" in the larger groups. Follow for a moment the differentiations within the various zones larger than the family. We cannot deal adequately with the world-wide burgeoning of economic structures and processes—hence we have, let us say, the neighborhood store, or, in these fantastic latter days, the suburban supermarket. We cannot deal adequately with the whole city; hence, at least since ancient Athens, we have the council or the court, and in more recent days the town or city council and the municipal court, in which, if we do not deal with the city, the city deals with us. On the progressively larger scale, there are state legislatures and national congresses and parliaments, composed of relatively few men who meet face to face and to whom we delegate more or less authority. The same principle may be observed operative in still broader groups which are difficult to observe in their entirety; it is no wonder that MacIver calls society invisible.[32] We cannot comprehend all the marvelous data which Nature and society present to us; hence we have, with all their failings, schools, universities, and academies. Humanity speaks to us in the humanities and, if we know how to listen, in the technologies. We cannot have access to or contemplate all the beauty of the world; hence we have societies of fine arts, subgroups which maintain the treasure houses of our museums. And, beyond all this, we cannot unaided face the whole mystery of things; hence we have temples and synagogues and churches on a scale where something of the face-to-face quality of the family is preserved. Where euthenic processes are necessary to remedy deficiencies or repair damage, these, too, are

30 G. Simmel, *Soziologie* (Leipzig: Duncker und Humblot, 1908), pp. 80 ff.
31 Contra, Eubank, *op. cit.*, p. 156, and references.
32 MacIver, 1937, p. 143; cf. MacIver, 1949, p. 136.

specialized and delegated to various organizations, boards, and committees. Such secondary groups or subgroups, we argue, are the true institutions; if this goes too much against traditions and common usage, they may be designated by the neat compromise term, "institutionalized groups."[33]

V.

The societal structures which are correlated with societal processes can be rendered still more evident if we examine some of the "zones" in more detail. Particularly we need to study the economic data, though, as we said, they transgress the sixteenth century's zonal boundaries. Here again, we cannot hope for utter precision or avoid overlapping, though we may account for much of this by the fact that the larger groups work their less complicated representative subgroups back into society on a scale commensurate with the face-to-face groups of the early zones. With these provisions, we may say that what men are doing is zoned or subzoned. When these subzones are studied in their natural setting, the natural environment, they are something more than metaphorical; there is in them a trace of natural stratification, not dependent on social privilege or degree of economic achievement. To sketch or suggest the subzones we shall need to mention ten or more, and these without hoping for a complete account.

1. First, there are those procedures which are merely *extractive*. To say nothing of men's indispensable use of air and water, there are undertakings in which they merely appropriate, with relatively little change, things which the environment provides. Primitive tribes gather food or hunt and fish. Miners dig in the ground.

2. Next, the environment is utilized in activities which are *productive*. These include agriculture and animal breeding, in which what the environment provides is selected and caused to increase and multiply. Everything from now on is dependent on these activities, which we call extractive and productive.

3. Closely allied with the foregoing are almost countless *processings*. We extract air and water freely from the environment, but air is processed all the way from the air-conditioned Lascaux cavern to the pressurized cabins of the jet planes, and water is filtered or chlorinated. Everywhere raw materials must be cleaned, shaped, combined in manifold ways, in the intricate processes of manufacture by the aid of animal, water, steam, electric, and atomic power, and the beginnings of utilization of solar energy.

4. The products extracted, produced, and processed must be *transported* from one societal group to another by various familiar means.

5. Closely allied with transportation is *distribution*—in a society of some complexity, the function of the often excoriated but indispensable "middle man."

[33] See Gurvitch and Moore, eds., *op. cit.*, p. 212.

6. As all this goes on, the need for *communication* increases, and some individuals engage in these activities, which cut across the boundaries which we have indicated or adumbrated.

7. Other functions and activities cut across the boundaries. Prominent among them are processes of *maintenance*, particularly of the machinery necessary for the operations noted above or to be noted presently.

8. As economic activities pass beyond their early boundaries of family or neighborhood or village, the devices of *exchange and finance* are contrived to facilitate the flow.

9. Gradually, too, *controls* have to be devised and imposed, and manifold subgroups are formed, so that officials and administrators come to operate more or less in accordance with law. Armed forces are organized and equipped.

10. Looking back over such zones and subzones, we find various groups of persons whose function it is to *enhance or correct* the above more or less workaday activities. Many of us work hard to entertain the rest of us. Historians assemble and interpret the data of the past. Teachers impart what they can to the younger generations. Research men, inventors, and explorers press into the unknown. Artists try to disentangle some beauties from the drabness of the world. Humanitarians try to stir the consciences of their fellow humans. Leaders of the religions try to penetrate the mystery of things.

11. To come anywhere near completing the picture, it should be added that scattered through all the groups or subgroups are associations based on occupational or professional or recreational interests of many sorts and many sizes.

Thus the plot thickens, but the plot is one of structures and processes. Each of us, in private or in some representative or delegated capacity, moves every day in some of these groups or among them. The family requires the carpenter and the plumber. The teacher makes a loan at the bank. The grocer is elected to the legislature. Someone gets an award and travels abroad. A select few are beginning to be groomed for space travel. There are not merely such individual, small-scale movements to and fro but also massive movements of great groups, acting through their representatives. Economic and political interests get more and more entangled; governments impose price controls or tariffs or set up foreign aid. Labor and capital enter more or less openly into politics. Economic and political and euthenic interests become entangled; a community cannot pay for its free schools or freeways without federal aid. Races blend or antagonize one another. Religions—that is, great cultural groups, carrying subgroups with them—sanction or fail to sanction economic and political and euthenic goods or evils. Here, as so often, the processes obscure the structures, and everything is complicated by psychology.

VI.

Let us try to look a little more closely at some of the data of psychology, data which the sociologists are inclined to take over from the psychologists without stopping to analyze them, or to see whether the psychologists have analyzed them or not. Time and again, as we said, societal structures are treated psychologically, as if the structuration itself were the work of minds. These interpretations commonly cite men's needs, wants, interests, and values. There is general agreement about needs and wants, but interests and values are hardly given adequate scrutiny. It is obvious enough that each individual, whatever his group or subgroup, works for some more or less clearly apprehended end or number of ends or purposes, but the structures which are involved in these processes are frequently obscured. There are various reasons for this. First, the operations of minds, especially when they are at all complex, are so out of reach of either observation or experiment that they seem to be intangible, and in anything intangible the process tends to be more conspicuous than the structure. Again, there is a widely prevalent tendency to rely on abstractions and to hypostasize or reify "values," make them overly mysterious, and either to rhapsodize about them or, not without emotion, to deplore them for their emotive appeals.

For a matter-of-fact psychology, or, let us say, a psychology not dissected away from neuropsychology, there need be no great mystery about values; all that is necessary is not to confuse a *value* and a *valuation*. A valuation is easily thought of as a process; we need to consider it in its structural aspect. Beginning well back in the evolutionary sequence, let us say that along with the tactile receptors, whereby objects are touched or smelled, the higher organisms are equipped with distance receptors, eyes and ears, which by means of light or sound waves can receive stimuli from objects with which they are not in immediate contact. These distance receptors are of great importance for survival. By means of them a desired or a dangerous object can be detected while it is still at a distance, and the requisite adjustment can be made in the temporal and spatial interval involved. The animal, by what Sherrington distinguishes as precurrent reactions, can go toward the desired object until in a consummatory reaction the object is attained.[34] Similar adjustments occur where an object is to be attacked or avoided. Precurrent and consummatory reactions together constitute what may be called means-end complexes.

Next come processes of conditioning, whereby one object can be substituted for another, or where a sign can function in place of an object. Thus language begins, and facilitates division of labor in a societal group. The whole flock of crows, let us say, does not see the hunter approaching, but the crow on the margin of the flock, perhaps the "sentinel," does see the hunter, takes flight, and, by a cry, which serves as a substitute for the hunter stimulus, induces the rest of the flock to take flight. As experience develops in human groups, language becomes more and more complex and articulate. It is, of course, a process; syntax or grammar reflects its structure.

As experience and behavior become still more complex, distance reception with its precurrent reactions involves circular responses. That is to say, before the final consummatory adjustment to the stimulus object can be effected, in-

[34] C. S. Sherrington, *The Integrative Action of the Nervous System* (New Haven: Yale University Press, 1947), pp. 326, 329, 332.

termediate adjustments have to be made, and intervening obstacles removed. Each step in this process serves as a stimulus for the succeeding step. With or without feedback, one obstacle after another is passed; finally, with the removal or overcoming of the penultimate obstacle, the way is clear for the consummatory reaction which with closure concludes that turn of events.

In the meantime, fragments of experience-behavior come by "redintegration" to serve as stimuli. Especially after the development of language, this makes possible abstraction and concomitant generalization. An abstraction, "dragged away from" its concrete setting, loses its moorings and easily drifts into a generalization indefinite in range and often too hastily called a universal. In the process here studied, ends which at first referred merely to objects discerned at a distance give way to abstractions which, if they are relatively difficult, remote, and actually or potentially approved by the group, constitute ideals. Ideals such as justice are often called values, but due attention to the sequence of structures and processes just indicated inclines us to prefer the term "valuations."

A glance at the terminology commonly employed and understood for the analogous and simpler process of perception helps in the argument. We have no great difficulty in distinguishing a perception, a perceiver, perceiving, a perceived object, a perceivable object, and, let us add, a more elusive "perceptual quality." Correspondingly, we may well distinguish a valuation, a valuer, valuing, a valued object, a valuable object, and, let us now add, "value." The last-named should not be used indiscriminately for any or all of the preceding; it should be restricted to mean the essential quality of a valuation. It has to be apprehended inwardly, subjectively, introspectively, intuitively. Objective measures for it may be devised; the question will be: Is what they measure valuational quality or some of its concomitants.

So, psychologically, what is happening in our societal procedures is a reciprocal adjustment of valuations to situations—Confucius might have said, of one set of structures to another. The activities of men, as they join or leave one subgroup or another, are registered, if they are not regulated, by these psychological valuations. Are they merely registered, or are they also, at least in part, regulated? This is the problem of freedom, and beyond the scope of the present paper. We can say that valuations structured in time register or determine men's groupings structured in space.

VII.

In this conference on Eastern and Western philosophies it is peculiarly in place to notice the roles of structure and process in the respective cultures and the philosophies which interpret them. The roles become clear when extreme cases are cited. The long-enduring caste system in India comes at once to mind as one of the clearest examples; it should be noted that ideally Hindu society was organized, not merely in castes and subcastes, but also in the four stages of life; the *varṇas,* combined with the *āśramas,* blended structures and processes in such ways that, when the prescriptions were followed, each individual knew where he stood and what he was to do in the respective groups and subgroups. In China, the family system imposed both structure and process upon the generations. Concerning the Chinese mainland, now cut off from us, one hesitates to speak, but from this distance it looks as if the communes are a grimly compulsive structure which must have profound effect on the processes of Chinese life. As for the West, there is small need to detail the role of change and process. There are enough automobiles in the United States to take the whole population on the gargantuan excursion seriously proposed by those who plan, if they do not envisage, the evacuation of the cities in time of danger. Automation, coming by leaps and bounds, is the industrial revolution in reverse; instead of pressing individuals into the factories, it is edging them out. The rural population is being drained off into towns and cities, and the cities are almost exploding into suburbs. Bound books are giving way to paperbacks. Universities are beginning to teach credit courses by television. And so it goes. There are, of course, comparable changes in Eastern civilizations. Primitive Buddhism's account of the world was founded on change—"All the constituents of being are transitory"—but primitive Buddhism never envisaged the structures which would exemplify the process. Heraclitus of Ephesus lived long ago on the threshold of Western civilization. Declaring that "everything flows," he deposited his book, they say, in the temple of Great Diana, but now even the successor of that temple is a few fragments of marble in a swamp.

VIII.

From such a study as this it should begin to appear that one reason for the baffling confusion in present-day ethics, Eastern and Western, is that sociology and social philosophy have not sufficiently emphasized the intricate relationships of structures and processes in society. The very intricacy makes it hard to distinguish the factors or aspects. The threads of the social network, where they are not tangled almost beyond hope, are always closely interwoven, and a change in the fabric at one point changes it at other points, not always for the best. To solve one problem is to raise another. Automation in industry increases the output of the makers of machines, but throws workers out of work. Reforms in anything from commercialized vice to government spending dislodge some members of the societal structure. The question is always: What structures should be made to give way to what processes? Or, what processes will remedy the defects in what structures?

With such concrete detail as we have been able to consider filled in, let us go back to our abstractions, to certain abstract and general relations of structures and processes which in one way or another apply to societal situations. One clue to those relations appears in what we may call a time differential. Everything is in process; everything changes, but things measured in a given frame do not all change at the same rate. Some component structures shift more rapidly than others, and leave more slowly changing component structures behind. The latter linger where they are left, and, accumulating, constitute modifications of structure.[35] Structure, let us say, is slowed process; process is accelerated structure. Corollaries follow. Anything which slows a process piles up structure; anything which piles up structure slows some process; anything which loosens a structure hastens some process; anything which hastens a process loosens some structure.

There can be no doubt that some structures are so rigid that they hamper the free and valuable flow of process. When we come to concrete examples we find room for controversy, but let us hazard the opinion that racial groupings in the southern United States, with their resistance to integration in the schools, and certain linguistic minorities in India, with their insistence upon linguistic bases for political organization, furnish two examples of such rigidity. Other examples may be seen in official and ecclesiastical traditions and policies with regard to divorce in England, and in the refusal of some nations—perhaps, in a test case, of all—to submit to United Nations over-all directives. "Cultural lag"[36] is familiar in social theories and practices.

On the other hand, consider processes which, as far as one can judge, lack structures adequate to implement them. Utopian projects are of this sort. Sometimes the process is as yet only mental, a dreaming in the mind of a dreamer, but it is nevertheless a process, and the lack of structure is patent and critical. One of the great questions of the day is whether communism can become permanently structured. Whatever is to be said about pacifism and non-violence, it is clear that they are not adequately structured in the world as of now. Immature nationalisms in various parts of the world insist on striving for independence, but many revolutions prove to be abortive. But let us remind ourselves again that ethics is not an exact science. Along with cultural lags which are hard to overcome, there are "cultural leaps" which carry with them some of mankind's highest hopes. Who can tell the true prophets from the false, or determine under whose banners to enlist?

IX.

When we come to sum up this study, we find that the authors whom we have cited furnish some particular insights into the facts of societal structure. Examples are the time differential by which processes, so to speak, deposit structures, and the fact that a societal group tends to be "nucleated," especially around emerging leaders, and to have distinctive features at its borders. Some authors have favored and some have opposed the definition of institutions in human rather than abstract terms.[37]

More generally, as suggestions coming more directly from the study, we may put first the point that the analysis offers a way of stating problems. Whether the solutions are apparent or obscure, at all events a clear emphasis on societal

[35] Cf. J. Dewey, *Experience and Nature* (Chicago: Open Court Publishing Company, 1926), p. 72.
[36] W. F. Ogburn, *op. cit.*, p. 200.
[37] G. L. Coyle, *op. cit.*, pp. 95, 111.

structures offers a frame or mold into which solutions may be poured. The problems may be stated, not so much in terms of psychological processes or logical relations or abstractions about interests and values as in human terms, involving groups made up of men and women and children in various configurations and adjustments. For example, take the problem of defining "the public interest." Such an approach as this should make it clear that there are several, if not many, "publics" of various sizes and that they have many, many different interests. When these are viewed concretely, "the public interest" is seen to be a highly abstract and general term which, like other remotely abstract and general terms, offers a point of view from which data may be considered without coming too closely to grips with them. Something is gained when we turn from reification to reality. Humanizing our problems does something to offset otherwise overly academic discussions and inadequately based conclusions. The study may go further and suggest a way of solving problems: dissolve the hard groups by working on individuals. Here is a task for education and personal example.

Secondly, our analysis may suggest a definition of liberalism. In a world where conservatives cherish structure and radicals throw themselves into processes, liberalism, in economics or politics or religion or anywhere else, is an attempt to adjust a set of persistent structures to a set of insistent processes. True, this definition is not precise; it may still be asked, What structures? What processes? What adjustments? But liberalism, like liberty itself, is by its very nature not precise. Its genius is to be indefinite. Anything which can be precisely defined, we may say, is thereby confined, and to be confined is by just so much to be deprived of liberty. This helps to show how hard it is for any liberal movement to formulate its platform or its policies. It is no wonder that democracy means one thing in one system and another in another. It is no wonder that Protestantism ramifies into hundreds of denominations or sects, and liberal tendencies in Hinduism and Buddhism are marked by similar ramifications.

Above all, how may we hope to find answers to the problems of society? The literature of sociology shows that empirical investigations are being pushed further and further, but, as the intricate data are more and more disentangled, the problem of putting them together again in any effective combination becomes more and more baffling. Rationalism may come to the rescue of empiricism, but cannot keep up with its output or provide adequate answers for its sharp questions. It looks as if we must turn to pragmatism, and rely on answers which may be said, albeit only provisionally, to "work." Pragmatism's emphasis on change, however, tends to deliver us all to the mercies of process. We must insist that structures are essential, and that pragmatism as a method or procedure applies in a structured world which pragmatism does not constitute or create. Pragmatism is practical, and in its place indispensable, but there are lingering questions about it. Pluralism lurks in the offing, and pluralism is hardly an answer to problems. It is more like a statement of them.

Should we mention one other possibility, whether or not we like it, and whether or not we know how to use it? Is there a word to be said for intuition? Intuitive solutions of societal problems are open to questions which haunt conferences like this and might haunt many others. One thing at least may be said here: intuition, the seizing together of large arrays of data with respect to their value-quality, granting that it is possible, is not a disembodied process, floating in a world that never was. It is, rather, an adjustment of one comprehensive set of structures, the structures of human personality, to another comprehensive set of structures, the structures of society, or, in still larger problems, the structures of the universe. Perhaps, if we knew fully how to develop our empirical and rational and pragmatic methods and resources, the answers to societal problems would be seen to be, not altogether in observation or experiment or thought or activity or feeling taken one by one, but in the union of them all, which is *valued and valuing life*. And life is most fully itself when it is the process proper to interrelated structured human groups. In life, structures and processes are maintained in a labile equilibrium. Perhaps this affords a formula and an ideal for societal adjustments.

At all events, let us not forget those words of Aristotle and Confucius. Together they tell us that, though a constructive ethics is not a natural science, it can be developed into a naturalistic discipline.

S. K. SAKSENA

Relation of Philosophical Theories to the Practical Affairs of Men

I. PRACTICAL AFFAIRS AND RELIGIOUS AND SCIENTIFIC BELIEFS

Before we inquire into the relation which philosophical theories as a class may have with the practical affairs of men, it may be worth while to ask what it is which generally guides and determines our conduct. The answer would probably be that it is by our beliefs, religious or secular, that we generally live and act. As the *Gītā* says, "Man is of the nature of his faith: what his faith is, that, verily, he is."[1] These beliefs may or may not be true, but, in the last analysis, it is these true or false beliefs which determine our conduct. While beliefs may be acquired in different ways, their chief sources are either the religious experiences of mankind, transmitted through theological knowledge, or the scientific knowledge of the day. These two sources of our beliefs cover almost the entire range of man's activities.

1. *Inadequacy of scientific and religious beliefs.*

While the above two sources of our beliefs, religious and scientific, are practically the originators and modifiers of our conduct, there is a philosophical unsatisfactoriness about each of them. Scientific beliefs, which have the merit of objective validity, have, nevertheless, a grave defect inasmuch as they do not refer to man's deepest questions regarding the meaning and purpose of life, nor do they deal with questions of valuation and worth. Scientific knowledge, which deals with the true, ignores the good, and theological beliefs, which have the opposite merit of being practically useful by virtue of their relevance to the practical aspirations of man, have the great defect of lacking objective validity

[1] *Bhagavad Gītā* XVII. 3, in S. Radhakrishnan and Charles A. Moore, eds., *A Source Book in Indian Philosophy* (Princeton: Princeton University Press, 1957), p. 155. All quotations cited from Indian sources are taken from this volume, hereafter referred to as *Source Book*.

and rational appeal. In other words, while theological beliefs are practical without being always true, scientific beliefs are true without being practical in the sense that, while they ascertain for us the relationship of ends and means, they do not tell us anything of the ends to be pursued for us. The realization that scientific knowledge and beliefs are not adequate since they do not touch even the fringe of man's problems of life and that the religious beliefs of one individual are of no use to another unless they percolate through his own rational thinking leaves the thoughtful man with a sense of vacuity and despair in the matter of the proper guidance of his life. While some have made their peace with science or religion, a large number are unable to do so. Nor is the mental vacuum thus created intellectually tolerable. The question, therefore, is: Can we find in philosophy grounds for satisfactory belief-formations and, if so, with what success and how?

2. *Contemporary skepticism about philosophical knowledge.*

It is obvious that the task of philosophy is more difficult than that of science or religion; for, while philosophy is unable to accept the unproven beliefs of theology, it is not aided by science in its quest for the good and the valuable. Nevertheless, philosophical knowledge, if it is to fill the gap, must combine the virtues of both science and theology without the defects of either. It must furnish us with beliefs about the real nature of the world and the meaning and the purpose of our lives which will not only possess the subjective certainty of the religious consciousness but also the objective validity of the sciences.

A glance at the balance sheet of contemporary philosophical performance with special reference to its practical utility will no doubt show that philosophy has drifted far away from life and that men no longer look to it for guidance in their daily lives. Deprived of both the subjective certainty of theological knowledge and of the objective certainty of the sciences, philosophical knowledge today seems to have surrendered its role of providing men with any fundamental or basic system of beliefs to live by, leaving men to be guided in their practical affairs by such beliefs as they may chance to have or not to have. Russell, in this respect the most pessimistic of modern philosophers, says, "To teach how to live without certainty . . . is perhaps the chief thing that philosophy, in our age, can still do for those who study it."[2] This opinion of philosophy and philosophical knowledge by one of the greatest philosophers of the age reveals the extent to which the modern mind has despaired of philosophical knowledge. One hopes, however, that things are not as bad as that, and that Russell himself will admit that he is not without at least the belief that he should continue to behave and conduct himself according to his reason and conscience and be free to propagate his views irrespective of their consequences to himself and to his reputation. This itself is a rational belief which has not only guided Russell but also influenced a large number of his admirers and followers in this age of philosophic uncertainty. It may be true that our philos-

[2] Bertrand Russell, *A History of Western Philosophy* (New York: Simon and Schuster, 1945), p. xiv.

ophers have so far made only a negative contribution to our systems of beliefs, yet our philosophical beliefs or our lack of them is all that we as rational human beings have to depend upon and live by. In being contemptuous of the role of philosophy in the determination of our beliefs we should not forget that the contempt applies, not to philosophical knowledge as such, but only to particular varieties of it, which, by and large, may deserve the condemnation.

But there is no denying the fact that philosophy has today stepped down from its high calling and has been progressively withdrawing itself from the practical problems of life and straying into both a rarified realm and a stultifying method in which, by the very nature of the case, no conviction or faith is either possible or even desired. To quote Russell again, "The philosophy, therefore, which is to be genuinely inspired by the scientific spirit, must deal with somewhat dry and abstract matters, and must not hope to find an answer to the practical problems of life."[3] It appears that philosophy, now by ridiculing religion, now by imitating science, and in turn being ridiculed by both, has itself become ridiculous without being able to correct the faults of either. From ancient times to modern and from modern times to contemporary, the journey of philosophical reflection in the West has been, broadly speaking, from the "practical" to the "useless" and from the "useless" to the "nonsensical." This may appear as too unsympathetic an oversimplification, but the element of truth in it cannot be denied. There is little relation today between philosophical theories and the practical affairs of our lives, and such little relation as might seem to exist between political or economic theories, which have practical results, and their philosophical background is due more to the demands of respectability and propaganda than to any logical relation between them and their philosophical counterpart.

3. *Need of philosophical knowledge in the formation of beliefs.*

That philosophy should have come to such a predicament in the matter of providing certainties and conviction for the guidance of our daily life is regrettable and is certainly not in keeping with its best traditions throughout its history of more than twenty-five centuries. Philosophical reflection throughout the world was the earliest and has been the boldest effort of man's reason and thought to face the mystery and complexity of life and existence without passion or attachment to any particular creed or dogma. So long as man has an awakened mind whose energies and function exceed his biological and economic needs, there is no relinquishing of philosophical pursuit, which by nature must seek the real behind the apparent and not rest until man has attained to the highest truth and the destiny of his being. Man was, thus, never without a metaphysics or a philosophy about the world, or without some ideals for his life. The choice, for man, as Bradley said, has never been between metaphysics and no metaphysics but only between a good metaphysics and a bad

[3] Bertrand Russell, *Our Knowledge of the External World* (Chicago and London: The Open Court Publishing Company, 1929), p. 31.

metaphysics. He must have a metaphysics of life, of right and wrong, and must, from time to time, undertake a revision of this conceptual or ideal framework with which he necessarily thinks about the world. This drawing or the re-drawing, in the world of his thought, of the map of total reality and integrating it with his life, this ideational framework of the highest possible generality, which constitutes his metaphysics, is inevitable for him, for a thoughtful life is not possible without it. This is not to say that philosophical theories are merely inevitable and do not have their uses. The metaphysics of Hegel had a great effect on historical studies in the nineteenth century, and the philosophical ideas of the Renaissance were responsible for the political and social revolutions of the eighteenth century. Nor have scientific discoveries and religious faiths been without inspiration from metaphysical insights and presuppositions, as is evident from the lives of a number of scientists and saints. If the purpose and function of philosophy are understood properly, there is no reason philosophical theories and knowledge should lack conviction and fail to supply men with a rational and comprehensive system of beliefs for a better guidance of their lives. In decrying philosophy and philosophical knowledge we are prone to forget that we are criticizing thought by thought. If it is through our philosophical reasoning that we are critical of either theological or scientific knowledge, the same philosophical reasoning should also provide us with positive beliefs for the guidance of our lives. The alternative to philosophical beliefs is either to allow the practical affairs of our lives to be governed by the haphazard uncertainties of a skeptical age or to surrender our minds to men who have "power without knowledge" (the politicians), "faith without truth" (the theologians), or "knowledge without purpose" (the scientists). This would be a sign more of our mental regression than of our intellectual advancement.

There is still another reason philosophy should not only step in but also be specially fitted for the task of belief-formation for the guidance of life. Looking at the map of world thought today, we find that the unity of man and his being is torn into numerous separate, disintegrated, and autonomous fields of reason and passion, persuasion and coercion, simultaneously pulling him in mutually contradictory directions without at the same time supplying him with any integrated view of life or of the ends to be pursued. While knowledge in these separate fields is constantly expanding, man's belief and conviction are progressively receding, because truth and knowledge gained in one direction are negated and contradicted by knowledge acquired in another. Lack of unified knowledge weakens belief, and it is philosophical knowledge alone which can stand for comprehensive and unified knowledge. The need of a synoptic vision was never so imperative and urgent as it is today, for, if, in these days of increasing multiplicity of fields of narrower and narrower specialization, philosophy also is to succumb to the temptation of specialization, all hope of a unitary knowledge is lost. Philosophy or philosophical reflection, which is distinctive of man's nature, should, therefore, be resurrected from its present plight and helped to undertake and perform its proper function.

4. *Causes of general skepticism about philosophical knowledge.*

What is wrong with philosophy and philosophical knowledge today? Why does it fail to supply us with a system of beliefs to live by?

a. Lack of a synoptic outlook. The first cause of skepticism about our philosophical pursuit is that philosophy, in its subject-matter, has tended toward an increasing alienation from life. To be a philosopher is no longer to know anything about the business of life. It is always the other fellow, the non-philosopher, who is the expert in the art of living and who must take care of the philosopher's own problems of life. Knowing and living have become two separate compartments of life, so that a philosopher can live in a world of ideas and knowledge, while others inhabit a world of life quite unknown to the philosopher. Philosophy no longer means a philosophy of life but only analysis and clarification of terms and propositions which have no reference to beliefs or conduct. Its outlook is no longer either practical or synoptic. The tragedy of the theoretical or the abstract philosopher is that the end sought by him is often lost in the activity itself. Seeking itself comes to occupy the place of finding. His aim is no longer truth but knowing. This is a paradoxical situation but not quite unlike an abstract philosophic search. Little wonder, therefore, that philosophical pursuit should be devoid of conviction and inspire philosophers like the Buddha to declare: "The Tathāgata, O Vaccha, is free from all theories."[4] Knowledge for the sake of knowledge has never been the proper function of the philosophical pursuit. As the *Gītā* says, "Insight into the *end* of the knowledge of Truth—this is declared to be true knowledge, and all that is different from it is non-knowledge."[5] The true philosophical endeavor is not just one theoretical discipline among others but one supreme quest for the whole of truth, which is both known and lived in the soul of man. A philosophy which is not of life and practiced in life is barren. How can our philosophical theories inspire us to belief and action when we find philosophers who have made great intellectual strides in their theoretical fields suffer in their own daily lives from almost all the failings of common man? Philosophy should be no more divorced from life by reason of its rational approach than religion should be bereft of philosophical truth by virtue of its insistence on the life of realization.

b. Lack of an integralist epistemology. The other and more important reason which makes philosophical knowledge and theories unconvincing is what Charles Morris[6] has called its intellectual excessiveness and what I should prefer to call its intellectual exclusiveness. Here I refer to a fundamental defect in the epistemological belief of philosophy itself. It has been too long assumed by philosophers that man has one or more cognitive faculties such as sense, reason, and intuition, each of which separately and appropriate to its own nature and function reveals to him knowledge of the outside and the inside world. He has

[4] *Majjhima Nikāya* I. 483–488. *Source Book,* p. 290.
[5] *Bhagavad Gītā* XIII. 11. *Source Book,* p. 146. Italics mine.
[6] Charles Morris, *The Open Self* (New York: Prentice-Hall, Inc., 1948).

senses for external objects, reason for objects not to be grasped by the senses, and intuition for the reality not to be grasped by either. The common assumption about philosophical knowledge has been that reason alone is its cognitive apparatus and that whatever belongs to or comes through the realm of the heart, feeling, will, or vision is an unphilosophical blend. This analytic view of man and his epistemological tools is a great blunder, for, in reality, the integral cognitive-affective-conative man is never so completely abstracted as to be all sense without reason, or all reason without feeling. Even if he were so abstracted for a moment, we have no reason for thinking that the truth or the reality revealed to him by any one of his absolutely pure and exclusive apertures is for that reason more reliable. In fact, it should be the less trustworthy. While the atomistic view of the faculties of man stands condemned by modern psychology, it is not a little surprising that this analytic division of man still persists in philosophical discussions. What, then, should be the source of philosophical knowledge? It is neither sense, nor reason, nor intuition, but the whole of the man. Philosophy is the reaction of the whole of man to the whole of reality. Man is a spirit, an integral whole, consisting of his body, mind, intellect, passion, and will, and his reason alone can no more exhaust him than his animality can encompass his reason. Reason or rational thought is only a part of his being. Purely rational knowledge, therefore, militates against and contradicts the affirmations of the rest of a man's being and receives acceptance only by a corner of his self.

Moreover, to know is to believe in what one knows. It does not make sense to say that one knows something but does not believe in what one knows. What one believes in may not be true, but what one knows has to be believed in so long as that knowledge lasts. That seems to be true of all knowledge except philosophical knowledge. The question should therefore be asked as to why is it that, of all kinds of knowledge, only philosophical knowledge should lack conviction in what is thus known. Is it because of the object of philosophical knowledge or because of the method of philosophical knowledge or because of both? To a certain extent, it can be said that, since philosophical knowledge concerns itself with the ultimate origin and end of the whole of reality and wants to grasp it with man's finite mind, an ultimate skepticism about it is involved in the very nature of the rational situation. This may be so, but still there is no reason to suppose that in the ultimate scheme of things this rational skepticism is not overcome in an integral vision (*darśana*) within the philosophical endeavor itself, an integral vision such as was attempted by the earlier philosophies of India and the West.

The real misfortune of philosophy seems to have been that philosophers themselves have misunderstood the function and the purpose of philosophy. They have generally agreed in calling it a rational and intellectual search, and, today, when the results of this rational quest are before us in the form of philosophical skepticism and lack of any reliable system of philosophical beliefs, it is time that we re-examine our premises and presuppositions and begin anew.

As Montague says, "The problem of validating belief is intimately associated with the problem of ascertaining the sources of belief."[7] Philosophy, therefore, should not be conceived as merely a rational or intellectual quest, but a spiritual endeavor of the whole of a man's being. It is only of a knowledge born in the whole of a man's being that we can say that to know is to believe. In this way alone does a man acquire the additional authority and power to speak with the language of reality and fact. As the Yoga says: "Truth-bearing is, then, knowledge."[8] In the last analysis, it is this psychologically integral quality of the Indian epistemology which gives it an intuitive (or, technically, the *"sākṣātkāra"*) attitude, which Northrop calls an aesthetic twist and which it has never lost. According to Northrop, this integralist standpoint, or the necessity of a unified epistemic correlation between the subjective and the objective, has remained a characteristic, not only of the Hindu, the Buddhist, and the Jaina theories of philosophy and knowledge, but also of all Western philosophies which have not been purely speculative or concerned with abstractions alone.[9]

Closely related to the integralist theory of knowledge is the question of the immediacy of knowledge. When philosophical knowledge is not grounded in the direct experience of the whole of a man's being, it lacks a necessary union of the knower and the known. The distance that is thus produced by the separation of the two and the inevitable mediation of thought which thinks out the things are also not conducive to conviction and belief. In revealed or self-discovered knowledge the knower feels an identity with what he knows as true without any shadow of doubt. The case of scientific knowledge is similar. I do not think anyone will seriously maintain that scientific knowledge is either mediate knowledge or purely deductive. If scientific knowledge is a blend of many elements such as imagination, hypothesis, generalization, verification, and perception, it is at least the most integrated knowledge that we know of where the knower is so related to what is known that knowledge is equal to faith in what is thus known. And theological and scientific knowledge, which are responsible for our beliefs, have this characteristic in common: they both carry instant conviction. This may also be due to the fact that, in both cases, there is neither mediation between the knowing subject and the known reality, nor any dialectics of thought making doubt possible. In this they both differ from philosophical knowledge in which what is thus known can be doubted at the very moment of knowing and the truth of knowledge depends either on another knowledge or on something outside knowledge, and hence fails to carry conviction. Knowledge as we understand it today can hardly yield conviction or certainty about what is thus known unless a state of identity of the subjective and the objective is reached at some stage of our endeavor in knowing. As Bradley admits, "Ideal or perfect knowledge would not be anything like what we mean by knowledge, it would be more like feeling, in that the distinction between the knower and the known would have disappeared altogether,

[7] W. P. Montague, *The Ways of Knowing* (London: George Allen & Unwin Ltd., 1928), p. 34.
[8] *Yoga Sūtra* I. 48. *Source Book,* p. 461.
[9] F. S. C. Northrop, *The Meeting of East and West* (New York: The Macmillan Co., 1946).

and knowledge would no longer be mediated through the forms of language or through our limited categories of thought. It would be direct and intuitive, an identification of mind with reality.... For this reason ... the use of these mystical phrases is the necessary consequence of following an entirely rational line of argument, as a kind of last chapter, of metaphysical systems."[10] Purely rational and mediate theories of knowledge have lacked conviction, and hence only such philosophical theories as have been based on some form of the unitary theories of knowledge, such as that of the mystic, the *sufi,* and the Upaniṣads, have carried conviction and certainty and have been successful in influencing conduct. Also, pure thought, by its very nature, works in dialectics: it creates and develops its own antithesis. It is one of the characteristics of rational and discursive thinking that it is at the same time aware of the other side also, and therefore an element of doubt is always there in the thinker's mind. No stable convictions can be built on mere dialectics. No true philosopher would ever be sure that there could not be another viewpoint or argument which has escaped him. It is of this kind of partial and unconvincing knowledge that the *Īśa Upaniṣad* speaks:

> *Into blind darkness enter they*
> *That worship ignorance;*
> *Into darkness greater than that, as it were, they*
> *That delight in knowledge.*[11]

It would thus appear that whatever is immediately or intuitively known is believed in at least for the moment, and, the more the mind of man takes to a discursive, an inferential, and a mediate way of knowing, the more there is skepticism or lack of conviction in what is thus known even at the time of knowing. Belief or conviction and an immediate theory of knowledge seem somehow to be related to each other, as also mediate theories of knowledge and skepticism seem necessarily to go together. For philosophical theories and knowledge to be practical, it is necessary that they should be believed in, and, in order to be believed in, they should have a basis in some form of immediacy.

Knowledge, therefore, before it can lead to action, must be accompanied by a conviction about its truth: knowledge without conviction is practically useless, and man without faith, as the *Gītā* says, perishes: "But the man who is ignorant, who has no faith, who is of a doubting nature, perishes. For the doubting soul [*ātman*] there is neither this world nor the world beyond, nor any happiness."[12]

In addition to the fact that philosophy has not adopted an integralist theory of knowledge, it has barred valid sources of knowledge other than reason or perception, as, for example, the testimony of a reliable person, which exclusion is not justifiable, especially from the point of view of its role of belief-formation. Indian philosophy, besides admitting the two kinds of perceptual knowl-

[10] D. F. Pearce, ed., *The Nature of Metaphysics* (London: Macmillan and Co., Ltd., 1957), p. 32.
[11] *Īśa Upaniṣad* IX. *Source Book,* p. 40.
[12] *Bhagavad Gītā* IV. 40. *Source Book,* p. 119.

edge, sensory and non-sensory, acknowledges testimony also as a means of true knowledge. It also subordinates other valid means of knowledge, such as inference, analogy, and others, to the two primary ones of perception and testimony, and perhaps much can be said in support of their being included within the purview of legitimate epistemological sources for philosophical knowledge. Of course, it is possible to say that for that reason it is not philosophy, but the point is that to the extent it relies on immediate knowledge philosophy influences man's conduct, and, if this is not to be thought of as philosophy, then whatever is philosophy can neither produce beliefs nor be practical.

Philosophical knowledge and theories will assuredly achieve all that they can—namely, critical acumen, sharpening of wit, even occasional insight—but will ever lack conviction so long as they confine themselves to inferential and ratiocinative knowledge as the only valid knowledge. In other words, philosophy, before it can affect men's conduct, must revise its ideas about the exclusive validity of its accepted sources of knowledge and include once again what it excluded when it separated from theology.

What has been said above about philosophical knowledge does not apply to the validity or the truth of that knowledge but only to its quality of being psychologically believed. What is maintained here is that philosophical knowledge and theories will carry conviction and give man a system of beliefs to live by only when philosophical knowledge stands for knowledge acquired by the whole of a man's self and by no single part of him. The truth-quality of such philosophical knowledge will depend upon the all-round perfection of the integrated being of the knowing self. It follows that, if philosophical knowledge is the result of the whole of the integrated personality of a man, the more perfect the soul of the knower, the purer his mind, senses, reason, and heart, the greater will be the philosophical truth revealed to him. No man will claim to have the true knowledge in any sphere if he believes his instruments of cognition to be defective. Similarly, no philosopher can hope to attain the truth except in proportion to the perfection of his soul. Ultimately, therefore, it is the intellectual, the moral, and the spiritual perfection of the man which reveals the perfect truth. The ideal philosopher, therefore, will be the *yogin,* in the sense of the most integrated and spiritually the most perfected individual.

I have been at pains in this section to clarify two separate but related points, the recognition of both of which is considered important if philosophical knowledge is to be both convincing and true. The first refers to the standpoint and the second to the conviction-value of philosophic knowledge, i.e., a synoptic outlook and an integralist epistemology for the philosophic quest. One reason philosophical knowledge has been open to doubt is found in its too narrow and exclusive epistemology—in its acceptance of only perception and reason (and that, too, in its too obvious and superficial meaning), to the exclusion of other parts of a man's being. It is suggested that sound sources of knowledge other than reason should also be admitted by philosophy in its integral search for total reality. This relates only to the valid sources of knowledge and not to their validity.

The second point deals with the criterion and validity of knowledge. Here it is suggested that the criterion of philosophical knowledge cannot be merely cognitive. For philosophical truths to be valid, the cognized material should have come through perfect receptacles. Philosophy does not seem to recognize the necessity of any moral or spiritual development on the part of its seekers after truth and seems to think that a developed intellect or reason is competent by itself to achieve its objectives. This is open to doubt: an integralist epistemology for the sources of knowledge and an ethical or spiritual perfection for the validity of knowledge seem to be two neglected requirements of the philosophical pursuit without which philosophical knowledge will neither produce conviction nor be true.

II. RELATION OF INDIAN PHILOSOPHICAL THEORIES TO PRACTICAL AFFAIRS

Indian thinkers of the past have left behind some fundamental philosophical beliefs which have not only governed the lives of the Indian people for ages but have not lost much of their hold on men even today. But, before we pass on to these beliefs and see their intimate relation to conduct, we might look at the origin itself of the Indian philosophic endeavor. This is rooted in the indubitable experience of suffering in the affair of living itself as contrasted with the origin of philosophy in the West, which lies in the intellectual possibility of doubting the nature and the existence of anything whatever. This reaction of the whole of a man's being to the experience of suffering is common to almost all the schools of philosophy in India. Philosophical endeavor in India thus began with a practical aim and purpose, which is not merely understanding the why and the wherefore of suffering but an absolute and final elimination of the curse of it all, of the tiring bondage of the causal chain of desire, and of the attainment of a state of liberation from even the possibility of suffering in this life as well as hereafter. This concept of liberation (*mokṣa*) for men from suffering from all bonds or fears whatever is not only a common *summum bonum* of all the different systems of Hindu philosophy, Buddhism, and Jainism, but is also a philosophical concept which is not to be dismissed as merely a theological or religious dogma. The Upaniṣadic philosophers, who were at the same time sages, arrived at this concept by their reflections on the nature of the one and the many, and founded their doctrine of freedom from pain and death—to be more precise, from fear as such (of any sort whatever)—on the truth of the oneness of reality to be realized within their own and irrefutable direct experience. The systems of the Nyāya-Vaiśeṣika, the Sāṁkhya-Yoga, and the two forms of the Vedānta have been led to the same goal of liberation by not being able to accept philosophically the conditioned and empirical existence of man as his true state, which is declared to be that of a state of freedom from all limitations. These systems have differed among themselves by emphasizing one or the other of the three ways for the attainment of *mokṣa* —knowledge, devotion, or action. They also differed concerning the exact nature of the liberated state in terms of its positive or negative character. But what is of significance for us to note here is that all the different schools and systems of philosophy have been occupied with this practical problem of man and with the practical means for its resolution. With all of them, it has not been merely the problem of knowing or of solving an intellectual puzzle but of finding a more satisfactory way of living. Even if all of Indian philosophy had given different answers to the questions of the true nature of man and of the means to its realization, it would have been entitled to the claim of a practical philosophy by virtue of its adherence to the practical problems of man and his life on earth.

It is also significant that, among the different systems of Indian philosophy, tradition should have given the highest place to the Yoga. Patañjali's Yoga, and his school, is through and through a system of psychological discipline, and its being a necessary practical counterpart of the theoretical philosophy of Sāṁkhya has never been doubted. We do not know of any system of philosophical reflection in which a course of conduct has been classified under philosophy. This shows how theory and practice, or knowledge and conviction, went hand in hand and influenced men's conduct in the past. As Huston Smith has pointed out, India's specialization has been in psychological wisdom as against the natural and the social of the West and the Chinese.[13] The Vedānta has quite another kind of peculiarity in this respect but with an identical result. Here, what is primarily claimed is not that any practical discipline is required for the attainment of the highest but that the attainment of true knowledge or the annulment of obstinate and inborn nescience itself constitutes the miracle of the attainment of the highest; for, in reality, nothing is to be attained or approximated except the lifting of the veil of *māyā,* or partial knowledge, something like the claim of modern psychoanalysis in the attainment of freedom from neurosis.[14] Here again, knowledge and action are not separated or even distinguished. The Vedānta came to this conclusion of the unity of theory and practice, knowledge and action, through criticism and analysis of the process of knowledge itself. All knowledge at the empirical level is conceived of as a mixture of both true and false knowledge, which is the cause of all striving and activity at that level. Complete and pure knowledge was found to be all that there is. Thus, while the Yoga is practical in the psychological sense of the term, the Vedānta is so in a metaphysical sense. By its insistence on the absolute reality of pure and absolute knowledge alone, it reduces all activity to the removal of nescience, or the lack of true knowledge.

The philosophical distinction between the partial reality of this world and the absolute reality of quite another kind of world has had perhaps the most profound and most durable influence on the conduct of men in India. While in all philosophizing a distinction has always been made between the sensory and the ideational, the empirical and the transcendental, or, at least, between

[13] Huston Smith, "Accents of the World's Philosophies," *Philosophy East and West,* VII, Nos. 1–2 (April–July, 1957), 16.

[14] *Brahma Sūtra* III.iv.1. *Source Book,* p. 539.

appearance and reality and, while all the scientists and philosophers in all parts of the world have had to start from a distinction of a "this" world and a "that," the distinction has remained practically a dead letter in the conduct of our daily lives. In spite of Plato's "world of ideas," Hegel's "Absolute," Kant's "Transcendental Ego," Husserl's or Hartmann's "Essences," or even in spite of the "original" or the "neutral stuff" of the realists and their distinction between the primary and the secondary qualities of matter, the practical affairs of men have proceeded as if these theories did not exist. But, in India, it would not be correct to say that this distinction is altogether erased from the daily conduct of men, even today, when philosophy, traditional or living, is not playing the dominant role it has played in the past.

That the theory of *māyā* is believed to have altered the outlook and the life of its believers in India is clear from the reproach Indian thought has received from the Western world. That the cause of India's present backwardness, political and economic, should have been put on the shoulders of the philosophical theory of *māyā* is an evidence of the fact that the theory was believed to have been followed in life. The point here is not whether a particular philosophical theory is correct, but only whether it is believed in and guides conduct. We are concerned only with the question as to whether philosophical theories can be believed and acted upon and, if so, how?

Again, that the philosophical pursuit was not conceived of as merely an intellectual excellence but was meant to be integrally related to the personality and the life of the philosopher is shown from the Indian doctrine of *adhikāra,* or of the merit and qualifications of the aspirant to philosophical wisdom. One of the repeated strains of Indian philosophical thought is that true knowledge and wisdom can be acquired only by the pure in heart, by one who has already attained the requisite moral virtues and is free from the psychologically and morally undesirable traits of personality and character. He should have controlled certain ignoble emotions and should be free from unworthy motives and desires. Mere mental gifts or intellectual abilities are not enough for the attainment of the highest truth.

Not he who has not ceased from bad conduct,
Not he who is not tranquil, not he who is not composed,
Not he who is not of peaceful mind
Can obtain Him by intelligence.[15]

Indian philosophical literature abounds in its repeated emphasis on the fourfold discipline (*sādhana catuṣṭhya*) for aspirants to philosophical wisdom.[16]

This blend of virtue and knowledge, of thought and moral practice, may seem to be a distasteful superfluity to the modern mind, which cannot understand the reason things clearly separate could not be treated as separate. But the view that philosophical wisdom should be ethically conditioned should cause no surprise to anyone today, when it is being increasingly realized that

[15] *Kaṭha Upaniṣad* II. 24. *Source Book,* p. 46.
[16] *Ibid.,* I. 20–24. *Source Book,* pp. 45–46. See also *Bhagavad Gītā* II and III.

the intellectual and the moral cannot be separated in any ideal system of instruction and learning. If this is true of everyday knowledge, how much more true it would seem to hold that, for the realization of the highest truth of reality, adequate moral and spiritual preparation should be necessary. After all, what is it to be intelligent or rational? Is it really possible to be intelligent or rational without being moral? If we analyze the behavior of a truly rational man, we are sure to find a number of qualities in him which will prove to be moral. To be rational, for instance, is not to be partisan, or to have prejudices, or to be swayed by passions or self-interest, or to falsify truth, or to have double standards, but it is to stand for truth under all conditions, etc. These are moral qualities. In fact, to be rational is to be moral, and to be completely rational is to be completely moral. The moral and spiritual qualification of a philosopher is, therefore, a condition of his philosophizing properly. Passion or ethical failings cannot but distort the vision, even of a philosopher. In fact, what is called intuition is not so much an independent faculty as a purity of the moral being of the knower which itself constitutes enlightenment. As the Upanisad says, "Therefore let a *brāhmin* become disgusted with learning and desire to live as a child."[17] It is one of the merits of Indian philosophical thought to have insisted on virtue for knowledge, for it is only thus that knowledge leading to belief and action can be acquired.

The Indian doctrine of *karma,* which is the extension of the universal principle of causation in the realm of the inward as well as in the outward life of man, also illustrates the application of philosophical theory to life. The belief that there is no escape from the welcome or the unwelcome effects of our minutest thoughts and deeds has had the most profound effect upon the practical affairs of men in India. It has saved men from temptations and has provided great consolation in their hour of misfortune. Related to this doctrine of *karma,* which provides an Indian with a practical and ready reckoner of the deeds of his life, is the corresponding theory of non-attached living (*niṣkāma karma*), which is believed to undo what the law of *karma* does. The law of *niṣkāma karma* is a philosophical antidote to the evil of bondage to the law of *karma.* While the law of *karma* binds the doer to the fruits of his deeds, the practice of *niṣkāma karma* frees him from this thraldom. As is said,

> *Thus on thee—not otherwise than this is it—*
> *The deed adheres not on the man.*[18]

It is one of the characteristics of Indian philosophical thought that corresponding to every law that binds man it discovers a law that liberates him. In the realm of action, if our deeds bind us through their fruits, we can so act as to free ourselves from that chain of causal action and reaction by acting in disregard of that chain. We can act and yet not be attached to any thought of our act's consequences. In *niṣkāma karma,* action having been started unilaterally and with no thought of its consequences, the fangs, as it were, of the

[17] *Bṛhadāraṇyaka Upaniṣad* III.v. *Source Book,* p. 83.
[18] *Iśa Upaniṣad* II. *Source Book,* p. 40. See also *Bhagavad Gītā* II. 47–48. *Source Book,* p. 110.

law of action and reaction to touch or hurt us are removed. The non-attached man, who performs actions only because he considers it his duty and not because he has bargained for results, has liberated himself from the chain of action and consequences to himself. It may be interesting to recall here that the same psychology applies to the practice of non-violence, where it is the violence of the other party which is to be disregarded. The idea is coming to be gradually appreciated in the West, especially through its psychological and sociological studies of the types of personality and leadership, if not in strictly philosophical fields. It is not merely a moral ideal but a philosophical theory arrived at by deep reflection on the psychology of desiring or striving and its effect on the reasoning purity of the knowing mind. The theory of *niṣkāma karma* is the counterpart in the sphere of action to the theory of the non-attached mind (*niṣkāma citta*) in the realm of knowledge. A *kāmya* (end-seeking or purposeful) mind, a mind that is infected and tarnished by low personal desires and aspirations, can with difficulty see the truth as it is. The *niṣkāma karma* can flow only from a *niṣkāma* mind, which appears to be a necessary qualification of an ideal philosopher, whose task is to perceive the truth about reality with undefective and clean instruments of reason and heart. While, for all practical purposes, the analogous moral theory of Kant's conscientious living and action is only of historical interest in the West, the theory of *niṣkāma karma* is still significant in India because it is a philosophy of action which lays down an ethical determinant to the epistemological validity of knowledge as well. As referred to above, a philosopher who is not otherwise ideal or perfect, i.e., in his practical outlook and action, is, by the very nature of his psychological situation, not entitled to true knowledge or to any reliability of his cognitive theories. Just as Kant deduces his theory from the principle of the pure reason in man, the theory of non-attachment in India is the outcome not only of a philosophical theory of the true nature of the pure or non-attached *puruṣa* or *ātman* (person or self) but also of a theory of relationship of knowledge to personality. And, though in the Buddhist theory of *anātma vāda* there is no corresponding non-attached *puruṣa* or *ātman,* it is philosophically interesting to note that this absence makes little difference to the mechanism and the framework of the possibility of the attainment of philosophical enlightenment as the outcome of freedom from attachment in both Buddhism and Hinduism. The non-attached *yogin* or *sannyāsin,* in whom the ideal of *niṣkāma karma* is exemplified, is not only a perfect or ideal man but is also more truly a philosopher, having attained true philosophical knowledge (*prajñā*), because in his life is typified the completest identity of philosophical knowledge and practice.

The above reflections should have shown how Indian philosophical theories of suffering, ultimate freedom, non-attachment, the unreality of the apparent, and of moral requirements for intellectual attainments have produced conviction and belief which have not only altered the outlook of their believers but have also given a different turn to their style of living. This could be attained because these philosophic theories not only originated by reflection on the practical affairs of life but were also founded on the direct experience of the whole of the being of man and were not based on any single, sensory, rational, or intuitive part of his being.

Through sages and saints these philosophical systems of belief came to be so crystallized into the common heritage of India that today it does not require a philosopher in India to proclaim that the world is but another name for the unceasing changes of creation and dissolution, the rise and fall of civilizations and cultures, or of birth and death, health and disease, richness and poverty—which is believed to be the very nature of the world and is picturesquely characterized as the wheel of life and death (*saṁsāra cakra*), in which man is caught. Further, it takes ages of tireless effort for the individual to emerge unscarred, as it were, by the ravages of the wheel. The fact that these beliefs came to Indians through their sages and saints, not only does not make them less philosophic, but is actually the reason for their being believed, showing once more the integral and unitary character of knowledge and action. Even today, when these traditional philosophical beliefs have dimmed in the stress and strife of modern life, it is difficult to say that an Indian goes through his daily life of birth, marriage, and death unimpressed and unaffected by these beliefs, the truth of which he seems to feel in his very bones.

How is it that these philosophical truths in India have permeated the entire population irrespective of the mental calibre or intellectual status of its people, while elsewhere philosophical truths are supposed to be the mental furnishings only of the intellectually gifted and informed minds? The answer is that these truths not only had their roots in the total experience of man but have, at the same time, served as the foundation of their religious beliefs as well. Ultimately, philosophical truths and religious intuitions are arrived at by the same integral, direct, ethical, and psychological process. It is the same truths arrived at philosophically by the learned which have filtered down to the unlettered masses through their religious beliefs. That is perhaps the only way we know in which philosophical knowledge and beliefs can influence and guide the practical affairs of men, i.e., by being philosophic and religious at the same time.

Many a scholar interested in Indian and comparative philosophies has complained of the dimness of the borderline between Indian philosophical truths and Indian religious beliefs. They have been puzzled to find that there is very little distinction between the two, and have wished it were not so. This is symptomatic of the modern analytical trends of breaking up the unity of man into separate and autonomous compartments of reason and faith. The chief merit of Indian philosophical thought lies in its unitary vision of man and life, in its intimate relation to religious beliefs, which gives it its practical character. Philosophy and religion are aspects of the same human activity. Philosophy is the theory of religion, as religion is the realization of that theory in practice. A philosophy which is not lived is as barren a pastime as a religion that is not founded on valid truths is a meaningless ritual. Where theory is divorced from life, reason from conduct, what expectation may one have that such theories can or will influence the practical affairs of men?

III. DISTINCTION IN THE MEANING OF THE "PRACTICAL" IN INDIA AND THE WEST

Incidentally, the above remarks about the practicality of Indian philosophy also show that the term "practical" itself has been understood in India in a sense not quite the same as that which it carries in the West, at least in the modern period. In the West, the term "practical" has referred to man's relation with his environment and to changes and alterations in it. It has not been so in India, where the term has referred to just the opposite meaning of effecting change and alteration within one's own self, where the entire effort has been concentrated on transforming the empirical ego into the pure self, or the egoity itself into non-egoity or mere "thusness." In short, the emphasis on the practical in India has been with reference to the inner transformation of man rather than to any socialized transformation in his style of living. The world of objective Nature is to be used only as the material for this inner change. The need to become his true self rather than to conquer outer Nature has been his deepest aspiration. His practicality has consisted in a constant effort toward self-discovery, self-discipline, and self-development.

It is heartening to note that one of the great American sociological thinkers, Lewis Mumford, while commenting upon the exclusively horizontal socialization of our present civilization, which equates life with property and power, comes to a similar conclusion about the need of richness and depth in the individual's own personality rather than in externals. "The progressive exchange of his natural, biological, and psychological self to his truly human self is what man alone can effect and create and he is human only in so far as this has been effected *by him in his own person*."[19] The more a man becomes externally socialized, the less is his depth within himself. This value attributed to the inward depth of the individual in Indian thought continues up to the present time, as is evident from the response of the people to the philosophies of Tagore, Gandhi, and Aurobindo, in which all practical programs of action in political, social, and economic fields are to conform to the belief that no achievement in any sphere is in itself worth while unless it leads at the same time to a desired transformation in the psychological quality of the inner nature of man, the individual.

IV. THE PRESENT SITUATION

Though India is free politically, its best minds are occupied in an attempt to catch up with economic targets in national living. *Pari passu,* there is to be noticed a general revival of the arts, literature, and other cultural activities—about which it is too early to form any opinion as to what it will achieve and in which direction. But indications are not lacking to show that it will be in the direction of a synthesis of the best in the West and the Indian cultural tradition. So far as philosophy is concerned, there is evidence, not only of an

[19] L. Mumford, *The Transformations of Man* (New York: Harper & Brothers, 1956), p. 24. Italics mine.

increased awareness of the philosophical knowledge of India's own past, but also of contemporary trends in Western philosophical thought. From the philosophical writings of Indians today one gains the impression that Indian thinkers are either critical or unenthusiastic about the modern Western philosophical trends of logical positivism, existentialism, and the philosophy of mere analysis. Whether this is due to traditional bias or to genuine philosophical insight is hard to determine. In recent times, the only philosophers of fame have been Aurobindo Ghose and Radhakrishnan, whose philosophies are both integral and practical. For the rest, there has been no philosophical reflection or theory which has yet crystallized into being properly called the contemporary Indian philosophical theory. The place of philosophy and philosophical thought in India consists at present of the ideas and ideals which are in general the products of its spiritual and moral leaders, such as Ramakrishna, Tagore, and Gandhi. What India still retains today of its past philosophical tradition after centuries of inactivity is not any development or modification of its earlier philosophy or philosophical theories, but perhaps a philosophical attitude and outlook which is more critical than creative. If philosophy is a product of the general climate of ideas (as it certainly is), it seems safe to predict that India's future philosophical activity will be in the direction of a philosophy of the co-existence of the ideas of the West and the East, of the old and the new, and in the discovery of the largest measure of agreement and compatability between the two. It would be a pity if Indian philosophers, too, adopt the view of an autonomous realm of philosophical pursuit divorced from the practical problems of life. Any approach toward life and the universe which is not integral, synoptic, or unitary, but divides and cuts life and its problems into compartments which tend to be autonomous, is likely to be skeptical in the end. If India can retain an integral attitude, something of value may well result from its re-emergence in the arena of creative thought.

QUESTION: I do not see any logical connection between intellectual attainments and ethical perfection. Consequently I do not see why a perfect philosopher has to be ethically perfect—or a *yogin,* etc.

ANSWER: It is psychologically a fact and quite obvious that a man's desires, emotions, passions, ambitions, etc., do affect his logical thinking and that a would-be philosopher is not immune from this danger—as anyone can look around and see for himself. What I meant was only an extension of this same psychological fact to a philosopher's thinking.

HERBERT W. SCHNEIDER

Western Philosophy and Practical Affairs

INTRODUCTION: THE PRACTICAL NATURE OF PHILOSOPHY

Philosophy should be the love of wisdom. It meant precisely this to the ancient Greeks, who spoke Greek and to whom the word "philosophy" did not mean an academic subject-matter or a speculative natural science; it meant literally and quite non-technically "loving wisdom." A philosopher was distinguished from a sage (*sophos*), of whom there were a few in ancient Greece, and from a sophist or teacher of wisdom, of whom there were too many when Socrates began his attack on them. There is, at least in the Western tradition, something pretentious about being either a sage or a sophist, and this attitude prejudices many Western philosophers against the traditional Indian *guru,* who seems to them a synthesis of sage and sophist. A philosopher is no more than a lover of wisdom; he neither knows what he wants to know nor teaches what he does not know. He is, if we may take Socrates as the classic model, a person who loves to know what he is doing and saying, who knows that he is not wise, and who knows that he ought to know wisdom when he finds it. This critical conception of philosophy, which has been a dominant influence ever since the Platonic Socrates made it so admirable, is evidently humanistic. One does not criticize the world or Nature (at least it is not wise to do so); one criticizes what is done by man. Hence, the primary subject-matter of the love of wisdom is human action and human production.

This emphasis on human affairs in Western philosophy received its first classic formulation in the Dialogues of Plato, who invented them, not as mere literary devices to combine comedy and tragedy (though this idea, too, seems to have occurred to him), but as a formalization of critical conversation. Running through them as a basic theme is Plato's insistence that the critical love of man is more important than the speculative love of Nature. The shift from cosmology to idealism in the Socratic Dialogues of Plato has left a permanent imprint on Western philosophy. "Platonic love" is not love of speculation; it is the dialogical pursuit of human ideals. Platonic idealism is a form of humanism and rests on concern for the perfection of man universally. All serious love idealizes. Photographs of the beloved are notoriously unsatisfactory and were scorned by Plato as mere "opinions." Portraits, if painted by a lover, may be better, since they are at least expressions of love. But love is never content with knowledge. There is always an element of longing in its enjoyments and of trust in its possessions. This is especially evident when there is life in the object loved, and when there is a reciprocity in love. It is from this point of view that philosophers contrast the pursuit of truth as it is found in science with philosophy as it is exhibited in philosophical literature and in philosophical persons. Truth may be quite cold, and its pursuit may be more like a life of devotion than like a life of love, whereas there is a kind of living warmth in wisdom which makes philosophers appear to be engaged in a kind of reciprocity or participation. Philosophical truth is found only in the context of human life, and hence the philosophical mind must have a genuine concern for human affairs and a readiness to remain in human fellowship. Both the pursuit of truth and the pursuit of wisdom may be endless, but they are endless in different ways. Truth remains eventual; it comes at the end. But wisdom is more analogous to happiness, which is found along the way and not at the end of the road. Wisdom and happiness are not objects; they are ways of being human.

The life-span of a philosophy must be measured culturally and historically in terms of the philosophy's relevance to a particular human environment. We are accustomed, for example, to refer as a matter of course to Eastern and Western philosophies, not because we believe, as some do, that "East" and "West" designate philosophical differences, but merely in order to designate vaguely the cultural fields of operation in which particular philosophies have their existence and meaning. Similarly, we speak of ancient and modern, French and German, pagan and Christian, philosophies, not in order to define them, but in order to locate them existentially. Such discriminations are decidedly accidental for science, but for philosophy they are necessary, for in relating philosophy to social practice we are not applying knowledge gained in abstraction to practical affairs externally, as applied science may be said to be external to pure science. Philosophy is not pure when it is pure theory; its very essence is to operate critically in human affairs. Philosophy originates in "the problems of men" and must return to them for its validation and justification. Such a conception of philosophy is not a mere sermon on what philosophy ought to be, but is a factual statement of how philosophy has existed historically and how it actually manages to make itself felt as a power in life and as a form of love.

This paper, which is introductory to the more specialized examinations of the practical aspects of philosophy, will confine itself to a few of the most important Western conceptions of civilization as a whole, of the entire complex of human arts, and it will try to show that these conceptions had their origins and also their aims in major turning points within human affairs. A theory of civilization or of history is usually symptomatic of a crisis in human affairs; it attempts to justify a certain type of civilization which may be threatened, or it looks ahead to a new civilization which seems to be coming. Like the Prophets of Israel, philosophers of history and civilization survey the whole course of human affairs in order to give their contemporaries a proper perspective for understanding their collective duties and destinies.

1. THE GREEK THEORY OF CIVILIZATION

The ancient Greek poets and philosophers were guided in their reflection by a basic distinction between natural processes and human construction, between physical movements and the creations of human art. Mankind lives in two worlds: Nature and art. To be a natural being means to have a destiny. The gods or the forces that govern Nature, whatever they may be, give to each human being a lot which is governed by universal necessity or destiny; he is put into a particular environment, given specific bodily resources, and assigned a span of years. Over these circumstances an individual has no control, and if he is prudent he will accept them as his fate. To try to escape one's natural fate is the height of folly and ends in tragedy. Insofar as a man attempts to defy the gods or protest against the reign of inexorable power, he falls victim to the pride which is heroic but tragic. Even the Titans fell on account of this hopeless defiance. But there is a certain majesty and dignity in this Promethean heroic bearing, for Nature and the gods are tyrants.

In barbarous societies, the attitude of resignation to the powers that be is universal; there is no heroism, merely a combination of tyranny and slavery. But, among the Greeks, who from their point of view were the only civil or civilized people, men were accustomed to distinguish between their natural relations and their social relations. Men are not naturally, inevitably destined to be subject to other men, as they are to the gods. Within the limits permitted by Nature, men can build cities, institute laws, and pursue their arts; this political communal existence is the realm in which man can be a creator and self-governor. To be governed by man-made laws or human reason was to the Greeks the very essence of freedom. The invention of general norms, impersonal imperatives, was the beginning of civilization and the foundation of all the arts. The submission to *Logos,* to the rules of reason, is a very different kind of submission from submission to destiny. Living under destiny is human tragedy; living under reason is both logic and freedom.

This conception of man's double existence in natural necessity and in free civility or art is the basic intellectual framework for the classic tragedies, the Platonic Dialogues, and the Aristotelian treatises. Greek philosophy rested on the attempt to define what it means to be civilized in an uncivilized world. It rested on a growing confidence in the arts and sciences; it is man who is the creator, the maker, the doer (in Greek, the "poet"). It is he who brings order, knowledge, and beauty into the world, and he unites all these creative enterprises into the one "architectonic"[1] art of living in communal freedom, in City-States.

The collection of treatises that were composed in the school of Aristotle was not a mere encyclopedia of current knowledge; it was the *corpus* of a philosophy which became for centuries "the teachings of the master." This philosophy integrated all the sciences and arts under the general "architectonic art" of communal welfare. In order to do this, Aristotle had to attempt a general house cleaning of the sciences, examining in detail the theories of his predecessors to determine which of them were speculative and which could be verified factually. In this way Aristotle continued the love of systematic criticism which Socrates and Plato had established in order to "live a life worth living."

The cities of the Greeks were the culmination of all the Greek arts. Their temples, theaters, forums, monuments were the correlate in stone of their poetry and philosophy; their sculptures were the memorials to their athletics, and, in general, their arts were the evidence of their intelligence. This attitude toward their civilization was consciously promoted by the Greek philosophical leaders. Such a portrait of Greek life is an idealization, not an accurate, historical account, as students of Greek history must know. To paint such a portrait was itself a great philosophic art; it made the Greeks self-conscious, proud, free. Without such a philosophic self-consciousness they would have been less impressive than they still are. Their philosophy was eminently practical.

But the wars of the Greeks were the evidence of their tragic destiny and the ruin of their brilliant culture. Alexander of Macedon, inspired by the philosophic enthusiasm for Greek art and Greek cities, conceived the bold idea of carrying the Greek ideals throughout the world, thus making Greek culture a world civilization. With this tragic pride to justify his military conquests, he set out in the direction of India. He soon met his due fate, and, with his doom, Greek culture was dissipated. In the absence of Greek City-States and Greek communal arts, Greek culture, and with it Greek philosophy, had to try to survive on an entirely new basis. It had to be a philosophy for Greek ruins.

II. STOICISM AND HELLENISTIC CIVILIZATION

What is known as the Hellenistic culture in the Roman world was a very different affair, in practice and in theory. The scattered Greeks survived as merchants, bankers, teachers, slaves. They lived as individuals, and their spirit became that of businessmen, or slave-teachers to wealthy Romans, or hired artists. They had to accommodate themselves to all kinds of "barbarians" and had to revise radically their conception of themselves. One of the philosophies

[1] See Aristotle's *Ethics*, Bk. I, chap. 1.

which tried to meet this Hellenistic situation was Stoicism. I shall use it as an illustration to show the new ways philosophy found of being practical.

Stoicism was essentially a gospel of comfort. In the confusion of cultures within the Roman Empire and in the growing fears for the *Pax Romana,* the Stoics developed the doctrine that those who felt lost in the Roman world might feel at home in Nature—they could be world citizens. The world itself was now conceived as a well-ordered city—a cosmopolis. Such cosmopolitanism had an intensely practical appeal. Over and above Roman rule and Roman law, proclaimed the Stoics, there is a universal rational administration to which any reasonable soul can gladly submit. Membership in what Emperor Marcus Aurelius addressed as "Dear City of the World"[2] meant participation in a universal community whose foundations are laid in peace and justice. "We are all made for co-operation," he said, and "even in a palace life can be lived well." Anyone who reads his meditations will note at once their intensely practical purpose and content. The same is true of the letters and essays of the Roman Senator Seneca, who was persecuted by another emperor, or of the Greek slave Epictetus, whose discourses were clearly a compensation for the miseries of his slavery and an attempt to practice complete detachment and equanimity in suffering. The doctrines of Hellenistic Stoicism were the complete opposite of those of the classic Greeks, and yet they were equally practical, for they were addressed to Greeks whose lives were the complete opposite. The appeal of Stoicism was felt for centuries. Note, for example, the *Consolations* of Boethius, written in prison and in terms of the Christian religion, and yet replete with the Stoic spirit and faith.

III. DANTE'S THEORY OF A UNIVERSAL CHRISTENDOM

I come now to one of the great philosophies of civilization which the West has produced, Dante Alighieri's theory of Christendom as a world-wide theocracy.[3] It will be best to expound the theory in his own words because he attempted to put his argument into the syllogistic form which St. Thomas, as a teacher of Aristotle's philosophy, had taught Dante to respect as essential to all science. In other words, Dante is here attempting to bring together Aristotle, Thomas Aquinas, and the Christian faith in the service of a plan for world-wide peace and intelligence.

In matters of action the final goal is the principle and cause of all, for by it the agent is first moved. It follows that any reasons for actions directed to this goal must be themselves derived from it.... Whatever, then, is the universal goal of human civilization, if there be such a goal, will serve as a first principle and will make sufficiently clear all the derivative propositions that follow. Now, it would be foolish to admit that one civilization may have one

[2] See the *Meditations* of Marcus Aurelius, which were written "to himself" during his military campaigns. They were composed in Greek and were not intended for publication.

[3] This is contained in his *De Monarchia,* written while he was in exile from Florence, probably about 1320. The following excerpts are made from the translation by Herbert W. Schneider, published in 1949 by The Liberal Arts Press, New York, under the title *On World Government.*

goal and another, another, and not to admit one goal for all. Accordingly, we must now see what the whole of human civilization aims at. . . .

God and Nature make nothing in vain, and whatever is produced serves some function. . . . There is therefore some proper function for the whole of mankind as an organized multitude which cannot be achieved by any single man, or family, or neighborhood, or city, or state. What that may be would be plain if we could see what the basic capacity of the whole of humanity is. Now, I would say that no capacity which several different species have in common can be the basic power of any one of them. . . . Accordingly, man's basic power is not mere being, for he shares being with the elements; nor is it to be compounded, for this is found in minerals, too; nor is it to be alive, for so are plants; nor is it to be sensitive, for other animals share this power; but it is to be sensitive to intellectual growth, for this trait is not found in beings either below or above man. . . . Therefore, it is clear that man's basic capacity is to have a potentiality or power for being intellectual. And since this power cannot be completely actualized in a single man or in any of the particular communities of men, there must be a multitude in mankind through whom this power can be wholly actualized. . . . This intellectual power of which I am speaking is directed not only toward universals or species, but also by a sort of extension to particulars. Hence it is commonly said that the speculative intellect becomes practical by extension, and acquires thus the aims of action and production. I distinguish between matters of action which are governed by political prudence, and matters of production which are governed by the arts; but all of them are extensions of theoretical intellect, which is the best function for which the Primal Goodness brought mankind into being. . . .

I have now made clear enough that the proper work of mankind taken as a whole is to exercise continually its entire capacity for intellectual growth, first, in theoretical matters, and, secondarily, as an extension of theory, in practice. And since the part is a sample of the whole, and, since individual men find that they grow in prudence and wisdom when they can sit quietly, it is evident that mankind, too, is most free and easy to carry on its work when it enjoys the quiet and tranquility of peace. Man's work is almost divine and it is clear that of all the things that have been ordained for our happiness, the greatest is universal peace. . . .

And consequently it is also clear what way we must take to attain that final goal set for all our work, which is universal peace. Let this, then, be our principle underlying all our subsequent arguments, and let it serve as a standard set before us by which to test the truth of whatever we shall try to prove. . . .

Mankind exists at its best when it resembles God as much as it can. But mankind resembles God most when it is most unified, for the true ground of unity exists in Him alone. . . . But mankind is then most one when it is unified into a single whole, which is possible only when it submits wholly to a single government, as is self-evident. Therefore mankind in submitting to a single government most resembles God and most nearly exists according to the divine intention, which is the same as enjoying well-being. . . .

Thus it seems necessary for the well-being of the world that there be world-government, that is, a single power, called Empire. This reasoning inspired Boethius when he said:

O happy race of men,
If like heaven your hearts
Were ruled by love!

Here Dante is carrying the concept of Christendom to its logical conclusion, applying it to all mankind and to a universal civilization. This was not an idle speculation on Dante's part, as his opening remarks make clear. It is conceived as a philosophical program for action. The problem of peace was as urgent then as it is now, and Dante was doing his utmost to provide a philosophical solution to the political evils of his day. He hoped for a holy Roman Empire to bring God's peace to all mankind.

IV. THE THEORY OF AN INTERNATIONAL COMMUNITY OF LAW

The conception of the unity of civilization under God, which inspired Western philosophy from Dante to Erasmus, was shattered by the rise of national cultures, national States, and national Churches. In the place of a philosophy of world government, there arose the ideal of the possibility of an international legal order or a universal community of nations. The first important practical application of this idea was made by Hugo Grotius in his work *The Law of War and Peace* (1625). In his Introduction he restates the Stoic and Christian faith in the existence of a natural moral law which is the basis of all positive law, and which may serve as a universal norm in the absence of positive law. Then he derives from this universal law norms for a positive law governing international relations and guiding diplomatic negotiations and treaties. Following Grotius came several other notable attempts to formulate principles for an international order. Chief of these were Puffendorf's *On the Law of Nature and Nations* (1672), Leibniz' *Diplomatic Codification of the Law of Nations* (1693–1700), Christian Wolff's *Institutions of the Law of Nature and of Nations* (about 1740), and Vattel's *The Law of Nations* (1758). The gradual shift in this literature from an emphasis on the law of Nature to an emphasis on the law of nations (adapted from the Roman *ius gentium)* is evidence of the desire underlying such works to make them of practical use in developing international law among modern States. But unfortunately they were used more for the purpose of justifying declarations of war than for regulating international differences peacefully. Recently, however, with the growth of international tribunals and leagues of nations these classics have been put to practical use, and gradually a body of positive international law is developing which governments respect, but which owes its beginnings to the more speculative works of philosophers.

More speculative and utopian than these seventeenth- and eighteenth-century treatises were the "sketches" for enduring or perpetual peace by Abbé de St. Pierre, Jean-Jacques Rousseau, and Immanuel Kant. We ought to consider here especially Kant's tract *On Perpetual Peace* (1795), coming as it did closely after the foundation of the United States on a federal basis, during the French Revolution, and at the outbreak of the Napoleonic Wars. It is an excellent example of a speculative and rationalistic philosophy being used to meet an urgent practical situation. Kant begins by listing six concrete, practical principles for governing international relations, hoping that there might be a willingness to accept such principles among powers that could not subscribe formally to the books of international law. Then he constructs a philosophical argument to show that these principles are right and hence impose a moral duty of obedience on all rational beings. From this argument I cite a few passages to show how insistent Kant is on the inherent relation between theoretical right and practical duty:

Reason, from her throne of the supreme lawgiving moral power, absolutely condemns war as a morally lawful proceeding and makes a state of peace, on the other hand, an immediate duty. Without a compact between the nations, however, this state of peace cannot be established or assured. Hence there must be an alliance of a particular kind which we may call a covenant of peace (*foedus pacificum*), which would differ from a treaty of peace (*pactum pacis*) in this respect that the latter merely puts an end to one war, while the former would seek to put an end to war forever....

In an objective sense, morals is a practical science, as the sum of laws exacting unconditional obedience, in accordance with which we *ought* to act. Now, once we have admitted the authority of this idea of duty, it is evidently inconsistent that we should think of saying that we *cannot* act thus. For, in this case, the idea of duty falls to the ground of itself.... That is, theory cannot come into conflict with practice. For, in that case, we would need to understand under the term "ethics" or "morals" a universal doctrine of expediency, or, in other words, a theory of precepts which may guide us in choosing the best means for attaining ends calculated for our advantage. This is to deny that a science of morals exists....

The moralist can cut asunder the knot which politics is unable to untie. Right must be held sacred by man, however great the cost and sacrifice to the ruling power. Here there is no half-way course. We cannot devise a happy medium between right and expediency—a right pragmatically conditioned. But all politics must bend the knee to the principle of right, and may, in that way, hope to reach, although slowly perhaps, a level whence it may shine upon men for all time.[4]

The idea that a covenant to outlaw war on moral grounds might be a practical idea for governments to adopt was revived after the First World War, under United States leadership, but it proved that a merely moral covenant was not enough. The faith in universal law as a basis for an international community of mankind depended for its strength on the strength of what was called "natural religion." During the seventeenth and eighteenth centuries natural religion was a growing philosophical faith. During this so-called Enlightenment in the West the philosophers, being rationalists, believed firmly that morality is one of the strongest evidences of the unity of mankind. Chris-

[4] The translation here used is by M. Campbell Smith, published by The Liberal Arts Press, New York, 1948, pp. 16–17, 32, 44.

tian Wolff, for example, wrote extensively on Confucianism in order to prove that moral knowledge independent of revelation is universal and absolute. Unfortunately for the covenant of peace, Kant was one of the last philosophers who were faithful to the Enlightenment's theory of ethics.

V. THE THEORY OF UNIVERSAL PROGRESS

The concept of natural law underwent a radical transformation during the Romantic era around and after the French Revolution. The natural moral order had been conceived as an eternal, unchanging foundation of morals and right, but now a more revolutionary idea dawned. The natural order is temporal, an evolutionary order, in continual development. A natural law of universal progress was supposed to govern both natural and human history. There followed a long list of evolutionary philosophies, each trying in its own way to demonstrate the existence of necessary, lawful progress. Civilization was conceived as developing by necessary stages. Some of these theories were more speculative than others: Hegel's theory of historical dialectic was more speculative than the Marxian, and Spengler's system was a more romantic ideology than is Toynbee's. But the great majority of these philosophies attempted to represent some practical movement as a natural stage in a universal progress. I select only two of these, one French, the other English; both of them were rationalizations of the triumph of industrial society.

Claude Henri de Rouvroy Saint-Simon (1760–1825) belonged to the lesser French gentry, who had turned their attention from agriculture to industry, from feudal society to the urban bourgeoisie. He saw clearly that French capital was following in the steps of the British and that the lords of the coming era would be not the landed aristocrats but the "captains of industry." Saint-Simonianism was a movement as well as a philosophy. The philosophy was more than a rationalization of the movement; it was both cause and effect, both inspiration and interpretation. According to this philosophy, civilization is in the process of transformation from the era of war to an era of peace and moral obedience, from an ethics of antagonism to one of co-operation, from a politics of anarchy to association, from a spirit of egotism to one of devotion, from critical negative philosophy to organic constructive thinking. Saint-Simon imagined himself as combining the efforts of René Descartes, Francis Bacon, and Isaac Newton; he was establishing the science of organic humanity, of the transformation of the individual from a self-sufficient being to a member of a socialist civilization. When he fought with the French forces in behalf of the American Rebellion at the Battle of Yorktown he represented himself as a soldier of "industrial liberty." All the signs of the times, to his mind, pointed to the emergence of a new type of civilization in which universal association would be directed by modern science, putting an end to war and using technology to organize labor for the most genuine production. This new world-order he expounded in a book entitled *The New Christianity*; this renewed religion would "organize society for the amelioration of the moral and physical existence of the poorest class." The instruments of labor would be "socially funded" by the State and administered by industrial chiefs. Such a scientifically planned society, he reasoned, would command the voluntary support and obedience of all to a hierarchy of benevolent captains of industry. Saint-Simon himself set to work in this spirit: one of his major interests was the planning of the Suez Canal. Another interest, after the defeat of Napoleon, was to organize a politico-economic league of Europe (similar to the one now taking shape). In fact, Saint-Simon became so absorbed in practical schemes that his secretary, Auguste Comte, resigned in protest, charging him with neglect of philosophy. When Saint-Simon died in 1825, his disciples, under the leadership of Enfentin, became more religious and formed a sect for "the rehabilitation of the flesh." The practical as well as the philosophical work of the group declined, and the sect came to an end in 1832.

Meanwhile a young Englishman, Herbert Spencer (1820–1903), was beginning to formulate another version of the theory of universal progress. He seems to have been inspired by a German philosopher who formulated what was known as Von Baer's Law, which stated that there is a universal process which moves from the homogeneous to the heterogeneous, from uniformity to diversity, and from military to industrial rivalry. In 1857, Spencer published his *Progress, its Law and Cause,* in which this conception of the progress of civilization was explained as an aspect of the first principles of evolution generally. By increasingly adapting "internal to external relations" mankind would arrive, so he reasoned, at a state of perfect equilibrium which would render government by coercion unnecessary. In its place would arise an industrial civilization in which peaceful competition would rule.

It is evident that neither Saint-Simon nor Herbert Spencer was indulging in mere speculation; their philosophies were directly related to the practical concerns of their times and were intended to help men understand the basic changes which were taking place, not only in their own countries, but, so they thought, in civilization as a whole. I have concentrated attention on these Western theories of civilization and progress in order to show that in even this widest of all human fields of speculation the philosophers were thinking, not in a spirit of detachment, but in a spirit of involvement. They were making their contributions to the most urgent and basic problems in the practical affairs of their own times. These theories were visions, to be sure, but these visions, even when obviously visionary, were realistic attempts to clarify and direct the thinking of practical men about their basic affairs.

VI. CONTEMPORARY EVALUATION OF INDUSTRIAL CIVILIZATION

To show that this is still true, I close with a few paragraphs from a recent work which brings the speculation about industrial society up to date. This work, too, is clearly an attempt to help men understand what is happening to them now and to direct their action along constructive channels. It is entitled "The Theory of the Present Epoch,"[5] and its author, Hans Freyer, is a well-known writer on European world history. After surveying contemporary "trends," "models," and "resistances," he describes the "present world-historical situation." His analysis is particularly significant as a commentary on the glowing hopes which Saint-Simon and Spencer had for industrial society. His reduction of history to a succession of "world-historical situations" is in line with the general tendencies among philosophers today to deny any continuous and inevitable evolution of civilization.

The whole course of human history so far has been a manifold of projects, achievements, and mistakes, a plurality of peoples taking shape and disintegrating, of cultures blossoming and wilting, of kingdoms established and destroyed. We can no longer believe in Hegel's image of a single world-historical day, whose sun rose in the ancient East, whose high noon was spent around the Mediterranean Sea, and whose evening twilight is gathering in the West. Nor can we believe that mankind was childlike in the ancient cultures of Asia, youthful in ancient Greece and Rome, and is reaching a mature old age in Christian Europe. This classical picture of world-history . . . has become classic in the same sense in which Newtonian physics is a classic, valid in its particular domain, but worthless as a formula for the whole. . . .

The second, third, and fourth millenniums B.C. can no longer be looked upon as "mankind's cradle" . . . or as "the dawn of history." . . . These millenniums have taken form as the age of many peoples whose names and destinies we now know, of many empires which had their distinctive traits. Thus the unity of world history has disappeared. . . . Instead, there have existed many distinctive world-historical situations, situations in which various centers of energy and dynamic fields are distinct but interacting; what each center does can be understood only in relation to the whole situation. . . . In such situations isolated peoples and cultures are thrown together or at least interrelated. All are permeated by a civilization and possibly transformed by it. All are faced with a common task or at least share a common fate.

Again and again in human history there have been centuries which had such a world-historical atmosphere. Their dominant situations were literally "projected." There were ideas which could interpret events beyond and above the particular historical areas in which they arose, and these ideas were not submerged by their own situations; there were powers that were not organic parts of the life of their times; and there were institutions which in many ways were foreign to the individuals who lived in them, because these institutions had been impositions, creatures of coercion or bureaucracy. But these situations were projected in the special sense that the energies which were to prove capable of dealing with them had to come from reserves or heritages of various peoples and regions of the earth, stored up in the course of their own historical experience. In every world-situation which embraces much of the globe there is always a return to the varied and limited achievements of many diversified elements. The world-historical manifold is always prepared to ap-

[5] These passages are translated from Hans Freyer, *Theorie des Gegenwärtigen Zeitalters* (Stuttgart: Deutsche Verlags-Anstalt, 1955), pp. 248–259 *passim*. His best-known work on the interpretation of European history is *Weltgeschichte Europas* (2d rev. ed., Stuttgart: Deutsche Verlags-Anstalt, 1950).

propriate and absorb whatever may have been achieved in the way of a universal order; only by being thus absorbed into the particular can anything universal gain historical meaning and duration. . . .

The industrial revolution that took place about 1800 in little Europe has created a world situation in which all continents are thrown together into a single dynamic field. . . . Infinite hopes had been projected into this situation, hopes for a mankind at peace, united by the humane bonds of morals and world commerce. These hopes have not been satisfied. It is evident today that in a thoroughly industrialized world there are more conflicts than ever, that world commerce is not unambiguously an instrument of peace, and that the politics of "One World" is a field of enormous tensions. But the faith in progress was justified insofar as it implied the universal spread of industrialized society. This universal situation is now here or is at least inevitably in the making. . . .

However, the peoples and continents of the earth are already well engaged in the process of appropriating this projected situation to themselves. The pluralism in world history is showing itself again in this instance, though it may be overshadowed somewhat. On all levels of activity, diversified world-historical forces are at work adapting themselves to the universal system, facing it boldly, and asserting themselves confidently. With their population pressures, their potential manpowers, their demands for freedom, their urge to go ahead, and many other ancient resources for adaptation, the peoples of the earth are rushing to the opportunities and tasks which the industrial system offers them. We had always taken for granted that this upsurge of the heritages and energies derived from the past is an element in all historical events. But now, in our world-situation, we are faced with it as the dominant reality, as the exciting competition of continents. We do not exaggerate if we regard it as the real theme of current world history and of the near future. This intercontinental competition will decide not merely what equilibriums and tensions will dominate the globe during the next century, but also what will be the destiny of the industrial system itself. . . . As always in history, so the future of the industrial system must be nourished by the reserve energies of the heritages of many peoples. . . . It has already been demonstrated by the process of the industrialization of peoples that the machine and mechanical labor are end products of civilization, which can be appropriated even by those peoples whose mental equipment was of an entirely different character. These possibilities will be realized more fully when the hundreds of millions of the earth will all be drawn into the industrial system, a process which is well under way. . . . And so it might be that one or another people with an ancient culture plunges into industrialism with all its traditional virtues of cleverness, silence, asceticism, reliability, and fidelity, and applies these disciplines with sovereign assurance to the new labor of factory and office as they had been devoted to ancient forms of labor. The qualities of "old" and "young" when applied to people are ambiguous attributes and tell us nothing about the values of culturally inherited traits. All depends on their adaptability to change. What India and China will be able to show in the way of virtues when they mobilize their millions of laborers is an open question. There may be much in their heritages that is immune to the ravages of the industrial system and much that may prove to be a distinct asset. The traits commonly called "American" are no longer adequate criteria for measuring the abilities which various peoples will show as they adjust in their special ways to industrial production.

The situation and the task of the West rest on the same principles. The West is one instance among many. Here, too, the question is whether Western history, which has been no less diversified than those of India and China, will reveal actual possibilities of making the industrial system serve humane ends. The fact that the industrial system has become primary in the West whereas it is secondary elsewhere is not so much an advantage to the West as a liability. . . . The theoretical subordination of industrialism to its secondary role in civilization is now a global problem, and hence the case of Europe is merely one special case among others. Anyone who observes current world history philosophically must eventually come to the question: How will the various streams meet that have been historically separate and that are now tributary to the world situation, and what actual powers will they bring with them for mastering the problems of this situation? Put in this way, the case of the West is but one among several, more difficult perhaps than others, but no more hopeless.

Hans Freyer, too, is a philosopher. We all speculate; we go far beyond our actual knowledge, and we pretend to understand not only the past and present but a bit of the future as well. Such imaginative generalization is essential to philosophy. But it is also a genuine contribution toward living well in our own times. The attempt to achieve historical perspective, world orientation, and self-knowledge is an enterprise essential to culture, and without it our practical affairs would be even more chaotic than they are. Speculative imagination is no sin, provided it keeps a critical eye on the actual problems of life, and aims at clarification, not at mystification.

QUESTION: In China, where the concept "philosophy" is foreign, the history of practical wisdom is dominated by a few great *sages* and their teachings, and it is generally believed that to become "sage-ly" is the greatest of virtues. Does not this Chinese tradition do more justice to the practical nature of philosophy than does the Socratic Western model?

ANSWER: China's great sages indeed illustrate well the conception of philosophy which I am defending. Their wisdom was built on experience and was formulated in such a way that it could be used for practical guidance by the people generally. They were neither pretentious nor enigmatic, and they took for granted that their wisdom would be validated in human experience. This is genuine practical philosophy. But there has been a popular tendency to represent their teachings as not systematic but proverbial—collections of wise "sayings." The effect is to make these sages appear to foreigners as prophets for the Chinese rather than as philosophers of mankind—as authorities rather than as "extenders of investigation." They seem to have been primarily systematic moralists, whose doctrines on other aspects of human life are less philosophical than their ethics. Such concepts as "heaven," "Tao," *"yin-yang"* seem to be taken over from ancient lore without sufficient systematic, critical evaluation; and hence Chinese philosophy has been more practical in the realm of morality than in other practical affairs. An adequate practical philosophy should include much more than moral theory; it should embrace the arts, the vocations, the religions, and all beliefs that are important for coherence and intelligence in human conduct.

QUESTION: Western theories of civilization and history, such as those selected for this paper, evidently have a relation to practical affairs, but could the same be said of metaphysical speculations and methodological controversies?

ANSWER: I do not deny that philosophies linger idly after they have ceased working, but a philosophy in its prime does not operate as a loose aggregate of metaphysics, epistemology, ethics, and aesthetics—it has genuine coherence and practical integrity. I have intentionally selected philosophies which attempt conspicuously to "ground" their practical propositions in basic, so-called "metaphysical," beliefs and reflections. The Greek theory of natural universal necessity was to them no mere cosmology or metaphysics but, rather, the essential correlate to the concept of human art; it was an attempt to define the limits set to human ambition and planning. As such, it was basic to all practical affairs. Similarly, Aristotle's so-called "metaphysics" was conceived by him as a "primary science" which, together with logic, consitutes a reflective post-script to the natural sciences and a normative pre-script for the arts. The problem of what-it-means-to-be was as urgent for him and his generation as it was for Hamlet and the princes of Shakespeare's time, and it is reappearing in our own generation as something more than mere speculation. Hellenistic cosmopolitanism was a practical movement because of its faith in a real, universal order or *Logos,* and this faith in turn appeared well founded in view of the practical achievements of Roman law and empire. Dante's faith in *Pax Romana* and in world government generally was more than religious; it was part of an attempt to develop the *logical* implications of man's obligation to live reasonably and peacefully. Here, science, logic, politics, religion, and art are all aspects of a unitary intellectual enterprise whose propositions may appear today as idle speculation but which in their historical lifetime were intensely practical. Similarly, any reader of the rationalist systems of Grotius, Hobbes, Spinoza, Leibniz, and Kant will readily discover that even the most metaphysical and theological propositions of these exponents of the Enlightenment were involved in their attempts to be practical moralists. The same could be said for such reformers as Descartes, Locke, Hegel, Nietzsche, Mill, Bergson, Croce, and Dewey. Turn where you will, you will find that any philosophy worth attention has a historical environment and practical relevance which account for its mission and vitality and which when gone leave a philosophy to exhibit its skeletal remains in classrooms, libraries, and museums, where it joins the immortal dead. It is only then that philosophies can be dissected into metaphysics, theology, and other disciplines which happen to be the objects of current abuse by those philosophers whose ambition it is to be more practical than they really are.

WING-TSIT CHAN[a]

Chinese Theory and Practice

In order to understand the relation between Chinese philosophical theories and practical affairs, it is necessary, first, to see what the Chinese have conceived that relation to be, and then to see how theory is related to actual practice. This paper is therefore divided into two parts: (1) the Chinese concepts of truth, and (2) humanism in practice, humanism being taken as the most dominant doctrine.

It is often said that there is a closer relationship between philosophical theories and practice in China than in other lands. Whether this is true or not, it is certainly a fact that the relationship between philosophical doctrines and actual practice in China has been very close indeed. As to why this has been the case, it is sometimes said that the system that has dominated Chinese thought throughout most of Chinese history, namely, Confucianism, is the same system that has controlled Chinese education, society, and government for some 2,000 years, and therefore there has been an unusually close affinity between theory and practice. It is also suggested that Chinese philosophers have not been much interested in abstract theories, and have, instead, directed their thinking chiefly to practical problems. There is also the theory that Chinese philosophy is essentially pragmatic and devoid of absolute, inflexible theories and is therefore more easily applicable to human affairs.

There is some element of truth in each of these assertions, but the matter goes much deeper. In order to find an adequate explanation of the practical character of Chinese philosophy, we must understand the Chinese concept of truth. First of all, truth is not understood as something revealed from above or as an abstract principle, however logically consistent, but as a discoverable and demonstrable principle in human affairs. In other words, the real test of truth is in human history. Therefore, when Confucius (551–479 B.C.) frequently referred to the legendary sage-emperors Yao and Shun[b] and when he repeatedly looked to the past, he was looking for historical evidence of truth. If that was conservatism, it was only incidental to that search. The fact that China has had a long and continuous history in which Confucianism has had a long and continuous domination makes the belief in the close relationship between theory and practice all the more certain. In the history of Chinese philosophy, there has been a continuing controversy over the question whether principles are transcendent to or immanent in events. Roughly speaking, the school of Chu Hsi[c] (1130–1200), which represents the rationalistic wing of Neo-Confucianism, insists that principles are inherent in things and events, while the school of Wang Yang-ming[d] (Wang Shou-jen, 1472–1529), which represents the idealistic wing of Neo-Confucianism, insists that principles are inherent in the mind. However, they both agree that the validity of principles can be tested only in actual events. As a matter of fact, Chinese philosophers generally do not distinguish between reality and actuality. From the point of view of technical philosophy, this Chinese position lacks refinement, but the Chinese spirit of stressing the affinity of theories and practical affairs is clear.

Since truth can be discovered and tested only in events—and that means chiefly human events—it follows that the records of truth are found in historical documents. Confucius repeatedly looked to such records, whether written or not. Eventually these records came to constitute what may be called the Chinese Canon, notably the Four Books and the Five Classics.[1] It is generally understood that these Classics are the foundation stones of Confucian teachings. It is not so generally understood, however, that they have been regarded by most Confucians as histories also. They are not merely histories of changing human events but histories of events as the unfolding and functioning of eternal principles. The Chinese word for Classics, *"ching,"*[e] means constancy, that is, what is immutable and invariable. As Dr. Hu Shih[f] has aptly remarked, the Chinese Classics have served for China as a Natural Law, for they have exercised supreme authority over government, society, religion, and other aspects of Chinese culture.[2] Historically, the Classics were set up as authority by Confucian scholars in the second century B.C. for the purpose of checking the power of the emperor. They were advanced as the highest authority, even over and above that of the sovereign, whose power had been supposed to be absolute. In 124 B.C., a national university was established with five colleges corresponding to the Five Classics, each with fifty nationally prominent scholars attached to it. The simpler of the Four Books were required as texts in school education. From the beginning of the fourteenth century, the Classics were accepted as standard texts for the civil service examinations, on the basis of which civil officials were selected. Until 1905 they were regarded as the norm for all aspects

[1] The Four Books are the *Analects,* the *Great Learning,* the *Doctrine of the Mean,* and the *Book of Mencius,* and the Five Classics are the *Book of History,* the *Book of Odes,* the *Book of Changes,* the *Book of Rites,* and the *Spring and Autumn Annals.*

[2] "The Natural Law in the Chinese Tradition," *Natural Law Institute Proceedings,* V (1953), 133–141.

of life. As such, they have provided China with a set of standards which are open to discussion and examination at all times. They have maintained the unity and harmony of Chinese culture and life for a remarkably long period. Most important of all, they have been living testimonies of the conviction that truth finds its validity primarily in history, and, as a Confucian would say, "can wait a hundred generations for a sage [to confirm it] without doubt."[3] At the same time, they grew to be so powerful as to dominate Chinese thought, restrict creative philosophical thinking, and discourage intellectual variety. At times, their study even degenerated into pure scholasticism. There can be no doubt that the belief in the supreme authority of the Classics delayed the advent of both the intellectual renaissance and natural science in China.

The fact that the Classics have been accepted as the highest standards for human activity implies that the eternal truths which they embody are essentially moral. This is another important aspect of the Chinese concept of truth. The Natural Law covers all events, so that all events, whether human or natural, have a moral character. When the Confucian of the second century B.C. advocated a philosophy of correspondence between political events and astronomical phenomena, they were not believers in astrology. To a great extent they were politically motivated, for they purposely utilized certain objective laws and events to control the emperor. Behind this political activity, however, there was the fundamental conviction about truth that it is essentially moral. That is to say, all truths, whether evident in Nature or in human history, are meant for the purpose of moral cultivation. The Chinese make no absolute distinction between physical things and human activities, both being represented by the word *"shih."*[g] (Only the Whiteheadian term "event" approximates this word.) They both obey the same set of laws, of which the moral law is considered the ultimate. As a result, there has been very little discussion on the problem of truth and falsehood but much discussion on the problem of good and evil. In fact, the question of good and evil has been one of the most important in philosophical inquiry throughout Chinese history, whether in Confucianism, Taoism, or Buddhism. On the transcendental level, Buddhism denies the distinction between good and evil. Taoism to some extent does the same. And, under the influence of Buddhism and Taoism, Neo-Confucianism made similar assertions. But Chinese philosophers have been quick to add that the having of no distinction of good and evil in the transcendental state is itself good. As Ch'eng Hao's[h] (Ch'eng Ming-tao, 1032–1085) famous saying has it, "Good and evil are all natural principles. What is called evil is not originally evil."[4] And Chu Hsi added, "All natural principles are good."[5] It is significant to note that the term *"shih-fei"*[i] (true or false) almost invariably has moral connotations.

However, it is not enough simply to read the Classics and learn the moral

[3] *Doctrine of the Mean* XXIX. For an English translation, see Lin Yutang,[ak] ed., *The Wisdom of Confucius* (New York: The Modern Library, 1938), p. 29.

[4] *I-shu*[al] ("Surviving Works"), IIA.1b; *Ts'ui-yen*[am] ("Pure Words"), I.9b, II.13a–b, both in the *Erh-Ch'eng ch'üan-shu*[an] ("Complete Works of the Ch'eng Brothers"), Ssu-pu pei-yao[ao] edition.

[5] *Yü-lei*[ap] ("Classified Conversations"), IV.12b.

truths contained therein. Truth comes to life only when it is genuinely and concretely realized by one's person through actual polishing and training in human affairs. This is the concept of *t'i-jen,*[j] or personally realizing and witnessing truth, a term that defies simple translation. It involves a critical and rational understanding of things, a personal conviction as to their meaning and significance, and, finally, an intuition of their ultimate reality. Such realization can come about only after rich experience in human affairs. One of the strongest advocates of such realization was the idealistic Neo-Confucian Wang Yang-ming. He was no Meditation Buddhist in Confucian disguise, as has been charged, for he always insisted that realization must be preceded by "always making endeavor in things."[6] To him, ultimate truth is to be realized in the midst of human affairs and can be understood only in the light of human affairs. Of course, Wang, Ch'eng, and Chu were all talking about moral truths. But, then, to most Chinese philosophers, no truth is amoral.

This close relation between truth and experience is expressed in yet another concept, namely, the close relation between action and words. Confucius was one of the very first Chinese thinkers to lay equal emphasis on both. He always insisted that words and actions should correspond. He said, "I listen to a person's words and watch his action."[7] He also said, "What the superior man says can be carried out."[8] In the *Doctrine of the Mean* it is said, "A superior man's words correspond to his action, and his action corresponds to his words."[9] The whole doctrine of the rectification of names in ancient Chinese philosophy, as well as the whole extensive discussion on the correspondence between names and actuality[10] in ancient China, was ethical in intent rather than epistemological or metaphysical. In the entire Neo-Confucian movement, this equal emphasis on words and action was faithfully maintained. According to Ch'eng I[k] (Ch'eng I-ch'uan, 1033–1107) and his elder brother Ming-tao, the efforts for extension of knowledge (of which words are but expressions) and actual demonstration are to be exerted simultaneously.[11] Chu Hsi said, "Knowledge and action always require each other. It is like a person who cannot walk without legs although he has eyes, and who cannot see without eyes although he has legs. With respect to order, knowledge comes first, and, with respect to importance, action is more important."[12] Again, he said, "The efforts of both knowledge and action must be exerted to the utmost. As one knows more clearly, he acts more earnestly, and, as he acts more earnestly, he knows more clearly."[13] The final result was Wang Yang-ming's famous doctrine of the unity of knowledge and action. He said, "Knowledge is the crystallization of the will to

[6] *Ch'üan-hsi lu*[aq] ("Records of Instructions for Practical Living"), secs. 87, 145, 147, 163, 170, 186, 188. For realization, see secs. 31, 66, 76, etc.

[7] *Analects* V.9. For an English translation, see Arthur Waley, trans., *The Analects of Confucius* (London: Allen & Unwin Ltd., 1938).

[8] *Ibid.*, XIII.4. Similar equal emphasis on words and action is found in *ibid.*, XIV.4; XV.5; XVIII.8.

[9] VIII.

[10] See Fung Yu-lan,[ar] *A History of Chinese Philosophy*, Vol. I (Princeton: Princeton University Press, 1952), pp. 54, 59–63, 173, 204–206, 253–255, 302–311, 323–325, 332–335.

[11] *Ts'ui-yen*, I.16.

[12] *Chu Tzu ch'üan-shu*[as] ("Complete Works of Chu Hsi"), III.8a–b.

[13] *Ibid.*

act, and action is the task of carrying out that knowledge; knowledge is the beginning of action, and action is the completion of knowledge."[14] Wang is usually credited with the innovation of the doctrine, but, while he was the first one to identify knowledge and action, the stress on their equal importance, and by implication on their mutual involvement, is an ancient one. Actually, in all this emphasis on the equality or identity of knowledge and action, the stress has always been on the side of action. This tradition can be traced to the *Book of History,* where it is said, "It is not difficult to know but difficult to act."[15] It was continued by Confucius, who taught that "the superior man acts before he speaks and afterwards speaks according to his actions."[16] We have already noted that to Chu Hsi action is more important than knowledge. When Sun Yat-sen turned the ancient doctrine around and said that "it is difficult to know but easy to act," he was really upholding the long tradition of emphasizing action.

From the above it is clear that in the Chinese tradition theories and practice have been thought of as complementary, interdependent, mutually penetrating, and even identical. Along with this conviction, or perhaps because of it, several significant developments have taken place in the history of Chinese thought. One is that in traditional China philosophy never became a separate discipline of study. This discipline came into existence only as a result of Western influence. Not that there has been no metaphysics. Neo-Taoist philosophy and much of Buddhist philosophy are highly metaphysical. But they are outside the main currents of Chinese thought. In the major tradition, philosophy was not set aside as an independent discipline but was regarded as a study of all human affairs in all their connections and ramifications. The word for philosophy, *"che,"*[1] means the same as the Greek *"sophia."* Etymologically it consists of the "mouth" and the "hand" (or the axe) as integral parts, thus suggesting words and action. But we are not sure of this etymology. At any rate, philosophy has been understood basically as wisdom. Among the Confucian Classics, the book that corresponds to philosophy is the *Book of Changes,* which was originally used for divination. To interpret Chinese philosophy as an outgrowth of ancient oracles is to miss the essential point. The connection between Chinese philosophy and divination has nothing to do with supernaturalism or revelation. Rather, divination performed the function of philosophy in early Chinese society because divination was a search for decisions for action, which is the very purpose of Chinese philosophy as the Chinese have understood it. In short, philosophy is dedicated to everyday life and ordinary action. Consequently, the Chinese did not develop a special terminology for philosophy different from everyday language and beyond the understanding of the simple man. As the *Doctrine of the Mean* puts it, the Way of the superior man "can be understood by the men and women of simple intelligence."[17] Major terms

[14] *Ch'üan-hsi lu,* sec. 5; see Frederick Goodrich Henke, trans., *The Philosophy of Wang Yang-ming* (Chicago: Open Court Publishing House, 1916), p. 55.
[15] See James Legge, trans., *The Shoo King*[at] (Hong Kong: Henry Frowde, 1865), p. 258.
[16] *Analects* II.13. See also IV.24; IV.22; XIV.29.
[17] XII.

such as *"li"*[m] (principle), *"ch'i"*[n] (material force or matter-energy), *"yin,"*[o] *"yang,"*[p] *"jen"*[q] (humanity), and so forth are ordinary words connected with various aspects of life, including art, government, medicine, and even cooking. To be sure, the Neo-Taoists and Buddhists used very technical philosophical terms, and terms like *"ch'i"* can become very technical, but they are exceptions rather than the rule.

Another interesting development parallel with or growing out of the close relation between theories and practice is that, aside from a few philosophers, notably Chuang Tzu[r] (between 399 and 295 B.C.), the Taoist Kuo Hsiang[s] (d. 312 A.D.), and Neo-Taoist and Buddhist philosophers, all have been men active in social and political affairs. Confucius was, of course, the one who set the pattern. As was said of him, "If for three months he was not in government employment he would be at a loss,"[18] so anxious was he for an active life. From Tung Chung-shu[t] (*ca.* 174–104 B.C.) through Chu Hsi down to K'ang Yu-wei[u] (1857–1927), with only a few exceptions, all prominent scholars have been active public figures. A typical case is that of Wang Yang-ming. After he started his public career at twenty-eight, all the rest of his life, with the exception of seven or eight years, was devoted to government service—as a magistrate, a governor, a minister of military affairs, or a military governor suppressing several rebellions, and so forth. In our own day, Chinese philosophers have been intimately involved in social and political movements.

Because Chinese philosophers have emphasized action more than words, and because they themselves were dedicated to social and political action, few have shut themselves up in an ivory tower to write long treatises on philosophy or any theoretical subject. This explains the scarcity of such materials in the huge body of Chinese literature. More often than not, they have propounded their doctrines in conversations, letters, and official documents. Hence, the teachings of Confucius, Lao Tzu,[v] and others are found in conversations. Books like the *Chuang Tzu* seem to consist of systematic essays. Actually, they are series of conversations. The two most important works of Ch'eng Ming-tao are his "On Calming Human Nature"[w] and "On Understanding *Jen* (Humanity)."[x] [19] The former is part of a letter, and the latter is a conversation. Similarly, the most important piece of work by Wang Yang-ming is his *Records of Instructions for Practical Living,* which is recorded dialogues, especially the essay on "Pulling up the Root and Stopping up the Source,"[y] which is part of a letter included in the *Records.*[20] The source of Chu Hsi's philosophy is his conversations, recorded and published in 140 chapters.

These facts, that Chinese Philosophy finds its being and expression in the common life and common speech of the Chinese, that most Chinese philosophers have been active men, and that their philosophical works have been chiefly writings connected with actual living, should convince us that the close relationship between theories and practice is not just a conviction in China but

[18] *Book of Mencius* IIIB.3.
[19] *I-shu,* IIA.3a–b, and *Wen-chi*[au] ("Literary Works"), III.1a–b, in the *Erh-ch'eng ch'üan-shu.*
[20] *Ch'uan-hsi lu,* secs. 142–143.

a demonstrated fact. However, we need to examine at least one basic doctrine and see how it has actually been applied to practical affairs. In order to do so, we must find the most representative doctrine, one that has been prevalent over a long period of time and has been characteristic not only of Confucianism but of Taoism and Buddhism as well. Fortunately, such a doctrine is not difficult to find. Most students of Chinese thought will immediately mention humanism, for humanism is evident in all aspects of Chinese life, is characteristic of all three traditional systems, and has prevailed in China for many centuries.

The emergence of man as of supreme importance took place very early in Chinese history, probably before Confucius. During the Shang Dynasty (1751–1112 B.C.), spiritual beings exercised direct control over men and their affairs. By the Chou period (1111–256 B.C.), however, their influence gradually declined. The mandate of Heaven, by which a ruler obtained his power to rule, used to be absolute but now came to be looked upon with misgiving. "The mandate of Heaven is not constant," an early Chou poet declared.[21] He also said, "Never mind your ancestors! Cultivate your virtue."[22] The new emphasis was now on man and his moral character. The emphasis on human virtue instead of on the powers of spirits or the might of the Lord-on-High represented a radical transition from the Shang to the Chou. The conquest of the Shang must have required a great deal of ingenuity and ability, and the importance of man could not have failed to impress thinking men. New talents were needed for new trades and the building of new towns. Thus, the role of man became greater and greater. The time finally came when a slave became a prime minister. By 645 B.C., a prime minister had declared that "The Way of heaven is far away and the Way of man is near,"[23] and, in 547 B.C., some famous words were uttered that were to become the established expression for the traditional Chinese concept of immortality. "The best is to establish virtue," so went the words, "the next best is to establish achievement, and still the next best is to establish words. When these are not abandoned with time, it may be called immortality."[24]

It was Confucius, of course, who brought Chinese humanism to its climax. When he was asked about knowledge, he said it was to know man.[25] When he was asked about serving spirits, he answered, "If you cannot serve man, how can you know to serve spirits?"[26] When he was asked about wisdom, he said it was "to attend to the welfare of the people."[27] Confucius was so concerned with man that, when a stable was burned down, he asked only if any person was hurt and did not ask about the horses.[28] In government, he shifted its center from the rulers to the people, urging the feeding and educating of the people as the primary functions of government.[29] The traditional concept of the superior man meant superiority in blood, for the term *"chün-tzu"*[z] literally meant sons of rulers. Confucius changed it to mean superiority in character.

[21] *Book of Odes,* ode no. 235. For an English translation, see Arthur Waley, trans., *The Book of Songs* (New York: Houghton Mifflin Co., 1937). [22] *Ibid.*

[23] *Tso chuan*[av] ("Tso's Commentary on the *Spring and Autumn Annals*"), Duke Chao, 18th year. See James Legge, trans., *The Ch'un-Ts'ew*[aw] (Hong Kong: Henry Frowde, 1872).

[24] *Ibid.,* Duke Hsiang,[ax] 24th year. [25] *Analects* XII.22.

[26] Ibid., XI.11. [27] *Ibid.,* VI.20. [28] *Ibid.,* X.12. [29] *Ibid.,* XIII.9.

This radical change in concept practically amounted to a social revolution, and it definitely contributed to the steady decline of feudalism, which finally collapsed in the third century B.C. The climax of humanism can be summed up in this celebrated saying of Confucius: "It is man that can make the Way great and not the Way that can make man great."[30] His humanism is complete.

At this point we must immediately add that Confucian humanism does not imply in the least that the Supreme Being is either non-existent or unimportant. When he said, "Respect the spirits but keep them at a distance,"[31] he merely wanted people to solve their own problems and direct their own destiny instead of depending on spirits or ancestors. Confucius clearly said that the superior man stands in awe of Heaven.[32] He said that at fifty he knew the will of Heaven.[33] The matter of religion will be discussed in a later session. Suffice it to say that, while genuinely believing in a Supreme Being, Confucianism unmistakably teaches that man is the center of things.

It may be objected that, while Confucianism is unmistakably humanistic, Taoism is certainly naturalistic and Buddhism otherworldly. No one can deny naturalism in Taoism or otherworldliness in Buddhism. It is not generally realized, however, that both Taoism and Buddhism are humanistic also. It may be surprising, but it is true.

On the surface, the *Lao Tzu* (*Tao-te ching*[aa]) seems to teach withdrawal from the human world. Actually, at least a third of the book deals with the art of governing, including a few chapters on military operations.[34] Chuang Tzu did say that "man, compared to the myriad things, is like the tip of a hair upon a horse's skin."[35] He also urged us "not to violate the Way with the human heart nor to assist Nature with man."[36] But three of the seven so-called "inner" chapters of the *Chuang Tzu,* which are considered to be the authentic chapters, deal with the mundane world, the ideal teacher, and the ideal ruler. The ideal being, to him as to Lao Tzu, is the sage, and is not one who withdraws from the human world. He takes no action (*wu-wei*[ab]), but, according to Kuo Hsiang, "By taking no action is not meant folding up one's arms and closing one's mouth."[37] He also said, "Although the sage is in the midst of government, his mind seems to be in the mountain forest. . . . His abode is in the myriad things, but it does not mean that he does not wander freely."[38] His ideal is what the Taoists have called "sageliness within and kingliness without."[39] This ideal was accepted in later Confucianism as well. By following Nature, then, Taoism simply means to be natural, which does not mean to be any less human. After all, the main theme in the long development of Taoism, both as a philosophy and as a religion, has been the cultivation of a long life, an everlasting life if possible. This theme is prominent in both Lao Tzu and Chuang Tzu, and was

[30] *Ibid.,* XV.28.
[31] *Ibid.,* VI.20.
[32] *Ibid.,* XVI.8; see also VI.26; IX.11; XIV.37.
[33] *Ibid.,* XII.4.
[34] XXXVI, LVII, LXVIII, LXIX, LXXVI.
[35] *Chuang Tzu* XVI; see Herbert A. Giles, trans., *Chuang Tzu, Mystic, Moralist, and Social Reformer* (2nd ed., rev., Shanghai: Kelly and Walsh, 1926), p. 202.
[36] *Chuang Tzu* VI; see Fung Yu-lan, trans., *Chuang Tzu, A New Selected Translation with an Exposition of the Philosophy of Kuo Hsiang* (Shanghai: Commercial Press, 1933), p. 113.
[37] Commentary on the *Chuang Tzu* XI.
[38] *Ibid.,* I.
[39] *Chuang Tzu* XXXIII; cf. Giles, *op. cit.,* p. 439.

even translated into action in the Taoist religion. For centuries, it tried various ways and means, including exercise, diets, medicine, and alchemy, in an effort to prolong life on earth.

As to Buddhism, most people agree that it has its otherworldly aspects. It is important to point out, however, that it was in an intensively humanistic atmosphere that Buddhism entered China and thrived. Consequently, from the very beginning, the Buddha was understood in human terms. In the well-known treatise, "The Disposition of Error" (*Li-huo lun*[ac]) by Mou Tzu[ad] (2nd cent. A.D.?), perhaps the first Chinese treatise on Buddhism, there is repeated emphasis on the Buddha as a man of moral achievements, claiming that he "accumulated many virtues," "aimed at virtue," "was the progenitor of virtue," etc.[40] The Chinese translation for the Buddha's name, Śākyamuni, was *"Neng-jen,"*[ae] literally "the ability to be good." Temples dedicated to him were called *"jen-tz'u,"*[af] "temples of goodness."

To be sure, the Buddha has been worshipped in China as a deity. In fact, the Chinese people worship three Buddhas, or, rather, the Buddha in Three Bodies or three aspects. But the most popular Buddhist deity in China has been Avalokiteśvara or Kuan-yin,[ag] and Kuan-yin has been almost humanized. In India, from the third to the twelfth century, and in Japan today, he retains his transcendental and heavenly features, but in China he has been devoid of these qualities and has become a human figure, and, from the T'ang period (618–907) on, a woman, or Goddess of Mercy, "Mother" to millions of devotees. In pictorial representations, the Indian rosaries are still present, but, more often than not, they are carried by a crane, a Chinese symbol for longevity. Kuan-yin holds a flower vase from which all kinds of blessings are poured over all of humanity. And these blessings are not *nirvāṇa,* a world transcending our own, but such human blessings as health, wealth, long life, and, most important of all, children. Instead of sitting in the high heavens looking upon us with compassion, she is likely to be sitting by a bamboo grove, carrying a baby or holding a fish basket. A story was even invented in the eleventh century that she was originally a girl who became a goddess because of her filial piety. Kuan-yin is so close to mankind as to be almost human.

The story of Chinese Buddhism is too complicated to go into here. It is often said, however, that the Pure Land and Meditation schools have provided Chinese Buddhism with a general pattern of practice. It is significant that in both these schools Buddhism has been humanized.

It sounds strange to say that the Pure Land school is humanistic, for to pray to be reborn in Paradise means to get away from the human world. Nevertheless, man occupies a central position in this movement. Technically speaking, the school is not indigenous to China, for the doctrine was taught in India and the basic texts are Indian. But in spirit and character it is truly Chinese, and it now exists nowhere else but in China and Japan, in both of which it is the most popular Buddhist sect. While in India rebirth in the Pure Land meant a

[40] Seng-yu,[ay] ed., *Hung-ming chi*[az] ("Essays Elucidating the Doctrine"), I.1B.2a. Ssu-pu pei-yao edition.

complete break with earthly life, which was considered a life of suffering, in the Chinese Pure Land school it means an extension of earthly living. There is no deprecation of mundane life. Human relations are continued in the Pure Land. This is why one should transfer his merits to his ancestors, and to the Buddhists this act is considered one of the most meritorious. One cannot help hearing here the ring of a Confucian note.

In the Meditation school the most important tenet is the belief that Buddha-nature is inherent in one's own mind and that the best means to salvation is to look into one's mind to see Buddha-nature there. This is what later Buddhists called "directly pointing to the human mind and becoming a Buddha by seeing one's own nature." The result is the doctrine of salvation by oneself. What is more interesting, salvation is to be achieved here and now. And, most interesting of all, it is to be achieved "in this very body." One cannot help recalling that Confucians have always regarded the body as a gift from parents and, as such, as a sacred trust and therefore to be well taken care of, and, that for centuries, as has already been noted, the Taoists tried many ways to make the body suitable for everlasting life on earth.[41]

From the above it is clear that in China the note of humanism has been strong not only in Confucianism but in Taoism and Buddhism also. It is not necessary to argue any further that humanism is the keynote in Chinese thought. That keynote vibrates throughout Chinese history. What we need to do now is to see how this uncompromising humanism has affected Chinese practices and institutions. For this purpose we shall concentrate on two questions: (1) Has man in fact occupied a central position in Chinese institutions? (2) Has man in fact been regarded as important?

With respect to the central position of man in Chinese life, it is significant to note that man, rather than law, has been the controlling factor in Chinese political life. The subject of government will be discussed in a later session. It suffices to point out that, as early as Confucius, man was considered the most important element in government. "The administration of government depends on men," declared the Sage. "Let there be men and the government will flourish," he said, "but, without men, government will decay and cease."[42] Up to our own time, government in Chinese history has been based on man rather than law or systems. Not that there were no laws or systems, but man was considered the deciding factor. Consequently, government officials were selected through an open competitive civil service examination which resulted in the institution of government by scholar-gentlemen, that is, government by the elite. Generally speaking, the record of these scholar-gentlemen has been a worthy one. It was good enough to be praised and imitated in eighteenth-century Europe. Nevertheless, it has given China a tremendous handicap in her transition from government by men to government by law, and personal considerations in Chinese government have been a curse.

[41] For a more extensive discussion on the Chinese humanization of Buddhism, see the writer's article, "Transformation of Buddhism in China," *Philosophy East and West*, VII, Nos. 3 & 4 (October, 1957–January, 1958), 107–116.

[42] *Doctrine of the Mean* XX.

Not only in government but also in art has man been the center in China. From its earliest days, Chinese poetry has been concerned with man's fortune and misfortune, his joys and sorrows, and his family and friends. It is man's sentiments that poets strive to express. This idea is stated more than once in the Classics. In the *Book of History* it is said that "poetry is to express the will."[43] This dictum is repeated in Tso's[ah] *Commentary* on the *Spring and Autumn Annals*.[44] And in the *Book of Rites* it is declared that "poetry is to express the will."[45] When Confucius said that the odes can arouse the mind, can help us observe social conditions, can assist us in living as a group, can express our feelings of dissatisfaction, and can help us fulfill the more immediate duty of serving our fathers and the remoter one of serving one's ruler, as well as becoming acquainted with the names of birds, animals, and plants,[46] he was describing the function of Chinese poetry that has been accepted in Chinese history ever since his time. It is true that there have been Nature poetry and religious poetry in China, but they are exceptions rather than the rule. While it has been the convention for poets to devote the first half of a poem to the description of natural scenery, the purpose is chiefly to create a mood for the expression of human sentiments in the latter half.

Like drama in many lands, Chinese drama had a religious origin and, consequently, in its early stages had supernatural characters and supernatural themes. But, as it developed, it quickly gave way to the portrayal of historical events and social life and the expression of sentiments. What is true of Chinese poetry and drama is also true of Chinese music, for it has always been a part of the poetic and dramatic arts.

It may be argued that in Chinese painting man occupies a rather insignificant place. In the traditional classification of painting, landscape and flowers-and-birds precede people-and-things. Landscape is the crowning art of China, in which the fundamental principles of art are embraced and the greatest artistic talents have been immortalized. It is truly the representative art of China. Here man seems to be subordinated to Nature, for human figures are usually very small, often incidental, and sometimes totally absent. This fact has led some Western writers to conclude that man is not important in China.

To understand the true meaning of Chinese landscape painting, however, one must understand its relation to poetry. It is well known to students of Chinese art that in Chinese painting there is poetry and in Chinese poetry there is painting, or, as Kuo Hsi[ai] (*ca.* 1085) put it, "Poetry is formless painting, and painting is poetry in visual form." In short, the two arts are not only related but identical as far as their ultimate functions are concerned. What is their function? It is none other than to express human sentiments of joy and sorrow, happiness and anger, and feelings of peace, nobility, loneliness, and so on. Chinese artists paint landscape for the same reason poets describe scenery in their poems. Their purpose is to refine the feelings, stimulate the mind, and create a mood so that when the reader or onlooker emerges from the mood,

[43] See Legge, trans., *Shoo King,* p. 48.
[44] Duke Hsiang, 27th year.
[45] XIX.
[46] *Analects* XVII.9.

he becomes a nobler soul, a loftier spirit, a friendlier neighbor, a more pious son, in short, a better human being. There is no subordination of man to Nature in Chinese landscape painting. Neither is there escape from the human world.

Not only is man central in Chinese government and the arts, but even in religion, which is supposed to be otherworldly and transcendental. This is not to deny that most Chinese Buddhists aspire to go to Paradise, the "Pure Land." But, significantly, one of the most important transformations of Buddhism in China has been the change from the doctrine of salvation in *nirvāṇa* after death to the doctrine of salvation on earth and "in this very body," as we have pointed out. In spite of its acceptance of Buddhist concepts of heavens and hells, the Taoist religion has always held to the goal of everlasting life on earth. Immortals are believed to inhabit the high mountains. They may ascend to heaven, but, more often than not, they roam this earth and move among men, guiding them and helping them. The center of religion is the human world, where even man's own body becomes important.

These observations are quite general, but they are based on such broad facts as to convince us that man in fact occupies a central place in the various aspects of Chinese culture.

As to the importance of man as such, it is often asked why, if man is so important, has the idea of the individual not been developed in Chinese thought? In answer to this it must be stressed that the Western impression that the individual is undermined in traditional Chinese society comes partly from limited observation of Chinese social and political life and partly from an inadequate understanding of Chinese thought. Since marriage has traditionally been arranged by parents, property held in the name of the family, and for a long time in Chinese history the family, rather than the individual, was treated as a unit, it would seem that China has had no respect for the individual. Furthermore, since both Taoism and Buddhism deny the self and Confucianism teaches obedience, it seems that Chinese thought attaches little importance to the individual as such.

Such observations are superficial. While in traditional China the Chinese has had no personal choice in marriage, he has enjoyed absolute freedom in the choice of religion. There is a general regard for privacy, in religion as in other spheres of life. While property has been held in common, each son has had his inalienable right to inheritance. There was no individual vote guaranteed by a constitution, and yet in village meetings every male adult was a voting member by natural right. In the thirteen-century-long tradition of civil service examinations, the basis for the selection of government officials was individual merit rather than race, creed, economic status, sex, or age.

Whether Buddhism denies the individual is a moot point. However, in the Mahāyāna concept of *nirvāṇa,* it is described in terms of permanence, joy, the ego, and purity. The self is not really denied. Certainly most Chinese Buddhists aspire to individual, eternal existence in Paradise. Taoism does advocate "having no self," and teaches that one must lose one's life in order to find it. Yet, the Taoist is the most rugged individualist among the Chinese. He would have as little government as possible. He would not be swayed by fear of other people's opinions. He meditates on Nature, not to overcome himself by it but to enjoy himself therein. Under Taoist influence Nature does seem to dominate in Chinese landscape painting where the human figure is dwarfed in the shadow of majestic mountains and rivers. But it is wrong to say that in Chinese landscape painting man is subjugated by Nature; the perspective is not intended to put man into oblivion, but to purify and harmonize his emotions and make him a better man. As to Confucianism, suffice it to quote from Confucius, who said, "Although the leader of three armies can be captured, the will of a common man cannot be destroyed,"[47] and from Mencius, who declared, "All things are complete in the self."[48] Some years ago a group of Oxford scholars, being disturbed by the popular but mistaken belief that the individual was respected in the West but suppressed in the East, examined the idea in all cultures. This is what the editor of the symposium had to say: "It was stated that the individual had been discovered by Christianity. Now, apart from the question of what the Christian religion has done for the individual—admittedly a very great deal—there can be no doubt that the statement is not true to historical facts. The India that produced Buddhism, not to speak of the greater part of the *Bhagavadgita,* in the centuries before the Christian era, had plainly been awake to the individual and his soul. In China, from the fifth century [B.C.] on, there were remarkable discoveries made by all sorts of thinkers as to the nature of personality and its value to society."[49]

Actually, one of China's chief troubles in recent decades has been an excess of individualism. Everyone has his own opinion. There have been far too many individualists who think they are above society. Teamwork and co-operative enterprise have been conspicuously lacking. This is the type of thing the communists have set out to destroy. The problem is whether they will destroy the individual himself in the process.

However, while the individual is fully considered as important, his importance is not to overshadow that of society. A balance of the two has to be maintained. In fact, the goal of moral discipline is exactly this balance. The highest ethical goal is humanity *(jen).* As Confucius taught, "The man of *jen,* wishing to establish his own character, also tries to help others to succeed."[50] This is an exceedingly important saying, one that is well known to any student of Confucianism. It is important, not only because it is a positive statement of the golden rule, but also because it expresses the central Chinese idea that a good man must also be a good member of society. Significantly the Chinese character for *jen* consists of two parts, one meaning man himself and the other meaning many, that is, society. The interest of the individual and that of society are fully recognized, and so is the necessity of their adjustment. A basic institution has existed for centuries for this purpose, namely, the family. Among the func-

[47] *Ibid.,* IX.25.
[48] *Book of Mencius* VIIB.14.
[49] E. R. Hughes, ed., *The Individual in East and West* (London: Oxford University Press, 1937), pp. 3–4.
[50] *Analects* VI.28.

tions of the family, surely one of the most important is its position as the intermediate point between the individual and the larger society. It is here that one is trained in the adjustments he will have to make throughout life as between himself and other men. This is the reason harmony has been stressed as a cardinal virtue for the family. How well the Chinese have succeeded in maintaining the balance between the individual and society and whether the family should continue to be the training ground for this adjustment in a modern democracy are important and interesting questions for discussions.

So far as our immediate question is concerned, the above observations cannot fail to lead to the conclusion that Chinese philosophy and practical affairs have been close both in theory and in fact.

In summary, from the Chinese concepts that truth can be discovered and tested only in events, that eternal truths are essentially moral, and that action and words are virtually identified, and from the fact that these concepts have resulted in humanism as the dominant system of Chinese thought, we are forced to the conclusion that Chinese philosophy and practical affairs have been close both in theory and in fact.

QUESTION: In your paper you have discussed Buddhism and Taoism at some length, and their place in Chinese life and thought is recognized. Nevertheless, it is hard to avoid the feeling that you have considered Confucianism the dominant system in Chinese history. Does this agree with the usual saying that the Three Systems of Confucianism, Buddhism, and Taoism have prevailed in parallel throughout much of Chinese history?

ANSWER: It is difficult to measure the influence of philosophical systems. Surely Taoism has exercised tremendous influence on Chinese art, religion, government, and philosophy of life, and Buddhism has contributed substantially to Chinese religion, philosophy, and art, especially sculpture. But there is no question that Confucianism, or, rather, Neo-Confucianism, has been the dominant system in China during the last 800 years. It has been the controlling system so far as government, education, literature, society, ethics, and noninstitutional religion are concerned. It went through many phases and has various aspects, but its fundamental tenets have remained throughout the centuries. In all these, both Buddhism and Taoism have played a secondary role. Furthermore, the metaphysics, espistemology, and psychology of medieval Buddhism and Taoism were assimilated into Confucianism to constitute Neo-Confucianism in the eleventh and twelfth centuries. Finally, there has been no significant Buddhist or Taoist development in the last 800 years whether in institutions or in thought.

QUESTION: You have emphasized the Confucian teaching of correspondence between theory and practice, and yet it seems that Confucius taught occasional departure from theory. In *Analects* XIII. 18, for example, Confucius taught that it is not upright for a son to bear witness against his father's stealing a sheep but upright for him to conceal the misconduct of his father. How do you explain that?

ANSWER: This and other teachings have given rise to the impression that Confucian ethics is relative or determined by circumstances, especially family relatives. This is not true. Actually, Confucians and Neo-Confucians have always strongly stressed eternal moral principles. At the same time, they have been practical enough to take care of special situations. They have done this with the twofold doctrine of Standard and Expedient. Eternal principles are Standard, while special situations require expedient measures. It is Standard to be forthright and honest, but in this case it is expedient to conceal the father's misconduct. The reason for this is not to sacrifice moral principles in order to be filial or to submit to the father's will. Rather, it is to sacrifice honesty to preserve the greater value of family harmony. This is permissible as an expedient when small issues are involved, so long as the total human values are preserved. However, when fundamental issues are involved, even family relations must be sacrificed. This is illustrated by the classical example of Confucius' hero, Duke Chou (d. 1094 B.C.). He executed his own older and younger brothers who were plotting for the overthrow of the Chou Dynasty (1111–256 B.C.). The principle "to annihilate relatives for the sake of great moral principles" (*ta-i mieh-ch'in*[aj]) has been a fundamental one in Confucianism.[51]

(The Chinese characters for this article are on the following page.)

[a] 陳榮捷
[b] 堯舜
[c] 朱熹
[d] 王陽明，守仁
[e] 經
[f] 胡適
[g] 事
[h] 程明道，顥
[i] 是非
[j] 體認
[k] 程伊川，頤
[l] 哲
[m] 理
[n] 氣
[o] 陰
[p] 陽
[q] 仁
[r] 莊子
[s] 郭象
[t] 董仲舒
[u] 康有爲
[v] 老子
[w] 定性書
[x] 識仁篇
[y] 拔本塞源論
[z] 君子
[aa] 道德經
[ab] 無爲
[ac] 理惑論
[ad] 牟子
[ae] 能仁
[af] 仁祠
[ag] 觀音
[ah] 左
[ai] 郭熙
[aj] 大義滅親
[ak] 林語堂
[al] 遺書
[am] 萃言
[an] 二程全書
[ao] 四部備要
[ap] 語類
[aq] 傳習錄
[ar] 馮友蘭
[as] 朱子全書
[at] 書經
[au] 文集
[av] 左傳
[aw] 春秋
[ax] 襄
[ay] 僧祐
[az] 弘明集

SHOSON MIYAMOTO[a]

The Relation of Philosophical Theory to Practical Affairs in Japan

I. PRINCE SHŌTOKU'S[b] IDEAL OF A NATIONAL STATE[1]

Prior to the introduction of Buddhism into Japan in the sixth century, there was no philosophical activity in the country. The people of the time were nurtured in the traditional Shinto[c] awe for Nature and its simplicity. That tradition still remains as an "exact reproduction of the ancient creed, just as the wooden temples of Ise[d] which are rebuilt every twenty years preserve the architecture of almost prehistoric times." The beauty of its simplicity in the form of straight lines is viewed in the quietness of the precincts. The aged trees and serene streams represent the beauty of the primitive life. Early Japan had a quite natural life. This way of life was decidedly practical, although not so conducive to conceptual reasoning. Influence from China by way of Korea changed this simplicity.

The contact with the Asian mainland was to effect a tremendous change and complex development in Japanese thought and culture. An ancient record states:

> In 538 [the *Nihongi*[e] says 552], the King of Paekche,[f] Syöng-Myöng,[g] sent a mission to Kimmei,[h] the Emperor of Japan, with presents consisting of an image of Shaka Butsu[i] in gold and copper, several flags and umbrellas and a number of Sūtras, saying: "This is the most excellent among all doctrines, but it is hard to explain and hard to understand. Even the Duke of Chou[j] and Confucius did not attain to a knowledge of it. It can give merit and reward

[1] Shoson Miyamoto, *Chūdō-shisō oyobi sono Hattatsu*[dq] ("Middle-Way Thought and Its Development") (Kyoto: Hozokan, 1944), pp. 854–911. This first part of this paper is re-constructed mostly from my article, "Kokka-riso to Kojin-jinkaku," or "Taigi to Shiji"[dr] ("Prince Shōtoku's Ideal of a National State and His Personal Individuality"), which was originally published in *Nihon Bukkyō no Kenkyū*[ds] ("Studies on Japanese Buddhism"), a special issue of the Journal, *Bukkyō Kenkyū*,[dt] II, No. 5 (September–October, 1938), 13–61.

without measure and without bounds and thus leads to a grasp of highest wisdom. Imagine a man possessing treasures to his heart's content and able to satisfy all his wishes. So it is with this wonderful doctrine. Every prayer is fulfilled and naught is wanting. Moreover, it has spread from distant India to the Three Han (Korea), where all receive it with reverence. Your servant therefore has humbly dispatched his retainer to transmit it to the Imperial Court and to spread it throughout the home provinces, in order to fulfill the words of the Buddha: "My Dharma shall spread to the East."[2]

The Emperor admired profoundly the *beauty* of the Buddha statue. This is a very important event for understanding the reason for the swift spread of Buddhism among the Japanese and for its impact on the practical affairs of their life. Ancient Shinto art and ceremonial worship had no images, while Buddhism inspired sculpture and painting of the image of the Buddha in India, Central Asia, China, and Korea. The great Graeco-*gandhāra* Buddhist art had for several hundred years, up to the year 538 during the reign of Emperor Kimmei, already cultivated deep spiritual realization in the countries of its influence.

By the end of the sixth century, a great crisis developed in Japan as the result of losing the ancient Japanese domains on the Korean Peninsula and also the defeat of her ally, the Kingdom of Paekche. But Japan was favored with a large number of Korean refugees, including many Buddhist artists and artisans, just as at the time of the crisis caused by the Mongol invasions many Zen masters fled to Japan during the Kamakura period (1192–1331) from the China of the Southern Sung Dynasty (1127–1279). The revolution wrought by Buddhism was moral as well as literary and artistic. It was the wish of Shōtoku Taishi (574–622), who may be regarded as the real founder of Japanese Buddhism, to give his people a better moral code. He was the type of genius and philosopher-statesman needed to mold the form and feature of the Japanese national State in the most critical period of her debut into the civilized nations of the world.

Prince Shōtoku[3] (*"shōtoku"* literally means "sovereign moral power"), a contemporary of Augustine of Canterbury and Muhammad of Arabia, was a prince regent of Empress Suiko.[k] He took office in 593, which is approximately half a century following the official introduction of Buddhism into Japan. Buddhism was at this time mainly a religion of immigrants, refugees, diplomats, those involved in commercial trade, and the royal family, who sought to utilize foreign economic, political, religious, and cultural means to gain distinction over powerful clans and feudal lords. The common people remained ignorant of Buddhism. The Japanese royal family in those days had yet to achieve its hegemony, and the clans and feudal lords were almost equal in distinction with the royal family.

[2] Sir Charles Eliot, *Japanese Buddhism* (London: Edward Arnold & Co., 1935), pp. 198–199. S. Miyamoto, "Waga-hō Tōru,"[au] in *Chūdō-shisō, op. cit.*, pp. 841–848.

[3] See Masaharu Anesaki,[av] *History of Japanese Religion* (London: Kegan Paul, Trench, Trübner & Co., 1930), p. 57, n. 1. See translation of *"shōtoku"* as "sovereign moral power," in Wm. Theodore de Bary, ed., *Sources of Japanese Tradition* (New York: Columbia University Press, 1958), p. 37.

The Buddhist idea of Mahāyāna (Great Vehicle) and Ekayāna (One Vehicle) of truth, and of the enlightened spirit of humanity, was conducive to the consolidation of the royal family as the sovereign power. This is the first attempt to apply philosophic thought to practical affairs.

From the earliest times it has been characteristic of Japanese Buddhism to worship the Buddha, rather than the *Dharma* (Law) or the *Saṅgha* (Assembly), of the Three Treasures. With the exception of the Zen (Ch'an[l]) sects, which worship Śākyamuni Buddha, the principal object of worship (*honzon*[m]) has been the cosmic or eternal Buddha. And this was always connected intimately with emperor-worship and ancestor-worship. This is the reason Buddhism became so much more pietistic and nationalistic in character than in either China or India, which emphasized the *Dharma* as philosophical thought and the *Saṅgha* in monastic life. Later the unbroken imperial lineage influenced the Shin[n] sect to adopt blood-succession, rather than *dharma*-succession, as was traditional in Buddhism, and so the eldest in the succession of the lineage of Shinran[o] becomes the head, the pope, of the Shin sect. We may find a clue to this unusual system when we consider the reason for Shinran's paying special homage to Prince Shōtoku, dedicating many songs of praise (*wasan*) to him, saying: "*Wakoku no Kyōshu Shōtoku-wo*"[p] ("Shōtoku is really the Buddha of Japan"). Prince Shōtoku "found in Buddhism a universal basis for the relationship of the ruler and the ruled. His inspiration helped in achieving national unity and in subduing the clannish spirit under it."[4]

Prince Shōtoku also utilized the Confucian idea of Heaven, Earth, and Man to establish the central authority of the court. It is reflected in the famous third Article of his *Seventeen Articles Constitution*:[5]

III. When you receive the imperial commands, fail not scrupulously to obey them. The lord is Heaven, the vassal is Earth. Heaven overspreads, and Earth upbears. When this is so, the four seasons follow their due course, and the powers of Nature obtain their efficacy. If the Earth attempted to overspread, Heaven would simply fall in ruin. Therefore it is that, when lord speaks, the vassal listens; when the superior acts, the inferior yields compliance. Consequently, when you receive the imperial commands, fail not to carry them out scrupulously. Let there be want of care in this matter, and ruin is the natural consequence.

He neglected, however, the idea that Heaven's will and movements may remove the Imperial Sovereignty if it becomes unsuitable. The emphasis on the need of public discussions and the people's co-operation is due to the influences of the Taoist *yin-yang*[q] reciprocal-circulation principle, the Confucian principle of the Mean, the Buddhist democratic equality; for example, as follows:

[4] "Prince Shōtoku," *op. cit.*, p. 17.

[5] See Sir George Sansom, *A History of Japan to 1334* (Stanford: Stanford University Press, 1958), pp. 51–52. "It is an important document and one of considerable historical interest, but it is today not generally accepted by Japanese scholars as Shōtoku Taishi's own work. It was most probably written as a tribute to his memory a generation or more after his death, when some of the reforms which he desired had at last been introduced; and this was a not unnatural act of piety, since he did beyond doubt play a leading part in the importation of ideas and things from China, thus leading the way towards an enrichment of Japanese life."

X. Let us cease from wrath, and refrain from angry looks. Nor let us be resentful when others differ with us, for all men have hearts, and each heart has its own leanings. Their right is our wrong, and our right is their wrong. We are not unquestionably sages, nor are they unquestionably fools. Both of us are simply ordinary men. How can anyone lay down a rule by which to distinguish right from wrong? For we are all, one with another, wise and foolish, like a ring which has no end. Therefore, although others give way to anger, let us on the contrary dread our own faults, and, though we alone may be in the right, let us follow the multitude and act like them.

XV. To turn away from that which is private, and to set our faces toward that which is public—this is the path of a minister. Now, if a man is influenced by private motives, he will assuredly feel resentment, and, if he is influenced by resentful feelings, he will assuredly fail to act harmoniously with others. If he fails to act harmoniously with others, he will assuredly sacrifice the public interest to his private feelings. When resentment arises, it interferes with order, and is subversive of law. Therefore, in the first clause it was said that superiors and inferiors should agree. The purport is the same as this.

Shōtoku sought to maintain harmony under the imperial throne, as seen in the First Article:

I. Harmony is to be valued, and an avoidance of wanton opposition is to be honored. All men are influenced by partisanship, and there are few who are intelligent. Hence, there are some who disobey their lords and fathers, or who maintain feuds with the neighboring villages. But, when those above are harmonious and those below are friendly, and there is concord in the discussion of business, right views of things spontaneously gain acceptance. Then, what is there which cannot be accomplished?

Prince Shōtoku contributed much to enrich the nation's life. The arts and sciences known on the continent were introduced and adapted, and it is interesting but not unnatural "that in the later ages, architects, and carpenters, sculptors and painters, artists of flower arrangements, masters of archery, adored the Prince as their patron saint, by organizing *Taishi-kō,*[r] i.e., *Shōtoku Taishi Union,* each according to the groups and localities, and by celebrating their Taishi festivals."[6]

Prince Shōtoku died in the year 622 at the age of 49. His wife died a year later. His eldest son, Yamashiro,[s] was popular as the heir apparent, but he and his wife committed tragic suicides when attacked by the arrogant Soga[t] clan, who were merciless to exclude any power which would prove an obstacle to their clannish ambition. It is to be noted that the Shōtoku family was of the closest kinship relation with the Soga family. "He died like a martyr, amid celestial portents, as we are told, and worthy of his father. 'If,' he said, 'I had raised an army and attacked Soga I should certainly have conquered. But for the sake of one person, I was unwilling to destroy the people'!" Thus he and his family took their lives before the statue of the Buddha. The whole family

[6] "Prince Shōtoku," *op. cit.*, p. 28.

of Shōtoku had kept the motto: "Everything is evanescent, and the only truth is the Buddha's teaching." This motto can be seen embroidered in the *tenju-koku*[u] *maṇḍala*[7] (*maṇḍala* depicting the land of Heavenly Life) tapestry, which was made in his memory by Lady Tachibana-no-Ōiratsume.[v] In this early period of the introduction of Buddhism, the life and the way of conduct of the Shōtoku family were extraordinary examples in which we can see how Buddhist teachings guided practical affairs.

Many historians and scholars of the present think that Prince Shōtoku is the founder of Japanese civilization, for to him is ascribed the *Seventeen Articles Constitution,* the commentaries on the *Saddharmapuṇḍarīka,* the *Śrīmālā,* and the *Vimalakīrti Sūtra(s)* and so on. The reason for ascribing these achievements to Prince Shōtoku, though they might be of later composition, is that his personality, his tragedy, and his sacrifice of his whole family led the people to worship him. Japan as a nation was not unified before this time, for she lacked an ideal personality for the unification of the country. Since that time Prince Shōtoku has been the idol of Japan, from whom everything ideal and cultural is believed to have originated. Seven great temples are also ascribed to him, namely, Hōryū-ji,[w] Shitennō-ji,[x] Chūgū-ji,[y] Hachioka-dera[z] (Kōryū-ji[aa]), Ikejiri-dera[ab] (Hōki-ji[ac]), Tachibana-dera,[ad] and Katsuragi-dera.[ae]

> Shitennō-ji was a Buddhist sanctuary, a place of worship, which remains even today the central temple of Osaka. Originally, it included four institutions: (1) Kyoden-in[af] (literally, "temple of reverence-field")... for discipline and learning; (2) Seyaku-in[ag] ("temple of the dispensary"); (3) Hiden-in[ah] ("temple of compassion-field"), and asylum for the helpless; (4) Ryōbyō-in[ai] ("temple of the hospital or sanatorium"). It was erected on a hillside on the eastern end of the Inland Sea. The Inland Sea was and is the maritime highway connecting central Japan with the western provinces and with Korea and China. Thus, the temple was erected at the post where the immigrants, artisans, missionaries, and envoys coming from the Continent finished their sea routes and landed in central Japan.... We can imagine how those newcomers from the Continent on landing at this port were impressed by the all-embracing spirit of the Buddha embodied in this sanctuary established by the ruler of the land.... Shitennō-ji was partly intended for the reception of the foreigners.[8]

II. BUDDHISM AS A GUARDIAN RELIGION OF JAPAN—AND THE PERSECUTION OF ITS CRITICS

In describing Japanese Buddhism, the terms "State religion" and "guardian religion" are often used, but it is important to know that, when a nation is still in its formative stages, the meanings of these terms are quite different from what we might understand them to be. The first form of Japanese Buddhism was a complex of faiths held by immigrants, a religion imported from abroad,

[7] The tapestry is preserved in the nunnery, Chūgū-ji, in the precinct of Hōryū-ji. The statue of "Thinking Maitreya Bodhisattva" is very famous, together with the Maitreya statue of Kōryū-ji at Uzumasa,[dw] in Kyoto.

[8] "Prince Shōtoku," *op. cit.*, pp. 21–23.

a source of material and worldly blessings, etc. The emphasis was on the worldly gains and benefits to be derived from praising the Buddha's virtues, and there was an almost total lack of real faith in or understanding of the teachings. A popular idea was that by worshipping the Buddha "calamities will be avoided and happiness will be brought about." This basic attitude continued even after Buddhism gained popular approval by the imperial courts and eventually came to have a determining influence upon the ceremonies of the State. Even today, the new post-war religions which promise the healing of sickness and the abolishing of poverty in return for oblation reveal the basic attitude which made the Japanese worship the Buddha for the sake of worldly blessings. This is not a trait of the primitive religious consciousness of the Japanese alone, for throughout the world, even in this modern scientific age, faith has a worldly and material attraction for the masses of the people. It is human nature to want a long life, a life free of sickness and disease, days filled with happiness, etc. The important thing is whether this basic desire of man is developed to include blessings for all of humanity. In Japanese Buddhism, prayer and worship are generally directed to the Buddha, not only for the sake of self, but for the sake of all people, for the country as a whole, and for society. In the early stages of the introduction of Buddhism into Japan there was no imperial or national State. With the introduction of Chinese culture, the people attempted to establish a society based upon the T'ang (618–907) court, and, though they attempted to utilize the ideals of Buddhist philosophy to establish a peaceful society, using such statements as "protecting and strengthening the country by the true *dharma*" (*shōbō-gokoku*[aj]), what actually happened was that prayers in ceremonies and rituals were offered for the prosperity and weal of society and the elimination of calamities and sickness.

Those who engaged in such pursuits consisted mainly of the upper classes connected with the imperial court, and thus it can be said that Japan was formed by the activities of the aristocracy, rather than by the lower stratum of society. This is evident in the famous statement: *"Kyūchū Shingon Kuge Tendai"*[ak]; that is, "Esoteric Shingon for the imperial court ritualism, and Esoteric Tendai for aristocratic ritualism."

Gradually, the structure of society changes as the imperial State is solidified, and in the Kamakura period the lower stratum of society becomes dominant and in control of the reins of government. In the beginning of the modern period, at the time of the Meiji Restoration (1868), the powers of government were returned to the imperial household.

In the Kamakura period, radical changes in Japanese society occurred. Kamakura is the new capital of the militarist Shōgunate.[al] The military are quite close to the farming class, who constitute 70 to 80 per cent of the Japanese population. This marks the new era—the era of the masses—warriors, peasants, and merchants, all of whom are non-aristocratic. This is especially true of the areas in the eastern part of Japan. This was the expansion of Japanese colonization; and Kamakura Buddhism was the frontier culture. The royal family and aristocracy in Kyoto became weakened. It is also interesting that such leaders of new religions as Hōnen[am] (1133–1212), Shinran (1173–1262), and Nichiren[an] (1222–1282) (except Dōgen,[ao] 1200–1253, who went to China for Buddhist studies) were all persecuted and exiled by the pressure of the old, established churches in Kyoto and Nara, giving them the opportunity to make contact with the common people. Although Hōnen, Shinran, Dōgen, and Nichiren achieved their religious reform in different ways, there was one way in which they were united: in the common cause of reformation and in the spirit which demands a religion of simplicity, practicality, absolute faith, individual spiritual awakening, and a new and vital aspiration.

It is interesting to note the reason for the persecution of the reformers, Hōnen and Shinran, by the traditional sects of the ancient city of Nara to the south and the monastery of Hiei[ap] to the north. They claimed[9] that Hōnen and Shinran disgraced the various deities and *buddhas;* that they were anti-socials who acknowledged the evil acts of men; and that they were anti-nationalistic. The traditional priests criticized Hōnen and Shinran as responsible for the weakening and disintegration of the imperial State, and advocated their banishment to distant and remote places and the promotion of the "various sects which would guard and strengthen the nation." They looked upon the

[9] In October, 1204, the priests of Mt. Hiei gathered for the purpose of petitioning for the suspension of the "single practice of the *Nembutsu*" (*senju-nembutsu*[dx]), that is, *Nembutsu*-absolutism. On hearing of this, in November, Hōnen wrote a "document in seven articles" (*shichikajō-kishomon*[dy]), as a solemn pledge and guarantee for the future generation, signed jointly by 190 disciples, and presented it to the Archibishop of Mt. Hiei: (1) to refrain from criticism of both Shingon and Tendai practices and to disregard other *buddhas* and *bodhisattvas;* (2) never to get into angry disputes with other Buddhists; (3) never to insist on people of a different faith and practice; and (4) in the name of the *Nembutsu,* which we say requires no *śīla,* discipline, not to encourage people to indulge in meat-eating, wine-drinking, or improper sexual intercourse. Never to say of people, by their sect, that they belong to the so-called "people of sundry practices," nor to say that those who trust in the Buddha's Original Vow need not be afraid of sin; (5, 6, and 7 are omitted here). Harper H. Coates and Rhūgaku Ishizuka,[dz] *Hōnen, the Buddhist Saint* (Kyoto: Chion-in, 1949), pp. 550–553.

In October, 1205, there came the [Nara]-Kōbuku-ji official petition for the suspension of the practice of *Nembutsu*-absolutism listing nine faults: (1) establish a new sect without Imperial sanction; (2) promulgate salvation by a new *maṇḍala;* (3) disregard for Śākyamuni Buddha; (4) disturb good deeds and virtues; (5) revolt against the national deities; (6) obscure the realities of the Pure-realm; (7) misinterpret *Nembutsu;* (8) corrupt public morals; (9) the partisanship of *Nembutsu*-absolutism ruins the harmony of state churches. Zennosuke Tsuji,[ea] *Nihon Bukkyō-shi*[eb] ("History of Japanese Buddhism"), Medieval Period, Vol. I (Tokyo: Iwanami-shoten, 1947), pp. 319–324.

Two years later, in 1207, Hōnen, Shinran, and others were persecuted and exiled. In May, 1224, the priests of Mt. Hiei, in a petition of the same kind, enumerated six faults, repeating the old ones except the fourth, which attacked the socio-historical view of the age of degeneration (*mappō*[ec]). "*Mappō*" literally means decrease or destruction of the Truth (Law), but it was used as the "Law of the Latter Days," a dark age full of vices and strife. This petition is found in the MSS: *Teishi-ikkō-senju-ki*[ed] ("Suspension of the Practice of *Nembutsu*-absolutism"). The text is reproduced in Kazuo Kasahara's[ee] *Shinran to Tōgoku Nōmin*[ef] ("Shinran and Farmers of East Japan") (Tokyo: Yamakawa-shuppansha, 1957), pp. 229–235; Junko Matsuno,[eg] *Shinran, sono Shōgai to Shisō no Tenkai-katei*[eh] ("Shinran: Historical Studies of Life and Thought") (Tokyo: Sanseido, 1959), pp. 81–96.

The doctrine of Three Periods (*shō-zō-matsu*[ei] or *-mappō*) has been commonly used in China and Japan. See Eliot, *Japanese Buddhism,* pp. 279, 424; Anesaki, *History of Japanese Religion,* p. 150, and *Nichiren, The Buddhist Prophet* (Cambridge: Harvard University Press, 1949), p. 4. But among Sanskrit texts, for instance, the *Vajracchedikā-prajñāpāramitā Sūtra,* says only "in the future, in the latter age, in the latter time, five hundred years later, when the good Law (Truth) becomes ruined." Further, the *Saddharmapuṇḍarīka Sūtra* says that "when his true law disappeared and the counterfeit of the true law (*saddharma-pratirūpaka*) was fading, when the reign (of the law) was being oppressed by proud monks, there was a monk, Bodhisattva Mahāsattva, called Sadāparibhūta." H. Kern, trans., *The Saddharma-puṇḍarīka, or The Lotus of the True Law,* Sacred Books of the East, Vol. XXI (Oxford, At the Clarendon Press, 1909), pp. 355–356. Sanskrit *saddharma* and *pratirūpaka* correspond to Pali *saddhamma* and *paṭirupaka,* but neither *paścima-kāla* nor *paścima-samaya* corresponds to "*mappō* as the third period." I may conclude that there is no Sanskrit or Pali word for *mappō,* and henceforth such an apocalyptic theory of *mappō* seems to have gained ground in Central Asia, China, and Japan. Especially Hōnen and Shinran, more particularly Nichiren, thought that this very *mappō* period was the right time to proclaim their own true doctrine.

reformers as mere agitators and not as men who attempted to develop new spiritual insights. A famous statement of Shinran reads: "Even the good man is saved; how much more so the evil man." The "evil man" (*akunin*[aq]) was a deep spiritual realization of Shinran, but the critics saw this as mere acknowledgment of the evil tendencies of men. Scholars say that this concept of "evil man" refers to the warrior class, the *bushi*[ar] or samurais,[as10] and others hold that it refers to the merchants[11] and workers of the day; but what is clear is that it does not refer to the aristocrats of olden days, who were upholders of the "guardian religion."

Shinran's name is not included in the traditional histories of Japan, though historically it can be shown that he was banished to Echigo,[at] spent a number of years in this remote northern province, then went to eastern Japan, and later returned to Kyoto, where he spent the remainder of his 20-odd years. Today, however, Shinshū, or Jōdo-shinshū,[au] the sect founded by Shinran, who mingled only with the masses, is the most aristocratic of the Buddhist sects. The aristocratic coloring of this sect began with Rennyo[av] (1415–1499) and is developed along this line in the Tokugawa period (1571–1867).

Dōgen, who also propagated a new type of Buddhism, avoided contacts with the imperial court, although he was of aristocratic birth. He practiced meditation and the disciplines of Buddhism away from the cultural center of Japan, deep in the remote hills of Eihei.[aw] Both Eisai[ax] and Dōgen studied in China and, respecting the tradition of Buddhism, transmitted the Rinzai[ay] and Sōtō[az] sects of Zen Buddhism. Shinran and Nichiren never went abroad, and they can be considered pure Japanese in the development of their thought.

Shinran, however, selected as the transmitter of his Buddhism two thinkers from India, Nāgārjuna and Vasubandhu; three from China, T'an-lüan,[ba] Tao-ch'o,[bb] and Shan-tao,[bc] and two from Japan, Genshin[bd] and Hōnen. He selected Prince Shōtoku and called him the "Buddha of Japan," and thus maintained a balanced view of Japanese culture. His consideration of the Original Vow of Amida as "non-dual" is in accord with Dōgen's non-duality of practice and *satori*,[be] original Buddhism's Middle Way, and Mahāyāna Buddhism's ideal of non-duality.

As opposed to this, Nichiren had as the principle object of worship the phrase, *"Namu Myōhō Renge Kyō,"*[bf] the *Saddharmapuṇḍarīka Sūtra,* and the four guardians of the nation in the four quarters, and placed alongside it Tendai Daishi[bg] and Dengyō Daishi,[bh] and also Hachiman Daibosatsu[bi] and Amaterasu Ōmikami.[bj] This is significantly different from Shinran, who revered Prince Shōtoku as the founder of Japanese Buddhism, for Nichiren worshipped the national god, or *kami*,[bk] Amaterasu Ōmikami. This is the reason that Nichiren is closely connected with modern Japanese nationalism and Shinto-

[10] Saburo Ienaga,[ej] *Nihon Dōtoku Shisoō shi*[ek] ("History of Japanese Moral Thought") (Tokyo: Iwanami-shoten, 1954), pp. 98–100; Junko Matsuno, "Shinran: Historical Studies of Life and Thought," pp. 108, 436–444.

[11] Toshihide Akamatsu,[el] *Kamakura Bukkyō no Kenkyū*[em] ("Studies on Kamakura Buddhism") (Kyoto: Heirakuji-shoten, 1957), p. 71.

ism. In modern Japan there have been many military men, scholars, and politicians who have followed the faith of Nichiren. It is an interesting sidelight that the great majority of the "new religions" in Japan have their origin in Nichiren's Buddhism.

III. SHINRAN'S NATURALNESS (JINEN HŌNI[bl])

The most outstanding figure among the leaders of new religions in the Kamakura period was Hōnen. He was "the real founder of Japanese Amidism. It is true that his followers were not officially recognized as a sect until the time of Tokugawa Ieyasu[bm] (1542–1616), though in practice they formed a religious body from Hōnen's lifetime onwards, and also that Shinran developed with great precision."[12]

His name originated in the saying *"Hōnen dōri no hijiri,"*[bn] [13] that is, the saint of *dharmatā-yukti,* or the saint as he really was. It means that by nature he embodied the reasoning of reality, or the principle of naturalness.

Hōnen dōri or *Hōni dōri* (*tao-li,*[bo] *yukti*) is the fourth reasoning among the four reasonings, which are as follows: (1) relation (*apekṣā*); (2) effect and cause (*kārya-kāraṇa*); (3) logical recognition (*upapatti-sādhana*); (4) ultimate reality or naturalness (*dharmatā-yukti*).

These reasonings were gradually formulated in the course of Abhidharmic studies. It was the idealist scholars who put them into a system. But I found out recently that their systematization is incomplete, and their interpretations differ from each other.[14] And, again, it is worth while to notice the fact that, practically, in Japan only the fourth reasoning became very popular. Although Hōnen was named after this reasoning, as the founder of a new sect, he was much occupied with the practical promulgation of the new teaching of salvation by *Nembutsu*[bp] (the repetition of the *Namu-Amida-Butsu*[bq]), and left the task of theorizing to his disciples.

Shinran, one of his disciples and founder of the Shin sect, interpreted this *dharmatā-yukti* from three angles: (1) *dharmatā* as the altruistic necessity of Amida's vow (*praṇidhāna*); (2) *dharmatā* as the unconditioned and absolute *nirvāṇa;* (3) *dharmatā* as the view from the *nirvāṇa* of no-abode (*apratiṣṭhita-nirvāṇa*). Most people know that Shinran taught that the one all-important thing is faith in the vow of Amida, but there are few who know that, after deep studies of long standing throughout his life of adversity, he succeeded in recording his own words about *dharmatā-yukti* at the age of eighty-six. His work is generally known as an essay on naturalness (*jinen hōnishō* or *no*

[12] *Japanese Buddhism,* pp. 363–364.

[13] *Hōnen, The Buddhist Saint,* p. 133. *"Hōnen"* means "Nature's saint" or "natural-born saint"; *"hōnenbō,"* means "Nature's own priest."

[14] *Nanjio* 247, *Samdhinirmocana Sūtra, chüan* 5, *Taishō* No. 676, Vol. 16, p. 709b; *Nanjio* 1170, *Yogācārabhūmi-śāstra, chüan* 25, *Taishō* No. 579, Vol. 30, p. 419b; *Nanjio,* 1177, *Prakaraṇāryavācā-śāstra, chüan* 20, *Taishō* No. 1602, Vol. 31, p. 582b; *Nanjio,* 1190, *Mahāyāna-sūtrālamkāra, chüan* 12, *Taishō* No. 1604, Vol. 31, p. 653b; *Nanjio* 1199, *Mahāyāna-abhidharma-samuccaya, chüan* 6, *Taishō* No. 1605, Vol. 31, p. 687a; *Nanjio* 1178, *Mahāyāna-abhidharma-samuccaya-vyākhya, chüan* 11, *Taishō* No. 1606, Vol. 31, p. 745b. The references of the Tibetan equivalents are omitted here.

koto[br]).[15] Therein Shinran developed a unique interpretation of *dharmatā yukti,* synthesizing the Mādhyamika interpretation of Donran (T'an-lüan, 476–542) of China and the Buddhist idealist theory of Vasubandhu (*ca.* 400–480) of India.[16] He adeptly made the best use of both sides of reality, that is, the unconditioned nature and the altruistic intermediary nature.

Shinran's *Jinen Hōni no koto*[bs] ("Essay on Dharmatā-yukti") runs as follows:

"*Ji*"[bt] means "of itself" or "by itself." "*Nen*"[bu] means to cause to be as it is. It is not due to the devotee's designing but to Nyorai's[bv] vow (*Tathāgata-praṇidhāna*) [that man is born in the Realm of *Dharmatā* to attain *nirvāṇa-satori*]. *Hōni,* or *dharmatā,* means that such *satori* is due wholly to the working of Nyorai's vow-power, without any devotee's contrivance. Being utterly devoid of the designing of man, all is caused by virtue of *dharma*-reality (*hō*[bw]). Therefore you should know that "no meaning is meaning" [in the faith in the Other Power].

"*Jinen*" is the term which means "to cause to be so because it is so." Amida vows and designs to make man trust in the Name "*Namu-Amida-Butsu*" and come to "his Realm of *satori.*" There is nothing left at all for the devotee to design, but all is left to Amida. As far as the devotee is concerned, he does not know what is good or bad for him. Such spontaneity of Amida is called vow-power-*jinen.* This is what I have heard.

Amida's vow is meant to make us all achieve Supreme Buddhahood (*mujō-butsu*[bx]). The Supreme Buddha is formless, and because of his formlessness he is known as "all by itself." [This means "unconditioned *jinen.*"] If he had a form to conform to, he would not be said to be abiding in the realm of "absolute *nirvāṇa*" (*mujō-nehan*[by]). It is because of his designing to let us know how formless he is that he can be called Amida. This is what I have learnt.

Amida is the "means" (*ryō*[bz]) by which we come to know what reality by itself is like (*jinen no yō*[ca]). When you have once attained this "logic" (*dōri,*[cb] reasoning), you need not think further about *jinen.* Should you still think about *jinen,* then the very realm of "meaningless meaning" would assume a meaning again.

All this comes from the *Bucchi,*[cc] or Buddha's Wisdom, which is beyond thinking.

Shinran, at the age of eighty-six years old.
December 14th, 2nd year of Shōka (1258).[17]

Zonkaku[cd] (1290–1373), Shinran's great-grandson and the most authoritative

[15] There are three sources: (1) *Jinen hōni no koto,* or *Jinen hōni shō:* the fifth chapter of the *Mattō-shō*[en] ("The Light to the Latter Days"), *Taishō* No. 2659, Vol. 83, p. 713. (2) *Kenchi Kikigaki*[eo] ("The Record by Kenchi"). Kenchi (1226–1310) was Shinran's chief disciple and secretary—as Ānanda was to the Buddha. It says that Kenchi heard it from Shinran, who was eighty-six years old at the time, at the home of Shinran's brother in Kyoto in 1258. The manuscript is extant. *Shinran Shōnin Zenshū,*[ep] ("Collected Works of Saint Shinran") (Kyoto: Zenshu Kankokai, 1956), pp. 54–56. (3) Appendix to Shinran's *Sanjō Wasan*[eq] ("Hymns in Three Volumes"), edited by Rennyo (1415–1495), the eighth patriarch, *Taishō* No. 2652, Vol. 83, p. 668bc. The contents of the second and third are the same, but the first two lines are missing in the first Text.

[16] Shinran is a combination of "*shin*" and "*ran*": "*shin*" of Tenjin[er] ("*Ten-shin,*" Chinese name for Vasubandhu) and "*ran*" of Don-"*ran.*"[es]

[17] *Taishō* No. 2659, Vol. 83, p. 713; *Shinshū-Shōgyō Zensho,* Vol. II, p. 663–664. See note 15.

commentator of Shinran's masterpiece, *Kyōgyōshinshō*,[ce] opined as follows: "The principle of *nirvāṇa* and the Amida Buddha coincide with each other. *Nirvāṇa* is named from noumenon and the *logos*-name of Amida from phenomenon. Phenomenon and noumenon differ from each other, but, non-dual in essence, they are one and the same. Amida is the *logos*-name of *nirvāṇa;* therefore, commentaries here and there reveal that *nirvāṇa* and Amida are nothing but the profundity of the Oneness."[18] It is obvious that Shinran and Zonkaku stood on the Mahāyāna idealist *advaya* theory of *nirvāṇa* of no-abode (*apratiṣṭhita-nirvāṇa*).[19] The theistic tendencies of the idealist *bodhisattvas*[20] and their artificial middle-way constructions admit this *nirvāṇa* of no-abode as the highest form of altruistic activity. *Bodhisattvas* neither abide in *saṁsāra* because of wisdom (*jñāna*), nor abide in *nirvāṇa* because of compassion (*karuṇā*), so as (because they wish) to devote themselves to a life of beneficent activity.

Shinran's view on *jinen hōni,* according to my recent studies, is based precisely on the old Abhidharmic definition, but his enlightened view marked a step in the progress of Buddhist philosophical thought. There are several idealist texts which supply different types of *dharmatā-yukti* definition: *Saṁdhinirmocana Sūtra, Yogācārabhūmi-Śāstra, Prakaraṇāryavācā-Śāstra, Mahāyāna-abhidharma-samuccaya,* its *Vyākhya* (commentary), *Mahāyāna Sūtrālaṁkāra,* etc. Among these, what largely coincides with Shinran's *jinen hōni* is the *Sūtrālaṁkāra*'s definition. It runs as follows: "*Dharmatā-yukti* means the realm beyond thinking. It is because *dharmatā*-reality, once attained, need not be thought about again: such as why does right view arise from reasoned thinking? Why does the elimination of defilement as an effect arise from right view? etc."[21]

Although there are several vital points in Shinran's view of *jinen hōno,* I will mention here only two most important points which concern the matter at issue. First, the context: "Amida is the 'means' (*ryō*) by which we come to know 'what reality by itself is (*jinen no yō*[cf]).' "[22] Modern scholars generally lack

[18] Shinran, *Kyōgyōshinshō-Rokuyōshō-Ehon*[et] ("Collated Text of the Doctrine, Work, Faith, and Attainment") (Kyoto: Zeniya and Chōjiya, 1779), Vol. VII, p. 15b; Vol. V, p. 55a; Vol. VII, pp. 10b, 25a. There are several recent Otani editions of the above-mentioned by Kikuya, Chōjiya, Hōbunkan, Bukkyōtaikei, etc.; *Rokuyōshō*[eu] ("Essentials of Six Volumes") (Kyoto: Shinshū-Shōgyō-Zensho, 1940), Vol. II, p. 148; Vol. III, p. 112; Vol. V, pp. 146, 149.

[19] Louis de La Vallée-Poussin, *Vijñaptimātratā-siddhi,* Traduite et Annotée (Paris: Paul Geuthner, 1929), Vol. VII, p. 671; Chinese Text, *Taishō* No. 1585, Vol. 31, p. 55b; Johannes Rahder, *Daśabhūmika-sūtra et Bodhisattvabhūmi* (Paris: Paul Geuthner, 1926), p. xxiv, *"Il n'est pas séparé du samsāra, ni ne se réjouit du nirvāṇa; il n'éprouve ni augmentation ni diminution."*

[20] There is a certain similarity between B. H. Streeter's interpretation of the identification of the Buddha and Nirvāṇa through the "Adoptionist view" of Christian theology and that of Zonkaku, which stood on the Mahāyāna idealist *advaya* (non-duality) theory of *apratiṣṭhita-nirvāṇa* (*nirvāṇa* without residue or *nirvāṇa* of no-abode). B. H. Streeter, *The Buddha and the Christ* (London: Macmillan and Company, 1932), p. 85; Shoson Miyamoto, "Freedom, Independence, and Peace in Buddhism," *Philosophy East and West,* II, No. 3 (October, 1952), 223; Th. Stcherbatsky, *The Conception of Buddhist Nirvāṇa* (Leningrad: The Academy of Sciences of the USSR, 1927), p. 232: "Its seeming contradiction with strict Monism."

[21] Sylvain Lévi, trans., *Mahāyāna-sūtrālamkāra,* Tome 1, *Texte* (Paris: Librairie Honoré Champion, 1907), p. 168; Tome II, *Traduction,* 1911, pp. 275–276. *"Le Raisonnement d'Idéalité, c'est le Lieu Hors-réflexion; car l'Idéalité, une fois atteinte, échappe à la réflexion qui n'a plus à se demander: "De quel Acte mental à fond vient la Vue régulière? ou le rejet des Souillures ensuite comme fruit?* . . . "Chinese Text, *Taishō* No. 1604, Vol. 31 (*Nanjio* 1190), p. 653.

[22] Sōyō[ev] (1723–1783), *Mattōshō-Kankiroku*[ew] (6 vols.), Vol. III, in *Shinshū-Zensho*[ex] ("Complete Collection of Shinshū Books") (74 vols.) (Kyoto: Jikiryō Tsumaki, 1913–1916), Vol. 17, pp. 326–327; Senmyō,[ey] *Mattōshō-Setsugi*[ez] ("The Gist of Mattōshō") (3 vols.), Vol. I, in *Shinshū-Taikei*[fa] ("A Great System of Shinshū Books") (37 vols.), (Tokyo: Shinshū Scriptures Publishing Society, 1916–1925; new series, 1953),

definiteness[23] about this point. Besides, once there was a certain Shin sect historian by the name of Ryōshō[cf] (1788–1842), of Mikawa[cg] province, who classed *jinen hōni shō* as unorthodox[24] from his personal point of view. But his seeming scholarship is not only far-fetched, but quite wrong from the present-day standard of Shinran study. On the basis of Donran tradition, Shinran holds the view that Amida is the Buddha as altruistic means of salvation (*upāyakauśalya-dharmakāya*). This *upāya-dharmakāya* (*hōben-hossin*, or *fang-pien fa-shen*[ch]) corresponds to *sambhoga-kāya* (enjoyment body, *hōjin*, or *fa-shen*[ci]) of the idealist three-*kāya* (*san shen*[cj]) theory (*dharma-kāya, sambhoga-kāya, nirmāṇa-kāya*). And Shinran's view of Amida as "means" is firmly based on the Buddhist middle-way principle, which is the common cause for both Mādhyamika (of Donran) and the idealist school (of Vasubandhu).

The rational process involved in reaching the principle of non-duality is strongly indicated by Shinran's enumeration of forty-eight pairs of opposites in the *Kyōgyōshinshō*:[25] abrupt and gradual, horizontal and vertical, superior and inferior, pure and mixed, straightway and roundabout, rational and non-rational, unbroken and broken, continuation and non-continuation, following one's own will and following another's will, transference and non-transference, self-power and other-power, etc. Thus describing the Original Saving Vow of Amida as non-duality, he means that the designing of Amida's vow is as boundless, unfathomable, and all-embracing as the sea. It is an interesting fact that it was only Zonkaku who inherited Shinran's philosophical culture and wisdom of non-duality.[26] But by reason of his distinguished ability and of his great

Vol. 23, pp. 36–42; Hōkai[fb] (1768–1834), *Mattōshō-Jinshinki*[fc] ("Notes of Mattōshō in the year of North Monkey [*jen shen*, 1812]") (4 vols.), Vol. II, in *Shinshū-Taikei*, Vol. 23 (new series), pp. 189–206; Eken[fd] (–1830), *Shōzōmatsu-Wasan-Kankiroku*[fe] ("Views on Shōzōmatsu-Wasan") (6 vols.), Vol. VI, in *Shinshū-Taikei*, Vol. 20 (Tokyo, 1920), pp. 261, 296; Tokuryū[ff] (1772–1858), *Shōzōmatsu-Wasan-Kōgi*[fg] ("Lectures on Shōzōmatsu-Wasan") (3 vols.), Vol. III, in *Shinshū Zensho*, Vol. 43 (Kyoto, 1913–1916), pp. 59–64. All of them say that "*ryō*" means "*tame*"[fh] ("for the sake of"). Eken and Hōkai mention examples of *ryō* from the *Tales of Genji*. We can mention some more examples from Shinran's letters, *Shokanshū*,[fi] ("Collected Letters"), *op. cit.*, pp. 128 (second letter), 152, 153 (eighth letter). But the true meaning of the context will not be clearly expressed unless "*ryō*" is translated as "means."

[23] Kosho Yamamoto,[fj] *Shinshū-Seiten*[fk] ("Holy Scriptures of the Shinshū Sect") (Honolulu: The Honpa Hongwanji Mission, 1955), p. 254. "We hear of Amida Buddha. This is but to make us know of this 'jinen' " (*Midabutsu wa jinen no yo wo shirasen 'ryō' nari*[fl]); D. T. Suzuki,[fm] *Mysticism, Christian and Buddhist*, (London: George Allen & Unwin Ltd., 1957), p. 155. We owe much to his fine English translation. But the line at issue is totally missing; Rev. Shinryū Umehara,[fn] "Jinen Hōni no Kaiken" ("Shinran's Concept of '*Jinen Hōni*' "), in Shoson Miyamoto, ed., *Bukkyō no Kompon Shinri*[fo] ("The Fundamental Truth of Buddhism") (Tokyo: Sanseido, 1956), pp. 1113–1126. Notwithstanding his excellent scholarly contribution, there is no comment at all on the subject-matter.

Gesshō Sasaki,[fp] late President of Otani University, who invited D. T. Suzuki to Otani University, *Busshin to sono Hyōgen*[fq] ("Buddha-mind and Its Revelation"). (Originally, Kyoto: Gohōkan, 1919); now in *Busshin to Bunka*[fr] ("Buddha-mind and Culture"), in *Gesshō Sasaki Zenshū*[fs] ("The Complete Works of Gesshō Sasaki") (Kyoto: Zenshū-Kankokai, 1928), Vol. V, pp. 105–190. In the passages on "*jinen hōni*" (p. 156), he says that "*ryō*" means "for the sake of," and that this very passage carries weight with it and could have been expressed only by Shinran among the disciples under Hōnen, but not by those disciples who understood Amida only as the external object of worship or as the object for petitions; Daitō Shimaji[ft] (1875–1927), famous Buddhist scholar and authority on Shinshū, "*Jinen-hōni*," originally published in the journal, *Hōni*,[fu] 1918; now in his *Shisō to Shinkō*[fv] ("Thought and Faith") (Tokyo: Meiji-shoin, 1928), pp. 407–412. He harbored a doubt for a long time as to why the section on *jinen-hōni-shō* is of such rationalistic bias and so full of philosophical jargon. But, later, he discovered that his opinion was wrong, and realized that the whole passage accorded well with *dharmatā* as the altruistic necessity of Amida's vow-power.

[24] *Igishū*[fw] ("Collection of Unorthodox Doctrines") in *Shinshū-Taikei*, Vol. 36, 1917, pp. 30–31.

[25] *Kyōgyōshinshō* ("Teachings, Practice, Faith, and Attainment") (Kyoto: Shinran-Shōnin-Zenshu-Kankōkai, 1958), Vol. II, Section on Practice, p. 61.

[26] "Freedom, Independence and Peace in Buddhism," *op. cit.*, p. 223; *Kyōgyōshinshō-shōkan-Kōdoku*[fx] ("Lectures on the chapter 'Attainment' of *Kyōgyō-shinshō*") (Kyoto: Hōzōkan, 1957), pp. 27–28; *Fundamental Truths in Buddhism: The Middle Way and Nirvāṇa*, p. 26.

fame and popularity Zonkaku was subjected to great pressure and remained all his life in exile from the Ōtani[ck] and Hongwanji[cl] patriarchal succession.[27] It is stranger that his succession has not been restored. The situation was so peculiar that the person who suppressed him was his father, Kakunyo[cm] (1270–1351), the actual founder of the Hongwanji Order. In the cause of Hongwanji centralization,[28] what was needed was the creation of Shinshū[cn] prominence and distinctness:[29] for instance, the formulation of the new Shinshū catechism, by which Shinshū Hongwanji as a newly established Order could be distinctive from Jōdoshū and at the same time from other Shinshū Orders, such as Takada Senjuji,[co] Bukkōji,[cp] Kinshokuji,[cq] etc.; the "idolization" of Shinran as the Hongwanji founder;[30] the ritualization of the Hongwanji cult; a movement and campaign for Hongwanji centralization; the suppressing of local Shinshū centers; the promulgation of the new dogma: "faith for salvation, *Nembutsu* with gratitude," that is to say, faith as heart-union; and daily life as thanksgiving, etc. After Kakunyo, for about seventy years under the successive patriarchs (Zennyo,[cr] Shakunyo,[cs] Gyōnyo,[ct] Zonnyo[cu]), Hongwanji was in a great depression. It was only when Rennyo (1415–1499) succeeded the eighth patriarch that Hongwanji extended its influence throughout the country through his evangelistic and propagandist personality. By such *practical peculiarities* as these—the prominence of the marriage system and blood lineage; the distinction of worshipping Amida *only;* regarding all one's activities in daily life as expressions of gratitude; whole-hearted worship of Amida consisting of nothing but thanksgiving with no room for prayers for health, temporal welfare, or any such petitions; mass communication through epistles and creed, etc.—Hongwanji was successful in creating quite a *uniquely practical religion,* and henceforth became one of the most influential sects in Japan.

Second, I should like to point out that Shinran's definition of *"dharmatā"* wholly coincides with that of the *Sūtrālaṁkāra:* "When you have *once attained* this reasoning (*dōri*), you *need no longer think about jinen.*" *"Dharmatā*-reality, once attained, need not be thought about again." While *"hōni"* expresses reality's positive side, revealing Amida's vow-power designing, *"jinen"* expresses its negative side, not only to shut out the devotee's designing, but

[27] Senshō Murakami,[fy] *Shinshū Zenshi*[fz] ("The Complete History of Shinshū) (Tokyo: Heigo-shuppansha, 1916), pp. 380, 384–388, 391–396; Yūsetsu Fujiwara,[ga] *Kakushin-nikō Gyōjitsu no Kenkyū*[gb] ("Life of Kakushin, the Youngest Daughter of Shinran") (Tokyo: Sankibo, 1932), pp. 107–135; Y. Fujiwara, *Shinran-Shōnin-den-e no Kenkyū*[gc] ("Studies of the Illustrated Life of Shinran-shōnin") (Kyoto: Hōzōkan, 1943), pp. 171, 175; Bunshō Yamada,[gd] *Shinshūshi no Kenkyū*[ge] ("Studies on Shinshū History") (Nagoya: Hajinkaku, 1934), pp. 114–123. The article referred to was originally printed in the journal *Mujintō*[gf] ("Unlimited Light"), IX, No. 2 (19B). It was at this time that the historical studies of Shinshū by modern scientific methods gradually began; Rev. Ichimu Tanishita,[gg] *Zonkaku-Ichigoki no Kenkyū narabini Kaisetsu*[gh] ("Study and Explanation of the Life of Zonkaku") (Kyoto: Shinshūgaku-Kenkyūjo, 1943), pp. 111–114.

[28] Junkō Matsuno, *Shinran: Historical Studies of Life and Thought,* pp. 457–590; Genchi Sasaki,[gi] *Tannishō seiritsu-kō*[gj] ("On the Formation of *Tannishō*") (Tokyo: Nihon-gakujutsu-shinkōkai, 1950), pp. 41–49; Kenmyō Nakazawa,[gk] *Shijō no Shinran*[gl] ("Historical Life of Shinran") (Kyoto: Rakutō-shoin, 1922), pp. 3–46; Y. Fujiwara, *Kakushin-niko Gyōjitsu no Kenkyū,* 93–135; B. Yamada, *Shinshūshi no Kenkyū,* pp. 24–113.

[29] *Shinran: Historical Studies of Life and Thought,* pp. 457–490; *Tannishō seiritsu-kō,* pp. 41–49.

[30] Kakunyo named Shinran's biography *Hongwanji-Shōnin Shinran den-e*[gm] ("Illustrated Life of Shinran the Saint"), *Taishō* No. 2664, Vol. 83, pp. 750, 753. The author, Kakunyo, idolized Shinran as the founder of Hongwanji in order to consolidate its authoritative tradition of their blood lineage. *Soshi Shinran denjyu-sōjō*[gn] ("The Founder Shinran's Transmitted Orthodoxy"), in *Shinran Shōnin Zenshū, op. cit.,* pp. 146, 156, 160. *"Shōnin no Gohonbyō-Hongwanji"*[go] ("Shinran's Mausoleum-Hongwanji"), *ibid.,* p. 173.

also to exclude phenomenal forms. Shinran was thus very faithful to the Buddhist cause, keeping the middle-way principle. Zonkaku also followed the old Buddhist way described above. But Kakunyo started to direct every possible effort to frame a new Shinshū cult and doctrine conformable to the ideal of the greater Hongwanji. Through the efforts and abilities of Rennyo, Kennyo[cv] (1543–1592), etc., Hongwanji became a major power in Japanese society. And, practically speaking, the devotee's worshipping cult centers upon the idolized Shinran statue and Amida Nyorai[cw] of *hōben hosshin* as *honzon* (principal object of worship). Later, Shinshū survived two crises, the first at the Meiji Restoration (1868), and the second at the defeat in World War II (1945). Each time, Shinshū did not and could not recover the old Buddhist way to which Shinran and Zonkaku were faithful. This new situation is filled with new problems concerning the relation of philosophical theory to practical affairs in Japan, but these must await future consideration.

IV. VARIOUS ATTITUDES TOWARD THE DEAD

The treatment of the dead will be discussed as one illustration of how Buddhism gave spiritual meaning to the traditional practices of Japan. Sir Charles Eliot writes:

In Japan as in all Far Eastern countries Buddhism is closely connected with the veneration of the dead. Until the Meiji era all funerals were performed by Buddhist priests, and even now many Japanese who have little to do with Buddhism during their lives are buried according to its rites. Some of the older sects seem to be literally religions of the dead. For instance, it seemed to me when I was visiting the great temple of Tennō-ji[cx] at Osaka that the priests and the numerous worshippers were all engaged in intercessory or commemorative ceremonies on behalf of the departed. In Buddhist families the mortuary tablets are placed before the household shrine, which occupies a shelf in one of the inner apartments, and the dead are commonly spoken of as *buddhas* (*hotoke-sama*[cy]). This bold language is, so far as I know, peculiar to Japan and is an imitation of Shinto. The Shinto dead become (it is not explained how) *kami* or superhuman beings, for the translation "gods" is an exaggeration: it could hardly be allowed that the Buddhist dead had an inferior status and they were therefore termed *buddhas, buddha* and *kami* being, according to popular ideas, much the same.[31]

He then says:

Further, the notion that everyone, nay even every grain of dust, can become a *buddha*,[32] though not unknown to Indian Buddhism, is more popular in Japan than elsewhere, and to Japanese politeness it does not seem an exaggera-

[31] Sir Charles Eliot, *Japanese Buddhism*, p. 185.

[32] Quite a few know the motto: "All *sentient* beings have Buddha-nature" (*Issai Shujō Shittsu Busshō*[gp]), and that therein the ultimate purpose of the Buddha is well expressed. But few know that this motto was coined for the first time in the *Mahāparinirvāṇa Sūtra*, belonging to the later Mahāyāna texts of the 3rd or 4th century, A.D. Still fewer people know the new motto: "Herbs, Trees, and Earth—All (sentient and insentient) beings have Buddhahood" (*Sōmoku-kokudo-Shikkai-jōbutsu*[gq]) by a certain scholar of Medieval

tion to speak of the commonplace dead as having achieved the highest destiny. This close connection with family and national sentiment has preserved Buddhism from many dangers, particularly during its lethargy under the Tokugawa régime. It is remarkable how in the various religions of the world sentiment and practice vary with regard to intercessory and commemorative services on behalf of the dead.

In Japan today, the mourning period is known as *"kichū."*[cz] The term *"ki"* expresses the ancient sentiment of looking upon the dead as an impurity or corruption. The custom today is that families of the recent dead avoid the compounds of temples and also avoid passing in front of temples. The mortuaries turn the screen (*byōbu*[da]) upside down and fold the paper of the guest-book in reverse. The family Buddhist shrine and the family Shinto altar are concealed with white paper. In this way the spirits of the dead are not violated but consoled.

These practices have continued from ancient times, but Buddhism relates them with the idea of the salvation of the dead. The idea of gratitude to all life (*hō-on*[db]) appears in these practices. Through Buddhism, the traditional funeral services take on a spiritual and religious significance which was lacking in the traditional treatment of the dead.

In the various sects of Buddhism, the rituals involved in the funeral service are called "transference of merit to the dead" (*kudoku ekō*[dc]). That is, by the merits accumulated through the expression of faith in the Buddha, scripture chanting, incense offering, etc., the dead are thought to be liberated into a peaceful state of existence. At the funeral, the people pray that the dead will reach Buddhahood. This is called "services in honor or memory of the dead" (*tsuizen-kuyō*[dd]) and "giving to the hungry devils" (*segaki*[de]).

In Shinshū, however, these activities related to the funeral service which are meant as transference of merits for the dead are termed transference of "non-transference" (*fu-ekō*[df]). Although even in Shinshū the priests chant invocations to Śākyamuni and various other *buddhas,* since the basic teaching is in the absolute power of the one Buddha, Amida, there is no transference of merit from the side of man. Thus non-transference (*fu-ekō*) is meant. Thus, although the mortuary tablet is placed before the Buddhist shrine on the occasion of funerals and memorial days on the 7th, 35th, and 49th days; and the first-, third-, and seventh-year memorials, the service is an expression of gratitude to the transference of Amida's compassion or merits to man. This concept of *shinjin-hō-on*[dg] (faith and the repayment of grace) is traditionally described thus: "the abandoning of (relative) gratitude and entering into the absolute are the true repayments of the Buddha's grace."

Tendai at Mt. Hiei, and later adopted by the *Noh*[gr] dramatists of the Muromachi-Sengoku[gs] period (1338–1568) as a most favorite phrase. After that it became very popular. Sir Charles Eliot says, "Grass, trees, land and earth will become Buddha, though not unknown to Indian Buddhism, is more popular in Japan than elsewhere, and to Japanese politeness it does not seem an exaggeration to speak of the common-place dead as having achieved the highest destiny" (*Japanese Buddhism,* p. 185). But he did not know how this motto was coined. See my recent essay, *"Sōmoku-kokudo-Shikkai-jōbutsu no Busshōron-teki igi to sono Sakusha"*[gt] ("On the Cultural Meaning of the Buddhist Motto 'Earth, Herbs, and Trees, all attain Buddhahood' and its Author"), *Journal of Indian and Buddhist Studies,* IX, No. 2 (March, 1961), 262–291.

In the various sects, the *o-Bon*[dh] service is the time for the dead to return to their temples to receive offerings and then take leave again, but in Shinshū the practice is different in that the chanting of *sūtras* is conducted at the family shrine in the homes of the dead. This practice is called *"tana-gyō,"*[di] and the emphasis is on the religious aspect of repaying grace by faith in Amida Buddha. That is why *o-Bon* is called *"kangi-e,"*[dj] or the gathering of joy. *"Kangi"* comes from *"Shinjin-kangi."*[dk] In this way the spiritual influence of Shinshū on what was a matter of practice is, indeed, very great in many aspects of Japanese life.

Another important tradition in Japan, known as bean-scattering (*mame-maki*[dl]),[33] a ceremony on the first day of spring, which is one of three great festivals along with *o-Bon* and New Year's and which is observed to keep away the evil spirits, shouting: "In with fortune; Out with the demon (evil)," is not practiced in the Shinshū temples. The reason for this is the religious absolutism of Shinshū faith, which believes in one absolute Amida Buddha, and in the repaying of grace, wh·ch, naturally, precludes any relationship with the spirits and gives no room for petitions.

> . . . a most remarkable step was taken to popularize the new creed [in the reign of Tenmu[dm]], which had hitherto flourished mainly in the immediate vicinity of the Court. "Orders were sent to all the provinces," says the Nihongi, "that in every house a Buddhist shrine should be provided and an image of Buddha with Buddhist sculptures placed there. Worship was to be paid and offerings of food made at these shrines." "Every house" doubtless means every official house, but in time the practice spread to private dwellings, and this edict is probably the origin of the Butsudan,[dn] or family oratory, still to be found in Japanese households.[34]

It is also to be noted that we have a number of statues from these days and most of them bear an inscription dedicating it to the memory of the dead parents. This practice (called *ekō,*[do] *pariṇāmanā*), means the dedication of a meritorious work to the memory, and for the spiritual welfare, of parents and others. The spread of this practice is a significant sign of Buddhist influence as combined with the ancient cult of the dead, broadening its scope and elevating its ideal aim. The cult used to be the worship of the dead, mingled with the superstitious practices of propitiating them and asking their help for the welfare of the living. Now, this was modified to the worship of the Buddha for the sake of the deceased, so that the departed and the living together could advance on their way to Buddhist perfection on account of the merit of the work. Consequently, the dedication could be extended to any beings besides one's relatives who should be induced to the communion of the Buddhist saints. This

[33] Fortune-seekers crowd around and wave at the famous temples and shrines. Nowadays, stars, prima donnas, actors, actresses, *sumō* and baseball champions, and even noted statesmen participate in the ceremonies. It seems to have originated in the popular belief of Shinto-Buddhist syncretism at Naritasan Shinshōji[gu] (Temple of the New Victory) to connect the auspicious victory over the usurper Taira Masakado[gv] in 940 A.D. with the prayer for the prosperity of New Spring. *Naritasanshi*[gw] ("History of Naritasan Temple") (Narita: Shinshōji, 1938), pp. 13–15, 166–168. Rev. Takudō Kuruma,[gx] *Risshun Zenwa*[gy] ("New Spring Talk of Zen") (Tokyo: Asakusa Banryūji, 1953), pp. 1–16.

[34] Eliot, *Japanese Buddhism*, p. 208.

proved to be the lasting influence of Buddhism and prevailed throughout the coming ages.

A conspicuous example of this dedication is the inscription on the back of the Buddha's statue made in memory of Prince Shōtoku and installed in the Hōryū-ji. On giving an account of how the statue was made, it says:

Let us, on account of this humble merit, attain the faith in the Way and enlightenment in it; let us secure peace in the present world and, on departing from life and entering death, follow the three (deceased) Lordships. Let this contribute to the promotion of the Three Treasures [*Sanbō*[dp]] and finally to the communion hereafter. Let the merit universally pervade the six resorts (of transmigration), and let all the sentient beings in the world (*dharma-dhātu*) be able to get out of the tormenting entanglements (of *karma*) and all together attain *bodhi* (enlightenment).[35]

Herein we see, in conjunction with the practice of dedication, a change in the idea of life and death, and consequently of the life beyond. In fact, the idea of the life beyond had been vague in the ancient cult. It was now replaced and enlarged by the definite Buddhist ideas of paradise and the resorts of transmigration, which were based on the teaching of *karma*. *Karma* means moral causation and retribution which rule one's existence throughout his lives, past, present, and future, and which bring together those beings of similar *karma* to live in groups of various types and qualities.

"Ancestor-worship led on the one hand to loyalty and patriotism and on the other to the idea of the family system. From early times to the present day, Buddhism cultivated these tendencies and widened their scope from the standpoint of humanitarian morality. Even in modern Japan, there are not a few sincere families who read the Scriptures and offer prayers to the Buddha of the family shrine every morning and night. They offer their daily rice to the Buddha at this shrine in the early morning, and they take their meal as a gift from the Buddha with thankfulness. This is the latent power of Buddhist influence upon the Japanese."[36]

(The Chinese characters for this article are on the following pages.)

[35] "Prince Shōtoku," *op. cit.*, pp. 23–24.

[36] Shoson Miyamoto, "Mahāyāna Buddhism," in William Loftus Hare, ed., with an introduction by Sir E. Denison Ross, *Religions of the Empire, a Conference on Some Living Religions within the Empire* (held at the Imperial Institute, London, September 22 to October 3, 1924, under the auspices of the School of Oriental Studies, University of London, and the Sociological Society) (London: Duckworth, 1925), p. 192.

[a]宮本正尊
[b]聖徳太子
[c]神道
[d]伊勢神宮
[e]日本紀
[f]百濟
[g]聖明
[h]欽明
[i]釋迦佛
[j]周公
[k]推古
[l]禪
[m]本尊
[n]眞宗
[o]親鸞
[p]和讃, 和国の教主聖徳皇
[q]陰陽
[r]太子講
[s]山背
[t]蘇我
[u]天壽國曼荼羅
[v]橘大郎女
[w]法隆寺
[x]四天皇寺
[y]中宮寺
[z]蜂岡寺
[aa]廣隆寺
[ab]池後寺
[ac]法起寺
[ad]橘寺
[ae]葛木寺
[af]敬田院
[ag]施藥院
[ah]悲田院
[ai]療病院
[aj]正法護國
[ak]宮中眞言公卿天台
[al]將軍
[am]法然
[an]日蓮
[ao]道元
[ap]比叡
[aq]悪人
[ar]武士
[as]侍
[at]越後
[au]淨土眞宗
[av]蓮如
[aw]永平
[ax]榮西
[ay]臨濟
[az]曹洞
[ba]曇鸞
[bb]道綽
[bc]善導
[bd]源信
[be]さとり, 悟
[bf]南無妙法蓮華經
[bg]天台大師
[bh]傳教大師
[bi]八幡大菩薩
[bj]天照大神

[bk] かみ, 神
[bl] 自然法爾
[bm] 徳川家康
[bn] 法然道理の聖 (ひじり)
[bo] 法爾道理
[bp] 念佛
[bq] 南無阿彌陀佛
[br] 自然法爾章 自然法爾事
[bs] 自然法爾事
[bt] 自
[bu] 然
[bv] 如来
[bw] 法
[bx] 無上佛
[by] 無上涅槃
[bz] 料
[ca] 自然のやう
[cb] 道理
[cc] 佛智
[cd] 存覺
[ce] 教行信證
[cf] 了祥
[cg] 三河
[ch] 方便法身
[ci] 報身
[cj] 三身
[ck] 大谷
[cl] 本願寺
[cm] 覺如
[cn] 眞宗
[co] 高田專修寺
[cp] 佛光寺
[cq] 錦織寺
[cr] 善如
[cs] 綽如
[ct] 巧如
[cu] 存如
[cv] 顯如
[cw] 阿彌陀如來
[cx] 天王寺
[cy] ほとけさま, 佛樣
[cz] 忌中
[da] 屏風
[db] 報恩
[dc] 功徳廻向
[dd] 追善供養
[de] 施餓鬼
[df] 不廻向
[dg] 信心報恩
[dh] お盆
[di] 棚經
[dj] 歓喜會
[dk] 信心歓喜
[dl] 經撒き
[dm] 天武
[dn] 佛檀
[do] 廻向
[dp] 三寶
[dq] 中道思想及びその發達
[dr] 國家理想と個人人格, 大義と私事
[ds] 日本佛教の研究
[dt] 佛教研究
[du] 我法東流
[dv] 姉崎正治
[dw] 太秦
[dx] 專修念佛
[dy] 七箇條起請文
[dz] 石塚龍學
[ea] 辻善之助
[eb] 日本佛教史
[ec] 末法
[ed] 停止一向專修記
[ee] 笠原一男
[ef] 親鸞と東國農民
[eg] 松野純孝
[eh] 親鸞, その生涯と思想の展開過程
[ei] 正像末の三時
[ej] 家永三郎
[ek] 日本道德思想史
[el] 赤松俊秀
[em] 鎌倉佛教の研究
[en] 末燈鈔
[eo] 顯智聞書
[ep] 親鸞聖人全集
[eq] 三帖和讃
[er] 天親
[es] 鸞

et 教行信證六要鈔會本
eu 六要鈔
ev 僧鎔
ew 末燈鈔管窺録
ex 眞宗全書
ey 宣明
ez 末燈鈔節義
fa 眞宗大系
fb 法海
fc 末燈鈔壬申記
fd 慧劍
fe 正像末和讃管窺録
ff 德龍
fg 正像末和讃講義
fh ため，爲
fi 書簡集
fj 山本晃紹
fk 眞宗聖典
fl 彌陀佛は自然のやうをしらせんれう（料）なり
fm 鈴木大拙貞太郎
fn 梅原眞隆
fo 佛教の根本眞理
fp 佐々木月樵
fq 佛心と其表現
fr 佛心と文化
fs 佐々木月樵全集
ft 島地大等
fu 法爾
fv 思想と信仰
fw 異義集
fx 教行信證證巻講讀
fy 村上專精
fz 眞宗全史
ga 藤原猶雪
gb 覺信尼公行實の研究
gc 親鸞聖人傳繪の研究
gd 山田文昭
ge 眞宗史之研究
gf 無盡燈
gg 谷下一夢
gh 存覺一期記の研究並に解説
gi 佐々木玄智
gj 歎異抄成立考
gk 中澤見明
gl 史上の親鸞
gm 本願寺聖人親鸞傳繪
gn 祖師親鸞傳授相承
go 聖人の御本廟本願寺
gp 一切衆生悉有佛性
gq 草木國土悉皆成佛
gr 能
gs 室町戰國
gt 「草木國土悉皆成佛」の佛性論的意義とその作者
gu 成田山新勝寺
gv 平將門
gw 成田山史
gx 來馬琢道
gy 立春禪話

ROBERT ROSSOW, JR.

*Natural Man, Philosophy, and Behavior**

This paper had its origins in an assignment given me by the State Department about five years ago, to devise and establish a course of training for Foreign Service Officers in mid-career. There was no precedent or formal tradition for such a course, and the first problem was to develop a conceptual rationale of the profession of foreign affairs on which a curriculum could be based.

One point was clear from the outset—that the traditional European continental and British imperial conceptions of diplomacy were not sufficiently pertinent to the practice of American diplomacy or to the American political system to afford a satisfactory conceptual base.

Another point became equally clear in our early experiments with the course—that a descriptive-survey approach to international problems was not particularly conducive to the professional development of officers in middle age and mid-career with highly varied backgrounds of expertise. At this stage of their lives they already had a surfeit of professional problems, and to present more merely added to the surfeit, or bored them if they were already familiar with them.

After considerable experimentation, a three-phased curriculum was settled upon. The first phase was devoted to a probing in depth of representative patterns of human culture and value. The treatments of these deliberately combined the historical, behavioral, and philosophical approaches, and the traditions covered included the Sinic, the Indic, the Islamic, the Judaeo-Christian, the Hellenic, and the recent European. The climax of this phase, and indeed a crisis point in the entire course, was reached when their attention was

* Responsibility for the data and analysis presented herein rests solely with the author and not with the United States or the Department of State.

turned finally to the American culture and behavior pattern. It is not difficult to demonstrate to the student the stuff and form of an alien culture which he can observe at arm's length. There comes a moment of critical enlightenment, however, when he is induced to probe his own psyche, to dredge up for critical inspection his own subliminated values and primitive concepts, usually somewhat hardened in middle age, and to recognize that they are of the same ephemeral substance and changeable form as those embodied in alien cultures. The technique used to produce this awareness was to have the class do its own anthropological research, using its own members as informants. The lesson invariably produced a severe shock effect on the class, broke the crust of ethnocentrism, and left them in a receptive mood for the next phase, which was designed to enable them to climb out of the morass of cultural and moral relativism that the first phase alone would have left them in.

The reference frame that was finally settled upon to facilitate the achievement of this purpose best was provided by the new theories of information and communication. The use of the message-processing communications system as an analogic model for a government and for the network of international relations proved highly useful and heuristic. The second phase of the course was thus devoted to the study of communications systems in the abstract and through controlled experiments drawn mostly from the field of social psychology, and to the elaboration of their universal characteristics and functional behavior.

The third phase of the course was devoted to professional seminars in which the students analyzed and "solved" a variety of professional problems in the light of the preceding exercise in rather abstract theory. The purpose of this final phase was to require the student to apply abstract theory—and one new to all of them—to practical professional problems, both to demonstrate the relation of theory to practice and also to demonstrate a new conception of the Foreign Service as a part of a vast message-processing communications system, whose professional function is the two-way transmission of messages across national and cultural boundaries.

While the effort in developing this course was limited to the establishment of a training regimen for the Foreign Service that would tend to improve professional performance and that was compatible with the American tradition, it was clearly apparent that the philosophical implications of information and communications theory and the related neurological theory went far beyond this limited application to Foreign Service operations, that it offered the scientific basis for a new and badly needed general philosophy, and that it had application to practical matters of a far greater magnitude, such as man's ability to live together in harmony on the same planet, his relation to a rapidly changing environment, and his patterns of social and political behavior. It is to this larger theme that I have devoted my paper.

These theories, and their philosophical implications, it is submitted, afford the relegation of many of the old paradoxes to the limbo of badly posed questions. They account for uncertainty, difference, change, and growth, yet afford clear criteria that provide escape from relativism. They provide a framework for harmonizing normative theory with the concepts of the new science and for reconciling and accommodating culture difference. They tend to dampen the harmful fear and anger that condition so much of man's behavior in the world today. They invoke an allegiance to man as a patterned legacy of information struggling for survival and dominion against the entropy of his environment.

Out of the derivative normative implications of these theories come also standards and concepts of political organization and behavior that are of the utmost practical urgency in this angry, tension-ridden age of political ferment and nuclear weapons.

As these new ideas seem so germane to the problems of cross-cultural relations, as their very essence is the relation of the theoretical to the practical, and as their normative implications have such pervasive application to perhaps the most pressing practical problems of the age—those of international relations and political unrest—it has seemed most fitting that an attempt should be made to give at least an introduction to them in a conference of philosophers from varied cultural traditions convening at a moment in history when the world so needs a new approach to its problems and new ideas to live by. It is this that I have attempted to do in my paper.

Never has the world so needed a new philosophy, a new way to conceptualize the nature of man and his relation to his social and physical environment.

The writer, as a professional in the field of international affairs, tends to conceive the urgency of this need in terms of the countless frictions, issues, and conflicts within and among nations, and the awesome forces at their command. But it is equally pressing in terms of each man's need to adapt forthrightly and constructively to this new technological age in all its manifold aspects, and to find peace of mind in the process.

The traditional philosophies of the West, whose well-traveled paths have for centuries led only to paradox, have been much discredited under the onslaught of the critical attack of the positivist-empiricist movement, and can contribute little in this quest for a new philosophy.

The positivist-empiricist movement had a beneficial effect on human thought, eradicating the crust of prejudice, challenging myth and arbitrary dogma, and generally liberating the mind. But its excessive reliance on the particulars of sense-data and its reduction of the role of the "observer" to little more than that of a mobile, sensitized photographic plate prevent it from being a satisfactory answer to the need for a new way of thinking. In its concentration on particulars and its disdain for the relations between the several fields of inquiry the very effort itself to formulate a general conceptual pattern is a virtual heresy in its own terms.

Its limitations in the field of human relations are even more serious in that its social relativism fails to provide any criteria of conduct other than social approval and power to effectuate. It is not to deny or minimize these criteria in human behavior to suggest that, alone, they leave man relativistically divided among cultural tribes, with only the law of the jungle prevailing between them. Buttressed as it is by residues of traditional dogma and myth, this conceptual pattern hardly affords the basis for a suitable standard of conduct in a world of missiles and nuclear bombs.

A brief examination of the neurology of sensation should suffice to demonstrate that the positivist-empiricist concept of sense-perception requires purification. When a sensory neuron on the periphery of the body is stimulated by energy of a particular frequency it will discharge a small electrical current across a synaptic gap to an adjacent neuron, which will fire in turn, and so on down a chain sequence. The sense-datum consists only in the firing or not-firing of a particular sensory neuron, according to the all-or-nothing principle of conduction. It is thus an isolated, particular event. It is capable of producing a reflex response, but, without further processing, which would take it out of the category of pure sensation, it is not capable of yielding concepts that endure in time and that have the same meaning for two or more people. Thus, while sense retains its vital role as man's only incoming link with his surroundings, the nature and extent of its contribution to human information must be more modestly conceived.[1]

The search for a new philosophy that is neither relativistic nor dogmatic, neither mythogenic nor dehumanized, and that avoids the dualistic paradoxes must start out afresh, and the first area of exploration, as suggested by the brief excursion above, must be in the natural sciences, especially in those fields that deal with man and his behavior.

We are very fortunate today in that for the first time in the history of thought a comprehensive natural-science theory of mind—theory of theory, as it were—exists. It is the product of the cross-fertilization of concepts between the neurologists and the communications and computer engineers. The development of computers and automatic-control mechanisms required the invention of physical techniques that would enable these machines to perform functions which are analogous to memory, ideation, purpose, and learning. Working on their own, and later with the suggestive stimulus of the achievements in the field of automation, the neurologists have established that the human nervous system operates in comparable ways, and, indeed, their own discoveries have stimulated even further achievement in the field of automation. Thus, one of the most productive cross-disciplinary ventures in the history of science is well under way and promises momentous implications for the behavioral sciences and for philosophy as well.[2]

[1] J. Z. Young, *Doubt and Certainty in Science* (London: Oxford University Press, 1951), pp. 25–28, 37, 40–47; F. S. C. Northrop, "Ideological Man in His Relation to Scientifically Known Natural Man," in F. S. C. Northrop, ed., *Ideological Differences and World Order* (New Haven: Yale University Press, 1949), pp. 411–414; Arturo Rosenblueth, Norbert Wiener, and Julian Bigelow, "Behavior, Purpose and Teleology," *Philosophy of Science*, X (1943), 18–24.

[2] Norbert Wiener, *Cybernetics* (New York: The Technology Press, John Wiley & Sons, Inc., 1948), pp. 7–56; Young, *op. cit.*, pp. 15–23, 131–142.

It is an ambitious undertaking to attempt to present even the bare essentials of this theory in a short paper such as this, and it requires the development of a few rather technical concepts. But it is so directly germane to the subject of this portion of the conference—"The Relation of Philosophical Theory to Practical Affairs"—that the writer is emboldened to make the attempt.

I. THE NATURE OF IDEAS

As von Neumann has said, the wiring diagram of the central nervous system is—in accordance with the analogy principle—the simplest logical expression of the total syndrome of human behavior.[3] In Wiener's words, ". . . the structure of the machine or of the organism is an index of the performance that may be expected of it."[4]

The 15 billion or so neurons in the human nervous system are arranged in an intricate network, on whose functioning the light of successful scientific inquiry is only beginning to shine. Enough has already been established, however, to explain in natural terms many things heretofore in the misty realm of myth.

The old stimulus-response concept of behavior could never adequately explain memory, words, and ideas. It is now well established that there are several ways that the nervous system can trap and preserve impulses and derivatives therefrom. One of the best known of these is by the reverberating neural loop. Here an incoming impulse fires a neuron in a loop circuit, which in turn fires the next neuron in the loop, and so on round to the first-loop neuron, which will fire again if its energy has been restored by the metabolic process, and the next will fire again and so on round and round the loop as long as the metabolic process continues. When such a trapping stands not merely for one particular momentarily experienced fact but for a class of similar momentarily experienced facts, it is the formal equivalent of a symbol which the logician terms a universal. Hence, it has been termed a "trapped universal."[5]

The human nervous system contains innumerable such loops, intricately interconnected with one another by linking chains. Many of the loops are derivative from other loops and represent abstract concepts. Also, many of the neurons in the system have multiple feed-ins and feed-outs, which require simultaneous multiple firing to pass the impulse and which make possible complex concepts. Some of them are capable of an inhibiting, or circuit-breaking, effect. The sequence of the loop connections and the pattern of the wiring have the effect of establishing a hierarchical relationship among the loops, some of them more dominant and pervasive than others.[6]

[3] John von Neumann, "The General and Logical Theory of Automata," in Lloyd A. Jeffress, ed., *Cerebral Mechanisms in Human Behavior,* The Hixon Symposium (New York: John Wiley & Sons, Inc., 1951), pp. 22–24.

[4] Norbert Wiener, *The Human Use of Human Beings; Cybernetics and Society,* Anchor Books (New York: Doubleday & Company, Inc., 1956), p. 57.

[5] Northrop, *op. cit.,* pp. 414–418; Warren S. McCulloch and Walter Pitts, "How We Know Universals," *Bulletin of Mathematical Biophysics,* V (1943), 115–133.

[6] *Ibid.*

Thus, according to the theorem of McCulloch and Pitts, any robot or organism constructed of regenerative loops possessing certain formal properties "can compute any computable number, or, what is the same thing mathematically, can deduce any legitimate conclusion from a finite set of premises"; or, as put conversely by von Neumann, "anything that can be put in words completely and unambiguously is *ipso facto* realizable by a finite neural net." Very simple neural nets of this character have been demonstrated by McCulloch and Pitts to have all the formal properties of the prime concepts of mathematics and deductive reasoning as set forth in Russell and Whitehead's *Principia Mathematica*.[7]

The elaborate electronic computers of the age are proof of the validity of the theorem, but for philosophical purposes the important conclusion is not only that ideas are explicable in terms of natural science but also that their functional mechanics determines and is of the essence of human behavior.

Before proceeding further, it should be noted that there are two different but related ways in which ideas, or the information they contain, are represented. Probably the more fundamental way is by analogy, whereby the configuration and dimensions of a physical object represent the information transmitted. Language and art, of course, are of the essence of analogy. So, also, philosophy depends on analogy, as, for example, in its use of models—the wheel, the clock-like mechanism, the living organism; indeed, as will be further elaborated later, the philosophy here expounded conceives the information-processing, goal-oriented communications network as an analogic model for man and society. The slide rule is another example of analogy in that it represents numerical quantities by analogy to physical extension. So, also, in application of the analogy principle, neural loops embody ideas, and the wiring diagram of the central nervous system is the simplest logical expression of the total syndrome of human behavior.[8]

The neuron, considered electrochemically, is an analogy machine as is the slide rule. So, also, is the vacuum tube or electromagnetic relay in a computer. Yet, these last three, under certain operating conditions, which happen to be normal ones, have the characteristic of functioning on the all-or-nothing principle, which means that they are digital machines, operating by number or count rather than by physical correspondence. The rational process involves both these techniques, the second being a special case of the first.[9]

These two ways of representing ideas have been briefly developed here somewhat parenthetically mainly because of their at least partial correspondence with certain ontological concepts in Eastern thought. An understanding of them also tends to dissolve much of the old one-many paradox of Western traditional philosophy.

[7] *Ibid.*

[8] Wiener, *The Human Use of Human Beings*, pp. 63–66; John von Neumann, *op. cit.*, pp. 5–9; Herbert A. Simon (and Allen Newell), "Models: Their Uses and Limitations," in Leonard D. White, ed., *The State of the Social Sciences* (Chicago: University of Chicago Press, 1956); Karl Deutsch, "Some Notes on Research on the Role of Models in the Natural and Social Sciences," in *Synthese*, VII (1948–1949), No. 6B.

[9] *Ibid.*

II. THE SOURCES OF IDEAS

If the central nervous system is the physical stuff of ideas, the question then arises as to whence comes its content. The answer is that it comes out of the system's past; there is thus an existential quality about it.

The structuring of the body, which—it has been asserted above—is a prime determinant of behavior, is governed by the genetic code-script which determines biological form and specialization, and sets the outer limits and basic patterns of behavior.[10]

But, in dynamo the system's ideas are formed for the most part by the educational conditioning process, by enculturation. From the very moment of birth the family and culture group begin to form the world about the child. He is taught to objectify his environment, and to see things selectively, to formalize them, and to name them. He is taught to identify with certain groups, to orient his affections in certain ways. He is taught a particular space-time frame and set of values.[11]

In the dispersal of the race there is wide variety in the formal patterns of culture, so that two men from different culture groups looking at the same phenomena will see them quite differently. Yet, in each individual there is a relentless quest for internal consistency required by the very functioning of the nervous system, which by its nature strives to relate its many concepts hierarchically and harmoniously one to another. When new data presented to the system are incompatible with the ideas already trapped in it, a breaking of the original circuitry can result, which will be followed by a searching and scanning process leading eventually to the formation of a new circuitry that accommodates the new data. This may be termed the eureka process; it differs from the enculturation process—both of them being types of learning—in that it results in new conceptual forms, rather than the mere transmission of old ones. It is exemplified in scientific inquiry and is the basis for man's capacity to adapt to new situations. It is the essence of human growth whereby man increases his knowledge and ultimately his mastery over his environment.[12]

In the learning process, concepts are made to conform to the data presented by the environment through the senses. Some ideas, however, resist contradictory data and impel the system to try to make the environment conform to their own intent. These are the determinants of purposive and moral behavior. These are what motivate the engineer in molding the earth to man's desires, the entrepreneur, the political exhorter, the teacher (in contrast to the student), the moralist generally. All these are motivated by a desire to change (improve) the world from its actual state. These are the ideas relating to what "should be," and may be termed normative, in contrast to those relating to what "is,"

[10] Erwin Schrödinger, *What Is Life? and Other Essays*, Anchor Books (New York: Doubleday & Company, Inc., 1956), pp. 66–73.

[11] Young, *op. cit.*, pp. 61–66, 89–99, 113–129.

[12] Wiener, *The Human Use of Human Beings*, pp. 61–69; Wiener, *Cybernetics*, pp. 141–147; Karl Deutsch, *op. cit.*

which may be called factual—bearing in mind that any of them may be good or bad, true or false.[13]

The relation between normative and factual concepts is essentially a matter of the hierarchy of concepts. Normative ideas are derivative from high-order factual concepts, such as those concerning the essential nature of man and the cosmos, and will override contradictory data of a lower order. When the high-order factual concepts are successfully contradicted, then the derivative normative concept must be modified accordingly.[14]

Thus, ideas—or theory, which is a complex of ideas—are of the very essence of man's conscious, purposive behavior, used constantly, if unwittingly, even in the most trivial day-to-day behavior. Man's world is informed in his central nervous system, conditioned by his past, modified by learning, and subject within limits to his purpose. This is a far cry from the simple, direct stimulus-response concept of behavior common to the positivist-empiricist.

III. THE CRITERIA OF IDEAS

Any theory, or complex of ideas, to be accepted as valid, must satisfy certain conditions. First, it must reflect the structure and functional dynamics of the organism. This will *ipso facto* assure compatibility with other ideas in the system, and, therefore, a suitable link with the system's past. It will assure internal consistency and economy, as the system in its natural functioning must relate ideas one to another, and, in so doing, pursues a quest for economy of concepts. It will also assure a logical ordering, as it must be fitted into the hierarchical pattern of the ideas in the system.

In the case of factual theory, any implication therein predicting the occurrence of particular events external to the system must correlate with the sense-data reporting those events, which is to say that it must be empirically verified.[15]

Normative theory, on the other hand, is not directly subject to the empirical test. Rather, it must be consistent with the high-order factual theory from which it derives; but the latter is subject to the empirical test.[16]

There are, moreover, very definite limits to the certainty provided by the empirical test. It yields one of two syllogisms: 1) If A then B; B is not the case; therefore A is not the case; or 2) If A then B; B is the case; therefore A is the case. It is clear that the negative statement in 1 is formally valid, whereas the positive statement in 2 commits the logical fallacy of affirming the consequent. Thus the empirical test can deny a theory with logical certainty, but it can yield only a tentative "perhaps" with regard to its affirmation.[17]

The limitations on certainty in theory are inherent in the nature of the

[13] Northrop, *op. cit.*, pp. 421–427; F. S. C. Northrop, *The Logic of the Sciences and the Humanities* (New York: The Macmillan Company, 1948), pp. 278–289.
[14] Northrop, *ibid.*, pp. 119–131.
[15] *Ibid.*
[16] Same as Note 13.
[17] Northrop, *The Logic of the Sciences and the Humanities*, pp. 144–148.

rational process. Theory is no less vital to man nor less productive—for it is with theory alone that man has achieved his position of supremacy on the planet. He can be just as decisive in his conduct with awareness of this element of uncertainty as he can be without it, and clearly more wisely so, for false certainties are disruptive of the rational process.

Considering the wide and manifold variations in conceptual patterns among the many culture groups in the world, the awareness of this uncertainty bespeaks an attitude of tolerance and restraint. Indeed, so long as a theory is logically structured internally and not empirically denied, it is perfectly acceptable as a basis for behavior. To the extent that it is accepted at the social level, it provides a tautological type of certainty within its frame of reference, by which men may live and for which they may even die.

Life may be conceived of as an almost rhythmical process of evolution from the tautological certainties preserved in form derived from the past, through doubt, search, and growth, to the creative formulation of new, if limited, certainties that modify and improve the old ones, in the sense of increasing man's range of self-determination.[18] It is a process that has no end, so long as it remains successful.

IV. THE PATHOLOGY OF IDEAS

There is a mechanism in the central nervous system that encourages and favors the ideational activity of man, and registers disapproval of frustration in that activity. It is known technically as the affective-tone totalizer, and its function is to receive messages from all parts of the body and report out its net condition in terms of pleasure or unpleasure (not to be confused with pain or grief, which are manifestations of different physical systems). The activity of the affective-tone totalizer is such that, if the tone increases, that is, is positive in the direction of pleasure, it has the effect of lowering all the synaptic thresholds in the system, so that all processes in the system at the time are favored. But if the tone decreases, or becomes negative in the direction of unpleasure, it raises the thresholds, thus tending to inhibit all the processes then in the system. The magnitude of the effect depends on the hierarchical level of the goals at stake, so that, if self-preservation is involved, the affective tone is powerful, while, if lesser goals are at stake, it can be relatively weak. It is a powerful adjunct to the learning process, and it governs the condition we know as happiness. It also acts as an impediment when ideational efforts are unsuccessful.[19]

More permanent and serious damage can result, however, when directly conflicting theories become trapped in the system at the same time, particularly if these are normative or factual theories of a high hierarchical order. The system is so structured that it cannot healthily tolerate conflicting theories without modification of the circuitry as in the learning process. When the

[18] Young, *op. cit.*, pp. 153–154, 160–163.
[19] *Ibid.*, pp. 118–120; Wiener, *Cybernetics*, pp. 149–173.

theories in conflict are of a high hierarchical order and affectively charged, permanent disabling damage to the system in the form of nervous breakdown can result. This happens to automatons as well as to humans, and is a phenomenon familiar to the psychiatrist.[20]

Another fundamental characteristic of the system is that it must have goals to which to orient its behavior. If no legitimate goal presents itself, the system will either invent a false goal or go into a frenetic behavior-pattern ending, again, in a form of nervous breakdown. This, too, is as much a trait of automatic mechanisms as of humans.[21]

Perhaps the ideational malfunction most dangerous to society, however, is the development of obsessive concepts and goals, leading to compulsive and aggressive social behavior. These are usually the consequence of the hyperactivity of another mechanism adjunct to the central nervous system, the sympathico-adrenal system. This is a humoral, rather than a neural, type of system with the massive effect of greatly increasing the gross-energy potential of the total body, acting to intensify and reinforce the initial output. Once activated, it tends to override the low-energy messages in the neural system, including any corrective feedback therein. It travels a one-way path, boosting the output until the gross energy built up is discharged in one way or another. It is the system which when activated by a message of alarm readies the body to meet, or flee, or conceal itself from, physical attack, and as such has been a vital mechanism for man's survival. But as civilization has reduced the amount of physical peril in the environment, it has tended to become a goal-oriented system without enough legitimate goals to occupy it. Thus it tends to orient itself to the protection of abstract and derivative concepts rather than to the defense of the physical body and to become activated by illusory concepts of peril. In this process it tends to become hyperactive and to endow the concepts it seeks to protect with an obsessive character, leading in turn to compulsion and aggression.[22]

V. THE PHILOSOPHIC MAN

History demonstrates that there are periods when great and massive changes occur in men's basic concepts, their surroundings, and their patterns of association, which changes result in powerful strains and pressures as old ways and ideas are expunged and new ones are groped for in an atmosphere of conflict and confusion. Between these revolutionary periods are longer time-spans of relative stability when life follows a more settled course.

There can be little doubt that we are today in one of those periods of change, and that as a consequence pathological symptoms abound. Contemporary man is plagued with anxieties, and in his confusion many false goals have arisen to confound behavior further. The new ideas on which rest the science

[20] Wiener, *ibid.*, pp. 168–180.
[21] *Ibid.*
[22] Arthur Koestler, *Insight and Outlook: An Inquiry into the Common Foundations of Science, Art and Social Ethics* (London: Macmillan & Co., 1949), pp. 113–116, 277–282.

and technology of the day conflict with the old concepts which continue to govern most of man's social and political behavior. As technology has shrunk the world, culture patterns have lost much of their insularity, and cultural cross-fusion is on the increase. This can result in benefit and growth if a new philosophy can be formulated that reconciles old and new, native and alien. But, until that is done, confusion and internal conflict are the result. But probably the most pathological phenomenon of the day lies in the prevalence of aggressive and compulsive behavior, which stems from the obsessions generated by hyperactive adrenals oriented toward mixed and false goals.

The way to salvation from this morass of confusion lies in the development of a new philosophy derived from a new concept of the nature of man. Such a concept, it is submitted, is that of man as a communications system, with feedback links among its parts and with its surroundings.[23] The internal and external feedbacks, the pulsations of looped neurons, the secretions of humoral systems, the motor actions—speech and ocular focus as well as gross muscular output, the wiring diagram itelf—are thus all forms of message.

Man lives in a cosmic environment which tends, as an arrow of time, toward entropy—disorganization, randomness, equilibrium. Information, which is the stuff of messages, is a measure of organization and the negative of entropy. Entropy tends constantly to encroach on the communications system in the form of noise—the anxieties, confusions, distortions, and obsessions described above.[24] It is in the very nature of man that he seek, not only to preserve and protect against this noise the pattern of information that is his essence and that is bequeathed him by his past, but also to seek to elaborate and improve that message in such a way as to extend it farther into the cosmic ocean of entropy.

From this factual theory of man there derives a normative theory that bespeaks a new kind of man—Philosophic Man. He is one who understands the role of idea and theory in informing his world and determining his behavior. He is respectful of concepts presented out of his past, yet subjects them to critical review. When feedback denies the validity of old concepts, he is prepared to repattern his conceptual configurations and hierarchies, striving always for compatibility, economy, and logical relation. He recognizes the limits of certainty and is thus tolerant of difference. He is also one who recognizes and opposes the encroachment of noise, and whose primary allegiance is to man as a patterned legacy of information struggling for survival and dominion against the entropy of his environment. It is a theory which essentially embodies uncertainty, difference, change, and growth, yet at the same time affords clear

[23] Feedback is defined as the return of some of the output of the system as input, so as to perform the function of tell-tale or monitor. Automatic-control mechanisms depend on feedback. The interlinks between neural loops and other parts of the central nervous system provide internal feedback. Goal-directed and goal-changing behavior depend entirely on external feedback. Most feedback is negative in that it acts to correct the behavior of the system relative to a defined goal. An example of positive feedback is found in the sympathico-adrenal system, which governs fear-and-rage behavior, the feedback reinforcing the initial output, rather than correcting it. Northrop, "Ideological Man in His Relation to Scientifically Known Natural Man," in Northrop, ed., *Ideological Differences and World Order*, pp. 418–421; Wiener, *Cybernetics*, pp. 113–116, 131–136; Wiener, *The Human Use of Human Beings*, pp. 23–27, 50–69, 151–153; Young, *op. cit.*, pp. 16–19, 76–78.

[24] Wiener, *The Human Use of Human Beings*, pp. 12, 21, 30–32, 39–42; Erwin Schrödinger, *op. cit.*, pp. 67–73.

criteria that make possible escape from the morass of relativism. As such, it provides a framework for harmonizing normative theory with the concepts of the new science, and for reconciling and accommodating culture difference. It should also tend to dampen the harmful fear and anger that condition so much of man's behavior today.

The world needs this new kind of man urgently in leadership and laity. Indeed, the need is so great that far more of the world's abundant communications facilities should be turned to the educational end of stimulating and producing him. So, also, special efforts are needed in the educational system to build bridges across disciplinary chasms, and to restore idea and theory to a primary status as vehicles of information and prime determinants of deliberate behavior.

If mankind cannot achieve this adjustment by the peaceful learning process, then the alternative is crisis with all its attendant traumas and destruction.

VI. THE PHILOSOPHIC STATE

Man does not exist in isolation, of course, being essentially a social animal. It has already been noted in passing how he is divided among culture groups, which are defined by the range of sharing of learned patterns of behavior. Men also function as parts of corporate systems and organizations. These are defined by specific foci of common purpose which are goal-determining, trapped universals embodied in the hierarchy of reverberating neural loops and engrams in the cortices of the membership.[25]

As such, a corporation may be conceived of as an information-processing communications system analagous to the individual man. It depends on the communication of messages, and its behavior is a function, not only of the goal-determining purposes trapped in the minds of its membership, but also of the wiring diagram of the channels that handle feedback messages both within and from outside the system.[26]

In using the analogy to individual man, however, it is important to bear in mind certain points of difference, which stem from the fact that the corporation is a communications system whose parts are integral communications systems in themselves. This makes for a far higher order of complexity and a greater volume of noise in the channels with consequent loss of message. By the same token, the parts are more prone to deviation, and, indeed, to actual conflict among themselves. Moreover, it must never be forgotten that the corporate system has no essential existence outside the common purpose in the minds of its individual members.

The national State is such a corporate system, and, indeed, in a less formalized degree, the community of nations, as well. They are susceptible to the

[25] F. S. C. Northrop, *The Taming of the Nations* (New York: The Macmillan Company, 1952), pp. 3–7.

[26] Richard C. Snyder, H. W. Bruck, and Burton Sapin, *Decision-Making as an Approach to the Study of International Politics* (Princeton: Foreign Policy Analysis Series No. 3, Organizational Behavior Section, Princeton University, June, 1954), pp. 82–91.

same kind of pathological conditions as is individual man, especially conflict among parts of the system, and the development of false and obsessive goals.

While it may also have secondary functions, the prime defining characteristic of the State is its monopoly of the force of the community. If it is accepted that the essential nature of man is that of an information-processing communications system in a social context, as described, then it follows derivatively as a virtual natural law that the State's proper purpose in exercising the force it monopolizes is to protect the channels of social communication from willful and compulsive disruption within or from without.

The compulsive authority of the State stems from the fact that each man, from the mere fact he is a man, enjoys a natural right to protection against disruptive types of social activity, is mandatorily enjoined from indulging in such activity himself, and has an obligation to contribute to the protective instrumentality.

It should be made clear that this natural right does not extend to protection against natural forces, or against the consequences of one's own actions or omissions, though the State may well have non-compulsory auxiliary purposes to these ends. Again, this does not mean that an individual or group has any right of immunity from free proposal and debate, or from adverse consequences of its adherence to a particular way of life. The natural rights here postulated pertain only to rights of protection against social activities which destroy, or induce malfunction in, the rational process and disrupt communications patterns by compulsive means.

As the State, or any other type of corporate system, is entirely derivative from the trapped universals in the minds of its individual members, it follows that the State's authority is also thus derived from its membership. This is inevitable so long as compulsive disruptive activity is eliminated from the community, for the only way a minority can hold authority against the will of the majority is by resort to compulsive disruptive techniques. This contrasts with theories that hold that law is imposed from above by a sovereign or his legislative agent, and that its only criterion is capacity to enforce.

Also derivative from this conception of man are certain considerations applicable to the relations among States. Considering the vast increase in the volume of intercourse and the intricacy of inter-involvement among nations, it is questionable whether the notion of the sovereign ultimacy of the authority of the national State can much longer be tolerated. So long as it endures, the military function tends to be supreme. It is to state the obvious to observe that, with the weaponry of the day, the contest of arms is a disastrous method of settling international difference. It would be the height of unrealism to think that mankind can merely wish away the threat of military force. It is not so unrealistic, however, to conceive of a higher authority—primarily judicial—than the national State, exercising a police power according to the natural-law principles adumbrated above, which would render unnecessary the military function of the subordinated national State. Steps in this direction have already been taken, of course, but there is a long way to go.

The great obstacle to progress in this direction lies in the prevalence of an obsessive kind of nationalism which infects every nation in the world today, large and small, new and old. It is exacerbated by the compulsive and aggressive behavior on the part of certain powers which initiates an oscillating fear-and-rage reaction throughout the community that operates as a positive feedback tending always to increase, blocking or overriding corrective tendencies toward adjustment of difference. In the process, original issues tend to become lost or distorted, and conflict more and more centers on side issues, and sometimes even on false ones.

About the only approach to correcting this dangerous tendency lies in what might be called "philosophic diplomacy," as exemplified by this very conference. The effort here is to strive to reconcile difference by illuminating it and lifting it above the level of passion, and endeavoring by cool reason to formulate new concepts that encompass or adjust the difference and lead to harmony. It is to be regretted that more and better effort is not being made along these lines.

No one, looking at the state of the world today, can fail to see that imminent disaster threatens. Yet, one also sees the possibility of a new Golden Age. The choice of which it will be depends on whether or not men can find a way to live and work together in harmony, reconciling their differences by mutual adjustment rather than by killing one another. This requires some profound changes and adaptations in the normative concepts in the minds of men, and only the philosopher can find and show the way. This most practical of all problems squarely challenges the philosopher, and time is of the essence. The author suggests that the new concept of natural man as an information-processing communications system, and the derivative normative concepts of the Philosophic Man and Philosophic State, offer a basis for meeting the challenge. There has been no more than a beginning, though, in developing these concepts into a full philosophy that would be effective in modifying behavior on the massive scale required. It is an awesome challenge for man to be required to meet, and one may well question whether it can be met. But the stakes are so high that one cannot permit the doubt to delay or weaken the effort.

QUESTION: Is not this theory a form of reductionism; does it not reduce man to the level of a machine?

ANSWER: It does not in any way derogate from man's dignity, nor deny his emotions and feelings, to conceive his central nervous system as a form of machine. The strongly negative reaction commonly evoked by such a suggestion is actually the result of a holdover of animistic ways of thinking. Animism has long since been displaced by science in our views of most natural phenomena, but it clings stubbornly in our conception of the subjective "I." The displacement of animistic with scientific ways of thinking about the heavens and about natural earthly events did not in any way detract from their dignity and significance; indeed it made them even more important and useful to man, and enabled him to expand his range of self-determination. It need no more derogate from the dignity and significance of man for him to think of the "I" in objective, scientific terms and to compare its behavior to that of a machine.

Let me make clear, however, that the alternative to animism is not just a simple stimulus-response kind of mechanism or materialism. The alternative must account for all the phenomena and "feelings" that make us want so desperately to cling to animism. I believe that this theory does that, and that it accounts as well for uncertainty, difference, growth, and change, and that indeed it even evokes an awe at the marvel of man, conceived as machine, and the timeless heritage he thus embodies.

QUESTION: Is this not a form of what Professor Werkmeister describes in his paper as "scientism"? (Professor Werkmeister confirmed that, in his opinion, this theory was the rankest form of "scientism.")

ANSWER: This is Professor Werkmeister's term, and it is his privilege to define it as he wishes. I do not believe that this theory need be so construed. I have already explained why I do not feel that it is reductionistic. Apart from that, I believe Professor Werkmeister's term is, in effect, a counsel against mixing universes of discourse. I heartily agree with him in this counsel, and I do not believe that in expounding this theory I have committed such an error. This is a deductive scientific theory in epistemic correlation with phenomenal man. It makes no pretense at being the only way man can be conceived. Indeed, there are thousands of different ways one can meaningfully discourse about man; this is but one. It is true that I have attempted to travel from factual to normative theory, but I believe the shift was made with care and rigor. I refer to the body of the paper on this score.

QUESTION: This is a very fine theory as to the nature of the central nervous system, but its relation to problems of ethics and political behavior is not clear.

ANSWER: Certainly this theory makes no pretense at providing the basis for solution of every kind of ethical or behavioral problem. What it does do is twofold:

First, it affords an explanation of the nature and sources of norms, and, therefore, enables one to conceptualize normative problems more usefully and accurately.

Secondly, it argues that normative theory is logically implied by, and therefore derived from, high-order factual theory. Some of the specific norms implied by the factual theory of information and communication are suggested in the last two sections of the paper. It is true that the vast majority of people are not conscious of this relationship, and that many can and do hold inconsistent beliefs. Such inconsistencies can be conceived, as demonstrated in the paper, as pathological in nature. These facts prove merely that people are prone to ignorance and error, and in no way deny the existence of the relation. That such a relationship does in fact exist is best and most fully expounded in the works of our colleague, F. S. C. Northrop.

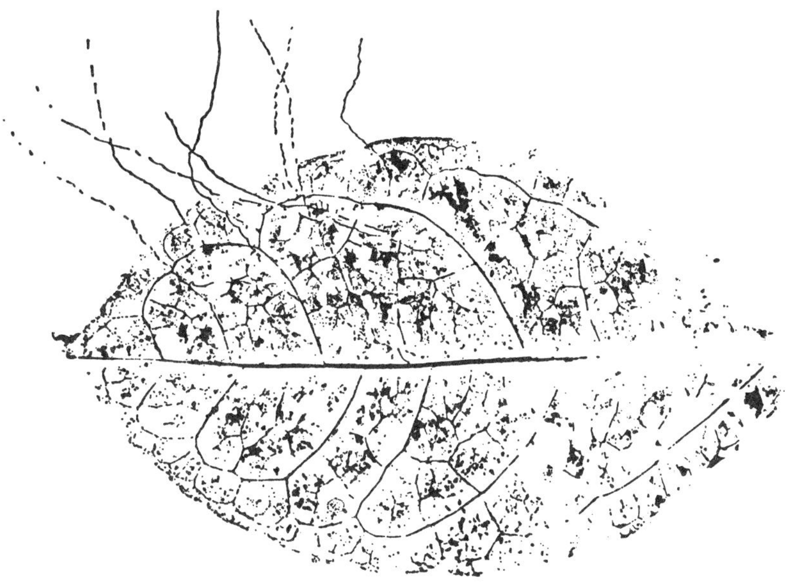

II. Natural Science and Technology in Relation to Cultural Institutions and Social Practice

W. H. WERKMEISTER

Scientism and the Problem of Man

I.

The papers and reports presented at the first and second East-West Philosophers' conferences reflect admirably the attempts hitherto made to establish a better understanding between East and West and to work toward greater co-operation in the solving of ultimate problems. If one fact stands out above all others, it is that all participants in these conferences earnestly have endeavored to find basic agreements—and to find them despite all diversities of cultural traditions and despite all variations in points of view.

Two approaches seem to have dominated the attempts at mutual understanding and co-operation, and both are important. The first approach is that of generalized surveys emphasizing common tendencies but recognizing also the crucial diversities—the assumption here being that only when divergent positions are reduced to their essentials can a fruitful comparison be made. That this procedure has its advantages is obvious, although there is danger that misunderstandings will occur so long as the basic terms germane to the comparisons have not been standardized. The second approach, therefore, aims at a standardization of key terms and at a reduction of whole traditions to these standardized terms. But here, again, immense difficulties arise, for the terms have as yet not been standardized even within a particular tradition—either East or West. Any attempts at standardization, therefore, must always be arbitrary. Moreover, rigid definitions of terms either destroy the living context of thought or falsify the picture by oversimplifying and, therefore, distorting the facts.[1]

[1] The work done by The Institute for Philosophical Research in San Francisco in tracing the development of the "idea of freedom" in the West is proof of the difficulty of any standardization of terms. See Mortimer J. Adler, *The Idea of Freedom: A Dialectical Examination of the Conception of Freedom* (Garden City: Doubleday and Company, Inc., 1958).

In view of this situation, I now propose to follow still another method in reaching an understanding between East and West. I shall examine rather critically certain trends in contemporary Western culture and shall point up problems which are crucial for any philosophy—East or West, or East-West. More specifically, it will be my aim to show in what sense, and to what extent, an exaggerated interest in, and devotion to, science leads to metaphysical "boundary transgressions" and, therefore, to "scientism" as a quasi-philosophical attitude which, in the last analysis, is destructive of human values. My thesis will thus be concerned with the nature of science and the status of values in our human world.

It must not be assumed, however, that Western philosophy is, or has been, all "scientific." The reduction of philosophy—be it the philosophy of the East or that of the West—to a simple "ism" or two merely falsifies the picture. Nevertheless, a few basic generalizations seem possible. Since they are relevant to my argument, I shall state them here briefly.

The most striking feature of Oriental philosophy, it seems to me, is its concern with the status of man in this world (China) and with man's ultimate goal (India). It is my impression that this interest in man clearly predominates over any interest in Nature or in God. As a result of this man-centered orientation, the philosophies of the East are primarily practical—designed to provide a guide for life, for the attainment of peace of mind. Theoretical considerations, as we find them in the scientifically minded West, play only a secondary part. That is to say, Oriental philosophy seems to be concerned pre-eminently with ultimate goals rather than with means of transforming the actual or of shaping it "closer to the heart's desire." However—and this seems to me to be crucial—the negative attitude toward the world of things is but a reflection of a positive valuation of something more profoundly human: peace of mind and contentment. The "Faustian ideal" is essentially absent from the philosophies of the East.

It must be noted, however, that, despite the great diversity of Western philosophy, certain basic orientations are readily discernible even here. In fact, three traditions determine what Western philosophy is today. There is, first, the classic tradition which stems from the Greeks. Most of the basic themes of Western philosophy found their first formulations in the statements of some ancient Greek; and it is largely true that "at heart we are still Greeks." But we must not overlook the importance for Western philosophy of the Judaeo-Christian tradition, which for centuries completely dominated the West. It is only after the Renaissance that the rise of modern science again changed the picture by shifting the emphasis from man's concern with the destiny of his own soul to the world around him, to the facts and forces of Nature.

If the Greek ideal was that of the wise man harmoniously adjusted to the cosmos around him, and the ideal of the medievalist was the saint glorifying his God, the ideal of modern man is the Faustian thirst for knowledge and for power over Nature (Francis Bacon). Science and scientism alike embody this ideal. However, it is important to keep in mind that, ever since the days of Greek philosophy, the concern for moral values, for the nature of man, and for his place in the universe has also been part and parcel of the Western tradition. To overlook this fact entails a distortion of history and a misconception of Western philosophy.

Still, it is true that Western philosophy today shows increasingly the impact of modern science. But it does so in a twofold way. On the one hand, problems arising out of scientific concerns—problems, that is, of logic, of methodology, and of an empiricistic epistemology—are in the forefront of philosophical discussion. The development of a special field, designated philosophy of science, is symptomatic of this fact. On the other hand, the existentialist rebellion against this very trend underscores the fact that in our concern for science we tend to neglect the value aspects of human existence and, thus, to falsify the position of man in his world.

My reference here to existentialism must not be taken to mean, however, that I regard existentialism as the answer to scientism and, therefore, as the solution of our philosophical dilemma. It is not, and cannot be, the solution. Nevertheless, in its own peculiar way, existentialism effectively calls attention to crucial deficiencies in the scientistically oriented philosophy of the West. In order to make my point quite clear and draw the conclusions which may—and, I hope, will—contribute to a rapprochement of East and West, I shall now take a closer look at science itself, at its methods, its assumptions, and its implications, and, having examined legitimate science, I shall define more specifically what I mean by scientism and shall show in what sense, and to what extent—philosophically and practically—this scientism is a real threat to human values and, therefore, to the status of man in the world.

As the foundation of modern medicine and modern technology, science is, of course, one of the great forces molding contemporary culture. The discovery of new methods of preventing and curing diseases—the discovery of antibiotics and "wonder drugs," of new vaccines, of radiation therapy, and of various other means of combating the ailments of the body and the mind—has contributed immeasurably to the prolongation of life and to relief from suffering. The ever-increasing understanding of, and control over, the forces of Nature—together with all the inventions and developments in technology made possible by such knowledge and control—have relieved man of many of the burdens which have been his lot since time immemorial. I am sure that we can all agree that great advances have been made, and are being made, along the lines here indicated. And we can all agree also on the fact that, without science, these developments would not have been possible.

But, surely, the same sciences which made possible the advances just mentioned have made possible also the new and hitherto unparalleled threats to man's very existence. Thus, the problems arising because of a rapidly expanding world-population are at least intensified because of man's success in combating diseases and expanding his life span; and the nightmarish possibilities of destruction of life and property inherent in hydrogen bombs and other devices are the direct result of an application of modern science. Although it is being argued that the very destructiveness of modern weapons is the greatest deterrent to war which we have, the problems which may lead to war are not solved simply by inspiring fear. The solution—if one is to be found—lies in a field far removed from applied science. It lies in the field of human values and in the realm of moral responsibility. Here science, being but instrumental, has its obvious limitations.

And there is a third area in which science—or at least industry and commerce built around the achievements of science—greatly affects human existence. Technological advancements have made possible mass production, our modern factory system, and the development of industrialized urban centers. With this development have come large corporations and "the organization man"—the "idolatry of the system," of material goods, and the misuse of science to achieve certain ends.[2] Even here, therefore, man himself is at stake as a person, and science provides no way out of his dilemma. The problem we face is one of values and valuations—of a threatening dehumanization of man, of a change in his status and stature as a person, and of his place in the world.

If this analysis is correct, science itself plays an ambiguous part in Western culture. On the one hand, it gives us dependable knowledge of the world we live in, thus satisfying our desire to know and control the forces of Nature. On the other hand, however, this very knowledge and this power to control are but instrumental in the practical affairs of living. When they are taken as more than this, our human values and, with them, we ourselves are at stake and, most importantly, are at stake as human beings, as morally responsible persons.

One thing, however, remains true even so: the truths of science are the same the world over. The laws of physics which hold in the United States hold in India and in China as well; and the laboratory techniques which are employed in the discovery and the testing of these laws are also the same. In a very real sense, therefore, science is universal. No national or geographical considerations affect its truths. Dealing with the specific subject-matter of their specialties, scientists from all over the world easily and readily understand one another. They speak a common language (even though some of them converse in English, others in Chinese, still others in Hindustani or in Russian), and their criteria of truth are the same. Even when they disagree on some facts or points of interpretation in their respective fields of research, they acknowledge common standards and test procedures which, in time, will lead to results on which all can agree. The community of research scientists is, thus, international —and it is so in a crucial sense. There is no physics of the West and an entirely different physics of the East; and there is no chemistry of the West and a quite different chemistry of the East. So long as we remain within the fields of the sciences themselves, the problem of an East-West separation cannot even arise.

[2] William H. Whyte, Jr., *The Organization Man* (New York: Simon and Schuster, Inc., 1956), p. 189.

Herein lies the great unifying power of science. But the uses to which science is being put in different countries and within the frameworks of widely differing cultures are another matter. It is here, in the differing cultural perspectives, that the divisive factors become evident—factors of value-commitments and valuations.

It must be realized also, however, that the universality of science itself entails consequences which are similar everywhere and which, in the aggregate, intensify the problems of human existence. The threat of hydrogen warfare, for example, is intensified by the fact that the same laws of atomic fission and atomic fusion hold in the free world and in the communist-dominated world. The laws of Nature are no respecter of national boundaries. Moreover, the technological applications of scientific knowledge, wherever made, lead to essentially the same forms of production and industrial organization and become the same sort of culture-determining factors everywhere. Thus, once the automobile is generally accepted as a means of transportation—to use an obvious illustration—we need roads, filling stations, and repair shops to make its use possible and to maintain it. We need large factories in which to manufacture cars, and we need refineries to produce the necessary fuel. If we add to the automobile some of the other "conveniences" of "modern living"—home appliances, frozen and packaged food, television, jet planes (to mention but a few)—it is evident that life adjusted to science and technology tends to assume similar forms everywhere and that the problems of human existence and human valuations likewise tend to be the same. That is to say, once mankind has entered the Age of Technology, cultural differences in various parts of the world are differences of degree, not of kind, and are the remnants of an older tradition or of meta-scientific considerations, i.e., they are of political, religious, or broadly cultural significance.

Thus, science plays a double role when we consider the over-all problem of man in his world. On the one hand, it provides dependable knowledge of the world around us and, in consequence, a better control over the forces of Nature; and scientific truths are universal. Science, therefore, could be a great unifying force encompassing all mankind. On the other hand, however, because of its purely instrumental nature, science tends to intensify problems on a world-wide scale which, without science, might have been restricted to local situations and local conditions.

One further difficulty is involved here. Science ultimately aims at the explanation of quantized observational data, and it aims at explanation in terms of integrated and integrative theories. Such theories, as I have shown elsewhere,[3] consist of a Set A of definitions and postulates from which a Set B of theorems or laws descriptive of the facts of observation can be derived by means of certain (logical and mathematical) rules of transformation. The def-

[3] W. H. Werkmeister, *The Basis and Structure of Knowledge* (New York: Harper & Brothers, 1948), chaps. VI, VII, VIII. W. H. Werkmeister, "Theory Construction and the Problem of Objectivity," in Llewellyn Gross, ed., *Symposium on Sociological Theory* (Evanston: Row, Peterson and Co., 1959), pp. 483–508.

initions and postulates comprising the Set A are stipulations made for the specific purpose of deriving the laws which, as generalized descriptions, account for the facts. Underlying the whole explanatory scheme is the assumption that all events in Nature are conditioned, caused, or determined exclusively by factors external to themselves or resolvable into external factors, and that the basic categories are quantity and relation. Whatsoever cannot be reduced to quantitative and/or relational terms cannot be explained scientifically.

But, if all scientific explanations are given in terms of definitions and postulates and if these are but stipulations,[4] then it follows that alternative stipulations may serve equally well the purpose of deriving the descriptive laws of science.[5] What this means, however, is that, no matter how far science advances, it must stipulate, or assume, certain conditions which themselves remain unexplained by the theory. Here we are confronted with problems of a meta-scientific, i.e., of a philosophical, nature. As von Weizsäcker has put it: "Physics cannot be expected to give answers to questions that cannot be answered in terms of physics."[6]

That questions concerning the nature of ultimate reality transcend the reach of the sciences becomes evident even when we consider the much more limited question of the nature of physical reality. Are electrons *ideational complexes*, or are they in some important sense *real things*, entities which may be said to exist irrespective of their being perceived or thought?[7] Are psi-functions ultimate, or are particles ultimate? Or are references to psi-functions and to particles, respectively, but "a manner of speaking"?[8] The answer to these questions can be given only in terms of presuppositions which transcend physics and which legitimately belong to the domain of philosophy. Moreover, if, on grounds of a consistent principle of causality, elementary particles must be regarded as "causally efficacious"[9] (since Geiger counters detect but "do not create them"[10]), the question now recurs: how are we to understand and explain them? Can the physicist, as physicist, provide the final answer?

Speaking as a physicist, Werner Heisenberg has stated that "all particles are basically nothing but different stationary states of one and the same stuff"; that "there is only one kind of matter but [that] it can exist in different discrete stationary conditions."[11] However, this statement evades rather than answers

[4] For some typical examples see P. A. M. Dirac, *The Principles of Quantum Mechanics* (3d ed., Oxford: Clarendon Press, 1947); George Willard Wheland, *The Theory of Resonance* (New York: John Wiley & Sons, Inc., 1944); Noel B. Slater, *The Development and Meaning of Eddington's "Fundamental Theory"* (Cambridge: Cambridge University Press, 1957).

[5] For example, Lemaître's theory of the "expanding universe" and Hoyle's theory of "continuous creation and annihilation" account equally well for all relevant facts.

[6] C. F. von Weizsäcker, *The History of Nature* (Chicago: University of Chicago Press, 1949), p. 125.

[7] For an extensive discussion of the problem from different perspectives see Henry Margenau, *The Nature of Physical Reality* (New York: McGraw-Hill Book Company, Inc., 1950), pp. 70–71, 99, 105, 296, 450; W. H. Werkmeister, "Professor Margenau and the Problem of Physical Reality," *Philosophy of Science*, XVIII, No. 3 (July, 1951), 183–192.

[8] Philipp Frank, *Philosophy of Science* (Englewood Cliffs: Prentice-Hall, Inc., 1957), p. 247.

[9] W. H. Werkmeister, "The Problem of Physical Reality," *Philosophy of Science*, XIX, No. 3 (July, 1952), 214–224.

[10] Louis O. Kattsoff, *Physical Science and Physical Reality* (The Hague: Martinus Nijohoff, 1957), pp. 295, 303.

[11] Werner Heisenberg, *The Physicist's Conception of Nature* (New York: Harcourt, Brace and Company, 1958), p. 46.

our question, and Heisenberg is well aware of this fact. In his Gifford Lectures he returned to the problem, asserting that "the elementary particles . . . form a world of potentialities or possibilities rather than one of things or facts."[12] But even this answer cannot put an end to all questions. In fact, physics itself is currently undergoing a basic change and, in the words of Heisenberg, the most characteristic trait of this change is "a return to its [physics'] original self-limitation"[13]—a return to a self-limitation, that is, as a science operating within a broader epistemologico-metaphysical framework and dealing with but one aspect of the real. The truth of physics, in other words, is by no means the whole truth. In fact, as Schrödinger (himself a distinguished physicist) has pointed out: "The material world has only been constructed at the price of taking the self, that is, mind, out of it, removing it."[14] As a result, the world of physics is colorless, soundless, unpalpable. It lacks, or is deprived of, values of any kind—utilitarian and instrumental as well as aesthetic and moral. Anything related to meaning and purpose is not only absent from, but can never be an integral part of, the world as described by physics.[15] That the same is true of the world described and interpreted by the chemist follows at once from the nature of chemical theory and chemical explanation.[16]

But when we turn to the social sciences, a new factor enters the picture. Here are sciences—anthropology, sociology, psychology—whose specific subject-matter is man himself and his social behavior. This means, however, that values and valuations are part—and an essential part—of the factual data to be interpreted and explained.[17] One might expect, therefore, that, in any explanatory theory, the key valuations would be included in the Set A of definitions and postulates from which the Set B of laws governing the phenomena can be derived. However, the trend in the social sciences is otherwise.[18]

To be sure, the social scientist aspires to give us an adequate description and an explanation of the facts of man's social existence; but he, unlike the physicist, faces a problem of "naturalistic reductionism," which may impair both his procedures and his theories. That this problem is a serious one cannot well be denied. That the reductionism which ensues falsifies the picture of man and of his position in the universe is also a fact, for the aim is the systematic elimination of values and categories of purpose from the theoretical structure

[12] Werner Heisenberg, *Physics and Philosophy* (New York: Harper & Brothers, 1958), p. 186.

[13] Heisenberg, *The Physicist's Conception of Nature*, p. 180; *Physics and Philosophy*, p. 201.

[14] Erwin Schrödinger, *Mind and Matter* (Cambridge: Cambridge University Press, 1958), p. 39.

[15] W. H. Werkmeister, *A Philosophy of Science* (New York: Harper & Brothers, 1940), p. 79; Schrödinger, *op. cit.*

[16] Werkmeister, *Basis and Structure of Knowledge*, pp. 331–369.

[17] Werkmeister, "Theory Construction and Objectivity," in Llewellyn Gross, ed., *op. cit.*, pp. 499–500.

[18] See, for example, the following books: Bernard Barber, *Science and the Social Order* (Glencoe: Free Press, 1952); F. J. Brown, *Psychology and the Social Order* (New York: The Macmillan Co., 1939); George A. Lundberg, *Foundations of Sociology* (New York: The Macmillan Co., 1939); Stuart C. Dodd, *Dimensions of Society: Quantitative Systematics for the Social Sciences* (New York: The Macmillan Co., 1942); I. Stuart Chapin, *Experimental Designs in Social Research* (New York: Harper & Brothers, 1947); Talcott Parsons, *The Social System* (Glencoe: Free Press, 1949); Harold D. Lasswell and Abraham Kaplan, *Power and Society: A Framework for Political Inquiry* (New Haven: Yale University Press, 1950); Nicolas Rashevsky, *Mathematical Biology of Social Behavior* (Chicago: University of Chicago Press, 1951); Marmon J. Levy, *The Structure of Society* (Princeton: Princeton University Press, 1952); Paul F. Lazarsfeld, ed., *Mathematical Thinking in the Social Sciences* (Glencoe: Free Press, 1952); Roy R. Grinker, ed., *Toward a Unified Theory of Human Behavior* (New York: Basic Books, Inc., 1956); Herbert A. Simon, *Models of Man: Social and Rational* (New York: John Wiley & Sons, Inc., 1957).

of the social sciences and, thus, the achievement of a positive "natural" science of society. As Llewellyn Gross puts it:

Particular aspects of sociological theory may be fruitfully reconstructed along lines that represent analogical approximations of positivistic methods in the natural sciences. In principle, such an endeavor is no different from what has come to be acceptable procedure in thousands of studies where fundamental measurement is simulated.[19]

Inherent in this approach to man are the assumptions—well known from, and justified in, physics—that all basic categories are forms of quantity, and that all factors determining the course of events are "environmental" conditions or forces external to the events themselves. Behaviorism in psychology and social determinism in sociology are representative of this very trend. Their aim is to understand and control "Nature"—including man and society—in terms, and by means, of categories other than those of value or purpose. In fact, values themselves are to be dissolved in the "real" forces which determine human events, biologico-environmental factors susceptible to measurement. As Lundberg put it: A value-neutral social science must disregard "the goals of striving" and must, instead, concentrate on the means only, for science, strictly conceived, is not concerned with ends.[20] To be sure, as Karl Mannheim saw it,[21] "a human being, regarded as part of the social machine, is to a certain extent stabilized in his reactions by training and education, and all his recently acquired activities are co-ordinated according to a definite principle of efficiency within an organized framework," and, presumably, the social sciences must discover the laws inherent in, or constitutive of, this structure—just as the natural sciences discover the laws of physical Nature. But is it not true also that in this process of developing a "naturalistic" science of man and of his society the real character of man and the true meaning of society are lost, that a social science so conceived is scientistic rather than adequate to the facts of human existence?—for those facts include values and valuations, and the projection of ideals which determine more than do environmental conditions the real stature of man in his world. The "total truth"—and this alone—(to borrow Professor Moore's apt phrase), and not "scientism" or "scientistic reductionism," is "the essential need of the world."[22]

I have spoken of "scientism" as distinguished from legitimate science; and this distinction is crucial. Science as such is an admirable enterprise of careful observation, meticulous experimentation, and judicious theory-construction aiming at the best possible and most dependable explanation of events in terms of quantity and external determinants. Scientism, on the other hand, is a brash

[19] Llewellyn Gross, "Theory Construction in Sociology: A Methodological Inquiry," in Llewellyn Gross, ed., *op. cit.*, p. 559. A number of other contributions in this Symposium indicate the same trend.

[20] George A. Lundberg, "The Future of the Social Sciences," *Scientific Monthly,* LIII, No. 4 (October, 1941), 240–244.

[21] Karl Mannheim, *Man and Society in an Age of Reconstruction* (New York: Harcourt, Brace and Co., 1951), p. 244.

[22] Charles A. Moore, "An Attempt at World Philosophical Synthesis," in Charles A. Moore, ed., *Essays in East-West Philosophy* (Honolulu: University of Hawaii Press, 1951), p. 1.

"boundary transgression," and the unjustifiable claim that the methods and categories of science are adequate to account for all facts of human existence no less than for all events in Nature and that phenomena not accessible to scientific methods or not subsumable under the categories of science are either irrelevant or illusory, or both.[23] Scientism thus implies that "the great ideals for which humanity has fought and suffered—the Good, the Beautiful, and the True—honor, love, and sacrifice—the eightfold path of the Buddha, the Christian vision of redemption, the Muslim communion with God—all these inspired revelations and ideals are just illusions on the surface of reality."[24] The conception of man inherent in scientism is thus essentially the same as that entailed by dialectical materialism.

This fact, however, points up better than anything else the crucial importance of the problem of scientism for philosophy and for the future of the world. Eastern philosophers, I am sure, will understand full well what is at stake. They will understand that the really great, the overriding, issue of our times is and remains the problem of man. We can arm ourselves to the utmost and can prepare to fight the biggest, the most devastating, war in history. But of what significance is all this—of what significance is even victory in such a war—if, in the process, we lose sight of man himself and of human values? After all, the scientistic "ideal" is as nihilistic in its consequences as is any form of materialistic reductionism. The present age calls for—nay, it demands—a philosophical reappraisal of our human situation and our human valuations.

We can all agree, I am sure, on the value of science for our modern world if the knowledge obtained in and through science is put to constructive ends. We can all agree also on what is essential to the enterprise of science: observation and measurement, experimentation, the formulation of descriptive but quantitative laws, and the construction of explanatory theories from which those laws may be derived.[25] We can agree, furthermore, that, in its legitimate employment and functioning, science has specific limitations. In no case does it provide "ultimate" explanations, and its key categories pertain to operationally determinable quantities only. We can also agree, I am sure, that scientism is a "boundary transgression" which distorts rather than clarifies the most important issues concerning the nature of man and man's position in the world, that it falsifies the problem of values, of moral responsibility, and, therefore, of human existence. We can all agree, therefore, that, having reached a common understanding with respect to science and scientism, we now face the more difficult, the crucial, problem of determining the value-framework within which man selects his goals, makes his commitments, and assumes moral responsibilities.[26] But basic to this is our conception of man himself.

[23] Cf. Whyte, *op. cit.*, p. 26. Note especially the quotation from Eric Voegelin's article in *Social Research,* XV, No. 4 (December, 1948).

[24] Russell W. Davenport, *The Dignity of Man* (New York: Harper & Brothers, 1955), p. 176.

[25] For an excellent discussion of the philosophical aspects of legitimate science see Pravas Jivan Chaudhury, *The Philosophy of Science* (Calcutta: Progressive Publishers, 1955).

[26] For the most concise statement of my own point of view see W. H. Werkmeister, "The Meaning and Being of Values Within the Framework of an Empirically Oriented Value Theory," in Richard Wisser, ed., *Sinn und Sein, Ein philosophisches Symposion* (Tübingen: Max Niemeyer Verlag, 1959).

II.

Having thus stated the problem, I shall now attempt a constructive interpretation of the nature of man which, though keyed to the best of our scientific knowledge, will yet do full justice to the unique and creative aspects of that nature and will place man into proper perspective relative to the world in which he lives. I thus enter the field of philosophical anthropology.

Although it is not my intention to consider all aspects of the complex and intricate problems before us, it will be necessary to discuss a number of facts pertaining to man as we have come to know them in the various fields of inquiry. I shall therefore not hesitate to turn to biology,[27] psychology,[28] anthropology,[29] and philosophy[30] in order to get before us a picture of man that is as complete and as comprehensive as the facts of human existence demand and the space at my disposal permits. This picture will reflect both the major traditions of Western philosophy and the best in contemporary science and, therefore, should provide a broad basis for fruitful discussion.

Human experience is essentially dual in nature, involving, on the one hand, a context or realm of objects[31] and, on the other hand, the experiencing of these objects as an awareness of, a being-concerned-with, an intending and an acting.[32] As far as the objects and their interrelations are concerned, we know them in the external mode characteristic of science. But we know ourselves in another way also—in the intimate self-disclosure of reflective experience. We experience ourselves as ourselves, as the unique and personal center of our experience.

[27] A. Portmann, *Biologische Fragmente zu einer Lehre vom Menschen* (Basel: B. Schwabe, 1952).

[28] D. M. Allen, *The Realm of Personality* (New York: Abingdon Cokesbury, 1947); G. W. Allport, *The Nature of Personality* (Cambridge: Addison-Wesley, 1950); G. W. Allport, *Becoming: Basic Considerations for a Psychology of Personality* (New Haven: Yale University Press, 1955); A. Angyal, *Foundations for a Science of Personality* (New York: Commonwealth Foundation, 1941); H. Cantril, *The "Why" of Man's Experience* (New York: The Macmillan Co., 1950); Henry P. David and Helmut von Bracken, *Perspectives in Personality Theory* (New York: Basic Books, Inc., 1957); S. Freud, *The Basic Writings of Sigmund Freud*, A. A. Brill, trans. and ed. (New York: The Modern Library, 1938); S. Freud, *An Outline of Psychoanalysis*, J. Strachey, trans. (New York: W. W. Norton & Co., Inc., 1949); E. Fromm, *Man for Himself: An Inquiry into the Psychology of Ethics* (New York: Rinehart & Co., Inc., 1947); K. Goldstein, *Human Nature in the Light of Psychopathology* (Cambridge: Harvard University Press, 1940); K. Horney, *Neurosis and Human Growth: The Struggle Toward Self-Realization* (New York: W. W. Norton & Co., Inc., 1950); W. Keller, *Vom Wesen des Menschen, Jahrbuch der Schweizerischen Philosophischen Gesellschaft*, Vol. III (Basel: Ernest Reinhardt Verlag, 1943); W. Keller, *Psychologie und Philosophie des Wollens* (Basel: Ernest Reinhardt Verlag, 1954); P. Lecky, *Self-Consistency: A Theory of Personality* (New York: Island Press, 1945); Ph. Lersch, *Der Aufbau der Person* (Munich: Barth, 1954); K. Lewin, *A Dynamic Theory of Personality* (New York: McGraw-Hill Book Company, Inc., 1935); A. H. Maslow, *Motivation and Personality* (New York: Harper and Brothers, 1954); G. Murphy, *Personality: A Biosocial Approach to Origins and Structure* (New York: Harper and Brothers, 1947); G. Murphy, *Human Potentialities* (New York: Basic Books, Inc., 1958); E. Rothacker, *Die Schichten der Persoenlichkeit* (Leipzig: Johann Ambrosius Barth, 1938).

[29] C. Kluckhohn and H. A. Murray, *Personality in Nature, Society, and Culture* (New York: Alfred A. Knopf, 1949); R. Linton, *The Cultural Background of Personality* (New York: Appleton-Century-Crofts, 1945); S. S. Sargent and M. W. Smith, eds., *Culture and Personality* (New York: Viking Fund, 1949).

[30] R. T. Flewelling, *The Person* (Los Angeles: The Ward Ritchie Press, 1952); M. Heidegger, *Sein und Zeit* (1926) (4th ed., Halle: Max Niemeyer, 1935); M. Heidegger, *Kant und das Problem der Metaphysik* (Frankfurt: Gerhard Schulte-Bulmke, 1934); E. Mounier, *The Character of Man*, Cynthia Rowland, trans. (New York: Harper and Brothers, 1956); A. Pfänder, *Die Seele des Menschen* (Halle: Max Niemeyer, 1933); J.-P. Sartre, *L'Etre et le Néant: Essai d'Ontologie Phénomènologique* (Paris: Gallimard, 1943); M. Scheler, *Die Stellung des Menschen im Kosmos* (Rev. ed., Darmstadt: O. Reichl, 1928); R. Ulich, *The Human Career: A Philosophy of Self-Transcendence* (New York: Harper and Brothers, 1955).

[31] Werkmeister, *The Basis and Structure of Knowledge.*

[32] W. H. Werkmeister, "On 'Describing a World,'" *Philosophy and Phenomenological Research*, XI, No. 3 (March, 1951), 303–326.

Our mode of existence is, thus, complex. For others and, in certain cognitive perspectives, even for ourselves, we exist in the objective and external sense in which all things in the world exist. But, at the same time, and in indissoluble connection with the first mode of existence, we also exist as the self-disclosed subject-pole of all our experience. In fact, human existence, insofar as it is truly human, is terminally encountered only as self-disclosure. To understand the nature of man means, therefore, to understand him in this complex mode of his self-revealed existence.

Still, we can learn much about the nature of man from the various sciences, for, in a fundamental sense, man is but a part of the cosmos which surrounds him, his body re-echoing but some of the physico-chemical aspects of that universe. Moreover, insofar as man is a living organism, his very existence, like that of every other organism, is conditioned by his assimilative interactions with his environment; and through the process of evolution he is kin to all forms of life, sharing with them some of his functions, his needs, his drives. Whatever specifically human traits man possesses, they appear only as embedded in the matrix of his biological existence.

But man *is* unique and differs from all other forms of life. His cultural achievements alone are proof that here is a being which surpasses all others in self-directed activities and in creative accomplishments. Man may be a creature of Nature, but, also, with man something unique and distinctive came into existence. The question is: How are we to interpret these facts?

In Western philosophy two contradictory traditions prevail. One assumes a radical dualism in the nature of man; the other attempts to interpret human existence within the framework of Nature itself. The first alternative has at all times led to insurmountable difficulties. I shall therefore follow the second, being fully aware, however, of the difficulties besetting my path also.

As a living organism, man shares with other forms of life certain dynamic and functional aspects of existence. He is never a merely static entity, and his development, beginning with the fertilized ovum and culminating in adulthood, is a process of functionally directed growth, and is essentially epigenetic.[33] But the human organism, even when fully developed, is constantly in a state of "equilibration"—in process, that is, of maintaining itself in the midst of and

[33] E. F. Adolph, *Physiological Regulations* (Lancaster, Pa.: Jacques Cattell Press, 1943); W. E. Agar, *A Contribution to the Theory of the Living Organism* (New York: Oxford University Press, 1943); C. M. Child, *Patterns and Problems of Development* (Chicago: University of Chicago Press, 1941); H. Driesch, *The Science and Philosophy of the Organism* (1908) (2d ed., London: Adam and Charles Black, 1929); J. S. Huxley and G. R. De Beer, *Elements of Experimental Embryology* (Cambridge: Cambridge University Press, 1934); R. S. Lillie, "Directive Action and Life," *Philosophy of Science*, IV, No. 2 (April, 1937), 202–226; R. S. Lillie, "Biological Causation," *Philosophy of Science*, VII, No. 3 (July, 1940), 314–336; R. S. Lillie, *General Biology and Philosophy of Organism* (Chicago: University of Chicago Press, 1945); T. H. Morgan, *Regeneration* (New York: The Macmillan Co., 1901); J. Needham, *Order and Life* (New Haven: Yale University Press, 1936); J. Needham, *Biochemistry and Morphogenesis* (Cambridge: Cambridge University Press, 1942); W. E. Ritter, *The Unity of the Organism* (Boston: R. G. Badger, 1919); J. Schultz, *Die Maschinen-theorie des Lebens* (Göttingen: Vandenhoeck & Ruprecht, 1909); H. Spemann, *Embryonic Development and Induction* (New Haven: Yale University Press, 1938); F. Strecker, *Das Kausalitätsprinzip der Biologie* (Leipzig: W. Engelmann, 1907); L. von Bertalanffy, *Theoretische Biologie II* (2d ed., Bern: A. Francke, 1951); L. von Bertalanffy, *Problems of Life: An Evaluation of Modern Biological Thoughts* (New York: John Wiley & Sons, Inc., 1952); Werkmeister, *A Philosophy of Science;* Werkmeister, *The Basis and Structure of Knowledge.*

despite interactions with his environment.[34] And this organismic activity provides the framework and the dynamic pattern within which the distinctly human activities are rooted.

But as we inspect and analyze our own experience of ourselves, we encounter here, too, a complex process of "equilibration," of adjusting and readjusting to manifold internal and external situations. The innermost reality of our self-disclosed being is a dynamic interplay of felt needs, felt urges, felt desires, of wishes, intentions, interests, cognitions, emotions, attitudes, and the like. That is to say, we are concerned with "something" that involves us existentially as active, cognitive, self-directive beings, responding to a physico-biological and social environment. We experience ourselves as beings which seek to maintain and to "actualize" themselves in the sense that they seek to satisfy their needs and to realize their innate possibilities. Whenever we fall short of satisfying our needs, we experience tensions and, ultimately, a feeling of frustration. Conversely, when we satisfy our needs and realize our potentialities, we experience a sense of fulfillment; we exist "authentically" as *we*.

In this experience of ourselves as *we*, as this unique, biographically definable center of experience, we thus apprehend the inward counterpart of the active and centrally regulative organism we call our body. We experience ourselves as a "body-mind" unity—as a *minded* organism. Physiological and psychological processes interpenetrate and fuse in the dynamics of the psycho-physiological whole which is at the core of human existence.[35]

But there is still another aspect to this wholeness and unity of the minded organism which is the human being. Although it has been customary to speak of cognition, feeling, and volition as if these broad ranges of human experience were independent of one another and could therefore be treated with impunity as separate "faculties" of man, human nature is essentially otherwise. Cognitive, affective, and volitional aspects of human experience are intricately and indissolubly interrelated at all times. Although in any given situation some one of these modes of experience—each one being itself diversified in many ways and degrees—may predominate, it is never completely separated from its manifold interrelations with other modes. To regard it as isolated is to abstract it from the living context of experience itself which falsifies the picture.[36]

[34] W. B. Cannon, *The Wisdom of the Body* (New York: W. W. Norton & Co., Inc., 1932); C. Bernard, *Leçons sur les Phénomènes de la Vie*, 2 vols. (Paris: G. B. Baillière et fils, 1878–1879); J. S. Haldane, *Respiration* (New Haven: Yale University Press, 1922); J. S. Haldane, *The Sciences and Philosophy* (Garden City: Doubleday, Doran & Co., Inc., 1931); I. Kant, *Kritik der Urteilskraft*, Reclam edition by Karl Kehrbach (Leipzig: Philipp Reolam, Jr., n.d.); C. S. Sherrington, *The Integrative Action of the Nervous System* (New York: Charles Scribner's Sons, 1906).

[35] Allport, *The Nature of Personality;* R. B. Cattel, *Personality* (New York: McGraw-Hill Book Company, Inc., 1950); J. C. Eccles, *The Neurophysiological Basis of Mind* (Oxford: Clarendon Press, 1953); A. E. Fessard, "Mechanisms of Nervous Integration and Conscious Experience," in Jean F. Delafresnaye, ed., *Brain Mechanisms and Consciousness* (Oxford: Blackwell's, ·954); J. M. Fletcher, "Homeostasis as an Explanatory Principle in Psychology," *Psychological Review* (1942), 80–87; R. Miller, *Aufbau der Persönlichkeit* (Berlin: Müller & Kiepenheuer, 1934); Murphy, *Personality: A Biosocial Approach to Origins and Structure;* H. Selye, *Stress: The Physiology and Pathology of Exposure to Stress* (Montreal: Acta, 1950); R. Stagner, "Homeostasis as a Unifying Concept in Personality Theory," *Psychological Review*, LVIII, No. 1 (January, 1951), 5–17; H. Thomae, *Persönlichkeit: Eine dynamische Interpretation* (Bonn: Bouvier, 1951); H. G. Wolff, "Life Stress and Bodily Disease," in A. Weider, ed., *Contributions Toward Medical Psychology* (New York: Ronald Press, 1953).

[36] E. W. Sinnott, *Cell and Psyche* (Chapel Hill: University of North Carolina Press, 1950).

The essential unity of man as minded organism, as a dynamic whole, is evident in still another respect. At the human level organismic growth finds its continuation and extension in psychological growth—a process which is essentially a spontaneous and non-coerced unfolding of potentialities with which the human embryo is endowed.[37] Theoretically, of course, there are biological and hereditary limits beyond which a given individual cannot grow. In the case of organismic growth this is an obvious fact. In the case of psychological growth, however, it is difficult to say when any given individual has reached his limit of development or whether anybody ever has. Within each multi-dimensional genetic framework of potentialities and limitations, and under diverse and varying environmental and cultural conditions, the possibilities of human growth appear to be boundless.[38]

At this point, however, additional facts must be considered. In the animal kingdom each species has its own distinctive characteristics, its own genetically determined species-specific pattern of behavior. The human species, of course, has its own propensities, its own hereditarily determined characteristics, which provide a framework for the development of the individual.[39] The instinctual and species-specific pattern of behavior, rooted in biological needs and initiated, sustained, and directed from levels far below that of consciousness, provides the background against and from which all psychic phenomena—all conscious desires, volitions, emotions, and insights—arise. Here, at the unfathomable depth of organismic needs and requirements, we encounter the irreducible core of our existence; and here, too, we encounter the potentialities and innate limitations of human development.

This irreducible core of our existence is that intangible *psychoidal* condition or state in which biological phenomena, being potentially mind in the making, are no longer biological only but are also not psychological or mental. The potentialities of the minded organism are as yet unrealized. Still, because of the potentialities and limitations it contains, this psychoidal core of our existence conditions the lifelong process of our growth and development as a person. It is, in fact, our "psychoidal proto-self," pressing for realization of its potentialities in continuation beyond mere organismic growth. Man, the actual, living human being—being always a self in process, in development—exists somewhere between his biologically conditioned and given proto-self and the ideal in which all his potentialities would find harmonious realization.

So far I have emphasized the fact that man is essentially a functionally integrated whole. But he is also, and perhaps even more fundamentally, a center of action. His "dark promptings," his urges and drives, deeply rooted in the psy-

[37] Fromm, *Man for Himself: An Inquiry into the Psychology of Ethics;* K. Goldstein, *The Organism* (New York: American Book Co., 1939); K. Horney, *New Ways in Psychoanalysis* (New York: W. W. Norton & Co., Inc., 1939); K. Horney, *Our Inner Conflicts* (New York: W. W. Norton & Co., Inc., 1945); Murphy, *Personality: A Biosocial Approach to Origins and Structure;* H. S. Sullivan, *Conceptions of Modern Psychiatry* (Washington: William Alanson White Psychiatric Foundation, 1947).

[38] Allport, *Personality;* Murphy, *Personality: A Biosocial Approach to Origins and Structure;* Thomae, *Persönlichkeit: Eine dynamische Interpretation.*

[39] C. G. Jung, "The Spirit of Psychology," in *Spirit and Nature: Papers from the Eranos Yearbooks,* Series I. Bollingen Series No. 3, I (New York: Pantheon Books, 1954).

choidal core of his being as they are, are the first revelations of his proto-self, of the primary pattern of his growth and development as a person. This dynamic oneness of human existence is essential to an understanding of the nature of man. But to insist upon this fact is not the same as to maintain that man, like any animal, is nothing but a complexus of elementary drives and that there is nothing unique about human existence, for there is. In fact, man's basic drives are not simply the promptings and drives of mere animal nature. They are what they are only because they are manifestations of the proto-self, of man's potentialities as a human being. It is only in their relation to the integrative and equilibrating wholeness of the living organism, as represented by the psychoidal proto-self, that man's drives find their true significance. In the last analysis, it is always the organism as a whole—the minded organism—which lives in and through those drives.

But man is, and experiences himself as being, an individual who is aware not only of himself as acting, as being "engaged" in various situations, but also as determining in a large measure his relation to the surrounding world and of finding or realizing himself in and through such self-determination. That is to say, man exists essentially as a "becoming" rather than as a mere "being," as a "task" to be fulfilled through his own efforts rather than as something definitively given or predetermined; and he experiences himself as a "task" despite the determining potentialities and limitations of his psychoidal proto-self.

The combination of two facts, I believe, makes this unique mode of existence not only possible but inevitable in the course of evolution. The first fact is man's awareness of his own drives. No matter how faint this awareness or how vague the discernment may be, the fact remains that man is aware of tensions and drives which prompt him into action. This awareness, however, discloses an inner duality of man's self-reflective experience which characterizes the whole of human existence. And only upon this basis of an inner duality is a self-directed "becoming" possible at all, for this experienced duality sets off the experienced tensions and drives from our experiencing of them, making it possible to see any particular drive in context with other drives and with things and situations in the surrounding world. It thus entails the possibility of "taking an attitude" toward that drive, of guiding, opposing, or redirecting it.

The second fact which, in combination with the duality of our self-revealing experience, makes possible, and even inevitable, man's unique mode of existence is the biological "immaturity" and consequent plasticity of the human individual at birth.[40] By the time the human infant reaches the stage of maturity possessed by many animals almost at birth, socially conditioned patterns have been superimposed upon his instinctive drives so that the latter can function only within a framework which is not biologically fixed. But what this really means is that his own immaturity at birth literally forces man to develop "himself" in a world of things and human situations. In this crucial fact lie his greatest opportunities and his dangers.

[40] A. Partmann, *Biologische Fragmente zu einer Lehre vom Menschen.*

As the human infant slowly develops from embryonic but postnatal immaturity to the relative independence of a small child he gradually awakens to a full awareness of himself as a center of experience and action, and as "other" than the objects with which he is concerned. He begins to respond, and respond ever more selectively, to the world around him, and he gradually "awakens" into full consciousness of himself and his world, adjusting to his world in manifold ways, prompted and guided by feelings of pleasure and displeasure, of satisfaction and frustration, no less than by perceptual experiences and a dawning apprehension of cause-and-effect relationships. The whole process is essentially an active "equilibrating" and thus, in a radical sense, a manifestation of that dynamic expansiveness which is life itself.

In this process of maturing, man's basic drives undergo manifold changes. The body-building and body-preserving drives, for example, may transcend their basic needs, so that the drive for food becomes an interest in, and desire for, cultivating the soil and domesticating animals, and, given certain conditions of plenty, for the culinary delights of a gourmet. And man's affiliative needs, which find their first expression in the child's dependence upon his mother, can still be traced in family and friendship groups and in the increasingly more complex co-operative enterprises of cultural living. Such development, initiated and sustained by the potentialities of the proto-self, takes place under social pressures but also in the light of an ever-increasing understanding of the world we live in and of the function and relative importance of our drives in that world.

But the central control of man's normal development, deeply rooted as it is in the "equilibrating" wholeness of the living organism, is indicative of still another drive that is basic to the nature of man. This is the drive toward self-fulfillment, toward the realization of his own proper potentialities. It is the drive which emanates from the potentialities of the psychoidal proto-self as a whole but which sustains even man's highest ambitions with respect to himself.

What is involved here is the fact that in every "normal" development of an individual as a person, and in intricate connection with his biologically conditioned needs and potentialities, there takes place a half-conscious, half-unconscious "self-molding" in accordance with some more or less clearly conceived "ideal self-image" (Karen Horney), which, for the individual, is a symbol of the very meaning and goal of his life. The ideal itself, whatever its origin, is always a valuational pattern which, transcending the actualities of our existence, can and does serve as a guide in whatever we do or do not do; and it is all the more effective as a guide when, at the subconscious level of our existence, it pervades our habits as well as our thoughts. The drive toward self-fulfillment finds its culmination in this ideal.

In each individual there is thus an inner tension—a tension complicated and intensified many times by the manifold interactions of our more specialized drives and by the pressures and demands of a social environment—which finds relief only in a process of "becoming" that brings us closer to our ideal. In this fluid state of adjusting tensions and pressures and conflicts, the individual becomes a "task" for himself, for it is he, as a person, who is constantly at stake. It is he who is "engaged" in his own development—in his own individuation as a person. And it is he himself who largely determines the kind of person—the manner of man—he is going to be.

Much of the process—comprising psychoidal developments, adjustments of drives, and adaptations to a social environment—is and remains deeply unconscious. At the level of consciousness, however, individuation is "a psychological task to be undertaken and carried through as a way of life"[41] in the deliberate effort to realize a self that will bring into harmony our "ideal self-image" and the potentialities of our proto-self and that will be adjusted to the realities of a social order. In this task of harmonious self-development we may not succeed, and our drive for self-fulfillment may be frustrated; but, by subjecting ourselves to an "ideal self-image," we impose upon ourselves demands for our own realization, for our own "inner validity," and for our authentic existence as a person.

That the drive for self-fulfillment may find realization in many different ways is obvious, for the complexly varied and diversified special drives may be combined in manifold ways and in countless variations of intensity, each combination being unique to a particular individual. The drive for self-fulfillment is, thus, not simply a drive for "more" life, in the purely quantitative sense of "more," but a drive toward qualitatively distinct manifestations of life. Each individual strives toward his own self-realization in his own individual way; and he does so in the light of his own projection of, and commitment to, an "ideal self-image."

That the commitment to, and pursuit of, an "ideal self-image" assumes a measure of personal freedom is obvious. But it is also obvious, I believe, that, experientially, the difference between compulsion and freedom, between drives and voluntary actions, is clear—no matter how many transitional experiences there may be in which elements of both feelings, compulsion and freedom, are present. What makes our voluntary actions possible is essentially our self-awareness and our insight into relationships. Our insight into cause-and-effect relations, in particular, augments all mere drives by providing a rational basis for their guidance and central control. We are free, therefore, not in the negative sense of being free from all determining factors, but in the positive sense of being able to act in accordance with our insights into relationships and laws. And only as free agents in this sense can we achieve self-fulfillment in any significant sense. Only as free agents can we have authentic existence as a person, and only as such agents can we be truly creative—envisioning new goals and transforming imaginative anticipations into actualities of human existence. And only thus do we reach our full stature as a man.[42]

[41] I. Progoff, *The Death and Rebirth of Psychology* (New York: The Julian Press, Inc., 1956).

[42] O. Rank, *Psychology and the Soul,* William D. Turner, trans. (Philadelphia: University of Pennsylvania Press, 1950).

However, human existence is essentially a cultural existence. A person is what he is only because of his contacts with other human beings. These contacts, however, are ambivalent. There is, on the one hand, the fundamental "we"-experience with its inherent sympathies and basic affinities, the community of men which is no longer a "side by side" but a *"with"* one another of individuals. There is, in other words, the *"we* of love" (Binswanger).[43] But there is also "a very primitive intolerance of others at the very roots of personality" (Mounier), for "the other" is experienced as "something alien," and the relation between "myself" and "the other" is "essentially not a 'being-with' but a conflict" (Sartre).[44] Only the two realities together, the *"we* of love" and the *"we* of conflict," in their manifold shadings and interrelations, account for the actual facts of man's communal living—the *"we* of love" satisfying our affiliative needs, the *"we* of conflict" requiring the imposition of laws to regulate human behavior.

From this point of view, moral imperatives and norms are but projected ways of avoiding or alleviating conflicts; positive law, tribal or written, is society's effort to deal specifically with actual conflicts of specific types. That, ideally, positive law presupposes and rests upon moral imperatives is therefore not difficult to understand; nor should it surprise us to find that moral imperatives imply the idea of an ideal society—such as Kant's "kingdom of ends," Royce's "beloved community," and the Christian conception of a "community of saints."

Membership in such a society—that is, by implication, membership in a moral society—imposes upon the individual certain requirements of self-discipline and modes of behavior consonant with the principles that are constitutive of the ideal society. And in accepting this discipline, i.e., in and through his explicit or implicit commitment to the group, the individual himself develops into a moral being.

It is true, of course, that each individual grows up in a social environment within which certain patterns of conduct and valuation prevail which may fall far short of the ideal, and that, in his own development, he must and does adjust to these patterns.[45] But it is also true that an individual achieves self-fulfillment even under these conditions either by specifically accepting the prevailing patterns and valuations as his own, or by responding to them critically and opposing to them his own vision or view of human living. In actual fact,

[43] L. Binswanger, *Grundformen und Erkenntnis des menschlichen Daseins* (Zurich: Max Niehans, 1942); M. Buber, *Between Man and Man* (New York: The Macmillan Co., 1948); M. Buber, *Das Problem des Menschen* (Heidelberg: Lambert Schneider, 1948); Th. Litt, *Individuum und Gemeinschaft: Grundlegung der Kulturphilosophie* (2d ed., Leipzig: B. G. Teubner, 1923); K. Löwith, *Das Individuum in der Rolle des Mitmenschen* (Munich: Drei Masken Verlag, 1928); G. H. Mead, *Mind, Self and Society,* C. W. Morris, ed. (Chicago: University of Chicago Press, 1934); P. E. Pfuetze, *The Social Self* (New York: Bookman Associates, 1954); M. Scheler, *Nature of Sympathy,* Peter Heath, trans. (London: Routledge & Kegan Paul, 1954).

[44] W. Desan, *The Strange Finale: An Essay on the Philosophy of Jean-Paul Sartre* (Cambridge: Harvard University Press, 1954); E. Mounier, *The Character of Man;* M. Natanson, *A Critique of Jean-Paul Sartre's Ontology,* University of Nebraska Studies, New Series, No. 6 (Lincoln: University of Nebraska Press, 1951); J.-P. Sartre, *L'Etre et le Néant.*

[45] R. Benedict, *Patterns of Culture* (Boston: Houghton Mifflin, 1946); E. Fromm, *The Sane Society* (New York: Rinehart & Co., Inc., 1955); J. J. Honigman, *Culture and Personality* (New York: Harper and Brothers, 1954); R. Linton, *The Cultural Background of Personality.*

the response of an individual is always a mixture of both attitudes, although the weight or prevalence of each may vary greatly from person to person and, for the same person, in the course of a lifetime. There is the person who gladly and wholeheartedly accepts the established pattern because he finds it congenial to his own potentialities; and there is the "born" rebel who finds self-fulfillment only in breaking away from, and transcending, the given pattern of valuations. One may be a rebel, however, in one of two radically different ways. One may be a rebel, for instance, because of perverted sensibilities, misdirected drives, and a distorted sense of frustration. The record of criminals is proof of this fact. But one may also be a rebel because of a new vision of man, a deeper insight into his potentialities and needs and the requirements for his fullest development. The great innovators, the reformers and "prophets," have at all times been rebels in this sense. In the slow process of man's cultural evolution, they have been, and still are, the pathfinders, the guides, the anticipators of his greatest achievements.

In becoming part of a social group, an individual accepts the pattern of valuations of that group. The better "adjusted" he is, the more has the group pattern become his own mode of living. Tensions arise only when the individual's own needs, own potentialities, and own insights come into conflict with the pattern. These very tensions, however, entail the possibilities of progress for the individual himself no less than for the group as a whole.

One indication of the growth of an individual under such conditions is the subtle transformation of conscience; and this transformation, it must be observed, is but a further manifestation of the drive toward self-fulfillment.

In its beginnings, conscience may indeed be but the repository of socially approved valuations and modes of behavior, and, in the beginning also, it may reflect merely fear of punishment. In the beginning, therefore, conscience may speak with the force of external authority, human or divine. But, as we mature, our conscience reflects ever more fully our own insights and value-commitments, and the *ought* which it imposes is essentially a self-imposed value-related obligation, not a compulsive *must*. It is an ought which demands the control of "transitory impulse and opportunistic adjustment in the interests of long-range aim and consistency with the [ideal] self-image" (Allport). A guilty conscience still means poignant suffering, but the suffering now stems from a sense of failure, of having forsaken one's own values, of having fallen short of the ideal. It is not fear of punishment.

If the feeling of guilt is thus a measure of the extent to which we live up to our "ideal self-image," the choice of that ideal is itself an index of our maturity as a person. It is a choice which we must make in full consideration of our own limitations. But, since our understanding of ourselves changes with deeper insight and wider experience, self-development requires that we adjust and readjust our aims and ideals themselves in harmony with our new insights. It is in this sense that the examined life is the truly mature life, the life of self-fulfillment.

It is true, of course, that man's culture also is in development. A perpetual "becoming," it is always in transition. It would be both interesting and important to consider the implications and ramifications of this fact, mindful of the further fact, however, that no real understanding of history is possible if in our interpretations we restrict ourselves exclusively to the past—no matter how distant or how recent. Not even in their daily affairs do human beings act simply by responding to stimuli immediately present to them. The cumulative experience of the past and the projection of goals into the future are part and parcel of their decisions, of their activities. In fact, the projection and pursuit of goals are the typically human mode of action—for the individuals as well as for the "subjects of history."[46] And the goals or projections of any given moment may have to be revised and, at times, revised radically, in the light of consequences which were not or could not have been foreseen, in the light of new value-commitments, of new aims, which transcend and replace the old. In this respect, history (as the "biography" of "subjects of history") and personal biography are mutually elucidating events.

In our history, however, the whole of man's journey on earth is involved. To understand man in the midst of his journey we must go back at least to the time of the Neanderthal man, who—his ritual burials prove it—must have wondered about the mysteries of his own existence. The fact is that, with man, an entirely new kind of creature came into the world, a being who was a problem to himself. His self-awareness, his ability to think and to reason, and his imagination which permitted him to transcend the immediately given, to relive the past, to anticipate the future—though all of these faculties matured but slowly, they were the factors which disrupted his inner harmony, his instinctive adjustment to Nature. At the same time, however, they also prevented him from ever returning to the unproblematic existence of a mere animal. On the one hand, man had become alienated from Nature; on the other hand, he had not yet found his place in a truly human world. His own development had set him adrift upon an ocean of unfathomed and unfathomable possibilities, had left him to himself without the sure guidance of animal instincts. Now that he was no longer a mere animal, tranquilly living in his own instincts the life of the species, there was only one hope for man, namely, to create for himself a new world, a human world, within which he could once again feel harmoniously at home and, in the process, become himself truly human.[47] His efforts to accomplish this—though the goal was felt rather than understood and the efforts were often misdirected and distorted because he did not understand either himself or the world around him—are the mainsprings of the noblest as well as the most pathetic and the most cruel events in history. They bespeak, however, also the

[46] W. H. Werkmeister, "History and Human Destiny," *The Personalist,* XXXVIII, No. 2 (Spring, 1957), 116–129; N. Hartmann, "Sinngebung und Sinnerfüllung," in *Kleinere Schriften,* I (Berlin: Walter de Gruyter & Co., 1955); Ortega y Gasset, *The Modern Theme,* James Cleugh, trans. (New York: W. W. Norton & Co., Inc., 1933); Ortega y Gasset, *Toward a Philosophy of History,* Helene Weyl, trans. (New York: W. W. Norton & Co., Inc., 1941).

[47] Buber, *Das Problem des Menschen;* N. Hartmann, "Naturphilosophie und Anthropologie" (1944), in *Kleinere Schriften,* I, 1955; H. W. Schneider, *Three Dimensions of Public Morality* (Bloomington: Indiana University Press, 1956).

basic meaning of history as the slow, the circuitous, the agonizing process of man finding a way to his own true humanity. What is at stake in this process is not only the individual as a person in the full sense of the integrated realization of his highest values, but also, and especially, the development of the "subjects of history" to the highest level of moral responsibility commensurate with the security, the freedom, and the dignity of the individual, so that in and through his society, in and through the culture in which he shares and to which he contributes creatively, the individual himself may realize to the fullest his own possibilities as a human being.

Such, at least, are the perspectives of a philosophical anthropology consonant with the facts disclosed in the various relevant sciences. It is my hope that on at least some of the crucial points philosophers of East *and* West can reach understanding and agreement. And since the ideas here presented reflect not only major trends in Western philosophy but the findings of modern science as well, agreement on these crucial points would mean also a rapprochement between East and West. It would entail an East-West conception of man.

QUESTION: Just what do you mean by "scientism"?

ANSWER: I use the term "scientism" to designate certain misuses and misconceptions of science. Specifically, I have in mind a form of reductionism (paralleling or replacing materialistic reductionism) which insists that *all* facts of human experience can ultimately be interpreted in terms of quantitative categories and/or external causal conditions, and which insists also that the methods of science are the only methods we have for discovering truth. That there are facts of human experience which cannot be reduced to the categories of science should be evident as soon as we consider the nature of moral obligation, the character of aesthetic experience, the meaning of logical entailment, and the whole range of affective valuations. And it is but a compounding of the confusion when the term "science" is used so loosely that it covers any empirically oriented and rational interpretation of experience. If, for example, the clarification of ideas aimed at in philosophy (which, in my paper, I called dialectic) is also to be called "scientific," then the term "scientific method" loses its distinctive meaning and may as well be discarded—along with the term "science." It is because I respect science that I wish to save it from those who, because of basic confusions, take its name in vain.

QUESTION: Does your repudiation of scientism mean that there is no connection between science and value—that science cannot aid us in clarifying our values?

ANSWER: It does not. But we must distinguish between (a) value of science, (b) value in science, and (c) value for science. As far as the value of science is concerned, it is obvious that cultural context determines the value placed upon science both as an instrument for the realization of human ends and as satisfying man's desire to know; and it is also obvious that changes in the cultural context entail changes in the value placed upon science. The transition from the Middle Ages to our times is proof of this fact. That science itself helps bring about changes in the cultural pattern is no proof to the contrary.

As far as value in science is concerned, we encounter no difficulty. What is meant here is simply that in some of the social sciences, e.g., anthropology, values are part of the facts of human existence which are to be analyzed and interpreted. That scientific investigations of the value-patterns of different cultures can be important even for our own value-commitments is, of course, not to be denied. What must be denied, however, is that the scientific study of values is in itself a commitment to the values studied, for a commitment is the acceptance of certain values as norms, not their study as given facts. Science, being but instrumental, does not prescribe norms.

Lastly, with respect to value for science, suffice it to say that the value-framework within which science operates is normative for science itself and is therefore neither a part of the content nor a part of the method of science. To be sure, this value-framework—including such values as freedom of inquiry, intellectual honesty, open-mindedness, and respect for facts—is foundational to the whole enterprise of science. The values involved here spell out norms entailed by the desire to discover truth in certain prescribed ways. They are character qualities of the scientists but not categories of science or of scientific method.

It is obvious that in our discussions of "science and value" we must first of all specify just what it is that we are talking about: value of science, value in science, or value for science. Loose talk about "science and value" leads only to confusion.[48] But insofar as science gives us factual knowledge and an insight into dependencies and causal relations; insofar, in other words, as it gives us a better understanding of the world in which we live, it can at least contribute to a better understanding of what is valuable, what is being valued, and what ought to be valued. It can do so without transgressing upon our valuations as such and without displacing the entirely different approach of value-theory.

QUESTION: Much has been said about "building bridges" between East and West. What is your reaction to the various suggestions that have been made?

ANSWER: Ultimately these suggestions all culminate in the one problem which is at the center of things: the problem of man. Kant pointed out that the three questions, What can I know? What ought I to do? What may I hope? really amount to the question, What is man? And, even if we add another question: What do I enjoy aesthetically? we come back to the question, What is man? Here, then, is the crucial problem. It is a problem, by the way, which is basic to any interpretation of social institutions, to our ideal of democracy, and, therefore, to our present world-situation. And, if we want to build bridges, then we ought to study intensively the problem of man, viewing man in the varying perspectives of our various cultures but keeping in mind the ideal of a common humanity.

[48] For a detailed discussion of this problem see W. H. Werkmeister, "Theory Construction and the Problem of Objectivity," in Llewellyn Gross, *op. cit.;* and W. H. Werkmeister, "Social Science and the Problem of Value," in Helmut Schoeck and James W. Wiggins, eds., *Scientism and Values* (Princeton: D. Van Nostrand Co., Inc., 1960), pp. 1–21.

STELLA KRAMRISCH

Natural Science and Technology in Relation to Cultural Patterns and Social Practices in India

Natural science deals with Nature. Nature, from the Indian point of view, is this world, the universe (the macrocosm), and man (the microcosm). The one comprises the other and corresponds to it. Nature is contingent and knowable. It has for its polarity the non-contingent and unknowable, the indeterminate Absolute, called Brahman (or *adṛṣṭaṁ,* that which cannot be seen or known).

The homology of microcosm and macrocosm, on the one hand, and their polarity, the indeterminate Absolute, on the other, are the contents of consciousness. They engender a triple attitude toward any object. The object is beheld in its physical, contingent reality; it is experienced in its psychological relevance; and it is valued in its metaphysical significance. These three aspects of an object are called the concrete or gross (*sthūla*), the subtle (*sūkṣma*) and the metaphysical (*parā*). While each of these aspects requires a special approach, the object in its totality impinges on consciousness.

The several branches of natural science in India are classified as theoretical knowledge and source of power (*vidyā*) and as art (*kalā*). Techniques and skills or arts are *done,* while a *vidyā* is *known.* The sciences and the arts are different but interconnected creative operations. They evolved their methods with reference to each of the three aspects of their object. The Indian natural sciences developed by experiment, by which they found or aimed at finding proof. They were basic for Western science through the Arabs and for Chinese science. In some respects the natural sciences in India anticipated or contributed to modern Western science. Indian mathematics knew indeterminate equations of the second degree centuries before they were rediscovered in Europe in the seventeenth and nineteenth centuries. Only a few years ago, Indian pharmacology contributed its anciently used drug *rauwolfia serpentina* to Western medicine, and a sixth-century Indian recipe for the preparation of adamantine plaster (*vajralepa*) was standardized by the German color industry as the formula for indelibly colored cement.

However, it is not so much the practical achievements of Indian sciences but their specifically Indian thought-processes which form the subject of this paper.

Indian mathematics invented the signs for the numerals whose fundamental concept is the number One. The number One is the architectural principle of the series of natural numbers. To the atomistic school of Indian philosophy, Vaiśeṣika, unity alone is an objectively real quality inhering in substances. The mathematical principle *and* the atomistic viewpoint have their background in the *Ṛg Veda,* the most sacred and ancient Indian text. There the *one* (*tad ekam*) is the creative principle evolving in the Uncreate. This one is the creative momentum and the germ of all things. But, because it is the source and origin of the existent to a later school of Indian thought, the one in its very nature is illusion (*eka śabdātmika māyā*). It can be singled out, as no longer the whole prior to and beyond creation, which is indeterminate, void of any *specific* content.

The concept of the Void (*śūnya*), an indeterminate plenum, is one in name with the Indian mathematical symbol for zero. The mathematical zero—the blank space for it was known to the Sumerians—was given in India in the seventh century its pragmatic and relational definition as the sum of two equal and opposite quantities. The use of the zero in Indian mathematics gives place value to the numbers. To their symbols were added those of plus and minus, the signs for square and cube roots and for the powers, for surds, for infinity. The infinite is demonstrated by the equation: $\infty - \infty = \infty$. This mathematical formula is anticipated philosophically in the *Bṛhadāraṇyaka Upaniṣad* (V. i. 1). Infinite is that Brahman, the indeterminate Absolute; infinite is this Brahman, the manifest Brahman, the cosmos. From the infinite proceeds the infinite. On taking the manifest infinite from the unmanifest infinite, the infinite is left.

Mathematical principles formulate in scientific terms intuitional insight, to which the philosophical theories give different evaluations.

Indian *physics,* proceeding from Sāṁkhya doctrine, knows that all objects are evolved forms from the same ultimate energy. The law of the conservation of energy results in India from a reduction of the multiple to the one. Similarly, the phenomena of sound, light, and heat are reduced or led back to *motion* by all schools of Indian philosophy. The first motion is attributed by the Vaiśeṣika school to an unknown or not-as-yet-known cause (*adṛṣṭaṁ*).

In the realm of *acoustics,* the theory of sound includes that of language. The Mīmāṁsā school distinguishes the physical basis of audible sound (*nāda*), sound as heard (*dhvani*), and intelligible sound (*sphoṭa*), which represents the eternal and ubiquitous essence of that sound. This is without physical support, noumenal. The three aspects of worded sound accord with those of any given thing, as mentioned before.

The science of *medicine* is particularly concerned with the microcosm. The matter of the body of man is constituted in the same way as is the macrocosm.

Of the five elements (earth, water, fire, air, and ether), three, that is, water, fire, and wind, are the main agents in the circulation of the sap and the movement of breath. Breath, the exponent of the life movement, moves throughout the body in currents and channels. These converge along the spine in vital centers (*marmā*) or centers of inner realization (*cakra*). The science of medicine is called "*āyurveda*," the science of longevity. It prevents and cures disease. Akin to *āyurveda* but further developed in its knowledge of the neurophysical body is the medicine of *yoga*. There the techniques of regulating the breath and of controlling voluntary and involuntary muscular movement are linked with a mental discipline by which the mind withdraws from objects and concentrates in progressive states of consciousness—allocated to the *cakras*—states of consciousness including and beyond those of the waking, dreaming, and sleeping consciousness. In these states, the psycho-physical body is mastered; contingency and individuation, the human predicament, are overcome. Consciousness attains to the indeterminate Absolute.

Science as mastery of human nature reached an unrivaled position in India. The technique of *yoga*, the technique of inner freedom, though practiced in solitude, acts as a leaven and sets up a standard in the society in which it was evolved. Man's material endeavors and success, his sensory satisfaction and moral code are measured against the status of the *yogin*, the state of mastery over natural man.

Parallel to the technique of *yoga* are the lesser techniques of alchemy and magic. These practices aim at powers over death. They are interlinked with medicine, *āyurveda*, the science of longevity, longevity being the next best substitute for immortality. Technological results of the desire for eternity are the discovery of the adamantine medium or cement (*vajralepa*) already referred to and of imperishable, unfading colors for painting and for the textile industry.

Over and above these practical results, the will to overcome death and destruction—the fatalities of Nature—created works of art. The Vedic altar, the Buddhist *stūpa*, and the Hindu temple are monumental symbols of the transformation of man from the mortal to the deathless state. The form of these monuments ranging over 2500 years has a continuity of purpose and a logic of evolving styles. Visually and kinetically these monuments convey a philosophy of existence by which man lives integrally in this phenomenal world of time and space, in which he realizes the Absolute, the state of freedom.

The monuments are concrete results achieved by technological methods. They were the centers of the cultural life of India. The innumerable carved and modeled images in which India conceived the more-than-human are also *concrete*. This is implied in their name, "*mūrti*," which means a concrete thing. The images of the gods, says the *Viṣṇusaṁhitā*, are concrete, subtle, and metaphysical at the same time.

The craftsman-technician artist, who works in forms and transforms this world of time and space, has his myth in the *Ṛg Veda*. In this initial and initiatory myth, the Indian mind accounts to itself for its creativeness.

The Ṛg Vedic myth of the Ṛbhus is the myth of creative man, the artist and scientist who makes this world in which man lives. This myth, hardly known and not understood today, will here be dwelt on first.

The Ṛbhus were three brothers. They were called Saudhanvana, "Sons of the Skilled Archer," after their father, Sudhanvan, the Skilled Archer. It was only later that they became known by their names, Ṛbhu, Vibhvan, and Vāja. The Ṛbhus were artisans. That is what "Ṛbhu" seems to imply (from *rabh,* to be skilled).[1] It may be that they inherited their skill from their father, the Skilled Archer. It is said that they were mortals, sons of man (*manor napātaḥ;* III. lx. 3), although the name of their father evokes the connection with one who does not miss his aim. The god Rudra is called Sudhanvan, the Skilled Archer (V. xlii. 11).

The Archer aimed well when his arrow hit the Father (I. lxxi. 5) at the dawn of creation, at the moment when the Father spent himself into creation by embracing the Virgin, his daughter, the Dawn (X. lxi. 3, 5–6). When this happened, the gods, in their concern (*svādhī*), fashioned, out of a numinous potency (*brahman*), Vāstoṣpati, the Lord of the Existent, the Protector of Law (Vratapā; X. lxi. 7). Vāstoṣpati is Rudra (*Taittirīya Saṁhitā* III. iv. 10.4), the Skilled Archer, Sudhanvan.[2]

As soon as he was born,[3] the Archer performed his task. His arrow hit the Father during the embrace. The Father withdrew from the Daughter. His seed fell on the highest peak of the Earth, on the place of the Sacrifice (X. lxi. 6).

Agni, the Fire, had prepared the seminal fluid (*rasa*) for the Great Father Heaven (I. lxxi. 5). From the pure seed that Heaven had shed, Agni brought to birth the Aṅgirases, the First Sacrificers and archetypal god-men (I. lxxi. 8).

Later Vedic texts[4] see incest in the primal embrace of the Father and the Daughter, but the *Ṛg Veda* applies no moral code to an ontological symbol. The images of this symbol refer to self-contained Wholeness and to its spending itself into creation. Agni, the creative Fire, had made ready the "sap" for the Father. In his heat (I. lxi. 8), the Father sought for a second. He remained close to his identity by seeking the nearest affinity, the Virgin-Daughter.

[1] Cf. M. Mayerhofer, *Kurzgefasstes Etymologisches Wörterbuch des Altindischen* (Heidelberg: Karl Winter Universitätsverlag, 1953), s.v.

[2] Cf. *Aitareya Brāhmaṇa* V.xiv; III.xxxiv.3; *Taittirīya Saṁhitā* III.i.9.6. The identity of Rudra and Vāstoṣpati has been overlooked by Western scholars. K. F. Geldner, *Der Rig Veda* (Cambridge, Mass.: Harvard University Press, 1951), Vol. III, p. 226, finds it difficult to say why the Hymn X.lxi begins by saying that it is a "Raudra Brahman," a sacred empowered word and an enigma concerning Rudra [taking here the word "*brahman*" in the sense interpreted by L. Renou, "Sur la notion de Brahman," *Journal Asiatique,* CCXXXVII (1949), fasc. 7, p. 7], and, on the other hand, by J. Gonda, *Notes on Brahman* (Utrecht: Beyers, 1950), pp. 14, 58.

E. Arbman, *Rudra* (Uppsala: Uppsala Universitets Arsskrift, 1922), p. 2, altogether overlooks the identity of Rudra, the archer, and Vāstoṣpati which is established in *Ṛg Veda* I.lxxi and X.lxi; see *Rudra,* pp. 30–31, 281; also A. A. Macdonell, *Vedic Mythology,* Grundriss der Indo-Arischen Philologie und Altertumskunde, Vol. III (Strassburg: Karl Trübner, 1897), pp. 74–77. The key to the understanding of Rudra is his action "as soon as born." Geldner, *loc. cit.,* senses this when he remarks that the name of Rudra is "*anirukta,*" that is, remains unexpressed in X.lxi.

[3] "As soon as born," Indra drinks the Soma (III.xlviii.1); as soon as born, he seizes his bow; as soon as born, he surpasses the gods (VIII.xlv.4); as soon as born, he makes panicky heaven and earth (I.lxiii.1).

As soon as born, a god shows his power and fulfills his mission. "As soon as born, he is an adult so as to go at once the great way of his message," it is said of Agni (X.cxv.1).

[4] *Satapatha Brāhmaṇa* I.vii.4.3; *Aitareya Brāhmaṇa* III.xxxiii.

Rudra-Vāstoṣpati is a "*brahman*," a numinous power who owes his existence to the celestial intelligence—the gods—operative at the moment of the primordial Wholeness of the Father spending itself into generation. The coming into existence of Vāstoṣpati is motivated by the wisdom and benevolence (*svādhī;* X. lxi. 7) of the gods.[5] But the first act of the Archer is one of wrath.

At the beginning of things, all this happened simultaneously, the desire of the Father, the embrace, the falling of the seed to Earth, on the one side, and, on the other, the wisdom of the gods which made Vāstoṣpati-Rudra come into existence, and Rudra, the Skilled Archer, discharging the arrow and wounding the Father.

Rudra, the Skilled Archer, the terrible and numinous power of Existence, resents the fact of existence apart from Being. He has to exist in order to protect the divine ordinances (*vrata-pā;* X. lxi. 7), for the seed of creation had already fallen on the summit of the earth. In the conflict of this situation, Rudra discharges the arrow. The conflict is in the fact itself of conscious existence which has to hit its target, pure Being—the Father—though no longer pure and whole, but self-infringed by desire.

The Ṛbhus, sons of the Skilled Archer, Sudhanvan, were born as mortals and as artists.[6] Their masterworks and feats are five in number. They created the chariot of the Aśvins that traverses space on three wheels and is horseless and reinless (IV. xxxvi. 1; X. xxxix. 12). They fashioned the bay steeds of Indra (III. lx. 2; I. xx. 2, etc.).[7] Thirdly, they produced for Bṛhaspati the cow Viśvarūpā (IV. xxxiii. 8; I. cx. 8; I. clxi. 7), the omniform, the all-vivifying one (Viśvajūvā)—the Dawn of the World, from the skin of primordial darkness. They tended the cow (IV. xxxiii. 4; I. clxi. 10) each day, for a year—and created the units of time. Fourthly, they made young again the ancient parents, Heaven and Earth (IV. xxxiii. 3; IV. xxxvi. 3) in the spring of the year and brought about the cycles of time. The most astounding of their masterworks is the making of four cups out of one cup.[8] This once "new and unique cup" (I. xx. 6; I. cx. 3) had been made by Tvaṣṭar.

[5] *Brahman* as a numinous power or "*Zauberwesen.*" Cf. J. Charpentier, *Brahman* (Uppsala: Almquist and Wiksells, 1932), p. 134. It is generated by the gods (*ajanayan*) in the shape of Vāstoṣpati, whom the gods carved out to the *brahman* (*nir atakṣan*). Vāstoṣpati, however, is also Soma (*indu*, VII.liv.2).

[6] The Ṛbhus are sons of man (*manor napātaḥ*) (III.lx.3), and they are sons of strength (*śavaso napāta*) (IV.xxxv.1). The "parents"—of the Ṛbhus—are also and ultimately Heaven and Earth, the ancient parents, whom they rejuvenate (I.xx.4; I.cx.8; I.cxi.1; I.clxi.3, 7; IV.xxxiii.2, 3; IV.xxxv.5; IV.xxxvi.3). Paternity in the *Ṛg Veda* is not restricted to one "father." "Dyaus (Heaven) was considered the father (generator) of Indra. His maker (*kartā*) was the great artist who generated him" (IV.xvii.4). The great artist is Tvaṣṭar. In IV.xxxvii.4, the Ṛbhus collectively or Ṛbhu (Ṛbhukṣan) are addressed as "Son of Indra, children of strength (*Indrasya sūno śavaso napāto*)—Indra is also called Ṛbhu or Ṛbhukṣan (III.xxxvi.2). Cf. X.xciii.8; I.cx.7; and A. Bergaigne, *La Religion Védique*, Bibliothèque de l'École des Hautes Études, 52 [Paris, 1882], Vol. II, p. 412, inasmuch as the Ṛbhus serve him as their chief. A. W. Ryder, *Die Ṛbhus im Ṛg Veda* (Gütersloh: Bertelsmann, 1901), pp. 21, 22, discusses the parentage of the Ṛbhus, but, following Yāska (*Nirukta* XI.xvi), he sees no connection between Sudhanvan-Rudra and the Ṛbhus.

The Maruts, similarly, are the sons of Rudra I.lxxxv.1; V.xlll.15; V.lii.16; VI.L.4; VI.lxvi.3; VIII.xx.17). Rudra is their Father (I.cxiv.6; V.lx.5)—and Vāyu has generated them (I.cxxxiv.4).

[7] The chariot of the Aśvins and the bay steeds of Indra are the means by which these powers move in the cosmos. The Ṛbhus effect their movement (cf. I.clxi.14).

The artistry of the Ṛbhus distinguishes them as sacrificers. Their craftsmanship supplies the driving power to the gods, the vehicles in which they move. These vehicles are the hymns and the sacrificial offerings (as shown by A. Bergaigne, *La Religion Védique, passim*).

[8] *Ṛg Veda* V.xlii.11, praises Rudra, the Skilled Archer, and it is not by accident that V.xlii.12 invokes "the artists with skilled hands" (the Ṛbhus) of whom Vibhvan particularly is named in this stanza. See also I.xx.6; clx.3,5; clxi.2,4; IV.xxxiii.5; IV.xxxv.2,3.

Tvaṣṭar is the first form-giving Principle, the Shaper of all that is to be (cf. X. cx. 9). He had made the new cup (*camasaṁ navam*) out of which the Asura drinks (I. cx. 3) and which holds the drink of the gods (*camasaṁ devapānam*; I. clxi. 5; IV. xxxv. 5), the drink of immortality. Now, its uniqueness, its wholeness, its fitness for the Asura and the gods to drink from has been profaned (I. clxi. 5). There are now four cups instead of one.

Tvaṣṭar first watched the Ṛbhus, then grew jealous (*avenat;* IV. xxxiii. 6) as he saw them make one cup after another (IV. xxxiii. 5), and, finally, in his resentment, he wanted to kill the Ṛbhus (I. clxi. 5).[9]

The new cup made by Tvaṣṭar for the gods to drink the elixir of immortality, the Soma (*amṛta*), this one cup, is the Moon. It is not the moon as mortals see it, but the Moon in its being in timeless, undiminished fullness, in the pristine secret of its substance (cf. I. lxxxiv. 15). Soma, the mead of Tvaṣṭar (I. cxvii. 22), the heavenly Soma (X. cxvi. 3), is in the Moon (I. lxxxiv. 15).[10] Tvaṣṭar carries this bowl full of mead (X. liii. 9). When the gods drink the Soma, this unique cup becomes replenished (cf. x. lxxxv. 5). The moon is the new and unique cup which Tvaṣṭar made for his elixir of immortality. The cup was new when the gods became immortal (IX. cvi. 8; IX. cviii. 3; X. liii. 10; X. lxiii. 4). Tvaṣṭar made the Moon—the chalice of the Holy Grail—before the beginning of time, when immortality came to be,[11] when the gods came to be, for they could drink from the new and ever-full cup the drink of immortality.

This miraculous cup, this "yawning chalice," the Ṛbhus "measured with their rod like a field" (I. cx. 5). They made the one cup into four cups, one after the other. By refashioning the cup of the pristine Moon, they partitioned its wholeness into the four cups, or aspects, of the moon, seen by the eyes of mortals when the moon replenishes its contents, not instantly, but in time. "The moon is the prototypal form (*akṛti*) of the years" (X. lxxxv. 5).

The one cup of Tvaṣṭar was of timeless Moon substance throughout. This substance is Soma, the elixir of life and immortality. None had it but Tvaṣṭar, who is called the greatest of all artists (I. clx. 4; X. liii. 9), for he made the cup before the beginning of things. It held the origin of Form. Thus, Tvaṣṭar made the form to hold it. The form was new (I. xx. 6). There had been no form before it. It was shining in its fullness. Its contents remained undiminished; it was the aeviternal source whence Tvaṣṭar "adorned with form (*rūpa*) heaven and earth and all the worlds" (X. cx. 9).

[9] A. Bergaigne, *op. cit.*, Vol. III, p. 55, sees ambiguity in Tvaṣṭar's nature as represented in IV.xxxiii.6 and I.clxi.5. In IV.xxxiii.5, Tvaṣṭar takes the Ṛbhus at their word (*panayad vaco*) when the oldest of them says he would make two cups, and the younger one that he would make three, while the youngest proposed to make four. Then, when Tvaṣṭar sees the cups (IV.xxxiii.6), he becomes jealous (*avenat*). Bergaigne translates "*avenat*" as "was charmed."

[10] The heavenly Soma is in the "house of the Moon" (I.lxxxiv.15), or it is the Moon (X.lxxxv.3–5). The receptacle and its contents are the same.

[11] This refers to the first act of creation. Beyond and before it there is neither time (=death) nor immortality (cf. X.cxxix.2).

With the help of the Soma, which Indra drank in the house of the Father (i.e., Tvaṣṭar, IV.xviii.3) and which he took from Tvaṣṭar (III.xlviii.4), he opened the rock in which the cows (=light) were hidden and released them (IV.xxviii.5). He discovered the lost light and let the sun rise in the sky (I.li.4) for all to see.

Indra, the creator of this cosmos, discovers the sun through Soma ("Indra-Soma broke open the hiding place of the cows"; IV.xxviii.5) by means of the creative Moon-substance, which is the secret of Tvaṣṭar.

The Moon-cup of Tvaṣṭar, the source of the principle of form, is his work, and, like Soma itself, it is his secret (*nāma apīcyam;* I. lxxxiv. 15). Tvaṣṭar is the master craftsman of creative form. Its secret must not be divulged, for its power would then be depleted and would not be the same. When the contents were appropriated by Indra, they made of Indra the creator of a new world-order. In Indra, the "drop" (*indu*)[12] of Soma, the elixir of life and immortality, when imbibed again and again in inexhaustible quantity, swelled the strength of the creator of this new world of ours. It was then that the one cup was made into four, and the sun arose on the firmament for men to behold (III. xxxix. 5; II. xvii. 4).

The Ṛbhus were craftsmen, and they were mortal. When, by their work, they gave proof of their skill, they were raised to the gods and became immortal (I. cx. 3, 4; III. lx. 2). The Ṛbhus as mortal artists gave a foretoken of their divine nature when they made bloom the old parents, Heaven and Earth (IV. xxxvi. 1). They exerted themselves in the service of these ancient parents (IV. xxxiii. 2). Their service (*veṣana, pariviṣṭi*) to Heaven and Earth, the parents, and their skill in serving them won for the Ṛbhus the friendship of the gods (IV. xxxiii. 2). They worked with penetrating perseverance (*taraṇitva;* I. cx. 4, 6; IV. xxxiii. 1), with the same penetrating perseverance by which Tvaṣṭar had carved his one cup (I. cx. 6). They worked with application and willingness to serve by their work (*śruṣṭi;* IV. xxxvi. 4). Their forming energy (*śacībhir apiṅśata;* III. lx. 2) made their intuition (*dhī;* III. lx. 2; IV. xxxvi. 2, 4) and mental conception (*manasā nirataksata;* III. lx. 2) come true. They took the hard way to immortality. Only after much wandering—in the years' course—did these "journey-men" reach the house in the beyond, of Savitar, the "Impeller" (I. cx. 2), the *Primus Movens,* and win the friendship of the gods (IV. xxxiii. 2). "Not without effort does one make the gods one's friends" (IV. xxxiii. 11).

They made the gods their friends. Savitar gave them immortality. For twelve days they slept in his hospitable house. But, by their masterwork, they had estranged Tvaṣṭar, for they had broken the secret of the cup and damaged its wholeness. They had profaned the cup for the drink of the gods (I. clxi. 5) by making four cups out of it. Tvaṣṭar meant to kill them for this (I. clxi. 5), so greatly was he outraged. Instead, he hid amongst the Gnās (I. clxi. 4), the women of the gods—to practice creation *per generationem* as a substitute for creation *per artem.*

Tvaṣṭar, the creator of all Form, being the creator of the formative principle itself, sees the secret of his art betrayed and profaned, vulgarized by repetition and partition, and brought within the reach of man's effort and purview. Now it can be seen here on earth, in the atmosphere and the sky, the triple world of man's perception, which the Ṛbhus represent inasmuch as their number is three.

They act unitedly. Not one of their feats is the work of any one of them

[12] The name "Indra" is traditionally, if not etymologically, derived from "*indu.*"

in particular. They are one energy working on the three levels on which the creative fire burns. In this concentrated endeavor of theirs, they see and confront themselves as Agni, the creative Fire. Aware of Agni, who is the messenger of the gods, they speak to him. They confront their creative conscience by asking Agni, "Has the oldest, has the youngest, come to us?" (I. clxi. 1). The oldest, the most ancient is the divine Fire in heaven; the youngest is the fire that burns on earth (III. i. 20; I. xcv. 3). They confront their inner creative fire. What will it create, and what will it destroy? Does it burn in them here on earth or illumine them from heaven? Which is it that burns in them and drives them to change the cup of Tvaṣṭar? They reply, "We did not criticize (*nindima*) the cup of transcendental stuff (*mahākula*).[13] We only spoke of the nature (*bhūti*) of the wood" (I. clxi. 1).[14]

It is the nature of the wood which provokes and excites these craftsmen as they proceed to carve the cups. "Water is [its] most essential nature (*bhūyiṣṭha;* I. clxi. 9), thus spoke one of them. Fire is [its] most essential nature, said the other. One [the third] spoke of the 'Death-bringer' (*vadharyantī*)[15] rather than of any other" (I. clxi. 9).

As craftsmen, the Ṛbhus are concerned with the "material" of the cup, with the substance they see and feel when working on it. Fire and water are the essential nature of the cup, which is the vessel of Soma, the elixir, the fiery water of life and immortality. The Ṛbhus work on the cup of Tvaṣṭar, the pristine Moon before all time, beheld by them in the fullness of its content, for they are creative artists. But, being mortals, the Ṛbhus, as they go to work on it, and carve the cups, see it wane. There is less and less of it as they go on with their work. When they look at it, they see the "Death-bringer's" work as out of the unique cup they make one cup after another until there are four cups, the four phases of the moon which mortals see.

Thus the Ṛbhus spoke truth (I. clxi. 9)[16] when they carved and discussed

[13] *Kula* in the sense of "family" or "community" as well as "nest" refers here to the contents and the container.

[14] Wood (*dru*) is here an equivalent of the Greek *hyle.* It is asked in another context (X.lxxxi.4): "What was the wood of which they fashioned Heaven and Earth?" The answer is: *Brahman* was the wood. (*Taittirīya Brāhmaṇa* II.viii.9.6.)

[15] *"Vadharyantī"* occurs in this passage only. Sāyaṇa thinks of the clouds or of the earth desirous of lightning. Hermann Grassmann, *Wörterbuch zum Rig-Veda* (Wiesbaden: Otto Harrasowitz, 1955), s.v., translates *"vadhary"* with "to hurl weapons" (*vadhar*) and suggests "lightning" for *vadharyantī,* but equates *vadhar* with *vadha,* which means killing, mortal and killer; death and destruction. Geldner, *Der Rig Veda,* Vol. I, p. 220, translates *"vadharyantī"* as *"Gewitterzeit"* and suggests (*ibid.,* note 9), following Sāyaṇa, the earth as the third element of which the cup was made.

Vadharyantī, the Death-bringer, though he or she is not mentioned in any other context as an embodiment of the dark moon, is an evil power which causes the dwindling of the moon. This power found no personification, whereas the auspicious phases of the moon, the full moon and the new moon, are represented in later Vedic texts by the goddesses Sinīvālī, Rākā, and Kuhū (A. A. Macdonell, *Vedic Mythology,* p. 125; cf. p. 144). Cf. also the goddess Anumati, L. Renou, *Vedic India* (Calcutta: S. Gupta, 1957), p. 74. Cf. *Ṛg Veda* II.xxxii.8, Guṅgū, Sinīvālī, and Rākā. *Ṛg Veda* X.lv.5, however, speaks of the hoary one (*palitaḥ*) who devours the moon.

The hoary one is the Death-bringer. Vadharyantī, the Death-bringer in the moon, is the power which makes Cyavāna aged and decrepit. Cyavāna is the Soma substance of the Moon (Bergaigne, *op. cit.,* Vol. II, p. 482).

A. W. Ryder, *Die Ṛbhus im Ṛg Veda,* p. 30, sensed an "esoteric meaning" of Vadharyantī.

[16] The truth which the Ṛbhus spoke is the "truth utterance" of hymn IV.xxxiii.5–6. W. Norman Brown, "The Basis for the Hindu Act of Truth," *Review of Religion,* V (1940), 42 ff., reconstructs the *"satya mantra"* (IV.xxxiii.5) in this way, "As so and so is true, let this cup become two; as so and so is true, let this cup become three . . ." The *satya mantra,* it appears, would have for its base the assertions of I.clxi.9 concerning the nature of the substance (*druṇa bhūti;* I.clxi.1) of the cup. The *mantra* could then be com-

the nature of the cup and made the four cups, the four phases of the moon that shines on this sublunary world. It is contingent truth which they spoke about the order of the phenomenal world. Tvaṣṭar, the greatest artist, the creator and preserver of the one cup, of the unspent wholeness of creative form, was outraged by and shrunk away from the *"hybris"* of the Ṛbhus. He became absorbed by the crowd of the women of the gods, who generate in the waters.

When Tvaṣṭar had threatened to kill the Ṛbhus, they were "brought into safety by the Virgin" (*kanyā*; I. clxi. 5). The Virgin[17] here is Sūryā, the Sun Maiden, who was to become the bride of Soma. She was to leave the house of the Father when her bridal cortege had taken leave of Savitar (X. lxxxv. 13).

At the moment when the Virgin brought the Ṛbhus into safety, the Ṛbhus had made their names by accomplishing the feat of making four cups out of one. "As Ṛbhu, Vibhvan, and Vāja, they went to the gods; as artists, they attained their share of the sacrifice" (I. clxi. 5–6). They came to the hospitable house of Savitar, the Impeller. He allowed them to rest. They slept twelve days, and, when they awoke, the earth was green once more. They had slept the creative sleep in the fullness of time, the same time during which they had served the ancient parents, Heaven and Earth, and had made them young again, the same time during which they ministered to the cow, the year. Twelve days in the house of the fountainhead are twelve months in the manifest cosmos.

Before they had reached the house of Savitar, the Rbhus had ministered with unrelenting effort to the old parents, Heaven and Earth, by creating the order of days, months, and the years—the order of time—of which the moon is the measure (X. lxxxv. 5).

As soon as they create the division of time, the sons of Sudhanvan are given their separate names.[18] They become immortal as artists and receive their share in the evening sacrifices. By their creative work, they have earned the hospitality of Savitar, who receives them in his house, which is at the creative source beyond creation. Unlike Tvaṣṭar, the Former, Savitar, the Impeller, does not shun the Ṛbhus. He receives at the source the three god-men, the workmen of creative ingenuity and perseverance. Savitar is the Impeller, whose impulsion reverberates from the uncreate throughout creation. Tvaṣṭar, who is the Maker of Form, of the pre-established mold of all that is to be, is the essential artist, who cannot tolerate an infringement of the wholeness of his work, which is his very substance, the germinal, form-holding power of the fiery water of life.

pleted: If it is true that water is the essential nature of the cup, let this cup become two; if it is true that fire is the essential nature of the cup, let this cup become three; if it is true that the "Death-bringer" determines its nature, let this cup become four.

[17] The Virgin is the Daughter of the Father (X.lxi.5). As daughter of the Father, she is Dawn. As daughter of the Father in his aspect of Tvaṣṭar, she is Saraṇyū. As daughter of the Father in his aspect of Savitar-Sūrya, she is Sūryā, the Sun-Maiden.

[18] If Sudhanvan is Rudra—who later was to become Mahākāla—this God of "Transcendental Time" had for his sons the makers of contingent time.

Bergaigne, *op. cit.*, Vol. III, p. 54, speaks of the diffusion of Soma—hidden in the mysterious sojourn of Savitar—by the three Ṛbhus, in the three worlds.

When the Ṛbhus had slept twelve days, when they dreamed with closed eyes that they "had moved around the worlds" (I. clxi. 12–13), they were awakened from their dream and sleep. Who awakened them? They asked Savitar, from whom nothing is hidden (*agohya*). He said it was the dog who had taken hold of their arm. The Ṛbhus cursed him who had taken hold of their arm.[19] (The Ṛbhus are thought of here as one entity. They represent the archetypal craftsmen.)

Savitar, whom the Ṛbhus see when rudely aroused from their sleep, speaks to them in the shape of the Ram (I. clxi. 13). Ram and Goat are cognate symbols. As Ram, Savitar is the Goat Aja Ekapād, the one-footed Uncreate, at the fountainhead, beyond the cosmos.[20] In manifestation, the one-footed Goat is the fiery axial pillar between the peak of manifestation and the pit. The fiery pillar traverses the three worlds. In each of them, Agni is active, in the flame on earth, the lightning in the atmosphere, and the sun in the sky. When Savitar, in his house, speaks as the Ram to the awakening Ṛbhus, they face him as the creative Fire at its source and speak to him (I. clxi. 12).

It is not for the first time that they speak to the Fire, that they account to themselves for their mission. Agni had come to them as a messenger of the gods (I. clxi. I) when the nature of Tvaṣṭar's cup first aroused their interest and prompted them—for thus they were bid by Agni, the Fire, the messenger of the gods—to make four cups out of the one (I. clxi. 2). When they had completed their feat, the messenger had gone (I. clxi. 4).[21]

Tvaṣṭar awakened the Ṛbhus, taking them by their arm. In the shape of a dog he did this (I. clxi. 13).[22] He took hold of their arm—the creative limb of the craftsman—of the Ṛbhus with their able hands (IV. xxxiii. 8). As a dog, and following his instinct as shaper of Form, Tvaṣṭar awakens these artists to the practice of their skill down in the triple world, whose activity in time they regulate.

Tvaṣṭar's instinctual "vengeance" is to shake the Ṛbhus out of their creative sleep and the dream-vision of their work into renewed activity. This activity is their proper domain, which they have created for themselves in this time world of change and movement, down below the changeless, quiet source of undivided form and wholeness. From their creative vision, in which they dreamed and slept at the source, in the house of Savitar, they must go down to work in this moving time-world, where "the Maruts move in the sky, the wind moves in the air space, and Varuṇa moves in the Waters, seeking [the Ṛbhus], the sons of Strength" (I. clxi. 14).

[19] *Ṛg Veda* I.clxi.12–13 names only Agohya, whom the Ṛbhus ask, "who had awakened them. The Ram named the Dog as awakener." The Ram (cf. Aja Ekapād, the one-footed Goat) ultimately refers to Savitar. This was recognized by Bergaigne, *op. cit.*, Vol. III, p. 54, as meaning also that the Dog refers to Tvaṣṭar. Cf. also *ibid.*, p. 60.

The Ṛbhus had no reason to be afraid of the Dog, for their jaws were of metal (IV.xxxvii.4).

[20] Ram and goat are closely linked as the symbols of the fiery cosmic axis. The ram stands for Savitar, the fountainhead, beyond the cosmos. The ram is the vehicle of Agni in later Indian myths.

[21] Cf. III.v.6. Agni acquired the dear name of Ṛbhu.

[22] In the myth of Indra, it is the entrails of Tvaṣṭar—the dog—which Indra cooks in the hour of greatest need (IV.xviii.13). See Bergaigne, *op. cit.*, Vol. II, p. 270.

The connection of the symbols of the dog and the moon persists in Hinduism in their association with Śiva.

Tvaṣṭar, the Dog who takes hold of the arm of the sleeping Ṛbhus, is instinctual creativeness, the itch of the craftsman to put his hand to his work.

The three Ṛbhus are immortal, as are the gods, for they have proved their valor as artists. Their greatest patron is Indra, the Creator of this cosmos. He is their friend (III. lx. 3; IV. xxxv. 7), and, as their patron, he is their father and carries their name (IV. xxxvii. 4; I. cxi. 4; I. clxvii. 10; X. xxiii. 2), Ṛbhu or Ṛbhukṣan. The names of the Saudhanvanas, the sons of the Skilled Archer which they received on becoming gods, Ṛbhu or Ṛbhukṣan, Vibhvan, and Vāja (IV. xxxiii. 3, 4), signify the skill, distinction, and power of the artist. These artists made their name when they built into the cosmos the order of time.

They brought time into the world and to the gods and earned the loathing of the Asura, of Tvaṣṭar, the greatest artist, who had created the wholeness of form, on which is based the uniqueness of each organism. Because Tvaṣṭar had prefigured all form and had given to it his very substance, however, he finally comes to see the feat of the Ṛbhus, no longer as an effrontery and interference with his own work, but as itself forming part of the pattern whose germ was his secret. Seeing the Ṛbhus asleep at the creative source, after they had done their work and proved their immortal calling, Tvaṣṭar, unseen by the Ṛbhus, has to awaken these godlike technicians of the clockwork of time. They must proceed with their work so as to fit and keep going this world below sun and moon according to the Form laid down by him. In taking the shape of the Dog, Tvaṣṭar follows his instinct, which allows this greatest of all artists to tease the artists born as sons of man.

The Ṛbhus are three in number, for they create the rhythms and figure of time in this triple and triune cosmos. They performed their work as one team, as the sons of Sudhanvan. The three of them are also spoken of in the plural, either as Ṛbhus, or as the Vibhvas or Vājas.[23] Although they are three, they act as one. They are the creative energy which keeps on making the rhythmical sequences on the face of the moon and the earth. In their masterwork of the four cups, the Ṛbhus shape the figure of a fourfold rhythm. By its numerical value, their work proves that it was seen by the eye of the sons of man. Their mental perspective belongs to those who live on this four-cornered (*caturbhṛṣṭi;* X. lviii. 3) earth. The completeness of the number four, its very form, is that of the pair of the pairs of opposites. The four corners of the earth are marked by the course of the sun, by the four orients, east and west, sunrise and sunset, and by the north and south, which stand for summer and winter. These corners impress the square of polarities in the course of the daily and annual movement of the sun on this circular earth.

The power of the opposites was intuited by the Ṛbhus when they pondered over the nature (*bhūti*) of the substance (*dru;* I. clxi. 1) of the cup of Tvaṣṭar. Fire and water were its substance under one aspect, and Vadharyantī, their

[23] Bergaigne, *op. cit.*, Vol. II, p. 405.

visible Destruction, under the other. Together, they formed the rhythm of the phases of the moon in the pattern of four.

The moon as module of the year in this triple world of time measures time out in twelve months. The twelve months do not exist in the beyond at the source where the Ṛbhus are allowed to sleep and dream twelve days,[24] twelve units of their working time during which they tend the Cow, the year, and the old parents, Heaven and Earth are made young by them.

The number three, which is the number of the vertical structure of the cosmos in its triple division of earth, atmosphere, and sky, operates through the fiery-creative activity of the three Ṛbhus in the dimension of time. The number four, as the number of the horizontal extent of manifestation, is seen by the Ṛbhus in the succeeding changes of the face of the moon. The transfer of the numbers three and four, denoting cosmic extent in the vertical and in the horizontal by the agency of the Ṛbhus into the dimension of time, is operating beyond even space and time in the number twelve as the number of time irrespective of duration.[25] This number denotes the sleep and dream of the Ṛbhus as subsisting in the realm beyond time during their active, creative work.

The favor of the Sun Maiden shines on them. The Father—as Savitar—gives them immortality; as Tvaṣṭar—in the shape of the dog—he awakens them to active work. In his own form, as the greatest artist, his dismay at their skill, in carving out of the secret and timeless wholeness of form the changing face of the moon and the time-world, threatened to kill them.

Although the Sun Maiden smiles on the Ṛbhus and their work of creation, the taint of Sudhanvan's, their father's, shot adheres to their activity. In the attitude of the Existent as against Being there is resentment and assertiveness. The dart of Existence had to pierce Being in the shape of the Father, who had already—through the act of creation—ceased to be pure Being. The shot of Existence infused its numinous power into a particle of the creator himself.

The sons of the Skilled Archer, sons of man, in their masterwork of the four cups, create visible form by violating the wholeness of the supreme Form as it is in the beyond, prior to the beginning of things.

Ironically, their greatest masterwork, the making of four cups out of one, is an act of separation of the original wholeness. From the metaphysical point of view—which is that of Tvaṣṭar and also of Rudra—disruption of the original wholeness is "original sin." From the point of view of creation *per artem*, however, the wholeness is restored by the creative act when the artist, on the level of his competence, produces the self-contained completeness of the work of art. Tvaṣṭar, therefore, as dog, awakens the Ṛbhus to their work in progress.

The myth of the god-men who establish time and continuity in this world is shot across with numbers and their significance in the structure of the cosmos. Numbers as symbols of cosmic structure regulate the layout and the piling

[24] Cf. the later mythical measures of time counted in years of the gods and in years of man; *Viṣṇupurāṇa* I.3.

[25] Cf.I.clxiv.12 and the respective allocation of time and space that side and this side of heaven.

of the Vedic altar. The altar for the Soma sacrifice is the most important. It has five layers, for five are the Indian seasons of the year. In the center of each alternate layer is a specific brick or stone (*svayamātṛṇṇā*). These three architectural units in their vertical sequence are symbols of the three strata of earth, mid-air (*antarikṣa*), and heaven, of which the sky is the figure. In building up such an altar, the cosmos is symbolically reconstructed. These and the other sacred numbers must be kept intact in the construction of any altar, that is, the shape of the altar must remain the same whatever its size. Certain altars (*kāmya agni*) were built for the attainment of specific ends, such as the attainment of heaven or the subduing of an enemy. Each particular purpose demanded an altar of a particular shape. Moreover, at each subsequent performance, altars of this "wish-fulfilling" kind had to be increased in area by the same square unit of measurement (one *puruṣa*).[26] This posed two geometrical problems. The one is how to construct figures of different shapes, square or circular or of the shape of a bird or of that of a turtle, having the same area, and the second is how to increase the area of a figure without changing its shape. Furthermore, the area of the several layers of the altar had to be divided differently so as to avoid the possibility of fission by the bricks of adjacent layers terminating at the same place. This involved a number of geometrical operations, such as the construction of a square having a given side, the combination of areas, and the transformation of areas. The theorem of the square of the diagonal was elaborated. More rational rectangles were known than those covered by Pythagoras (for instance, $7^2+24^2=25^2$ or $8^2+15^2=17^2$). Geometrical algebra goes back to the *Śatapatha Brāhmaṇa* (X. xxiii. 17), where the complete quadratic equation $ax^2+bx=c$ is demonstrated. An elementary treatment of surds allowed the determination of the approximate value of $\sqrt{2}=1+\frac{1}{3}+\frac{1}{3.4}-\frac{1}{3.4.34}$ and the knowledge of its irrationality. There are instances of progressive series. It is probable that it was known in the *Śatapatha Brāhmaṇa* (X. v. 4. 7) how to sum up a series. The same ancient, sacred text (X. iv. 2. 2–17) makes an attempt at factorization on the basis of the altar's having 360 enclosing stones—360 being the number of the days in the year, the year being the unit of cyclical time, the construction of the unit of cyclical time being a symbol of the mastery over time, a symbol of deathlessness.

The will for transcendence, the desire for deathlessness, compelled the construction of symbolic figures, and this necessitated a geometry and resulted in a science of mathematics. Scientific truth subserved and evolved within the pursuit of metaphysical truth. The institution of the sacrifice and the practice of setting up altars for daily and seasonal as well as for special rites were central and basic for the evolution of the sciences and the arts. Foremost among these are architecture and magic.

The science of architecture (*vāstuśāstra*) makes civilized existence possible.

[26] B. B. Datta, *The Science of the Sulba* (Calcutta: University of Calcutta, 1932), p. 24. Cf. Durgādatta Tripāṭī, "The 32 Sciences and 64 Arts," *Journal of the Indian Society of Oriental Art*, XI (1943), 40.

The name *"vāstu"* is derived from *"vas,"* to exist. Architecture is primarily a ritual which is practiced by the art of building in conjunction with other rites, like that of the banishment of evil influence (*śānti*), by ablutions, bathing, and other apotropaic means. Being a ritual, the science and art of architecture has magic efficacy. Magic (*kṛtyā*), the "act" par excellence, is an art (*kalā*) and a science (*vidyā*),[27] according to Indian definition. The magic which is harnessed prior to any building operation is that of the soil. A center of pilgrimage and religious practice is a seat of magical power and action (*tīrtha*). The harnessing and acquisition of more-than-human powers, though not the end, is a means of Indian spirituality, not so much for the purpose of dominating but of overcoming physical reality.

The plan (*vāstu-maṇḍala*) of a Hindu temple is a magical chart, a square compass. It symbolizes at the same time the apparent daily movement of the sun and the apparent monthly and annual movements of the moon and the sun.[28] This compass is divided into 28 equal sections. These represent the mansions of the moon (*nakṣatra*). To these 28 positions are added 4 divisions or compartments symbolic of the 4 cardinal points of the equinoxes and solstices. The architectural ground-plan or site-plan is a helio-planetary cosmogram, the place of the adjustment of solar and lunar cycles.

The 32 divisions are marked along the perimeter of the square (*vāstu-maṇḍala*). The area of the square *vāstu* is divided into subsquares. The main types of the *vāstu* are that of 64 squares, which is sacred to *brāhmins,* and that of 81 squares, which is sacred to *kṣatriyas.* A cycle of 5 lunar-solar years is a *samvatsara.* If these figures are multiplied, they yield 25,920, which is the number of years in the period of the precession of the equinoxes. By another factorization, 25,920 is 9×8×360, the figures representing the length of the two main types of the *vāstu-maṇḍala,* or plan, multiplied by the number of days of the lunar-solar year. The architectural ground or site-plan as chart of the cycles of time is not so much a figure of the wish that the house be built for eternity as that it is the place of coincidence of all times, the *hic et nunc,* the place of realization of the eternal moment. But the house which will be built on the plan is also the place where man is fitted into the social and the cosmic order. The position and orientation of a building are ascertained by a calculation parallel to the astronomical method by which the place of the sun or moon or any of the planets is found in the cycle of the *nakṣatras.* The longitude of the heavenly body expressed in minutes is divided by 800. The quotient gives the number of *nakṣatras* through which the planet has already passed and the remainder gives the traversed part of the *nakṣatra* in which it is at present. By a similar calculation, the remainder indicates the direction which a building is to face. This direction is called the *yoni,* the birthplace of the building.[29] Death and destruction will befall the builder if the building faces a wrong direction. Disorder will result not only in the body of the builder but also in

[27] L. Renou et J. Filliozat, *L'Inde Classique* (Paris, Payot, 1947), Vol. I, p. 611.
[28] Stella Kramrisch, *The Hindu Temple* (Calcutta: University of Calcutta, 1946), p. 31.
[29] *Bṛhat Saṁhitā* LII.lxxiii (comm. Utpala).

the kingdom. Astronomy converted into applied astrology will further determine the day and month on which it will be favorable to build that particular building.

Astronomy and astrology are not linked only in architectural practices. Prophecies from stars, planets, and eclipses were born of religious needs and became political instruments or served personal interests—in forecasting, for example, falling or rising prices.

Magic, prophecy, demonology, and the "science of signs," furthermore, are interlinked with physics, meteorology, zoology, and medicine. The correspondence of man and cosmos is a premise of Indian thought and experience. A disorder in Nature is held to correspond to a moral shortcoming. The correspondence works both ways. Crime upsets the order of Nature, while favorable stars beget good men. The king is a thaumaturge; he moves in a magic circle—and it is he who makes the wheel turn (*cakravartin*) as world ruler.

Dream interpretation developed its own key, whose scientific validity is paralleled by the role of dream interpretation today in the Western world. It was known that dreams give access to a more real world than that of waking consciousness. Psychology is a science which was developed in India to a degree which only modern Western science can assess. Apart from having been a science, it evolved a discipline, that of *yoga*.

Indian science does not start from a study of phenomena in order to discover successively more and more general laws. It sets out from general laws and finds them exemplified, not in one field of reference only, but on corresponding, antithetic levels. Man and cosmos are the basic levels of reference; manifestation and the unmanifest are their superstructure. The science of physics thus is part of a system of philosophy, called Vaiśeṣika. Vaiśesika is a system of discrimination, which determines by eliminating. It is an atomism which distinguishes and eliminates the four kinds of atoms, earth, water, fire, and wind, from the non-atomic categories of ether, time, space, soul (*ātman*), and mind (*manas*). *Ātman* is all that constitutes neuropsychic activity. The substantiality of *ātman*, however, is proved in the same manner as is that of the wind (*vāyu*). Bhāskara, the great astronomer, who lived in the twelfth century, saw in the power of the (cosmic) wind (*pravaha*) the cause of celestial movements. Indian medicine, the science of longevity (*āyurveda*), identifies the soul (*ātman*) with the wind (*sarvātman*) in a homology of man and cosmos.

Cosmic conscience is stronger than social conscience in India. Sin is a miasma that acts on the health of the person and on the cosmic order. Cleanliness is a pre-condition of ritual, not only cleanliness of the physical body but also of the psyche or subtle body (cf. the rites of *śoṣaṇa* and *bhūtaśuddhi,* the rites of drying up the impurities of the subtle body and of purifying the bodily elements). Water purifies by the act of bathing and as symbol. The great baths connected with temples or by themselves are public monuments of bodily and psychological hygiene—from the bath on the acropolis of Mohenjo-daro of the Indus civilization to the ponds in villages of the contemporary scene.

The ultimate concern of any philosophy or science in India is *mokṣa,* release. *Mokṣa* is attained by a sustained effort which requires a healthy body. Hence the necessity of preserving, increasing, and renewing health by hygiene, medical therapy, pharmacology, and alchemy.

Medicine, the science of longevity, knows that the body consists of the same elements as does the cosmos. The active elementary principles are fire, water, and wind or breath. These are conducted throughout the body by channels (*śirā, nāḍī*). They cross in the vital centers called *marmās,* which are vasculo-nervous bundles. Indian pathology knows the cause of illness as a disturbance of the three elementary principles. Although the anatomy and physiology of *yoga* differ from those of *āyurveda,* they are based on the same principles. The breath, the life movement (*prāṇa*), circulates in channels (*nāḍī*) and is concentrated in the vital centers (*marmā*) known in *yoga* as centers of inner realization (*cakra*). This physiology and anatomy, moreover, form part of the architectural plan. This helio-planetary diagram is also conceived with reference to the body of man. The perpendicular lines and diagonals, respectively, are *śirās* and *nāḍīs;* their intersections are *marmās.* No building should be set up on these, on the site plan; no corner or pillar should be raised where the *marmās* are in the ground plan of a building; otherwise, the existence itself of, and in, the building would be obstructed.[30]

The relation of medicine and architecture is not expressed in India by the building of hospitals only. These two sciences, or arts, medicine and architecture, are deeply concerned with man's being on all levels and not with his physical existence only. Man's body is the term of reference in common, because fire and water, the sun, the moon, and the gale of the spirit are also the inner active principles of the body. The elements which constitute the universe build up the body. The helio-planetary cosmogram, which is the architectural ground or site plan, is also a medical chart. On its correctness depend the quality of a building and the well-being of the builder. If the builder of a temple is the king, the welfare of the kingdom and the stability of the cosmos are the responsibility of the architect.

The science of architecture was codified by the sixth century A.D., and its tradition has lasted practically to this day. The temple has been at all times the main monument of Indian architecture. From it the mode of building, the science of architecture, radiated into every building enterprise, from the palace of a king to his encampment, from a *brāhmin's* house to the dwelling of a *śūdra,* and from the building of a house to the construction of its furniture and the carriage of the owner. Wherever man dwelt, the science and technology of his day confirmed and made him conscious of his rapport with the cosmos and, through it, of his human responsibility.

[30] Kramrisch, *op. cit.*, pp. 51–57.

N. BAMMATE

The Status of Science and Technique in Islamic Civilization

The first part of this paper is mostly descriptive. It attempts to review some characteristics of scientific research in Islamic civilization.

The second part is an interpretation of those data, as related to Islamic philosophy. The wide field of science in Islamic history has been hardly explored, and the time has not come—far from it—to outline a general survey. As a contribution to a comparative study of Eastern and Western cultures, these notes introduce some preliminary remarks on the specific style of scientific thinking in Islam, more particularly the methods of investigation applied by Muslim scientists.

I. THE MAIN CHARACTERS OF SCIENTIFIC RESEARCH IN CLASSICAL ISLAMIC CIVILIZATION

1. *The plurality of sources; the international character.*

The first and most evident aspect of science in Islamic civilization is, from the outset, the plurality of its sources. This, in turn, is a result of the suddenness and amplitude of the Muslim expansion in the second half of the seventh century. Covering, within a few years, a great diversity of scholarly centers, from the Hellenistic schools, across the Middle East, to the Persian schools, and ranging as far as the areas of Indian science, it kept those traditional centers alive, while providing them with a new framework. Closer connections were thus established between regions which, throughout antiquity, had only casual scientific contacts. Henceforth, science will decidedly be an international endeavor, and it will be transmitted as such to the Christian West.

The most important single influence was undoubtedly the Hellenistic one.

In this respect, circumstances had singularly favored the newly growing Islamic empire. In fact, during the period which had preceded the Arab conquest, there had been a decisive shift of Greek science, a migration of scholars, eastward. This migration was due mainly to persecution directed by the Byzantine orthodoxy against the Nestorians and the Monophysites. In 489, Emperor Zeno closed the great Nestorian school in Edessa, and the monks took refuge in Persia, where the Sassanid emperor settled them in Gundishapur. This city, which was already a noted seat for Persian medical studies, became then a center for the translation of Greek sources into Oriental languages, especially Syriac and Pehlvi. Gundishapur being located in the southwest of Persia, its proximity to India also enhanced its cultural significance.

Later, in 525, when Justinian closed the Platonic school in Athens, a new wave of refugee scholars followed. But the most eventful migration was probably the transfer of the Hellenistic school from Alexandria to Baghdad, some years after the new Islamic caliphate had settled there.

On the other hand, Indian influences upon Islamic science seem to have appeared at an early stage, as evidenced by the translation into Arabic, in 773, under the name of Sindhind, of the Indian Siddhānta, which became one of the foundations of the developing Muslim science of astronomy. More Indian elements were introduced later, when al-Battānī, one of the greatest names in Islamic thought, brought back from his journeys a large book of observations on Indian science, philosophy, geography, and customs.

The same diversity in national origins persisted even after Islamic religion had molded together and given cultural unity to the various peoples of its territory. The great scientists of Islam originated from every territory, from North Africa to Central Asia. This feature was again stressed by the easy communications which permitted scientists to travel extensively. In fact, the biographies of a great many of them lead us throughout the empire.

Baghdad can still be located as the main center of Islamic science, after the creation, in 830, of the *Dar al-Hikmat* (House of Learning or Wisdom). This was a combination of an academy of science, a library, and a translation office, where the main effort was concentrated upon the translation of Greek scientific and philosophical classics, such as those of Hippocrates, Galen, Plato, Aristotle.

In the course of history it is possible to discern a gradual shift of the scientific centers toward the West, a slow return of the wave. In 966, a *Dar al-Hikmat,* on the model of the Baghdad Academy, was founded in Cairo. In the twelfth century, the emphasis rested upon Cordova and Muslim Spain. Toward the end of that century, the scientific heritage thus preserved and developed was transmitted to the West, through Spain and the south of Italy. The period of Muslim leadership in science came to an end. It had lasted approximately five centuries, from the eighth to the twelfth.

2. *Borrowed characters; the translations.*

Being open to so many simultaneous influences, Islamic science necessarily appears with a composite nature. Intense translation activities, and the hunt for

Greek manuscripts long stood in the foreground and exercised a deep influence upon subsequent evolution. This feature of Islamic science has led many critics to challenge its originality. And, indeed, historically, its merit appears in co-ordination and transmission rather than creation of new doctrines.

Still it must be pointed out that the very process of translation from the Greek to a Semitic language, Syriac or Arabic, reveals such a difference of approach to objective reality that this confrontation is one of the most stimulating which may be proposed for the study of comparative linguistics or cultural anthropology. Under the superficial appearances of Hellenization, Semitic forms which had deep and lasting effects reveal themselves. The translators themselves had constantly to apply acute criticism. More than often they had to turn into philosophers as a new foreign concept opened up problems of epistemology to their minds.

Besides the language, it is necessary to consider two other unifying factors which have given original style to Islamic scientific thinking: the influence of the Muslim religion and the specific methods of investigation. In fact, those methods may prove to be the most important contribution of Islamic civilization to science.

3. *Encyclopedic character.*

Muslim scholars have always shown a keen taste for the classification of sciences. Many of their treatises appear as a catalogue of knowledge, a register of scientific data. This attitude was, no doubt, due partly to the fact that, when the Arabs met with Greek culture, science appeared to them as a given quantity, a full-fledged body of knowledge.

The systems were at hand. The main task seemed to be to assimilate, to recapitulate. This use of classification meant a change in perspective. Systematization, in the Aristotelian or Neo-Platonic sources, was an intellectual construction, a doctrine; but to the Arabs it presented itself as a reference table to consult, a program of study. It took on a pedagogic value and stimulated their investigation. Moreover, the certitude that science was a coherent, harmonious whole to be discovered, with sufficient care and accurate methods, gave an optimistic character to Islamic research.

On the other hand, the encyclopedic tendency gradually inclined Islamic scholars to consolidate scientific systems within a general explanation of the universe. Science became a part of philosophy. The results of experience took place, whether they fitted or not, within a doctrinal construction made of Aristotelianism, but deeply modified by Neo-Platonic adjuncts.

Muslim science, like medieval Christian science, became scholastic.

4. *Experimental character.*

But, here again, investigation should not stop at first appearances. The systematization according to Greek structures was often superficial. The encyclopedic presentation and the organization within a scholastic system were mostly the façade, the working up, the elaboration of scientific results which had been reached through entirely different methods. They do not contradict the essential feature of scientific research in Islamic civilization, which is its experimental character.

The primacy of the experimental method is repeatedly stressed by the most representative scientists of Islam. Its first important philosopher, al-Kindī (d. 872), writes in his *Rasa'il al falsafa* ("Epistles on Philosophy"): "There is perhaps no greater ignorant person than he who makes his observations in the learned books of antiquity, especially in the science of Nature."[1] Then, a few pages later, after having started to present a theory of heat, as explained through Aristotelian theories of circular movement, he suddenly changes his approach altogether and launches into a series of empirical observations, taking the commonplace example of baths in various experimental conditions.

In another of his "Epistles," al-Kindī goes further, connecting the description of an experiment and its reduction to mathematical expression: "He who wants to know a logical demonstration must attach himself to mathematical and geometrical demonstrations inasmuch as they are easier to understand since they fit exactly with perceptible demonstration."[2]

This combination of experimentation in physics closely associated with analysis of results through mathematics was brought to even more systematic expression, and thoroughly applied in his research by Ibn al-Haythām (Alhuzen), whose works and methods directly influenced Robert Grosseteste, Bishop of Lincoln, and, through him, his pupil Roger Bacon. Ibn al-Haythām's "Optics," still reprinted in Basle in 1572, represents, in fact, a typical illustration of the experimental approach, with support from geometry and practical observation. On one hand, the study of optics is based upon a thoroughgoing mathematical study of refraction. On the other hand, great care is taken in the construction and description of various plane and parabolic mirrors used for demonstration. The same minute details as regards the construction and operation of his hydrostatic balances are listed by al-Bīruni when he presents his investigations on specific gravity. In chemistry, too, Rāzī indulges in technical recipes and, although he is, no doubt, the greatest Muslim theoretician on the subject, he often appears as a manipulator painstakingly testing various processes of sublimation, crystallization, coagulation, cupellation, etc.

A good example of lucidity in observation and strictness in deduction is also shown by Avicenna, in this passage, typical of his sober scientific style: "The mountains may originate from two causes, either from an upheaval such as that produced by earthquakes, or through the action of flowing waters and winds, which dig valleys through soft stones. Such changes may have taken a very long time. Indeed, we may assume that water has been the chief agent in those changes, since we can observe the presence in some stones of prints left

[1] Abū Yūsuf Ya'qub ibn Ishaq ibn al-Sabbāh al-Kindī, *Rasa'il al falsafa* ("Epistles on Philosophy"), German translation by Albino Nagy, *Die philosophischen Abhandlungen des Jaqūb ben Ishāq al-Kindī, Beiträge zur Geschichte des Philosophie der Mittelalters,* II, 5 (Münster: Aschendorff, 1897).

[2] *Ibid.*

by aquatic animals. The yellow earth on the surface must not have the same origin as the central hard rock, but comes apparently from the destruction of vegetal remains mixed with earth carried by waters. Originally, those materials must have been under the sea which covered the earth."[3]

But even more illuminating, perhaps, since it shows a clear and conscious insight into the very process and scope of experimental method, is the following passage from al-Fārābī's classification of sciences (*Iḥṣā al'ulūm*). Al-Fārābī mentions Aristotle's distinction between natural and artificial bodies. But then he starts a rather original discussion about this distinction. "Scientific intelligibility, which cannot be reached through speculation on pure substances, may on the contrary be reached through the study of material combinations in artificial bodies. In fact, man may skillfully provoke such combinations." And al-Fārābī takes the example of chemical medicaments.[4] "Medicaments act through forces which are released by their composition and decomposition. . . . Although the causes of such mutations are not perceptible to the senses, still the senses may perceive their effects and make deductions therefrom."[5] Then he takes the example of a tree, noting that the strength which makes it grow is unreachable to us, since it is a natural process; but it may be reconstructed by analogy through the study of fermentation in wine, for instance, which is equally unreachable in itself, but which we can easily enough produce, control, and alter, at our will, creating various operational conditions. Continuing in that direction, Islamic civilization was to reach the concept of a science which would understand its object in relation to a set of operations whereby the experimenter makes calculated interventions within a given process. In a word, it was to be an operational science, containing the elements of laboratory research.

No wonder that Alexander von Humboldt stated: "The Arabs must be considered as the real creators of physical sciences."[6] G. Sarton, no doubt the most eminent historian of science, wrote: "However much one may admire Greek science, one must recognize that it was sadly deficient with regard to the experimental point of view. . . . The main as well as the least obvious achievement of the Middle Ages was the creation of the experimental spirit, and this was primarily due to the Moslems, down to the XIIth century."[7]

5. *Analytical character.*

The analytical character of Islamic science is, of course, directly connected with its experimental approach. The former is the intellectual attitude which commanded the latter as a scientific method. But, it may be useful to single

[3] Abū Alā al-Husain ibn Abdullah ibn Sīnā (Avicenna), *Kitāb al-shifā* ("The Book of Recovery"), German translation by Max Joseph Heinrich Horten, *Das Buch der Genesung der Seele* (Halle und New York: R. Haupt, 1907).

[4] Abū Naṣr Muhammad ibn Muhammad al-Fārābī, *Kitāb iḥṣā al 'ulum* ("Classification of Sciences"), Arabic text with Latin version (Madrid, 1932). Spanish translation, *Catálogo de las Ciencias.* Edición y traducción castellana de A. González Palencìa (Madrid: Facultad de Filosofía y Letras, 1933).

[5] *Ibid.*

[6] Alexander von Humboldt, *Kosmos* (Berlin, 1845–1858), Vol. II.

[7] George Sarton, *Introduction to the History of Sciences* (Baltimore: Published for the Carnegie Institution of Washington by the Williams & Wilkins Co., 1927), Vol. I.

out this analytical tendency, since it is related in a way to some essential aspects of Islamic thought and is strengthened, as we shall find out, by the very structure of the Arabic language.

At this stage, it will be sufficient to take notice of this phenomenon. The examples are numerous: in astronomy, one of their main fields of study, the Muslims have not devised any great cosmographic theory—they generally follow Ptolemy; but their strongest contribution consists in collections of factual observations, calculating tables of extreme scientific accuracy, such as the "Verified Table," established in Baghdad by Yahyā ibn Abi Manṣur (d. 830), the "Hakemite Tables," established by 'Ali ibn Yūnis, around 1010 in Cairo, the "Ilkhan Tables," established in Maragha, in 1272, by Naṣr ed-Dine Thūsī.

In medical science, the Muslims did not improve much upon Greek theory, accepted as a corpus, from Hippocrates to Galen; but their outstanding qualities appear in the analysis of individual sicknesses (like Rāzī's classical monograph[8] on smallpox, still reprinted in the West in the middle of the eighteenth century), or in surgical practice, or in the transcription of clinical cases, real diaries of various stages in the evolution of specific sicknesses. Those qualities gave Muslim medical science its pre-eminence in the Middle Ages.

In geometry, a comparison of al-Khwarezmī, perhaps the greatest Muslim mathematician, with Euclid would be revealing. He has practically no a priori general definitions, axioms, or postulates in the Euclidian manner. Euclid wanted simultaneously to construct a geometry and also to set up a model of correct reasoning, a structure of logic. Although Euclid was available to al-Khwarezmī, in a good Arabic translation made by al-Hajjaj, his colleague at the Baghdad Academy, still he presents his work as a plain treatise on measurement, a set of rules for the practical purposes of land surveyors. This is a deliberate purpose, as appears from the introduction to his treatise, where he emphasizes that, in contradistinction to the Greek theoretical mathematics, his own will serve practical ends and needs of the people. And the treatise, so poor in geometrical construction, appears as an amazing wealth of specific problems, elegantly solved through unexpected simplifications.

This basic analytical trend of Islamic science, even when it is later integrated within a philosophical survey or an encyclopedic work, is strikingly defined by a lesser-known astronomer, al-Asturlabi (d. 1140), in his "Treatise on the Use of the Spherical Astrolabe," one of those numerous Islamic books on the improvement of scientific instruments for accurate measurement: "The ancients distinguished themselves through their discovery of basic principles and the invention of ideas. Modern scholars, on the other hand, distinguish themselves through the discovery of a multitude of scientific details, the simplification of difficulties, the combination of the miscellaneous."[9]

[8] Abū Bakr Muhammad al-Rāzī, *Kitāb aljadār wal hasba* (*A Treatise on the Small-pox and the Measles*), William Alexander Greenhill, trans. (London: The Sydenham Society, 1848).

[9] 'Alī Ibn *'Isa al-Asturlābī, 'Treatise on the Use of the Spherical Astrolabe,'* Arabic text edited by L. Scheicho (Beyrouth, 1913). German translation by C. Schoy, "Alī Ibn 'Isā, Das Astrolab und sein Gebrauch," *Isis*, IX, No. 2 (August, 1926), 239–254.

As stated by H. A. R. Gibb, one of the leading authorities in Islamic studies: "The concentration of thought upon individual events permitted the Moslem scholars to push experimental method much further than their predecessors in Greece and in Alexandria."[10]

6. *Practical character. Relations between science and technology in Islamic civilization.*

Contrasting with the Greek notion of "knowledge for the sake of knowledge," a great part of the scientific effort in Islam was closely related to the practical needs of technology and handicrafts.

Even as abstract a study as mathematics was affected, as may be seen from al-Khwarezmī's conceptions just referred to, by practical problems. And many other such problems resulted from the life of the Islamic community: assessment of taxes, assessment of legal alms, division of heritage according to Qur'ānic law. They have given a specific style to some areas of mathematics in Islamic civilization.

It is partly for similar practical reasons that astronomy reached an eminent status: it was connected with ritual necessities such as the determination of the proper time and orientation for prayer, or the calculation of the periods for fasting.

There, again, a desire for simplification led to the development of trigonometry, a science which started as a branch of astronomy and was later greatly developed by the Muslims. Al-Bāttānī, the most eminent specialist in that field, wrote: "Hipparchos used entire cords; but we, *for the facility of demonstration,* have taken the half of double arcs,"[11] i.e., the sine, probably borrowed from the Indians. Later, amplifying al-Bāttānī's work, Ferghānī spread the use of the tangent, which made calculation still easier.

A contrary evidence of this trend toward the practical may also be given. For instance, zoology and botany were not especially promoted as natural sciences unless they dealt with actual needs. In zoology the main attention was for horse and cattle breeding. Botany was fostered either as an aid to pharmaceutics or as an aspect of agriculture, essentially important in a generally dry and hot climate, where irrigation was an acute problem and the care of soil was confined to gardening. Hence the variety of fruits and vegetables later transmitted to Europe through the Spanish channel.

The main alterations to Ptolemy's cartography were due to commercial and administrative needs, and were most frequently introduced not by scholars but by tradesmen and other travelers who often enriched Arabic literature with extremely precise descriptions of foreign lands and habits.

In the course of commercial contacts, paper, gunpowder, and the magnetic needle, for instance, were adapted from the Chinese and put to practical use.

[10] H. A. R. Gibb, *Modern Trends in Islam* (Chicago: University of Chicago Press, 1947).

[11] Abū 'Abdallāh Muhammad ibn Jābir al-Battānī, *Kitāb al-Zij al-Sābī* ("Opus Astronomicum"), Arabic text with Latin translation by C. A. Nallino, *Al-Battānī sive Albatenii opus astronomicum.* 3 vols. (Milano: Ulrico Hoepli, 1899–1907).

Those trade relations were vital for the Islamic world. Since it lacked mineral resources and was practically deprived of that most important good, timber, and, since vast areas of its territory were barren or desert, improper for agriculture, it developed into an essentially urban civilization which derived its wealth out of trade or handicrafts. Since the urban centers were sometimes far apart and the trade routes stretched over the sea or over long caravan tracks, it was an advantage to concentrate the highest value in relatively small bulk. This meant spices, incense, and perfume. But it also meant products of industry which had great technological value. Thus, some of the reasons which, in modern times, caused investment in precision machines in Switzerland, for instance, can also account for the development of technical crafts in the Muslim world.

Damascus blades and embroideries, Mosul fabrics, Cordova leather, Persian enamels, carpets, and all kinds of copperware and glassware were constantly improved. This fundamental urban and commercial aspect of Islamic civilization, based upon luxury handicraft and its long-range exportation, explains the relative fragility of the system. The rupture in the lines of communication caused by invasions, the closure of Mediterranean trade to Islam as a result of Western expansion, and, even more, the discovery of new routes which shifted world trade toward the Atlantic were important elements in the decline of the Muslim empire.

But, as long as the system flourished, it caused peerless stimulation, lively mutual intercourse between science and technology.

It would be hard to determine the borderline between pure and applied science in Islam. In this, again, the difference from Greece is obvious. It also appears in the different status granted to the craftsman, the technician. In Greece, the ideal was the free citizen, and the real scientist was a philosopher; the craftsman was often a slave. In Islamic society, the craftsman had an economic influence through the corporations. But the corporative structure also possessed some political significance and it often had a religious and ethical character, through its initiation aspects. Thereby, through technique, science was deeply woven into the social pattern of the community. Through technical skills and devices in the crafts it even projects into art. A copper basin or a faïence earthenware belongs simultaneously to art, to technique, and to science. For, it must be stressed again, Islamic science had a great part to play in connection with all aspects of medieval technology. Reciprocally, the progress of physics and chemistry was due largely to the necessity of promoting new methods for dyeing, new alloys, new glazes for pottery, etc. The great philosopher Avicenna devoted much of his attention to medicine, but also to techniques such as coloring processes.

Even in the earliest stages of Islamic civilization, it is interesting to notice how the initiator of chemistry, Jaber ibn Haiyān, replaces the sense qualities of Aristotelian science (hot, cold, dry, humid) by operational properties (ductility, fusibility) favoring such handicraft processes as hammering, pulverizing, stretching, etc.

In al-Fārābī's classification, speculative knowledge is closely connected with technology. For instance, the science of weight is defined simultaneously as a study of weights as measures but also as a "study of the various apparatus which may lift heavy objects and transport them from one point to another." Similarly, mechanics is equally "the science of bodies according to mathematical relations and the art to produce such relations between bodies." The two aspects receive the same stress. Science (*'ilm*) and technical know-how (*sina'a*) are expressly related.

II. ELEMENTS FOR AN INTRODUCTION TO THE PHILOSOPHY OF SCIENCE IN ISLAM

7. *Islamic religion and science.*

Islam, as a religion, essentially consists in the recognition of the unity and transcendence of God. Apparently, these dogmas might preclude the very possibility of any knowledge of the scientific type. The unity of ultimate truth would make any relative, finite, transient experience illusory. And transcendence would put reality beyond human reach. But, although the world is not an end in itself, as a creation of God it is not an illusion either. The world is not a game (*laghib*); it is in earnest. God has instituted the creation in truth and mercy. And, according to this theology, natural objects are to be considered as "signs" (*"ayat"*) or "remembrances" (*"dhikr"*) of God. Properly interpreted, they are manifestations of truth, mercy, harmony, and power, which are in God. Therefore, the Qur'ān repeatedly exhorts man to consider the "signs" around him, in the natural world. Several verses remind him of the signs which are "in the heavens and in his own soul." Thereby, a correspondence is also shown between the natural and the human being. There is no estrangement between the essential nature of man and the structure of the universe.

Moreover, as expressed in the Qur'ān, man is the "caliph," which means the vicar of God upon earth. The world is not only a network of signs to be understood for self-realization but also a matter, a substance, to be grasped, handled, and organized by man, in self-assertion on earth. As an individual soul, responsible as a person before God, his mission is not only to unify his being but also to project this unity into society and into Nature. The singleness of the human soul, the coherence of the community, and the rule of man's mind established over Nature are but various aspects of this *"ordinatio ad unum."* This is the reason why *"'ilm,"* science, as a means of reaching these aims, enjoys a privileged status in Islamic civilization. Of course, it has to be interpreted as meaning "knowledge," essentially spiritual, and "wisdom," essentially ethical, more than "science" in the present Western sense. But, the spiritual being united with the worldly, in Islam *"'ilm"* is also used to designate secular science. The modernists, nowadays, constantly refer to it in their attempt to restore a scientific feeling in Muslim society. And it would hardly be sustained that the word *"'ilm,"* in the famous and often-quoted Islamic tradition: "Go in search of *''ilm'* (science) even to China," would mean anything but secular science.

As things are, the importance of science, in the rational sense, has often been stressed by religious tradition and also by the major philosophies in Islam. Let it suffice to quote the two most important figures perhaps, one for orthodox theology, al-Ghazzālī, and the other for "Greek philosophy," Ibn-Rushd, or Averroës.

Al-Ghazzālī, author of, among other works, the *Tahāfut al falsafa* ("Refutation of Philosophy"), aimed against Avicenna's Aristotelianism, writes in another of his works, *Munqidh min al-dalāl*[12] ("Escape from Error"), that: "A grievous crime indeed against religion has been committed by the man who imagined that Islam is defended by the denial of mathematical science, seeing that there is nothing in revealed truth opposed to those sciences and reciprocally."

On the other hand, Averroës, who wrote, among other works, one entitled *Tahāfut al-tahāfut*[13] ("Refutation of the Refutation"), against al-Ghazzālī, still agrees, in his "Decisive Treaty," that: "Divine Law invites to rational observation and rational knowledge of existing beings, and this is evident from many verses in the Qur'ān."

So, the heritage of the prophets and the heritage of Greek reason both point toward the same conclusion. There is a dual basis to the scientific optimism of Islamic civilization. In the beginning we noted the confidence and the youthful dynamism which were inspired in the new searchers by the very structure of Greek science, its philosophical synthesis, and its encyclopedic prospects. We can see now that the same attitude can be rooted equally in the traditional faith in God's mercy and man's mission in the universe.

But this happy conjunction, nevertheless, hides a deep-set misunderstanding between the Hellenic and the Semitic outlooks. Science, for the Arab, is not a system of concepts and theories. Even in his scholarly activity, scholastic philosophy, the doctrinal apparatus is chiefly a framework: the fundamental, the living element is the direct, meaningful experience of a specific fact or event. Perception is not so much a "vision" of the mind, but, rather, an "action" of the whole being, totally engaged in its experience. Rather than a conceptual structure, thought has an operational tempo. The "Promethean" boldness of Greek science, with its sense of "creating laws" and its underlying philosophy of essences, is likely to appear as mere rebellion or idolatry. For a Semitic mind, a scientific law is never set up by man. But, to an inquisitive, intense, righteous searcher, a part of the reality may occasionally be disclosed, unveiled (*kashf*) for a momentary glimpse.

Finally, Islamic science appears experimental, practical, analytical, and dis-

[12] Abū Hāmid Muhammad ibn Muhammad al-Ghazzālī, *Munqidh min al dalāl* ("Escape from Error"), Arabic text with French translation by F. Jabre (Beyrouth, 1959).

[13] Abūl Walēd Muhammad ibn Rushd (Averroës), *Kitāb fasl al-maqāl,* 7th ed., Arabic text edited by Marcus Joseph Müller, 1859; German translation by Marcus Joseph Müller, *Philosophie und Theologie von Averroës* (München: G. Franz, 1875).

junctive more or less in the same way as are Islamic religion, philosophy, and law, and largely for the same reasons.

8. *The intellectual equipment.*

We shall briefly examine in this category some of the "tools" applied to reality in order to investigate it scientifically. We shall successively consider the Arabic language, as an instrument of analysis; the Islamic notions of time and space; and the process of demonstration. Finally, we shall consider two sciences, which were especially developed in Islam: algebra and chemistry.

9. *The Arabic language as an instrument of analysis.*

Arabic soon became the universal scientific language of the various peoples who belonged to Islamic civilization. It molded, with its very peculiar structure, some of the most significant aspects of Muslim thinking. Even Greek concepts, passing through this mold, underwent deep modification.

Indeed, there are momentous differences between Semitic languages, such as Arabic, and Indo-European, such as Greek, Sanskrit, and modern Western languages. Scarcely anything in the Arabic sentence would remind us of the architecture of Indo-European languages, that compact stonework of Latin or German, for instance, where causes and consequences, inductions and deductions are solidly imbricated, and determine each other, where thought is constantly based on the various modalities of speech. On the contrary, Arabic has very few subordinate sentences. It does not incline to express relations of causality or temporality. It proceeds through a juxtaposition of principal sentences simply drawn in a line through conjunctions: "and," "and then," etc. It contacts ideas in a direct, often abrupt, manner.

In European languages the subject of the sentence is always definitely expressed and omnipresent. Any subordinate fact or action is related to the subject, seen, judged from his point of view. Nothing of the sort in Arabic. The sentence lies bare. The subject is seldom isolated. It is generally integrated within the verb, as an inflection thereof. In contrast to European languages, the action is more important than the agent, the participation more important than the assessment; the emphasis is on the immediate experience itself, not on the subject.

In fact, the essential components of Arabic sentences are neither whole propositions, nor nouns or pronouns, but verbs. And, even within the verb, the ultimate living cell, the core, is a group of letters, generally three, which form the root, the "soul" of speech. The meaning concentrates around those roots. Ideas are thus further condensed. So, the Arabic language stresses the general tendency toward analytical, particularizing, experimental thought. Those were the very characteristics of Islamic science.

10. *Islamic notions of time and space.*

One of the most strenuous endeavors of Islamic science was to assimilate the Greek notions of time and space constructed as categories.

For traditional Muslim thought, time is neither a flow, nor a historical duration, nor a mechanical chain of successive moments. The most characteristic doctrine is that of "the renewal of creation at every moment." While professing creation *ex nihilo,* through a unique act of God, this doctrine considers, however, that the divine act of creation is not extinct, and that it reverberates, alive, actual, in every moment of our existence—so that every minute reflects the miracle of creation in its spontaneity, while retaining, in its novelty itself, an echo from eternity. All is always possible if it pleases God, *"in sha Allah."* Every second is ripe with promise and with threat. And this is why a "linear" conception of time, stretched out as a measure, is difficult to admit. We cannot be "located" in time; time is within us as a most intimate experience, inseparable from our personality.

In fact, such "spatialization" of time, which is characteristic of Greek thought, was contrary to the most spontaneous feelings of the Arab. In the Arabic language we can observe a quite different tendency: concepts of space are often indicated with locations pertaining to time. For instance, in *"asbaha,"* "to arrive in the morning," the emphasis does not bear on the fact of arrival but on the idea of "becoming one with the morning" as expressed by the root form.

While the Greeks had a natural sense of finite space, the ancient Arabs generally had to observe space stretching around them as a more or less shapeless continuum. The eye could not easily find a place to rest. By crossing, this continuum could best be filled and measured through movement, through rhythmical repetition: footsteps, the shuffle of the caravan, the chanting of litanies, which all generate contact, mark time. The outside perception is transferred inward, converted into a subjective, vital feeling.

On one side, we can observe a projection, an objectivization of time into space. On the other, we have a reabsorption, an interiorization of space within a personal, incommunicable experience of time. Here, again, a parallel could be made with the observations gathered while examining the original characters of Islamic science.

11. *The process of demonstration.*

Differing from Indian and Chinese forms of demonstration, the Islamic knows the Greek syllogism. The familiar three terms are there, it is true. But they are differently used. The stress put upon the various terms is not identical; reasoning does not base itself upon the same elements for demonstration.

The emphasis rests upon the minor term, which comes first, rather than the major. Once again, Islamic philosophy does not start with a general idea, "All humans are mortal," but finds insurance in the specific individual truth expressed in the minor term in "Socrates is human," in the Greek syllogism.

Further, the passage from one term to another is not enacted in the same way. Moving between the general and the particular, Greek thought remains on the same level of intellectual experience; the prospect gets only broader or narrower.

In the Oriental syllogism, there is a break in the process. Indeed, the passage is not between more and less, between the general and the particular, but between direct individual perception and information from some other, extraneous source. There is a leap to be made from one type of experience to another, from an experimental position to the data of revelation, tradition, authority, etc. After "Socrates is human" comes an explicit or implicit "and *on the other hand . . .* "; then comes the other proposition, "all humans are mortal," which brings the obvious conclusion.

But this syllogism, even altered, is still not the most characteristic form of demonstration in Islamic thought. The genuine form, used also in the Jewish tradition, has only two terms, two branches. This is the dilemma form. It is "either/or," sometimes "nothing except." Each term in the dilemma is felt in its full contradictory value. They are two poles rather than two dialectical moments. The mind has been compelled to adhere or to refuse. Deduction is replaced by a choice or decision; dialectical balance gives room to an act of will or an act of faith. Man has to commit himself with the whole of his human experience.

12. *Two sciences in Islamic civilization: algebra and chemistry.*

Algebra: The observations made under Section I and the interpretations given under Section II may now be grouped together and applied to a special case—algebra. Among all fields of knowledge this is certainly one where the contribution of Islamic scientists has been decisive. It may therefore give us the best clue as to the specific style of Islamic sciences.

Algebra resulted in great part from the reluctance of the Muslims to consider negative numbers, which were quite familiar to Indians. Therefore, an equation with a negative number was considered as incomplete. The permutation of negative quantities, turning them into positive, was called *"al-jabr"* (re-establishment), hence the name algebra. Then homologue quantities are suppressed in both members, and this operation was called *"muqabala"* (compensation), the full name of the new science being *"al-jabr wa al-muqabala,"* the title of al-Khwarezmī's leading treatise. With al-Khwarezmī, who really initiated algebra at the beginning of the ninth century, the most important name in that field is that of Omar Khayyam, better known in the West as a poet.

Algebra started as an introduction to calculus. It had been first associated with geometrical figures, then grew gradually autonomous. From the start, algebra corresponded to some of the main characteristics of Islamic science. It has a practical aspect, originates in empirical simplifications, and displays its analytical character by the importance given to the solution of individual cases or problems.

But algebra also corresponds to some of the essential features of Islamic civilization as a whole. Against a philosophy of essence, accidents, and virtues, expressed in science by Greek geometry, algebra introduces a purely operational science, where number has been made immaterial. Algebraic numbers have no substance, only properties. While geometry works on forms, the algebraic process is mobility itself.

For Islamic science, ultimate reality should be respected. There must be no attempt to describe it with concepts. But it may be alluded to, pointed at, through signs (*ayats*). Algebra is precisely a combination of signs, a most allusive, elliptical science. It does not pretend to structure reality as geometry does. Rather, it reveals, it unveils a reality which has always been there, but as an unknown term. It does not project numbers in the spatial, static continuum of the Greeks, but into an open network of forces. It does not establish a hierarchy of forms, but an interplay of equivalent phenomena.

There are parallels to be made, not only between algebra and Muslim philosophy, but also between algebra and Arabic literature, algebra and Islamic arts, especially the arabesque decoration. A description of the language could be given in algebraic terms. As opposed to the conceptual geometry of the Greek language, which seems to extend its dialectical avenues through space, Arabic reduces speech to abstract formulas, rhythmically rather than logically connected, separated by grammatical voids and unknown quantities, and expanded out in the manner of a linear algebraical series.

Chemistry: In the same way, again, Islam was attracted by the atomistic theories it could trace in Greek sources. Those theories reached far into orthodox thinking. In fact, the main "pagan" danger was to oppose Nature or essences to God. One possible escape was to dissolve Nature in atomism. And this, in turn, leads us to chemistry, which satisfies a similar urge. It connects and disconnects matter into ever-shifting combinations. The operational fluidity of chemistry, like the operational fluidity of algebra, or the fluidity of arabesque design over a hidden mathematical pattern, all present the same guarantee of impermanence.

Beyond this ever-moving appearance, the principle of stability remains, signified sometimes, but always transcendent.

13. *The downfall of Islamic science. The crisis in respect to Western science.*

Islamic science starts sinking into decay toward the end of the twelfth century, precisely when Europe is taking over the heritage it had maintained. It would go beyond the scope of this paper to study the channels through which Muslim knowledge and the precious Greek heritage it contained have been transmitted. Neither would it be the place to study the political and economic reasons which brought the downfall of Islamic science, together with the stagnation of Islamic civilization.

But some of the inner, intellectual causes of the downfall might still be briefly considered:

(a) The lack of unity of Islamic scientific sources has been pointed out. In spite of spectacular examples of a synthesis, the "Greek tendency" and the "prophetic tendency" did not really merge into a coherent scientific movement. As long as intellectual enthusiasm and vitality existed, the tension between the two tendencies, expressing different psychological approaches and different styles of culture, proved fruitful. When the impulse lagged, the two went apart. "Greek science" desiccated itself. "Muslim science" turned toward religion, law, and literature.

(b) The scientist had no definite status in society. Moreover, he was sometimes a scientist and a physician, a philosopher, a technologist, a statesman, or a courtier. As long as the connection between science and technology was maintained, the situation was a healthy one. When it changed, due mainly to adverse trade conditions affecting technology, the status of the scientist deteriorated. The ideal of learning was then exclusively set by the literary man (*adib*) or by the jurist (*faqih*).

(c) The tendency to consider phenomena as "signs" caused many specifically Muslim improvements in the field of science, mainly through algebra and chemistry. But the notion of "sign" was also degraded. It often led to astrological and alchemical dead ends.

(d) The experimental character, one of the main features of Islamic science, now boasted of by apologists, did not bring exclusively happy effects. We have seen how it could be related to a basic tendency in Islamic civilization to respect the unity and transcendence of ultimate reality. This very limitation often brought original creative results in science, since it concentrated research on experience rather than on theory. But it induced science to become satisfied with plain technique and, accordingly, to decay.

(e) The two points which have just been mentioned raise some questions about Western science. First, it appears that the experimental analytical method would not really distinguish Western science. Islamic civilization had developed it earlier, to a considerable degree. More specific aspects of Western science, when it took its impulse, may have been: (1) the reduction of qualitative data to measurable quantities and (2) a philosophy which recognized the expansion of the individual and his creative faculties. This fullness of the individual, the "Promethean" philosophy of Western man, may have been most important.

It would appear, then, that one of the main factors in Western scientific development has not been technological, but consisted in philosophy, Western philosophy of science.

(f) Its meeting and conflicts with an advanced Western science caused deep crisis in Islamic thought. As a result, one of the most frequent pleas was to accept Western techniques, while safeguarding Oriental values. This appeared hardly possible in the long run. But it is interesting to compare this basic reaction with the spontaneous movement which carried Islamic science toward the experimental and empirical, rather than to the elaboration of great theories. In both cases, values had to be preserved. In both cases, ancient and modern, popular attitudes seem to have been similar, greeting the technique, mistrusting scientific systems.

(g) A curious interchange seems to have occurred during the meeting of Western science and Islamic civilization in recent times. For a great number of Oriental modernists, science seems to have stopped with nineteenth-century concepts. It is materialist, positivist, rational, comforting. During the same period, Western science was baffling common sense, dematerializing matter, and reducing things to mathematical abstractions.

Such want of synchronism does not necessarily result from lack of knowledge or of information. But, in mass education, the type of science which Oriental leaders want to spread is precisely meant to give the picture of a coherent world, which science can well explain and technique safely transform, for this is the kind of moral certitudes and positivist truths which, to their judgment, appear most needed as a reaction against traditional teachings.

(h) Science has now become international, and there seems to be no place for an Islamic conception of science, or any other cultural or regional conception of science. But it may be interesting to note that science again tends to become more and more "operational." Roughly speaking, the spirit of "algebra" is again facing the "spirit of geometry." One may ask what consequences this could entail for all cultures, Eastern as well as Western.

HIDEKI YUKAWA[a]

Modern Trend of Western Civilization and Cultural Peculiarities in Japan

As a theoretical physicist I shall first analyze, mainly from a scientific point of view, the general trend that seems now to me to be prevailing in the recent development of Western civilization. The pecularities of Japanese culture will then be examined from a more general standpoint, and in this connection the possibility will be investigated for some of these peculiarities to contribute in mitigating the distortions that, as the result of the above development, will in the future become more and more serious in every stage of human activity.

Standing at the beginning of a new age of technology, we are confronted inevitably with a hitherto unexperienced change in every aspect of human civilization. This change is produced mainly by the liberation of a vast amount of energy and also by rapid development in the means of transmission and accumulation of information. This change is especially remarkable in the domain of physics. Dividing this branch of research into two parts, the experimental and the theoretical, it is already well known that the progress of the former has always been rendered possible by a corresponding progress on the technical side. But insofar as theoretical physics is concerned, our conviction has been that we are in a so-called safety zone avoiding the attack of technology. Of course, this attitude rests on the classical ideal that the rational, autonomous, and active power of human thinking discovers the fundamental laws in the chaos of natural phenomena. In the last analysis, theoretical physics is nothing but the endeavor to reconstruct this actual universe on the basis of the ensemble of possibilities. The process of postulation, succeeded by selection of the fit by means of trial and error, is the essence of the mental activities of all theoretical physicists. Experimental physics represents our outer activities, whereas theoretical physics represents our inner activities, to understand natural phenomena in a rational fashion.

But now we must take the possibility into account that, quite in the same way as human labor and skill have been almost completely replaced by mechanistic apparatus in the domain of experimental physics, most of the labor and skill of the human brain is to be replaced by electronic computers. Originally, these were devised for the purpose of numerical solution of various kinds of equations. But I want to point out that the essentially human process of creativity can be replaced, to a considerable extent, by mechanistic processes occurring in these computers. The validity or invalidity of any postulated fundamental physical law will, in many cases, more easily be determined by judging the outcome from the computers. The process of selection from among possible fundamental laws may well reduce to the level of mechanistic operations, shifting the real problem in theoretical physics to the stage of technology. The rational understanding of the physical data obtained by experimentation has long been conceived as being essentially a problem of the inner activity of the human power of thinking. It has become possible that many of the problems may be projected outside the realm of inner human activity.

The tendency discussed above will probably culminate in the following. The electronic computers can be thought of as a kind of experimental apparatus, wherein any electro-mechanical input is designed to be transformed into a definite electro-mechanical output in quite the same way as any physical object reacts to external conditions in a definite fashion prescribed by fundamental laws. Then the task of theoretical physics may well be reduced to that of setting up a unique correspondence between two kinds of mechanistic processes, one occurring in experimental apparatus and the other on computers. In this branch of research not much room will be left for the autonomous power of human thinking. The human intellect and insight will in the future play less and less part in the act of theorization, and accordingly mankind will be able to be proud only of the human ability of devising complicated computing mechanisms. In short, we may characterize such a tendency as the prevailing of empiricism or positivism in a broad sense.

The above tendency is not peculiar to physical science only, but common to all aspects of human civilization. Not only is the worship of the mystery of the physical universe in the process of decay, but, as for the dignity of human existence itself, the part properly played by activities of human origin seems to be less and less important. Now we wonder what will be left in future for mankind to perform without the aid of mechanistic apparatus. Technocracy is now threatening the nucleus of the human spirit. This is a natural and at the same time necessary outcome of the European mode of rational thinking, which has so far been so effective in establishing the machine civilization. In the process of this development, the Eastern mode of thinking was evidently destined to exert a negative influence. But, now that the future of Western rationalism seems not to be a pleasant one, we notice the rise of the hope that the Eastern tradition will play a complementary part in the future development of world civilization.

It is certainly beyond my ability to make in detail a comparative study of the Eastern and the Western modes of thinking and, in addition to this, to point out the specialities of Japanese culture in the Oriental background. However, it may, at least, be said that the Western mode of human living is characterized, in a broad sense, by confrontation with external environments, whereas the Eastern mode is characterized by adaptation to these. According to the former attitude, human living is destined to be, in every respect, positive or adventurous both in action and in thought. This was the very origin of the rational and abstract mode of thinking, and, moreover, the active and dynamic approach to natural phenomena by experimentation gave rise to modern scientific civilization. Though Eastern culture is characterized as being passive and static in its essence, in contrast with the above, we may say, disregarding differences in many respects and an exceptional case of Japan, that rationalism is a common factor in both of the two contrasting civilizations. In short, rationalism is a pattern of thinking which inquires into everything in the background of an ensemble of complementary possibilities. The peculiarity of the Japanese mode of thinking lies in its complete neglect of complementary alternatives. This we may term Japanese irrationalism. Of course, this is completely foreign to any form of scientific spirit, but it is identical neither with absolutism nor with skepticism. Moreover, this is akin to an optimistic rather than a pessmistic point of view. Nevertheless, it is well known that Japanese mentality is very far from any kind of insensibility. The subject of the following analysis will therefore be the irrationalism of the Japanese way of thinking, which is so peculiar and contradictory that even a Japanese himself finds it hard to understand.

In the first place, we can distinguish Western culture from Eastern by the fact that the former is far more adventurous in nature than the latter. The tribes that settled in the Eastern zone preferred stability in life to drastic changes. In other words, they have long been satisfied with the existing conditions imposed on them from the outside. Of course, the Japanese cannot be an exception to this. Though it has experienced short periods of outward extension, its political history has been dominated by stability. In this sense, Japanese culture holds a conspicuous position, even among those of the Orient.

Such a speciality of the culture of Japan may be attributed to its natural conditions, its geographical isolation and the mild climate. The Japanese have escaped invasions from outside and famines on a large scale. As has already been pointed out, Western and Eastern modes of human life are characterized, roughly speaking, by conquest of natural conditions and adaptation to them, respectively. In other words, these attitudes are those of hostility and reconciliation to Nature. But, in Japan, there was originally no such thing as alienation between man and Nature. Man's physical existence has been relatively easy in Japan because a small amount of compromise on man's part has sufficed for adaptation to physical conditions. In Japan, therefore, there has been little need for adventure either in action or in thought.

Under the severe circumstances of the Western zone, adventurous effort to secure survival leads to the establishment of artificial environments for human living and consequently gives rise to a dynamic idea of a non-directional progress. In order to compromise with Nature, man stands in need, not only of his autonomous action to modify external conditions, but also of effort to modify himself. This implies that some existing conceptions are renounced and then one is to conform to a new concept selected from an ensemble of alternative possibilities. This is the very origin of the rational mode of thinking, and furthermore, of the scientific spirit to discover physical laws in natural phenomena. Science is the outcome of the rational contact of man with external Nature.

In Oriental culture, examples of adventures of human thought are seen in various systems of fantastic cosmology. Then among the main themes in the systems of Eastern philosophy we notice that of transmigration. In this the recurrence of approximately the same pattern is essential. This tendency seems to be reflected in the Oriental speciality that after destruction reconstruction is made with little modification and no drastic change.

Now let us analyze the dominant pattern in the Japanese mentality. It has the tendency to sidestep as far as possible any kind of confrontation. This, in turn, leads to the tendency to retain the existing stability with the least amount of modification at the sacrifice of a thoroughgoing solution. It seems to avoid any form of rational compromise based on a selection from alternative possibilities. If a prejudice exists, it is therefore in danger of dashing into collapse. But it must be noted that this is not a simple renouncement of rationality. Originally speaking, rationality takes an interest in the permanent and universal order transcending the narrow scope of space and time. But Japanese thought is concerned mainly about the local and temporary order restricted in space and time. This may be termed, for convenience, Japanese rationality. As an illustration, we here cite the fact that among various forms of human association a conspicuous importance has so far been given to the one between father and son or to that among the members of a family. Even at present the morals of a human group are apt to be molded in conformity with this same pattern —the relationship between a boss and his henchmen. Generally speaking, the Japanese is out of his element in long-range and abstract thinking. This tendency is completely foreign to adventurous and drastic changes. The remarkable stagnation and the conservatism noticed in various stages of Japanese culture are explained by the fact that temporary neglect of a succession of difficulties ensures the stability of a once established system.

The Japanese mentality is, in most cases, unfit for abstract thinking and takes interest merely in tangible things. This is the origin of the Japanese excellence in technical art and the fine arts. The unconscious recognition of their own defect in abstraction seems to drive the Japanese to the uncritical adoration and the unconditional adoption of the religious and philosophical systems brought in from the outside. Such is a task relatively easy for the high-level Japanese intellect. But, in these systems, only the elements familiar to the Japanese clime are assimilated and the unfamiliar ones are left unappreciated. Thus, existing conditions remain untouched and unchanged, ensuring the conspicuous stability of traditional elements. The abstract mode of thinking will continue to be foreign to the Japanese. And to them any rational system of thought, generally speaking, will not be able to be more than something mystical, satisfying their intellectual curiosity.

In the history of Japan, we can cite numerous examples of the above. As was seen in the instances of the introduction of Buddhism and of Confucianism, the Japanese were very progressive in the assimilation of high-level cultural assets. But, among these, only the ones were appreciated that were effective in regulating and maintaining the social and political order. Hence, a thoroughgoing rationalism, such as the philosophy of Lao Tzu[b] and Chuang Tzu,[c] escaped general comprehension and found sympathy in the intellectual minority alone. This indifferent mode of life, standing aloof from the world, is symbolized by the seven wise men in the bamboo grove. The elements of thought common to this have, from ancient times, been found in the West—especially in Greece and Rome. This higher form of epicureanism is still seen in Western Europe and, in particular, in France, but may be regarded as a kind of vice in America and Soviet Russia. Properly speaking, this element is also foreign to the Japanese mentality, and the minority's longing for it finds no chance of actualization, being hindered by the disposition of the majority. Furthermore, even in the Eastern zone, the trend of transmigrationism is more remarkable in India, and there we find fakirs instead of Chinese hermits.

In the philosophy of Lao Tzu and Chuang Tzu we notice an element of thought similar to that characterizing science. This recognizes the insensate aspect of Nature, as was symbolized by Lao Tzu's saying, "The law of the universe is insensate, for it regards everything as a straw effigy," and, moreover, contains an element of the negation of human existence itself. In contrast with this, the Japanese mentality has a regard for ideas having concrete applicability to human living. The indifferent pursuit of the truth, made independently of such implications, did not and cannot appeal to most of the Japanese. For example, at the time of the introduction of Western civilization in the Meiji[d] era (1867–1945), the practical sciences of Anglo-American origin were dominant. In spite of this, it was curious that thereafter the philosophical systems of German origin became most popular in Japan, whereas the ones of Anglo-American origin lost ground. This is due to the fact that the German systems were looked upon as something like mysticism or as akin to religious thought, aiming at the salvation of the human being. We may say that their rational character, as systems of learning, escaped the general understanding of the Japanese. This is also true of the Nishida[e] philosophy, the unique system of philosophy in Japan. In the last analysis, the introduction of alien culture has been characterized, in Japan, by a peculiar action of transmutation.

In Japanese thought, the most conspicuous part has been played by moral principles which may be termed as the Way. But this is somewhat different in meaning from the one seen in Confucius'[f] saying, "If a man in the morning learns the Way, he may in the evening die without regret." This is similar neither to the philosophy inquiring into absolute truth nor to the religious creed aiming at human salvation. This is, in a sense, a thoroughgoing passiveness that submits to the irrationalities omnipresent in the universe by regarding them as inevitable. Moreover, this represents a kind of enlightenment by subsuming in one's self all the irrational elements of the universe. This is of a purely individual nature and requires no universality. In Japan, this has been regarded as the ideal for character building, and the Japanese multitude has shown regard for followers of Stoic discipline who pursue the Way. The status of Buddhism and Confucianism in Japan must be estimated in connection with the Japanese Way. In this sense, the Zen[g] school plays an essential part in Japanese thought.

In the region of science, the Japanese mentality discussed above is reflected in laying stress on applied science and correspondingly in the negligence of rationalistic, abstract, and fundamental study. The multitude pays due regard to the dignity and mystery of scientific research, but cannot appreciate the essence of academic freedom, which is primarily of European origin.

As was discussed in the beginning of this paper, European rationalism has led, of necessity, to the world-wide predicament of today. The Orient has hitherto been compelled to accept Western culture in a passive manner, has utilized it, and has reconstructed its own culture so as to conform to the Western pattern. Here we admit that among the elements indigenous to Japan there have been many which have been inconvenient for such a purpose. But we must also note that the rationalistic and systematic aspects of European thinking cannot be the whole of the measure of value in human life. The elements of thought completely foreign to those in European culture or complementary to these are abundantly preserved in the tradition of Eastern thought and especially Japanese thought. This state of affairs has hitherto escaped the attention of the Oriental himself, and, moreover, has not been of much importance, judging from the current of the world. But now, in the light of the present-day world predicament, close examination of the possibilities contained in Oriental thought is essential.

The Western mode of living is characterized by confrontation with external circumstances and by man's being armed against them. This isolation of an individual is the very origin of European individualism. But we find in Western civilization a note of stiffness and uneasiness. In contrast with this, the Oriental has the subtle wisdom to devise comfortable conditions of human living by adapting himself to natural conditions.

The spiritual predicament of Western civilization is certainly caused by its too much dependence on artificial conditions. Generally speaking, the happiness of human life is the less stable the more it depends on external conditions. Therefore, the Japanese mode of thinking is more closely allied to happiness, since it makes an ideal of attaining a complete union of man and Nature, and, accordingly, of resolving any kind of alienation between them. This Japanese peculiarity gave rise to no rationalistic systems of science and philosophy, to be sure, but has led to a high degree of excellence in the fine arts. By nature, the Japanese are interested in the fine arts, both new and old, and also are always ready to appreciate their value. The feeling of fineness is reflected in every aspect of human living in Japan.

Unique in world history is the fact that in a corner of the Orient a distinguishing form of culture has been cultivated which suffers the least amount of disturbance from the outside. But modern Japan is in the process of incessant transfiguration. At present, we note the dangerous tendency in Japan to disregard uncritically the peculiar elements of its own culture in order to conform to patterns of Western civilization. We believe that we are in urgent need of searching out the possible ways in which Japanese cultural elements may contribute to the dissolving of the world-wide predicament of today.

[a] 湯川秀樹
[b] 老子
[c] 荘子
[d] 明治
[e] 西田幾多郎
[f] 孔子
[g] 禅

COMMENTS ON HIDEKI YUKAWA'S[a] PAPER, BY SHOSON MIYAMOTO[b]

I should like to add a few comments on Dr. Yukawa's paper for the purpose of discussion. Unfortunately, he is not here to reply. The first concerns his statement:

> Japanese mentality is, in most cases, unfit for abstract thinking and takes interest only in tangible things. This is the origin of the Japanese excellence in technical art and the fine arts.

Elsewhere, Yukawa speaks of "Japanese irrationality" and "defect in abstraction." In order to avoid any misconception among the non-Japanese members of the conference, I want to point out the inadequacy of this presentation and show that the greatness of Japanese art does not lie merely in "irrationality." By this I mean that any great art is based upon a balanced and exact observation of environment and a penetration into the depth of Nature. A certain amount of abstraction and rational thought-process is necessary for the conception and expression of art.[1]

[1] K. Tomita[w] and C. Horioka,[x] of the Boston Museum of Fine Arts, related to me an interesting episode about Motonobu when I visited them on June 16, 1959. In Japan there are no tigers, but Motonobu drew many masterpieces of tigers. Motonobu envisioned tigers by studying carefully the hair of a cat. I also saw many drafts of different subject-compositions in which I could see the artists' painstaking endeavors to mold a vision.

In Japanese art, for example *dharma-cakṣu* (*hōgen*,[c] in Japanese), which means the eye which penetrates the *dharma*, is considered to be essential to art. In fact, great artists, such as Kano Motonobu[d] and his successors, used *dharma-cakṣu* as part of their name.

In Buddhism *dharma-cakṣu* is the first stage of a *bhikkhu* entering the stream of the Buddha's *satori*.[e] It is to see and realize things in their true nature just as they are; in the original, it is *yathābhūtañānadassana*. This is not mere irrationalism or intuition, but, as I said, a balanced and exact observation of Nature. Art, which is universal, is based upon this, and in the deepest source of human culture there is neither East nor West, but only Truth, Goodness, and Beauty.

This universal basis of Japanese art must be taken into consideration for a balanced view of the subject. It was this universal element which attracted men like E. Fenollosa, the American professor of logic and later aesthetics at the Imperial University of Tokyo in 1878, and Dr. W. S. Bigelow, the Western art-patron, to Japanese art. They taught the Japanese the inherent value of their art at the time of the Meiji Restoration, when traditional cultures of Japan were being abandoned for Western culture, and Buddhist art and sculpture were being disposed of at ridiculously cheap prices.[2] From this awakening to its own rich aesthetic past the Japanese established the Academy of Japanese Art, which produced many great artists.[3] Incidentally, Fenollosa and Bigelow are peacefully enshrined in Hōmyoin[f] of the Miidera[g] Temple, belonging to the Tendai[h] school, near the ancient capital, Kyoto.

The point is, however, that they saw the *universal* in Japanese art, and this aspect, beyond East and West, Japanese and non-Japanese, must not be overlooked in the enthusiasm to show what traits are peculiar to the Japanese mind.

The second point on which I wish to comment is this: Yukawa states that the peculiarity of "Japanese irrationality" is "a complete neglect of complementary alternatives" and that, because of the utter lack of the abstract mode of thinking among the Japanese, "any rational system of thought, generally speaking, will not be able to be more than something mystical, satisfying their intellectual curiosity."

Now, Buddhism in Japan took 300 years, after its introduction in A.D. 538, to produce the philosophical doctrines of Shingon[i] and Tendai, and more than 600 years to produce original Japanese Buddhist thinkers such as Hōnen,[j] Shinran,[k] Dōgen,[l] and Nichiren.[m] But, since the modernization of Japan, which began in 1868, it took *less than 90 years* to master the ways of Western civilization and attain a level of rational, scientific thought which developed scientists, such as Noguchi,[n] Yukawa, and others. What is the reason for this relatively swift accomplishment? It is because the Japanese mind has been

[2] For Fenollosa and Bigelow, the Japanese deprecation of their own art was a blessing, since they could purchase priceless objects of art for almost nothing. Their world-famous collection is now in the Boston Museum.

[3] The world-renowned painters Hōgai Kano[y] and Gahō Hashimoto[z] were Fenollosa's collaborators, and, under his influence, Kakuzō Okakura,[aa] the author of the *Book of Tea*, and such famous artists as Kwanzan Shimomura[ab] and Taikwan Yokoyama[ac] and others were "born."

trained and developed, consciously and unconsciously—I may say, *existentially* —by the streams of Buddhist rationalistic ways of thinking. Aside from Tendai and Shingon, Rinzai Zen[o] greatly influenced the statesman, the warrior, and the intelligentsia; and Sōtō Zen,[p] founded by Dōgen, and the Shin[q] school, founded by Shinran, deeply affected the pattern of thought and life of the common people.

As an example of the fact that Buddhism cultivates rational thinking and does not rely merely upon intuition, I wish to discuss briefly one of the most important terms in Japanese Buddhist thought, namely, *dōri*,[r] [4] which may be translated as rational, reason, or principle.

Dōri is derived from the fourfold *dōri* or *yukti* of the Vijñānavāda School. ("*Yukti*" means "unity" or "way of union.") The fourfold *dōri* is:

1. *apekṣā,* the Mādhyamika's principle of relation;
2. *kārya-kāraṇa,* the Buddhist causal principle of relation which stresses conditions of conditional functioning. This thought runs through the Abhidharma schools down to Vijñānavāda and the Hua-yen[s] (Kegon) schools;
3. *upapatti-sādhana,* which concerns Buddhist logic and refers to the logical method of recognition; and
4. *dharmatā,* the most essential principle in Mahāyāna Buddhism, known in Japanese as *hōni-dōri*[t] (*dharmatā-yukti*).

Although the fourfold *dōri,* or the four ways of philosophical thinking, influenced the Japanese way of life, it is the fourth, *hōni-dōri,* which I wish to discuss.

Shinran, for example, wrote an essay on this subject, "Essay on *Dharmatā*" (*Jinen-hōni-shō*[u]). He pointed out that "this *Dharmatā* is the Saving Vow of Amida itself," and that "Amida Buddha is the means by which we come to realize the principle (*dōri*) of *Dharmatā*." Shinran also describes the Original Saving Vow of Amida as non-duality.

The Middle Way is a practical principle of life which sees the living value of things themselves in their rightful place and at their opportune moment. Based upon an open point of view, it makes possible an infinite range of insight. The term "intuition" alone does not cover the insight which penetrates the vital fact in a balanced view of the whole, nor does it strike the truth of the thing itself by analysis. In order to grasp the changing, real moment, the rational analysis of the whole, an untiring activity of the will, continued

[4] *Dō* of *dōri* is the Chinese character Tao,[ad] and *ri*[ae] is the reason or law of things. Professor Wing-tsit Chan defines the character *ri* (read *li* in Chinese pronunciation) most aptly, as follows: "*li* has come to mean the form, texture, quality, or nature of things, and acquires the meaning of the reason or the law of a thing or things." (*Philosophy East and West,* IV, No. 4 [January, 1955], 328). Chan is also in agreement with Joseph Needham's interpretation of *li* as "organization" and "principle of organization." In Japan, to give two illustrations: the famous historian, Kitabatake Chikafusa[af] (1293–1354), author of *Jinnō Shōtōki*[ag] (or "The Records of the Legitimate Succession of the Divine Sovereigns"), used *dōri* as the basic concept in formulating his philosophy of history; and, in the contemporary age, Dr. Amano Teiyū,[ah] a colleague of Nishida[ai] at Kyoto University and one-time Minister of Education, used this as the main theme in the book entitled *Dōri no Kankaku*[aj] ("The Sense of Reason"). "*Dōri*" was a word of common use among all Buddhist scholars of those days, not to mention Hōnen, Shinran, Dōgen, Nichiren, etc.

with fortitude and perseverance is of absolute necessity. The Middle Way is such a practical principle of synthesis.

Non-duality (*advaya*) is the rejection of opposites and contradictory viewpoints, but it is also a rejection of nihilistic negation. This "no-position" is called Voidness (*śūnyatā*), but this is not nihilism. This is a dynamic principle of life which permits a becoming of infinite progression. Non-duality is so called because it negates the pairs of opposites, but the opposites themselves are also in infinite progression; and, therefore, though it is a function of the process of negation, there are involved comparison, measurement, elimination, abstraction, postulation, and universalization.

Non-duality is not the name for mere intuition, because it is vital not to become attached to intuition itself. Since there is this comprehensive and total aspect to the Middle Way, Non-duality, and Voidness, they are sometimes termed "inexpressible," and yet none is absolutism. This is the most important point and vital thing to remember. The rational process involved in reaching the principle of Non-duality is indicated by Shinran's enumeration of 48 pairs of opposites; abrupt and gradual, horizontal and vertical, superior and inferior, pure and mixed, straightway and roundabout, rational and non-rational, unbroken and broken, continuation and non-continuation, one's own will and following another's will, transference and non-transference, self-power and other-power, etc. In the *Sūtra of Wei Lang*,[v] thirty-six pairs of opposites are enumerated.[5] Thus, Shinran followed the basic stream of Buddhist thinking on *Dharmatā*, Middle Way, and Non-duality.

Dōgen speaks of the non-duality of practice and *satori*, and he dedicated his life to seeking the true philosophical meaning of *Dharmatā*.

Shinran, though he relentlessly sought the good, had a deep insight into the existential evil of man's nature. Consequently his exposition of *dharmatā-yukti* has a strong tinge of religious practice and vow; whereas Dōgen pushed toward the living realization of *dharmatā*, the true nature of things, and engraved a philosophical poem in the realm of truth to be remembered as a poet-philosopher. The former is spiritual in its realistic faith; and the latter philosophical in its realized actuality. Both, however, are rational in their understanding of *dharmatā-yukti*, and both touch the aesthetic sense of reality.

Dr. Suzuki has expounded the intuition of Rinzai Zen for many years, but the philosophical, rational thought of Shinran and Dōgen await interpreters for the West.[6]

In conclusion, my point is that, although there has not been a rational *system* of philosophy and science in Japan as in the West, nevertheless, it is true that the Japanese mind has been trained in *rational thinking* by Buddhism for many centuries.

(The Chinese characters for this article are on the following page.)

[5] See Christmas Humphreys, *Studies in the Middle Way* (London: Luzac & Company, 1948), p. 90.
[6] The Sōtō Zen sect, founded by Dōgen, supports the Komazawa Buddhist University in Tokyo.

[a] 湯川秀樹
[b] 宮本正尊
[c] 法眼
[d] 狩野元信
[e] 悟
[f] 法明院
[g] 三井寺
[h] 天台宗
[i] 眞言宗
[j] 法然
[k] 親鸞
[l] 道元
[m] 日蓮
[n] 野口英世
[o] 臨濟宗
[p] 曹洞宗
[q] 眞宗
[r] 道理
[s] 華嚴宗
[t] 法爾道理
[u] 自然法爾章
[v] 六祖大師法寶壇經
[w] 富田
[x] 堀岡智明
[y] 狩野芳崖
[z] 橋本雅邦
[aa] 岡倉覺三
[ab] 下村觀山
[ac] 横山大觀
[ad] 道
[ae] 理
[af] 北畠親房
[ag] 神皇正統記
[ah] 天野貞祐
[ai] 西田幾多郎
[aj] 道理の感覺

HU SHIH[a]

The Scientific Spirit and Method in Chinese Philosophy

I.

In the course of the past conferences on East-West philosophy, the question has been raised as to whether there was science in the East, and why the East developed little or no science.

To the first question, some of the answers seem definitely in the negative. "So the West generated the natural sciences, as the East did not," said Professor Wilmon Henry Sheldon.[1] And Professor Filmer S. C. Northrop said, "there is very little science [in the East] beyond the most obvious and elementary information of the natural history type."[2]

To the second question as to why there was very little or no science in the East, the answers vary. But the most challenging and provocative answer has come from Northrop, who declares, "A culture which admits only concepts by intuition is automatically prevented from developing science of the Western type beyond the most elementary, inductive, natural history stage."[3] As defined by Northrop, concepts by intuition are those "which denote, and the complete meaning of which is given by, something which is immediately apprehended."[4] This is Northrop's theory:

> Formal reasoning and deductive science are not necessary if only concepts by intuition are used in a given culture. If what science and philosophy attempt to designate is immediately apprehended, then obviously all that one

[1] "Main Contrasts Between Eastern and Western Philosophy," in Charles A. Moore, ed., *Essays in East-West Philosophy* (Honolulu: University of Hawaii Press, 1951), p. 291.
[2] "The Complementary Emphases of Eastern Intuitive and Western Scientific Philosophy," in Charles A. Moore, ed., *Philosophy—East and West* (Princeton: Princeton University Press, 1944), p. 212.
[3] *Ibid.*
[4] *Ibid.*, p. 173.

has to do in order to know it is to observe and contemplate it. The methods of intuition and contemplation become the sole trustworthy modes of inquiry. It is precisely this which the East affirms and precisely why its science has never progressed for long beyond the initial natural history stage of development to which concepts by intuition restrict one.[5]

This theory is concisely expressed in these words: "The East used doctrine built out of concepts by intuition, whereas Western doctrine has tended to be constructed out of concepts by postulation."[6]

I have no intention to go into the details of this Northropean theory, which must have been familiar to us who have followed our philosopher-friend all these 20 years.

I only wish to point out that this theory of bifurcation of East and West is unhistorical and untrue as far as the intellectual history of the East is concerned.

In the first place, there is no race or culture "which admits only concepts by intuition." Indeed, there is no man who "admits only concepts by intuition." Man is by nature a thinking animal, whose daily practical needs compel him to make inferences for better or for worse, and he often learns to make better and surer inferences. It has been truly said that inference is the business man never ceases to engage in. And, in making inferences, man must make use of all his powers of perception, observation, imagination, generalization and postulation, induction and deduction. In that way, man develops his common sense, his stock of empirical knowledge, his wisdom, his civilization and culture. And, in the few centers of continuous intellectual and cultural tradition, man of the East and of the West, in the course of time, has developed his science, religion, and philosophy. I repeat, there is no culture "which admits only (the so-called) concepts by intuition," and which "is automatically prevented from developing science of the Western type."

In the second place, I wish to point out that, in attempting to understand the East and the West, what is needed is a historical approach, a historical attitude of mind, rather than a "technical terminology for comparative philosophy." Northrop includes among his examples of "concepts by postulation" these items: Centaurs,[7] the opening sentence of the Fourth Gospel, the concept of God the father, the Christianity of St. Paul, of St. Augustine, and St. Thomas Aquinas,[8] as well as the atoms of Democritus, the atomic models of Bohr's and Rutherford's classical atomic physics,[9] and the space-time continuum of Einstein's physics.[10] Surely, one can find a thousand imaginary concepts in the mythological and religious literature of India and China that can compare with the Greek concept of "Centaurs." And, surely, one can point to many scores of religious ideas in India and China that can compare

[5] *Ibid.*, p. 223.
[6] F. S. C. Northrop, *The Meeting of East and West* (New York: The Macmillan Co., 1946), p. 448.
[7] *Philosophy—East and West*, p. 183.
[8] *Ibid.*, p. 216.
[9] *Ibid.*, p. 183.
[10] *Ibid.*, p. 185.

with the concept of God contained in the first sentence of the Fourth Gospel.[11] Are we not justified in calling a halt to such "bifurcating" terminology, which tends to emphasize a difference between East and West which historically does not exist?

I would like very much, therefore, to present here what I mean by the historical approach to the comparative study of philosophy. Briefly, the historical approach means that all past differences in the intellectual, philosophical, and religious activities of man, East and West, have been *historical* differences, produced, conditioned, shaped, grooved, and often seemingly perpetuated by geographical, climatic, economic, social and political, and even individual or biographical factors, all of which are capable of being studied and understood historically, rationally, and intelligently. Through this historical approach, patient and fruitful studies and researches can then be conducted, always seeking to be understood, never merely to laugh, or to cry, or to despair. It may be that, through this historical approach, we may find that, after all, there are more similarities than differences in the philosophies and religions of East and West; and that whatever striking differences have existed are no more than differences in the degree of emphasis brought about by a peculiar combination of historical factors. It may be that, through this historical approach, we may better understand the rise and rapid development of what has been called "science of the Western type"—not as an isolated or exclusive creation of any chosen people, but only as the natural product of an unusually happy combination of many historical forces. It may be that, as a result of patient historical researches, we may better understand that none of those historical forces, nor a combination of them, will ever "automatically prevent" or permanently incapacitate any race or culture from learning, adopting, developing—and even excelling in—the intellectual activities historically initiated and developed by any other race.

To say that any culture "is automatically prevented from developing science of the Western type" is to despair prematurely. But to seek to understand what historical forces have conspired to give the nations of Europe the glory of leading the entire world by at least fully four hundred years in the development of modern science, and, on the other hand, what other historical forces or what combinations of such forces have been largely responsible for retarding or even crushing such scientific development by any race or culture throughout historic times, not excepting the Graeco-Roman-Christian culture throughout the Middle Ages—that would be a legitimate ambition not unworthy of such a learned assembly of philosophers and historians of philosophy.

[11] Northrop may be interested to know that the *"Logos"* in the opening sentence of the Fourth Gospel has been translated "Tao"—the same Tao as appears in the first sentence of the *Lao Tzu* (*Tao-te ching*). A scholar trained in modern linguistics will probably translate *"logos"* as *"ming"* (the Word)—the same *"ming"* which appears in the second sentence of the *Lao Tzu* and which is erroneously translated as "the name," as quoted by Northrop. *Ibid.*, p. 204.

II.

It is in the direction of suggesting some such a historical approach to comparative philosophy that I have prepared this paper with the rather immodest title: "The Scientific Spirit and Method in Chinese Philosophy."

I have deliberately left out the scientific *content* of Chinese philosophy, not merely for the obvious reason that that content seems so insignificant compared with the achievement of Western science in the last four centuries, but also because I am of the opinion that, in the historical development of science, the scientific spirit or attitude of mind and the scientific method are of far more primary importance than any practical or empirical results of the astronomer, the calendar-reformer, the alchemist, the physician, or the horticulturist.

This point of view has been eloquently presented by Dr. James B. Conant, former President of Harvard University, and a first-rank scientist in his own right, in his Lectures, *On Understanding Science.* Let me, therefore, quote him:

> Who were the precursors of those early investigators who in the sixteenth and seventeenth centuries set the standards for exact and impartial inquiries? Who were the spiritual ancestors of Copernicus, Galileo and Vesalius? Not the casual experimenter or the artful contrivers of new mechanical devices who gradually increased our empirical knowledge of physics and chemistry during the Middle Ages. These men passed on to subsequent generations many facts and valuable methods of attaining practical ends but not the spirit of scientific inquiry.
>
> For the burst of new ardor in disciplined intellectual inquiry we must turn to a few minds steeped in the Socratic tradition, and to those early scholars who first recaptured the culture of Greece and Rome by primitive methods of archaeology. In the first period of the Renaissance, the love of dispassionate search for the truth was carried forward by those who were concerned with man and his works rather than with inanimate or animate nature. During the Middle Ages, interest in attempts to use the human reason critically and without prejudice, to probe deeply without fear and favor, was kept alive by those who wrote about human problems. In the early days of the Revival of Learning, it was the humanist's exploration of antiquity that came nearest to exemplifying our modern ideas of impartial inquiry....
>
> Petrarch, Boccaccio, Machiavelli, and Erasmus, far more than the Alchemists, must be considered the precursors of the modern scientific investigator. Likewise, Rabelais and Montaigne who carried forward the critical philosophic spirit must be counted, it seems to me, among the forerunners of the modern scientists.[12]

I believe that the position taken by President Conant is essentially correct. It is interesting to note that he gave his lectures a sub-title: "An Historical Approach."

[12] James B. Conant, *On Understanding Science* (New York: Mentor Books, 1951), pp. 23–24. See also, Conant, *Science and Common Sense* (New Haven: Yale University Press, 1951), pp. 10–13.

From this historical standpoint, "the love of dispassionate search for the truth," the "interest in attempts to use the human reason critically and without prejudice, to probe deeply without fear and favor," "the ardor in disciplined intellectual inquiry," "the setting of standards for exact and impartial inquiry"—these are characteristics of the spirit and method of scientific inquiry. It is these aspects of the scientific spirit and method, as they are found in the intellectual and philosophical history of China, that shall form the main body of my paper.

III.

To begin with, there was undoubtedly a "Socratic tradition" in the intellectual heritage of ancient China. The tradition of free question and answer, of free discussion, independent thinking, and doubting, and of eager and dispassionate search for knowledge was maintained in the school of Confucius (551–479 B.C.). Confucius often described himself as one who "learns without satiety and teaches without being wearied," and as one who "loves antiquity and is earnest in seeking to know it."* On one occasion, he spoke of himself as one "who is so eager to know that he forgets to eat, whose cares are lost in moments of rapturous triumph, unmindful of the coming of old age."

That was the man who founded and molded the orthodoxy of the Chinese intellectual life of the past twenty-five centuries. There was much in Confucius that reminds us of Socrates. Like Socrates, Confucius always professed that he was not a "wise man" but a man who loved knowledge. He said: "He who knows does not rank with him who loves knowledge; and he who loves knowledge does not rank with him who really delights in it."

An interesting feature in the Confucian tradition is a deliberate encouragement of independent thinking and doubt. Thus Confucius spoke of his most gifted student, Yen Hui,[b] "Hui is no help to me: he is always satisfied with what I say." But he also said, "I often talk to Hui for a whole day, and he, like a dullard, never raises an objection. But when he is gone and I examine his private life, I find him fully capable of developing [my ideas]. Hui is no dullard." Confucius apparently wanted no docile disciples who would feel pleased with everything he said. He wanted to encourage them to doubt and raise objections. This spirit of doubt and questioning was best shown in Mencius, who openly declared that to accept the whole *Book of History* as trustworthy is worse than to have no *Book of History* at all, and that, of the book *Wu-ch'eng*[c] (a section of the *Book of History*), he would accept no more than two or three (bamboo) pages. Mencius also suggested a free and independent attitude of mind as a necessary prerequisite to the understanding of the *Book of Odes* (*Shih ching*[d]).

* Editor's note: Because of two serious illnesses which have hospitalized and incapacitated Dr. Hu for several months (he is now recuperating) it has been impossible to provide complete references for some of his quotations from classical texts.

The best-known Confucian dictum is: "Learning without thinking is labor lost; thinking without learning is perilous." He himself, however, seemed to be always inclined to the side of learning. He said of himself: "I have often spent a whole day without food and a whole night without sleep—to think. But it was of no use. It is better to study." "Study as if life were too short and you were on the point of missing it." "He who learns the truth in the morning, may die in the evening without regret." That was China's Socratic tradition.

Intellectual honesty was an important part of this tradition. "Yu," said Confucius to one of his students, "shall I tell you what knowledge is? To hold that you know a thing when you know it, and to hold that you do not know when you really do not know: that is knowledge." When on another occasion the same student asked Confucius how to serve the spirits and the gods, Confucius said, "We have not yet learned to serve men, how can we serve the spirits?" The questioner then asked about death, and the Master said, "We do not yet know life, how do we know death?" This was not evading the questions; it was an injunction to be intellectually honest about things one does not really know. Such an agnostic position about death and the gods and spirits has had lasting influence on Chinese thought in subsequent ages. That, too, was China's Socratic tradition.

In recent decades, doubt has been raised about the historicity of the man Lao Tzu,[e] or Lao Tan,[f] and about the authenticity and the dating of the ancient book known as the *Book of Lao Tzu*. But I, for one, still believe that Confucius was at one time a student of and apprentice to the older philosopher, Lao Tzu, whose influence in the direction of a naturalistic conception of the universe and of a *laissez-faire* (*wu-wei*[g]) philosophy of government can be observed in the thinking of Confucius himself.

To have postulated a naturalistic view of the universe at so early a date (the sixth century B.C.) was a truly revolutionary act. The ancient Chinese notion of *T'ien*[h] (Heaven) or *Ti*[i] (Supreme God), as represented in the songs and hymns of the *Book of Odes*, was that of a knowing, feeling, loving, and hating supreme ruler of men and the universe. And the fate of men was also supposed to be in the hands of all kinds of gods and spirits. In place of such an anthropomorphic deity or deities, an entirely new philosophic concept was proposed.

> *There is something of indeterminate origin,*
> *And born before heaven and earth.*
> *Without voice and without body,*
> *It stands alone and does not change;*
> *It moves everywhere but is never exhausted.*
> *It may be regarded as the mother of the universe.*
> *I do not know its name:*
> *I call it "the Way"* (Tao[j]),
> *And perforce designate it "the Great"* (ta[k]).

So the new principle was postulated as the Way (Tao), that is, a process, an all-pervading and everlasting process. The Way becomes so of itself (*tzu-jan*[l]), and all things become so of themselves.

"The Way (Tao) does nothing, yet it leaves nothing undone." That is the central idea of this naturalistic conception of the universe. It became the cornerstone of a political theory of non-activity, non-interference, *laissez faire* (*wu-wei*). "The best ruler is one whose existence is scarcely noticed by the people." And the same idea was developed into a moral philosophy of humility, of non-resistance to evil and violence. "The supreme good is likened to water which benefits all things and resists none." "The weak and yielding always wins over the hard and strong." "There is always the Great Executioner that executes. [That is the great Way, which does nothing but leaves nothing undone.] To do the executing for the Great Executioner is like doing the chopping for the master carpenter. He who does the chopping for the master carpenter rarely escapes injuring his own hand."

Such was the naturalistic tradition formed by Lao Tzu, the teacher of Confucius. But there was a fundamental difference between the teacher and his student. Confucius was a historically minded scholar and a great teacher and educator, whereas Lao Tzu was a nihilist in his conception of knowledge and civilization. The ideal utopia of Lao Tzu was a small State with a small population, where all the inventions of civilization, such as ships carriages "which multiplied human power by ten times and a hundred times are not to be put in use; and where the people would restore the use of knotted cords instead of writing!" "Always let the people have no knowledge, and therefore no desires." How different is this intellectual nihilism from Confucius' democratic philosophy of education, which says, "With education there will be no classes!"

But the naturalistic conception of the universe, as it was germinated in the *Book of Lao Tzu* and more fully developed in subsequent centuries, has been a most important philosophical heritage from the Classical Age. Naturalism itself best exemplifies the spirit of courageous doubt and constructive postulation. Its historical importance fully equals that of the humanist heritage left by Confucius. Whenever China had sunk deep into irrationality, superstition, and otherworldliness, as she has done several times in her long history, it was always the naturalism of Lao Tzu and the philosophical Taoists, or the humanism of Confucius, or a combination of the two, that would arise and try to rescue her from her sluggish slumbers.

The first great movement "to use the human reason critically and to probe deeply without fear and favor" in the face of the State Religion of the Han Empire was such a combination of the naturalistic philosophy of Taoism and the spirit of doubt and intellectual honesty that was the most valuable heritage handed down from Confucius and Mencius. The greatest representative of that movement of criticism was Wang Ch'ung[m] (A.D. 27–*ca.* 100), author of a book of 85 essays called *Lun-heng*,[n] "Essays in Criticism."

Wang Ch'ung spoke of his own essays in these words, "One sentence sums up my essays: I hate falsehood." "Right is made to appear wrong, and falsehood is regarded as truth. How can I remain silent! . . . When I read current books of this kind, when I see truth overshadowed by falsehood, my heart beats violently, and my brush trembles in my hand. How can I be silent! When I criticize them, I examine them in my reasoning power, check them against facts, and show up their falsehood by setting up proofs."[13]

He was criticizing the superstitions and falsehoods of his age, of which the greatest and most powerful were the central doctrines of Catastrophes (*tsai*[o]) and Anomalies (*i*[p]), which the State Religion of the Han Empire, under the name of Confucianism, interpreted as warnings sent by a benevolent and all-seeing God (*T'ien*) to terrify the rulers and governments so that they might repent and reform their acts of misrule. This religion of Han Confucianism had been formulated by a number of philosopher-statesmen of the second and first centuries B.C., who were justifiably worried by the real problem of how to deal with the unlimited power of the absolute monarchy in a vast unified empire, and who, consciously or semiconsciously, had hit upon the religious weapon and had worked out an elaborate theology of "reciprocal relationship between Heaven (*T'ien*) and the rulers of men" which seemed to have been able to hold the absolute sovereigns in awe throughout the several centuries of the Han dynasties.

This theology of the State Religion of catastrophes and anomalies was best expressed by Tung Chung-shu[q] (*ca.* 179–*ca.* 104 B.C.), who spoke like a prophet and with authority: "The action of man, when it reaches the highest level of good and evil [that is, when it becomes government action affecting vast numbers], will flow into the course of Heaven and Earth and cause reciprocal reverberations in their manifestations." "When a State is on the verge of ruin, Heaven will cause catastrophes [such as floods, famines, great fires] to befall earth as warnings to the ruler. When these are not hearkened to, Heaven will cause strange anomalies [such as sun eclipses, comets, unusual movements of planets] to appear to terrify the ruler into repentance. But, when even these anomalies fail to check his misrule, then ruin will come. All this shows that Heaven is always kind to the ruler and anxious to protect him from destruction." This theology of intimate reciprocal reverberations between Heaven and the rulers of men was supposedly based on an elaborate interpretation of the pre-Confucian *Book of History* and the Confucian *Ch'un-ch'iu*[r] Annals (*Spring and Autumn Annals,* which recorded numerous unusual events on earth and in the heavens, including thirty-six eclipses of the sun and five earthquakes between 722 and 481 B.C.). But the canonical Classics of established Confucianism were not enough for the support of this fanatic and fantastic theology, which had to be reinforced by an ever-increasing crop of apocryphal works known as the *wei*[s] (woofs or interweaving aids to the Canon) and the *ch'an*[t] (prophecies), which are collections of bits of

[13] *Lun Heng,* chap. 24.

empirical knowledge intermixed with hundreds of astrological fantasies.

It is a historical fact that this State Religion of pseudo-Confucianism, at the height of its glory, was taken so seriously that many a Prime Minister was dismissed and one was forced by the Emperor to commit suicide, all because of the belief in Heaven's warning in the form of catastrophes and abnormalities. One of the three great medieval religions was in full sway over the empire.

It was against the basic idea of a reciprocal responsive relationship between a teleological God and the rulers of men that Wang Ch'ung was directing his main criticism. He was criticizing the theology of the established religion of the empire. The world view with which he set out to attack the current theology was the naturalistic philosophy of Lao Tzu and the Taoists. He said:

> The Way Tao of Heaven is that it does nothing and all things become so by themselves. If Heaven were to give warnings to men or mete out punishments, that would be "doing" things and not things "becoming so of themselves." . . . Those who hold that catastrophic and abnormal occurrences were purposeful warnings from Heaven are in reality degrading the dignity of the great Heaven by interpreting natural phenomena in terms of human action. They are therefore not convincing at all.[14]

For, he pointed out,

> Heaven is most exalted, and man is tiny. Man's place between heaven and earth is like that of a flea inside one's clothes, or that of an ant in an anthill. . . . Surely it is absolutely impossible for man with his tiny body of seven feet to hope to bring about any response from the vast atmosphere of the great firmament.[15]

That is why Wang Ch'ung said that the doctrine of reciprocal response between Heaven and man was in reality "degrading the dignity of the great Heaven."

And he offered to prove that man and all things in the universe were *never purposefully* (*ku*[u]) produced by Heaven and Earth, but were *accidentally* (*ngou, ou*[v]) so, of themselves:

> It is wrong to hold that man is born of Heaven and Earth purposely. Certain fluids are combined, and man is born accidentally. . . . All things are formed of fluid (*ch'i*[w]), and each species reproduces itself. . . . If it were true that Heaven purposely produced all living things in the world, then Heaven should make them all love each other and not allow them to injure or prey on each other. . . . But there are tigers and wolves, poisonous snakes and insects, which prey on man. Can we say that it is the purpose of Heaven to create man for the use of those ferocious and poisonous animals?[16]

[14] *Ibid.*, chap. 42.
[15] *Ibid.*, chap. 43.
[16] *Ibid.*, chap. 14.

The first century of the Christian era was a period of calendar reform under the Han Empire. And Wang Ch'ung made full use of the astronomical knowledge of his age to expose the folly of the current theological doctrine of catastrophes and anomalies as warnings from Heaven against the evil acts or policies of the rulers of the empire. He said:

There is one eclipse of the sun in about forty-one or forty-two months, and there is one eclipse of the moon in about six months. Solar and lunar eclipses are regular occurrences which have nothing to do with government policies. And this is true of the hundreds of anomalies and thousands of calamities, none of which is necessarily caused by the action of the rulers of men.[17]

But Wang Ch'ung more frequently cited facts of everyday experience as proofs or evidences in his numerous criticisms of the superstitions or falsehoods of his age. He offered five "tests" (*nien*[x]) to prove that thunder was not the wrath of Heaven but only a kind of fire generated by the friction of the *yin*[y] and *yang*[z] fluids in the air. And he produced many a proof to support his thesis that there were no ghosts or spirits. One of those proofs is most ingenious and so far irrefutable: "If a ghost is the spirit of the dead man, then the ghost should be seen only in naked form and could not be seen with clothes on his body. For surely the cloth or silk can have no soul or spirit to survive destruction. How can it be explained that ghosts have never been seen in naked form, but always with clothes on?"[18]

So much for my favorite philosopher, Wang Ch'ung. I have told his story to show how the spirit of courageous doubt and intellectual honesty of the Classical Age of Chinese philosophy could survive centuries of oblivion and would arise to carry on the fight of human reason against ignorance and falsehood, of creative doubt and constructive criticism against superstition and blind authority. To dare to doubt and question without fear and favor is the spirit of science. "To check falsehoods against facts and to expose them by setting up proofs" constitute the procedure of science.

IV.

The rest of my paper will be devoted to a brief interpretative report on a great movement in the history of Chinese thought which started out with the ambitious slogan of "investigation of the reason of all things and extension of human knowledge to the utmost" but which ended in improving and perfecting a critical method of historical research and thereby opening up a new age of revival of classical learning.

That great movement has been called the Neo-Confucian movement, because it was a conscious movement to revive the thought and culture of pre-Buddhist China, to go back directly to the humanist teaching of Confucius and his school, in order to overthrow and replace the much Indianized, and therefore un-

[17] *Ibid.*, chap. 53.
[18] *Ibid.*, chap. 62.

Chinese, thought and culture of medieval China. It was essentially a Confucian movement, but it must be noted that the Neo-Confucian philosophers frankly accepted a naturalistic cosmology which was at least partially of Taoist origin and which was preferred probably because it was considered to be more acceptable than the theological and teleological cosmology of the "Confucian" religion since the Han Dynasty (206 B.C.–A.D. 220). Here was another case of a combination of the naturalism of Lao Tzu and the philosophical Taoists and the humanism of Confucius once more rising in protest and rebellion against what were considered as the un-Chinese otherworldly religions of medieval China.

This new Confucian movement needed a new logical method, a *"novum organum,"* which it found in a little essay of post-Confucian origin entitled the *Great Learning,* an essay of about 1,700 Chinese characters. From that little essay, the founders of Neo-Confucianism picked out one statement which they understood to mean that "the extension of knowledge lies in the investigation of things." That soon became one of the central doctrines in the philosophy of the school of the Ch'eng brothers (Ch'eng Hao,[aa] also called Ch'eng Ming-tao, 1032–1085, and Ch'eng I,[ab] also called Ch'eng I-ch'uan, 1033–1107), especially as that philosophy was interpreted and reorganized by the great Chu Hsi[ac] (1130–1200). The investigation of things was further interpreted to mean "seeking exhaustively to investigate the reason (*li*[ad]) in all things."

What are "things"? According to the Ch'eng-Chu school, the scope of "things" was as extensive as Nature itself, including "every grass and every shrub" as well as "the height of the heavens and the thickness of the earth." But such a conception of the "things" to be investigated was beyond the capability of the philosophers, who were men of affairs and politicians as well as thinkers and teachers of men. They were more vitally interested in the moral and political problems of men than in the investigation of the reason or law in every grass or shrub. So Ch'eng I himself began to narrow down the scope of "things" to three categories: the study of books, the study of men of the past and the present, and the study of what is right in dealing with practical affairs. "Always begin with what is nearest to you," he said. And Chu Hsi, the greatest of the Sung philosophers and the most eloquent and untiring exponent of the philosophy of the investigation of the reason in all things, devoted his whole life to the study and exposition of the Classics of Confucianism. His Commentary on the *Four Books* (the "New Testament" of Neo-Confucianism) and his Commentaries on the *Book of Odes* and the *Book of Changes* were accepted as the standard texts for seven centuries. The philosophy of the investigation of the reason in all things was now definitely applied to the limited field of classical studies.

Truly inspired by the "Socratic tradition" of Confucius, Chu Hsi worked out a set of principles on the spirit, the method, and the procedure of investigation and research. He said, "Investigate with an open mind. Try to see the reason (*li*) with an open mind. And with an open mind follow reason wherever it leads you." What is an open mind? Chu Hsi said, "Retreat one step back, and think it over: that is the open mind." "Do not press your own opinion too much forward. Suppose you put your own opinion aside for a while, and try to see what the other side has to say. Just as in hearing a case of litigation, the mind is sometimes prejudiced in favor of A, and you are inclined to seek evidences against his opponent B, or vice versa. It is better to step aside and calmly and slowly study what both sides have to say. Only when you can step aside can you see things more clearly. The Master Chang Tsai[ae] (also called Chang Heng-ch'ü, 1020–1077) said: 'Wash away your old ideas to let new ideas come in.' If you do not put aside your preconceived notions, where and how can you get new ideas?"

The Neo-Confucians of the eleventh century had often stressed the importance of doubt in thinking. Chang Tsai had said, "The student must first learn to be able to doubt. If he can find doubt where no doubt was found before, then he is making progress." As an experienced worker in textual and semantic researches, Chu Hsi was able to develop a more practical and constructive methodology out of the idea of doubt. He realized that doubt did not arise of itself, but would come only when a situation of perplexity or difficulty was present. He said: "I used to tell students to think and to seek points of doubt. But I have come to understand that it is not fruitful to start out with the intention to find things to doubt. Just study with an open mind. After working hard at a text, there will be places which block your path and cause you perplexity. That's where doubts naturally come up for you to compare, to weigh, to ponder over." "The student [as it has been said] should learn to find doubt where no doubt had previously existed, but he should also learn to resolve the doubt after it has arisen. Then he is making real progress."

Doubt would arise in a situation in which conflicting theories simultaneously claimed credulity and acceptance. Chu Hsi told of his early doubts when he found "the same passage in the *Analects* had been given widely different explanations by various commentators." "That," said he, "led me to doubt." How is doubt to be resolved? "By keeping one's mind open," he said. "You may have your own view, but it may not be the correct view. Do not hold it dogmatically. Put it aside for a while, and search for more and more instances to be placed side by side, so that they may be compared. Then you may see through and understand." In one of his letters to his friend and philosophical opponent, Lu Chiu-yüan[af] (also called Lu Hsiang-shan, 1139–1193), he again used the example of the judge trying a case of litigation: "Just like the judge trying a difficult case, one should keep his mind open and impartial, and must not let his own inclination or disinclination influence his thinking. He can then carefully listen to the pleading of both sides, seek evidences for cross-checking, and arrive at a correct judgment of right and wrong."

What Chu Hsi was saying amounts to a method of resolving doubt by first suggesting a hypothetical view and then searching for more instances or evidences for comparison and for checking the hypothesis "which may not be correct" and which Chu Hsi sometimes described as "a temporarily formed doubting thesis" (*ch'üan-li i-i*[ag]). In short, the method of doubt and resolution of doubt was the method of hypothesis and verification by evidence.

Chu Hsi told his students: "The trouble with you is that you are not capable of doubting; that's why you do not make progress. As for myself, I have my doubt even in the least significant matters. As soon as one begins to doubt, one has to go on [thinking] until the doubt is completely resolved."

It was because of this inner urge to resolve doubts that Chu Hsi often confessed that, from his younger years on, he was fond of making investigations based on evidences (*k'ao-cheng*[ah]). He was one of the most brilliant minds in human history, yet he was never tired of hard work and patient researches.

His great achievement lies in two directions. In the first place, he was never tired of preaching the importance of doubt in thinking and investigation—doubt in the sense of a "tentatively formed doubting thesis," doubt, not as an end in itself, but as a perplexity to be overcome, as a puzzling problem to be solved, as a challenge to be satisfactorily met. In the second place, he had the courage to apply this technique of doubt and resolution of doubt to the major Classics of the Confucian Canon, thereby opening up a new era of classical scholarship which did not attain its full development until many centuries after his death.

He did not produce a commentary on the *Book of History,* but he made epoch-making contributions to the study of that classic by his great courage to doubt the authenticity of its so-called "ancient-script" portion consisting of 25 books which were apparently unknown to the classical scholars of the Han Dynasty, but which seemed first to appear in the fourth century A.D., and came to be accepted as an integral part of the *Book of History* after the seventh century. The 28 (actually 29) books that were officially recognized in the Doctors' College of the Han Empire had been transmitted orally through an old scholar, Fu[ai] (who survived the book-burning of 213 B.C.), and had been transcribed in the "modern script" of the second century B.C.

Chu Hsi started out with a great doubt: "There are two distinct languages in these books—some of them are difficult to read and understand, others can be read and understood quite easily. It is very strange that the books which were transmitted from memory by the old scholar Fu are all hard to read, whereas the other books, which made their appearance much later, should all turn out to be quite easy to understand. How can we explain the strange fact that the old scholar Fu could memorize only those most difficult texts but could not transmit those that are so easy to read?"

In his *Chu Tzu yü-lei*[aj] ("Classified Sayings"), he kept repeating this great doubt to every student who asked him about the *Book of History.*[19] "All the books easy to understand are the 'ancient-script' texts; all those most difficult to read are the 'modern-script' texts." Chu Hsi did not openly say that the former group of texts were later forgeries. He merely wanted to impress upon his students this most puzzling linguistic distinction. Sometimes he suggested

[19] Chap. 78.

a very mild explanation to the effect that those books most difficult to read probably represented the language actually spoken to the people in those public proclamations, whereas the books easy to read were the work of official historians who probably did some revising or even rewriting.

Naturally such a mild theory did not explain away the doubt which, once raised, has persisted for many centuries to plague classical scholars.

A century later, under the Mongol (Yüan) Dynasty (1279–1368), Wu Ch'eng[ak] (1247–1331) took up Chu Hsi's challenge and drew the logical conclusion that the so-called "ancient-script" books were not genuine parts of the *Book of History*, but were forgeries of a much later age. So, Wu Ch'eng, in writing a Commentary on that classic, accepted only 28 "modern-script" books, and excluded the 25 "ancient-script" books.

In the sixteenth century, another scholar, Mei Tsu,[al] also took up the question, and published in 1543 a book to prove that the "ancient-script" portion of the *Book of History* was a forgery by a fourth-century writer, who apparently based his forgeries on the numerous passages found in ancient works wherein specific titles of "lost" books were mentioned as sources of the quotations. And Mei Tsu took the trouble to check the sources of those quotations which formed the kernel of the forged books.

But it took another and greater scholar of the seventeenth century, Yen Jo-chü[am] (1636–1704), to put a finishing touch to the task of resolving the doubt raised by Chu Hsi in the twelfth century about the "ancient-script" portion of the *Book of History*. Yen devoted thirty years to the writing of a great book entitled "Inquiry into the Authenticity of the Ancient-Script Portion of the *Book of History*." With his wonderful memory and great learning, Yen proved these books to be deliberate forgeries by tracing almost every sentence in them to its source and by showing how the forger had misquoted or misunderstood the meaning of the original passages. Altogether, Yen offered over a hundred proofs to expose the forgery. Although his views were vehemently attacked by conservative scholars of his day, it is now considered that Yen Jo-chü's book has convincingly rendered a final verdict, and that nearly one-half of a major book of the Confucian Canon, which had been accepted as sacred scripture for a thousand years, must be recognized as a proven forgery.

And for this intellectual revolution of no small magnitude credit must be given to our philosopher Chu Hsi, who in the twelfth century expressed a courageous doubt and proposed a meaningful question which he himself was not yet fully prepared to answer.

Chu Hsi's treatment of the *I-ching*[an] *(Book of Changes)*, another of the "sacred scriptures," was even more daring, so daring indeed that it was never accepted and developed during the last seven centuries.

He published a Commentary on the *I-ching* and a little book entitled "A Primer on the Study of the *I-ching*." And he left a number of letters and discussions on that classic.[20]

[20] *Ibid.*, chaps. 66–67.

His most daring thesis about the *I-ching* was that that book, which had always been regarded as a sacred book of profound philosophical truth, was originally devised as a text of divination and fortune-telling, and could be understood only if it were studied as a book of divination and *no more than a book of divination.* "The sentences or judgments for every *kua*[ao] (hexagram), of which there were 64, and every line (of which there were 384) were meant to be used as answers to people who wanted to know whether it was propitious to do such-and-such a thing or not. Some answers were for sacrifices, others for hunting, others for traveling, or for war, or emigration. If the sages had intended to talk about philosophy, why should they not simply write a philosophy book; why should they talk always in terms of fortune-telling?" "If the book is studied merely as a text for the diviner, then so many passages which had been wrongly explained as mysterious and profound wisdom immediately become quite plain, simple, and intelligible."

This common-sense theory was the most courageous doubt ever uttered about that strange book. But it was rejected by his friends as an "oversimplification." But Chu Hsi replied: "It is just like this big lantern. Every strip of bamboo added to the lantern frame simply takes away that much of the light. If we could only get rid of all those light-covering devices, how much more light would there be, and how much better it would be for all of us!"

That was a truly revolutionary theory which illustrates one of his great remarks that "the simplest theory is usually the true theory." But Chu Hsi realized that his view of the *I-ching* as nothing more than a text for divination was too radical for his time. He sadly said, "It is difficult to talk to people about this theory. They would not believe it. Many distinguished people have argued so vehemently against me, and I have spent so much energy to explain and analyze my view to them. As I now look back, it is better to say nothing more. I shall leave it here, regardless of whether people believe it or not. I shall waste no more strength to argue for it."

Chu Hsi was justly proud of his Commentary on the *Book of Odes* (1177) which was to remain a standard text for many centuries after him. Two features of this work have been fruitful in leading to future developments in research. One was his courageous discarding of the traditional interpretation as represented in the so-called "Prefaces to the Poems" and his insistence that the songs and poems should be read with an open mind and independent judgment. The other feature was his recognition of the "ancient pronunciation" of the end-rhymes, a recognition that was at least indirectly responsible for the future development of a more exact study of the entire field of ancient pronunciation, leading to the beginnings of a science of Chinese phonology.

When the *Book of Odes* became a major Classic of the Confucian Canon under the Han Empire, there were four different schools of textual reading and interpretation. After the first two centuries of the Christian era, only one school, the Mao[ap] school, was in the ascendency, overshadowing all the other schools. This Mao school claimed to have based its interpretation of the poems on the authority of the "Prefaces," which were supposedly handed down from Tzu-hsia,[aq] a great disciple of Confucius, but which were probably the work of some Han scholar who had taken the trouble to assign each poem to some historical occasion or event, or even to some historic personage as its author. Some of the historical assignments were taken from the *Tso-chuan,*[ar] one of the three commentaries of the Confucian *Ch'un-ch'iu* Annals, in which the origin of a few "Poems" was specifically mentioned. This display of historical erudition was quite impressive and probably accounted for the success of the Mao school in gradually winning general acceptance and official recognition. "The Prefaces of the Poems," therefore, were regarded as having sacrosanct authority throughout more than a millennium before the time of Chu Hsi.

Chu Hsi's senior contemporary, Cheng Ch'iao[as] (1104–1162), the learned author of the encyclopedic *T'ung-chih,*[at] published a little book with the title, "An Examination of the Absurdities about the *Book of Odes,*" in which he strongly attacked the "Prefaces" as absurd interpretations by vulgar and ignorant persons with no sense of literary and poetic appreciation. Cheng Ch'iao's vehemence of language at first shocked our philosopher Chu Hsi, but, he confessed, "after reading several of his criticisms and checking them with historical works, I soon came to the conclusion that the 'Prefaces' of those poems were really not reliable. When I went on to compare some other poems with their Prefaces, I found the content and meaning of the poems did not tally at all with their Prefaces. I was finally convinced that most of the 'Prefaces' were not trustworthy."

Here was a good illustration of conflicting ideas leading to doubt, and also of an open mind being receptive to new ideas and successful in resolving the doubt by evidence. Chu Hsi told how he had tried unsuccessfully to persuade his life-long friend and philosophical comrade, Lü Tsu-ch'ien[au] (1137–1181), to reject the Prefaces. He pointed out to Lü that only a few Prefaces were confirmed by clear references in the *Tso-chuan,* but most of them were grounded on no evidences. "But my friend said: 'How can one expect to find so many documentary evidences!' I said: 'In that case, we shall have to leave out all those Prefaces not based on evidences. We cannot use the Prefaces as evidences for the interpretation of the poems.' 'But,' said my friend Lü, 'the Prefaces themselves *are* evidences!' From our discussion, I realized that many people prefer to explain each poem by its Preface, and refuse to seek understanding by reading the poem itself."

In his courageous fight to overthrow the authority of the Prefaces and seek to understand the meaning of the poems by reading each poem with an open mind, Chu Hsi was only partially successful, both in his own new commentary and in leading future workers to go farther in the same direction. The weight of tradition was still too great for Chu Hsi himself and for future generations. But the great and creative doubt of Cheng Ch'iao and Chu Hsi will always be remembered whenever modern and unprejudiced scholarship undertakes to work on the *Book of Odes* with new tools and in an entirely free spirit.

For the second new feature of Chu Hsi's work on the *Book of Odes,* namely, the aspect of the ancient pronunciation of the rhymes, he was inspired and aided by the work of another learned contemporary of his, Wu Yü,[av] who died in 1153 or 1154. Wu Yü was the real pioneer in the study of Chinese phonology in working out an inductive method of comparing rhymed lines in that ancient Classic among themselves and with other ancient and medieval rhymed poetry. He wrote quite a few books, including "A Supplement on the Rhymes of the *Book of Odes,*" "Explaining the Rhymes in the *Ch'u-t'zu,*"[aw] and "A Supplement to the Standard Rhyme-Book" (*Yün-pu*[ax]). Only the last-named has survived to this day, through reprints.

There is no doubt that Wu Yü had discovered that those many end-rhymes in the *Book of Odes* which did not seem to rhyme according to "modern" pronunciation were natural rhymes in ancient times and were to be read according to their "ancient pronunciation." He therefore carefully listed all the end-rhymes in the 300-odd poems of the *Book of Odes* and worked out their ancient pronunciation with the aid of ancient and medieval dictionaries and rhyme-books. A preface written by Hsü Ch'an,[ay] a friend and distant relative of his, clearly described his patient method of collecting and comparing the vast number of instances. "The word now pronounced *'fu'*[az] appears 16 times in the *Book of Odes,* all, without exception, pronounced *'bek'* [or *'b'iuk,'* according to Bernard Karlgren]. The word now pronounced *'yu'*[ba] appears 11 times in the *Book of Odes,* all, without exception, rhymed with words ending *-i.*"

This strict methodology impressed Chu Hsi so much that he decided to accept Wu Yü's system of "ancient pronunciation" throughout his own Commentary. Probably with a view to the avoidance of unnecessary controversy, Chu Hsi did not call it "ancient pronunciation" but "rhyming pronunciation" —that is to say, a certain word should be pronounced in such a way as to rhyme with the other end-rhymes the pronunciation of which had apparently remained unchanged.

But, in his conversation with his students, he frankly said that he had followed Wu Yü in most cases, making additions or modifications in only a few instances; and that the rhyming pronunciations were the natural pronunciations of the ancient poets, who, "like us in modern times, composed their songs in natural rhymes." That is to say, the rhyming pronunciations were ancient pronunciations.

When asked whether there was any ground for the rhyming pronunciation, Chu Hsi answered: "Mr. Wu produced proofs for all his pronunciations. His books can be found in Ch'üan-chou.[bb] For one word he sometimes quoted as many as over ten proofs, but at least two or three proofs. He said that he originally had even more evidences, but had to leave out many [in order to reduce the cost of copying and printing]." And in those cases in which Chu Hsi found it necessary to differ with Wu, he also cited examples for comparison in his "Classified Sayings" and in the *Ch'u-t'zu chi-chu*[bc] ("An Annotated Edition of the Ch'u-t'zu").

But because Chu Hsi used the term "rhyming pronunciation" throughout his Commentary on the *Book of Odes* without ever referring to the term "ancient pronunciation," and because Wu Yü's books were long lost or inaccessible, a discussion was started early in the sixteenth century in the form of a severe criticism of Chu Hsi's improper use of the term "rhyming pronunciation." In 1580, Chiao Hung[bd] (1541–1620), a great scholar and philosopher, published in his "Notes" (*Pi-ch'eng*[be]) a brief statement of a theory (probably his friend Ch'en Ti's[bf] [1541–1617] theory) that those end-rhymes in ancient songs and poems that did not fit into modern schemes of rhyming were all natural rhymes whose pronunciations happened to have changed in the course of time. He cited a number of instances to show that the words would rhyme perfectly if pronounced as the ancients sang them.

It was Chiao Hung's friend, Ch'en Ti, who undertook many years of patient research and published a series of books on the ancient pronunciation of hundreds of rhyming words in many ancient books of rhymed poetry. The first of these works was published in 1616 under the title: *Mao-shih ku-yin k'ao*[bg] ("An Inquiry into the Ancient Pronunciation of the *Book of Odes*"), with a preface by Chiao Hung.

In his own preface, Ch'en Ti proclaimed his main thesis that the end-rhymes in the *Book of Odes* were naturally rhymed in their original pronunciation, and that it was only the natural change of pronunciation which made some of them appear not to rhyme at all. What had been suggested by Chu Hsi as "rhyming pronunciations," said Ch'en Ti, were in most cases the ancient or original pronunciations.

"I have done some evidential investigation (*k'ao-chü*[bh])," he said, "and have grouped the evidences into two classes: internal evidences (*pen-cheng*[bi]) and collateral evidences (*p'ang-cheng*[bj]). Internal evidences are taken from the *Book of Odes* itself. Collateral evidences are taken from other ancient rhymed works of approximately the same age."

To show how the word *"fu"* was invariably rhymed in its original archaic pronunciation (*bek,* or *b'iuk*), he listed 14 internal evidences and 10 collateral evidences, a total of 24. The same inductive method was applied to the study of ancient pronunciation in other rhymed literature of ancient China. To prove the ancient pronunciation of the word *"hsing,"*[bk] he cited 44 instances from the rhymed sections of the *Book of Changes,* all rhyming with words ending in *-ang*. For the word *"ming,"*[bl] he cited 17 evidences from the same book.

Nearly half a century later, the patriot-scholar Ku Yen-wu[bm] (1614–1682) completed his *Yin-hsüeh wu-shu*[bn] ("Five Books of Phonology"). One of them was on "The Original Pronunciation of the *Book of Odes*"; another on "The

[21] *Ibid.*, chap. 80, pp. 15–17; also *Ch'u-t'zu chi-chu* III, p. 21.

Pronunciation of the *Book of Changes*"; and another on "The Rhyming Groups of the T'ang period," which is an attempt to compare the ancient pronunciation with that of the Middle Ages. Ku acknowledged his indebtedness to Ch'en Ti and adopted his method in classifying his proofs into internal and collateral evidences.

Let us again use the word *"fu"* as an example. In his "Original Pronunciations of the *Book of Odes,"* Ku Yen-wu cited 17 internal evidences and 15 collateral evidences, a total of 32. In his larger work on the rhyming groups of the T'ang Dynasty (618–907), he listed a total of 162 evidences from available ancient rhymed literature to show how that word was rhymed and pronounced in ancient times!

Such patient collecting and counting of instances was intended to serve a twofold purpose. In the first place, that was the only way to ascertain the ancient pronunciation of the words and also to find possible exceptions which may challenge the rule and demand explanation. Ku Yen-wu acknowledged that some exceptions could be explained by the possibility of local and dialectal deviations in pronunciation.

But the most valuable use of this vast statistical material was to form a basis for systematic reconstruction of the actual groupings of ancient sounds. On the basis of his study of the rhymed literature of ancient China, Ku Yen-wu concluded that ancient pronunciations could be analyzed into ten general rhyming groups (*yün p'u*).

Thus was begun the deductive and constructive part of Chinese phonetics, namely, the continuous attempts, first, to understand the ancient "finals" (rhyming groups), and, in a later period, to understand the nature of the ancient initial consonants.

Ku Yen-wu proposed ten general rhyming groups in 1667. In the following century, a number of scholars continued to work on the same problem and by the same inductive and deductive methods of evidential research. Chiang Yung[bo] (1681–1762) suggested 13 rhyming groups. Tuan Yü-ts'ai[bp] (1735–1815) increased the number to 17. His teacher and friend, Tai Chen[bq] (1724–1777), further increased it to 19. Wang Nien-sun[br] (1744–1832) and Chiang Yu-kao[bs] (died in 1851), working independently, arrived at a more or less similar system of 21 rhyming groups.

Ch'ien Ta-hsin[bt] (1728–1804), one of the most scientifically minded men of the eighteenth century, published in 1799 his "Notes," which include two papers on the results of his studies of ancient initial labials and dentals. These two papers are outstanding examples of the method of evidential investigation at its best. He collected over 60 groups of instances for the labials, and about the same number for the dentals. In the identifying of the ancient sound of the words in each group, every step was a skillful combination of induction and deduction, of generalization from particulars and application of general rules to particular instances. The final outcome was the formulation of two general laws of phonological change regarding labials and dentals.

It is important for us to remind ourselves that those Chinese scholars working in the field of Chinese phonetics were so greatly handicapped that they seemed almost from the outset to be doomed to failure. They were without the minimum aid of an alphabet for the Chinese language. They had no benefit of the comparative study of the various dialects, especially of the older dialects in southern, southeastern, and southwestern China. Nor had they any knowledge of such neighboring languages as Korean, Vietnamese, and Japanese. Without any of these useful tools, those Chinese scholars, seeking to understand the phonetic changes of their language, were actually faced with an almost impossible task. Their successes or failures, therefore, must be evaluated in the light of their numerous and important disadvantages.

The only dependable tool of those great men was their strict method of patiently collecting, comparing, and classifying what they recognized as facts or evidences, and an equally strict method of applying formulated generalizations to test the particular instances within the classified groups. It was indeed very largely this meticulous application of a rigorous method that enabled Wu Yü and Chu Hsi in the twelfth century, Ch'en Ti and Ku Yen-wu in the seventeenth century, and their successors in the eighteenth and nineteenth centuries to carry on their systematic study of Chinese phonetic problems and to develop it into something of a science—into a body of knowledge answering to the rigorous canons of evidence, exactitude, and logical systematization.

I have briefly sketched what I have conceived as the story of the development of the scientific spirit and method in the Chinese thought of the past eight centuries. It began in the eleventh century with the ambitious ideal of extending human knowledge to the utmost by investigating the reason or law in all things of the universe. That grandiose ideal was by necessity narrowed down to the investigation of books—to the patient and courageous study of the few great books which formed the "sacred scripture" of the Chinese classical tradition. History saw the gradual development of a new spirit and a new method based on doubt and the resolution of doubt. The spirit was the moral courage to doubt even on questions touching sacred matters, and the insistence on the importance of an open mind and impartial and dispassionate search for truth. The method was the method of evidential thinking and evidential investigation (*k'ao-chü* and *k'ao-cheng*).

I have cited a few examples of this spirit and method at work, notably in the development of a "Higher Criticism" in the form of investigations of the authenticity and dating of a part of the scriptures and in the development of a scientific study of the problems of Chinese phonology. But, as a matter of history, this method was fruitfully and effectually applied to many other fields of historical and humanistic research, such as textual criticism, semantics (in the original sense as the study of the historical changes of the meaning of words), history, historical geography, and archeology.

The method of evidential investigation was made fully conscious by such men as Ch'en Ti and Ku Yen-wu in the seventeenth century, who first used the terms "internal evidences" and "collateral evidences." The efficacy of the method was so clearly demonstrated in the scientific works of the two great masters of the seventeenth century, Ku Yen-wu and Yen Jo-ch'ü, that by the eighteenth and nineteenth centuries practically all first-class minds in intellectual China were attracted to it and were devoting their lives to its application to all fields of classical and humanistic study. The result was a new age of Revival of Learning which has also been called the Age of Evidential Investigation.

Even the most violent critics of this new learning had to admit the scientific nature of its rigorous and effective method. One such violent critic was Fang Tung-shu[bu] (1772–1851), who published in 1826 a book which was a vehement criticism and condemnation of the whole movement. Even Fang had to pay high tribute to the rigorous method as it was used by two of his contemporaries, Wang Nien-sun and his son, Wang Yin-chih[bv] (1766–1834). Fang said: "As a linguistic approach to the classics, there is nothing that surpasses the *Ching-i shu-wen*[bw] ("Notes on the Classics As I Have Heard from My Father") of the Wangs of Kao-yu.[bx] That work could actually make the great Cheng Hsüan[by] (d. 200) and Chu Hsi bow their heads (in humble acknowledgment of their errors). Ever since the Han Dynasty, there has never been anything that could compare with it." Such a tribute coming from a violent critic of the whole movement is the best proof that the meticulous application of a scientific method of research is the most effective means to disarm opposition, to undermine authority and conservatism, and to win recognition and credence for the new scholarship.

What was the historical significance of this spirit and method of "exact and impartial inquiry"?

A brief but factual answer must be: It succeeded in replacing an age of subjective, idealistic, and moralizing philosophy (from the eleventh to the sixteenth century) by making it seem outmoded, "empty," unfruitful, and no longer attractive to the best minds of the age. It succeeded in creating a new age of Revival of Learning (1600–1900) based on disciplined and dispassionate research. But it did not produce an age of natural science. The spirit of exact and impartial inquiry, as exemplified in Ku Yen-wu, Tai Chen, Ch'ien Ta-hsin, and Wang Nien-sun, did not lead to an age of Galileo, Vesalius, and Newton in China.

Why? Why did this scientific spirit and method not result in producing natural science?

More than a quarter of a century ago, I tried to offer a historical explanation by making a comparative chronology of the works of the intellectual leaders of China and of Europe in the seventeenth century. I said:

If we make a comparative chronology of the leaders of Chinese and European learning during the seventeenth century—the formative period both for the new science in modern Europe and the new learning in China—we shall see that four years before Ku Yen-wu was born (1613), Galileo had invented his telescope and was using it to revolutionize the science of astronomy, and Kepler was publishing his revolutionary studies of Mars and his new laws of the movements of the planets. When Ku Yen-wu worked on his philological studies and reconstructed the archaic pronunciations, Harvey had published his great work on the circulation of blood [1628], and Galileo his two great works on astronomy and the new science [1630]. Eleven years before Yen Jo-chü began his critical study of the *Book of History,* Torricelli had completed his great experiment on the pressure of air [1644]. Shortly after, Boyle announced the results of his experiments in Chemistry, and formulated the law that bears his name [1660–61]. The year before Ku Yen-wu completed his epoch-making *Five Books* on philological studies [1667] Newton had worked out his calculus and his analysis of white light. In 1680, Ku wrote his preface to the final texts of his philological works; in 1687, Newton published his *Principia.*

The striking similarity in the scientific spirit and method of these great leaders of the age of new learning in their respective countries makes the fundamental difference between their fields of work all the more conspicuous. Galileo, Kepler, Boyle, Harvey, and Newton worked with the objects of nature, with stars, balls, inclining planes, telescopes, microscopes, prisms, chemicals, and numbers and astronomical tables. And their Chinese contemporaries worked with books, words, and documentary evidences. The latter created three hundred years of scientific book learning; the former created a new science and a new world.[22]

That was a historical explanation, but was a little unfair to those great Chinese scholars of the seventeenth century. It was not enough to say, as I did, that "the purely literary training of the intellectual class in China has tended to limit its activities to the field of books and documents." It should be pointed out that the books they worked on were books of tremendous importance to the moral, religious, and philosophical life of the entire nation. Those great men considered it their sacred duty to find out what each and every one of those ancient books actually meant. As Robert Browning sang of the Grammarian:

"What's in the scroll," quoth he, "thou keepest furled?
Show me their shaping,
Theirs who most studied man, the bard and sage,—
Give."—So, he gowned him,
Straight got by heart that book to its last page. . . .
"Let me know all! . . .
Even to the last crumbs I'd fain eat up the feast." . . .
"What's time? leave Now for dogs and apes!
Man has Forever." . . .

Browning's tribute to the spirit of the humanist age was: "This man decided not to Live but Know."

The same spirit was expressed by Confucius: "Study as if life were too short and you were on the point of missing it." "He who learns the truth in the

[22] *The Chinese Renaissance* (Chicago: University of Chicago Press, 1934), pp. 70–71.

morning, may die in the evening without regret." The same spirit was expressed by Chu Hsi in his age: "There is no end to knowledge. I can only devote my whole energy to study: death alone will end my toil."

But Chu Hsi went further: "My friends, you are not making progress, because you have not learned to doubt. As soon as you begin to doubt, you will never stop until your doubt is resolved at last." And his true successors, the founders and workers of the new age of Revival of Learning, were men who had learned to doubt—to doubt with an open mind and to seek ways and means to resolve the doubt, to dare to doubt even when they were dealing with the great books of the Sacred Canon. And, precisely because they were all their lives dealing with the great books of the Sacred Canon, they were forced always to stand on solid ground: they had to learn to doubt with evidence and resolve doubt with evidence. That, I think, is the historical explanation of the remarkable fact that those great men working with only "books, words, and documents" have actually succeeded in leaving to posterity a scientific tradition of dispassionate and disciplined inquiry, of rigorous evidential thinking and investigation, of boldness in doubt and hypotheses coupled with a meticulous care in seeking verification—a great heritage of scientific spirit and method which makes us, sons and daughters of present-day China, feel not entirely at sea, but rather at home, in the new age of modern science.

[a] 胡適
[b] 顏回
[c] 武成
[d] 詩經
[e] 老子
[f] 老聃
[g] 無爲
[h] 天
[i] 帝
[j] 道
[k] 大
[l] 自然
[m] 王充
[n] 論衡
[o] 災
[p] 異
[q] 董仲舒
[r] 春秋
[s] 緯
[t] 讖
[u] 故
[v] 偶
[w] 氣
[x] 驗
[y] 陰
[z] 陽
[aa] 程顥，明道
[ab] 程頤，伊川
[ac] 朱熹
[ad] 理
[ae] 張載，橫渠
[af] 陸九淵，象山

[ag] 權立疑義
[ah] 考證
[ai] 伏生
[aj] 朱子語類
[ak] 吳澄
[al] 梅鷟
[am] 閻若璩
[an] 易經
[ao] 卦
[ap] 毛詩
[aq] 子夏
[ar] 左傳
[as] 鄭樵
[at] 通志
[au] 呂祖謙
[av] 吳棫
[aw] 楚辭釋音
[ax] 韻補
[ay] 徐蕆
[az] 服
[ba] 友
[bb] 泉州
[bc] 楚辭集註
[bd] 焦竑
[be] 筆乘
[bf] 陳第
[bg] 毛氏古音考
[bh] 考據
[bi] 本證
[bj] 旁證
[bk] 行
[bl] 明
[bm] 顧炎武
[bn] 音學五書
[bo] 江永
[bp] 段玉裁
[bq] 戴震
[br] 王念孫
[bs] 江有誥
[bt] 錢大昕
[bu] 方東樹
[bv] 王引之
[bw] 經義述聞
[bx] 高郵
[by] 鄭玄

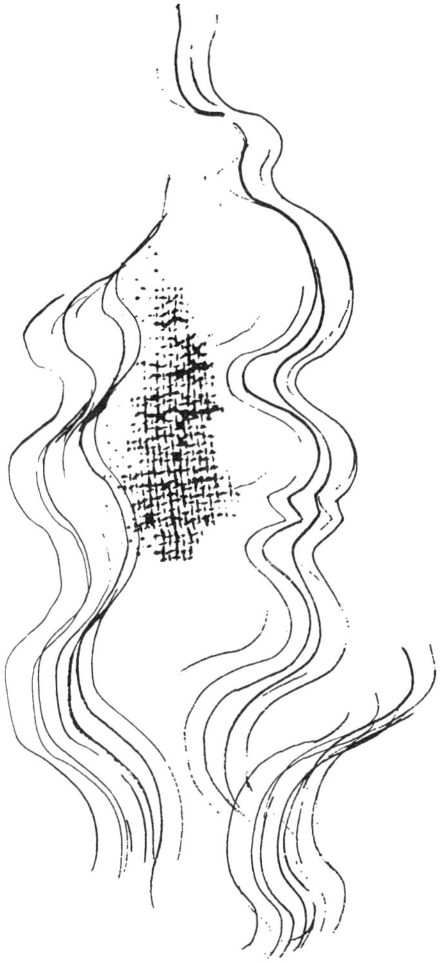

III. Religion and Spiritual Values

T'ANG CHÜN-I[a]

The Development of Ideas of Spiritual Value in Chinese Philosophy

I. A TENTATIVE DEFINITION OF SPIRITUAL VALUE

Before I talk about the ideas of spiritual value in Chinese philosophy, I will define what I call spiritual value.

By the word "spirit" I mean any self-conscious subject and its activities which are initiated by self-conscious ideas. Any value which has the following characteristics is called spiritual: (1) created or realized "by the spirit"; (2) presented or revealed to the spirit, that is, "for the spirit"; (3) self-consciously recognized as such in (1) and (2), and then the value can be predicated on the spirit, that is, "of the spirit."

According to (1) of the above definition, we can differentiate spiritual values from the values of outer natural objects and from the values of the satisfaction of our natural instincts. Outer natural objects usually have the value of utility, for they are instrumental in the realization or attainment of spiritual aims or purposes. Sometimes, outer natural objects may have some aesthetic values which are presented to our enjoying spirit, too. However, at least at the moment when we say these values are created or originated or manifested by outer Nature and belong to outer Nature they are not spiritual values. It is generally agreed, too, that, when our instinctive desires are satisfied in instinctive ways, there is the realization of natural values which need not be taken as spiritual.

According to (2) of the definition, we can differentiate spiritual values from a certain kind of social values which come from the effects of a certain action (or actions) of a person (or persons) on other persons and the whole historical society. As the chain of effects of human action may stretch and extend to an indefinite number of persons, areas of society, and even ages in history, the social values of a human action cannot all be presented and known by any personal spiritual subject except God. These values are always realized outside the self-consciousness of the person who performs the action. Therefore, the existential status of these values should be said to be in the historical society as a whole and not within any particular personal spirit.

According to (3) of the definition, we may differentiate a genuine spiritual value from a certain quasi-spiritual value, which is created by a certain spirit and then presented to that same spirit but is not self-consciously recognized as such. For example, the imagery of a dream may be merely symbols of a spiritual idea we have had before. Thus, it is created by our spirit and presented to our spirit. However, when we are dreaming, the aesthetic value of the imagery seems to belong to the imagery itself and is not self-consciously recognized as created "by the spirit," "for the spirit," and "of the spirit." This is not a genuine spiritual value. So, any value of human activity, though originally created by the spirit and presented to the spirit, if its origin is forgotten and taken as belonging to the world outside the spirit, is only a quasi-spiritual value, which is alienated from the originating spirit itself.

From the above, we may say that the first group of spiritual values are the values of moral and religious activities. Generally speaking, in moral and religious activities, one is self-consciously commanding himself how to act, to meditate, or to pray. All such activities are initiated, at least to some degree, by one's spiritual subject in the very beginning, and their values, such as goodness, peace of mind, holiness, and so on, are more or less taken as created or realized by the spiritual subject and presented for the spiritual subject, and can be taken as inhering in, and then predicated of, the same spiritual subject.

The second kind of spiritual values consists of those of the artistic and intellectual activities of man. It is doubtless that there are values of beauty and truth realized by, and presented to, the spiritual subject through one's spiritual activities, such as speculative thinking, experimental observation, and creative imagination. Yet, the truth-value or beauty-value is not only capable of describing the spiritual activities of man but also can be predicated of aesthetic objects or the objective realities as outside of the spirit of men. It is much more difficult to say that moral goodness and peace of mind exist in themselves outside the spirit or personality of man, even when we believe in a Platonic metaphysics of value. Thus, the spiritual values of artistic and intellectual activities are differentiated from the moral and religious values, and they may not have the same degree of spirituality.

The third kind of spiritual values consists of natural values and social values, defined above as non-spiritual, which are transformed into spiritual values. These transformations are achieved usually by highly exalted spiritual activities. For example, the utility or beauty of natural objects is generally taken as having originated from the objects themselves. If we, as some poets, religious men, and metaphysicians have done, take man and Nature as created by some absolute spirit, such as God or Brahman, or as the manifestation of some absolute spirit, then all the utilitarian aesthetic values of natural objects may be taken as having originated from the same spiritual substance of man, in which case the values of natural objects can be taken as transformed into spiritual values.

On the question as to how social value also can be transformed into spiritual value, the crucial point is that any social value of one's action which is taken as outside the personal spirit can also be taken as inside the spirit by the more fully developed moral consciousness of the subject. For example, a discovery in the theoretical study of a scientist may benefit mankind in the indefinite future and generate infinite social values which are beyond the expectation of the theoretical consciousness of the scientist. Yet, if the moral consciousness of the scientist is fully developed into infinite love of mankind, such as the love of Jesus or the *jen*[b] (humanity, love, benevolence) of Confucius (551–479 B.C.), then he understands that all the social values generated from his inventive action are by principle such as can satisfy his love of mankind, although all the details of all the effects of his action could never be foretold by him. If the satisfaction of this love is purely spiritual and has spiritual value, then the actual realization of any social value of his present discovery any time in the future is at the same time a realization of the spiritual value of his present love of mankind. The realizations of these two kinds of values are co-extensive and equivalent in domain, at least in his present lofty moral consciousness. Therefore, for this consciousness, all social values which are not taken as external values become internalized, immanently present to the spiritual subject, and thus transformed into spiritual values. Needless to say, outside such a lofty moral consciousness, the social value is just a social value, just as, outside the consciousness of poets, religious men, and metaphysicians, as mentioned above, natural value is merely a natural value.

II. SPIRITUAL VALUES IN CONFUCIAN MORAL TEACHINGS AND THE KEY CONCEPT OF "SEARCHING IN ONESELF"

The Confucian school and the Taoist school are the main currents of thought of native Chinese philosophy. They and Buddhism have usually been mentioned together and called *"san-chiao,"*[c] three teachings or three religions. Generally speaking, these three teachings all intend to deepen spiritual experience, cultivate the spiritual life of man, and have much social-cultural influence on the Chinese historical society. Hence, if we wish to know the main ideas of spiritual value in Chinese philosophy, we have to study them in the Confucian and Taoist and Buddhist philosophies.

It is held by some writers that there are no really spiritual values in Confucianism. It is said that in the body of Confucianism dealing with the virtues of men in definite relations only social values can be realized. Some contend that when Confucius talked about the importance of the cultivation of these virtues he always said this is a way for preserving the social solidarity of the nation or the peace of the world or for training the people to be contented with their circumstances and not to offend their superiors. These values are therefore alleged to be only socio-political and not spiritual values as defined above. Others contend that when Confucius talked about the values of the virtues he was considering the values as a means to the achieving of harmony and order in human relations, which were taken as a part of the harmony and order of the natural universe. Yet, the harmony and order of the natural universe may have a natural value only and not necessarily a spiritual value.[1]

The views which efface the ideas of spiritual value from the Confucian ethical system are not without some justification. Actually, many Confucians in the course of Chinese history, such as those of the Yung-k'ang school[d] and Yung-chia school[e] of the Sung Dynasty (960–1279), and Yen Yüan[f] (1635–1704) and Tai Chen[g] (1723–1777) of the Ch'ing Dynasty (1644–1912), laid their emphasis on the exposition of the social utilitarian value of ethical actions. Many Confucians in the Han Dynasty (206 B.C.–A.D. 220) emphasized the natural value of ethical action.

But, from our point of view, the values of the virtues in Confucian ethics should be considered essentially spiritual values. The central idea of virtue peculiar to Confucius, Mencius (371–289 B.C. ?), and the Neo-Confucianism of the Sung-Ming period (960–1644) is to consider the virtues as the inner essence of one's personality, and their values as intrinsic to one's moral consciousness and tinged with a certain religious meaning, and thus as definitely spiritual values. The key concept in this interpretation is the concept of "searching in oneself," which is a teaching handed down from Confucius himself and developed by all later Confucians. I shall explain its meaning from three aspects.

(1) In the first aspect, "searching in oneself" means that in all ethical relations one has to do his duty to others, but not require others to do their duties to him, reciprocally, though the others should do their duties of their own accord. In order to explain this we have to know that there are three ways to develop one's spiritual life to the fullest extent, and all three may be called in a certain sense "backward ways."

The first way is to get real freedom from all the instinctive and irrational desires in human life. The extreme of this is what Schopenhauer called the denial or mortification of the will. This way is practiced, more or less, by all ascetics and mystics, as a negative step in the very beginning of spiritual cultivation for the higher positive spiritual development.

The second way searches for some kind of higher or highest Idea or Existence in the very beginning of spiritual cultivation which is supernatural and transcendent, such as the Idea of the Good in Plato and the self-existent God in the otherworldly religions. We may call this the way of leaving the mundane world behind, in our process of spiritual ascent.

The third way is to live in definite ethical relations with others in the actual world, practicing the morality of doing one's duty to others but not asking them to do their duties, reciprocally, as taught in Confucianism. This way of

[1] Many writers, such as Ch'en Tu-hsiu[al] (1879–1942) in the period of the New Culture movement at the beginning of the Republic of China, took the utilitarian point of view to interpret the ethical value of Confucian teachings, and some missionaries and naturalism-biased Chinese scholars usually interpret the ethical values of Confucian teachings as just natural values in contrast with the supernatural or spiritual values.

life may be called the way of thinking or acting morally just for oneself, which is opposite to the "forward way of asking others to do something morally for me," as in the common attitude of our daily life. It is a "backward" way of life and is as difficult to put into practice as the other two ways.

The difficulties of this third way arise from the fact that when one does his duty to others he naturally supposes that others are moral beings like himself. According to the universal principle of reason, man naturally expects others to do their duties in response to his action. Thus, he naturally thinks he has the right to demand that others do their duties. Actually, social justice and legislation are based upon the reciprocity of rights and duties. One who does his duty without asking others to do theirs is the same as one who has only duty-consciousness without right-consciousness and lives beyond the idea of social justice. In duty-consciousness, one does what his conscience commands him to do, and never goes beyond his conscience to see what happens in other consciences, and so the value realized is completely internal to his conscience and is therefore a purely spiritual moral value. If I have this kind of duty-consciousness in full degree, then, the less others do their duty to me, the more I shall do my duty to others. That is to say, the more my expectation from others is disappointed, the more intensified is my self-expectation from myself. The value of social justice, which is offended and lost because others do not do their duty, is recompensed and satisfied by the moral values of my fulfillment, which is purely spiritual and belongs to my inward life. Yet, this kind of duty-consciousness is the most difficult for human beings, because we have to do to others more than they deserve. What we do to others is the same as the grace of deity conferred on man though man may not be aware of it or respond to it with a sense of thanksgiving. It is significant that Christians translate the word "grace" with the Chinese word *"en"*[h] in the term *"en-i,"*[i] which means that one does his duty without reciprocation, and so confers something which is absolutely beyond what others deserve. Therefore, we may say that in the first meaning of "searching in oneself" in Confucianism a deification of human life is implied and has religious and spiritual meanings.

(2) The second meaning of "searching in oneself" is that one ought to cultivate his virtues and abilities without asking praise from others. This is also very difficult to practice due to the fact that men, motivated by the universal principle of reason, naturally want others to appreciate or approve what they themselves have appreciated or approved. This desire may not be morally bad, if it is accompanied by a moral feeling of respect when we request it from others and accompanied by our gratitude when we receive it from others. But, leaving the desire for praise itself alone and as unconditionally right, then we may simply take the praise of others as personal gratification. When we are anxious to receive this kind of gratification, many modes of moral evils, such as ambition, or the will to power to control the will of others, or disloyalty to one's original ideals in flattering others and then receiving praise in return, can be generated in different circumstances. When I ask the praise of others, I

am taking my virtues, and abilities and their expressions in actions and speech as a means, and they then have only instrumental or utilitarian value, which is non-spiritual social value or quasi-spiritual value as defined in Section I, above.[2]

If our ordinary outward desire of gaining others' praise is diminished, we may live a life which is directed by our moral conscience itself. We can then eradicate the roots of our desire to control the will of others; we will never be disloyal to the moral ideal in order to please men, and, at the same time, never have any complaint or grudge against others or Heaven. This is the meaning of the Confucian saying: "There is no one that knows me. . . . I do not murmur against Heaven. I do not grumble against men. . . . But it is Heaven that knows me."[3] This is a kind of deified human life.

(3) The third meaning of "searching in oneself" is that all the moral principles, moral ideals, and moral values of our actions and intentions can be discovered by self-reflection. This is strongly implied in the teaching of Confucius, and is explicitly stated and elaborated in the teaching of Mencius and many later Confucians, as in the thesis that "human nature is good."

The thesis that "human nature is good" has had various interpretations in the various schools of Confucianism. In the teaching of Mencius, the first exponent of this thesis, the doctrine does not say that all men's actions or intentions are actually good enough. It says simply that there are good tendencies or good beginnings in human nature and, most important, that, when we have good intentions or do good actions, there is usually an accompanying feeling of self-satisfaction or self-joy or self-peace.[4] This may be said to be deep self-praise when I find my intention or action is really good. This deep self-praise is usually concealed when we are eager to ask for praise from others or when we lack deep self-reflection. Yet, when we withdraw the desire to ask others for praise and have deep reflection, then everybody can find the deep self-praise which accompanies all good intentions or good actions. However, this deep self-praise is a result of my deepest self-evaluation, which immediately follows my intention or action. This self-evaluation reveals to me what is good as good and what is not good as not good, and from the former I feel self-satisfaction, self-joy, and self-peace, but from the latter I feel disquieted, unjoyful, and dissatisfied. As my mind feels self-peace or self-joy or self-satisfaction in the good only, so my human nature is disclosed as essentially good. I shall take this as the orthodox doctrine of the thesis that "human nature is good," which was morally expounded in Mencius' teaching, was metaphysically explained by Chu Hsi's[j] (1130–1200) theory of *Li*[k] (Principle, Reason, or Law), and culminated in the teaching of *liang-chih*[l] (almost the same as conscience) in Wang Shou-jen's (Wang Yang-ming,[m] 1472–1529) philosophy.

If we take human nature as essentially good, moral ideals and moral prin-

[2] Cf. my essay, *Tsai ching-shen sheng-huo fa-chan chung chih hui-yü i-shih*[am] ("A Phenomenological Study of the Consciousness of Praise and Defamation in the Development of Spiritual Life"), *Jen-sheng,*[an] X, No. 1 (1954).

[3] Cf. Legge's translation: *Confucian Analects* XXXVII.

[4] The Chinese words are "*chih-te*"[ao] for self-satisfaction, "*yüeh*"[ap] for self-joy, "*an*"[aq] for self-peace.

ciples are nothing other than the norms or standards awakened within or originating in the nature of our mind and immanently presented to our moral self-consciousness for self-evaluation. Consequently, our moral training and moral cultivation have no other purpose than to preserve and extend what is judged or evaluated as good, and all the achievements of moral life and the formation of a moral personality express no more than the desire to conform to these immanent norms or standards, to realize what originates from the nature of the mind, and to know to the maximum what is implicitly contained in the nature of the mind.

However, in the development of our moral life, any phase of our ordinary life which is taken by common sense as non-moral or immoral can be evaluated as either good or evil. So, every phase of our life has moral meaning, can be moralized by a certain cultivation, and then has moral value, which can be presented immediately to our self-reflection, as defined above, and become a purely internal value. It is not difficult to see that if we resolve to have all the phases of our life moralized, then our self-evaluations and self-reflections may arise successfully and co-extensively with the extensions of all phases of life, including those phases of our life which are considered by common sense as merely directing to, or dealing with, the so-called external environment.

Hence, self-evaluation and self-reflection should not be taken as subjective and self-closed, but should also be taken as objective and self-open to all the other social and natural objects of the universe as our whole environment. Here the "investigation of things" as taught by Confucianism has not only intellectual value but also moral value, and then we may have the wisdom that all the objects in the universe can be taken as the occasions for the realization of spiritual moral values, and that all may be lighted and permeated by spiritual and moral values as well. This is the vision of the moral man, who realizes his good nature, develops his moral life to the fullest extent, attains unity of the inner world and the outer world, and achieves the grandeur and beauty of personality as expounded in the *Doctrine of the Mean*[5] and the *Book of Mencius*.

III. (1) HUMAN NATURE AS GOOD, (2) HEAVEN, (3) MIND, AND (4) THE UNIVERSAL ATTAINABILITY OF SAGEHOOD

If we compare the thesis that human nature is good with the idea of original sin in Christianity or the *karma* theory and the *avidyā* theory of Buddhism, there are many pros and cons worthy of discussion. Yet, if we acknowledge the existence of original sin or impure *karma* in the depth of our mind, we may still believe that human nature is essentially good. We may hold that original sin and impure *karma* are not derived from real human nature, but that the feeling of unrest that arises when we are told we have original sin or impure *karma* originates from our real human nature. This nature, as revealed in unrest, is the same as the nature revealed in our unpeacefulness in our evils,

[5] Cf. the *Doctrine of the Mean* XXV.

and is absolutely good. In the feeling of unrest, of course, I may find at the same time that I am so weak as to try to set myself free from the bondage of original sin or impure *karma,* and I may pray to some transcendent being, such as God, Brahman, or Amida Buddha, to save me. In this type of religious consciousness, we think our nature is not good enough. Yet, the very confession of our weakness and our praying come from our nature, too. Our very confession may not be weak, and our praying must be good in itself. If it is objected that the very confession and words of prayer do not come from our human nature, but are the result of human nature as affected by a transcendent being or receiving grace from above, then we reply that our capacity for being (and our unconscious willingness to be) affected and receiving grace are additional evidences that human nature is essentially good. If we deny this, then how is it possible that men can be saved? The thesis that human nature is good does not fundamentally oppose the ultimate teachings of Christianity or Brahmanism or Buddhism, which believe either that man is the image of God, or that man is Brahman, or that the Buddha is a sentient being awakened to the fullest extent. Therefore, the thesis that human nature is good cannot be denied, even if we concede the existence of original sin or impure *karma,* because we can reassert our nature as good again in the very self-reflection of our unrest or unpeacefulness in our evils and our very unwillingness to be bound by them. However, the Confucian thesis that human nature is good is still different from many religious points of view which take the evil origin of human actions much more seriously and believe that only a transcendent being can save man from evil. The crucial point is that men who hold the latter point of view always look at human nature as a mere potentiality and insist that the principle of its actuality resides in some transcendent being. Yet, from the thesis that human nature is good the principle of actualization is seen to be immanent in human nature.[6]

What we have said above does not imply that Confucian thought lacks the idea of a transcendent reality, such as God, the Mind of Heaven, or the Universal Mind. In fact, many Confucians have these ideas. The real difference between the Confucian point of view and the above religious point of view is that, in the latter, the idea of a transcendent being, such as God, Brahman, etc., is more easily brought to light by contrasting it with our sin or impure *karma* or bondage; while, in the former, the idea of the Mind of Heaven, the Universal Mind, God, or Heaven is usually brought to light by the positive development of our moral life to the fullest extent, with the knowledge that the transcendent being is at the same time immanent in our moral life. How is it possible to have these ideas brought to light by the positive development of our moral lives? The answer was suggested in the teaching of Mencius and culminated in the Neo-Confucians of the Sung-Ming period, who had a deep understanding of the thesis that human nature is good.

Briefly, the central theme of this trend of thought is that when we develop

[6] For example, in Aristotelian-Thomian metaphysical and religious thought, human nature is usually taken as a potentiality in contrast with God, which is pure actuality.

our moral life to the fullest extent, as a sage does, the essence of our good nature is wholly actualized in, presented to, and known by, our self-consciousness. The essence of our good nature may be said to be *jen,* which is love, beginning with filial piety, and flowing out as universal love to all the men with whom I have definite ethical relations, to all the people under Heaven, and to all natural things. So, the moral consciousness of *jen,* in its fullest extent, is all-embracing love, which pervades, permeates, and fills heaven and earth as a whole. So, Mencius said: "The virtuous man transforms all experiences he passes through and abides in holiness or deity-nature. His virtues are confluent with heaven above and with earth below."[7] Chang Tsai (Chang Heng-ch'ü,[n] 1020–1077), Ch'eng Hao (Ch'eng Ming-tao,[o] 1032–1085), Ch'eng I (Ch'eng I-ch'uan,[p] 1033–1107), and Chu Hsi had the same idea, namely, that the man who realizes *jen* considers Heaven, Earth, and the ten thousand things as one body. Lu Chiu yüan (Lu Hsiang-shan,[q] 1139–1193) said: "The universe is my mind and my mind is the universe." Wang Shou-jen said: "Pervading Heaven and Earth is just this spiritual light—my spiritual light—which is not separated by, or separated from, Heaven, Earth, deities, and the ten thousand things."[8] But is this mind only my own? In the mind which identifies itself with the universe, where is the dividing point between what is mine and what is not mine? When selfish ideas and motives are transformed into universal and all-pervading love, where is the borderline or the boundary between our mind and the universe? Why can I not take this type of mind as belonging to me and also to Heaven? Why can I not take this type of mind both as created and presented by myself and as revealed and descended to me from Heaven? Is its belonging-to-me incompatible with its belonging-to-Heaven? If I take this kind of mind as mine and not of Heaven, does this not simply contradict the very nature of this kind of mind, which has no borderline to differentiate itself from what is not itself and which is felt as a universal and all-pervading mind? Therefore, when I have this kind of mind and know its nature truly, I shall never take this mind merely as my own; I shall know that this kind of mind is conferred by Heaven as much as it is mine and I shall know Heaven (which was originally synonymous with the word "God" in the Chinese Classics). As this kind of mind is the mind of one who develops his moral life to the fullest extent, and whose *jen* is wholly actualized as a sage, so the sage is said to be the same as Heaven, and human nature is therefore sometimes called Heaven-nature, and the human mind is called the mind of Heaven in some Confucian literature. So, Mencius said: "To have our mind preserved and Nature nourished is the way to serve Heaven" and "The man who has passed through the stage of completing his virtues and sheds forth his spiritual light brilliantly, and then can transform the world, is called a sage. The sage, unfathomable by intellect, is called holy or divine."[9]

Yet, the highest teaching of Confucianism is not merely the realization that

[7] This is my own translation of the *Book of Mencius* VIB.13.
[8] Wang Shou-jen: *Ch'uan-hsi lu*[ar] ("Records of Instructions for Practice"), III.
[9] My free translation of the *Book of Mencius* VIIB. 25, from 5 to 9, and condensed into two sentences.

the sage is the same as Heaven, but the realization of the universal attainability of sagehood for all men and what is implied by it. The universal attainability of sagehood is a logical consequence of the belief that human nature is good. The sage is the man who has fully realized his nature. If all men have the same good human nature, surely all can realize their nature and attain sagehood. Furthermore, the universal attainability of sagehood is itself an immanent belief of the mind of the sage. Since the mind of the sage is full of love and unselfishness in the fullest extent, he could not have any idea that he is the only sage, because this is selfish and contradictory to the very nature of his mind. He must love to see, expect, and hope that everyone else shall be a sage. Therefore, the universal attainability of sagehood is a belief immanently involved in the mind of the sage. If I believe there is a sage, or if I can be a sage, then I have to think of the idea of the sage through the mind of the sage, and thus the universal attainability of sagehood is also involved in my idea. Yet, according to the thesis that human nature is good, I must believe there is a sage and that I can be one, because sagehood is nothing more than my own nature, *jen,* wholly realized. So, I must believe in the universal attainability of sagehood.[10]

According to the idea of the universal attainability of sagehood, an actual sage can be born at any time and any place in the world, and no one sage of any particular place or particular time has the privilege to be the only sage. As all sages have the same fundamental virtue, *jen,* or universal love, so all sages go in the same way, and are of the same spirit of mind, and live with the same principle or the same Tao.[r] [11] This idea led the Chinese people to believe that there can be sages in different religions of different peoples.[12] This is one reason there were no religious wars or large-scale religious persecutions in Chinese history. So, this idea has its religious value.

Furthermore, when we know there is a single spirit, or a single mind, or a single principle, or a single Tao in the world of sages, we have to know one thing more. This is: "I can know all this in my here-and-now mind." This is to say that I can comprehend what is universal and all-pervading in the world of sages in my here-and-now mind. So, the world of sages is as much immanent in my here-and-now spiritual world as it is transcendent to my here-and-now

[10] Cf. on the spiritual aspect of forgiving, chap. 12, sec. 9, of my book: *Chung-kuo jen-wen ching-shen chih fa-chan*[as] ("The Development of the Chinese Humanistic Spirit").

[11] About the universal attainability of sagehood, we may cite the saying of Mencius and Lu Chiu-yüan. Mencius said: "Those regions (of Shun and King Wen,[at] reigned 1171–1122 B.C.) were distant from one another more than a thousand *li*[au] (about a third of a mile) and the age of one sage was later than that of the other by more than a thousand years. But . . . the principles of the earlier sage and the later sage are the same." (Legge's translation, *Book of Mencius* IVA.1.) Lu Chiu-yüan said: "The universe is my mind and my mind is the universe. If in the Eastern Sea there were to appear a sage, he would have this same mind and this principle (*Li*). If in the Western Sea, there were to appear a sage, he would have this same mind and same principle. If in the Southern or Northern Seas, there were to appear sages, they, too, would have this same mind and this same principle. If a hundred or a thousand generations ago, or a hundred or a thousand generations hence, sages were to appear, they (likewise) would have this same mind and this same principle." Fung Yu-lan,[av] *A History of Chinese Philosophy,* Derk Bodde, trans. (Princeton: Princeton University Press, 1953), Vol. II, p. 537.

[12] In the *Lieh Tzu,*[aw] supposedly written by a Taoist philosopher of the pre-Ch'in period, there is a paragraph about the sage of the West which was originally taken as an argument to convince Chinese people that the Buddha is a Western sage. Yet, when Jesuits came to China during the Ming Dynasty, this sentence was reinterpreted by Matteo Ricci in his book, *T'ien-chu shih-i,*[ax] as the prophecy of Jesus Christ as a Western sage.

actual existence. When I am awakened to this idea, then all that is remote, such as the highest ideals or holy virtues of sages, is nearest to my here-and-now mind, and all the values of the highest ideals and holy virtues belong to my mind as much as they do to the minds of sages themselves. This is perhaps the highest idea of human spiritual life expounded by the thinkers of the late Ming (1368–1644) after Wang Shou-jen. It is too subtle to explain all its meanings here.[13]

IV. SPIRITUAL VALUES IN TAOISM

The Taoist ideas about spiritual life were usually expounded as in contrast with the life of worldly man. Such names as "real man," "Heavenly man," "spirit-man" or "divine man," "perfect man," and "sage man" were used by Taoist philosophers to differentiate their ideal man from the worldly man.

The Taoist philosophers, who looked aloof at everything here, felt some fatigue in worldly affairs and sought spiritual quiescence and tranquillity, and then, withdrawing their minds from worldly things, were men who had a transcendent mentality. The Taoist philosophers usually thought and spoke about their ideals of human life *negatively*, unlike the Confucians, who usually thought and spoke *positively*. Lao Tzu[s] (6th century B.C.) taught men to be weak, soft, quiet, and foolish, instead of strong, hard, active, and wise. Chuang Tzu[t] (399–295 B.C. ?) taught man not to seek reputation, honor, or social success, to forget himself and be indifferent to worldly gain and loss, happiness and misery, and life and death. They taught people to live a way of life which is neither driven by instinctive desires nor motivated by calculation, forgetting worldly benefits. So, the value of their ideal life is quite beyond the category of the satisfaction of natural desires and utilitarian value as defined in Section I, above. But what is the spiritual value of this kind of life, which seems purely negative and from which we can derive nothing?

The answer is twofold. First, the Taoist ideal of life has its positive side. Second, this positive value of life can be realized by living in a negative way. I shall begin with the latter point.

The reason the positive value of life can be realized by living in a negative way is very simple. If our ordinary way of living is considered of no value or of disvalue, then not living in this way is a positive value. For example, if the toil of the whole day is considered to be disvalue, is not rest itself a positive value? The important thing is that the negating of disvalue should be presented to the spiritual subject. If the negating of disvalue is presented to a spiritual subject, the value of the negating itself is positively presented to the spiritual subject, immanently exists in the subject, and becomes positive spiritual value. So, when I am not seeking worldly wealth, reputation, and honor, which are considered to be of disvalue, the very quiescence and tranquillity in my non-

[13] The sayings of Wang Lung-ch'i[ay] (1498–1583), Lo Chin-ch'i[az] (1515–1588), Lo Nien-an[ba] (1504–1564), and Liu Ch'i-shan, [bb] (1578–1645) are available in *Ming-jü hsüeh-an*[bc] ("Writings of Ming Confucians"), edited and written by Huang Tsung-hsi.

seeking can be presented to my spiritual self as full of positive value (just as rest after a day of toil can be presented as of positive value).

If we understand this clearly, then we know there are as many kinds of values experienced by the men who want to transcend worldly things as by men who cling to worldly things. The sense of tranquillity and quiescence of the men who transcend worldly things successfully seems homogeneously extended. Yet, under this homogeneous extension, the heterogeneous worldly things are transcended co-extensively. So, the spiritual content of the life of the man who transcends worldly things is as full as the life of the worldly man, the difference being that all worldly things are transcended and superseded in his mind. From this point we may proceed to the reason many Eastern and Western mystics who see the transcendent world as Divine Nothing estimate the value of the Divine Nothing as higher than everything, full of everything that has been superseded, and as a Divine All-Being.

The problem of all mystics, who want to transcend worldly things, is that the deep quiescence or tranquillity of the spirit is not easily preserved, and the Divine Nothing is not easily revealed. So, it may be easily concluded that, without faith in a transcendent savior who descends from above to help us ascend to the transcendent world, we can never raise ourselves. However, in Oriental religious and metaphysical thought there is an idea which is most important: that it is not necessary for us to have faith in a transcendent savior to help us transcend the mundane world. Instead, we may have wisdom to see that worldly things are themselves sunk down and have no power to disturb our tranquillity and quiescence of mind and that the world is itself a place where something like the Divine Nothing reveals itself. This is the wisdom of Nothing in Taoist philosophy.

This wisdom is very simple in essence. It is the realization that any worldly thing begins in or comes from "where it is not," or "Nothing," through a process of transformation or change, and ends at or goes back to "where it is not." Then, "beginning and ending in Nothing" is the general nature of all things and the Great Way, or Tao, where all things pass through. This idea is based primarily on our everyday experience. Everybody agrees, at least from the point of view of phenomena, that the future is what has not "yet been" and is now nothing, and that the present, which was the future and becomes the past, may be said to come from Nothing and go to Nothing. If we know deeply that everything comes from the Nothing and goes back to Nothing, then all things may be taken as involved in a Great Nothing,[14] or as floating out from the Great Nothing, only to sink into it again. Then not anything can really constitute bondage or disturb our spirit. When its very nature of "shall-be-sinking" is really presented to me in the immediate present, it is already nothing and has no effect as a disturbance or bondage for me even now.

[14]Taoist philosophers used the word *"wu,"*[bd] which has not actually the same sense of "nothing." *"Wu"* means nothing or non-being in phemomena but may not mean nothing or non-being in reality. We use the phrase "Great Nothing" here as the translation of the word *"wu"* to indicate that it is like nothing in the phenomenal world, yet it may be something in reality.

The two great founders of Taoist philosophy, Lao Tzu and Chuang Tzu, both present the wisdom of Nothing in metaphysics as the theoretical basis for the development of the spiritual life of tranquillity and quiescence so as to achieve an actual transcendence over worldly things. This is the negative side of their teachings. On the positive side, there are differences in their teachings on the spiritual life. When Lao Tzu thought about the relation of worldly things to the "Nothing," he usually thought that worldly things were involved and contained in the Nothing. The ideal spiritual life, corresponding to this metaphysical vision, is identified in our mind or spirit with the Nothing and is free from all the limitations of finite particular worldly things. Thus we can comprehend and embrace all things without partiality. When this kind of mind is used in political philosophy, it is the mind of a sage-king, which has no special reaction to any particular thing, but is glad to see all things and actions of all people well done, and embraces all people as his children. This kind of mind is mild, kind, soft, as broad as Heaven or the Void, always wishing for all things to go their own way, and tolerating them, following them, and never interfering with them. This is the first aspect of Lao Tzu's teaching, which has cultivated the virtue of tolerance and broad-mindedness in the Chinese people, and has provided Chinese government with the political ideals of non-interference with people, concession to the will of the people, and so on.

In the second aspect of Lao Tzu's teaching, the mind, which is identified with Nothing and is as broad as Heaven or the Void, may simply contemplate the "coming and going," "birth and death," and "prosperity and decay" of all things without affection or mercy. It is the mind of a spectator of the universe. It is neither morally bad, nor morally good, and maintains ethical neutrality. The metaphysical truth is thus presented to this mind with a kind of intellectual value.

In the third aspect of Lao Tzu's teaching, the mind, which knows that what is prosperous shall decay, that what is strong shall become weak, and that what is born shall die, can generalize all these into a principle: Everything moves in a curve which represents the natural law of all things. According to this principle, when a thing reaches the top of the curve it is destined to fall. Therefore, if we do not want to be a victim of this natural law, the only way is never to progress to the top of the curve, or, when we do approach the top, to go back to the beginning of the curve again, for then the top of the curve will always be in our purview, but we shall never arrive there, and so we shall never fall. So, Lao Tzu taught us to go backward, to learn the way of the child or the female, and to be humble and modest, in order to preserve our vitality and other powers to prevent falling down. This is the utilitarian aspect of Lao Tzu's philosophy, which is neither morally good nor morally bad and may not include any spiritual value to be realized by this kind of mind.

In contrast with Lao Tzu, when Chuang Tzu thought about the things of the world, he did not hold that all things are contained in the Great Nothing, but paid more attention to the great process of incessant change or transformation of all things in the Infinite Heaven. In this process, all definite forms and colors of things come into being and pass away. So, this process can also be taken as a great change or transformation of a Great Ether or Air, which is itself formless and colorless, being combined with non-being. Since Chuang Tzu paid more attention to the process of transformation in the universe, his view of human life placed more emphasis on the spiritual transformation of human life itself. If one wants to be a real man or a man of Heaven, free from one's past habits or ordinary self, one ought to live a life of spiritual flight, or spiritual wandering, through the process of the infinite transformations in the universe. He should also take all things as equals when they are presented and enjoyed by one's spirit, yet without judging them as good or bad from one's partial, personal point of view. In its flight or wandering in the universe, one's spirit sees everything with empathy and takes the myriad forms as the forms of things which it encounters, yet without attachment to any one, and lets the forms successfully be taken and then left. When the form of anything is left, then nothing remains and nothing needs to be remembered. When the form of anything is being taken, it is absolutely new, just as the world which is present to the new-born child or new-born animal is preceded by nothing, and, as we may not expect anything from it, is followed by nothing. It is immediately presented and enjoyed, as if it were floating in an infinite Void or Heaven as its background. This is the way of life of the real man, the man of Heaven, or the spirit-man of Chuang Tzu. Therefore, the word "spirit" (*shen*[u]), which originally meant an invisible spirit which existed objectively, was used by Chuang Tzu as the name of the spiritual mood or activity of the spirit-man which extends his spirit beyond the limitation of the universe. He used "*shen-yü*"[v] (literally, spirit-meeting) as the term for the way of the ideal man when he encounters anything immediately with empathy for the moment, without attachment.[15]

From the above, we may conclude that the spirit of Chuang Tzu's way of life is more aesthetic than Lao Tzu's way of life, which comprehends all things from above, but is, rather, a universal way of all things in heaven and earth, and so can appreciate with empathy the beauties of all things or the "beauty of heaven and earth," as he called it.[16] Yet, this kind of beauty does not consist simply in the forms of things. As every form exists in the process of "transformation of ether or air," so the most beautiful forms should never be clear-cut and should be permeated by the flow of ether and become ethereal forms. As the forms pass through the ether and return, they create rhythms. Ethereal rhythm (*ch'i-yün*[w]) is a key term of Chinese aesthetics; it has the Infinite Void or Heaven as its background. It permeates the whole universe charged with life.[17]

[15] The whole paragraph is my elaboration of Chuang Tzu's idea of spiritual life. It would require much space to cite all the documents concerned with comments which are omitted.

[16] Cf. *Chuang Tzu* XXII.

[17] This is just a way of deducing an idea of Chinese aesthetics from the philosophy of Chuang Tzu. Historically speaking, the idea of Chinese aesthetics has its origin in the philosophy of Confucianism, too. But, as we know that almost all the later Chinese artists liked to read Chuang Tzu, we have more reason to suppose that the philosophy of Chuang Tzu influenced the aesthetic ideas of later artists prominently.

V. BUDDHIST IDEAS AS A SUPPLEMENT TO CHINESE PHILOSOPHY

From the Chinese point of view, the Buddhist theory of the non-permanence of everything is very similar to the Taoist idea that everything is in a process of change, as coming from Nothing and returning to Nothing. Yet, impermanence in Buddhism is based on the principle of *yüan-sheng,*[x] sometimes translated as causal or dependent origination, meaning that everything is a combination of conditions. (It was never consciously posited by Lao Tzu or Chuang Tzu.) The meaning of *yüan-sheng* is simple in itself. It leads our thinking from the assertion that "a thing is generated by its conditions and has no 'self' concealed in it to sustain its existence" to the assertion that "the self-nature or self-essence of a thing is emptiness," that is, that there is no such self-nature.

To show that *śūnyatā* is the nature of everything, according to the theory of *yüan-sheng,* the Buddhists argue that, if we know a thing is generated by its conditions, then there is absolutely nothing which exists as such, before or after all conditions have met together. Since all the conditions which come together can be separated, nothing has any permanence, and what is existing can also be non-existing. Therefore, the existing thing has no self-nature or self-essence to sustain its existence, and the possibility of its non-existence is the very nature of its existence. (This is *śūnyatā.*) Yet, when we really know this starting point and other, further theories of *śūnyatā,* we have to see directly and intuitively the *śūnyatā* of all things. This requires strict training in spiritual concentration, spiritual quiescence, and spiritual wisdom. When we understand *śūnyatā,* then all things of the world become clear to us. Then all is enlightened by non-being, and non-being is enlightened by being. This is, of course, an awakening which is beyond the self-consciousness of the layman and the speculation of philosophers.

The idea of *yüan-sheng* in Buddhism, especially in the Mādhyamika school, never requires us to know merely the conditions of a thing. On the contrary, its main purpose is to direct our consciousness to *depart* negatively from the false idea of self-nature or self-essence, and to look to the conditions of a thing. As every existing condition has its various conditions, too, so the idea of *yüan-sheng* directs our consciousness to depart from the thing as a center, to extend its light to the conditions, to the conditions of conditions, and to go beyond the thing itself. Then the self-nature or self-essence of anything can be cancelled and the *śūnyatā* of all things may be revealed.

In the cultivation of spiritual life, the value of the teaching of *śūnyatā* is tremendous. Since all the bonds of our spiritual life and the infinite evils of human life come from clinging to the apparent realities of worldly things, these teachings remove the roots of all bonds and evils. Infinite merits can be achieved and infinite virtues or spiritual values can then be realized by us. This is the ideal of Buddhahood.

Buddhist demonstrations of the *śūnyatā* of all things are based upon the conditional relations of things, which are acknowledged as actually existing in the intellect of common sense and science. Therefore, all these demonstrations can logically be carried out as in the Mādhyamika school of Buddhism.

Another point to be discussed is the idea of the *ālaya* (storehouse) consciousness and its seeds as expounded by the Yogācāra school of Buddhism. These ideas come from our spiritual light reaching into the unconscious nether world. From the teachings of the Yogācāra school, we can understand the world of *ālaya* and its seeds through indirect and mediate reasoning only, though they can be consciously known directly and immediately by deep contemplation of the *bodhisattva* or the Buddha. In the teachings of this school, many layers and aspects of the world of unconsciousness are elucidated and analyzed, and so are many ways of *yoga* for the self-transformation of the whole personality in order to attain the vision of the *bodhisattva* or the Buddha. These were all new teachings of spiritual cultivation for the Chinese people.

The ultimate purpose of Buddhism is to teach man to attain Buddhahood and to see the *śūnyatā* of all things, which is super-intellectual. This is different from Taoist philosophy, which usually uses metaphorical symbolism or aesthetic imagination to attain the super-intellectual. The combination of the spirit of the teaching of Buddhism, mainly the Mādhyamika school, and the spirit of Taoist philosophers is the way of Ch'an[y] (Zen), which may be taken as the free use of intellectual ideas to cancel other ideas and let the vision of *śūnyatā* of Ch'an experience be expressed by symbolic language and actions.

VI. NEW ORIENTATION OF VALUE-CONSCIOUSNESS IN THE NEO-CONFUCIANISM OF THE SUNG-MING PERIOD

It is generally agreed that the Neo-Confucians of the Sung and Ming dynasties were men of an introvert type. They propounded the values of quiescence, serenity, reverence, self-reflection, and self-examination. They even adopted static sitting as a way to spiritual cultivation. All this seems quite different from the pre-Ch'in (220–206 B.C.) Confucians, who were more active in social, political, and cultural activities. So, the Confucians of the Ch'ing (1644–1912) criticized the Confucians of the Sung and Ming dynasties as Buddhists or Taoists in disguise. This is an exaggeration. Almost all the Confucians of the Sung and Ming dynasties most sincerely opposed many teachings of the Buddhists and Taoists. Their ideas of the ethical relations and of the sacrificial ceremonies for ancestors, sages, and worthies and their many other historical, cultural, political, and economic ideas are all of Confucian origin. So, we have to explain why they laid more emphasis on the self-reflective or quietistic way of spiritual cultivation through the influence of Buddhism and Taoism, plus the development of Confucianism itself.

Compared with the earlier Confucians, the Neo-Confucians were more conscientious about the inner obstructions to the development of spiritual life. These obstructions, such as the evil elements of *karma* and *ālaya,* had not been taken seriously by earlier Confucians. It is usually the case that the higher in spiritual life one wants to ascend, the more inner obstructions one finds. The more self-reflective one is, the more faults or potential inner motive of faults one finds deep in his mind. The Neo-Confucians called these inner obstructions insincere ideas, e.g., selfish desires, habitual materialistic tendencies, obstinate opinions, variegated temperaments, and the manipulative or calculating mind, which are all deeply rooted and always concealed in our minds. Only deep inner meditation or self-reflection can illuminate and reveal the way to eradicate the roots of these obstructions. In order to eradicate these ideas, which are all purely negative to the development of spiritual life, we have to avoid absolutely doing certain things and let the negative things be arrested, appeased, and transformed, and thus our spiritual life may be purified. In these cases, all our ways of life must be quiet and static, at least in appearance.

Secondly, the Neo-Confucians were more metaphysical and religious than the earlier Confucians, and consequently they usually had a sense of life, both moral and super-moral. The ideas of Heaven, God, the Reason of Heaven, and the Mind of Heaven, as mentioned before, were always discussed by them. They always talked of man from the point of view of Heaven and had a belief in the eternal Tao. These were somewhat similar to Taoist thought. Ch'eng Hao said that "the achievements of the sage-emperors, such as Yao[z] and Shun,[aa] may be like a floating cloud in an infinite void,"[18] since the eternal Tao of the universe has no addition by "the achievements of Yao or Shun, the sage-emperors," nor is there any loss by all the evils done by Chieh[ab] or Chou,[ac] the worst kings. When a pupil of Lu Chiu-yüan regretted that Chu Hsi (an opponent of his master) did not know the Tao rightly, Lu reproached his pupil and regretted that he had made no improvement and said, "The Tao shall neither be added nor subtracted whether there are Lu Hsiang-shan (Lu Chiu-yüan) and Chu Yüan-hui[ad] (another name of Chu Hsi)."[19] All these sayings took the standpoint of Heaven and originated from a metaphysical and religious faith in the eternal existence of Tao, or a spiritual mood which is, at least in a sense, beyond the distinction of the good and evil of conduct and the right and wrong ideas of man. In the philosophy of Wang Shou-jen, *liang-chih* (conscience) is sometimes said to be beyond good and evil. This is based upon the fact that, in the practice of *liang-chih,* when evil is wholly undone, no evil is left, and, when good is done, no good is left. So, in the practice of *liang-chih* we can pass beyond good and evil, and the nature of *liang-chih* is neither good nor evil, and this is called the chief good of *liang-chih*. Here we find Wang's view to be moral thought combined with the super-moral idea, and this may be said to be a combination of the moral ideas of earlier Confucians and the super-moral ideas of the Buddhists and Taoists.

However, the Tao and the *liang-chih* of the Neo-Confucians are still essentially moral concepts. "To see man from the point of view of Heaven" is itself a phase of moral life, according to the Neo-Confucians. When Wang Shou-jen said that "*liang-chih* is neither good nor evil, and this is called the chief good,"

[18] *Erh-Ch'eng ch'üan-shu*[be] ("The Complete Works of the Ch'eng Brothers"), chap. 4.
[19] *Hsiang-shan ch'üan-chi*[bf] ("The Collected Works of Lu Hsiang-shan"), chap. 8.

it is still beyond mere evil and ordinary good, but never beyond the chief good. So, the super-moral ideas of the Neo-Confucians should be taken as the expressions of their highest moral experience, though, in the profundity and depth of this moral experience, they may exceed all the earlier Confucians in certain respects.

VII. SPIRITUAL, SOCIAL, AND NATURAL VALUES DURING THE PAST THREE CENTURIES

In the development of Chinese thought there has been a great change since the end of the Ming Dynasty. During this period, generally speaking, the trends of thought have moved from depth of thought to extent of thought, from inward reflection to comprehensive understanding, from meditation on the spiritual and moral life to a consideration of natural and social life, and from the gaining of material for thought from personal experience to the gaining of material for thought from historical documents and relics. At the end of the Ming Dynasty, great scholars, such as Wang Fu-chih[ae] (1619–1692), Ku Yen-wu[af] (1613–1682), and Huang Tsung-hsi[ag] (1610–1695), even though they were erudite and usually based their ideas upon documentary evidence, all held a lofty idea of culture and had high personal characters, to which their knowledge was subordinated, and the spiritual and moral values of all social, political, and cultural life was expounded by them. From the school of Yen Yüan and Li Kung[ah] (1659–1733), a new current of thought began to flourish, which laid more emphasis on the social utilitarian values. Even the values of music and of the moral virtues were considered by them according to a utilitarian standard. From the middle of the Ch'ing Dynasty, in the thought of Tai Chen and Chiao Hsün[ai] (1768–1820), much attention was paid to the satisfaction of men's natural feelings and desires. The moral values of benevolence and social justice were interpreted to be the results of men's mutual consideration of the satisfaction of natural feelings and desires. So, the ideas of moral value, social utilitarian value, and natural values were combined into one homogeneous system. The most important current of thought late in the Ch'ing Dynasty was the thought of the Kung-yang[aj] school, which gradually laid more emphasis on the political and economic problems of the time (and found its justification in the commentaries on the Classics). These currents of thought finally joined with the thoughts of social construction from the West and resulted in the thought of K'ang Yu-wei[ak] (1858–1927). In recent decades, the spirit of searching the documentary evidence of the scholars of the Ch'ing Dynasty has become gradually connected with the Western scientific spirit and transformed into the popular high estimation of all things of scientific value. The two watchwords of the so-called new cultural movement at the beginning of the Republic of China were democracy and science, which were taken to have a very high social utilitarian value and truth value. Other spiritual values were generally neglected. When Marxism attracted the minds of the young generation, a communist party was organized and now has gained political power on the mainland of China. The communists' sense of value has further narrowed down to the political and social sphere. Only the technical value of science has been emphasized by them.

From the above, it is clear that the direction of the development of Chinese thought, from the end of the Ming Dynasty to recent years, has gradually left the spirit of Neo-Confucianism, which paid more attention to the spiritual values of human life, and now pays more attention to the importance of the social, utilitarian, technical, and natural values of human life. Since the nineteenth century, the value-consciousness of Westerners has gradually concentrated on the social, utilitarian, and technical sphere and on the values of satisfaction of natural desire. Here is a meeting of the value-consciousnesses of East and West, which represents a *Zeitgeist*. On its good side, this *"Zeitgeist"* may be taken as an extensive development of human value-consciousness for the preparation of the spiritual ground of the coming age, which should pay more intensive attention to the importance of spiritual values. But when and how the various kinds of natural value, social values, and spiritual values can be integrated into a great harmony in the new age is a complicated problem which is quite beyond the sphere of this essay.

QUESTION: You talk about spiritual life in Taoist philosophy and you identify the wisdom of Lao Tzu with the wisdom of Nothing in metaphysics as the theoretical basis for the development of spiritual life. It seems to me that the Tao of Lao Tzu is a metaphysical being, the primordial mover of the universe or the Godhead. How can the wisdom of Lao Tzu be identified with the wisdom of Nothing?

ANSWER: The wisdom of Lao Tzu is not identified simply with the wisdom of Nothing. I did not use the word "identified." Surely, the Tao of Lao Tzu may be interpreted as a metaphysical being or primordial mover of the universe, perhaps something like the Godhead. However, in this paper, I had to stress the Nothingness side of Lao Tzu's Tao. One reason for this is that the Tao of Lao Tzu as a metaphysical being is said to be revealed to us through the transiency of natural things. The transiency of things is explained as their coming from Nothing and sinking into Nothing. The other reason is that the meditation on Tao as metaphysical must begin with the thought of worldly things themselves as nothing. "Nothing" is a mediation between the thought of worldly things and meditation on Tao. When we want to ascend to Tao, we must transcend worldly things and encounter Nothing first, and the very transcending is itself a "nothing-ing" activity initiating from the Tao. This is explicitly stated in Lao Tzu's thought also. When we talk about Lao Tzu's idea of spiritual value as a higher value transcending worldly values, as my paper does, the wisdom of Nothing in Lao Tzu must be stressed.

(The Chinese characters are on the following page.)

a 唐君毅
b 仁
c 三教
d 永康
e 永嘉
f 顏元
g 戴震
h 恩
i 恩義
j 朱熹
k 理
l 良知
m 王守仁, 陽明
n 張載, 橫渠
o 程顥, 明道
p 程頤, 伊川
q 陸九淵, 象山
r 道
s 老子
t 莊子
u 神
v 神遇
w 氣韻
x 緣生
y 禪
z 堯
aa 舜
ab 桀
ac 紂
ad 朱元晦
ae 王夫之
af 顧炎武
ag 黃宗羲
ah 李塨
ai 焦循
aj 公羊
ak 康有為
al 陳獨秀
am 在精神生活發展中之毀譽意識
an 人生
ao 自得
ap 悅
aq 安
ar 傳習錄
as 中國人文精神之進展
at 文
au 里
av 馮友蘭
aw 列子
ax 天主實義
ay 王龍溪
az 羅近溪
ba 羅念菴
bb 劉蕺山
bc 明儒學案
bd 無
be 二程全書
bf 象山全集

HIDEO KISHIMOTO[a]

Some Japanese Cultural Traits and Religions

I.

Suppose a man is taking a walk in the countryside of Japan. He is surrounded by quiet autumnal scenery. Some sentiment comes to his mind. He feels it and wants to express it. To express the sentiment, he would say, "*Samishii*"[b] (lonesome).

What he says, on such an occasion, can be simply one word, as above. This single word can well be regarded as a complete statement in the Japanese language. For the Japanese language, a full sentence in the Western grammatical sense is not ordinarily called for. The nature or structure of its syntax has its own peculiarity. A complete statement can be made just by saying "lonesome," and nothing else.

It is not necessary in Japanese to specify the subject by explicitly stating whether "I" am feeling lonesome, or "the scenery" is lonesome. Without such analysis, one's sentiment can be projected there in its immediate form. Analytically, the sentiment is the result of the collaboration of the subject and the object. No doubt, both are taking part in it. But, what is actually coming up in his mind is the sentiment of lonesomeness, working in the domain of an immediate experience. It is in-between. One of the characteristics of the Japanese language is to be able to project man's experience in its immediate and unanalyzed form.

No doubt, in modern Western languages, also, people can say things in short abbreviated form. But, when they use such a simple form, they are always conscious of the fact that what is being said is only the abbreviated part of the more complete full statement. The syntax of Western languages requests, in their construction, more distinct and full indication of the subject-object relation than does the Japanese. So, a full statement of the subject-object relation is expected in English, while the Japanese language is more closely connected with man's immediate experience.

This peculiarity is not limited to the language alone. It is rooted deeper in Japanese culture. It seems to be reflected in the way the Japanese people think. This is a more fundamental problem. A subtle but significant difference between the Japanese mind and that of Western people seems to be betrayed there.

To the Japanese, the Western mind seems to be making a sharper distinction between subject and object. The first reaction of Western people to any given situation seems to be in contrast to the Japanese, more inclined in the direction of analysis, analyzing the situation into a subject-object-predicate relation. To the Western mind, these composite elements of experience immediately arise. Based on them, the instinctive reaction of the Westerner is to achieve an analytical grasp. They use many more "I's," "you's," and "it's" than would Japanese. Of course, on similar occasions, the Japanese are also aware of the subject-object relation. But the Japanese seem to direct their interest more to the domain of immediate experience.

This cultural trait seems to have some bearing on the nature of Japanese thought. It is often said that the general trend of Japanese thinking is idealistic. It certainly is strongly tinged with introspective tendencies. The Japanese usually do not show too much interest in the exact details of factual events and objects. In this sense it seems idealistic. But, in spite of that, it could be asked whether it is really idealistic in the Western sense of the term.

In the West, the distinction between the two types of thought, realism and idealism, is more distinct. Realism is factual. It puts its focus on objective facts. Idealism is conceptual. It puts its emphasis on subjective ideas. Japanese thinking may seem idealistic because it is introspective and takes less interest in factual objects. But it has seldom taken the form of conceptual idealism. It should be noticed that, in the course of cultural history, the Japanese have never shown their strength in speculative thinking. The system of formal logic or abstract concepts has made little progress in Japan. Outstanding thinkers are rather few in Japan. Buddhism has been equipped with deep and complicated philosophical systems, such as Tendai[c] and Hossō.[d] But they had developed in India and China. Japanese Buddhism in turn has grown more as a practical religion. Confucianism also prevailed in Japan. But no leader like Chu Hsi[e] (1130–1200) or Wang Yang-ming[f] (1473–1529) appeared in Japan. To repeat, the Japanese have been more interested in the domain of immediate experience. So, if one wants to call Japanese thinking idealistic, it might be better to call it empirical idealism. It should be distinguished from conceptual idealism of the Western type.

Immediate experience plays a very important role in Japanese life. The Japanese people introspectively ponder and feel around in the domain of immediate experience. This is a very concrete domain for a Japanese. If conceptual speculation goes too far into abstract thinking, a Japanese quickly loses interest. And he wants to be less abstract and more concrete and realistic. But to be realistic does not necessarily mean, for a Japanese, to go back to factual realism, but to be realistic to the reality of immediate experience.

In the philosophical trends of the West, there is a third general trend which may not be as influential as the other two. It is the trend which is more concerned with immediate experience, such as Bergsonian intuitionism, the radical empiricism of William James, and recent existentialism. It is not unnatural that such trends in philosophy should have a strong appeal to the Japanese mind.

The characteristic mentioned above may be called the "radically empirical trait" of the Japanese, in contrast to the "analytical trait" of the Western mind. Why has this peculiarity developed in Japanese culture? The indigenous intuitive nature of the Japanese people must be credited with that, as well as the cultural influence of Buddhism. In the long course of history, the introvert nature of Buddhism must have accelerated this tendency a good deal. This is a subtle trait. But it seems to have fundamental importance. It is so basic that various features of Japanese culture may be interpreted from this point of view. Taking this as a clue, I should like to make a brief observation on some features of religions and other spiritual values in Japanese culture.

II.

There are many religions in Japan. Various different religions are flourishing side by side, such as Shinto[g], Buddhism, Christianity, and others.

Among them, Shinto is an age-old native religion of the Japanese people. It originated in Japan and has grown along with the development of her culture. Buddhism came from India by way of China. The transmission of Buddhism to Japan was in the middle of the sixth century. It spread all over Japan, and also penetrated Japanese culture. Christianity entered Japan once, briefly, in the fifteenth century. Present-day Christianity, including both Catholic and Protestant, is the second entrance, which was about one hundred years ago. Besides these, there are many independent religions which have been founded by individual spiritual leaders. Some of them are Sectarian Shinto, and there are still other new religions. New religions are abundant. Within the span of a decade of post-war Japan, statistics say about six hundred religions came into being.

The variety of religions is broad and extensive in Japan. But, excepting Christianity, most of them share a common general characteristic. This seems to be rooted in the basic empirical trait of Japanese culture.

The common concern of all these religions is the internal problems of man. Their main focus is on immediate experience. How to remove worries and anxieties from man's mind is their main task. Various devices are suggested for that purpose. They generally try to remold man's mind. This constitutes the central part of the religious activities. Mental training is the indispensable element in those religions. Religious experience of a mystical nature is also cherished by them. But those religions do not show too much interest in the social life of the people. They do not put special emphasis on the ethical problems of man. Such religions present a fairly different picture as compared to those of the Western religious tradition.

For instance, Shinto has a strong tinge of Nature mysticism. Shinto has long maintained that there should not be a rational interpretation of it. It has no sacred scripture corresponding to the Bible of Christianity or the holy *Sūtras* of Buddhism. A faithful believer would come to the simple hall of a Shinto sanctuary, which is located in a grove with a quiet and holy atmosphere. He may stand still quite a while in front of the sanctuary, clap his hands, bow deeply, and try to feel the deity in his heart. He would not try to build up a rational proof for the existence of an invisible deity. For him, the proof of divine existence depends on whether or not he can feel the deity directly in his heart. Shinto being a polytheistic religion, each sanctuary has its own particular deity. But seldom do the believers know the individual name of the deity whom they are worshipping. They do not care about it. It is not a matter of importance for them. The more important point for them is whether or not they feel the existence of deity directly in their hearts.

In the case of Japanese Buddhism, its supreme aim is to emancipate man from the miseries of life. Most of the miseries of life are undoubtedly caused by the difficulties of environmental situations. But such environmental difficulties themselves are not the direct cause of the real miseries of life. They become the real miseries of life only if the mind is affected and disturbed by such difficulties. In the disturbed mind, conflicting desires arise, and they combat each other in the mind. Such a state of mind causes worries and anxieties, and man is tormented by agonies. Therefore, the key to the real miseries of life is how a man accepts a given situation. Thus, this key point is closely connected with immediate experience. Buddhism can check the miseries of life. In such a way, Buddhism focuses its interest on the internal problem of man. Worries and anxieties in the domain of immediate experience have become its main concern.

To discover the ultimate means for overcoming the miseries of life, the Buddha made introspective inquiries, deep in the psychology of man. What is the main cause of worries and anxieties in man's mind? According to Buddhist teachings, it is the basic desire within man. Stimulated by the environmental situations, conflicting desires flare up in the mind. Unfulfilled desires become the further cause of disorder in the mind. This is the main cause of worries and anxieties. So, the task of emancipating man from them develops in Buddhism into the problem of how to handle basic desire in man.

Indian Buddhism, reflecting the extremely speculative mind of the Indian people, went far. It carried the solution of the problem to the goal of logical conclusions. If the basic desire in man is the cause of the miseries of life, the most effective means to check them is to exterminate such basic desire. Then worries and anxieties should disappear. But utter extermination of desires would mean no life at all. The metaphysical theory of Indian Buddhism logically puts its ultimate goal on the disappearance of man from this worldly cycle of life. Such an ideal of life-negation, however, was too much for the Japanese people. The Japanese are apparently life-enjoying people. They want to take a more affirmative attitude toward life.

Buddhism in Japan shows radical differences from such life-negating Buddhism. It is Mahāyāna Buddhism. It also aims at remolding man's mind. But there is an important shift in the purpose of such remolding. It does not try to exterminate basic desire, but it tries to correct the desire-structure of man. Conflicting desires are the cause of worries and anxieties. Desires as such are not only the cause of worries and anxieties, but are also the cause for all life-activities. Only the wrong desire-structure becomes the cause of worries and anxieties. So, desires as such should not be exterminated. But desires should be given a right structure. Following the teaching of the Buddha, Japanese Buddhists believe man can remold his mind to give his desire-system a right structure. Enlightenment means that a man has a right structure of mind. The stimulations of environmental situations will no longer make conflicting desires arise. His worries and anxieties disappear. He suffers from no miseries of life. The environmental world may remain the same, but, for him, the life of miseries changes into the life of happiness. After having achieved enlightenment, a man will still enjoy earthly life. Buddhism, for the Japanese people, is thus a life-affirming religion.

Buddhism, with its influence penetrating very deeply into Japanese culture, has made the Japanese mind more and more introverted. Turning inward, the radically empirical trait of the Japanese people was further strengthened. But Japanese philosophy did not develop into abstract conceptual idealism.

In this way, both Shinto and Buddhism focus their main concern on the domain of immediate experience. The role of religions in Japan is to teach people how to accept the given environmental situation. If man's mental state is well adjusted, his grasp of situations will be well-balanced and conflicting desires will not arise. Thus, the radically empirical trait of Japanese culture seems to be effective as the basic factor of Japanese religions.

III.

The peculiar nature of Japanese religions has brought forth two conspicuous cultural features. One is a distinct separation in the sphere of activities between the religious system and the ethical system. The other is the close relation between religious value and aesthetic value.

All through the history of Japan, Japanese religions have been steeped in the inner problem of man. The inner problem has exclusively occupied the interest of Japanese religions. They were not active in providing ethical principles for man's social conduct. What should man's respectable social conduct be? How should a man endeavor to reform society according to his religious ideal? Such a problem did not develop within the domain of religion. The problem whether a man's conduct is good or bad is different by nature from the problem of how to emancipate man from worries and anxieties. In Japan, religion has concentrated upon the latter problem. Neither Buddhism nor Shinto has had much concern for the ethical problem. In the well-known words of Shinran[h] (1173–1262), "Even a righteous man can be saved, why not a sinner."

Because of the peculiar nature of Japanese religions, they have tried to deal with the sphere of man's problem which is beyond the sphere of good and evil conduct.

But the fact that Japanese religions had not supplied any ethical principles to Japanese society did not mean that the Japanese society was not in need of ethical principles. In earlier days, because of the homogeneous social structure of Japan, the need for an established system of ethical principles might not have been as serious as in other nations. But the society grew and became more complicated. It could not do without some kind of ethical system. Confucianism, transmitted from China, came to fulfill this need. From the beginning of the seventeenth century, by the time of the Tokugawa[i] government, the Confucian system was taken over as the ethical code of Japan. This has been the social role of Confucianism in Japan. As a result of this, a kind of division of labor was developed. For principles of moral conduct, people rely on the Confucian code. The domain of inner problems is left to Shinto and Buddhism. In other words, Confucianism functions for ethics, and Shinto and Buddhism for religion.

This dualism of religion and ethics in Japanese culture is often misunderstood by Western people. It is not too easy for them to grasp. Western visitors to Japan often ask the Buddhist or Shintoist what is his moral code. The answer is often weak and negative. Interpreting the weakness of such an answer in the Western fashion, they draw the conclusion that these religions in Japan are either half dead or out of date. They take the moral code of religion as the index of its vitality. The Japanese religions may well be getting out of date, but the judgment of their vitality should not be based upon this. A religion of the Japanese type can be vitally active without being equipped with a full-fledged moral code. In fact, this is the characteristic nature of Japanese religions.

The introduction of Christianity into Japan is particularly interesting in this connection. Christianity is new to Japanese culture, not only in its monotheistic structure, but in its tight integration of religious principles with its ethical principles. It is for the Japanese people a religion with a new structure.

Professor Friedrick Heiler and Professor Gustav Mensching say that there are two different types of religion. They would say that Buddhism and Shinto are religions of the mystical type, and that Christianity is the prophetic type. It is not that Buddhism and Shinto are out of date, or undeveloped, or do not have an effective moral code, but that they are a different kind of religion.

While the ethical system and the religious system are divided, on the other hand, the aesthetic value and religious value are regarded as having a close relationship in the Japanese cultural tradition. In their achievements religious values and aesthetic values are not two different things. Ultimately, they are one for the Japanese.

This close relationship between religion and the arts does not simply mean that Japanese religions specifically base their expression upon an abundant use of artistic representations. It goes deeper into the basic problem.

As has been mentioned above, the main concern of Japanese religions, especially Buddhism, has not been so much with the good and evil of man's conduct, but with the attitude of man, that is, how to accept the given environment. In other words, they put stronger emphasis on the mental aspect of man than on the behavioral aspect. They instruct man how to reach a tranquil and balanced state of mind. Then man can see things just as they are, without any disturbance or bias in his mind. Such mental emphasis on the part of religion makes its relationship to aesthetic value very close.

When we turn to aesthetic value, we find that the general attitude of Japanese artists also reflects the basic empirical trait of Japanese culture. They believe that the artist's mind must be calm and tranquil. A polished mirror can reflect things as they are. Only when the artist's mind is as calm as the surface of a mirror can the real nature of the outside object be grasped.

In the mind of the artist, nothing but an exact image of the object should exist. In this sense, the mind of the artist must become one with the object. To achieve this, the artist must practice mental training along with his technical training in art. This will explain why so many artists practice Zen[j] training. And, also, why many Zen monks became master artists.

Religion tries to emancipate man from worries and anxieties. Art tries to grasp beauty and represent it. But both religion and art try to achieve tranquillity of mind and to grasp objects as they are. On this point, religious value and aesthetic value become one.

IV.

In Japanese society, also, among the people as a matter of social custom, it has been regarded as a high virtue to be able to keep the mind tranquil and calm. This was mainly the influence of Buddhism. Confucianism also helped to encourage people to subdue their emotional excitement. Anger and sorrow should not appear on the countenance. Tears should be suppressed with full effort. For the Japanese, tears cannot be seen by others without some feeling of embarrassment. Generally speaking, the more subdued in emotion a man is, the more he is respected.

There is a prevailing interest among the people in practicing mental training. *"Shugyō"*[k] is the Japanese term for mental training. Various kinds of systematic training–such as waterfall ablution, mountain climbing, fasting, and others–have been offered by religions and other systems of culture. Zen, which is distinctly Buddhist, may be taken as the typical example of these. Flower arrangement and calligraphy are also taught for that purpose.

Naturally, in such circumstances, the Japanese have developed a complicated emotional structure of personality–probably to the degree that it is not easy for the outsider to understand it fully. The so-called Japanese "poker face" typically symbolizes it. The Japanese "poker face" is not because there is a lack of emotion. Strong and powerful emotional feelings are hidden behind it. The long cultural tradition has given the people the mental power to control the expression of their emotions.

This complexity of the Japanese mind often brings forth a peculiar form of emotional reaction. It is a familiar scene in which a Japanese champion at the Olympic Games stands on the victor's platform with a golden trophy in his hand, and, although he is expected to laugh happily, tears are in his eyes, as if he has just come away from a Greek tragedy. It is not that he is unhappy. In actuality, a feeling of joy is welling up within him, but he tries rigorously to suppress it. As the result, a complicated combination of emotions brings happy, warm tears.

Suppose a Japanese woman makes a small commotion by falling down on the street. As she struggles to get up, one may notice a faint smile on her face. In spite of her inner disturbance, she instinctively tries to keep her mind calm and balanced, and to observe the situation objectively. With great effort she tries to say to herself: "What a blunder you are making," and tries to smile at herself. This whole reaction can occur in an instant, because of long cultural tradition.

The emphasis on balanced tranquillity of mind has cultivated among the Japanese a peculiar ability to meet difficult situations; the attitude of accepting any difficulty quietly and courageously is regarded as a high virtue.

The most difficult problem of all for man to face is the oncoming of death. The problem as to how to face death has developed in Japan as a peculiar pattern of culture. It makes the Japanese feel that they must meet death squarely, rather than avoid it. The cultural tradition encourages them to be prepared to accept death with courage and with tranquillity. So, how one faces death has come to be regarded as an important feature of life. Death is not a mere end of life for the Japanese. It has been given a positive place in life. Facing death properly is one of the most important features of life. In that sense, it may well be said that for the Japanese death is within life.

Thus, cultural tradition has developed to the extent of establishing an etiquette for committing suicide. The ceremonial performance of *seppuku*[l] (often called *harakiri* by Westerners), which has aroused the curiosity of the Western people, is a very interesting cultural phenomenon. It was officially observed until the end of feudalistic days in the middle of the last century.

It was not a blind admiration of suicide. It was the last honor given to a samurai whose conduct deserved death.

In Japanese society, committing suicide has never been regarded as a sin, or a shame. The point of concern was the manner of committing it. If one could commit suicide in a fine self-composed manner, it could be taken as a respectable achievement. This will explain the Banzai[m] attacks and the Kamikaze[n] attacks during the recent war. The Japanese could do such daring acts, not because the Japanese have emotionally less fear of death, but as a result of cultural tradition. From childhood, consciously and unconsciously, they have been trained to meet death courageously.

Emphasis on tranquillity and a balanced state of mind may thus be taken as another expression of the empirical trait of the Japanese culture.

V.

During the last one hundred years, modern Western culture has been penetrating Japan. No other countries on the globe have ever met Western culture and Eastern culture in such an overwhelming way. Japanese culture is changing rapidly. A new Japanese culture, modernized and Westernized, is coming into being. But, in the case of Japanese religions, it is still too early to make any appraisal of these changes. The traditional religions are not affected. In spite of the vigorous trend of modernization and actual changes of other aspects of culture, they remain little changed.

Modern Western culture came into Japan as an integral whole. But it consisted of two different elements. These were Western culture and modern culture. These two have had very different effects upon Japanese culture. One has Westernized Japanese culture, and the other modernized it. But, the Japanese accepted them as an integral whole. The Japanese could not clearly distinguish the difference between these two elements. The problem as to whether a Japanese should learn English in addition to the indigenous Japanese language involves Westernization. To learn how to use the modern equipment of technology is modernization. The Japanese could not distinguish the difference between these two. This indiscriminate acceptance has caused deep confusion.

For the Japanese religions, it was fatal to become Westernized. Buddhism and Shinto could not take monotheistic form without losing their fundamental trait. Confucianism could not easily abandon its theory of benevolence. The empirical trait of Japanese culture could not change suddenly into a rational trait. They therefore resisted Westernization. But they could not resist Westernization alone. Modernization and Westernization were thought of as one. Resisting Westernization, they were unconsciously resisting modernization at the same time. As a result of this, while all other aspects of culture in Japan were making rapid progress toward modernization, Japanese religions and other indigenous cultural institutions lagged behind. The lag in the steps of modernizing religions is one aspect of present-day confusion.

But, now, Japan seems to be coming to the turning point. As the result of one hundred years' effort, though it was a difficult struggle, Japan has been modernized rather successfully. Having achieved this, the Japanese people are now, for the first time, realizing the distinction between Westernization and modernization. Japanese culture can be modernized without being Westernized. Now the Japanese people are able to see that their religions can be safely modernized, and that there is no need for infringement upon their intrinsic nature by Westernization. This turning point means the starting point for the modernization of Japanese religions and other indigenous institutions. We must watch their course of development.

[a] 岸本英夫
[b] 寂しい
[c] 天台
[d] 法相
[e] 朱子、朱熹
[f] 王陽明
[g] 神道
[h] 親鸞
[i] 德川
[j] 禪
[k] 修行
[l] 切腹
[m] 萬歳
[n] 神風

S. RADHAKRISHNAN

The Indian Approach to the Religious Problem

I. EAST AND WEST

There is no reason to believe that there are fundamental differences between the East and the West. Human beings are everywhere human and hold the same deepest values. The differences which are, no doubt, significant are related to external, temporary social conditions and are alterable with them.

East and West are relative terms. They are geographical expressions and not cultural types. The differences among countries like China, Japan, and India are quite as significant as those among European or American countries. Specific cultural patterns with distinctive beliefs and habits developed in different regions in relative isolation from one another. There were periods when China and India were pre-eminent in cultural affairs, others when Western nations became dominant. For the last four centuries Western nations aided by scientific development have dominated the East.

The world has now reached a stage of intercommunication. All societies are fast becoming industrialized, and new sets of values are springing up. We are called upon to participate in the painful birth of a new civilization. If we are to live together in peace we must develop international co-operation and understanding.

It is for the political leaders to determine the practical steps by which the sources of power and communication now available to us can be used for closer co-operation and friendliness among the peoples of the world. No political understanding can be made permanent without understanding at the cultural level. Apart from its intrinsic importance, such understanding contributes to the enrichment of human experience. Facile generalizations which are highly misleading are made by philosophers of history. Hegel in his *Lectures on the*

Philosophy of History says that "Persia is the land of light; Greece the land of grace; India the land of dream; Rome the land of Empire."[1]

If we glance at the long history of India covering nearly five millenniums, we are struck by the contrasts of extreme situations, summits and chasms. The country rises, wavers, falls, shrinks into herself, tears herself to shreds and pieces, and again endeavors to regain her greatness. She passes through different moods of pride, resignation, shame, detachment, excitement, and adventure. Yet, all through runs an idea which she is attempting to realize, a kind of equilibrium, a wholeness of human nature, which events and vicissitudes inseparable from all forms of life shake but do not shatter. The country is mobile on the surface but constant in the depths. India is a complex equilibrium with an extremely rich diversity. The country is not defined by any dominant race or religious doctrine or economic circumstances. She has a remarkable mixture of ethnic elements, but the great tradition which has affected all her people is the work of human hands.

In a conference of East-West philosophers, it will be useful to consider briefly the metaphysical presuppositions which are the formative forces of any civilization. Metaphysics is not an esoteric pursuit. It has an important place in the life of every reflecting person.

Philosophy is a wide term including logic, ethics, aesthetics, social philosophy, and metaphysics. The last is concerned with the ultimate nature of things. The search for metaphysical certainty has been the source of much that is profound and significant in the history of thought. Metaphysics comprises two main fields: ontology, derived from the Greek word for "being"—what is the reality which exists in its own right and is not dependent on anything else?—and epistemology, which is derived from the Greek word for "knowledge." What can the human mind know with certainty? How does opinion differ from knowledge? What is real? What can be known? These are the problems with which metaphysics deals.

In Indian philosophical circles, a ferment has been caused by the impact of Western thought on the traditional doctrines. Generally speaking, this has not resulted in any major changes of outlook though the methods of approach have been affected. There are a few who have abandoned the Indian tradition and adopted the ideas of some Western thinkers, but, unfortunately, they have not made any deep impression either on Indian thought or on Western philosophy. The most effective development is in the presentation of India's fundamental thought in the idiom of our age and its development in new directions. One may indicate the Indian approach to the problem of religion by a reference to the first four aphorisms of the *Brahma Sūtra,* which is said to give the main purport of the Upaniṣads, which are a part of the Vedas. The four *sūtras* deal with (1) the need for knowledge of Ultimate Reality, (2) a rational approach to it, (3) the experience of Reality, and (4) the reconciliation of seemingly conflicting formulations of the nature of Ultimate Reality.

[1] G. Hegel, *Lectures on the Philosophy of History,* translated from the 3d German ed. by J. Sibree (London: H. G. Bohn, 1861).

II. DESIRE FOR KNOWLEDGE OF REALITY

The theme of the first *sūtra* is *brahma-jijñāsā*. It indicates man's desire to know the Real. There is dissatisfaction with the world. History, astronomical, geological, pre-human, and human, appears to be an aimless process of creations and perishings from which no meaning for the individual human existence can be derived. We discern no principle in the whole chain of being which demands man's meaningful participation in the adventure of time. The world seems to be meaningless, vain, and futile. It is *anitya,* transitory, and *asukha,* painful. Animals are subject to disease and decay but are not capable of distress. The Buddha bases his way of life on the fact of suffering. St. Augustine speaks of "the ceaseless unrest which marks the temporal life of the individual." The consciousness of death is the cause of anxiety. Confucius says (*Shih chi,* 47):

The great mountain must crumble.
The strong beam must break,
And the wise man wither away like a plant.

If man loses himself in the world and its diversions, his anxiety may be a brief fleeting fear. But man is a thinking being. When he reflects on the finite and limited character of his existence, he is overcome by fear, which is, as Heidegger says, "more primordial than man himself." When the fear becomes conscious of itself, it becomes anguish. The tragedy of the soul is added to the contemplation of the world as mortal.

The consciousness of the finiteness and mortality of all our achievements makes us ask whether there is anything beyond and behind the world process. If there were not a Beyond, we should have been satisfied with the world process. The suffering individual cries out in the words of the Upaniṣad—

Lead me from the unreal to the real,
Lead me from darkness to light,
Lead me from death to eternal life.

It is the presence of the Infinite that makes us dissatisfied with the finite. We are reminded of the word of God that Pascal believed he had heard: "You would not seek me if you had not already found me." Compare the confession in Romans, "We do not know how to pray as we ought but the Spirit himself intercedes for us with sighs too deaf for words."[2] The suffering is the result of the conflict in us. Man belongs to two worlds, the spiritual and the natural. He is Being and non-being (*sad-asad-ātmaka*).

Existence is essentially a process in time. It is perched on a razor's edge, as it were, which divides being from non-being. Human being is involved in non-being. We were not; we will not be. What is the nature of being? What is the mystery of non-being which surrounds and conditions existence as we know it? Being needs non-being for its manifestation. St. Augustine, in the first chapter

[2] Romans 8:26.

of his *Confessions,* asks what his longing for God means. Does it mean that he has found God or has not found God? If he had not found God, he would not know of God, since it is God who gives him the yearning for God. If he had found God and knew him fully, he would be incapable of yearning, since he would be fulfilled and so would not have to struggle and suffer.

Karl Barth in *The Epistle to the Romans* has a notable passage relating to the inner, invisible conflict: "Men suffer, because bearing within them . . . an invisible world, they find this unobservable, inner world met by the tangible, foreign, other, outer world, desperately visible, dislocated, its fragments jostling one another, yet mightily powerful, and strangely menacing and hostile."[2a] Life is a perpetual drama between the visible and the invisible.

III. REASONED FAITH

The problem of meaninglessness cannot be solved by religious faith alone. The faith has to be sustained by metaphysical knowledge. We have to think out the metaphysical presuppositions and attain personal experience of the religious *a priori* from which all living faith starts. We need intellectual effort and spiritual apprehension, metaphysics and religion. Only reasoned faith can give coherence to life and thought.

The idea suggested by the Scriptures requires to be clarified by the use of reason. The worlds of reason and religion do not turn in different orbits. Indian thought is firm in its conviction that religious propositions should be grounded in reason.

The second *sūtra* makes out that God is the world ground, the source from which the world proceeds, by which it is maintained and ended (*janmādy asya yataḥ*). How does it happen that there is something rather than nothing? Being is already there without reason or justification. It is not exhausted by any or all of its appearances, though it is there in each one of its appearances. The world with its order, design, and evidence of purpose cannot be traced to non-intelligent matter. Materialism is the theory which regards all the facts of the universe as explicable in terms of matter and motion. It explains all psychical processes by physical and chemical changes in the nervous system.

Though there are a few Christian theologians like Karl Barth who protest against the intrusion of reason into the realm of religious faith, the main tendency in Catholic and many Protestant forms of Christianity is, however, to use reason for the defense of faith. In his Epilogue to *My Life and Thought,* Dr. Schweitzer writes: "Christianity cannot take the place of thinking, but it has to be founded on it. . . . I know that I myself owe it to thinking that I was able to retain my faith in religion and Christianity."[3]

The *Brahma Sūtra* (I.i.2) takes its stand on the *Taittirīya Upaniṣad,* which distinguishes matter, life, mind, intelligence, and spirit in the world process. In the world, to use Leibniz' words, "there is nothing fallow, nothing sterile,

[2a] Edwyn C. Hoskins, trans. (London: Oxford University Press, 1933).

[3] Albert Schweitzer, *Out of My Life and Thought,* an autobiography translated by C. T. Campion. Postscript by Everett Skillings (New York: Henry Holt & Co., 1949).

nothing dead." There are no sharp cleavages. The gradation from one order of being to another is so imperceptible that it is impossible to draw the line that shall distinctly mark the boundaries of each. Everything in Nature is linked together. All beings are connected by a chain of which we perceive some parts as continuous and others escape our attention.

We cannot account for this cosmic process if we do not assume the Divine Reality which sustains and inspires the process. Even as we admit a mystery behind the cosmic process, we recognize a mystery behind the flux of mental states.

Existentialism is not a phenomenon of modern times. It is one of the basic types of thought which appear in the history of philosophy whenever we stress the difference between the individual being of man and the being of objects in Nature. There is a difference between the being of self and the being of things. Man not only *is* but he *knows* that he is. His being is open to himself. Knowledge is confined to the world of objects, but the self is comprehended from within. There is objective knowledge as well as subjective comprehension.

Metaphysical thinking, which bases itself on experience, holds that Nature is grasped with the concept of necessity and the nature of the self by that of freedom. Without this concept, our understanding of man's nature will be deficient and distorted. While both man and Nature are the creation of God, the being of man is made in the image of God[4] and is therefore quite distinct from the being of Nature. Man is not a *res cogitans,* which, though distinct from *res extensa,* is still a *res,* an objective concept and not the personal "I." We cannot understand man scientifically, as if he were only an unusually complicated object of Nature. An objective account de-personalizes man and reduces him to a heterogeneous mass of fragments, which are studied by the different sciences. There is the biological man, the social man, the political man, and also the individual man, who feels pain and joy, bears responsibility, does good or evil, and is conscious of his alienation from himself when he ceases to be subject and becomes an object.[5]

IV. RELIGION AS EXPERIENCE

A philosopher's loyalty to reason does not commit him to the proposition that the nature of Ultimate Reality can be apprehended only as an object of reason. Many philosophers in both the East and the West have reached the conclusion that reality is supra-rational, that it is not in its ultimate nature accessible to conceptual understanding, that religious insights are also genuine revelations of Ultimate Reality.

The third *sūtra, śāstra-yonityāt,* may mean that the Supreme is the source of Scriptures, or that we obtain the knowledge of Reality from Scripture. All

[4] Genesis 1:26.
[5] But I have that within which passeth show;
These but the trappings and the suits of woe. (*Hamlet* I.2)

philosophy starts from experience and returns to experience. Religion is not the mere affirmation of propositions. It is not simply an exercise of intelligence. It is the response of the whole man. It claims total allegiance though it may not always command it. The Real is not an idea or a hypothesis. It should become an experienced fact. A non-discursive immediate cognition of the Real (*aprokṣānubhūti lokottarajñāna*) is possible. This is not a mere glimpse into Reality but a steady communion with it. As Boehme says, it is "the country which is no mere vision but a home." In spiritual experience we pass from time to eternity. This does not mean an extinction of the limited ego; it is liberation into the cosmic and transcendent consciousness.

The *Śāstras,* or Scriptures, are the records of the experiences of the seers who have grappled with the problem of Reality. Their claim to acceptance does not rest on the logical validity of a set of propositions about God or the historical validity of the reports about the activities of God. Such statements may be shaken by scientific or historical discoveries. The experience may be gained by anyone who is willing to undergo a certain discipline and put forth effort.

Those who have the experience are the pioneers in the world of spirit. They walk by sight, not by faith. Authentic religion is based on the consciousness of being in direct relationship with the Supreme. This experience transcends all forms, all images, and all concepts. The union is effected in the central self, which is the root of intellect and will alike. All religious utterances are vain attempts to deal justly with the meaning of the experience which has been attained.

The Buddha is called the Lord of mysteries (*guhya-pati*). He stresses enlightenment (*bodhi*). In all its forms Buddhism insists on intuitive insight. The Zen discipline asks us to cut through the complexities of conceptual thought to reach a radical transformation of being and consciousness.

V. SAMANVĀYA OR RECONCILIATION

The fourth *sūtra* deals with the reconciliation of the different reports of the seers about the nature of Reality as recorded in the Scriptures. Science leads to a reverent acceptance of mystery. Religion tells us that we can have a personal experience of the Ultimate Mystery. Philosophy of religion is based primarily on the data gained by religious men rather than on the rational concepts of abstract philosophers. We try to create out of the experience something that will save the memory of it. St. Augustine says, "We believe we know the inner mysteries, but we are still in the outer court." Whitehead tells us, "Words do not convey it except feebly; we are aware of having been in communication with infinitude and we know that no finite form we can give can convey it." Our descriptions are all partial truths and not whole truths. What is implicit in the Scriptural statements is exhibited in a connected system of thought.

There are two forms of the Supreme Reality, *nirguṇa* and *saguṇa,* qualityless and qualitied. When, in I.i.2, we lead up to the Supreme from the observed data, the Supreme is conceived to be the Cosmic Lord, creator, governor, and guide of the universe. When we experience the Supreme, it is understood to be transcendent to the world, lifted above all its categories, is described only in negative terms. A great deal of zeal, passion, and ingenuity has been spent on the attempt to resolve the problems to which silence or adoration would seem to be the most adequate response. The nature of the Absolute is manifested by the comment of silence.[6] The Supreme is conceived in a twofold way, according to Śaṁkara.[7]

In the *Mahā Upaniṣad,* Brahman is described as void, as trivial, as unmanifested, unseen, inconceivable, and qualityless.[8] The Buddha says: "Verily, there is a realm where there is neither the solid nor the fluid, neither heat nor motion, neither this world nor any other world, neither sun nor moon. This I call neither arising nor passing away, neither standing still nor being born nor dying. This is the end of all."[9] St. Augustine, steeped in Neo-Platonism, defined the Absolute in negative terms. "God is not even to be called ineffable, for to say this is to make an assertion about him." The Real is an unconditioned transcendent and cannot be grasped by a language without symbols.[10]

Organized religions strive to inspire the common man with a faith in the existence of God as revealed in or by the founder of a religious system. They also prescribe a discipline by which one can reach the Supreme. The Indian thinker wishes us to remember that God is above all religious systems. He is without end or limit, though theologians attempt to set limits to him.

The way in which we describe the Supreme is determined by the presupposition of our age, our tradition, and our personal upbringing. Time consecrates, and what is gray with age becomes sacred to us. In this way the gods and goddesses of the people of India were identified with the Supreme. The insistence throughout has been on the inward vision and transformation.

The significant limitation of the competence of reason to understand Reality is not inconsistent with a rational investigation of the nature of experience. When F. H. Bradley said in a jesting mood that "metaphysics is the finding

[6] *mauna-vyākhya prakatita para-brahma-tattvam.*
Dakṣiṇāmūrti stotra.

[7] *dvirūpam hi brahmāvagamyate.*
nāma-rūpa-vikāra-bhedopādhiviśiṣṭam, tad viparītam sarvopādhivarjitam.

[8] *eṣa hy eva śūnya eṣa hy eva tuccha eṣa hy evā 'vyakto 'dṛṣyo 'cintyo nirguṇaś ca.*

[9] *Udāna* 80. In F. L. Woodward, trans., *The Minor Anthologies of the Pali Canon,* Part II (London: Oxford University Press, 1935).

[10] Professor Paul Tillich in his article on "The Religious Symbol" in *Daedalus* (1958), 14–15, observes: "The divine beings and the Supreme Being, God, are representations of that which is ultimately referred to in the religious act. They are representations, for the unconditioned transcendent surpasses every possible conception of a being, including even the conception of a Supreme Being. In so far as any such being is assumed as existent, it is again annihilated in the religious act. In this annihilation, in this atheism immanent in the religious act, the profoundest aspect of the religious act is manifest." Shelley said in "Queen Mab" that "There is no God" but added a note: "This negation must be understood solely to affect a creative deity. The hypothesis of a pervading Spirit co-eternal with the universe remains unshaken." *The Poetical Works of Percy Bysshe Shelley,* Vol. I, Ernest Rhys, ed., *Lyrics & Shorter Poems* (1st ed., London: J. M. Dent & Sons, Ltd.; New York: E. P. Dutton & Co., 1907; reprint, 1930), pp. 96, 126 (Everyman ed., Vol. I).

of bad reasons for what we believe by instinct," he suggested that our deepest convictions required to be vindicated by reason. It is the only way by which we can have a sure foundation for our beliefs. The revelations, though self-certifying to the experiencer, may be only subjective wish-fulfillments, objects projected by the individual. As for the deities to whom offerings are made, some Mīmāṁsakas contend that they are of the nature of words only and are cognized through words or are mental projections.[11] Mutually contradictory experiences are accompanied by strong subjective convictions. Hobbes is right in his observation that for a man to say that God "hath spoken to him in a dream, is no more than to say that he dreamed that God spake to him."[12] The authenticity of an experience has to be judged by rational considerations.

Many people all over the world have clung with passionate intensity to beliefs in fiendish demons which never existed save in their imagination. It is by the employment of reason that we can repudiate such beliefs. Professor H. de Wolf writes about "the worship of such fiendish deities," "There has been no lack of existential faith in them. In obedience to their supposed commands thousands have fasted, burned themselves, cast themselves from precipices, endured shame, fought fanatically, and offered their own children as bloody sacrifices. Will we condemn the use of reason by which great multitudes have learned that such gods did not exist, and hence have been freed from their tyranny?"[13] Though reason may not be adequate as an organ for the apprehension of the Divine, it is useful as a critic of claims to such apprehension.

By the use of reason, Indian religious thought strives to rid religion of obscurantism and lifts faith above superstition. If we practice diabolisms and condemn others, it is like Satan rebuking sin. The mythologic beliefs and dogmas form the content of a closed, static religion. The intuitive vision of Reality, which transcends the objective and formal elements, gives life and meaning to them.

In an ancient Upaniṣad, it is said that we should attain an insight into Reality by hearing (*śravaṇa*), reflection (*manana*), and meditation (*nididhyāsanā*). The first gives us scriptural teaching, the second a rational approach, and the third the way to assimilate the truth heard and reflected on into our being. These three are considered in the first three *sūtras* of the *Brahma Sūtra*. The reconciliation of authority, logic, and life is suggested in the fourth *sūtra*.

[11] *śabdātmakā eva devatā śabdabodhya vā manaḥ kalpita-rūpā vā devatāḥ svīkāryāḥ. Mīmāṁsā Sūtra* II.i.22.

[12] *Leviathan,* Everyman ed. (New York: E. P. Dutton & Co., 1950), p. 200.

[13] *The Religious Revolt Against Reason* (New York: Harper & Brothers, 1949), p. 115.

P. T. RAJU

Religion and Spiritual Values in Indian Thought[1]

I. INTRODUCTION

"A spiritual view," says Radhakrishnan, "is sustained not only by insight but also by a rational philosophy and sound social institutions."[2] If "spiritual view" means "religious view," then every religious view must be capable of being sustained by a rational philosophy and also of being embodied in social institutions. But we hear it often said that all social life should be detached from its religious origins, that social and political thought should be secularized by being based on a scientific study of man, of his nature, needs, and activities. Thus the thought of our age contains contradictory opposites, each pointing to the defects and dangers of the other. On the one hand, religion is treated as superstition, and our age is prone to relegate it to the limbo of human error; on the other, there are protests from leaders of thought who say that science by itself can lead us nowhere, if the ethical and spiritual nature of man does not make equal progress. Again, there is a crisis in world history. In the most advanced countries of the world, not only has science come into conflict with religion but also the reality and individuality of the person apart from society has been questioned. The attempt to plan and organize national and also international societies has produced one line of thought for which the individual is a mere cog in the machine, a mere means

[1] As my paper, "The Concept of the Spiritual in Indian Thought," *Philosophy East and West,* IV, No. 3 (October, 1954), was used at the conference as a basic supplementary paper, I have not repeated here what I wrote there. Therefore, an acquaintance with the ideas presented there is assumed. It would also be useful if the reader were acquainted with my "Activism in Indian Thought" (Anniversary Address, Bhandarkar Oriental Research Institute, Poona, September 17, 1958, published in the *Annals of the Bhandarkar Oriental Research Institute,* Vol. XXXI, Parts III–IV, October, 1958), which deals with the thought of the Brahmaṇical religion, the Mīmāṁsā. The activism of the Mīmāṁsā and the inward realization of the Vedānta are the two primary opposites in Vedic thought.

[2] *Eastern Religions and Western Thought* (Oxford: Oxford University Press, 1940), p. 76.

for the progress of national and international societies, and is considered to have no destiny of his own lying in his inward relation to the divine spirit. Humanism, in its history, has fought several battles with superstitious religions when they became oppressive, particularly during the time of Socrates and Plato, and, later, during the Renaissance in Europe. It has now to put up equal resistance to equally oppressive and materialistic ideologies advocated in the name of science. But, unfortunately, humanism has no deep spiritual and philosophical foundations, and is unable to withstand the sweeping onslaughts of the so-called scientific outlook; the child it brought up in its revolt against religion. The modern outlook and modern thought are unable to defend the reality of man's inwardness and freedom from this outward social and material embodiment.

How will Indian religion react to this situation? What help can India's religious thought give to a solution of these problems? This paper will bear upon these questions. Besides, it will be a reflection and revaluation of Indian religious thought in the light of the criticisms of some of the West's great thinkers who say that Indian thought is inimical to social thought and action and that it supplies no basis, and no incentive to any ethical action.

II. NATURE OF INDIAN RELIGION

First, it should be borne in mind that Indian religion does not mean a fixed set of dogmas, doctrines, creeds, and rituals. There are several Indian religions, the old Aryan *Dharma* or Brahmanism, the religions of the Vedānta, Jainism, Buddhism, Śaivism, Vaiṣṇavism, Śaktism, Sikhism, and the modern Brāhmo Samāj and Ārya Samāj. They have both common and differing features. Many of their doctrines and rituals are different. All except Buddhism and Jainism owe allegiance to the Vedas in some form or another. Even Jainism and Buddhism originated in the atmosphere of Vedic thought.

Second, the word "religion" is an English word. Etymologically it means that which binds a man back or holds him onto the source from which he derived his being. This meaning can apply to every philosophy and practice, even undiluted materialism, in which man has to go back to his material origins. Somewhat corresponding to this word is the Sanskrit word *"yoga,"*[3] meaning that which unites and therefore that which unites man to the divine spirit. But the English word is usually translated by the Sanskrit word *"dharma"* (*dhamma* in Pali), which etymologically means that which supports. In this sense, the word is philosophically understood as law—natural, ethical, and legal. Natural law sustains Nature; the other laws sustain man and society. At the human level, the word carries the meaning of duty. But religion, which contains creeds and ritual, obedience to which is required of all its followers, is also called *dharma*.

[3] In its narrower meaning, which is given by Patañjali, *yoga* is the stopping of the functioning of mind. In its wider meaning, it means all forms of activity leading to communion with the Divine Spirit. In its widest meaning, it is skillfulness in action (*yogaḥ karmasu kauśalam*), as the *Bhagavad Gītā* explains (II.50).

Third, Indian religions have retained some of the most primitive forms of worship, giving them a symbolic value, and yet have developed the highest forms of religious thought and spiritual philosophy, culminating in the nondualism (*advaita*)—often called monism—of Śaṁkara. Śaṁkara's monism is not only a philosophy but also a religion.

Fourth, according to the Indian tradition, it is not necessary for a philosophy to accept the reality of God in order to be called spiritual. Even if Śaṁkara's Brahman, the Mādhyamika's *Śūnya* (Void), and the Vijñānavādin's *Ālayavijñāna* (unperishing consciousness) are said to correspond to God in some way, the main Sāṁkhya, the early Mīmāṁsā, Jainism, and the other schools of Buddhism argued against the reality of God—yet they are great religious philosophies. Not even belief in the *ātman* (self) is an essential requirement: most of the Buddhists reject the reality of the *ātman* also. Yet, taking all these philosophies together, if we ask: What is their common characteristic that entitles them to being called religious?—the answer is: the conviction about the inwardness of man's conscious being. The inward, as I pointed out elsewhere,[4] is not the same as the inner. For all these philosophies, there is something deeply inward to man, and it is called *Ātman* (Self), *Śūnya* (Void), Brahman (Absolute), Īśvara (God), etc. Man's conscious being has two directions, the inward and the outward. Each direction has a limit. The inward limit is called by the above names; the outward is called matter, whatever be the definition given to it by scientists. Indian philosophers could go only so far as to say that it consists of five elements: earth, water, fire, air, and ether. But the understanding of man with two directions of conscious being is not alien and unacceptable to Western religion and philosophy.

Fifth, none of the Indian religions is a revealed religion. A revealed religion is one for which the divine truth is revealed to a single founder; others must know it only through him. The Indian religions are reflective. The Buddha and Mahāvīra are the founders of Buddhism and Jainism, respectively; but they do not claim that the truth was revealed to them alone; everyone who cares to go through the necessary discipline and reflects on his experiences can reach the truth. This reflective nature of Indian religions prevents the conflict between science and religion. There has been no development of dogmatics and theology in India.

Sixth, none of the Indian religions is a tribal religion. Yahveh is said to have been originally a local divinty,[5] worshipped by a tribe; he later became the God of Israel, and still later the universal God. It is characteristic of tribal religion to insist upon a particular social and ethical code, which was originally the code of the tribe. A reflective religion does not insist upon a single code, but allows every group to follow its own code. Buddhist reflectiveness emancipated its spirituality from all social codes, and it could therefore suit itself to the social forms of India, Tibet, Mongolia, China, Japan, and

[4] "The Concept of the Spiritual in Indian Thought," *op. cit.*, p. 210.

[5] A. J. Toynbee, *A Study of History*, abridged by D. C. Somerwell (New York: Oxford University Press, 1951), p. 501.

the countries of Southeast Asia. Even tribal religion becomes reflective after a time. But, so far as the Vedic religious ideas are concerned, they developed out of Nature and Nature-gods, Nature including both man and the material world. It is said that Indra (who later became the god of clouds and the thunderbolt) was originally a tribal god. But he was turned into a Nature-god. Nature-religions, when they develop, do not involve a social code to impose upon their converts. Max Müller calls Indian religion psychological religion; Hocking calls it reflective religion. If Nature means everything that exists, then we may call Indian religion natural religion, as Nature includes spirit, mind, and matter.

Seventh, it is said that some religions are universal, and others are particularist. Christianity and Islam are called universal, because they accept converts; Judaism and Hinduism are called particularist, because they do not accept converts.[6] But there is another principle of distinction which is important. If inward spirituality is the essential meaning of religion, then every religion in which every man can realize God through his own inwardness should be called universal, and every religion which holds that such realization is possible only through faith in its own founder should be called particularist.[7] Conversion means conferring communal membership; it does not mean the conferring of, or initiation into, inwardness. Truth, whether scientific or religious, is open to all; it is not the monopoly of an individual or group. In this sense, Hinduism is a universal religion.

III. THE GROWTH OF INDIAN RELIGION AND ITS THOUGHT

It has already been said that all the Hindu religions grew out of Vedic thought. The Vedas themselves contain four parts, of which the second part, Brāhmaṇas, and the fourth part, Upaniṣads, are considered to be primary by the Mīmāṁsakas and the Vedāntins, respectively. The former uphold the religion of Brahmanism, which is the religion of sacrifices; and the latter uphold the Vedāntic religion, which is the religion of self-realization. Sacrifice is activity, but self-realization is meditation on one's self. Activity must conform to the injunctions of the Brāhmaṇas; and the idea of this conforming developed into that of duty. Thus, not only the ritualistic activities of sacrifice but also other activities, such as the social, became duties. And duty was defined as action according to Vedic injunctions. On this idea of duty was raised the superstructure of the Mīmāṁsā religion and philosophy, which was first propounded by Jaimini. It is a system of rigorous ethical activism, accepting a pluralistic world—a world of a plurality of atoms and a plurality of selves as agents of action. Sacrifices are addressed to different gods, who were at first regarded as capable of bestowing rewards and punishments but later as mental creations, when ethical action was raised to the

[6] The Ārya Samāj, a modern reform movement, is converting non-Hindus.

[7] See the author's *India's Culture and Her Problems* (Jaipur: University of Rajputana, 1951), p. 33.

level of the Supreme and was considered to be capable of bringing the fruit without outside help. The original meaning of *karma* is action, not fate; and the Mīmāṁsā is a philosophy of *karma*.

The growth of the Vedāntic religion may also be briefly indicated. Western scholars usually interpret Vedic religion as the growth from polytheism (animatism and animism), through henotheism and monotheism, to monism (religion of the impersonal Brahman). But this description belongs to an outward point of view. The truth of this growth lies in the transformation of outward polytheism into inward monism. The early Aryans in India realized that the physical elements and psychical activities are correlated.[8] Earth is the correlate of smell, water of taste, fire of sight, air of touch, and ether of sound. The presiding deities of the elements (which polytheism accepted) became the presiding deities of the senses also. Then it was thought that the same deity must have polarized itself into the sense and the corresponding element. Next, the Supreme Deity controlling the activities of these gods was considered to be the Supreme *Ātman* controlling the senses. Similarly, the organs of action such as the hands and feet and the internal organs such as the mind and speech were each assigned a deity, and the organs themselves were considered to be transformations of the deities. In religious language, man was considered to be the vehicle of the subjective poles of the deities, and man's field of action the field of action of the deities for their enjoyment. His action and enjoyment were in essence the action and enjoyment of the deities.[9]

The above account, though semi-mythological, has deep spiritual and philosophical import. First, the Supreme Spirit residing inwardly[10] in man became the Supreme God controlling the objective natural forces. Second, a clear path for the realization of God as the inward spirit within man was laid. Third, man, with his senses, organs of action, and mind, became the subjective pole of the universe, the objective pole being the external world; and both a religious and a philosophical explanation were offered for man's being what in Western philosophy is called the microcosm of the macrocosm that is the universe. Fourth, the creation of the world was explained as the self-objectification of the deities and the Supreme Spirit through self-polarization. Creativity thus becomes, not the transformation of God's being, as of milk into sour milk, but the projection of objectivity out of one's self without at the same time losing oneself in the process. But, as these projections are

[8] Among Greek philosophers, Democritus held a similar view.

[9] See the *Aitareya Upaniṣad* I and II, for an account of creation according to this correlation.

[10] The importance of the conception of inwardness and outwardness can be seen from another angle also, namely, that of the evolutionists. Lloyd Morgan, for instance, says that God is present in matter from the beginning as the upward nisus. But is God creating qualities out of matter or manifesting himself in different forms in matter? Mind as an active agent cannot be a mere quality of matter. God can be better conceived as the inward dynamism of matter. Similarly, when Spinoza says that mind and matter are attributes of God (Substance), he recognizes the dependence of the attributes on substance, but not the latter's inwardness to the two attributes. Even in the Vedāntic literature, the long controversy over the doctrine that the world is produced by the Brahman transforming part of itself would have been avoided had it been recognized that the creation of the world by God cannot be the transformation of his substance into matter but a peculiar activity analogous to the image-projecting activity of our mind. Spirit is not a quality of matter, but its inwardness; and inwardness is not a passive quality, but a dynamic agency.

made by the Supreme Spirit and the deities, not by man himself, man experiences them as objects which he cannot create at will. Fifth, this account made all Vedānta idealistic in the sense that the world is ultimately due to the self-polarization of the Supreme Spirit. If idealism means that objects are wholly states of the mind, then the Vedānta (except for one Advaita subschool) is not idealism.

But, when God projects the world out of himself, he does not identify himself with it. Two Vedāntins, Rāmānuja and Śrīkaṇṭha, say that the world is the body of Brahman. But none of the other Vedāntins accept this position, since it would require that God is affected by the imperfections of the world, his body. The position of Śaṁkara has this advantage: *māyā*, which is the source of the world, is an object (*viṣaya*) of God (Īśvara), who does not identify himself with it. None identifies himself with his object, but only with his body. God is lower than the pure Brahman, which does not have any objectivity to encounter.

The Vedas thus gave rise to two kinds of religion and philosophy, the Mīmāṁsā giving all importance to active life and upholding a pluralistic philosophy and the Vedānta giving all importance to meditative life and upholding, on the whole, a monistic philosophy. There has been no proper reconciliation of the two,[11] though as Vedic philosophies they are equally important and orthodox. It is also important to remember that the early Mīmāṁsā denied the reality of God, but not of the *ātman*. Some of the essential and relevant features of these two major Hindu religions and philosophies may be noted.

Mīmāṁsā religion and philosophy: This is also called Brahmanism, since it is based on the Brāhmaṇa texts of the Veda. For it, only those sentences of the Veda which enjoin action are primary; the rest are secondary. For instance, the sentence "The *ātman* has to be realized" is not of primary validity, as it does not lead to any action. *Dharma* (right action) is more important than *mokṣa* (salvation, liberation). The Vedas are eternal, and the world is without beginning and end and was never created. So, God as creator is not necessary. Actions performed by man control the universe and its processes. There is a universal, single, unitary activity (*karma*), of which the different kinds of action are forms.[12]

Adequate thought has not been given to the interpretation of the Mīmāṁsā. But it contains one of the major activistic philosophies and religions of the world. Without action, nothing can be achieved. Existence is endless activity and continuous enjoyment of the fruits of action. This philosophy never thought of being tired of action and of retreating from it into liberation. Some of its followers even ridiculed those who thought of such retreat. Now, actions are of various kinds. Some are performed for otherworldly fruit, others for results in this world. Some of the latter are directed, again, toward

[11] See the author's "Activism in Indian Thought."

[12] See *ibid.*

society and its members. But all are duties, or *dharmas,* without the performance of which no good can be achieved. The Vedas and the Mīmāṁsā explain those *dharmas* the performance of which produces results in a way not understood by man's intelligence. The Dharmaśāstras (ethical and legal codes) explain those which can be understood by man. But, in them all, *dharma* is the same and works in the same way as far as the inward nature of man is concerned.

How does *dharma* (right action) work? How does it produce its results? *Dharma,* or duty, is action.[13] Action may or may not produce its results immediately. Then how is it connected with the results? How are the results related to the agent? According to the Mīmāṁsā, ethical and religious action, when it is completed, does not die out but assumes a subtle latent form called *apūrva*[14] (extraordinary) and resides in the *ātman* of the agent. From there it works with or without his knowledge. Thus, action becomes an unconscious force or will, producing results for the agent when proper conditions appear, and controlling his destinies and those of the universe. External action, then, is not only the result of will, but also produces it and modifies it. Thus, man becomes the master of his destiny through his own action, and consciously or unconsciously chooses what he will be through ethical action. If, as J. H. Muirhead says, will is self which is directed toward action,[15] then the Mīmāṁsā conception of the *ātman* is essentially that of the will. Action is meant and is necessary for producing the right kind of will, and will can produce results. Then what are called merit and demerit are not adjectival attributes of the *ātman* but its dynamic potencies.

The Mīmāṁsā understanding of action has two important aspects. On the one hand, action produces a chain of effects in the objective world; and, on the other hand, it adds new potencies to the will of the agent and transforms it. The latter aspect points to the spiritual significance of ethical action. Furthermore, the Mīmāṁsā view implies the truth of the correlation through action between our outward existence and our inward. Without this correlation, our inward life may become imaginary, fanciful, and isolated, not necessarily connected with, or based upon, the realities of the world. The modern man may not accept the Mīmāṁsā doctrine of sacrifices, but the underlying doctrine of action seems to be important for ethical and religious philosophies of action and has much in common with pragmatism.[16]

As mentioned earlier, by postulating a unitary eternal *karma* (action) in place of God, the Mīmāṁsā not only dispenses with God as the bestower of the rewards of ethical action, but also rejects the reality of minor gods, saying that they are only mental creations. Action, by becoming a kind of unconscious will with latent potencies, spontaneously produces the required forms in the

[13] This is Kumārila's view, generally accepted by most of the Mīmāṁsakas; but Prabhākara's view is that *dharma* is the potential merit produced by action.

[14] According to Kumārila. According to Prabhākara, as *dharma* itself is *apūrva,* it is produced by action.

[15] *Elements of Ethics* (London: John Murray, 1910), p. 55.

[16] Prabhākara's view that the meaning of a word is understood only when associated with action is practically that of the pragmatists.

external world in which the agent of action enjoys its fruit. The question as to how a non-intelligent principle such as action can have the discriminative power of apportioning fruit according to the type of action done by the agent is not answered by the Mīmāṁsakas satisfactorily. Some of the later Mīmāṁsakas and those Vedāntins who hold that action is necessary for salvation postulate a supremely intelligent God for the purpose. But the Nairuktas, whose philosophy is regarded as subsidiary to the Mīmāṁsā, maintain that action is the essential nature of the *ātman,* which is conscious, and that, therefore, action, as the *ātman,* can produce the results intelligently. But the Mīmāṁsakas do not seem to accept this view of the Nairuktas.

Vedāntic religion and philosophy: Though some scholars believe that the Vedas should be interpreted as presenting one philosophy and one religion, it is difficult to show that the classical Mīmāṁsā is the same as the classical Vedānta. The usual interpretation that the two are meant for two different levels of intellectual maturity is unsatisfactory because, when any metaphysical system claims to be true, it claims to be the absolute truth. But neither of these two systems admits that it is only relatively true. And, if both are true for particular intellectual levels, then man, the possessor of intellect, must be ultimately real. But then it is the Mīmāṁsā, not the Vedānta, that confers ultimate reality on man. For the Mīmāṁsā, *dharma,* or ethical action, and enjoyment are the highest ideals of man's life. *Mokṣa,* or liberation, is meant for the tired soul and is not even commendable, since it is only a neutral state of no pain and no pleasure.[17] Of course, man may choose whatever ideal he likes.

The absolute opposite of the activism of the Mīmāṁsā is the Advaita Vedānta of Śaṁkara, who teaches that salvation (liberation) is the highest aim of life and that it can be achieved through renunciation of action and through the inward realization of one's identity with the Supreme Spirit (Brahman). Right action (*dharma*) and the religion of sacrifices have only an instrumental value, that of purifying the mind.[18] One cannot know the truth through action, but only through reflection.[19] (As we shall see, what Śaṁkara calls reflection resembles the analysis of modern existentialists such as Gabriel Marcel and Karl Jaspers.)

Śaṁkara's contention that one cannot know the truth through action is contested by many. At least so far as empirical truth goes, action confirms cognition, which is as weak as action in giving certainty. Each confirms the other. The Naiyāyikas, the Buddhist Vijñānavādins, and Rāmānuja hold that empirical truth is known through action; that is, a cognition is true if its object is known to serve the purpose for which it is meant.[20] From the modern point of view, we may say that without action we may be living in our private subjective

[17] See "Activism in Indian Thought."

[18] Śaṁkara, *Vivekacūḍāmaṇi,* 10, 11 (Bombay: Lakshmi Venkateswar Press, 1949).

[19] *Vastusiddhirvicāreṇa na kiñcit karmakoṭibhih.*

[20] The Vijñānavādins say that all cognitions are false, whereas Rāmānuja says that all cognitions are true. But both say that, in our mundane experience, the cognition which leads to expected results in action is true, otherwise false. This means that action enables us to know truth.

world of imagination and dream, but in action we live in the world of reality. The truth in Śaṁkara's view is that we cannot know our inward reality through actions pertaining to outward reality.

Śaṁkara does not discuss how right action (*dharma*) purifies the mind. Rāmānuja also holds this view, insisting in addition that one should lead a life of action until death.[21] But what is meant by purification of the mind? If action is successful when it is in accordance with reality and the object cognized is a true object, then purification of the mind must mean bringing it into accord with reality. A "true" object, which is the same for all minds, means that the perceiving subject is similar and therefore universal in all agents. This implication, in its turn, means, particularly in ethics, the ridding of the mind of egoistic impulses and ideas. As long as there is the danger of man's falling into egoistic particularity, he has to perform right actions. Rāmānuja thinks that this danger exists up to death; but Śaṁkara thinks otherwise. Rāmānuja defends the utility of the Mīmāṁsā doctrine of right action as leading to the right knowledge of Brahman, and says that right knowledge leads to the love of the Lord. But Śaṁkara rejects this view as self-contradictory.[22]

Rāmānuja occupies a middle position between the Mīmāṁsā and the Advaita in reconciling right action (*dharma*) with liberation (*mokṣa*). The ideal of life presented by the Mīmāṁsā is made a necessary instrument to the ideal of the Vedānta. But Śaṁkara treats it as a dispensable instrument.

The *Bṛhadāraṇyaka*, the earliest of the Upaniṣads, reinterprets sacrifice as the sacrifice of outward reality by the sacrificer. Renunciation of outwardness is necessary for gaining inwardness. Here, the modern objection will be that inwardness is a fluid, amorphous expanse, the distinctions in which are hard to define. The individual is not a defined part of the inward-outward continuum, but a creative part with an independence and privacy of his own, and he may mistake his imaginative projections for actualities of inwardness. He has to keep his mind in exact tune with actuality, whether inward or outward, in order to know the truth as it is. Inwardness has its own objectivity, that is, independence of the subject's privacy, as outwardness has its own independence of the subject. Just as material objects are common to our outward cognitions, God, or the Divine Spirit, is common to our inward knowledge. When we rightly perceive an external object, our mind is in tune with external objectivity; similarly, our mind has to be in tune with inward objectivity, if it is to see spiritual reality. Mind is pure when it becomes one with reason and transcends its egoistic particularity. This is the reason Pythagoras thought that mathematics leads us near to God. The *Logos* as Reason is the first evolute of God for the Greeks. The Sāṁkhya and the Vedāntic schools maintain the *Mahat*[23] (the Great, Reason, *Mahān Ātmā*,

[21] Rāmānuja, *Śrī-Bhāṣya* I.i.l. See M. Rangāchārya and M. V. Varadarāja Aiyangār, trans., *The Vedānta-Sūtras with the Śrī-Bhāshya of Rāmānujāchārya* (Madras: The Brahmavādin Press, 1899), Vol. I, p. 22.

[22] *Ibid.*, p. 10. For the controversy, see pp. 8–26.

[23] As the Sāṁkhya does not accept the Supreme Spirit, it treats the individual's reason itself as cosmic. But the Vedānta calls the individual's reason "*buddhi*" and Cosmic Reason "*Mahat*," or "*Mahān Ātmā*." See the *Kaṭha Upaniṣad* I.ii.10 and 11.

Buddhi) is close to the spirit. Reason transcends the ego and lifts man to the level of cosmic universality. But more effective than cognitive reason in lifting man above his egoistic particularity is ethical action, in which man not only knows what is true but also does what is good. Man's selfish interest in the external world is through his ego. Selfless action is ethical action that lifts man to a universal standpoint without at the same time depriving him of his actuality and without turning his existence into an imaginary and false dream. Selfless action is action according to universal *dharma,* the law of the universe controlling human destiny.

The philosophy of action according to the Bhagavad Gītā. It is selfless action that is called "desireless action" by the *Bhagavad Gītā. Niṣkāma karma* has been variously misunderstood as desireless action, motiveless action, disinterested action, and so forth. There have been classical interpretations of this type, particularly by the Advaitins, who extol desirelessness (*ataraxia*), the killing of all desires, under the influence of the ideas propagated by monastic Buddhism and Jainism. But this negative form of desirelessness is not really advocated by the *Bhagavad Gītā.* Kṛṣṇa exhorts Arjuna not to have anything to do with non-action.[24] The lower *karma* (action), that is, the egoistic *karma,* is far removed from reason (*buddhi*), and so one should take refuge in reason.[25] One who acts according to the dictates of reason, the *Logos,* is not touched by the merits or demerits of his action.[26] Reason is higher than the ego (*ahaṁkāra*), according to both the Sāṁkhya and the Vedānta; and, when actions are performed by man after he has risen to the universality of reason, they become non-egoistic and he is not touched by their merit or demerit. Such actions are called "desireless actions" because they are not motivated by egoistic desires but by desires in tune with the processes and dispensations of the Cosmic Person (Virāt), or the *Logos,* the World Reason. Kṛṣṇa does not ask Arjuna to kill all desires; on the contrary, he says that he himself is desire which is not opposed to *dharma,*[27] the universal ethical order or law. Thereby Kṛṣṇa asks Arjuna to attune his desires with the processes of the universal ethical order, which he later revealed to Arjuna by showing his Cosmic Person. In fact, the universe is created out of the desire of the Supreme Spirit,[28] and works according to that desire. That desire is *dharma.* Man is not to kill all desire, but to channel desire according to the laws of the universal spirit by lifting himself to the level of Reason or universality.

Buddhism and Jainism: Before the rise of Buddhism and Jainism, right action was understood in terms of the Mīmāṁsā principle as action according to the injunctions of the Veda. The injunctions are contained in the Brāhmaṇas (ritual texts), which treat performance of sacrifices as a duty. The

[24] *Bhagavad Gītā* II.47. [25] *Ibid.,* II.49. [26] *Ibid.,* II.50.
[27] *Ibid.,* VII.11. [28] See *Bṛhadāraṇyaka Upaniṣad* I.ii.4f.

ethical inward transformation which the performance of action produced was lost sight of; and the popular mind attached all importance to external action and its pomp and paraphernalia. It was thought that the wider the scale of sacrifice, the better would be the result. The Upaniṣadic teaching of inwardness and self-realization was already current, but did not appeal much to the popular mind, which cared little for the amount of bloodshed in the sacrifices. The Buddha and Mahāvīra developed the idea that religion was meant for spiritual realization, which is inward, that external acts of worship and sacrifice were by themselves meaningless as religion, and that true ethics did not lie in literal obedience to the Vedic injunctions but in those forms of discipline and self-control which enabled man to reach his inward depths. In preaching their views, they had to turn against the Upaniṣads also, since they were part of the Vedas, which preached the religion of sacrifices. The Buddha was not really opposed to the spiritual teachings of the Upaniṣads, but only to the sacrificial religion. For instance, it is said in the *Dhammapada* that a true *brāhmin* is one of high ethical and spiritual qualities, but not one who was at that time merely following the Brāhmaṇas. Thus, Buddhism and Jainism were reform movements within the *ārya Dharma* (the Aryan religion or way), as it was called, though later they came to be regarded as separate religions. It is relevant to note that, like the early Mīmāṁsā, neither Buddhism nor Jainism accepted the reality of God, and both gave all importance to man's own effort and exertion. Furthermore, the brunt of opposition to the Mīmāṁsā seems to have been borne by the Buddha, who enunciated a new philosophy of *dharma* as opposed to that of the Mīmāṁsā.[29] *Dharma,* the Buddha maintains, is not literal obedience to the Vedic commands, but the law of ethical and spiritual discipline, and the bearing of this law is inward, not outward. Again, the Mīmāṁsakas maintain that man cannot understand how the performance of ethical actions produces results through the agent, because they are produced by an unseen potency (*apūrva,* will). But the Buddha said that *dharma,* the law of ethical action, falls within man's experience and can be realized in experience. Thus, the word "*dharma*" was given a new meaning: at first, it meant action and its potency; now it means ethical and spiritual inwardness. The law of this inwardness and discipline is not a command from a book, but a law of the nature of man's inwardness itself.

The Upaniṣads do not speak of the *ātman* as the *dharma* of man. But the Buddha, had he propounded the reality of the *ātman,* would have called it *dharma. Dharma* in Buddhism is not only the law and nature of man's inward being, but also the inward being itself. The Mīmāṁsakas and many Vedāntins reject the idea that self-realization is a *dharma* (right action), because it is no action at all. But the Buddhists will accept it, if we substitute *vijñāna* (consciousness) or *śūnya* (void) for the *ātman.* It was perhaps by

[29] The significance of the *Dhammapada* can be estimated in this context in delineating the growth of Indian religion. This paper does not present Buddhism in any detail, as fellow members from Buddhist areas deal with it separately.

following Buddhism that the Vaiśeṣikas regarded self-realization as a *dharma* (duty) and *vidhi* (injunction). Later, the word *"dharma"* came to acquire the meanings of ethics, religion, law, and Nature—and many other meanings besides, which are not relevant here.

The chief ways of God-realization. In the Upaniṣads, man was understood, not only horizontally, as one of the objects of the world, but also vertically, as consisting of several layers of reality—matter, life, mind (*manas*), reason (*buddhi*), and spirit (*ātman*),[30] and his goal and destiny were not to be found on the horizontal level but in the vertical. The teachings of the Buddha resulted in placing almost exclusive emphasis on the vertical in India. With Bosanquet, the Indian philosophers would agree in saying that the world is the vale of soul-making, but would add that it is also the vale of soul-finding.[31] But a way for discovering the soul has itself to be found. Hence, the idea of the way (*mārga*) and of man as the wayfarer entered India's religious thought. The goal is the inward spiritual essence of man, however it may be called by the different schools. But the Buddha's insistence that it can be realized by analysis of man's conscious existence (existential self-analysis) gave rise to the doctrine of *jñānamārga,* the way of knowledge. This seems to have been adopted *mutatis mutandis* by the Vedāntins. But the orthodox schools did not give up the way preached by the Mīmāṁsā, and called it *karmamārga,* the way of self-realization through action.

Although, for the early Mīmāṁsā, self-realization was not the primary goal of man, after the idea of salvation later entered its thought, its followers held that action, if non-egoistic, would lead to salvation. We have already explained the meaning of non-egoistic action. The ordinary man, who cannot understand this philosophical import of ethical action, is asked to surrender himself and his actions to God and to act without desires of a selfish nature. This is the way of action, the religion of the Mīmāṁsā reinterpreted in the light of theism.

But neither the way of knowledge nor the way of action satisfies man's needs for love, confidence, and faith. Man is not only an intellectual and active being but also an emotional creature. If he is to treat the Supreme Being as the source of his intellect and as the goal of his action, he is to treat it as the object of his love also. Surrender is easier through love than through knowledge and obedience. The Supreme Being is of the nature of intense bliss, and can satisfy emotional needs also. Besides the Brāhmaṇical and the Upaniṣadic religious thought, there were Śaivism, Vaiṣṇavism, and Śāktism, which teach that the Supreme Spirit is like father and mother, always ready to forgive and love. Thus, another way was made open to man, the way of love or devotion (*bhaktimārga*). Rāmānuja says that *dharma* (right

[30] These levels are different for Buddhism and are understood by it as *skandhas,* aggregates.

[31] The English word "soul" does not really correspond to *ātman,* but to what the Indian writers call *jīva.* The *jīva* is the psycho-ethical individual, but the *ātman* transcends it. Indian religion is really in search of the *ātman.* But I use the word "soul-finding" in a very general sense to correspond to Bosanquet's word "soul-making."

action) leads to *jñāna* (knowledge), and knowledge leads to *bhakti* (love, devotion). Śaṁkara says that love of the Lord leads to knowledge. The main characteristic of all the three ways is the transition from outwardness to inwardness.

The wayfarer and his opportunities. Man's opportunities to obtain salvation are not limited to one life. Birth and death are not the limits of existence. Man can have several lives for obtaining salvation; and, if he does not care for salvation, he can choose an infinite number of lives, one after another, for enjoyment through ethical action. The doctrine of reincarnation is accepted by all schools, except the Cārvāka, which can hardly be called religious. It is difficult, however, to prove or disprove the theory of reincarnation.

Again, all schools, except the Cārvāka, believe that the nature of future birth is determined by past and present ethical action. Patañjali says that it determines one's caste or race (i.e., the family in which his birth takes place), his facilities for enjoyment, and the duration of his life.

The doctrine of *karma* has been wrongly interpreted as fatalism. Indian writers divide *karma* into three kinds. It has been mentioned above that *karma* (action) assumes a potential form immediately after the action is completed. This potency also is called *karma* and is of three kinds: the whole accumulated potency of *karma,* the potency that has started to bear fruit, and the potency that has not yet begun fructifying. The latter two are parts of the first. The second cannot be thwarted, but the third can be prevented by performing a stronger *karma* of the opposite type or by complete renunciation of all *karma* and self-realization. It is difficult to verify these ideas thoroughly. However, the doctrine of *karma* and that of reincarnation have acted as ethical checks on the conduct of man, and the latter doctrine offers endless opportunities and hope for salvation.

The problem of evil: The question whether human nature is essentially evil or good did not attract the attention of the classical Indian thinkers as much as it attracted that of the classical Chinese thinkers. But the question whether the world itself is inherently good or evil occupied the minds of the Indians. Only the Buddhists say that the world is misery, but the others say that it contains misery along with pleasure. Again, whereas the Christian thinkers were obsessed by the doctrine of original sin, the Indians were obsessed by the doctrine of original ignorance. Even Rāmānuja is concerned about ignorance and says that *karma* (both right and wrong action) is ignorance, probably meaning that we have to perform ethically right *karma* only so long as we are ignorant of the essential nature of ourselves and of the Lord. Ignorance is the cause of evil. And evil is real for those schools for which the world is real; and even for the other schools it is real as long as the world is real. One can rise above evil through self-realization. The Mīmāṁsā alone says that one can rise above evil through right action.

IV. ĀTMAN AND ITS REALIZATION

Ātman-realization is called self-realization, because the word "*ātman*" is generally translated by the word "self." According to the Mīmāṁsā and the Nyāya-Vaiśeṣika, this realization is not very covetable because the pure *ātman* is only existence and has neither consciousness nor bliss, which the *ātman* obtains incidentally when reason comes into contact with it. But the *ātman* is detached from reason in the liberated state. According to the Sāṁkhya and the Yoga, the *ātman* is both existence and consciousness, but not bliss; it obtains bliss only so long as it is connected with reason (*buddhi*). According to the Vedānta, the *ātman* is existence, consciousness, and bliss (*sat, cit,* and *ānanda*). Most of the Buddhist schools reject the reality of the *ātman,* and differ in describing the essential nature of man's conscious being. For all, it is a state of pure non-disturbance (*nirvāṇa*). Some Buddhists, the Vijñānavādins, hold that it is *vijñāna* (consciousness). But that it is bliss also is not asserted. In this section, we shall present mainly the view of the Vedāntins.

Realization of the *ātman* is often understood as mysticism; but mysticism is a blanket term that means many things, irrational, vague, and mysterious. The *Bṛhadāraṇyaka Upaniṣad* says that the *ātman* has to be heard about from a teacher, then reflected upon, and meditated upon by oneself, and then perceived directly.[32] According to Rāmānuja, it is the I-consciousness itself (*ahamdhī*) ; but, according to Śaṁkara, it is the support of I-consciousness and transcends it. Meditation is recommended in order to retain the experience of the pure *ātman* once it is obtained.[33]

Like modern Western existentialists of the theistic persuasion, the Vedāntins showed great skill in the analysis of the I-consciousness, and with the help of yogic methods they could go even deeper. No one will come forward and say: "I do not exist." If he does, we treat him as a lunatic. Then what is the nature of the "I"? This question was of the deepest interest to the Vedāntins, because salvation is meant for the "I," but not for the physical body. The "I" is not the physical body, since the latter is its object and since the "I" is continuous in the waking, dream, and deep-sleep states,[34] although the objects of these states have no such continuity. The pre-occupation of the Western mind with the object and with the determination of its truth and reality in the world of waking consciousness led it to treat the "I" as merely subjective, unimportant, and even false, at least as something the experience of which cannot be trusted and relied upon. If Socrates, Plato, and the Upaniṣadic thinkers were alive now, they would say that the modern Western thinker distrusts his very self and would wonder how he could accept the deliverances of a distrusted self. The existentialists are right, therefore, in saying that the methods of explaining the nature of the object are not

[32] II.iv.5. But the *Upaniṣad* immediately asks: How can one know the knower? II.iv.14.
[33] Rāmānuja, *Śrī-Bhāṣya* I.i.1. See *op. cit.,* Vol. I, p. 18.
[34] For a detailed presentation, see the author's "The Concept of the Spiritual in Indian Thought."

applicable to explanations of the subject. The Vedāntins would say that the "I" is not even the ordinary subject when fully analyzed. It has various stages, going deeper and deeper. Śaṁkara would say that the deepest is both the subject and the object, and to it the ego is surrendered.

The "I" is the knower, and cannot be the object known.[35] The physical body, senses, mind, and reason are objects of consciousness, and therefore cannot be the "I." The I-consciousness transcends everything that can be made its object. Here Rāmānuja says that the I-consciousness itself (*ahamdhī*) is the *ātman,* and is different from the ego (*ahaṁkāra*),[36] which is derivative and identifies itself with the physical body, etc., and appropriates to itself all actions, their merits and demerits, and suffers and enjoys. The *ātman* is essentially an on-looker, but, through identification with the ego, becomes involved in the activities of the ego. Śaṁkara often speaks of the "I" as the perceiver, but when giving a technical explanation he treats it as the knowing consciousness without the "I" (*aham*). For him, the I-consciousness (*ahamdhī*) and the ego (*ahaṁkāra*) are the same. The *ātman* is pure self-consciousness. The "I" is the result of gradual contraction of unlimited consciousness into a center of experience. The subject-object polarization develops through this contraction. This contraction should not be imagined spatially. It is the development of a projective focus, the development of pure self-consciousness into a knower-consciousness, the projection in the outward direction out of pure existential inward self-contained consciousness. The ego is part of the inner sense (*antaḥkaraṇa*) and is lower than reason, which also is a part. The word *"ātman"* is translated as "self" in order to distinguish it from the ego. But there is continuity of the consciousness of the latter into the former.

According to Śaṁkara, the *ātman* is the same as the Supreme Spirit. But, according to Rāmānuja, the Supreme Spirit is the *Ātman* within our *ātmans.* Now, the Western thinker may find it difficult to understand Śaṁkara's view that pure consciousness, which is the Supreme Spirit, can be creative, can be a dynamic force. Even in understanding Rāmānuja's view, this difficulty may be felt, for, in the above analysis, the *ātman* is shown as the consciousness which transcends the body, senses, mind, and reason. In Western thought, consciousness, except for the existentialists, is a pale light not integrally related to the existing world and thus deprived of existence. The Advaita Vedāntins also treat conscious processes (*vṛttis*) in this way. But they treat the *ātman* as consciousness that is existent. And existence is not necessarily material existence. How, then, are we to understand that the realization of the *ātman* does not deprive us of existence, and that it is the highest goal of life? According to Śaṁkara, the consciousness that is the *ātman* and is not directed toward the objects of the world is one with the whole reality, subjective and objective. Reality understood inwardly is the Supreme Spirit and

[35] Śaṁkara, *Vākyavṛtti,* and *Ātmajñānopadeśavidhi* I.2–6. See Swami Jagadananda, ed. (Madras: Sri Ramakrishna Math, 1953). Cf. Gabriel Marcel's view that being cannot be made objective. *Journal Métaphysique;* Bernard Wall, trans., *Metaphysical Journal* (Chicago: Henry Regnery Company, 1952), p. viii.

[36] Rāmānuja, *Śrī-Bhāṣya* I.i.1. See *op. cit.,* Vol. I, p. 94.

understood outwardly it is the physical universe. According to Rāmānuja, the *ātman,* though atomic (*aṇu*) and different from the Supreme Spirit, can be identical with God, matter, and other spirits through its attribute-consciousness (*dharmabhūtajñāna*). But this identity is not existential identity, although the existential consciousness of the atomic *ātman* and its attribute-consciousness are both existent (*sat*). Śaṁkara does not hold that the *ātman* has attribute-consciousness in its essential being; this is only its projective power. The existence of both is the same. Like Marcel, he would distinguish between "to be" and "to have." What I am is different from what I have. I have the attribute-consciousness, but I am not the attribute-consciousness, and I project it out of myself as I project mental images out of myself. For Śaṁkara this attribute-consciousness has no existence of its own apart from the existential consciousness of the *ātman,* at the highest stage of realization. But, for Rāmānuja, it has its own existence.

In general, Western philosophy—and even Western psychology—studies only what the Vedāntins call attribute-consciousness, not existential consciousness. Hence the difficulty for Western philosophers. Now, the peculiarity of the *ātman* (existential consciousness) is that it can identify itself with some of the objects of its own consciousness. Though the physical body is an object of my consciousness, and therefore different from the subject of that consciousness, I say, "I am so many feet tall." I identify myself with my mind and say, "I am happy," and so on. Through this kind of identification with objects which I have before me, my *ātman* alienates itself from its original nature, is diffused through existential *diaspora,* spread out through senses and mind. But its original nature can be realized by reversing this process, by dis-identification, by dis-alienation. And the several kinds of *yoga* are prescribed for this purpose.

V. SUPREME REALIZATION IN BUDDHISM AND JAINISM

The general principle underlying the *yoga* of all the Indian religious schools is the same: it is retraversing the process of identification and alienation. According to Buddhism, the psycho-physical individual is an aggregate of five aggregates: matter, feelings, ideas, instincts (*vāsanas, saṁskāras*), and consciousness; or twelve bases (*āyatanas*) of being: the five senses and their objects, and mind and its objects. When man analyzes himself into these elements, he finds there is no remainder. And that state is *śūnya* (void) and *nirvāṇa* (non-disturbance).

Jainism, unlike Buddhism, believes in the reality of the *ātman,* which it calls *jīva.* The spirit is bound by its *karma* (action) and becomes finite. Salvation lies in weeding out *karma*—understood by Jainism as consisting of particles—from the spirit, when it becomes pure and perfect in knowledge. Such a spirit becomes omniscient. All spirits are independent of each other and form a plurality. Salvation is not transformation of outwardness but giving up outwardness altogether. In this belief, Jainism is at one with the

Nyāya-Vaiśeṣika and the Sāṁkhya. The difference is that for both the Sāṁkhya and Jainism the spirit in its pure state is consciousness, whereas for the Nyāya-Vaiśeṣika it is not conscious.

VI. RELIGION AND ETHICAL VALUES[37]

For all Indian systems, except for the early Mīmāṁsā and the Cārvāka, ethical discipline is geared to salvation, and it is difficult to separate completely ethical from spiritual discipline. Yet, their moral teachings, except those of the Cārvāka, are as rigorous as those of any. The Cārvāka is no religion; and its ethics is individualistic, hedonistic, and opportunistic. The Mīmāṁsā ethics is more or less like the Jewish, a set of commands issued by the Veda. Practically every virtue upheld by Western writers is upheld by the Indians also; but the supporting reasons are different. Ethics is not developed with the problems of social organization in view, as it was by the Greeks, or by a study of social relationships, as by the Chinese. The Mīmāṁsā developed ethics for the happiest life of man in terms of the invisible potentiality of action. Only the ethical codes (Dharmaśāstras) have social organization in view in terms of castes and stages of life (*āśramas*). But the codes cannot be called systems of ethics; they are only lists of guiding principles or, rather, laws and rules codified for ready use in social life and courts of justice.

Mīmāṁsā and the ethical codes. We have already mentioned the Mīmāṁsā concept of *dharma.* It has two main interpretations, given by the two leading Mīmāṁsakas, Kumārila and Prabhākara. According to Kumārila, *dharma* is action enjoined by the Veda; and it enters the *ātman* as a latent force, called *apūrva,* before producing its fruit. According to Prabhākara, *dharma* is the potency produced by action, not the action itself. For both, however, there is, first, action and then the latent force produced in the *ātman.* This force is really a kind of unconscious will. But the Mīmāṁsā is interested mainly in the production of the will that produces otherworldly fruit,[38] and does not discuss the forms of activity in the social context. This task is left to the ethical codes (Dharmaśāstras). And, according to the times and conditions, the authors of these codes observed the customs and practices of the different groups living in the country, codified them, and gave the laws. All the authors accepted the Mīmāṁsā concept of *dharma,* but they extended the concept to this-worldly activity also.

But, by the time the ethical codes were written, the ideas of the Supreme Spirit and of salvation entered the Mīmāṁsā. God was introduced as the

[37] As another member of the conference is writing on the ethics of India, I do not discuss ethical values in any detail, but very briefly present the relation of Indian religion to ethical values in order to preserve the unity of the presentation of the relation of religion to spiritual values.

[38] It is interesting to note that, whereas this will has cosmic significance for the Mīmāṁsā in that it controls the processes of the cosmos to suit its workings, reason has cosmic significance for the Sāṁkhya and the Vedānta, which assign conative qualities also to it.

intelligent agent who apportions the fruits of actions according to merit and demerit. It is also said that the latent potency which action assumes does not reside in the *ātman* but in the Supreme Spirit, as Rāmānuja maintained. But some of the Mīmāṁsakas still continue to hold that the potency resides in the *ātman*. If one performs his duties according to his caste and stage of life, and surrenders himself and his activities to God, one obtains salvation. The idea of the fourth stage of life (*āśrama*), namely, that of renunciation, was also introduced by the codes. But the question was not raised as to how the life of renunciation and the way of action can be reconciled. In fact, Manu calls his work *Karmayogaśāstra* (science of the way of action). But the codes remained codifications of the laws of conduct for the different castes and stages of life.

As the codes accept the Mīmāṁsā concept of *dharma,* they involve the ethics of the will.[39] Law is not meant merely to put a check on man's liberty of action, but to exhort him to produce a will, the potency of the *ātman,* its power to produce and enjoy the fruit. Will is not mere wish or intention, but must result in action. The peculiarity of the Mīmāṁsā conception is that will and action are invariably related. Without action, the will cannot be produced; and, without the will, the fruit cannot be obtained. The violation of a positive law is a violation of *dharma,* like the violation of a Vedic injunction. The Indian writers did not draw a line between the "ought" and the "should." The "ought" is a "should," if one wants a particular result such as heaven. It is a "should" to refrain from evil, if one wants to avoid hell. But man has freedom of choice.

Ethical values in the Bhagavad Gītā: The *Bhagavad Gītā* is a reconciliation of the ideal of the early Mīmāṁsā with that of the Vedānta by expounding the doctrine of selfless action, called *karmayoga.* It discredits the pure Mīmāṁsā theory of action and the idea of life in heaven, and says that action according to reason, whether the result be pain or pleasure, is the only right way. True reason is always steadfast and unwavering; those who do not attain that level are infirm and wavering.[40] Firmness in being one with reason is the main virtue. In order to obtain it, selfish desires, lust, anger, etc., have to be given up, because in steadiness there is no disturbance or agitation. When one's reason is destroyed, one is destroyed. When one's reason becomes steadfast, one can enter one's pure *ātman* in what is called *samādhi* (concentrated or collected consciousness).

Ethical discipline in the Vedānta. For the Vedānta, the highest ideal of life is salvation. To attain it, Śaṁkara says that one must develop the following four virtues: (1) discrimination between the eternal and the transient; (2) renunciation of all enjoyment here and hereafter; (3) the six qualities of (a)

[39] See "Activism in Indian Thought."
[40] II. 41.

tranquillity, (b) restraint of the senses from their objects, (c) withdrawing the mind from outer objects; (d) endurance of all pains without complaint; (e) faith in what is rationally understood from the teacher and the scriptures; and (f) keeping the mind always directed toward the Brahman; and (4) passionate desire for liberation by understanding the true nature of the ego, mind, and the senses and their objects.[41] The performance of other duties is only a means for purifying the mind.

For Śaṁkara, the way of knowledge is the highest. But, for Rāmānuja, the way of love or devotion is the highest. He defines love as the continuity of knowledge without effort.[42] This is possible only in passionate love and desire for communion. Hence, knowledge is only a means to love. Rāmānuja insists that one should lead a life of action until death, after which one obtains salvation; and the life of action should be according to the Mīmāṁsā and the codes. Love or devotion (*bhakti*), defined as continuity of knowledge, is difficult to practice; and therefore self-surrender to God is also preached.[43] In Rāmānuja's philosophy, the doctrines of grace and of God's love for his devotees play an important part. Self-surrender will be explained by the followers of Śaṁkara as non-egoistic activity. The ethical discipline of the other orthodox schools is more or less the same as that of the Vedānta. That the early Mīmāṁsā is an exception has already been mentioned.

Ethical discipline in Buddhism and Jainism. The Buddha preached the Noble Eightfold Path as the ethical discipline necessary for spiritual realization. The eightfold way consists of right views, right intention, right speech, right action, right livelihood, right effort, right mindfulness, and right meditation. In the Mahāyāna literature, the ideal man is conceived to be the *bodhisattva*. This word may be etymologically rendered as the person whose being is knowledge. It is interesting to note that the *Bhagavad Gītā* calls the ideal man the *sthitaprajñā,* which may be translated as the person whose reason is firmly settled. Literally, the words come to mean the same, because *prajñā* is a synonym of *buddhi* or *bodhi*.[44] The *Bhagavad Gītā* describes its ideal man as one "who is steadfast in his reason, is without selfish desires, unagitated by pains and unattached to pleasures, without fear and anger; he neither hates nor favors any. He controls his senses and does not allow them to run after pleasures. . . ." The Mahāyāna describes its ideal man as one who possesses the six main virtues: charity, morality (character, *śīla*), patience, energy, meditative power, and knowledge. All virtues are precipitated into these six; and, of the six, again, knowledge is regarded as the highest.[45]

[41] *Vivekacūḍāmaṇi, op. cit.*, pp. 18 ff.

[42] For instance, a girl in love remembers her paramour continuously and without effort.

[43] Cp. *prapatti* (self-surrender). See Śrīnivāsācārya, *Yatīndramatadīpikā*, Swami Adidevananda, ed. and trans. (Madras: Sri Ramakrishna Math, 1949), pp. 94 ff.

[44] See the lexicon, *Amarakośa*.

[45] See Prajñākaramati's *Bodhicaryāvatāra-pañcikā* and also the author's *Idealistic Thought of India* (Cambridge, Mass.: Harvard University Press, 1953), p. 230. Further details are not given, as other members of the conference deal with Buddhism.

The ethical discipline of Jainism is the severest of all schools. Its main point is that salvation can be had only by weeding out all *karma* particles from the soul (*jīva*), at which time it regains its pure state. This can be achieved through faith in Jaina teachings, true knowledge, and character.[46] Of all the Indian schools, Jainism attaches the greatest importance to *ahiṁsā* (non-injury) and vegetarianism. The highest character is that which has developed complete indifference to the objects of the world.[47]

VII. RELIGION AND INTELLECTUAL VALUES

Because of the reflective nature of all Indian religions, there has been no conflict between science and religion in the cultural history of India. True, the Vedāntins and the Buddhists maintain that reason cannot give certainty of the spirit. But that is because the rational methods used for studying objective Nature cannot be applied to the inward reality of man. The methods for studying the latter have to be different. But, though different, whether it is reasoning about the objective world or reflection on one's inner being, the work has to be performed by the same mind. That which does the work is *buddhi*, or reason.[48] It is not a function of mind. From the time of the Upaniṣads, the different levels of man's inward being have been demarcated by Indian thinkers, and the stages are not regarded as functions of mind but as levels of inward being, mind itself being the lowest level. In the classification of these stages, there is no unanimity;[49] but, on the whole, the levels are three: mind (*manas*), ego (*ahaṁkāra*), and reason (*buddhi*). The function of mind is to analyze and synthesize the impressions and carry them to the ego, and also to cognize pains and pleasures and convey them to the ego. The ego appropriates them in saying, "I see, I enjoy." Reason is beyond the ego, deeper and higher. It interrelates the several results from a universal point of view, not from the point of view of the particular ego. But the ego and reason have a continuity of being. The ego rises to the level of reason in the process and loses its particularity. Reason is always objective, universal, and cosmic in its processes and nature. It commits no mistakes when it is pure and does not get involved in egocentricity.[50] When the ego intrudes

[46] Mādhava Ācārya, *Sarva-darśana-saṁgraha* (Poona: Anandasrama Press, 1928), pp. 25 ff.

[47] S. Radhakrishnan, *Indian Philosophy* (London: George Allen & Unwin Ltd., 1928), Vol. I, p. 325.

[48] H. H. Price saw some similarity between the Indian conception of the Self (*Ātman*) and Kant's conception of the transcendental ego (*The Hibbert Journal*, LIII, No. 3 [April, 1955], 228). But closer examination shows that the transcendental ego corresponds to the *Mahat* of the Sāṁkhya and the *Mahān Ātmā* of the *Kaṭha Upaniṣad* and is more or less the *Logos* of the Greeks. This may be treated as the Pure Reason of the *Critique of Pure Reason*, but Kant seems to be somewhat hesitant to identify this Pure Reason with the Practical Reason of the *Critique of Practical Reason* and the Aesthetic Reason of the *Critique of Judgment*. The *Sattva* (*Mahat, Mahān Ātmā*) of the Sāṁkhya and the Vedānta performs all the three functions; it is above the ego, but below the *Ātman*.

It may also be noted here that the modern existentialists' hostility to reason deprived them of the use of the *Logos* and prevented them from seeing its existential nature. The result is that they have generally tended to be shut up in subjectivity, and are unable to explain how reason has validity even for the objective world.

[49] See the author's "The Nature of Mind and its Activities," in *The Cultural Heritage of India* (Calcutta: The Ramakrishna Mission Institute of Culture, 1953), Vol. III, pp. 507 ff.

[50] For this reason the *Kaṭha Upaniṣad* differentiates between the individual's reason and Cosmic Reason (between *buddhi* and *Mahān Ātmā*). The Sāṁkhya uses the word *"mahat"* for the individual's reason.

into the universality of reason, the latter commits mistakes. Indian philosophers would accept the Pythagorean contention[51] that reason in man is nearer the Supreme Spirit than mind or senses, and the Heraclitean view[52] that the *Logos* is common to all.

It is necessary to keep these psychological distinctions in view in order to appreciate how Indian spirituality incorporates intellectual values. If intellectual values are values achieved by the intellect or reason in the form of scientific discoveries in the objective world, Indian philosophy is not opposed to them, though it will add that they are not the highest in life, but only instrumental. Yet, understanding the true nature of the world is necessary in order to know what the highest values are. If "intellectual values" mean that the attitude of man to the world and to himself is to be rational, then Indian philosophy will support them and say that man should raise his ego to the universality of reason. The highest intellectual value, from the standpoint of religion, is reason itself, and the highest intellectual attainment is to become one with reason, which is a higher state of the self than the ego. Man's reason is really part of the Cosmic Reason, and the two are essentially continuous and one. In no other philosophical tradition is the idea of truth more admired than in the Indian. Gandhi said that God is Truth, with a capital T. If writing Truth with a capital T is a philosophical error, then the error is committed by many Western philosophers and religious thinkers as well.

But the highest truth for Indian thinkers is not reason or the *Logos,* but something still higher, namely, the Brahman. The Greeks generally accept the *Logos* as the highest, although there are indications in Plato's thought that there is something still higher. One synonym for *buddhi* (reason) often used by the Upaniṣads is *vijñāna,* which also means mundane science and arts.[53] *Jñāna* is knowledge for salvation, and *vijñāna* is knowledge about sciences and arts. This distinction corresponds to the distinction made in the Upaniṣads between higher and lower knowledge. What is meant by calling the realization of truth a spiritual value? If one realizes that the object in front of him is a fly, is this attainment of truth a spiritual value? Has it even moral significance in the context of the development of one's personality? What is spiritually valuable in this context is that aspect of man's personality which is characterized by his readiness for and susceptibility to truth or the receptivity to universality and objectivity. It is the purity of reason, its readiness to be above ego-involvements. It is the development of this aspect of

[51] The Pythagoreans believed that mathematics takes man near God.

[52] Georg Misch: *The Dawn of Philosophy,* R. F. C. Hull, trans. (Cambridge, Mass.: Harvard University Press, 1951), pp. 258–259. It is interesting to note that Heraclitus identified the *Logos* with fire, and the Indian philosophers treated the god of Fire as the deity of speech. The speech which directly issues from the god of Fire is said never to be false.

[53] See *Amarakośa.* Buddhist scholars usually translate the word "*vijñāna*" as consciousness, mind, etc., and Indian scholars translate the word "*buddhi*" as intellect, intelligence, and understanding. If we study the words, which are synonyms, in their contexts and connotations, we find that they have the significance of reason and *Logos* in Greek philosophy. It is better to translate the words by "reason," which has many shades of meaning in Western thought as in the Indian, than by intellect, intelligence, or understanding.

personality that is a spiritual value. Thus, reason, as part of the *Logos* present in us, is itself the value. It is a value, not only for intellectual work, but also for ethical uplift, as the *Bhagavad Gītā* teaches.

VIII. RELIGION AND AESTHETIC VALUES

For an understanding of the doctrine of the beautiful in Indian thought, as for understanding the doctrines of the true and the good, the clue lies in the conception of *buddhi* (reason).[54] Aesthesis (*rasa*), or aesthetic pleasure, like truth and goodness, belongs to *buddhi*. The Sāṁkhya attributes to *buddhi* the qualities of determination (certainty, assertion, will), *dharma* (virtue), knowledge, dispassion, and power.[55] But these qualities belong to it when it is pure.[56] When it is impure, the opposite qualities belong to it.[57] Impurity means ego-involvement. Generally, when the word is used it is understood in its pure state. Thus truth and goodness are its attributes. Now, when the Sāṁkhya explains aesthetic pleasure, it again attributes it to *buddhi* (reason). In fact, all orthodox schools attribute it to *buddhi*, however it is conceived. According to the Sāṁkhya and the Yoga, aesthetic pleasure cannot belong to the *ātman*, which is only existential consciousness, but not bliss (*ānanda, rasa*); it belongs to *buddhi* only. According to the Nyāya and the Vaiśeṣika, the *ātman* is only existence but not consciousness or bliss; *buddhi* has no substantial status, but is an adventitious quality which the *ātman* acquires when mind (*manas*) comes into contact with it. However, it is the *buddhi* that contains aesthetic pleasure and conveys it to the *ātman*. But the Advaitins say that the *ātman* is essentially bliss also and is aesthetic (*rasa*); and the aesthetic pleasure experienced in the world is a reflection of the bliss aspect of the *ātman* in pure *buddhi* (reason). This is the view of practically all the Vedāntins. Taking all these views together, we may say that the general tendency of Indian thought is to assign what we generally call aesthetic value to reason itself. The Vedāntic schools have more religious significance than the others.[58] The common point in their arguments comes to this: The experience of aesthetic pleasure belongs to *buddhi*, or reason, freed from ego-involvements, that is, with egoistic motives held back. But when I say, "I experience that pleasure," my ego connects that experience to itself as it connects to itself the experiences of dream and deep sleep. I am able to do this because my ego is continuous and essentially identical with reason (*buddhi*). And there are no ego-involvements in the experience of aesthetic pleasure, because, as Kant says, there is no urge in the ego at that time to appropriate the object and to work on it in a possessive activity, but only

[54] For a detailed account, see K. C. Pandey, *Indian Aesthetics* (Banaras: Chowkhamba Sanscrit Series, 1950), and P. N. Srinivasacari; *The Philosophy of the Beautiful* (Madras: Thompson and Co., 1942).

[55] *Sāṁkhyakārikā* XXIII (Poona: Oriental Book Agency, 1934).

[56] *Sāttvika.*

[57] *Tāmasika.*

[58] Buddhism and Jainism do not seem to have devoted much thought to aesthetics. There are important differences between the orthodox schools; but they are not discussed here for want of space. Not even all the Vedāntic schools can be presented here. Only the general trend is given.

to appropriate the pleasure derived from it. Of course, the desire to have that pleasure exists.

Abhinavagupta (10th century), Bhoja (11th century), and Jagannātha (17th century) are the foremost exponents of aesthetics in India, although Bharata was the founder of the theory first associated with dance. All explain aesthetic pleasure in terms of sentiments.[59] Whether the aesthetic activity is painting, music, dance, or drama, it is due to the working out of a sentiment such as love, dread, anger, etc. In actual life, when the sentiments arise in our mind, they result in action toward the object, and there is ego-involvement. In the aesthetic situation, however, they do not result in the usual action, but in representation in color or sound, in movements in dance, or in the working out of a dramatic plot. Aesthetic activity, like play, is a creative activity, which, when completed, satisfies the mind. Then *buddhi* (reason) assumes the state of equanimity, or harmony (*samatā*). According to the Sāṁkhya, this emotional equanimity is itself aesthetic pleasure; according to the Vedānta, this equanimity, because it becomes pure (*sāttvika*), reflects the bliss aspect of the *ātman* and becomes pleasure. In music, the different notes combined properly in different forms called tunes (*rāgās*) stir up different emotional components and, when the last note is reached, the stirrings readjust themselves into a placid state, which is aesthetic pleasure. In this state, particularity is submerged, and the ego rises above itself. The higher stage is *buddhi* (reason) in its pure (*sāttvika*) aspect. Thus man can lift himself above the ego and nearer the Divine not only in the realization of truth and goodness, but also of the beautiful. If so, God can be realized by systematic aesthetic cultivation.

God-realization through aesthetic cultivation has been developed into a *yoga*. The philosophy of music, for instance, is based on a study of the Sound Brahman (the Word, *Nādabrahman*), which is called an evolute of the Supreme Brahman. The Sound Brahman is not the origin of speech only but also of music. One who practices music in the right way finally obtains communion with the Brahman. Tyāgarāja is said to have made music his path of God-realization. This is the reason for the depth and perfection which music reached in India and also for the importance of music in temples. All fine arts are spiritual disciplines in India, although many who study them do so for secular reasons.

Abhinavagupta maintains that all sentiments have their source in the sentiment of peace (*śānti*), rise out of it like waves out of the ocean, and enter it again. Peace is a positive sentiment or emotion, not the absence of emotions. It is the harmony of all, a state in which *buddhi* (reason) becomes completely pure and aesthetic pleasure is intense and undisturbed. Images of the Buddha, for instance, produce this state in us. Bhoja maintains that the highest form of aesthetic pleasure is love (*śṛṅgāra*), and all the others are only its forms. He defines love as the purest form of the *ātman* at its peak. Only Bhavabhūti,

[59] "Sentiment" is the English word used for "*bhāva*." But some of the *bhāvas* listed by Indian writers are emotions.

perhaps under the influence of Buddhism, says that compassion (pity, tenderness, *karuṇa*) is the highest aesthetic pleasure; the others are its forms appearing under different conditions. But this view has not been worked out either by him or by others.

Clearly, then, Indian religion and philosophy not only encouraged the realization of aesthetic values but also made them important ingredients of spiritual discipline. And what should strike any student of Indian thought is that the *Logos* is not only rational and ethical but also aesthetic.[60] The realization of each of these aspects leads to the same goal, although, as far as mundane life is concerned, they remain separate. Thus there has been no hostility of religion toward the values of truth, beauty, and goodness, because they have been made spiritual values, though instrumental, in the literal sense of the term. But, when their spiritual significance is forgotten and man pursues them for other purposes, they become secular values. Even then, when pursuing them he is unknowingly pursuing spiritual values. And all three are aspects of reason, which belongs to man's inward being, is cosmic in its nature and reference, and is above the subjectivity of the ego.

IX. CONCLUSION

So far, a general description of the nature of Indian religious thought and its attitude to spiritual values has been given. Many schools have been referred to incidentally; many Vedāntic schools have been omitted; and, even of the two Vedāntic philosophies of Śaṁkara and Rāmānuja, many details have been left out for want of space. One must have seen that the Mīmāṁsā religion supplied the real counterpart of the Vedānta by advocating ethical activism as the highest philosophy. Together, the Mīmāṁsā and the Vedānta have guided the life of Indians for centuries. After the rise and spread of Jainism and Buddhism, the philosophies of salvation became dominant, and the activistic philosophy and religion of the Veda was left, comparatively, in the background. Also, the political conditions from about A.D. 1100 until India attained her independence contributed to the neglect of activism. But it is not dead, since it is an undeniable aspect of India's Vedic culture, as can be seen by any student of Indian thought and culture, if he approaches the subject without contrary preconceptions. Half of the Veda cannot be denied as non-existent.

[60] Even the science of language or linguistics is traced to the *Logos* as the Word, *Nādabrahman*. The more one studies and thinks about the concepts of Indian thought, the more does one realize the importance of the role of *sattva* (*mahat, Mahān Ātmā, buddhi, Nādabrahman*) for interpreting Indian spiritual values and culture. It is a mistake to think that these concepts are only speculative. They are primarily existential concepts of man's inward being, and secondarily concepts of constructive philosophy. If this feature is ignored, the spirit of Indian thought, particularly that of the Vedānta, the Sāṁkhya-Yoga, and Buddhism, and also the truth of these schools as religions, will be missed. The quarrels between the schools are not so important for the modern man as the correlation of their concepts. The first and primary task of the modern student of Indian philosophy who seeks the importance of philosophy for life should be to correlate the concepts of the Indian schools after a critical study. If he wants to do comparative philosophy, he should then correlate them with the concepts of Western philosophy. The tendency of Western interpreters is to treat them as concepts of speculative metaphysics, which is a purely outward approach. The Western man also has his inwardness over which he should reflect when interpreting Indian concepts.

It is wrong to think that Indian thought, particularly the Vedānta, leads to totalitarian philosophies, in which the individual is submerged in the Brahman, and that Eastern despotism is due to this outlook. One may as well say that any philosophy for which God is the Supreme Controller of the universe leads to autocracy and despotism in political thought and that only a philosophy like that of Leibniz, for which God is merely a monad among monads and gets the position of God by election, can support democracy. But no application of religious philosophy to political thought was made in India. It was made in the West and China. But the truth is that it cannot be made. Only those philosophies and cultures which have not been able to recognize the peculiarity and reality of inwardness would attempt to apply the concepts of the Absolute, God, Supreme Controller, etc., to outward society and the objective world. Even supposing that Śaṁkara's philosophy is true, then, since everyone is essentially the Brahman, there can be no difference between the despot and his subjects. If the despot wishes to "absorb" (rule, suppress) his subjects, then every one of his subjects, since he is the same as the Brahman, can have the same wish. Then the result will be either a war of all against all or equality and democracy. Śaṁkara, however, was not interested in this deduction. He knew, of course, that his philosophy confers sacredness and dignity on the individual, because the essential core of each individual is the Brahman. He knew also that the recognition of inwardness is the same as the recognition of the freedom of the individual.

But the recognition of inwardness—and the interpretation of intellectual, ethical, and aesthetic values with reference to inward transformation—is not the same as preaching absorption in subjectivity. If man's essential nature is intimately connected with the objective world—some Western philosophers have explained this relation as the relation between the microcosm and the macrocosm—then man's true inwardness can be realized only through proper correlation with outwardness. None can have aesthetic pleasure without seeing the aesthetic object; none can be good without ethical activity in the objective realm; and none can know truth without knowing the objects as they are. And, ultimately, what are these values for? They are for the inward transformation of man. They are not meant for the dissipation of man in external objectivity. If dissipated in objectivity, man's soul is wasted and lost. Like Christ, Indian philosophers would ask: Of what use will it be if a man conquers the world and loses his soul? But man's true spirit can be realized only through activity, intellectual, ethical, and aesthetic.

The contribution of Indian religious thought, then, is the recognition and explication of the inwardness of man, of its freedom, dignity, sacredness, and importance. It is certainly true that India has not produced great ethical systems and political philosophies. The only attempts are that of the Mīmāṁsā and the ethical codes. Social ethics and political thought were not regarded as important by the classical philosophers. This, indeed, has to be admitted and may be traced to the classical philosophers' deeper interest in the inward reality than in the outward.

But, it is difficult to accept the view of Dr. Haas,[61] for example, that, although the Eastern mind is engrossed in subjectivity and the Western is diffused in objectivity and each is reaching a danger point, they cannot be synthesized. Very few will admit that China is at present engrossed in subjectivity. Even taking India, the Mīmāṁsā—therefore, half of the Veda—was not engrossed in subjectivity but in the conquest of objectivity through ethical action. This school had no idea of scientific and technological conquest, but a philosophy that belonged to a period twelve centuries ago can hardly be expected to think of science and technology. However, even leaving out the Mīmāṁsā, as this paper might have shown, this subjectivity is not a closed, windowless subjectivity, but a subjectivity that has not cared so far to look through the windows with microscopes and telescopes. Similarly, one may say that the Western mind has not been lost in objectivity, but it tends to forget itself. Truth is never lost, but may be undiscovered or forgotten. It can therefore be discovered or recovered. Neither man's inwardness nor his outwardness can ever be lost. "Losing one's soul" is a metaphorical phrase. Man's inwardness and outwardness are the two directions of his very being; he can never lose either. The shock of reality will awaken him to each. But, instead of being roused by a devastating shock, the Eastern mind may be awakened by a friendly touch of the Western mind and vice versa. Each is a complement of the other, and each can enter into a synthesis of the two. Mutual understanding leads to assimilation of each other's values, and this assimilation is synthesis, not enforced by an external agent but spontaneously developed by life's becoming conscious of what it has missed.

Then, if the contemporary demand, voiced by Radhakrishnan, that a spiritual view should be sustained by sound social institutions is true, then social institutions cannot be considered to be sound if they do not make possible the realization of the spiritual ideal. And society can make this possible by offering the individual scope for the development of his spiritual qualities and activities—intellectual, ethical, and aesthetic. These presuppose the inwardness, freedom, dignity, and sacredness of the individual. Freedom, dignity, and sacredness are due to his inwardness, without which the physical body is nothing but dirt and filth. There is, in every living body, a skeleton which frightens us, but does not endear us to itself; the human form is divine because the inward spiritual qualities are expressed through it. It is the expression of these qualities that makes social life worth living. Indian religious thought did not have the necessity, at the time when it was formulated, to devote itself to the problems of social organization and the study of social relationships, which have become intimately connected with economic and political problems, the forms of which are fast changing on account of scientific and technological progress. But, whatever be the changes, man

[61] S. S. Haas: *The Destiny of Mind: East and West* (London: Faber and Faber Ltd., 1956). The strength of inwardness can be used for outward conquest, as evidenced by the adoption of Zen Buddhism by the samurai of Japan. See Joachim Wach, *Sociology of Religion* (London: Kegan Paul, Trench, Trübner and Co., Ltd., 1947), pp. 261–262.

should not be lost in them by losing his inwardness and its freedom; and this inwardness should not disenable him for reacting appropriately to the changing complexities of outward existence. Here, East and West have much to learn from each other. True inwardness is not privacy, or mere subjectivity, or loneliness. Whitehead said that religion is what man does in his loneliness; but Hocking said that religion is not private. True inwardness, as this paper might have shown, is the sacrifice of privacy and subjectivity.

QUESTION: You have represented Indian religion as teaching mere inwardness, and as engrossed in mere subjectivity. Is this true? Do you accept the idea that Indian thought does not recognize the reality of the objective world, and do you accept Dr. Northrop's view that Indian philosophy is concerned with only the intuitive aesthetic continuum?

ANSWER: My answer is in the negative to all these questions. True inwardness can be developed only in correlation with outwardness. None can be good without performing good acts; no one's cognition can be true without his knowing the true object, perceptual or conceptual; and no one can have aesthetic pleasure without experiencing the aesthetic object (*ālambana*). The correlation between the inward and the outward is essential. So, objectivity is as essential as subjectivity.

Neither the word "intuition" nor the word "inwardness" has a definite meaning in Western philosophical literature. Contemporary Western thought, particularly that of America and England, tends to understand the words to mean subjectivity. And the subjective is regarded as unimportant in determining the nature of reality, and often as even false. There has been an indiscriminate use of the words "subject" and "subjective." Even a true object is that which is determined to be true by a true subject. As writers on science such as James B. Conant say, a true object is one that is fitted into a conceptual pattern or scheme. So, there must be a subject that fits the object into that scheme. Insofar as the subject is true, we usually say that the subject is right. In the process of this fitting, the structure of the subject undergoes a change toward truth as much as the structure (the what) of the object undergoes a change toward its truth. The change toward truth is what may be called the change toward universalization, because, like the object, the subject also must then become common to all the percipients and thinkers. This is what Socrates and Plato call, one may say, the cultivation and realization of the rational part of or reason in the soul of man. And reason is universal. There is nothing that is not understandable in this cultivation. So far as religion goes—I am talking of religion in this paper—spiritual values are meant for lifting man's ego to the level of universality. There can be nothing egoistic in intellectual activity, just as there can be nothing egoistic in ethical and aesthetic activities. Now, Greek thought attributes both truth and goodness to reason. But Indian thought attributes to it aesthetic pleasure also. Philosophers like Russell say that this attribution introduces confusion into philosophy. But they understand reason as ratiocination, whereas Greek and Indian philosophers have understood it as a level of our conscious being higher than our ego, the ego being the real subject, which is particular and separate from other subjects. But reason is also our very being, lifted to the level of universality. The question, of course, will be whether there is such a level. We may study the question now independently of what the Greeks and the Indians have said. But the Western use of the word "subject" for all the levels of our conscious being is misleading. Even the existentialists are committing this mistake.

Now, for what purpose is the realization of spiritual values meant except for the spiritual or inward transformation of man's conscious being? It is this point that Indian religious thought brings to the fore. As Christ said, man should not lose his soul in the conquest of the objective world. Its conquest through intellectual, ethical, and aesthetic activities has to result in the inward transformation of our particular ego into the truth of the spirit, if the activities have any spiritual significance at all. These activities presuppose the reality of the objective world; without them, the ego cannot be transformed into spirit. The objective world is the forge in which the ego is wrought into spirit through such activities. Modern industrial and technological society, with its preoccupation with the mere object, is tending to forget man's inwardness and its freedom. The complaint is made in different forms by Western writers such as Spengler, Schweitzer, and Toynbee.

Man's reason, though inward, is as objective as atoms, electrons, and protons. Essentially, it is public, not private.

QUESTION: You are speaking of some inwardness as objective. How can inwardness be objective? The objective is the external world.

ANSWER: There is inwardness that is private to each individual and inwardness that is public to all. We call the latter reason, although it is found in each man. We may remember what the Kantians and the Hegelians say in this connection, namely, that it is reason that confers objectivity even on the objects perceived externally to us. This view is in accord with Conant's view that a true object is the one fitted into a conceptual scheme, which is rational and which, therefore, belongs to reason. Reason is the public property of all rational beings and is, therefore, objective in its essence. Yet, it is continuous with the subject, or the ego, and belongs to a higher level. For instance, Plato and Aristotle call it the highest part of the soul and treat it as immortal. We may leave out the question of immortality but we have to recognize that it is higher than the ego. What is merely private to any individual cannot be fitted into a conceptual scheme which belongs to all. The private is what is merely subjective. What is public is truly objective. As reason is public, we may call it objective.

I do not know how to improve upon these words. Even the word "real" has ambiguity. Are illusions real? This is an ambiguous question. It may mean: Are there illusions? Or, can the objects seen in illusions be fitted into the conceptual scheme of the physical world?

[62] See the article, "Being, Existence, Reality, and Truth," *Journal of Philosophy and Phenomenological Research,* XVII, No. 3 (March, 1957), 291–315.

QUESTION: You seem to say that Indian philosophy teaches immersion in subjectivity and indifference to the objective world. Is this true?

ANSWER: No. Indian philosophy does not teach immersion in subjectivity. My paper concerns religion. Religion is essentially inward experience, and so I have written on the nature of inward experience and on how the realization of spiritual values transforms the inwardness of man for the better. True inwardness is essentially correlated to true outwardness. The recognition of their correlation is important. One can easily see that the Mīmāṁsā, which is a philosophy of half of the Veda, is opposed to any immersion in subjectivity.

QUESTION: In Western philosophy, too, we often speak of inwardness. But Indian philosophy seems to have a clearer and more detailed conception of it. Will you explain, in brief, what you mean by inwardness?

ANSWER: The senses know the objects, but the objects cannot know the senses; the mind knows the senses, but the senses cannot know the mind; reason knows the mind, but the mind cannot know the reason; the *ātman* knows the reason, but the reason cannot know the *ātman*. Yet, all of these are involved in perceiving any object. This is one way of explaining inwardness. It would require a long discussion to explain details.

QUESTION: You present the growth of Vedic religion as a growth from the worship of the natural forces to the spiritual religion of the Vedānta. But some scholars say that, even originally, the gods were not physical elements, but psychic forces. How do you defend your position?

ANSWER: Either position depends on the method of interpretation of the Veda. If we adopt the position that the Veda is one and has no historical growth, then we may read the latest ideas of the Upaniṣads into the earliest hymns of the *Rg Veda,* and say that the gods of Fire, Wind, etc., are symbolic of the psychic forces even for the hymns. But, if, after our knowledge of the primitive religions of Africa and Australia, we accept the idea that religion, even in India, has a historical growth and that even the early Aryans belonged to primitive tribes and worshipped the natural forces directly —which is said to be historically true—we have to say that spiritual inwardness was gradually recognized after generations of reflection, and that only toward the end of the Āraṇyaka period did the Indian Aryans correlate the Nature-gods with psychical and spiritual forces, and finally identify the two. I follow the latter method. Even then, as I have indicated in my paper, the delineation of the growth from polytheism to monism is less important for Indian religion than that of the growth from outward worship to inward realization.

NOTE

Dr. Werkmeister suggested that the word "mysticism" should not be used as representing Indian religion, for "mysticism" means everything from witchcraft, necromancy, medieval alchemy, and self-hypnosis to inward realization.

I do not know what other single word there is in English for better representing Indian religion. Perhaps "inward realization" is a more suitable phrase. One can see by reading Bradley's ethics that even "self-realization" becomes an ambiguous word to express the Indian spiritual ideal. One may like to use the term "*ātman*-realization"; but the reality of the *ātman* is not accepted by Buddhists. In Western literature, the word "mysticism" is used in both a respectful and a disrespectful sense. In the disrespectful sense, we may agree that it is, as Dr. Hu says, psycho-pathological. But, if reason belongs to the inward being of man, just on that ground it cannot be called pathological. Reason, on the contrary, confers sanity. On the other hand, if one denies the reality of the inward being of man on the basis of what one considers to be science, we may call him "scientio-pathological." The words "scientism" and "historicism" are already current in depreciatory meanings also. As there is the "naturalistic fallacy" (G. E. Moore's term), there can also be the "scientific fallacy," the fallacy committed by some scientists who think that with the help of the method of a particular science everything in the universe can be explained and that whatever cannot be so explained has no reality. And, to make matters worse, "science," although etymologically it means knowledge, has come to mean particularly the physical sciences.

M. M. SHARIF

Islam and Spiritual Values

Before making an attempt to write on Islam and spiritual values, one must make two things clear.

First, it must be clearly understood that in Islam there is no priesthood and no organized Church. No class has the monopoly on spirituality. There is no division of society between the Church and the State and between secular and religious laws or their ministers. It is not the business of any class but of believing men and believing women in general to enjoin what is right and forbid what is wrong,[1] and such believing men and women are not only Muslims but are also found among non-Muslims.[2] Let there be a band of persons who discharge this function more efficiently than others,[3] but such persons do not form an organized class mediating between God and man and attending exclusively to this work.

Second, in Islam there is no distinction between the religious and the secular, the spiritual and the mundane. The spiritual and the temporal are not two distinct domains, and the nature of an act however secular in its import becomes spiritual if inspired by the whole indivisible complexity of life.[4] The distinction arises out of the bifurcation of the unity of man into two distinct and separate entities—matter and spirit. The truth is that matter is nothing but spirit in space-time reference.[5] The ultimate reality, according to the Qur'ān is spiritual, and its life, besides being transcendent, is immanent in the temporal.[6] The spirit finds its opportunities in the natural, the material, the

1 Qur'ān 9:71. 2 *Ibid.*, 3:110. 3 *Ibid.*, 3:104.

4 M. Iqbal, *Reconstruction of Religious Thought in Islam* (Lahore: Shaikh Muhammad Ashraf, 1960), p. 154.

5 *Ibid.*

6 Qur'ān 24:35–36; 43:84.

secular. All that is secular is therefore sacred in the roots of its being.[7] All values are both spiritual and secular, and they unfold themselves in life, social as well as personal. They determine man's relation to his fellow beings as well as to his God. In Islam, there is no asceticism.[8] It is opposed to renunciation or otherworldliness which claims to achieve unalloyed spiritual values in monasteries or sanctuaries cut off from society.[9] All ascetic practices which involve hardship, pain, and torture to the body are prohibited.

Islam is not, however, against a period of temporary withdrawal from society and devotion to spiritual discipline.[10] There is a rhythm inherent within the soul of a prophet, a mystic, or a great genius. First, he lives his normal life. Then he retires within himself and undergoes a soul-illuminating discipline until he gets a soul-shaking moment, often a moment of ecstasy—a moment which, as Ibn Khaldun says, "comes and goes as swiftly as the flicker of an eyelid"—in which he receives an illumination, message, or inspiration. In the third stage of his spiritual progress, he returns to himself to live a transformed life. There is a similar rhythm in his relation to society. He first lives his normal life in the midst of his fellow men. Then there comes a period when he withdraws from society, and his personality acquires its creative power, and, thus transfigured, he returns to his social milieu with added spiritual force. The life of the philosopher-king which Plato describes in the *Republic,* Book V, is marked by the same rhythm, and the same rhythm of life characterizes the personal and social lives of all great leaders of men in different fields of life. No achievement is possible without undergoing a rigorous discipline in a period of comparative retirement from life around—be it in a mystic's cave, a scientist's laboratory, a technician's workshop, an artist's studio, or a scholar's den—and, after having thus acquired fresh powers, joining that life again. Such a rhythm marks even their daily lives.

All values together, call them spiritual or mundane as you like, form the very goal of man, situated as he is in the universe around him.

According to Islamic ideology, the universe in which man is placed is not created for idle sport;[11] it is not without a purpose or a goal; it is throughout teleological, and to this universal teleology human beings are no exception. For every one of them there is a goal,[12] and that goal is God himself.[13] He is the beginning and the end.[14] As al-Ghazzālī has explained, God is the beginning as the cause and the source of our existence, and is the end as an ideal—or, rather, the Ideal. God as a goal in his full beauty and grandeur cannot be seen by us finite beings,[15] but for our understanding he has described his attributes by similitude in terms of our highest values.[16] In order that we may apprehend what we cannot comprehend, God uses similitudes from our experience.[17] As

[7] Iqbal, *op. cit.*, p. 155.
[8] Ahmad ibn Hanbal, *Musnad* ("Authenticated Sayings") (Cairo: al-Matbaat al-Maimaniyah, Idarat al-Sayyid Rahmat al-Babi al-Halabi, 1313 H. [1895 A.C.]), Vol. VI, p. 226.
[9] Qur'ān 57:27.
[10] Muhammad's own life illustrates such withdrawal.
[11] Qur'ān 15:85.
[12] *Ibid.*, 2:148.
[13] *Ibid.*, 53:42.
[14] *Ibid.*, 57:3.
[15] *Ibid.*, 6:103.
[16] *Ibid.*, 30:27.
[17] *Ibid.*, 30:28.

compared to the essence of God, these attributes are only finite approaches, symbols, or pointers to reality, and serve as the ultimate human ideals.

Man is not a mere animal. He is the highest of all that is created.[18] God has created him in the best of molds.[19] According to the Qur'ān, he is born with the divine spirit breathed into him,[20] even as for Christians and Greek sages he is made in the image of God. Man's highest perfection, therefore, consists in being dyed in divine colors[21]—in the achievement and assimilation of divine attributes.[22] It is this capture of divine attributes to which Iqbal refers when he exhorts: "Catch the Lord with a noose, O Manly Courage."

God desires nothing but the perfection of his own light,[23] the perfection of these attributes. The sole aim of man is, therefore, a progressive achievement of life divine, which consists in the gradual acquisition of all divine attributes —all intrinsic values.[24]

These divine attributes or intrinsic values are connoted by the different names of God,[25] but they can all be summarized under a few essential heads: life, unity, power, truth, beauty, justice, love, and goodness. God is one; he is a free creative activity, which is living, all-powerful, all-knowing, all-beauty, most just, most loving, and all-good.

God, as described by the Qur'ān for the understanding of man, is not an indeterminate entity, a blind force, or an empty self. He is living,[26] and man, by living in this world and the next, realizes one of God's attributes. The taking of life (one's own or another's) destroys this basic value and is therefore a crime.[27] It is permissible only for realizing a greater good or avoiding a greater evil.[28]

Since the time of Plato, goodness, beauty, and truth have been universally recognized as the essential facets of reality and as the ultimate values of life. Plato could not think of God as free creativeness, nor could he conceive the ultimate unity of all existence, first and last, seen and unseen.[29] The bringing to light of these two ultimate values is among the greatest achievements of Islam.

Nothing is more emphasized by Islam than unity as an attribute of God.[30] Unity is therefore a basic human ideal or value.

Unity, as one of the ideals of man, implies both internal and external unity. Internal unity relates to what falls within the human mind. It means unity of thought, passion, and action; of practice and profession; and integration of the self as a whole. Externally, it means organization of society; inter-communication, toleration, family harmony, and fraternity; national solidarity and in-

[18] *Ashraf al-Makhluqat.*
[19] Qur'ān 95:4.
[20] *Ibid.*, 38:72.
[21] *Ibid.*, 2:138.
[22] *Takhallaqu bi akhlaq-Allah—Hadith.* R. A. Nicholson, *Secrets of the Self,* English translation of M. Iqbal, *Asrar-i-Khudi* (Lahore: Shaikh Muhammad Ashraf, 1961), Introduction, p. 19.
[23] Qur'ān 9:32.
[24] *Ibid.*, 84:6, 19.
[25] *Ibid.*, 59:24.
[26] *Ibid.*, 2:55; 40:65.
[27] *Mishkat* ("Niche" [symbolically meaning source of light]), Urdu translation by Mirza Hairat Dehlvi (Karachi: Karkhana-i-Tijarat-i-Kutub, n.d.), Nos. 3288–3290, 3297–3301.
[28] Qur'ān 5:35.
[29] *Ibid.*, 57:3.
[30] *Ibid.*, 2:163; 5:75; 6:19; 16:22, 51; 23:90–92; 37:1–5; 38:65–68; 112:1–4.

ternational brotherhood;[31] and, finally, identification of the personal with the universal will, i.e., direction of the personal will to eternal values, and communion and union with God.

In general terms, unity means integration of life in all areas of experience, unity of the personal and the general, and unity of the worlds of phenomena and noumena,[32] transcendent God being also immanent in Nature and man.

Power is also a divine attribute.[33] As a human ideal, this attribute is also both internal and external. Internally, it means the power of the will, the power of choosing, pursuing, and carrying out a truly worthy end, and, in reaching this end, facing opposition, mastering difficulties, and defying discouragement. It thus signifies perseverance, fearlessness, courage, and physical strength; initiative, interest, and zest; drive, resolution, and control over passions and temptation; and subordination of the personal to the common good, thought-creation, and personality building.

Externally, it implies destruction of evil, conquest of Nature, plans of action, and schemes of social construction; national freedom, personal liberty (which means freedom of thought, worship, belief, expression, and socially desirable action), and social democracy. Equally, it includes production and means of production and all creative activity manifesting itself in literature, music, architecture, and other fine arts, embodying itself in museums, art galleries, universities, towns, and other great monuments of human endeavor, and consolidating itself in all forms of world culture. Briefly stated, it means the dynamism of life without which no progress is possible and the presence of which is a guarantee of all development and expansion. "When the self gathers strength, the streamlet of life expands into an ocean."[34] It is this value which, with some poetic exaggeration, Iqbal sometimes calls the sole harvest of life, and "by means of which you can penetrate all regions of the heavens and the earth."[35]

Both the individual and society are thus dynamic unities with infinite possibilities of integration and action. But both the human mind and society, besides their unity and general dynamism, have three special aspects: intellectual, emotional, and volitional. The ideal of the first is to know truth from error. Broadly speaking, truth is the same as knowledge or wisdom. Like power, wisdom is also a divine attribute.[36]

As an ideal or a basic value for man, it means the knowledge of facts, ideals, and values, while error or untruth means their misapprehension. There are three degrees of knowledge in the ascending scale of certitude: (1) knowledge

[31] As for human brotherhood, the Prophet says, "O people, verily, your Lord is one and your father is one. All of you belong to Adam." Oration delivered during his Farewell Pilgrimage at Mina on Friday, Zil-Hijja 10 H. (631 A.C.).

[32] Qur'ān 57:3.

[33] *Ibid.*, 2:29, 117, 284; 3:29; 6:12–13, 65, 73; 7:54; 10:55; 11:6–7; 13:16–17; 16:72–81; 21:30–33; 25:61–62; 29:60–62; 48:7; 51:58; 53:42–54; 66:2–3; 85:12–16.

[34] M. Iqbal, *Asrar-i-Khudi* (Lahore: Shaikh Mubarak Ali, 1959), p. 15.

[35] Qur'ān 55:33; Iqbal, *Reconstruction of Religious Thought in Islam*, p. 131.

[36] Qur'ān 2:284; 3:5, 29; 4:26; 6:3; 18; 117; 10:61; 13:8–10; 16:23; 20:114; 21:4; 31:34; 34:2; 64:4; 67:14; 95:8.

by inference,[37] (2) knowledge by perception or observation,[38] and (3) knowledge by personal experience or intuition[39]—a distinction which may be exemplified by my certitude of (a) fire always burns, (b) it has burnt John's fingers, and (c) it has burnt my fingers. Likewise, there are three types of error: (1) errors of reasoning, (2) errors of observation, and (3) errors of intuition.

The exact quantitative determination of facts by observation and experiment and the discovery of the laws of their relations constitute scientific knowledge—the content of physical and biological sciences; the exact quantitative determination of events and their trends and the evaluation or qualitative appraisal of these events and trends constitute the content of social sciences such as history, economics, sociology, etc.; and the apprehension of values as means and ends is the knowledge of the humanities, i.e., the knowledge yielded by such studies as literature, fine arts, ethics, logic, philosophy, and religion. To discover truth in all the three fields, to communicate it through spoken and written word, and to accumulate it as a traditional heritage of ideas and public opinion, libraries, and archives constitute the function of the seeker after truth. The ideal of human knowledge is the completion of truth in all its grandeur. But, of course, the degree of its achievement depends on natural abilities, environmental conditions, and the maturity of the individual and the society concerned.

Like knowledge, beauty is a divine attribute and therefore another basic value.[40] Just as truth is the ideal of the intellect, so is beauty the ideal of the receptive and emotional side of life. It expresses itself both in contemplation and in art creation. When beauty is combined with vastness of power, it becomes sublime. Beauty is not only of physical objects, but also of mental qualities. When corporeal beauty is combined with beauty of character, we have something superb in its splendor. Beauty is the manifestation of a poise, equilibrium, or repose, besides enjoyment for the creating and contemplating minds. If poetry is the noblest of arts, it is nobler far to make one's life a perfect poem or song, to convert life itself into a work of art and live it with the same equilibrium or repose. Beauty arouses tender and noble emotions. It enhances our whole psychical life in a harmoniously integrated way and as a vital stimulant stirs us to great actions. It reflects ever-new aspects of delight and bliss. It widens our horizons, gratifies our senses, chastens our taste, elates our emotions, enlightens our cognition, informs our lives, and helps in the better integration of our being. But, apart from all that it does, it is a value-in-itself, a divine attribute, an ultimate goal, to be enjoyed in our religious experience, contemplated when found in Nature, and progressively realized in our bodies and minds, in our surroundings and society.

Two other attributes of God and our corresponding basic values are always mentioned together in the Qur'ān. These are justice and love, the latter includ-

[37] *Ibid.*, 102:5.
[38] *Ibid.*, 102:7.
[39] *Ibid.*, 69:51.
[40] *Ibid.*, 7:180; 17:110; 20:8.

ing, among other attributes, the attributes of munificence, mercy, and forgiveness.

God is the best to judge[41] and is never unjust.[42] On the Day of Judgment, he will set up the scales of justice, and even the smallest action will be taken into account.[43] He is swift in taking account[44] and punishes with exemplary punishment.[45] He commands people to be just[46] and loves those who are just.[47] Justice is one of the highest socio-spiritual values. In matters of dispute between men and men, people must decide with justice[48] and never be influenced by sheer advocacy.[49] They must "stand out firmly for justice as witness to God, even as against themselves or their parents or their kin and whether it be against the rich or the poor,"[50] and should not let even the hatred of others make them swerve to wrong and depart from justice.[51] Their lives, their properties, their honor, and their skins are sacred and inviolable.[52] Violation of any of these is a punishable crime. All agreements and treaties[53] must be honored and all promises fulfilled.[54] All men must be treated as equal. "There is no superiority for an Arab over a non-Arab, and for a non-Arab over an Arab; nor for a red-colored over a black-colored and for a black-skinned over a red-skinned except in piety. The noblest is he who is the most pious."[55] "Even if a manacled Abyssinian slave becomes your chief, hearken to him."[56]

For those who refrain from wrong and do what is right there is great reward,[57] and God suffers no reward to be lost.[58] People's good deeds are inscribed to their credit so that they may be requited with the best award.[59]

Divine punishment is equal to the evil done. It may be less (for, besides being most just, God is most loving and most merciful), but it is never more.[60] Such is not, however, the case with his reward. He is most munificent and bountiful and therefore multiplies rewards for good deeds manifold.[61] These rewards are of both this life and the hereafter.[62]

Islam, no less than Christianity, lays emphasis on the basic value of love. Whenever the Qur'ān speaks of good Christians, it recalls their love and mercy. God is loving[63] and he exercises his love in creating, sustaining, nourishing, sheltering, helping, and guiding his creatures; in attending to their needs; in showing them grace, kindness, compassion, mercy, and forgiveness, when, having done some wrong, they turn to him for that; and in extending the benefits of his unlimited bounty to the sinners no less than the virtuous among

41 *Ibid.*, 10:109.
42 *Ibid.*, 4:40.
43 *Ibid.*, 21:47.
44 *Ibid.*, 7:167; 24:39.
45 *Ibid.*, 13:6.
46 *Ibid.*, 7:29; 16:90; 57:25.
47 *Ibid.*, 5:45.
48 *Ibid.*, 4:58.
49 *Ibid.*, 4:105.
50 *Ibid.*, 4:135.
51 *Ibid.*, 5:9.
52 Oration delivered by the Prophet during his Farewell Pilgrimage at Mina, Zil-Hijja 10 H. (A.D. 631); Bukhari, *Sahih* (Urdu translation) (Karachi: Karkhana-i-Tijarat-i-Kutub, n.d.), pp. 236, 632, 833, 1048; *ZAD*, Vol. I, p. 245; *Bayan*, Vol. II, p. 24; also Muslim, Tirmidhi, Ibn Hisham, and Ibn Sa'd.
53 Qur'ān 2:283–284; 9:4, 7–10.
54 *Ibid.*, 2:177; 3:76.
55 Oration delivered by the Prophet during his Farewell Pilgrimage at Mina, Zil-Hijja 10 H. (A.D. 631).
56 *Ibid.*
57 Qur'ān 3:172.
58 *Ibid.*, 9:120.
59 *Ibid.*, 9:121.
60 *Ibid.*, 6:160.
61 *Ibid.*
62 *Ibid.*, 4:134.
63 *Ibid.*, 4:28, 45; 6:17, 64, 77, 88, 122; 10:57; 17:20, 21; 19:96; 85:14; 87:3; 92:12; 93:7; 96:3.

them.[64] Among human beings, no love is greater than that of a mother for her child, and God's love for his creatures is immensely greater than that.[65] Love among human beings expresses itself in a variety of forms. It is the golden thread that runs through the warp and woof of life and lends it such strength, richness, and luster as no other sentiment can. While ignoble sentiments cut us asunder, love unites. It is the motive force that can bring real unity among individuals and nations. In man it expresses itself in devotion, friendship, kinship, neighborliness, helpfulness, kindness, benevolence, mercy, and self-sacrifice, in both the personal and international fields. Expediency, the principle which is generally followed nowadays in international relations (though not professedly), can at best establish a weak and fragile bond which is easily broken at moments of tension. Real brotherhood of mankind is impossible to achieve without maximizing the socio-spiritual values of justice and love.

God is all-good, free from all evil.[66] He is also the source of all good[67] and worthy of all praise.[68]

Human good is the same thing as value, and goodness is the subordination of the personal will to the universal will—the free direction of the will to eternal values. This free direction of the human will to values is itself an ultimate value. Just as truth is the ideal of the intellectual side of our minds, and beauty and love are the ideal of the emotional side, even so is goodness, no less than power, the goal of the volitional aspect of our nature. It is the ideal of our practical activity. Nobility of character arises from the will that has the quality of goodness, that has worthy aims and always chooses and endeavors to achieve ultimate values. It is character that determines our preferences. In our daily lives, we are swayed by motives, desires, and passions. It is character that helps us to determine which of these ought to be satisfied and which checked, channelized, or sublimated. Every moment we are faced with alternative courses of action, and it is only under the guidance of character that we make our choices. A noble character expresses itself in right conduct or righteousness, which is the sum total of all our right actions—actions which aim at realizing the ultimate ends of life. Righteousness implies virtue, for virtue is the habit of doing right action and is formed by the repetition of these actions. The most significant of all virtues is justice, which, as explained before, implies equality of all human beings in the eyes of law—equality of all without any distinction of status, caste, color, race, or creed in natural rights and in claims to the protection of these natural rights. Our choice of things is seldom a cold choice. It is always accompanied with the warmth of feelings. These feelings become so strong and intimate that when anything happens to the objects of our choice, persons, things, places, or animals we feel intense emotion about them. Some of these emotional attachments or sentiments integrate the mind, others distintegrate it. The most significant of all the sentiments that integrate the mind is

[64] *Ibid.*, 2:150, 174; 4:25–27, 45; 5:77; 6:12, 17, 54, 63–64, 133, 162; 7:151; 9:117–118; 10:21, 32, 57; 12:64, 92; 14:32–34; 15:49; 16:119; 17:20, 21; 21:83; 23:109, 118; 29:60–62; 35:2–3; 39:153; 40:51; 52:28; 55:27; 86:14; 93:6, 8; 96:3.

[65] Bukhari, *Sahih*, "Kitab al-Adab" ("Book of Manners"), Cairo: 1345 H. (A.D. 1926), Vol. VIII, p. 9.

[66] Qur'ān 59:23.

[67] *Ibid.*, 16:53.

[68] *Ibid.*, 31:26.

love. It is the most important aspect of goodness—so important that it has sometimes been regarded as the same thing as the good. For mankind, it means complete devotion to the objects that are esteemed as good. Besides the right type of character, conduct, virtues, and sentiments, goodness implies integrity of purpose, clarity of conscience, and a sense of duty and responsibility.

The unrestricted achievement of these goals for a long time gives a value-tone to the whole of personality. This value-tone is called peace, bliss, or happiness.[69] Paradise is called by the Qur'ān the abode of peace.

These eternal and ultimate spiritual-secular values are, then, the ultimate goals of man. Each of them is related to some aspect of the human mind and has a special significance in relation to it.

Man, however, is not a purely spiritual entity. His spirit carries with it a physical organism as well. Ultimate spiritual values cannot be realized unless the needs of the physical organism are also satisfied. These needs relate to a man's organic life expressed in appetites such as hunger, thirst, sex, and wants such as clothing, shelter, etc. In their satisfaction lie man's economic values. These economic values, though not ultimate, are necessary for the realization of all ultimate aims. Therefore, for both society and the individual they are values of a secondary and yet a necessary order. No value of the higher order can be realized without the achievement of economic values as means. Economic values are in no sense ultimate and yet they are the necessities of life, and the seeker after ultimate values has to be a seeker after these as well. Satisfaction of man's economic need is an indispensable condition for his spiritual growth.

Corresponding to ultimate values, there are ultimate disvalues or evils. These are disunity, weakness, error, ugliness, injustice, hatred, vice, and misery. Disunity may take the form of disintegration or chaos. Weakness may appear as indiscipline, disease, stagnation, regression, or retrogression. Error may be due to wrong perception, bad reasoning, or ignorance. Ugliness may be of body, mind, or environment; and viciousness may entail hatred, injustice, or general misery (misery may mean physical pain or mental torture). Similarly, corresponding to economic values there are economic disvalues. These are poverty and starvation. Hunger, thirst, lack of shelter, and sex-starvation may lead to personal slavery, moral degradation, mental derangement, and even death.

Social or individual life directed to disvalue is chaotic and disintegrated life, not welling up in its natural course, but stagnating and ultimately receding into disappearance. To follow the path of value is to follow the right path,[70] the path of the blessed.[71] To follow the path of disvalue is to take the wrong path, the path of transgression. Values express our creative abilities; disvalues disclose and foster our destructive impulses militating against values.

Each intrinsic value can be used as a means for the advancement of evil rather than good. Unity among gangsters becomes a source of social injustice. Power in the service of passion and greed leads to the slavery of nations, disastrous wars, and endless human suffering. Knowledge is a dangerous weapon in

[69] *Ibid.*, 89:27. [70] *Ibid.*, 1:6. [71] *Ibid.*, 1:7.

the hands of people having no moral scruples. Beauty can conceal the hideousness of vice. Hence for the achievement of each value or good the necessity of avoiding all disvalues and using all ultimate values as means.

We cannot speak exclusively of our cognitive response to truth. Nor can we speak exclusively of our emotional response to beauty, or exclusively of the response of our will to goodness. And the same is true of our response to other values. They are all interwoven currents of the same life-process. Likewise, the goals of economic satisfactions and the ideals of unity, power, truth, beauty, justice, love, and goodness are not isolated ideals. In reality, they are all interrelated phases of the same ideal. Each ultimate value is a good-in-itself, but none is complete-by-itself. Each is supplemented by the luster of the others. No beauty will survive in a sphere of immorality. No morality will develop where no sense of beauty exists, where there is no knowledge of good and evil, right and wrong, and where economic needs absorb all or most of our time. The appreciation of a great work of art enhances our knowledge, and, by stimulating our will and conditioning our motives, lends support to our goodness. Values can be preserved and advanced only in harmony with one another. All of them converge and merge into one Ultimate End, the *Summum Bonum,* the value of all values, the end of all ends. They must all be aimed at as one unified ideal—the Ideal.

When the human will is directed to ultimate values in their unity, it is said to have surrendered itself to the will of God, and its success in this course is always accompanied by happiness, bliss, or peace, by whatever name we may call it. It is in this sense that Islam means both obedience and peace, and claims to be the core of all true belief from the days of the first man down to the end of time.

WALTER T. STACE

The Mystical Form of Western Spirituality

I.

It may be said, I believe, that in the West there is more than one concept of what is meant by "spiritual." There are at least two concepts, and we may designate them roughly as the mystical and the non-mystical. In one of his books Burtt has observed that, while mysticism is a major strand in the religions of the East, it is a minor strand in the religions of the West. This may be true. But for that very reason the mystical type of spirituality as it appears in the West is in danger of being neglected at a conference like this, although it plainly has a right to be represented. I am by temperament more suited to undertake the task of discussing the contribution of mystical spirituality to Western religion than the task of representing the non-mystical type. I shall therefore take this form as being, so to speak, my niche in this conference. I have little doubt that the non-mystical types of Western spirituality will receive adequate treatment at the hands of my colleagues. And in this way we can co-operate to produce a more complete picture of the whole Western situation to present to the conference.

For my limited purposes in this paper, therefore, I mean by spirituality simply mysticism, and especially that kind of spiritual experience which is called mystical experience. But by this identification we learn nothing unless we are able to give a more precise specification of what this spiritual experience is. There are two kinds of mystical experience, which I call, respectively, the extrovertive and the introvertive. The latter is the kind which is of importance to us here, and I shall speak only of it, and not at all of the extrovertive experience.

I am willing to take as my model of the introvertive experience a famous Indian description of it which occurs in the *Māṇḍūkya Upaniṣad*. For I shall maintain that the same type of experience is found in the West, and one could start at once with a Western model; but there are many advantages from the point of view of the purposes of this paper in starting with the statement in the *Māṇḍūkya Upaniṣad,* and then switching to the West. In that Upaniṣad we read that the experience is "beyond the senses, beyond the understanding, beyond all expression . . . it is the unitary consciousness wherein awareness of the world and of multiplicity is completely obliterated. It is ineffable peace. It is the Supreme Good. It is the One without a second. It is the Self."[1]

I think it may be of interest to the Asian members of this conference to show that this type of experience, thus described, is very well known in the West, and that it has a long history there, some of the high points of which I shall try to outline. I shall go on to show that, although the experience itself is well known in the West, the interpretation given to it there has been very different from the interpretations given it in Hinduism and Buddhism. I shall try to show what the essential philosophical and religious differences are.

But, before I do any of these things, I must try to explain a little further what I understand the essence of this experience, as it is found both in the East and in the West, is supposed to be, and to make some further comments and remarks on the matter.

The core of the experience both in the East and in the West is evidently that it is an *undifferentiated unity.* The key words of the passage I quoted from the *Māṇḍūkya Upaniṣad* are these: "It is pure unitary consciousness wherein awareness of multiplicity is completely obliterated." Our ordinary consciousness is always a multiplicity of various items, sensations, images, thoughts, volitions, etc. This multiplicity constitutes the empirical content of our minds. Because it is always changing and flowing it is sometimes called the stream of consciousness. Now, the experience described in the Upaniṣad is said to be one from which all this multiplicity has been completely obliterated. What is left is the pure unity of the self.

The more you consider it, the more completely extraordinary and paradoxical this claim appears. All over the world, East and West, the instructions for attaining this state of consciousness are basically the same, although details differ in different cultures. If you wish to attain it, you must suppress all sensations, images, thoughts, volitions—the entire multiplicity of the empirical contents of consciousness. When you have done this, what will be left is the pure unity of the self, the pure ego.

Consider how extraordinary this is. If you could perform the enormously difficult feat of emptying your mind of all sensations and images and of stopping all thoughts, volitions, and other empirical contents, one would naturally suppose that you would become unconscious or fall asleep. But the claim is that this is not what happens. What emerges is a pure consciousness, a consciousness without any objects.

[1] *The Upanishads,* Swami Prabhavananda and Frederick Manchester, trans., Mentor Paperback (New York: New American Library, 1957), p. 51.

The basic paradox here is that this consciousness is simultaneously both positive and negative. Since the mind has been emptied of all contents, since it has no objects, this consciousness is a mere nothingness, a complete vacuum, emptiness, or void. It is the void, the *śūnyatā* of Buddhist thought. And yet, it is not unconsciousness but a positive state of consciousness, pure consciousness. The metaphors of light and darkness are commonly used for the positive and negative aspects, respectively. Thus, Henry Suso, one of the German Catholic mystics of the thirteenth century, brings together the negative and positive sides of the experience in a single phrase by calling it a "dazzling obscurity." And in *The Tibetan Book of the Dead* the expression used to combine both sides of the paradox is "the clear light of the void," which means the same as Suso's "dazzling obscurity."

We should realize also that all this flatly contradicts David Hume, who asserted there is no self to be found except the stream of consciousness. That is why, with Hume in mind, you would expect that if you obliterate the stream of consciousness there will be nothing left except blank unconsciousness. But Hume, according to what we are discussing, was making a plain factual or empirical mistake. It should be noted, however, that the self which is here said to emerge is not a substance, or thing, but a pure undifferentiated unity. To all intents and purposes, it is the same as what Kant called "the transcendental unity of apperception."

There is also another important preliminary point to be made. Practically all mystics, excluding the Theravāda Buddhists, who constitute a special case, having experienced the undifferentiated unity, interpret it as being the pure unity of the self. In the first instance this means the finite individual self. But mystics usually tend to take a further step. They identify this personal and private self with the Universal or Cosmic Self. This is the special lesson of the Upaniṣads. But in a different form it also appears in Western mysticism, where it gives rise to the conception of the mystical union with God. We have, therefore, everywhere to distinguish three stages or steps. The first is the actual experience of the undifferentiated unity. The second is the interpretation of this as being the pure self of the individual. The third, which may or may not be taken, is the further interpretation of the pure individual self as being either identical with, or in some sense merged in union with, the Universal Self, the Cosmic One, God. It is only this last step which brings mysticism into the sphere of religion. The experience of the undifferentiated unity would not of itself be religious, nor would the discovery therein of the unity of the individual self. Only when we take the third step to the Self of the universe have we arrived at anything which most people would call religious. That is why Theravāda Buddhism, which is based on the undifferentiated unity but yet refuses to recognize that this is the unity of the self or indeed that there is any self, is by some thinkers classed as being a philosophy and not a religion.

In spite of anything that Hume may have said, in spite of anything that the orthodox empiricists or naturalistic philosophers may think *a priori* obvious, the evidence is overwhelming, from all cultures, from all over the world, that this kind of experience is an actual psychological fact. And I return to the point that its essence is that it is an undifferentiated unity.

I now turn to the task of exhibiting a few of the main points of the history of this pure consciousness as it has appeared in Western religions and philosophies and how it has been interpreted in the West.

It is important to keep clearly before our minds the distinction between the experience itself and the interpretations which the intellect puts upon it. For the main point is that the experience has been by and large the same all over the world, but that Eastern and Western interpretations of it have been widely divergent.

II.

Unless we go back into ancient Greek times, we may say that the history of Western mysticism begins with Plotinus. Plotinus cannot be said to have been a follower of any of the recognized religions. But his thought profoundly influenced Christianity, and we have to begin with him. I shall discuss a few of the major Christian mystics, and then I shall at the end, for reasons which will become evident as we go along, mention one famous modern Jewish philosopher, Martin Buber. I shall add a little more about Judaism. I shall also make a brief reference to Islamic mysticism.

To begin with Plotinus, we find him writing as follows:

> No doubt we should not speak of seeing but, instead of seen and seer, speak boldly of a simple unity. For in this seeing we neither distinguish nor are there two. The man . . . is merged with the Supreme, one with it. . . . Beholder has become the unity, having no diversity either in relation to himself or anything else . . . reason is in abeyance and intellection, and even the very self, caught away, God-possessed, in perfect stillness, all the being calmed. . . .
>
> This is the life of gods and of god-like and blessed men . . . a flight of the alone to the Alone.[2]

In the first sentence, we hear that the experience is "a simple unity." The word "simple," of course, means indivisible into parts, which is the same as undifferentiated. This is reinforced by the subsequent description of the unity as "having no diversity either in relation to [itself] or anything else." This, then, is the core of the experience, which agrees with the description in the *Māṇḍūkya Upaniṣad,* where it is called "the unitary consciousness wherein awareness . . . of multiplicity is completely obliterated."

Coming to the interpretation which Plotinus gives to this experience, we find that, while he does not specially emphasize the second step of the identification of the undifferentiated unity with the individual self, it is nevertheless implied in his statement that the seer and the seen are one. What he empha-

[2] Plotinus, *The Enneads,* Stephen McKenna, trans. 2d ed. rev. by B. S. Page, with a foreword by E. R. Dodds and an introduction by Paul Henry (New York: Pantheon Books, 1957), VI. lx. 11.

sizes is the third step. "The man," he says, "is merged with the Supreme," and "the very self caught away, God-possessed."

The interpretation here does not really differ from that of the Upaniṣads. Plotinus, therefore, so far as his thought is concerned, is just as much Eastern as Western. The split, the differentiation between Eastern and Western modes of interpretation, comes only when Christianity has taken charge of the mysticism of Plotinus and transformed it into the specialized Western theistic variety, which I shall explain later.

Plotinian mysticism becomes Christianized in the unknown author who passed himself off under the name of Dionysius the Areopagite. This name was apparently intended to imply that he was a contemporary and follower of St. Paul. But internal evidence in his writings shows clearly that he cannot have lived and written before the fifth century.

He emphasizes the negative view of God as wholly beyond conception, comprehension, or language. Thus, he writes of the Divine:

> It is not soul, or mind. . . . It is not order or greatness or littleness. . . . It is not immovable nor in motion nor at rest, and has no power, and is not power or light, and does not live and is not life . . . nor is it one, nor is it Godhead or goodness . . . nor does it belong to the category of non-existence or to that of existence . . . nor can any affirmation or negation apply to it.[3]

This is plainly the same as the *śūnyatā* of the Buddhists. It necessarily follows from the description of the experience as undifferentiated unity. If you empty your mind of all empirical predicates, leaving only the blank unity, it follows, of course, that none of the empirical predicates which you have removed from it can now be applied to it. It is therefore completely incomprehensible, unknowable, beyond all conceptions, beyond all words. It makes no difference whether you call it the void or whether you call it incomprehensible. They are the same. It is the *"neti, neti"* of the Upaniṣads. It is the *śūnyatā* of the Buddhists. It is the Being, or non-Being, or the non-non-Being, or the non-non-non-Being, etc., of which Dionysius is speaking.

Dionysius may be regarded as one of the earliest exponents of the linguistic school of philosophy—a fact which ought to endear him to many of the most up-to-date philosophers of the present day. This appears in his book *The Divine Names*, in which he institutes an inquiry into the nature of religious language. The problem, of course, is that, if the Divine is utterly beyond all thoughts and all language, how is it that the mystic can use any language about it, even the string of negatives to which Dionysius treats us. Dionysius comes up with a version of the theory that all words as applied to the Divine are symbolic. Any symbolic theory of religious language, intrinsically and as such, runs into what may perhaps be insurmountable difficulties. But, even if we discount these inherent difficulties of the theory, the version put forward by Dionysius must be regarded, even in its own terms, as a failure. His general

[3] Dionysius the Areopagite, *On the Divine Names and the Mystical Theology*, C. E. Rolt, trans. (New York: The Macmillan Company, 1920; reprint, 1957), p. 200.

line is to argue that, although God cannot be in himself good, or possessed of power, or will, or consciousness, or personality, or wisdom, or even of existence or non-existence, yet he is called good, powerful, wise, personal, existent, etc., because he is the cause of those empirical existences to which these empirical predicates apply. Obviously, this theory will not do at all, but we need not pursue Dionysius' speculations further. The main point is that these speculations are all interpretations of the experience of the undifferentiated unity.

It is true of Dionysius, as it was of Plotinus, that the differentiation of mysticism into those specifically divergent forms which distinguish Western mystical spirituality from that of the East has not yet taken place. Although Dionysius writes from within the fold of Christianity, and was perhaps, apart from his mysticism, an orthodox Christian believer, there is nothing specifically Christian about what he says of the nature of the Divine and the nature of mystical union. For this we have to wait until Christianity has had time to enforce its own special interpretations upon the experience of its mystics.

Passing from Dionysius, we must skip over something like eight centuries in order to come to that supreme flowering of the mystical consciousness which, in Roman Catholic Christianity, reached its peak around the thirteenth century. And here, out of the many famous names which press their claims upon us, we have room to discuss only three, Meister Eckhart, the German, Jan van Ruysbroeck, the Fleming, and St. John of the Cross, the Spaniard. Chronologically, Eckhart comes before Ruysbroeck and exerted a strong influence upon the thought of the latter. Much of what Ruysbroeck says has its source in the genius of Eckhart. Nevertheless, I shall find it more convenient to speak of Ruysbroeck first.

Consider the following quotation:

> The God-seeing man . . . can always enter, naked and unencumbered with images, into the inmost part of his spirit. There he finds revealed an Eternal Light. . . . It (his spirit) is undifferentiated and without distinction, and therefore it feels nothing but the unity.[4]

The first sentence says that the mystic's experience is "unencumbered with images," and that it is "naked." The word "naked" means that it is not clothed in sensuous imagery or thought. The expression "unencumbered with images" is very characteristic of Ruysbroeck. He is constantly emphasizing the absence of sensuous images. He does not in this passage mention the absence of actual physical sensations, but this can be taken for granted. Nor does he here speak of the absence of conceptual thought, but in many other passages he makes it clear that this is included. What all this refers to is the emptying of the mind of all empirical contents, whether sensations, images, or thoughts. In the present quotation, he says that by means of this process the mystic enters into "the inmost part of his spirit," in other words, the pure ego. This, he says, "is

[4] Jan van Ruysbroeck, *The Adornment of the Spiritual Marriage, The Sparkling Stone, The Book of Supreme Truth,* translated from the Flemish by C. A. Wynschenk Dom, edited with an introduction and notes by Evelyn Underhill (London: J. M. Dent & Sons, Ltd., 1916; London: Watkins, 1951), pp. 185–186.

undifferentiated and without distinction, and therefore it feels nothing but the unity."

This is almost the same language as that used in the *Māṇḍūkya Upaniṣad,* and I do not see how it can be doubted that it refers to the same experience.

Now consider the following remarkable passage from Ruysbroeck:

> There follows the union *without distinction.* Enlightened men have found within themselves an essential contemplation which is above reason and beyond *reason,* and a fruitive tendency which pierces through every condition and all being, and in which they immerse themselves in a *wayless abyss* of *fathomless* beatitude where the Trinity of the Divine Persons possess their nature in the *essential unity.* Behold this beatitude is *so onefold* and *so wayless* that in it every . . . *creaturely distinction ceases and passes away. . . .* There *all light is turned to darkness;* there the three Persons give place to the essential unity and abide without distinction. . . . For that beatific state . . . is so simple and so onefold that neither Father, nor Son, nor Holy Ghost is distinct according to Persons.[5]

Thus Ruysbroeck tells us that in the experience to which he refers "every creaturely distinction ceases and passes away." That is to say, all multiplicity is obliterated, and there is left nothing but the "essential unity." It is "onefold," i.e., there is no two-ness or many-ness in it. Also, it is described as "wayless." A way is a track across an area which divides the area into two parts. "Wayless" therefore means undivided, or undifferentiated.

So much for the description of the experience. Now look at the interpretation. Ruysbroeck interprets it in terms of the doctrine of the Trinity; and this idea I think he got from Eckhart. The Trinity is a three-in-one. Now, according to both Ruysbroeck and Eckhart, the Godhead is an undifferentiated unity which, however, differentiates itself into the three Persons, the Father, the Son, and the Holy Ghost. And what Ruysbroeck is saying in the last part of the passage is that the mystic in his experience enters into the ultimate unity of the Godhead, wherein there is no distinction, no multiplicity, not even the distinctions among the three Persons.

Notice the statement that "all light is turned to darkness." Darkness, we have observed, is the characteristic Christian metaphor for the unity in which all distinctions disappear. This metaphor is used, of course, because all distinctions do disappear in the dark. Elsewhere Ruysbroeck says, "This is the dark silence in which all lovers lose themselves." By lovers, of course, he means lovers of God.

Let us now turn to a passage from Eckhart:

> If you are to experience this noble birth you must depart from all crowds. . . . The crowds are the agents of the soul and their activities: memory, understanding and will in all their diversifications. You must leave them all: sense-

[5] *Ibid.,* pp. 244–245. Italics mine.

perceptions, imagination.... After that you may experience this birth—not otherwise.[6]

By "this noble birth" Eckhart means the birth of God in the soul, that is, the mystical experience. He tells us that it is only to be reached by getting rid of all crowds. "Crowd" is his word for multiplicity. But he specifies further what the multiplicity is. It is the activities of memory, understanding, and will, of sense-perceptions, and imagination. In other words, it is the entire content of empirical consciousness. This is the emptying process which is everywhere the same and leaves nothing but the pure unity of the ego. Eckhart has several names of his own for this. He calls it the "apex of the soul," "the aristocrat," etc.

Eckhart interprets the experience of a unity beyond all multiplicity in terms of the doctrine of the Trinity in the same way as Ruysbroeck does.

Exactly the same lessons can be drawn from an examination of the writings of St. John of the Cross, except in regard to the interpretation in terms of the doctrine of the Trinity. St. John, too, speaks of the emptying of the mind of its empirical contents and the resulting simple unity. It is worth noting that St. John lived in a different century and culture from Eckhart and Ruysbroeck. He belongs to Spain two and a half centuries later. Yet, his evidence is the same as theirs.

III.

I shall very briefly document the same conclusions with regard to Islamic mystics. I have space for only two quotations.

Says the great al-Ghazzālī:

When the mystic enters the pure and absolute unicity of the One and Alone, mortals reach the end of their ascent. For there is no ascent beyond it since ascent involves multiplicity implying... an ascent from somewhere... to somewhere, and when multiplicity has been eliminated, Unity is established and relationship ceases.[7]

My other quotation is from Mahmud Shabistari, who says:

In God there is no duality. In that Presence "I" and "we" and "you" do not exist. "I" and "you" and "we" and "he" become one.... Since in the unity there is no distinction, the Quest and the Way and the Seeker become one.[8]

I shall not comment in detail on these quotations beyond noting that the undifferentiated unity and the absence of all distinctions in it are emphasized.

[6] Meister Eckhart, *Meister Eckhart: A Modern Translation,* R. B. Blackney, trans. (New York: Harper & Brothers, 1957), p. 118.

[7] In Margaret Smith, *Readings from the Mystics of Islām* (London: Luzac & Co., Ltd., 1950), p. 70.

[8] *Ibid.*, p. 110.

IV.

I shall make a brief reference later to the general Jewish tradition. But meanwhile I want to quote a most remarkable and important passage from Martin Buber:

> Now from my own unforgettable experience I know well that there is a state in which the bonds of the personal nature of life seem to have fallen away and we experience an undivided unity. But I do not know—what the soul willingly imagines and is indeed bound to imagine (mine too once did it)—that in this I had attained to a union with the primal being or the Godhead. . . . In the honest and sober account of the responsible understanding this unity is nothing but the unity of this soul of mine, whose "ground" I have reached, so much so . . . that my spirit has no choice but to understand it as the groundless. But the basic unity of my own soul is certainly beyond the reach of all the multiplicity it has hitherto received from life, though not in the least beyond individuation, or the multiplicity of all the souls in the world of which it is one—existing but once, single, unique, irreducible, this creaturely one: one of the human souls and not "the soul of the All."[9]

The first thing to notice about this is that he describes his experience in language almost identical with that of the *Māṇḍūkya Upaniṣad.* It is, he says, the experience of an "undivided unity." It is "beyond the reach of all the multiplicity it has hitherto received from life." It is, in short, the undifferentiated unity. But now the remarkable thing is that he gives two interpretations of the experience which are incompatible with one another, but of which he at first accepted one and then later repudiated it and adopted the other. We have the first step, the actual experience of the undivided unity. Immediately after he has had the experience, he takes the second and third steps, that is, he interprets the experience not only as reaching the ground of his own pure ego but as attaining union with God. But, later he retreats from this third stage and goes back to the second. That is, he interprets the unity as being only the unity of his individual self, the pure ego.

Why does he do this? In my opinion he does it because of the pressure of the Jewish culture to which he belongs. In that culture the claim to actual union with God is generally frowned on and thought to be presumptuous if not blasphemous.

V.

This brings us to a profoundly important cleavage between Eastern and Western religions in general. In the major Indian tradition, from the Upaniṣads through Śaṁkara, the experience is interpreted in terms of the category of identity. That is to say, the individual self is found in the experience to be

[9] Martin Buber, *Between Man and Man,* Roland Gregor Smith, trans. (London: Macmillan & Co., Ltd., 1948), pp. 24–25.

identical with the Universal Self. But against this conception the three Western theistic religions, Christianity, Judaism, and Islam, take a determined stand. They have the same experience of the undivided unity as the Indian does, but they insist that between God and man, Creator and creature, there is a great gulf fixed, so that the creature can never be, or become, the Creator. On the other hand, the mystics of the West tend to show a clear drift toward the Indian idea of identity. This produces tension between the mystics and the ecclesiastical authorities, who sternly repress this tendency, which they label as a pantheistic "heresy." In Baghdad in the year 922 a Sufi mystic named al-Hallaj was crucified for using language which was thought to amount to claiming identity with God. For similar reasons a long series of charges of heresy was brought by the Church against Meister Eckhart, who wrote an elaborate defense but died before the issue came to trial.

Thus it becomes an important question how the mystics of the West, those, that is, who accept from the theologians the belief that it is impossible for the creature to be, or become, identical with the Creator, interpret their experience of the undivided unity. We have seen how Buber reacts to it. He shows at first the usual drift of the mystic toward pantheistic identity, but then retreats from this in obedience to the pressure of his culture. But apart from Buber as an individual we want to know where the three Western theistic religions in general stand in the matter.

The Christian point of view is extremely interesting. The experience is interpreted, of course, as "union with God." But the word "union" is ambiguous. It may mean either identity or similarity. After the union of the Mississippi and the Missouri, the two rivers become one river. This may be called identity. But in a trade union the members remain distinct persons. The union means only that they all have similar purposes. This enables us to understand the orthodox Christian conception of "union with God." It is to be understood in terms of the category of similarity, not identity. A single example will be sufficient to show this. Says St. John of the Cross:

> If we speak of the union of the soul with God we do not have in mind . . . substantial union, but we do mean that union of the soul with God . . . which can come about only when the soul attains to a *likeness* with God by virtue of love. We shall therefore call this the *union of likeness. . . . Union comes about when the two wills—that of the soul and that of God*—are conformed in one, so that there is nothing in the one that is repugnant to the other.[10]

To my mind, the analysis of the mystical union as similarity between two distinct and separate wills is a very inadequate interpretation of it, and compares unfavorably with the Indian concept of identity, which is the free and natural meaning given to it by the mystic, if he is not interfered with by the theologians. In India, this is taken as a matter of course. But, in the West, it is likely to lead to the mystic's being crucified.

[10] St. John of the Cross, *The Dark Night of the Soul*, Kurt F. Reinhardt, trans. (New York: Ungar Publishing Co., 1957), p. 34.

I shall add a word about Judaism. Here, also, the gulf between the creature and the Creator is emphasized. Moreover, its implications are carried much further than in Christianity. In Christian mysticism, the concept of union with God, in the special sense explained, is allowed. But, in orthodox Judaism, the concept of union in any sense tends to be rejected, although it is true that we find it in the later Hasidim and in some other instances. The orthodox Jewish concept of mysticism is, so I understand, conveyed by the word *"devekuth,"* which means adhesion or immediate contact between God and the human soul. In other words, the direct vision of God in some sense is allowed by the orthodox, but not union with God. The seer remains distinct from the seen.

VI.

The general conclusions which I wish to draw are as follows:

(1) The introvertive type of mystical experience is the same in the East and the West. It is the experience of an undifferentiated unity. But different interpretations are given to it by different cultures and even by different individuals.

(2) There is evidence that the experience tends to be interpreted in terms of pre-existing beliefs and that it does not produce the beliefs. Thus it can be combined with any philosophy or theological doctrine, and is generally fitted by the mystic into his already existing framework of ideas. For instance, in Buddhism it can accommodate itself to the denial of both the self and a Supreme Being. At the other extreme, Eckhart and Ruysbroeck interpret it in terms of the doctrine of the Trinity.

(3) In the East, the mystic is allowed to follow his natural bent and to speak in terms of the category of identity. In the West, the mystic's interpretation is dominated by ecclesiastical or theological authorities, who are governed by the idea of the gulf between God and man. Hence, in Christianity the notion of union has been whittled down to mean similarity. And Judaism is in this respect more extreme than Christianity, the whole concept of union being regarded with disfavor.

VII.

I shall now speak briefly about the consequences of Western mysticism for practical living.

Perhaps the commonest moral accusation against mysticism is that it functions in practice merely as an escape from the active duties of life into an emotional ecstasy of bliss which is then selfishly enjoyed for its own sake. On this view, mystical experience is sought only because of the feelings of peace, blessedness, and joy which it brings. The mystic wallows as in a bath of delicious emotions. And this, it is charged, is a mere flight from life and from the urgent work of the world. It may even be suggested, by those who cultivate so-called depth psychology, that what the mystic is "really" trying to do is to go back into the warmth of his mother's womb. I have put the criticism in its strongest possible terms, perhaps exaggerating it in a way which no one who has any knowledge of the actual history of mysticism would endorse. But, whether we express the criticism in stronger or weaker language, the essence of it is that, in greater or less degree, the mystic pursues his own salvation, his own beatitude, in a selfish way, while other men, whom he does not help, suffer.

The danger of resting selfishly in mystical contemplation as an end in itself is clearly recognized by the great Western mystics. For instance, Eckhart writes:

> What a man takes in contemplation he must pour out in love.
> If a man was in rapture such as St. Paul experienced, and if he knew a person who needed something of him, I think it would be far better out of love to leave the rapture and serve the needy man.
> It is better to feed the hungry than to see even such visions as St. Paul saw.[11]

In another passage he writes:

> Those who are out for "feelings" or for "great experiences" and only wish to have this pleasant side: that is self-will and nothing else.[12]

Ruysbroeck expresses the same certainty that the highest mystical experiences must overflow in love into the world. He writes:

> The man who is sent down by God from those heights . . . possesses a rich and generous ground, which is set in the richness of God: and therefore he must always spend himself on those who have need of him. . . . And by this he possesses a universal life, for he is ready alike for contemplation and for action and is perfect in both of them.[13]

The moral force of the Christian mystics has certainly been impressive. It is in this that the great strength of the Christian mystics lies, not in either their purely spiritual or their speculative profundity. In these, it seems to me we have to award the palm to the mystics of India, China, Japan, and perhaps of the East generally. Whether the moral and social activities of the Christian mystics have been of much actual value to their fellow men is more questionable. St. Teresa spent her life in the founding or reforming of convents. A modern social reformer or philanthropist is not likely to be much impressed by this. But this kind of activity was no doubt the medieval conception of the highest Christian virtue; and we have to take account of the times.

It is true that one who has mystical experience *can* treat it as a means of selfish enjoyment. And this has no doubt often happened. But this is an abuse of mysticism and is no part of its essential nature. Perhaps every ideal has its own characteristic abuse or form of degeneration. For instance, mob rule is the characteristic evil which tends to disfigure the ideals of democracy. Learning

[11] Quoted by Rufus M. Jones, *Studies in Mystical Religion* (London: Macmillan & Co., Ltd., 1909), p. 238.
[12] Quoted in Rudolph Otto, *Mysticism East and West: A Comparative Analysis of the Nature of Mysticism*, Bertha L. Bracey and Richenda C. Payne, trans. (New York: Meridian Books, 1957), p. 73.
[13] *Op. cit.*, pp. 220–221.

tends to degenerate into pedantry, religion into priestcraft. But it is of prime importance to understand that no ideal is to be judged by its abuses, but, rather, by its inherent nature. The nature of democracy, its ideal, is not mob rule; the ideal of learning is not pedantry; the ideal of religion is not priestcraft. Similarly, the ideal of mysticism is not escapism. Perhaps we might use here the idea of a besetting sin or temptation. The besetting temptation of the mystic may no doubt be to enjoy his ecstatic experiences for their own sakes, to indulge in what St. John of the Cross calls "spiritual gluttony." Departures from an ideal must not be blamed on the ideal but on the failures and defects of human nature. That Christians do evil is basically because they are fallible human beings. And, if mystics do evil, this also is because they are human. The essential tendency of mysticism is, therefore, toward the moral life, the social life, the life of altruistic action, not away from these things.

But perhaps we ought to face the question: Can mysticism be shown actually to have made men better? Has it been in practice an incentive toward feeding the hungry, healing the sick, curing or alleviating the monstrous mass of human misery? And it may be objected that we have defended only the ideal of mysticism, but not answered the question about its actual historical results. But this seems to me to be a question which it is almost useless to try to answer. Consider the parallel question whether religion—insofar as it can be distinguished from mysticism—has done good in the world or not, or more good than harm. Those who disbelieve in the truth of any religion, the skeptics and unbelievers, tend to say that religion has never made men morally better and that in fact it has done harm. Believers in religion take the opposite view. Neither opinion is based, I believe, on an impartial survey of the facts. Both are founded on little but the predilections and preconceived ideas of those who argue pro or con. And for this there is good reason. The empirical facts of history are so complex that the strands of good and evil tendency cannot be disentangled from the vast mass of events. The same must be said of mysticism. Those who dislike it will abuse it as escapism, or say that little or no good can be traced to it. Those who favor it will contend that it has made men better. Some have become saints whose influence for good has been incalculable. It has introduced lofty aspirations into the world, and these have infiltrated all civilizations. I have little inclination to be drawn into this battle of prejudices. I can only point to the fact that in its essence mysticism contains the love which is the ultimate motivation of all good deeds, that its tendency must therefore presumably be toward the good—however much this ideal tendency may be smirched by the evils and weaknesses and follies of human nature.

QUESTION: Should not Western mysticism begin with Jesus Christ, as presented in the Gospel of John, not with Plotinus?

ANSWER: Some people might want to go back to the Pythagoreans or the Greek mysteries for the origin of Western mysticism, but there is no positive evidence of the occurrence of the mystical consciousness *as understood in my paper* among the Greeks. They may have been mystical in some looser and vaguer sense. In the same way, I see no evidence that Jesus Christ possessed that consciousness. His religion, being Judaic, was of the prophetic or objective, not the mystical, kind. Mysticism came into Christianity later on from other sources. Mysticism is not a major strain in Christianity.

This question refers to the Gospel of St. John. It is true that the author of that Gospel put into the mouth of Jesus a number of phrases which suggest the idea of the mystical union with God. But since there is no trace of such mysticism in the Synoptic Gospels I cannot accept these phrases as historical utterances of Jesus. Nor do they show that the author of the Gospel himself possessed the mystical consciousness. Quite possibly he did possess it. But the use of a few mystical-sounding phrases which after all anyone, including the present writer, can pick up and use sympathetically, is not sufficient evidence of actual possession of mystical consciousness.

QUESTION: Since mysticism is an experience of the whole personality, is not universal love, rather than undifferentiated unity, the essence of the mystical consciousness?

ANSWER: By the "essence" of mystical experience I mean those characteristics which are definitive of it in the sense of marking it off from all other kinds of experience. Love would not fill that role, but undifferentiated consciousness does. I hold that the introvertive mystical consciousness is in essence identical in all cultures, but that there are two variable factors which cause mysticism to take different forms from culture to culture. One is the *intellectual interpretation* put upon the experience. The other is the *emotional reaction* to it. Suzuki has observed, "There is no reference whatever in Buddhist satori to such personal . . . relationships as are to be gleaned from these terms: flame of love, a wonderful love shed in the heart, embrace, the beloved, bride, bridegroom, spiritual matrimony, Father, God, the Son of God, God's child, etc."[14] This is admirably written. But I shall make two remarks concerning it. First, what he says about it can be generalized as explaining the differences between mysticisms in all cultures, and not merely the difference between Buddhist and Christian mysticism. Second, Suzuki does not distinguish between intellectual interpretation and emotional reaction. Examples of both are mixed together in his list. The questioner gives as a reason for his view that "mysticism is an experience of the whole personality." But this statement, though frequently made, is, I believe, incorrect. The mystical consciousness, on the contrary, depends on the total wiping out of all personality.

[14] D. T. Suzuki, *Zen Buddhism, Selected Writings*, William Barrett, ed., Anchor Paperback A90 (New York: Doubleday & Co., 1956), p. 106.

CONSTANTIN REGAMEY

The Meaning and Significance of Spirituality in Europe and in India

I.

I will not conceal the fact that the task of describing and discussing at this conference the main trends and characteristics of Western, and particularly European, spirituality inspires me with some apprehension. I am an Orientalist, and when acting as a spokesman for Western doctrines I can do it rather as a European, whose mentality and culture have been shaped by the traditions of his continent, than as representative of any particular Western philosophical school. I hope that professional philosophers will excuse some deficiencies of my erudition and consider me, rather, as a product of a cultural tradition than as one of its active animators. This position may give me greater freedom in embracing as a whole innumerable currents of European life and thought, as they are reflected in the mind of an average representative of its culture—and perhaps it will also give me greater courage in dealing with doctrines and problems which Western technicians of philosophy seem to avoid as not sufficiently scientific and up to date.

In fact, when reading the proceedings of the former conferences held at this same place, one is struck by the obvious disparity of approach in Western and Eastern papers. While Eastern authors defend with deep and sincere conviction even the extreme spiritual attitudes of their philosophies and religions and do not hestitate to appeal to the authorities of their whole history, most of their Western colleagues seem to confine themselves to some modern technically scientific analysis and, when referring from time to time to great metaphysical or religious traditions of the West, do it with utmost discretion, as if they feared to lose the solid ground of scientifically controllable discussion.

This fact has not been overlooked by the participants of the former conference, as pointed out by Mr. Moore in a note to the "Seminar Reports"[1]: "Emphasis was placed upon Western naturalism for strategic reasons, because it was felt that in the contrast of this doctrine and several Oriental systems lay the basic cleavage between East and West.... There was no need to reconcile the 'idealisms' of East and West, since their affinities have been abundantly demonstrated by scholars on both sides.... There was no intent to regard Western naturalism as *the* present-day philosophy of the West, nor were Christian and Western idealistic ethics neglected in the Seminar discussions." In spite of this final remark, it is a fact that the West has been represented at these discussions rather one-sidedly. For an attempt at world philosophical synthesis such a strategic experiment was somewhat misleading. There are really few possibilities of finding a common language between Western naturalism and, e.g., the general trends of Indian thought. Although "recent Western naturalism ... in its present development does not wish to exclude any actually experienced value or insight,"[2] and consequently may accept as real facts the spiritual experiences of Eastern religions and philosophies, yet it would consider them rather as new data for psychological or psychoanalytical research or, at most, as the extending of the notion of experience to that of dreamless sleep or of trance more or less provoked by appropriate techniques of concentration. But this way of viewing the facts can neither justify the exceptional value attached to these experiences in the East nor explain why they are considered as man's unique access to the ultimate reality, as the irrefutable proof of the existence of a spiritual reality with regard to which all other evidence is secondary or simply illusory. The reaction of our Eastern colleagues was unanimous: they refused to examine the higher insight of the ultimate at the same level as sensorial, phychological, or purely empirical evidence.[3] On the other side, naturalism can admit the evidence of infra-psychic or para-psychic phenomena; it cannot recognize in them spiritual facts, that is, facts in our life which cannot be explained by purely physical or psychological causes and which, therefore, are considered as more or less direct proofs of the existence of a higher, non-scientifically controllable principle or power.

Now, the attitude which admits such a higher sphere of reality without which most facts of human life would remain unexplained is by no means the monopoly of the East. In spite of violent criticism of some modern schools of Western philosophy against the "romantic vagaries of idealism" or of "meaningless metaphysical judgments," an objective and impartial glance at the whole history of Western thought and culture will reveal, not only that the spiritual attitude was prevalent until the middle of the nineteenth century, but also that it is by no means absent or secondary in our times. The most representative philosophical schools of present-day Europe—neo-idealism, phenom-

[1] Charles A. Moore, ed., *Essays in East-West Philosophy* (hereafter, *EEWP*) (Honolulu: University of Hawaii Press, 1951), p. 440, note 6.

[2] *Ibid.*, p. 437.

[3] So much more are they opposed to the psychoanalytical methods of viewing the spiritual experience. Cf. the violent condemnation of such methods by Sri Aurobindo or Sri Ramana Maharshi.

enology, existentialism, French spiritualism, personalism, and, last but not least, different varieties of modern "schools of metaphysics" (Alexander, Whitehead, Nicolai Hartmann, Neo-Thomism)—are all much nearer the spiritual attitude than the scientificism of different kinds of postivism. And, what is more important, this attitude is not limited to academic discussions of philosophers, but continues to mold the mentality of millions of Westerners, to inspire and guide their activity, to stimulate them to creative or heroic deeds, to self-sacrifice for the sake of ideals which by no means could be identified with the materialistic greed of personal or social welfare.

Yet, if Westerners themselves do not find it necessary to emphasize this side of their life and culture, we cannot be astonished that even the most open-minded among our Eastern friends have such a narrow conception of the dominant trends of Western mentality. If it were not our own fault, would it be possible that, e.g., Mr. Raju would affirm that "Western philosophers might find it useful to understand man . . . as a spiritual being far transcending his relations to matter and society,"[4] as if it were not only one of the basic beliefs of Christian religion but also one of the fundamental problems of present-day European philosophy. Similarly, the conviction that "higher and higher forms of being rule the lower and lower ones"[5] has been since the Greek philosophers the main source of the whole of European spiritualism.

It seems, therefore, that we can achieve a more fruitful result when comparing Eastern doctrines with Western spiritual conceptions and not with Western systems which in their methodology find no place for the idea of the spiritual. This comparison is not at all superfluous. The affinities of idealisms of East and West which "have been abundantly demonstrated by scholars on both sides" are mostly concerned with single points, and their similitudes appear often to be quite superficial when considered in a broader context. As a whole, these "idealisms" *do need* to be reconciled, if we want to avoid misunderstandings, since the fundamental differences between them are more important than convergencies. And before we try to reconcile these two attitudes—or at least to make them mutually transparent—we ought to clarify the basic differences. Moreover, Western spirituality is by no means limited to idealisms or even to Christianity. Both in theoretical and practical fields, it finds expressions which are for us highly spiritual but often appear to Easterners as self-sufficient humanism or as sterile, purely academic, or dogmatic speculations.

My intent is neither to defend Western spirituality (which, after all, is much more attacked in the West than in the East) nor to examine which of them—that of the East or that of the West—deserves in a higher degree the qualification of spiritual. It has often been stated at former conferences that it is dangerous to oppose East and West *en bloc* and to forget how numerous and far-reaching are the divergencies *within* each of these areas. It would be a hopeless task to try to give even an approximate description of the extremely

[4] *EEWP*, p. 227.
[5] *Ibid.*, p. 229.

multifarious expressions of the spiritual attitude in Western thought and culture, all the more since even the perspectives in which the historic development of this attitude can be viewed are also very divergent and never quite objective. I shall merely try to emphasize some basic tendencies which have given Western culture and mentality their particular style and which in most obvious ways differ from the Eastern approach to the spiritual. Here, too, I shall take into consideration, above all, the most representative aspects of Eastern spirituality: those of Hinduism, of Mahāyāna Buddhism, and occasionally of Taoism.[6]

II.

A thorough examination of some constant reproaches made to the West by the Easterners leads often to paradoxical results. Thus Mr. Moore twenty years ago very judiciously showed[7] that the alleged hedonism, considered as a typical Western attitude, is much more characteristic of the East where even the highest spiritual aspirations are less disinterested than in the West.[8] More consistent is the reproach of the scientificism of Western culture, though it is often improperly confounded with materialism and mechanicalism; there remains almost nothing of the naive conception of matter in modern science and pure mechanicalism is also abandoned by present-day physics. What remains is the method of studying reality by means of exact conceptual reasoning based on experience and tested by experiment. Now, this method cannot be a motive of reproach, since in India it is applied even to spiritual facts; even the intuition of the ultimate requires experimental testing. As Swami Nikhilananda says, "Untested philosophical beliefs are no more trustworthy than untested scientific hypotheses." And on the same page he says: "through Yoga it can be demonstrated that genuine religious experiences are as valid as scientific truths." We find here the same postulate of empiric testing as in Western science, the only distinction being that this method is applied to a non-material subject and consequently cannot be expressed in exact relational formulas or explicitly described. But we find even there our postulate of interpreting raw experience and controlling it in order to avoid delusion: "personal experience may very well be self-deception"[9] and must be tested by scriptural evidence and severe reasoning.

[6] Neo-Confucianism, with its concept of determinate *li* (organic principle) accessible to reason, with its method of *ko chih*, which is rational intuition without a "leap," and with its emphasis upon action, is much nearer to Western patterns than to Buddhism or Taoism. As for Islam, I fully agree with the well-known thesis of Northrop (*The Taming of the Nations* [New York: The Macmillan Co., 1952], chaps. V, VI) that with regard to its spiritual foundations it belongs much more to the West than to the East.

[7] Charles A. Moore, ed., *Philosophy—East and West* (Princeton: Princeton University Press, 1946), pp. 309–311.

[8] Although the Indian, and especially the Buddhist, spiritual way requires a fully disinterested attitude of self-denial and self-sacrifice, it has to be practiced for the sake of one's own *mokṣa*. Indian ethics is pre-eminently soteriological, whereas the ideal of the good as an imperative, as a moral duty independent of reward or other advantages, has been developed in the West.

Professor Mahadevan points out in his paper, "Indian Ethics and Social Practice," in this volume, that this concept of the ought-to-be-done (*kāryatā-jñāna*) has been sponsored by the Prabhākara Mīmāṁsakas. But this was a school that had no influence on the general aspect of Indian thought, and—as Mahadevan admits (*ibid.*, p. 5)—"most of the systems of Indian philosophy would agree with the Nyāya in holding the view of ethics as instrumental to the desired end."

[9] *EEWP*, p. 234.

Reasoning is here only auxiliary, a method which prepares the proper experience and controls it. On the contrary, the West alone has discovered in reason the source of knowledge *which needs no external testing at all,* since every experience is automatically interpreted by and consequently dependent on our intelligence. This evaluation of reason as the final instance of knowledge is one of the pillars of Western spirituality: the feeling of *certainty* and *universality* of rational truth, which cannot be deduced from experimental data, presupposes, if not necessarily a higher intellect modeling our consciousness, at least the existence in ourselves of a universally valid mental faculty irreducible to sensorial perceptions.

This distinction in the hierarchy of our highest sources of truthful knowledge brings us back to the famous opposition, established by Mr. Northrop, of "theoretically formulated and indirectly tested concepts by postulation" in the West and "directly tested concepts by intuition" in the East. In the perspective of Western spirituality, especially important are concepts by postulation and rational relations, which do not need any experimental verification and can be tested only by reason itself. Though absolute confidence in such omnipotence of abstract rational truth is not and has not been shared by all Western currents of thought, it remains one of the most original and distinctive features which have shaped Western mentality. It can be opposed both to Western experimentally scientific method and to the general Indian attitude.

In fact, in India, this Western rational approach is considered as an antithesis of the spiritual. It is from that point of view that Radhakrishnan opposes Eastern *Religion* to Western *Thought* and reproaches the West with having conceptualized in abstract formulas life, mind, man, society, and spirit. We know that a strong reaction against this one-sided deification of reason has arisen also in the West and has led to a considerable extension of the notion of the spiritual. Nevertheless, this reaction has very rarely been accompanied by a radical disavowal of the spiritual origin and significance of reason. The Indian reaction is based on other arguments: Knowledge by concepts is knowledge *about* reality; it is mediacy, while Eastern and especially Indian sages strive for immediacy, for direct identification with fundamental reality. Now, the Western response to this argument (which, however, is not shared by all Westerners) is that we, too, strive for immediacy, but we find it in a higher degree in reason than in experience. Let us quote the postulate of immediacy as it has been developed by Mr. Raju in the beginning of his paper presented at the former conference, "if self-sufficiency or self-validation is needed somewhere, if we are to get it in some cognition, then why not acknowledge it in every cognition? That is, the truth of every judgment must be self-revealing, and reality or existence must be self-revealing. But what would be the nature of a reality that is self-revealing? It cannot be anything but Self."[10] Then the Western response would be, "It cannot be anything but the Cartesian *cogito,*" where the immediate statement of the fact of reasoning is primary to the de-

[10] *Ibid.,* p. 211.

duction *ergo sum*.[11] And the conviction of the existence of some reality being an "other" to knowledge is a further deduction, a postulate of reason which will avoid the solipsism of the consequent *esse est percipi vel percipere*. But our only faculty which not only is able to reveal itself but can correct its errors within itself and through transcendency can validate itself without appealing to external sources of knowledge—is reason. Why not consider it as reality?

This step has been taken by Western thinkers, and it is of secondary importance whether they consider reason as being the exclusive reality (as post-Kantian idealists have done) or as the essential part of reality, the intelligible, existing in things outside the mind, but yet in accordance with the laws of reason (as, since Greek philosophy, different schools of Western realism have done). The latter will add to this intelligible and rational essence the mysterious existence which, as already stated, is also a postulate of reason much more than a product of objective evidence, since it can be neither verified experimentally nor felt outside the subject. What is really important for the particular development of conceptual thought in the West is the fact that it discovered in reason the method of attaining universally valid certitude and that this sense of certitude gives the impression of grasping reality immediately[12] and in its very essence. The sense of certitude produced in the discoverers of rational truths the same rapture and ecstasy that the intuition of *Ātman-Brahman* gave to the sages of the Upaniṣads. And it is not surprising that ancient Greek philosophers, when discovering, in the mathematical rules empirically elaborated by the Egyptians, universally valid laws, independent of any sensorial and common-life experience, saw in this rationality the presence in their minds and in Nature of some higher, spiritual principle.

The process is the same in the West as in the East: the spiritual value is discovered inwardly and put in relation to the psychical faculty which affords certitude free from any contingency. We have no right to deny that Eastern and Western mystics do experience the sense of absolute certitude when they reach the direct insight of the ultimate. But this insight is indescribable and incommunicable, known only to him who has attained it. It is a characteristic feature of every experience, both worldly and trans-worldly, that it cannot be directly communicated unless it is rationally elaborated and interpreted. This is possible with worldly experience; the trans-worldly insight can at most be metaphorically or negatively alluded to: in its essence it remains ineffable. And this is the paradox of every mystic realization, that it leads to an immediate apprehension of an all-embracing universal unity in which all

[11] Indian philosophy knows a strikingly similar exordium in the beginning of Vasubandhu's *Viṁśatikā*, in which the author finds the proof of the reality of consciousness in the fact of doubting. The absoluteness and self-sufficiency of consciousness is here even much more emphasized than in Descartes, since Vasubandhu does not infer from *cogito* either the *sum* or even the subjectivity of thinking. His formula is, rather: *cogito ergo cogitatio est*. Yet, the conviction of the superiority of undifferentiated immediacy is, even in this extreme Indian idealism, so powerful that, in spite of such rational premises, Vasubandhu, in his final conclusions, deprives the pure consciousness of any trace of conceptual or discursive thought.

[12] Here, "immediately" does not mean "instantaneously." Rational truth very often requires a long chain of reasoning, but this chain is based on the same assurance of the validity of reasoning. Rational certitude is immediate to the extent that it requires no other tests than those contained in reason itself. It is precisely self-revealing and self-validating.

individuality is absorbed and dissolved, and at the same time it is based on an absolutely individual experience.

The West has always felt the same longing for an all-embracing unity, but it achieves it in the reason which permits unequivocal communication and does not dissolve the particular. It is the way of grasping the world as a whole without destroying it and with the possibility of sharing this universal grasp with every other being endowed with reason. In the East, the ultimate unity is realized through *elimination* of every distinction; in the West, the distinctions are carefully emphasized, and the unity has to be achieved through their *harmonization*. In its search for unity, the East attains the *One* through negation of the individual and the personal, and yet realizes it in an exclusively individual mental operation; the West in its search for unity discovers the *totality* which maintains individual and personal distinctions and yet succeeds in securing universal union through the communicability of the truth and the generalizing power of reason.

These basic distinctions will leave ineffaceable traces on the whole spiritual development of both West and East and will have important practical consequences. They will solidify the characteristic Western attitude which we may call "spiritual pluralism," and they are also at the basis of one of the most fundamental metaphysical divergencies between Europe and India: in the West, the generalizing reason is the principle of universality, and being is considered as *principium individuationis* (there are very few exceptions to this general attitude, e.g., Duns Scotus); in the East, being is considered as universal and undifferentiated, and all individualization is the product of rational determinations.

I know that the identification of Indian philosophy with intuition and of Western thought with reason is a commonplace and, like all such theses, is an oversimplified one. The opposition against the rationalization of reality has been and is still quite important in the West, where we have also purely intuitionistic currents, much more anti-intellectual than India has ever had. On the other hand, the dialectical and logical skill of Indian philosophy is well known. We can certainly agree with Mr. Datta when he concludes[13] that reason is the common method of philosophy in India as it is in the West. But we can ask: On what level? In the West, reason rises to the highest regions of reality; it has been considered as the unique faculty which can lead not only to the threshold of the Absolute but to the Absolute itself. In India, it has to disappear at this threshold. No rational approach to *Nirguṇa Brahman* is possible; there is a gap which cannot be crossed by anything other than supreme insight. The Mahāyānist *prajñā* seems to be nearer the concept of the absolute reason of Western idealists; it is the foundation of discursive reason (*vijñāna*), and in the relation *vijñāna-prajñā* we may find some analogy with the hierarchy of reason in post-Kantian schools. Yet, in Western idealism this ascension is achieved through subsequent degrees of transcendency which include lower

[13] *EEWP*, pp. 87, 88. Cf. also the remarks of Raju, *ibid.*, p. 440, note 3.

forms of reason and do not eliminate them. There appears a dialectic continuity, whereas between *vijñāna* and *prajñā* no transition is possible. As in the case of *Nirguṇa Brahman,* "there is a leap, an existential leap."[14]

Here we touch the key problem of our discussion. The absence of continuity in the hierarchy of mental faculties as accepted by Indian and related doctrines affords the clearest explanation of the fundamental differences which separate the conceptions of the spiritual in India and in the West. In India, the limit between the spiritual and the non-spiritual is identified with the leap which has to be achieved when passing from reason to the direct insight of the ultimate. *All that lies below that gap is non-spiritual,* is material. According to Hindu psychology based on the Sāṁkhya system, even cosmic reason (*buddhi*), as much as the ego (*ahaṁkāra*) and the mind (*manas*), "are not different from external material objects, such as trees or stones, as far as their essential nature is concerned."[15] All the variety of our psychical life that even Western naturalism does not reduce to physical processes is conceived in this psychology as effects of more or less subtle forms of matter. The only spiritual fact in a human being is his experience of the ultimate; the activities of man can be considered as spiritual only when they are directed toward the realization of *ātman.*[16]

This Indian conception does not disqualify psychical life in such a degree as would appear to us in the West. But, when discussing the problems of spiritual values, it is necessary to be aware of the much narrower meaning of the word "spiritual" in India. There is some terminological misuse in the translation of *ātman* by "spirit." This equivalence would be fairly correct, if we take into consideration the original, mythological meaning of these terms when both *ātman* and πνευμα = *spiritus* denoted "breath." In their further development, both terms have assumed such divergent meanings that the translation of *"adhyātma"* by the word "spiritual" is today rather misleading. The

[14] Cf. D. T. Suzuki, "Reason and Intuition in Buddhism," in *EEWP,* p. 43 (cf. also, above, note 11). In the same passage, Suzuki explains that there can be no continuous progress from *vijñāna* to *prajñā,* because, if there were, *"prajñā* would cease to be *prajñā;* it would become another form of *vijñāna."* This statement shows the difference between the Western and Indian notions of transcendency. Western thought has discovered in reason, and in reason alone, the capacity of transcending itself and analyzing itself. In India, the ancient denial of this capacity ("You cannot know that which is the knower of knowledge," *Bṛhadāraṇyaka Upaniṣad* II.iv.14) has always remained valid; if reason is transcended, it can be so only by a totally different principle. Hence the leap which creates problems unknown to the West: How can the ultimate be the foundation of rational developments if it is in full transcendency with regard to reason and to any determination? And, in the religious aspect, how can Brahman be the cause of the world, if it cannot be affected by any process of acting or transformation? Hence the doctrine of *māyā* and *śakti,* which, though accepted by Śaṁkara, are considered by him as logically and ontologically inexplicable (cf. Raju, *EEWP,* p. 222). Here lies the source of the conception of *vivarta* (illusory transformation), which saves the transcendency of Brahman but at the cost of rendering the world illusory. The extremely illuminating paper of Paul Mus, "The Problematic of the Self, West and East, and the Maṇḍala Pattern," in this volume, gives further precision to this fundamental problem of transcendency in Indian thought. In India, transcendency is a method of reaching a higher level through a "non-additive integration," a kind of coalescence of lower elements into unity, which in itself represents no supplementary "entity" added to the total of the integrated elements; "It is all of them, without being any of them." The lower elements are not subordinated to the integrating unity, but identified with it. This unity is coextensive with its parts, which are also coextensive among them.

[15] Cf. Swami Nikhilananda, *EEWP,* p. 102.

[16] In the discussion of my paper, Raju objected that there is no radical discrimination between *buddhi* and *ātman, buddhi* being the principle nearest the ultimate. I can answer with Raju's own words ("The Concept of the Spiritual in Indian Thought," *Philosophy East and West,* IV, No. 3, October, 1954), where it is stated that *buddhi,* compared with *Logos,* is not the same as the Highest Spirit, that *antaḥkaraṇa,* which, according to the Sāṁkhya and most of the Vedāntic schools, encompasses reason, ego, and mind, "is not the same as spirit." "Spirit is beyond the principle of reason."

Western term is here mechanically applied to a notion already codified and having in the East a long tradition. In the West, the connotations of this term are far more complex, since, from the beginning, the notion of spirit has not been limited to a single peculiar psychical power and it has been considerably enlarged during the history of Western spirituality.

III.

Let us sum up briefly the history of the origin of Western spirituality in those two cradles of Western civilization that are the Graeco-Roman world and the Hebrew-Christian religion. The basic motive for the distinction of two spheres of reality, matter and spirit, has been everywhere the same: the more or less intuitively felt essential irreducibility of some facts of our life either to physical or sensorial processes or to the merely physiological needs of food, shelter, procreation, pleasure, etc. Disinterested moral feelings, demands for order, responsibility, freedom, justice, longing for immortality or unity with the whole, intuitions of beauty or of truth, mental faculties such as attention, abstraction, coherent reasoning, and quite generally the notion of non-utilitarian values—these were facts which distinguished man from the animals and required at least a radical distinction between physical and psychical components of human personality. Yet, the profound feeling of disproportion between the imperative attraction of these aspirations, which often induced men to act against their instincts or egoistic needs, and the limitations and contingency even of our psychical life, led to the assumption of some higher source of these intuitions and demands. The ancient religions, with their mythological, cosmogonic, ritualistic, or magical schemes, could but partly justify these aspirations and explain these intuitions. In nearly all the great civilizations of the ancient world they were completed or sublimated by the discovery of principles, laws, or entities—often placed above the gods or even substituted for traditional pantheons—which have appeared as models or norms for human conduct and as the supreme goal of man's aspirations. I say "discovery," since they had to be found as explanations of our higher faculties and demands. The latter being considered as reflections or projections of the Supreme Entity or Norm, our only way leading to this supernatural principle was to scrutinize in our psychical data those which gave the feeling of greatest certainty and universality.

The East, and especially India, found this feeling in the mystical experience of immediacy. The "leap" that this experience required marked the sharp limit between higher and lower components of human nature and, *per analogiam,* between the ultimate and the relative in the ontological perspective. The way of the Greeks was different. Their daily half-cosmogonic, half-scientific conceptions of Nature have often been compared with Indian doctrines: Parmenides with Upaniṣadic monism, Heraclitus with Buddhism. But the similarities here are rather external, since these pre-Socratic doctrines were no projections of internal experience into the ontological field, but speculatively elaborated constructions. For these philosophers man was an object of inquiry only as a part of Nature, and they did not seek within him the principle which would explain the world. Consequently, they did not try to establish a definite limit between his lower and higher components, or to emphasize a particular faculty. They did it indirectly, however, through the discovery of a new kind of theoretically formulated conceptual knowledge. And when Pythagoras found out that universal validity lies not in the things but in pure relations, he did not hesitate to recognize in mathematical laws the ruling principle of the world. By the same token, and in spite of all mythological hypostases with which he enveloped his discovery, he opened the way to the conviction that among all human faculties reason alone can attain the universal norm.

With Socrates, this faculty assumes the full value of a spiritual principle opposed to our physical and sensorial components. It is reason which forces us to act against our desires and instincts and in conformity with universal norms. It can dominate our body and give a real freedom of choice. It serves as the link between all men. But it is not an undifferentiated static element infused in every being which has to be discovered. "Know thyself" differs in both words from the Oriental "Self-realization": it does not mean the immediate insight into a supra-personal Self, but the gradual penetration through reflection into one's own self with all its psychical complexity and the transformation of this self into a more perfect individuality conforming itself to universally valid norms. These norms, again, are neither given from outside nor grasped in an act of instantaneous intuition. They are elaborated by the same reflection, in a free inquiry which may be achieved collectively in discussions. As Northrop has pointed out,[17] the Sophists had already shown that determinate knowledge given with immediacy varied from person to person. This discovery caused Socrates to return to the speculatively inferred, theoretically constructed, and mutually, from person to person, tested method of knowledge. Only then could one escape sophistry and find determinate laws the same for all men.

The further ascension of reason in Greek philosophy is well known: its deified hypostasis as νους, its formulation as λόγος, its principle of determinate coherence and universal order opposed to confusion, formlessness, and chaos of direct experience, and, finally, its magnificent apotheosis in the Platonic world of ideas. In spite of such exaltation of one single component of the human psyche, *there appeared no gap between it and other mental faculties.* Both our moral intuitions (the Good received the dignity of the supreme Idea) and even sensorial perceptions, spiritualized in the contemplation of Beauty, were included by Plato in his world of spiritual values. The mysterious capacity of art—that no naturalistic or utilitarian theory can ever explain or justify—to express spiritual values through concrete elements grasped by our

[17] *The Taming of the Nations*, p. 206.

senses was particularly emphasized in his doctrine. But all these elements are conceived as spiritual only because they express a rational perfection.

With Aristotle, to whom humanity is indebted for the first precise formulation of the very functioning of conceptual reason, this reason is to a certain extent despiritualized: the rational no longer has its source in a higher principle, not even in our higher mental faculties, but in things; the intellect is supplanted by the intelligible. And, with the Stoics, the spiritual principles will become material: *πνευμα*, which is the prototype of our term "spirit," is for them a material breath, and reason is identified with fire. And yet, with the same Stoics appears the first intuition of the spiritual significance of the *person* as the center of free accepted universal law and the ideals of freedom, justice, and equality of all men before the law. Through the practical applications of these ideals in Roman legal science, the Western world will receive a set of principles which belong to its basic spiritual foundations. At the same time, the Graeco-Roman process of discovery of spiritual values seems to be closed and petrified. Having centered their inquiry exclusively on the conceptual power of reason, the philosophers of antiquity stopped before the deeper faculties of reason: they did not discover transcendency, and they disregarded the intuitions of the infinite, which troubled the magnificent but rigid rational construction. This rigidity will be overthrown by a new force appearing suddenly at their horizon: the message of Christianity.

Coming from the East, Christianity brings with it new conceptions of the divine and spiritual. Yet, the genuinely Oriental elements of its message—the religion of the Old Testament—were not basically distinct from those infused in the minds of the Greeks and Romans by five centuries of philosophical research: the unity of God and a moral law based on determinate principles and having, even more than in Stoicism, the character of a contract, a covenant between God and men. But in Christianity—which, as has been frequently pointed out,[18] is as Greek as it is Hebrew in its roots—the still tribal and natural, though divinely inspired, concept of law was transformed into the ideal of universal law, which met the Greek conception of man as a "citizen of the universe." And this law was no longer based on the Commandments of God codifying in determinate moral statutes the natural social order, but it appealed to the λόγος, which is exalted in the famous climax of the opening words of the Fourth Gospel more than it had ever been in Greek philosophy: It is at the beginning of the whole, it is with God, it *is* God.

This λόγος is no undifferentiated all-embracing unity but an ideal, a theoretically conceivable pattern, determining a law of absolutely universal validity equal for all men, prior to the creation and infinitely superior to it.[19] And it is at the same time a Person. The very conception of universal reason and law was familiar to the Graeco-Roman world. But the origin of this reason,

[18] Cf., among others, F. S. C. Northrop, *The Taming of the Nations*, p. 189.

[19] Cf. Luke 16:16, 17: "And it is easier for heaven and earth to pass, than one tittle of the law to fail," and Paul, Romans 17:12, 14: "The law is holy," "the law is spiritual." The universality of this law based on λόγος is also the pattern of every right reasoning; hence Jesus' condemnation of the vain and futile speculations of the scribes and Pharisees, which resembles so much the condemnation of sophistry by Socrates.

the practical implications of the new law, and its "non-prudential" ethics were in many respects to appear to antiquity as overthrowing the established habits and shocking their common sense. The values of the determinate and the infinite were here turned upside-down. Christianity directed man toward the infinite, no longer presented as synonymous with disorder and confusion, but as the source of transcendent grace and as the supreme goal of man's aspirations.

The link between the infinite and the finite is not reason but love of God for man and of man for God. It is no longer the Stoics' intellectual love of God but a feeling that captured hearts directly, thanks to the event that was, as Kierkegaard will say, "folly for the Greeks, scandal for the Jews": the Incarnation. It is neither an *avatāra* (incarnated being) nor a *nirmāṇakāya* (transformation-body), but total acceptance of man's fate, with its simplicity, its deficiencies, and its sufferings, and even martyrdom.

The power of love testified by this supreme exaltation of man's nature by God, the central role that it will play not only in revolutionary Christian ethics but also in the very essence of the new religion, provided a new dimension of the spiritual: it opened the path to the supernatural through emotional faculties and suddenly gave to this component of human psychical life a rank higher than that of reason.

This new path is *faith*—the discovery in one's emotional life of a subjective certitude more powerful and evident than that given by reason—not an immediate experience of the ultimate which proceeds through gradual elimination of sensorial, emotional, and cognitive processes, but *confidence based on love to God,* which engages and permeates all psychical faculties of man and which has as its object, not an undifferentiated and ineffable reality, but a set of revealed truths, determinable and describable though not spontaneously attainable through "natural" reasoning. This way of knowledge was so new for the philosophically trained minds of the Greeks and Romans that not only the revelation but also the very faculty of faith has been conceived as a supernatural gift of grace granted by God in his infinite love for creation.

The fact that faith appeals to all mental faculties explains also the variety of approaches to God in Christianity. We find there the passive and almost exclusively emotional surrender to the Divine, and the tendency to rise to the mysteries of God through reason (since the scriptural authority did not exclude this possibility),[20] and also the way of mystical approach much more frequent and important than is generally admitted in the Orient. All these ways are by no means exclusively Christian and can be found in other great religions. Especially in the mystical approach the similarities seem to be striking throughout the world. Yet, though it is not easy to analyze and describe mystical experiences, it seems that there are some characteristic differences between Christian mysticism and that of Hinduism or Buddhism. The first

[20] Paul, Romans 1:19, 20: "Because that which may be known of God is manifest in them; for God hath shewed it unto them. For the invisible things of him from the creation of the world are clearly seen, being understood by the things that are made, even his eternal power and Godhead. . . ."

is preceded by faith, is not its source; far from being an experience prepared by appropriate methods and training[21] and leading to an impersonalized bliss, in which all distinctions and relations disappear, Christian mysticism has, rather, the character of contemplation guided by love and striving for communion with the Divine in the perspective of "me" and "Thou." In India, we find this form of mystical approach with Caitanya, Ramakrishna, and Aurobindo, rather than with the ancient sages of the Upaniṣads or with the consequent Advaitins. And, as for spirituality based on love of God, the quasi-identity between the Indian religions of *bhakti* (devotion) and the Christian approach is recognized even by the most exclusive Christian theologians.[22] The difference lies in only two essential points: in the personal though infinite nature of God and in the status of man, who is created by God but is neither part nor attribute of him.[23]

Christianity takes over the Old Testament concept of man as created as a being distinct from God but in his image, which means that man is endowed with moral principles and personal responsibility in the temporal world. But it adds more: the grace of the Holy Spirit, giving man the possibility of achieving his eternal destiny. Since then the expression "spiritual nature of man" is no longer a metaphor. The Holy Spirit working in man is not the presence of an ontological all-embracing principle that it is sufficient to discover in the innermost region of one's being, but the inspiration of the divine λόγος, infinite virtuality of creative activity that man not only can but must develop through all his faculties. In contrast to Indian religions, which, in one way or another, consider the cultivation of individual personality as a hindrance in the path of spiritual progress, Christianity bestows on man's person a dignity and a value that it never had before. Man is no longer an instance of universal law, but a unique value in itself, a creature which received from God its being but also the potentiality to create by itself, freely, its own spiritual person.[24] And the community of men united in the ἐκκλησια, the mystical Body of Christ, is called to fulfill, in the temporal sphere, God's designs.

[21] Yet, the methods and elaborated techniques of concentration are also known in Christian practice; the recent studies of the Byzantine Hesychasm have shown striking similarities with *yoga*.

[22] Cf., e.g., F. Pierre Johanns, S. J., *La pensée religieuse de l'Inde* (Paris: Bibliothèque de la Faculté de philosophie et de lettres de Namur, 1952).

[23] God as person is known to the *bhakti* religions, but he is in final conclusions conceived still as a kind of manifestation, a secondary nature of the ultimate. In spite of the Indian anti-dogmatic attitude, there exist in India, as well as in the West, some constant patterns, which cannot be completely rejected or explained away. To such dogmas belongs the deep conviction that man and the universe are not outside God but within him. In spite of various efforts displayed by Rāmānuja, Madhva, Nimbārka, etc., in order to reconcile the personal relation between God and man with the dogma of *sṛṣṭi* (creation), the latter could never be ignored in the Indian tradition. This point remains one of the paramount divergencies between the Indian and the Western religious outlooks.

The authority on both sides is the scriptural evidence. But in this respect, too, there are characteristic differences between India and the West. In Hinduism scriptural evidence represents the sum of the experiences of ancient sages, as much as of modern inspired men; it is a kind of collective spiritual patrimony. In Christianty it is considered as revelation, supreme and final truth given to the finite man directly by God. Hence its more rigid and exclusive character.

[24] Person is not an equivalent of individual; it is an ideal of spiritual fulfillment that man has to achieve. This is "self-realization" in the Christian sense. The very presence of this ideal in our mind is considered as a proof of the existence of the prototype of person in God. To those who object to the anthropomorphism of the idea of a personal God one can reply, with Max Scheler, that it is, rather, a question of the theomorphism of the ideal of person.

Creation is not a once-achieved static fact; it goes on perpetually, and the temporal world, God's work and God's realization, is neither negligible nor to be rejected altogether. It is in this sphere that God creates through man. Man cannot create being, but he is free in the domain of spirit and he can transform reality, strive to develop and perfect in it all that is not pure being. This activity is as important as his spiritual and personal progress toward eternity. "Thy will be *done on Earth* as it is in Heaven." But, in order that man's activity be really creative and responsible, he must be endowed with free-will; he can do right or wrong; he is not deprived of his creative power, even if he does not submit to the will of God.[25]

These Christian conceptions of spirituality, which do not disclaim the tendencies developed by the Hebrews and Greeks, but enrich them in the perspective of the infinite, do not exhaust the totality of the new message, nor have they always been explicitly emphasized. On the contrary, they were often narrowed, forgotten, or misinterpreted by the Christians themselves and applied to the wrong ends. But the ideal of a determinate and exclusive truth, not liable to various and contradictory interpretations, of universality which does not eliminate individuality, of the full realization of the many-sided nature of man, and of the creative activity striving for the world's betterment or displayed for the sake of creativity—will remain deeply anchored in the mentality of Western man and will determine the attitude even of those who will turn aside from Christianity, will deny trans-worldly perspectives, and will no longer recognize the origins of their ideals and their dynamism.

IV.

Those who reproach Western civilization with its lack of a deep religious outlook, its ideological relativism and fragmentation, too easily overlook fifteen centuries of its history during which the Western world enjoyed spiritual unity

[25] With regard to this specifically Western ideal of action conceived as the expression of the will of God, one can quote for India the *Bhagavad Gītā*, which exalts action as the way to God. But, in the *Gītā*, action must be free from motives and personal purpose, and those who act should not consider themselves as doers, but as performers of the will of God: *"As the unlearned act from attachment to their work, so should the learned also act, but without any attachment, with the desire to maintain the world-order"* (III.25).

In the Western and Christian conception, he who acts should know that he is a free and responsible doer, and, if he acts according to God's will, it is not with the desire to *maintain* the existing order, but to create a new and better one. He has and ought to have both motives and purposes for his action.

In a very interesting paper, "Activism in Indian Thought," in *Annals, Bhandarkar O. R. Institute,* Vol. 39, Parts III–IV, pp. 185–226, Raju brings out new data concerned with a very different approach to the problem of action in the ancient tradition of India. As it was for the problem of non-instrumental ethics (cf. note 8), he finds it again in the Mīmāṁsā. In this doctrine, *ātman* is considered both as agent and as enjoyer. According to Kumārila, no one acts without a purpose; man is the master of his destiny, and *vairāgya,* disinterest in the values of the world, is condemned as escapism. The Nairuktas go even farther in their doctrine of activism and process: in striking contrast with the views of other schools, they consider pure becoming (*bhāva*) as the essence of *ātman.* Though this Indian activism has not the creative aspect of Western attitudes, it leads to an exalted humanism ("Man is the Brahman acting *in this world*" [*ibid.,* p. 213]) closely related to Western conceptions. The existence of such tendencies in ancient India, in the doctrines rooted in pre-Upaniṣadic traditions, is undoubtedly of great interest for modern Indian thinkers, anxious, under Western influence, to liberate India from its traditional contemplative quietism in order to have a balanced view of life. But the stress laid upon such tendencies is an evidence of modern evolution in India toward the practical aspects of social life, an evolution that appears clearly among the representatives of India at this conference. Yet, it would be difficult to claim that the above-mentioned doctrines confined to secondary philosophical schools (the activism of the Nairuktas is in fact a theory of grammar) have actually molded Indian mentality in its long history. The revival of interest for these long-forgotten theories is the result of the confrontation of Indian life with the Western world.

of such an intensity that all forms of human life were deeply and naturally permeated with religion. There was a time when the Middle Ages was considered as a period of stagnation and obscurantism; confronted by the masterpieces of its art, literature, philosophy—nobody could today charge the Middle Ages with being devoid of culture and creative spirit. And, as for the reproach of the absence of scientific research, of rigid dogmatism and intolerance, one forgets that this era was one of certainty and universality of faith and that the facts of Christian revelation were for the people of the Middle Ages *direct evidence* as natural and general as is for a Western man of today the scientifically interpreted image of the world.

This evidence was thoroughly subjective but communicable, and even if not always explicable (mysteries of the revelation) yet formulated in terms of conceptual description. And this similarity of formulations between theological and philosophical matters encouraged thinkers, after St. Anselm and Abelard, to try to understand and to demonstrate the revealed dogmas. The boldness and richness of these attempts to rationalize the facts of faith are surprising. If medieval philosophy was *ancilla theologiae,* it was so in the same measure that modern science is servant to experimental facts. And, even if revelation was the main object of its investigations, it cannot be said that medieval philosophy was one-sided. On the contrary, in the Middle Ages, Western civilization reaches an astonishing equilibrium between faith and reason, between aspirations toward heaven and the full recognition of this world, between the spiritual and the material. This equilibrium finds its most cogent expression in the imposing synthesis of St. Thomas, a synthesis of the two sources of Western culture, and the only ancient philosophical system in the West which still remains alive. The main points of Christian revelation find in this synthesis their support in Aristotle, whose doctrine, in its turn, is enhanced by the spiritual outlook which it had lacked. Nature receives here its full recognition, but, while it conserves its material existence, it is spiritualized through the form which pervades it; man is presented neither as pure spirit nor as an animal but as mind-body in one individual. Spirit and matter are no longer considered as mutually hostile or contradictory, but as two complementary aspects of reality: essence and existence, Grace and Nature, miracle and natural law, Church and State. They are different but equally important stages in the realization of a single purpose of God, in whom essence and existence are identical.

This sense of harmony and unity between the spiritual and the material, the eternal and the temporal, is not the result of philosophical synthesis alone. It is felt naively and spontaneously by St. Francis, who embraces in his love for God the whole of God's creation, including its humblest forms, and to whom not only animals but even phenomena of Nature, fire, wind, and earth are brothers and sisters, objects and subjects of universal love. The same sense of balance between trans-worldly and worldly affairs appears with those medieval monks who know how to harmonize the *via contemplativa* with active participation in social works, who are practically the pioneers of organized social relief.

The medieval equilibrium was a new way of accomplishing unity without doing away with distinctions, unity toward which the Greeks had striven and which was based on a much more immediate certainty of faith. Thanks to the spontaneous acceptance of a single and unique truth by the whole Christian world, the Middle Ages could establish a real spiritual unity—no longer a postulate, but a tangible fact. This universality, without peer in the history of the Western world, will remain one of the dominant ideals of Western man, even when faith, which provided its foundation, will no longer have the same intensity and the same character of unshaken certainty. This ideal lives in the postulate of scientific universality, which is fulfilled in our time. And the medieval conception of the *Civitas Dei,* of a world-wide society united by the acceptance of the same and unique truth, will reappear in diverse, even frankly antireligious, cultural, social, and political activities of the modern world. Greece had created the concept of man as "citizen of the universe." But it is the spiritual community of the Middle Ages that prepared the way for the concept of "mankind."

Yet, these great achievements of the Middle Ages contained in themselves the ferments which were to shatter them. Equilibrium and universality, accomplished in a practical way, ended in a certain fixity of ideal. But this ideal encompassed also principles—freedom of the human spirit and its dynamism, which was to operate not only with the view toward eternity but also here, "on earth"—which were in contradiction with any definitely achieved and immutable state of being. And the tendency of emphasizing these trends, which since the last centuries of the Middle Ages are considered as inseparable from the spiritual dignity of man and from its lofty mission, will lead, in the fifteenth and sixteenth centuries, to the collapse of the imposing—but static and reduced to a limited area—spiritual, cultural, and social medieval unity.

The real foundation of the medieval universality and equilibrium was a harmonious synthesis of faith and reason, and irrational and subjective certitude, shared by all Christians ever since it was formulated in objectively determinate terms as communicable as the concepts of reason. The universality of this conceptual expression of the credo was similar to "Socratic" rational universality, since it resulted from a *collective* agreement, the dogmas having been elaborated and mutually tested at the Councils and placed under the guard of the unique authority of the Church. As long as the evolution of the creative thought of medieval philosophers took place in its own field and was not concerned with the basic truths of the revelation, the boldest speculations were allowed (in spite of numerous official condemnations, which were as often revoked, as e.g., the Aristotelianism which, after having been condemned with Abelard, later became the basis of the official Christian philosophy), and even extreme divergencies between the doctrines could not shake the universality of religious certitude.

But it was undermined at the very moment when the right to *individual* free inquiry was extended to revelation itself. This happened in conjunction with both the Renaissance and the Reformation. It behooves us to emphasize that this revolution, decisive in the history of Western spirituality, was not due to the weakening of faith or of confidence in reason, but, quite on the contrary, it happened in the name of the autonomy of faith and reason. In all the Protestant movements, the emphasis was placed upon the sovereignty of faith as not having to bow before any collective authority. Yet, this claim for the rights of subjectivity and of faith independent of rational inquiry did not result in a purely emotional, indeterminable attitude; though hostile to Scholastic speculations, the new subjective faiths have been formulated again in conceptual terms, so that divergencies between them did not represent different ways of saying the same thing but real divergencies of religious and moral principles. Hence violent conflicts between the denominations which broke out in the name of a religion of peace and universal love, but which were the unavoidable expression of spiritual ardor, and the sincerity of Western man accustomed to the idea of a unique determinate supreme truth admitting no polyvalent interpretations.

By the same token, revelation could no longer be considered as direct evidence common to all people. They felt the need of seeking another source of universal certitude for their knowledge and even for their faith. The philosophers of the Italian Renaissance, again taking up Greek traditions, hoped to find it in the universality of reason. This time, however, the method has been reversed: reason had not to explain or demonstrate the truth given with certainty by faith, but it had to take the place of faith and provide the rational foundation of it. And the Renaissance was not a mere return to antiquity; owing to the imposing philosophical work achieved in the Middle Ages, confidence in reason has considerably increased. A need for collective search for truth and mutual testing was no longer felt as being necessary; individual reason appeared self-sufficient even in the perspective of the divine. Hence the plurality of mutually irreducible systems, each of them claiming to be universal.

Thus, the same era which inaugurated an extraordinary expansion of man's knowledge and a sudden widening of his horizons, which in a few centuries brought about the swiftest and most radical transformations of life, culture, and science that the history of mankind had ever witnessed, produced an explosion which disintegrated the medieval equilibrium in all domains. While getting to know new worlds, Europe was losing its own cohesion. The religious fragmentation provoked by the Reformation was followed by the appearance of modern nationalisms,[26] shattering the medieval social and political community. The astonishing progress of science, which after the failure of rational attempts to justify religion turned exclusively to Nature, shook the balance between the spiritual and material. And, while discovering in himself unlimited potentialities, modern man was losing the inner equilibrium in which all his faculties had been directed toward a single supreme goal. There arise conflicts between faith and reason (Pascal), between reason and experience (Hume). But it is,

[26] Cf. F. S. C. Northrop, *The Taming of the Nations*, chap. XI.

above all, the crisis of the criterion of truth which can serve as guarantee both for knowledge and for conduct.

No longer sure of the universal validity of the inwardly felt spiritual source of certitude, Western man searches for it outside of himself, in the experience furnished by Nature. This evidence—not only purely physical but also psychological and social, as well as other observable facts—has been and still is considered as the final instance both in science and in philosophical naturalism. Though this new method of knowledge has not restored universality of truth,[27] it would be senseless to deny its extraordinary result for our lives and to see merely the wrong side of this particular evolution of Western science. But it would be an equally superficial view to maintain that the scientific and technological progress of the modern world is due exclusively to the abandonment of the trans-worldly outlook and to the adoption of the experimental method. Observation as such cannot constitute the basis of any coherent cognition whatsoever. For it to become scientific knowledge it has to be interpreted, i.e., to be supported by the faculty of reason independent of experience. The fall of the apple would never have led to the discovery of the law of gravity if it had not coincided with Newton's rational postulates. And these postulates had not been originated by mere empirical observations. It is really striking that the thinkers who gave Western science its precise methodology—Descartes, Newton, Leibniz—did it much more with a spiritual purpose than out of desire to describe Nature. And the tremendous technological application of the results of scientific discoveries is, in spite of its utilitarian effects, above all the result of the same longing for creative activity which was one of the basic elements of the Western spiritual attitude.

Neither a scientific theory nor a technological invention can be explained without the intervention of the creative spirit of man. It is not, as Raju says, "stubborn resolve to analyze and reconstruct the world conceptually at all levels, starting with the lowest concepts at the material level and gradually building up the concepts at higher levels."[28] Scientific method can appear as such only in its didactic presentation, but the very act of scientific discovery is a creative act which starts at the level of reason. And the proof that this kind of reasoning is not a merely academic exercise of our intellect is the transformation of the world it has produced and goes on producing.

The objections of Raju can be concerned, rather, with modern Western materialism, which indeed tries to explain "the higher by the lower." But materialism is not based on the experience of the outer world, since matter as such is not observable and is a postulate of reason. And, as for the conviction that matter is the *only* component of reality, it is simply a fact of irrational *faith* as unprovable by sensorial evidence as is faith in the existence of spiritual values. We find here the same postulate of a unique principle being the source of real-

[27] We have already mentioned the modern ideal of scientific universality. But it is necessary to distinguish practical results of applied science—in which indeed there has been achieved a far-reaching universality—and science as interpretation of the world, as *source of truth*. For the latter, in all the fields of scientific research we are still very far from a *consensus omnium*.

[28] *EEWP*, p. 231.

ity as in most religions—a postulate that no observation can even suggest. It is one more instance of the fact that tendencies and aspirations developed in Western mentality by spiritual doctrines remain alive even when the very notion of the spiritual has been flatly denied.

But precisely in the fact that attitudes of Western man, formed through centuries of spiritual training—the need of an absolutely valid faith or knowledge and consciousness of man's creative power enabling him to transform the world according to these principles—persist in spite of the loss of a universally recognized truth lie the great dangers of our time. The ancient universal spiritual goal has been replaced by particular and contradictory scientific, national, social, and political ideals, which people, nevertheless, seek to put into practice and to impose with the same conviction or even fanaticism. The troubles which result from this evolution of the Western world and which also begin to contaminate the East are evident. They explain the desire of numerous Westerners to look for the model of spirituality no longer in their own traditions but in the East.

V.

Yet, as I emphasized at the beginning of my paper, to view modern Western culture only in the light of the above-mentioned facts is definitely one-sided. The crisis of the fragmentation of our culture has been extremely grave, and we have not recovered our unity. But it cannot be seriously stated that the fragmentation of Christian faith has completely undermined the religious outlook of the Western world. It is obvious what an enormous influence Christian religion still exercises today on the hearts and in the thought of men throughout the world, and this, not only among the common people, but in the most prominent representatives of Western culture. And, parallel with the faithful adherence to traditional ideals of Christianity, we must recognize also an extraordinary evolution of thought which, within the Christian tradition or outside of it, not only looks for new bases of spiritual unity, but at the same time fully exercises the creative faculties of the human spirit allowing man to avoid the danger of the fixity and the immutability of the Middle Ages.

The main stages of this evolution are generally known, and it is not necessary to describe them in detail. My purpose will be merely to try to show that there is some continuity in this maze of apparently contradictory and independent doctrines. No longer able to depend upon an authority shaken by the crisis of the Renaissance and the Reformation, Western thinkers, with admirable courage, begin anew and at the very beginning. To a certain extent, they begin even at the stages which never had been examined by ancient thinkers: the criteria of any knowledge are now submitted to a severe criticism. And, as in ancient times, modern philosophers seek a path to the spiritual inwardly, trying, one by one, single psychical faculties. The sensorial perceptions, newly discovered as the reliable evidence for the knowledge of Nature, have provided the basis of science only in close union with reason. Pure empiricism could not withstand criticism and ended either in Hume's skepticism or—by a surprising quirk of history—in Berkeley's mystical faith. Once more in the evolution of Western thought it appeared that reason could not be eliminated. It could withstand the criticism; the very fact that there was no other way to test the validity of reason than to use reason as criterion and tool of control was already a sufficient confirmation. With the Cartesian *cogito,* the problem of the self-sufficiency of reason (admitted since antiquity without proof) has been, for the first time in the history of Western philosophy, put to the test and has emerged victoriously from this trial. And in the Cartesian distinction of *res extensae* and *res cogitantes* the difference between spirit and matter has been for the first time emphasized with precision. But what was determining in this distinction—and what allowed all the subsequent developments of Western idealism—was that reason, identified with spirit, was no longer considered as an element superposed on matter, neither as an attribute of the latter (the intelligible) nor as a faculty which grasps matter, but as an independent reality. Though Descartes himself did not draw all the conclusions of his thesis, the way was opened for the doctrines which will admit the reality of pure thought *needing no support of being* or, rather, prior to being, since the latter will be identified either with rational necessity (Spinoza) or with thought grasping itself as object. In this concept of reality not based on being lies a very important difference between modern Western thought and both the whole of Eastern philosophy and Western thought before Descartes.

A further important step leading to the exaltation of reason was achieved with the great scientific discoveries of Newton and Leibniz, especially with the invention of differential calculus, which proved that reason was able to conceptualize with precision even the realm of the infinite, which had been previously considered as accessible only by intuition.[29] Hence, the conclusion has been drawn that experience cannot constitute the basis of universally valid knowledge, but that laws precisely formulated by reason lay the foundations of experience, and that truth is truth by itself and not because it corresponds to anything being outside reason. And, since reason could grasp even the infinite, the traditional Western equation, rational=spiritual, has now been reversed: the spiritual became synonymous exclusively with the rational.

For Leibniz, intelligence is the unique and fundamental characteristic of the spirit. The whole spiritual tradition of the West is now reduced to rational principles. Virtues such as goodness, justice, and perfection are no longer considered as effects of God's will (as Descartes still admitted) but as reflections of his reason, which in himself dominates his will. The notion of person is now reduced to merely rational elements of remembrance and consciousness of what we are. Freedom of the spirit is identified with the state in which man is guided

[29] This great discovery of the capacity of reason to penetrate even into the apparently irrational domains will reveal itself as very fruitful. In its further development mathematics will conceptualize relations and ideas, defying any imagination, and mathematical logic will be able to grasp in precise formulas translogical intuitions, even those of Eastern philosophy, such as the notion of *śūnyatā* (cf. Hajime Nakamura, "Buddhist Logic Expounded by Means of Symbolic Logic," *Journal of Indian and Buddhist Studies,* VII, No. 1 [December, 1958]).

exclusively by reason. And, since the fundamental characteristic of reason is its independence, the human mind cannot be considered as a passive reproduction of God's reason: "Man cannot think with the ideas of another." Thus, in Leibniz' monadology representing the whole reality as a "republic of spirits governed by God" Western spiritual pluralism finds its extreme expression.

The great rational systems of the seventeenth and eighteenth centuries tended anew to be a kind of definitely established synthesis. But, once more, Western thought did not accept fixity; as in previous cases, the onset came from within: the perfect coherence of rational constructions postulating universality of reason was contradicted by the plurality of irreducible systems appealing to the same reason. There came also the inexorable criticism of Hume demonstrating the limitations of human thought. And once more the failure was a fruitful one: it led to the discovery of the *dynamic character of reason.* The plurality of systems could be explained as the unavoidable consequence of the finite nature of the human mind, which cannot grasp in any definitely achieved system the infinite features of the Supreme Spirit. But, in contrast with the Indian approach to the ultimate, the infinite does not mean in the West the indeterminable: there is a possibility for finite spirits to come near this infinitude, but only by collective efforts and by stages.[30] And the proof that these stages are not a mere succession of new speculative constructions but can represent a real progress has been furnished by Kant. He succeeded in overarching rationalism and empiricism, not by a mere amalgamation of the two opposed methods, but by the discovery of the transcendental method, which allowed reason to rise above itself and to reach a level which embraced both reason and experience.

The consequences of this discovery are well known. It was not Kant's skepticism as to the possibility of knowing reality in itself by reason which determined the further development of philosophy, but his discovery of the fact that the knowable is to be sought within us and not in things. The rationalists of the seventeenth century emphasized the self-sufficiency of reason as being a part of reality independent of experience. Now, with the post-Kantian idealists, reality itself was no longer considered as the source of knowledge but as the product of reason. The creative spirit became the unique origin of reality conceived as process and not as an eternally given, static, and immutable ultimate. The discovery of transcendency permitted man to overcome the limitations of finite spirit and gave him the ladder by which he was now able to attain the infinite, since the infinite was also a creation of spirit.[31] By means of successive transcendental syntheses, the post-Kantian idealists attain the notion of absolute reason, the ultimate self-creating principle and the source of reality represent-

[30] Such is, e.g., in our time Brunschvicg's conception of *Deus interior,* who is conceived as a constant progress achieved by the totality of human minds. Though they are finite, their number in space and in time is infinite.

[31] It is the reversal of Leibniz' approach. In his mathematical discoveries, Leibniz found the means to reduce the infinite to the finite. Now, the infinite has proved to be, not an intuitional vision that discursive thought could conceptualize by means of finite formulas, but the product itself of reason, the expression of its infinite possibility of unfolding itself.

ing its inner objectivation. With Hegel, this inner activity becomes the very essence of the Absolute Spirit, which exists insofar as it maintains the process of self-creation, being at the same time the creation of reality. As soon as it defines itself as "being," as an achieved result, it dies as an abstraction of knowledge.[32]

It would be a commonplace to mention the enormous influence exercised by Hegel, not only in the history of Western thought, but also in the practical aspect, which led to the paradoxical result that this supreme exaltation of the spiritual inspired also radically anti-spiritual dialectical materialism. On the other hand, this summit of Western rationalism was also to collapse and to produce by reaction a series of positivistic doctrines which, while disavowing the work of the most productive centuries of European philosophy, more than ever denied the validity of any aprioristic creation of reason and, by the same token, for the first time in the history of the West, eliminated as unprovable the very notion of the spiritual.

But, also, in the camp of those who continued to believe that the spiritual aspirations and activities of man (which even from the positivistic point of view were *facts*) could not be explained by anything other than spirit the Hegelian approach was abandoned. This time, there was no possibility of reproaching with fixity and rigidity one of the most dynamic systems of Western philosophy. For European spiritualists, self-sufficiency of spirit and its creative dynamism were unquestionable characteristics of the spiritual. But they reproached Hegel because of the one-sidedness of his system: spirit appeared to be much more than pure reason. Thus a large proportion of Christian thinkers preferred to return to the well-balanced tradition of Thomism which was enriched by philosophical investigation of modern times, and which has never denied the creative capacity of the human mind, but has limited it to the domain of the temporal. But at the same time there appeared numerous tendencies, faithful to the *élan* of post-Kantian idealists, but trying to attain the spiritual through faculties of the human psyche other than reason.

These tendencies have been initiated already by post-Kantian philosophers. Kant himself opened the way to this enrichment of the spiritual approach, since he emphasized the impossibility for exclusively rational metaphysics to explain both human free-will and the intuition of God or of the immortal soul. The profound feeling of certitude peculiar to this intuition has, according to

[32] The affinities of post-Kantian idealism with Advaita Vedānta or with Vijñānavāda have often been emphasized. Yet, the divergencies seem to be more striking than the similarities. In India, to know = to identify oneself with the object of knowledge; in post-Kantian idealism, to know = to create. Indian philosophy also knows the creative power of reason (*kalpanā*), but its products are considered as the source of error and delusion, since they superpose artificial hypostases upon the unknowable reality. There can be no dynamic process in the Indian Absolute (cf. Raju, *EEWP*, p. 226: "Deepest truths are eternally accomplished facts"). One can compare the Hegelian unfolding Absolute with Śaṁkarian *vivarta;* yet, *vivarta* is not the product of Brahman. And, even in the ancient Upaniṣad, *ātman* "dies" when it unfolds empiric plurality, when it loses its static transcendency. For Hegel, spirit reveals and enriches its absolute nature when it creates reality. The dynamic conception of the Absolute, which will be predominant in the West also after the collapse of Hegelianism, does not necessarily mean the absolutization of time (though this consequence will also appear in some modern schools of metaphysics). The infinite unfolding of its inner nature by the Absolute is, in Hegel, a logical process, which is accomplished beyond time, the latter being itself the product of reason: it is only necessary for the finite spirit to apprehend this process in temporal succession.

Kant, its source in a psychical faculty distinct from reason and called practical reason. This faculty, the very projection of the spiritual in human nature, is the same which much more imperatively, as rational justifications, dictates to us the lines of moral conduct. For Fichte, the moral ego is already the absolute expression of the spiritual. With Schelling, intuition receives a status as important as reason: and its object is being, conceived, not as an all-embracing ultimate, but, on the contrary, as the unique residue of every cognition which escapes reason, the absolutely individual "to be there," which defies any generalization.

Each of these rediscovered approaches to reality, intuition and immediacy of being, will appear for important philosophical schools of our century as unique ways to the spiritual and will supplant reason in this function. In the system of Schelling, intuition and reason were complementary. Bergson, James, Dilthey, and their followers will oppose intuition to reason as the unique faculty grasping reality directly, while reason through abstraction artificially falsifies its qualitative richness and continuity. These philosophers—especially Bergson, who preached also the mystical approach to the spiritual—are often considered as having the most striking affinities with the Eastern philosophical attitude. But even here the differences between the West and the East appear clearly. The final results of the intuitional approach are on the two sides completely divergent. Bergson rejects the intellectual analysis because of its rigidity. According to him, intuition alone can unveil the dynamic character of reality, which is *action and process*. Indian intuitive insight into reality discovers its static immobility and ascribes action and dynamism to the mind or *māyā*, which is not the ultimate.

It seems that a much greater affinity to the Indian approach can be found with the existentialists. They try to attain concrete reality lying beyond reason, not in the outer world, but in the deepest regions of man's psychical life, and at the end of their scrutiny they find being. Yet, in this scrutiny they are not guided by any mystic insight but by an emotional reaction that no rational interpretation can justify: by feelings of anxiety, of disgust, of the solitude of man in the world. And what they find is not all-embracing universal certitude, but, on the contrary, the frailest part of the human being, that which in him is absolutely subjective and individual, his existence prior to any determination and synonymous with total freedom to give itself its essence.[33] But precisely in this feeling of the frailty of our existence lies the proof of the presence of being which transcends existence and which escapes any attempt to define it. And precisely the fact that it is ontologically concealed emphasizes the responsibility and autonomy of the human being and constitutes an appeal to free self-transcendence.

[33] Mus points out in his paper in this volume the parallels to Vedānta or Buddhism in Sartre's assertion: "We shall never see that center . . . for we are it," and in that of Mme S. de Beauvoir: "Never shall I become to myself a solid object; what I am experiencing within myself is just that emptiness that is myself." The parallel in itself is very impressive, but the practical implications of this basic indetermination of "myself" are completely different in existentialism, when they lead to total freedom, and in Buddhism or Hinduism.

Thus, even the philosophical approach which reduces the origin of the spiritual life of man to mere existence (a fact which causes existentialists considerable difficulties in the method of philosophical development of their basic principles—they try to avoid abstraction when applying some kind of aesthetic description which has to supplant logical deduction[34]) ends in the West with emphasis placed upon the free, dynamic, self-creative character of the individual. And we find the same conception with modern doctrines of personalism, which can be considered as the widest synthesis of all Western attempts to grasp and to justify the spiritual aspirations of man. For the personalists, the really mysterious and yet fundamental insight is not man's *existence* but *his* existence, the *immediately felt unity of all components* of his personality, a unity which does not suppress any of them. Only this richness and variety of human nature can explain its spiritual activities. The doctrines which limit man's activity to merely psycho-physical processes cannot explain its creative originality; and theories which reduce the spiritual to a single higher psychical power forget that man fulfills his self-realization by means of his lower faculties. He has to act in this way because he is the free spirit + being, which latter does not depend on him and determines his individuality and "situation" in the world. As being, he is individual; as spirit, he strives for participation in the universal. As such, he is more than an individual: he is or, rather, has to be a person. And person is not an achieved thing: it is a goal, a steady aspiration for self-transcendence. The spirit realizes himself through reason—in science and philosophy; through will—in moral conduct and practical life; through sensibility—in art. In all these fields he enters into contact with the world, but he reveals himself. Reason allows him to introduce through abstract conceptual constructions his own unity in the multifarious and in themselves unorganized data of existence; in art, he reveals to himself the same unity of multiplicity by means of concrete constructions of the sensuous, the unique domain where he can be fully free and creative. In his moral, juridical, social, and political activity, he strives for the same universality and is guided neither by sensibility (by what he merely likes) nor by reason (the intelligent utility of conduct) but by a direct and irreducible-to-other-psychical-approaches intuition of *value*. If the spirit constantly strives to surpass itself, it is because it feels its insufficiency and is conscious of a Supreme Spirit, which is the model and goal of its aspirations. This feeling finds its deepest direct emotional expression in religion.

As long as our spiritual components are identified with one single faculty—reason, intuition, immediacy of existence, etc.—the ultimate prototype of it can be conceived as a principle, an impersonal reality. But, when the spirituality of the human being appears as the development and harmony of all its components, the Supreme Model and Source of the spiritual appears as a Person, as God. He is infinitely superior to all we can think or feel about him,

[34] Here lies another striking similarity between Indian and existentialist method, since the Indian pattern of thinking leads also to artistic and symbolic expressions by the means of *maṇḍalas* (cf. the above-mentioned paper by Mus).

but he is not indeterminate. He is more than a synthesis because he surpasses every possible synthesis. He is not a static, once-for-eternity-achieved and essentially unknowable and ineffable ultimate, but an infinite richness of eternally expanding expressions which appear to us as models of our own constant and never-achieved self-realization. This is for finite spirits the way to participation in the infinite. The simple discovery of God's presence and passive surrender to his will, or the tendency to be absorbed by his infinitude, constitute abdication and betrayal of the spiritual energy which he bestows on us.

Thus, after a long evolution, after many deviations, Western spiritualism constantly returns to this fundamental idea of the dynamic realization of the full nature of man, to the ideal of a person whose purpose and very essence are to surpass itself without ever being satisfied with an achieved perfection. The interpretations and applications of this basic Western tendency can be and have been very many. But it seems impossible for Western man, as long as he is conscious of his spiritual mission, to change this attitude. There appears undoubtedly a radical divergence from the conception of spiritual evolution found in the East. But the constant effort to achieve ever-wider and richer syntheses, as well as the capacity of harmonizing opposites through ever-higher transcendencies, is the basic characteristic of Western spirituality. Perhaps here lies the possibility of finding a point of meeting between the East and the West: not an orchestrated and artificial unity, nor a compromise, but a higher synthesis in the Western way, which has always striven for universality which does not eliminate distinctions.

QUESTION: Referring to the last sentence of your paper, when trying to reconcile Eastern and Western approaches to spirituality, why must we do it only in the Western way? Does not this preference given to Western methods only stagger the equilibrium and compromise *a priori* the synthesis we are trying to establish?

ANSWER: I think the answer is already included in my statement about the Western way of achieving unity through transcendency, of reconciling opposite views without the elimination of distinctions. With regard to opposite spiritual attitudes, the Western religious approach (of Judaism, Christianity, and Islam) is generally considered as being that of exclusivism, whereas the Eastern approach is predominantly that of universalism. It is evident that, from the exclusivistic point of view, we cannot achieve any spiritual synthesis. And, at first inspection, it seems that the Eastern universalistic way, which we find, e.g., in Japanese religious syncretism, in Hinduism, in Ramakrishna's integration of all religions, in the attempts of A. K. Coomaraswamy, in Vietnamese Cao-dai, etc., may lead much closer to a spiritual synthesis. In fact, it cannot be denied that since Romanticism a great many Westerners looking for a universal spiritual approach have been inclined to choose the Eastern way. But they are not aware of the fact that in this way they do not achieve a true synthesis, since in such attempts the essential features and values of opposite attitudes are irretrievably lost. No Christian can become a true

Vedāntin, Sufi, or sincere adept of Zen without renouncing the basic foundations of his spiritual attitude; and, for a Hindu, it is not sufficient to recognize Christ as an incarnation of the ultimate or adopt Christian ethical norms for becoming truly Christian. Let us examine the most striking example of Ramakrishna, who did not strive for spiritual syncretism, who was not satisfied with solutions proposed, e.g., by the Brāhmo Samāj combining common trends of different religions but by the same token devoiding them of their essential contents, who wanted to live *in concreto* any spiritual experience and who actually had visions of Christ. Yet, what he experienced was a purely Hindu *samādhi* directed on Christ conceived as a manifestation of the ultimate, a mystical identification essentially different from the interpersonal relation between God and man, which is at the basis of the Western religious attitude. I have already pointed out the fundamental distinction between the Christian concept of incarnation (which is not a manifestation, but the full acceptance of human nature by God) and the Indian concept of *avatāra.*

Thus, the two attitudes do not lead to a real spiritual contact which can enrich and deepen the opposite approaches without depriving them of their basic values. But there exist other ways to fulfill that task. I cannot affirm that in Eastern thought such a way cannot be found. But till now, in the traditionally bound development of this thought, I do not know any successful attempt for achieving this purpose. On the contrary, some Western philosophical methods allow us to hope that it can be done. I have already pointed out the achievements of transcendental synthesis. May I be allowed to quote in this context another interesting attempt, by Jacques-Albert Cuttat, to apply the Husserlian method of *epoché,* of phenomenological reduction, to the problem of the confrontation of religious attitudes of the main civilizations of the world. Without reaching far-going syntheses, the author succeeds in delimiting, by this method, an "inter-religious field" which allows the discovery of essential common bases of different religions and the specifying of criteria which make it possible to avoid spiritual relativism and to deepen the comprehension of one's own religious attitude. See his *Recontre des Religions* (Paris: Aubier, 1957) and "Phänomenologie und Begegnung der Religionen," *Studia Philosophica,* XVIII (1958), 45–89.

VAN METER AMES

Aesthetic Values in East and West

I. INTRODUCTION

Philosophical interest in art in the West goes back to Plato, but many Western philosophers have not taken art seriously. They have regarded cognitive and moral questions as more worthy of their attention. When Western thinkers have found art important they have often been formalists, seeing the value of art as divorced from other and (to them) lesser values of life. For a second group, art has not had spiritual value in its own form but in serving to express the values of a religion or ideology, as for Thomas Aquinas and the dialectical materialists. Still another way of conceiving the spiritual value of art is that of men who hold with John Dewey that all normal human interests can attain a spiritual level through the techniques of artistic expression. The spiritual value of art, then, inheres in clarifying and intensifying values which are already there in life.

There is no one philosophical attitude toward art which is distinctively or characteristically Western. But, since the eighteenth century, when modern aesthetics arose, most notably with Kant, Western philosophers have taken art more and more seriously, and have considerably broadened their outlook. It may be emphasized that for them, in the twentieth century, art is seldom made spiritual by exalting it to a higher realm, or by having it subservient to other than artistic values instead of being fused with them.

The different ways in which the spiritual value of art has been understood in the West, in relation to other values, can be explained with reference to form. Although form may be thought of as only one aspect of art, it is such a basic and inclusive term in Western aesthetics that to follow out the meanings of form will constitute a comprehensive approach to aesthetic values in the West.

Form has meant the shape of the work of art. But the effort to confine an art object to its own outline has been met by the realization that a thing of art reaches beyond its surface to the response of the appreciator, expresses the values of life, and may have influence throughout a culture. Some philosophers have continued to emphasize form in the formal sense of the structure of an object. They belong to the school of art for art's sake. They have a way of assuming that to disagree with them is not to appreciate art, not seeing how it belongs apart from life and the ordinary world.

But this has not been the only approach to art in the West. For such a culminating philosopher as Dewey art is not an escape from what is temporal, hence disagreeable, to the eternal, which alone is lovely, but an organizing, expressing, and celebrating activity in the midst of the ongoing affairs of every day. Art, for Dewey, is not spiritual because it is out of this world, but spiritual because it brings freshness, freedom, creativity into the world. Art is life-giving as opposed to all that is dead and deadening. Art is a release from unseeing and unfeeling ways that smother spark and spontaneity, not by turning away from life but by enlivening it.

Philosophy of art in the West, both on the side of art for itself as self-contained form, and on the side of art for life as the form of life most alive, has been the work of many centuries and of many thinkers, not only of Plato, Hegel, Croce, and Dewey. And choosing sides, for life or beyond life, has given vitality to aesthetics. The position taken in this paper is that the aesthetic belongs with the other spiritual values, the good and the true. The aesthetic, in being social, is inseparable from the scientific and the religious. Not only do all these values go together—a deepening understanding of them is bringing East and West together.

The meeting of East and West comes easily in science, subtly in art. In mathematics and natural science there are no cultural differences, whereas in social science such cultural differences may be the field of study, and they are prominent in art. When a Westerner looks at a Japanese temple or watches a Nō play, he is struck by a feeling for life that he wants to understand. Far Eastern collections in Boston and other Western cities have been passing the language barrier. It goes down before art, with the exception of literature. There translators and interpreters smooth the way. The influence of Japanese poetry upon Western poets is comparable to that of Japanese painters upon Western artists.

Foreign thought and religion need to be studied. Strangeness may grow with knowledge, so that the learned become so aware of differences under apparent sameness that they distrust comparisons. But the forms of art are there for all to see, especially in the good light of modern photography. Anyone familiar with the structures of his own culture may go from West to East or from East to West and become sensitive to what he finds. He will begin to see that other sculpture, painting, architecture, and music are formulations of human experience. He will realize that, the world over, there is common endeavor to achieve satisfactory forms. In Japan, the influence of Zen has spread the importance of forms that are fresh, not set or conventional. But, with or without Zen, the West also appreciates creativity. Although hurry, slackness, lack of energy or insight lead men to stereotypes, the zest for expression is perennial. The question is whether art comes to the full in the design of the art work itself, as formalists hold, or whether form that is vital serves to organize and order thought and feeling about the human situation, to focus and *form* the values of life that, in becoming artistic, do not cease to be social, scientific, and religious.

II. FORM VERSUS SENSUOUS AND EMOTIONAL APPEAL

The idea of beauty as pure form, simply to be contemplated, goes all the way back to Plato in the West. But so does the idea that art is sensuous and emotionally moving. In the *Philebus* Plato says he means lines, curves, surfaces, and solid forms which "have their proper pleasures, no way depending on the itch of desire."[1] When he comes to condemn art it is for turning from beauty as pure form to imitation or representation of gross things, especially in poetry and the theater where far from ideal characters are presented, stirring the feelings and indulging the irrational nature of man.[2]

The Romantic Germans in the eighteenth century, in their *Sturm und Drang,* idealized Greek sculpture (which Plato did not discuss) as exemplifying the beauty of form free of sensuous and emotional appeal. Winckelmann was not able to confine beauty to the abstract unity and variety of a geometrical pattern.[3] Neither was Hogarth, with his preference for the serpentine line.[4] But Kant carried through to its consequences the ancient idea of formal beauty, emptying it of all content, and of any hold on sense or desire.[5] He would even rule out color from the beauty of a flower shape. This is the line followed more or less strictly by later formalists.

It also serves to place anti-formalists. Charles Guyau maintained that every agreeable sensation "can take on aesthetic character in acquiring a certain degree of intensity, of reverberation in consciousness."[6] He cited the feel of ice on a fevered forehead, a glass of milk in the mountains, as supremely aesthetic without benefit of form, through sheer intensity of sensuousness, and recalled the Song of Songs as further evidence. Santayana was in essential agreement that enjoyment of sensuous qualities may be aesthetic without grasp of form, and considered that all the vital functions may contribute to what he significantly called the sense of beauty.[7] D. W. Prall also considers the sensuous surface of experience as aesthetic, and stresses the need of appreciating the sensu-

[1] Plato, *Philebus* 51B, in E. F. Carritt, *Philosophies of Beauty* (Oxford: Clarendon Press, 1931), p. 30.
[2] Plato, *Republic* 605.
[3] J. J. Winckelmann, *Geschichte der Kunst des Alterthums* (1764), G. Henry Lodge, trans., *The History of Ancient Art.* 2 vols. (London: Sampson Low, Marston, Searle, & Rivington, 1881).
[4] William Hogarth, *The Analysis of Beauty* (1753), Joseph Burke, ed. (Oxford: Clarendon Press, 1955).
[5] I. Kant, *Kritik der Urtheilskraft* (1790), J. H. Bernard, trans., *Critique of Judgment* (New York: Haefner Publishing Co., Inc., 1951).
[6] Charles Guyau, *Les Problèmes de l'Esthétique Contemporaine* (Paris, 1884) (12th ed., Paris: Librairie Félix Alcan, 1929), p. 61.
[7] George Santayana, *The Sense of Beauty* (New York: Scribner, 1896), Part III.

ous aspect as necessary to appreciation of other aspects of art.[8] But both he and Santayana think of sensuous elements as the materials of beauty, instead of saying that they can constitute a full aesthetic experience in themselves. Frances Herring's remarkable article, "Touch,"[9] is closer to Guyau. He was anticipated by the ancient Chinese who passed delicate fabrics to guests for them to feel. The aromas of coffee and tobacco seem to be enjoyed aesthetically in the West, too, as well as incense, apart from any formal structure.

In the Italian Renaissance, art was associated with the sensuous and the sumptuous. Form was not absent but dyed with the color of stuffs and flesh in painting, overlaid with costly materials in palaces and churches, most flamboyantly in Venice. Comparison may be made with the Heian period in Japan (794–1192), if one thinks of the colorful richness suggested in Lady Murasaki's *The Tale of Genji,*[10] and the imagery in poetry of the time which has carried over ever since in the Japanese love of flowering trees and autumn leaves.[11]

Here, sensuous merges with emotional appeal, which also has been opposed to pure form, notably by Eugène Véron, who put the transmission of emotion above beauty as formal perfection.[12] So did Tolstoy.[13] Dewey, discussing this theory, pointed out that emotional discharge is a necessary but not sufficient condition of expression.[14] To have art there must be transformation of blind impulsion. Aesthetic expression is more than pouring out.

III. FORM VERSUS EXPRESSION

Emphasis on the sensuous and emotional appeal of art leads to recognition of expression as more than the beauty of pure form. When Kant saw, after reading Edmund Burke's *The Sublime and the Beautiful,*[15] that beauty as form detached from existence needed to be supplemented by the sublime, he made room in the aesthetic for the frightful and the overwhelming. He required that fear be offset by the surging up of a response to face it. But the safety of form was exploded with its prettiness; the infinite was let in. Aestheticians still tried to tame the influx by maintaining that in the end there was reconciliation, transcendence, a resolution not unbeautiful. Bosanquet suggested a distinction between easy and difficult beauty.

The conventionally beautiful became insipid. Max Dessoir admitted that the ugly must be brought in to keep beauty from being too safe and tame.[16]

[8] D. W. Prall, *Aesthetic Judgment* (New York: Thomas Y. Crowell Company, 1929).

[9] Frances Herring, "Touch: The Neglected Sense," *The Journal of Aesthetics and Art Criticism,* VII, No. 3 (March, 1949), 199–215.

[10] Shikibu Murasaki, *The Tale of Genji,* Arthur Waley, trans. (1-vol. ed., London: Allen & Unwin Ltd., 1935).

[11] Ryusaku Tsunoda, Wm. Theodore de Bary, Donald Keene, eds. and compilers, *Sources of Japanese Tradition* (New York: Columbia University Press, 1958), chap. IX.

[12] Eugène Véron, *L'Esthétique* (Paris, 1878) (4th ed., Paris: Schleicher Frères et Cie., 1904).

[13] L. Tolstoy, *What Is Art?* (1896), Alymer Maude, trans. (Oxford: Oxford University Press, 1930).

[14] John Dewey, *Art As Experience* (New York: Minton, Balch & Co., 1934; G. P. Putnam's Sons, Capricorn Books, 1958), chap. IV.

[15] Edmund Burke, *The Sublime and the Beautiful* (1756), in *Works,* Vol. I (Boston: Little, Brown & Co., 1871).

[16] Max Dessoir, *Aesthetik und Allgemeine Kunstwissenschaft* (1906) (2d ed., Stuttgart: Verlag von Ferdinand Enke, 1923).

There must be a place in aesthetic experience for the wild ungovernable forces of Nature, and for the tragic in human life. Aristotle's theory of catharsis, that in tragedy the emotions of pity and terror are so stirred that they are cleaned out, had been relied upon to offset Plato's fear of indulging the irrational side of man's nature in art. But Dessoir felt that tragedy is irreconcilable with the cultural ideal of the finest souls. The contradiction at the heart of things cannot be resolved into the non-contradictory. Santayana felt that it is false to hold that life or art is better for having pain and evil in it, though he came later, after reflecting on Freud, to admit that many people crave the painful.

DeWitt H. Parker noted that there is too much ugliness in art to be ignored or explained away, citing such examples as Goya's "Massacre of the Inhabitants of Madrid," but he tried to think of ugliness in art as "oblique representation of beauty," and of tragedy as redeemed by heroism or religious faith.[17] There may be, as in Gide, the feeling that people are too complacent about social evils and need to be shocked into seeing how things are. Faulkner and Sartre have presented horror that may be hard to square with moral purpose, unless this age of violence needs such writing, and such painting as Picasso's "Guernica," to express man's inhumanity to man. If we cannot make the world nice, we may at least have the satisfaction of saying what we do not like.

If the pure form of pure beauty was not an adequate idea of aesthetic experience for Kant, it certainly is not for modern man. Even popular literature is no longer addicted to the happy ending. Yet, there still is a welcome for beauty and for what is felt to be pure or abstract form. Kant suggested that beauty as form, even though not expressive in itself, might become the occasion of expression. Thus he spoke of form as beautiful when it calls out a harmonious play of man's subjective powers, permitting him to express his ideal, imaginative make-up, free of desire or "interest."

This was abstract, but with this hint Schiller was able to launch the play theory of art.[18] He gave sense and feeling their due in the idea of play, holding that man's sensuous nature is not hopelessly selfish, as Kant thought, and that sense might enter in as well as reason, as long as play was free of control by either. But Schiller was still close to Kant in explaining that man is free in art because there, removed from practical purpose, he can *play* with appearance. For all the insights in subsequent developments of the play theory, it was discredited because it did not recognize the full seriousness of art.

Hegel took art seriously enough, treating it as more than formal or playful in being the sensuous vehicle of the "Idea," the most comprehensive thought. But, while elevating art, he also marked it down below philosophy and religion, since he gave art the impossible assignment of rivaling them intellectually. For him, art has a special function, however, in being as expressive as possible in the medium of sense, and thereby meaning more to many people than pure philosophy or high religion could without the help of art. He in-

[17] DeWitt H. Parker, *The Principles of Aesthetics* (New York: Silver Burdett & Company, 1920, 1946).
[18] Friedrich Schiller, *Letters on the Aesthetic Education of Mankind* (1795), Reginald Snell, trans. (New Haven: Yale University Press, 1954).

sisted that the best that art can do is to point beyond itself to spiritual realities.[19] He did not shy like Kant from seeing that art is addressed to the senses. The purpose of art for Hegel is to show in sensuous form how all oppositions are overcome in the truth of the Absolute. But in Romantic art sensuous presentation is most effective when felt to be inadequate.

This is in the tradition of Plato's thought in the *Symposium* and the *Phaedrus,* that the high use of beauty is to hint the ideal through sense, with the corollary that the artist should strive to elevate the mind. In Book X of the *Republic* he regrets that, instead of doing this, the artist is prone to imitate mundane things, including the most unworthy, even misrepresenting the gods, thereby indulging man's irrational nature. But in Book III he saw the possibility of artists "gifted to discern the true nature of the beautiful and graceful." Through such artists "will our youth dwell in a land of health, . . . and beauty, the effluence of fair works, shall glow into the eye and ear, like a health-giving breeze from a pure region."[20]

Here form is more than for its own sake. It is for inspiration, for opening the soul to philosophy, if not exactly to the philosophy of Hegel. At least, Hegel shared with the "Platonic" Plato the view that form and its beauty are for expressing something beyond. Dewey objected to the interpretation of art as pointing to a harmonious whole above life, because it has borrowed the traits of the complete, the coherent, and the integrated "from esthetic experience, where they do have application, and has then illegitimately extended them till they became categories of the universe at large, endowed with cosmic import."[21]

When Hegel stretched the aesthetic to the frame of the Absolute he burst its form. He settled any conflict between form and expression by sacrificing form. Hegelian Croce was equally drastic in simply identifying form with intuition, which, for him, was a synonym for expression. This reversed Santayana's willingness to consider expression aesthetic when felt to be fused with the sensuous and formal qualities of an object. Expression, for Croce, is not the third but the first and sole consideration. This involves depreciation of technique in handling materials. The real work of expression is an affair of inspiration, after which the work of the hand is no problem. This is like the Japanese concept of *yūgen,* as the high achievement of an actor or other artist beyond what is attainable by technical means. But it is a common notion in the West that technique is not all, that a personal or spiritual quality makes a great difference. Croce carried to the extreme the idea calmly put by Kant that creative work is beyond rules, hence beyond form in any formal sense.

Much the same idea has developed in India around the term *rasa,* used by Bharata (first century A.D.) and by Abhinavagupta (tenth century) to mean the taste or essence of poetry and drama at the level of ideal beauty, enjoyed intuitively, above ordinary pleasure and any naturalistic attitude, in a contem-

[19] G. W. F. Hegel, *The Philosophy of Fine Art* (published as *Aesthetik,* Berlin, 1835), F. P. B. Osmaston, trans. (London: G. Bell & Sons, 1920), Vol. I, sec. 1.

[20] Plato, *Republic* 401.

[21] P. A. Schilpp, *The Philosophy of John Dewey* (Evanston and Chicago: Northwestern University Press, 1939), p. 553.

plative mood evoked by various idealizing devices. *Raga,* in every Indian art, means the (natural and divine) factors of emotion and technique which stimulate the response of *rasa.*[22] For Radhakrishnan, art expresses religious and moral truth at a level at which the self is most uniquely itself, because also universal.[23] He distinguishes between the artist's vision (which is an intuition of ultimate reality) and the work of putting this vision into words or other terms, and holds, unlike Croce, that the vision is not merely personal or it would not be significant to other men.[24] For Sri Aurobindo, aesthetic experience enables divided beings (which men are) to glimpse the universal harmony, the beauty beheld by the divine soul.[25] This is Abhinavagupta's conception of beauty, which dominates Indian aesthetics to this day. In Abhinavagupta's theory, aesthetic experience rises from sense (sight and hearing) to a transcendental Universal, imaginatively and emotionally grasped, which improves the appreciator morally by lifting him into the bliss of the higher Self. This experience is brought about by the artist's creative work, which is freed from the particular limitations of natural objects in time and space, and is appreciated only through contemplative realization of what is suggested by what is physically presented. The appropriate attitude in aesthetic experience "differs from the practical attitude in ordinary life inasmuch as it is marked by total absence of expectation of being called upon to act in reality."[26] Yet, the sensuous level is not left behind. Indian art often presents the divine in frankly sensuous forms, with the conviction that all life is one, in being and becoming, and in the dualism of masculine and feminine.

In China, the conception of beauty has been more naturalistic and humanistic. Much Chinese poetry is casual recording of daily doings and happenings, apparently without emotion, fitting right into a poet's biography, such as Arthur Waley's *The Life and Times of Po Chü-I.*[27] The wonder of the outdoors and the pleasures of solitude are celebrated with appropriate feeling, along with comments on political events, expression of the horror of war, and denunciation of social injustice. In poetry, the Chinese share with the Japanese a recurring emphasis on the basic human relationships, especially in the pain of parting and the joy of homecoming. But Japanese poets adhere more steadily to personal emotion, usually melancholy, in very short poems appealing to the reader to fill in what is suggested.

In China and Japan, the brush stroke unites painting and writing, with delicate and powerful variations. The void surrounds the strokes in a painting or poem, and the emptiness counts as much as what is indicated. Architectural

[22] Cf. Pravas Jivan Chaudhury, "The Theory of Rasa," and W. G. Raffé, "Ragas and Raginis: A Key to Hindu Aesthetics," *The Journal of Aesthetics and Art Criticism,* XI, No. 2 (December, 1952), 147–150, 105–117; and Ananda K. Coomaraswamy, *The Transformation of Nature in Art* (New York: Dover Publications, Inc., 1956), pp. 47, 49, 55.

[23] Cf. Robert W. Browning, "Reason and Types of Intuition in Radhakrishnan's Philosophy," in P. A. Schilpp, ed., *The Philosophy of Sarvepalli Radhakrishnan* (New York: Tudor Publishing Co., 1952), p. 208.

[24] *Ibid.,* p. 212.

[25] Cf. Sri Aurobindo, *The Life Divine* (New York: Sri Aurobindo Library, 1949, 1951), pp. 101–102.

[26] K. C. Pandey, *Comparative Aesthetics,* Vol. I, *Indian Aesthetics* (Banaras: Vidya Vilas Press, 1950), p. 154.

[27] Arthur Waley, *The Life and Times of Po Chü-I* (New York: The Macmillan Co., 1949).

lines also approach calligraphy. The ancient controversy between Confucius and Mo Tzu about music goes to the heart of Chinese aesthetics. For Mo Tzu, music (including everything artistic) is wasteful in having no such productive use as feeding and housing people. For Confucius, the beauty of music and other art, as of ceremony and propriety, lies in the higher social use of fulfilling and completing human life.[28]

Related as Chinese and Japanese art are, the differences require careful study. Professor Richard Edwards, comparing Chinese and Japanese painting and asking whether a work is a Chinese original or a Japanese copy, finds that he is comparing two civilizations. To distinguish between the original and the copy it is necessary to know that the Chinese would paint one way, the Japanese another. This is not easy in the Nara period (710–794), since there is only a fine distinction between a Horyuji fresco and a T'ang (618–907) painting. In relation to Western art, he suggests that Chinese painting is nineteenth-century in its wholeness and completeness, Japanese art twentieth-century in its emphasis upon the detailed and the fragmentary. There are sharpness and abruptness in Japanese ink painting. Chinese painting is softer, and the gradations are more gradual. The popularity of Zen in Japan, in contrast to its dying out in China, is related to the stern abruptness of the Japanese representations of a monk or other Buddhist figure.[29]

The conclusion to be drawn from this is that, important as form is in the art of India, China, and Japan, it has never been all-important but has been subordinate to expression.

The bravest attempt to justify formal form was in the theory of *Einfühlung*, or empathy, which is a variation of the play theory. According to Theodor Lipps,[30] the self, taken as a unity, seeks to grasp every manifold as a unity, and therefore likes forms which facilitate such grasping, forms in which the self can deploy and play with its unifying powers. But no physical sensations enter into aesthetic empathy. This theory, which seems to promise explanation of the attraction of abstract forms, specifically rules out any appeal to the biological or social self. The self set up to enjoy abstractness is an abstraction. Form turns out not to be the expression of anything human. Kinaesthetic sensations are ruled out along with all practical interests. All that comes into play aesthetically is said by Lipps to be a kind of disembodied, disfranchized, thinned out "inner" activity. So, form-as-form for Lipps is as otherworldly as form-turned-expression for Croce, who banishes from what is truly aesthetic anything physical, intellectual, utilitarian, or moral. Instead of explaining the interest in aesthetic experience, these aestheticians are as paradoxical as Kant when he said that the beautiful is what interests without interest: "*Was interesst ohne alles Interesse . . . das ist schön.*"[31] Aesthetic *Einfühlung* goes back to

[28] Cf. Y. P. Mei, *Motse The Neglected Rival of Confucius* (London: Arthur Probsthain, 1934), pp. 140–142.

[29] Richard Edwards, of Washington University, in discussion at Fulbright Conference at Atami, Japan, March, 1959.

[30] Theodor Lipps, *Aesthetik,* 2 vols. (Leipzig: Verlag von Leopold Voss, 1903–1920).

[31] Kant, *Critique of Judgment,* sec. 5.

the standpoint of the pure spectator, reducing expression to airy nothing to fit empty form.

Freud would seem to leave formalism for a serious theory of expression, in stressing the role of erotic wishes and ambitious daydreaming as motivating art, but he admittedly does not explain why some men can put their dreams into artistic form while others continue to dream. He is more concerned with art which reproduces the artist's experience than with art which is more creative.

The idea of the creative came to be closely associated with the symbolism of Poe and the literary movement launched by Baudelaire's translation of Poe in the mid-nineteenth century, spreading through Mallarmé and Rimbaud to a number of later writers. Symbolism here is a vague suggestiveness, coming to be linked with free association à la Freud, an escape from the ugliness of the industrial revolution, the vulgarities of the bourgeoisie, and the supposed reduction by science of the human to a level meaner than dreams. Proust, Kafka, James Joyce, Gide, Thomas Mann all were fascinated with the dream side of life, breaking over set forms in search of a freer and more expressive form. This quest for emancipation is not always opposed to science, which itself has stimulated new departures in art. Charles E. Gauss[32] relates the experiments of the impressionist and neo-impressionist painters to experimental science, in their effort to get closer to the real appearance of the world until, with the symbolist Gauguin, there was a switch from interest in outer reality to the artist's own soul.

But even irrational developments in art recognized at least indirectly that science had destroyed traditional conceptions. About 1910, futurism sprang up in France and Italy in a desperate effort to be original, followed by the deliberate nonsense of Dada from Switzerland and eventually by the anti-rational and professedly personal expressionism of surrealism and existentialism. More recently, Zen's stress on creativity is attracting artists. Not only the Japanese woodblock artist Munakata but also the French painter Braque credits Zen for inspiration. In Zen, the stress on technical skill, which goes with putting form first, is relegated to second place. Thus D. T. Suzuki says that when the artist has "the breath of heaven and earth" in his work he can "neglect the technical details." That is why there have been famous Zen artists who had no professional training.[33] Hoseki Shin'ichi Hisamatsu makes the same point in speaking of "detachment" as freedom from rules, standards, and conventions, and from any *mere* logic or rationality except as used freely.[34] The idea is to achieve unstudied vividness, which will register the deep freedom of Zen living. Yet, admittedly, it is a way of using the brush; it is an expressive style or form.

[32] Charles E. Gauss, *The Aesthetic Theories of French Artists* (Baltimore: The Johns Hopkins Press, 1949).

[33] D. T. Suzuki, "Sengai: Zen and Art," *Art News Annual*, XXVII (November, 1957), Part II, 193.

[34] H. S. Hisamatsu, *Zen and Fine Arts* (Kyoto: Bokubi-Sha, 1958), pp. 34–36.

IV. FORM VERSUS ASSOCIATION AND REPRESENTATION

Form as self-contained may be thought of as opposed, not only to sensuous and emotional appeal, and to the suggestion of feelings or insights beyond words or other embodiment, but also to any associations of life or representation of objects and situations in life. Here the opposition is not between form and what expressionists and symbolists feel to be more than form, in being too much for it, but between form and what could very well be given form but supposedly should not properly be included in form or added to it. The content of Hegel's "Idea" is more than artistic form could formulate, although imagined to have organic integration. Now, the question is similar to that of the exclusion of sensuous pleasure and the itch of desire from form, which could perfectly well be given form if it were seemly. The question now is the related but somewhat different one of whether to include in art and the proper appreciation of it more that may be associated with it or represented by it, not in the high metaphysical sense of Hegel's "Idea" or the vague irrational or supra-rational sense of the symbolists and surrealists, but in the more commonplace reaches of everyday activities and interests.

Clive Bell, in reaction against sentimentality in nineteenth-century painting, insists that abstract formal qualities alone are aesthetic.[35] Since he considers representation irrelevant to art, he can say: "To appreciate a work of art we need bring with us nothing from life, no knowledge of its ideas and affairs, no familiarity with its emotions."[36] He has painting especially in mind. This position of Kant (and of Plato in the *Philebus*) was applied to music by Gurney[37] and Eduard Hanslick,[38] who were out of patience with what they regarded as the sentimental excesses of program music and opera. They considered music as properly only tones and their relations and would rule out any association, representation, or message. Vernon Lee distinguished *listeners*, who concentrate upon the "music itself," from *hearers*, "whose comparative poverty from the musical side is eked out and compensated by . . . a shallow tide of . . . memories, associations, suggestions, visual images and emotional states." Yet, she found that the musical experience of the hearers was "far more various, more complicated and in many ways more interesting."[39]

What happens when the aesthetic is strictly defined, in terms of what can be directly experienced in a work itself, is that much of what makes the experience interesting and important is left out. But if the aesthetic is construed loosely it may become confused with the merely agreeable or the interesting. Santayana's solution is useful, including in the aesthetic any expression which is felt to be fused with the qualities of the art object. Otherwise, as Prall admits, we must say that the value of art is often not aesthetic but in the presentation

[35] Clive Bell, *Art* (London: Chatto & Windus, 1914).
[36] *Ibid.*, p. 25.
[37] Edmund Gurney, *The Power of Sound*, Gustav Cohen, trans. (London: Smith, Elder & Co., 1880).
[38] Eduard Hanslick, *The Beautiful in Music* (London: Novello, 1891).
[39] Violet Paget (Vernon Lee), *Music and Its Lovers* (New York: E. P. Dutton & Co., Inc., 1933), pp. 32, 35.

of wider human interests and satisfactions.[40] This becomes obvious in literature, unless one is to say that novels, plays, etc., which are full of life are not truly art, leaving perhaps such poetry as is unintelligible to be enjoyed for its sonority.

Perhaps the persistence of the formalist approach to art is explained as reaction against both sentimental and crude realism or representationism. But there is a growing endeavor to understand art in a more adequate fashion than in reduction to abstract design.[41] The tendency (as in Dewey's *Art As Experience*) is to assimilate the form of art to the form of freely controlled experiences in life—as these are brought to expression. But when what is more than the sensed-as-formed art object itself is regarded as its message, it may be easy for the formalist to deny that this is part of what is *there*. Instead of speaking of a message or meaning, which might be put in a statement, it is more accurate to say that something may be conveyed by music which, although it cannot be put into words, is suggestive, perhaps through association with a kind of occasion such as a wedding, a funeral, or other recognized event.

To regard the bare sensuous structure of a piece of music as the "real" work is like regarding sense-data as the essential elements of any experience, whereas the sensuous form is an abstraction from the whole work, as sense-data are arrived at by analysis instead of being all that is there to begin with. To take out whatever can be picked out from the whole may help, as analysis usually helps, to appreciate the whole, but not if supposed to be the whole.

We may smile at Plato's objection to instrumental music and rhythm without words.[42] But it violated his sense of wholeness and fitness to sever music from poetry and choric movements, with their story and moral. He denounced as "exceedingly coarse and tasteless" the sort of thing "which aims only at swiftness and smoothness and a brutish noise, and uses the flute and the lyre not as the mere accompaniments of the dance and song."[43]

The Japanese Nō play is like what he had in mind. Derived from ancient folk and temple dances, it is imbued with Buddhism, especially Zen. The bareness of the stage, the masked figure in a dance slowing to only breathing, the pausing poetry, the deep harmony of the chorus subsiding into silence—all this suggests the enveloping emptiness, the pregnant nothingness of Zen. The calm of a Nō play also comes through the clack and thump of drums and the shrill insistence of the flute, as the quiet of the mind should be attained "amid the din of things." The primitive yowls of drummers and the chanting of the chorus somehow go together, though the drums do not seem to keep the measure, and the notes of the flute slide between tones known to the West.

Modern composers in the West depart from their own tradition, too. John Cage, with his "prepared piano," is influenced by Zen: in reproducing noises from ordinary life and spacing them to be heard for their own sake, without

[40] D. W. Prall, *Aesthetic Judgment* (New York: Thomas Y. Crowell Company, 1929), chap. X.
[41] V. M. Ames, "The Trend Away from Formalism in the Arts," in *Proceedings of the Third International Congress of Aesthetics* (Turin: University of Turin, 1957).
[42] Plato, *Laws*, Book II.
[43] Plato, *Republic* 669.

benefit of any pattern from the past, also setting off the ensuing silence by their isolated and startling impact. The playing of a Webern quartet and the experiments with electronic sound also raise again the question of Plato: how tones alone compare with the large form of Greek (or Japanese) music-and-dance drama, uniting art to art and art to life. But in "music itself," or in sophisticated elaboration of noise pure and simple, there may after all be a life-relation or rejection.

The formalist is given undue advantage when the alternative to his concentration upon what appears to be there is presented after a rather literal semantic model, as simply adding a sign function to form. If a work of art is not insulated within its own outline but rises above its surface, it is not adequate to think of this as sending out a message. Art often is not cognitive in the sense of stating propositions to be understood apart from the art behind them, as if it were only for launching them. Nor does it do justice to art to say that instead of statable propositions it has truth claims embedded in it. Moreover, denying that art is literally or subtly cognitive need not mean that it is emotive, in the sense of just stimulating the appreciator subjectively without actually conveying anything to him. Without being strictly cognitive or merely emotive, art may so go with an attitude, so fit a mood, so belong to a sort of occasion, that without being exactly semantic it is much more than sensuous and formal. Art may have the *bodhisattva*-function of helping to save people from being only half alive, through seeing how free and creative human experience can be.

The formalist approach remains important as one way of getting at a work of art. But that is no reason for abandoning other approaches. The formalist might be justified in using his method exclusively if the significance of an art work were sealed up in a metaphysical essence within it. But, if art is human work, it owes something to the worker, to the occasion and motivation of his work, and to the uses made of it. Art then is multi-functional. In understanding and criticizing it, the social side of its creation and appreciation should count. The formalist attempt to concentrate upon an essential ontological object, to the exclusion of wider considerations, provides less scope for criticism than recognizing the many relations between art and life.

One may still ask what the work of art itself is at the center of all its radii. Stephen C. Pepper developed the rather unsettling implications of the fact that a work is what it is experienced to be.[44] Croce had anticipated Pepper in contending that the real work is an intuitive expression, not to be confused with the physical object which somehow is convenient for conveying the artist's inner work to the appreciator. For Pepper, the work is between the maker and the taker, and appears somewhat differently each time it is perceived by the same appreciator (not to mention the complication of different appreciators). Presumably there is a cumulation of perceptions successively becoming more adequate. But, if there is no end to this, a work of art, instead of being some-

[44] Stephen C. Pepper, *The Basis of Criticism in the Arts* (Cambridge: Harvard University Press, 1946).

thing objective and obvious within its outline, dissolves into an ideal never realized, though criticism may promote further and fuller realization.

The formalist would guard against the deliquescence of the art object into fluctuating perceptions of it and its fading into social relationships. He would scold, as Clive Bell and Hanslick do, the person who uses a painting or a symphony as a reminder of life, an opportunity to enjoy free association, instead of as an invitation to discover what has been uniquely added to reality by creative imagination and skill in the mastery of a particular medium. The formalist opposes the sentimentalist, who will enjoy the "beauty of Nature," which makes no formal demands upon him, as much as any art, and turns to art only as a substitute for what it represents. When art is not representative he probably can "make nothing of it." There is a case here, and it has been well argued. But it has not been settled except to the satisfaction of its advocates.

In contrast is Dewey's *Art As Experience,* emphasizing the continuity of art and life, regarding art as the clarification and completion of what experience normally is or tends to be. This view has the support of primitive art and of most of the art in various cultures, except for the art-for-art's-sake movement of the West in the nineteenth century, in reaction against the industrial revolution. But even this movement uses art for life in cherishing the freedom threatened by mass production, or by any inhuman organization of society. The traditional defenders of pure form did not anticipate its acquiring social significance. But condemnation of modern art in Hitler Germany and Soviet Russia made non-representational work represent the free human spirit.

Rapprochement between form and association or representation is more understandable when it is realized that "abstract" form need not be geometric or rigid. Absence of machine precision, even slips and uncertainties of the hand, remaining in finished work, instead of being felt as flaws, can be precious signs of men at work, on their own, guided by their own taste. So, improvisation in true jazz is not purely formal in the sense of having no connection with the pathos of the Negro's situation in American life and his need to recover freedom if only in expressing its loss.

Freedom felt in art not only is conducive to freedom in living but flows from life to art. This is clear in Japan in the influence of Zen upon culture through art, and upon art through Zen living, as brought out by Suzuki, and also by Hisamatsu in his book on *Zen and Fine Arts,* in emphasis on the fresh and vivid dynamism of Zen experience, and the continuity of man's form-free self with Nature's forms and form-transcending vastness. In Zen life and art there is the sense of depth, of power in reserve, and vital freedom. In culture permeated by Zen it is impossible to draw a line between art and life, between art forms and art associations, between life brought into art and art carried into life and Nature. Love of Nature in Japan includes taking care of forests and cherishing tiny gardens. A tree in a pot or outdoors will be trained to be asymmetrical, as if weather-beaten, made by man to look as if more than man had a hand in it. The old pine tree painted at the back of the Nō stage has scraggly dead branches here and there, as if left to the neglect of Nature. Rocks in a garden should be mossy, as if they had always been there, the tea hut unpainted, as if ancient. Parts of a garden count more than the whole, being planned to make it impossible to see them all at once, suggesting more than is ever present. The gardens of the Japanese bring near the far, the vast, the unexplored, mountains, waterfalls, forest, whereas in America there would be a yard inside a prosaic fence. So, in their poetry, however brief, feeling is deep, beginning with feeling for the time of year and for other years at the same season. Even when the moment seems to be all, it has a lift above the given image. This is notably true of the *haiku* (seventeen-syllable poem). And the extent to which poetry is enjoyed and written by the Japanese people is only one sign of how life for them is also art.

V. FORM VERSUS FUNCTIONAL AND MORAL ASPECTS

The over-reach of art beyond the given takes another turn in the common Greek notion held by Plato, in one of his ways of thinking about art, that its beauty is in the exercise of skill in performance of a function. In the *Hippias Major* the argument is that efficiency is beauty and inefficiency ugliness. In Book X of the *Republic* form is simply a matter of use and usefulness. The painter will paint reins and bit, the worker in leather and brass will make them, but these persons do not know the right form of bit and reins. "Only the horseman who knows how to use them—he knows their right form."[45]

This conception of art and beauty applies the world over to early pots, weapons, blankets, canoes, and all manner of things to work and fight and live with, down to automobiles and airplanes. Design has been guided by use, and also by delight. If delight goes beyond use, it is hard to say where either gives way to the other. It seems vital that the look and feel of what is functional should be pleasing, while the function of much ornament and decoration is to please. Men want not only to survive but to live with some style and flourish. Their well-being is enhanced by shaping and touching-up what they use, not only to fit the hand but to meet the eye with a balance, a rhythm, a finish that is more than useful and is most human.

Architecture has served practical ends, being too expensive and too much needed to be purely formal, although often unfunctional to an uncomfortable degree. For Ruskin,[46] honest and imaginative treatment of materials and functions was of a piece with respect for one's fellows. In spite of his anachronistic attachment to Gothic and his loathing of the machine,[47] his spirit was reborn in Louis Sullivan and his Chicago colleagues who started the world movement which has gone far to correct what Carl W. Condit called the failure of society "to achieve a formal, aesthetic discipline of the chief cultural phenomena of

[45] Plato, *Republic* 601.

[46] John Ruskin, *The Seven Lamps of Architecture* (1849) (New York: John Wiley & Son, 1876).

[47] Bertram Morris, "Ruskin and the Moral Imagination in Architecture," *The University of Colorado Studies, Series in Language and Literature,* No. 6, January, 1957.

the time, science, technology, and industrialization," by achieving a new unity of form with structural and utilitarian elements.[48]

Here was anticipation, both in theory and practice, of the Chicago School of philosophy, which, at the turn of the century, under the leadership of Dewey, would bring all the spiritual values together in creative intelligence: the aesthetic with the moral and religious, the scientific and the social. These would be the new terms for the beautiful in relation to what Plato called the good and the true. In the same year that Dewey published his social and scientific study of art (*Art As Experience*) he published his equally social and scientific view of religion (*A Common Faith*).[49] He thought of living religiously as striving, in the face of risk and odds, to realize social ideals, as he thought of living aesthetically as also belonging to the joint enterprise of creative intelligence: the co-religious and co-scientific enterprise of helping people to realize what a full life can be. Thus the good becomes a question of practical morality and religion, in terms of science and democracy, as the modern aspects of truth and love. At the same time, the traditional, abstract value of the beautiful, contemplated outside life, gives way to a more scientific and social interest in what artists are doing and how their work can aid people to make their lives more creative.

VI. FORM VERSUS THE SOCIAL AND SCIENTIFIC APPROACH TO ART

The return of art to its ancient and almost universal relation with life, after separation in the West for a century or so, was marked by a shift from aesthetics centered on the appreciator (supposedly passive) to study of the artist in action. This transition was announced and aided by Max Dessoir in his book *Aesthetik und Allgemeine Kunstwissenschaft*[50] and the *Zeitschrift* with the same name which he founded in the same year and edited for thirty years. The double title calls attention to dissatisfaction with isolationist, form-bound aesthetics, and the need to supplement it with a less speculative, more scientific and social kind of investigation. This would get away from the abstract shapefast concept of beauty and move on to the dynamic ways of making and taking art. Traditional aesthetics, since the eighteenth century, had been about an experience imagined to be free of pain and unstained by intellectual, ethical, religious, sexual, or any other concern of actual human life. Emil Utitz summed it up in observing that, while the beautiful may be the "purest form of the aesthetic, this is not to say that it is the one most full of value, or the only justified one, or that art should be merely beautiful and nothing else."[51]

In 1913, Dessoir launched the first International Congress for Aesthetics and

[48] Carl W. Condit, "The Chicago School and the Modern Movement in Architecture," *Art in America*, XXXVI (January, 1948), 20, 34. Cf. also Carl W. Condit, *The Rise of the Skyscraper* (Chicago: The University of Chicago Press, 1956).

[49] John Dewey, *A Common Faith* (New Haven: Yale University Press, 1934).

[50] Max Dessoir, *Aesthetik und Allgemeine Kunstwissenschaft.*

[51] Emil Utitz, *Grundlegung der Allgemeinen Kunstwissenschaft* (Stuttgart: F. Enke, 1914–1920), Vol. I, p. 120.

the General Science of Art. War and world dislocations slowed the movement, but in time it spread to other countries, as can be seen in the founding of journals inspired by his: the American *Journal of Aesthetics and Art Criticism,* 1941; the Spanish *Revista de Ideas Estéticas,* 1943; the French *Revue d'Esthétique,* 1948; the Japanese *Bigaku,* 1950; the Indian *Aesthetics,* 1951; and the Italian *Rivista di Estetica,* 1956. The term "aesthetics" in these titles does not indicate a return to contemplation of form-fettered beauty but, rather, a broadening of the word to include what Dessoir thought another term was needed to designate.

Thomas Munro, the editor of the *Journal* published for the American Society for Aesthetics, has well stated what it means to be scientific and social in aesthetics.[52] To be scientific does not mean reducing aesthetic experience to measurable responses to isolated shapes or colors in a laboratory, with all due respect to what can be learned there. It does mean using various techniques, with resourcefulness and imagination as well as with care, to illuminate the many aspects of the complex transaction of producing and appreciating art. To have a social approach means taking art museums out of the artificial glass-case conception of culture, having classes for children and adults in the processes of art-making, having exhibitions of current work, presenting things with maps showing where they come from and explanations of the culture behind them, with the help of illustrated lectures. There is also the increase of attention to art in colleges and universities, where exciting things are going on in theater, painting, architecture, ceramics, and music, as well as in creative writing, even in "appreciation" as now linked to original work. Munro calls upon the high schools to do more with the natural art-interest of adolescence, which is intimately bound up with drives that should be given a creative and idealizing direction.

What the scientific and social approach to art means, in contrast to what it opposes, may be represented by Munro's review[53] of *The Voices of Silence* by André Malraux.[54] Munro notes that Malraux passes over architecture, city planning, and industrial design, where art is allied with science. "By excluding the arts which have reached a wide public, he is able to say that artists have isolated themselves from society." He speaks of the Oriental's "groveling before a fear-compelling Presence," ignoring, as Munro observes, "Chinese naturalism and insouciance in religious matters." Malraux even says that Buddhism, though Asian, is not Oriental, because it does not grovel! And he is worse than unappreciative of primitive art.

To be as unscientific as he is in this book seems to involve being undemocratic, too. Being cavalier with facts goes with being unfair to people, as taking

[52] Thomas Munro, *Toward Science in Aesthetics* (New York: Liberal Arts Press, 1956); *Art Education: Its Philosophy and Psychology* (New York: Liberal Arts Press, 1956).

[53] Thomas Munro, review of *The Voices of Silence, The Journal of Aesthetics and Art Criticism,* XV, No. 4 (June, 1957), 481.

[54] André Malraux, *The Voices of Silence* (New York: Doubleday & Company, Inc., 1953), based on Stuart Gilbert, trans., *Psychology of Art.* 3 vols. (New York: Pantheon Books, 1949), from *Psychologie de l'art,* 3 vols. (Geneva: Albert Skira, 1947–1950).

care to get things straight is akin to treating people with respect. Not to see what there is to art, beyond form which can be abstracted, is not to acknowledge the artist or his public.

If aesthetic appreciation were as purely personal an experience of form as purists have assumed, the scientific and social approach would not come close. How wrong the purist can be is shown by Etienne Souriau in his "General Methodology for the Scientific Study of Aesthetic Appreciation."[55] He makes clear that it is no less unscientific than unfair to judge the aesthetic sensibility of a child or of an untutored adult by looking for the responses of a cultivated person to reproductions of art works. Another important French study, by David Victoroff, considers the varying occasions of applause, bringing out the connection between the response to art and the surrounding culture.[56] Gillo Dorfles of Italy also shows how art and aesthetics are involved in life, in the present split between "two distinct kinds of taste: one of the experts and one of the uninitiated."[57]

VII. CONCLUSION

Form in the restricted meaning of a pattern of abstract relations leaves out the sensuous and emotional appeal of art, with the expressive, moral, functional, and social dimensions which are more than bare design. Then, for a whole view of art, in the usual experience of it, these other aspects would have to be added, like color to a statue, whether regarded as non-aesthetic or not. But it seems more adequate to regard form in the broad and vital way of interfusing sensuous materials, expression, function, and the rest. Then form, instead of being an isolated element in aesthetic experience, while supposed to be all there is to it, becomes the organization of all that is actually involved. "Pure" form is only part of complete and vital form, and need not be opposed to it, since it belongs to it.

The idea of pure form was only one of Plato's approaches to beauty and art. Winckelmann and Kant, though committed to the romantic glorification of pure form, when they saw how it bottled up the beautiful in its outline, had to add a more expressive notion for the dynamic and human side of art. Attention to the structure or design of an art work need not rule out its wider aspects, unless form is taken to be a sealed-in metaphysical essence. Then the outer aspects would be unessential and negligible. When the wider ranges of art are included in the aesthetic, however, the formalist fears that form is reduced to a blank to be filled out by anyone to suit himself. A blank is neither form for a formalist nor expression for anyone. But when the devotees of form try to explain why it interests them, it is clear that form, which is important to them, is full of significance, even of vitality.

[55] Etienne Souriau, "General Methodology for the Scientific Study of Aesthetic Appreciation," *The Journal of Aesthetics and Art Criticism,* XIV, No. 1 (September, 1955), 1–18.

[56] David Victoroff, "L'Applaudissement: Une Conduite Sociale," in *L'Année Sociologique,* 1955–1956 (Paris: Presses Universitaires de France, 1957), pp. 131–171.

[57] Gillo Dorfles, "Art and the Public: Education for Mutual Understanding," *The Journal of Aesthetics and Art Criticism,* XVI, No. 4 (June, 1958), 491.

The way form is spoken of in athletics, to mean how a man swims or runs, how smoothly his muscles and breathing function, is revealing for aesthetics—if art is not regarded as something finished and done, and to be contemplated otiosely, but is appreciated as an activity, a process, a way of attacking marble or canvas. Form can also mean the stiff forms of convention. But form that makes life and art worth while is a rhythm of organizing energies, of meeting situations freely and resourcefully, as an animal does in hunting or escaping, or as a man does when solving problems in the line of his work or relationships, in the light of experience and skill. Then form is not something isolated or abstracted but the feel of a career. Then sense and emotion, expression, association, and function are not added to form or detachable from it, but inherent in it, constitutive of it. Then form is the way something is done when done well, with all that it comes to.

This is the sum and substance of recent aesthetics in the West, especially in the United States. Traditional Western aesthetics shared the dualism inherited from the Greeks in philosophy, religion, and literature: between a timeless realm of perfection and the dust of daily living, the messiness of generation and decay. Man's high achievement was to contemplate changeless truth, goodness, and beauty. In British and American thought, this dualistic orientation of Europe has been largely given up for interest in the going world men live in, as it is known, shared, and enjoyed.

What the scientists are doing and enabling others to do is taking the place of "pure" knowing. Contemplation is superseded by creative intelligence. Instead of the ancient and medieval subject-knower, timelessly confronting an object to be known, there is the research worker. He does not "know" in any high and final way. His "logic of inquiry" is tentative. But it is self-corrective and increasingly reliable.

In a science-centered age what was called the good has become the better: in seeking better ways of making things, doing things, and improving human relationships. A democracy, dedicated to a better life for everyone, especially needs science. And science needs democracy, since genuine inquiry depends upon freedom of direction, publication, and discussion. In return, science contributes more than materially to a democratic society in the moral qualities which science inculcates and must have: honesty, patience, co-operativeness, resistance to superstition and also to pure rationality—since science will use trial and error, and hunches subject to test. The spirit and method of science seem as important as its achievements. Its main result is that morality is made a matter of sharing the world with all people, through what men more rapidly come to know and know how to do. Science, by unbelievably increasing human power for good and evil, makes the religious attitudes of neighborliness and good will imperative. Science makes the moral and social side of religion paramount. In spite of belated efforts to revive theology, American philosophy has moved away from it to interest in the practical, social, and aesthetic aspects of religion.

While the true becomes a matter of what scientists are doing, and the good what morally or religiously motivated people do about social problems in a practical and co-scientific way, the beautiful, as once contemplated in a subject-object relation, becomes what artists make and other people make of their making. As the logic which counts for Dewey is not that of the contemplator but of the researcher, the agent, and the doer, so in religion and art he turns to the attitudes and activities which are creative. Doing, making, and remaking are much the same in art, science, and society. So, American philosophy of art joins with the philosophy of science, with ethics and philosophy of religion, in social philosophy.[58]

If this blurs distinctions between religion, science, and art, it is better to see how they overlap in life than to separate them academically. For Plato, the values of the good, the true, and the beautiful were indissoluble. Today, the religious, the scientific, and the aesthetic belong together as the social or spiritual values. These are the free and interweaving reaches of life when it is creative, appreciative, and critical. Neither religion, nor science, nor art would be spiritual in and by itself, apart from human use and fulfillment. Religion or science or art would be unspiritual if confined to church, laboratory, or museum instead of being diffused in society. The spiritual loses its value unless fused with what men do and feel when they do the best they can with the energies and disabilities they have, to make what they can of it all, on their own and together. Spiritual values are the vital interests and activities of human beings when criticized and tested in knowing, sharing, and recreating the world.

The great cleavage for Western philosophers of art is between those who hold that spiritual value is transcendent in pure form and those who see the spiritual as immanent in human experience, when it is fulfilled and deepened through art. On one side is the feeling that what is really fine is too good for this world and must belong to a higher sphere. On the other side is the conviction that what is good, true, and beautiful for men is the best of this world, and that this world is at its best when it has the benefit of art, when the form of art is the form of life, when art has life and life attains art.

While the physical sciences and technology are releasing people from age-old necessities, we are in need of social sciences and techniques, and the work of religion and art, to help people keep from wasting the freedom thrust upon them. The pressing, practical, and actual question, next to that of avoiding universal catastrophe, is the use of leisure: not only in the Utopia which science may fail to bring, but in the world which the sciences have already made over. Leisure is a problem for the rich and the retired, but also for the young. Violence is rising for sheer lack of imagination, the inability to see an appealing alternative way of using energies and urges. William James spoke of the need for a moral equivalent of war. We also need an aesthetic alternative to boredom.

[58] With credit to Professor Max H. Fisch of the University of Illinois, fellow Fulbrighter, who made this point in addressing the Japan-America Society, Tokyo, December 11, 1958.

Many people in the West are discovering the life-transforming value of working at art themselves, beyond just "appreciating" it: in the so-called fine arts and in art-related sports, in gardening, cooking, household decoration, conversation. For some, there is growing interest in the aesthetic aspects of religion and of science. If the West in general does not wake up to the widening opportunity to pursue artistic interests, then, instead of demanding that our Oriental friends explain why their countries did not develop science sooner, we in the West must explain why, even later, with the leisure provided by science, we do not write more and better poetry, and why we do not find in the forms of art the inspiration to *form* our lives more humanly.

Question: Must art be moral?

Answer: All art is moral in organizing impulses and urges in creative work—directly for the artist, vicariously for the appreciator. But the question is most pertinent to literary art. It is moral in the further sense of producing both good and evil effects upon attitudes. Plato condemned poetry because poets could not be trusted to use its power for good. Whatever the quality of a poem, a drama, or a novel in its intrinsic sensuous and formal aspects, the meaning conveyed may be wrong and reprehensible. A work of which this is true must be inferior to a work of equal inherent excellence which fosters a more admirable and acceptable view. A moral idea may not be well presented, and the result may be inartistic in the narrower meaning of form. But, of two works equally masterful in the restricted sense, the greater will be the one superior in the broad social and moral dimension; not simply in carrying a better message; rather, in so dealing with the values of life as to arouse a deeper, more reflective awareness.

IV. Ethics and Social Practice

VIRGIL C. ALDRICH

Beyond Ethics?

I. BEYOND BEING

Plato, after having described essence as Being at its best or as pure Being, made a remark that set the stage for centuries of subsequent metaphysics, ethics, and theory of value. He said that "the good . . . far exceeds essence in dignity and power."[1] On the whole, the mighty opposites that, until the turn of our own century, issued from this distinction between Being and something beyond Being can be put under two very general heads, naturalism and supernaturalism.

In this opposition, the naturalists tended to identify "what is" or Being with Nature, and to take arms against the notion of *anything* else. Even ideals and values—the good—were assigned a derivative and dependent natural status in the realm of essential Being. Essence comes first and determines everything, was the slogan of these naturalists. Beginning with the seventeenth century, in the flush of the scientific era, naturalism portrayed essence or Being as consisting of "primary qualities," those most congenial to the mathematical conception of the exact natural sciences. Beyond such Being there are only the secondary and tertiary qualities of sensation and valuation, which were thought of as subjective and only "in the mind." Remember Descartes and Galileo and Locke.

The supernaturalists reacted to this with a vengeance, but on the basis of a surprising agreement with the naturalists. They agreed on the conception of Nature as primarily the domain of the objects of scientific observation and understanding, and that the rest is indeed "in the mind." But what a mind! Metaphysical and objective idealism emerged to declare that Absolute Mind or Spirit is the comprehensive ground of the Being of everything, including

[1] B. Jowett, trans., *The Republic* (New York: Modern Library, Inc., 1941), p. 250.

Nature, transcending it and far exceeding it in dignity and power. Thus was Plato's good reinstated with a vengeance, as something beyond and better than *natural* essence or Being. The ought-to-be, the ideal (with ontological import), took precedence over what is. Kant's cautious and critical statement of this position is perhaps the best, less embarrassed with confusions than the heavy post-Kantian development culminating in Hegel.

This is an old story which the West knows and loves, and it reminds one of the similar wonderful Eastern story of the plunge from Being into Non-Being. But my concern and my present duty are to pass on to another story of the twentieth century which is not so generally well known—or loved. The nerve of the old or classical story of opposition had to do with the conflict between Being and something better than Being. Up to the turn of our century, the philosophical theses and antitheses made it look as if there were a cosmic conflict—or at least a distinction—between Being and the Good, where *even the Good is construed as an extraordinary kind or way of Being—a something* that is better than ordinary, natural existence. The Oriental story, with its beautiful and expressive paradoxes, about Non-Being approached via *neti-neti* renunciation also confirms this remark. This whole issue takes on another complexion in the twentieth century, to the account of which I now anxiously turn. We must first patiently refresh our memories of twentieth-century developments in ethics and value-theory in the West, noticing especially what has happened in that area since our last conference of a decade ago. Then I shall be equipped to deal with the main issue, the question of whether philosophy is taking us "beyond ethics."

II. CONSPECTUS OF RECENT WESTERN DEVELOPMENTS IN MORAL THOUGHT

For Anglo-American philosophers, G. E. Moore is the Plato of the twentieth century, on the following count. In his *Principia Ethica,* of 1903, we find a proposition comparable to Plato's quoted above; and mighty opposites have issued from it since then, the polar opposition being similar in form to the classical, but very different in content. We must first get a bird's-eye view of this in its inception.

Moore's proposition, declared at the beginning of the century, is that good is a non-natural quality.[2] This sounds like Plato and the modern metaphysical idealists, but let us look cautiously at Moore's meaning. In the first place, he does *not* mean that something called "good" is better than natural qualities, such as pleasant, intelligent, or even cool and sweet and bright blue. Though he calls good a non-natural quality, his main concern is *not* to assert the extraordinary being of something that far exceeds natural qualities in dignity and power. His point is a logical one, not an ontological. He is analyzing the meaning of any expression of the form "x is good," where x is any natural

[2] G. E. Moore, *Principia Ethica* (Cambridge: University Press, 1903), chap. I.

quality, thing, or state of affairs. He has noticed that one can significantly ask of *anything* natural, "Is it good?" and this to him is evidence that good cannot itself be simply identified with, or defined as, anything natural. So, he persists in taking good as a simple, unanalyzable, non-natural quality, which may or may not qualify anything in Nature. He is distinguishing the predicate "good," as of a different logical type, from any "natural" predicate, such as those listed above. To suppose that it is not this sort of non-natural predicable, and to identify it with some natural quality, such as pleasant, or object-of-interest, are to commit the "naturalistic fallacy." All philosophers who define "good" in this way—indeed, who attempt to define or analyze it in *any* way—commit this fallacy. Good is good, and that is that. Anything may be qualified by this non-natural quality, but must not be identified with it. (What it qualifies may *also* be pleasant or desired, etc., and these things will be "the goods" of life.) Moore is saying in effect that the adjective "good" has a peculiar meaning inasmuch as it does not name (stand for, refer to) any natural quality. But it *does,* he asserts, name a non-natural quality—something beyond the being of anything natural.

Such a position is apparently pregnant with a new and vexing sort of Platonism. It soon generated critical questions. How is *this* distinction between natural and non-natural to be interpreted, with its veiled logical instead of ontological concern? Is the question still the old one, about *what* "good" means and the nature of this element, or is it not now in effect a new question, namely, *how* this value-predicate and others mean? Are value-terms descriptive predicates, such as "pleasant" and "cool"? In short, are they to be treated as "cognitively" significant terms, in expressions that are true (or false) of "values"?

A great division formed around this issue, but this time it was not the old naturalism vs. supernaturalism; it was naturalism vs. non-naturalism, where *both* of these opposites were primarily concerned with the logic of valuation—the question of *how* value-expressions signify or under what controls. And so, the period of "meta-ethics" began. The new naturalists in ethics and theory of value argued that the logic of moral judgment and valuation is identical with that of the factual, natural sciences. And, to set the stage for this demonstration, they rejected Moore's notion of good as a non-natural quality intuitively prehended. The presence of such a quality would spoil the performance of ordinary empirical method, which depends on controlled observations and predictions. Values can be known, according to the twentieth-century naturalists. This means that knowledge-claims can appropriately be made in this connection; and this involved holding that "x is good" is of the same logical type as "x is edible," where both "edible" and "good" are "constructs" of the sort that are under the nice cognitive controls operative in the empirical sciences.

Before mentioning some of these naturalists, and the opposing non-naturalists, let us remember that this growing logic-and-language consciousness was not confined to philosophy. The scientists had also been jarred into this new method-consciousness by developments in physics—Einstein's special and general theories of relativity in 1905 and 1915. These, together with the strange quantum mechanics, made the scientists also wonder about *how* the language of science signifies instead of just *what* it means. The same phenomenon appeared in art, with the new formalism or abstractionism. Art analysts became obsessed with the question of how a work of art means—poem, painting, or musical composition. It is as if another stage of the self-conscious had been reached, where the "self" seemed to be man as a symbolizing animal, to use Cassirer's phrase.

But, back to the new naturalists. R. B. Perry,[3] influenced by behavioral psychology with its concern to bring psychological statements under observational controls, defined value as the object of any interest, construing interest non-introspectively. He hoped thus not only to make "good" observable but especially to make value-judgments confirmable. A valuation makes cognitive sense, under the established logic of factual inquiry. Notice that the primary concern here is not pointedly to say what value is as a quality of an object. The aim is, rather, to give an analysis of valuations which will subject them to standard confirmation, as if the question of what good "essentially" is had been outmoded.

The same motive is conspicuous in John Dewey's treatment. He argues that good is a "construction,"[4] meaning to make a methodological point rather than an ontological one. This is why this sort of naturalism is ontologically so accommodating—it leaves *that* question open. He is anxious lest moral judgments and value-judgments be exempted from the control of the ordinary logic of inquiry and decision. He notices how we cannot be said to know anything until we form a construct or concept of it which connects it with conditions of its occurrence and permits its stabilization or production at will. This is the difference featured between "having" or simply experiencing a *desired* something, on the one hand, and knowing it under controls that define it as *desirable,* on the other, with a premium being placed on the latter.

Similar remarks apply to another prominent naturalist in value-theory, C. I. Lewis.[5] The "expressive statements" which simply announce the presence of a "had" or immediate quality *(quale)* of enjoyment are not value-judgments. They make no claims to knowledge: they do not make cognitive sense. (Note what happens, on this ground, to Moore's expression of a simply intuited quality of good.) Only when value is *construed* as an objective property of something does it become knowable, and it is then expressed in "non-terminating judgments," which formulate definite expectations of various consequences of the knowledge-claim, and these either confirm the judgment or upset it—as in the case of any factual ascription of any property. Lewis goes further than Dewey in making it explicit that he is deliberately ambiguous about the description of value as a quality. He calls it vaguely a "dimension-like mode or

[3] *General Theory of Value* (New York: Longmans, Green & Co., 1926).
[4] *The Quest for Certainty* (New York: Milton Balch & Co., 1929).
[5] *Analysis of Knowledge and Valuation* (Chicago: Open Court Publishing Co., 1946), especially pp. 373–396.

quality," something like enjoyment but not to be exclusively identified with this. It is worth noticing, finally, that Lewis, unlike Dewey, distinguishes such *valuations* from *ethical* imperatives of a more Kantian sort. These, he acknowledges significantly, are *not* empirical statements, subject to cumulative experiential testing. With this distinction I shall be much concerned later, in a more general context.

These samples suffice to show that the new school of thought is appropriately called "logical naturalism," to distinguish it from the earlier metaphysical or ontological variety. I turn now to an account of its opposition, calling it "logical non-naturalism" in ethics and theory of value.

The first conspicuous (and notorious) version of this is the logical positivists', with which I shall not stay long, since it is so well known the world over. It emerged in the twenties of our century. R. Carnap and A. J. Ayer, operating under the spell of the language of physics as the paradigm, accept Moore's pronouncement that "good" (in fact, any value-term) does not denote any natural quality. But, they add that it is not used to describe or name *any* quality. Its meaning is not descriptive at all. One misinterprets its sense if he thinks it functions as an adjective of factual assertion. Such a mistake tempts one to look for a quality called "goodness" in things or in the subjective response—e.g., pleasure—of people, and the search never succeeds. This is because value-terms and ethical terms signify in a different mode or way from terms in true or false statements. They signify expressively exactly as smiles or frowns do. Their meaning is thus "emotive," and value-judgments are pseudo-statements. According to the non-naturalists, the supposition that these are confirmable propositions is the mistake of the logical naturalists, who are still haunted by the ghost of the traditional assumption that valuations are true or false by reference to something or other.[6] This concept of emotive meaning of valuations was occasionally extended to include a "motivational" or imperative dimension, making them something like grammatically veiled commands or requests. Thus, "This is wrong" would mean "Don't do this," on this interpretation.

The bible of emotivism is C. L. Stevenson's *Ethics and Language* (1944).[7] Stevenson was motivated more by models in psychology than in physics, under the influence of Ogden and Richard's *Meaning of Meaning*.[8] Though his analysis of any expression of the form "x is good" resolves it into two components, "I approve of x; do so as well"—one a factual statement, the other an imperative—yet Stevenson is an astute enough psychologist to know that this complex expression lacks the *emotive* force of the simpler "x is good," since "good" is a dynamic term that kindles favorable feelings and attitudes, and triggers action. The concept of conditioned response is prominent here. Value-terms evoke feelings and modify attitudes, without the necessary intervention

[6] A. J. Ayer, *Language, Truth and Logic* (London: Gollanz, Ltd., 1936); R. Carnap, *Philosophy and Logical Syntax* (London: K. Paul, Trench, Trübner Co., Ltd., 1935).

[7] New Haven: Yale University Press, 1944.

[8] C. R. Ogden and J. A. Richards (New York: Harcourt, Brace & Co., Inc., 1923).

of ideas, though these may incidentally intervene in the process of emotive communication. Stevenson's method of "persuasive definition" is not as well known in this context as it should be. It is in some respects his most sensitive contribution. Value-terms may be "persuasively" defined. Given a sufficiently vague term with emotive (valuational) meaning, such as "cultured," it may be connected with other terms having descriptive or cognitive meaning, such as "intelligent," "erudite," "imaginative," etc., in a persuasive definition. The effect will be to evoke a favorable response to people having such characteristics, since to be "cultured" is already granted as "good." "Cultured" means emotively, as does "good," and thus tends to confer favor on anything to which it is applied. This is the way all value-terms mean; and *how* they mean is the main question, not *what* they mean. It will be seen that defining value-terms this way certainly does not get at, or expose, the "essence" of anything for what this meant in the classical tradition. And let us remember again that it was Moore's suggestion that "good" is an indefinable, non-natural quality which was bearing this kind of meta-ethical fruit, with the spotlight of attention turned on questions of *how* expressions mean.[9]

Our story of recent positivism, also called logical empiricism, ends with a brief mention of another psychologically oriented member of the movement, C. W. Morris.[10] For him, signs or expressions signify in (at least) three "modes of signifying": designative, appraisive, and prescriptive. Valuational expressions are interpreted as signifying mainly in the two latter. What distinguishes this account from the others in this group is Morris' attempt to fix a sense of "true" which allows even appraisals and prescriptions to be capable of truth or falsity—though they do not make designative or descriptive sense. The treatment is in the framework of behavioral psychology. But the significant thing in this connection is the first sign of a breakdown of the sharp positivistic distinction between the cognitive and non-cognitive functions of language, with respect to valuational discourse. Morris' theory is also significant for its classification of "types of discourse"—metaphysical, religious, poetic, scientific—which gives it a cosmopolitan complexion, an interest which was revealed earlier in his *Paths of Life* (1942),[11] well known to many Eastern philosophers.

The deck has been cleared for the presentation of the remaining branch of this tree of logical non-naturalism, another development whose growth has by now all but hidden the positivistic ramification under its foliage, and whose contributions to *moral* philosophy have been made only in the last decade, since our last East-West conference. It is a much more subtle approach to our problems, with suggestions that do greater justice to the multifarious spirit of man as a language-using agent. This development is, on the whole, much less understood, especially in the East, than the logical positivism it is superseding with *éclat*. In fact, critics commonly make the mistake of supposing that these

[9] Moore's concessions to Stevenson are startling: see his reply in P. Schilpp, ed., *The Philosophy of G. E. Moore* (Menasha, Wisconsin: Banta Publications Co., 1942).
[10] *Signs, Language, and Behavior* (New York: Prentice-Hall, Inc., 1946).
[11] C. W. Morris, *The Paths of Life* (New York: Harper & Brothers, 1942).

new "Oxford philosophers"—conveniently called this for short—are still positivists, while what actually defines the new approach is its rejection of the logical-positivistic verification theory of meaning together with the earlier logical atomism and the tendency to hold scientific method up as the model for all serious discourse. The genius of the new philosophy is the *later* Wittgenstein, expressed at first in the nineteen-thirties in the *Blue and Brown Books*[12] (published later in 1958) and in *Philosophical Investigations* (1953).[13] The chief and the best points are made in the form of mercurial aphorisms or enigmatic suggestions which tax the imagination. We turn now to a short survey of this new current, which in the area of ethics is only a decade old, and which by all odds is the most conspicuous development in the Anglo-American world and Scandinavia during the decade.

The keynote of the Oxford philosophy is that people do all sorts of things with their living language, and these various uses are the meanings. This highlights the concept of "performatory meaning," a good first approximation to which we get in Margaret Macdonald's treatment.[14] Here the outlook is partly anthropological, like that of Malinowski in his studies of the primitive uses of language; so, the model of ritualistic performance or expression looms large, as the standard of interpretation for ethical utterance.

Macdonald rejects emotivism in ethics as featuring too lyrical, subjective, or private a mode or expression. The model of true-false factual statement must be put aside, she agrees with the emotivists, as against Moore; to say "x is good" does not describe any quality of anything. But the affair of making moral judgments is too serious, fraught with public sanction, to be characterized as emotive. They must be treated "ceremonially" and invested "with an authority to affect action. . . . Moral judgments are thus impersonal verdicts of a common moral ritual . . . they are the language of a rite in which we are all lifelong performers."[15] The analogy is with verdicts of guilty or not guilty formally uttered in a court of law. This, according to Macdonald, is *how* moral utterances mean—without making any (true-false) statement of "objective fact" or without describing any properties at all, natural or non-natural.

This theme of "performatory" meaning, fathered in the special Oxford way mainly by J. L. Austin,[16] is given a variation by H. L. A. Hart, who portrays moral discourse as having a sort of "ascriptive" sense. To say, "Fred *did* it," speaking morally, is in effect *not* simply a description or even report of an action, but the *ascription* of a responsibility, in relation to certain rights.[17] But the variation on this theme that has drawn most attention is the concept of "commendatory" meaning. To say "This is good" or "Slandering is wrong"

[12] Oxford: B. Blackwell, 1958.
[13] Oxford: B. Blackwell, 1953.
[14] "Ethics and the Ceremonial Use of Language," in Max Black, ed., *Philosophical Analysis* (Ithaca: Cornell University Press, 1950).
[15] *Ibid.*, p. 229.
[16] See his "Other Minds," in Anthony G. Flew, ed., *Essays in Logic and Language*, Second Series (New York: Philosophical Library, 1953).
[17] "The Ascription of Responsibility and Rights," in Anthony G. Flew, ed., *Essays in Logic and Language*, First Series (New York: Philosophical Library, 1951).

is to perform the act of commending or condemning something, not to describe or further characterize it. Such judgments serve to *guide* choice, and to encourage or deter actions. (They do not *goad* choice by psychological incitement, as the emotivists believe.) Reasons may be given supporting the judgments, and the reasons will generally be factual or descriptive statements about properties of things or actual social patterns of conduct. But these are not to be mistaken as "defining the meaning" of the moral judgments, since a commendation is never a (true-false) description. That value-terms have also a dimension of descriptive meaning, in addition to their primary commendatory sense, is suggested (with reservations) by R. M. Hare.[18] But the earmark of valuations is consistently held to what, in the main, is done with them, their job of commending. And this is their performatory meaning. Like C. I. Lewis, these thinkers also tend to distinguish value-terms ("good") from ethical ("right"), and both of these from duty terms ("ought")—the point I converge on later.

The more important considerations come up in connection with the question of "justification" of moral judgments in this context of the new philosophy of the language of morals and values. S. Toulmin's treatment[19] is a fair sample, culminating in a dramatic view of the logic of ultimate valuational "decisions"—a view shared by others in the movement, and one which makes it akin to other ethical philosophies on the European continent and in the Orient. I shall elaborate on this important fact later, central as it is to the concern of this, our third conference.

According to Toulmin, elementary moral judgments (commending this or that) fall under a hierarchy of rules, appeal to which justifies the judgments. There are first (moving up) the general maxims or rules of thumb governing right conduct, such as that telling lies is wrong. If these maxims themselves come under fire or are challenged, they are justified in turn by checking on their power to "harmonize" the satisfactions of members of the society. Now, if the whole "way of life" of the society is questioned, with other forms of life in view, something besides *moral* reasoning must be appealed to and a "personal decision" made, influenced by supra-moral considerations of the alternative patterns or cultures. Such an examination may comprise persuasive presentations of the alternatives, as in a great novel that gives the reader the feel of the total situations, or the agent may actually install himself in them one after another—trying them out. Choice of a way of life will not, at this level, be simply an act of *moral* decision. It will involve a crucial commitment or plunge, beyond the guidance of moral reason and will. Hare sounds a similar note, making the individual's decision look even more detached from rational considerations. Toulmin says there are traces of the existentialist mood in Hare's account. Yet, these Oxford philosophers do not intend to favor relativism in moral matters.[20] It is as if reality or Being were a character that things have

[18] *The Language of Morals* (Oxford: Clarendon Press, 1952).
[19] *The Place of Reason in Ethics* (Cambridge: University Press, 1950).
[20] Hare, *op. cit.*, p. 143. Toulmin, *op. cit.*, pp. 206–209.

only in the articulate framework of a "form of life" and its language. Things are objectively what they are only in such a reference-frame.

This subtle concept of a "form of life" is Wittgenstein's[21] in his later, more influential, phase. He associates this closely with the logic of the language, and this reminds one of Cassirer and Whorf.[22] But Wittgenstein's followers are not underwriting that kind of metaphysical idealism. Their point about language as a form of life is related to Wittgenstein's theory of aspects.[23] This tremendously fruitful concept needs to be elaborated in something like a descriptive metaphysics, and there now seems to be some recognition of the need, even among the Wittgensteinians.[24] Austin, for example, is beginning to speak of the philosopher's subject as "phenomenology of language." But more of this theme later.

On the whole, this new Oxford movement is the liveliest and most promising in current Anglo-American ethical thought. One remembers Nowell-Smith's book *Ethics*[25] also in this connection (1954). Before passing on rapidly through some other strands in the texture of the present-day moral mentality of the West, toward my main concern about East-West comparisons and constructive suggestions, let me just mention some recent efforts among sympathizers with the Oxford approach to transcend the strict individualism of the "personal-decision" idea just mentioned,[26] in favor of an intercultural principle governing these ultimate decisions, thus giving them a moral rationale, after all. Even some recent naturalists, who are not sympathizers but only begrudgingly give recognition to the new anti-descriptivists and admit that value-terms are not simply descriptive, are co-operating in this effort to find a common ground for decision by *all* moral agents.[27]

Having raised this issue of whether there is a critical stage at which the individual is thrown back on his own resources, making the act of personal decision appear to be one of creative option *in vacuo,* we are in a position to look beyond the Anglo-American scene to the European continent, at existentialism. Though this philosophy is waning, and something like a more analytical phenomenology (Husserl, Hartmann, Scheler) is being revived there, it is still sufficiently viable to demand notice. An existentialist *ethics* would be an anomaly, since the focal point of *Existenz* thinking is a metaphysical one about Being vs. Non-Being. This is just what Heidegger argues in justifying his failure to produce a specific ethics. The lack of such special ethical concern is characteristic of German thought of the last decade or more. Heidegger's dialectical metaphysics of Being provides a nook for the phenomenon called "conscience," connecting it with authenticity, but leaves it little chance to

[21] Ludwig Wittgenstein, *Philosophical Investigations* (Oxford: B. Blackwell, 1953), p. 88c.
[22] See Harry Hoyer, ed., *Language in Culture* (Chicago: University of Chicago Press, 1954).
[23] *Op. cit.*, pp. 193–215.
[24] See P. F. Strawson, *Individuals* (London: Methuen, 1959); also V. C. Aldrich, "Chess Not Without the Queen," *Proceedings of the American Philosophical Association,* 1958.
[25] P. H. Nowell-Smith, Pelican Books (Baltimore: Penguin Books, Inc., 1954).
[26] K. Baier, "The Point of View of Morality," *Australian Journal of Philosophy,* 1954, 104–135; J. Rawls, "Outline of a Decision Procedure for Ethics," *Philosophical Review,* LX, No. 2 (April, 1951), 177–197.
[27] E.g., P. B. Rice, *On The Knowledge of Good and Evil* (New York: Random House, 1955).

operate in the arena of existential conflicts, since it contains no useful regulations for conduct. Authenticity is demanded, but with a view more to *being* something than *doing* anything. Jasper's moral philosophy is comparable. The suggestion is that, as long as one loves, he may do as he pleases. "Love" here has a religio-metaphysical ring: a submissive rapport with what transcends the whole human scene of action—God as a metaphysical Absolute. A high commitment to this Absolute will give an indirect, ambiguous, provisional direction for authentic people below who are trying to do their duty. The act of commitment itself is supra-rational; there is no *logic* of obligation to this process. (Compare this with Eastern pronouncements.)

One might say, in view of such recent utterances (and earlier Hegelian ones), that the German consciousness is an a-moral one, or tends toward this. Remember also Nietzsche's *Beyond Good and Evil.*[28] And it is this spirit that has permeated much of the East, on the professional philosophical level. I think first of Nishida and Nishitani in Japan, as just two star examples. In the creative literature of our period—the last decade—there is dramatic evidence of this tendency of existentialism to put a red pencil through morality in its ethical dimension, as something to be superseded. And, again, I mention only one prime example: *The Mandarins,* by Simone de Beauvoir,[29] a devoted propagator of the existentialist faith of Jean-Paul Sartre, who is supposed to have long been working out a specific existentialist ethics but has not yet produced one. There the chief characters are portrayed as by-passing ethical constraints (under sad necessity, to be sure) in favor of liberation and progress, according to an "ethics of ambiguity." This is man's tragic circumstance. But this view has connections with communist ideology, whose position relative to ethics I shall come to later. Here, too, we are beyond ethics, with a vengeance. So much for what is being called "Situation Ethics."

Akin to this outlook is something outside professional philosophy, the new Protestant theology of Paul Tillich, consideration of which gets us back to the American scene, without breaking ties with the European. It is difficult to pick out any book of his which is specifically on ethics. The one that comes closest to qualifying is perhaps his *The Courage to Be*[30] (1952), and the very title shows that it is a metaphysical treatise on Being—with Non-Being threatening to get the better of it. Tillich's existentialism began by having some of the theological and generally religious color one would expect under the brush-strokes of a professed theologian, and some bearing on Christian morals. It has of late passed more openly over into the camp of straight metaphysics, and other theologians are at last finding this out, to their dismay. In a recent pronouncement,[31] Tillich professed a return to Essence or Being, as deserving more notice than the incipient nihilism of his previous existentialism had given it. This "essentialism" is a revival of the thought of Hegel in his earlier stage,

[28] Helen Zimmern, trans. (New York: Boni and Liveright, Inc., 1917).
[29] Cleveland: World Publishing Company, 1956.
[30] New Haven: Yale University Press, 1952.
[31] Kenyon College Lecture, 1959.

before even *The Phenomenology of Mind*,[32] though with affinities to this. And what of ethical principles? Tillich's answer is, at bottom, the old one of dialectical idealism. You get beyond them.

Reinhold Niebuhr does much better as a Christian and religious moralist[33] than his protégé Tillich. Both share the notion that the language of religion is mythic in some true or important sense of "myth," but Niebuhr does not forget this when he gets down to doing Christian ethics and theology. He is not just a philosopher as Tillich is. Man is caught in the "historical situation" and must tragically act, of necessity, at times, participating in evil with others. But over him arches the rainbow of a humanly impossible perfection, an ideal of the perfect life symbolized by Christ, functioning as a catalyst that activates as righteous a life as possible here below. Again, the idea of absolute transcendence.

The difficulty of achieving a genuine moral community of highly civilized individuals, and of disclosing its rationale if any, is also featured by the depth psychologists in the wake of Freud. Freud's own thinking on this issue is concentrated in his *Massenpsychologie* (1921),[34] in which the idea of such a society is left tense with an inner conflict. On the one hand, he makes the ruler or ruling faction look like a hypnotist with sadistic impulses, subjecting the people to a tranced obedience whose masochism permits, even invites, it. One would think, then, that he favors democratic individualism, but not so. In such a State, individuals are lonely, lost, and insecure. So, they tend naturally to escape from freedom (Erich Fromm), into the over-all social control of the Super-Ego imaged in the ruler. Yet, though Freud distrusts democracy as the final condition of well-being for the society, he hates dictatorship and is groping for a concept of individualism of some sort—individualism without optimistic liberalism or the old idea of salvation-by-education-for-democracy associated with American pragmatism. This is the problem that now preoccupies social psychologists who apply the psychoanalytic techniques to whole societies or culture-patterns. For example, David Riesman[35] characterized the earlier or rugged individual as "inner-directed" and not intelligently coordinated with the social pattern except in the limited conditions of "open capitalism," which has been outgrown. Now, another pressure-group pattern has emerged in which individuals have no core of individuality left. They are "other-directed." There is something "compulsive" about the behavior of both of these kinds of individuals. Then there are individuals who are still striving toward "autonomy"—the "saving remnant." The autonomous individual does not compulsively follow others, nor does he operate under a compulsion to flout them as does the primitive rugged individual. But, if we ask Riesman for the formula of this intelligent form of individualism, he will give the reply of

[32] J. B. Baillie, trans., 2 vols. (London: S. Sonnenschein & Co., Ltd.; New York: The Macmillan Co., 1910).

[33] *An Interpretation of Christian Ethics* (New York: Harper & Brothers, 1935).

[34] *Massenpsychologie und Ich-Analyse* (Wien: Internationale & Psychoanalytischer Verlag, 1921).

[35] *Individualism Reconsidered* (Glencoe, Ill.: Free Press, 1954), esp. chap. VI. See also, Herbert Marcuse, *Eros and Civilization* (Boston: Beacon Press, 1955) for a prospectus with a more Jungian flavor.

a man on the threshold of unfamiliar ground: "We know almost nothing about the factors that make for such positive results; it is easier to understand the sick than to understand why some stay well."[36] This uncertainty is characteristic of others in the same camp, as is the general agreement that a new concept of a sound individualism is in the air, and needs to be captured and formulated.

In another camp, with a more religious and traditional orientation, this something new is being called, not the new individualism, but the "new conservatism," whose hero in social, political, and religious thought is Edmund Burke, in his *Reflections on the Revolution in France* (1790).[37] Russell Kirk's recent *The Conservative Mind* (1953)[38] is the bible of the present-day group of new conservatives.[39] Their outlook is comparable to Toynbee's in history (in his middle period) and to Eliot's in literature. (Eliot is known to have said that he is an Anglo-Catholic in religion, a royalist in politics, and a classicist in literature.)

These theorists, most of whom are in the United States, find the depth-psychology approach objectionable, but they share with those psychologists the concern to reach an adequate concept of individuality and freedom and the conviction that "reason" is hedged in on all sides by factors that make it fairly impotent. Like Burke, they see the well-being of the individual as thoroughly dependent on institutions, the more hallowed by tradition the better; and the political institution of the State is subordinate to the religious one of the Church, all under God. The wise individual will be institution-directed. The rational intelligence of the individual is suspect, and is demoted to the position of servant of something higher, in which service is perfect freedom. "The rationalist or liberal frames his decisions in accordance with some theory derived from an abstract notion of universal truth; the conservative takes into consideration an extremely wide range of concrete acts. . . ."[40] The new conservative, in short, eschews rational constructions in favor of devout action under spiritual regulation from on high, manifest in crucial events and interpreted by an institutional élite. The recrudescence of this sort of spiritual élitism favors *some* form of aristocracy. (Compare Indian thought on this count.) It should be noted that not all the new conservatives stress religious fundamentals. For example, Walter Lippmann, pandit of the *New York Times*, has taken, on the whole, a more secular stand in favor of a new conservative view of man's good, making the theory look more like a new humanism. *All* of them fear the possible "tyranny of the majority," which threatens most in democracy as usually conceived. And it is this that has created the need for a new concept of individualism—beyond even the best insights of Dewey's once-influential social philosophy. The New Conservatism at present is itself not

36 *Op. cit.*, p. 116.

37 London: J. Dodsley, 1790.

38 *The Conservative Mind, from Burke to Santayana* (Chicago: H. Regnery Co., 1953).

39 Others in or associated with this movement are: Walter Lippmann, Clinton Rossiter, and Francis Wilson. See F. Wilson, *The Case for Conservatism* (Seattle: University of Washington Press, 1951). Also, Peter R. E. Viereck, *Conservatism from John Adams to Churchill* (Princeton: D. Van Nostrand Co., Inc., 1956), a good short survey of the whole movement since Burke.

40 Viereck, *op. cit.*, p. 108.

widely influential—it appeals mainly to church and university leaders and professors of political science—except as an expression (not a cause) of the world-wide worry about the place of reason in human affairs.

Some of the omissions in this brief survey will be made good in the general interpretations and comparisons that follow. To this task, including reflections on the bearing of the theories on actual social practices in the West, I now turn.

III. BEYOND ETHICS?

There is a position already magnificently outlined which sets the stage for my final consideration about the present moral mentality of East and West. This is the one that F. S. C. Northrop takes in his *The Meeting of East and West* (1946),[41] and especially his *The Taming of the Nations* (1952).[42]

Northrop's position is too well known to call for elaboration here. Let me be brief. There is, for him, a very general distinction between the genius of the East and that of the West. The mind of the Orient is intuitive, spiritually sensitive to the "undifferentiated continuum," as ultimate reality. So, the Eastern sage will tend to void the personal identity of his ego in the vastness of the real, and not to make much of differences in theories and rules of conduct, all of which are superficial. To achieve this, one must not be preoccupied with activity in the framework of ideas, desires, and goals of action. Calling the blessed result thus arrived at either Being or Non-Being makes only a terminological difference—Brahman, Nirvāṇa, Tao, Jen. But, moral or ethical striving presupposes this framework of unreal distinctions. So, ethics and morality will be tentative, to be finally dissolved in the solvent of the Absolute Vastness. There can be no ultimate concern to take a definite ethical stand. The moral function of a wise man, in this view, will be that of the mediator seeking compromise, without himself having a fixed ethical position.

The Western mind is logical. Its genius is the Word, the "theoretically given logos of the classical West."[43] In its pristine purity and first intention, this is the principle of universalism in theoretical constructions, which are the fruits of ideational intelligence. In principle, there is one true theory, one law, one institution (political or religious) for all men. There has been a fragmentation of this by unfortunate mistakes in the West: dogmatic absolutism instead of constitutionalism in politics, half-baked Protestantism instead of genuine Catholicism in religion, misconceptions in philosophies leading to a pluralism of conflicting theories of Nature and man, etc. This has been the "fall from grace," symbolized by the story of the Garden of Eden and its misappropriated Tree of Knowledge.

To be moral, under this aegis, is to know and to respect in action the Law Universal. This taxes both the intellect and the will of the ethical person more than his intuitive sensibilities. Anyway, this is the characteristic *tendency* of

[41] New York: The Macmillan Co., 1946.
[42] New York: The Macmillan Co., 1952.
[43] *The Taming of the Nations*, p. 226. See also chap. V.

the Western mind in moral action. Moral obligation is a fixed and ultimate thing.

Northrop's conception of Eastern morality as provisional is underwritten by our representative from India, Mahadevan, both in his essay of a decade ago at the East-West Conference[44] and in his "Beyond Ethics" (1953).[45] "One cannot attain the goal [of life] so long as one remains merely moral."[46] Being moral is too closely tied in with the intellectual machinery of theoretical constructs and the drive of desires influencing the will. To be sure, there are duties to be fulfilled, but with as little desire as possible and with the sustained realization that true guidance comes from a supra-moral source, not from the etiquette or the imperatives of moral intelligence. From a different angle, a Zen Buddhist concurs: "In Buddha-mind there is nothing good, nothing bad; nothing to be called right, nothing to be called wrong."[47]

Now, as I take on the role of moderator, I first remember with gratitude Radhakrishnan's warning that all "immense simplifications of the complicated pattern of reality are misleading."[48] Then I bare my forehead to the light of what seems to be the dawn of a new philosophical entente between East and West, and proceed.

I find Northrop's metaphysical scheme too general to serve as an instrument of exposition or correction that does justice to either the Occidental or the Oriental mind. But he has tempered this by recognizing the diversities on both sides of the fence, and this description of the mentality of the East with respect to morality or ethics is significant and true. (Whether this is *explained* by his metaphysics of theoretic (determinate) and aesthetic (indeterminate) components of reality remains, however, an interesting question.) There is little doubt that, according to the Oriental view, though man is *in* a stratum of ethical being and action, he is not essentially *of* it. The result of our second East-West conference may seem to deny this; it does not really. The Asian is provisional and compromising in his moral conduct. He is head, shoulders, and heart above the plane of *ethical* concern, while his nether parts are caught in its substructure of *karma-yoga*. In this connection, it appears that Charles A. Moore's argument to the effect that the Easterner is fundamentally moral is an overstatement,[49] while Northrop, backed by Mahadevan, is nearer the truth.

To unsnarl this complex issue, I must conclude by distinguishing the various ways of getting and being beyond ethics, in theory and social practice, noticing cases both in the Eastern and in the Western camps. Surprising parallels and differences will emerge, with some suggestion of a new over-all concept of morality. These ways are:

[44] In Charles A. Moore, ed., *Essays in East-West Philosophy* (Honolulu: University of Hawaii Press, 1951), pp. 317–335.

[45] Mahadevan, "Beyond Ethics," in T. M. P. Mahadevan, *et al*, eds., *The Indian Philosophical Congress*, Silver Jubilee Volume (Madras: Indian Philosophical Congress, 1950), pp. 43–54.

[46] In Moore, ed., *Essays in East-West Philosophy*, p. 322.

[47] Nyogen Senzaki, "Mentorgarten Dialogue," *Chicago Review*, XII, No. 2 (Summer, 1958), 37–40.

[48] S. Radhakrishnan, *Eastern Religions and Western Thought* (2nd ed., London: Oxford University Press, 1940), p. 74.

[49] Moore, ed., *Essays in East-West Philosophy*, chap. XXII.

A. We might notice, first, in passing, a way to get beyond ethics that is trivial in some respects, and becomes a bore if dwelt with too long. This is the way of meta-ethics, the study of the use or function of ethical expressions. But we must remember that even this movement, cavalierly overlooked by the tradition-minded philosopher, was and is motivated by a question of cardinal philosophical importance moving us all, namely, the problem of the place of reason in moral experience, thought, and action. The new language-philosophers of the Oxford ilk make this explicit, in a more profound consideration than that of the logical positivists. This has already been suggested. Also, such an approach, conscious of the various ways expressions mean even within the single area of moral judgment and valuation, clears the path for more progress in substantive ethics or ethics proper, the study of the non-linguistic conditions of morality. Metaphysicians, mystics, and theologians have themselves suggested *some* such distinctions from the beginning. Remember, too, that the findings of the new meta-ethicists do not support subjectivism in moral theory or the old relativism—though neither does it aid and abet traditional rationalism or objectivism.

B. Then there is the way of existentialism, with its metaphysics of the vacuum in which lonely men exist (*Existenz*), act, and choose, *before* essence and order are realized by creative fiat, under no cosmic regulation. Schopenhauer's vision of the irrational will, hungrily and desperately "objectifying" itself to get *something* to cope with and to depend on for provisional satisfactions, provides a classical frame for the current existentialist picture. This existentialist consciousness or mood is nihilistic, in which *everything* is provisional, including certainly the ethical concern with its objectives. The spirit of Hīnayāna Buddhism is conspicuously akin to this, as also is Taoism on some counts. All this, of course, does not mean that men will not take any ethical action. It means, rather, that they will act under concocted rules. The religious or Kierkegaardian existentialists provide a transcendent principle in God, the approach to which, however, is thoroughly irrational and supra-moral—a notion that brings Tillich into this camp. In fact, Tillich's manner of thinking and speaking about this suggests that man's final and highest comprehension places him above even religious theism—something that any good Hegelian (or Buddhist) would assert. So, one's ethical (to say nothing of religious) procedure is indeed quite tentative. A definite ethical regulation is not to be had, or a specifically ethical theory. The human spirit is left as a pulsation between Being and Non-Being, with the "courage to be" as its only moral directive.

C. Mysticism's way of transcending ethics is classically exhibited in the East, and on this I have already touched. The metaphor may be either that of up or down. The former I have already used—head and heart above, etc.—as have most of the great Oriental mystics. But the below-ethics picture is also powerfully suggestive and frequently used. The image then is of sinking into the universal deep, and of dissolving the limitations of the finite ego there—though this will be something like "pouring milk into milk." The experience of sinking into a profound sleep is a favorite example. In the Upaniṣads, Āruni says to his son, "Now, when one is sound asleep; composed, serene, and knows no dream. . . . That is Brahman."[50] This has the true ring of any consistent and final mysticism, and carries with it the suggestion of a condition beyond the wakeful and strident concerns of the ethical consciousness of the individual-in-action. Of course, there is the paradoxical notion of the possibility of being wisely asleep even while one acts, in a kind of trance of detachment, and there is some genuine wisdom in practicing this. But, even then, the point of the mystic is that there is something ultimate one had better keep in mind if he is not to become the slave of ethical concern. And this, too, as I shall finally argue, is important to realize. But with a different emphasis.

D. The metaphor of depth reminds us of depth psychology and its way of getting beyond ethics. In its Freudian form, the theory is clearly distinguishable from mysticism. Its method requires it to eschew *normative* standards of evaluation and moral judgment in favor of a clinical one. What psychoanalysis does is simply to uncover causes or motives of the conscious behavior of the ego, sandwiched between the dark subliminal Id beneath and the Super-Ego above, whose social pressure tames or civilizes the beast below as much as possible, in the wakeful personal performance of the individual. As Riesman said, these psychologists cure sick people, without exactly knowing what the norm of health is—and without meaning to make moral judgments or develop an ethical theory. In the Jungian version, the concepts (archetypal images, etc.) become even more metaphysical, and so the color is more congenial both to religion and to a mystical theory, though still without explicit bearing on what one *ought* to do in an ethical sense of the term. Zimmer's interpretation of the philosophical mind of India in these terms is a significant example.[51]

E. What might be called evolutionary-goal philosophies also tend to get beyond ethics, in a characteristic way. And I do not mean primarily the old Darwinian and Spencerian naturalism, as formulated in Huxley's *Evolution and Ethics* (translated into Chinese in 1898).[52] Nietzsche's case is much more significant, and so is that of communism under the spell of Marx and Lenin. It is the analysis of such more ideological and romantic cases that discloses what we now need most to do as moral philosophers, in a meeting of Eastern and Western minds.

To make this final crucial point, I must first remind you of the grand distinction, in the history of moral philosophy, between respect-for-law theories (deontic), on the one hand, and value-realization (axiological and telic), on the other. Generally speaking, the former have been "formalistic," stressing ethical rectitude even where this is at the expense of valuable goals that might have been realized without the ethical restrictions. They have defined duty as the requirement of conformity to rules or forms of *correct* procedure, in a law-

[50] S. Radhakrishnan and Charles A. Moore, eds., *A Source Book in Indian Philosophy* (Princeton: Princeton University Press, 1957), p. 68.
[51] Heinrich Zimmer, *Philosophies of India* (New York: Pantheon Books, 1956).
[52] T. H. Huxley, *Evolution and Ethics, and Other Essays* (New York: D. Appleton and Company, 1896).

abiding spirit and for the sake of moral character-building. The value-realization theories have, on the other hand, subordinated such rectitude (rightness, righteousness, virtue) to the goods of life or at least to a good *something,* defining duty primarily in the light of attaining the latter (the "good" vs. the "right"). Thus does the *ethical* (right) appear antithetical to the *valuable* (good), and the question of duty or what one ought to do becomes problematic, sometimes agonizingly so in specific cases. That the right and the good are independent and occasionally incompatible principles of duty is not just an appearance. It is a fact, structuring the theater of human existence, generating there the tragic sense of life and the penitent appeal to a transcendental source for forgiveness and a final redemption beyond our power as human beings. When Gautama Buddha left his wife and child for the sake of the *good,* he violated a rule of *right* action. He broke a promise. He was being unethical, which he sadly sensed, though it was his genius to fulfill his duty in but one of its dimensions, the axiological. Attempts to make one of these principles derivative from, or to define one in terms of, the other have failed. So, J. S. Mill fails in his conception of the foundations of *right* conduct (duty) under ethical rules, by a too exclusive featuring of the goal of striving—the *good* as the general happiness. He was reacting against Kant, who made the opposite mistake of leaving valuable consequences (goals) of action completely out of the consideration of dutiful conduct.

I am suggesting that moral philosophy has two distinct, irreducible, and co-ordinate principles to keep in view while developing a concept of Duty (this time with a capital). Questions about the *good* or the valuable, and the logic of value-judgments, are about a property or state of being as the goal of conduct. Questions about the *right* or the ethical, and the logic of ethical judgments, concern the imperatives of correct procedure in the attainment of the goal, to the point of ignoring the latter if necessary to ethical righteousness. And Duty is to be conceived and defined by reference to the demands of *both* distinct sets of imperatives: ethical imperatives and value-imperatives, there being no pre-established harmony between them on the plane of actual human striving ("right" and "good," with "ought" as the tantalizing connective).

Let us look at the communist mentality and practice in the framework of this suggestion. There the goal-oriented value-imperatives dominate, and duty is conceived mainly under this head, at the expense of the ethical. This is the communist's way of getting beyond *ethics*—not beyond values. This ideology plainly favors amoralism (in the form of non-ethical concern) in conduct, even explicitly in some of its literature (e.g., *The Mandarins,* and Arthur Koestler's *Darkness at Noon*[53]), invoking evolution and revolution in support of a swift and ruthless drive toward the realization of values. And the ultimate goal is pictured as a social condition in which the need for institutionalized ethical regulation will have withered away completely. When men are quite good, they

[53] New York: The Macmillan Company, 1941.

are quite beyond ethics; and they are eventually going to be quite good. Ethical considerations should not be allowed to slow up progress toward that goal.

This is a lopsided philosophy of duty, nourished by a sentimental and optimistic metaphysics of human nature. Human nature demands that action be both ethical and valuable, though this does produce tension and conflict in sensitive moral experience. Being a man can be *defined* by this dual demand. The recognition of either set of imperatives in the human situation may tend to minimize the other, yet the total demand of Duty makes both mandatory. To operate too exclusively under just one principle or the other tends to make monsters of men. The Puritan mind[54] has been guilty of the mistake of conceiving duty too much in the dimension of ethical rectitude under a Kantian pattern, while the communist mentality has sinned in the direction of value-realization beyond ethics. The classic lament of Boris Pasternak's *Dr. Zhivago*[55] is to the point. Larissa sadly notices Strelnikov's face become an abstract symbol of an impersonal collective drive toward a valuable goal which The Party aims to realize, flouting ethical or moral considerations of persons as individuals along the way. The communist does this with the sense of doing his duty. And he cannot be *simply* refuted. He is doing his duty (little d), but not his Duty (capital), which requires more than the urgent and sincere reaching for values. It demands also that the action taken to realize them be ethical, even where this slows progress toward the goal. The rules governing this matter of human life-and-death make a sort of ultimate game of living wisely. You can win only by obeying the dual requirement of Duty. It is rather like another game that can be imagined. Suppose there are roses (values) in a box with a small aperture (ethical restrictions). One has a short time to get the roses out through the opening, and he wins the game who gets most out without injury to the flowers. The game of Duty is like that: there are values which can be possessed only under the restriction of ethical imperatives, such as prohibit lying, cheating, slandering. Above all, they prohibit using individual persons as mere means to ends, howsoever valuable the ends. Disregarding this rule deforms the values that are too ruthlessly possessed.

As Mahadevan has said, the mind of India is value-oriented in practically all of its thinking. "Indian philosophy is essentially a philosophy of values."[56] But what this means to the mystical Indian is different in a very significant respect from what it means to a Chinese communist who was conditioned by the Neo-Confucianism of, say, K'ang Yu-wei (of the latter half of the nineteenth century) to receive the Marxist idea of a secular, social goal as the final value, the supreme good.[57] What the Indian philosophy of values calls the final or supreme value redeems it from requiring harsh treatment of individuals. It is, rather, a compassionate plea for a higher mode of being, transcending the

[54] See Herbert W. Schneider, *The Puritan Mind* (Ann Arbor: University of Michigan Press, 1957) for an excellent, sympathetic account.

[55] Max Hayward and Manya Harari, trans. (New York: Pantheon Books, 1958).

[56] Moore, ed., *Essays in East-West Philosophy*, p. 317.

[57] O. Brière, *Fifty Years of Chinese Philosophy*, L. G. Thompson, trans. (London: George Allen & Unwin Ltd., 1956).

painful or sorrowful distinction between the ethical and the valuable.[58] In this light, if we still call the Most High "good" or "valuable," we must realize that we are using these terms not in their ordinary signification but as Spinoza used them, in application to the Absolute. Such meaning as they then retain, if any, is open only to mystical or religious insight, and closed to philosophical *statement*.

Spinoza also called this human wisdom at its height the "intellectual love of God." I suggest that the voice of Duty at its transcendent apex, above the ramification into the two little voices of ethical and valuational imperatives, which regulate us here below, is the voice of Love moving us to that compassionate, trans-rational understanding of one another which tempers the tragic complications into which men are born, and among which they live and die. Our ultimate task, as philosophers of East and West, is the dedicated study of this concept of Duty, especially in its tantalizing dual requirement that men live with a respect for both values *and* ethics—since this is how we must live as men, if not as gods. The formula that respects and resolves this duality is the one that, on the whole, the Western mind in moral action is *trying* to abide by, without a clear understanding of what the formula is. The West is *not* content, as the East *tends* to be despite its demurrers, with the solution of salvation by transcendence of physical existence. We Westerners continue to love *this* world, though our love has in recent decades become somewhat desperate. This-worldliness is what, by and large, distinguishes us from our Eastern colleagues. We like the expression of a modern Western painter who loved colorful things: "This earth . . . the paradise of gods"—though hell encroach upon and darken it as it quite certainly does. Or, a line from Handel's *Messiah* may do, if the mood is religious: "Though worms destroy my body, yet *in my flesh* shall I see God." To the Westerner, bodies are wonderful, though a source of corruption. He wants a formula that saves him in the flesh, while bringing his spirit to full flower. And he believes that no Easterner really means to reject such a formula. The real problem is to find it.

QUESTION: This distinction between the ethical (right) and the valuable (good) is not clear. For example, deception is not only unethical but is at the same time a disvalue. Or, if you want a positive example, telling the truth is valuable (though also ethical). Why separate these moral concepts?

ANSWER: Deceiving is a disvalue (bad) only in relation to its unfortunate consequences, such as fear, ill-health, impoverishment, etc. These latter are disvalues, strictly speaking, or "in themselves," whereas deception, in itself, as an action, is unethical (wrong) by violating the ethical imperative of veracity. Similar remarks hold for the positive example. If you do not separate these concepts, you cannot adequately account for the agonizing duality of moral endeavor.

[58] P. T. Raju refers to the Most High as "the Great Spirit . . . transcending his relations to matter and society," which nicely marks off the Indian philosophy from the communistic, though both are goal-oriented in *some* sense. In Moore, ed., *Essays in East-West Philosophy*, p. 227.

HERBERT W. SCHNEIDER

American Traits and Principles

The peoples who settled in America brought with them much of the cultural heritage which the nations of Europe share. The filling up of the so-called "New World" has been referred to by historians as "the expansion of Europe." Today the various American peoples represent something more than merely the expansion of Europe, but they are still tied to Europe. Americans would not dream of detaching themselves from their European heritage, despite their political independence, for without it they would be unintelligible to themselves. Neither their history nor their present, neither their traditions nor their aims could be what they are without this continuity and community with Europeans. But the new environments under which wandering Europeans have found themselves in the Americas have added to the complexities of Western life and thought; they have created new applications for old ideas, new experiments in living, and new interpretations of traditional values. In addition, we must take into account the substantial non-European elements that have been introduced into American cultures, some of them borrowed from the American natives, others from Africa and Asia.

I shall try to indicate in summary fashion the dominant intellectual and moral traits and ideas that have emerged within the relatively brief history of the United States of America as guiding principles and ideals of thought-in-action. I shall describe seven such factors in American life. They are not necessarily distinctive of American culture (other peoples share some of them), but together they constitute a specialized pattern of practical philosophy. They do not form a single school or system of philosophy, for they bring together elements from various -isms. They are more indebted to idealism than to materialism, more realistic than pragmatic, more empirical than positivist. In any case, they live together loosely, forming no coherent system; they are compatible enough to practice, but not rationally unified.

I. INTERNATIONAL CHARACTER OF THE AMERICAN PEOPLE

Until about a century ago there were many philosophers and politicians, both Northern and Southern, who hesitated to speak of "the people of the United States." They insisted that the United States is composed of many peoples, united, or, rather, federated politically, but not welded culturally into a single people. The Americans, they said, may be a nation but not yet a people.[1] This is not a merely verbal issue. The important fact is that in all the United States, especially and notably here in the State of Hawaii, there live, all mixed together, people who elsewhere would live separated. In Europe, Germans, Swedes, Italians, and Spanish live side by side, segregated, whereas here they live mingled inextricably. And not only Europeans but Africans and Asians. It never was true, in spite of what Europeans may think, that the Americans are an Anglo-Saxon people. The Spanish and French were here before the English. There were Russians on the Pacific Coast. African slaves were brought in early. During the nineteenth century the country quickly filled up with families from all corners of the earth and of the most varied cultures. The majority soon learned to speak a variety of English, but English has never been the exclusive language of Americans in their daily life; many languages are still current. And, even where the English language is used, there survive all kinds of non-English cultural traits—moral, religious, artistic. American folk arts are variations on varieties of various other peoples. To be international is an essential aspect of what it means to be American. Here, international relations are no longer external; they are internal relations.

This does not mean that Americans are cosmopolitan—far from it. There have been noted Americans who were notably cosmopolitan—Benjamin Franklin, Thomas Jefferson, William James, Henry Adams, J. P. Morgan, to mention a few of them. Abroad, these men have been regarded as 100% Americans, and justly so, but they themselves thought of themselves as citizens of the world and thought of America as a member of the community of nations with a "decent respect for the opinion of mankind." But the great majority of Americans, like the great majority of any country, are foreign to foreigners; their horizons are limited. They are not "men of the world," but usually without being conscious of it they are cultural pluralists. National solidarity among Americans does not imply cultural uniformity. Europeans accuse Americans of being conformists, all exhibiting the same "mass culture" or mass lack of culture, but no

[1] On this subject, see the later writings of John C. Calhoun; Francis Lieber, "On Nationalism and Internationalism," in *The Miscellaneous Writings of Francis Lieber* (Philadelphia: J. B. Lippincott & Co., 1881), Vol. II, p. 221; John C. Hurd, *The Theory of our National Existence* (Boston: Little, Brown & Co., 1881), and *The Union-State* (New York: D. Van Nostrand Co., 1890); T. I. Cook and A. B. Leavelle, "German Idealism and American Theories of the Democratic Community," *Journal of Politics*, V, No. 4 (October, 1943), 213–236.

careful observer of American life and thought could come to such a conclusion.[2] American diversity is not merely a fact of historical origins but a present reality which has deep moral and philosophical implications. Speculation about a future race of robots is still speculation and applies not merely to Americans. The mere geographical diversity of the United States produces significant regional differences, quite apart from the historical factors which have been mentioned. From the European view and with European conceptions of what a "country" is, the United States, like India, is more of a "sub-continent" than a country. A wide range of tolerance and sympathy is here a necessity; without it sociability would be impossible. The French conception of *fraternité*, implying a general agreement on basic values, is here an impractical ideal: diversity goes deep, to the very bottom, and Americans in both city and country must be neighborly with fellow citizens whose ideas, faiths, and customs may be quite foreign to them, and for whom they may have little respect. Consequently, among the very first principles of American society must be respect for diversity itself. It is possible that this may change soon and that Americans will become as stereotyped as they are supposed to be, but, for the present, American habits and ideals must be those of an international community and culture. These facts have been father to the ideals, and social necessity the mother of moral invention.

This inter-cultural mixture is not an unmixed blessing: it creates moral and aesthetic difficulties. Such a culture lacks authenticity and integrity; it is confused and confusing. But it may be creative, for it has many possibilities which more stable and unified cultures lack. And it need not be superficial, for variety and conflict naturally stimulate reflection, criticism, experimentation, and progress. Whatever be the values and defects of American society, in it are thrown together human beings from the whole world who are physically compelled to have a sense of human rights; it thus becomes a laboratory in international relations for the whole of mankind. Here in Hawaii it is needless to dwell on this fact; sociologists and anthropologists long ago pointed to these Islands as a very significant and successful experiment in international living and thinking.

The most serious problem which the American mixture of peoples has produced is the problem of transforming large numbers of Negroes, descendants of slaves, into citizens with equal rights. The presence of a large slave population in early America threatened to create a permanent caste system in the slave-holding States. Since the whole republican tradition of the European settlers was in opposition to class society, and since the Constitution of the Federal Union and those of many of the States presupposed such republican equality as a basic political principle, it soon became apparent to most American leaders and moralists, including those of the South, that there was a flat contradiction between the economics of slavery and the politics of the republic, and that in

[2] For a judicious discussion of this problem by a British student of American life, see D. W. Brogan, *The American Character* (New York: A. A. Knopf, 1944).

some way or other slaves would have to be transformed into citizens. Whatever may be said about the economic classes in the United States, there has been from the early days a persistent opposition not only to the introduction of feudal classes but to the whole idea of classes or castes as a social and legal institution. But the large slave population created a large problem which is still unsolved. The Civil War, Lincoln's Emancipation Proclamation, and the ensuing Constitutional Amendments settled the legal principle, but the practical and moral problem of creating equal rights and classless communities is still troubling the country. The decision of the Supreme Court in 1954 prohibiting racially segregated public schools, in which the three Southern Justices concurred, not only made the legal issue clear, but also reasserted the determination of the people as a whole to overcome racial discrimination in fact as well as in principle. Just because there seems to be this general determination, both legal and moral, to solve the problem thoroughly and not to permit racial castes to take shape in any way, the whole ideal of inter-cultural and international pluralism is being put to a severe test. There is little doubt in the minds of most Americans that this pluralism will be vindicated in practice, but the inherent difficulties to be faced will probably plague the country for several generations, especially the Southern villages and the Northern cities. Industrialization is aiding in the solution of social desegregation—in America as everywhere else in the world, including Asia—but it has its own dangers in regard to economic segregation.

The practical and theoretical acceptance of cultural pluralism in the United States tends to generate habits and ideals for internationalism generally. At least, it serves as a concrete demonstration that a single world-culture is neither necessary nor desirable. Men with very different traditions and interests can live together in peace and community without sacrificing their diversity. Differences are a cultural asset if they are treated as such. The United States' motto, *E Pluribus Unum,* refers only to its federal type of government; culturally the United States stands for *In Pluribus Unum.* A composite culture may nonetheless be a genuine composition.

II. FAITH IN THE LAW OF THE LAND

The written American Constitution was framed consciously on the basis of considerable practical experience, but it was justified to the people by its framers on the ground of painstaking philosophical reflection and criticism. It was intended to be more than British Common Law; it was not to be a natural, slow growth, habitually respected though not formulated; it was to be an institution, made to order. Thomas Jefferson, who was a disciple of Montesquieu, knew perfectly well that according to the philosophical principles of Montesquieu the law of the land must conform to the spirit of the people, but he hoped, sometimes desperately, that the spirit of the American people could be molded by the law of the land. And this hope has been partially justified. It was Jefferson, more than any other of the founding fathers, who insisted on the first ten amendments and who believed that amendments should come frequently. He conceived the Constitution as something formative, and not absolute or rigid; people and law must adapt their "spirits" to each other. Jefferson's theory has proved correct. The Constitution has been amended and adapted to other American institutions which have developed less consciously than the law. But basic to the system of amendment is a spirit of loyalty to the Constitution and respect for the Supreme Court. These are deeply ingrained in the American conscience, and conflicts centering about the Supreme Court are morally supreme conflicts for American citizens. Even the Supreme Court is subject to "amendment" or "packing" (depending on your point of view), but such tampering must not endanger the institution itself. An attack on the Supreme Court is a revolutionary gesture, and is treated as such.

Lacking the European concept of "the State," being content with an unorthodox federation of States that have ceased to be States, the political consciousness and philosophy of Americans demand a basic legal framework to carry the burden which is usually placed upon an all-inclusive, cultural order or State in the traditional sense. The concept of *Kulturstaat,* developed in nineteenth-century Germany and used as an ideal in many countries is foreign to American philosophy and inapplicable to American institutions. Americans do not think of their political union as the sum and substance of all their institutions; their political ideas must be adapted to the pluralistic nature of their society and culture. They think of Society not as "the social order" but as a collective name for societies, which are more or less autonomous, held together, not by a State or *central* government, but by a legal framework to which the federal government itself is subject. This framework, being merely legal, is constitutive of the public moral order, but this order is one of several and does not constitute the whole of American society.

There is a danger, to be sure, that the Constitution and its Supreme Court become a fetish; but Americans, like any other people, must hold something sacred and inviolable; otherwise peace is impossible, as anyone who has eyes and ears must be convinced. But what is held in sacred trust is not a document or a decision but the law of the land as a *process* of adjudication. Jurisdiction is trusted because it is adjustment. And adjustment must be carried on continually. This trust in formalized law as morally basic goes back historically to the Greeks in the West, but it has found a revival and a vitality in the United States which comes, not from history, but from philosophy, and the philosophy comes from hard experience and practical need. Just because the American people is loosely constituted and American culture is carelessly composed, the citizens must put their common faith in something very common, which is "the law of the land" conceived as the very essence of their community. Americans hold together, not by friendship, not by *solidarité,* not by a *volonté générale,* not by public spirit, not by a common good or goal, but by an unshaken determination to live "under law." Jurists and philosophers have tried to justify this determination by preaching that justice and peace themselves are "under law" rather than above it. By this doctrine they do not mean, or should not mean, that the only justice is legal justice and the only rights civil rights. They must concede that peace and justice are the ends and that law is the means. But they are convinced, on empirical grounds, that law must be *the* means. As Emerson said, "The end pre-exists in the means." It is a basic duty to pursue justice and peace lawfully. This is moral philosophy; whether it is also the theory of freedom is a debated question.

Such considerations prove that American respect for the law of the land is more than a legal matter. They prove that there exists in the American people a moral bond of union or "common faith" which is conceived in secular terms but operates as a religious commitment. This basic morale, for which the Constitution is more a symbol than a cause, is what Montesquieu conceived as "the spirit of the laws." It cannot be defined in terms of "the American way of life," which is largely a European myth, nor does it presuppose a unity of ends or ideals. It is a moral bond in the narrower sense, a community of responsibilities, a sharing of burdens, a democracy of labor. This secular morality, grounded in daily life, can be and must be a genuine union for a people which is not united in religious communion, nor in political policy, nor in economic interests. To use philosophical jargon, it is not a teleological structure, but a deontological order. It is not a community of ends and means, but of reciprocity. It is a working agreement to tolerate division of labor—not merely division of responsibilities within a process of co-operation, but division in the sense of diversified production. Such a working democracy does not depend on universal co-operation, in the sense that a co-operative enterprise implies unity of aim, but, rather, on the willingness to maintain a public environment in which variegated labor can thrive in freedom and peace. Some such moralistic explanation must be given to the spirit and structure of American democracy. It does not imply a rigid conformity to the Constitution or a conformism in taste and manners. It is an "uncovenanted society of free spirits" whose union is not in their freedom of spirit but in their concern for each other's freedom. As James Thurber has put it humorously, "*Laissez faire* and let *laissez faire*" is not a principle of anarchy, but an agreement to promote liberty. Such secular morality can find expression in a wide variety of religious communions, and explains what often puzzles foreign observers, how Americans can live religiously in such a profusion of sects and cults. The secular common faith is common to many religious faiths, and not derived from them.

Americans are well aware that their Constitution is now operating quite differently from the way its framers intended it to operate, and they know, too, that the Amendments are being used for purposes which they were not intended to serve. They are compelled to admit that law itself is fallible, at best an experimental art. Nevertheless, they are committed morally to making this experiment a success, and the criterion of its success is, as I have just said, its ability to promote peace, justice, and freedom. For this reason, Americans are also committed to taking very seriously their agreement to enforce as if it were the law of the land the extension of the Bill of Rights which is contained in the United Nations' Universal Declaration of Human Rights, for in this declaration there is a more explicit definition of the ends which law is supposed to serve.

III. THE LOVE OF FREEDOM

The effectiveness of bills of rights depends ultimately on the love of freedom; unless freedom is cherished, rights will not be respected. To love freedom is an elementary human trait on which Americans have no monopoly. But an American is taught to be conscious of the need for freedom and aware of the dangers which threaten the enjoyment of traditional liberties. In the beginning, America was largely an escape mechanism for Europeans who expected to be able to live in the new world or "wilderness" a life of complete liberty—each minding his own affairs. This romantic conception of American freedom received its most ardent expressions during the first half of the nineteenth century, when Europe felt the throes of reaction and when immigration to America seemed the only and the universal panacea. I cite two examples: one taken from a description of American democracy before the French Revolution, the other from 1838, when democracy was growing in America and suffering setbacks in Europe.

In 1782 there appeared in London a small volume of *Letters from an American Farmer*,[3] written to his British friends but also intended for translation into French. The author was a French gentleman named Michel-Guillaume Jean de Crèvecoeur, who had emigrated to England and assumed the name of J. Hector St. John de Crèvecoeur and who then became a gentleman farmer in America. In one of his letters he attempts to answer the question, What is an American? His answer is as follows:

> Whence came all these people? They are a mixture of English, Scotch, Irish, French, Dutch, Germans, and Swedes. From this promiscuous breed, that race now called Americans have arisen.... In this great American asylum, the poor of Europe have by some means met together, and in consequence of various causes; to what purpose should they ask one another what countrymen they are? Alas, two thirds of them had no country. Can a wretch who wanders about, who works and starves, whose life is a continual scene of sore affliction or pinching penury; can that man call England or any other kingdom his country? A country that had no bread for him, whose fields procured him no harvest, who met with nothing but the frowns of the rich, the severity of the laws, with jails and punishments; who owned not a single foot of the extensive surface of this planet? No! urged by a variety of motives, here they came. Everything has tended to regenerate them; new laws, a new mode of living, a new social system; here they are become men....
>
> We are a people of cultivators, scattered over an immense territory, com-

[3] Michel Guillaume Jean de Crèvecoeur (J. Hector St. John de Crèvecour), *Letters from an American Farmer* (London, 1782), pp. 52–55.

municating with each other by means of good roads and navigable rivers, united by the silken bands of mild government, all respecting the laws, without dreading their power, because they are equitable. We are all animated with the spirit of an industry which is unfettered and unrestrained, because each person works for himself. . . .

Here the rewards of his industry follow with equal steps the progress of his labour; this labour is founded on the basis of nature, *self-interest;* can it want a stronger allurement? Wives and children, who before in vain demanded of him a morsel of bread, now, fat and frolicsome, gladly help their father to clear those fields whence exuberant crops are to arise to feed and clothe them all; without any part being claimed, either by a despotic prince, a rich abbot, or a mighty lord. Here religion demands but little of him; a small voluntary salary to the minister, and gratitude to God; can he refuse these? The American is a new man, who acts upon new principles; he must therefore entertain new ideas, and form new opinions. From involuntary idleness, servile dependence, penury, and useless labour, he has passed to toils of a very different nature, rewarded by ample subsistence.—This is an American. . . .

Europe has no such class of men; the early knowledge they acquire, the early bargains they make, give them a great degree of sagacity. As freemen they will be litigious; pride and obstinacy are often the cause of law suits; the nature of our laws and governments may be another. As citizens it is easy to imagine that they will carefully read the newspapers, enter into every political disquisition, freely blame or censure governors and others. As farmers they will be careful and anxious to get as much as they can, because what they get is their own. As northern men they will love the cheerful cup. As Christians, religion curbs them not in their opinions; the general indulgence leaves everyone to think for themselves in spiritual matters; the laws inspect our actions, our thoughts are left to God. Industry, good living, selfishness, litigiousness, country politics, the pride of freemen, religious indifference, are their characteristics. . . .

Judge what an alteration there must arise in the mind and thoughts of a European: he begins to forget his former servitude and dependence . . . he begins to form some little scheme, the first, alas, he ever formed in his life. If he is wise he thus spends two or three years, in which time he acquires knowledge. . . . I only repeat what I have heard many say, and no wonder their hearts should glow, and be agitated with a multitude of feelings, not easy to describe. From nothing to start into being.

This dream was quickly dispelled, and immigrants who still come with this dream, imagining that they can live in plenty and in complete personal liberty, are being increasingly disillusioned as they feel the increasing burdens and obligations which free institutions impose on them. Americans, therefore, both old and new, are peculiarly emotional and tense in facing the problems of freedom. The need to feel free is primarily a concern for one's own liberty—freedom to work, to move, to own property, freedom of conscience, speech, and assembly, the right to self-government, security against violence. But one learns early that one's claim to freedom and one's love of it are worthless without a respect for the freedom of others. Consequently the *love* of one's own freedom is moralized into the general *obligation* to maintain institutions of freedom.

By 1838, when James Fenimore Cooper wrote his *The American Democrat,*[4] a more sober picture of American life was becoming evident. Cooper gives us a critical estimate of what democracy means when it has become generalized and moralized:

> It must be an equivocal freedom, under which everyone is not the master of his own innocent acts and associations, and he is a sneaking democrat, indeed, who will submit to be dictated to, in those habits over which neither law nor morality assumes a right to control. . . .
>
> All that democracy means, is as equal a participation in rights as is practicable; and to pretend that social equality is a condition of popular institutions, is to assume that the latter are destructive of civilization, for, as nothing is more self-evident than the impossibility of raising all men to the highest standards of tastes and refinement, the alternative would be to reduce the entire community to the lowest. The whole embarrassment on this point exists in the difficulty of making men comprehend qualities they do not themselves possess. We can all perceive the difference between ourselves and our inferiors, but when it comes to a question of the difference between us and our superiors, we fail to appreciate merits of which we have no proper conceptions. In face of this obvious difficulty, there is the safe and just governing rule of permitting everyone to be the undisturbed judge of his own habits and associations, so long as they are innocent, and do not impair the rights of others to be equally judges for themselves. It follows, that socal intercourse must regulate itself, independently of institutions, with the exception that the latter, while they withhold no natural, bestow no fictitious advantages beyond those which are inseparable from the rights of property, and general civilization. . . .
>
> The democrat, recognizing the right of all to participate in power, will be more liberal in his general sentiments, a quality of superiority in itself; but, in conceding this much to his fellow man, he will proudly maintain his own independence of vulgar domination, as indispensable to his personal habits. The same principles and manliness that would induce him to depose a royal despot, would induce him to resist a vulgar tyrant.
>
> There is no more capital, though more common error, than to suppose him an aristocrat who maintains his independence of habits, for democracy asserts the control of the majority only in matters of law, and not in matters of custom. The very object of the institution is the utmost practicable personal liberty, and to affirm the contrary, would be sacrificing the end to the means.

The task of maintaining general, institutional freedom is becoming increasingly difficult in the world, since it involves both domestic and foreign policies and it imposes increasing burdens and obligations on the individual citizen. Consequently, the love of freedom is strained, and American public affairs are in a state of continual tension. The tension is both emotional and intellectual; it is difficult to determine how the essence of freedom can be maintained by means of growing restrictions on traditional and personal liberties. No one can fail to appreciate now that freedom is problematical; the high cost of freedom is beginning to give men a realistic sense of its value. But it is also

[4] James Fenimore Cooper, *The American Democrat* (New York: H. & E. Phinney, 1838), pp. 93–96.

creating a popular demand for a more critical philosophy of freedom than those in vogue a century or more ago.

It is at this point that the European philosophical and practical experience is extremely important. The freedom that is possible, whether it is lovable or not, is a civilized freedom, an institutional freedom, a moralized freedom toward which many generations of men throughout the world have been struggling. And the history of this struggle is becoming increasingly meaningful to Americans as they appreciate increasingly how closely their own experience is related to that of other peoples, ancient and modern.

One illustration taken from this long history may be useful at this point. In his remarkable little treatise, *On The Athenian Constitution,* Aristotle tells us that the beginning of genuine freedom for the people of Athens was when Solon abolished the penalty of imprisonment for debt. This was the beginning of bankruptcy legislation. Today, Americans, especially Americans who are creditors, realize that what Solon did for the Athenians is now being done for citizens throughout the world by inflation of credit and currency. Debtors and creditors today, instead of facing periodic bankruptcies, experience the gradual relief from debt by the liberalization of credit or the devaluation of money. According to Aristotle, this means the people's freedom; according to modern individualists, this means governmental robbery. It is clear that the theory of freedom is bound to be difficult and confusing under such circumstances. Debtors and creditors are not apt to agree on the meaning and means of freedom. This is but one of the many circumstances which make the theory of freedom today a difficult and a supremely important task. It is evident to all today that the philosophy of liberty must take into account the redefinition of property rights, the principles of equity, the facts of political economy, the obligations of international community, as well as the traditional theories of self-government. The four or five or six freedoms may be given separate names, but they all hang together or stand together. Here is a major problem not only for the social sciences but also for moral philosophy, not only for Americans but for citizens the world over. The more freedom is threatened, the more it is cherished; and the more urgent the problem is, the greater is the practical responsibility that faces scientists and philosophers in clarifying the ideal, for the situation is hopeless so long as freedom is not understood.

IV. THE OBLIGATION TO COMPROMISE

A direct consequence of the three traits mentioned so far is the principle of conscientious compromise. T. V. Smith has called the American ethics of compromise "the legislative way of life."[5] This principle underlies the two-party political system to which Americans have become accustomed and which

[5] See Thomas Vernor Smith, *The Legislative Way of Life* (Chicago: The University of Chicago Press, 1940). The theory is further developed in two of his other books: *Beyond Conscience* (New York and London: Whittlesey House, McGraw-Hill Book Co., Inc., 1934), and *Discipline for Democracy* (Chapel Hill: The University of North Carolina Press, 1942).

they now regard as an essential element in freedom. The British reliance on "His Majesty's Opposition" is similar, but there is both a theoretical and a practical difference between the two systems. In Great Britain, one party is definitely in power; in the United States, it has become quite common to have the two parties sharing power, one being dominant in the legislative branch (or in one of the Houses of Congress) and the other in the executive branch of the government. Under these circumstances, government must be carried on by continually compromising, bargaining, making "deals." The need for inter-party negotiation then becomes a matter of principle—a principle that takes priority over the principle of party loyalty and opposition policies. In a crisis, this spirit of give-and-take may lead to formal coalition and co-operation. But such coalitions must be emergency measures, and, when the storm blows over, there must be a return to the art of party compromise. The government must always face organized criticism. This has become a fundamental principle in American conceptions of free government, though there is not a word of it in the Constitution. The Italian fascists invented the slogan, "We welcome criticism but not opposition." In the United States and Great Britain and other free countries, the government must always face organized opposition, on the theory that where there is freedom there is competition, but in the case of the United States the process of compromise and bargaining is becoming an inherent aspect of the process of governing and not merely a party of opposition.

The so-called "ethics of bargaining power" seems to be the American substitute for the class-struggle. This theory of "fair play" takes for granted that there is a legitimate use of reciprocal intimidation and threat, but never to the extent of violence. When negotiation uses violence, it becomes a "racket," and rackets are America's Public Enemy No. 1. They exist and are a real menace to American democracy; the effort to stamp them out wherever they can be detected is sure to find general approval in public opinion and staunch support in the courts. Corruption in public and private business is serious enough, but violent corruption is generally regarded as intolerable. As far as possible, the process of compromise is supposed to be carried on in public; secret deals are dishonorable. But the whole art of negotiation, diplomacy, and bargaining, and the whole strategy of the professional politician, are regarded by most citizens as a necessary evil, morally contemptible, tolerated only because the alternatives would be worse evils.

The enormous growth of bureaucracy and corruption in both public and private business has nourished the ancient prejudice against government as such. "The less government the better" is still a common point of view among Americans, even though no one now attempts to justify *laissez faire* as a philosophical principle. In general, Americans do not look upon their government as their "superiors" nor upon the State as the highest embodiment of their freedom. Political organization is looked upon as one of the more utilitarian institutions of culture, necessary but not noble. Nevertheless, there is a general acceptance of legal authority and discipline and a habitual law-abidingness which is good evidence of the general morale and civic morality of the people. Americans are seldom satisfied with their government, or, as they say, they usually vote against rather than for; but they are not apt to look elsewhere with envy or agitate for a different kind of constitution. They are always ready for a "new deal" within the game, but not for a new game; there is little interest in revolution. Occasionally there are voices of rebellion, but, on the whole, the memory of the Rebellion a century ago is still too vivid and terrible to permit Americans to hope for an improvement by such means. The temper of Americans is decidedly post-revolutionary.

V. THE SUBORDINATION OF MILITARY TO CIVIL AUTHORITY

The subordination of military to civil authority comes down as a classical doctrine from the Greeks and Romans, but it needs to be reasserted in view of the many violations of the principle among the neighbors of the United States, and in view of the growth of military influence within the country in these times of war. Any weakening of this principle of Constitutional Law would be recognized as a tragedy by the people as a whole and just cause for revolt.[6] Compulsory military service is accepted in good faith as a democratic way of meeting the needs of war. But there is general resentment over the prospect of an indefinite state of war and of an army for international police purposes. To have overwhelming military power is a distinct embarrassment to the American people, for it might gradually lead to a militarization of American politics generally. Americans become alarmed when they see large numbers of the youth of the land in uniform, when every boy must sacrifice a year or more of his best and most critical years to military service, and when the military budget reaches the enormous proportions which it now has reached and threatens to maintain. For such an existence the American mind and temper are not prepared. A "cold" war of such proportions does not leave Americans cold. To them, this is not collective security but global folly. In short, the present state of international affairs is not apt to impress Americans as an extension of bargaining techniques on a world-wide scale or as a process of political negotiation. These are police tactics to meet a police-State enemy. If such tactics were to become prolonged and normal, the tragedy would threaten all of the principles and ideals to which Americans now cling.

VI. THE PLURALISTIC PHILOSOPHY OF THE PUBLIC

The pluralistic philosophy of the public amounts to a theoretical recognition of the great vested interests as public, corporate persons, each of which

[6] For a good exposition of this conviction by an American philosopher see the concluding chapter, "The Future of War," of J. Glenn Gray's *The Warriors* (New York: Harcourt, Brace & Co., 1959). See also the detailed account of a significant contest in recent American politics, Joseph Garner Anthony's *Hawaii Under Army Rule* (Stanford: Stanford University Press, 1955).

has a public responsibility. Such a theory tries to do justice to the network of basic institutions which compose society. Society is not primarily political, even if the Constitutional framework of law serves as society's skeleton; the community's interests embrace the interests of its major, regular, incorporated institutions. In addition to family, there are school, church, sciences and arts, labor unions, industry, trade, banks, insurance, agriculture, recreation, communication, etc. To label every interest that is not governmental as "private" and to regard what is private as not inherent in the community structure is a highly unrealistic theory. The public *is* the network of vested interests (including law and government), and the proper functioning of these organizations in view of the commonwealth or general welfare is obviously the community's concern and moral responsibility. The general principle of pluralism implies that each corporate or institutional interest shall be as self-governing as possible, but that none can claim exemption from the force of public interest and judgment.[7] The methods by which these various interests are regulated and integrated will depend on the types of problems and conflicts which are generated. Legal regulation, to which they are all more or less subject, is only one of the ways in which a community can exercise control. All interests, especially those that are most personal, deserve as much autonomy as possible, and there is no interest, not even the political, which can claim an over-all sovereignty. A community is a federation of interests in which regulation and control pass from one institution to another, depending on circumstances and subject-matters. These interests do not constitute a hierarchy or scale of values, nor is the so-called public interest a definable, concrete, all-inclusive interest. To attempt to make a distinction between interest and will, as the idealistic theories do and as certain corporative theories do in order to give priority to a few "basic" institutions,[8] is not fair to the facts of American society but is based on certain speculative considerations and categories which are not relevant to the subject. Co-ordination, co-operation, toleration, equity, reciprocity, and relative autonomy—these are the basic elements in American community structure. They are in clear contrast to totalitarian integration and hierarchy.

I do not mean to assert that all Americans would subscribe to such a pluralistic philosophy, for there is no philosophy on which all Americans would agree. All that can be asserted is that this philosophy tries to take account of the fact that vested interests are now recognized as having a right to lobbies and to representation in legislative debates and enactments.

[7] The moral and philosophical aspects of this principle are discussed critically in a document prepared by Wayne A. R. Leys and Charner M. Perry for the American Philosophical Association, under the title, *Philosophy and the Public Interest* (Chicago, 1959).

[8] See, for example, Elijah Jordan's analysis in *The Good Life* (Chicago: The University of Chicago Press, 1949), a work which otherwise is an important and objective exposition of American corporate organization. The pluralistic nature of the public is discussed in John Dewey, *The Public and Its Problems* (New York: H. Holt and Co., 1927), and Walter Lippmann, *The Public Philosophy* (Boston: Little, Brown & Co., 1955).

VII. THE RIGHT TO LIBERAL EDUCATION

Lastly, I call attention to the importance which is assigned in American life to education for all in the sciences and arts. This principle of public education is really a corollary of the preceding principle that there is a public concern for the reasonable promotion of all institutions and interests. The chief aim of such a general program of education is to give to each a decent acquaintance with the interests of all. The knowledge of certain sciences and skills has professional value, and professional or technological training is, of course, a major concern of the community. But underlying the public concern for the arts and professions by which citizens earn their livelihoods is the public concern for the opportunity of all to have some intelligent understanding of and share in the varied interests and the cultural heritage of the community. This has become a major feature of American democracy. To what extent this education is administered by tax-financed institutions and to what extent the various interested institutions can supply it is a minor and technical question. General education is a general responsibility in whatever way it may be provided.

Let this suffice as a survey of American ideas in action. Philosophy has become only recently an academic subject and a professional speculation. As one looks back over the history of American thought, one is impressed by the fact that it has been carried on, for the most part, until very recently, by men of practical affairs and experience. Philosophical reflection and practical affairs were not divorced; each made the other meaningful and responsible. I cite, in closing, one famous illustration of this general fact. During the thick of the Civil War, while President Lincoln was planning his Declaration emancipating the slaves, Ralph Waldo Emerson was writing an essay, *American Civilization*. From it I quote a few passages to illustrate the union of critical reflection and deliberate courageous action:

> Labor: a man coins himself into his labor; turns his day, his strength, his thought, his affection into some product which remains as the visible sign of his power; and to protect that, to secure that to him, to secure his past self to his future self, is the object of all government. There is no interest in any country so imperative as that of labor; it covers all, the constitutions and governments exist for that—to protect and insure it to the laborer. All honest men are daily striving to earn their bread by their industry. And who is this who tosses his empty head at this blessing in disguise, the constitution of human nature, and calls labor vile, and insults the faithful workman at his daily toil? . . .
>
> In this national crisis, it is not argument that we want, but that rare courage which dares commit itself to a principle, believing that Nature is its ally, and will create the instruments it requires, and more than make good any petty and injurious profit which it may disturb. There never was such a combination as this of ours, and the rules to meet it are not set down in any history. We want men of original perception and original action, who can open their eyes

wider than to a nationality, namely, to considerations of benefit to the human race, who can act in the interest of civilization....

It looks as if we held the fate of the fairest possession of mankind in our hands, to be saved by our firmness or to be lost by hesitation.... Emancipation is the demand of civilization. This is a principle; everything else is an intrigue....

The weapon is slipping out of our hands. "Time," say the Indian Scriptures, "drinketh up the essence of every great and noble action which ought to be performed, and which is delayed in the execution."...

The end of all political struggle is to establish morality as the basis of all legislation. It is not free institutions, it is not a republic, it is not a democracy, that is the end—no, but only the means. Morality is the object of government. . . . Nature works through her appointed elements; and ideas must work through the brains and arms of good and brave men, or they are no better than dreams.[9]

QUESTION: Are there no basic or positive values or goals to which Americans as a people are committed?

ANSWER: I agree that there are very positive and definite commitments which Americans share and which are *basic* to their community life, but I would distinguish these from *values* in the sense of ultimate ends or goals. I have referred to internationalism, law-abidingness, pluralism of institutions and faiths, the obligation to compromise, the subordination of military to civil authority, and public education as *basic* aspects of American life and thought. These are not ideals in the sense of goals, but principles, postulates, or axiomatic needs for the successful functioning of American practical affairs. They are positive foundations. My thesis is that Americans are more solidly united by their awareness of these basic needs than in their striving toward common ends.

In Section II, I have referred, almost incidentally, to "peace, justice, and freedom" as ultimate criteria in terms of which the American experiment must be judged. Whether these three be regarded as prerequisites or as ultimate ends seems to me to raise a speculative rather than a practical issue, for all three are both means and ends, constitutive principles as well as intrinsic goods. I have refrained from singing the praises of this trinity because I regard it as a universal moral standard rather than as a set of values which it is the peculiar virtue of Americans to cherish. I cannot imagine any nation which would repudiate these ideals, and I know of none that has denied them. The tragedy is that, though all proclaim their loyalty to them, each makes his own interpretation and fails to join a co-operative pursuit.

Consequently, the important issue for Americans is, rather, to be fully, philosophically aware of the experimental nature of their own particular devotion to mankind's general commitment to the ideals of peace, justice, and freedom; and to be ever ready to judge themselves and others by their practical success in approaching these universal norms. To conceive this so-called "American way of life" as an ultimate end in itself would be philosophical dogmatism

[9] *The Complete Works of Ralph Waldo Emerson*, Vol. XI, *Miscellanies*, Edward Waldo Emerson, ed. (Cambridge: At the Riverside Press, 1904), p. 295.

and political folly. One of the principles which is by this time fairly well established in American philosophy and morals is the habit of continually evaluating principles in terms of ideal criteria, and to conceive these criteria themselves in terms of the varying successes and failures which men in all times and places have experienced in their efforts to give ideals concrete and co-operative embodiment.

BIBLIOGRAPHY

In addition to the works mentioned in footnotes 5, 7, and 8, the following are useful references:

Charles A. Beard, *The American Spirit.* New York: The Macmillan Co., 1942.

J. L. Blau, *Men and Movements in American Philosophy.* New York: Prentice-Hall, 1952.

D. W. Brogan, *The American Character.* New York: A. A. Knopf, 1944.

Merli Curti, *The Growth of American Thought.* New York and London: Harper and Brothers, 1943.

Joseph Dorfman, *The Economic Mind in American Civilization.* 2 vols. New York: The Viking Press, 1946.

R. H. Gabriel, *The Course of American Democratic Thought.* New York: The Ronald Press Co., 1940.

Hamilton, Madison and Jay on the Constitution: Selections from the Federalist Papers, with a critical introduction by R. H. Gabriel. The American Heritage Series. New York: Liberal Arts Press, 1956. (This whole series of paperbacks is a good reference library.)

Sidney Hook, ed., *American Philosophers at Work.* New York: Criterion Books, 1956.

E. W. Lefever, *Ethics and United States Foreign Policy.* New York: Living Age Books, 1957.

Max Lerner, "Christian Culture and American Democracy," *American Quarterly,* VI, No. 2 (Summer, 1954).

A. T. Mason, *The Supreme Court from Taft to Warren.* Baton Rouge: Louisiana State University Press, 1959.

G. H. Mead, "The Philosophies of Royce, James, and Dewey in their American Setting," *The International Journal of Ethics,* XL, No. 2 (January, 1930).

R. B. Perry, *Puritanism and Democracy.* New York: The Vanguard Press, 1944.

Stow Persons, *Public Opinion—A Democratic Dilemma.* (Merrill Lecture, "Stetson University Bulletin.") Deland, Florida, October, 1958.

H. W. Schneider, *A History of American Philosophy.* New York: Columbia University Press, 1946; Oriental edition, 1958.

FRITZ-JOACHIM VON RINTELEN

Values as a Foundation for Encounter

The object of our inquiry is the problem of an encounter between East and West—an encounter between two very different cultural spheres: the Asian sensibility and, let us say, Occidental-European conceptual thought that has also spread to those parts of the world to which many Europeans have emigrated in the past. But what do we mean by "encounter"? It signifies a reciprocal meeting of minds (*Verstehen*). But it signifies also something more than this, namely, an inner human contact which reveals that even in apparently different attitudes and situations there are venerable spiritual qualities to be discovered. When this much is gained, then a reciprocal fertilization can follow. Encounter is not realized in and through abstract and universal notions or conceptual thinking, as was believed by the men of the Enlightenment. It is not sufficient to say that certain universal conceptions are common to all men. Such an attitude would simply destroy the specific character of the various cultures, depriving them of their distinctive qualities, and we would remain on the surface of the problem. Each culture can retain its life, its productivity, its profundity and intensity, its power to form men, only in accordance with the manner and the law of action which first brought it forth in history. Genuine encounter does not mean, therefore, that we must give up our ultimate understanding of, and our attitude toward, the essence of our human existence and of the world in which we live. Rather, it means that we must cultivate a loving readiness to apprehend the particular perspective and the type of human greatness proper to each mode of thought and each culture. The same is true in the encounter of man and man—referred to today by the philosopher Jaspers as "communication." It is precisely in conversation that each one of us manifests his readiness to understand the other—a readiness which results in a unity of the two and engenders mutual respect, so that, with Goethe, we can say that in the encounter each individual catches "a breath of the spirit of the other." Even though their opinions may differ, the participants in the conversation remain open for a deeper unity, for an agreement on a more fundamental plane. We may also discover that similar basic human problems, when seen in different perspectives, do arrive at diverse and yet profoundly different answers—which not only complement and cross-fertilize one another but also lead to mutual contacts in such a way that a reciprocal inner gain results from the encounter. This is the type of encounter between individuals and, ultimately, between representatives of cultures, which I have in mind here, and the principles of which I intend to examine.

(1) Our first basic principle should be the following: An encounter is possible only on the grounds of a mutual respect for our cultures and through insight into their ultimate motives and ideals. This does not imply surrendering one's own convictions, for each participant in the encounter should remain true to himself; nor does it mean the establishment of abstract, formal principles which fail to appeal to man's innermost existence.

(2) It seems a *datum* to me, therefore, that the desired mutual understanding should be possible first and primarily within the domain of philosophy, mainly because in all parts of the world philosophy originates in religious intuition, in the creation of language, and, thus, in the primal attitudes of mankind. Without doubt, cultures today have an extraordinarily great deal in common. But this mutual contact is found chiefly in the sphere of the consequences of the physical and mathematical sciences and in the development of international commerce. As a result, the world has, in a large measure, become uniform. But natural science and technology are independent of cultural attitudes. They do not often bring people together or resolve the contradictions between various cultures. In fact, more often than not, they accentuate these contradictions, and they are often servants of political conflicts. Although a most remarkable manifestation of the human intellect, facilitating manifold exchanges among cultures and making the world smaller, natural science and technology remain more or less neutral in the actual human encounter.

They are achievements which depend on functions of the empirical, rational-analytic, and merely human intellect only—an intellect which restricts itself to the so-called exact sciences and which is capable of promoting a "scientific world-orientation" (*wissenschaftliche Weltorientierung*). But this purely intellectual activity does not have much relation to the inner existence of man and the ethos attributed to him. On the contrary, the characteristics which decisively mark the nature of man are his humanitarian achievements and his ultimate and profound interpretation of life and the world. In the realm of technology, an individual can produce astonishing intellectual results, and we marvel at the acumen of his intellect. As a human being, however, this same individual can pursue either very noble or very base goals, putting science itself, for example, to the service of coercion and the utter disregard of basic human rights. In human society, therefore, quite different factors are decisive. An inner encounter is difficult to imagine in terms of rational-technical respects only.

We must endeavor, therefore, to penetrate to the quite different and more decisive levels of spiritual life in order to carry on a discussion of essentials. We thus arrive at our second basic principle: Mutual encounter demands more than an exchange of ideas on problems extending no further than progress in natural and technical sciences, praiseworthy as such progress may be.

(3) Once again we return to our proper theme. The cultures of the various peoples of the earth can be traced back to much more primordial activities than those of rational-technical functions, that is, they can be traced back to basic experiences which inwardly determine modes and manners of perception and basic feelings. These primal experiences disclose the soul of any culture—the most sublime form of its thinking, its peculiar attributes, its comprehension of the world, and its sense and meaning of life. Here we can still encounter the ultimate motives which are often not immediately in the forefront of consciousness. To a large degree, they stem from a long historical tradition and receive from it their sanction. These motives should never be depreciated if we wish to avoid talking at cross-purposes. Briefly, what is involved is a question of what are the *basic values* around which life centers. As Nietzsche puts it: "The world revolves upon the awakening of values; inaudibly it revolves," to quote freely. Tell me the values which you avow, and I shall tell you who you are.

These values emerge continually in our attitudes toward others, toward the community, and toward objects of culture—toward the goals we pursue; and they emerge in the manner in which we approach life, in our ethos, and, last, in our religious experience. Are not the contradictions in the contemporary world the result of diverse valuations by mankind—of the person as well as the worth attributed to it, the *dignitas hominis?* Are not humanitarian values of such a kind as to make demands on all men, even though historically the effects of experiencing them have been different, and even though the character of their particular demands has a different significance in different cultural spheres?

I do not wish to present here a contrived and specialized theory of values. I wish, rather, to state that at all times and in all cultures the decisive impulses in human behavior proceed from basic valuations, that any period is conditioned by the value-aspirations dominant at the time, and that the values involved are rooted in man's ultimate understanding of Being (*Seinsverständnis*). This seems to be a simple historical fact, and a philosophy intent on being world-embracing can evade or overlook this fact only on pain of disregarding its inner responsibility. Such a philosophy dare not dismiss the basic valuations as being merely contingent, completely relative, and thus of no importance. On the contrary, we face here a problem which today occupies thoughtful minds everywhere. For here we meet that which is essential to mankind, that which moves man inwardly, that toward which he strives and of which he will not allow himself to be deprived. When a man appears to us to embody a certain worth or value, we esteem and respect him. When the immanent values of a spiritual movement reveal an inner richness that is capable of advancing man's self-fulfillment, we approve and affirm it.

The values involved may be of a completely external nature, extending only to material things. Still, they can also grip us inwardly; they can gladden, elevate, and enrich us, and give life a definite meaning. This last fact in particular is linked to mutual understanding, to an "encounter" and a helpful readiness to understand. However, the whole question has nothing to do with abstract theories. It involves, rather, the lives of all of us. I shall speak, therefore, of "value-realism" (*Wertrealismus*)—using the term as pertaining to the real fulfillment of human aspirations. It is in this context that the whole problem of value arises.

Let us take simple examples from life. A medical doctor fulfills his life especially through his professional duties. A mother obtains happiness in the education and welfare of her children. A scientist finds satisfaction in the discovery of new facts or new laws. An engineer derives satisfaction from designing some new construction which will serve the community. And an artist finds self-fulfillment in the creation of a great work of art which is meant to enrich others. The examples could be multiplied endlessly. Why does their activity appear meaningful to the various individuals? It appears so because the result of their efforts is something containing in itself value. But let us be more general in our statement. What are the decisive value-experiences which are proper to the various cultures? If we are able to find an answer to this question, then an inner encounter is possible. Our third basic principle, therefore, is: The exchange of ideas must be related to the dominant modes of valuation encountered in mankind as a whole.

(4) Professor Charles Morris (University of Chicago) has written a book about the distinctions of valuations in East and West, disclosing the urgency of this problem.[1] Margaret Mead, in her comprehensive comparative work,[2] has shown us the radical differences among primitive peoples. Is there nothing unifying to be said in regard to these peoples? This problem played an important role in philosophical "historicism," expounded in Germany by Wilhelm Dilthey (died 1911) in his *Methode der Geisteswissenschaften,*[3] and by Ernst Troeltsch[4] (died 1923). It is thanks to Dilthey that we better understand the inner development in past and present cultures. He taught us that, first of all, we must submerge ourselves with "loving sympathy" (*Einfühlung*) into the

[1] See Charles Morris, *Varieties of Human Values* (Chicago: University of Chicago Press, 1956), pp. 41 ff.

[2] See Margaret Mead, *Cooperation and Competition among Primitive People* (New York: McGraw-Hill Book Company, Inc., 1937).

[3] Wilhelm Dilthey, *Gesammelte Schriften* (Leipzig and Berlin: B. G. Teubner, 1921), Vol. I, *Einleitung in die Geisteswissenschaften,* Book I, *Methode der Geisteswissenschaften,* pp. 4 ff.

[4] Ernst Troeltsch, *Gesammelte Schriften,* Vol. III, *Der Historismus und seine Probleme,* Book I, *Das logische Problem der Geschichtsphilosophie* (Tübingen: J. C. B. Mohr, 1922). F. J. von Rintelen, "Der Versuch einer Überwindung des Historismus bei Ernst Troeltsch," *Deutsche Vierteljahrsschrift für Literaturwissenschaft und Geistesgeschichte,* VIII (1930), No. 2, 320 ff.

other culture and try to view it from its own perspective. We must re-live its thoughts, aims, and experiences, in short, its value-ideas, and must attempt to reproduce these endogenically, and, so far as possible, we must not let our own presuppositions interfere. This means that we must allow the "inner experiences" of the culture in question to enter into us, for only then will we possess a faithful picture of that culture. In Troeltsch's work we find the further idea that every epoch and its culture are derivable from a more or less closed "totality of meaning" (*Sinntotalität*).

Men, individually or communally, repeatedly seek a content of meaning which will justify their existence. This content is often a very complex configuration in which all parts are interconnected. If we pick out only one part, we run the risk of falsely isolating it and of never penetrating to the totality of the soul of the epoch or culture. It is also to be noted that certain particular modes of behavior which occasionally appear as anti-values can take on understandable meaning when viewed within the totality of an ethos or culture.

In comparing cultures, however, does not the fact of the contradictoriness or changeability of valuations force us to admit the relativity of all valuations? But, then, would not that be admitting that every one of us has the right to release himself from the inward obligation of certain value-demands since such demands have a merely historical origin which establishes their validity for only a short time? May they not be superseded tomorrow? As an individual, I stand only accidentally in this or that situation—a situation determined, perhaps, by the community which today arbitrarily prescribes certain demands and tomorrow prescribes others. The disdain shown in our own days for humanitarian values illustrates my point, making judgments in the light of humanitarian values impossible. We shall see later whether or not such subjectivism is justified. For the moment let us be satisfied with our fourth basic principle: Valuations made by individuals can, by and large, be completely understood only from the point of view of the totality of a given culture. Unless we enter into this totality, we can never fully grasp the ultimate roots of these valuations.

(5) I believe that in contemporary philosophy we have passed both through and beyond the situation of absolute historicism. The fact that there are many kinds of valuations is, of course, obvious. But perhaps out of insecurity and an excessive criticism, we are far too much inclined to bring under one heading contrary historical data, thereby losing the over-all picture of history. This is the more understandable as far as values are concerned, for we are dealing here with attitudes toward individually concrete and historical occurrences, and not, as in the natural sciences, with universal laws. But Leibniz, in accordance with his *principium identitatis indiscernibilium,* has already told us that in Nature there is no perfect identity. If at any one time we place all historical events side by side, we are not able to attain detachment of observation. It is fitting here to refer to Fichte's words of wisdom, "satisfaction is never produced by the historical but only by the metaphysical."[5]

[5] Johann Gottlieb Fichte, *Werke,* Fritz Medicus, ed., Vol. V (Leipzig: F. Eckardt Verlag, 1910), p. 197.

But let us not call upon such ultimate questions to aid us here. Let us listen, instead, to simple experience. In 1957, as Visiting Professor at the University of Southern California, I had classes consisting of people from the most diverse cultures and religious leanings, but, to my profound amazement, it was possible to attain far-reaching agreement—particularly as regards values in human character. We need but think of fidelity, courage, trust, genuineness, nobility, veracity, loyalty to oneself, and helpfulness, of the awe of man in the face of those possibilities of this life which affect him most profoundly—death, aesthetic elevation and the expression of it, and religious calling or experience, however manifold it be.

Perhaps I may be allowed to refer here to a personal experience. During the first World War, serving as a young soldier at the front, I was in the thick of battle. Because of the fighting, I did not receive any rations for three days—a fact most disagreeable to a young person. But then, completely spontaneously, a fellow soldier gave me a most marvelous present—ham and eggs—something which I had not seen for years because of the dreadfully poor food distribution. This was a precious deed of good will and would in all ages and in all nations be regarded as good in itself in a situation in which only the *do ut des* is obeyed. The goodness of the action cannot be explained by the fact that I found it useful, because, as a soldier, I could have been killed at any moment. I never saw that man again, for he belonged to another company.

Examples can be multiplied easily, together with examples of base attitudes, of crime and misdeeds. I wish to illustrate merely that there are essential human values which transcend all temporal bounds. To quote Garcia Máynez of Mexico, "There is a common source of convictions and sentiments about value."[6] And this gives us our fifth basic principle: In spite of all diversity in valuations, we can point to certain fundamental characteristics common to the various cultures. These characteristics, as I see it, are fundamental values which may serve as the basis for real communication and an inner encounter. Without these values, inter-personal contact would be completely impossible. But we can observe daily that this contact is most certainly there, quite independent of specific cultures.

(6) However, our argument now requires a short evaluative interpretation. What is meant when I say that this or that is valuable or that it carries its value within itself? As far as life is concerned, it seems to mean accomplishment or content capable of fulfillment, "a fulfillment of life," something which we value highly and attempt to attain. The realization of such fulfillment reveals itself in our actual experience; and for this reason I speak of "value-realism." The concrete real value embraces a certain fulfillment of value, thus explaining its being directly experienced. It is not an abstract idea.

Yet, by means of mental exertion, I am also able to isolate at any time the essential characteristics and to speak of value-contents (such as justice, love,

[6] Eduardo Garcia Máynez, "Vom Wesenssinn des Rechtes," in R. Wisser, ed., *Sinn und Sein. Ein Philosophisches Symposion* (Tuebingen: M. Niemeyer, 1960), p. 604.

beauty) as value concepts, keeping in mind at all times, however, their basic relation to reality. In this reality it is the concrete person, for instance, which in itself carries the value; I do not merely attribute the value to the person. So much, at least, is implied by a value-judgment which embraces the very being of the person, his or her human existence. And it may be said as well that concept-formation takes place continually in the language context and against our cultural background, a fact which accounts for its marked historical limitation. I prefer, therefore, to speak of *meaning* (*Sinn*), of qualitative value-meaning, which, as that which is commonly meant, can assume very different conceptual designations depending upon the varying accents and characteristics important in each separate culture. Despite these linguistic differences, however, the fundamental intentions remain the same, and they comprise the invitation, if not the duty, to fulfill evaluative goals.

But here another decisive factor appears in the problem of values. One and the same value-tendency can attain various degrees of actual fulfillment because of the possibility of comparative and superlative gradation (*Steigerung*). We speak of the value of the beautiful, of the value of goodness, of the value of a person, of the value of help, of loyalty to oneself. But that which is meant by the value of a person, for example, can be realized on completely different levels, all of which are embodied in *individuals*. No perspective is broad enough to enable us to grasp fully the content of essential values. I would, therefore, prefer to speak of the varying dimensions of profundity of a value-possibility (*Tiefendimension*). With a mere survey of Being it is completely different. As a botanist, I can concentrate on single plant forms and be interested in their general form only and not in the individual object. It is a matter of complete indifference to me if a particular specimen is a more perfect or a less perfect plant—a fact seen most clearly by Goethe.

Yet, precisely the fact that the degrees of fulfillment of anything of value lie in the realm of the concrete individual leads to the conclusion that we, because of our habit of perceiving only a single factor at any one time in our cultural and historical surveys, tended toward a historical relativism. In contrast to the other sciences, we neglected the supra-individual phenomena which might be realized in a diversely individualized manner. This variability of dimensions of profundity exceeds purely conceptual abstraction.

But even this method of procedure is not satisfactory. The scientist of culture could reply that, in addition to the individual designations of value in their state of gradation in history, there exist extraordinarily many varieties of evaluating attitudes. Let us think, for example, of the differences in the essential value of love as it was seen in the Greek *eros*, in the brotherly love of Christianity, in humanitarian love, or, at the present time, in social love. In spite of all this, however, I would still maintain that, in the last analysis, all of these attitudes have as a basis a common value-tendency which historically manifests itself in a spectrum of variations (*Variationsbreite*), just as the concepts are different in the different languages. We are concerned with the self-same value which has received in reality its historical character because of diverse gradations and diverse emphasis or importance (Rothacker's term is *Bedeutungscharakter*[7]). It is characteristic and important for contemporary thinkers to stress that which is more or less general and common to all, for we already know accurately enough the diversity which may enrich our historical outlook. One would never now contest the fact that during certain periods of history certain fundamental values of human existence were almost overshadowed. The value of freedom is a case in point. Situations were created which resulted in "value-blindness" (Scheler), and often indeed in a warping of value which led in the end to value-error. This fact leads to our sixth basic principle: We encounter the phenomenon of value in the real occurrence of life, in Being itself. It may find individual fulfillment in varying stages of gradation. Yet, the various degrees of fulfillment may be regarded as but the modes in which trans-temporal fundamental values find expression and are revealed to us historically in their range of variations. To be able to fuse one's life into these variations and to become conscious of them is the reliable path to mutual understanding.

(7) We have now reached our last point: How can we demonstrate all this? It cannot be proved in the sense of natural scientific method, which relates sensory data to mathematical-rational descriptions, because here, where we deal with values, we are concerned with intellectual-spiritual phenomena. However, we may turn to *de facto* exhibition and the intellectual insight within it —that is, we may turn to inner experience, to the qualitative content of experience with which phenomenological method has been concerned so successfully. This method depends on the authenticity and conscientiousness, the scientific responsibility, of the analysis. How are we able to show the value-content of the life's real experiences? We inwardly emulate the fulfillment of an actual occurrence. It is possible to do so because we are human and can convince ourselves that, because we are human, we must achieve it. This procedure can be found wherever there is insight into values that possess immediate character. But phenomenological analysis requires a thorough justification.

When I say, with Kant, that man is never to be regarded as a means to an end but always as an end in himself (*Selbstzweck*), I thereby utter a social demand for value. To a certain degree, this demand was always there. We can perceive it, for example, in religions which demand reverence for the inwardness of the encounter between man and God, that is, before an inner realm of distinctively human values peculiar to man (Augustine)—and this even when religions themselves did not always heed it. Such a demand embraces a value-progression, and the justification of such a demand appears in the form of an insight into the idea of man as the idea is cultivated by us.

In this analysis a specific value of character as such is ascribed to the human person which, when fully developed, also includes, conformable to nature, a

[7] Erich Rothacker, *Geschichtsphilosophie* (Munich and Berlin: R. Oldenbourg, 1934), pp. 94 ff., 101, 107, 130 ff.

relational or utilitarian value insofar as the human being is capable of becoming a useful member of society. True understanding of value will, therefore, always reveal that all efforts as to ends and utility can be understood only as standing, in the last analysis, in the service of intrinsic values (*Eigenwerte*). The latter alone are able to fulfill life. Each sacrifice which I make for anyone else—a sacrifice which an artist or scientist would ordinarily make only with extreme effort—has meaning only if my effort is directed at something regarded as in itself valuable and thus worth attaining—something which is simply there and which we know is worth living for.

However, this brief reference to the demonstration of intrinsic values is not central to mutual understanding. It is simply a fact of human existence that all cultures and human societies, together with the single human being himself, proceed every day afresh from accepted value-goals which, as a single unity, present themselves historically in the form of a system of values susceptible to analysis. These values shed light upon man's innermost aspirations. And, if we seek a true encounter, we must attempt to penetrate into these values and to exchange them in earnest discussion.

I shall thus close with the seventh and last basic principle: Profound human understanding seems especially attainable in the sphere of valuation because only there does man speak to us in his completeness and entirety. His most secret impulses are revealed there. The reason for this is precisely that values are grounded in the most profound spiritual insights, in the innermost human intentions. This is not to deny their historical character. But inherently they possess a claim to inner obligation. Let us inquire, therefore, in our meeting of minds, how far values are unconditioned and find out how a true encounter is possible within the perspectives of valuation. And let us consider, too, the ultimate horizons of the meaning of human life which these perspectives reveal.

QUESTION: What do you understand by value-realism? Should spiritual values be thought of as real, or do you connect the good with concrete being? And what do you understand by spiritual values as far as they contain something eternal?

ANSWER: (1) Why do we ask about values? Because we judge of real actions. Is this action or the individual being good or valuable? Why do we condemn a crime? That is the decisive question, the first aspect, why we speak about values at all. Professor Regamey spoke, for instance, about the realization of spiritual creations.

(2) But what is reality? Ultimately, we cannot give a definite answer. I would say: Reality is that which is concrete in space and time, in the world of finitude. You can understand reality as things or as matter. But for physicists that is not sufficient. It is too one-sided. It seems to me that psychological acts, consciousness, deeds, and spiritual acts in us also have existence. They are not nothing. We can say that reality is always a combination of material conditions

with an inner order. For instance, a law as such in Nature is not reality. It is an intelligible interpretation. But law is really effective in Nature. It is the real and inner condition for the development of Nature. And we can transfer or carry over this idea to the problem of values. But personal values are not necessary laws, rather an invitation, a summons to us.

(3) We develop an abstraction, spiritual concepts, and then we speak about spiritual values. The concepts, however, are very dependent on language and cultural background. Therefore, I prefer to ask for the inner meaning, the signification by means of phenomenological analysis, what it is that I understand with my concepts. And these significations (*Sinnbedeutungen*) are more or less independent of the concepts which we construct. My opinion is a reaction to that sort of phenomenology which attempts to recognize only general essences and bracket out the problem of real existence. You can find this reaction also in existentialism, but with the other extreme which denies all objective obligatory answers.

(4) And we have to add another idea. The fact that a value-realization can be realized only in different qualitative degrees, in the sense of comparative and superlative: for instance, the value of personality can be realized more or less perfectly. That is not the case if we have only the aspect of being. One table cannot be more a table than another. But the value-degrees are given in reality. A value-idea has infinite possibility for variation and different dimensions of depth in realization. An absolute realization is not possible in our world. This recognition could lead us to the problem of transcendence.

(5) Other philosophers have spoken about a proper ideal sphere of spiritual values which includes obligation: Nicolai Hartmann, the Neo-Kantians and, to a degree, Scheler. They recognize an ideal being (*Idealsein*). This sphere is not concrete reality. We can say with them that this spiritual being has its foundation in God or in a transcendent realm or—not metaphysical—in supra-temporal ideas of validity. But to obtain a mutual understanding we must first show the inner value-content in a good realization. This is possible for us all. There, we can analyze and explain what is the realization of a value, perhaps of an objective value or eternal, unconditional value in itself.

QUESTION: What do you mean by historicism, and do you believe that in the face of historical change relativism can be overcome?

ANSWER: Philosophical historicism comes from the historical interpretation of cultures beginning in the period of Romanticism, in Germany of the historical juridical school of Savigny (Historische Schule), then more developed by Dilthey and today by Rothacker. It means that all concepts in general and the concepts of value are only a historical development, as Hegel said about the spirit in general. Yes, that is right and not right. We cannot deny historical development. But is the consequence an absolute relativity? Then we could not speak about an inner obligation beyond the historical situation. It seems to me that this relativity is only a relative relativity. It is understandable that the historians came to historicism because they had to do only with the concrete individual situations which always change. And I said that the most important aspect of valuation is to disclose the gradation of *individual* value-realization, e.g., great works of art. But the philosophical question is: Can we show that in the development of history we can point out general fundamental valuations realized in different variations? For instance, love as *eros, caritas,* humanitarian love, and social love. Here we can see that the realization can have a different dimension of depth. We can demonstrate many opinions in the field of valuation which are more or less common in all cultures and times, but always with different accent. In this way I want to overcome the absolute relativity of historicism.

QUESTION: What is the meaning of your quotation from Fichte: "Satisfaction is never produced by the historical but only by the metaphysical?"

ANSWER: The meaning of Fichte's phrase is that from history you can derive many different and opposite opinions. Everything is possible in history. A historical fact is not a proof for or against a philosophical question. With history alone we remain in an absolute relativism. You can then deny all positions and can accept all opinions. Men cannot live this way. Therefore, we have to go beyond this confusion and ask about the metaphysical question; in other words, we have to give a philosophical answer, which asks for definitive unconditionality.

HSIEH YU-WEI[a]

Filial Piety and Chinese Society

This paper will discuss the practicality of Chinese ethics and explain the doctrine of filial piety (*hsiao*[b]) and its place in the Chinese ethical realm. We shall then discuss the far-reaching influence of this doctrine in Chinese society, including family life, religious worship, social activities, and political affairs generally. Finally, this paper will shed some light upon what the doctrine of filial piety may contribute to the peace and welfare of the world.

Since the Confucian teaching of filial piety has held for four thousand years the most important place in Chinese ethics, I have selected it as the leading Chinese moral principle. In terms of this teaching, I shall explain the characteristics of Chinese society in the light of the relationship between these principles and the realistic life of the Chinese people.

I.

The *Great Learning,* as the words of Confucius (551–479 B.C.) taken down by his disciple Tseng Tzu,[c] has this leading passage: "What the *Great Learning* teaches is: to demonstrate illustrious virtue; to renovate the people; and to rest in the highest excellence attainable."[1] This sentence forms the central thought of Chinese philosophy. What most ancient Chinese philosophers strived for generally was put under these three items: "demonstrating illustrious virtues," "renovating the people," and "resting in the highest excellence." These three objectives form the focus of most ancient Chinese philosophers. It starts with the cultivating of one's personal virtues, progresses in stabilizing

[1] *Great Learning* I. 1.

the social order, and then culminates in the perfection of one's personality. Hence, Liang Ch'i-ch'ao[d] (1873–1929), a renowned Chinese scholar, remarked that:

...most Chinese learning has been the study of human behavior rather than theoretical knowledge. The pursuit of theoretical knowledge is neither the starting point nor the final goal. The literal translation of Chinese academic thought as philosophy is rather misleading. If we borrow the term it should be qualified as "philosophy of life." Chinese philosophy took for its starting point the study of human beings, in which the most important subject was how to behave as a man, how one can truly be called a man, and what kind of relationship exists among men.[2]

Even though I cannot agree with Liang Ch'i-ch'ao in treating Chinese philosophy merely as a philosophy of life or ethics, it is still correct to say that the main theme of Chinese philosophy has centered around ethics, which also formed its starting point. The Chinese philosophical domain includes metaphysics and epistemology, but these were shaped on the basis of ethics. They derived their source from ethical principles, and were systematized through ethical interpretation. Starting from the standpoint of "demonstrating illustrious virtue," the philosopher advances to the study of human nature, in which the virtue of benevolence (*jen*[e]) is inherent; by this the philosopher tries to reveal the "Mind of Heaven" and the "natural laws" by deduction in order to "assist the transforming and nourishing powers of Heaven and Earth." As the *Doctrine of the Mean* has said:

It is only he who possesses the most complete sincerity that can exist under Heaven and who can give full development to his nature. Able to give full development to his own nature, one can do the same to the nature of other men. Able to give full development to the nature of other men, he can give full development to the natures of animals and things. Able to give full development to the natures of creatures and things, he can assist in the transforming and nourishing powers of Heaven and Earth. Able to perform this latest feat, he may with Heaven and Earth form a trinity.[3]

If man can thoroughly understand physical laws and heavenly matters and even join himself with Heaven and Earth as in a trinity only by developing his own nature to the utmost, does this metaphysical theory not proceed from Chinese ethics?

Ancient Chinese philosophers had also discussed ways and means for the "perfecting of knowledge through the investigation of things," which in turn was conducive to "making one's thoughts sincere" and "rectifying the mind" in everyday living conditions. As the aim of investigating the nature of things was primarily "making the thoughts sincere" and "rectifying the mind," this theory dwells upon the necessity for action after the acquiring of knowledge.

[2] Liang Ch'i-ch'ao, *Ju-chia che-hsüeh*[e] ("The Confucian Philosophy"), Yin-ping shih ho-chi[f] (Shanghai: Chung-hua Shu-chu, 1936), Vol. 34, p. 2.

[3] *Doctrine of the Mean* XXII.

Any and all knowledge is worth while only when it is applicable in action in daily life with goodness as its result. The ancient savants then pursued epistemological discussion of the relationship of knowledge and practice. Hence, Wang Yang-ming (Wang Shou-jen,[f] 1474–1529) urged the "unity of knowledge and action," whereas Dr. Sun Yat-sen[g] advocated the theory that "knowledge-acquiring is hard, but practice may be easy." These two views were set forth in epistemological studies on an ethical basis.

Hence, in the eyes of Chinese philosophers, the establishment of ethics rested, not in its theoretical system, nor in mere language or words, but in energetic striving for practice. That is one distinctive point by which Oriental ethics is to be differentiated from the Western pattern. The latter more or less concentrates its discussion especially on the question as to what constitutes "right" or "good." Most Western philosophers treat ethics in a sense as a science or a line of thought rather than a way of life or as a kind of conduct; they separate ethical thinking from the actual practice of the thinker. Hence, some authors of ethical works who may be highly learned in the scientific expounding of what is good in morality may actually be ignorant as to how to bring about goodness in daily life, and their own behavior may also have gone astray, because they treat ethics merely as one aspect of thought and possibly as having nothing to do with conduct. Such a concept or attitude is not acceptable to the orthodox Chinese philosopher.

Mencius (371–289 B.C.?) said, "Why should I be fond of disputing? I am compelled to do it!"[4] Such an attitude of speaking with reluctance and only when it is absolutely necessary has been a tradition handed down by Confucius to the Sung-Ming (960–1644) Neo-Confucian scholars.

II.

As Chinese ethics stresses the practicality of moral teachings, its central idea is benevolence, on the one hand, and filial piety, on the other. They are correlated, the latter serving as the basic requirement of the former. As Confucius' disciple Yu Tzu[h] said, in the Confucian *Analects,* "Filial piety and fraternal submission!—are they not the root of all benevolent actions?"[5]

Why should benevolence and filial piety be joined? And why should the latter serve as the foundation of all benevolent actions? This point may be generally overlooked or misunderstood, not only by Western Sinologists, but also by many Chinese students. Some intellectuals in the New Cultural Movement in the early years of the Chinese Republic went so far as to vow against filial piety. Such a radical campaign demonstrated that in modern China there are many literati who are ignorant of the meaning of this traditional virtue. In fact, the tenet of filial piety has always held the most important place in Chinese ethics and also in the Chinese cultural tradition as a whole.

[4] *Book of Mencius* IIIB. 9.
[5] *Analects* I. 2.

The Confucian scholar often linked filial piety with benevolence, and did not regard it as an incidental expediency. There are two weighty reasons for this. First, benevolence as a paramount and comprehensive Chinese virtue must have its roots. And, second, benevolence must have its application in human society.

Where may we find any root of benevolence? As Mencius put it: "Every human being is endowed with the sense of commiseration."[6] And he added, "The feeling of commiseration is the starting point of benevolence."[7] As everyone possesses an inherent feeling of commiseration, this is the evidence that everyone is endowed with the virtue of benevolence. Mencius also said: "The ability possessed by men without having been acquired by learning is their 'intuitive ability,' and the knowledge possessed by them without the exercise of thought is their 'intuitive knowledge.' Children carried in arms all know to love their parents; and, when they are grown up, they all know to respect their elder brothers."[8] This is to emphasize that human love toward one's own parents is innate, as in the case of little children, without any need of being acquired through study. This inherent love-and-respect toward parents is the feeling of filial piety. And this is the fountainhead of benevolence. It is the germination or starting point of the gradually expanding virtue, the universal love of mankind.

However, the seed of benevolence as sown in filial piety still needs timely cultivation, without which it tends to wither away or completely disappear, and then the great virtue of benevolence, even though it may have been developing in other directions, will be rootless, whereas it should have been a foundation. Or, the drifting virtue of benevolence may soon dry up like a tree without a root or a stream without a source. In order to keep benevolence durable and expanding, cultivation of the feeling of filial piety as its fountainhead is indispensable. This is one essential reason explaining why Confucians had all along championed the correlation between benevolence and filial piety.

Another reason lies in the fact that benevolence needs realization through actual practice. But then how should men practice benevolence? The Confucian *Analects* related, "Fan Ch'ih[i] asked about benevolence. The Master said, 'It is to love all human beings.' "[9] And Mencius also asserted, "The benevolent man loves others."[10] Then, whom should everyone love? Theoretically, he should love all others throughout the world as a matter of course. In such a great love, how should one start and whom should he love first of all? Is it not correct to say that he should love his parents to start with? As everyone has an inherent love toward his parents, is it not right that this filial piety should be observed as the starting point of one's practice of benevolence?

To all such questions, the answers of Confucian scholars were in the affirm-

[6] *Book of Mencius* VIB. 11.
[7] *Ibid.*, IIA. 6.
[8] *Ibid.*, VIIA. 15.
[9] *Analects* XII. 22.
[10] *Book of Mencius* IVB. 28.

ative. They agreed unanimously that the realization of benevolence must begin with the love of children toward their parents. This means that, in the complicated relations among men, filial piety forms the primary and most fundamental unit of mutual connection between two or more persons, in which the practice of benevolence must first be fulfilled. By inference, all other relations among human beings should emanate from this basic virtue as their source; otherwise they may not stay on the right course of benevolence for the attainment of peace and prosperity.

Meanwhile, it is possible that if one ignores his duty of showing love to his own parents, he will also be apt to neglect the practice of benevolence toward other people. Hence, the Confucian tenet "The benevolent man loves others" must be interpreted in the light of filial piety to the effect that "The benevolent man loves others, with his own parents as the starting point." This is a sound postulate because of its factual basis and indisputable reasoning.

It is a universal fact that every human being loves his parents from the beginning. If one should love others instead of his own parents, this would be a treacherous act. The *Classic of Filial Piety* thus set the warning: "Therefore to be without love of parents and to love other men [in their place] means to be a 'rebel against virtue'; to be without reverence for parents and to reverence other men means to be a 'rebel against sacred custom.' "[11] Actually, such moral rebels are rare in any civilized country. And eventually those who do not love their own parents will also have no love toward others; those who do not respect their own parents will not respect others in the proper way. Therefore, even though fraternal love may be prevalent, any biased practice of benevolence is vacillating and void if it is not rooted in the prime sense of filial piety. As Mencius pointed out, "The substantiation of benevolence begins with service to one's parents."[12] This, again, means that the observance of filial piety is one phase of the practice of benevolence, if not its starting point. This is another reason to explain why the Confucian so closely related these two virtues.

Accordingly, the doctrine of filial piety was recognized as primary among Chinese ethical principles, with the virtue thus shaped also taking the paramount position in Chinese morality. After the Han Dynasty (206 B.C.–A.D. 220), from the early part of third century B.C., in which the *Classic of Filial Piety* was supposed to have been "drastically revised by some Han filial pietist," this human virtue firmly established itself as the foundation of Chinese ethics. One can hardly understand Chinese ethics, and to some extent even Chinese political activities, if he cannot grasp the true import of this filial doctrine with its practical application in Chinese society.

Western philosophers generally appeal to reason, to conscience, to sympathy, or to the idealism of universal love of mankind in order to discover or ex-

[11] *Book of Filial Piety* (or *Classic of Filial Piety*) IX.
[12] *Book of Mencius* IVA. 27.

pound the source of morality. All these are important, of course, in the exploration of this ethical domain. And yet, without filial piety as their mainstay, all go adrift in confusion or are limited in their development and application. In other words, if one's love toward his parents withers away due to negligence of cultivation, where can he find better soil for developing reason, conscience, sympathy, and fraternal love? In this case, his conscience or sympathy may go astray or even die. His moral sense, then, is liable to become twisted into an abnormal state.

It is plain that the ideal development of good morality must derive from its true source, that is, filial piety in its enlightened and broad interpretation. This explains why ancient Chinese philosophers emphasized the doctrine of filial piety as the fountain of all good conduct.

Nevertheless, the foregoing observations do not mean that filial piety is all-embracing as the exclusive virtue. It is merely the starting point, not the final goal, of moral practice. Most Confucian scholars well understood this basic principle. As the *Classic of Filial Piety* put it: "Filial piety at the outset consists in service to one's parents; in the middle of one's path, in service to his sovereign; and, in the end, in establishing himself as a mature man."[13] Mencius further extended this virtue, saying, "The superior man should love his parents and be lovingly disposed to the people in general; and so he should also be kind to all living creatures."[14] He had previously pointed out, "Treat with reverence the elders in your own family, so that the elders in other families shall be similarly treated; treat with kindness the young in your own family, so that the young in other families shall be similarly treated."[15] All such passages show that filial duties toward one's parents must be expanded to the whole society. With the broad view in mind, the developing process may be pushed on step by step. The *Doctrine of the Mean* points out: "The ways of the superior man may be compared to what takes place in traveling, when to go to a distance we must first traverse the space that is near; and, in ascending a height, we must begin from the lower ground."[16] This way marks out the general process which is to start with one's loving and serving his own parents. Otherwise, by following the roundabout and difficult way, there may be "too much putting of things in confusion, fear, and sorrow, which may result in a standstill."[17] For this reason, it is plain why Mo Tzu's[j] (5th cent. B.C.) "principle of all-embracing love" and Jesus' doctrine of universal love have not been readily acceptable to the Chinese masses.

The Chinese ethical principle is not opposed to the doctrine of universal love, however. In embracing the latter, the former insists on starting with the observance of filial piety. That is the easiest approach. And then, step by step, its expanding process might readily be directed toward the goal of universal

[13] *Book of Filial Piety* I.
[14] *Book of Mencius* VIIA. 45.
[15] *Ibid.*, IA. 7.
[16] *Doctrine of the Mean* XV.
[17] *The Works of Chuang Tzu*, chap. IV.

love. The Confucian advocacy of this tenet definitely indicates the easy and practical way from filial service to moral practice in general.

All of the human virtues, therefore, should be born through observance of filial piety, which serves as the dynamic force of all other virtues. With genuine and comprehensive love toward one's own parents in its developing process, one may naturally learn to be benevolent to all living creatures, affectionate toward mankind as a whole, loyal to his country and to the duties of a free citizen, faithful in keeping obligations, righteous in action, peaceful in behavior, and just in all dealings. All these eight virtues, moral items, together with many others, may emanate from filial piety through its expansion. The *Classic of Filial Piety* says, "It is filial piety which forms the root of all virtues, and with it all enlightening studies come into existence."[18]

As the Confucian scholars always taught, in the learning of filial piety there should be concurrently the cultivation of other virtues for its supplementation. The main virtue must be endowed with benevolence and righteousness as well as loyalty to country and courage in justifiable actions. Hence, Tseng Tzu, the chief exponent of the Confucian doctrine of filial piety and one of the most learned disciples of the Sage, once said: "Those who lack propriety in private life, loyalty in serving the sovereign, or seriousness in discharging official duties, or faithfulness in treating friends, or bravery in waging war, are all found wanting in filial piety."[19] Therefore, for the fulfillment of the paramount virtue of filial piety many more moral aptitudes are required as its necessary supplementation. And, in this sense, filial piety has been extended far and wide to embrace all virtues. Since all virtues derive from filial piety, they all are also contained within the full development of filial piety.

There was no independent treatise on benevolence in Chinese classical works, but there was the distinguished filial-piety classic. By inference, it is unmistakable how important the feeling as well as the practice of filial piety was considered in Chinese ethics. It serves as both the fountainhead and the accomplished state of Chinese morality as a whole.

III.

We are now in a position to appreciate the paramount virtue of filial piety in its relation to Chinese society as a whole.

What influence has the doctrine of filial piety had on Chinese society? During the past several thousand years, how has the Chinese world been affected by this moral concept as its basic virtue? And how was Chinese society built up on the doctrine of filial piety as the cornerstone of Chinese ethics?

Chinese society has always been thoroughly under the sway of the ethical concept of filial piety. In other words, it was built up on the basis of filial piety, which has penetrated into every corner of Chinese life and society,

[18] *Book of Filial Piety* I.
[19] *Book of Rites* VIII. 24.

permeating all the activities of the Chinese people. Its influence has been all-prevailing. All traditional habits and customs of the people, collectively as well as individually, show the influence of the practice of this ethical principle. This observation may be verified through a careful survey of the family life, religious life, social life, and political life of the Chinese people.

First, with reference to family life, Chinese society, which has laid special emphasis on the integrity of household relations, treats the family as the foundation and the unit of society. Mencius held it to be true that "The root of the empire is in the State, and the root of the State is in the family."[20] The *Great Learning* advocated that "in order rightly to govern the State, it is necessary first to regulate the family; in order to put the empire in peace and prosperity, it is necessary first to regulate the State."[21]

Prior to the setting up of a community or a State, there must be the social unit called the family. Therefore, to put one's household in good order is the primary stage to demonstrate one's ability to hold a public office in such a way as to bring well-being to the State and peace to the empire. The primary stage, according to the Confucian view, was absolutely important as a prerequisite for the attainment of the latter. The logical reasoning was based on the premise: "What is meant by 'In order rightly to govern the State, it is necessary first to regulate the family,' is this: It is not possible for one to teach others if he cannot teach his own family."[22] As everyone's parents, and by inference also his ancestors, are the source of his life, this fundamental blood relationship legally as well as morally dictates the imperative rule that one owes certain unavoidable obligations to his parents. Taking for granted that he is endowed with the virtue of love, he must first show it toward his parents. Otherwise, how can he be expected to show kindness to society at large or to the country in which he lives? He must first be able to uphold his responsibility to his parents and his family as a social unit before he can shoulder his heavier, though remoter, responsibility toward society and the State. The logical conclusion of this reasoning on the importance of the family obviously revolves around the theme of filial piety.

Chinese society has therefore laid its emphasis upon the family system, in which the relationship between parents and children assumes the top priority, and filial respect and love toward one's elders are held to be urgently required even after their death. Mencius put it emphatically: "Of services which is the greatest? Service toward parents is the greatest. . . ."[23] Failing to perform this service, the root of all other services, one cannot be expected to do good to others.

But, how can one perform well the greatest service in one's life—to teach and to cultivate? This was what Chinese ethics and all other related learning, such as rituals and music, concentrated their efforts upon. From the emperor

[20] *Book of Mencius* IVA. 5.
[21] *Great Learning* I. 4.
[22] *Ibid.*, IX. 1.
[23] *Book of Mencius* IVA. 19.

and his ranking officials down to the common people, such as peddlers and hirelings, all without exception were taught and urged to practice filial piety. The teaching of their tutors, the inspiration drawn from customs and illustrations, and praise by the literati all emphasized filial piety. As the *Classic of Filial Piety* has taught, "Filial piety is the unchanging truth of Heaven, the unfailing equity of Earth, the [universal] practice of man."[24] Before the dawning of the twentieth century, most Chinese had actually observed this text and translated it into practice, though deviations may be found, of course, in certain respects.

Later, during the past half-century, since Western culture seeped into Chinese society with some ill effects, the former Chinese large-family system was gradually dissolved and the virtue of filial piety was also gradually relegated to obscurity. Nevertheless, most Chinese families still maintain reverential service to their elders as the Heaven-ordained obligation of all children. In practically all Chinese households elderly parents are living with their married son or daughter in harmony. Such a condition may be found less often in the Western world. This characteristic of the Chinese family system unmistakably demonstrates the practice of filial piety, which prevails in Chinese society.

Next to the parent-son relationship is the marriage relation, which in ancient China was held to be inviolable except in the case of certain adequately prescribed conditions. Again, with the doctrine of filial piety as the nucleus of the family system, the Chinese nuptial relationship was evolved. For the purpose of continuing the blood line as one important phase of filial piety, one must first of all keep oneself in sound physical condition. It was taught by the *Classic of Filial Piety* that "the body with its limbs and hair and skin comes to a person from father and mother, and one dares not spoil or injure it without justifiable cause."[25] This precept reaffirmed the importance of one's life as handed down by his ancestors. Then, as a necessary tribute to his forefathers, it is one's duty to perpetuate the blood line by producing offspring through wedlock. The marriage between man and wife was not an affair forged through instinctive desire alone but was based also on the higher concept of creating new life or lives so as to prolong those of one's ancestors including one's parents. Therefore, the Chinese family system placed great importance on marriage, not only because of the husband and the wife themselves, but also because of their children.

It is plain that, on the premise of filial piety, there were at least three essential points governing traditional Chinese marriage. First, the wedlock once formed was not to be dissolved without adequate reasons strictly prescribed. Second, the parents should see to it that their children were properly married, though not necessarily in terms of mutual love prior to the nuptial ceremony. And, third, the younger couple had the inherent obligation to produce offspring, and again bore of themselves the responsibility of getting their children

[24] *Book of Filial Piety* VII.
[25] *Ibid.*, I.

married when they became of marriageable age. Consequently, many of the ancient Chinese families have been propagated for thousands of years down to the present era in innumerable descendants.

Love counts after the nuptial ceremony of a couple and seldom before it. Such an ancient custom in China might seem absurd and even ridiculous to Westerners. The principal mission of marriage, then, lay in the perpetuation of the family line. If the couple failed to produce a male descendant, it was permissible for the husband to divorce his wife, or, as an alternative, for the husband to take one or more concubines. Even though such a practice is, from the modern viewpoint, unreasonable or unjust to womanhood, the ancient custom might be understood better in terms of practicing filial piety in its historical sense.

Aside from the vertical line of lineage involved in the Chinese family system, there is also the horizontal as represented by the brotherly relationship. Between father and son, filial piety was highly emphasized, while between the elder and the younger brothers mutual respect was the keynote. Chinese ethics urged the younger to respect his elder brother with submission, whereas the elder must love and take good care of the younger. Their connection was like that of hands and feet, with close co-operation as their reciprocal obligation.

Brotherly love in China may, nevertheless, be attributed to esteem for the source of their lives, which in turn had recourse to the filial-piety doctrine. As we highly esteem our parents, by inference we must also esteem their creatures. Hence, the fraternal duty was correlated with filial piety. As Mencius emphasized, "The great course in life of Yao and Shun[k] [emperors of antiquity] was simply that of filial piety and fraternal love."[26] Those who can perform the former well would, of course, know how to perform the latter. In many old Chinese families, brothers persistently shared the same household, even though they had themselves married and raised a host of children. And they retained the same household as long as either one or both of their parents remained alive. Some Chinese took pride in sharing the same household with several generations of the same paternal line. The large-family system thus brought about was gradually abandoned, for there were various drawbacks. But, as the origin of this system is explained, it is seen to be derived from the practice of filial piety.

Aside from the Chinese family system, which was built upon the practice of filial piety, Chinese religious life also had much to do with the doctrine of filial duties.

Apparently most Confucian scholars seldom touched upon religious subjects. They seemed to have behaved complacently toward the issue of life and death. They also slighted such controversial topics as the existence of God and the immortality of the soul, which have been so extensively discussed by Western philosophers. The Confucian *Analects* took the following stand: "Chi-lu[l] [a disciple of Confucius] asked about serving the spirits [of the dead]. The

[26] *Book of Mencius* VIB. 2.

Master said, 'While you are not able to serve men, how can you serve their spirits?' Chi-lu added, 'I venture to ask about death?' He got the answer, 'While you do not know life, how can you know about death?' "[27] This attitude of avoiding the issue of the unknown world was later almost unanimously adopted by Confucian followers. Some even openly disparaged the prevalent Taoist and Buddhist religions. What is the reason for this? Was there no need for a Confucian to have some sort of religious belief?

It is to be noted that most Confucian followers, though not openly professing religious worship, actually had faith in some basic principle in place of religion. This substitute was the observance of filial piety. The Confucian religion was intrinsically involved with the doctrine of filial piety.

How can this doctrine take the place of religion? Or, how can the doctrine of filial piety be formulated as a doctrine of religious worship? These two questions can be answered only by considering the essential elements of religion and the religious value of filial piety. Definitions of religion are varied. The essentials of any religion should consist of at least the following three points: first, faith in a supernatural being or a supernatural force; second, the hope for salvation from extinction; and, third, consolation for sentimental cravings. Since no religion can lack these three elements, any emotional or intellectual belief abounding with them may be called a religion or a substitute for religion. The doctrine of filial piety therefore transformed itself into a kind of religious worship, with beliefs and practices, or at least a substitute for them, and with all their essentials provided for.

Filial piety involves paying due respect not only to one's living parents but also to the deceased and to remote ancestors. Therefore, ancestor worship took place as a natural sequence of paying tribute to one's parents. The *Classic of Filial Piety* states:

> In filial piety there is nothing so great as honoring the father. In doing this, there is no achievement so great as making him an "Associate of Heaven": and Duke Chou[m] (d. 1094 B.C.) was the man who succeeded in this achievement. In ancient times Duke Chou offered sacrifice to his high ancestor Hou-chi[n] in the suburbs as an "Associate of Heaven," and set up King Wen's[o] (reigned, 1171–1122 B.C.) [his father's] tablet in the Ming-t'ang[p] [the Illustrious Hall] as an "Associate of Shang-ti"[q] [God-on-High]. The result was that from all the lands within the Four Seas came princes each with tribute to join in the sacrificial ceremony.[28]

Though some contemporary scholars, such as E. R. Hughes, doubt the interpretation given for these terms, "Associate of Heaven" and "Associate of Shang-ti," as being tinted with exaggeration, the quoted passage nevertheless portrays the sentiment of identifying the deceased father with a sort of superhuman force which deserved worship in the expanded expression of the feeling of filial piety. Hence, the Confucians laid particular emphasis on the solemniza-

[27] *Analects* XI. 11.
[28] *Book of Filial Piety* IX.

tion of the rites in ancestral worship, including funeral rites for deceased parents.

Before offering sacrifice to one's ancestors, the most rigorous vigil was kept inwardly by the pious offspring, while outwardly he fasted and bathed for at least one or more days.

On the day of the sacrifice when he enters the apartment [in the ancestral temple], he gasps: Surely there is a vision by the spirit tablet! After he has moved here and there [in making his sacrifice] and comes to the threshold, he is struck with awe: Surely he hears the particular tones of the deceased parents' voices! Then, as he hears and listens, he catches his breath: Surely he hears the sound of the deceased parents' sighing![29]

All such descriptions show Chinese ancestral worship to be laden with so much care and awe that it might even have surpassed the similar attitudes and practices of Christians in their church service. As ancestral worship had provided all the essentials of a religion, though in certain respects it differed from most of the regular religious sects, its essential meaning or significance may still be identical with that of, say, Christianity.

Chinese ancestor-worship had its main sentiment laid in commemoration of one's origin—the fountain of his life—and in repaying the debt that he owes to his ancestors, yet without much praying for blessings. To a certain extent, however, the rituals of worship may involve praying for blessings. As Confucius once put it, "When I wage war I will win the victory, and when offering sacrifice I will gain blessings, because I have practiced the right way."[30] He also pointed out, "For offering sacrifice, there are many purposes: one for praying for blessings, another for paying obligations, and still another for purification from sin."[31] Hence, Confucian ancestral worship did not conceal the desire for blessings from some supernatural force or forces, on the one hand, and to avoid calamity, on the other. When facing some critical moment—for example, prior to waging war or making important decisions on State affairs—ancient Chinese emperors or kings appealed to their ancestors for oracular revelations and blessings.

Later, the Chinese geomancy practiced by the common people in another form of ancestral worship laid even more emphasis upon the seeking of blessings from the supernatural power through the intermediary grace of ancestors who, in certain respects, were looked upon as identical to Buddhist or Taoist deities.

Next, the doctrine of filial piety played even a greater role in the search for emotional consolation through ancestral worship. Human beings cannot avoid death. Practically all religions have been built upon the sentiment that even after passing into the unknown world the human soul will be taken care of by some supernatural force, with deserved reward or punishment awaiting it.

[29] *Book of Rites* VIII. 24.
[30] *Ibid.*, V. 10.
[31] *Ibid.*, V. 11.

However, if there is another way to dispose of the soul without the need of the help of such abstract faith, there is no need to seek help from any religious sect.

The Confucians had their own particular way of disposing of this problem. Their way hinged upon the doctrine of filial piety. Mencius said, "There are three things which are unfilial, and having no posterity is the greatest of them."[32] This utterance may seem enigmatic to many, especially Westerners. Why was it so important for one to have posterity? To Confucians, one's offspring are the continuation of his own and also of his ancestors' lives. With such continuation, his and his ancestors' lives are looked upon as being immortal. Therefore, anyone who has cut short the flow of his ancestors' lives would be condemned as having committed the gravest sin of being unfilial.

On the other hand, anyone who has generations of offspring to prolong his lineage—especially one who has "father-like sons" to continue and, better still, to develop his father's academic attainment or industrial enterprise or other honorable pursuit—might take great consolation and pride in that fact. He may also deem it to be the immortality of his own life in succession to those of his ancestors. In this respect, the filially pious son is always cautioned to take good care of his own body and his own mental and moral attainments. Thus, the *Classic of Filial Piety* says, "The body with its limbs and hair and skin comes to a man from his father and mother, and it is on no account to be spoiled or injured."[33] The Confucian *Analects* also teaches, "If the son for three years does not alter from the way of his father, he may be called filial."[34]

As the continuous flow of one's life in his offspring, together with his trade or mental achievement, was looked upon by Confucians as the perpetuity of his own life, then the question concerning the continued existence of the soul (and where his soul will be) is unimportant. It was said, "When one has a son or sons, he will be satisfied with all in his life."[35] Professor T'ang Chün-i[r] has said: "As the life of one's offspring comes from his, the survival of one's life in future generations proves directly that his own life will never . . . perish. . . . Hence, in the preponderant love of one's offspring there will be only slight desire for immortality of his own soul after death."[36] Such a view undoubtedly was derived from the doctrine of filial piety. So, Chinese religious life virtually consists in the practice of filial piety.

Regarding social life, the Chinese people essentially expanded or extended family life into a larger area. This was an expansion of the practice of filial piety. In the Chinese community, kinship was formed through the marriage relationship, clans were established through blood relationship, and villages were built up through the regional relationship in which one was born and brought up. One's ancestors, and, still further, tutors and friends, were linked together through academic pursuit or mutual attraction or other causes—all

[32] *Book of Mencius* IVA. 26.

[33] *Book of Filial Piety* I.

[34] *Analects* IV. 20.

[35] A common adage in ancient China.

[36] T'ang Chün-i, *Chung-kuo wen-hua chih ching-shen chia-chih*[u] ("The Spiritual Worth of Chinese Culture") the Cheng Chung edition of 1953, p. 322.

these revolved around the center of gravity of the practice of filial piety. In Confucian ethics, the position of the tutor was particularly respected, ranking next to the father's position in every household. In a series of worshipped, more or less personified, objects, as stated in a simple tablet in the family alcove, there were "Heaven, Earth, Sovereign, Father, and Tutor." It was then observed that, as the parents had given birth to the physical body of the son, it was the teacher who had much to do in formulating the pupil's spiritual and cultural life. By expanding the view that one must honor his physical-life giver, he must also honor his cultural-life giver. By the same reasoning, one treats his bosom friends with high respect, too. Confucius' disciple Tseng Tzu therefore said, "The superior man on grounds of culture meets with his friends, and by their friendship helps to establish his virtue."[37]

While the Chinese respect for the tutor was an extension of filial piety, the respect of friendship was, as an expansion of the tutorship, also an extension of filial piety. The closely knit patterns of relatives, clansmen, fellow countrymen, and tutors, together with friends, were all interwoven around the filial axis in the Chinese community. Such a condition still prevails in some conservative groups of overseas Chinese residents.

Finally, in regard to the Chinese people's political life in its traditional form, it may be said that the Chinese seem to have shown little interest in politics as viewed in the West. The traditional political life of the Chinese was different from that of Westerners. It emphasized the principle of *laissez-faire,* because in every community or every village and in every trade organization the local self-government, based on the social relationship as stated above, usually functioned instead of higher administrative regulation. From the filial viewpoint, everyone was exhorted to respect the elder in the family in the management of family affairs and in the settlement of intra-family disputes, if any serious dispute arose; and then, in case of inter-family controversies, the village chief was at hand to settle them as amicably as possible. The *Book of Rites* emphasized, "As the people are taught filial piety and brotherly love at home, with reverence toward the elder and diligent care for the aged in the community, they constitute the way of a great king; and it is along this line that States as well as families will become peaceful."[38]

In the traditional local government of China, the village elder took the place of the administrator and the judge, and the observance of the traditional rituals or ceremonies also considerably eliminated the function of legal provisions. It was said, "The power which the rituals have of transforming by instruction is not on the surface. They put a stop to evil before it takes form. They cause men day by day to travel toward the good and leave wrong-doing far behind."[39] Thereupon, Confucius remarked that there is no more excellent method than the rituals for making those in authority secure and the people

[37] *Analects,* XII. 24.
[38] *Book of Rites* X. 45.
[39] *Ibid.,* II.

well-ordered. If every village is kept in good order, the whole State will naturally be in good order. Confucius said, "By reviewing the local rule in the villages, I comprehend that the King's Way should be easy."[40] Even though the whole empire might collapse, with the ruling house changing hands sometimes frequently, yet the people might still take advantage of the local village rule which, as stated above, was an expansion of the practice of filial piety in every good household.

For several thousand years, the Chinese people thus enjoyed their family life, religious life, social life, and political life—all involving, directly or indirectly, the practice of filial piety. Chinese society is thus seen to have been under the sway of the doctrine of filial piety and to have been built virtually upon the basis of filial piety as its essential foundation.

IV.

One of the outstanding characteristics which have marked the difference of social and cultural patterns between the Chinese and the Western countries is, therefore, the Chinese emphasis upon filial piety.

Chinese society and its cultural flow have been based on the doctrine of filial piety, which was derived from the intrinsic love of human beings in its natural course of development. The working principle may be found in the theme of extending such virtue beyond the household into society at large, with pure, true, and durable love, devoid of any consideration of selfish profit. By the practice of such a virtue as filial piety, although still far from being perfect, Chinese society and its culture could therefore endure throughout the past several thousand years up to the present. The unity of every family, the solidarity of the community, and the unification of the whole nation all depend upon the strengthening of such love.

The problem which now demands careful consideration is whether the present Chinese nation may still resort to the application of filial piety as one means to its rejuvenation *and* whether the ethical sense and practical value of filial piety still may hold its position in Chinese society. And, ultimately, in the synthetic or comparative point of view, whether the doctrine of filial piety still is worth being preserved and expanded in the cultural interflow between the East and the West in the light of philosophical examination and scrutiny. Before the paper is concluded, it is befitting that these questions should be answered, though only briefly.

It is to be noted that Chinese society has been undergoing drastic change. The ancient large-family system is collapsing, while filial piety as a paramount virtue is also being ignored progressively and gradually by the younger generation. In the face of such a critical period, will the modern philosophers of China sail with the tide that seems formidable enough to sweep people off their feet, or will they put up a gallant stand against this trend?

[40] *Ibid.*, X. 45.

As ethics must not bend itself to any evil force, what it should emphasize is not what the fact unwarrantedly dictates, but what the moral law discerns as the best for the world. There should be no expediency, submitting what ought to be to what society blindly prefers. Further, the Chinese ethics of today must take upon itself the responsibility of correcting the wrong and championing the right.

Therefore, the doctrine of filial piety must be propagated and put into practice in Chinese society and in other communities—though revision and modernization of certain phases of it are desirable. The intrinsic love which is inherent in the filial doctrine is most valuable to mankind.

Why should filial piety be preserved in the modern world? The import of this virtue is the affirmation of affection for human life and society, if not exactly love; and it is an essentially consolidating factor of society. As its starting point is the children's love of their parents, it is conceivable that the inherent nature of life must be good and of intrinsic value. Hence, the filially pious son should highly esteem the origin of his life, should carefully cherish his own life and the name of his family, and then create the next generation so as to maintain the flow of life without interruption. This is the full affirmation of the value of life. And this is the most fundamental attitude of the Chinese toward life, indicating that life is worth living.

By use of the filial doctrine to solidify human society, with the correlated virtues of mankind, such as benevolence, righteousness, justice, faithfulness, and the love of peace, together with bravery in fighting against the aggression of brutes, all brought up to the fullest possible extent, then and only then may the world achieve the blessings of durable peace.

In this regard, the fundamental premise to be definitely and universally recognized should be mutual love of all men in place of jealousy and hatred. Only through mutual love may human beings come together, with reciprocal co-ordination and co-operation of efforts for the common good. This is only common sense—for all mankind.

QUESTION: What is the relation of justice to filial piety? In case there is a conflict, how can you reconcile them? What about the story in Confucius' *Analects* in which the father stole the goat and the son refused to appear as a witness in the court against him.

ANSWER: Such conflicts between virtues, especially between loyalty and filial piety, were frequently found in the history of the Chinese ethical thought. There is no simple solution to such conflicts, that is, no fixed general rule for settling them. The only solution is that you have to consider the situation in which you are. In other words, you have to consider what F. H. Bradley called "My Station and its Duties." For example, if you are an official, you will decide in favor of justice, but, if you are an ordinary person, then you will decide in favor of filial piety. In the case of the father who stole the goat, the son should not appear as witness against his father. In not appearing as witness, the son is not violating justice. For, whether his father is guilty or not, the son is not in the position to judge. If you judged your own father, you wouldn't feel easy in your heart. Thus, the Confucian ethical point of view is that, in case of such conflicts, though there is no fixed rule, you should do what is proper in your heart, that is, what you will feel easy about when you have done it.

QUESTION: Why should we love and respect our ancestors? The important thing for us to do is to educate the young.

ANSWER: If anyone doesn't like his ancestors, how can he like the man in the street? The doctrine of filial piety is aimed at the cultivation of love toward your parents, your ancestors, and then extending your love toward others. If you don't like your ancestors, there is the end of the matter. But my advice is that you should like your ancestors. That is all.

COMMENT BY T'ANG CHÜN-I

A parent's love of his child is strictly biological, whereas filial piety, love and respect for one's parents, is not biological but is moral, being based upon a sense of obligation or a debt of gratitude, and is therefore spiritual.

[a] 謝幼偉
[b] 孝
[c] 曾子
[d] 梁啟超
[e] 仁
[f] 王陽明, 守仁
[g] 孫逸仙 (中山)
[h] 有子
[i] 樊遲
[j] 墨子
[k] 堯舜
[l] 季路
[m] 周公
[n] 后稷
[o] 文王
[p] 明堂
[q] 上帝
[r] 唐君毅
[s] 儒家哲學
[t] 飲冰室合集
[u] 中國文化之精神價值

DAISETZ T. SUZUKI[a]

Basic Thoughts Underlying Eastern Ethical and Social Practice

I.

To understand what lies underneath Eastern* culture and moral practice it is necessary to know the three principal forms of thought prevailing in the East: Confucianism, Taoism, and Buddhism. The first two are native to China, whereas the last is an importation from the neighboring country, India, in the first century of the Christian era.

Confucianism is concerned chiefly with moral life and politics, that is, with worldly affairs so called. While Taoism is also politically minded, there is much of religion in it, for instance, when it refers to the "Mysterious Mother" (*hsüan p'in*[b]).[1] Buddhism, when it was first transplanted to China, encountered some resistance from the native scholars, chiefly the Confucians, but proved itself strong enough to be gradually recognized not only by the people but also by the intellectuals. The reason is that Buddhism has what the Chinese mind lacks —metaphysics and spiritual feelings. This fact first repelled the Chinese but later attracted them.

Besides, in the Taoist way of thinking and feeling there is something closely related to the Buddhist trends of thought: love of Nature, poetic imagination, transcendentalism, a mystic appreciation of reality. Buddhism also has much thought affiliating itself with Confucianism, for instance, when it is not so amoralistic as Taoism. But it was the Taoists who first approached Buddhism and adopted a great deal of its way of life and finally developed a religious system akin to it. Not only that, but, when the Chinese began in the seventh century to establish their own forms of Buddhism, they exhibited a great deal

* This term will be used here in a very narrow sense, for I wish to limit the applicability of my thought to the Far Eastern area, that is, China and Japan.

[1] Lao Tzu, *Tao-te ching* VI.

of originality. The Ching-t'u[c] (Jōdo), Hua-yen[d] (Kegon), Ch'an[e] (Zen), and T'ien-t'ai[f] (Tendai) are such forms. In them we can detect the imaginative depths of the Chinese mind as well as its speculative penetration. The Chinese perhaps did not realize that all these qualities lay dormant in them until the qualities were finally brought brilliantly to the surface of their consciousness.

As I consider the Zen form of Buddhism more important in many ways than the other forms, such as the Jōdo, I wish to regard Zen as representing Buddhism generally when I talk about the Buddhist influence over Eastern, and especially Japanese, moral life.

Zen flourished in China from the seventh century throughout the T'ang (610–905) and the Sung (960–1278), and even down to the Ming (1369–1628). In Zen we find the best that Chinese culture can offer to the world harmoniously blended with the best of the Indian speculative mind.

In the following, let me take up the Buddhist philosophy of Emptiness and contrast it with the Western way of thinking, for Zen also bases its *Welt-* and *Lebens-Anschauung* on it.

II.

One, at least, of the most fundamental differences between East and West as far as their way of thinking is concerned is that the Western mind emphasizes the dualistic aspect of reality while the Eastern mind basically tends to be advaitist. Advaitism is not the same as monism; it simply asserts that reality is non-dualistic. Monism limits, whereas advaitism leaves the question open, and refuses to make any definite statement about reality. It is not-two, which is not the same as one. It is both yes and no, yet it is neither the one nor the other.

The West lives in a world separated into two terms: subject and object, self and not-self, yes and no, good and evil, right and wrong, true and false. It is therefore more logical or scientific, where yes cannot be no and no cannot be yes, where a square is not a triangle, where one is not two, where "I" and "thou" are eternally separated and can never be merged, where God creates and the creature forever remains created, where "our Father . . . art in heaven" and we mortals are groveling on earth. The Western mind abhors paradoxes, contradictions, absurdities, obscurantism, emptiness, in short, anything that is not clear, well-defined, and capable of determination.

Advaitism is not a very clear concept, however, and I should like to have another term to make my position better defined. When I say that reality is not dualistic, that a world of subject and object is not final, and that there is a something which is neither subjective nor objective, and further that this something is not to be subsumed under any category born of the dualistic concept of subject and object, I may be stamped as a mystic with all his scientifically unacceptable qualifications. Whatever this may mean, the mystic has a very concrete and therefore a very positive experience of ultimate reality which according to him cannot be conceptualized after the ordinary rules of logical thinking. Logic, as we understand it, has its limitation and cannot expect to catch every fish in its net.

All our sense-experiences are limited and definite, and the intellect based on them is also limited and definable. They all belong in the world of subject and object, seeing and seen, thinking and thought, that is, in the world of dualities. Here reality is always subjected to a separation; it is never grasped in its suchness or isness, or in its totality. Logicians and scientists deal with reality in its inevitably separated and therefore limited aspect. Therefore, there is always a something left over after their studies and measurements. They are not conscious of this something; in fact, they insist that there is nothing left behind, that they have everything they want to study. They go even so far as to declare that if there is anything left they have nothing to do with it, for it can never be scooped up with their logical shovel.

In fact, there are some minds that can never be satisfied with so-called logical accuracies and mathematical measurements, for they have the feeling or sense of a something which persistently claims their attention and which can never be "accurately" determined. This something is described by Baudelaire as "the steely barb of the infinite." They cannot rest until this disquieting something is actually held in their hands in the same way as we pick up a piece of stone or listen to a singing bird. Whatever name we may give to this mysterious something—God, or Ultimate Reality, or the Absolute, or the *Ātman,* or the Self, or Brahman, or Tao, or Heaven, or Reason, or the Infinite, or Emptiness, or Nothing—it is always bafflingly before us or behind the duality of "I and thou," or of the self and not-self, or subject and object, or God and the creation.

I may provisionally call this mysterious something the First Person, "I." It cannot be logically determined, temporally chronicled, spatially located. You might say, "That is too vague, too obscure, and we cannot deal with such an unknowable." Naturally, it cannot be clear and definable as far as our intellection is concerned. It is "O taste and see."[2] The tasting-and-seeing is not intellectual; it is perceptual and personal and cannot be brought out to the open market of conceptualization. But its presence in our mind is undeniable and its persistent call for our conscious attention is authentically attested in the history of thought. For this no specifications are needed.

Let me repeat: the First Person, "I," is not the subject standing in contrast to the object; it is not the self opposing the not-self; nor is it the creator looking at his creation. It can never be caught up in any form of intellectual duality, because it is that which produces all dualities and which hides itself somewhere as soon as dualities are taken notice of. It is, therefore, outside the pale of our logical comprehension. The only way to catch it is by means of a paradox or contrary diction—"the clear light of the void," or "rays of darkness," or "eternal present," or "pure darkness is pure light," or *"todo y nada"* (all and nothing), or $0 = \infty$, and so on.

[2] Psalms 34:8.

Zen is rich in this kind of vocabulary, as is explained in my works on Zen.

There is no doubt that this mysterious First Person is not an object of knowledge. But, if it is not, how can one take hold of it so that one can say, "I have it now!"? An "intuition" does not seem to be an adequate term for this kind of experience. "Feeling" is liable to be misunderstood, unless a specifically defined sense is given to it. I like to take it in the most primary sense, somewhat in the way the eye sees and the ear hears.

The difference between sense-perception and "primary" feeling-experience is: in the former there is a sense-subject and its object, but, in the latter, subject and object are not differentiated—subject is object, and object is subject, and yet there is no particularizable substance to be known as such, as a something. What I can state, though only tentatively, in this "primary" experience is that, when I hear or see, it is my whole being wherein hearing is seeing and seeing is hearing, because in the totality of my being there are no such sense-differentiations as one observes in one's sense-perception.

That is to say, one's whole being is there where the hearing or the seeing takes place and there is no sense-particularization. One's whole being is the ear or the eye, and with it the totality of being hears or sees itself in the hearing or seeing. There is nothing in it that is vague or obscure or chaotic. In truth, the ear then hears and the eye sees in the real sense of the term.

Daitō Kokushi,[g] [3] one of the greatest Zen masters of Japan, composed a poem on the subject:

> *When the ear sees,*
> *And the eye hears,*
> *One cherishes no doubts:*
> *How naturally the rain drips*
> *From the eaves!*

This is a typically Zen poem, one might say. How could the raindrops from the eaves be heard as natural when the sense functions in such a crazily confused manner as stated above? But we must remember that our ordinary hearing or seeing is a specialized sense-function taking place at a specified area where a specified set of nerves converge for the performance of a particular limited form of activity. A totalistic hearing or seeing, on the other hand, eventuates at the deepest level of one's being, where hearing is seeing and seeing hearing. If this functional interfusion should come to pass at the localized terminal, there would be an utter confusion of the senses. What might be called the totalization of particular senses, including intellection, transforms all the brutal mechanistic laws of "necessity" into something full of meaning. Life then ceases to be a mere repetition of biological events governed by the so-called laws of Nature.

This may be called Eastern subjectivism, though the term frequently lends itself to gross misinterpretation. What I mean by subjectivism is not opposed

[3] Daitō Kokushi or "Daitō the National Teacher" (1282–1337) is the honorary title given by the Emperor Godaigo but he is otherwise known as Shūhō Myōchō. The thirty-one syllable poem quoted here is a well-known one ascribed to him. Unfortunately, I am so far unable to locate its source.

to objectivism, which generally characterizes Western thought. Eastern subjectivity is an absolute one. It is a position transcending all forms of opposition and separation. Buddhist philosophy designates it as "Emptiness" (*śūnyatā* in Sanskrit, *k'ung*[h] in Chinese, and *kū* in Japanese). I understand there was a Western philosopher who called it "subjectum," which corresponds to the "First Person" or Lin-chi's[i] [4] *jen*[j] ("person" or "I").

III.

The philosophy of Emptiness is full of meaning. As I state repeatedly, it is not the philosophy of sheer nothingness; it is the philosophy of infinite possibilities, of a nothing filled with fullness of things, in which "nothing is lost and nothing is added." And there is no contradiction whatever when I say that "Emptiness" is the First Person, "I," and that the First Person, "I," is Emptiness. The identity can be expressed also in the following formulas:

zero = infinity,
infinity = zero.

In the familiar Buddhist phraseology:

rūpam = *śūnyatā*,
śūnyatā = *rūpam*.[5]

I have no time here to explore all the implications that can be discovered in the philosophy of Emptiness. Suffice it to give two of the most significant: (1) Being and becoming are one. (2) Necessity and freedom are one. As long as we hold to the dualistic way of thinking, statements like these are highly contradictory or utterly impossible, and, psychologically as well as morally, we shall find ourselves constantly in one form or another of nervous tension and asked to come to a decision. Fortunately, Buddhism is not a system of philosophy; it simply makes use of philosophy in order to satisfy our intellectual requirements. It tells us that there is a higher field of discipline where we can find our original home. I may call it an ethico-aesthetic experience of reality. Judaeo-Christian mythology will supply us with an illuminating parallel to illustrate what I mean by the "ethico-aesthetic."

When God as creator came out of the Godhead (as Emptiness), he did not ask the question "Why?," nor did he complain about the task of looking after his work. He saw light separating itself from darkness, and said, "Good!"

[4] That is, Lin-chi I-hsüan (Rinzai Gigen, d. 867 A.D.). *Rinzai Roku* ("Sayings of Rinzai").

[5] In Chinese the formula is: *shih*[bq]*=k'ung,*[br] *k'ung=shih;* in Japanese: *shiki=kū, kū=shiki;* in English: *form=emptiness, emptiness=form.* Literally, it is: "Form is not different from emptiness, emptiness is not different from form; what is form is no other than emptiness, what is emptiness is no other than form." This is the basic philosophy of the "Prajñā-pāramitā" group of Buddhist *Sūtras*. In the original Sanskrit the phrase runs:

Iha, Śāriputra, rūpaṁ śūnyatā, śūnyatā eva rūpaṁ;
rūpan na pṛthak śūnyatā, śūnyatā yā na pṛthag
rūpaṁ; yad rūpaṁ sā śūnyatā, yā śūnyatā tad rūpaṁ.

Cf. D. T. Suzuki, *Manual of Buddhism* (London: Rider and Company, 1950), p. 26.

It is not our business as human beings to fathom the meaning of this utterance on the part of the creator, for it is the most mystically pregnant exclamation anyone endowed with the power of expressing himself can make while viewing any work, human or divine.

The eye confronts a mass of spring foliage and declares it green. Insofar as we cannot go any further than that, we are still on the logically mechanistic level of necessity. We may be human but are far from being divine. It is only when we can pronounce, "Good!" that we can approach the "psychology" of the creator, which is what I term "ethico-aesthetic." The "good" here has no moral implication pure and simple. It corresponds to what we call in the East *myō* in Japanese (*miao*[k] in Chinese). When we understand it, the whole universe, including everything in it, good and evil, right and wrong, subject and object, you and me, goes through a transformation, which is marvelously phenomenal.

Advaitism, or the philosophy of Emptiness, is still an intellectual and therefore a conceptual term and does not mean much to the Oriental mind, which is ever yearning for the deepest and most fundamental in the world we live in. The logically true or the morally good is never satisfactory, never fully thirst-quenching. We must come to the realization of the *myō,* the ultimately good, while surveying the creation in its infinite wholeness. Let us study the *myō* for a while.

To understand what the *myō* means is to understand the working of Japanese psychology, or that which lies behind Japanese culture and Japanese behavior. The term appears in Lao Tzu's *Tao-te ching* and also in Chuang Tzu's work. Perhaps it is originally Taoist. Buddhism adopted it, and *saddharma* (true law) was translated as *miao-fa*[l] (*myōhō*) in A.D. 407 by Kumārajīva. The best English equivalent one can find for this term *"myō"* is "mystery" or "mysterious." But "mystery" or "mysterious" has certain intellectual overtones, which is inevitable, seeing that the Western mind is not so well acquainted with the realm of discipline where the idea of the *myō* plays a predominant role.

The *myō* being a Taoist term, it is best for us to know something more about Lao Tzu. It is possible that the *myō* was used before his time,[6] but it was he who made the most of it. In the first chapter of the *Tao-te ching* the author refers to the *myō* as something characteristic of Tao. Tao is beyond any form of designation or definition. As soon as one begins to define it, Tao ceases to be Tao. But, as we cannot leave it without designating it somehow, we call it Tao and make it manifest as "being" and "non-being," as something contradicting itself. This is Tao determining itself.

[6] A commentator of the *Tao-te ching* says that the character *miao* first appears in the *I ching* (*Shuo kua,* Eighth Wing), where it is verbalized. (Cf. Carl F. Baynes, trans., *The I ching,* or *Book of Changes.* The Richard Wilhelm translation rendered into English by Carl F. Baynes. Foreword by C. G. Jung. Bollingen Series No. 19. 2 vols. [New York: Pantheon Books, 1950], Vol. I, p. 291.) It is generally used either as a noun or as a modifier; it is unusual to see it turned into a verb as in *miao wan-wu*[bs] "the ten thousand things [acquire the quality of the] *myō* (or *miao*)." The *miao* may be said to be our human response to a situation in which the finites are harmoniously blended with the Infinite, or we can state that here the absolute present touches on Eternity. It is interesting to note that *miao* in the *I ching* is identified with the Spirit (*shen*[bt]) that moves behind the ten thousand things. The Infinite is "the unmoved mover" behind the ten thousand things, behind the constant flowing stream of all things.

By means of "non-being" we have a glimpse of the *myō,* and by means of "being" we have an objective world of multiplicities and limitations (*chiao,*[m] *kyō*). The world of being is subject to quantitative measurements, whereas the world of non-being is unlimited. Unlimited and therefore infinite is this world of absolute non-being. We human beings live in two worlds, limited and yet unlimited, finite and yet infinite. This living in two worlds is called *gen* (*hsüan*[n] in Chinese).[7] And for this reason Lao Tzu's philosophy is known as the teaching of the *hsüan* (*gen*), and we have compounds like these: *hsüan-hsüeh*[o] (doctrine of the *hsüan*), *hsüan-lan*[p] (survey of the *hsüan*), *hsüan-t'an*[q] (discussion on the *hsüan*), *hsüan-chih*[r] (principle of the *hsüan*), *hsüan-men*[s] (doorway to the *hsüan*), etc. When Taoism was made a pseudo State-religion early in the T'ang, Lao Tzu was canonized in A.D. 666 as Hsüan-yüan huang-ti[t] (the emperor of the most abstruse philosophy).

Gen (*hsüan*) literally means "dark," "reddish black," "the color of the sky," which derivatively came to signify "impenetrable," "unfathomable," "inexpressible," "mysterious," etc. When this *gen* is personified, it is called the "Mother." All things come from the Mother and return to her. The Mother is "the creator of the ten thousand things." In the West, the creator is the Father, the Heavenly Father, the Almighty God of wrath and jealousy, but in the East the creator is the Mother, the Mother Earth, the Great Earth, or, as Lao Tzu has it, the "Valley Spirit," or the "Mysterious Female."[8] (This difference between East and West provides us with a number of interesting topics for discussion.)

Gen (*hsüan*) and *myō* (*miao*) are largely synonymous, with perhaps this distinction: *gen* has a more objective sense, while *myō* is more subjective; *myō* is more psychological and *gen* more ontological; *myō* is the way human minds react to the presence of *gen*. When we see a wonderfully executed, most inspiring work of art, we describe it as *myō* and not *gen*. The impenetrable depths of the sky are *gen* but not *myō*. All things designable can be designated as *myō* issue from what is *gen*. Sometimes the two characters form a compound. In this case, *genmyō* may be tentatively translated as "deeply (or unfathomably) mysterious."

The character *myō* (*miao*) was originally written as a composite of *gen* (*hsüan*[u]) and *shō* (*shao*[v]), which latter means "young," "small," "weak," "wanting," etc. But later the *gen* was replaced by the character *jo* (*nü*[w]), meaning "a woman," and then *myō* came to be associated with a young maiden. But the original meaning was never lost, that is, an aesthetic appreciation of something immeasurably deep and defying description of any kind. The *myō* is thus not to be caught up by the analytical meshes, however fine, of scientific study, for there is something warm and living and full of creativity, which can only be experienced individually, personally, and is not to be conceptualized.

The *myō* is, then, definable as the feeling reflecting the mystic experience of Identity (*gendō, hsüan-tung*[x]), in which nothingness (*jōmu, chang-wu*[y]) and

[7] *Tao-te ching* I.
[8] *Ibid.*, VI.

somethingness (*jōu, chang-yu*[z]) are indistinguishably merged as one, though differentiated in name. The *gen* is its ontological name, and the *myō* is its psychological, or, rather, aesthetic reaction. When the mystic experience of Identity is actually attained in its pure totalistic aspect, each particular experience one may have in the realm of finites will participate in the general *myō* feeling for "the mystery of being" (*hsüan chih yu hsüan*[aa]). Hence "the doorway of all *myō* (*shūmyō no mon, chung-miao chih men*[ab])."

In ordinary language, the *myō* experience is essentially the outcome of understanding the obscurest depths of eternal Tao (*jōdō, chang-tao*[ac]) or eternal *Logos* (*jōmei, chang-ming*[ad]), which expresses itself in the finite world of particulars (*yūmei, yu-ming*[ae]). The finite, namable world of particulars ultimately returns to the infinite Nameless (*mumei, wu-ming*[af]), which is called by Lao Tzu "the Mother of all things." By "returning," however, is not meant "to stay returned"; it means that there is a close interrelationship between the Infinite and the finites, the Mother and the child (*eiji, ying-erh*[ag] or *eigai, ying-hai*). So, says Lao Tzu, the Mother and the child are not to be separated.[9] The understanding of this Identity constitutes the feeling of *myō*. It goes without saying that the Identity is not to be numerically conceived, but is on the transcendental level of the Nameless. We may call it the mystical experience of the Darkness. It would be a great mistake to try to treat it along the line of intellectual analysis.

The serious oversight which is likely to be committed by scientists or logicians is to reduce everything to mathematical measurements and give the result in numbers or in signs. They forget altogether that the essential nature of the feeling is subjective and that when it is objectified it ceases to be itself and turns into a concept which has no life whatever. The feeling that is not alive is no feeling. Especially is this the case with the feeling that arises in connection with the totality of things, which cannot be finitely comprehended. A circle with an infinitely extending circumference is one of such cases; an infinite series of finite numbers is another. A serial infinity may be mathematically symbolized and treated accordingly. An infinity as a concrete totality is not only beyond the pale of intellection but incapable of becoming an object of feeling in the ordinary sense. An infinite totality may be symbolized to a certain degree or may have its analogical representation. As long as our intellect and senses are limited to finite experiences, an infinity must be said to be altogether outside their comprehension. Yet, we have a feeling for the Infinite, and this feeling is at the basis of all finite and particular feelings. We only "vaguely" feel its presence, though we ordinarily fail to bring it to the surface of our consciousness.

When I say a feeling of the Infinite, I use the term "feeling" in its deepest and most fundamental sense. I often used "intuition" in such cases, but I now find it somewhat inaccurate because intuition has still an epistemological taint, as I stated before, while an experience of the Infinite is not to be subsumed

[9] *Ibid.*, XVI, XX, XXV, XXVIII.

under the same category. It is *sui generis.* It is no wonder that so-called religious-minded people ascribe this experience to a power higher than themselves.

Western people try to approach Tao objectively, as I said before, and therefore inevitably epistemologically. On the other hand, the Eastern approach is from the inside; that is, it is subjective, and by "subjective" I mean from the point of view of the thing-in-itself-ness of a thing, or simply its isness. To see a thing subjectively, therefore, means to see it as it is, in its suchness, in its just-so-ness. What we ordinarily call "subjective" is, strictly speaking, not subjective, for it is still objective inasmuch as it is conceived in opposition to an object. No subject is possible without its object, and to this extent there is in the subject something of objectivity. I like to point out that there is a something, though not definitely designable as this or that, even before the differentiation of subject and object. This is one of the first questions the Zen master would require us to answer: "What does your face which you had even before you were born look like?" This "face" which every one of us has, or this something which transcends all forms of dualistic opposition, is that which creates "the ten thousand things." It may be called the Absolute or Ultimate Reality, or Emptiness (as Buddhists have it). Those who hold this view cannot be called subjectivists as the term is commonly understood.

I may add one more word and say that the identification of subject and object where self-knowledge or self-realization takes place is in actuality the self-determining of Emptiness, or the Godhead's turning into God as the creator. By this turning, the Godhead becomes self-conscious in the way Emptiness comes to self-realization.

When I make this kind of statement, I am said to be vague, approaching nonsense. But, when you actually have it, you know what it is and will realize that there is nothing clearer, simpler, and, at the same time, deeper.

When one asserts that the seer is the seen and the seen is the seer, we may declare him nonsensical, because logically A is A and is never not-A. Moreover, practically speaking, the eye cannot see itself—it requires a mirror to see itself. But, in actuality this kind of seeing is not at all seeing itself, but seeing its reflection, which is by no means its self, as it is in its isness, or in its nakedness.

The West excels in describing an object in its relatedness to others, in analyzing it epistemologically, following logical steps one after another, and in coming to a certain form of conclusion, which, however, is not a conclusion, because it is never conclusive or final. One "conclusion" reached by one philosopher is sure to be contested by another, indefinitely.

The East excels in seeing reality or Tao from the inside, from within, in its just-so-ness, without doing any violence to it. Easterners have been so trained since the first awakening of consciousness.

This awakening has taken two separate courses in its development: the one is the Western way and the other the Eastern. We can say that the West is extrovert, while the East is introvert or introspective or self-analyzing or not at all analyzing. The West is not unconscious of this self-analyzing process, the discipline prevailing in the East. But the West has been doing this cursorily, sporadically, or spasmodically. We see in the West some splendid specimens of it, such as Plato, Plotinus, Eckhart, St. John of the Cross, and so on. But they have been looked upon as abnormal, eccentric, and unacceptable.

A system of discipline more or less methodical has been going on since of old in China as well as in India. To give an example from the *Chuang Tzu*[10]:

Yen-ch'eng Tzu-yu[ah] said to Tung-kuo Tzu-chi[ai]: Since I received your instruction, in one year I gained simplicity; in the second year I knew how to adjust myself as demanded; in the third I felt no impediments; in the fourth I objectified myself; in the fifth I had an attainment; in the sixth the spirit came to me; in the seventh I was in conformity with Heaven; in the eighth I had no thought of life and death; finally, in the ninth year, I attained to Great *Miao*.

As long as we are in a dualistic world of birth and death, right and wrong, good and evil, subject and object, we cannot realize what the *myō* is; we feel it only when we come in contact with the Infinite, where we are free from all forms of restriction and inhibition. To accomplish this, it may take nine years or more, but one will attain it if one does not relax his efforts.

Instantaneity and eternity, *saṁsāra* and Nirvāṇa, this world of transiency and the Pure Land of permanent peace, are great contrasts. We live in the former and desire the latter. The desire is strong, but its object is at a great distance. It is impossible to cross the distance. Some say that this distance is the soul of the beautiful and to contemplate the beautiful is bliss. This view, however, is not the one held by Eastern thinkers. Chuang Tzu would advise us to attain what is known as *tso-wang*,[aj] "sitting-forgetting," or *sang-wou*,[ak] "losing the self."[11] Chuang Tzu is not a Buddhist; therefore, he does not go any further than to state that the self is to be lost or forgotten. Buddhists declare that there is no self from the beginning, that the mirror has never been soiled with dust, and that therefore there is no need of trying to clean it. When we get rid of the delusions arising from finite existences, the "self" is purified, and the "Original Person" reveals himself. It is he who enjoys the ethico-aesthetic feeling of the *myō*.

Tso-wang[12] is defined by Chuang Tzu: "It is freeing oneself from the body, getting rid of the intelligence, and, further, thus, by separating oneself from form and removing the intellect, identifying with the Great Thoroughfare (*ta-t'ung*[al])."[13] *Sang-wou*[14] is given the following description: It is "as if absent-mindedly going beyond the opposition of subject and object, as if the body were like a dead tree and the mind like cold ashes, and no longer looking like

[10] Book XXVII, "Yü-yen."[bu] "*Yü-yen*" means "a talk ascribed to somebody else." It is a fable, or legend, or parable. Most of the stories found in the *Chuang Tzu* are of this nature.
[11] *Ibid.*, II, "On Equalizing Contraries."
[12] *Ibid.*, VI, "The Great Teacher."
[13] This may also be translated as "Great Identity" and interpreted as equivalent to "Great Emptiness."
[14] *Chuang Tzu* II.

one's former self." According to Chuang Tzu, when this state of mind is attained, one is in communion with *t'ien-chün*[am] (heavenly equity), or *t'ien-i*[an] (heavenly unity),[15] which means that one goes beyond the humanly finite discrimination of good and bad, right and wrong, and lives in the field of infinity, where things move in their just-so-ness. Everything has its place, its destiny, its function, and, so long as it does its work in the way its nature requires though it may not be conscious of it, there is nothing that will interfere with its movements.

In regard to the experience of Identity of Heavenly Unity, Chuang Tzu has the following to say about the wise man who achieves such transcendence of dualistic difficulties:

It is only the wise man who knows how to make use of the principle of Identity through the maze of contrary ideas. He does not uphold his own views as absolutely correct; he surrenders himself to that which transcends all individual differences. By so doing he objectifies himself. By objectifying himself he passes over obstacles. By passing over obstacles he attains Identity and with this he is contented. He has no cravings for anything else. He rests with himself now, and he does not know why it is so. This is Tao.[16]

This is one of the difficult and obscure passages in the *Chuang Tzu,* and I have added a few words to make it more intelligible to modern readers. The translation is inevitably an interpretation and open to discussion.

The principle of Identity to which Chuang Tzu resorts in order to unify or merge the controversies that have been going on around him has its concrete symbolization in the person of Nan-kuo Tzu-chi.[ao] This person is introduced at the beginning of Chuang Tzu's discourse on the subject, that is, in Book II of his work. Nan-kuo Tzu-chi is probably Chuang Tzu's imaginary creation. He is found to be leaning against the table as if lost to the whole world. He looks so absent-minded that he is no longer like his former self, which was involved in the whirlpools of subject and object, right and wrong, good and bad.

To such a one, metaphysically speaking, the whole universe is no bigger than the tip of a hair; P'eng Tsu,[ap] historically renowned for his long life of 800 years, is not any older than the baby who dies even before weaning; "heaven-and-earth and I are of the same age; the ten thousand things and I are all one." From the moral point of view, he is a wise man or a perfect man. He is not concerned with worldly affairs of gain and loss; he lives outside the dust and filth of a finite life; he is the living example of *miao-tao*.[aq] [17]

[15] *Ibid., T'ien-chün* and *t'ien-i* are interchangeable; they both refer to the heavenly reason (*t'ien-li*[bv]), in which all inequalities and contradictions we encounter in this world of finites are wiped out, or rather, merge, though not indiscriminately.

[16] *Ibid.*

[17] *Ibid.*

IV.

Living is the art of creativity demonstrating itself. Creativity is objectively seen as necessity, but from the inner point of view of Emptiness it is "just-so-ness" (*jinen* or *shizen* in Japanese and *tzu-jan*[ar] in Chinese). *Jinen*[18] is literally "by-itself-so" and may be regarded as equivalent to spontaneity or naturalness, but in *jinen* we see the innerliness of things more emphatically brought out. When the human mind is perfectly attuned to this innerliness, the feeling of the *myō* is awakened in a manner somewhat as when the tongue touching sugar tastes it sweet.

Objectively speaking, the *myō* may be represented as the straight line of time drawn tangent to a circumferenceless circle of Emptiness. The point at which the time-line touches the curve is the absolute present, or eternal now, or here-now. All the past converges here and all the future issues from here, but the "here," which is really "here-now," is Emptiness itself—Emptiness infinitely rich in content and inexhaustibly creative. Chuang Tzu calls it the "heavenly storehouse" (*tenfu, t'ien-fu*[as]). The *myō* is the human way of expressing this experience.

Emptiness, like the Godhead, being the source of inexhaustible creativity, is not to be conceived as empty nothingness, inert, inane, and eternally quiescent, and absorbed in aesthetic contemplation. The *myō* is not such a state of contemplation. It is in every form of motion, in every phase of action, not only individually but totalistically in it. When this is experienced, necessity is freedom, and freedom is necessity. When hungry I eat, when thirsty I drink. "Tao is no more than our everyday-mindedness."[19] "What does Heaven say?" asks Confucius, "yet the four seasons go on, and the ten thousand things grow up. What does Heaven say?"[20] Thus everything goes on along the line of "just-so-ness."

The *myō* is also applied to works of art. However technically perfect, they do not awaken in us the sense of the *myō;* there must be something that goes beyond the technique, that is to say, something that enlivens every display of skill. When this enlivening agency of creativity is present, we have the *myō.*

Life, as long as it is confined to the animal and to the vegetative, is neces-

[18] I wonder if Lao Tzu was not the first philosopher who used the term. Buddhists have adopted it and coupled it with *hōni* (*fa-erh*[bw]), "as-it-is-ness."

[19] *Ching-te chüan-teng lu*[bx] (*Keitoku Dentōroku*) ("The Record of the Transmission of the Lamp"), J. Takakusu and K. Watanabe, eds., *The Tripitaka* (Tokyo: The Taishō Issai-kyo Kanko Kwai, 1928), Vol. LI, No. 2076, Bk. XXIX, fasc. 28. Under "Daijaku Dōichi" (Ta-chi Tao-i,[by] Ma-tsu Tao-i, Baso Dōichi, d. 788).

"The Transmission of the Lamp," consisting of thirty fascicles, is generally ascribed to Tao-yüan,[bz] Zen monk of Wu Province. The work was completed during the Ching-te[ca] era (1004–1007) of the Sung (960–1279). The Record begins with the stories of the seven Buddhas prior to Śākyamuni Buddha and goes on to the twenty-eight patriarchs of India. These are followed by accounts of the six Chinese patriarchs, including Bodhidharma, who is the Twentieth Patriarch of India and the First in Chinese Zen Buddhism. After the Sixth Patriarch, Hui-neng,[cb] the line of "transmission" breaks into two and then into five. The Record includes down to the followers of the Fa-yen[cc] (Hōgen) school in the early Sung Dynasty. Altogether, 1701 masters of 52 generations after Bodhidharma find here their short biographical notes and mainly their sayings and sermons.

[20] The *Analects* XVII.

sity; but man is free and creative and proceeds to make the universe look beautiful and lovable. To man, the universe is not something rigidly, mercilessly, and altogether impersonally controlled by so-called laws of Nature.

Beauty is not primarily objective. Nature, symbolic of necessity, becomes beautiful and the source of joy when man's mind rises above things finite, and, soaring up to the Infinite, surveys the world therefrom. It is a mistake to think that what is beautiful is limited to a human work of imagination. The universe is also a work of art, though not human; it is beautiful when it is seen from the point of view where the iron chain of necessity and obedience, of law and irresistibility, is shattered, that is to say, when one enters into the spirit of creativity, as "God makes himself necessity," to use the terminology of Simone Weil.[21]

When this takes place, we have the *myō,* the feeling of beauty, not objectively perceived but innerly growing out of one's being. The *myō,* therefore, is a subjective and psychological term. It is the sense of harmony, which is not necessarily objectively demonstrable, but which is felt innerly when all the finites are seen in something infinitely transcending them while not losing their particularization. When this *myō* is felt in the way one lives we have a life of no-striving (*wu-kung-yung-hsing*[at] or *anābhogacaryā*),[22] which Buddhists consider as superseding all the moral values we finite beings esteem.

It is not quite true that the East looks upon ethical values as insignificant because the absolute reality is above all forms of relativity. The East, no doubt, pays the highest regard to the Ultimate, but that does not mean that ethics is neglected. In this respect, Chinese Buddhism is eloquent in disproving the charge, in that Chinese mentality is firmly rooted in the Great Mother Earth. The Chinese look up to Heaven as much as the people in the West, but they never forget the Earth. Confucius as well as Lao Tzu and Chuang Tzu and other Taoists make frequent references to Heaven and Heavenly Reason, but for that reason they never neglect relating it to our earthly affairs and human relations. Their Heaven always remains in intimate communion with things going on on earth. Indeed, it is Heaven that looks down upon us below instead of our looking up to it.

Buddhism made its start in India and was known for being ethically minded. But, as it developed into the Mahāyāna system of thought, it became more speculative and transcendental and showed a decided tendency to flee from the world. But, when it struck root deeply in China, we find it intimately affiliated with Confucianism as well as with Taoism, supplying them with what they needed, that is, a philosophical background. In Chinese Buddhism, we thus discover the best in Indian Buddhism organically functioning in the Chinese practical mind. For instance, Zen Buddhism, which swayed China from the early T'ang (618–907) to the late Ming (1368–1644), for about nine hun-

[21] *Gravity and Grace* (London: Routledge and Kegan Paul, 1952), p. 38.

[22] *The Lankāvatāra Sūtra,* Bunyū Nanjō, editor (Kyoto: The Otani University Press, 1923), pp. 42, 43, 89, etc.

dred years, is the embodiment of Chinese and Indian thought happily amalgamated.

Buddhism does not try to find meaning outside of life, for living itself is meaning. Meaning is not added to life from the outside. When one knows what life is, one knows that there is nothing of value beyond the living of it. How to live, however, is an art. In this respect every one of us is an artist, a creative artist. The painter may need brushes, canvas, paints, and other materials to produce fine specimens of art. So with sculptors and others known as artists. But we, most ordinary and probably prosaic people, deeply concerned with worldly affairs and far from being artists of any denomination whatever, are also artists in the genuine sense of the term. Besides, we have no need for such external materials as are required by professional artists. Everything we wish to have is already in us, with us, and waiting to be utilized. We are each and all born artists. We are creators of the *myō*.

Inasmuch as life, or how to live it, is an art and every one of us is meant to be an artist of high grade—and who knows we are not already such!—we must try our best to attain the *myō* in our daily living. When a Zen master was asked what Tao is, the answer was "Everyday-mindedness." When another master was further asked, "What is the meaning of it?" he said, "When you wish to sleep you sleep, when you wish to sit up you sit up."[23] Is this not leading a life of "just-so-ness," following the natural order of things in our daily life? Where is the *myō*? Where is the art? This is the very point, however, where the *myō* is beyond our intellection.

Some may ask, "There are many people who cannot eat even when hungry, cannot sleep even when tired. What about them?" Such questions are asked because the questioner is still groveling in the mud of finitudes and dualities. The *myō* is appreciated only when one can stand at the highest peak of the Himalayas and at the same time walk along the very bottom of the Pacific Ocean.[24] The idea, in modern expression, is that a world of finites is to be understood as the Infinite limiting itself, or, in Buddhist terminology, as the self-determination of Emptiness. The following incident extracted from the history of Zen, I hope, will, to a certain extent, illustrate the point.

Yakusan (Yüeh-shan Wei-yen[au]) once gave the sermon: "Where the intellect fails to reach, do not try to make any statement [on the matter]. If you do, the horns will grow on your head."[25]

[23] "Transmission of the Lamp," fasc. 10. Under "Chōsha Keishin" (Ch'ang-sha Ching-ch'en,[cd] a disciple of Nan-ch'üan P'u-yüan,[ce] 748–834).

[24] "Transmission of the Lamp," fasc. 28. Under "Yakusan Igen" (Yüeh-shan Wei-yen).

[25] Yüeh-shan Wei-yen, 751–834. *Ku-tsun-su Yü-lu*[cf] (*Kosonshuku Goroku*), ("Sayings of the Ancient Worthies"), fasc. 25. "Transmission of the Lamp," fasc. 14, under "Dōgo Yenchi" (Tao-wu Yüan-chih), gives a somewhat different version.

The "Sayings of the Ancient Worthies," consisting of 48 fascicles contains sermons, *mondōs*, and sayings of 36 Zen masters beginning with Nan-yüeh Huaijang[cg] (Nangaku Ejo) and down to Sung master Busshō Tokkō (Fuchao Te-kuang[ch]). Compiled by Ii (Wei-i[ci]) of the Sung. The first edition appeared in 1267, a later one in 1617. I have used the Japanese edition popularly known as the "Ōbaku." Tetsugen, the Zen master of the Obaku Monastery, carried out this gigantic task of printing 7334 fascicles of the Buddhist Tripiṭaka in thirteen years (1669–1681).

Dōgo (Tao-wu Yüan-chih[av]) [or brother Chih][26] then left the room.

Ungan (Yün-yen T'an-ch'eng[aw]) later asked the master, "Why did not Brother Chih react to your remark, O Master?"

Said the master, "It is Chih the monk who knows all about it. Go and ask him."

Ungan, following the master's advice, came to Brother Chih and said, "How is it that you did not react at all to our master's remark the other day?"

Dōgo responded, "I have a headache today. You had better ask the master himself."

When Ungan passed, Dōgo remarked, "Ungan did not know what's what, after all. I regret that I did not tell him all about it then. In spite of all this, he deserves to be called a disciple of our master, Yakusan."

Daigu Shūshi (Ta-yü Shou-chih[ax]) of Kinshū later gave this comment: "Ungan did not know what's what. As for Dōgo's knowing it, he regrets that he did not at the time tell Ungan all about it. Tell me now whether or not Dōgo really had it?"[27]

This Zen story may not seem to be very intelligible. The only reference to anything abstract, and perhaps intelligible, is Yakusan's statement about the intellect. Though he does not expressly mention the subject about which he is talking, we know that it is about the final reality or the ultimate truth, and he goes on to say that it is beyond one's intellectual grasp and that if one attempts to give it anything approaching a conceptual definition one will surely miss it. The rest of the story makes no reference whatever to the main subject except one's having a headache and the other's regretting and the third's evading.[28] As for the commentator, he is anxious to know whether or not Dōgo understood the whole affair. All that we can get out of the whole transaction is what seems to be a trivial episode in the life of a monastery. But is this really so? What is there in it that makes Zen people so concerned with it?

I will give another example to elucidate what makes Zen masters so concerned with details of our daily life, which passes on without attracting much attention on our part. It may be necessary for the philosopher to maneuver an imposing army of abstract ideas and erudite references when he wants to demonstrate the truth of a proposition, to establish the significance of human values, to confirm the objectivity of knowledge, etc. But, to the Zen master, such a parade of concepts does not mean very much. He is content with offering tea to a visitor, with bidding a fare-thee-well to a departing friend. When a philosopher comes to the master ready to discuss with him something weighty, the master has no hesitation in telling the intruder that he has a headache. The

[26] Dōgo, whose other name was Enchi, is referred to as "Chih the Elder" by his fellow monks and as "Brother Chih" by the master.

[27] Shou-chih of Ta-yü Shan was a disciple of Fen-yang Shan-chao[cj] (Funyō Zenshō, 947–1024).

[28] When this inner feeling of *myō* is objectively demonstrated in our daily life, we have a life of *anābhogacaryā*—the life that is free and creative, transcending all moral values we finite beings discriminatingly estimate. Buddhists, especially Zen Buddhists, do not use words such as "spiritual," "saintly," or "divine"; they designate this kind of life as "leaving no traces", "productive of no merits," "doing nothing, yet doing everything," "using the spade empty-handedly," "riding horse-back while walking," "like the moon serenely reflecting itself in the stream without any thought of doing so," or "like the stone-woman dancing while the wood-man sings," etc.

headache is really the answer to whatever question may be coming. If the philosopher understands it, it is all right with him and he may be grateful for the master's kindness. If not, woe unto him!—he has "another thirty years" to ponder the matter.

When Ryūtan Sōshin (Sung-t'an Ch'ung-Hsin[ay])[29] first came to Dōgo to study Zen, Dōgo gave him no special teaching about it. Some time passed, and Sōshin grew impatient and approached the master and asked him about Zen. Dōgo said, "Ever since you came to me, I have been teaching you in Zen every day." Sōshin was puzzled and wished to be enlightened on the matter. Dōgo said, "When you bring me a cup of tea in the morning, do I not take it gratefully? When you give me something to eat when mealtime comes, do I not accept it? When you greet me, do I not return it? When have I not instructed you in the essentials of Zen?" Sōshin dropped his head and began to reflect. The master lost no time in saying, "When you want to see, see at once—no deliberation whatever!" This instantly helped Sōshin open his mind. Sōshin then asked how to nourish it further. Dōgo's answer was: "Saunter along self-sufficiently in accordance with your nature; be free and uninhibited in response to the situation in which you find yourself. Only do away with thoughts arising from your limited knowledge, and there is no realization specifically to be termed supreme."

"To do away with one's limited thoughts" means to recognize rightly the relativity of all knowledge and, further, to see deeply into the source of being or to survey the open field of Emptiness. There is no other revelation to be known as supreme or divine. As Buddhists say, the moon of Suchness shines by itself when the clouds of ignorance (i.e., *wu-ming,*[az] or *avidyā,* that is relative knowledge) are dispersed. A life cleansed of all accretions is one of *anābhoga-caryā,* a life of no-striving.

Baso's (Ma-tsu[ba]) saying, "Everyday-mindedness," is explained by himself in the following way:[30]

Tao does not need any form of discipline, only have it not defiled. What are the defilements? Have no thought of birth and death. Have no contrivances. Have no purposiveness. These are the defilements.

If one wishes to understand instantly what Tao is, everyday-mindedness is Tao. What is "everyday-mindedness?" It is not to strive after anything. It is neither right nor wrong. It is neither to take up nor to let go. It is to be neither nihilistic nor positivistic. It is not to make any distinction between the commoner and the wise man.

In the *sūtra* we read: "It is not the life of the ordinary man, it is not the life of the saint—that is the life of the *bodhisattva.*" As we at present walk, rest, sit, lie down, respond to various situations, or meet people of all classes—Tao is in all this.

[29] Lung-t'an Ch'ung-hsin (Ryūtan Sōshin) was a disciple of T'ien-huang Tao-wu[ck] (Tennō Dōgo, 748–807). "Transmission of the Lamp," fasc. 14, under "Ryūtan Sōshin."

[30] See footnote 19.

To recapitulate: *Anābhogacaryā* is, as one Chinese translator has it, a life of no strivings, of no usefulness, of no effectiveness. This corresponds to: Lao Tzu's *wu-wei*[bb] or *wu-wei erh wu-pu-wei*[bc] (By doing nothing, all things are done," or "Everything is done by non-doing)[31]; Chuang Tzu's *wu-yung chih yung*[bd] (usefulness of non-usefulness)[32]; Chao-chou Ts'ung-shen's[be] "Stone-bridge which carries horses as well as donkeys"[bf 33]; Lin-chi's[bg] *wu-shih chih jên*[bh] (a man of no-work)[34]; Hakuin's[bi] "Hiring an idiotic wise man who tries to fill the well with snow[bj 35]; Bankei's[bk] *pu-sheng jen*[bl] ("Man of the Unborn")[36] and the *chieh-k'ung jen*[bm] ("Man of Emptiness"), to the exposition of which the whole Prajñā-pāramitā literature is devoted.

A man of *anābhogacaryā,* then, is one who lives the *myō* in its ethico-aesthetic sense, as well as in its ontological sense. All the moral values and social practice, Buddhists claim, come out of this life of no-strivings, of just-so-ness, of Suchness, which is Emptiness. When all the defilements and accretions are wiped away, purged, purified, the original light of creativity will illumine one's whole being, and whatever one does will be "good."

The Dhammapada reads:

> *Not to do any evil,*
> *To promote the good,*
> *To purify one's own mind,—*
> *This is the Buddha's teaching.*[37]

QUESTION: Jean-Paul Sartre says that the world constantly presents to us "an object that can never be an object for us, as it is what we have to be." Simone de Beauvoir says that in the middle of herself she "only finds the emptiness that is myself." What would be the comment of a Zen master on these two mental attitudes?

ANSWER: Both views are equally far from the Zen experience, and there is no choice between them, because they are both on the plane of intellectual quest. Let me quote a *mondō* between Enkwan Saian[bn] (of the eighth century) and a monk.[38] The monk asked, "What is the primal body of Vairocana Buddha?" (i.e., What is the Self?). The master said, "Will you pass me that pitcher over there?" The monk did what he was asked to do. The master then said, "Thank you. Now take it back where you got it." The monk returned it to the original place. Then the monk repeated the first question regarding Vairocana Buddha and waited for an answer. The master nonchalantly said, "The old Buddha left a long time ago." Too bad that "the old Buddha" also eludes both of the French philosophers.

[31] *Tao-te ching* XXXXVIII.
[32] *Chuang Tzu* IV.
[33] "Transmission of the Lamp," fasc. 10. Under "Jōshū Jūshin" (Chao-chou Ts'ung-shen, 778–897).
[34] *Rinzai Roku* ("Sayings of Rinzai" or *Lin-chi lu*).
[35] *Dokugo Chū Shingyō*[cl] ("Poisonous Comments on the *Prajñā-paramitā Hṛidaya Sūtra*"), published 1861.
[36] *Bankei Zenji Goroku* ("Sayings of Bankei"[cm]), compiled by D. T. Suzuki (Tokyo: Iwanami Shoten, 1941).
[37] Verse 183.
[38] "Transmission of the Lamp," fasc. 7.

Question: What significance does Zen have for the practical matter of maintaining a productive, peaceful order in society?

Answer: Disorderliness of society is caused by not understanding Zen. Zen proposes to bring a peaceful state of mind to every individual. There cannot be any disorderliness in a group of individuals whose minds are quiet, peaceful, orderly, well-behaving, and therefore creative.

Question: If a Kantian were to reach an understanding of Buddhism, would you consider it a useful analogy to say that Zen is the surprising of reality before it is properly clothed in the forms of space and time and the categories of the understanding?

Answer: Yes, "surprising," but this is on your side and not on reality's. This reminds me of Eckhart's reference to God as being all stripped off as when we go to a bath.

Question: When Zen keeps Buddhist terminology and imagery to express how wonderful the life of every day can be in its just-so-ness and suchness, what becomes of its iconoclastic aspect? Then, how about its naturalism without striving for anything beyond?

Answer: Zen tells us first to "kill" everything we come across: *buddhas,* patriarchs, *arhats, bodhisattvas,* humans, and non-humans; and then to serve others with your "face and head covered with dirt and ashes," and this quietly and "secretly" as when you pray in a closet. As to striving, the door will never open without it; but, as long as you are relying on *your* striving, that is, as long as your *pride* subsists, the door will forever remain closed to you.

Question: Regarding the Zen experience: (1) Is it available to everybody? (2) Can one be sure of having it? (3) Does it endure forever?

Answer: (1) The Zen experience may not be available to those who are mentally defective. Otherwise, anybody can have it if he makes up his mind to experience it. (2) The strange thing about Zen is that when you have it you know you have it. The assurance is sometimes so overwhelming that the man who has it is led to ascribe it to someone above or beyond him. The idea of revelation is probably based on this psychological fact. (3) The experience once gained has no "dry period." But, human psychology being as it is, a constant watch over what you have gained is needed. They call it "the maturing process."

Question: How can one make the connection between *śūnya* and *karuṇā-garbha* (repository of compassion) intelligible?

Answer: From the human point of view, the ultimate reality which is Emptiness has two aspects: *prajñā* and *karuṇā,* substance (*t'i*[bo]) and activity (*yung*[bp]). The one is static and the other dynamic. The center remains immovable, like the eye of a cyclone, while the surrounding air is activity itself. *Karuṇā* is activity, "knowledge" in contrast to "innocence" and to the principle of differentiation. In the equation, $O = \infty$, zero corresponds to nothingness or Emptiness, which is immanent in the multiplicity of things, but, because of *karuṇā* or love or *agape,* an infinity (∞) of resourceful activities known as "skillful means" (*upāya*) are produced to lead all beings to enlightenment (*bodhi*). When the *bodhisattva* says that he postpones his entering into *nirvāṇa* because of his love for his fellow beings, he may appear to be separating *karuṇā* from *prajñā,* but in actuality his *karuṇā* is *prajñā* itself, for the two cannot be separated as if they were merely two connected parts of one thing. The one thing is *prajñā* as well as *karuṇā.*

This may not be very understandable when it is taken out of context. In one of the following paragraphs, reference was made to the "everyday-mindedness" of Great Tao. The phrase is characteristic of the Zen philosophy of life. "Having a headache," expressing "regrets" of any kind, or "evading a definite answer on certain occasions"—all these are everyday occurrences, that is, the demonstration of "everyday-mindedness." The ultimate reality is not limited to a highly abstract concept. It is to be experienced or intuited in the raising of a finger or in walking in the street or exchanging greetings, saying, "A Happy New Year" or "A Merry Christmas." Relying unconditionally on the "omnipotency" of intellectual analysis is a sign of stupidity. Those who are addicted to it are to be born as animals "with two horns on the head."

[a] 鈴木大拙
[b] 玄牝
[c] 淨土
[d] 華嚴
[e] 禪
[f] 天台
[g] 大燈國師
[h] 空
[i] 臨濟
[j] 人
[k] 妙
[l] 妙法
[m] 徼
[n] 玄
[o] 玄學
[p] 玄覽
[q] 玄談
[r] 玄旨
[s] 玄門
[t] 玄元皇帝
[u] 玄
[v] 少
[w] 女
[x] 玄同
[y] 常無
[z] 常有
[aa] 玄之又玄
[ab] 衆妙之門
[ac] 常道
[ad] 常名

ae 有名
af 無名
ag 嬰兒 or 嬰孩
ah 顏成子遊
ai 東郭子綦
aj 坐忘
ak 喪我
al 大通
am 天鈞
an 天倪
ao 南郭子綦
ap 彭祖
aq 妙道
ar 自然
as 天府
at 無功用行
au 藥山惟儼
av 道吾圓智
aw 雲巖曇晟
ax 大愚守芝
ay 龍潭崇信
az 無明
ba 馬祖
bb 無爲
bc 無爲而無不爲
bd 無用之用
be 趙州從諗
bf 僧云，如何是石橋
州云，渡驢渡馬
bg 臨濟義玄
bh 無事之人
bi 白隱
bj 傭他癡聖人，擔雪共塡井
bk 盤珪
bl 不生人
bm 解空人
bn 鹽官齊安
bo 體
bp 用
bq 色
br 空
bs 妙萬物
bt 神
bu 寓言
bv 天理
bw 法爾
bx 景德傳燈錄
by 大寂道一
bz 道原
ca 景德
cb 慧能
cc 法眼
cd 長沙景岑
ce 南泉普願
cf 古尊宿語錄
cg 南嶽懷讓
ch 佛照德光
ci 渭頤
cj 汾陽善昭
ck 天皇道悟
cl 毒語註心經
cm 盤珪禪師語錄

NIYAZI BERKES

Ethics and Social Practice in Islam

I. INTRODUCTION

Discussions of the ethical aspect of Islamic life may vary considerably in content, emphasis, and even conclusions, depending upon the attitude taken initially in defining the term "Islam." At least three understandings of the term are current.

The term is commonly used with reference to a particular civilization existing in the past as a whole and yet partially manifest in many lands scattered between the Atlantic and Pacific shores. In this understanding, it is the civilization or the system of society possessing features distinctive from other civilizations that makes Islam what it is.

Another understanding of the term refers only to a particular faith shared by many people irrespective of the system of society or the civilization to which they happen to belong. According to this understanding, it is only a particular system of beliefs that makes Muslims Muslims.

To many Muslims of today, however, Islam means something that, perhaps, combines or includes the other two understandings. Islam means a unique system of beliefs differing from all other systems both in the conception of life in its totality and in the content—hence the meaning—of that totality. In other words, Islam is, first, all-comprehensive, that is, it leaves nothing in life outside the scope of an over-all religious outlook. It recognizes no part of life as irrelevant to its ultimate principles. Even those aspects of life unregulated by enjoined norms are left to individual choice, not because of their accepted irrelevance to the beliefs or because of their autonomy from the principles, but because these aspects are approved of only within a certain range of alternatives set by the principles themselves in a value-scale. Second, Islam is characterized by its worldliness, by its claim to rationalize life. The conduct of the individual has to be in harmony with its principles. This is not only to save the soul in the other world or to elevate the soul above the mundane, but also in order to build a worldly society in terms of its principles—a society capable of achieving that harmony. One can find two ideas in this last view that appeal greatly to many Muslims in the present world of competing ideologies, each claiming hold over the entire life of men: comprehensiveness and rationalism. Also, it sounds modern and has even been conceived of as a modern *ideology* to parallel democracy, socialism, communism, and fascism because of these two features.

Thus, we have three understandings of Islam, all of which may be implicit in the usage of the term by both Muslims and non-Muslims: Islam as a civilization, Islam as a faith, and Islam as an ideology. We must treat here all three of these understandings because of the peculiar connections among them both logically and historically.

A search for the ethical principles implied in or derived from an over-all philosophical outlook attributable to Islam or entertained by philosophically minded Muslims is relevant and possible in terms of the first understanding. In fact, this is the only legitimate approach, if we accept the view that philosophy is a search (autonomous from religion) for the nature and meaning of the universe and life. But, interesting as it may be in terms of the history of philosophy, confining our discussion within the dictates of this first view of Islam will provide an incomplete, if not misleading, understanding of the mutual interactions of the religious, social, political, and philosophical problems in the past as well as at present. We would also miss those fundamental questions having vital implications for ethics and conduct.

Were we to approach our discussion in terms of the second view of Islam, still we would be forced to tackle the problems raised by the first and third views, especially in terms of contemporary Islam. For, although historical Islam as a civilization exists no longer, all Muslims are faced with the problem of reconciling their religious tradition to the new conditions of modern civilization. This problem, common to Muslims, is far greater than the same question is for Christians and for the non-Muslim peoples of the East who are also challenged by contemporary civilization because the Muslims are facing not only a religious or metaphysical challenge but one which involves every aspect of life, from the economic to the ethical. The second view, then, will entitle us to discuss the ethical problems of Islam on religious as contrasted with philosophical grounds. This is essential because, as we shall see later, the basic ethical question is the question of the unity or separation of the two.

Taking the second approach inevitably involves discussing our subject in terms of the third view of Islam. In spite of its claim to be the only correct view of Islam, logically as well as historically, the latter view is of modern origination, even though it is not entirely devoid of historical foundations; it is beset by fundamental problems, with which Muslim thinkers sought to grapple in the past when the conditions were far different from those with which the contemporary exponents of the view must deal.

The problem of defining life attitudes in a religion becomes serious when all of life is brought within the scope of religion. Then, religion must produce a clear economic ethics, for example. It has to enjoin rules for building up a polity. It has to shape philosophy, science, and technology in terms of its own principles. It has to regulate aesthetic and sexual attitudes and the personal relationships of the individual. Because of its worldly attitude and rationalism, it can neither reject nor ignore these areas of life insofar as they are necessary expressions of the "natural" forces in the world. Religion, therefore, has to develop its own metaphysical view of the world. Here lies the difficulty encountered by Muslims today, as it was encountered when Islam was yet in its formative stages—for the ultimate instrument for determining ultimate truth and values will be either reason or revelation.

It may appear easy to solve the question of reason versus revelation by ignoring it, by asserting that the two are compatible, or, as the more daring have tried, by claiming that the two are identical. Muslim theologians and philosophers have tried all three solutions. Not a single theologian or philosopher today, insofar as he has remained true to his original position, has been able to provide a solution even slightly better than his predecessors. Moreover, the task of the theologian and philosopher was relatively easy and their solutions tenable, because initially they had been charged with building up theological or philosophical systems in terms of the conditions under which the Islamic attitude faced the world for the first time. Today, on the other hand, the Islamic life values are no longer in the process of formation. They have been in existence for many centuries and (quite naturally in terms of the position taken) Islam has become identified with these values, whose sanctioning powers are derived no longer from revelation or reason but from tradition. Questioning or rejecting these values, even temporarily, in order to build anew in terms of contemporary life conditions is regarded as tantamount to secularism or heresy. But, to re-examine the world concept of Islam necessitates an objective and historical approach which is nothing but secularistic, because such an approach shows that the all-comprehensive concept of Islam is a latter-day historical product rather than something inherent in Islam as a faith or concomitant with Islam as a civilization.

In order to derive conclusions from our discussion of the past for the present and, if possible, for the future, we must free ourselves from three common tendencies in viewing Islam: that Islam represents a single historical tradition woven in monochrome of one quality of thread as distinct from the multi-colored and multi-patterned Western tradition; that Islam is an Eastern tradition outside and independent of, even alien to, Western civilization; and that the contemporary Islam can be understood in terms of one simple and closed tradition. We have just noted that we can look at Islam in three ways—as a civilization, as a religion, and as an ideology—and that our choice would have different implications for our subject. This is not an arbitrary view, because history presents Islam to us in each of these three appearances. Islam as a religion originated on the periphery of the civilized world, that is, at the meeting-place of the older traditions of the Graeco-Roman, Persian, and Egyptian civilizations. Because of its worldly impulse, it quickly turned into a political power. It established its supremacy over a large area before Islam as a religion succeeded in transforming the "world," that is, the pagan Arab society against which it first sprang. The teachings of the Qur'ān created, not a church hostile or indifferent to the world, but the ethics of a worldly State. At the same time, however, this ethics met the challenges of the "world" of civilizations into which it penetrated. This "world" was very different from the original home of Islam. From the interaction of the two there gradually emerged the Islamic civilization; historical Islam took its fundamental features within that Islamic civilization, and these features later came to be identified with the religion of Islam. This last happened when Islam penetrated farther and farther outside the germinal ground. The soil of the civilization in which that Islamic civilization developed out of the Islamic ethics was the germinal soil of what we now call Western civilization. The affinity between Islam and the West which has been forgotten by both Muslims and Westerners was exceedingly great, for Islam was connected with the West at both ends, the Hellenistic and the modern.[1] Islam represented a complex tradition that was a link between the West and the East. This was so, not only politically, economically, and technologically, but also ethically and philosophically. Historical Islam as a civilization was perhaps the only one in its time to be in the cross-currents and cross-winds, East-West and West-East. Its tradition was as dynamic and variegated as that of the West.

The above observation will help us to realize why the inner structure of Islam has been affected so deeply by the revolutionary changes in post-medieval Western civilization and why we can hardly speak of an Islamic tradition as one in the past or as one which is as alive today as it was in the past. We shall illustrate these features of dynamism and variety, as well as the role of the links between Islam and the West in producing these features, in the following discussion of the sources of the basic ideational attitudes that may be identified as Islamic and of their implications for ethics and actual conduct.

II. THE QUR'ĀN

The Qur'ān has been the ultimate source of the Muslims' religious and moral world-view. It is a collection of the Prophet's recitations, and consists of moral teachings, arguments against those rejecting God's Law, injunctions relating to economic, familial, civil, and personal relationships, and commentaries or reflections on current affairs. The fact that its constituent parts made their appearance over about twenty years and, therefore, underwent literary,

[1] C. H. Becker has given perhaps the best discussion of the affinity between the West and Islam in his *Islamstudien,* Bd. I (Leipzig: Quelle & Meyer, 1924), pp. 24–39. There he points out that neither Islamic nor Western history can be understood adequately without a proper appreciation of this affinity.

contextual, and religious evolution made the Qur'ān difficult to understand. Add to this the Qur'ān's poetical and symbolic quality (which can be appreciated best from the Arabic text), its emphasis upon spontaneity rather than intellectualized internal consistency, and, finally, the method of arranging the parts utilized by the compilers of the definitive version (a method still baffling those who would make a textual criticism). The total gave rise to controversy when Muslims began to develop theological, metaphysical, moral, and legal systematizations of Islam (within the first century and a half). Like all great books, the Qur'ān was a mine from which legitimization for conflicting doctrines, especially those basic to every attempt at a rational systematization of a religious message upon a metaphysical foundation, could be derived. Theologians, philosophers, lawyers, and moralists quoted the Qur'ān constantly, to the extent that a phrase was seen adequate substantiation for a particular doctrine or thesis. But, the Prophet was a layman. The Book in its entirety does not take a friendly attitude toward priests, legalists, magicians, skeptics, and philosophers. The Qur'ān did not claim to offer intellectual knowledge concerning what is or what should be. It claimed to uncover the meaning of the world, not by means of the intellect, but by virtue of a direct realization of the presence of God. Religion believed that the abstractions of the intellect were irrelevant to salvation.

The novelty of the Qur'ān's moral message lay in its being, perhaps, the most typical of the prophetic messages offering an ultimate stand regarding the world by virtue of a direct grasp of the world's meaning. This may be illustrated in terms of three points.

1. The Qur'ān introduced the idea of *dīn* in the meaning of acting in accordance with the truths revealed by God. It is to be contrasted with the idea of *sunna*, that is, the ethos of a community in which men act in accordance with the traditions and usages of the ancestors. *Dīn*, righteousness, manifests itself only in the fulfilling of God's will.[2] In the Qur'ān it was nothing but what was understood by Islam. Its exclusive use for Islam as a religious system did not begin until much later.

In the Qur'ān the traditional connotation of *dīn* as action according to tradition gave way to action according to revelation. Revelation and tradition were thus contrasted. The new conception put the Prophet in conflict with tradition and with society. *Dīn* did not consist only of performing the rites of the ancestors. Traditionally, a man who conformed perfectly with *dīn* was considered righteous even though he usurped the rights of orphans, widows, and the poor, used fraudulent weights and measures, practiced usury, and so forth.

[2] The word "*dīn*" was used in pre-Islamic Arabic, and meant custom, habit, a "system of usages and rites and ceremonies inherited from a series of ancestors." It was used in numerous passages of the Qur'ān in that sense. Modern scholarship is far from agreed on the origin and exact meaning of the word. Meanings such as "compensation," "reciprocity," and "obligation" are said to be implied, in addition to "custom." It seems that "*dīn*" was used in all of these senses before and after the Qur'ān gave a new meaning to it. See H. Birkeland, "The Interpretation of Surah 107," *Studia Islamica*, IX (1958), pp. 21–22; also Arthur Jeffery, *The Foreign Vocabulary of the Qur'ān*. Gaekwad's Oriental Series, No. 79 (Baroda: Oriental Institute, 1938), pp. 131 ff.

This was not righteousness but hypocrisy. A requisite of righteousness is being good and just throughout.

2. The contrast between the traditional and Qur'ānic understanding of *dīn* may be illustrated further by the theism of the Qur'ān as opposed to the atheistic fatalism of the traditional society.[3] The dominant note of the Qur'ān was theism set in opposition to ancient pagan atheism. The Qur'ān rejected the pagan concept of *dahr,* the inescapable course of events, the impersonal Time-Fate. As against *dahr,* it put the idea of the power and compassion of one God. It attacked the disbelief in one God, in the Day of Judgment, and in the reality of the afterlife. If the great emphasis given to these matters in the Qur'ān is viewed as a protest against the pagan conception of *dahr,* polytheism, and the disbelief in the moral significance of an afterlife, the Qur'ān would appear to be aiming at a new moral rationalization of man's life. Man was not precluded from doing good works by a predestined fate. There were forces in the universe to assist him. His moral strivings would not be in vain. The Qur'ān's message, then, was for man to make this moral effort. It gave assurance against the fate that had been believed to control man's life. This did not mean, however, that the Qur'ān rejected the idea that man's life was destined. It brought the idea, the most characteristic of prophetic religions, that the destining power is not the impersonal Time-Fate stripped of all moral attributes, but, rather, a God who is just and righteous to those who order their conduct according to his Law, and merciless only to those who do not obey him. God gives men the chance of attaining eternal bliss by sending his promise through his messenger: whosoever resigns himself to God's power and mercy can look to his destiny with assurance and will be free from the whims of Fate.[4]

3. The above did not necessarily imply resignation in the sense of inactivity or flight from and abnegation of the world. Despite its consistent reference to the other world, despite its claim that "the life of this world is but comfort of illusion," the Qur'ān was occupied primarily with the attitudes of the here and now. The futility of the world is accepted only in the sense that the "world" is an imperfect one because of the existence of evil in it. God is eternal, timeless, and perfect. His rules are also eternal and perfect. What the revelation aimed at was the subordination of the transitory, imperfect world to the values of that which is eternal and perfect. This would provide men with happiness in this world and eternal salvation in the other world. Thus, it is not the world itself that was rejected by the Qur'ān as inherently wicked and evil, but, rather, *that* world denying God's commands. God destined men to live in the world he created. Consequently, he gave a Law to show men how to live in the world and how to build a righteous society. In keeping with God's compassion, the world is not necessarily sinful. God has always sent his message and has given his guidance in every age. The substance of his revela-

[3] For a fuller discussion see W. Montgomery Watt, *Free Will and Predestination in Early Islam* (London: Luzac & Company, Ltd., 1948), pp. 165–172.

[4] *Loc. cit.*

tions was to provide direction for the pursuit of sacred values. These revelations aimed at giving a meaning to life that the world lacked in itself and that the pagan denied.

The Qur'ān imposes duties and expects action in the world in accordance with God's Law. Its teaching is decisively worldly. Islam should undertake to rationalize mundane life ethically and generally against the existing society. The Qur'ān's fiercest attacks are directed against traditional society and those who have deviated from God's earlier revelations. God is not to be outdone. No evil-doer can escape God's punishment as he is all-powerful and all-knowing. Man, on the other hand, is not always capable of establishing an equilibrium between his inclinations toward good and temptations toward evil. He can save himself from evil through his own effort, but his capacity for this is not unlimited. Satan, in the Qur'ān a rebellious angel envious of God's concern for men and dedicated to tempting them, has made men even more dependent upon God's guidance. Only thus may man walk on the straight path. This path can be traversed by none but the righteous armed with the directives contained in the revealed Book. Man either errs, which is due to correctable ignorance, or commits moral offence, which is far more serious and requires efforts to obtain forgiveness. Man, therefore, is morally responsible. The basis of this is good intention. The Qur'ān invites the believer to surrender to the commands of conscience.

The Qur'ān, then, neither abnegated nor sought to revolutionize the world. It urged a worldly society and even recognized several aspects of the ancient mores. But, with its new conception of *dīn,* it was turned against the moral foundations of the ancient society. What the Qur'ān attacked was the whole way of life based on the denial of one God, Judgment, and afterlife. The necessity of belief in these is taken as evidenced by the events of life and the universe and, thus, as not requiring metaphysical justification.[6]

What was specifically Islamic in the Qur'ān, therefore, was its ethical view. The ultimate ideal was submission to the will of God. This is the real meaning of the word "Islam," in which ethics and religion are one and the same. It was a religious determination of life-conduct. Its ethics, the practical impulses for action that are found in the psychological and pragmatic context of the Qur'ān, exercised the greatest influence in the formation and worldly success of the community of believers.

We may here ask the extent to which the two ideas that have played the greatest role in shaping the historical Islamic civilization and the modern Islamic ideology (i.e., the idea that Islam enjoined formal norms regulatory of every detail of human action and the idea that God predestined everything in the world) existed in the Qur'ān. In conformity with the general tendency in the evolution of religions, as noted by Max Weber, the enunciations of the Qur'ān were reinterpreted fundamentally to "adjust the revelation to the

[5] Qur'ān 3:185.
[6] Qur'ān 45:20–27; 36:47; 10:17.

needs of the religious community."[7] The Qur'ān has been used repeatedly to uphold contradictory doctrines regarding the ethical and metaphysical foundations of Islam.[8]

The source of divergent views probably lay in the fact that the Qur'ān did not contain an explicitly stated metaphysical system as the basis for its moral teachings. Similarly, there was not a systematic or categorical legal structure therein to serve for the codification of rules to cover all aspects of individual and community life. The attempts to systematize a rational theology as the metaphysics of the Qur'ān and to codify its teachings as a law seem to have been reciprocally influential. The theoretical as well as practical difficulties in deriving consistent world outlooks from it impelled later generations to reinterpret it fundamentally.

The Qur'ān contains, for example, a number of rules of conduct regarding matters that could become matters of law in a politically organized society. But, as the Qur'ān was not revolutionizing in a political sense, it envisaged these rules within the framework of the ancient society in such a way as to make these serve as *the* moral foundations of *a* worldly economic, legal, and political system. The Qur'ān decidedly ignored the world as politically constituted. None of its injunctions concerning worldly affairs has any sanction other than the ethical or religious. There are even in the oldest parts of the Qur'ān a number of injunctions relating to economic matters,[9] but in none of these is there a legislative formulation or anything other than moral injunctions. The text of the Qur'ān, its tone, and its general hostility to law and tradition do not warrant the direct derivation of legalism from it. This leads us to look elsewhere for the basis of the legalism of historical Islam as it developed. The aim pursued does not seem to be that of laying down a system of law, but, rather, that of teaching man how to act within the existing framework so as to meet the test of the Day of Judgment.[10]

The Qur'ān sounds conservative or indifferent toward legal and political institutions, even toward economic institutions, because it never dealt with such matters as parts of a social system but only insofar as they concerned the moral conduct and ultimate salvation of the individual. The virtues demanded of men as members of communities, cities, or States are recognized as matters

[7] "Religious Rejections of the World and Their Directions," in Hans Gerth and C. W. Mills, trans.. *Essays from Max Weber* (London and New York: Oxford University Press, 1946), p. 270.

[8] Even modern scholarship is not unanimous in assigning support for one or the other doctrine to the Qur'ān. The view changes in the case of law and ethics, according to whether one looks at the Meccan or at the Medinan *surahs,* or verses, which are known to have been mixed in the traditional edition. A great deal depends upon viewing the Qur'ān as a historical scripture, reflecting the prophetic career of Muhammad, or as the word of God, revealed piecemeal but pre-existing in its totality, as orthodox Muslim doctrine affirms. For the various views current among modern scholars, see J. Schacht, "Foreign Elements in Ancient Islamic Law," *The Journal of Comparative Legislation and International Law,* Third Series, XXXII, Parts III and IV (November, 1950), 9–17; S. Vesey Fitzgerald, "The Alleged Debt of Islamic to Roman Law," *Law Quarterly Review,* LXVII, No. 265 (January, 1951), 81–102; S. D. Goitein, "The Birth-hour of Muslim Law," in Zeki Velidi Togan, ed., *Proceedings of the Twenty-Second Congress of Orientalists* (Leiden: E. J. Brill, 1957), pp. 247–252.

[9] Such as loyalty to the given word, contract, and witness (7:32–33), just weights and measures (83:1–3), the avoidance of usury (10:30–39).

[10] See, in general, J. Schacht, "The Law," in G. von Grunebaum, ed., *Unity and Variety in Muslim Civilization.* Chicago University Comparative Studies of Cultures and Civilizations, No. 7 (Chicago: University of Chicago Press, 1955), pp. 68 ff.

of practical political ethics, but all of these matters are regarded as affairs to be settled by the communities themselves. The Qur'ān appears to have accepted the existing political, legal, and economic institutions, as no specific alternatives were offered. Arab institutions such as *ijma'* (referendum) and *mashwara* (deliberation and council) were praised. Such acceptance does not seem, however, to be viewed as falling within the scope of a Qur'ānic legislation. The legal autonomy of even non-Muslim communities (Christian and Jewish) was recognized. The really legislating aspects of the Qur'ān, that is, where it modified or changed the Arab mores,[11] were announced as in accordance with the same injunctions in the ancient Judaic law, with the exception of those regarding inheritance. In other words, there was very little in them that was new in content and there was nothing new in form. It can hardly be said, therefore, that a desire to reform the society in the economic, legal, or political sphere was manifest.

The exceptions were the efforts to make certain changes in the Arab mores, such as in the customs of infanticide and polygamy, and the attempt to put restrictions on sexual behavior. These all concerned moral innovations incompatible with the ethics of manliness (*muruwwa*) of the Arab.[12] Even the codification of the obligations within the field or ritual is secondary, vague, and general.[13] All the formal rules, ritualistic as well as legal, seem to have been the product, not of the revealed Book, but of the practices taking shape within the Islamic community—a fact that reflected itself later in the controversy over the question of reason versus revelation as the source of ethics and law.

The indifference of the Qur'ān to sociological questions is manifest in its acceptance of a pagan terminology in establishing a formula for distinguishing between good and evil. In the ancient pagan conception, whatever was known, customary, and socially approved (*ma'rūf*) was accepted as good; whatever was socially rejected (*munkar*) was evil. The Qur'ān rejected tradition as the source of the criteria involved in this formula. Instead, it brought God's rule as the criterion according to which what is approved is good and what is rejected is evil. Hence, the Qur'ān commanded the execution of the *ma'rūf* and the persecution of the *munkar,* on the basis of God's moral law.[14]

Let us come to the second idea. The Qur'ān contained both the idea of the responsibility of man, or the freedom of will, and the idea of the omnipotence of God. The Qur'ān did not contain a metaphysical discussion of either

[11] Such as matters pertaining to food, intermarriage, the nursing of infants, almsgiving, ablution, and sacrifice.

[12] On this concept, see Ignaz Goldziher, "Dīn and Muruwwa," in *Muhammedanische Studien* (Halle: M. Niemayer, 1888), Vol. I, chap. 1. The pre-Islamic conception of virtue implied retribution, whereas the Qur'ān preached forgiveness, security for the guest, kindness to the orphan. Real virtue and nobility lay in forgiveness.

[13] The most important ritualistic duties were not specified (Qur'ān 50:38 f.; 17:80 f.; 11:16; 2:239). It looks as if these were left to the choice of the Muslims within the framework of the existing ritual practices. For example, the number and hours of the daily prayers, so elaborately specified in historical Islam as, perhaps, the chief duty, seem not to have been so for one or two centuries. The ambiguity seems to have been even greater with regard to such matters as food, drink, and inheritance.

[14] See, for example, 2:176.

the scope of God's revealed Law in worldly affairs or the relationship between God's will and man's freedom. Its preoccupation is with faith as a duty; conduct is viewed as a necessary corollary. Like other scriptures, the Qur'ān was not concerned with an abstract presentation of law and moral values. Neither did it provide the theoretical criteria or the metaphysical grounds for a rational differentiation between right and wrong or good and evil.

III. THE SHARI'A: FIQH AND KALĀM

The transformation of the community believing in the Qur'ānic morality into a political community took place rapidly at an early stage. It introduced strife and deep-seated controversy over political, as well as several other worldly affairs. As, true to its spirit, the Book set no rules on such matters, the question of religion versus the "world" became the cardinal issue for the believers. We find, therefore, the gradual interfusion of the "world" and religion on a plane different from the context of the Qur'ānic teachings in the first century and a half.

The most salient feature of this interfusion was the fusion brought about between the religious ethics and the law. There came into existence as a result what is known as the knowledge and practical system of *sharī'a*—a formalized code of conduct extending over all of life. A second tradition, the *sharī'a* Islam, took the place of the first, the Qur'ānic Islam. As the *sharī'a* was one of the unique phenomena in the history of morals, and as it became the core of the historical Islam as well as the source of the Islamic ideology, a brief discussion of its make-up is warranted.

The development of the *sharī'a* was the product of the attempt to rationalize the "world" on the basis of the spirit of the Qur'ān. Actually, it was a systematization of worldly practices—some derived from pagan Arab times, some from Prophetic tradition, some from Roman and Persian practices, plus the early experiences of the Muslim community—into a "sacred" law. It was never a legal code enacted or legislated by a temporal organ. Two features must be noted: (a) the process of "sacredizing" the "world" and (b) the code of conduct emerging from this.

The first was the product of the view that life should be regulated by an all-embracing Divine Law, the ultimate source and criterion of what is good. It was also the result of an effort to find a mundane sociological framework that would serve as the substratum for the Qur'ānic formula of commanding the good and rejecting the evil. The spirit justifying such an approach was present in the Qur'ān undoubtedly, although the rules developed and systematized as the *sharī'a* were not derived from the Qur'ān itself for the most part.[15] What the architects of the *sharī'a* did was simply to extrapolate the

[15] As a Western jurist pointed out, of the 6,236 verses of the Qur'ān, only about 500, that is, less than one twelfth, can be said to have legal relevance; L. Ostroróg, *The Angora Reform* (London: University of London Press, Ltd., 1927), p. 19. See also Goitein, *op. cit.*

view of Divine Law to cover all life in the community. Law could be enunciated by the prophetic lawgiver only on the basis of the truth revealed to him. Law could not be other than the will of God. Human will and thought had to be excluded from legislating the rules of conduct for man. They were the work of God's wisdom. Man was incapable of knowing their reason. Man had only to obey, for the rules were willed by God for man's well-being. But since the Qur'ān did not legislate law or rules of conduct, how could this be done in such a way as to be accepted as God's Law and as derived from his revelation?

In actuality, as modern scholarship has proven,[16] the *sharī'a* has been the product of a long process that does not seem to have begun directly upon the completion of the Qur'ān. The Muslims acted for about one century in accordance with the prevalent institutions by interpreting and adapting them experimentally within the framework of the religious and moral teachings of the Qur'ān taken simply and pragmatically.

The "sacredization of the world" was the result of the old pagan method of sanctioning a rule on the basis of custom, *sunna*. This was rejected by the Qur'ān. The *sunna* began to assert itself as a source of legitimization as against the use of reason. This time, however, the *sunna* was not the tradition of the pagan community but, first, the tradition of the Prophet and, then, the tradition of the Muslim society itself. An enormous number of *hadīths,* reports concerning the Phophet's exemplary acts or sayings (overt or implicit), accumulated.[17] All contained direct or indirect precepts regarding ethical, political, economic, sexual, and other matters, and indicated traditions showing what was good and evil in these. Most of these *hadīths* actually embodied the ideas and assumptions as well as the habits and interests of the generations of the intervening two centuries. The *hadīths* became the vehicle through which the mind of the community as evidenced in its accumulated practices was recorded.

The rise and accumulation of the *hadīths* are events as important as the revelation of the Qur'ān in view of the fact that historical Islam is their creation. The recurring underlying viewpoint in them was astoundingly different from that in the Qur'ān.[18] First of all, the *hadīths* covered a far wider range of ritualistic, legal, and moral matters which had remained on a secondary plane in the Qur'ān. The *hadīths* contained judgments concerning faith, ritual, and civil and criminal matters, in addition to judgments concerning economic, aesthetic, and sexual affairs and personal and civil ethics. Second, the predominant note in the *hadīths* was the emphasis upon the duty to follow the exemplary Prophet. There was also a greater emphasis upon actions and formal rules than upon good intentions and inner moral predisposition. Finally, there was a metaphysical conception of the world underlying the *hadīths* that was not in accordance with the Qur'ānic view of man and the world.[19]

[16] The latest example is the work of J. Schacht, *The Origins of Muhammadan Jurisprudence* (Oxford: Clarendon Press, 1950).

[17] The *hadīths* were recorded and stabilized finally in the middle of the third century of Islam. Their study became an important object of religious and legal learning.

[18] For a full discussion, see Watt, *op. cit.*, pp. 19–29.

[19] *Loc. cit.*

In time, the conduct implied in the alleged Prophetic actions or utterances began to be called the *sunna*, or the way or habit of the Prophet. Just one further step was needed to make it the *sunna*, or tradition, of the community. First, the *sunna* began to be viewed as mores or as the ethos of the society acting according to the Prophetic authority implied in the *hadīths*, not according to the custom of the ancestors. The establishment of a justificatory link between the *sunna* and the Qur'ān would then complete the process of reintroducing the traditions indirectly. This was done on the basis of the principle of consensus (*ijmā'*). This completed the chain in the sacredization of an ethical system of action by giving binding authority to the injunctions of the scholars of *fiqh*, the science of the *sharī'a*. Any rule that came into existence through the exercise of opinion, analogy, or practice and was proven to be in accordance with the Qur'ān through the *hadīths* was accepted as binding by a consensus of the learned of the community. A consensus once reached on a given point was considered to be binding forever. Thus it was not the Qur'ān that had the last word—it was the *ijmā'*. It ruled over and above the Qur'ān. The latter was interpreted through the science of exegesis (*tafsīr*) by the later generations. These read the practices that had become matters of consensus into the verses of the Qur'ān. Later on, the unreasoned acceptance of the final state of the doctrine as laid down by the precedents (*taqlīd*) replaced the *ijmā'*.[20]

The *sharī'a* was a code of conduct, a system of action. It was ethical, religious, and legal all at once. It was not so much a law as a systematization of the rights and duties of the Muslim. It was still equally ethical and legal at its base, although it was formal and all-inclusive, sacred and immutable. Our impression of it as a legal code is derived largely from its formalism rather than from its content. It covered all of life in the absence of other codes powerful enough to claim certain sectors of the lives of the believers, for whom faith was itself the first of all duties. Its main subject was an ideal righteousness. The conduct was regulated in terms of a value-scale ranging from absolute obligation to absolute prohibition. There were five categories: matters in which a choice could be made were designated between two degrees of obligation and two of avoidance. The contents were matters of belief and ritual, and of civil, penal, political, economic, ethical, intellectual, and aesthetic activity—all differentiated, not on the basis of autonomous realms, but on the basis of a single value-hierarchy, that of the five categories. The *sharī'a* was believed to be the self-sufficient and sole regulator of human action.

Would not this mean that ultimately two areas of life were differentiated implicitly—those minima that were subject to categorical command or prohibition and the maxima left to the choice of the individual? The first would be religious-legal, the second moral.

In practice, the first also split into the "religious" and the "legal," the latter being those the temporal authority chose to enforce as its law. The second also

[20] See J. Schacht, "The Law," *op. cit.*, pp. 76–77.

split into the "customary" (*'ādat*) and the "ethical." The *sharī'a* lives on today to the extent that its injunctions in the past found currency in the forms of ritual, law, custom, individual ethics, and social ethics—meaning that it was far from self-sufficient. Some of the rules were never practiced, such as those relating to the political authority (*imamate*). Some remained largely obsolete, such as the application of the *qiṣas* (talion). The *fiqh* literature claims that the *sharī'a* comprises all precise rules regulating man's relations with God (*'ibādāt*) and with man or the world (*mu'āmalāt*). The *sharī'a,* however, never made the distinction that we make between the sacred and the secular, among the religious, moral, ethical, and legal. Commercial rules were mixed both with legal injunctions and with ritual, moral, and ethical matters. Rigidity and conservatism, the inherent tendencies of every legal system, were accentuated in the case of the *sharī'a,* perhaps in view of its dissociation from deliberate legislation. Its rigidity served to guarantee its stability and enabled it to survive even when it did not have the backing of a strong political authority or when the political institutions began to decay.[21] In setting up an eternal, unchanging, divinely sanctioned standard of conduct, it became a decisive factor in creating a stable community of widely diverse peoples, as well as in repelling the impact of secularizing factors coming from internal changes and external contacts.

The most important implication of all this, from the standpoint of our particular concern, was the danger it brought to the autonomy of ethical action. Is there a question of ethical action if individuals are expected merely to perform what is obligatory and avoid what is prohibited? Would ethics not become merely a catechism? In the *sharī'a* tradition, the moral teachings of Islam would tend to consist of an integral part of a general code aimed at showing the path the believer should follow. In time, faith and righteousness (*dīn*) became a matter of externalities. It was against these tendencies that philosophy and mysticism revolted. Before discussing them, however, we must discuss the *kalām,* the dogmatic side of the *sharī'a* tradition.

While life was being reduced to rules by *fiqh,* the faith was in the process of being formulated in terms of dogmas. This process was the product of a series of controversies over the metaphysical foundations of the Islamic faith presented in the Qur'ān in unresolved antinomies. Two major schools fought in attempting to produce a consistent theodicy for Islam out of the Qur'ān.

We shall not discuss the early phases of the controversy. There were upholders of the idea of free-will; there were the predestinarians, the ethical conformists (emphasizing faith over conduct), and the strict followers of Islam in action as well as in belief. The first great theological school, that of the Mu'tazila, arose in response to the controversies involving these early theological views. Its members discussed matters of faith in the dialectical terms of Greek philosophy. The Mu'tazila made the first attempt to bring the dogmas of religion into agreement with contemporary philosophy. This was at the

[21] *Ibid.,* p. 77.

time when Greek thought was beginning to be known among the Muslims.[22]

Throughout the early development of Islamic theology the contrasts between the Qur'ānic conception of God's omnipotence and human responsibility, on the one hand, and between the religious and moral attitudes of the pre-Islamic fatalism and the Qur'ānic sense of creatureliness or dependence upon God, on the other, were the main points of dispute.[23] The irreconcilable tendencies were bound to clash in discussing God's nature, man's relation to him, and the questions of man's reason and free-will before God's revealed word. The Mu'tazila discussed questions such as to what extent postulating God's righteousness puts limits on his power, to what extent man is responsible for his doings, whether God creates evil, and whether the Qur'ān is created or eternal.

As Max Weber points out,[24] producing a consistent theodicy in monistic religions is a difficult matter. In the Qur'ānic view, the absolute power of God triumphs over evil, and yet evil is not eradicated. Once God's omnipotence is accepted, it becomes difficult to accept the existence of evil, and especially the inconsistency between God's compassion and his preparation of a hell to punish his own creatures eternally for their sins. These dogmas necessitate sacrificing part of God's absolute power or compassion that the responsibility may be put on man's shoulders. Only thus may God be absolved from acting unrighteously.

The Mu'tazila believed in the freedom of human will and held that it was the only doctrine compatible with the righteousness of God. God could not create evil. The Mu'tazila denied the properties attributed to him by the fatalists and the traditionalists. The Qur'ān was created; the belief in its eternity was idolatory. Reason had greater weight than revelation. The Mu'tazila reached a conception of natural religion. "This was built up on the basis of an inborn knowledge, universally necessary, that there is one God, who, as a wise Creator, has produced the world, and also endowed Man with reason that he may know his Creator and distinguish between Good and Evil."[25] Good and evil are not differentiated, since they were made arbitrarily so by God. "God who is wise does only that which is salutary and good." It is because good and evil are in themselves good or evil that God has declared them to be so. Even God's will and decree should be in harmony with reason. Since God could not be responsible for evil, man must be responsible for his own actions. The knowledge enabling man to distinguish between good and evil existed before revelation; hence, the Qur'ān is created, although its spirit existed before it was revealed. Justice and truth, then, existed *a priori* even above God.

The second theodicy was provided by the doctrine of predestination. As it

[22] Translations from Greek philosophy were made mostly at the beginning of the ninth century. The Mu'tazila flourished from the middle of the eighth to the middle of the ninth century. At first, their doctrines enjoyed political support. They were declared heretical after 847.

[23] The relevant statements in the Qur'ān (2:136; 3:139; 9:51; 13:27, 30; 14:4, 32; 24:31; 39:9; 54:49) seem far from providing coherent doctrines on these matters; they gave little with which to reconcile the apparent contradictions.

[24] *Op. cit.*, p. 358.

[25] T. J. de Boer, *The History of Philosophy in Islam,* E. R. Jones, trans., Luzac's Oriental Religions Series, Vol. II (London: Luzac & Company, Ltd., 1903, 1933), p. 49.

was with the development of the *sharī'a* doctrine of conduct, here, also, *hadīths* emphasizing a diametrically opposite view were being stored up to burn out the relationalism of the Mu'tazila. A return to them as the ultimate source of the faith triumphed.[26] The idea of the determined and inescapable course of events, recurrent in the *hadīths,* was, as Montgomery Watt shows, very close to the pre-Islamic idea of *dahr.* As Watt points out with surprise, few Muslims noted the difference between the anti-fatalism of the Qur'ān and the pronounced fatalism underlying the *hadīths.*

The foundations of the doctrine accepted later on as the orthodox theology of Islam were laid down toward the end of the tenth century by the opponents of the Mu'tazila doctrine when they applied the same Greek logic used by the Mu'tazila to the data of the Qur'ān and *hadīths.*[27] I need not elaborate the details of the Ash'arite theology, as they were the exact opposite of the Mu'tazila doctrine at every point. Briefly stated, they concerned God's omnipotence, universal agency, and omniscience, and man's acquisition of, or ability to give, assent to the acts done by God's agency: God possesses infinite power and absolute freedom to punish or reward as he likes. All events are the product of his decree. This settled all things before the creation of the world, and what we perceive as the sensible world is made up of passing accidents. Reason is dependent upon revelation—whatever is incumbent upon the believer is in the revelation. Reason by itself cannot determine good and evil—these derive from the prescriptions of the Lawgiver. Man's capacity to act consists only of accompanying an act, not choosing an alternative. Man's responsibility derives from this acquisition or assent.

The triumph of the predestinarian theology over the Mu'tazila doctrine marked, according to some,[28] a return to the ancient Arab *dīn* through the purging of the doctrine of faith of all foreign elements, that is, of ideas such as the law of Nature, natural causation, and justice (which came from Greek philosophy). The rationalist and naturalist approaches to religion and ethics were defeated by a fatalistic and occasionalistic theology. The Qur'ān's resignation to God (Islam) became man's absolute dependence upon God's will and decree. The latter marked the rejection of a differentiation between the secular and religious in the doctrine of the *sharī'a* and between God's will and individual freedom in the orthodox doctrine of *kalām.*

IV. THE PHILOSOPHERS

It was against this religious and theological background that philosophy, the third element in the Islamic tradition, came forward to tackle the ethical question with a powerful metaphysical foundation, derived, not from the Qur'ān or Islamic theology, but directly from Greek philosophy.

[26] A. J. Wensinck, *The Muslim Creed* (Cambridge: Cambridge University Press, 1932), pp. 85 f.

[27] The success of the orthodox school of theology, named after its greatest representative, al-Ash'arī (893–935), was due largely to the support given it by Caliph Mutawakkil (847–861). On the Ash'arites in general, see Watt, *op. cit.*, pp. 135–162.

[28] See *ibid.*, p. 147.

Islamic thinking had not yet exhausted its potentialities by the formulation of the orthodox doctrines of belief and conduct. Through *fiqh* the gap between human law (*sharī'a*) and the Divine Law (revelation) seemed to have been bridged. The Qur'ānic law and that of man's reason were combined. The Divine Law was made the worldly law of the *sharī'a*. Orthodox *kalām* accepted the dogma that the Divine Law covered these matters that could not be proven by rational demonstration and that demanded acceptance on faith. The objective was the justification of faith. Reason was deemed subordinate to revelation. If law is essentially an attempt to rationalize the "world" by intellectually devised rules, and if theology is basically concerned with presenting the "world" as an ethically oriented order, the Islamic *sharī'a* succeeded in merging the two by transforming religion into a "law" in which rules were made the means of attaining the moral ends of the world.

When born in the ninth century, Muslim philosophy was making the attempt to derive or justify this "Law" from a metaphysical conception of the world through reason, which conceives the world in terms of causality. The philosophers attempted during the tenth and eleventh centuries to relate the Aristotelian philosophy to faith. In order to harmonize the doctrines of Aristotle with the tenets of faith, they were compelled to incorporate a number of Neo-Platonic ideas. Their difference from the orthodox theologians was that, while the latter viewed the world through a moral order, the former viewed the moral order through the causal terms of the mechanism of the universe. Just as the latter in the end sacrificed reason to faith, so the former were compelled to sacrifice faith to reason.

Muslim philosophy, like Greek philosophy, was concerned mainly with politics, ethics, and metaphysics. All Muslim philosophers took for granted that human happiness and perfection are to be realized only in an ideal State or society governed by the Divine Law. The law of the ideal society is the *sharī'a*; politics must be based on this in order that man's happiness may be safeguarded. The Muslim philosophers' preoccupation with the ideal State, the ideal ruler, and the Divine Law was a reflection of the fact that the ideal unity aimed at by the *sharī'a* was seen to fail most clearly in the realm of politics, where the constitutional theories of the scholars of *fiqh* were constantly being contradicted by the facts. The more the theocratic idea of the *sharī'a* was approached in fact, the greater the deviation from the theory. In the long run, the view was accepted that a non-sharī'atic State could be tolerated as long as the Muslims acted in accordance with the *sharī'a* in religion and morality. Then what would that State be? Dispute over the ideal rulership pervaded the history of Islamic political thinking. The philosophers attempted to devise a new approach as to how to establish that rulership as the ideal State, irrespective of the theocratic speculations of the scholars of *fiqh*.

The search for the ideal polity led the philosophers to the search for the ideal man. The union between God and man, faith and reason, was sought by the philosophers in the concept of the Perfect Man. Their speculations on this concept inevitably led them to a discussion of the Prophet and the Philosopher, or of the law and knowledge based on Revelation and Reason. The ideal lawgiver should have reached the philosophical truth embodied in the message of Islam. Truth, however, had been enunciated there in the form of formal and legal terms and doctrines understandable to the common intelligence. The Divine Law was based on certain convictions concerning God, the world, and the after-world. These convictions, however, were not the very self of the pure truth reached by philosophy. They were only symbolized expressions of it. Therefore, the law as a means of realization of these convictions was necessarily on a level below that of philosophy. This, the philosophers claimed, did not mean that there was a fundamental opposition between philosophy and revelation. The philosophers engaged in their speculations in order to make the revelation and the law it brought identical with the absolute truth.

Religion consists of articles of faith and rules of conduct given through revelation. The philosophical truth is the expression of the understanding by the intellect of the mechanism of the universe in terms of a causal structure. The Muslim philosophers tried in vain to reduce the first to the second. Some, like Ibn Sīnā (908–1037), attempted to give a naturalistic interpretation, through a psychological theory, of revelation and prophecy—a phenomenon accepted by the theologians as a miracle, and, hence, absolutely incomprehensible through reason.[29] Despite their efforts, these philosophers could not escape the conclusion that God had given to his revelation an anthropomorphic appearance in order to make his commands comprehensible and acceptable to the masses who were unable to understand him philosophically. The true meaning underlying the revelation could be understood only by the wise. It became common for the Muslim philosophers to distinguish between the worded-historical scripture and the spiritual-timeless scripture. The philosopher seeks the real truth behind religion, while positive religion is necessary for and understandable to the masses. Philosophy and religion, though identical in content, are distinct in their ways of teaching and expressing the truth.

It was obvious that the fundamental differences between theology and philosophy lay in their viewing the universe from different angles. Philosophy strove to explain the moral imperatives in terms of a metaphysical view of the world, while theology explained the world as a purposive, God-ordained order in terms of moral imperatives.

These speculations put the philosophers at variance with the convictions of the theologians at two points. One concerned the respective areas of faith and reason. Despite their efforts to prove that the difference between the two was only in appearance, reason was still the basis of all possible knowledge for the philosophers. Only Ibn Rushd (1126–1198) tried to avoid the difficulty by delimiting the respective areas of the two and refusing to reconcile them. He not only rejected the primacy of the faith but also denied harmony between

[29] For a detailed discussion, see F. Rahman, *Prophecy in Islam—Philosophy and Theology*. Ethical and Religious Classics of East and West, No. 2 (London: George Allen & Unwin Ltd., 1958).

the two. Faith and reason operated at different levels. What was valid for faith was unsuited to philosophical understanding. Religion was for its moral aim; it was the moral law and not knowledge. Those who had attained to the highest state of wisdom could discard it in discussing the truth. Religion could not be understood intellectually; it was to be believed in. The evidence brought forward by the theologians to prove the existence of God could not stand up to the philosophic test. Philosophy did not reject faith, but it is itself the highest form of truth; it is the knowledge of all that exists.

The philosophers also failed to satisfy the theologians by refusing to provide a supernatural source of religion. The metaphysical grounds of the philosophers differed fundamentally from those of the theologians. While the latter laid the main emphasis on God's will, the former regarded the essence of God to be thought. There remained an irreconcilable difference between the two in their general outlook toward God, the universe, and the soul. The God as the Idea at the apex of the Aristotelian universe was unacceptable to the theologians, for whom God was the Act, eternal and self-existing. The unacceptability of the philosophic stand toward religion may be illustrated best, perhaps, by a view shared by philosophers such as al-Fārābī (d. 950) and Ibn Sīnā. They reached the conclusion that there is a single active intellect for all humanity. The spiritual content and background of all religion are identical.

The rise of this view, as Windelband notes,[30] seems to be preliminary to an intellectual awakening brought about by contacts among the philosophers of the three monotheistic religions of the West. The more Christianity and Islam clashed on the level of historical reality (during the Crusades), the less sharp the differences between their doctrines began to appear. In order to reach some common element behind the differences, the idea of a universal religion could be achieved by screening all forms of historical revelation and bringing in their place those that were universally valid through reason and knowledge. Thus, with the help of Neo-Platonic teachings, the idea of a universal religion based on science began to take form and to be transmitted to European philosophy.[31]

V. THEORETICAL AND PRACTICAL ETHICS: MYSTICISM

Having noted their general outlook, we can now review the ethical views of the Muslim philosophers.

The criteria of good and evil, the philosophers held, were determined by reason. A blending of Plato and Aristotle was brought into the field of ethical

[30] Wilhelm Windelband, *A History of Philosophy*, J. H. Tufts, trans. (2nd ed., London: Macmillan & Co., Ltd., 1914), p. 319.

[31] The idea took one direction among the Muslim Sufis and another among Christian thinkers such as Abelard and also Roger Bacon, who, under Muslim influence, pioneered in viewing ethics as the content of the universal religion. In the later Islamic development, the idea was eclipsed by a new reassurance of the *kalām* against philosophy. It took a long time to mature in the West, doing so only in the eighteenth-century philosophy of the Enlightenment.

theory. The Muslim philosophers differed among themselves and from their Greek masters in matters of detail, but their ethical views were essentially Greek. We find the rationalistic approach to ethics in practically all Muslim philosophical schools. Al-Fārābī, the greatest Aristotelian among the Muslim philosophers, was the first thinker who viewed the problem of ethics in a spirit different from that of *fiqh*. Every human, he claimed, has rational and animal parts, each of which impels him in its own direction. The animal side leads to sensual pleasures, the rational to virtues. It is man's reason that can decide between the good and the evil. Man has freedom of choice, the basis of which is rational consideration. Just as logic has to give an account of the principles of knowledge, so ethics has to deal with the fundamental rules of conduct. Reason should determine conduct just because the highest good or virtue consists of knowing. Pure thought is the sphere of freedom—a position perfectly in accord with Platonic and Aristotelian ethics, but utterly incompatible with the sharī'atic view, which rejected rules of conduct provided by reason.

Despite his treatment of ethics only within the framework of his general philosophy, Ibn Sīnā gave more space to ethics in his writings than did al-Fārābī. He divided philosophy into the theoretical and the practical. The latter dealt with worldly affairs from the point of view of *fiqh* and comprised ethics, politics, and economics. The philosopher was concerned with the theory of ethics. For man seeking the philosophical truth Ibn Sīnā resorts to Neo-Platonism rather than the *sharī'a*. He conceives of a moral progress of man through a combination and cultivation of courage, temperance, and knowledge (Plato's three faculties of the soul) toward an ultimate union with God's universal soul. Such is the happy and perfect man, the man who worships God with a spiritual love and without any consideration for reward or punishment, hope or fear, and whose greatest happiness lies in contemplating the essence of God. This is an experience, though, whose secret cannot be disclosed or communicated to the masses; they should remain content to obey the *sharī'a*.

We find more or less the same philosophical view of ethics in the celebrated philosophical novel of Ibn Tufail (d. 1185), *Hayy Ibn Yaqazān* ("Hayy, Son of the Valiant"), a work that seems in the Latin translation to have inspired *Robinson Crusoe*. In this novel, the state of Nature is an imaginary island inhabited only by Hayy. This island is contrasted with the civil society on another imaginary island. On the latter, one man controlled the religion of the masses by practical means; another man reached the truth by rational knowledge. When the second man escapes to the former island, he finds that Hayy has discovered the same truth in Nature and through the mystic vision of God. The two return to the inhabited island to teach the truth. Soon disillusioned, Hayy returns to his island of Nature.

The philosophic contemplation reached in the writings of the philosophers became a matter of practice in the conduct of the Muslim believer when it was transformed into a mystic doctrine. Through mysticism, philosophy provided an esoteric ethical compensation for the formalistic and exoteric *sharī'a*. The more *fiqh* extended itself into the area of the ethical, the wider the gap became between the actual and the ideal. The soul needed the guidance of an inner experience and training. Thus it was that the Sufis came into the closest contact with the realm of the inner moral experience lying between the formalism of the orthodox law and theology and the loftiness of the philosophers. The practice of Sufism was the real ethical field in which the humble man could find satisfaction for his soul as well as cultivation for his innate virtues.

Early *taṣawwuf* (Islamic mysticism) appeared as an asceticism in response to the worldliness current in early Islam. It was dominated by the idea of the fear of God and the renunciation of the world. Later, with the spread of the collective organizations of the Sufis in the eighth century among the middle classes, especially among the artisans and in the urban centers, the idea of fear gave way to the idea of the love of God. This brought a social element over against the spread of orthodoxy as a religious movement. The Sufi orders began to show congregational characteristics from the eleventh and twelfth centuries; they became the real centers of religious experience. Despite the suspiciousness of the "learned," the Sufis won the respect of the rulers and the veneration of the masses as "saints."

It is impossible here to give an account of the doctrines of the Sufis and yet do justice to their varieties and their degree of orthodoxy or heterodoxy.

The Sufis were, perhaps, those Muslims most alive to the question of the place of ethics *vis-à-vis* the Law. They stood for inner sincerity as against formalism and the externalities. They preached a higher motive for human conduct than the rewards and punishments of the theologians and legalists. The fundamental premise of true faith was not the fulfillment of duties alone, but also man's capacity for spiritual development. Some (like Junaid of Baghdad) believed that the Sufis should be bound by the Qur'ān and the *hadīth*, hence, to the *sharī'a*. The true path of the Sufi could not be found without these, as God's Law was the avenue toward supreme morality. Obedience to the Divine Law was a step on the pathway to the celestial world of spheres. Others (like Quashairī) accentuated the tendency toward evil in human nature and regarded the Sufi path with its "states" or "stages" as a succession of efforts to conquer Nature by renouncing worldly temptations. This path was the one of resignation and self-surrender to the predestination of God (*tawakkul*). For such, asceticism or piety (*zuhd*) was the supreme virtue; true morality would mean the avoidance, not only of that prohibited by law, but also of that permitted by law. This implied a withdrawal from society and the world as well. Still others, those closest to the artisan associations (in fact, their orders became fused with the medieval guilds in many cases) preached a morality of virtuous work consisting of hope, serenity, brotherhood, solidarity, modesty, moderation, honesty, equity, and trust in God (the *futuwwa*). This was the worldly variety of the Sufi asceticism.

In general, however, the Sufis, because of their monistic tendencies, were faced with the need to reconcile divine power with divine goodness. They resorted to the theory of non-being (*adam*) of Plotinus in the attempt to do this. This eventually carried them to pantheistic speculations. In their attempt to discover the mysteries of the religious symbols—of which the philosophers said so much—they were aided by Neo-Platonic doctrines. They accepted the pantheistic doctrine that God is all in all. The theologians' Unity of God became with them the Universal Unity of Existence. However, the Sufi antinomianism did not mean freedom of man in Nature and society. It meant freedom *from* them. Thus, just as the theologians sacrified the "world" for the sake of the complete freedom of God, the Sufis forsook the "world" for the sake of the loving nature of the Divine Being.

Many Sufis adhered, too, to the philosophers' doctrine of a double standard. They believed that those who had reached the Love of God were absolved of obligations to the law. Law was for the ordinary man—the raw souls. Elevating oneself above mere obedience to Law required longing for what was above. The highest virtue is Love, which strives after union with God and is evinced in this life as self-abnegation. Those who reach perfection and contemplation, the men tempered in their search for God, are above the external law. Ultimate happiness lay in understanding and eventually reaching the Supreme Being. Needless to say, there was a profound difference between the Sufis' understanding of God and the theologians' conception of him. For the Sufis, it is neither the hope of reward and Paradise nor the fear of the Law and Hell that elevates man to God, but Love. Happiness is neither in knowing the Law nor in acting according to the Law, but in union with the Beloved. Thus, the Sufis reached some conception of freedom for moral action. The freedom of man meant loving God so perfectly that one's will was one with the Divine Will. Man's capacities were seen to receive divine qualities through the Sufi path.

We may say in general that the more extreme the orthodox theology became in its transcendentalism, the more the *taṣawwuf* went to the extreme of pantheism. As H. A. R. Gibb remarks, "To judge from the books, one would suppose that the Muslim must be either a complete transcendentalist or a complete pantheist."[32] Although the two clashed severely at times, many of orthodox persuasion and many Sufis found common ground. The two were complementary in the actual conduct of the medieval Muslim.

The ideas of the philosophers and the mystics were indications of the desire to break away from the restrictions found in the accepted doctrines or orthodoxy. Their effort to work out a metaphysical groundwork for faith and ethics brought a reassertion of the dogmatic theology, with the incorporation of certain mystical elements, by al-Ghazzālī (1058–1111). A skillful dialectician, al-Ghazzālī has been regarded by many as the greatest Muslim thinker. The pantheistic tendencies of the Sufis, the rationalism of the philosophers, and the thinking of the theologians which left no room for inner experience evoked

[32] *Modern Trends in Islam.* University of Chicago Haskell Lectures in Comparative Religion, 1945 (Chicago: University of Chicago Press, 1947), p. 21.

a reaction from him. His significance lay in his refutation of the metaphysics of the philosophers in favor of a dogmatic theology, and in his reconciliation of mysticism with theology. It was he who gave the final stamp to Muslim orthodoxy.

Al-Ghazzālī's was the strongest attempt to save the orthodox faith from the pantheistic mystics and the philosophers. The ultimate problem before him was to show that the categorical imperatives implied by faith in the revealed law were not open to argument by demonstrative evidences. His *Incoherence of the Philosophers*[33] was aimed at refuting the Aristotelianism of the Muslim philosophers; it evinced thorough skepticism toward philosophical speculation and reasserted the unfettered sovereignty of God. His ideas were in opposition to those of the philosophers, and at the core of his views on God, the universe, and the spirit was still the Ash'arite theology. His metaphysics was designed to justify a voluntarism that would restore the absolute moral imperatives of the *sharī'a* in the life of men and society. The rationalist approach of the philosophers was shown to be destructive of the absolute character of the moral imperative. It was the moral imperative of the *sharī'a* that al-Ghazzālī sought to restore against the philosophers and heretics (pantheists). The essence of life was duty; philosophy was the poison of faith. Combining the teachings of the *taṣawwuf* with the preachings of the *sharī'a,* he developed an Islamic ethics oriented toward formalism. In his *Iḥya' 'ulūm al-dīn* ("Revivification of the Religious Sciences") he gave a comprehensive system of practical ethics, in which every aspect of the Muslim's life, from ritual to intimate relationships, was covered.[34] The criterion was the attitude of the soul toward God. Love of the world and of self and the absence of love and fear of God are the roots of all vice. Love and fear of God and the absence of love of self and this world are the sources of all virtue.

God is the motive-force for al-Ghazzālī's entire system of morality. This motive-force not only leads the individual to eternal salvation but also ensures the best and loftiest moral virtues. The highest consideration for the ethical education of man is the purification of the heart through severing all ties with the world, in spirit at least, by subordinating action to that spirit. The final abode of man is the grave. The present world is only a passage. Therefore, one must take from the world only what is necessary.

It is on these principles that al-Ghazzālī surveys all of life and gives a picture of the economic, sexual, civic, and private ethics of the medieval Muslim. In spite of his refutation of the stand of the philosophers and his tremendous influence throughout time, the philosophical tradition continued. Ibn Rushd wrote a very powerful refutation of the *Incoherence of the Philosophers.* The stream of creative philosophical speculation had dried up, however, by the thirteenth century. The successors to the philosophers introduced nothing

[33] *Tahāfut al-Falāsifah,* S. A. Kamali, trans. (Lahore: Pakistan Philosophical Congress Publications, 1958).

[34] For a synopsis of this work in French, see G. H. Bousquet, *Ih'ya 'Ouloûm ed-Dīn ou Vivification des Sciences de la foi,* 4 vols. (Paris: Gustave Paul Maisonneuve, Besson, 1955).

new. They remained in opposition to the theologians, who also merely repeated the stand of their precursors, up to our times.

Although the outstanding philosophers did not write separate treatises on ethics, their classification of philosophy into the theoretical and practical, and the latter into the fields of economics, politics, and ethics, led to the treatment of the last in the form of manuals on practical ethics. These treatises combined in their theoretical foundations the teachings of *fiqh, kalām,* philosophy, and *taṣawwuf,* to which were added numerous rules and precepts taken over from the pre-Islamic Persian and Greek traditions. They were eclectic in nature and practical in the sense that they aimed at classifying and describing virtues and vices in order to show how to cultivate and/or acquire the first, how to avoid the second, and, in short, how to turn human nature (*khulq*) into a virtuous disposition (*akhlāq*). They were practical also in the sense of attempting to cure or correct the afflictions of the soul. They were written by men who cannot be called philosophers and whose reputations were not, in most cases, based on their ethical treatises. These treatises or manuals of ethics were first written in the eleventh century. The work continued to the sixteenth century. Such works continued to be read down to the end of the nineteenth century—a fact showing that Muslim ethics in practical life was molded of all the major traditions discussed herein.

The earliest known treatise of this kind was written by Ibn Misakawaih (d. 1030). His treatise[35] shows the influence of Plato and Aristotle and Greek, Syrian, and Arabic books. It became the model after which other treatises were patterned. According to this, the basis of morality is knowledge. Among living creatures, man is distinguished by his volition. Man has the ability to distinguish, choose, and think. Thus, man is confronted with the problem of distinguishing the good from the evil. The "good" is chosen by man's own will and effort. A certain disposition directed toward an end is requisite in order to be good. Only a few are good by nature. Those who are neither good nor evil by nature can be turned in the direction of either good or evil. Good is general or particular. The absolute good is the supreme good and is identical with knowledge. For each individual there is a particular good. This appears to him as happiness or pleasure, and it is but the active manifestation of his own nature. Good and happiness are, therefore, not the same for everyone. Since not every individual can attain the good in this way, men have to live in society. Man can attain happiness and perfection in society. The basis of all virtues, the supreme duty, then becomes "a general love for mankind."[36] Morality is social, and real virtue is social virtue. Individuals, like organs of the body, associate and co-operate. The good belongs to all. Social virtue is attainable, but in society and not in isolation. The person who renounces the world may be religious and pious, but his action is not an ethical action.

[35] *Al-tahdhīb al-akhlāq wa taṭhīr al-'araq* ("Doctrine of Dispositions and the Cleansing of Veins"), summarized by D. M. Donaldson, in *Studies in Muslim Ethics* (London: Society for Promoting Christian Knowledge, 1953), pp. 121–137.

[36] Known as *Sa'ādatnāma* ("The Book of Happiness").

Apart from these theoretical considerations, Ibn Miskawaih's treatise is concerned with how to cultivate predispositions, acquire virtues, and avoid vices. Here we find an echo of the classical Greek (Platonic) ethical theory. The soul is composed of four faculties. Their cultivation together creates the four main virtues: wisdom, temperance, courage, and justice. Virtue is the golden mean in each of these—that is, the middle way between the extremes of each (Aristotle). The first five chapters of the treatise deal with this topic, the virtues and the vices, and the cultivation of the virtues and the avoidance of the vices. Then follow chapters on the way to ameliorate the moral diseases of the soul: conceit, vanity, jocularity, boastfulness, perfidy, unfairness, fear, etc.

Another treatise on ethics, by Nāṣir Khusraw (d. 1061),[37] falls within the same genre of practical philosophy. It, too, was influenced to a large degree by Greek ethical ideas. The rise of an interest in writing ethical treatises seems to have been associated with the climax of the Graeco-Hellenistic philosophical impact, on the one hand, and with the fall of the jurists' ideal of an Islamic State (before the decline of the Caliphate and the rise of temporal States), on the other. However, the revival by Nāṣir al-Dīn al-Tūsī (1201–1274) of Ibn Miskawaih's treatises after two centuries of oblivion shows that their real day came with the thirteenth century.

Al-Tūsī's treatise on ethics[38] was also deeply influenced by Greek philosophy, although eclecticism with the *sharī'a* is even more apparent in it. Its major concern, however, is directed toward the obtaining of the virtues that are the sources of perfection and happiness.

Jalāl al-Dīn Dawwānī (1427–1501), another thinker of the same bent, wrote, two centuries later and on the basis of al-Tūsī's work, perhaps the most widely used treatise on ethics.[39] It, too, was concerned with practical politics and ethics, with the kinds of virtues and vices, with the cultivation of the former and the avoidance of the latter, and with the means of curing mental aberrations and maintaining the moral health of the soul.

Despite the eclectic nature of these treatises, their continued use up to recent times is indicative of the permanence of the ethical ideas of Greek and Hellenistic origin before the pressure of orthodox theology against philosophy. Their eclecticism played an important role in shaping the medieval Muslim practical ethics.

[37] Known as *Akhlāq-i Nāṣirī* ("The Ethics of Nāṣirī").

[38] The treatise is known as *Akhlāq-i Jalālī;* the full title, *Lawami' al-ishrāq fī makārim al-akhlāq* ("Flashes of Splendour Concerning Excellencies of Dispositions"), W. F. Thompson, trans., *The Practical Philosophy of Muhammadan People* (London: Printed for the Oriental Translation Fund of Great Britain and Ireland; sold by W. H. Allen and Co., 1839).

[39] Several treatises of the same nature have been written since then in Arabic, Persian, and Turkish. Two may be mentioned as, perhaps, the most widely used. *Akhlāq-i Muhsinī* ("Muhsinī's Ethics"), written by Husain Wā'iz Kāshifī (d. 1504), was particularly favored in India; *Akhlāq-i 'Alā'ī* ("'Ali's Ethics") by Kinalizade Ali Chelebi (1510–1572), in Turkey. Both were used in the *madrasas* (colleges) down to the nineteenth century.

VI. CONCLUSIONS

We have completed our survey of the major traditions coursing through Islam—religious, legal, theological, philosophical, and mystic—and their implications for ethical and social practice. Now, what was the share of each in shaping the conduct of the Muslim in his religious, economic, political, professional, domestic, and aesthetic behavior? Did any of these establish its exclusive supremacy in the Islamic past?

We cannot say that any one of these ever became the exclusive mold for Muslim conduct. Each represented an approach in the attempt to combine belief and the "world." What was selected depended upon the interests of the time and place, politics, class, profession, and, perhaps, even nationality. It acquired a greater degree of authority and attractiveness to the disfavor of the other traditions under complex conditions. But, no one tradition ever succeeded in banishing all the others. Each of the major traditions, furthermore, had a greater or lesser share in the various departments of life. The *sharī'a,* for example, was always the code of the average Muslim in his ritual. At least in terms of its minimal obligations and prohibitions, it was the norm of his civil relations, too. The *sharī'a* never had currency in his political life. It fell short in a number of respects in his economic conduct. One may say, in general, that the *sharī'a* "worked" insofar as it adapted itself to the contingencies and necessities of a medieval civilization. The severity of the morality of the pious and the legalist conditioned the appeal and the authority of the scientific and mystic strands in Muslim life. Generally, the greater the rigidity in legalism or the strictness of the otherworldly asceticism, the less the appeal of science and the less it maintained contact with philosophy and had a function in the technology of the society. Where legalism was strong, philosophy and science were viewed as heretical or as esoteric—occultism, as it were.

All the major traditions surveyed had days when they enjoyed moral appeal and practical success. The Muslim *sharī'a* gave law and order, Islamic mysticism inspired great works of art and humanism in outlook and deed, and philosophy and science not only achieved much for the Islamic civilization itself but also played a far wider civilizational role. They kept the flame of the Greek-Hellenistic heritage kindled and handed the burning torch into the eager grasp of the awakening civilization of Western Europe.

But—be it the morality of the common man, of the pious, of the legalist, of the mystic, of the administrator, or of the artisan, it arrived at stagnation with the downfall of the medieval civilization. Being so close and akin, the medieval Islamic civilization was naturally exceptionally exposed to the impact of the new civilization arising out of the downfall of the medieval civilization in the West, especially since the balance among the various traditions had become highly tenuous through the loss of originality and vitality in each. The loss of the distinctive, and yet functional, role of each may be seen, for example, in the increasing eclecticism of the ethical manuals mentioned above. The originally distinct ethical principles underlying the Qur'ānic, legalist, orthodox, theological, philosophical, and mystic approaches to moral phenomena became so blended in these treatises that they have no appeal to the contemporary Muslim, faced, as he is, by a different constellation of traditions.

We have seen from this survey that Islam in the past constituted a civilization analogous to the Western civilization in which a number of life attitudes constituted various traditions. As in the West, all of these revolved about the understanding and interpretation of a system of supreme values. We have seen that the view called Islamic ideology today was not the only and exclusive tradition.[40] All of these traditions ceased to live with the downfall of the Islamic civilization. There is no question of taking any one of them as the only Islamic tradition and of reviving it as it is presumed to have been or as it was. Just as is the Western world, the closely akin Islamic world is confronted with the task of entering a new phase of world history. Its task is one of creating, not of turning to, tradition. And this act of creating will probably go not in one direction only but in a plurality of directions—just as was the case in the past. We may get a hint of the general direction to be taken if we ascertain the factors instrumental in damaging its pluralistic development long ago.

The most important factor, in our view, was the replacement of the attempt to provide a metaphysical foundation for ethical values with the attempt to provide a metaphysical view of the world based upon and determined by fixed ethical values. The result of this was the penetration of essentially religious values into all spheres of life, including those pertaining to philosophy and science. The major task confronting Islam in the ethical realm under the conditions of today is that of freeing philosophical thinking from dogma. The failure to do this in the the past resulted in two conditions detrimental to the very existence of the Islamic civilization—the annihilation of philosophy and science and the cessation of contacts with other civilizations, especially with the Western civilization. These contacts had been kept alive constantly in the past by Islamic philosophy and mysticism. Islam became stagnant in its way of thought and action from the time that the prejudices of religious supremacy, both in relation to its internal life and in relation to the external world, triumphed and established the belief that Islam had reached the culmination of its own essence. Islam became stagnant when it found itself impervious to external stimuli at the time when it was exposed to the rest of the world in the form of new relationships.[41] It was then that the Muslins suffered the conse-

[40] Sir Paul Rycaut, in a survey of the seventeenth-century Ottoman Empire, *The Present State of the Ottoman Empire* (London, 1687), p. 67, expresses to his English readers his amazement at the variety of the religious, mystical, and philosophical trends he observed among the Muslims. This is significant if we remember that he wrote at a time when Islamic civilization had reached stagnation and Great Britain was the scene of numerous religious and philosophical trends.

[41] See Bernard Lewis, "The Muslim Discovery of Europe," *Bulletin of the School of Oriental and African Studies* XX (1957), 415. For a good survey of the gradual decline in the contacts with the West and the consequences of this, see pp. 409–416.

quences of having deadened the philosophical tradition. Through the poverty of a philosophical culture, they failed to understand and appraise the problems raised by modern conditions. They revived and clung ever more strongly to the theocratic conception of life. They mistook this for a new philosophy.[42] They became possessed with the idea that this was the unique aspect of Islam. The obsession was such that they misread Islamic history and also failed to see the spread of political and economic and ethical crises as a result of the disintegration of the medieval ethics that was unsuited to the economic, political, and intellectual demands of modern times. When, finally, the crisis could be ignored no longer, it was perceived as the result of a threat directed against the allegedly inherent features of Islam. This led to enmity for everything new, especially for everything coming from the rest of the world. The ethical question was viewed as a religious one. On the other hand, secularization and the progressive failure of medieval ethics to govern conduct continued in almost every department of life, especially in the areas of economic, political, personal, and sexual relationships, until the state of anomy—political, social, and moral—that we can see clearly today was reached. It was only when and wherever the tenacious hold upon the theocratic view was loosed that there was an attempt to revive the philosophical affinity between Islam and the West.

The greatest task is that of Islam's adapting itself to a secular mentality. Just as the adaptation of religion to the "world" was a long and tedious task once in the past, so this is and will be a tedious task.

QUESTION: What are the aspects which distinguish Islamic thought from Western thought? What makes Islam more Eastern than Western?

ANSWER: It would be easier for me to give an answer which would be more specific than that given in my paper if we had an objective definition of East and West. In a philosophical conference, these terms should not be used in their geographical, diplomatic, and journalistic senses. The need for a philosophical understanding of these terms is greater when we study the Islamic tradition which lies on a line that may belong to one or the other side of the fence, depending upon one's understanding of the two terms. Even geographically it is difficult to say whether Islam is East or West unless we delimit these terms beforehand. We must, therefore, know what we mean by the terms we use or we must make explicit what we consider implicit.

In this conference, speakers have attributed certain features to the Eastern tradition or to the Western tradition. In each case, anything incompatible with the assumed features of the one was implicitly attributed to its opposite. We can get a clue to your question from an observation of the implicit definitions made by this procedure. Whenever one (to be specific, a Western member) referred to the tradition or the philosophy of the nations that he did not believe belonged to Western civilization, he invariably identified the philosophical tradition of these nations with their religious tradition. When talking

[42] The man most responsible for and influential in initiating the new theocratic view of life was the controversial Jamāl al-Dīn al-Afgānī (1839–1897). Under the influence of his anti-colonialist zeal, his writings and agitations indirectly hampered the growth of a genuine philosophical approach among the Muslims of the late nineteenth and twentieth centuries.

of the Western tradition, he seldom did this, and even when he did he took the religion only as a part of that tradition. For example, different persons spoke of Buddhism sometimes as a religion, sometimes as a philosophy, more frequently as both, and sometimes as a form of world view or a way of life, that is to say, as neither a philosophy nor a religion. One could speak of the philosophical convictions of the Buddhist faith, but if one ever spoke of the philosophical convictions of the Christian faith he would merely be speaking of a part of Western tradition and not a very important one at that if the philosophical tradition was under consideration. In other words, in talking of Western tradition one does not identify its religion with its philosophy; often they are even believed to clash.

This attitude observed generally in the conference discloses to us the essential differences between the East and the West that were at the back of our mind as the "ideal-types" of two world outlooks. What distinguishes Western thinking from Eastern is its secularized outlook in which the ideas of Natural Law and human reason transcend those of faith and its values. Such an attitude is unacceptable to the Eastern mind, as has been illustrated by our Indian colleagues, who believe that a separation between philosophy and religion renders them both meaningless and functionless in life.

In this sense, I believe that it is possible to speak philosophically of the East and the West. I am critical only of the use of these terms as stereotypes reflecting our national or religious or racial sentiments. I do not believe, further, that they are immutable and inherent attributes of the groups of nations of one geographical area or even of cultures or civilizations. The two modes of approaching reality may co-exist, or one may succeed the other, or one may predominate over against the other, if we look at each tradition not as a static but as a dynamic unity.

In my paper I claimed that the Islamic philosophical tradition belonged to the Western tradition rather than to the Eastern. This sounds incredible to you. It is not possible for a Westerner to believe that Muslims, who emphatically claim to be non-Western, could be taken as belonging to the Western tradition. In my paper, I did not claim that the Muslims of today belonged to the Western tradition, and I tried to explain why. The crucial question is: to what extent was the shift from the Western attitude to the Eastern determined by or inherent in their religion? There is nothing in the origin or in the essence of Islam to make the philosophical orientation of the Muslims Eastern or Western, any more or any less than in the cases of Judaism and Christianity. Philosophy, science, literature, law, and government in Islam did not derive exclusively from the teachings of the Qur'ān, which, incidentally, said, perhaps symbolically, that turning to the East or to the West would not make one a believer.

It takes long to explain the historical, not intrinsic, difference between Islam and the West. In terms of the relationships between religion and philosophy their respective directions have been reversed. Philosophy became the victim of the battle between the East and the West within Islam. In present-day religious and philosophical movements observed among the Muslim nations, we find the battle still going on. We find there the Eastern as much as the Western outlook although neither can be taken absolutely as typical of Islam.

T. M. P. MAHADEVAN

Indian Ethics and Social Practice

Indian philosophy is not merely a way of thought but also a way of life. As between the speculative and the practical, it is the latter that is considered to be the more important factor in philosophy. "Take care of the way you live, and the vision of truth will follow" seems to be the teaching of all the philosophers. Conduct counts, not creed. Reform your life, mold your character, and the ability to think and understand will then develop along right lines and lead to fruitful consequences. That without moral purity metaphysical insight cannot be gained is a generally accepted principle. As the *Kaṭha Upaniṣad* puts it, "Not he who has not ceased from evil conduct; not he who is not tranquil; not he who cannot concentrate his mind; nor even he whose mind is not composed can reach this (Self) through knowledge."[1] And there is a saying of the Mīmāṁsakas, "The Vedas cleanse not the unrighteous."[2]

In view of the pronounced practical outlook of Indian philosophy, it is rather strange that some critics should have leveled against it the charge of unethicality or—less uncharitably—of insufficient emphasis on ethics. Especially Vedic philosophy—what is inaptly referred to as "Brahmanism"—has faced severe attack, even by understanding Orientalists. A. B. Keith, for instance, observes that "in comparison with the intellectual activities of the Brahmins the ethical content of the Upaniṣads must be said to be negligible and valueless" and that "the aims of the Brahmin were bent on things which are not ethical

[1] *Kaṭha Upaniṣad* II. 24.

[2] *Ācārahīnam na punanti vedāḥ*. Also, see *Nārada-purāṇa* IV. 25: *Vedo vā haribhaktir vā bhaktir vā maheśvare ācārāt patitam mūḍhaṁ na punāti dvijottama*. And Plotinus: "God on the lips without good conduct of life is a word."

at all."[3] Two reasons seem to weigh with those who offer this criticism: (1) The Indian philosophical texts discuss mostly the nature of reality and the modes of realizing it, and seldom the problems of life. In the Upaniṣads, for example, or in the classics of the schools, metaphysical topics are elaborately dealt with, but very little consideration of ethical questions is to be found. (2) The goal of Indian philosophy is said to be beyond ethics. The ethical value which is goodness (*dharma*) is not the highest value. However useful ethics may be to one who is striving to reach the goal, to the one who has reached it it has no meaning at all. Commenting on such texts of the Upaniṣads as the one from the *Kauṣītakī,* "He who understands me [Indra is the speaker, representing *Ātman*]–by no deed whatsoever of his is his world injured, not by stealing, not by killing an embryo, not by the murder of his mother, not by the murder of his father; if he has done any evil, the dark color departs not from his face."[4] R. E. Hume remarks that "the possession of metaphysical knowledge actually cancels all past sins and even permits the knower unblushingly to continue in 'what seems to be much evil' with perfect impunity."[5] If perfection, as envisaged in Indian philosophy, is a state beyond good and evil, the distinction between right and wrong, the "ought" and the "ought not," does not apply to the conduct of the perfect one. As a Vedāntic text asks: "For one who walks in the path of the distinctionless reality, what injunction is there and what prohibition?"[6]

These reasons adduced by the critics will not bear scrutiny. (1) It is true that the metaphysical texts which expound the nature of reality and the ways of knowing it do not discuss ethical questions in great detail. For a discussion of these questions one must turn to the Dharmaśāstras, whose especial domain is the good life. It is these texts that deal with conventional morals as well as ideal morality, define the moral code, and determine the moral principle that lies behind it. The conduct of men, both as individuals and in groups, constitutes the theme of these Śāstras. The metaphysical texts assume an acquaintance with the Dharmaśāstras, and have no need to repeat their theme. Even so, they do indicate, on occasions, the importance of ethical principles and the nature of the conduct that should be based on them. The Upaniṣads, for example, teach the fundamentals of the good life. In a well-known context, the *Bṛhadāraṇyaka* summarizes a whole philosophy of ethics in the three commands, "Cultivate self-control" (*dāmyata*), "Be generous" (*datta*), and "Have compassion (*dayadhvam*), given to gods, men, and demons, respectively.[7] In the *Taittirīya,* there is one whole section devoted to detailed moral instruction imparted to a student at the conclusion of his scholastic studies.[8] To cite another instance, a philosophical text, that is, the *Vaiśeṣika Sūtra,* whose sole concern is the exposition of the categories, begins with the statement, "Now,

[3] A. B. Keith, *The Religion and Philosophy of the Veda and Upanishads* (Cambridge, Massachusetts: Harvard University Press, 1925), pp. 584–586.

[4] *Kauṣītakī Upaniṣad* III. 1.

[5] R. E. Hume, *The Thirteen Principal Upanishads* (London: Oxford University Press, 1934), p. 60.

[6] *Nistraiguṇye pathi vicaratāṁ ko vidhiḥ ko niṣedhaḥ.*

[7] *Bṛhadāraṇyaka Upaniṣad* V. ii. 3.

[8] *Taittirīya Upaniṣad* I. xi.

therefore, we shall explain *dharma* (righteousness)," and proceeds to define *dharma* as that from which results the accomplishment of exaltation and of the supreme good.[9] Besides the metaphysical texts (Darśanaśāstras) and the ethical codes (Dharmaśāstras), there are several books of applied philosophy, such as the *Bhagavad Gītā,* the *Dhammapada,* and the *Tirukkuṛaḷ,* each of which expounds a metaphysic of morals.

We have now given evidence to show that ethical teaching does figure in a significant way even in purely philosophical texts. We would like to repeat what we have observed already, that is, that fruitful philosophizing demands, not only a sharp intellect, but also moral excellence. Without proper ethical training there is no use philosophizing. Commenting on the first word, "Then" (*atha*), in the first aphorism of the *Brahma Sūtra,* Śaṁkara prescribes for the prospective philosophical student the following fourfold qualification: (1) discrimination between the eternal and the non-eternal, (2) non-attachment to the pleasures of this world and the next, (3) cultivation of the cardinal virtues, and (4) a longing for liberation (*mumukṣutva*). Of these four qualifications, it will be seen that, while the first refers to intellectual competence, the other three constitute the practical requirement consisting in the disciplining of the emotions and the will of the aspirant. He should never lose sight of the goal of his inquiry. He should desire nothing else but that, i.e., *mokṣa.* Consequently, he should develop a distaste for the pleasures of this world and the next. And he should prepare himself morally for a life of metaphysical contemplation by cultivating such qualities as calmness, self-control, and contentment. The insistence on the acquisition of moral excellence as a condition for effective philosophizing is not peculiar to Vedānta; it is common to all the systems, including Jainism and Buddhism.

(2) As for the other reason offered by the critics to the effect that, since the goal of Indian philosophy is beyond ethics, ethical value is not important and the distinction between good and evil has no meaning for the man who has reached the goal, the critics here are guilty of gross misjudgment. It is true that the ultimate value is *mokṣa,* spiritual freedom, and not *dharma,* righteousness. According to all the schools of Indian philosophy, empirical life is, and is bound to be, a region of imperfection. Bondage (*bandha*) consists in the soul's being involved in this region. Identifying itself with a psychophysical complex, it finds itself caught in a cycle of birth and death. Freedom from this erroneous identification, liberation from the wheel of empirical existence, is called *mokṣa,* and by several other names such as *apavarga, niḥśreyasa, kaivalya,* and *nirvāṇa.* Some schools conceive of *mokṣa* as a state of total absence of misery; others regard it as the plenary experience of unexcelled bliss. Many systems believe that *mokṣa* is a state which is yet to be; a few, such as Advaita Vedānta, teach that it is the eternal state of the Self, which has never really been lost, and that all one has to do is to realize this fact. All the philosophical

[9] S. Radhakrishnan and Charles A. Moore, eds., *A Source Book in Indian Philosophy* (Princeton: Princeton University Press, 1957) (hereafter, *Source Book*), p. 387.

points of view, however, recognize that the goal of life is to be absolutely free from the need to be reborn.

While it is admitted that *mokṣa,* and not *dharma,* is the supreme end, the sole intrinsic value, it is clearly and undoubtedly taught by all Indian thinkers that, without *dharma, mokṣa* cannot be gained. What is contrary to *dharma,* i.e., *adharma* (unrighteousness), is a great hindrance to *mokṣa.* So, *mokṣa* is not opposed to *dharma,* as it is to *adharma.*[10] What is more, what fulfills cannot be antagonistic to or subversive of what is less. If *mokṣa* is the end, *dharma* is the means.[11] Sometimes the analogies of the ladder and the boat are given to show that the end exceeds the means. One makes use of a ladder to reach a terrace, but does not cling to it after achieving his end. The boat is employed for crossing a river, but, after the crossing, the boat is left behind.[12] Such analogies should be understood with care. The man of perfection, the one who has reached the goal, has no need to be moral under compulsion. He does not function as if impelled by a sense of obligation. He is not a slave of the "ought"; he has risen above formal rules and mechanical regulations. Texts like the one quoted from the *Kauṣītakī* do say that the perfect man may perform actions such as stealing, killing, etc., and is not affected thereby. Before clearing up the misunderstanding of such texts, it is worth while to note that similar statements are to be found in the books of the other traditions, too, such as the Bauddha. The *Dhammapada,* for example, defines a *brāhmin* as one who "goes scatheless though he have killed father and mother and two kings of the warrior caste and a kingdom with all its subjects."[13] Anyone conversant with Indian philosophical texts will admit that these passages should not be understood literally. They are figurative statements (*arthavāda*). *Arthavāda* texts are those which praise and condemn what they approve and disapprove, respectively. When a text declares, for instance, "The sun, verily, is the sacrificial post," the meaning is not that the sun and the post are the same. Obviously, the two cannot be the same; the evidence of perception is against their identity. So, the statement is to be regarded as a figure of speech, intended as praise of the sacrificial post. Similarly, when a father says, "Eat poison," to his son who has accepted a dinner engagement which is not to his liking, it does not mean that he wants his son actually to take poison and perish; all that is meant is that the son should cancel the engagement. The statement is a condemnation of the intended act. Thus, the *arthavāda* texts are not assertions of facts; they have figurative meaning only. When a text declares that even such heinous crimes as matricide, patricide, theft, and infanticide do not affect him who is released, it does not imply that the released person will perform these crimes. To imagine that it does is like looking for a mane and claws in the case of a

[10] J. A. B. van Buitenen does not seem to be quite right when he says that *mokṣa* is opposed to *dharma,* but not as *adharma.* See his "Dharma and Mokṣa," *Philosophy East and West,* VII, Nos. 1 and 2 (April-July, 1957), 37.

[11] Ernest W. Lefever, *Christian Ethics and United States Foreign Policy; An Annotated Reading List and Guide to Current Information.* (New York, Department of International Justice and Goodwill, National Council of Churches of Christ in the United States, 1953), p. 10: "Ethics is a discipline of means, not of ends."

[12] See the *Uttara Gītā* V. 18.

[13] *Source Book,* p. 315.

man who is described as a lion. One who has become perfect cannot, certainly, be immoral. To say that he transcends morality is not to say that he can be a libertine or a moral rake. He does not take leave of the cardinal virtues after reaching the goal. These become now his embellishments or adornments. No longer does he strive to be good; goodness becomes his very nature. So, it is well to remember that, according to Indian philosophers, ethical value is not discarded in *mokṣa* but conserved and sublimated.

Why should not the goodness as evisaged in ethics, it may be asked, be regarded as the highest value? The reason Indian philosophy aims at a goal which lies beyond ethics is that ethics belongs to the world of relativity—a world of claims and counter-claims with its contradictions and imperfections—and so long as one is content to belong here one cannot realize perfection. One need not even go so far as to say that perfection is not gained at the level of mere morality; even the solution to moral problems is not found at this level. Let us take two typical questions: (1) the question of form versus content in ethics, and (2) the question of fate versus free will.

(1) The issue between Kantian rationalism and hedonism in Western ethics is well known. The rationalism of Kant emphasizes the form of morality at the expense of content. Hedonism seeks content without paying due attention to form. The former gives us the *how* of morality when it teaches that we should so act that the principle of our action may be universalized. The latter is concerned with the *why* of morality when it sets forth pleasure or happiness as the goal of action. The issue is one between the rule and the goal, the right and the good. There are some schools of Indian thought which take sides on this issue. The question that is raised is: What prompts activity—is it the awareness of a deed as something *to be done* (*kāryatā-jñāna*), or is it the cognition of a deed as the means to some end to be gained (*iṣṭasādhanatā-jñāna*)? According to the Prābhākara Mīmāṁsakas, it is the knowledge that something is to be done that results in volition. What-is-to-be-done may mean either what can be done or what ought to be done. It is the latter sense that the Prābhākaras sponsor. The obligatoriness of duty lies, they say, in the awareness of the ought-to-be-done. Here, again, it is not the simple awareness of a deed as something to be done that constitutes obligation. The agent should be conscious of the fact that *he* ought to do it, that the deed ought to become *his* qualification. It is not only in the case of obligatory duties (*nitya-* and *naimittika-karmas*) that there is the sense of obligatoriness but also in the case of optional deeds (*kāmya-karmas*). Though in the latter case the desire for an end serves as a motive, the deed acquires the quality of oughtness by the end being regarded as a qualification of the agent. Thus, in the Prābhākara view, all willed action is prompted by the sense of oughtness. In their eagerness to universalize the law of duty, the Prābhākaras bring even optional deeds under its operation.

The Nyāya view, on the contrary, stresses the importance of the consciousness of end and means. In order that there may be a willed act, there must be the knowledge that the act is instrumental to the desired end. This is so, not only as regards the optional deeds, but also in the case of obligatory duties. It is the end that determines all voluntary action—but it is the end as chosen by the agent and not as an external impelling force conditioning his behavior.

Most of the systems of Indian philosophy would agree with the Nyāya in holding the instrumentalist view of ethics. Moral conduct is part of the means to *mokṣa*. It is not that any mode of conduct becomes moral if it leads to a desired end. The end cannot justify the means. As is the means, so will be the end. *Mokṣa,* which is the supreme end, requires on the part of the aspirant, as we have seen, the possession of the virtues and the practice of good deeds. All the systems accept this principle. In the highest reaches of Indian philosophy, such as Advaita and theistic Vedānta, however, it is held that the distinctions between end and means, content and form, etc., are transcended. The man who has realized the Self or God, as the case may be, is not tormented by any sense of obligation; nor does he harbor any desires. Neither *kāryatā* (obligatoriness) nor *iṣṭasādhanatā* (instrumentality to the desired) has any relevance for him. Of such a person, the Upaniṣads declare, "Such a one, verily, the thought does not torment: 'Why have I not done the good? Why have I done the evil?' He who knows this saves himself from these [thoughts]. For, truly, from both of these he saves himself—he who knows this!"[14] "Him [who knows this] these two do not overcome—neither the thought 'Hence I did wrong' nor the thought 'Hence I did right.' Verily he overcomes them both. What he has done and what he has not done do not affect him."[15] The *Bhagavad Gītā* says, "The man who revels in the Self, who is content in the Self, and who is satisfied only with the Self, for him there is no obligation."[16] "He in whom all desires subside, even as the waters subside in the ocean which, though ever being filled by them, never overflows—that man finds peace; not he who desires desires."[17]

(2) The conclusion that one has to go beyond ethics if one is to be free from all conflicting notions may be arrived at also by an examination of the vexed question of fate versus free will. The determinists and the indeterminists have waged battles royal on this issue, the former maintaining that man is completely a creature of circumstances, and the latter that he is the maker of his own destiny.

The various brands of naturalism regard man as part of Nature, as essentially the same in kind as any other species, subject to the same laws, behaving in the same way. The sense of freedom which he may feel is sometimes only imaginary and not real. The so-called moral behavior of man is not different from, say, the falling of a stone or the flight of a bird in pursuit. The consistent naturalist, who is a necessitarian or determinist, thinks, therefore, that there is no meaning in the "ought" of morality. Ethics is a natural science and not a normative study. Its task is to investigate what men do or tend to do, and not what they ought to do. To the evolutionary biologist, man is an item in the course of evolution, governed by the natural law of existence, survival, and

[14] *Taittirīya Upaniṣad* II. 9.
[15] *Bṛhadāraṇyaka Upaniṣad* IV. iv. 22.
[16] *Bhagavad Gītā* III. 17.
[17] *Ibid.,* II. 70.

supercession. To the behavioristic psychologist, man is a mechanism, though a complicated one, for receiving stimuli and responding to them. His brain thinks, even as his liver secretes bile. To the dialectical materialist, man appears as a product of economic forces, shaped or misshaped by his material conditions, and acting according to set patterns, urged by the primary needs of living. Thus, all determinists are agreed in denying to man initiative and freedom and in converting him into a robot or automaton. He can take credit for none of his actions; nor can he be blamed for any of his failings. He has no responsibility whatsoever. He is to be considered more a patient of external forces than an agent of actions.

There is a higher determinism which is that of the theologian, according to whom

There is a divinity that shapes our ends,
Rough-hew them how we will.

We are as nothing before the might and glory of God. Not a sparrow falleth without his consent. Our wills are ours only to make them his. It is in vain that man sometimes attempts to get out of God's plan. Man mistakenly thinks that he can make or mar his future. But one day or other he has to awake from this delusion and realize that God is the sole impeller of all things and the undisputed architect of the world.

The indeterminists or libertarians, who are mostly pluralists and personalists, will not brook the fettering of man's will either by Nature or by God. Their main argument is that, if man is not responsible for his actions and has no freedom to choose between alternative courses of conduct, he cannot be the subject of moral judgment, and thus there will be no distinction between good and evil. As Kant urged, there would be no meaning in an "ought" if it were not accompanied by a "can."[18] If man cannot do what he ought to do, morality is meaningless, and there can be neither praise nor blame for what he actually does. Weighing the pros and cons of the contending doctrines, William James states his conclusion thus: "While I freely admit that the pluralism and restlessness [of a universe with freedom in it] are repugnant and irrational in a certain way, I find that the alternative to them is irrational in a deeper way. The indeterminism offends only the native absolutism of my intellect—an absolutism which, after all, perhaps deserves to be snubbed and kept in check. But the determinism . . . violates my sense of moral reality through and through."[19] In order to safeguard the freedom of the individual, some modern pluralists even go to the extent of limiting the power of God. God, according to them, is not the Almighty. He is merciful, but not omnipotent.

There are some moralists who reject both determinism and indeterminism. Both freedom and necessity, they say, are essential to morals. There is no unrestricted or unlimited freedom, nor is there absolute necessity. "Necessity is the

[18] See J. S. Mackenzie, *A Manual of Ethics* (London: University Tutorial Press Ltd., 1929), p. 73.

[19] *The Will to Believe and Other Essays*, pp. 145–183. Quoted in James Seth, *A Study of Ethical Principles* (10th ed., Edinburgh: William Blackwood, 1908), p. 373.

inseparable condition, or, rather, let us say, *co-element,* of freedom. And without that co-element, freedom is as incapable of being construed to thought, is something as impossible as walking without ground to tread on, or flying without air to beat."[20] Man is conditioned by what he has inherited. What he has inherited depends on his own past. But, with this as his initial capital, he can build his future. A sculptor finds his material given. But how he shapes his material depends upon his own skill. Morality requires neither predestination nor indetermination, but self-determination.

It is in this sense that the *karma* doctrine is to be interpreted. *Karma* is not a relentless fate pushing man to a preordained destiny. It is what man has achieved in the past; and he is answerable to it. He has acquired also certain tendencies and dispositions which make him act in one way rather than in another. But he can change them in the present and shape his future according to his will. God in such a scheme would be the general ground for the operation of the law of *karma.* God, or destiny (*daiva*), is not opposed to human effort (*puruṣa-kāra*). Both are necessary for making morality possible and yield its result. *Reader's Digest* (September, 1953) provides an interesting illustration: "A widow, who had been left with six sons to bring up, was asked how she had managed to raise such exceptional sons alone and unaided. 'It did take grit and grace,' she said, 'but I wasn't exactly unaided—the Good Lord helped me. Every night I knelt and told him I'd furnish the grit if He would furnish the grace.' "

The will implies an ego that exercises the will. It is from the standpoint of the ego that the problem arises. If the ego is unobstructed in activity, it is believed to be free. If it is opposed by the non-ego, either in the form of Nature or in the form of God, and is conditioned thereby, obviously it cannot be free. The ethical "ought" is unmeaning without freedom. Yet, the limited ego finds itself in chains. So long as we refuse to go beyond the level of the ego, the problem cannot be solved.

What, then, is the solution? Self-knowledge. The ground of the ego and the non-ego is the Self. It is the ground of fate and free will. It is without peer because there is nothing besides it. It is the sphere of actionlessness. How, then, can there be the function of will? For those who have realized this truth, there is no problem to solve. As a modern Indian sage, Ramaṇa Maharshi, says, "The dispute as to what wins, fate or free will, is only for those who have not the knowledge of the ground of fate and free will. Those who have realized the peerless Self which is the ground of fate and free will are free from them."[21]

So far, we have endeavored to show the soundness of the view generally held in Indian philosophy that morality is not a realm which is self-sufficient and self-complete, that one has to go beyond ethics in order to reach the final goal, which is *mokṣa,* and that it is only in the plenary experience of spiritual freedom that all contradictions and all problems are resolved. Because Indian

[20] *Mind,* Old Series, V (1880), 252.

[21] *Forty Verses on Existence* (*Uḷḷadu Nārpadu*), V. 19. See T. M. P. Mahadevan, *Ramaṇa Maharshi and His Philosophy of Existence* (Madras: Sri Ramanasramam, 1951), pp. 85-89.

philosophy is *mokṣa*-oriented, some of its critics say that its ethical attitude is one of world-and-life negation rather than of world-and-life affirmation. The most prominent of such critics is Albert Schweitzer. There are two contrasted world-views, according to him: the view of world-and-life negation and the view of world-and-life affirmation. The representative of the former is the Indian, that of the latter is the modern European. World-and-life affirmation consists in regarding this world and life in it as valuable. Its opposite consists in regarding both the world and life as meaningless and sorrowful. Those who adopt the negative attitude resolve (a) to bring life to a standstill in themselves by mortifying their will-to-live, and (b) to renounce all activity which aims at improvement of the conditions of life in this world. Schweitzer admits that the twofold difference of world view has nothing to do with difference of race. This is not a case of an East-West rift. The Chinese and the Iranian, like the Westerner, lean to world-and-life affirmation. No tradition, again, is totally negative or completely affirmative in outlook. So, it is only a question of emphasis. What Schweitzer wishes to maintain is that, in Indian thought, world-and-life negation occupies a predominant place. In the teachings of Jesus, too, there is found a form of world-and-life negation, but this is not the same as the Indian form of negation. The Christian type "only denies the evil, imperfect world in expectance of a good and perfect world which is to come." It "does not preach the inactive ethic of perfecting the self alone, but active, enthusiastic love of one's neighbor." The Indian attitude, on the contrary, is escapist and non-activistic. The primary concern of the Indian is to seek his own inner perfection; he is not concerned about what happens to his neighbor. The Indian world-view, which is mystical and monistic, sponsors a non-active ethic, which is no ethic at all in the true sense of the term.[22]

Our reply to Schweitzer will consist of partial admission and correction. It is true that Indian philosophy advocates a withdrawal from the life of the flesh. But that is the price one has to pay if one desires the life eternal. What actually hinders progress in spirituality, however, is not physical existence in the world and participation in its affairs, but forgetfulness of the true aim of life. All that serves as a hindrance to the realization of that aim must naturally be renounced. There is no happiness, as the Upaniṣad says, in that which is narrow and small; true happiness lies in or is the Infinite.[23] Even those systems of Indian philosophy which hold a theistic view insist on the need for the destruction of egoism. As a modern Indian mystic, Sri Ramakrishna, puts it, the answer to the question "When shall I be free?" is "When 'I' shall cease to be." It is to lead the individual away from his small and petty self that the institution of stages in life (*āśramas*) was organized in India. As one completes his first stage in life, which is the period of studentship, and enters the second by marrying and founding a family, his circle of interests becomes wider, and he becomes less and less self-centered. But he is not to stop there. The exclusive

[22] Albert Schweitzer, *Indian Thought and Its Development,* Mrs. Charles E. B. Russell, trans. (London: Adam and Charles Black, 1951), chap. I.

[23] *Chāndogya Upaniṣad* VII. xxiii.

love of family and clannishness can be as crippling as narrow egoism. After the individual has received in his spiritual path the help that life as a householder can give him, he must march onward by taking to the life of a hermit, and finally by becoming a recluse (*sannyāsin*), leaving behind all affiliations that cramp and bind the soul. Kalidāsa, the great Indian poet, describes this ideal as "owning the whole world while disowning oneself." "It is a tribute to the high metaphysical capacity of the Indian people," observes Paul Deussen, "that the phenomenon of asceticism made its appearance among them earlier and occupied a larger place than among other known people."[24]

Indian negation, if it is to be called negation, is a significant negation. The ascetic attitude is not the barely negative attitude. It is the leaving off of the lower in order to pursue the higher. Two paths have been in vogue from time immemorial, says Śaṁkara in his Commentary on the *Bhagavad Gītā*, the path of activity (*pravṛtti*) and the way of withdrawal from action (*nivṛtti*). The former is meant for the householder, the latter for the recluse. *Pravṛtti*, by itself, will lead only to worldly welfare; *nivṛtti*, properly understood, is the means to release. Attempts have been made to introduce the spirit of *nivṛtti* into *pravṛtti*, so that *pravṛtti* may serve as a preparation for the higher life of renunciation. One such attempt is to be found in the *Laws of Manu*. Dealing with the question of food, permitted and forbidden, Manu says, "To act thus is natural to man; but conscious restraint leads to a higher goal."[25] This observation applies, not only to the taking of food, but to all actions that issue from inclination. Some of these are permissible in the case of the householder. But, turning away from them, says Manu, is a greater merit.[26] In other words, the householder, too, must practise *nivṛtti* as far as possible. In the *Bhagavad Gītā*, we have a more satisfactory reconcilation between *pravṛtti* and *nivṛtti*, in the doctrine of disinterested activity (*niṣkāma-karma*). "You have a right to the work alone, and not to the fruit thereof," says the *Gītā*. "Let not the fruit of action be your aim, nor let your attachment be to inaction."[27] The teaching is: Whatever be the activity, let it be performed without any selfish motive. This rule applies to all voluntary actions, and to all the *āśramas*. "Disinterested" activity, however, does not mean purposeless or aimless activity. What the *Gītā* teaches is that, instead of having a different end for each action, one should have one and the same motive for all action, i.e., the gaining of self-purification (*ātma-śuddhi*) leading to *mokṣa*. Since *mokṣa*, as conceived in the more important schools of Indian philosophy, is neither an isolated state of the individual nor a post-mortem experience, the pursuit of *mokṣa* involves neither desertion of life nor neglect of the interests of the world. The attitude behind this pursuit cannot better be described than in the words Schweitzer himself employs in defining what he calls the profoundest form of world-and-life

[24] Paul Deussen, *The Philosophy of the Upanishads*—Authorized English translation by A. S. Geden (Edinburgh: T. & T. Clark, 1906), p. 65.

[25] *Manu Smṛti* V. 56. Quoted by M. Hiriyanna, "A Neglected Ideal of Life," in T. M. P. Mahadevan *et al.*, eds., *The Indian Philosophical Congress, Silver Jubilee Volume* (Madras: Indian Philosophical Congress, 1950), p. 223.

[26] *Ibid.*, p. 224.

[27] *Gītā* II. 47.

affirmation, although he will not admit this: "In the profoundest form of world and life affirmation, in which man lives his life on the loftiest spiritual and ethical plane, he attains to inner freedom from the world and becomes capable of sacrificing his life for some end. This profoundest world and life affirmation can assume the appearance of world and life negation. But that does not make it world and life negation: it remains what it is—the loftiest form of world and life affirmation."[28]

Closely related to the criticism we have examined above is the one which says that the pursuit of *mokṣa* is a selfish one, although in an exalted sense. The individual is concerned with his own salvation, and is not worried about what happens to his neighbor. He has to practice harmlessness as part of his spiritual discipline, but is not obliged to love his fellow men. He is asked to refrain from destroying or damaging any living being, but active love is not demanded of him.[29]

In answer to this charge, we wish to point out that the Indian is not the particularly egotistic individualist he is made out to be. Self-interest is natural to man. What common morality aims to create in one is enlightened self-interest. The spiritual morality which Indian philosophy favors helps one in the sublimation of the lower self in order that the Supreme Self may be realized. The process of sublimation is effected by selfless service directed toward world welfare. Kṛṣṇa teaches Arjuna in the *Bhagavad Gītā* that one ought to work for the commonweal (*lokasaṁgraha*), and commends the examples of Janaka, the royal sage, and himself, the incarnation of God (*avatāra*).[30] The common good, however, should not be regarded as the *end* of action. What is called social service becomes at its best the worship of humanity. But humanity, too, is a finite object. So, the doctrine of *karma-yoga* as taught in the *Gītā* urges that in action all finite aims should be discarded, both narrow private ends and the so-called public good. The world is certainly benefited by the disinterested action of the *yogin,* but from his standpoint such benefit is only a *consequence* and not the *end.* There is a gradation of social values, each higher one being more expansive and more intensive than the lower one. The highest value, however, is the non-dual Self.

As for the pursuit of *mokṣa,* it can never be selfish in any sense of the term. It is only when all selfishness vanishes that *mokṣa* is realized. A necessary part of the discipline, as we saw above, is for one to transcend narrow affiliations and attachments by working for the welfare of the world as a whole. When the end is reached, according to Advaita Vedānta, which is the butt of all such criticisms, there is no individuality left. It is from the standpoint of the unreleased that the released appears to be an individual. In release itself there is no duality, no distinction. When one attains release, it is believed, the entire world is taken nearer perfection. And, according to one view in Advaita, no single individual soul is finally released until all souls are released. This is known as the doctrine of universal release (*sarva-mukti*). The wise ones who

[28] Albert Schweitzer, *op. cit.,* p. 6. [29] *Ibid.,* pp. 8–9. [30] *Gītā* III. 20–24.

play the role of teachers aim at helping others on the pathway to perfection. The Jaina prophets are called "ford-makers" (*tīrthaṁ-karas*), because they discovered the way to cross the sea of transmigration, not only for themselves but for all people. It is said of the Buddha that after achieving enlightenment his first inclination was to spend the rest of his life in utter retirement and isolation, and that he was dissuaded from adopting this easy course of spiritual lassitude by the deity Brahmā, who besought him to preach the truth to the world. And, according to tradition, he declared that he would willingly bear the burden of everyone's suffering if he could thereby bring relief to the world.[31]

Of the four values, called *puruṣārthas,* recognized in Indian philosophy, wealth (*artha*), pleasure (*kāma*), righteousness (*dharma*), and release (*mokṣa*), the first three are temporal or instrumental values, and the last is the eternal or intrinsic value. Sometimes, it is true, people mistake instrumental values for intrinsic ends. The miser, in his excessive attachment to wealth, may seek to acquire and preserve it, as if it were an end in itself. The old materialists of India, the Cārvākas, admitted no other end for man except pleasure. Some of the ritualist-philosophers taught that religious duty was an end-in-itself. But, in the clash of ideals that took place very early in the history of Indian thought, these three goods found their rightful places as stages, not necessarily successive, in the journey of the human spirit to its appointed destination, i.e., release from finitude and imperfection.

It is clear from this value-scheme that what are called this-worldly values have a place in man's life. Things like long life, robust health, good progeny, power, wealth, etc., are as much sought for in India as elsewhere. In the *Ṛg Veda,* for instance, there are prayers to the gods asking for earthly goods. A familiar formula that is uttered by the priest during the performance of any domestic rite asks that the householder be blessed with money, grain, cattle, children, and life for a hundred years. But what the great ones of India urge is that man should not become a slave to the goods that perish. Commenting on the word "then" in the *Taittirīya* text, "Then, bring me prosperity (*śrī*) in wool, along with cattle,"[32] Śaṁkara observes that prosperity should come after one has gained discriminative intelligence, for, he adds, prosperity makes for evil in the case of one who does not have this intelligence.

The Cārvāka recognizes only two values: wealth and pleasure. Of these, wealth is the means, and pleasure is the end. Pleasure that results from the attainment of the objects of one's desire is the aim of life; and by "objects" the Cārvāka means the contents of sense-enjoyment. It is not denied, of course, that there is no pleasure unmixed with pain. But, just because pain is mixed with pleasure, no sane person would reject pleasure. The part of wisdom lies in avoiding pain as much as possible and in acquiring the greatest amount of pleasure. "Men do not refrain from sowing paddy-seeds," argues the Cārvāka,

[31] Kumārila, *Tantra-vārttika* I. iii. 4.
[32] *Taittirīya Upaniṣad* I. iv. 3. Śaṁkara: *amedhaso hi śrīr anarthāyaiva.*

"because there are wild animals to devour them; nor do they refuse to set the cooking-pots on the fire, because there are beggars to pester them for a share of the contents." The ethics of pleasure advocated by the Cārvāka has for its basis his materialist philosophy. Nothing is real, according to him, which cannot be sense-perceived. There is no soul apart from the physical body, no God, no afterlife. Therefore—"While life remains let a man live happily; let him feed on ghee even though he runs into debt; / When once the body becomes ashes, how can it ever return again?"

A crude egoistic hedonism such as the Cārvāka's is self-stultifying. Pleasure in the sense of an agreeable feeling is not what is generally sought for. We seek objects of pleasure and not pleasure itself. The feeling of satisfaction, which is pleasure, is only an accompaniment or a consequent of the attainment of the desired object. Even granting that pleasure is desired by some people, it does not follow that pleasure is desirable. One may get all the pleasures imaginable, and yet one may not be happy. And, as has been pointed out by Western critics of hedonism, the chances of gaining pleasure are very slim if one consciously pursues it as the end. "The 'pursuit of pleasure' is a phrase which calls for a smile or a sigh," says the well-known British idealist Bradley, "since the world has learnt that, if pleasure is the end, it is an end which must not be made one, and is found there most where it is not sought."

The Cārvāka and the hedonist believe that the greatest quantity of pleasure is the human goal. But how is it possible to add one pleasure to another, where they are so disparate by nature? The pleasure of the table, for instance, cannot be added to the pleasure derived from contemplating a grand idea. Even at the cost of discontent and dissatisfaction, we prefer some pleasures to others. That is because we grade pleasures as higher and lower, and distinguish them qualitatively. Now, if one pleasure is better than another in spite of the fact that both are pleasures, then it is not pleasure as such that is valued but something in it which makes it good. Thus, at the slightest touch of analysis, the naive philosophy of pleasure crumbles. What has been called the "music-hall theory of life" can please man only for a while. The Cārvāka materialism is a passing mood of the human mind.

If the rule for man is "eat, drink, and multiply," what difference is there between him and the animal? In the matter of sense-gratification there seems to be no distinction between man and animal. The members of the animal species are attracted toward pleasant objects and repelled by unpleasant ones, even as we human beings are. Yet, there is something distinctive about man, and that is a sense of value. He is able to discriminate one value from another, and rate them as higher and lower. He can pierce through the appearances and get at the abiding reality. In the words of the *Aitareya Āraṇyaka*, "The *Ātman* is expanded only in man. He, indeed, is most endowed with intelligence. He gives expression to what is known. He sees what is known. He knows what is to come. He knows the visible and the invisible worlds. He perceives the immortal through the mortal. Thus is he endowed. But with the other animals, eating and drinking alone constitute the sphere of their knowledge." It is wrong, therefore, to believe that, in taking his pleasures, man must imitate the animal. The author of the *Kāma Sūtra,* Vātsyāyana, in spite of the fact that he adopts the positivistic attitude in the exposition of his theme, lays down at the outset that *artha, kāma,* and *dharma* should not clash with one another, and that they should find a harmony in a person's life.

There used to be current a view among some Vedāntins which bears the name *Kāmavilayavāda.* According to this view, the desire for enjoyment should be fulfilled. It is only when all desires are satisfied that one obtains eligibility for knowledge, and, through that, release. All desires, including that for heaven, should be first satisfied, and then there will be no more attachment to them. When there is complete non-attachment, one becomes fit for the path of knowledge. The Advaita Vedāntin would say, in reply, that desire is not destroyed by fulfillment, and that it only multiplies by being served. Never does desire cease by enjoyment; it increases like fire which flares up when ghee is poured into it. Therefore, one should turn away from desires, for they are not the means to release; and one should resort to the path of Self-knowledge through the taming of the passions.[33] It may be asked, "Is not the desire for *mokṣa* a case of attachment?" The reply is: Although the term "desire" is used with reference to *mokṣa,* it is not desire in the usual sense. More properly, it is an "interest" in the eternal Self, caused by discrimination. Similarly, when the Upaniṣads declare that the Self is the supreme object of love, it is not self-love that they teach. The meaning is this: We may start with loving what is perishable and finite; but we may not end there. Nothing that is limited can give us lasting happiness. The pleasure that we find in the objects of sense is but a reflection of the bliss that is the Self. It is the discovery of the Self or Self-realization that is the goal of the search for pleasure.

In our examination of the Cārvāka ethics we saw that there is a philosophy behind it, i.e., materialism. All the other schools of Indian thought are non-materialist in their outlook, but are of different types: pluralisms and monisms, realisms and idealisms, combinations of these, and some that are neither. Some are theistic and others non-theistic. Some are orthodox and others heterodox. In spite of these divergences, they support an identical ethic because of their basic attitude, which is spiritualistic. The ethical discipline that is prescribed in the several schools is in substance the same. There is a distinction between the moral code pertaining to the ascetic and that relating to the householder. In Jainism, for instance, the former consists of what are known as the "great vows" (*mahā-vratas*) and the latter as the "lesser vows" (*aṇu-vratas*). These two do not differ in kind, however, but only in degree. The vows in the case of the ascetic are: (1) not to injure any living being (*ahiṁsā*), (2) not to speak untruth (*satya*), (3) not to steal (*asteya*), (4) to lead a celibate life (*brahmacarya*), and (5) to possess nothing (*aparigraha*). In the case of the householder, the rules

[33] T. M. P. Mahadevan, *The Sambandha-vārttika of Sureśvarācārya* (Madras: University of Madras, 1958), pp. 176–178.

are the same except that the last two are amended to mean chastity and contentment, respectively.

It is because the systems agree on matters of ethics that all of them accept the teachings of the Dharmaśāstras. In order to understand the quintessence of *dharma,* let us turn to the *Mahābhārata,* whose place among the Hindu Śāstras is unique. It is encyclopedic in its sweep, covering all the important topics relating to man. There is no major problem which it does not consider, and no vital question which it does not seek to answer. One finds teachings in this Great Epic as to how one should strive for worldly prosperity and take one's pleasures without offending the moral principle. There are discourses about domestic and community life, about the professions and intergroup relations, about political strategy and rules of war. Spiritual disciplines, ways of overcoming sorrow, metaphysical truths—these are also taught. As the Epic itself puts it, "Concerning the four ends of life, one may find here all that is to be found elsewhere; and one cannot find elsewhere what is not to be found here."

The central concept around which every other revolves in the *Mahābhārata* is *dharma,* the good life. Yudhiṣṭhira, one of the main characters of the story, has the appellation, *"dharma-rāja"* (king of virtue) and *"dharma-putra"* (son of righteousness). He is often described as one who is the foremost among the bearers of virtue. He is said to have eclipsed his virtuous father, Pāṇḍu, by his character, conduct, and devotion to duty. Arjuna, the hero of the Epic, is also described as the paragon of virtue. The five Pāṇḍava princes in the story, in fact, represent the forces that make for goodness. Some of the elders who assume the role of teachers made *dharma* the main topic of their expositions; and they are themselves exemplars of virtue. Vidura knew the truth of *dharma,* and practiced it. Bhīṣma is referred to by Kṛṣṇa as "the greatest of those who know *dharma,"* and Yudhiṣṭhira is directed to seek wisdom from him when the war had ended, as he lay on a bed of arrows awaiting death. Kṛṣṇa, the great *avatāra,* the Lord incarnate, is *dharma* itself. In the Śāntiparvā of the *Mahābhārata,* Bhīṣma addresses Kṛṣṇa thus: "Obeisance to the great *Dharma,* obeisance to the creator Kṛṣṇa!" The *Mahābhārata* is not to be regarded as a mere story of intrigues and battles, but as an allegory of the struggle between good and evil, and of the ultimate triumph of the good. It is not political conquest that is the end of the Great War, but inner victory, which is victory over all that is base and narrow in man. Kṛṣṇa tells Yudhiṣṭhira in the Vanaparva that *dharma* is superior to gaining a dominion. In the Bhīṣmaparva, Arjuna reminds his king and brother that victory is to be achieved not so much by strength and valor as by truthfulness, benevolence, and righteous effort. This is the advice Bhīṣma gives in the Śāntiparva: Death through observing *dharma* is better than victory through sinful conduct. The Epic itself is called by the name *"jaya,"* which means victory and the great proclamation that it makes is: Where *dharma* is, there is victory.

It is not easy to define *dharma. "Dharma"* means, literally, one's nature—

not one's nature as it appears on the surface, but one's nature as it really *is* and *ought* to be. That is why it is said that the truth of *dharma* is hidden in a cave, as it were. It requires all the skill and wisdom of which man is capable to discover *dharma.*

In matters concerning *dharma,* scripture is said to be the authority. Kṛṣṇa says to Arjuna, in the *Bhagavad Gītā,* "Scripture, therefore, is the authority in regard to what ought to be done and what ought not to be done; knowing the way set forth in scripture, thou shouldst perform thy duty here." But many are not in a position to understand what scripture teaches. There are apparently contradictory scriptural commands. And so, another piece of advice is also given: Follow the pattern of conduct set by the great ones. But, even thus, one may not be truly moral. Obedience to an external code is not the highest morality. If the individual does not freely choose the good and strive to realize it, he does not progress morally. Hence it is that at the end of the *Bhagavad Gītā,* Kṛṣṇa tells Arjuna, "Pondering over all that I have taught thee, do as thou pleasest!" The purpose of Śāstra is to make one understand the truth, and not to impose on one any particular course of action. So each one should act responsibly, in order to be moral; and the morality of each action depends on its worthiness to lead the individual toward the goal of freedom.

The aspects of *dharma* which relate to the life of the individual in society are various. Each individual occupies a specific station in life by virtue of his character and constitution. He ought to perform the duties that pertain to that station. He passes through different stages in life; and each stage has its special responsibilities. But, in fulfilling his obligations, the individual should be inspired by the spirit of *dharma,* and not blindly follow some rigid code. Birth in a particular group, for instance, may condition the resources and abilities of a person. Yet, birth is not all. One may be born low and be noble; one may be born high and be of despicable character. Hence, character and conduct count, not lineage. Whether one is born low or high, says Vidura, one will excel a hundred high-born persons if one keeps to the moral law and is virtuous, gentle, and honorable. Vidura also declares: "I am of the view that lineage is no mark of respectability if one is lacking in character. Character alone excels even if one is born in the lowest class."

Different lists of virtues are given in the *Mahābhārata,* some short and others long. One of these lists mentions the following virtues: forbearance, fortitude, non-violence, equanimity, truthfulness, straightforwardness, conquest of the senses, skill in the performance of one's duties, mildness, a sense of shame in doing what ought not to be done, absence of fickleness, non-wretchedness, freedom from flurry, contentedness, sweetness of speech, refraining from hurting, and freedom from envy. The aim in cultivating all these virtues is that the individual should be made to progress toward perfection. What stands as a bar to perfection is his narrow self. This distorts his vision, puts in his heart distracting desires, makes him a slave of passions, and thus forges fresh bonds for him. Triple is the door to hell, as the *Gītā* teaches, which leads one to destruction: it is passionate desire, anger, and envy. In order that man may avoid entering this dreadful door, he must arm himself with virtues. He should cherish the divine in him, and sublimate the beastly, for that is the only way to realize the *Summum Bonum*. All that is base and wicked must be destroyed: the senses and mind must be subdued; the source of happiness which is within should be discovered.

The quintessence of *dharma,* i.e., what a man ought to do, may be found in the replies given by Yudhiṣṭhira to two of the questions put to him by the ghost in the Vanaparva. What is the most sacred bath? And what is the noblest gift? The reply was: "Cleansing the mind of its impurity is bath; safeguarding the welfare of all beings is gift." One can work for the well-being of all only when one is pure in heart. The Golden Rule is: Do not do unto others what is disagreeable to you (*na tat parasya sandadhyāt pratikūlam yadātmanaḥ*). But this is possible only when one succeeds in sublimating the ego. So long as one identifies oneself with the perishing psychophysical organism, so long as one takes plurality to be real, one cannot lead the good life in all its completeness. Self-interest must be given up. This can be accomplished only when the true Self is gained. *Dharma* is the path which one must pursue in order to gain the Supreme Self, which is also called God. And, in its higher meaning, *dharma is God*: it is the inner nature of all beings. Thus, *dharma, satya,* and Brahman are synonyms. "*Dharma* is the eternal truth; truth is the eternal Brahman."

There is no greater *dharma,* therefore, than the quest after perfection. The Epic boldly issues the command: Renounce the world for the sake of the Self. Only, the Self, which is the supreme end here, is not the ego, the lower nature in man. On no account is *dharma* in this sense to be neglected. Worldly prosperity and private pleasures are as nothing before *dharma*. Even empirical life has no value as against *dharma*. In the following words addressed by Vidura to Dhṛtarāṣṭra we have the highest teaching of the Dharmaśāstras: "Now I shall declare to you, O sire, what is superior to everything, what is most sacred, and supremely excellent. One should never give up *dharma* out of desire, fear, or covetousness—not even for the sake of life itself. *Dharma* is eternal; pleasure and pain are but transient. The soul is eternal; its circumstances are transitory. Discarding what is temporal, get firmly established in the eternal, and be happy. Indeed, it is only the good that are truly happy."

Between the ethical ideals and the social practice of a people there is inevitably a lag. In most cases, individuals make only an asymptotic approach to the highest ideals. A few succeed in winning the goal at any given time. The people as a whole have to rely for their conduct on institutions, on checks and balances. Since institutions are man-made, they tend to deteriorate, and have to be kept in constant repair. Those who can render this service are the proper leaders of mankind. India is fortunate in that at no time has it been without its spiritual leaders and moral exemplars. Undoubtedly there have been ups and downs in India's cultural history. When institutions and the people become corrupt, there is a downward curve. When, as a result of the teaching and example of the right type of leaders, the people are roused from their lethargy, there is real progress.

There will always be social ills and the endeavor to remove them. The long political subjection of India was responsible in a way for highlighting the defects in Hindu social organization, such as caste, untouchability, and the status of women. But it is pertinent to point out that from the earliest times of India's long history there have appeared leaders of vision who have roused the conscience of their fellow men against such evils. The Upaniṣadic seers, the Buddha, Mahāvīra, the teachers of the philosophical schools, the saints of the different traditions, the great preceptors of the Vedānta systems, and the reformers of modern India have all emphasized the need for exaltation of life through freedom from all kinds of narrowness. The present renaissance, which started in the nineteenth century, has had among its leaders such towering personalities as Ram Mohan Roy, Dayananda, Ramakrishna, Vivekananda, Tagore, Aurobindo, Ramana, and Gandhi. It is significant that, although these leaders were called to play different roles in the task of rebuilding Indian society, all of them stressed the same moral and spiritual values which have been the springs of inspiration in the country. It is also significant that under the leadership of Gandhi the Indian people won their freedom in 1947 through truthful and non-violent means. We have already seen that ethical discipline is considered to be essential for the student of philosophy. The same discipline, said Gandhi, is necessary for the social worker and the freedom fighter. *Satya* and *ahiṁsā* (truth and non-violence) became the key concepts of Gandhian politics. These are not only moral virtues but also metaphysical principles. It is Self-realization or spiritual perfection that is the goal even of politics, according to Gandhi. All this is in the truest tradition of Indian culture. In recent international politics Prime Minister Nehru has been pleading for the adoption of the five moral principles which have come to be called *Pañcaśīla*. Vinoba Bhave, who is walking in the footsteps of Gandhi, is working for a silent socio-economic revolution relying solely on the principles of truth and non-violence.

The contribution of Indian ethics to the moral conscience of man is this teaching: (1) A thorough discipline in morals is necessary for both thought and action, and (2) one should not stop with being moral; morality is but the steppingstone to spiritual perfection.

SWAMI NIKHILANANDA

The Realistic Aspect of Indian Spirituality

A widespread view persists among Western scholars that the spiritual perspective of Indian[1] philosophy[2] is incompatible with ethical practice and the ordinary values of life. In this view, Hinduism is, by and large, an otherworldly doctrine concerned with the salvation of the individual and leaves the great mass of humanity to its fate. This attitude, it is often alleged, accounts for India's poverty, illiteracy, and general backwardness. If the world is unreal, as the followers of non-dualism contend, why bother about it?

It will be my endeavor, in this paper, to show that Indian thinkers, including non-dualists, are not indifferent to the world; that, on the contrary, they take the world to be very real in a certain important sense; that they do not repudiate moral values, but, rather, point out that the fulfillment of social obligations is indispensable for the attainment of spiritual experience. To be sure, Indian leaders have often shown indifference to the welfare of the many; but this attitude is due either to their ignorance of the basic truths of Hinduism or to the distortion of these truths prompted by selfishness.

Indian culture has been molded in a special fashion by religion and philosophy. From time out of mind, spirituality has formed the backbone of India. It has left an indelible impression, not only upon her social structure, but also upon her many cultural achievements. Loyalty to certain spiritual concepts, moreover, has preserved Indian society during the many centuries of foreign

[1] The word "Indian" in this paper is generally used to signify "Hindu" because, despite the fact that during the past thousand years non-Hindu elements also entered into the thought-current of India, Indian culture has been largely created and influenced by Hindu philosophical and religious concepts.

[2] In the Hindu tradition there has been no sharp division between religion and philosophy. The former is the emotional and practical approach to reality, the latter is the intellectual. Both intellect and emotion, reason and faith, play important parts in the attainment of the knowledge of reality.

domination. During the darkest period of Indian history, great thinkers, saints, and prophets never failed to exhort the people to perform their social duties, face misfortune calmly, cultivate patience, and keep faith in the ultimate triumph of righteousness and truth. The cause of India's downfall was not her spirituality; on the contrary, spirituality has preserved the country's vitality up to modern times[3]—a fact amply demonstrated in recent years by her heroic struggle for political freedom and her strenuous efforts, along democratic lines, to rebuild the nation after centuries of stagnation.

India has not always been a land of poverty. When India was spiritually great, she was also materially prosperous and culturally creative. It was her fabulous wealth that invited foreign invaders, from Alexander to the English. The foundation of the edifice of the new India must rest on her past attainments; but she must keep her windows open for fresh air from outside to prevent inner pollution. If India abandons her traditional spiritual heritage and takes exclusively to politics, science, and technology to build her future, she will be courting disaster: this is the lesson of India's past. But the spiritual truths of Hinduism must be reformulated with the help of science, technology, and a modern philosophy to suit the conditions of our age.

TWO WAYS OF LIFE

Indian thinkers have always recognized two *dharmas,* or ways of life. One of these is "characterized by activity and the other by renunciation. This twofold *dharma* is the cause of the stability of the world order and also the means by which men attain prosperity and the highest good."[4] By means of activity one enjoys material happiness here and hereafter, and renunciation leads to the highest good. The desire for happiness is universal and persistent. At a certain stage of evolution, a man feels an equally irresistible urge for liberation of the spirit from all forms of attachment. Both the desire for worldly happiness and the desire for the highest good are legitimate desires, and they are always present.[5] The means to their fulfillment are the warp and the woof of the fabric of Indian thought. Both are accepted as valid in the Vedas, the Upaniṣads, the *Mahābhārata, the Rāmāyaṇa,* and the *Code of Manu.* The *Bhagavad Gītā* centers around a war fought for the preserving of the social order. Desire for the contemplative life, which is cherished at a certain stage of spiritual growth, arises only after a man has gone through all the material enjoyments provided by society. One cannot experience inner tranquillity without having first led an active life.[6] Very few, indeed, seek perfection, which is unattainable without inner peace. "Among thousands of men, one strives for perfection; and of those who strive and succeed, one perchance knows Me in truth."[7] The majority of men are satisfied with a worldly life. For them, reli-

[3] *Bhagavad Gītā* XVIII. 78.
[4] *Ibid., Śaṁkarācārya's* introduction to his commentary.
[5] *Kaṭha Upaniṣad* I. ii. 2.
[6] *Bhagavad Gītā* III. 4.
[7] *Ibid.,* VII. 3.

gion and philosophy are designed to awaken their desire for higher ideals and show them the means to their realization. For the enlightened, they are redundant: "The Vedas cease to be Vedas."[8]

According to the Vedic philosophers, material pleasures can be meaningfully enjoyed through gratifying the gods and discharging one's duties toward one's fellow men and sub-human creatures. The gods, in the Vedic tradition, are the controllers of such natural phenomena as rain, sunshine, and wind, and also of the activities of the mind and the sense-organs. Furthermore, they are jealous custodians of social welfare, obstructing the liberation of those mortals who seek liberation without fulfilling their social duties. Yama, the god of death, imparted the knowledge of self to Naciketas after the latter had discharged his duties to his father.[9] The *Muṇḍaka Upaniṣad* states that the god of fire severely punishes the man who performs the Agnihotra sacrifice without showing hospitality to guests.[10] According to Kauṭilya's *Arthaśāstra,* Varuṇa, the god of justice, punishes the king who neglects his kingly duties.[11] Agni, the god of fire in the Agnihotra sacrifice, keeps an eye upon the husband and wife to see that they perform properly their family duties. The Vedas regard the universe as a seamless garment in which all living beings have their appropriate places. Their interdependence is emphasized, the welfare of one being determined by the welfare of all. The Hindu scheme of life is not competitive but co-operative. It is by the ceaseless co-operative activity of both inanimate Nature and living beings that the wheel of creation is kept moving. "From food all creatures are born; from rain food is produced; from sacrifice comes rain; sacrifice is born of action. Know that action arises from the Vedas, and the Vedas from the Imperishable."[12] He who does not recognize this all-pervading co-operative spirit lives in vain.[13]

The Hindu scriptures speak of four kinds of spiritual discipline, called *yajña* (sacrifice). The sacrifice for the propitiation of the ancient seers, who are the creators of the spiritual culture, consists in daily recitation of the scriptures and the imparting of their instruction to pupils. By means of this sacrifice, the culture of the race is preserved and developed. Next comes the sacrifice for the propitiation of the Manes, who wield power over men and are interested in their welfare. They are propitiated by the regular offering of food and drink. There is also the sacrifice for one's fellow human beings, who, when in distress, should be helped by the gift of food, drink, and clothing. "He who cooks only for himself verily eats sin."[14] Another part of this sacrifice consists in digging wells, building roads, and planting fruit trees for the benefit of one's fellow men.

An embodied person receives various favors from the gods, the seers, and the Manes. They are called his debts (*ṛṇas*), which must be paid off before he

[8] *Ibid.,* II. 46; VI. 44.
[9] *Kaṭha Upaniṣad* I. i. 10–11.
[10] *Ibid.,* I. ii. 3.
[11] R. Shamasastry, trans., *Kauṭilya's Arthaśāstra* (Mysore: Wesleyan Mission Press, 1909), p. 307.
[12] *Bhagavad Gītā* III. 14–15.
[13] *Ibid.,* III. 16.
[14] *Ibid.,* III. 13.

is qualified for liberation. The debt to the gods is to be paid through offering oblations in the sacrificial fire, to the seers through scriptural study, and to the Manes through the procreation of children.[15]

SOCIAL VALUES IN THE VEDAS

The Vedic seers were exhilarated by the beauty and sublimity of Nature and composed moving songs in praise of the earth, the sun, fire, the dawn, and the wind.[16] They reflected deeply on the moral principles behind the universe and sang hymns in honor of the cosmic order, ethical laws, and social virtues.[17] Vedic philosophers never denied the physical world and the pleasures it offers. "This [the physical universe] is real."[18] "If a man wishes to live a hundred years, he should live performing action."[19]

The following quotations will show how keenly interested the Hindus in Vedic times were in marriage, procreation, morality, and other worldly concerns.

About marriage: "I take your hand in mine for a happy future, that you may reach old age with me as your husband."[20] "Be not parted; dwell here; reach the full term of human life. With sons and grandsons, sport and play, rejoice in your abode."[21] "I am this man, that woman are you; I am the psalm, you are the verse; I am the heavens, you are the earth. So will we dwell together here, parents of children yet to come."[22]

About procreation: "This woman has come like a fertile cornfield. There sow, O man, the seed of future harvest. She from her teeming side shall bear you children and feed them from the fountain of her bosom."[23]

About liberality: "They seek the fleet steed for the bounteous giver; the maid adorns herself and waits to meet him. His home is adorned and made splendid like a god-made lake with lotus blossoms."[24] "Let the rich satisfy the poor, and keep in view the long pathway. Riches come now to one, now to another, and like the wheels of cars are ever turning."[25]

About hospitality: "Now that man who eats before the guests eats up the sacrifice and the merit of the house. He devours the milk and the sap and the vigor and prosperity and the progeny and the cattle and the fame and reputation, the glory and understanding of the house. . . . When the guests have eaten he should eat. This is the rule for the success of sacrifice and the preservation of its continuity."[26]

About concord in council: "Walk together, speak together, let your minds

[15] *Manu Saṁhitā* VI. 35.
[16] Sarvepalli Radhakrishnan and Charles A. Moore, eds., *A Source Book in Indian Philosophy* (Princeton: Princeton University Press, 1957), pp. 5 ff.
[17] *Ibid.*, pp. 25 ff.
[18] *Muṇḍaka Upaniṣad* I. ii. 1.
[19] *Īśa Upaniṣad* II.
[20] *Ṛg Veda* X. lxxxv. 36.
[21] *Ibid.*, X. lxxxv. 42.
[22] *Atharva Veda* XIV. ii. 71.
[23] *Ibid.*, XIV. ii. 14.
[24] *Ṛg Veda* X. cvii. 10.
[25] *Ibid.*, X. cxvii. 5.
[26] *Atharva Veda* IX. vi. 31–38.

be all alike. May the purpose be common, common the assembly, common the mind; so be your thoughts united. . . . May your decision be unanimous, your minds being of one accord. May the thoughts of all be united so that there may be a happy agreement among us all."[27]

About longevity: "May we see a hundred years. May we live a hundred years. May we know a hundred years. May we progress a hundred years. May we prosper a hundred years. May we be a hundred years; may we assert our existence a hundred years; yea, even more than a hundred years."[28]

About health and vigor:

Power art Thou, give me power;
Might art Thou, give me might;
Strength art Thou, give me strength;
Life art Thou, give me life;
Eye art Thou, give me eyes;
Ear art Thou, give me hearing;
Shield art Thou, shield me well.[29]

"May I have voice in my mouth, breath in my nostrils, sight in my eyes, hearing in my ears, hair that hath not turned grey, teeth free from yellowness, and much strength in my arms. May I have power in my thighs, swiftness in my legs, steadfastness in my feet. May all my limbs be uninjured and my soul unimpaired."[30]

About the home: "I, full of strength, enlightened and happy, come home rejoicing in my spirit—home where joy and cheerfulness abide. May joy be ours, felicity and blessing."[31]

About being a householder: "Agni, may I become a good householder. Agni, mayest Thou become a good householder. O Agni, may our household matters be smoothly managed for a hundred years, not like a one-ox cart."[32]

About general prosperity: "O Lord, may there be born in the kingdom *brāhmins* distinguished for the knowledge of Brahman; heroic *kṣatriyas,* skilled marksmen, piercing with shafts mighty warriors; cows giving abundant milk, good at carrying weight; swift horses; and industrious women. May the clouds send rain according to our desire; may our fruit-trees ripen; may we secure and preserve property."[33]

About the welfare of the king: "Let him be the lord of endless treasures; let him as king be master of the people. Grant him great power and strength; let his enemies be deprived of strength and vigor."[34]

About battles and the attitude toward enemies, etc.: "May Indra aid us

[27] *Ṛg Veda* X. cxci. 2–4.
[28] *Atharva Veda* XIX. lxvii.
[29] *Ibid.,* II. xvii.
[30] *Ibid.,* XIX. lx.
[31] *Yajur Veda* III. 41–43.
[32] *Ibid.,* II. 27. (The phrase "one-ox cart" refers to a situation created by disagreement between husband and wife.)
[33] *Ibid.,* XXII. 22; see also *Ṛg Veda* I. xcvi. 8; II. xxi. 6; III. xvi. 5; IX. xcvii. 50.
[34] *Atharva Veda* IV. xxii. 3.

when our flags are out; may our arms be victorious. May our brave warriors come home with flying colors. O Lord, protect us in the din of battle."[35] "Confusing the minds of our enemies, seize their bodies; depart, O panic. Attack them, confound them. Let our foes abide in utter darkness."[36] "We do not hate the conquered enemy; may we enjoy peace and security."[37] Whoso with an ungodly mind tries to injure us, proud of his might among princes, let not his deadly blow reach us. May we humble the wrath of the proud miscreant."[38]

From these quotations it will be apparent that the Indo-Aryans of Vedic times lived a full and happy life and regarded the world as real. They communed with the gods and pursued the path of justice and truthfulness and discharged their social responsibilities. It was not a purely materialistic happiness that they sought, however; for them, worldly enjoyment was a means to a higher end, as will be presently shown. The sacrificial part of the Vedas is not devoid of philosophical speculation about ultimate reality. Mention is made of the non-dual Brahman.[39] The disciplines of continence,[40] self-control, and inner purification[41] are described, and knowledge and wisdom[42] extolled.

THE UPANIṢADS AND SOCIAL VALUES

The Upaniṣads form the concluding part of the Vedas and embody their essence; hence, they are called Vedānta. Here the philosophical inquiries of the Vedic seers reach their full depth. They raise the question: "Who am I?" and answer it with the statement: "That thou art."[43] When a man experiences his oneness with God and the universe, his philosophical thinking cannot go any farther. It should be stated here that the Vedas are made up of both the Mantra and the Brāhmaṇa sections, which apply to the two stages in man's evolution. The Mantra or sacrificial part is meant for those who still desire material happiness here and hereafter. The Upaniṣads, the philosophical part contained in the Brāhmaṇas, are for those who, weary of material happiness, seek the highest good or liberation.

The aim of the Upaniṣads is to establish the existence of Brahman, Absolute Reality; they have been interpreted in different ways by different schools of Indian philosophy. In the opinion of non-dualists like Gauḍapāda and Śaṁkara, Brahman is one and without a second; besides it, nothing else exists. It is to be realized by the method of negation. Here it may be noted that the followers of non-dualism in India are numerically fewer than those of the qualified non-dualistic and dualistic schools. These schools affirm the reality of living beings and the universe, as parts of Brahman or as independent of it, respectively. According to non-dualists, as long as a man regards the physical

[35] *Ṛg Veda* X. ciii. 11. [36] *Yajur Veda* XVII. 44.
[37] *Atharva Veda* XIX. xiv.
[38] *Ṛg Veda* II. xxiii. 12.
[39] *Ibid.*, I. clxiv. 46; VI. xlvii. 18; X. cxxxii. 3; *Atharva Veda* XIII. iv. 14–21; XIII. iv. 22–24.
[40] *Atharva Veda* XI. v. 1; XI. v. 10; XI. v. 17.
[41] *Ṛg Veda* I. lxxxix. 8; *Yajur Veda* XXXIV. iv. 6.
[42] *Ṛg Veda* I. clxiv. 37; *Atharva Veda* X. ii. 28–30; *Yajur Veda* XL. 6.
[43] *Chāndogya Upaniṣad* VI. vii. 7.

universe and the individual ego as real, he should regard himself as separate from or part of reality. Many non-dualists, at the beginning of their spiritual life, worship, pray, and perform their social duties like dualists.

The Upaniṣads do not deny the reality of the world. They allow it an empirical reality (*vyāvahārika sattva*). As long as a man is conscious of multiplicity, he must deal with it as real. He must accept social values and ethical laws. The householder must be hospitable to guests; otherwise, his "hopes and expectations, the reward of his intercourse with pious people, the merit of his kindly speech, the good results of his sacrifices and beneficial deeds, and his cattle and children are destroyed."[44] Unless he gratifies his father and propitiates the gods, he cannot attain the knowledge of Brahman.[45] The *Bṛhadāraṇyaka Upaniṣad* narrates the story of the Creator's exhorting the gods, men, and the demons (*asuras*) to cultivate, respectively, the virtues of self-control, charity, and compassion.[46] According to Śaṁkara, the "gods" represent here those men who are endowed with many noble and refined qualities but are lacking in self-control. Those men who are particularly greedy are here called "men." And the "demons" among men are those who are cruel and given to injuring others. Hence, the instruction imparted here applies to men alone.

In King Aśvapati's description of the state of his kingdom, in the *Chāndogya Upaniṣad,* are reflected the high standards of society in Upaniṣadic times: "In my kingdom there is no thief, no miser, no wine-bibber, no man without a sacrificial fire, no ignorant person, no adulterer, much less an adulteress."[47]

Again, that the importance of moral conduct is clearly recognized can be seen in the advice of a teacher to his students who have finished their education and are about to embrace the householder's life, as recorded in the *Taittirīya Upaniṣad:*

Speak the truth. Practice *dharma.* Do not neglect the study of the Vedas. Having brought to the teacher the gift desired by him, [enter the householder's life and see that] the line of progeny is not cut off. Do not swerve from the truth. Do not swerve from *dharma.* Do not neglect [personal] welfare [health and longevity]. . . . Do not neglect your duties to the gods and the Manes. Treat your mother as God. Treat your father as God. Treat your teacher as God. Whatever deeds are faultless, these are to be performed—not others. Whatever good works have been performed by us, these should be performed by you—not others. . . . Now, if there arises in your mind any doubt concerning any act, or any doubt concerning any conduct, you should conduct yourself in such matters as *brāhmins* would conduct themselves—*brāhmins* who are competent to judge, who [of their own accord] are devoted [to good deeds] and are not urged [to their performance] by others, and who are not too severe, but are lovers of *dharma.* . . . This is the rule. This is the teaching. This is the secret wisdom of the Vedas. This is the command. This you should observe. This alone should be observed.[48]

[44] *Kaṭha Upaniṣad* I. i. 8.
[45] *Ibid.,* I. i. 10–13.
[46] *Bṛhadāraṇyaka Upaniṣad* V. ii. 1–3.
[47] *Chāndogya Upaniṣad* V. xi. 5.
[48] *Taittirīya Upaniṣad* I. xi. 1–4.

The Indo-Aryans longed for sons endowed with noble qualities. The rituals of birth have been vividly described in the Upaniṣads.[49] A typical prayer for wealth, cattle, prosperity, and longevity is the following: "Bring me, without delay, fortune which will always provide me with clothes and cattle, food and drink.... May I become famous among men. May I become richer than the rich."[50] The desire for wealth, children, grandchildren, cattle, gold, long life, and happiness both here and hereafter is widely expressed in all the principal Upaniṣads. All the teachers of the major Upaniṣads were householders. Yājña-valkya renounced the world only after having entered into two marriages.

SOCIAL VALUES IN THE SECONDARY SCRIPTURES

We come, next, to the secondary scriptures of the Hindus, called the *Smṛtis,* among which may be listed the *Rāmāyaṇa,* the *Mahābhārata,* the various Purāṇas, the *Code of Manu,* the Tantra treatises, and the *Arthaśāstra* of Kauṭilya. They are based chiefly on the Vedic tradition. In contrast to the *Śruti,* or Vedas, the truths of which were discovered by the seers through their spiritual insight, the *Smṛtis* are ascribed to human authorship. They give a popular interpretation of the philosophic truths of the Upaniṣads and show how these may be applied in the life of the individual and of society. The *Smṛtis* change from time to time, according to the needs of the age, but they show the way to liberation. One interesting feature of Hinduism is that, though it is based upon certain immutable and universal philosophical truths, it recognizes that these must be adapted to peculiar social conditions of time and place. And this latter task falls to the *Smṛtis.*

The *Rāmāyaṇa,* India's earliest epic poem, describes the penetration of Indian culture into the south and the gradual assimilation of the non-Aryans by the Aryans. In its pages are expressed the Indian ideals of filial piety, the chastity of women, friendship, loyalty, kingly duties, and the courtesy to which inferiors are entitled from their superiors.

The *Mahābhārata* is a "miscellany of history and mythology, politics and law, philosophy and theology."[51] Both the *Rāmāyaṇa* and the *Mahābhārata* give the picture of a happy and prosperous society. In the *Mahābhārata,* one observes the gradual assimilation of different backward tribes into the Aryan family. The *Bhagavad Gītā,* which is part of this great work, is designated as a Mokṣaśāstra, a treatise showing the way to liberation. Arjuna, the hero of this poem, is faced with a moral dilemma. The stability and the ethical values of society are threatened, and can be preserved only by a war. Arjuna seeks an escape through the easy life of retirement from the world, but Kṛṣṇa characterizes his attitude as "lowness of spirit, unbecoming an Aryan, dishonorable, unmanly, and an obstacle to the attaining of heaven."[52] Since all attempts for

[49] *Bṛhadāraṇyaka Upaniṣad* VI. iv. 1 ff.
[50] *Taittirīya Upaniṣad* I. iv. 2–3.
[51] Sarvepalli Radhakrishnan and Charles A. Moore, *op. cit.,* p. 99.
[52] *Bhagavad Gītā* II. 2–3.

a just and peaceful settlement with the wicked enemies have failed, he urges Arjuna to fight. According to the *Bhagavad Gītā,* there is no conflict between spiritual enlightenment and the performance of social duties in a spirit of non-attachment. "Verily, by action alone men like Janaka attained perfection. Further, you should perform action with a view to guiding people along the right path."[53] An enlightened man, no doubt, is above duty. There is nothing in the three worlds he has not gained and nothing that he has to gain. Yet, he works, for, if he does not engage, unwearied, in action, men in every way will imitate his example. If he ceases to work, the world will perish.[54] Arjuna heeds Kṛṣṇa's advice, plunges into the war, witnesses, without being distracted, the death of his near and dear ones, and on the battlefield itself obtains a rare exalted spiritual experience.[55]

For many centuries the *Bhagavad Gītā* has inspired the lives of countless Hindus, whether monks or householders, recluses or social workers. In our own times, Mahatma Gandhi drew inspiration for his unceasing labors from this book. The method of non-violence and non-resistance to evil prescribed by Gandhi to win India's political freedom is not in accordance with the teachings of the Hindu scriptures such as the *Rāmāyaṇa,* the *Mahābhārata,* the *Bhagavad Gītā,* the *Candi,* and the *Code of Manu.* In Hindu society, the *kṣatriyas,* or the military people, occupy the second position. Śaṁkara says in his commentary on the *Bhagavad Gītā,*[56] that the lack of co-operation between the *brāhmins* and the *kṣatriyas* destroys the *yoga,* or the spiritual culture. According to the last verse of the *Bhagavad Gītā,* one sees good fortune, triumph, welfare, and firm morality where "Kṛṣṇa, the lord of *yoga,* and Arjuna, the wielder of the bow," co-operate with each other.[57] Righteous war, according to Indian thinkers, is justified when all reasonable efforts for peaceful settlement fail. Gandhi's advocacy of non-violence was his personal religious creed, not accepted by many even among his intimate followers. The latter approved of non-violence as an expediency dictated by the existing political condition of the country.

Another important part of the *Mahābhārata* is the section on Peace (Śanti-parva), which contains the instruction given on the battlefield by Bhīṣma, an elder statesman and military general, to the princes who participated in the war.[58] The teachings cover the duties of householders, kings, and monks, and also the rules of conduct to be observed as expediencies in times of crisis. Among the general ethical laws are mentioned truthfulness, justice, compassion, amiability, patience, and procreation of offspring with one's wife. Bhīṣma does not give any categorical definition of good and evil, righteousness and unrighteousness, the concepts of which vary according to time and place. A general principle seems to emphasize harmlessness to all creatures as good or virtuous, and injury to them as evil. But one meets with difficulty in the prac-

[53] *Ibid.,* III. 20.
[54] *Ibid.,* III. 21–24.
[55] *Ibid.,* XI.
[56] *Ibid.,* IV. 2.
[57] *Ibid.,* XVIII. 78.
[58] All the information regarding the *Mahābhārata,* the *Rāmāyaṇa,* the *Code of Manu,* and Kauṭilya's *Arthaśāstra* is based on *A Source Book in Indian Philosophy.* The quotations from these works are also taken from that book.

tical applications of this principle. Forgiveness is not extolled as the highest virtue under all circumstances. One need not always speak the truth. Under certain circumstances, "it is better to speak what is beneficial than what is true."[59] Though upholding the law of *karma,* Bhīṣma also stresses the virtue of self-effort. Destiny and exertion equally operate; yet exertion is superior, for "destiny is ascertained from what is begun with exertion."[60] The law of *karma* is often misinterpreted as fatalism. In reality, it is nothing but the law of cause and effect. "As one sows, so one reaps." The effect need not be confined to the present life alone; it is seen in a future life, too. The law of *karma,* according to Indian thinkers, supplies a man with a blueprint of life, as it were, at the time of his birth. His habits and attitudes are explained according to impressions left by his actions done in the previous life. What does he know of life who knows only one life? The law of *karma* teaches a man to regard his present misfortune as the result of his own past, and, at the same time, exhorts him to act now in such a way that he will avoid suffering in the future. Destiny (*adṛṣṭa*) is nothing but the accumulated impressions of a man's action in the past life, of which he is not aware in the present life. Bhīṣma condemns the renunciation of ascetics if it is not accompanied by knowledge: "Emancipation does not consist in poverty, nor is bondage to be found in affluence. One attains emancipation through knowledge alone, whether one is indigent or affluent."[61] He warns seekers of the highest good against worldly pleasures: "The desire for wealth can never be fraught with happiness. When acquired, great is the anxiety that the acquirer feels. If lost after acquisition, that is felt as death. Lastly, respecting acquisition itself there is uncertainty."[62]

The *Code of Manu* deals with the conduct of the individual as a member of society, the individual's ultimate goal being the attainment of the highest good. According to Manu, the purpose of the caste system is to encourage social harmony for the common good. A special feature of this work is the respect shown to women, though their dependence upon men is not overlooked.

Kauṭilya, who lived about three hundred years before Christ, is the author of the famous *Arthaśāstra,* a treatise on politics and diplomacy. Among other topics dealt with in this work are the duties of government superintendents, the conduct of courtiers, war and invasion, espionage, the plan of a treaty, the life of a saintly king, law, marriage, the source of authority of sovereign States, and the nature of political alliances.

The *Mahānirvāṇa Tantra,* a scripture esteemed especially by the followers of Tāntrika mysticism, discusses at length the duties of the householder. Some of its ideas are given below:

A householder should be devoted to God; yet he must work constantly, performing all his duties; he must give up the fruits of action to God. The great duty of a householder is to earn a living, but he must take care that he does not do this by telling lies or by cheating or by robbing others; and he must

[59] *Mahābhārata* (Śāntiparva) 329. 13.
[60] *Ibid.,* (Śāntiparva) 58. 14–15.
[61] *Ibid.,* (Śāntiparva) 321. 46–52.
[62] *Ibid.,* (Śāntiparva) 177. 26–28.

remember that his life is for the service of God and the poor.... Knowing that his mother and father are the visible representatives of God, the householder always and by all possible means must please them.... Equally important is his duty to his wife, and he must always maintain her as if she were his own mother. Even when he is in the greatest difficulties and troubles, he must not renounce his wife if she is chaste and devoted to him.... To his enemies the householder must be a hero. When threatened by them he must resist. He must not sit down in the corner and weep, and talk nonsense and non-resistance. If he does not show himself a hero to his enemies, he has not done his duty. And to his friends and relatives he must be as gentle as a lamb.... It is the duty of the householder not to pay reverence to the wicked, because, if he reverences them, he patronizes the wicked. And it will be a great mistake if he disregards those who are worthy of respect—the good people.... A householder must struggle hard to acquire two things: first, knowledge, and second, wealth. This is his duty, and if he does not do his duty he is nobody. A householder who does not struggle to acquire wealth is immoral. If he is lazy and content to lead an idle life, he is immoral, because upon him depend hundreds of other people. If he gets riches, hundreds of others will be supported. The householder is the center of life and society. It is a kind of worship for him to acquire and spend wealth nobly. The householder who struggles to become rich by good means and for good purposes is practically doing the same thing for the attainment of salvation as the anchorite does in his cell when he prays; for in them we see only different aspects of the same virtue of self-surrender and self-sacrifice prompted by the feeling of devotion to God and to human beings, who are His manifestations.

If the householder dies in battle, fighting for his country and religion, he comes to the same goal that the yogi attains through meditation.[63]

THE DARK AGE IN INDIA

A great change came over India when she lost her political freedom in the eleventh century. Muslim power was established in Delhi and gradually spread throughout the country. The new rulers brought with them a different outlook on life which profoundly disturbed the old concepts. During the seven hundred years of Muslim domination, Hindu society lost its creativeness and became conservative. Instead of producing original ideas, scholars preoccupied themselves with giving subtle interpretations to the ancient texts. The caste system became stratified, and social customs grew rigid. All this, however, brought about one good result: an almost impenetrable wall was thus erected around Hindu society, which foreign influence could not pierce. At the same time, it prevented fresh ideas from coming from the outside. But, even during the period of alien rule, Hinduism produced great religious leaders such as Rāmānuja, Kabir, the Mārhāttā saints, and Chaitanya of Bengal, who tried to improve the condition of the masses, especially the untouchables. What one sees in India today does not reflect the dynamic Indian culture of a thousand

[63] Swami Vivekananda, *Karma-Yoga* (New York: Ramakrishna-Vivekananda Center, 1955), pp. 20 ff.

years ago, but the continuation of many of the rigid social and religious practices prevalent during the long period of foreign domination.

During the British rule of one hundred and ninety years, India remained culturally sterile. But the introduction of English education brought educated Indians into contact with the rational, aggressive, and dynamic West. Through the notable efforts of Western Orientalists and British historians and archaeologists, the Indians again learned to value their past cultural achievements, though it is a fact that many of those who received English education became thoroughly Westernized in outlook. Christian missionaries also aroused the dormant social consciousness of the Indians. Thus there took place a new cultural revival with significant political and social implications.

SOCIAL VALUES IN MODERN INDIA

The Brāhmo Samāj, established in 1828, was founded by Rājā Rāmmohan Roy (1744–1833). A religious liberal, he drew ideas from Christianity, Buddhism, and Islam; but the main source of his inspiration remained the Vedas. The ethics of Christianity moved him deeply. The Brāhmo movement declared the supremacy of reason, advocated the ideals of the French Revolution, abolished the caste system among its members, sanctioned the remarriage of Hindu widows, stood for the emancipation of women, and agitated for the abolition of early marriages. Though a religious movement, the Brāhmo Samāj, under the influence of Western culture, advocated mainly social reform. Its influence was confined, however, to a comparatively small number of intellectuals.

The Ārya Samāj, founded by Swami Dayānanda (1824–1883), stood for Hindu orthodoxy and asserted the supremacy of the Vedas, especially the Vedic sacrifices. Its influence spread among the common people in northern India. Like the Brāhmo Samāj, it advocated social reform. Both these movements were natural reactions against the stagnation which had all but paralyzed India during its thousand years of foreign rule.

THE RAMAKRISHNA MISSION

The non-dualistic traditions of the Upaniṣads were revived in modern times by Ramakrishna and Vivekananda. The Ramakrishna Mission, founded in 1897 by Swami Vivekananda (1863–1902), has blended India's traditional spiritual disciplines with philanthropic activities, which are carried out through institutions organized on more or less Western lines. Vivekananda stated in the rules and regulations of the Ramakrishna Mission that his ideal was to turn the Belur Math, the headquarters of the organization, into a finished university where the traditional spiritual culture of India and the physical sciences of the modern West would be studied side by side.

Ramakrishna (1836–1886), unlike the leaders of the Brāhmo Samāj and Ārya Samāj, who were essentially social reformers, was a man of God. Diagnosing the cause of the human malady as spiritual, he exhorted people to realize God

—dwelling in all living beings as their inner spirit—as the only reality. According to his teaching, when a man knows God he rids himself of ego, which is the cause of greed, lust, anger, and the other vices. He did not explain away the world as unreal, as do some extreme non-dualists, but described it as a manifestation of God's creative power called *māyā*. He did not regard *māyā* as a sinister force, but gave it a spiritual status. For him, human relationships find true meaning only through the knowledge of men's relationship with the Godhead. Ramakrishna realized the divinity of the soul and thus pointed out where the true spiritual basis of individual freedom and democracy lies. By his experience of the oneness of existence and the solidarity of mankind, he showed the real foundation of ethics. Further, he realized that religions, in their essence, are not antagonistic but complementary. His spiritual experiences have great social implications. He dedicated his body, mind, and soul to the service of others.

Ramakrishna asked his foremost disciple, Swami Vivekananda, to see God, not merely with eyes closed, but with eyes open as well. The most effective way of worshipping God, he taught him, is to minister to the needs of people by bringing education to the illiterate, food to the hungry, and medicine to the sick. Needy people, however, should be served not as objects of pity but with respect as living images of God. Vivekananda said later: "You may invent an image through which to worship God, but a living image already exists—the living man. You may build a temple in which to worship God, and that may be good, but a better one, a much higher one, already exists—the human body."[64]

A social worker, according to Vivekananda, must fulfill three conditions: he must intensely feel the suffering of others, he must know the remedy for it, and he must be totally unselfish. Vivekananda felt deeply for the unfortunate masses of India: "The great national sin of India is the neglect of the masses, and that is one of the causes of our downfall. No amount of politics will be of any avail until the masses in India are once more well educated and well cared for. They pay for our education, they build our temples, but in return they get our kicks. They are practically our slaves. If we want to regenerate India, we must work for them." "Him I call a *mahātmā* [noble soul] whose heart bleeds for the poor; otherwise he is a *durātmā* [wicked soul]."[65] He strongly emphasized that "the national ideals of India are renunciation and service. Intensify her in those channels and the rest will take care of itself."[66] The monks of the Ramakrishna Mission take the twin vows of self-realization and service to humanity. To them, work is worship. Their lives alternate between meditation and social service. They are taught to feel the presence of the same God in the market place as in the cloister, in the laboratory as in the temple.

It is often said that Indian thinkers, on account of their preoccupation with

[64] Swami Vivekananda, *The Complete Works*, Vol. II (Mayavati: Mayavati Memorial edition, 1919), p. 311.

[65] *Ibid.*, Vol. V, p. 45.

[66] *Ibid.*, Vol. V, p. 157.

transcendental reality, neglect the visible universe. Even in ancient times, Indians made considerable progress in the positive sciences. They cultivated, among other things, knowledge of astronomy, chemistry, metallurgy, mathematics (including algebra), medicine and surgery, and logic and grammar.[67]

In the *Chāndogya Upaniṣad,* Nārada describes to his teacher, Sanatkumāra, the variety of subjects he has studied before seeking the knowledge of the self. He lists them as follows:

The Rig-Veda, the Yajur-Veda, the Sāma-Veda, the Atharva-Veda as the fourth [Veda], the epics and ancient lore as the fifth, grammar, the rules of sacrifice by which the Manes are gratified, the science of numbers, the science of portents, the science of time, logic, ethics, etymology, the science of pronunciation, ceremonials and prosody, the science of elemental spirits, the science of weapons, astronomy, the science of serpents, and the fine arts."[68]

Then Nārada adds: "But, venerable sir, with all this I know words only; I do not know the self. I have heard from men like you that he who knows the self overcomes sorrow. I am one afflicted with sorrow. Do you, venerable sir, help me to cross over to the other side of sorrow."[69] Evidently, even in Vedic times Indian thinkers cultivated the knowledge of both the physical sciences and the science of the soul.

JUSTIFICATION OF SOCIAL VALUES

In the foregoing pages I have tried to show that Indian thinkers have not been really otherworldly in their outlook, but, on the contrary, have taken a keen interest in the nature of the universe according to the information available in their times and also in moral and social values. In what follows I shall attempt to show that India's idealism is not in conflict with its realism.

Indian philosophers have investigated the nature of reality from two standpoints: the relative (*vyāvahārika*) and the Absolute (*paramārthika*). The relative reality of the physical world is based upon the undeniable evidence of the seers. The diversity of ego and non-ego is its very structure. Śaṁkara[70] refuted the doctrines of Buddhist nihilism and subjective idealism.[71] Again, undeniable experience of the seers reveals the fact that there is a reality which is absolute existence, knowledge, and bliss (*Saccidānanda*).[72] For Śaṁkara, this reality, called Brahman, is non-dual, eternal, immutable, relationless, and the unattached source of the creation, preservation, and dissolution of the universe.

That both the Absolute and the relative can be real, though under different conditions, has been illustrated by the examples of the desert and the mirage, waking and dreaming, the rope and the illusory snake superimposed upon it

[67] S. Radhakrishnan, *Indian Philosophy,* Vol. I (London: George Allen & Unwin, Ltd., 1923), pp. 29–30.

[68] *Chāndogya Upaniṣad* VII. i. 2; see also *Muṇḍaka Upaniṣad* I. i. 5.

[69] *Chāndogya Upaniṣad* VII. i. 3.

[70] Śaṁkarācārya is often called Śaṁkara.

[71] Commentary on *Bṛhadāraṇyaka Upaniṣad* IV. iii. 7.

[72] *Taittirīya Upaniṣad* II. i. 1; II. v. 1; III. vi. 1.

through ignorance. But they are not experienced as real from the same point of view. When you see the desert, you do not see the mirage. When you see the non-dual Brahman, you do not see the phenomenal universe. The universe is called *māyā*. *Māyā* is the power inherent in Brahman which accounts for the appearance of the universe. Owing to it, the appearance is taken for reality. But this apparent reality does not in any way affect the true nature of Brahman: the mirage does not moisten a grain of sand in the desert. At first, *māyā* hides the nature of reality; next it projects multiplicity. *Māyā* is neither real nor unreal. It is not unreal, because, under certain conditions, the effect, namely, multiplicity, is perceived to exist. It is not real, because multiplicity disappears when one achieves the knowledge of Brahman. According to Śaṁkara, the ultimate goal of the Upaniṣads is to prove that whatever exists is the non-dual Brahman. The Upaniṣads have condemned duality, but never non-duality. "By mind alone is Brahman to be realized; then one does not see in it any multiplicity whatsoever. He goes from death to death who sees multiplicity in it. This, verily, is that."[73] "Duality does not exist for one who knows reality." Brahman is "one without a second." Brahman, as absolute reality, always exists, even when the world is taken to be real, just as the desert alone really exists even when one sees the mirage. The reality of the sense-perceived universe is empirical. Social values cannot be derived by those who regard themselves as part of the relative world.

To the enlightened all that exists is Brahman.[74] Non-dualism is not illusionism (*māyāvāda*); it is an experience which sees the sole reality of Brahman (*Brahmāstitvavāda*). But the dualist person regards the universe of multiplicity as real; so, also, are the pairs of opposites such as ego and non-ego, pleasure and pain, good and evil, virtue and vice. Therefore, one cannot deny his relationships with others or his social obligations. He must pray, worship, work, and reap the fruit of action. For him the Personal God is real as the controller of his destiny and the universe. But, when the universe disappears in Brahman, the Personal God, heaven, and earth merge in it, too.

The Indian thinkers admit the inherent perfection of the soul, though this perfection may be distorted (according to the dualists) or hidden (according to the non-dualists) by the power of *māyā*. They also believe that every soul will eventually attain perfection. But, as it cannot be attained in one life, they postulate the doctrine of rebirth—which is governed by the law of *karma*. Birth, growth, decay, and death apply to the body and not to the soul.

The very divine nature of the soul, hidden or distorted though it may be, makes it seek absolute existence, knowledge, and bliss. Man wants to be, to know, and to enjoy bliss. He seeks the fulfillment of these three basic desires on earth and in heaven. To that end, he performs selfless action, propitiates God, or pursues knowledge. He assumes numberless bodies, but nowhere does he discover absolute existence, knowledge, and bliss. The knowledge that is acquired through the senses and the mind has a beginning and an end. There

[73] *Kaṭha Upaniṣad* II. i. 11.

[74] *Chāndogya Upaniṣad* III. xiv. 1.

is no abiding happiness in the finite. In creation nothing exists forever. The cause produces the effect, and in time the latter disappears. Absolute existence cannot be realized in the phenomenal world, in which one experiences constant birth and death. "Frail indeed are those rafts of sacrifices"[75] to take one across the ocean of interminable births and deaths, called *saṁsāra*. "Having enjoyed the vast heavenly world, they come back to the world of mortals when their merit is exhausted. Thus abiding by the injunctions of the three Vedas and desiring desires, they are subject to death and rebirth."[76]

> Let a *brāhmin,* after having examined all these worlds, acquire freedom from desires. Nothing that is eternal can be produced by that which is non-eternal. In order that he may understand what is eternal, let him, fuel in hand, approach a teacher who is well versed in the Vedas and always devoted to Brahman. To that pupil who has duly approached him, whose mind is completely serene, and whose senses are controlled, the wise teacher should rightly impart the knowledge of Brahman, through which one knows the immutable and all-pervading spirit.[77]

PRACTICE OF YOGA

Now the pupil begins in earnest the practice of spiritual discipline, which is known by the general name of *yoga*. For the active man, the discipline of action is prescribed.[78] Through selfless action the pupil acquires serenity of mind, remaining unruffled in pain and pleasure, success and failure. He discharges his social obligations, regarding himself as God's instrument, or always remaining conscious that the sense-organs perform the action, the spirit remaining a serene witness. He sees "action in non-action, and non-action in action,"[79] but never gives up action. "May you never be attached to non-action."[80]

The emotional man is asked to follow the discipline of the love of God, a love that knows no fear, a love that seeks no reward, a love that is cultivated for love's sake.[81] A dualist generally practices this discipline. He regards himself as an instrument in God's hands, and wholeheartedly serves both God and living beings, whom he regards as God's creatures. Chaitanya, a great dualist saint of the sixteenth century, exhorted his followers to cultivate taste for God's name, to show compassion to living beings, and to honor holy men for their realization of God. "By that devotion alone he knows Me, knows what, in truth, I am and who I am. Then having known Me in truth, he forthwith enters into Me."[82]

The discipline of concentration is recommended for the introspective.[83] Its goal is the isolation of the soul from the body through *samādhi,* or deep medi-

[75] *Muṇḍaka Upaniṣad* I. ii. 7.
[76] *Bhagavad Gītā* IX. 21.
[77] *Muṇḍaka Upaniṣad* I. ii. 12–13.
[78] Swami Nikhilananda, *Hinduism: Its Meaning for the Liberation of the Spirit* (New York: Harper & Brothers, 1958), pp. 94 ff.
[79] *Bhagavad Gītā* IV. 18.
[80] *Ibid.*, II. 47.
[81] Swami Nikhilananda, *op. cit.*, pp. 105 ff.
[82] *Bhagavad Gītā* XVIII. 55.
[83] Swami Nikhilananda, *op. cit.*, pp. 130 ff.

tation. Though a follower of this path confines himself to a minimum of social action, yet he is told that one of the means of controlling the restless mind is to show friendship toward the happy, compassion toward the unhappy, and gladness toward the good.[84]

The discipline of knowledge is meant for philosophic minds. Its followers—the non-dualistic monks—pursue the negative path of renunciation and give up exclusive or restricted attachment to all physical objects. These monks control all desires which spring from finite existence. "When all the desires that dwell in the heart are got rid of, then does the mortal [man] become immortal and attain Brahman in this body."[85] The Upaniṣads are emphatic that immortality cannot be attained without the total renunciation of attachment to the world, whose three chief pillars are offspring, wealth, and heaven. "The knowers of Brahman of olden times, it is said, did not wish for offspring [because they thought]: 'What shall we do with offspring—we who have attained this self, this world?' They gave up, it is said, their desire for sons, for wealth, and for the worlds, and led the life of [religious] mendicants."[86] "This self is dearer than a son, dearer than wealth, dearer than everything else [because] it is the innermost."[87] According to the *Muṇḍaka Upaniṣad,* renunciation must be accompanied by monastic vows.[88] Śaṁkara upholds this view; but, in the Purāṇas, mention is made of householders, such as the Emperor Janaka, a butcher, and a housewife, who attained to the knowledge of Brahman through the performance of their respective worldly duties. However, the practice of total non-attachment, both in action and in thought, is absolutely necessary prior to the direct knowledge of Brahman. Therefore, it is easier for monks to follow this discipline.

HINDU ETHICS[89]

Now I propose to discuss Hindu ethics, both in its personal and in its social aspects. According to Hindu philosophers, ethics is the steel-frame foundation of the spiritual life and the practice of *yoga.*

Ethical disciplines in Hinduism are derived from certain spiritual concepts. They are not justified on purely utilitarian or biological grounds. Indian thinkers have discussed ethics from both the social or objective and the personal or subjective standpoints, with emphasis on the latter, in consonance with the Hindu metaphysical view that the ultimate goal of life is liberation. The excellence of a culture, according to Indian thinkers, is to be judged, not by the material prosperity or creature-comforts it provides for the society or the individual, however important they may be, but by its upholding of the principle of plain living and high thinking. A man profits very little if he gains the whole world, but loses his soul, as the Bible says.

[84] Patañjali, *Yoga Sūtra* I. 33.
[85] *Bṛhadāraṇyaka Upaniṣad* IV. iv. 7.
[86] *Ibid.,* IV. iv. 22.
[87] *Ibid.,* I. iv. 8.
[88] *Muṇḍaka Upaniṣad* III. ii. 4.
[89] Swami Nikhilananda, *op. cit.,* pp. 68 ff; Nikhilananda, *The Upanishads,* Vol. II (New York: Harper & Brothers, 1952), pp. 1 ff.

Social ethics centers around the Hindu concept of *dharma*. Generally translated as "duty," "righteousness," or "religion," *dharma* means much more than what is connoted by any of these terms. The sanction of duty often comes from the outside. Many people take religion as a set of dogmas laid down in scriptures, through which a devotee can approach God, who is external to him. But, according to Indian philosophy, *dharma* is the law of inner growth, by which the embodied soul is supported in the present state of his evolution and also shown the way for his future development and ultimate liberation.

Dharma, formed by a man's past actions and thoughts, determines his attitude toward the outer world and governs his mental and physical reaction in a given situation. It constitutes his righteousness, his code of honor. Hindu thinkers recognize certain universal *dharmas,* such as truthfulness, non-injury to others, and compassion. There are also specific *dharmas,* relative to particular caste, stage in life, and circumstances. As already stated, nothing is absolutely good or evil in the ever-changing phenomenal world; evil may be defined as what is less good. One cannot stipulate what is absolutely good or evil for all men, or even for an individual, for all times or circumstances. The attempt to do so—and to judge all people by a single concept of *dharma* and to impose it upon all without paying attention to relative circumstances—has been a cause of much of the injustice and cruelty committed upon humanity. If one wants to give a comprehensive definition of *dharma,* one may say that what helps a man in establishing kinship with his fellow creatures is good, and its reverse is evil.

Social ethics, whose immediate purpose is the promotion of social welfare, has been enjoined upon householders who are conscious of their social responsibilities. Such people form the bulk of society. Through the observance of social ethics, an ideal society is created which affords individuals opportunities to realize their highest spiritual potentialities. The discharge of social duties in a large measure preserved Hindu society from utter collapse during the period of foreign domination. Their neglect, on the other hand, undermined its vitality.

The Hindu caste system is intimately connected with the social aspect of ethics. It has served various purposes. As long as its original meaning was followed, the caste system promoted harmony and co-operation between the divergent members of society. It eliminated friction and competition, and saved the weak from exploitation by the strong. It has helped Hindu society to absorb alien peoples according to their merits and aptitudes. Through it, men recognized renunciation, self-control, service, and sacrifice as cardinal virtues. The present state of the caste system of India is deplorable. Its true spirit has been practically forgotten; people are clinging merely to the outer forms.

The *brāhmins* are priests and teachers. They are men of knowledge and science, thought and learning, self-control and austerity, uprightness and forbearance.[90] The *kṣatriyas,* who are fighters, are endowed with the qualities of

[90] *Bhagavad Gītā* XVIII. 42.

heroism and high spirit, boldness and fortitude, firmness and dexterity, generosity and rulership.[91] According to Śaṁkara and the *Bhagavad Gītā,* through co-operation between the spiritual and the royal power, the spiritual culture is preserved and social welfare assured.[92] The *vaiśyas,* who are farmers and traders, are men of desires, possessions, and acquisitive enterprise.[93] The main duty of the *śūdras,* the laborers, is action in the form of service to the higher castes.[94] They are men of little intelligence, who cannot be educated beyond certain restricted limits, who are incapable of dealing with abstract ideas, and who are capable of only manual work. Men are not born equal, though all men should be regarded as equal before law and given equal opportunities to develop their latent powers. These four types exist in every organized society. It is Nature, and not the Vedas or Manu, that is responsible for divisions in society. The *Bhagavad Gītā* says that in the beginning the positions in the castes were determined by men's action and merit.[95] Each of the four castes has its own hygiene, its own domain of labor, its own sentiment of perfection, and its own special superiority. The rules regarding the castes sum up the social experience and sagacity of long centuries of Hindu thinkers. Regarding the caste system, Mahatma Gandhi said: "It is a law of spiritual economics and has nothing to do with superiority and inferiority."

The hierarchy in the caste system as originally formulated was determined by the degree of voluntary renunciation and poverty, self-control, and intellectual and spiritual attainment. The higher the position of a man in the caste system, the greater is his obligation to the members of the lower castes. *Noblesse oblige.* It is obligations that are the crux of the caste system, and not rights. Whatever right a person demands must be derived from the fulfillment of his obligations. Through the caste system India indicated the supremacy of spirituality and intellect over military power, wealth, and labor. In time, everything becomes corrupt. People of upper castes enjoyed power for a long time and became selfish and greedy. They demanded rights and privileges without fulfilling their obligations. Caste laws became rigid and stratified. Contact with the West, which prizes equality, democracy, freedom, and social justice, has revealed to thoughtful Indians many drawbacks in their caste system. Since India's attainment of freedom, laws have been enacted removing caste inequities. But there is no room for the caste system in a secular and industrialized society, which is controlled primarily by the power of machines, wealth, and labor. If India gives up the principles of the caste system and denies the supremacy of intellect and spirituality, she will surely lose her spiritual backbone. The leaders of society in free and democratic India must be endowed with the spiritual qualities of self-abnegation, understanding, justice, and compassion. These new *brāhmins* may be drawn from all sections of society.

[91] *Ibid.,* XVIII. 43.
[92] Śaṁkarācārya's commentary on *Bhagavad Gītā* IV. 1; *Bhagavad Gītā* XVIII. 78.
[93] *Bhagavad Gītā* XVIII. 44.
[94] *Ibid.,* XVIII. 44.
[95] *Ibid.,* IV. 13.

Untouchability is a blot upon Hindu society. It was originally introduced to protect the spiritual culture of the Indo-Aryans from contamination by contact with primitive people, who were uncouth and of low mental development. It also served the purpose of saving the aborigines from annihilation. The social or spiritual standard of the Aryans were not imposed upon them by force. On the other hand, efforts were made to assimilate these people gradually through education. But during the dark days of Hindu society the process of assimilation stopped, and great injury was done to these unfortunate people. Now free India is making atonement for her past sins. Laws have been passed removing discriminatory treatment toward the untouchables.

Apart from the caste laws, a man's *dharma* is formulated according to his stage in life. Hinduism speaks of four stages with their respective ideals, all of which are legitimate. During the student stage a man must study in order to acquire knowledge, lead an austere life, conserve energy, and protect himself from defilement of body and mind. During the second stage he marries. Marriage is obligatory for all except those who suffer from a dangerous ailment which may be transmitted to children, and also for those who at an early age forsake the world at the call of God. It may be mentioned here also that, in certain important religious sects, for instance, the one founded by Rāmānuja, a man is not entitled to the monastic life unless he has passed through the stage of a householder. Children endow marriage with social obligations; and family life provides the householder with a training ground for the practice of unselfishness. During the third stage he retires into a forest or a solitary place to contemplate the deepest problems of existence. During the fourth stage, when a householder renounces the world and becomes a *sannyāsin* (monk), a well-disciplined life attains its fullest development. For him, the call of the infinite becomes irresistible. He rises above narrow responsibilities of family or society, and regards himself as a citizen of the world. He becomes a living demonstration of the reality of God and the ultimate unreality of material existence. He acts as a teacher and monitor of mankind. According to Hindu injunction, a man should give up individuality for the sake of the family, the family for the sake of the country, the country for the sake of the world, and everything for the liberation of the self.[96] Through the discipline of the four stages, a man learns progressive non-attachment. Today, for all practical purposes, one sees in Hindu society only the two stages of the householders and the monks. Unfortunately, in modern times many monks do not lead the life expected of them. They renounce the world in order to escape the hard realities of life and to find means of sustenance from credulous people who respect the holy garb of the *sannyāsin*. Genuine monks can come only out of the householders who lead ideal lives. At any time they are few and far between. A healthy society, in the Indian tradition, should have at the top a few genuine monks, devoted to the life of renunciation and service, who are living examples of non-attachment and serenity.

[96] *Mahābhārata* (Ādiparva) 115. 38–39.

AFFIRMATIVE ATTITUDE TOWARD LIFE

The affirmative attitude of Hinduism toward life has also been emphasized by the four ideals or values which an intelligent and normal person should aspire to realize. First, *dharma,* or duty, which has already been discussed. This is the basis of society, where people must live together in harmony. Second, *artha,* or wealth, which is absolutely necessary in the present state of human evolution for preserving the physical body, promoting human welfare, and creating the leisure without which no culture can be built. Third, *kāma,* or the enjoyment of sense pleasures which cover a vast area, from the enjoyment of conjugal love to the appreciation of art, music, and literature. Life becomes drab and gray unless one cultivates aesthetic sensitivity. Both wealth and sense pleasures should be pursued according to *dharma;* otherwise, they will turn into greed and sensuality. The fourth ideal, equally forceful and legitimate, is the attainment of *mokṣa,* or spiritual freedom. How can a man enjoy peace, even though he performs his worldly duties, possesses wealth, and enjoys sense pleasures, if he is a slave of passion, anger, and greed?

In the *Kaṭha Upaniṣad,* when Naciketas is offered material pleasures to be enjoyed on earth or in heaven, he says: "These endure only till tomorrow. Furthermore, they exhaust the vigor of the sense-organs. Even the longest life is short indeed. Keep your horses, dances, and songs for yourself."[97] And in the *Bṛhadāraṇyaka Upaniṣad,* Yājñavalkya teaches Maitreyī that one can never expect to attain immortality through wealth.[98] Even when all the desires for individual happiness and social welfare are fulfilled, still he wants to know how to suppress inner restlessness. Suffering is due to man's estrangement from the universal life. The individual is like a bone dislocated from its socket or a wheel separated from its axle. The result is constant friction accompanied by pain. The fourth ideal shows a man the way to liberation. But the three other ideals are not to be neglected. Their rightful fulfillment prepares the way for the realization of the fourth. Now we come to the disciplines of personal ethics, which have a direct bearing upon liberation.

PERSONAL ETHICS

The chief disciplines of personal ethics are austerity, control of the body and mind, non-attachment, chastity, reverence, forbearance, and concentration. Their main purpose is the purification of the individual's mind, and has no direct bearing upon social welfare. These disciplines are more or less common to all the major religions.

A few words may be said here as to why the Hindu philosophers emphasize personal ethics more than social ethics. First, if the individuals who constitute society are righteous, the welfare of society will be easy to achieve. Unfortunately, India has often overlooked the fact that a good society is also necessary

[97] *Kaṭha Upaniṣad* I. i. 26.

[98] *Bṛhadāraṇyaka Upaniṣad* II. iv. 1–3.

to create good individuals. Second, the general moral tone in ancient Hindu society was high; everyone was expected to follow his own *dharma,* which asks him to help those who are in distress. The country was prosperous, and people were hospitable. Therefore, no special need was felt for organized charity. Third, the peculiar physical and cultural climate of India inclined Hindu minds more to an introspective than to an active life. Fourth, the Hindus regarded spiritual help as of more enduring value than physical help. A spiritual man can remain unruffled in pain and suffering, which are inevitable to a certain extent in our embodied existence. Finally, Indian thinkers have not accepted the modern idea of progress in the sense that evil and good are two completely different entities, of which one can be gradually eliminated and the other increased until in the end good alone will remain. The idea of progress applies to the individual and not to the world at large; it is the individual who attains liberation. The idea of world progress has been a rather recent development in the West, especially since the growth of science and technology. According to Hindu thinkers, "pain and pleasure constantly rotate like a wheel." The sum total of happiness and unhappiness remains constant. The cosmic process resembles the surface of the ocean, where every crest is followed by a trough. It may take many a century for the rise of the wave to reach the crest before it begins to fall. If a man takes a short-range view of existence and confines his view only to the rise, he may speak of some sort of progress, which idea also rests on faith and not on historical evidence. The Vedas speak of the *kalpa,* or world-duration. Each *kalpa* contains its golden age (*satya*), silver age (*tretā*), bronze age (*dvāpara*), and iron age (*kali*). The world process is sustained by the rotation of the *kalpas.* We live in a changing world, but it need not be a progressive world. Every age, in spite of its many drawbacks and superstitions, has shown sincere seekers the way to the highest goal. Indian philosophers, without encouraging the illusion of a perfect society to be created by human effort and intelligence, have urged people to do good to others as a part of their spiritual discipline. That is the essence of *karma-yoga* as taught in the *Bhagavad Gītā.* Though neither good nor evil of the relative world is the ultimate truth, yet we come nearer to truth by doing good than by doing evil or remaining indifferent to both. The world is a moral gymnasium where through constant exercise we go beyond evil and finally beyond good also. Doing good to others has an instrumental but not an ultimate value.

Social ethics should be encouraged in modern India. Times have changed. The old concept of *dharma* has lost its hold upon the people.

DUTY AND FREEDOM

An ethical person works from a sense of duty which generally implies compulsion or necessity. Duty often creates unpleasantness and friction. When stretched too far it can become a disease. Furthermore, if a man wishes to attain perfection, which is inherent in the soul, he should not always look outside. But ethical duties can be performed through love. This love does not mean sentimentality, but springs, for the dualist, from the consciousness that all living beings are children of God, and, for the non-dualist, from the perception of the oneness of existence. Love greases the wheel of duty and makes it run without friction. Thus duty paves the way to freedom.

A non-dualist can look upon ethical practices from both ascetic, or negative, and affirmative standpoints. The negative discipline consists in suppressing the craving of the ego or the I-consciousness, which separates a man from others. This separation is responsible for attachment to friends or aversion for enemies and indifference to the rest. A man yields to selfishness, which must be suppressed for the realization of a higher life. There lies the efficacy of ascetic disciplines. On the other hand, the affirmative ethical discipline of the non-dualist is based upon the recognition of Brahman as the self in all. He must always remain aware of this oneness and show his awareness by his action and thought. He must cultivate a feeling of kindliness for all. Broadly speaking, the ascetic discipline shrinks the ego, and the affirmative expands it. The final result is the same: the destruction of the finite ego that feels attachment or aversion, or remains indifferent.

The enlightened person goes beyond ethical thought. No more does he consciously practice ethical disciplines. But by no means can he perform an unethical act. Ethical virtues adorn him like jewels. However, when an enlightened person acts as a teacher he practices ethical disciplines to set an example for his pupils. According to Indian thinkers, ethics is not an end in itself, but a means to attain a higher state beyond the strife and struggle of the relative world.

THE ULTIMATE GOAL OF LIFE

What is the goal of life? It is the realization of freedom (*mokṣa*), also called perfection, enlightenment, or immortality. This is not a new acquisition, but the discovery of the true nature of the self, which was hidden by *māyā,* or cosmic ignorance. It is the highest state of understanding. The Vedic seers always sought this understanding. "May He awaken our understanding."[99] The enlightened man is free from doubt,[100] and always dwells in the self.[101] As he sees the Lord equally existent everywhere, he does not injure the self by the self and therefore attains the highest goal.[102] He gets rid of selfish desires.[103] It is not a case of escapism. He attains to reality, light, and immortality. The enlightened man enters into a new realm of consciousness; the chrysalis emerges as the butterfly. He is like the one who, having been blind, is now restored to eyesight; who, having been sick, is now made whole; who, having been asleep, is now awake. He has attained absolute existence, knowledge, and bliss (*Saccidānanda*), and has realized in its fullness a man's desire to exist, to know, and to be happy.

[99] *Ibid.,* VI. iii. 6.
[100] *Muṇḍaka Upaniṣad* II. ii. 8.
[101] *Bhagavad Gītā* XV. 5–6.
[102] *Ibid.,* XIII. 28.
[103] *Kaṭha Upaniṣad* II. iii. 14.

How does an enlightened man live and act?[104] It is difficult for one who has not attained enlightenment to understand. But certainly he does not lead a life of quietism or inactivity. He devotes himself to the welfare of all.[105] Saṁkara, the paragon of Indian non-dualists, was active every moment of his life—writing commentaries on the scriptures, establishing monasteries, and instructing people about the supreme wisdom. An enlightened man lives, works, and dies under the spell of the soul's immortality, non-duality, and divinity. After transcending his human limitations, he embraces again the whole of humanity. He returns to the world and sees it as the manifestation of Brahman. "With every state of mind he experiences *samādhi*."[106]

The enlightened man, as long as he dwells in the body, cherishes desires to promote human welfare. He exhorts the worldly-minded to perform their social duties. In cases of emergency, he himself undertakes those duties. Saṁkara, by his strong support of the caste system and the four stages of life (*varṇāśramadharma*) encourages social duties. In modern India many *sannyāsins* engage themselves in various kinds of humanitarian activities. Śaṁkara said somewhere that a man should first realize that he is Brahman and then regard all as the manifestation of the same Brahman.

Outwardly active or inactive, an enlightened person constantly seeks and works for the welfare humanity:

> May I be able to look upon all beings with the eye of a friend. May we look upon one another with the eye of a friend.[107]
>
> May the world be peaceful. May the wicked become gentle. May all creatures think of their mutual welfare. May their minds be engaged in what is auspicious. And may our hearts be immersed in selfless love of the Lord.[108]
>
> O Lord, I do not want any kingdom, nor heavenly pleasure, nor even escape from rebirth. But I do desire that the affliction of all beings tormented by the miseries of life may cease forever.
>
> May all be freed from danger. May all realize what is good. May all be animated by noble thoughts. May all rejoice everywhere.
>
> May all be happy. May all be free from disease. May all realize what is good. May none be subject to misery.
>
> O glorious Lord, urge even a miser to charity, and soften the heart of the niggard.[109]

In the short space of this paper I have tried to show that the religious and philosophical thought of India, from the earliest times, has harmonized realism with idealism. It is not otherworldly or anti-social in the usual sense of these words. Indian thinkers have come to grips with reality, the meaning of which changes at different levels of the evolution of the soul. They have reflected upon man's real problems of life from his first wandering into the realm of phenomena to his final liberation. Their teaching seems to be: first idealize the real, then realize the ideal.

[104] *Bhagavad Gītā* II. 54–72.
[105] *Ibid.*, XII. 3–4.
[106] *Ibid.*, II. 70.
[107] *Yajur Veda Saṁhitā* XXXVI. 18.
[108] *Bhāgavatam* V. xviii. 9.
[109] *Ṛg Veda* VI. liii. 3.

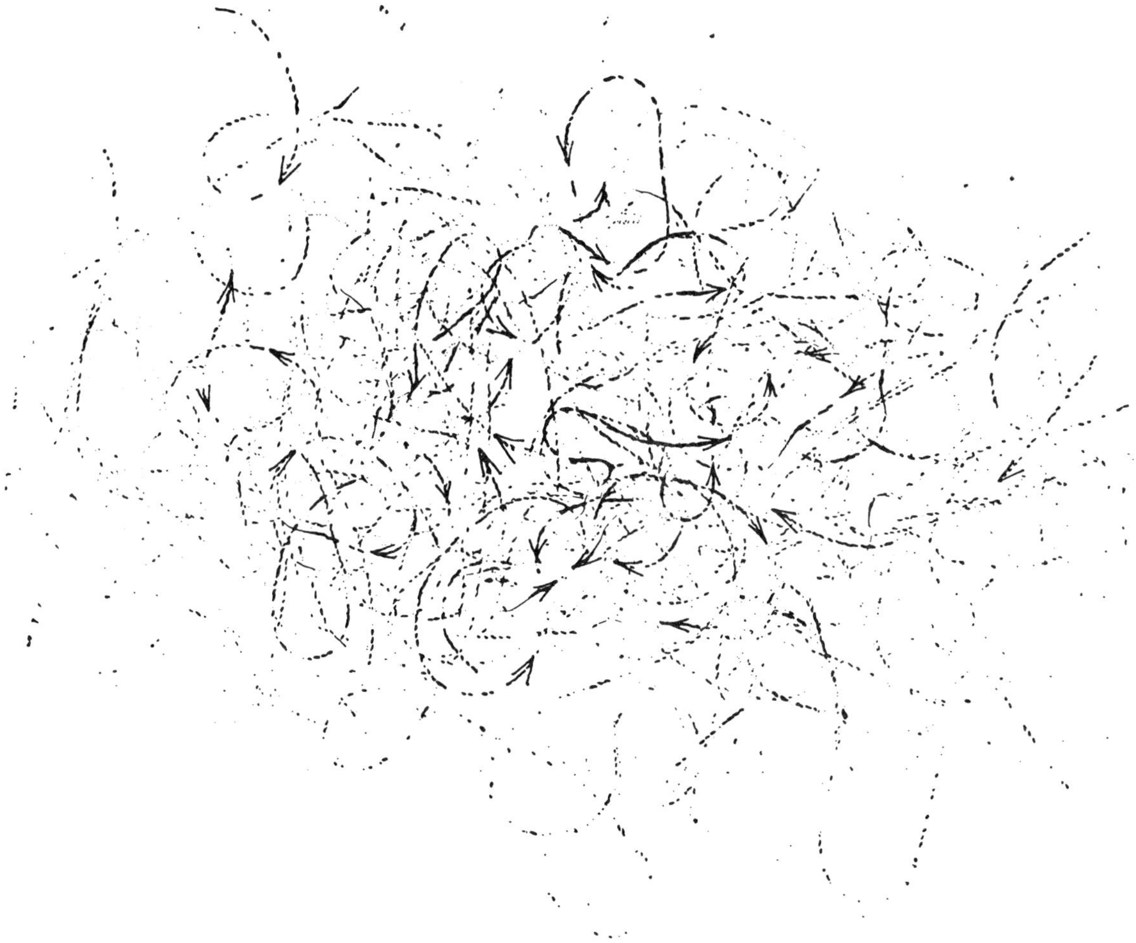

V. Legal, Political, and Economic Philosophy

F. S. C. NORTHROP

*Comparative Philosophy and Science in the Light of Comparative Law**

Every legal and ethical theory contains and requires for its validity epistemological and other non-normative assumptions. Since epistemological propositions are cognitively true or false, legal and ethical theory is, therefore, cognitively true or false also.[1]

The world's legal systems fall into three major species: (1) law of (biologically defined) status, (2) mediational dispute-settling, and (3) law of contract, where both status and contract are used in the sense of Sir Henry S. Maine's *Ancient Law*. Their corresponding epistemologies are: (1E) naive realism, (2E) radical empiricism, and (3E) radical empiricism in epistemic correlation with logical realism. Naive realism is to be distinguished from logical realism in the following way: Both affirm that one knows objects and events in public space and time, all the defining properties of which are independent of their relation to the perceiver. Naive realism, however, affirms that one knows such a public self and public world directly, i.e., naively with radical empirical immediacy; whereas logical realism, noting that all such properties and events are relative to physical frames of reference, to the perceiver, and even to different sense-organs of the same perceiver, affirms that public selves and a public world cannot be known by recourse merely to radically empirical concepts by intuition but require, in addition, logical constructs specified by a particular formally

* Due to a vote by the members of the conference limiting the length of the papers to be published in this proceedings volume, this is an abridged version of the paper submitted by the writer and discussed at the conference. A rewritten version of the latter paper which profits from the critique and suggestions of conference members has been published under the title "The Comparative Philosophy of Comparative Law," *Cornell Law Quarterly*, XLV, No. 4 (Summer, 1960), 617–658.

[1] For a lengthy elaboration of these statements, see the writer's *The Complexity of Legal and Ethical Experience* (Boston: Little, Brown and Co., 1959) and Part I of his *Philosophical Anthropology and Practical Politics* (New York: The Macmillan Co., 1960).

constructed set of postulates which, being imageless, this writer at the 1939 session of these conferences called "concepts by postulation which are concepts by intellection."[2] Because, moreover, the invariant, i.e., public selves, events, and objects designated by such concepts, being imageless, are not directly observable, the logical realist affirms that the empirical confirmation or disconfirmation of their existence must be indirect by way of epistemic correlations or epistemic rules of correspondence with directly observed and experimentally determined imageful data denoted by radically empirical concepts by intuition and their operational definitions.[3]

Most people in any culture, be it Oriental or Occidental, African, North European, or Polynesian, begin with law of biologically defined status[4] and its naive realistic epistemology. Their theories of natural science are also those of such an epistemology. Time, for example, means the time of directly sensed events, which is cyclical rather than linear. The most elemental immediately sensed cycle is that of darkness and light. This day-and-night cycle, by sensed counting, gives the larger cycle of the sensed colorfully differentiated seasons called "spring," "summer," "fall," and "winter." These sensed, annual cycles when counted give the human-sensed cycle of birth, youth, the maturity of life, and the decline of life and death, repeating itself over and over in each generation. This repetitive cyclical sequence is the causality of Hume's constant temporal succession which in Asian philosophy is sometimes called *"karma."* Similarly, the chemical elements are not imageless theoretical constructs epistemically correlated with sensed experimentally inspectable images, lines, qualities, and pointer readings, but are, instead, defined in terms of sensed qualities. Thus the atom or aggregate of atoms called fire is anything which is sensed as both hot and dry; the atom or aggregate of atoms called water is anything that is sensed as both cold and wet. It is to be noted that not merely Asian science, such as that of the Cārvākian materialists, but also Aristotelian science defined scientific objects in this naive realistic qualitative way.

Moreover, if their scientific theory of heredity is that the female functions merely as a receptacle in which the male places all the inherited traits, then, assuming there is no cultural diffusion, the codified law and politics are patriarchal; if, on the other hand, the female is thought of as contributing all the inherited traits, matriarchal law and politics occur.[5]

The distinguishing mark, however, of any law-of-status society, in the sense of Sir Henry Maine, is that religious, legal, moral, political, and familial rights and duties are defined by one's tribal ancestors, where tribe is related to sensed

[2] F. S. C. Northrop, "Complementary Emphases of Eastern Intuitive and Western Scientific Philosophy," in Charles A. Moore, ed., *Philosophy—East and West* (Princeton: Princeton University Press, 1944), chap. VIII; also F. S. C. Northrop, *The Logic of the Sciences and the Humanities* (New York: The Macmillan Co., 1947), chap. V.

[3] Northrop, *The Logic of the Sciences and the Humanities*, chap. VII.

[4] Sir Henry Maine defined a law-of-status society as one that "has for its units, not individuals, but groups of men united by the reality or the fiction of blood-relationship." Sir Henry S. Maine, *Ancient Law* (London: John Murray, 1908), p. 163. Status defined by "blood relationship" is clearly biologically defined status

[5] Cf. C. W. Westrup, *Introduction to Early Roman Law, Comparative Sociological Studies, The Patriarchal Joint Family*, Vol. III, *Patria Potestas: The Nascent Law* (London: Oxford University Press, 1939).

color of skin, one's genealogical table, one's sensed biological sex, and one's sensed temporal order of birth. The latter criterion of the personally, morally, and legally good expresses itself in that branch of law called inheritance as the rule of primogeniture. Hence, law of status when used in the sense of Sir Henry Maine and of this paper means biologically defined rather than economic or division-of-labor status, even though the latter type of status often arises over time as a consequence of the former.

In such naive realistic naturalistic and cultural societies, elaborate scientific and philosophical theories exist, but, as Professor Needham's lengthy recent studies of classical Chinese science clearly show, their concept of differentiated time is that of sensed cyclical time and their concept of mathematical number arises from the inductive counting of such sensed temporal cycles or the inductive counting of temporally simultaneous but spatially differentiated sensed qualities.

The ethics of a completely naive realistic law-of-biological-status society exhibits itself most markedly in the role which "nation" in the sense of "tribe" plays in such a society. As Dr. Suniti Kumar Chaterji has shown in his paper, "Krishna Dvaipāyana Vyāsa and Krishna Vāsudeva,"[6] the castes, for example, of Aryan Hindu Indian society represented originally people of different tribal origins. It is interesting in this connection to note that one of the Sanskrit words for "tribe" is also the word for "color." Hence, in law-of-status societies at the time of their origin, people fall into different nations and castes according to the color of skin of their tribal ancestors. In later generations, of course, when younger brothers break away from the joint family and its tribe to set up an independent familial and tribal line, there will be tribal nations without color differences. Fustel de Coulanges has shown in *The Ancient City*[7] that the early law of ancient Greece and Rome was of this patriarchal law-of-status type. In the more recent *Introduction to Early Roman Law*,[8] C. W. Westrup has reconfirmed Fustel de Coulanges' thesis in greater detail.

With time, scientists and philosophers arose in both classical Asia and the Graeco-Roman West who found that all sensed qualities are relative, not merely to the percipient, but to different sense-organs and different occasions of the same percipient. Like Berkeley in the modern West, they found that for primary as well as for secondary and tertiary qualities, *esse est percipi*. Then the self-contradictory character of a naive realistic epistemology becomes evident: Clearly, one cannot define realistic objects which purport to exist independently of their relation to the observer in terms of sensed objects, qualities, events, and relations, all of which are relative to the percipient.

Modern Western mathematical physics, for example, begins when Galilei rejects Aristotle's naive realistic epistemological theory of heat[9] for the directly

[6] Suniti Kumar Chaterji, "Krishna Dvaipāyana Vyāsa and Krishna Vāsudeva," *Journal of the Royal Asiatic Society of Bengal*, Letters, XVI, No. 1 (1950), 73–87.

[7] Numa Denis Fustel de Coulanges, *The Ancient City*, Anchor Books (New York: Doubleday & Company, Inc., 1956).

[8] Westrup, *op. cit.*, pp. 228–229.

[9] E. A. Burtt, *The Metaphysical Foundations of Modern Physical Science* (New York: Harcourt, Brace & Co., 1925), p. 75.

unobservable kinetic theory of heat and gases, according to which the atoms or molecules of the gas or solid are conceived as located in public, imageless, and hence unsensed, mathematically constructed invariant space and time. In other words, modern mathematical physics, like Democritean and Platonic Greek mathematical physics, rests on rejecting a naive realistic epistemology for that of logical realism in epistemic correlation with radical empiricism. Even the contemporary logical positivists, such as Carnap, who initially thought with Wittgenstein that scientific objects and invariant space-time could be defined in terms of sensed events, qualities, and objects or could be reduced by the Carnapian reduction-sentence technique to assertions about radically empirically known data are now in agreement with the mathematical physicist Einstein, Professor Margenau, and the writer upon this conclusion.[10]

When it is realized that a naive realistic epistemological theory is a self-contradictory theory and that a law-of-biological-status ethics requires naive realism for its validity, then the cognitive error of any law-of-status ethic becomes equally evident. Because universal affirmative propositions do not convert simply, it does not follow, as Professors Hook and Stace concluded, that modern laymen and philosophers who believe in a naive realistic epistemology must also believe in a law-of-status ethic. It is by no means certain, however, that, if any person believes in a naive realistic epistemology and does not believe in a law-of-status ethic, the latter conclusion does not result from the additional fact that he has been living for decades in a law-of-contract nation and in a law-of-contract Western civilization in which ethical and legal conceptions, which a naive realistic epistemology cannot justify or validate, have been influencing his moral intuitions and judgments.

In any event, when it becomes evident that a naive realistic epistemology is self-contradictory, two ways are possible. One can keep the naive, i.e., the radically empirical, factor in naive realism, and reject the realism. The result is the shift from law-of-status to mediational dispute-settling of the Confucian-Buddhist pre-Aryan and Gandhian non-dualistic Vedāntic Hindu ethic of the middle path; similar to the latter also is Professor Wesley Sturges' version of American legal realism.[11] Or one can retain the realism of naive realism, while rejecting its radically empirical naiveté, by finding a way to define realistic epistemological objects and their laws purely formally and axiomatically, making no use of either the undifferentiated aesthetic continuum of immediacy[12] or of any sensed or introspected images within it. The ancient Greek mathematical physics of Democritus and Plato (Aristotle returned ancient Greek science to a naive realistic epistemology and its traditional approval of law-of-status slaves) and modern science took this epistemological way, re-introducing concepts by postulation which in whole or part are concepts by intellection. The result for the normative sciences of ethics, law, and politics was the crea-

[10] R. M. Martin, "On Semantical Rules and Definable Predicates," *Philosophical Studies,* X (April, 1959), 33–38.

[11] F. S. C. Northrop, "The Mediational Approval Theory of Law in American Legal Realism," *Virginia Law Review,* XLIV (1958), 347–363.

[12] F. S. C. Northrop, *The Meeting of East and West* (New York: The Macmillan Co., 1946), chap. IX.

tion by the Stoic Romans of Western legal science and its "shift from status to contract,"[13] and its implementation, after Newton, by Jefferson.

This new concept of law and personal morality generates formally and contractually constructed laws which depend upon consent rather than biology and breeding for their authority. Its formal definition of the intrinsically good and just is:

For any person p and for any object of normative judgment x, to say that x is intrinsically good or intrinsically just is equivalent to saying that there exists a postulationally or contractually constructed determinate law to which the parties concerned have committed themselves, which is universally quantified for any person p and whose substantive content s is also universally quantified for any person p.

In other words, religious, legal, political, and moral man is universal, cosmopolitan, ecumenical, or catholic human being.

The significance of modern mathematical physics for the contemporary world as a whole is that with Galilei, Newton, and their successors, Maxwell, Gibbs, Planck, Einstein, Schrödinger, and Heisenberg, the naive realism of Aristotelian physics and metaphysics and of Thomistic Roman Catholic theology and natural law was rejected in favor of indirectly and experimentally confirmed logical realism in epistemic correlation with directly experienced radical empiricism. It is the technology of this logically realistic mathematical physics and the contractual legal and political institutions of logically realistic legal and political science which people the world over today are demanding for themselves. Since logical realism in epistemic correlation with radical empiricism contains the latter epistemology as part of itself, contractual legal and political science of the free democratic type is compatible with the radically empirical concept of the formless Nirvāṇa or *cit* consciousness self of Buddhist and Hindu Asia; it is incompatible only with the naive realistic law-of-status person of the Mīmāṁsā dualistic school of Hinduism and this Hindu factor in Hindu-Buddhist Southeast Asia generally. In fact, according to the most elemental Buddhist and Hindu concept of the person, all human beings are, not merely equal, but also identical in their essential nature. Clearly this belief is compatible with liberal contractual democracy.

REPLY TO CRITICISMS OF THE ABOVE

Dr. Hu Shih's friendly criticisms show that both the thesis and the epistemological method of the foregoing abridged paper are easy to misunderstand.[14] In fact, were my position what Hu interprets it to be, I would be as critical of both my previous writings and the present paper as he is. To see that there is misunderstanding, let us begin with the negative and the positive points of Hu.

[13] Sir Henry Maine, *Ancient Law*, p. 151, and Northrop, *The Complexity of Legal and Ethical Experience*, chaps. XVII and XXII.

[14] See his paper, above, "The Scientific Spirit and Method in Chinese Philosophy."

His negative point is that the epistemological analysis of the meaning of the abstract nouns which one finds in the historical texts of comparative philosophy is quite unnecessary. Does Hu really believe this? Certainly Locke, Hume, and Kant did not. Locke explicitly says that, before any philosopher can state or discuss normative philosophical theories or problems, he must first carry through an epistemological inquiry concerning the source and the nature of the meanings of the words that he uses.[15] Locke's classical *Essay* is an attempt to do this. Hume, similarly, in his *Treatise of Human Nature* begins with a determination "Of Ideas, Their Origin, Composition, Abstraction, Connexion, Etc."[16] Only after having thus made clear the criterion of a meaningful word does he turn to his philosophical conclusions concerning space, time, causality, goodness, and justice. Kant likewise begins with his *Critique of Pure Reason,* which is a specification of two different types and sources of the meaning of words. Reject this epistemology and his ethical and legal conclusions do not follow.

The plain fact is that every word we use has as many diverse meanings as there are different epistemological theories of the source of the meaning of any word. Consider, for example, the word "person." In its radical empirical meaning this word denotes the private introspected data of what James called one's "flow of consciousness." In its naive realistic epistemological meaning the person is the immediately sensed-color-of-skin, sexual, primogeniture-of-birth natural-history object. From the standpoint of a logically realistic epistemology in epistemic correlation with a radical empirical epistemology, the person is the formally constructed cybernetic nervous system with its trapped impulses in epistemic correlation with one's introspected Jamesian flow-of-consciousness private ideas. Clearly, the concept of person is quite different accordingly as one interprets this abstract noun from the standpoint of these three different epistemological theories of the meaning of any word.

It follows, therefore, that it is impossible to know what a given philosopher in a given historical text means by the words which he uses unless we first determine his particular epistemology by trying out different epistemological theories of what his words may mean or by finding his epistemological theory stated somewhere in his writings. The supposition that the historical method alone is sufficient in comparative philosophy will not, therefore, stand careful examination.

Hu's reference to the natural scientists as the justification for using the historical method and for the neglect of an epistemological analysis is somewhat unfortunate for his own thesis. Natural scientists are famous for their neglect of the history of their subject. Clearly, the historical method is not their method. The English mathematical physicist who made the major advance in quantum theory in his country once told the writer that he had never read Newton. Instead, Dirac began with the latest verified theory—namely, that of

[15] John Locke, *Essay Concerning Human Understanding,* Alexander C. Fraser, ed. (Oxford: The Clarendon Press, 1894), Vol. I, pp. xxxvi, 9.

[16] David A. Hume, *A Treatise of Human Nature,* T. H. Green and T. H. Grose, eds. (London: Longmans, Green & Co., Inc., 1886), Vol. I, Table of Contents.

quantum mechanics as it came from the minds of Planck, Schrödinger, and Heisenberg and went on from there. To be sure, as Hu notes, President Emeritus Conant, now turned pedagogue, is concerned with making historical discoveries in natural science more vivid for high school students in order to stimulate their interest in the subject, but this is hardly the basis for the method to be used either by mathematical physicists in analyzing the concepts of their theory or by scholars in comparative philosophy.

Nor does Hu's and the writer's admirable philosopher Dewey warrant Hu's conclusion that the historical method is the method of philosophy. The spirit of Dewey was one in which the dead were to be allowed to bury their dead and philosophical study was concentrated instead on a logical, semantic, and unrestricted philosophical analysis of today's problematic situations. To be sure, when today's international and national legal and political problems exhibit, under analysis, cultural and political conflicts between the law-of-status norms of medieval and ancient beliefs still persisting and the new technological, legal, and politically contractual norms derived from Stoic Roman law or modern secular legal and political philosophy, Dewey's way of philosophizing requires one to examine the ancient and medieval historical beliefs and the reasons for them. But to examine even them in a way that leads to an understanding of what they affirm requires that we pay attention to the epistemological meaning of the words the ancients used. Dewey's method requires also that we stop talking so much about what a marvelous philosopher Dewey was and get down to the hard philosophically analytic labor of determining the precise assumptions of the conflicting cultural customs and beliefs and of then proposing a constructive philosophical solution of the problems confronting us today. Clearly, more than merely going to some ancient texts with the historian's method and his philosophically and epistemologically unanalyzed abstract nouns is required to do this. Otherwise, the resort to the historical method is merely an escape mechanism for avoiding the Deweyian analysis and resolution of today's problems rather than the practice of his practical philosophy.

Hu's comments make it clear also that he, like Professors Needham, Datta, Mahadevan, and Raju before him, has misunderstood the writer's concepts by postulation. I am especially indebted to my good friend Hu for making clear precisely where I misguided him and perhaps also them. That the fault, however, is not entirely mine is shown by two considerations. First, other readers of my writings have grasped my meaning correctly. Second, even the word which I introduced that misguided him will not misguide if one pays meticulous attention to the original definitions of "concepts by intuition" and "concepts by postulation."[17]

The word which I used and which misled Hu was "centaur," when given without further qualifications being stated, as an example of that species of a "concept by postulation which is a concept by imagination." Considered by itself, apart from a careful reading of the definitions of concepts by intuition

[17] See note 2, above.

and concepts by postulation, "centaur" is a misleading example. It is misleading because, for most minds, the word has merely an imaginative, radically empirical meaning and hence is a concept by intuition. It is possible, however, to think of the construct "centaur" as a "mass" axiomatically constructed with the imageless relational properties of Euclidian space-time and the mechanical properties of an entity variable which is a relatum in the mathematical relations that are Newton's three laws of motion. "Centaur," in the sense of the introspected image epistemically correlated with this formal construct, is clearly an example of what the writer meant by a "concept by postulation that is a concept by imagination."

Were there images epistemically correlatable with all the constructs of mathematical physics, all the concepts of the latter science would be concepts by postulation which are concepts by imagination; for every mathematically constructed scientific object there would be an isomorphic imaginable model. We now know, however, from quantum mechanics and also from Einstein's general theory of relativity, that such is not the case. In other words, imaginable models for all scientific objects, properties, and relations or laws are no longer required; nor are such models possible in contemporary mathematical physics. This means that the latter science contains concepts by postulation which are wholly concepts by intellection. Quantum theory, for example, becomes self-contradictory if one insists upon assigning wave-like and particle-like images to its scientific constructs.

But, if imageful entities are always concepts by intuition, why, then, did I use the word "centaur" as an instance of a particular species of concept by postulation? Or, to put this same question in more general terms, why did I speak of concepts by postulation which are concepts by imagination and of concepts by postulation which are concepts by perception? The answer appears in the difference between the definition of concepts by intuition and concepts by postulation which was given first at the East-West Philosophers' Conference of 1939 and immediately afterward at the Unity of Science Congress at Harvard University and reprinted later in the writer's *The Logic of the Sciences and the Humanities*. In all these sources a concept by intuition was so defined as to be solely a concept by intuition. This is the significance of the words *"the complete meaning of which"* in their definition. A concept by postulation, however, was so stated as to be *in part or whole* an imageless construct, i.e., a concept by intellection. This is the significance of the words "in whole or part" in their definition. Hence, although any concept by postulation whatever has its imageless, formally constructed component and is, therefore, in part a concept by postulation which is a concept by intellection, only concepts by postulation which are completely concepts by intellection are scientific constructs for which there are no one-one imageful epistemic correlates. The words "whole or part" in this definition of concepts by postulation express the fact, therefore, that there are imageless concept-by-intellection constructs of different species some of which do have one-one epistemically correlated radically empirical, directly sensed or imagined images and some of which do not. When, however, one has a concept by postulation which is in part a concept by intellection for which there are epistemically correlated sensed or introspected images, the meaning of the image does not exhaust the meaning of the concept by postulation.

Unless these technical epistemological distinctions are correctly grasped and the definitions of concepts by intuition and concepts by postulation fully comprehended, the writer's thesis in his paper at this conference and his previous books with respect to the differences between the scientific and philosophical theories of classical Asia and those of the non-Aristotelian mathematical physics and contractual legal science of the West simply cannot be understood. Furthermore, there is nothing in anything Hu, Needham, Datta, Mahadevan, and Raju have written which shows that they have understood the writer's thesis. The plain fact is that it cannot be understood apart from the postulational techniques of pure mathematics and the contemporary symbolic logic of relations for creating imageless conceptual constructs. The writer has recently examined Needham's last volume on Chinese science. Near the end Needham concludes that everything in his volume goes to show that this writer's thesis that there are no concepts by postulation in Asian science is false. Yet, not once from one end of Needham's volume to the other does he give us a solitary text or even his own exposition of a text which presents an imageless, axiomatically constructed concept. Quite the contrary. Again and again Needham's texts show that scientific objects are defined in terms of sensed qualities. This means that the remarkable scientific knowledge of classical Chinese science contains very subtle and complex theories, but they are theories of objects defined in terms of concepts by intuition, since sensed qualities are not axiomatically constructed imageless things, but immediately, radically empirically sensed things. There is no evidence also in any of the law books of Hindu India or any of the codes that the writer has read of classical Chinese law which shows that they had the Western contractual legal concept of a corporation conceived as an imageless, contractual construct.

It may help the neutral reader to judge this issue if we consider what the situation would be were there no concepts by postulation even in Western mathematical physics as well as classical Asian science and philosophy. The situation would be what the early logical positivists, such as Carnap, first supposed[18]—namely, that all concepts in mathematical physics, referring to unobservable scientific objects, properties, events, and laws, could be defined in terms of sensed objects, properties, and relations. Note that this would mean that all the concepts of Western mathematical physics would be definable in terms of what the writer calls "concepts by intuition," since a concept which refers for its entire meaning to sensed entities and relations and numbers is a species of such a concept. Furthermore, were the Wittgensteinian or Carnapian reduction technique as given in Carnap's "Testability and Meaning"[19] a correct analysis of the concepts of mathematical physics, not only would there be no

[18] Rudolf Carnap, *Der logische Aufbau der Welt* (Berlin: Weltkreis; Leipzig: Felix Meiner Verlag, 1928).

[19] Rudolf Carnap, "Testability and Meaning," *Philosophy of Science*, III (October, 1936), 420–471, and IV (January, 1937), 1–40.

concepts by postulation in classical Asian science and philosophy, but there would be none in Western mathematical physics, either. Since philosophers of science as steeped in the use of imageless axiomatic methods as Carnap have come only recently to the admission that there are concepts by postulation in Western mathematical physics, the writer's thesis that pre-Western Asian scientific and philosophic theories do not contain such concepts is hardly a surprising one.

The latter thesis does not mean that ancient Asian science and philosophy do not possess very complex theory—even very complex mathematical theory. Of course they do. In fact, concept-by-intuition theory in mathematics, natural science, normative law, and philosophy is far more complex than theory of the concept-by-postulation imageless, axiomatically constructed type. As Ernst Mach noted, one of the merits of the latter type of theory, aside from its greater predictive power, is the fewer assumptions which it requires, i.e., the greater economy of thought which it provides. The reason for this greater simplicity and economy of thought is clear. Natural objects in their concept-by-intuition meaning, as directly sensed, are so different in their sensed properties and behavior as to require the assignment of different defining properties and different rules of behavior to them. Nevertheless, in their concept-by-postulation meaning they are found to be instances of a single construct, e.g., mass, and to fall under the same law.

The mathematics of concept-by-intuition number, space, and time is similarly different from the mathematics of axiomatically constructed numbers and space-time. From the plurality of sensed differentiations one can abstract, as did classical Asian mathematical science, the concept of sensed number; from the sensed cyclical sequences called day and night, by sensed counting one can get it also. From sensed spatial relations one can obtain a concept-by-intuition meaning for space. In a mathematics that defines its operations and concepts in such immediately inspectable ways elaborate scientific theories that are mathematical can be developed. But such mathematical science is quite different from the axiomatically constructed numbers of Definition 5, Book V, of Euclid or Peano's Fifth Postulate or the axiomatically constructed metrical space of Euclid's geometry or Einstein's four-dimensional space-time. That Asia, before the influence of Greek mathematics and mathematical physics, had mathematical science in the former of these two senses there is no doubt. Until, however, some student of the ancient Asian scientific treatises can present textual evidence of a deductively formulated set of imageless axioms such as Definition 5, Book V, of Euclid or Peano's Fifth Postulate, we have no alternative but to conclude that they did not discover mathematical concepts and theories which are those of concepts by postulation.

Professor Paul Kurtz raised the question of the relation between "natural and contractual law," restricting his usage of the latter two words to that philosophy of Western legal science called legal positivism, which arose in the eighteenth century and contrasts with earlier naturalistic philosophies of Western law such as those of Hobbes, Locke, Jefferson, St. Thomas, or the Stoic

Romans. This distinction between the positivistic and the naturalistic theories of Western contractual legal science is important but outside the scope of the present inquiry, since, as was emphasized at the outset, this paper is using the words "law of contract" in the comparative legal sense of Sir Henry Maine as referring to what distinguishes Western legal science since its creation by the Stoic Roman lawyers from other types of the world's law.

Kurtz raised the question also of the relation between (1) the epistemologies of the law of status and the law of contract and (2) "economic relations," suggesting that the former "reflect" the latter. In a society whose customs are those of the law of status in the sense of Sir Henry Maine, the traditional "economic relations" are determined by the decisions of the biologically-born head of the patriarchal family or of the tribe, and it does not occur to the other members in the community to question the authority of the head of one's own family or of the tribe of which one's family is a part, with respect to economic or other matters. When, however, the hypothetical constructs of a logically realistic way of thinking or knowing become available, as they did with the Stoic Roman lawyers in their creation of Western legal science, then it becomes possible to order the economic relations of people to one another in ways that never existed before and which may have little if any relation to the genealogical familial and tribal relations of biological breeding and birth. Individual persons can enter into economic, marital, and political relations directly *qua* individuals instead of being largely controlled by the heads of the family and the tribe. These considerations suggest that, instead of "economic relations" causally determining a people's epistemological and moral way of thinking, it is the other way around.

Professor Sharif raised the question whether revealed law should not be added to status, contractual, and mediational law as a fourth type. The reason for answering in the negative is that all three types have claimed revelation as their source or partial justification. Conversely, a comparative study of revealed law will show, I believe, that its content is one or another of these three types, or a combination of them.

I am especially indebted to Datta and Raju for their conference papers, which show that the law-of-status codes of classical Hindu law are the work of Hindu philosophers who were Mīmāṁsā dualists. It was evident from my previous reading of these codes that some such naive realistic ontologically dualistic philosophy is required to account for their sensuous biological and racial content with its emphasis on caste. It is equally evident also, however, in these codes, as exemplified in the *Laws of Manu,* that they are the product of a synthesis of non-dualistic philosophy and the philosophy of the self without differences of the earliest Vedas and the Upaniṣads which was later articulated by Gauḍapāda and Śaṁkara and given the name "non-dualistic Vedānta." This shows in the *Laws of Manu* and other Hindu law books in the following specific ways: First, the naive realistic law-of-status values of a Mīmāṁsā dualistic philosophy apply largely in the "householder stage" of any Hindu's life. In the other three stages, the Hindu's life is devoted to meditative acquaintance with and pursuit of the non-dualistic self without differences. There is no doubt left in the law books either, that of the two selves—the naive realistic Mīmāṁsā dualistic law-of-status self and the Vedāntic self without differences—it is the latter which is the one most to be sought and the true self. Second, in the caste system the person most expert in expressing the Mīmāṁsā dualistic law-of-status racial and tribal self is the maharaja ruler, who is housekeeper of the State, commander of the army, and administrator of the status-codified law. He, however, is given merely second-caste status, the highest-caste status going to the humble *guru* who, while teaching the respective duties and values of the four castes and the four stages of the Hindu's life, spends a major portion of his time in meditation, identifying himself with the non-dualistic true self without differences. Hence, even though Hindu law was codified by Mīmāṁsā dualistic philosophers, this law is a complex combination of Mīmāṁsā dualistic and Vedāntic non-dualistic values, in which the latter are regarded as the truer and given primacy of status and importance. The interested reader will find this thesis worked out in more detail in the writer's "The Comparative Philosophy of Comparative Law" in Volume XLV of the *Cornell Law Quarterly*.

The conference members also discussed the question of the portion (a) of Buddhist, Hindu, and Confucian societies that is characterized by determinate moral and legal norms which cannot be compromised and the portion (b) which is fluid, subject to the compromises of mediational peace-making. The answer of this paper to this question is that (a) is the law-of-status component with its naive realistic concept of the person and that (b) derives from the radically empirical self without differences. In Buddhism, the latter is called the Nirvāṇa state or one's *Buddha*-nature; in Hinduism, it is "the true self" in which Brahman and *Ātman* are one, and in Confucianism it is fostered by what Professor Chan referred to as "the universal [as distinct from the differentiatedly particular] factor in *jen*."

GRAY L. DORSEY

The Influence of Philosophy on Law and Politics in Western Civilization

In Western civilization, philosophy has had an influence upon the norms of law and politics and upon the attitudes toward legal and political questions and problems. The basic influence, as might be expected, occurred early in the course of Western civilization. It produced a central tradition of natural law and humanism that has had setbacks and various interpretations but is still the guide for law and politics in Western countries except for the communist ones, and for a time the Germans.[1] However, one of the characteristic attitudes has no present justification.

I. THE INFLUENCE UPON NORMS

In the last century of the Roman Republic and continuing into the Empire a social revolution of first magnitude occurred. C. H. McIlwain has said of this change in Roman life, "There is probably no other social revolution in recorded history so important, so complete, so continuous over so long a period."[2] McIlwain noted the transformation in every branch of Roman private law: property, marriage, testamentary succession, contracts, etc. These are the working-together and living-together relations of a society, and are political in the sense that they constitute the way in which the *polis* is organized for action. Why should such a complete change occur? We shall look first at the life and ideas of the earlier period and then at the life and ideas of the later period, and see if the reason for the change does not appear.

[1] Ernst Troeltsch, "The Ideas of Natural Law and Humanity in World Politics," in Otto Gierke, ed., *Natural Law and the Theory of Society,* translation and introduction by Ernest Barker (Cambridge: Cambridge University Press, 1950).

[2] Charles H. McIlwain, *Constitutionalism, Ancient and Modern* (Ithaca: Cornell University Press, 1940), p. 54. (Referred to hereafter as *Constitutionalism*).

Life in the early City-State of Rome (and in the early Greek City-States) is best seen through the pages of Fustel de Coulanges' *The Ancient City*.[3] Fustel, with what is today generally recognized as remarkable insight, stressed the importance of religion in the life of the family and of the City-State. The head of the family, the paterfamilias, had the sole right to carry on the family religion. It was his responsibility to see that the sacred fire on the hearth was never extinguished, or profaned by the presence of strangers. This fire was the constant symbol of the living soul of the original paterfamilias surviving in his descendants, partaking of the "immortality of generation."[4] The paterfamilias was also the lawgiver and judge, the economic manager, the leader in war.[5] When cities were formed by amalgamation of gens and tribes of families, it was thought necessary to establish a hearth and a sacred fire for the city.[6] Indeed, community was possible only on the basis of community of worship. Gods were local and exclusive.[7] Rights and duties existed only between those who had the same gods. Each family was autonomous until it joined with others in a gens, tribe, or city, which then shared a common worship.[8] In the face of threatened destruction, Athens could not extend her defensive league beyond the cities linked by common worship in the amphictyony of Delos.[9] The normal state of relations between the cities of Greece was war, and community of worship was the basis of such co-operation as they achieved.[10]

For our purposes, the significance of these facts about life in the early Roman and Greek City-States will become apparent when an implicit premise is stated and compared with one resulting from Greek natural philosophy. The later premise would be, "The universe is rational." The earlier, the implied, premise was, "The universe is whimsical." Events were not related by cause and effect. Events occurred, or did not occur, at the whim of the appropriate god. We speak of the mythical gods of ancient Greece and Rome. But they were not mythical then. They controlled events. In such a world the only way to plan ahead was to consult the gods. The only wise men were those who could consult the gods—and these were the heads of families, gens, tribes, and City-States, who had responsibility for the religion of the groups they headed.

It was common sense that authority should belong to the paterfamilias, or his counterparts in the City-State. Therefore, they were the judges, economic managers, and war leaders. It would be foolish to have decisions made by anyone else. Rostovtzeff has said, "The public life of Rome was inseparable from religion: every action of the state began and ended in a religious ceremony.... The *imperium* or executive power of the magistrate was closely connected with

[3] Numa Denis Fustel de Coulanges, *The Ancient City*, Willard Small, trans. (7th ed., Boston: Lee & Shepard, 1889).

[4] Plato, *Laws*, in *Dialogues of Plato*, B. Jowett, trans. (9th printing, New York: Random House, 1937), Bk. IV, p. 721.

[5] C. W. Westrup, *Introduction to Early Roman Law*, Vol. III (London: Humphrey Milford, Oxford University Press, 1939), pp. 148, *et seq*.

[6] Martin P. Nilsson, *Greek Piety*, Herbert J. Rose, trans. (Oxford: Clarendon Press, 1948), p. 6.

[7] A. H. J. Greenidge, *A Handbook of Greek Constitutional History* (London: Macmillan & Co., Ltd., 1896), pp. 6–7; Nilsson, *op. cit.*, p. 10; Fustel, *op. cit.*, pp. 162–163.

[8] Westrup, *op. cit.*, Vol. III, p. 143.

[9] Greenidge, *op. cit.*, pp. 48–51, 202.

[10] *Ibid.*, pp. 46, 60.

his exclusive right of ascertaining the will of the gods by auspices, of soliciting, in the name of the community, their protection, and lastly of propitiating them."[11]

The Stoic philosophers were the first to formulate the full implications of a rational universe for law and politics. Plato and Aristotle had believed that only the best men could know the rational order in the universe, and that other men were by nature fit only for lesser jobs than knowing the good and planning community affairs wisely. The Stoics taught in their physics that the universe is ruled by absolute rational law and that the essential nature of man is reason.[12] The implication of this was that all men are rational creatures. And when the Stoics in their ethics taught men to "Live according to Nature," they were building acceptance for their idea of a single Cosmopolis in which all men are equal because reason makes them equally able to know what justice requires in every relation of life.

Stoicism began to be taught in Rome a little less than a century before the fall of the Republic.[13] Ehrlich, one of the great students of Roman legal history, has said that the main root of Roman law is juristic law, and he claimed credit for having shown in his *Beiträge zur Theorie der Rechtsquellen* that the Roman jurists created their law independently, and not by interpretation of the earlier statutes and edicts.[14] About thirty years after Stoicism was first taught in Rome, the first of the great Roman jurists, Q. Mucius Scaevola (a Stoic), wrote the eighteen volumes on civil law which earned him recognition as the founder of Roman law.[15] Of fourteen jurists whom Jolowicz lists as laying the foundation for and developing Roman juristic science during the Republic, at least eleven can be found by perusal of Arnold's *Roman Stoicism* to have been Stoics.[16]

The Greek philosophers destroyed the world of whimsy. They posited a world of reason, and their evidence was so convincing that the gods who controlled events gradually faded from reality to myth. With them went community consensus in support of centering authority in men who had charge of religious auspices. The resulting changes can be traced in Roman private law, as McIlwain suggested.[17]

In the early City-States all property belonged to the family—conceived of as the continuity of generations, not as a community of living persons. The current paterfamilias could not alienate family property. He could not disinherit the son. The son could not refuse an inheritance that was a net liability. In fact, the paterfamilias possessed and passed on, not the property itself, but only the authority to act with respect to the property. Daughters, who

[11] M. I. Rostovtzeff, *A History of the Ancient World*, J. D. Duff, trans. (2nd ed., Oxford: Clarendon Press, 1930), Vol. II, pp. 53–54.

[12] Walter T. Stace, *A Critical History of Greek Philosophy* (London: Macmillan & Co., Ltd., 1934), p. 349.

[13] E. Vernon Arnold, *Roman Stoicism* (Cambridge: Cambridge University Press, 1911), chaps. XII–XV.

[14] Eugen Ehrlich, *Fundamental Principles of the Sociology of Law*, Walter L. Moll, trans. (Cambridge: Harvard University Press, 1936), pp. 260–261.

[15] Rudolf Sohm, *Institutes of Roman Law*, James C. Ledlie, trans. (3d English ed., based on 12th German ed., Cambridge: Clarendon Press, 1907), pp. 90–91. The time was about 100 B.C.

[16] Herbert F. Jolowicz, *Historical Introduction to the Study of Roman Law* (Cambridge: University Press, 1932), pp. 90–91.

[17] See above, note 2.

could never become the family head, could not inherit. With the influx of Greek thought, the idea of legal personality was divorced from religious authority. Family heads could alienate some of the family property. Sons could hold property and make contracts in their own right during their father's lifetime. Daughters could inherit. Sons could be disinherited, or could refuse an inheritance.[18] In short, the control by the succession of paterfamilias over all property from which members of the family derived benefit was completely broken through. The control of the paterfamilias over the persons of family members and even slaves was restricted.[19] Thus, it can be seen that the change in the content of the norms of the Roman *polis* was very great.

The change in the structure of norms was also great. The subjects of rights and duties are no longer men as understood in a common-sense way but conceptual entities defined within the hierarchically ordered body of norms covering all human relationships. Roman law had been a series of legal rules, such as one finds in the *Code of Hammurabi.* Suddenly it had the logical structure that caused Cuq to say that "the Romans have fixed for all times the categories of juristic thought."[20] This logical structure first appeared in the treatise of the Stoic Scaevola, referred to above. Sohm has said that Scaevola "was the first to determine, in clear outline, the nature of legal institutions (will, legacy, guardianship, partnership, sale, hiring, etc.), and their various kinds (genera)."[21] For the first time, there was a juristic science. Sohm succinctly states the significance of such a science:

> A scientific exposition, for example, would never run as follows: If a thing has been delivered to you under a contract of sale, you have the right to keep it, and a third party into whose possession it comes is bound to hand it over to you. [This is the kind of language you will find in Hammurabi's Code.] The scientific exposition would be in this fashion. First, ownership is a right, unlimited in its contents, to exercise control over a thing. Thus we get the conception of ownership. Secondly, ownership can be acquired by traditio, occupatio, usucapio, &c. (each of these terms being defined). Thus in place of a series of legal rules we have a number of abstract conceptions.[22]

The change with respect to the source of norms was equally great. With respect to private transactions, the change was from ritualistic formulas to formless juristic acts. With respect to public law—government—it was a change from the authority of those in charge of the auspices to the authority of the people. In private transactions the actual articles, such as cattle or grain (or symbols representing them), had been passed from hand to hand as the appropriate ritual was recited. If the ritual was faulty in any small detail, the transaction was not accomplished. With the change in Roman law, concepts rather than physical articles were manipulated. The modern transaction of

[18] Sohm, *op. cit.,* pp. 177–178, 186–193, 449–450, 482–488, 501–505.
[19] *Ibid.,* pp. 165–184.
[20] Édouard Cuq, *Les Institutions Juridiques des Romains* (Paris: Plon, Nourrit et Cie., 1904), Vol. I, p. xxiv.
[21] Sohm, *op. cit.,* p. 91.
[22] *Ibid.,* pp. 32–33.

mortgage replaced a physical exchange of land and money for a period of years. Ritual was replaced by the intent of the parties—not the will of the gods, invoked through ritual, but the will of rational men in a rational world was decisive as to whether the transaction was completed.[23]

The changes I have outlined above were some of the practical consequences of an idea that provided a basis for community beyond the community of worship. All men could enter into reciprocal rights and duties and receive justice with respect to their relationships because justice did not lie with any man's gods but was in the hands of professional jurists sworn to uphold the impersonal, universal law before which all men were equal. Men did not deal with one another *qua* men, but transactions were carried out between "seller" and "purchaser," "pledgor" and "pledgee," "mortgagor" and "mortgagee," etc., all of whom had definite, specific rights and duties set down in the hierarchically ordered body of legal norms.

Not only could community become larger, but also it could become much more complex. Since man as a legal person was not common-sense man, but legal-concept man, it was thus perceived that artificial legal persons could be created.[24] This is the basis for the modern corporation, so important today in accumulating the vast capital needed in modern economic enterprise.

Most important of all, here was the basis for the institutions of private property and free contract as the means of distributing the decision-making about the allocation and use of the natural resources of a society. Each person who has met the requirements to be recognized as the "owner" of property has the right to make the decisions about the use to which that property will be put. He uses it by contracting with others who have other property, or their own personal skills or labor. This method of distributing decision-making makes no sense at all unless man generally—any who may acquire property by this indiscriminate method—can be expected to make decisions about his piece of the resources that in the long run will be wise from the standpoint of the community as well as from the standpoint of personal gain. Society can not allow a man with no access to the gods to control a grain field if a god controls the productivity of that field. Society can allow a man who can learn about soil treatment and grain fertility to control a grain field if these matters affect the production of grain (and if the operation of the market will induce him to produce).

Naturally, the legal and political implementation of these basic ideas has had many ups and downs and curious twists of interpretation. One of the most ironical was the immediate result for public law in Rome. The people prevailed over the patricians in the Senate.[25] But recognition of the authority of the people to govern was little more than a formality. The emperors seldom conducted themselves as representatives. Any legal and political consequences of the rational faculty in man were subordinated for centuries to the official reason and revelation of the Church, and then of kings. The rational approach

[23] *Ibid.*, p. 69. [24] *Ibid.*, pp. 195–204. [25] McIlwain, *Constitutionalism*, chap. III.

has prevailed in periods when new institutions and political values were being created, such as the time of the creation of the modern Nation-States. The analytic approach has prevailed in periods of comparative social calm, as in England in the last century, and has made institutions more efficient and law less confusing and contradictory. The sociological approach has prevailed in periods when social change has outrun legal and political institutions, and it has secured re-interpretation of established principles in the light of their current social result, as in England and the United States after the Industrial Revolution. But, underlying all, Western law and politics still assume a rational universe and rational men trying to make their way about in it.[26] The conceptions of Greek natural philosophy provided the ideas for the basic legal institutions of private property, contract, rights in the person, and the right to have social institutions act to protect these rights; and, also, for the basic political institutions of representative government and of constitutionally limited government.

II. THE INFLUENCE UPON ATTITUDES

Northrop has called attention to the universalness, the absoluteness, and the determinateness of the legal and political norms engendered by the type of concepts that Greek natural philosophy produced. He has pointed out that, because of these attributes in its norms, Western society expects, demands, and uses police power to get a high degree of explicitness of behavior. He has pointed out that what the West would approve as "sticking up for one's rights" would be regarded in Asian societies as "trouble-making," and that some of the actions the West would approve as "law enforcement" (especially in the international sphere) would be viewed by members of Asian societies as unjustified resort to armed force, which will not help to settle disputes.[27]

I would agree completely with this characterization of Western legal and political norms. And there can be no question that the attitudes are generally held in the West. I believe, further, that the attitude of sticking up for one's rights is a likely and probably necessary result of the nature of the system of knowing from which the norms stem. Greek science examined objects as discrete entities having predicates of their own. This carried over into legal and political norms in the form of individual legal and political rights. Legal machinery for the protection of these rights is provided, but the machinery must be activated by complaint of an injured party. Justice will not be done if the injured person does not set the machinery in motion. This is true, to a

[26] Charles H. McIlwain, in his *The Growth of Political Thought in the West* (New York: The Macmillan Company, 1932), takes the rational nature of man as the main thread of the history of Western political thought. In his introductory paragraph (p. 1), he says: "Dominion if it is to be justified at all must be 'a condition of rational nature' as Wycliffe defined it, and in reason permanent government must have a justification sufficient to explain the historical fact of its continuous existence among rational beings. . . . [W]here does 'rational nature' require that the dominant power be lodged; . . . how does this 'rational nature' prescribe that this power shall be exercised, wherever lodged?"

[27] F. S. C. Northrop, *The Taming of the Nations* (New York: The Macmillan Company, 1954), chaps. II, III, VII, X.

considerable extent, even with respect to criminal justice because of the vital importance of the evidence given by the "complaining witness" (the victim of the criminal act). "Sticking up for one's rights" is necessary, therefore, to the successful operation of a Western society.

I want to suggest, however, that resort to force in the cause of justice is, in certain instances, not justified by the nature of Western norms and the Western way of knowing. I believe that, to some extent, the attitude of approving resort to force for justice is a holdover from the view of life held prior to Greek science. This would seem to be an area of study in which significance more easily becomes apparent by comparison. I will therefore compare early thought in the West with thought about the same questions in ancient China.

The very early lover of wisdom observed (as would a truly naive observer today) a sensed world of movement, changing colors, alternating periods of light and more or less absence of light, revolving seasons, opposition, communion, reproduction, growth, and death. Some vital power must animate and order this activity. To know the source and nature of this power could mean the difference between survival and death. The early inhabitants of the valleys of the Tigris, Euphrates, and Nile rivers, and the shores of the Aegean Sea generally ascribed an anthropomorphic source to this animating and ordering power.[28] The early Chinese generally did not.[29]

It is fascinating to speculate on why the early peoples in these two regions accepted different answers to this basic question, but the answer remains inconclusive. Possibly the geographical and ecological environment focused attention on different factors in experience. Chiang Yee says that China developed its civilization in the interior, under relatively easy conditions, which allowed isolated small groups to meet subsistence requirements, did not place a particular emphasis upon the unusually capable man, or create a need for close co-operation to meet the rigors of sea voyages and coastal storms. By contrast, he says that "sea-civilizations" were created in Egypt and Greece.[30] On the other hand, Toynbee says that the challenges of geography and ecology were the same in the two areas. He says that the "Egyptiac and Sumeric and Sinic civilizations were responses to the challenges of drought and flood and swamp and thicket."[31] Maspero takes a middle position, saying that, despite the similar fluvial orientation, the "two worlds" were "entirely different," "the soil, the climate, the flora, the fauna have nothing in common."[32]

Whatever the reason for the difference, the fact of the difference had remarkable consequences—certainly upon attitudes toward human actions, and probably upon the development of systems of knowing and consequent social norms. The anthropomorphic interpretation of the animating and ordering

[28] Westrup, *op. cit.*, Vol. III, pp. 216–217; J. L. Myres, "The Background of Greek Science," in *University of California Chronicle*, Vol. XVI, 1914, p. 396.

[29] Chiang Yee, "The Philosophical Basis of Chinese Painting," in F. S. C. Northrop, ed., *Ideological Differences and World Order* (New Haven: Yale University Press, 1949), p. 35; G. Lowes Dickinson, *An Essay on the Civilizations of India, China and Japan* (London: J. M. Dent & Sons, Ltd., 1914), p. 46.

[30] Chiang, *loc. cit.*, p. 36.

[31] Arnold J. Toynbee, *A Study of History* (London: Oxford University Press, 1934–1954), Vol. I, p. 321.

[32] Henri Maspero, *La Chine Antique* (Paris: E. de Boccard, 1927), p. 8.

power directed thought to (1) men as semi-autonomous entities, and (2) *control* of physical events. The non-anthropomorphic interpretation resulted in a system of knowing in which (1) man is merely one attribute of the only entity, the universe, and (2) attention is directed to preserving and promoting the natural harmony of the universe.

The personalizing of the animating and ordering power is seen in the concepts of the Roman *genius,* the Greek *daimon,* the Persian *fravashi,* the Egyptian *ka.*[33] Certain resourceful, powerful, and practically wise men were thought to be filled with the animating and ordering power to a higher degree than others. When such a "demi-god" died, it was thought, his soul lived on as a companion of and a protector to his descendants. Such a man was the founder of a family. He was the Greek eponymous hero, the Roman original paterfamilias. The hearth fire was the symbol of the continued presence of his living soul, and it burned upon "the hearth, the seat of the household gods, under the foundation stone of which the house-father had once been buried."[34] Not only did the genius of the original house-father remain near his grave to assist, guard, and guide those who supplicated it properly, but also his active power, or *mana,* was passed through the continuity of generations.[35] When the peoples ascribed personalized gods to natural events, these became family Manes and were as local and exclusive as the founding house-father or the eponymous hero.[36]

The beliefs just recited were the basis for the way of life and the legal and political norms of the early City-States that were described in Part I of this paper. At the moment, we are interested in their influence upon the system of knowing developed by the Greeks, and upon attitudes toward the use of force for justice. But, first, because we are comparing, we must look at the corresponding beliefs in early China.[37] If Granet is correct about early life and thought in China, it would appear that the most significant fact of experience for the Chinese was the feeling of oneness with the universe which was experienced at the festivals and hierogamies and which seemed to contain the efficacy that produced the different orders of life for men and women which alternated with the periods of communion at the festivals and hierogamies and corresponded with the rhythm of the seasons.[38] Time and space were immediately apprehended, yet were public (or more accurately *social,* because it was a group experience) and also normative. Time was composed of bits of the universal order of comportments that occurred in

[33] Westrup, *op. cit.,* Vol. III, pp. 216–217.

[34] *Ibid.,* p. 219.

[35] See above, note 4.

[36] See above, note 7.

[37] This is an uncertain enterprise because the Chinese system of knowing did not give rise to the kind of logical analysis produced by the Greek system of knowing. Accordingly, ancient records must be interpreted in the light of the Chinese concepts that analysis shows were implicit in early Chinese thought before valid comparison can be made with early Western concepts. Marcel Granet has attempted such an analytical statement of Chinese concepts in his *La Pensée Chinoise* (Paris: Albin Michel, 1934). It is not possible, of course, for one who is not a Sinologist to make a definitive judgment as to the success of Granet's attempt. However, a strong inference that he is generally correct can be drawn from the fact that, if he is correct, then many aspects of traditional Chinese society are seen as sensible implications of basic beliefs, whereas, if he is not correct, these aspects are inexplicable or are explained away as mystical foolishness—as many modern investigators, both Western and Chinese, have done.

[38] Granet, *op. cit.,* Bk. II.

the proper sequence. Space was composed of bits of the universal order of comportments that occurred in the right geometrical distribution with respect to each other. Time was weak or strong, depending upon whether or not it was composed of bits of comportment that restored the sensed experience of universal solidarity. "Duration is truly itself, entire and dense, only at occasions enriched by life in common which mark illustrious events and seem to establish time."[39] The festivals and hierogamies restored the vitality of time and renewed the rhythm of the universe. Space was full or diluted, depending upon whether the correct distribution of comportments occurred within it. Beyond the area of the civilizing influence of the proper order of comportments there existed only an "uncultivated space which supports only some imperfect beings."[40] Space and time, it will be noticed, contained, not just the comportments, but the proper *order* (sequence or distribution) of those comportments. "Time and space are always imagined as an ensemble of groupings, concrete and diverse, of *sites* and *occasions*" where and when it is proper for comportments to occur.[41]

The concepts of time and space show quite clearly that the source of the animating and ordering power was believed to be either in the sites and occasions where and when the universal oneness was experienced or in the total order that was only partially immanent in these particular events. The main stream of Chinese civilization has always centered attention on the social and the immediate, not upon withdrawing from the world in order to experience the timeless. Therefore, the latter is ruled out, and this makes it quite probable that the Chinese thought of the sites and occasions where and when universal oneness was experienced as the source of the animation and order in the universe.

We are now in a position to compare the answers of early Greek natural philosophy and the implicit answers of early Chinese thought to certain basic questions:

Question	*Greek Foundations of Western Civilization*	*Early China*
What is real?	The real is stuff (material).	The real is social.
Is it one or many?	A sensed one.	A sensed one.
Divided or undivided?	Divided.[42]	Undivided.[43]

These answers were to a great extent presaged by the differing answers given to the question of the source of the animating and ordering power. The answer that the real is stuff is likely among a people whose attention is directed to controlling their environment. The answer that the real is social is likely among a people whose attention is directed to the collective experience of sensed universal oneness. The answer that the real is divided is almost neces-

[39] *Ibid.*, p. 107. [40] *Ibid.*, p. 92. [41] *Ibid.*, p. 89.
[42] John Burnet, *Early Greek Philosophy* (London: A. & C. Black, 1892), pp. 10–11.
[43] Granet, *op. cit.*, pp. 147–148.

sary among a people who believe that the animating and ordering power over stuff is present in a high degree in particular men. The answer that the real is undivided is quite likely among a people who have a liturgical, social theory of time and space.

In turn, these answers, to a very great extent, presage the differences between Western civilization and Chinese civilization. When the real is believed to be properly ordered comportments, thought is likely to be concentrated more on "categories of relationship than on categories of substance."[44] Most important of all, when the real is believed to be undivided, lovers of wisdom are not driven by contradiction, as the philosophers of the West were, to posit objects other than sensed objects, or to examine objects as discrete entities with attributes of their own. If stuff is a one and divided, the question arises whether it is infinitely divisible. Logically, it should be. But Zeno's paradox shows this to be impossible. If points have extension, an infinite number of them could not be contained in a finite line. If they do not have extension an infinite number could not compose any line at all. But when it was said that the real is a material, sensed many, the contradiction of incommensurable magnitudes arose. If there are indivisibles with magnitude, and numbers refer to such objects, then every line must be composed of some whole number. Yet, it was discovered that the hypotenuses of certain right triangles cannot be expressed as whole numbers. Democritus proposed to avoid this contradiction by putting the incommensurability in the sensed world and positing a real world, known rationally, which contained the indivisibles with magnitude. Although this particular solution was soon rejected in favor of Plato's solution, which accounted for arithmetic incommensurables within the real world, yet the use of postulated objects has remained a unique feature of Western science.[45]

Because the Chinese never held that the real is divided, they never met the contradictions. There is evidence that they were aware of the right triangles whose hypotenuses bothered the Greeks, though the date is questionable.[46] Far from being a bothersome contradiction, however, these triangles were used by the Chinese in an ingenious demonstration of the way in which the actual dimensions of the universe were adjusted to the unchanging normative dimensions, by the dimension of the emperor used as a gnomen.[47] The Chinese investigation of Nature that was developed on this base was brilliant for its time. In fact, it was surpassed in the West only yesterday.[48] Its method was acute investigation of relationships between objects. I believe that Northrop is right in his characterization of the concepts of this system of knowing as being confined to the immediately sensed,[49] so far as objects are concerned.

[44] E. R. Hughes, "Epistemological Methods in Chinese Philosophy," in C. A. Moore, ed., *Essays in East-West Philosophy* (Honolulu: University of Hawaii Press, 1951), p. 57.

[45] Burnet, *op. cit.*

[46] Granet, *op. cit.*, pp. 261–262.

[47] *Ibid.*, pp. 263–267.

[48] Joseph Needham, *Science and Society in Ancient China* (pamphlet), Conway Memorial Lecture, London, 1947.

[49] F. S. C. Northrop, "The Complementary Emphases of Eastern Intuitive and Western Scientific Philosophy," in C. A. Moore, ed., *Philosophy—East and West* (Princeton: Princeton University Press, 1944), p. 168.

However, I am convinced, by a thorough study of Granet's account of the basic concepts of this system of knowing, that relationships that had not been observed were postulated (in rather crude ways, such as tables of correspondences or the play of numbers representing categories of related objects) and that the usefulness of relationships so discovered was a form of verification.[50]

The limitation on this way of knowing is strong evidence in support of Northrop that the Chinese never went behind sensed objects to postulated objects. All of the early discoveries made by the Chinese[51]—and which have occasioned much speculation as to why modern science did not develop in China—will be found to be based on relationships between objects, or combinations of objects, observable by the senses. The limitation of this type of system and the contrast between it and Western science with its postulation of objects and relationships is striking in the case of gunpowder. Gunpowder is a *mechanical* mixture of saltpeter, charcoal, and sulphur. By crude experimentation or accident one could discover gunpowder by dealing only with the proper comportments (proper ways, or *tao*) of sensed objects. The improved smokeless powder, or guncotton, of the West is another matter. Guncotton is "a series of cellulose nitrates, the highest and most explosive member of which may be represented by the formula $C_{12}H_{14}O_4(NO_3)6$."[52] Guncotton is a *chemical* compound, which can be fully understood only by knowing the *tao* of postulated objects behind the sensed objects.

We are now in a position to see the causes of the charteristic attitudes toward law and politics in the West and in China. From the earliest beginnings of Western civilization, a central purpose of society has been *power*. All authority was put in the hands of the house-fathers because they had the active power of the original house-fathers and had access to the gods who controlled physical events. When the universe and men became rational, the central problems of law and politics became, and remain, the just distribution of power and the effective maintenance of that distribution by corrective justice, as Aristotle foresaw.[53] The central purpose of Chinese society was the establishment and maintenance of universal *harmony*. Law and politics as separate pursuits or disciplines were little developed because the affairs of man did not receive a sharp focus of attention. Human activities ought to harmonize with the universal order of comportments. The river has its *tao*, the same as a man.

The desire to accomplish these central purposes naturally fostered the development of attitudes calculated to aid that accomplishment. In China, actions that violated norms were wrong because they disrupted the harmony of the universe. Injury caused others by such actions was not of primary concern. Therefore, the area that the West calls private law was almost non-

[50] Granet, *op. cit.*, especially Bks. II, III.

[51] Joseph Needham, *Science and Civilization in China* (Cambridge: Cambridge University Press, 1954–1956), Vol. II, pp. 327, *et seq.*

[52] Webster's New International Dictionary.

[53] Aristotle, *Nichomachean Ethics,* D. P. Chase, trans. (London: J. M. Dent & Sons, Ltd., 1911).

existent. The injured person who demanded compensation and took the wrong-doer to court to get it would only be further disrupting the harmony that ought to prevail—especially if close relatives were involved, such as brothers. John C. H. Wu reports, as typical of law in traditional China, the case of the neighbors who brought to court a dispute over the ownership of a chicken. The magistrate asked each party what the chicken had been fed that morning. One said beans, the other rice. Whereupon the magistrate ordered the chicken killed, and his stomach opened. There were beans in the stomach. The man who had said rice was punished.[54] The fact that the proper Chinese way would have been peaceful mediation and compromise does not mean that there should have been compromise as to the norms of ownership. It was simply that a second disruption of community harmony would not restore the harmony lost by the first disruption. Not only should the harmony of human relationships be maintained, but also the harmony of human activities with events of Nature. Severe punishments, especially death sentences, were not carried out in the spring, when life is awakening. They were carried out in the fall, when Nature is causing "the decline and the arrest of the forces of life."[55]

In the West, the just distribution of power is disrupted by actions that injure others. Since it is a primary purpose of law and politics to maintain this just distribution, the injury suffered by the victims of the wrong-doing is of primary concern in Western society. The logical corrective action is to restore the just distribution as nearly as possible. This is done by requiring the wrong-doer to compensate his victim in damages, or to return what he has taken, or to do certain acts that will stop or repair the injury. Since action by society to correct the injustice must be initiated by the injured person, and since that correction is a primary purpose of society, it is essential that an attitude of demanding justice, of "sticking up for one's rights," should prevail. Because a misuse of power has caused the injury, it is socially necessary, and appropriate, that the organized power of society should be brought to bear upon the wrong-doer to enforce the judicial decision and compel him to correct the injustice. Therefore, an attitude of approval of the use of force for *corrective* justice is necessary to the successful operation of Western-type legal and political norms. Indeed, it is the application of the organized power of the community to compel compliance with the explicit, public casuistry embodied in the legal norms that has produced man's best protection against the arbitrary use of power.

The use of force in support of distributive justice is another matter. In this area are the many difficult problems generally referred to under the rubrics of minority problems and revolution. When force is used in support of distributive justice, the purpose is to coerce compliance with norms held by those persons whose organized power is used. But the persons coerced are not willing, as a matter of principle, to accept those norms. This is radically different

[54] John C. H. Wu, *The Art of Law* (Shanghai: The Commercial Press, 1936), p. 50.
[55] Jean Escarra, *Le Droit Chinois* (Paris: Librarie de Recueil Sirey, 1936), pp. 11–12.

from the use of force against persons who are not principled dissidents but wrong-doers for selfish purposes.

I find nothing in the nature of the concepts resulting from Greek science that would support approval of the use of force to settle a dispute over which system of norms will be used to organize a society. I do find in the older tradition of the West support for such an attitude. If personal possession of the power that animates and orders the universe and access to the gods who control physical events is determinative of who is entitled to have authority, then success in battle proves the *right* to prevail, and not just the *power* to do so. Approval of the use of force to settle disputes over distributive justice is an attitude appropriate to the earliest stage of Western civilization. It is inappropriate in a mature stage, when the premises that fostered it have been long since rejected.

QUESTION: Is your characterization of Western society as power-seeking accurate, or is it a reading back of recent history? It would seem to be true of the past two or three centuries in the West, but did the people in the early period of Western civilization think of themselves as organizing society in order to achieve the power to control their environment? And is it not a distortion to speak of "distributive justice" as being concerned only with the distribution of power? Does not this idea include the just distribution of wealth, respect, and other values?

ANSWER: Let me say immediately that I was not seeking to set down an accurate summary of what Western legal and political writers have said about the nature of law and politics in the West. I wanted to confine myself to the philosophical ideas and the social ideals that captured the imagination of enough people so that they were acted upon and therefore had substantial effects in Western societies. We are discussing the relation of philosophy to practical affairs. For this purpose, philosophical ideas are irrelevant if they have never become the directing ideas in any society.

With this in mind, I believe there is reasonable accuracy in such statements, for instance, as that the West generally gave an anthropomorphic interpretation to the animating and ordering principles or forces and that China generally did not. This does not deny that contrary currents of thought existed in each instance. Of course, any evaluation of such complex data is a matter of judgment, and judgments of reasonable men may differ. I think that the nature and the central importance of the auspices show that a primary purpose of earliest Western society was to make the greatest use of the power over events that could be obtained. With the Greek classical writers, the central importance of power appears more in the discussion of human nature than in the discussion of social organization. While Aristotle originated the concept of distributive justice and discussed it to some extent in terms of the just distribution of power among members of the community, his primary discussion is in terms of the just distribution of the powers of the individual person to take actions that reason shows him to be right. It should be remembered, too, that Aristotle viewed ethics and politics as two parts of the same subject. With the Stoics, especially, but also with Aristotle, virtue (personal and political) comprises an element of will that executes the right actions learned through rational knowledge of the *Summun Bonum.*

Power as a purpose of society was doubtless quiescent during the Dark and Middle Ages. But the fundamental conceptions of human nature and the universe that sparked Greek natural philosophy are the same conceptions that sparked Western law and politics. The seeds of modern science, with its great potentialities for power over Nature, were planted by the Greeks though they lay quiescent for centuries. I believe the same is true of Western law and politics, and that a central purpose has always been—although for centuries more or less quiescent—the organization for power over natural and human events, and the development of effective controls over the power sought to be generated. For these reasons, then, I do not think the statement that a primary purpose of social organization in the West has been power is beyond the limits of inaccuracy necessarily present in any broad generalization.

As to the view that "distributive justice" refers to the distribution of other values than power, let me say that, from the legal and political points of view, the important thing is always whether persons do actually receive, use, and enjoy the goods that they have a right to receive, or whether someone who has the power to interfere—but no right to interfere—prevents that reception, use, and enjoyment. In this sense, all law and politics are concerned with using power to keep power within the boundaries of justice.

QUESTION: We have heard much of dichotomies—the West is rational, the East is not rational; Western norms are universal, Eastern norms are particular. Is there really such a sharp contrast between traditional Chinese law and Western law?

ANSWER: I believe there are fundamental differences between traditional Chinese law and Western law and that these differences stem from differences in fundamental conceptions accepted in the two instances. I am not asserting, however, such a sharp dichotomy as the question poses. I do not agree with Dr. Northrop that the norms of Chinese law were arrived at by mediation. Chinese ethics was highly developed, and its norms were taught in the home and in the school. The correct way for the son to act toward his father in a given situation was the correct way for all sons to act with respect to all fathers. If the son did not act in the way prescribed by the norm, he violated the norm. Everyone knew the norm and recognized the violation. The mediation that followed was concerned with what should be done about the violation; it was not concerned with establishing the norm for action of this son toward his father in this situation. Therefore, the norms were not mediational. They had universalness and absoluteness within the categories to which they applied. Mediation occurred after violation because universal harmony would be disrupted a second time if litigation were resorted to. Dr. Wu has stated the same thing a little differently in saying that China had a system of duties, but not a system of rights. The father did not have a right to compel his son to obey the norm, but the son had the duty to obey the norm. Therefore, the norm was established prior to a behavior situation between a particular son and a particular father.

QUESTION: Is Western law as rational as you suggest? Isn't the human element present at all?

ANSWER: I think the human element operates at two stages in the legal and political process. The first stage is in the adoption of legal and political norms. I do not believe that the relation between philosophical ideas and legal or political norms is a logical relation, that the latter are deduced from the former. I believe that, in a crisis situation, when things have become so bad that change has become acceptable, and someone gets the notion that a philosophical idea (which he may distort or be only vaguely familiar with) implies or requires some new social organization or action, and the apathy for the old and the asserted authority of the new result in its acceptance, then a social result of a philosophical idea is born. Later, as trained persons study the implications, corrections in the social result may be made if the society has provided institutions through which community wisdom of this sort can be utilized. In this way, a society, over a period of time, can be reorganized according to a radically different, technically complex system of knowing, although scholars who know the virtue of the new could never get the support of revolutionary masses, and revolutionary leaders could never fathom epistemology.

The other stage at which the human element operates in the legal and political process is in the application of legal and political norms to the affairs of daily life. In a practical sense, all law is made by humans and applied by humans. (Even "revealed" law is revealed to humans, to the best of my knowledge.) Therefore, the qualities of goodness, mercy, honesty, love, devotion to duty, etc., that make humans better humans will make judges better judges and lawyers better lawyers. The knowledge of human fallibility is a constant ameliorator of the rational rigor of the law. Further, I believe that in Western society, or in any society, men are rational only when they have to be. A lawyer argues his case step by logical step to the judges of the appellate court, who are trained to examine matters in this way. But the great trial lawyers talk to the jury in a seemingly rambling, disconnected way, telling ancedotes, drawing homely analogies, quoting the Bible and Shakespeare. They know that the average man is not accustomed to thinking in a logical, connected way.

There is a much more serious aspect to man's reluctance to be rational. I believe that legal and political norms are more often limits than initiating guides to the actions of men. I mean by this that the average man never thinks about the law as long as he is "doing all right" and is not made too uncomfortable about it. When injured persons or his conscience raise obstacles, he has consciously to decide whether to continue that course of action or take up another one. Then his own higher good, and the common good, as well as gain, may become factors in the decision. The decision will be affected by qualities of his character, by the pressure brought upon him by persons gaining or losing by his actions, and by persons whose only interest is in seeing that the norms of the society are obeyed. It is the task of this latter group, the "forces for law and order," to hold the balance and keep society from disintegrating into the chaos of unlimited struggle for selfish gain. This disinterested group can rally and prevail only when there is consensus as to the justice of the community's norms. And it often seems that the brink of chaos must be approached before enough persons will rise to perform this civic duty. Little Rock is a recent example. Law and order have to be preserved from day to day by enough persons rising above personal gain and convenience to act or support action in accordance with the common good as rationally discovered and culturally transmitted.

QUESTION: Why do you say that the common good is rationally discovered? One need not go through a process of reasoning to know that it is bad when large numbers of persons in industrial slums are starving because their wages are too low, or to know that legislation requiring minimum wages is good. What one needs is to care, not to know.

ANSWER: Certainly one needs to care, but the community needs also to have possible alternative actions related to accepted fundamental principles in order to preserve other values in the community. This is another instance of the way in which legal and political norms act as limits, and not as initiating guides to community action. In exactly the situation referred to, starvation wages and miserable working conditions in the wake of the industrial revolution, the Supreme Court of the United States required that it be proved that minimum-wage and maximum-hour laws have a real effect in protecting the health and welfare of workers and that the need for such protection was great. Only when it was convinced that these two facts were proven did the Supreme Court hold wage and hour laws valid. Until then the Court had held these laws an unconstitutional abridgment of the fundamental right of free contract.[56] Maximum-hour laws for women were held constitutional in 1908 in Muller v. Oregon, 208 U.S. 412. Minimum-wage laws, which the Court considered a more direct interference with the contract relation between employer and employee, were not held constitutional until 1937, in West Coast Hotel Co. v. Parrish, 300 U.S. 379.

It may be objected that the only purpose served by the Supreme Court's rational scrutiny of the proposed legislation was to delay remedial action and let many people suffer in the meantime. To answer this objection one must call attention to the potentialities of the alternative—no responsible weighing of proposed action against authoritative first principles. English legal and political history provides an instructive example. In the first half of the seventeenth century the English kings used their royal prerogative to prevent many injustices that would otherwise have resulted from the operation of the strict rules of the common law. For instance, a man ousted from his land could not plead in an action at law that the title had been taken from him by fraud, so he lost it to a defrauder. But, sitting in equity, and acting on natural justice, the Chancellor would order the defrauder in the King's name not to prevent the rightful owner from retaking and using his land on penalty of fine or imprisonment. There was a great growth of equity in this period, with great benefit to the people. However, a moment's reflection will lead to the realization that the first half of the seventeenth century was also the period of the infamous Star Chamber in England. The kings asserted that their prerogative could override the common law. They used it to do great good. They used it to do great evil. The English decided by revolution that they would rather have limited power in the monarchy.

[56] If it be questioned whether the principle of free contract was rationally discovered in the first place, I would say it was in the roundabout way outlined in the first part of my answer to the preceding questions.

FRANK H. KNIGHT

Philosophy and Social Institutions in the West

I.

Discussion of this topic is best approached in historical terms.* The variety of philosophic views held in either the East or the West makes it hard to speak of "the" philosophy of either region; the regions themselves have vague bounds as well as internal differences, and there have been important historical changes in both. But these have been vastly more "fundamental" in the West than in the historical East, before Westernization set in. The general history of culture in Europe—and particularly Western Europe (and its "colonies"), the region actually to be considered—has been distinguished by a fairly sharp periodization, recognized in the textbooks and treatises. Ignoring less important "breaks," account must be taken at least of classical antiquity (taken as a beginning), the Middle Ages, a period of monarchical States which has no familiar name better than mercantilist, and, finally, the age or period of "Liberalism." They were separated by fairly short and distinct intervals of revolutionary change—the "decline and fall" of the classical civilization, the Renascence, and the Enlightenment, or Age of Reason. Each of the four epochs was marked by fairly characteristic institutions and world view, more or less definitely expressed in its recorded philosophy.

My main concern will be the fourth epoch, as what I mean by "the West," and with the ideas and ethos embodied in liberal institutions, rather than explicit statements of philosophers. I shall pay little attention to classical antiquity, as its great advances in civilization were lost in the succeeding Dark Ages of extreme primitivism. And I shall argue that the resurgence of civilized life following the Middle Ages was less a literal "renascence," a

* Note: It is suggested that Part I of this paper (the first half) be regarded as "background" and only Part II as matter for discussion.

rebirth, than a new birth, a development along different lines. Of course, there were significant survivals, and more important revivals; but I think they served more as a stimulus than as a model for imitation. So, I shall use the term "renascence" chiefly in a chronological sense. I hold that—at least apart from the field of fine arts, which I do not discuss—importations from the East and creative innovation in the West itself were together more important for the major changes and the sweep of history than was the rediscovery of classical culture. The importations, about which more will be said presently, are a reminder that account should be taken of the Near or "Middle" East, from which the post-classical West took its dominant religion, out of which its philosophy slowly differentiated. And, incidentally, the more important revivals finally accepted in the field of ideas were largely transmitted to the West by Muslims and Jews.

History merges into evolution; and in that connection some further observations are in order, partly to indicate a personal position, which is bound to color more or less the whole presentation. There is much truth, along with literary exaggeration, in the statement of Ortega y Gassett (he was paraphrasing William Dilthey) that "man has no nature, what he has is, history." Philosophy must surely deal with "man," the human mentality, and should have cognitive truth and relevance to general human problems, intellectual and practical. It is not merely a form of entertainment or one of the fine arts. Looking at man as the resultant of age-long development, his nature clearly consists of "layers," which have been added more or less successively, one at a time, yielding, as it were, a stratified deposit. He is a physico-chemical body, a living organism, an animal—he is biologically the "highest" species, so far, in an ascending series. On all this, a uniquely human mental nature has been superposed by later evolution. One thing that strikes me as decisive about Eastern and Western thought (modern Western) is that the latter takes account of the fact that man is basically an animal, while the former fails to do so, or does it in a radically different way—in the idea of *saṁsāra*. However, this difference in particular is one of Western history rather than of geography: Plato believed in the transmigration of souls, and the doctrine seems to have been prevalent earlier in Greece.

It surely follows that the concept of reality, particularly as regards man, must be *pluralistic,* associated with the conception of "emergent" evolution. The essence of the emergent view is that "stages" of evolution introduced categorical novelties, somehow (usually) superposed upon what existed previously (rather than a replacement) but not to be accounted for in terms of the same concepts. A brief sketch may ignore the earlier breaks, even the appearance of organic life; but it must note the supreme discontinuity, the emergence of consciousness. This clearly cannot be explained in "physical" terms, nor in those of the main accepted theory of organic evolution—the chance occurrence of "mutations" and natural selection of those highly exceptional ones which happen to be favorable for the survival and increase of a species. Thus new strains arose, sometimes becoming distinct varieties, and occasionally new species. In the human species, when it was established, this had not occurred. There is much prejudice to the contrary, but truth-seeking students are dropping the conception of races of man, since no one can list them, or name any one that will be generally accepted as valid. The next emergent to be stressed is "culture" (in the anthropological meaning). Somehow, animal instincts were attenuated into vague "drives" and were replaced as to concrete content by "social inheritance," through imitation of their elders by the young of each new generation. This substantially achieved the advantages of "inheritance of acquired characters"; and these are so great, in flexibility and speed of adaptation, that biological evolution apparently ceased, many thousands of years ago—or may since have been more or less retrograde.

It is "culture" that primarily distinguishes man from other animals, particularly as associated with the acquisition of language, for there lie the differences most significant for the project of synthesizing or reconciling, or understanding, the divergent philosophies. In contrast with biological convergence, resulting in a practically uniform human species, culture has shown the opposite tendency, to wide divergence, which is illustrated by the multiplication of languages over the earth. Another vital fact about culture and the attending mentality is that its change and differentiation—again illustrated by language—cannot in the main be explained in terms of biological usefulness, for survival and increase. Human behavior comes to be motivated, taking the form of conduct, which commonly involves use of means to achieve ends. The mental attitude and activity of "reason," by which men adapt acts to ends, itself shows a limited tendency to universality. But more important for understanding human nature are the emotions, which provide the ends. These diverge widely and obstinately, particularly as they come to be less and less directly or visibly connected with the biological "ends." First, with advancing civilization, thinking tends to become less instrumental, in any realistic sense; more "playful" seems to be the best description. But, in addition, when men do think instrumentally, they rather typically use their minds to circumvent Nature, and also society and its laws, on which they are utterly dependent, for in them man lives and moves and has his being. Instrumentally, civilized man has largely inverted the natural and undoubtedly the original relation between his body and his mind. In place of the mind's serving the body, functionally, biologically, he treats the body and its life as a means to some preferred kind of mental experience.

All this cannot in general be termed "bad," as it involves the whole higher purposive life of man—good or bad according to the case and the standards of judgment—which exhibits the most important culture divergence. Greater uniformity of basic standards has now come to be imperative for world civilization or humanity; and that is, I suppose, what is practically meant by the project of "synthesizing" Eastern and Western philosophy. ("Reconciling" would seem to be a better term for it.) Certainly, culture differentiation, in relation to world-wide mobility and communication, with conflicting loyalties, has created "awful" problems, and so has the remarkable diversity among individuals in desires and ideals that has appeared in the "free" society of the modern West—no longer held in unison as formerly, though on a small scale, by the more disciplinary institutions of preceding epochs. (But it went far enough in Greece to cause decline, after a short century or so of brilliance achieved under comparative freedom—a fact that is ominously suggestive, in the light of kindred symptoms that the liberal epoch may be taking a similar course.)

Treatment of the body as the slave of the mind has often gone on to the repudiation of the body as far as possible—the notion of a "war" between the flesh and the spirit. This has had profound consequences, social as well as intellectual; it has been used to justify slavery, or an equivalent class or caste order, in which the "good life," that of the philosopher or priest, is essentially parasitic on the mass of society. Here one should go back of philosophy to religion and consider the relations between the two. What can be said is somewhat speculative, but it seems clear that religion is historically primary and philosophy differentiated out of it—much more fully in the West, until the separation is in practice essentially complete under Liberalism—another major contrast with the East. (In medieval Islam, philosophy grew out of medicine.) In the first epoch of Western thought, the Greeks made progress in this separation but it was lost in the Dark Ages, as philosophy disappeared in dogmatic theology, to reappear gradually as we approach modern times. Primitive religion was typically magic, and "crudely" utilitarian in conception and intention. (This is still seen in the West, in numerous superstitions—for an unbeliever including prayer, for any tangible result.) Religion is directly relevant for our "historical approach," because the West considered is Western Europe, which, at the close of the classical epoch, became a theocracy. Conditions were different in the Eastern part of the Mediterranean region, where the "Roman" Empire survived into the Renascence centuries, and under Islam, as this power took over there (and in much of what had been the Western Empire) and finally extinguished Byzantium (except for Russia). As far as I know, the nations of the (far) East have never been under ecclesiastical rule, and hence could not undergo a revolution against it; and the fact of such a reaction in the West goes far to account for its difference from the East, after it occurred.

As has been suggested, I find the best way to characterize (recent) Western thought and institutions is to contrast them with conditions in the Middle Ages, and to do that by summarily sketching the course of change through the transitional interval. I contend that "medievalism" was, in essentials, more "Eastern" than the culture of the East itself. In particular and first of all, it was more "religious" in several respects. In both, thought was "mystical," but in the West theistic-supernaturalistic, whereas the East was intuitional, in a sense that seems to me much like early-Christian gnosticism. Both systems (groups of systems) centered around the objective of "salvation," to be achieved through "believing" the "truth," and so being made "free" (for

Christendom, see John 8:32). Salvation was "from" the world of everyday experience, which was viewed in completely pessimistic terms, but "for" another life very differently conceived in East and West, as was the belief or knowledge instrumental to it. In the West, "faith" was equally independent of evidence, but had to be supported and supplemented by revelation, from an anthropomorphic Deity called Creator and Father of everything. The West had "Heaven" and "Hell" in place of reincarnation in a higher or lower order of life, or eventual "release," hard to distinguish from oblivion. It seems fair to describe the Eastern view as unworldly, in contrast with the Western as otherworldly. Any delineation pretending to accuracy would have to consider innumerable subdivisions of doctrine, and make subtle distinctions in the meanings of terms; and it should also go into the relations between scholastic theory and everyday practice—and between the lives of different orders in society.

Monasticism played a greater role in the life of "Christian" Europe, though the general pattern was imported from the East, and was given a more extreme interpretation in Eastern than in Western Christendom. Its devotees are necessarily parasitic, but the Roman Catholic version produced a dualistic ethic by which the masses could be saved in a life beyond by one of vicarious atonement in this world. In both regions, devotion to a religious ethic of renunciation allowed the utmost luxury of living on the part of potentates. The Roman Church invented the doctrine of Purgatory, with intercession by the living for the souls that had passed on; the agency of the Church was needful and its service in procuring forgiveness of sin came to be sold as "indulgences." This grew into the scandal that helped to precipitate the "Reformation." I have not run across any of this in accounts of Eastern thought, which was, in general individualistic and internalistic, while the Western (pre-liberal) system centered on a corporate body, "The Church," as the authoritative dispenser of salvation and custodian of all significant knowledge. Both powers, or missions, were held to have been conferred by a divine commission, with the revelation of truth. Another item, familiar in the West but seemingly not found in the East, is belief in miracles, in the past and as current events—another ground for the characterization of the West as differing from the East in being similar in principle but "more so."

The concrete transformation that occurred in the West, by which its modern culture is to be described, amounted to an inversion of fundamental values—an *Umwertung aller Werte,* to use a Nietzschean expression. Conformity-and-obedience in an essentially "static" spiritual and social order—the latter naturally one of more or less rigorous hereditary classes or castes—was replaced by another pair of intimately connected ideals, freedom-and-progress, i.e., freedom for progress and progress through freedom. Freedom is inherently individualistic, while social as well as individual progress was to result from individual freedom. India, if not China, had a more rigid class structure, but inheritance of status in Europe was similar in principle. The level of culture, for the masses, was in both regions about as low as possible, but the East had a far more cultivated aristocracy. The extreme character of the culture revolution in the West is no doubt partly explained as a "pendular" reaction; it was, of course, influenced by the surviving tradition of classical greatness, and more by increasing contact with the Byzantine and Islamic East, where much of the ancient culture had survived and received some further development.

As already indicated, the transformation, which I shall call the "Liberal Revolution," occurred in two fairly distinguishable stages. In the first, at the time of the Renascence, two major changes came about. The first was the secularization of political power—though the Roman Church had been as much a political as a religious body. Further, it was a partial secularization, but turned out to be crucial. The second event was a first step toward progress and freedom of thought, represented by the new scientific movement. Both need discussion at a length impossible in this paper. The fundamental achievement of the revolution as a whole was "Freedom of the Mind" (Professor Bury's phrase) from tradition and authority; but it came gradually and fitfully and in relation to several movements. The secularization, such as it was, came rather earlier than the liberation, as the culmination of a long struggle between political and ecclesiastical authorities (in Italy, Ghibellines versus Guelphs). Concentration of feudal power in the hands of territorial princes gave rise to "States" in something like the modern meaning, and these succeeding in securing domination over "The Church," or whatever churches survived the awful turmoil of the Wars of Religion following the so-called "Reformation"—the revolt of what came to be known as Protestantism. It is a puzzling fact that generally in history (prior to liberalism) the authority on which order was based has typically been exercised by an uneasy partnership of these two forms, contending about as much as they have cooperated, often in open war; and this is strikingly true of European and West-European history, since the "conversion" to "Christianity" marking the close of the classical era. This point has been stressed by J. N. Figgis; Gibbon called the conversion "the triumph of barbarism and religion," and Fr. Cumont has argued that classical polytheism had already disintegrated under the spread of "mystery cults," of which Christian "churchianity" was essentially one.

The victory of the States was about as definitive in countries that remained Catholic as in those that became Protestant; his Catholic majesty the King of Spain also kept a firm hand on his clergy. But, for other reasons, the sequel was very different in Britain and on most of the Continent. The secularization was limited in that everywhere the new States were absolute monarchies under dynasties ruling by divine right (*Dei gratia*) and they had no intention of being less autocratic than the prelates of The Church had been—and were much less "enlightened" than these were before the Protestant Revolt brought on the Counter-Reformation (Council of Trent), which took them back to medievalism. The partial secularization was important because the military competition in which the States found themselves forced them to tolerate and even quietly encourage both science and trade (science as the basis of a rational and progressive technology), as sources of new wealth, the sinews of war. Historically, too, the political authorities have tended to be less dogmatic in opposing change than the ecclesiastics, more disposed to consider ways and means to their ends—which centered in power, as in the case of The Church. In any case, in Britain after the Civil Wars (which were largely wars of religion) the course of history was set toward democracy, while, on the Continent, the settlement in the treaties of Westphalia (coincident with the execution of the Lord's anointed, Charles I) fastened on the peoples the twofold "sovereignty" of the State over the individual and of the prince in the State. Britain became the main home of the liberal movement. After the definitive triumph of Parliament over Stuart absolutism in Britain, there is not much for us to notice here, in politics; through most of the eighteenth century, Europe was preoccupied with dynastic and colonial wars. Toward the end of the century began the second stage of the "revolution." Trade and science progressed, chiefly in Britain, where they had much more freedom, and the two undoubtedly furnished the main dynamic of progress toward liberalism. There, too, the literal "renascence" was much less distinct from the Enlightenment, the enthusiasm for ancient learning and art less prominent in comparison with scientific and political interests.

The second great event of the Renascence period, and doubtless the definitive one in destroying and replacing the medieval system, was centered in science. In Britain in particular (Gilbert and Bacon) this was from the first bound up with applications, in sharp distinction from science in antiquity. But the first great specific step toward progress through the liberation of the mind was the "Copernican Revolution" in astronomy. Its importance lies, not, as commonly pictured, in the new picture of the solar system, but in the fact that it forced recognition of radically *new* knowledge, and so, finally, destroyed the belief in eternal and immutable truth, particularly as given once for all by revelation. (Copernicus had forerunners in antiquity, whom he recognized, and others in centuries then recent, which had been voices crying in the wilderness of a dogmatic-ritualistic religious culture.) As put forward by Copernicus, timidly and in a "half-baked" form, the new view might not have taken hold; that result may well be attributed to Galileo and his telescope, which revealed visual proof to anyone who would look that neither the Bible nor Aristotle could always be believed.

Incidentally, it is a puzzling fact that religions have had to teach weird mythologies, purporting to explain the origin of things and the whole past, taking the place now filled by science and history. But that raises the large question of what religion is "for" anyway, its "function," or "why" otherwise intelligent people strenuously hold one doctrine to be true and others false. But men's reasons for believing, or asserting, are not a cheering inquiry, and are too complex to go into here. I merely note that critical reflection is a late product of advancing civilization—when it occurs at all—and that human and social problems arise in large part because man is naturally more romantic than rational, and at least as much anti-social as social. (Hobbes is more right than Aristotle.) He is the lawbreaker of the known world, and the "liar," and shows strong anti-social traits even in the small-scale tribal society that is his natural milieu—and far more in the large and heterogeneous agglomeration of a modern nation—or the world, which increasingly has to become an orderly society, if civilization or the race is to survive. Man was evolved in, by, and for an environment very different from that which modern civilization has quite suddenly produced; to live in the latter he needs to learn many new things and new ways and acquire new attitudes.

It is significant that man first adopted the rational attitude toward Nature, and fields of natural phenomena about which he does not propose to do anything in the way of control, of changing the "natural" course of events. Astronomy is the type; and Vesalius' empirical treatment of anatomy, which is also practically unamenable to change, appeared in the same year, 1543. Also, about the same time came notable advances in mathematics, another subject-matter of the same character. That reminds us that underlying the new intellectual advance were many technological innovations, and many of the most important were imported from the East. The lens itself is said to have been long known in China, and it was the telescope and microscope that most directly forced the revolution in knowledge. Probably most important of all, in the long run, was the "Arabian" arithmetic and algebra; the former intellectual achievement was brought from India and introduced into Europe at the beginning of the thirteenth century (two decades before the birth of Thomas Aquinas, who gave its definitive form to "medieval" thought). In Europe it was put to practical use; without it, neither modern science nor modern business would be possible. Yet it made headway slowly; it was just coming into use in Britain three centuries later, when the "voyagers" were discovering "the world," previously unknown in Europe and its existence denied. Next in rank would be paper-and-printing (they should be associated) already known and used in China for many centuries; and there were gunpowder and the magnetic compass, and still other achievements.

The great original innovation of the West was the twofold tie-up of science with technology, and in science that of empiricism with measurement and mathematical analysis. Here the work of Copernicus had to be substantiated by Galileo and completed by Newton; and Francis Bacon must also be named—he was preaching progress through the mastery of Nature by science at roughly the same time that Galileo announced his discovery of the "Medicean Stars" (satellites of Jupiter) and the sunspots. It may have been the Reformation in Britain that saved him, and Newton also, from the fate of Giordano Bruno just a few years before—or at least that of Galileo, who was forced to recant, and spent his later years in house arrest under clerical surveillance. But none of these men looked toward democracy, or general freedom of the mind, or challenged the supreme place of religion in society. Newton spent his later years working out fantastic interpretations of the Book of Revelation; and Bacon wrote the famous pronouncement that "the more absurd and incredible any divine mystery is, the greater honor we do to God in believing it. . . . " That seems to be the essence of religion, in the tradition of Christendom; it is the duty of unquestioning belief, regardless of facts and logic, without asking why one should believe one doctrine rather than another. It is no wonder that the inquiring and critical attitude made headway slowly, even in the knowledge of Nature—or that the "war" started over again in 1859, when Darwin and Wallace promulgated the theory of biological evolution (where skirmishing still goes on)—or, especially, that a critically objective approach to social problems is still struggling to be born.

Nor is there anything surprising in the tooth-and-nail resistance to such progress put up by the custodians of "sacred" and (therefore) eternal and immutable truth. (Sacred truth cannot change unless God changes his mind, which seems to be a contradiction in terms.) In particular, believers in salvation by belief in a prescribed creed and performance of prescribed ritual will persecute, torture, and kill recalcitrant "heretics" if they have the power; any other course is a confession either of insincerity or of impotence. This practically applies to any belief in absolute right or truth; yet the "intellectuals" of the Western world still commonly repudiate the relativity of knowledge, which is simply one of the obvious facts of life. The idea that there is such truth need not be harmful, if not associated with belief that somebody knows what it is; but it seems to be virtually inevitable psychologically that those who believe in it go on to assert that they have it, or know who has. Then, in case of disagreement, it is surrender or fight, or the defeated party surrenders after a fight, if still alive. That obviously cannot be the meaning of freedom in society; final truth must be something to be pursued rather than possessed. This has come to be recognized in science, but it percolates slowly into men's minds with respect to truth about man, history, morals, or politics, where its own "truth" is much more obvious and important.

The more conspicuous changes came about in the second stage of the revolution, at the time of the Enlightenment. Most conspicuous of all were the democratization of the absolutist governments and radical economic changes resulting in part from what is referred to as the "Industrial Revolution," centered in Britain in the late eighteenth century. Another movement which is not much talked about but which I think contributed much to making that country the home of liberalism was the vogue of sports, before and after the seventeenth-century Restoration of the Stuart Dynasty. "Sportsmanship" seems to me actually and necessarily a fundamental moral ideal for a free-and-progressive society, and it is categorically alien to the main previous moral tradition, particularly as taught under Jewish-Christian religious auspices. Empirically viewed, the grand result for the nineteenth century was a dualistic social order of political democracy and the system of free markets and private enterprise as a largely independent "economic order" in that sector of men's active life. Both were manifestations of the general ideal of individualism (so-called), and there was a close connection between the two in the historical events of the period. These included commercial and colonial wars, particularly between Britain and France. The victory of the former, statistically a much smaller and weaker nation, was largely that of free enterprise over political bureaucracy; and it was the resources created by the new industries and commerce which made possible the defeat of Napoleon. Of course, many factors complicated the situation.

Outstanding in the political history of the period were the American and French revolutions. Of these, the former was surely the more important in the historical long-run and along with and in the light of other American happenings was probably decisive for the future of liberalism. The war was won with the aid of the French monarchy, but its result was a republic which grew rapidly in power and prestige, and was progressively liberalized. The suffrage was extended—finally made universal for normal adults—slavery was abolished, and free education introduced, now everywhere recognized as indispensable to free government. Another major American contribution was formally complete religious freedom, through separation of Church and State, which has been laggardly followed elsewhere, or hardly at all. A free society must be a secular order, since civilized men will not freely agree on supernatural dogmas. The problem is agreement where it is important, at least where it is necessary.

II.

With freedom of thought and expression goes freedom in conduct, virtually as a corollary. The libertarian world-view is this-worldly, centering largely in the effective use of means by individuals to achieve freely chosen ends, and so achieve a better life. Its moral essence is the right of each to be the final judge of his own ends, meaning both personal desires and ideal values, in a spirit of fair play; there is no implication of "self-interest" in a bad sense. In fact, the contrary is implied in the faith in progress through freedom. It means voluntary association, on terms fixed by agreement or assent of the parties. Each must, of course, respect the equal freedom of others; it cannot mean the right of one person to infringe on the freedom of any other. That restriction has always been taken for granted, to be enforced by compulsion where conscience and intelligence do not suffice. The "basic" freedom is that of discussion, in which ideally all meet as equals. Next most important is voluntary co-operation for the more effective use of means, which implies the organization of activity through free enterprise, already mentioned; but any plurality of people are free to arrange for any terms on which they may agree.

The whole change in the social ethos may be summed up as the replacement of the maxim "be good" by that of "be intelligent," taken primarily in the broad instrumental meaning of acting—choosing among the alternatives open—as individuals and groups, in such a way as to achieve the best results, selected by critical evaluation. In more comprehensive terms, the maxim is:

be good intelligently. In the intellectual life, it calls for believing only on the basis of a critical appraisal of evidence. Insofar as medievalism had a place for intelligence, it meant "rationalism," something very different from instrumental rationality. It purported to mean knowing by "intuition," plus a little deductive inference; the beliefs stressed actually arose in the creative imagination, were supported by wishful thinking, and became embedded in a tradition finally sanctified and enforced by the most cruel penalties that could be devised. Allegedly rational knowledge had to be supplemented by revelation, and both were declared and interpreted by the divinely commissioned Church, whose major premise in action was maintenance and extension of its own power. In morals and politics, "reason" meant "natural law." Whether this or "divine law" has a close parallel in Eastern thought, I do not know. The injunction to follow Nature permeates the thought of China, and could, I should say, be interpreted into the Indian systems by an appropriate definition of the concept of "Nature." (In the West it is vague enough to be used in a formula for promoting nearly any doctrine.) It is doubtless "natural" for any society to have *some* law; but, as to the relevant question of *what* law, the only one to be called natural is that which actually exists at a time and place—or perhaps a *jus gentium,* to be found in a number of systems somehow coming into contact. "Natural" is also used to distinguish between the fiat of a legislator and either customary law as a "growth" or the laws some writer thinks "necessary" for any social order to exist. In their enthusiasm for freedom from tradition and authority, the Enlightenment thinkers went to absurd extremes, to virtual anarchism, dominated as they were by an utterly "romantic" conception of the innate rationality and goodness of men. The result was a reaction, beginning at once, early in the nineteenth century; and it has been growing ever since, shifting the mainly negative view of the role of law and government over to more and more positive action. (More will presently be said about that.)

As to problems, medieval and Enlightenment theory alike had no room for any, in the strict sense, either individual or social, but the views rested on opposite grounds. The former envisaged a "static" moral and legal order; and, if laws are immutable, men will naturally know what is right, learning that as they learn their language. They would not, indeed, *do* right, because of original sin, and so needed rigorous control by authority—and to question its identity or jurisdiction was the worst of crimes. Also, the "given" laws, or the divine source of law and authority, provided the technique for enforcement as well as the norms to be sanctioned. Thus, only moral choices between good and bad were open to anyone, and the word "problem" refers to questions to be dealt with intellectually. Enlightenment inversion of the notion of original sin also endowed the individual in a different way with all necessary knowledge, and also with good will, logically leaving neither a role for authority nor problems for anyone to solve. The position logically implied the anarchist ideal. This, I understand, was the position of Confucius; but I am acutely aware of ignorance of the theory and practice of law in the

East—and that is where I think one finds the "true inwardness" of a social order.

Any serious inquiry into the philosophy of the West, from the Greeks to the present, would have to give extended consideration to the theory of knowledge, particularly from the standpoint of intelligent social action. Knowledge should be brought into relation with error and sin (intellectual with moral judgments) and with choice, or "the will"; and these should be considered in relation to aesthetic taste, the third member of the familiar value-triad. Aesthetic criticism is chiefly a creation of the modern West. Beauty is interesting in ways variously connected with social life, but has relatively minor practical importance for problems of community action. Disagreements in this field rarely give rise to serious conflicts. Beauty has not been considered an absolute, as have truth and right, nor in particular as divinely ordained and sanctioned—and the matter of taste hardly enters into the conception of the Deity, whose perfection in knowledge and goodness is so much stressed. The popular view is that of *"de gustibus non disputandum,"* which has only limited validity in that field, and has some, if less, in the other two. Investigation of values and value-theory might well start from the question, how far intelligent people ought to agree in their valuations, of the several species. It would soon appear that the distinction between facts and values also has limited validity—in both directions: values are facts, in a sense, and any serious question about facts is a question of values—of "evaluating" evidence. The important distinctions are those between different species of value. Again, for special reasons, but very different ones, disagreements in the field of "science" as knowledge of Nature also only exceptionally present serious social problems, in comparison with factual disagreements about man and society, which much more intricately involve value-judgments, though all matters of truth are value-problems.

What remains for this paper to undertake is a survey of nineteenth-century revisions of the institutions and the underlying and supporting philosophy that came out of the Enlightenment—changes forced by historical events. The theory of liberal society is "individualism," which is generally used as a close synonym for liberalism; and that is proper enough, logically and etymologically, since freedom pertains primarily to an individual mind and will. In fact, the "Anglo-Saxon" tradition in particular has carried repudiation of any "social-mind" concept to an indefensible extreme, for the reality of group will, choice, and action is inherently a part of the notion of a free society. Rousseau is famous for stressing this point, though he failed to work it out and apply it intelligibly to a workable social order. The theory of a society based on mutual agreement (misleadingly called "contract" by Sir H. S. Maine) between individuals began almost at once to break down in Britain, in a way that it seems would have been foreseen, and a reaction set in which has been extending itself ever since. It stands in manifest, not to say absurd, contradiction with unalterable facts of human life. The breakdown began at the most obvious point, in the relations between adults, or adult "society," and young children, where the theory itself is, to repeat the word, simply absurd. And this is more or less the case with some helpless men, and many wretched women; the scandal of women's work in mines, added to that of children in the textile mills, started official reaction with the first British factory-acts. Since that time, the movement has continued and expanded, through more and more political "interference" in the working of the "economic order." That has been the main current of such change as can at all be attributed to deliberate action promoted and directed by thinking on a national scale and with respect to internal policy. Action touching international relations must be ignored here, in spite of its current magnitude and the repercussions on internal policy of war and preparedness for war.

A major result of the liberal revolution, establishing the freedom of culture in its various aspects and of economic life and political democracy, is a revolution in the nature of thinking about social change. Very recently and suddenly, in historical terms, societies have begun to think, with general participation, about their own nature and problems and consciously to direct action to deal with the latter. Prior to the advent of the idea of progress, such serious thinking about society as was done at all was done by a few individuals, and was chiefly apologetic for the established order of things; it involved little historical explanation, and that of a very naive kind. Anything like modern objective and interpretive history, or especially culture-anthropology, is a very recent development. The idea of progress stimulated both study of the past in a new way and effort to look to the future with a view to prediction, adaptation, and control. Democratization of government expanded all this to the social scale and made it "responsible." Popular sovereignty virtually created the right to change the laws in any fundamental way, inhering in "the people," practically without limit. The revolution itself, particularly the second stage, which wrought the major changes, must be attributed in part to thinking and discussion of a sort, along with impersonal culture-historical forces. Even for the Renascence changes, one can find, or make, a theory with some validity, rooted in intelligible motives; and, at the Enlightenment stage, "individualism" has quite a simple theory. The difficulty is that in many respects it is out of accord with basic and unalterable facts of life.

The fundamental discrepancy, already suggested, is that individual liberty takes as "given," as making up society, individuals with their actual interests—desires and ideals, and their actual capacities for acting, including internal abilities and "property." The social theory, in short, is mutuality or reciprocity between given individuals. This is largely false to facts and impossible, on two obvious grounds. First, responsible individuals as they are, capable of active participation in social life, are not given; both their wants and their capacities are in concrete content products of the working of social processes. Second, an implication of the same fact, freedom has no meaning for infants, unformed and unendowed, or for other dependents, who make up half, more or less, of the population of a continuing society. Human beings are *not* born either equal or free—unless equal to zero; they have potentialities, which are highly unequal, but have "natural" rights only in the sense that any society does and must grant and secure to its members *some* rights, if it is to continue to exist as a society. (My right to life means only that no one has a right to kill me, unless he has that right!) The real question is: *what* rights, in detail, and how are they to be implemented? One general right required in order to be human is some degree and kind of freedom, together with some opportunity for action; and this must include some control of means, without which freedom is empty—and also some endowment with civilized tastes, implanted through culture contacts and education. Again, the question is: *what* freedom, and what power; both must exceed strict necessity, biological or social, if the future adult is to have a responsible part in the life of a free society, and a reasonable share in the benefits of advancing culture. In a democracy, with "government by discussion" (Lord Bryce's definition), fundamental equality is implied.

Neither freedom nor equality, nor even an effective right to life, comes to people by natural process. They are not found in animal societies, and only to a minimal degree in most human communities known to history. The common situation has been slavery or closely equivalent hereditary status. The American Declaration of Independence, famous for the principles cited, emanated from slave owners and was issued on behalf of a nation which maintained slavery for nearly a century afterward. This exemplifies the glaring inconsistencies that characterize the political thinking and practice of Western liberalism, making it hard to find any fairly definite and effective working philosophy. Its first pretension is to exclude inheritance of status in favor of equal opportunity for everyone born to find his own position in society. This presupposes an equal start in life, and no detailed analysis is needed to show that both are impossible. But no democracy tries very hard to live up to its professions. The necessity of compromises between ideal freedom-and-equality and other values or needs is aggravated in practice because the revolutionary struggles against tyranny made freedom a "word to conjure with." Its resulting potency for propaganda use has led to other goods and rights being fallaciously defined into the term—especially the right to possess and control economic means, which should be judged on its own merits as a different dimension of the field of voluntary action. In consequence, the meaning of the words "liberal" and "liberalism" has been inverted; they have largely had their original reference to liberty replaced by its opposite, State paternalism. The fallacy is evident: the correct *definition* of freedom is negative—no interference by others with anyone's doing what he wants to do and can do, or could do in the absence of "coercion," which is the term needing definition. "Positive freedom" implies *power*. But the definition does not mean that freedom will give people happiness or well-being, or the rights they "ought" to have and that a society ought to grant or secure. A Crusoe is entirely free, but is not therefore to be judged better off than he might be in a social order subjecting him to many restraints and obligations.

Ranking ahead of freedom and the means to make it effective is *order*: some form of "law" is essential for a human society to exist—though it may reject freedom by establishing a despotism. The latter has in fact been presented as the best possibility in post-medieval Western thought (by Thomas Hobbes, in mid-seventeenth-century Britain). The self-interest of a dictator would make it expedient for him to supply some other values. Every person would inevitably have some freedom, and some control over means—even a slave. A third requisite is some degree of *efficiency*, hence, a workable economic organization. A fourth is personal *security*, which is implied by order; but order and security come into conflict with freedom, and freedom's relation to efficiency is ambiguous—though freedom is empty without these complements. Fifth, as has been stressed, freedom is tied up with *progress*. The sixth essential is *justice*, a human craving that must be met in some form and degree if a society is to persist—especially a free society, which radically changes its nature, from a basis in hereditary status to chosen relations between individuals. In practice, those of economics set the most serious problems, more so than that of dealing with crime. Finally, for intelligent management of its affairs, a free society must consider "culture," in the meaning of a "high" civilization, with progress, aesthetic and "spiritual," and science for the sake of understanding as well as for use as a means.

Manifestly, the problems of a free society, now confronted in the West, can be met only through compromise, not merely between conflicting individual interests but between many "valid values," most of which must imperatively be recognized and implemented, up to some point. A society can be free only insofar as its members can freely agree on courses of action, or on some procedure for indirectly reaching agreement, beyond that produced by subconscious historical forces and "free" discussion. But, the problems and human nature being what they are, ideal discussion presents difficulties; and, worse, thinking has been *ad hoc*, opportunistic, a patchwork of expedients, largely misdirected. People "naturally" tend to deal with symptoms, evading serious diagnosis and a long-run view of consequences. Human nature, as it has evolved through the ages under utterly different conditions, is averse to the effort to solve problems through intellectual co-operation. The recognized need for agreement prompts trying to get others to agree with "me"—hence persuasion, sales talk, rather than real discussion. It tends to run into moralizing, blaming somebody, then into a quarrel and appeal to overt force. Modern liberalism makes the first serious attempt in history to base social order on free choice rather than tradition, and to minimize compulsion—especially in large units. The West (and the world) still fails to realize the difficulties raised by the commitment to freedom and related values.

The method of action, to repeat, is discussion; it is inherently "free and equal," the type for intelligent association. But discussion, regardless of the subject-matter, confronts severe limitations, even with "the best will in the world." First of all, it depends on *inter*-communication; but, while one person can (more or less effectively) communicate "to" a large number (with modern aids to any number who will pay attention), one can attend to only one other at a time, and no invention will change that fact. In consequence, discussion must be organized; but that presupposes both law—"rules of order"—and an authority with power to enforce the rules. Moreover, the knowledge, or the possibility of knowing, necessary for intelligent action, is very inadequate.

For group action, the members must *agree* on several items: first, on the ends to be sought, the social ideal envisaged for the future. (This means a *direction* of progress, not a "goal"; there is no "perfection" in human affairs.) Another requisite is agreement on what can and cannot be done. This depends on knowing historical laws of cultural change; but it is hard to know the facts of past history, and far harder to learn from them to distinguish what is inevitable and must be taken as given from what can be changed, still not mentioning the main use, to predict the future. A third necessity is knowledge predicting the consequences of any action considered, the difference it will or would make, in contrast with inaction. This is clearly relative to the "natural" course of future history, which hardly has definite meaning for human beings and especially for large political units. Only a very few "antinomian" anarchists contemplate absence of all politico-legal action by "States," and their picture of social life envisages quite primitive conditions. (When a theoretical anarchist gets a chance at power he usually strives to become a dictator; Marxism is an example, and its prototype, the historical Western Church, is essentially another.) However, common sense is not wholly in the dark about the effects of such laws as a democracy "can" enact and administer—it has surely been more right than wrong on the whole—and systematic fact-finding and analysis can add to such knowledge. The problem raised is that of the validity of "social science"; this, unfortunately but perhaps inevitably, is split up into several competing disciplines, vaguely defined and at best overlapping in content. Most directly relevant would be criminology and economics, with the others in an auxiliary though necessary role, while as to relevance all are auxiliary to jurisprudence, including "politics," as the master social science. (The possibility of a general science of "man," biological and psychological, or of society—sociology—is a problem too vast to be considered here.)

Criminology is less able than economics to predict the consequences of legislation in their respective fields. As to method, the latter is really two sciences, one abstract-deductive, based on axioms, the other empirical. Both yield solid and useful knowledge, though far less accurate and reliable than the physical sciences. The greater predictability of the results of political-economic action over criminal law is connected with a different technique of enforcement. A government in power can forcibly deprive individuals of property or income and use the proceeds to subsidize, or to conduct by its own officials, any activity that it judges needful and not performed (or not in the best way) by the market machinery. The distinction from punishment is not sharp, and may be "psychological." Pecuniary fines are used as a penalty for law-breaking, and the victims, even of a mild prison sentence, have sometimes described the sacrifice as the price paid for an indulgence, and averred that this was worth the cost.

The hardest knowledge-problem is the one first mentioned, agreement on ends—what institutional change is desirable, considering the cost. Intelligent social action must not only adjudicate conflicts between its living members, but must look to the distant future, to the living children, and beyond, to the well-being of the unborn and the level of civilization. The problem is "progress," and in particular moral progress, or progressive morality. This is so different from "morals," as a relation between "given" right and wrong, that a different name is imperative. "Ethics" might serve for this distinction. "Morals," in use as a close synonym, would be kept for its etymological meaning, conformity with the *"mores,"* or customary law, viewed as not subject to change. Ethics will then cover all the values entering into a "higher" civilization, standing for the best dynamic balance where these clash among themselves.

The most serious ethical problem actually calling for action is that of economic or "distributive" justice. It is the most controversial aspect of the relation between democratic politics and the economic order of markets and free enterprise—though it cannot be sharply separated from other aspects of this general problem. As already noted, freedom involves a radical redefinition of the concept of justice. In pre-liberal society, its final meaning was conformity to law, jural or moral, taken as given. (This meaning is embodied in the word, as *jus* means "law.") Liberalism poses the vastly harder problem of justice "of" the law itself, implying higher standards—not absolute, but subject to constant revision. Like other rights and duties, economic justice is no longer a matter of inherited status, but of relations between free individuals, all, in theory, equal before the law. As we have seen, such equality is impossible, notably as between adults and children. Inherited inequality is clearly unjust, by individualistic standards, but it can at best be minimized, not abolished. The family and social milieu into which anyone is born must largely affect the way of life open to him. And, in fact, democracies do not try as they might to reduce the injustice or provide "deserved" inequality or equality of opportunity.

The main thing to be said, at the end of a long paper, about distributive justice is that the problem is typical in having no possible "solution," other than the "best" compromise among conflicting ideal principles. The first of these is the norm of "productive contribution"—each participant in a social economy to receive what his activity adds to the total output. This result the enterprise economy will achieve, insofar as it works in accord with the theory of "perfect competition." This norm, that each shall receive the consequence of his acts, has moral-ethical validity: "What a man soweth that shall he also reap." Moreover, only limited divergence from it is possible, since only what is produced can be distributed and consumed. The market machinery actually works far from perfectly, and the first set of social problems arises in that connection. But far more serious are the ethical limitations of individualism as such—most obviously as regards the rights of unproductive dependents. A difficulty is presented by "property," especially inherited wealth. Too much has been made of this. There are other ways of accumulating productive capacity, and of passing it on to heirs, and, besides, there is no clear difference in principle between inheriting property and family advantages or contacts—or even genetic traits. The general problem roots in use of power in any form to acquire more power. Thus arise a tendency to cumulative growth of inequality ("To him that hath shall be given") and the unequal start in life that is the outstanding individual injustice. Much has been done to mitigate the evils—most notably through free education of the young, at the cost of the parents judged most able to meet it, and through inheritance taxation. Such action involves applying norms other than the productive contribution of individuals. The most obvious principles are "need," in relation to ability to meet others' needs, and "equality," at least reducing the extreme inequality that "naturally" results under free competition—much distorted as this is by various "machinations," power-seeking, monopoly, and "luck" or things beyond individual control. All three principles have to be taken into account, thus limiting any one; and there is no formula except good judgment, for the best balance, or for the best way to achieve it.

To conclude, I add some notes on the alternative to free association, particularly in markets—which is "politics." Government is the agency by which a democracy acts as a unit and takes responsibility for its destiny. The "first commandment" for intelligent action is "Compare the alternatives," beginning with understanding what they are. Much unnecessary evil comes from the disinclination of people to do that, particularly in this case. They commonly prefer subjective snap-judgments, rooted in self-interest, or some "romantic" prejudice—rather typically blaming uncritically the economic system and looking naively to "the government" to correct any alleged wrong. Objective comparison would show that the two organizations are much alike in basic respects—politics is much more irrationally motivated by competitive persuasion—while in others one or the other can do things or yield advantages the other cannot. Human nature being at all as it is, a primary objective must be to minimize the scope of necessary agreement. That obviously means two things: first, dismissing uniform belief about supernatural reality, and all compulsory dealings with supernatural powers; and, second, in matters economic, maximum reliance on the free market, except where political methods will *clearly* yield better results. The market order has the supreme merit of freedom. It provides for voluntary co-operation of individuals in using what means they have to achieve their freely chosen ends, without agreeing on ends or methods, and with "boundless" increase in effectiveness. In a competitive market, no party has arbitrary power over another, since each may choose between equally good opportunities, by dealing with the "other" who offers any better terms. Accordingly, it is a first task of society—not an easy one—to enforce by law and government a close approximation to effective competition. An exchange *is* an exchange, and is advantageous to both parties if they are competent to manage their own affairs. Only this system can provide freedom of choice to both producers and consumers. For reasons already suggested, by itself it falls far short of meeting even social necessities, still more of ideal justice; but further development would call for a treatise on elementary economics, which cannot be thought of here.

On the other hand, the most democratic government cannot afford comparable freedom. At the utmost, some majority dictates to minorities, and in political reality to express and enforce a majority opinion is often impossible. For freedom, there must be a presumption of voluntary association—in particular, the free market. However, many necessary things can be done only by society as a unit, and others political action can do better. One necessity is suppression of organization for power in contrast with efficiency. Beyond what has been said, further elaboration is impossible. The only general prescription is intelligent comparison of agencies on particular issues and adoption of the best method in each case. More of such effort would do good, especially in stopping much palpably stupid action.

Two important generalizations are very inadequately understood by the public. The first is that a free society under modern conditions is largely a tissue of *agency* relations. In particular, the personnel of government are the agents of the public in all matters delegated to them, and the "management" of business enterprises are the agents at once of the consumers and the final producers, those who supply the labor and property services employed in the operations. The problem is to find the best method of choosing agents and holding them responsible to their principals. In both business and politics, the method is competition; the difference lies between centralized decisions under rules hard to change and decentralization with flexibility. In both fields, the agency structure is required for effective management of the large and complex units needed to apply modern technology or to deal with its problems. But the agency relation prevails widely, is nearly universal, in consequence of the specialization of knowledge, required for its growth. An illustration, where no organization in the usual meaning is present, is the relation between a patient and his doctor. The latter is the agent, but, while the relation persists, he has *power* over his principal—in this case, power of life-and-death—and every agent has more or less discretionary power. The only freedom possible to the patient is that of choosing his doctor, and changing doctors at will; but—the second generalization—this choice cannot be made very intelligently. The patient would have to know extant medical science—annulling most of his need for the service—and also know both the technical and the moral qualifications of the available candidates.

All of these conditions apply to the employee-employer situation, and that of the consumer to the enterprise, and also, though not in quite the same sense, to the citizen and his representatives in the government. Everywhere, the freedom possible to the common man is that of selecting an agent who will be his "boss" to a greater or less extent, over a longer or shorter period.

Competition governs the selection, even in the case of the doctor, and fixes the delegated powers and the payment to be made. What needs to be understood is the severe restriction this ubiquitous agency-relation places on rational freedom in general—for similar considerations apply to the basic freedom, that of knowledge or belief. Most of what anyone knows, or thinks, if not an accident of tradition, is taken from some chosen authority. Thus, most serious questions place the free man in the paradoxical position of having to judge between others he recognizes as more competent on the issue than he is. But this limitation is the condition of having the residual freedom that is possible, with the vast progress in most fields of endeavor that has been seen to follow its establishment.

DHIRENDRA MOHAN DATTA

Political, Legal, and Economic Thought in Indian Perspective

I. THE PHILOSOPHICAL BACKGROUND

The basic philosophical concepts guiding Indian political, economic, and legal thought can be traced, partly in germinal forms, in the Vedic literature (the four Vedas, the Brāhmaṇas, and the Upaniṣads) and partly in the later-developed systems of philosophy, Vedic and anti-Vedic, numbering about a dozen. During at least 2,000 years before the Christian era, there must have been a struggle among the conflicting ideas of the different schools, and the ones that survived and were harmonious got practically adopted by society and social thinkers. The literature on social philosophy, including political, legal, and economic thought, began to evolve and took definite shape before the Christian era. Social philosophy is to be found chiefly in some parts of the voluminous Great Epic (the *Mahābhārata*), in the many works called the Dharmaśāstras (*Sūtras* and *Smṛtis*), of which Manu's is the most important, in the eighteen Purāṇas, and in the more technical later works on polity called the Nītiśāstras (the science of Statecraft), of which the *Śukrānītisāra* is the most important, and in the allied works called Arthaśāstras, of which Kauṭilya's is the most exhaustive one available now.[1]

The Moral Conception of Nature

With the exception of the materialists, all schools of Indian thought, including the Buddhists and the Jainas, have a moral conception of Nature.[2]

[1] For an exhaustive survey of the vast literature of polity, law, and economics, see P. V. Kane, *History of the Dharma-śāstras*, Vol. III (Bombay: Bhandarkar Research Institute, 1946). Indian chronology is uncertain. Some tentative dates are: Vedic period, 2500–600 B.C.; Epic period, 600 B.C.–A.D. 200; Dharmaśāstras, same period; Kauṭilya's *Arthaśāstra*, between 321 and 296 B.C. (See S. Radhakrishnan and C. A. Moore, eds., *A Source Book in Indian Philosophy* (Princeton: Princeton University Press, 1957), pp. 193-223. *The Śukranītisāra*, Jivānanda Vidyāsāgara, ed. (Calcutta: Narayana Press, n.d.) of Śukra is placed by different scholars from pre-Christian times to several centuries after Christ.

They hold that all natural phenomena are guided by inviolable laws that ensure the conservation of moral values, so that human actions, good and bad, can give rise to appropriate effects, within man and in the outer world in this life or hereafter. Nature helps and ensures the reaping of the fruits of human actions. Action *(karma)* includes, not only the gross overt act, but also its subtler causal states in mind and speech. Early in the *Ṛg Veda*[3] we find the concept of *Ṛta,* the inviolable, eternal law which makes for order, regularity, and harmony in the universe, the law which even the gods obey, and in accordance with which the god Varuṇa metes out justice to man. It should be noted that *Ṛta* combines here the idea of a positive, natural law and that of a moral principle.

This moral conception of Nature generates in the Indian mind a deep confidence in cosmic justice. We find it reflected in the oft-quoted maxims: "Truth alone prevails, not falsehood"[4]; "The righteous side will have the victory"[5]; "*Dharma* kills if it is killed; *dharma* protects if it is protected"[6]; "The entire world rests on *dharma.*"[7] *Dharma,* which has among its many senses the meaning of morality, is etymologically explained as the principle of preservation—that which holds together and preserves the people. "By unrighteousness man prospers, gains what appears desirable, conquers enemies, but perishes at the root," says Tagore, following Manu (4.174). This unity of moral outlook, in spite of the diversity of metaphysical theories, supplies the common background to Indian culture.

Human Life a Rare Opportunity

Counterbalancing the possible defeatist attitude springing from the thought of life's transitoriness there is the common belief that, though the present life is momentary, the individual has a beginningless existence continuing through successive lives; his action in the preceding lives determines the quality of the succeeding one. It is foolish, therefore, not to utilize the present life for improving the individual's future possibilities.

Human life is regarded, therefore, as a great opportunity. "Rare is human birth," says the *Bhāgavata.*[8] "The human status is hard to attain," says the Buddha.[9] In the evolutionary scale of living beings *(jīvas),* the status of man is the highest and is obtained after a long series of incarnations.

[2] D. M. Datta, "The Moral Conception of Nature in Indian Philosophy," *International Journal of Ethics,* XLVI, No. 2 (January, 1936).

[3] *Ṛgveda* (Ajmer: Vaidika Yantrālaya, 1900), I.lxviii.2; I.cv.12; I.cxxxvi.2, *et passim.* (The numerals refer successively to *maṇḍala,* hymn, and stanza.) See Kane, *op. cit.,* pp. 244–245.

[4] The motto now adopted by the Indian Government.

[5] *Mahābhārata* (Calcutta: Bangabasi Press edition, 1909), Salyaparva, 63.60. (The numerals refer successively to chapter and stanza.) (P. Tarkaratna, ed.)

[6] *Manusmṛti* (hereafter *Manu*) (Bombay: Nirṇayasāgara Press edition, 1920), 8.15. (Amendator, V. L. Paṇśīkara.)

[7] *Mahānārāyaṇa Upaniṣad* XXII.1 (in *A Compilation of 120 Upaniṣads;* Bombay: Nirṇayasāgara, 1948). *Taittirīya Āraṇyaka* (Calcutta: Asiatic Society of Bengal, 1872). (Editors: N. R. Acarya; R. L. Mitra.)

[8] *Śrīmadbhāgavatam* (Calcutta: Bangabasi Press edition, 1920), 11.2.29. (Numerals refer successively to *skandha,* chapter, and stanza.) (P. Tarkaratna, ed.)

[9] *Dhammapada,* S. Radhakrishnan ed. and trans. (London: Oxford University Press, 1950), XIV.4.

Dharma as Man's Differentia

The differentia of man is not the mere intellect, which lower animals also possess to some degree. The oft-quoted verse runs: "Hunger, sleep, fear, sex are common to all animals, human and sub-human. It is the additional attribute of *dharma* (morality) that differentiates man from the beast. Devoid of *dharma,* man is like a beast."

It is necessary to understand the meaning of *"dharma,"* which has many senses, as does the English "good" or "law." These are brought under one principle by Bhīṣma in the *Mahābhārata* (*Śāntiparva,* chap. 258), which anticipates Kant's moral maxim. This basic principle of *dharma* is put positively and negatively thus: "What you desire for yourself, you should desire for others" and "What you do not like others to do to you, you should not do to others." Bhīṣma shows that falsehood, cruelty, theft, and other vices would be suicidal in practice—making the doer the victim of his own bad action, and would make society, the State, or any corporate existence impossible. So, *dharma* comes to be regarded as the principle of preservation as well. Though one in the abstract, *dharma* expresses itself in many new forms in different spheres of life.

The *Mahābhārata*[10] holds that the essence of *dharma* is self-control (*dama*). The human self is often described figuratively as the occupant of the body, its chariot:[11] the sensory-motor organs are the horses, the sensuous mind *(manas)* is its rein, reason *(buddhi)* is the driver. Self-control thus comes to mean the rational control of the body, the senses, and the mind, guiding it along the desirable path. *Dharma* supplies the principles for good guidance. The irrational impulses of the body, senses, and senseward mind express themselves in the life of animal propensities *(pravṛtti)*—hunger, sex, fear, etc. It is the rational guidance of *dharma* that tames them and harnesses them and saves them from running riot and from conflicts of selfish desires which may lead to ruin.

The Individual

Emphasis on the importance of the individual is common to all the Indian systems of philosophy. It is worthy of special note that even those who believe in God as the creator do not hold that the individual soul is created by God. God creates only the material objects, including the human body. But the soul is co-eternal with God.

For the Sāṁkhya, the individual soul, though ignorantly identified with the finite body, is essentially pure, infinite consciousness. For the Advaitin (the Vedāntin of the school of Śaṁkara), the individual soul is nothing but *Brahman* itself illusorily identified with the finite body. For the Jaina, every individual soul has the potentiality for infinite knowledge, faith, power, and bliss. Even the Buddhist, who does not believe in a soul as such, believes in the potential Buddhahood of every individual. For theists in general, the in-

[10] Śāntiparva, 60.9.
[11] *Kaṭha Upaniṣad* III.3.

dividual can attain spiritual freedom and God. And, for all, it is by using the opportunities of this life that the individual can realize its high destiny.

Every individual, every living being, thus comes to be regarded as a sacred center of potential value, deserving of respect and possessing freedom for unhampered progress toward its goal. Non-injury to life (*ahiṁsā*) is universally enjoined, therefore, by all these schools of thought as a fundamental virtue. *The individual's right to life and freedom of development is recognized as a fundamental right.* It results in the universal maxim: Treat everyone as yourself (*ātmavat*). From *ahiṁsā* also follow logically the other virtues (or duties toward every individual), such as truthfulness (*satya*), non-stealing (*asteya*), kindness (*karuṇā*), friendliness (*maitrī*), forbearance (*upekṣā*), etc. As all these may be logically deduced from respect for life, *ahiṁsā* is often described[12] as the supreme virtue (*parama-dharma*). The altruistic virtues and duties lay the secure foundation for a harmonious society in which individuals can respect and help one another and work out their respective spiritual destinies.

Individual and Society

We should briefly consider here the Indian conception of the relation between the individual and society. Is the individual the basic and independent unit and society a mere collection of individuals? Is society the primary reality, of which individuals are mere parts? Or are they both equally real and organically related? It is difficult to bring all Indian views under one type. But perhaps they are in some respects nearer to the organic view, with some reservation. For a rough description, we can call the general Indian trend *spiritual individualism through social organicism.*

Insofar as the individual is a self, it is a distinct reality; its spiritual freedom is the ultimate end to which its entire life's activities should be directed. But insofar as the self is embodied, and all its activities are through the body, subtle and gross, and the body is an inseparable member and product of the world of Nature, out of which the bodies of other selves also have evolved, there is an indissoluble natural bond between the embodied individual and all other such individuals forming the social corpus. In this naturalistic, empirical perspective, the evolution of the world of objects and human society is conceived in the *Ṛg Veda*[13] as taking place out of the body of the Supreme Person (*puruṣa*), the four castes being differentiated as his mouth, arms, thighs, and feet. The Person, however, also transcends the manifested form. In the later theistic literature and also in the *Smṛtis* and Purāṇas, we find the analogy of the Cosmic Egg (*Brahmāṇḍa*), out of which the world evolves by internal organic differentiation. Judged in this naturalist perspective, human society is a part of the cosmic organism, the phenomenal manifestation of God, and the individual human being is a part of the social organism.

The empirical bond of the individual to Nature and other beings finds

[12] *Mahābhārata,* Anuśāsanaparva, 116.38.

[13] Puruṣa Sūkta. See Radhakrishnan and Moore, eds., *A Source Book,* p. 31.

recognition in various ways. Nature *(prakṛti)* comes to be regarded by some theists as the mother, the consort of the Supreme Self or God, who is the father of all beings, and so the entire universe is conceived as one's own country. Again, in the five daily rounds of duties for the householder is recognized the multiple duty of the individual to his parents, from whom the body derives its existence, to the sages, who conserve and propagate the cultural heritage, to the deities that govern Nature, to the stranger-guest as a man, and to lower animals as fellow beings.[14] The individual can advance only by gradual steps through the hard disciplines of the life of a student, a householder, a retired spiritual aspirant, and, finally (for a *brāhmin*), a life of renunciation.[15] Manu repeatedly warns that one who tries to rush to the last stage of life without discharging the prior obligations to family and society goes down.[16] The individual requires maintenance, protection, and help even for spiritual realization, and therefore the economic, political, and legal organizations of society are deemed necessary.

The Integral Outlook and the Golden Mean

All through Indian thought one comes across an integral outlook—a serious concern for the self's ultimate end (*sādhya*) combined with a realistic appreciation of the graduated series of means (*sādhana*) by the proper cultivation of which alone the ultimate end can be attained. This is so important for a correct appreciation of Indian thought and culture that we should dwell a little upon it. In education, we find this outlook reflected in the attempt of the Upaniṣadic teacher not to reveal the ultimate truth all at once, but through graduated steps in strict relation to the present fitness of the student. Brahman, or *Ātman,* is revealed first as the body, then vitality, then sense-mind, then pure reason, and then bliss. The real, present, physical, mental, moral nature (*svabhāva*) of the individual determines his particular aptitude or right to know and do (*adhikāra*); it also determines his own sphere of duty (*svadharma*).[17] The fourfold division of society into the sage, the warrior, the trader, and the laborer is a natural division based on the recognition of quality (*guṇa*) and *karma* (action),[18] so far as the justifiable ideal behind it is concerned. Each class has its own well-defined duties in accordance with its own nature. But at the same time all have also universal duties (*sādhāraṇa-dharmas*) and virtues to cultivate, because of their common human nature and obligations. "Each one can achieve the highest end by sticking to one's duty."[19] The preaching of an indiscriminate equality of rights and duties is considered an unrealistic confusion of thought leading to social chaos.

The *Īśa Upaniṣad* realizes the great harm and imbalance that one-sided concern for the knowledge (*vidyā*) of transcendent Brahman can cause to the necessary life of duty, and to the lower empirical knowledge (*avidyā*), on which

[14] *Manu* 3.70. [15] *Ibid.*, 7.97. [16] *Ibid.*, 6.35; 6.37.

[17] *Gītā* II.31; II.33; *et passim.* See also Sri Aurobindo, *Essays on the Gita* (Calcutta: Arya Publishing House, 1945), 2nd series, chap. XX.

[18] *Gītā* IV.13. [19] *Ibid.*, XVIII.45.

normal life depends. So, it gives a stern warning against *one-sided otherworldliness* as well as to *one-sided worldliness,* and balances the transcendent with the immanent aspects of Brahman. "Into a blind darkness they enter who follow after ignorance, they as if into a greater darkness who devote themselves to knowledge alone" (verse 9). "Doing verily works in this world one should wish to live a hundred years" (verse 2). "That moves and that moves not, That is far and at the same time near; That is within all this and That also is outside all this. But he who sees everywhere the Self in all existences and all existences in the Self shrinks not thereafter from aught" (verses 5–6).[20]

This golden mean, based on an integral view reconciling the eternal with the transitory, knowledge with action, the individual's spiritual freedom with an active life in society, is taught again in the *Gītā,* in the *Mahābhārata,* and also in the Dharmaśāstras.

It is by re-emphasizing this integral view that the leaders of the modern Indian social and political renascense try to arouse the people to the spiritual ideal and moral life. Tagore, Gandhi, Aurobindo, Vinoba–all go back again and again to the *Īśa Upaniṣad* for inspiration. B. G. Tilak, Gandhi, Aurobindo, and Vinoba all write commentaries to interpret the *Gītā* in their respective lights–but all in support of a harmonious life of knowledge, devotion, and action.

Unity in Diversity

Most of the modern Indian social and political leaders constantly emphasize the Indian spirit of unity in diversity in their attempts to understand and reconcile the ideas and interests of the divergent racial, religious, and linguistic groups that compose the population of India and the world. What are the philosophical roots of this attitude in classical Indian thought? We can find in the Vedas and the Upaniṣads the idea that the same reality manifests itself in various forms (just as the sun's one white light is diffused into many colors), that the same reality is called by the names of different gods, that differences are only matters of names and forms whereas the underlying reality is the same, that all are destined to find their way back into the same reality (just as rivers running in different courses and directions become one in the sea). These monistic ideas developed along different lines in the many schools of the Vedānta, which can be broadly divided into two: the Advaita (pure monism) of the Śaṁkara school and the non-Advaita schools of theistic Vedānta. The first, which is more known to Western scholars (and even today thought by some as *the* philosophy of India), regards the reality (Brahman) underlying all phenomena (including what is sometimes called the "undifferentiated aesthetic continuum"[21]) as devoid of all distinctions and assignable predicates. The perceived world of diverse objects is only an appearance. Yet,

[20] Sri Aurobindo's translation in his *Isha Upanishad* (Calcutta: Arya Publishing House, 1945).

[21] By F. S. C. Northrop, in his *The Meeting of East and West* (New York: The Macmillan Co., 1947), pp. 335, *et passim.*

this phenomenal world is not groundless; it is grounded in Brahman, and enjoys a lower status of practical (*vyāvahārika*) reality, which is, however, higher than the status of illusory objects of everyday life, and higher than the utterly unreal (like the son of a barren mother). In spite of their uncompromising monism, therefore, even Advaitins allow degrees of reality and value, and think in terms of identity-in-difference in respect to all phenomena, including social ones. Identity is the ultimate truth, but differences are its appearances; and to be able to realize identity through diversity is a necessary and valuable step toward the ultimate truth. It is nearer the truth than the naive contentment of resting in sheer diversity. The theistic Vedāntins (who command the largest following among the masses) hold, on the other hand, that the diverse manifestations of reality are also real. Brahman possesses eternally diverse elements which become manifest in creation. Unity in diversity is, therefore, true even of the ultimate.

Among the pluralists, we may mention the early Buddhists and the Jainas. In a sense, the early Buddhists, who consider everything as unique, and admit no common positive universal, are the most uncomprising particularists. But the later Buddhist thinkers of the Mahāyāna school approach in many respects the Absolutist Advaita point of view and try to understand all phenomena as the appearance *(saṁvṛti)* of an underlying indescribable Absolute *(Paramārtha).* The Jainas not only believe in many ultimate reals, but also discover the innumerable real aspects of each real. They develop, therefore, in epistemology a *realistic relativism,* with a scheme of seven different kinds of possible logical judgments at the same time in respect of the same thing viewed in different aspects. This *logic of the manifold truth*[22] (*anekāntavāda* and *syādvāda*) exposes the weakness of every cocksure dogmatism that tries to monopolize truth. It is a pluralistic way of understanding and appreciating the possibility of divergent true views and lays the foundation of practical social philosophy that tries to accommodate different views and interests. Gandhi, and following him now Vinoba, advocates this Jaina logic in practical politics.[23] India's present foreign policy of *Pañca-śīla* (five rules of mutual good conduct), or *peaceful co-existence,* can be thought to stem from this pluralistic, realistic, relativist logic.

On the whole, then, we find that there is sufficient philosophical support, both from the monists and from the pluralists, for the spirit of reconciliation and synthesis that we find in Indian social and political thought.

II. PHILOSOPHY AS EMBODIED IN INDIAN POLITICS, LAW, AND ECONOMICS

We can now try to understand how the foregoing ideas influenced Indian political, legal, and economic philosophy. The very first thing that strikes one

[22] See K. C. Bhattacharya, "The Jaina Theory of *Anekāntavāda,*" in his *Studies in Philosophy,* Vol. I (Calcutta: Progressive Publishers, 1956).

[23] See N. K. Bose, *Selections from Gandhi* (Ahmedabad: Navajivan Publishing House, 1948), pp. 4,20; *Young India,* January 21, 1926; *Bhūdāna-Yajña* (Banaras), November 15, 1957.

is the fact that *dharma* is taken as the only sound basis of personal life, as well as of all social institutions and organizations. A good State and good government can, therefore, be based only on the principles of *dharma.* Even the more secular works on politics and economics, such as the *Arthaśāstra* of Kauṭilya and the *Śukranītisāra,* generally recognize the soundness of this view in spite of their occasional deviation from high moral standards.

Origin of the State

We have seen previously that man, the embodied self, is conceived of as possessing potentiality for infinite perfection, but as hampered by his ignorance, passions, and immoral tendencies generated by his own past actions. As he is, he is both good and bad.[24] It is the duty of the ideal State to create conditions and opportunities that will gradually help man overcome his ignorance, selfishness, and immoral tendencies, so that a harmonious community may evolve in which every individual can advance toward the supreme goal of *spiritual freedom*—freedom from ignorance and selfishness and all the vices and sufferings that follow therefrom.

Man without society, or society without a State, is never contemplated as a historical possibility or as a desirable ideal. We find occasional hypothetical speculation as to what would have been the fate of individuals if the State did not exist. Manu (7.20) surmises that "if the king did not vigilantly inflict punishment on the guilty, the stronger would have roasted the weaker like fish," for, he frankly says, "an absolutely pure man is rare in this world." Similarly, in the *Mahābhārata* (Śāntiparva, 15.30), Arjuna says: "If there were no Sceptre in the world, people would have perished. The stronger would have devoured the weaker just as fish do in water." This analogy of the fish (*matsya-nyāya*) has been generally employed by all political thinkers in describing the probable fate of a hypothetical Stateless state of men. In the *Mahābhārata* (Śāntiparva, 59) there is the mythical account of a kingless society in the golden age, and a subsequent degradation of the people leading to the necessity of their entrusting the protection of the land to a king, selected, at their request, by God. Similar mythical accounts are found in Buddhist and Jaina works in slightly altered forms. All these would point to a kind of social contract theory.[25] But such a theory is not seriously advocated.

The Sceptre (Daṇḍa)

In Indian political literature, the figure of the Sceptre *(Daṇḍa)* has come to stand, by a kind of metonymy, for the State—with its awe-inspiring and irresistible authority that rules by law and punishment. So, like the word *"dharma," "daṇḍa"* has various associated meanings, e.g., political authority, rule of law, punishment, etc. Political philosophy itself is sometimes called "the principles of the Sceptre" *(daṇḍa-nīti).* The Sceptre is idealized by Manu (7.14) as an original creation of God, out of Brahman's radiant energy, it being nothing

[24] *Manu* 12.10.
[25] See A. S. Altekar, *State and Government in Ancient India* (Delhi: Motilal Banarasidas, 1958), chap. II.

but *dharma* itself, the child of God and the protector of all beings. It is the prototype of all earthly political authorities. In a similar manner, Manu (7.3) speaks of the ideal king, the prototype of all kings, as being created by God to protect all beings from fear resulting from anarchy.

The royalists have sometimes wrongly interpreted such statements as supporting the divine origin of kings, and for inculcating implicit loyalty to particular rulers. But that such an interpretation is unsound is evident from the fact that Manu (7.26–31) and other thinkers[26] repeatedly point out that only the righteous ruler is worthy of the Sceptre, which itself destroys an unrighteous king, and the *Mahābhārata* even holds that a tyrant should be destroyed, as King Veṇa was in olden times. Moreover, according to most authorities,[27] the king or the State is not even recognized as the owner of the country. Though revenue was paid by the people, in kind or cash, it was in lieu of the protection and welfare services rendered by the State. Manu would almost support the principle: *No protection, no taxation.*[28]

The Three Values Subserved by the State

The political literature of India generally speaks of the threefold human value (*trivarga*)—*dharma* (morality), *artha* (wealth), and *kāma* (enjoyment)—and omits the last one, *mokṣa* (liberation), which, along with the first three, constitutes the fourfold traditional value (*caturvarga*) of Indian philosophy. Even the *Mahābhārata* (Śāntiparva 15.3) and Manu (2.224) speak of the threefold value and omit spiritual freedom (*mokṣa*), the highest end. We can think of two reasons for this rather secular attitude: (1) Though liberation is recognized as the ultimate goal, it does not enter directly into the immediate objects of social and political organization. (2) The concept of spiritual freedom—and of the path leading to it—differs from school to school, and political philosophy need not necessarily be affiliated to any one of these. The reasonable object of a liberal political philosophy is to lay down the broadest principles, free from conflict with morality (*dharmāviruddha*), on which can be founded an ideal corporate life conducive to the free pursuit of the higher spiritual goals in accordance with the aptitude and choice of the individual concerned. While it is dangerous for the State to allow the violation of the essential laws of morality, the State need not interfere with the individual's spiritual life.

We find in India a peculiar blend of a strict demand for social morality and conformity and a wide latitude for freedom of thought and choice in ultimate matters. And it is here that we can find also the ancient pattern of a *secular, but morally grounded, State,* free from religious sectarianism—the ideal of Aśoka[29] and Gandhi[30] and professed by the present Indian constitution.

[26] *Mahābhārata,* Śāntiparva, 59.94; *Śukra,* 2.274–275.

[27] See U. N. Ghoshal, *Agrarian System in Ancient India* (Calcutta: University of Calcutta, 1930), Lecture V.

[28] *Manu* 8.304–309.

[29] See Aśoka's Rock Edicts XII, XIII, *et passim,* in D. C. Sircan, ed., *Inscriptions of Aśoka* (Delhi: Government of India Publication, 1957).

[30] Bose, *Selections,* p. 224: "Here religion does not mean sectarianism. It means belief in an ordered moral

One-sided Economics, Hedonism, and Asceticism Reconciled

Some materialist economists in ancient India, as in the West, claimed that all values ultimately depend on wealth. Their case was passionately advocated by Arjuna, the great fighter, in the *Mahābhārata.* His long lecture is summed up thus: "Performance of duty (*dharma*), enjoyment of pleasures (*kāma*), and even the attainment of heaven depends on wealth, on which life itself depends" (Śāntiparva 8. 17). Interpreting wealth (*artha*) in the widest sense of all objects, including the earth, which constitute the means of subsistence, Kauṭilya also thinks of "wealth" as the foundation of human existence and the basis of the other two goals. The other extreme side is revealed in the ascetic disgust for wealth expressed in the *Yoga-Bhāṣya* (II.30) and in the *Mahābhārata* by Bhīṣma. The earning of money, its preservation, its loss, its expenditure, are all said to be sources of suffering. So, wealth is a great evil.

Manu (2.224) rejects, however, the different views that *dharma* alone, or that *dharma and wealth,* or that *wealth and enjoyment* are the most important values. He holds that all three, harmoniously cultivated, jointly constitute the threefold end of human life. This is the balanced golden mean of Indian social thought, which rejects both one-sided hedonism and one-sided asceticism. It represents the most influential current of social thought, too.

The State and Society

The State is primarily a product of society, and, therefore, it reflects the ideas and beliefs that dominate the society of a particular place and time. The early Indian State accepted for the most part the established notions of the four classes and the four stages of life, and their respective duties, privileges, and obligations. The State had among its obligations the protection of the established social order and the helping of every individual in the performance of the duties of his caste and stage of life. The four classes were assigned different kinds of work. This also involved an economic organization based on the division of labor. The classes were not originally very rigid and were not hereditary, but were based more on the quality and work of the individual. The Dharmaśāstras and even the Arthaśāstras expect the State to maintain the social order. The State had to recognize and maintain whatever inequalities of opportunity were prevalent in society.

But it should be remembered that, though the higher castes enjoyed higher social prestige, in the ideal State this prestige had to be earned by a higher standard of knowledge and conduct, and a greater sacrifice of material advantages and creature comforts. That the sole criterion of birth is unsound is realized by political thinkers like Śukra (1.38), who advocates the assignment of duties in accordance with merit and work (*guṇa-karma*). Moreover, Śukra holds that, instead of submitting to the trends of the age, the king, as the head of the State, should take the initiative in ushering in a new era to solve

Government of the Universe." Also, Gandhi, *An Autobiography* (Ahmedabad: Navajivan Publishing House, 1948), p. 5: "... the essence of religion is morality."

new emergencies, and should introduce new practices. In this, Śukra was only making a new application of Manu's idea that the king should be the maker of his age.[31] Whether it is to be a golden, silver, copper, or iron age depends on his initiative.

The Constitution and Multiple Functions of the State

Though there are stray references to different kinds of States (*gaṇa,* people's State; *saṅgha,* community State; *rāṣṭra,* territorial State; and *rājya,* kingdom) in Indian literature, the works on politics discuss only the constitution and functions of monarchical States. In Vedic literature, we come across terms suggesting different kinds of States like monarchy (*rājya*), diarchy (*dvairājya*), empire (*sāmrājya*), and self-rule (*svārājya*). There is an ambiguous term, *"vairājya,"* which may mean either "kingless State" or "good State." Two northern States (Uttarakurus and Uttara-Madras) are said to have been kingless republics. There were also later some federal republics, such as the Yaudheyas and the Licchavi Mallas. But monarchy was always the general and dominant pattern.[32]

Kingdoms varied widely, however, from small village and city-states to far-flung empires covering major parts of India. "The Mauryan empire covered a territory certainly as wide as India and Pakistan"[33] (during *ca.* 324–232 B.C.). It supplied the background for Kauṭilya's work. A cursory glance at the contents of his book, and of the more elaborate work of Śukra, gives us detailed knowledge of the aims, constitution, and functions of the State, of which we have only broad outlines in the Dharmaśāstras. Among the subjects discussed are: the basic sciences and arts; the ends of life; the duties of the different classes; the duties and the training of civil and military officers; the training and management of soldiers, spies, ambassadors, horses, elephants, navy; the science and art of diplomacy, warfare, strategy; constructions of forts, tunnels, bridges, roads; arms and ammunitions; peace, treaty, fair and unfair expedients; raising of revenues from rents, taxes, mines, forests; seizing of enemy property; administration of justice through laws; removal of "thorns"; provision of welfare services for health; mental and moral education; irrigation, traffic, building of temples; celebration of festivities, etc.

The Constituents of the State

The seven essential elements constituting a monarchical State are described by Manu (9.294) in order of importance as: the king, the ministers and other officials, the fortified capital, the territory of the kingdom, the treasury, the forces of the Sceptre (army, cavalry, etc.), and the allies of the State. Though the king is regarded as the most important and supreme seat of authority, political thinkers constantly remind us that, however able he may be, the

[31] *Manu* 9.30 ff.
[32] See U. N. Ghoshal, *History of Hindu Public Life* (Calcutta: R. Ghoshal, n.d.), pp. 86–87; and Altekar, *op. cit.*, chap. II.
[33] Altekar, *op. cit.*, p. 320.

king should be helped by the counsel of good ministers in the daily administration of the State, in the administration of justice, in conducting wars, in negotiations for peace and treaties, etc. In a large State, as envisaged by Kauṭilya and Śukra, there were a legion of administrative departments with thousands of officers, composing a large hierarchy of delegated authority, and with a vigilant supervisory and co-ordinating staff.

But it would appear that the kingdom was a federation of different parts, down to the villages, which were more or less autonomous units internally ruled by the village elders. Allegiance to the center consisted primarily of the willingness to pay land revenues and taxes for different kinds of professional incomes and to co-operate with the State in the maintenance of peace and order and in the defense of the country against foreign attacks. The villages were grouped in hierarchies of tens, twenties, hundreds, and thousands; and there were chiefs and officers appointed by the State for each of such units.[34]

The King and His Officers

The foundation of an ethical State required a long process of careful training of princes, the heirs apparent, and the selection of honest and efficient officials. The king's cabinet consisted of from three to seven ministers, the royal priest, and a chief judge.

All political philosophers require the king and the high officials to have a sound training in the different Vedas (including their subsidiary disciplines), sciences, arts, logic, and philosophy. The reason the works on polity are so encyclopedic is perhaps to be sought in the fact that they were meant for the education of the young princes, and were used as manuals by administrators. It is of special interest for us to note that a high place is given by all to logic (*anvīkṣikī*), which, along with philosophy, is eulogized in the famous couplet of Kauṭilya thus: "The light to all branches of knowledge, the means to all activities, the eternal basis of all virtues."[35] Logic, with epistemology, is specially discussed in relation to the administration of law. Among the philosophies, Sāṁkhya, Yoga, and Vedānta are often mentioned as aids to the administrator's equanimity, detachment, and steadfast devotion to the ultimate goal of life.

Along with intellectual education, great stress is laid on enthusiasm, moral discipline, control of the senses, speech, thought, and action. Control of passions—such as anger, jealousy, unjust greed, egoism—is also thought necessary. Addiction to vicious hobbies is strongly condemned.

The net result of this all-round intellectual and moral culture is called *vinaya,* which connotes both discipline and genuine humility. Kings are advised to wait daily upon the learned and experienced for acquiring this quality. Again and again, the *Mahābhārata,* the lawgivers, and political philosophers cite a black list of mythical and historical rulers who lost their king-

[34] See *Manu* 7.115 ff.; and Kane, *op. cit.* pp. 153 ff.
[35] Kauṭilya's *Arthaśāstra* I.i.2, R. Shamasastry, trans. (2nd ed., Mysore: Wesleyan Mission Press, 1923).

doms owing to the lack of this quality and another list of worthy persons who rose to be great kings by virtue of it.[36]

The ceremony of the coronation of the young prince by the old king (retiring for spiritual pursuit) also gives us some glimpses of the philosophy of kingship.[37] The new king takes the solemn pledge of serving the Brahman manifested as the earth (*Bhauma Brahman*), in the presence of the subjects, who are described as Viṣṇu, the God manifest as the people. The Sceptre that the king assumes is regarded as an earthly emblem of the righteous rule of Varuṇa, the god of justice, over the world of Nature and living beings. The ideal king of the *Arthaśāstra* (15.19) is described thus: "In the happiness of his subjects lies his happiness; in their welfare his welfare; whatever pleases him he shall not consider as good, but whatever pleases his subjects he shall consider as good."

Needless to say, such ideals were extremely difficult of practical attainment. We hear of many kings who fall far short. Against tyrants, political thinkers provide checks such as mass migration by subjects deserting the king's territory, or the deposition of a bad king and the installation of his good son with the consent of the subjects. Along with such checks of visible consequences, there is the moral check of invisible consequences often cited as a warning; for example, a king who fails in his duty but takes his remuneration, namely, one-sixth of the land's proceeds, is warned that he will suffer for one-sixth of the vices of the subjects. Moreover, as we shall see later, the king has to atone for the miscarriage of justice, by starvation and privation.

We have not found in any of these ancient treatises, however, any instances of a positive moral check such as Gandhi's methods of *Satyāgraha,* non-violent non-co-operation, non-payment of unjust taxes and levies, and civil disobedience of immoral laws. These Gandhian experiments, developed under Eastern and Western influences, try to avoid the two extremes of passive resignation to the automatic law of *dharma,* on the one hand, and violent revolution and destruction of the tyrant, on the other. While Gandhi believed in the inviolable course of the moral truth, the inexorable law of *dharma,* he also believed in the truth of the moral effort of the individual, which can bring about desirable changes in accordance with that supreme moral law itself. The attempt to remove an evil by a wrong act of violence forgets the evil consequences which would also inevitably follow the bad attempt, if the moral law is inexorable. Gandhi's method therefore gives full recognition to the law of *dharma.* It follows the precept of the Buddha that evil cannot be conquered by evil; evil can be conquered only by good.[38] Gandhi also urges: "Conquer hate by love, untruth by truth, violence by self-suffering."[39]

[36] *Manu* 7.40–42; *Arthaśāstra* (T. G. Śastrī, ed.) I.i.2; *Mahābhārata,* Śāntiparva, 18.8; *Yājñavalkya-smṛti* (Trivandram: Government Press, 1922), I.304–306.

[37] See *Rājanīti-ratnākara* of Caṇḍeśvara, K. P. Jayaswal, ed. (Patna: Bihar and Orissa Research Society, 1924), chap. XVI.

[38] *Dhammapada* XVII.3; I.5.

[39] See Bose, *Selections,* p. 184.

The Ethics of Administration and Foreign Relations

The philosophy of internal administration is inspired by lofty ideas. But, in practical dealings, it is always remembered that human nature is both good and bad, that men are not all of the same nature and do not deserve the same kind of treatment. So, absolute trust and absolute distrust are both to be avoided, says the *Mahābhārata* (Śāntiparva 181.8–12), which recommends the golden mean and constant vigilance. Equity and justice—rather than indiscriminate equality—constitute, therefore, the aim of political behavior. Says Manu, "The king should be righteous in his own State, severe in punishing the enemy, candid to friends and allies, and lenient to the gentle *brāhmin*" (7.32). The same idea is clearer in Śukra's work (2.282): "The king should behave in three different ways: like the (pleasant) autumn moon to the learned, like the (scorching) summer sun to the enemy, like the (moderate) spring sun to his subjects."

While such internal policies are morally justifiable, foreign policies leave much to be desired. Four possible expedients are broadly distinguished: (1) Peace or conciliation by negotiation (*sāman*), (2) placating by giving (*dāna*), (3) fomenting dissension (*bheda*), and (4) punishment by attack (*daṇḍa*). These expedients (*upāyas*) are to be applied in accordance with one's own and the enemy's strength and weakness. Of these four, peace and punishment are better for the kingdom, says Manu (7.109). When war breaks out, any of the six kinds of alternative strategies (*ṣaḍguṇas*) can be judiciously resorted to, namely, peace-treaty, declaration of war, invasion, remaining in one's own country for self-defense and yet inflicting loss on the enemy, division of the forces to wage guerrilla warfare, or seeking asylum in a friendly country.

An elaborate diplomatic theory of the balance of power is developed by political thinkers who use their psychological and logical acumen in analyzing and naming technically about ten different kinds of relation that can possibly exist between an ambitious king, residing in a power zone (*maṇḍala*), and sixty or more different ways of tackling the enemy, the ally, the neutral, and so on.[40] The basic principle is to build power on common hatred, distrust, greed, and fear.

Righteous and Unrighteous War

If the cause is right and the means adopted is fair, war is called righteous. Righteous war (*dharma-yudda*) is justified by the *Mahābhārata,* the *Gītā,* and the works on *dharma,* e.g., Manu's.[41] It is regarded as the duty of the warrior caste; and battle fought without fear is commended as leading to the most desirable ends, fame here and heaven hereafter. An ethical code of personal chivalry and fearlessness is formulated. It forbids all unfair means and intrigue. Manu lays down, for example, that in a righteous battle no one should use secret weapons, poisonous and incendiary weapons; no one should kill

[40] See Kane, *op. cit.,* chap. IX.

[41] *Manu* 7.88–95.

a fighter who is unprepared, unarmed, begs pardon, surrenders himself, has lost his armor, is naked or unconscious, is a mere observer or a noncombatant companion of the enemy, or has turned back from the battle. One who kills such a man takes the burden of all his sins. An emissary, even if discourteous, is never to be killed.

Such a battle is confined to the battlefield, and to the conventional hours of the day; and striking is allowed only on particular parts of the body. Convention entitles the victor to the rightful ownership of the property of the defeated. But war does not much disturb the civil population or their peaceful occupations. Megasthenes and Hsüan Tsang were surprised to observe these good points during their sojourn in India.[42]

In addition to the righteous warfare described above, political thinkers, such as Kauṭilya,[43] describe the methods of unrighteous warfare (*kūtā-yuddha*), in which treachery, secret assassination, poisoning, and all kinds of satanic methods are employed to achieve victory. They remind us of the last two great wars of this century.

The Hypothetical Imperative of Śukra and Arjuna

The large gap between the ethics of internal administration and the ethics of international relations, particularly during war, rankles in the conscience of Śukra, who poses a hypothetical imperative: *If* you want success and *if* the State is to survive and prosper, you must fight when necessary, and also practice deceit and appropriate the wealth of the defeated enemy. He cynically observes: "Stealing is bad for a thief, but plundering is good for a king. We need not try to unravel the mystery of *dharma*. What is condemned by many is bad, what is praised by many is good (*dharma*)."[44]

This frank defense of the violation of the rules of inter-personal morality in war is an appeal to conventional morality, in which the modern world still believes. In ancient India, where the defense and protection of the country were left to the warrior class (*kṣatriyas*), for whom the fear of facing a fight was a sin, dying in bed meant hell. Elaborate rational justification of such a class morality is found in the *Mahābhārata* (Śāntiparva 15), mostly in the words of its greatest military leader, Arjuna, who presents together a philosophy of the State, wealth, and non-violence, which are interconnected. We give here the substance of his arguments:

Life is an undeniable value. But life and the realization of all its values, including spiritual freedom, depends on wealth, the means of subsistence. In the struggle for existence, the stronger try to oust the weaker. This is the universal law of Nature, too, as can be seen among animals. This can be prevented by a strong organization like the State, headed by a king and backed by soldiers capable of fighting back the intruders threatening the life and property of the subjects and capable of punishing and restraining the subjects themselves from

[42] See Altekar, *op. cit.*, p. 298.
[43] *Arthaśāstra* Bks. X, XIV.
[44] *Śukra*, 5.32–35.

encroaching upon one another's rights. If violence—the application of force and even killing—is necessary for such a sacred purpose, it is right. Absolute non-violence is both impossible and suicidal. It is impossible because even the ascetic who retires to the forest kills every day visible and invisible living beings in treading on the ground, drinking water, eating fruit, and even in breathing the air and moving the eye-lids. So, living means taking life. Total abstinence from violence is also suicidal because if the shepherd hesitates to kill the wolf he helps the destruction of the flock and himself. So, injury to life for the protection of life is permitted by classical texts. Such virtuous and dutiful violence (*sādhuhiṁsā*) is really a kind of non-violence (*ahiṁsā*), properly understood. If life, property, and spirituality are to be preserved, the State must resort to violence to prevent violence, if it is necessary.

The foregoing summary of Arjuna's arguments also sums up the main stream of religious and moral thought in India. This realistic golden mean of social, political, and international morality recognizes that harmlessness, truthfulness, and other universal virtues which should be practiced in thought, speech, and action can be practiced and reached only by degrees, in accordance with the capacity of the individual; and the possibility of practicing them in political and international fields is increasingly more difficult than in interpersonal behavior. Manu (8.350–351) permits, for self-defense, the killing of even "one's teacher, an old man, a child, a learned *brāhmin*." He also holds that killing, if necessary for carrying out the injunctions of the Vedas, should not be regarded as a sin (5.44). He also permits (8.104) the speaking of untruth if necessary for saving any life, and thus allows "pious perjury." Though he also allows war, and advises the king to fight and adopt various strategies, he places first peaceful, amicable inter-state relations (*sāman*).

The Higher Ideal

The highest practical effort for moral relations within the State and with other States was made, however, in the third century B.C., by the greatest emperor of India, Aśoka,[45] whose earlier experience of unrighteous war, causing untold suffering to the people, roused him to the truth of the noble teachings of Gautama, the Buddha. He not only established many kinds of welfare services for the people, and even hospitals for men and animals, but also abjured all intentions of war, even though he was the strongest. He realized the superiority of peaceful relations with other States, and concluded treaties for mutual non-aggression. He sent out good-will missions with medicines for men and animals, and ethical emissaries (*dharmamahāmātras*) to distant lands (as far away as Greece) to preach the universal human virtues and toleration of the faith of others as the best service to one's own.[46] It should not be forgotten, however, that even Aśoka had his army and that he had founded his empire on bloodshed and devastation. But the ideal of moral conquest (*dharma-vijaya*),

[45] See H. G. Wells, *The Outline of History* (New York: Garden City Books, 1949), pp. 402–404.
[46] See Aśoka's Rock Edicts XII, XIII, *et passim*, *op. cit.*, pp. 50–55.

rather than territorial conquest, which he conceived and subsequently tried to practice, has left a blazing trail for humanity's uphill struggle toward an ethical State and ethical international relations.

More than 2,000 years after Aśoka, Gandhi tried to relive his ideal of Truth and non-violence, and even took a step forward, by mass practice of morality, in political struggles.[47] He was influenced mainly by the Sermon on the Mount as interpreted by Tolstoi, the Friends, and Henry David Thoreau; the teachings of the Buddha and the Jainas; the philosophy of the *Gītā;* and the ideas of Ruskin. He interpreted the war in the *Gītā,* not as a historical fact, but as an allegory for the inner battle with desires and other evil forces which every individual spirit, like Arjuna, should overcome, as a spiritual duty, in order to attain God. He did not believe, therefore, that the *Gītā* teaches violence. He also thought, as did Tilak, Aurobindo, and Vivekananda, that liberation can be attained through work without attachment. He believed that selfless service to God's creatures is the best way of realizing God. So, politics became a religion for him. He differed, however, from all those ancient and modern Indian thinkers who regarded violence and untruth as justifiable by the good political ends which they might serve. He was aware that, as long as one is in the body, perfect non-violence is difficult to observe. Injury to life may be caused unknowingly, as Arjuna pointed out. But we are morally responsible only for our consciously performed actions. Moreover, the difficulty of attaining a high ideal does not justify its lowering, but demands, rather, the intensification of moral effort, which itself is more ennobling and important than success. "Full effort is full victory."

The modern age of democracy, Gandhi thought, has made the founding of the State on force and immoral principles an anachronism. Democracy is the way of social and political life which tries to raise every individual to a higher sense of moral dignity, responsibility, and freedom. Violence and untruth are precisely the denial of these higher principles. Only a State enjoying "moral authority" can advance democracy.

With a keen moral consciousness, Gandhi sees theft and violence in an economic organization of society which deprives the laborer of the rightful fruit of his labor and impairs thereby the economic basis of his life. He sees violence also in a society which denies equality of status and opportunity to any class of its members.

But, like Aśoka, Gandhi also has only blazed for humanity again a trail in the limited sphere of liberation from foreign domination. It has only dimly lighted the path of Western democracy, which free India has adopted.

[47] Bose, *Selections,* p. xi.

III. THE INDIAN PHILOSOPHY OF LAW

Dharma—as the Law of the State

One of the various later developments of the Vedic concept of *Ṛta,* the principle of cosmic order and harmony, is *dharma,* which is the principle of preservation and harmony in the human world. *Dharma* expresses itself in personal life as virtues and duties, and in political life as the laws of the State—just laws which restrain evil propensities and promote virtuous life. The king has to take the vow of protecting and maintaining the people with *dharma* on earth, as Varuṇa rules with *Ṛta* from heaven. *Dharma* as law is above the king, just as *Ṛta* is above the gods. The king obeys the law, or *dharma,* and inspires virtue and loyalty in the people by his own example.

Dr. Fritz Berolzheimer[48] holds that the Vedic idea of *Ṛta* and the concept of *dharma* influenced the legal and ethical theories of the Greeks and Romans. He holds: "What Augustine sets forth as Pax appears to have been a possession of all cultures. We may recall that, to the Vedic Aryans, the central philosophic conception of organized nature was 'rita,' which included the natural and human order. A closely related conception was dharma. The Greeks emphasizing the creative energy made of 'rita' φυσις and of the 'Dharma' Θεμις. The Romans, through the Greeks, derived from *rita,* their central conception *ratum, ratio, 'naturalis ratio'* and Augustine christianized *rita* into Pax."[49]

Whatever be the historical value of this view, there is, no doubt, a striking similarity between the Indian moral conception of Nature and the Greek concept, particularly of the Stoics, that Nature and men are both governed by a common moral law. Zeller thinks that the Stoics "may be said to be the real creators of the moral theory of the world."[50] But the *Ṛg Veda,* which conceives the moral law of *Ṛta,* is much earlier than the Stoics. The Indian conception of the evolution of law from the moral law governing the universe bears a striking resemblance to the evolution of law in ancient Greece and Rome from the Stoic conception of the law of Nature. Roman Natural Law (*ius naturale*) is the ideal law, to which the laws of the State should try to conform. In Western legal literature, "natural" thus comes to mean "ethical," "reasonable," "equitable," and "natural law" becomes, for some, an ideal basis for international law as well.

The Many Sources of Indian Law

Dharma, or morality, in the abstract, or, as expressed in basic moral precepts, is too general for judging the rightness of specific kinds of human relations and actions which the individual and the State should know how to deal with justly. Consistent with morality, there are different kinds of practices,

[48] Author of *The World's Legal Philosophies.* In the Introduction to the English translation of this German work, Sir John Macdonell says that it enables us to "ascend to a height from which we can see law as an ever-present part of an ever-flowing stream." (Boston: The Boston Book Company, 1912.)

[49] Quoted by R. B. Pal in *The Hindu Philosophy of Law* (Calcutta: Bishwabhandar Press, n.d.), pp. 1–2.

[50] Eduard Zeller, *Philosophie der Griechen* (Stoics, etc.). English translations by Oswald J. Reichel (London: Longmans, Green & Co., 1870), p. 178.

customs, conventions, and contracts, in respect of familial, social, economic, and other relations among members of the State, in different places, times, and classes. The individual and the State must recognize these as the specific embodiments of *dharma,* conducive to social stability and welfare.

Manu recognizes four chief sources of law: (1) The Vedas (which include the Brāhmaṇas and the Upaniṣads), (2) the *Smṛtis* (works on *dharma* like those of Manu himself, Yājñavalkya, and others), which expound the teachings of the Vedas, (3) the practice of the virtuous, and (4) the satisfaction of the self.[51] Of these four, the Vedas enjoy the highest authority, since they are believed to contain eternal truths directly perceived by the purest sages, the seers. In order to understand the Vedas, where they are obscure or silent, it is recommended that light should be sought from the *Smṛtis,* and also the *Mahābhārata,* the Purāṇas, etc., all of which follow the Vedic tradition. But, in cases of doubt still unresolved, light should be sought from the conduct of the virtuous, how they behave under the circumstances. Approved and good customs prevalent among a class, a guild, a family, in a particular region, and in a particular age thus come to be recognized by the State as laws in dealing with cases relating to them. (These compare with customary and conventional laws in the West.)

The interpretation of the scriptures, the resolution of conflicts between authorities, and decisions of what is just and right, when no light is available from the other sources, ultimately depend on the reason of the judge himself, and what satisfies him will have to be the law in application. Manu[52] lays great stress in different contexts on the satisfaction of the self, the inner self (*antarātman*), as a criterion for right decision. In the Vedāntic background of Manu, the inner self means the self as detached from its ordinary selfish identification with the outer body, the senses, and the lower sensuous mind, the self which judges things with the higher mind, the pure reason (*sāttvika-buddhi*).[53] Through pure reason the self can have integral comprehension of the worth of a thing in the widest of perspectives in relation to the cosmos. Its decision would, therefore, be in accord with the cosmic *Ṛta.*

The Turning but Steady Wheel of Law

It is seen thus that, though the Indian conception of law initially starts with an ethical monotone of *dharma,* it gradually assumes a variety of forms and taps a variety of sources to cover the various manifestations of *dharma* in the scriptures, customs, conduct, and the individual's reason. This makes Indian law a unity in diversity, rooted in the idea of *dharma,* yet progressively accommodative, and comparable to a steadily moving wheel. This idea can be seen in the following extract from a dialogue between Janaka, the model of India's philosopher-king, and *dharma,* disguised as a *brāhmin,* India's traditional wise man: "You [Janaka] are the person to turn the *wheel* [or *dharma* as law], the nave of which is the Brahman, the spoke, the *understanding,* and which *does*

[51] *Manu* 2.6; 2.12.

[52] *Ibid.,* 2.6; 2.12; 4.161; 8.84; 11.233.

[53] *Ibid.,* 12.27.

not turn back, and which is checked by the quality of *goodness* as its circumference."[54]

In addition to the earlier works, a vast literature—in the form of commentaries and digests and manuals—appeared in medieval times. Some of these specially recognized regional customs and conventions. So, the corpus of law was further expanded. But there was not much of positive law enacted by the State, except the occasional edicts (*śāsanas*) of kings, e.g., Aśoka's, as revealed by inscriptions. The British rulers enacted laws based partly on Roman and English principles and partly on Indian ones. Recently, free India has modified and codified the Hindu laws of marriage, divorce, succession, etc., which had for so long been left to the interpretation of the Dharmaśāstras by lawyers and judges.

Administration of Justice

In a large State there were many courts of justice, higher and lower. Many legal disputes and slight offences were dealt with by village elders, professional guilds, and regional courts established by the king. Major offences and appeals were dealt with by the king, assisted by from three to seven judges, among whom was the royal priest. The king, as well as his officers, was required to have unimpeachable character, good knowledge of the three Vedas, the other law books, and the subsidiary disciplines, particularly logic. The priest was expected to be able to guide the court on all points of law and custom and to be absolutely upright. Though the ultimate judgment was passed by the king, the entire court, called the *Sabhā,* had to contribute to the decision by ascertaining the facts, examining the evidence, and weighing the arguments in the light of relevant laws. They were all morally responsible for the decision. Manu says (8.18) that if any injustice is done to the complainant "one-fourth of the resulting sin goes to the respondent, one-fourth to the witness, one-fourth to the judges, and one-fourth to the king." The court is called "The house of *dharma*" (*dharmādhikaraṇa*), and the judges "men of *dharma*" (*dharmastha*).

Justice and Logic

It is of philosophical importance that the judicial process (*vyavahāra*) is conceived in terms of the Indian method of philosophical discussion aiming at truth, as described by Nyāya. Kātyāyana defines "*vyavahāra*" as "judgment aiming at the removal of doubts raised by the conflicting statements of the complainant and the defendant."[55] When we see how the Indian law books discuss the process of ascertaining truth by adopting all the technical terms of logic[56] (*hetu,* reason; *liṅga,* middle term; *pakṣa,* minor term; *pakṣābhāsa,* fallacious minor; *pramāṇa,* valid source of knowledge; *yukti,* reasoning; *anumāna,* inference; *tarka,* hypothetical reasoning) and epistemology, we understand why so much stress is laid on the king's and the judge's knowledge of

[54] Quoted by R. B. Pal in *The History of Hindu Law* (Calcutta: University of Calcutta, 1958), p. 194.
[55] Quoted by Kullūka on *Manu* 8.1.
[56] *Śukra,* 4.5.128 ff; *Arthaśāstra* III.i, Shamasastry, *op. cit.,* p. 150; Kane, *op. cit.,* pp. 304, 354–355.

logic. The picture of the king's court of justice gives us a concrete background against which we can place, and understand the utility of, Gautama's (author of the *Nyāya Sūtra*) methodology of debate, in which also two contending parties are conceived as presenting opposite points of view in a council presided over by learned and impartial judges, who declare defeat or victory for the proponent after weighing all arguments for and against him, supporting the decision with all relevant sources of knowledge. This would explain why justice itself is called *nyāya* (logic) and why the judicial process is called *vyavahāra* (application), and the king is asked to wield the Sceptre with reasoning.[57]

Cases for Decision

Cases for judicial decision are analyzed by Manu (8.4–7) into eighteen kinds, which give us a rough idea of the field of legal rights and legal action. They are: non-payment of debt, entrusted wealth, illegal sale, co-operative business, resumption of gifts, non-payment of remuneration, violation of contract, disputes between buyers and sellers, disputes between owners and tenders of flocks, boundary disputes, harshness in speech, and in physical handling, theft, audacious violent aggression defying the people and the Sceptre (e.g., robbery, arson, homicide), immoral sex-relation, conjugal disputes, division of inherited wealth, and gambling. These branch off into a hundred others, as Kātyāyana observes.

It is interesting to note that for failing to punish a culprit Vaśiṣṭha prescribes that the king shall fast one night, and the priest, his legal adviser, for three nights.[58] This shows that moral responsibility is in direct proportion to the prestige and position enjoyed in the system. Kauṭilya follows Yājñavalkya in holding that in fining an innocent person the king should atone for the sin by offering thirty times that fine to Varuṇa (the god of justice), and the priest by hard penance.[59]

Forms of Punishment

Forms of punishment varied from mild admonition, censure, fine, branding and parading in public places, mutilation of limbs and organs, fetters, imprisonment, exile, and confiscation of property, to death. In addition, some forms of expiation through repentance, austerity, and rituals are prescribed under certain conditions. Some of the forms of punishment, such as mutilation of limbs, appear to us too harsh, and even barbarous. That shows how our humane sentiments have developed; and it marks the unmistakable progress of man in civilized life. Historians of India point out by comparing the recorded impressions of the Greek envoy, Megasthenes, of the third century B.C., and those of the Chinese pilgrim, Fa Hsien, about seven hundred years later, that the harsher forms of punishment were gradually replaced by fines, imprisonment, etc. We may remember that as late as the beginning of the nine-

[57] *Mahābhārata*, Śāntiparva, 24.34. [58] *Ibid.*, 36.17.
[59] *Arthaśāstra*, Shamasastry, *op. cit.*, p. 307; *Rājanīti-ratnākara*, p. 73.

teenth century more than a hundred kinds of offences were punishable by death in England, and even in 1832 a child was hanged there for stealing a box of paints worth twopence.[60] How incredible it sounds. How incredibly fast our moral sentiments have developed.

As early as the *Mahābhārata*[61] we hear the protest against the unreasonableness of capital punishment. The sentiment and reasoning against capital punishment gather force in Śukra, who points out (4.1.92–108) that this bad practice violates the Vedic injunction against taking any life; it should be replaced by imprisonment for life, if necessary, and a natural criminal should be transported to an island, or fettered and made to repair the public roads. Brutality in punishment was gradually replaced. Fa Hsien reports that he did not find any capital punishment in India (A.D. 399–400), but fining was there, and mutilation in cases of treason.

Equity in Law

Were all individuals equal in the eyes of law? Manu tells us (8.335): The king should spare neither his father, nor his teacher, nor friend, nor mother, nor son, nor priest, if he or she violates the law. But in the very next stanza (8.326) he says: "Where an ordinary man is fined one coin, a king should be fined a thousand coins." Śukra (4.5.282) prescribes deterrent punishment for judges violating their duties. Again, not to speak of a child under five who is totally exempted from punishment, an old man above eighty, a boy below sixteen, and all women are given half-punishment compared to male adults. Women are exempted by Kātyāyana (487) from capital punishment; they suffer excision of a limb, instead. *Brāhmins* are exempted from physical mutilation and death by most authorities, though branding, fining, imprisonment, and exile are permitted. But, in case of theft, a *śūdra* (laborer) is punished the least, a trader above him is punished twice as much, a warrior four times, and a *brāhmin* eight times. Again, a *brāhmin,* but not the lower castes, is punished for drinking. Also, crimes against higher classes and against women are more severely punished than those against lower classes and against men. Crimes against lower animals are recognized and punished (Manu, 11.131 ff.).

Legal authorities try to reduce these apparent inequalities to a principle of equitable relativity. Manu (8.126) says punishment should be inflicted after examining the circumstances, place, and time, as well as the worth and offence of the culprit. Yājñavalkya (1.368) puts it more clearly: A culprit should be punished after considering the offence, place, time, strength, age, work, and economic condition. This list obviously does not cover all points of special treatment noted above, but the points mentioned would be found acceptable to modern conscience, though the leniency shown to hereditary higher castes would be objected to, as was done by Śukra (1.38) and others in India, so that legal privileges of caste gradually disappeared. Discrimination against backward classes in public places and in civil life has now been prohibited by legal

[60] Kane, *op. cit.*, pp. 390–391.

[61] *Mahābhārata,* Śāntiparva, chap. 266.

enactment. The underlying spirit behind ancient Indian law was to protect and promote a social system in which wisdom and goodness—the ultimate means to spiritual freedom—would receive the highest regard. But the spirit of the law became corrupted in practice.

The Objectives of Punishment

If we analyze the implied and explicit purposes of punishment, we find that punishment was conceived, first, as a *deterrent* measure calculated to strike fear into the hearts of the criminally minded and to check their immoral and anti-social passions. This purpose was served particularly by disproportionately severe punishment and by "branding," "parading," and publicizing punishment. The second object was the *prevention* of the possibility of the culprit's repeating the crime. So, the culprit was imprisoned, fettered, killed, or exiled. *Retribution* may be said to be the third motive of punishment in two different senses: retaliation, and making the wrongdoer suffer the fruits of his own *karma.* The first is particularly noticed in the mutilation of that very limb by which the wrong was done (e.g., cutting off fingers or hand of a thief, the tongue of a defamer). Punishments, fourthly, are conceived to be an *educative,* and, therefore, a *reformative* process also. Śukra points out that, consistent with the Vedic teaching of non-injury to life, a culprit should be educated *(śikṣayet)* and made to work. He takes a very modern socio-psychological view when he says (4.1.110): "Such persons were corrupted by bad company. The king should punish them and always educate them back onto the right path." But punishment was thought to be, not only reformative, but also *purificatory* in a moral sense. This is more evident in the fact that punishment also included different forms of repentance, confession, prayer, penitential starvation, and long periods of penance (e.g., a *brāhmin,* while spared capital punishment, had to live even as long as twelve years in the forest in austerity and celibacy to atone for murder).

It will also be seen that violation of law was regarded primarily as a crime against society and its guardian, the king, who was thought responsible for all preventable natural calamities and human vices threatening society.[62] Compensation for personal damages, torts, was also provided for, but even in such cases fines were payable to the State also.

Legal Rights

It has struck modern scholars that Indian social thinkers consider human relations in terms of duties rather than rights. This peculiar attitude follows perhaps from an emphasis on "what I should do to others" rather than on "what others should do to me." But, when duties are well defined and performed, rights are also determined, respected, and fulfilled thereby. The laws of the State, in punishing the violation of duties toward others, also safeguard

[62] See Kane, *op. cit.,* p. 387, and P. N. Sen, *Hindu Jurisprudence* (Calcutta: University of Calcutta, 1918). See Lecture XII, for refutation of Sir Henry Maine's theory that ancient law recognized only torts, not public crimes.

their rights. The duties of the king or the State to the people define the rights of the people. The necessity of a clear definition of political rights arises when the State is brought into existence after dispute, negotiation, and contract. But, as we saw, the State in ancient India was based neither on contract nor on enacted laws.

The conception of proprietary rights in respect of wealth is found, however, as early as the Vedic period; and there are even terms to distinguish between ownership (*svatva, svāmitva*) and mere possession (*bhoga*). The right to life, as recognized in the duty of non-injury to life, led logically to the recognition of the right to wealth as the means to the maintenance of life. Manu says that there are seven righteous sources of ownership, namely, inheritance, finding (unowned things), purchase, labor, victory (for the warrior), investment for increase (in case of the trader), and acceptance of gift (in the case of the *brāhmin*). Others add a few more. The king is not generally regarded as the owner of the lands. The *Bhāgavata* (17.14) raises the concept of ownership to a high plane: all wealth is God's; his creatures have a right to as much as will support life; one who claims more is a thief and deserves punishment. A similar idea is traceable in the *Īśa Upaniṣad.* Vinoba is utilizing this idea in his movement for voluntary gifts and sharing of land *(bhūdāna),* by which process he has collected above five million acres of land (including about five thousand whole villages now communally shared).

IV. CONCLUSION

India has now outwardly adopted from the West political democracy, industrial organization, and part of its legal system. But to understand why India still shows some strange inclinations and conflicting moods we must know the contending and indecisive forces inwardly active, for example, the cold, utilitarian realism of Kauṭilya and Śukra, the high idealism of Yudhiṣṭhira, Aśoka, and Gandhi, and the golden mean of Manu and Arjuna. It is hoped that this short account will throw some light on these divergent forces, and their general philosophical background, which still dominate Indian thought and action.

QUESTION: What would make a war righteous?

ANSWER: The question is answered partly in the section headed "Righteous and Unrighteous War," where the *means* of righteous warfare has been described according to Manu. The rightness of the *cause* justifying a war needs further elucidation, though it should be realized that the cases could be so divergent that nothing but a well-cultivated moral sense and a practical sagacity can determine the rightness of a particular cause. But, in the light of the teachings of Manu and others, it can be said roughly: A war is righteous if it is for the defense or recovery of *unquestionable rights,* when *all peaceful expedients* have failed, and the *means* adopted are *fair.*

QUESTION: What would Gandhi do if India were attacked?

ANSWER: Let Gandhi answer: "India must not submit to any aggressor or invader and must resist him."[63] "There are two ways of defense. The best and the most effective is not to defend at all, but to remain at one's post risking every danger. The next best but equally honourable method is to strike bravely in self-defense and put one's life in the most dangerous position. If we bear malice and hatred in our bosom and pretend not to retaliate, it must recoil upon us and lead to our destruction."[64] "I would rather have India resort to arms in order to defend her honour than that she should, in a cowardly manner, become or remain a helpless witness to her own dishonour."[65]

Gandhi thinks that violence springs from inner weakness, fear, and malice; it leads to more violence and demoralizes both parties. The meeting of violence by non-violence or love (the way of the Buddha, Mahāvīra, and Christ) ennobles both parties, quenches enmity, and, though it needs long moral training and entails great sacrifice, it is the best way consistent with the spiritual dignity and destiny of man, who must rise above the brute.[66]

[63] See Bose, *Selections*, p. 173.
[64] *Ibid.*, p. 154.
[65] *Ibid.*, p. 155.
[66] *Ibid.*, chap. XI.

PAUL MUS

The Problematic of the Self, West and East, and the Mandala Pattern

Modern Western philosophy has established itself to a large extent on problematical answers, constructive, if at times somewhat paradoxical. As a matter of fact, the resulting complex does not by any means lack practical, worldly applications. It closely parallels in that respect the perspective (better called, perhaps, *prospective*) of contemporary art. Each is a part of a new style of life–simplified, analytic, expeditive in its handling of tangible material, all the stress being put on the arabesque of mathematical probabilities. Mechanization and exploration actively support each other and keep open between them a process of "information." All this stands in marked contrast to the heavy equipment of classical logic, syllogisms and figures, attributes, predicates, and copula and subject, this last and basic element being commonly described as the grammatical counterpart of a substance (the designation of "created substance" took care of theological difficulties): its admittance of predicates could never be reversed in its being, as such, predicated of anything else.

In our universe of interdependent relations, where even the "atom" has become a world of its own, if not a galaxy of worlds, such a restrictive conception appears somewhat outmoded. Comparative studies, in the philosophical as well as in the philological field, suggest that there was little more in the whole construction than the hypostasis of a peculiarity of Western tradition: our own grammatical notation of the *substantive,* boldly, and, in fact, quite unduly generalized—there is, strictly speaking, no room for it in Chinese, Tibetan, or Malay grammar, among many others. It is typical of contemporary philosophical trends that the final answer of yesterday—the substantive, the subject, and the self—should have become the crux of today's cruxes. Actions, qualities, inflexions, all kinds of changing factors, we find ourselves free to observe and refer to ever perfectible frames; but what are we to put under that specious designation, "the substantive"? Classical approaches, insofar as they were established on that style of answers, appear in their turn all the more problematic as they have been less aware of being so.

Do, however, such remarks build a better case in favor of our own problematic solutions? What kind of logical satisfaction can one derive from a process whereby questions do not find their answers but are met by other questions? The difference is that modern usage brings in an all-important proviso: the second question should not be located at the same level as the first, but "emerge" at a higher one, so that the balance, even when short of an equational solution, should leave us with a logical benefit. Instead of a circle of inconsistencies, chasing one another, the process is thus made into a spiral.

In order to achieve this, a problematic answer has to insert a new logical —if not ontological—dimension; this implies an additional element, not to be found in the premises. It is up to the auditor, reader, or spectator to provide it. Was then the initial statement incomplete and, if so, why? What did the author or initiator of the question miss that he had to leave to his auditor, etc., to furnish? There is but one physical as well as logical possibility that can make sense in this respect: the additional element nobody but the auditor, etc., is in a position to provide must be himself or something of himself.

Along that line, Auguste Rodin's definition of architecture may be considered illuminating—he would make it an art of motion, the motion being in the visitor and commanding the sequence of the views he takes of the building.[1] Motion, however, can be found in the monument, built as it is so as to impress definite patterns of attitudes and movement, the ones that make it meaningful, on whomsoever approaches it. Chartres certainly has an answer to something it comes and seizes deep within us. But was that something really there before? Have we not, conversely, to reach for it in the structure and symbolism of the monument? This is a two-sided process in which a question meets a question, specifically. The answer that each of them gives the other is not conceptual, but concrete, deictic, reminding us of Michel Eyquem's description of his friendship with La Boétie: *"parce que c'estoit luy parce que c'estoit moy."*[2] To resort to the terminology of the Upaniṣads, it is hard to say in such a case which one it is that is seized and which one is the seizer.

Whether we meet "the other man" bodily, mentally, or indirectly in some structure bearing his mark—institution, pattern of thought or monument, in Montaigne's *Essays,* or at Chartres, Paestum, or Agra—it is only through and

[1] Auguste Rodin, *Les Cathédrales de France* (Paris: A. Colin, 1914), p. 33. *"Les photographies des monuments sont muettes pour moi. . . . Mais devant les pierres, je les sens! Je les touche partout du regard en me déplaçant, je les vois platfonner en tous sens sous le ciel et de tous les côtes je cherce leurs secrets."*

[2] Michel Eyquem de Montaigne. *Essais,* Livre Premier, chapitres XXVI à LVII, texte établi et presenté par Jean Plattard, Editions Fernand Roches (Paris: Les Textes Français Collection des Universités de France, publiér sous les auspices de l'Association Guillaume Budé, 1931), p. 68.

against *him* that we become fully aware of ourselves, in personal intention. In other terms, no communication-value can be ascribed to any proposition until it is established in a field of reciprocal implication, where the first person, ontologically as well as grammatically, becomes *the capacity of the second* (the capacity of assuming—mentally, but always with the help of some physical mimesis process—the other fellow's point of view) and vice versa. Man thus meets man but not after a tautological pattern, as their common access is to a collective, sociological reality, the exact kind and level of "reality" that happens to exist then and there, as a repository of the synthetic judgments on which is built a civilization. Man, in such a concrete setting, is not to man a metaphysical but a historical answer, and, by that very standard, the adequate answer. Taking into account the general solidity of such a situation, minor historical discrepancies, such as doctrinal disagreement, can be considered unimportant.

Even at the crudest, least philosophical level, reflexive self-consciousness has to be dug out of the massivity of this plain, symbiotic *"existing-in-the-world."* To quote Husserl's famous dictum, "all perception is an exception" (*das Erfassen ist ein Herausfassen*),[3] the exception of personality—in other words, the dramatic capture of what one has to be. Jean Wahl's thorough analysis runs: "Being may assume two forms, one of which occasionally appears as a hole dug into the other; on one hand, there is the immutability and compacity of plain being, on the other, being-for-oneself, which means incessant mutability, continual negation and, in the last resort, nothingness."[4]

This makes the self an effective but transient and ultimately evanescent construction, nesting, so to speak, in an occasional space of its own, which assigns it its scope and actual limits. The occasion is the matrix of the corresponding realization. Yet, a central *intention* is required, and a resulting tension, were it but to engross the occasion: an instance of the kinetics of elasticity, where action balances counteraction.

We get thus very close to John Dewey's fundamental comment on the contemporary Copernican Revolution: "The old center was mind knowing by means of an equipment of powers complete within itself and merely exercized upon an antecedent external material equally complete in itself. The new center is indefinite interactions taking place within a course of nature which is not fixed and complete but which is capable of direction to new and different results through the mediation of intentional operations.

"Neither self nor world, neither soul nor nature (in the sense of something isolated and finished in its isolation) is the center any more than either earth or sun is the absolute center of a single universal and necessary frame of reference. There is a moving whole of interacting parts; a center emerges wherever there is effort to change them in a particular direction."[5]

[3] Edmond Husserl, *Méditations Cartésiennes* (Paris: J. Vrin, 1947), pp. 38–39; cf. Paul Foulquié et Gérard Deledalle, *La Psychologie Contemporaine* (Paris: Presses Universitaires de France, 1951), p. 367.

[4] Jean Wahl, *Traité de Métaphysique*, Cours professé en Sorbonne (Paris: Payot, 1953), p. 121.

[5] John Dewey, *The Quest for Certainty: A Study of the Relation of Knowledge and Action* (New York: Minton-Balch, 1929), pp. 290–291.

This in a sense meets Indian, and especially Buddhist, thinking half way; were it not for the fact that Dewey's world welcomes "new and different results," in sharp contrast with the predelineated theoretical structure of the *dharmas,* the passage quoted could be taken as an exposition of the well-known Buddhist doctrine of Dependent Origination (*pratītyasamutpāda*). The classical Western notion of *natura naturans* and *naturata* had to be built on metaphysical assumptions. This is no longer the case, and contemporary phenomenology is less interested in any solid "substantive" than in transient syntheses, emerging from their elements, with no material addition to them, yet following a particular *intention.*

Such a process of ruptive stabilization, reshaping itself according to qualitative differences, would perhaps find its clearest Western formulation in Alexander's Principle of Emergence. With by no means inconsiderable disagreement in their final interpretation, the Brāhmaṇical as well as the Buddhist schools of thinking are equally familiar with the notion of such a critical moment, when, out of the interaction of various elements, a synthesis appears, whether, according to a "positive" doctrine of the self (*ātmavāda*), as the ultimate reality, or as the fundamental error on which is built the endless round of transmigration.

Is it, however, philosophically and philologically permissible to take Husserl, Dewey, and Alexander, and with them Buddhaghoṣa and Śaṁkarācārya all in the same stride? Putting aside such superficial similarities as their common acceptance of as vague a notation as that of a center, is there but one well-defined and indisputable concept they do agree on? It might be the touchstone of all comparisons, between East and West, for it is precisely where the new trends of Western philosophy show a fairly consistent agreement, not only among themselves, but with Asian tradition, in a common distrust of the specious but ultimately misleading serviceability of a too-rigid conceptual approach: abstraction, as the ultimate of comprehension, and generalization, projecting this abstract connotation into denoted extension. The stuff we have now to handle is far less formal and lies deeper in human nature: a discovery that it is only fair to observe that Western philosophy has largely made on its own, even if it finds powerful consonances in Eastern cultures.

We feel all the closer to these, now that a perspective of "patterns of behavior," with syntactic phenomenological "responses," tends to replace, in a world of adjustment and emergences, our previous commitment to a straight division and syllogistic deduction of concepts. The definition of a problematic answer would thus become: *a pattern plus a choice,* bringing action, as a choice, in the very center of our conception of the self. It is highly significant that a thinker in many respects as "classical" as Louis Lavelle should nevertheless have asserted that action (*karma,* in the well-known Indian terminology) is not an attribute, but the essence of the self. This, in his view, was neither flat determinism nor mere contingency: it implied an enveloping, if at first problematic, pattern and a choice that would remain open for a while:

the choice of the ingress, *engagement,* or commitment, as one now says. As soon as the subject has "chosen himself," the pattern closes on him.

Meaning—on what? What is the core, if any, of such a construction? How could we grasp that elusive center? It would appear at times to be the very center of ourselves were it not for its constantly escaping us, in order, so to speak, to jump wherever in space and time "our intention" builds a new standpoint from which to rebuild the world, just to drop it again by one more somersault. "More new-fangled than an ape," to quote from *As You Like It.*[6]

"We shall never *see* that center," observes Jean-Paul Sartre, "although it bears the whole structure of our perceptual field: for we *are* it. And this is why the objective order of the universe never stops throwing at us the image of an object which basically cannot be an object for us, as it is what we have to be"[7]—a quasi-Vedāntic statement; but it has found a more Buddhist echo in Mme de Beauvoir's *Pyrrhus et Cinéas:* "Never shall I become to myself a solid object: What I am experiencing within myself is just that emptiness that is myself: I discover that I am not."[8]

In addition to this evanescent, yet fundamental, center, the phenomenologist's ontological paraphernalia must include still another symbol, to make the set complete: the one Edmund Husserl calls *a halo* or *the horizon* of a given instance, Jean Wahl's *hole,* dug in plain existence-in-the-world, to give room to existing-for-*oneself;* in other words, the *matrix* of our choice. Maurice Merleau-Ponty has a graphic description of the way this peripheral construction is raised to its precarious state of "being":

"I am the absolute origin. My existence does not derive from antecedent factors, from my natural and social environment. On the contrary, it reaches for them and upholds them. No one but myself can assign existence-for-myself (the only meaning such a word can have *for me*) to any tradition I chose to support or to yonder horizon the distance of which to me would fall down and disintegrate, were I not here to take scope of it; for it does not *belong* there."[9]

Such statements, coming from leading American and European thinkers, have a bearing, for comparative purposes, East versus West, that a simple and direct remark may bring at once into full light. The self-situating pattern they so painstakingly describe, avoiding all references to any conceptual division or to the unsatisfactory distinction between soul and body (the pitfall of Western classical thinking), is just an Indian, or Tibetan, or Chinese Buddhist, or Japanese *maṇḍala*—for Buddhism has diffused this most effective of symbols throughout the Far Eastern world. To bring into our picture another field of modern Western thinking, the Jungian psychoanalysis (or *Tiefenpsy-*

[6] Cf. Pāli *kapicitta,* "monkey-minded." A thorough analysis of this symbolism with Buddhaghoṣa, *Visuddhimagga* ("The Path of Purity"), translated from the Pāli by Bhikkhu Ñāṇamoli (Colombo: Semage, 1956), p. 265.

[7] Jean-Paul Sartre, *L'Être et le Néant, Essai d'ontologie phénoménologique* (Paris: Librarie Gallimard, 1949), p. 381.

[8] Simone de Beauvoir, *Pyrrhus et Cinéas* (Paris: Librarie Gallimard, 1945), pp. 67–68.

[9] Maurice Merleau-Ponty *Phénoménologie de la Perception* (Paris: Librarie Gallimard, 1945), p. 111.

chologie), the joint efforts of the Sinologist Richard Wilhelm, as the translator, and of C. G. Jung, as the deep-reaching commentator, of a (rather late) Taoist treatise, *The Secret of the Golden Flower,* may help us to bridge what still subsists of the Eastern-Western "gap."[10] Jung gives a detailed account of how he met *maṇḍalas* in the routine of his psychoanalytic vocation, long before he himself knew the word.

"When the fantasies are chiefly expressed in thoughts, the results are intuitive formulations of the dimly felt laws and principles and these tend to be dramatized or personified. . . . If the fantasies are drawn, there appear symbols that are chiefly of the so-called *maṇḍala*-type. *Maṇḍala* means circle, more especially a magic circle, and this form of symbol is not only to be found all throughout the East, but also among us. *Maṇḍalas* are amply represented in the Middle Ages. The specifically Christian ones . . . [often] show Christ in the center, with the four Evangelists or their symbols at the cardinal points. . . ."[11]

"When my patients produce their *maṇḍala* pictures it is of course not through suggestion; similar pictures were being made long before I knew their meaning."[12]

In these "modern" Western drawings, as well as in the Asian samples, the vital part is always the center; the artists (not all of them could truly be described as "patients") often define it as "the center within their own self" marking it by an abstract symbol or leaving it empty, in close agreement with Mme de Beauvoir's philosophical "fantasy" and at the same time as a good tangible rendering of *the* problematic answer.

"Among my patients," goes on the famous analyst, "I have come across cases of women who did not draw *maṇḍala* symbols but danced them instead. In India this type is called *maṇḍala nṛtya* or *maṇḍala*-dance and the dance figures express the same meaning as the drawings.[13]

"Psychologically this circular course would be the turning in a circle about oneself, by which apparently all sides of the personality become implicated. The poles of light and darkness are made to rotate. . . . Thus the circular movement has also the moral significance of activating all the bright and dark forces of human nature and with them all the psychological opposites of whatever kind they may be. That means nothing else than self-knowledge by means of self-incubation. A similar primordial concept of an absolutely complete creature is that of the Platonic man, round on all sides and uniting within himself the two sexes."[14]

Strong arguments could be brought in support of this. The *yin-yang* diagram of the Chinese, the Indian bi-sexual conception of the cosmic male, Puruṣa, entering with his consort in what is technically called in the Upaniṣads a parity-by-adjusted-halves (*ardhabṛgalam,* adv.!, a vision later incorporated in the personage of Ardhanārīśvara = Pārvatī + Īśvara) or the cosmic pairing

[10] *The Secret of the Golden Flower: A Chinese Book of Life,* translated and explained by Richard Wilhelm, with a European Commentary by C. G. Jung (London: Kegan Paul, 1947).

[11] *Ibid.,* pp. 96–97.

[12] *Ibid.,* p. 99.

[13] *Ibid.,* pp. 97–98.

[14] *Ibid.,* p. 101.

of Geb and Nout in ancient Egypt, all bear witness to the universality of the symbol. Jung was unquestionably right to list it among his "archetypes," and in insisting on its connection with the human person, its elusive center and its mythical bi-partition; the whole import is usually inscribed in a self-supporting, self-limiting pattern, a circular symbol or image of the feminine organ: the matrix of the occasion!

Yet, from a strictly philological point of view, Jung's approach is open to some serious objections. He has not made clear why he should have selected, as a sample of the *maṇḍala* figure, so remote and so late a tradition as a Taoist treatise of the seventeenth century with vague reference to a sage of the T'ang period, said to have been born A.D. 755; this brings his interpretation too close, as far as I can see, to later Tantric developments, whereas the deeply rooted antecedents of the *maṇḍala* symbolism, apparent as early as in the *Ṛg Veda* collection, have escaped his attention.

It is not certain, however, that the demonstration has suffered from such omissions and shortcomings. Greater familiarity with the ancient sources would have brought on the renowned psychologist the suspicion that he was simply reading them in a late Taoist document, whereas, as the matter stands, a confirmatory cross-reference, bridging over so many centuries and cultural changes, is likely to carry all the more weight as it comes unprepared and unexpected.

It is easy to observe, by a direct comparison of their structures, how unequivocally the *maṇḍala* pattern identifies itself with the regular pattern of the Vedic sacrifice as it is minutely described and interpreted in the great Brāhmaṇas, a textual tradition which can be dated, at the latest, *ca.* 1000–700 B.C. But considering the cultural interval, a purely formal coincidence cannot present the same demonstrative value as the recognition of a strong analogy in the inner values and intention.

To go straight to the root of the question, then, let us state that the basic aim of this paper is to show that the entire system of the ancient Brāhmaṇical society, as pictured in the *Śatapatha Brāhmaṇa* and the *Aitareya Brāhmaṇa*, and in such Upaniṣads as the *Bṛhadāraṇyaka* and *Chāndogya*, was established on the precise and, in its own way, thoroughly rationalized apprehension of the very notion with which the preceding excerpts from contemporary Western thinkers have made us familiar: the emergence of a qualitative construct, rising, at a critical moment, above elements it presupposes and immediately integrates, but without being an addition to them. This non-additional integrating unit is the self (*ātman*). As analyzed, for instance, in a crucial passage, *Bṛhadāraṇyaka Upaniṣad* I.iv.17,[15] it is not given as being by itself a pre-established entity but as a living process, to be ritually completed by an integration of its psycho-physiological and sociological elements, viz.:

[15] *Bṛhadāraṇyaka Upaniṣad*, traduite et annotée par Emile Senart, Collection Emile Senart (Paris: Société d'Edition Les Belles Lettres, 1934), p. 15.

1a	mind	which is	the self (*ātman*)	1b
2a	speech	" '	the wife	2b
3a	breath	" "	progeny	3b
4a	sight (lit. the eye)	" "	wordly belongings	4b
5a	hearing (the ear)	" "	heavenly goods	5b
6A	the self (*ātman*)	" "	action (*karma*)	6B

On the analogy of *Manu* IX.45, stating that "he alone is a man who is wife, self and progeny," this has been considered a loose, somewhat confused enumeration. At closer examination it appears, on the contrary, as a fundamental *legal* (as well as *religious*) statement, expressed with mathematical thoroughness. The key to the real import is that the self (*ātman*) is mentioned twice, but (in strict agreement with the dialectic of a problematic answer) at two different levels. The item numbered 6A in the above tabulation is not just another term in the list of "psychological" functions; it is their integrating unit, as the same *Upaniṣad* clearly says, I.iv.7: "Forsooth, breath is he, when he breathes, voice when speaking, sight when seeing, ear when hearing, mind when thinking, through all these never integrally complete (*akṛtsna*), for they are but names to designate his functions (*karman*). Whosoever concentrates on them taken separately shall not know him, for through them, taken one by one, he does not integrate himself. It is just the self (*ātmety eva*) on which one must concentrate, for that is where they all originate together as *the one* (*ete sarva ekaṁ bhavanti;* for *bhū* — cf. φυω; 'to emerge' would not be an overstressed translation)."

It would be difficult to improve on this comprehensive presentation of an integrating non-additive process, except perhaps by introducing some kind of algebraic symbols. To make use of a handy style of notation, familiar to the ETC. school of semanticists, let, for instance, *ātman* I stand for the primary, physical self (1b, pairing with the wife, 2b, etc.) and *ātman* II for the synthetic, integrated construct (6A). The basic import of the *Upaniṣad* is then an equation between (6A), i.e., *ātman* II, and (6B), i.e., "action," meaning indubitably, in such a context, a complete program of the Vedic sacrificial actions, for these require, according to the standing religious rule, that one, in order to discharge himself of them, should be "completed" by wife, progeny, etc.: 1b + (2b + 3b + . . .). By analogy with the usual phrase, *"joint* or *extended family," ātman* II might be called *"joint* or *extended personality."* The complete self is thus established (in the above sketched topological table) just where the two branches of a fundamental "square" meet, hinging on each other; one of them corresponds to the psycho-physiological integration (6A) = $\int$ 1a, 2a . . . and the second to the ritual (which is tantamount to, say, the social) integration (6B) = $\int$ 1b, 2b. . . .

Keeping in mind the golden rule of semantic criticism, "never to credit a people, a period, or a context with any conception they would be unable to find a word to define," the question arises: Is there a Sanskrit equivalent to, let us say, Alexander's "emergence"? There *is* such a term, and as a matter of fact, a most prominent one: in Brāhmaṇical speculation; *atisṛṣṭi,* "super-creation," creation *beyond* (*ati-*) plain unintegrated existence (*sṛṣṭi*): the latter is the initial stage in the emission of the world, when the "cosmic" male Prajāpati (= Puruṣa) is said to have "fallen into pieces" (*vyasraṃsata*)—the result approximating what modern phenomenology calls existence-in-the-world.

The vital purpose of the Vedic ritual is the re-integration of those dispersed elements. It materializes in the establishment of the sacrificial ground, giving the measure (*mātra*) and showing the transcendental structure and intention of the sacrificer's ritual "body," further identified with the universe (microcosm = macrocosm). We meet there with very early samples of sacrificial *maṇḍalas,* to which can be traced the symbolic dispositions of the much later Hindu monuments, as shown in Professor Stella Kramrisch's admirable monograph, *The Hindu Temple.*[16] The establishment of the old Vedic altars was, as a side issue, connected with the symbolic "emergence," over the cosmic waters, of a lotus flower, and this is to the present day another expression of the *maṇḍala* pattern, never quite absent from an Indian's eye and mind.

The ways and means of this great accomplishment were represented as a sublimation of the cognitive and sensorial elements given in the psychological integer ∫ 1a, 2a . . ., i.e., breath, sight, etc.: these were separately and collectively transfigured into the transcendental unity of the integrated self (*ātman* II). Simultaneously, the sacrificer's social self or "joint personality," with all that "belonged" to it—wife, progeny, belongings—was projected to a higher divine level.

This evaluation of the philosophical conceptions exemplified in ancient Indian thinking strongly disagrees with the customary appreciations of Western Indologists, concerning the Brāhmaṇical doctrine of the self. According, for instance, to A. B. Keith's well-known exposition of *The Religion and Philosophy of the Vedas and Upaniṣads,* "when no clear distinction had been made between personal and impersonal and anything whatever might be conceived as active and living, it was inevitable that little progress could be made with formal definitions. We have instead endless identifications. . . . The love of numbers already appears as a dominant factor; the term *prāṇa,* breath, is subdivided into five elements among other divisions, and these five are obviously incapable of presenting any intelligible picture to the mind of the priests; moreover, under the same title (breath =) *prāṇa,* we find not only varieties of breathing, as is natural, but the quite different set of five: mind, speech, breath, sight and hearing."[17] A way of thinking where hearing and sight would appear as varieties of breathing, while retaining some historical interest, would certainly not, as the expression of a philosophy, be worth a moment's attention.

[16] Stella Kramrisch, *The Hindu Temple,* photos by Raymond Burnier (Calcutta: Calcutta University Press, 1946).

[17] Arthur Berriedale Keith, *The Religion and Philosophy of the Vedas and Upanishads,* Harvard Oriental Series, Vol. XXXI–XXXII (Cambridge: Harvard University Press, 1925), Vol. II, p. 484; cf. pp. 454, 598–599.

But this conclusion of Keith's is just a warning of the danger attached to a barely "lexical" translation of terms conveying, under cover of systematic metaphors, values of a very different purport, deeply connected, as they appear to be, upon attentive examination, with the structure of the corresponding society, as well as with a most elaborate analysis of the operations of the mind—the staging manager of such expressions. Professor Jean Filliozat, a prominent Indologist, with a medical instead of Keith's legal background, has claimed some consistent objective value for the first list of five *prāṇas* (*prāṇa, apāna,* etc.), a circumstance that makes all the more typical of Keith's mental blindness, in that matter, his lack of response to the true signification of the second sequence (mind, speech, etc.), which happens to be based on juridical considerations, as stated in the context. Mind, speech, etc., as the elements of the psychological integer $\int$ 1a, 2a . . ., placing in their middle the self (*ātman* II = life endowed with full consciousness and taking hold of its constituent elements), "entered" Him and so "became as many special aspects of Him." Here we meet one of the cruxes of Sanskrit philology. Who is "He"? It cannot be the breath (*prāṇa*), which has been defeated by Death, as well as the other elements. Yet, He is called *prāṇa,* with a further specification: "the breath that is in the [middle of the] mouth." Emile Senart and Otto von Böhtlingk as well as Arthur Berriedale Keith seem to have been baffled by that unaccounted-for "emergence" and to have accepted it—for want of any better interpretation—as identical with plain *prāṇa.* But the frequent identification of *prāṇa* with *ātman,* from various points of view, in the texts concerned, would seem to give a much better clue. "*Prāṇa* in the middle," as a synthesis of the other *prāṇas,* including breath (*prāṇa, stricto sensu*), is no more plain breath (*prāṇa* I, the breath of the physical unreflexive self, *ātman* I) but the commanding unity in which elementary functions coalesce: *prāṇa* II—the very action and "self" of *ātman* II. What has been said above of the synthetic unity of the self shows that *prāṇa*-in-the-middle-of-the-self, integrating its constitutive elements, should by no means be considered as a supplementary "entity" added to their total; the self, in its reflexive capacity, is all of them, without being any of them more specifically than any other, *de jure,* although a closer *de facto* connection is usually recognized between it and breathing (*prāṇa* I). As the text puts it: "They all became specified aspects of Him." This integrated unity of the self, experienced in and, so to speak, checked by the unity of consciousness (*prajñā, prajñā-ātman,* "the self as consciousness"), is, moreover, carefully described with the help of a consistent sociological analogy, for the self as consciousness is said to play in the structure of our personality the same role as the head (*pati,* same root as in Latin *potestas!*) of a group when he acts in the name of the community and "represents" it, as a conventional, authorized, and authoritative substitute for it. Or he may, on the contrary, *delegate* members of the community who, acting in *his* name, shall represent *him:* the same connection, taken from the other end. That is precisely why they bear his name.

"And that is why they are all called *prāṇas* after him. And whosoever has this knowledge, the family in which he is born shall in the same manner be named after him."[18] Nothing is more remote from such psycho-sociological speculations and practical dispositions than an alleged pre-logical or primitive mentality. Instead of Senart's[19] reference to Lucien Lévy-Bruhl's famous theories, such hierarchical relativity would, rather, lead toward Lord Russell's logistic and the notion of the class "that is not a member of itself," the simple, familiar equation of which takes the form:

$$A + B = B$$

The application usually given in textbooks in order to illustrate this formula is *Femininity* and *Humanity:* all female human creatures as included in the totality of human creatures:

$$F + H = H$$

The same holds, of course, of masculinity:

$$M + H = H,$$

so that $M + F = H$, $M + F + H = H$, etc., is a term-to-term rendering of the typical statement of the *Bṛhadāraṇyaka Upaniṣad*,[20] in which the cosmic male, Puruṣa, is said to have the precise measure of man + woman embracing in a parity-by-adjusted-halves, where the female is co-extensive with the male, whose non-additive, integrating measure she is (*mahiman*=*sva*=*anya ātman*) as he would not be himself, or even would not be at all, in her absence: *puruṣa* I + *jāyā* = *puruṣa* II. Each one of the two "symbolic" fragments (*bṛgala*) added to the self, or their integrated total, which is the self, added to the self, makes just the self.

Elaborating on social structures, rather than on mathematics and physical sciences, as was our case, to get an idea of the operation of our mind, the Indian thinkers appear to have hit, at a very early date, upon some of the fundamentals of our latest "logistic" conceptions—topology or *analysis situs* and the notion of functional connection. The fact that they had to reduce them to mythical instead of mathematical symbols did not impair the acuity of their perception, as may, for instance, be demonstratively shown by the exact parallel the *Śatapatha Brāhmaṇa* readily provides to Jean Wahl's phrase, *"un trou dans l'autre,"* as a bold picture of the insertion of being-for-oneself in plain being-in-the-world. When the gods dug out the clod of earth with which was to be made the fire-pan—considered as the most intimate symbol of the self of the sacrificer—they ritually established "for the sake of protection" the excavated hole as his "matrix" (*yoni* = womb) and "co-extensive [other] self" (*samambila*) as, for all magical and legal purposes, it had the

18 *Bṛhadāraṇyaka Upaniṣad* I.v.21; *loc. cit.*, p. 21.

19 *Chāndogya Upaniṣad,* traduite et annotée par Emile Senart, Collection Emile Senart (Paris: Société d'Edition Les Belles Lettres, 1930), p. 78, note 1, *in fine;* cf. p. 26, note 1.

20 I.iv.1; *loc. cit.*, p. 10.

same measure or gauge as himself.[21] One does not need to stress the similarity between this process, extracting the embryo of a "reflexive" self from the compacity of plain existence, and the correlative notations of figure and background, in the specific perspective of the Gestaltist theory. Vedic symbolism and modern attempts at non-syllogistic thinking operate along quite comparable lines; with the latter as well as with the former, *the matrix of the occasion phenomenologically co-determines the scope and limits of the corresponding realization.*

The problematic of the self, in contemporary Western thinking, has been summed up, in the first pages of this essay, as "a pattern plus a choice." Do our ancient Indian analogies cover the whole extent of this definition?

From Vedic times down to modern Hinduism, the *pattern* has always been pre-eminently sociological: the commanding image is that of the head and center of a closely-knit community. It is significant that the word *"maṇḍala"* should apply, not only to a structural circle (the aesthetic substitute for our conceptual analysis of a given "situation") with artistic, religious, and magical as well as physiological incidences, but also to administrative and political "circumscriptions" or "circles." It is normal that the life of such structures should appear pre-eminently located in the center. In the Indian "archetype," this position is occupied *par excellence* by Indra. The *Śatapatha Brāhmaṇa,* in a powerful myth, designed to describe our psycho-physiological constitution, "kindles" Indra in the middle of the other "functions" or breaths, as their synthetic integrating unity; the impact of such notions and images on the Indian mind is shown, with an additional confirmation of its sociological leanings, by the fact that the name of the "functions" accordingly shifted from *prāṇas* (breaths) to *indriyas* ("powers," "Indraic or Indra-like powers").[22] Further developments, fully analyzed in Kirfel's *Kosmographie der Inder* or Stella Kramrisch's *Hindu Temple,*[23] were to establish Indra, as king of the gods, in the center of a "cosmogram," where he is surrounded by 32 dependent Indras, the gods of the ancient Vedic lore now reduced to "forms" or "projections" of his transcendental self, just in the same manner as the psycho-physiological "functions" of the human self, ∫ 1a, 2a . . ., were said to have "entered" that self. The 32 Indras are seated, as it were, each on one of the 32 petals of a lotus-like diagram; the center "emerges" as the supreme "location," the synthetic—not barely additional—value of which is never lost sight of. In his *Weltbild und Bauform in Südostasien,* Robert von Heine-Geldern gives interesting samples of political and architectural applications of that pattern, in India and Further India.[24] In the Sanskrit Abhidharma texts may

[21] VI.iii.3.26. Cf. Julius Eggeling, *The Śatapatha Brāhmaṇa,* according to the text of the Mādhyandina school, translated . . . Part III, The Sacred Books of the East, Vol. XLI (Oxford: Clarendon Press, 1894), p. 213.

[22] VI.i.1.1. *Ibid.,* p. 143.

[23] Willibald Kirfel, *Die Kosmographie der Inder nach den Quellen dargestellt,* mit 18 Tafeln (Bonn und Leipzig: K. Schroeder, 1920), pp. 28, 173, etc. On the ground plan and cosmological iconography of the Hindu temple, see Kramrisch, *op. cit.,* Vol. I, p. 22; Vol. II, pp. 306, sqq.

[24] Robert von Heine-Geldern, "Weltbild und Bauform in Südastasien," in *Wiener Beiträge zur-Kunst-und Kulturgeschichte Asiens, IV* (1930), 48. Cf. P. Mus, *Barabuḍur Esquisse d'une histoire du Bouddhisme fondée sur la critique archéologique des textes,* Tome I (Hanoi: Imprimerie d'Extrême Orient, 1935), p. 297.

be found a description of how the 32 Indras, looking at the Great Indra, enthroned in the middle of their *maṇḍala,* are repeating, all and every one of them, *sotto voce,* "*I* am the one that sits in the middle."[25]

So much for the pattern. As for the choice, that problematic choice left open in the center of Mme de Beauvoir's intellectual construction, as well as in the sometimes naive and sometimes very elaborate *maṇḍalas* drawn by C. G. Jung's patients, it finds, in ancient Brāhmaṇical tradition, a mythical expression the quasi-mathematical precision of which bears comparison with the logistic accuracy of the other above-mentioned "integrations." The basic notion is the identification of two levels of understanding and correlative existence. The temporal, sensorial level, the level not for a *Critique* (for such is not the Indian style) but for a full *Establishment* of Practical Reason, is placed under the supreme authority of Indra. Yet, above that level, one has to visualize, mentally, a superior plane that might be called the realm of Pure Reason, for want of a better term to translate the notion of Brahman (nt.); in contrast with Indra's figure, it transcends all existence-in-the-world and appears as a repository of all the authentic forms which, by the cosmogonic operation of Speech, the Vedic Verb, it has the power of projecting in this world, yet without being, in any manner, *tainted* by them.

How does this adjust with Indra's supremacy? If Brahman means the Absolute and if Indra's power is limited to the material world, the problem thus formulated would sound familiar to the Western mind. Not, perhaps, that this brings us closer to a solution, but, at least, we believe that we know where to look for it, having been at it, though with little result, for such a time. But this would just be reading our own problems in an Indian context. The Brahman is not described by any term that our notion of the "Absolute" can represent; it is *avyākṛta* ("not developed in specific forms"), or *anirukta* ("not defined," "not enunciated," literally, "not spoken out"); the nearest approach would probably be "the ultimate" (*parārdham gataḥ,* "gone-over-there beyond").

It cannot be too much stressed that Indian thinking has no use for the clear-cut divisions of our concepts and operates instead with the help of *constructs*—patterns or scenarios—comparable, in some degree, with Kant's schematism, or with the "finality without concept" of the Third *Critique.* In the present case, the Brāhmaṇas give a detailed description of Prajāpati's (= the Brahman's) dual nature and of the corresponding "locations." Prajāpati "alone" was the universe (*idam* = "this whole," nt.)—in some undeveloped

[25] On that group of texts, cf. my *La Lumière sur les Six Voies,* Tableau de la Transmigration bouddhique d'après des sources sankrites, pāli, tibétaines, et chinoises, en majeure partie inédites. I. Introduction et Critique des Textes, Université de Paris, Travaux et Mémoires de l'Institut d'Ethnologie, XXXV (Paris: Université de Paris, 1939), chap. IV, *Les sources sanskrites du pāli birman;* and V, *La Lokapaññatti et l'Abhidharma Sarvāstivādin.* The descriptions of the Sudhammā Sabhā, i.e., the Hall where the Thirty-three Gods sit in state, a motto familiar to the Pāli Canon, too, is reproduced, e.g., in the corresponding chapter of the *Chagatidīpanī Aṭṭhakathā.,* Śakra, Lord of the Gods (Pāli: *Sakko devānaṁ indo*—the name of the Vedic god, Indra, Pāli. Inda, having been gradually reduced to a common appellation: "lord, chief, king"), sits in the middle of his 32 acolytes, each of them styled "an Indra" (so that *Sakko devānaṁ indo* approximates "King of Kings") sit around him. "To the mind of every one of them this thought occurs: I am the one that sits in the middle (*sabbesaṁ pana evaṁ hoti: ahaṁ majjhe nisinno ahaṁ majjhe nisinno*).

form, as the production of that same universe had still to take place. Speech was "his" (*sva*), i.e., his "scope" (*mahiman*) and thus his (alternative) self, (*anya ātman*), in some implicit form. The creative process started with Prajāpati's emission of Speech, which then "developed itself in all that exists." The implicit "scope" of Prajāpati thus became explicit in the universe which our sensorial and cognitive equipment makes us aware of. There are, accordingly, two and only two correlative and inseparable ways in which we may think and say something concerning him: as "undeveloped" or "not enunciated," he is that which is capable of becoming "all this"; and, on the other hand, as "all this," i.e., as *being* the world we are aware of, he is what we have to establish, in our mind, as the "logical" premises of "this all," if we are to find any meaning in it.

The crucial terms *"nirukta"/"anirukta"* (enunciated/not enunciated) can thus be more readily interpreted. Prajāpati might be called "unspecified" when, and only when and where the specific operation of Speech (productive of the world, as the explicit word) has not taken place. But such a condition destroys itself, as it leaves no spatial or temporal specification, no *where* and *when* to build on. All Western attempts at a metaphysical interpretation of the Absolute have had to face that fatal objection, and none of them can be demonstratively said to have survived it. Did the ancient Indian schools of thinking fare better in that respect? We can at least try to see in what direction they have sought their own answer. Philologically—the only safe basis for such explorations—Prajāpati is *not* to be described as "Absolute" (*absolutus*), which would denote either a dualistic situation, admitting of a distance between the Absolute and what it would then be conceived to be "solved" or "detached from," or, as the only alternative, a reductive monism dissolving the world in the (idealistic) Absolute or conversely this idealistic Absolute in a (materialistic) acceptation of "this" world. Prajāpati may be thought of as *anirukta,* either as still in his "unexpressed" stage, or as having again reabsorbed himself—i.e., the world, as his explicit self—into it. In both cases, nothing remains "here" from which to measure any distance up to him.

This brings us back to the logistic pattern of an integrating unity, nonadditive to its elements. Prajāpati I is this world in which we find or, rather, have to find ourselves; in the (Vedic) Word, *he* finds his meaning, measure (*mahiman*), and proper belongings (*sva*), and so finally emerges in his reflexive personality (Prapāpati II); this cosmic operation (*atisṛṣṭi*) is the integration of what happens "individually," by virtue of the Vedic sacrifice (*yajña*), to the "aryans"; consequently all the rest of the world bears a notation of religious and legal non-existence (*parabhūta,* which one might translate "outside the natural law," with due consideration to the semantic equations *bhū-* = φυω and *natura* = φυσις). Prajāpati, in his "ultimate" form, is the meaning of this world and as such is neither identical with it nor separable from it, except in words. Can one ask for a more specific anticipation of our phenomenological "patterns"? Wherever no Vedic thinker and sacrificer is present in order to assume a personality (*ātman* II) that would enable him to grasp the meaning of the world, chaos prevails. Maurice Merleau-Ponty's description is here fully adequate: the horizon in which a meaningful world has to be integrated has fallen down, annihilating a distance that belongs neither to it nor to us but to the bold construction of a being-for-oneself (*atisṛṣṭi,* the confirmed Aryan's way of life) amidst plain being-in-the-world (*sṛṣṭi,* the non-Aryan, demonian or savage way of life, outside the Aryan pale).

There is neither a primitive mentality nor just a sophisticated, decadent play on empty words behind the identification of Prajāpati with Speech, his daughter and consort, and with mind, his other, masculine, "form"—and the same may be said of the steady assertion that he is not to be conceived as any additional *thing.* All this is another instance of the logistic, inductive equation, $A + B = B$, of which the ancient Indian thinkers have made such an extensive and in many ways constructive usage. Prajāpati is the "support" (*dharma*) that gives a meaning to the joint operation of Mind and Speech, in other words, of physical "forms" and intelligible classifications and designations; he is, rather than any conceptual abstraction, the order proclaimed and extended by that type of civilization and in that historical setting of which, as presented in our texts, he is an active personification. A well-ordered world is neither identical with its order nor different from it; it may conversely be said to be both at the same time—but the identification has a stronger *meaningfulness,* as it embodies all authoritative values in the corresponding civilization, whereas the discrimination would appear as a much more theoretical—though philosophically indispensable—correction.

The positive aspect, in its massivity, is ruled and expressed by the lordly power, the *kṣatra,* Indra's might and sway; on the strength of the logistic equation which underlies all those ancient speculations—and institutions—the spiritual power, the Brahman, cannot be, in any tangible way, anything that the lordly power does not fully absorb and represent, and that is why, at the coronation ceremony, the king is addressed as *"brahman."* An old myth (once again the usual algorithm, in such a religious and sociological context) states that Indra, after his victory over the powers of evil, wanted to be and became "what Prajāpati was," that is, adds the Brāhmaṇas, "great (*mahant*)"; the juridical implication of such a terminology is now fairly easy to ascertain: Prajāpati's greatness (*mahiman*) is this world, with which his two "halves," Mind and Speech, are, each of them, as he is himself through them, co-extensive. The myth and status of Hindu kingship, in its developments, remained fundamentally established on that construction: the lordly power is co-extensive with the spiritual power, described as its "other self," its "self by [adjusted] half [and half]" (*ardhātma,* cf. *ardhabṛgalam*), and also with its "Royal Fortune" (Śrī, Lakṣmī), which extends as far as the word of the king is obeyed: the $M + H = H$, $F + H = H$, $M + F = H$ pattern is subjacent to these political rationalizations.

Predominant as these positive values may appear, the practical side of the negative aspect—to wit, that even a world in perfect order *is not* its order—should not be left unobserved. The Vedic legend has it that, Indra having become "all that Prajāpati was," the latter asked, who, then, he was to be, and met the answer, "Just what you have said: Who"—hence "his name, 'Who'? (*Kah?*)"—a problematic answer, if any![26] Yet its practical value cannot be overstressed, for it placed the *brāhmin,* as the image of an unfathomable spiritual power, above the reach of the king, as explicitly proclaimed by themselves at the consecration ceremony. The king, with their help, could identify himself with "all that was" under his sway—in the matrix of the occasion. He filled the latter with his impersonation of the ultimate (technically he was described as Prājāpateya). But the ultimate was not caught in the occasion thus defined. The ultimate was to remain just a question mark.

Deep and permanent (one would feel inclined to say: archetypical) psycho-sociological factors are at work behind these symbols. For, if the king was an impersonation of Indra, such was also the case, at a more modest level, of all sacrificers, or even, to some degree, of all such men as were not out of their "senses" (*indriya*). A king had to keep in harmony, not only with the world order, but with what of it was reflected in his dependents, under the omnipresent guidance of the *brāhmins.* Serious weight should be placed on Manu's warning that the latter retained the power to create "other worlds and other gods," i.e., to displace any king that would prove insane enough to try to injure their order in which was his "matrix." For no king, in the logistic perspective of these traditions, was such on his own right. The "occasion" had made him, and could undo him, for in the middle of his political *maṇḍala* there remained, with Prajāpati's evasiveness, the "open" value that modern Western *maṇḍalas* have been found to express no less significantly—though quite at another level.

This zero value (the zero class of modern logicians) explains why no addition is made to the ultimate, by any specification of it. It helps us to understand why Hinduism admits (in contrast with the complete integration of the Chinese Empire) as many "universal" kings, as many Indras, as circumstances require. Their universality is qualitative. It is not a materialization of what would be, in Alexander's terminology, an "emergence," i.e., being-for-themselves. Consequently, they are not building up their political personalities as conflicting values involving their kingdoms. The result is only a theoretical, cultural unity, wherein are included "universal" political units, which it tends to keep out of conflict, in a pattern of good neighborhood, reminding them, as it were, that they are fundamentally non-additional. Shall we say that the specific character of the Hindu Kingdom is a problematic universality? Let us leave open the question whether philosophical ideas, explicit or implicit, determine social and historical conditions or reflect them: in either case, the association is close enough to make them symbolic of each other.

[26] *Aitareya Brāhmaṇa* XII.x.1, quoted in Sylvain Lévi, *La Doctrine du Sacrifice dans les Brāhmaṇas.* Bibliothèque de l'École des Hautes Études, Sciences Religieuses, Onzième Volume (Paris: E. Leroux, 1898), p. 17.

The troubled state of present world affairs seems an ever-increasing challenge to the logical thinking of the West. On the contrary, such a situation has striking analogies with the kind of irrational turmoil India has more than once managed to survive under the impact of so many foreign invasions. When no constructive, unified conceptual order is attainable, tending toward some kind of world constitution that would satisfy our Aristotelian turn of mind, is it not wise to aim more modestly at some kind of provisional arrangement, built on a cultural denominator, rather than on our political moves and counter moves. Seen from that angle, Hinduism may appear to the historian, as well as to the philosopher, in a new light and, as has just been said, in sharp contrast to the imperialistic and bureaucratic unification of China. The Hindu pattern, as mirrored in the *Mahābhārata* and Purāṇas, and in Indian philosophy, has induced and helped neighbors to admit each other culturally, while leaving open the political questions. There, too, it was a pattern plus a choice. The pattern was cultural, the choice political. Such a hierarchy of values has made possible a positive predominance of the spiritual, the Brahman (one may use here the Western equivalent: The Humanities—UNESCO style!) over the *kṣatra,* "Caesar," as a political background of discriminative enterprise. The fate of local, dynastic pretensions depended to a large degree, in the eyes of their subjects and neighbors, on their conforming to a set pattern of behavior: the model of the gods rather than that of the Titans (Asuras). A political, historical "personage" had thus to be established in a dynamic, competitive prospective, rather than in our conceptual perspectives. In a world of action (*karman:* sacrificial, moral, and political action) one has first to build his own *ātman* in order to merit and meet his destiny: a problematic solution *par excellence!*

Could we not, then, read the new problematic trends of Western thinking as a sign that we are gradually reconciling ourselves with some of these historical Asian solutions, at the same time as we have to re-evaluate our own, in a fast-changing world? First, let us get rid of all cultural *apartheid!* "Tolerance" is not the word: what we need is a full, reciprocal understanding—by no means eccentric, but commencing the spiral process of progressive relativity.

JOHN C. H. WU[a]

Chinese Legal and Political Philosophy

It is impossible to cover the whole field of Chinese legal and political philosophy in a short discourse. I shall therefore confine myself to three basic questions: (1) the foundations of political authority, (2) the relations between law and ethics, and (3) the ultimate ideal of human society and the historical process of its realization.

I. FOUNDATIONS OF POLITICAL AUTHORITY

The sources of all political authority, according to the most ancient of Chinese documents, the *Book of History*,[1] are threefold: the mandate of Heaven, the people's good will, and the ruler's virtue.

It goes without saying that the mandate of Heaven is the real cornerstone. But it is worthy of note that the ancients did not think of the mandate as Fate. It is something that one must gain and maintain by constant virtue and effort. The ancients never tired of teaching that the mandate of Heaven is not fixed once for all in a single family and that it is subject to be forfeited should its incumbent prove unfaithful to the solemn trust.

It is further to be remembered that Heaven manifests its will in many ways. Natural calamities and other unusual phenomena were considered grave warnings of God to the reigning monarch. It is even more clearly revealed in the people's resentment against the abuses of power, particularly greed and injustice on the part of their rulers, and their spontaneous flocking to a newly arisen leader who knows their sufferings intimately. Besides possessing other qualities

[1] The *Book of History* has been translated into several European languages. The passages quoted in this paper are my own rendering, but I have consulted the translations of Legge, Couvreur, Old, and Karlgren.

of leadership, this new leader must be unselfish and capable of judging justly the conflicts among his followers. He must use the faults of the dying dynasty as a mirror in order to cultivate the virtues that present a clear contrast to them.

In ancient China, revolution was not regarded as a right, but as a solemn duty that the new leaders of the people owed to Heaven to rectify the abuses or perversions of its mandate, and to relieve the people from intolerable oppressions of the tyrant. As the great T'ang[b] [2] declared, on starting a revolution, "The ruler of Hsia [2183–1752 B.C.] has committed innumerable crimes, and it is the will of Heaven to slay him. . . . As I fear God on high, I dare not refrain from rectifying the perversion."[3] Even after T'ang had succeeded in overthrowing the Hsia Dynasty, a spokesman of the new dynasty, fearing lest T'ang's action might be misunderstood by later generations and even cited as a justification for ordinary rebellions, explained its underlying philosophy in clear and emphatic terms: "It is always necessary to remember the beginnings in order to secure a happy end. By protecting the law-abiding people and overthrowing the lawless oppressor, by carefully observing the dictates of the Natural Law, the mandate of Heaven will be perpetually kept intact."[4] The expeditionary forces of T'ang are said to have been welcomed by the people of the whole country, to such an extent that their only complaint was that he did not arrive earlier. In the graphic words of Mencius (371–289 B.C.?), "The people were hoping for his coming as they would hope to see the cloud in a time of great drought."[5]

The Shang Dynasty (1751–1112 B.C.) lasted six centuries. In the twelfth century B.C., another revolution was necessary. In the Grand Oath of King Wu[c] [6] (reigned 1121–1116 B.C.), he pointed out to the people that King Chou[d] (reigned 1175–1121 B.C.) of Shang was even worse than King Chieh[e] (reigned 1802–1752 B.C.) of Hsia. Just as the crimes of Chieh had moved Heaven to direct the great T'ang to deprive the Hsia of its mandate, so it now fell upon King Wu to execute the sentence of Heaven upon Chou. In the same oath he announced a great principle which has been quoted through the ages: "Heaven sees as our people see, and hears as our people hear."[7]

The Chinese philosophy of political authority may be summed up in a few words. Political authority is a trust conferred by the mandate of Heaven upon the government for the welfare of the people. The government is created for the people, not the people for the government. The whole philosophy finds its best exposition in the works of Mencius. I have dealt with it at some length elsewhere, but here I can only introduce a dialogue between Mencius and King Hsüan[f] of Ch'i[g] [8] (reigned 423–342 B.C.). "Suppose," he asked the king, "that

[2] T'ang was the founder of the Shang Dynasty (1751–1112 B.C.).

[3] See "The Oath of T'ang" in the *Book of History*. [4] See "The Counsels of Chung-hui,[ah]" *ibid.*

[5] See the *Book of Mencius* IB.5. [6] King Wu ascended the throne in 1121 B.C.

[7] See "The Grand Oath" of King Wu, second part, in the *Book of History*. It may be of interest to note that these words were quoted by Mencius.

[8] *Book of Mencius* IB.2. For a general discussion of Mencius' political and legal philosophy and its metaphysical foundations, see John C. H. Wu, "Mencius' Philosophy of Human Nature and Natural Law," *Chinese Culture Quarterly*, I, No. 1 -(July, 1957), 1–19.

one of Your Majesty's servants were to entrust his wife and children to the care of a friend, while he went to the State of Ch'u[h] for a trip, and that, on his return, he should find that his friend had caused his wife and children to suffer cold and hunger. How is such a one to be dealt with?" "He should be cast off as a friend," the king replied. Mencius proceeded, "Suppose that the minister of justice could not regulate his officers, how should he be dealt with?" "Dismiss him," was the ready answer. Mencius pursued further, "If within the four borders of the kingdom there is no order and peace, what is to be done?" The king is reported to have "looked to the right and to the left, speaking of other matters."

The idea that the ruler is a steward of the common good, who must forget his own interests, including his physical safety, is clearly brought out by Lao Tzu[i] (604–531 B.C.): "Only he who is willing to give his body for the sake of the world is fit to be entrusted with the world. Only he who can do it with love is worthy to be the steward of the world."[9] He even says, "To receive all the dirt of a country is to be the lord of its soil-shrines. To bear the calamities of a country is to be the king of the world."[10]

Thus, both Lao Tzu and the Confucians draw upon the *Book of History* as a common source of political wisdom. In spite of their differences on many points, they are in accord on some vital points. Both are emphatic on the ruler's virtue of humility toward the people. Take, for instance, the following song recorded in the *Book of History:*

The people should be cherished,
And should not be downtrodden.
The people are the root of a country,
And, if the root is firm, the country will be tranquil.[11]

This should bring to mind what Lao Tzu says:

Truly, humility is the root from which greatness springs,
And the high must be built upon the low.
That is why the dukes and princes style themselves as
"The Helpless One," "The Little One," and "The Worthless One."
Perhaps, they, too, realize their dependence upon the humble.[12]

Even the doctrine of *wu-wei*[j] (non-assertiveness) seems to have its seed in the famous song of Kao-yao:[k 13]

When the head is enlightened,
The arms and legs will function smoothly
And the people's well-being ensured.

[9] *Tao-te ching*[al] XIII.
[10] *Ibid.*, LXXVIII.
[11] See "The Songs of Five Brothers," in the *Book of History*. The translation is by Herbert Giles; see Giles, *History of Chinese Literature* (New York: D. Appleton & Co., 1931), p. 9.
[12] *Tao-te ching* XXXIX.
[13] Kao-yao was the chief judicial officer under Emperor Shun, who reigned, probably, in the twenty-third century B.C.

But if the head is fussy and meddlesome,
The arms and legs will become indolent,
And all affairs fall into decay.[14]

I need hardly point out that this is in entire consonance with the spirit of Lao Tzu. But even Confucius (551–479 B.C.) has praised the *wu-wei* of Emperor Shun[l] of antiquity: "May not Shun be said to have governed by non-assertiveness? For what assertion was there? All that he did was to control himself with great care and reign reverently with his face toward the south."[15] On another occasion, he said, "Sublime were Shun and Yu[m] [founders of Hsia Dynasty]! They possessed the whole world, but were not possessed by it."[16] This is Confucius' notion of *wu-wei,* and I submit that it cannot be very far from what Lao Tzu himself had in mind.

Confucius and Lao Tzu are in agreement in maintaining that punishment must not be relied upon as a policy of government, that the ruler must guard against luxury, against the lust of power, against giving rein to his arbitrary will, against violence and extreme measures, especially against pride and self-complacency. Both stress the necessity of self-denial, although there are some differences in their ideas of self-denial.[17]

True enough, Confucius thinks of reality in terms of the Will of Heaven, while Lao Tzu thinks of it in terms of the Way of Heaven or the Way of Nature. But, for our present purposes, this makes little or no difference, for in both cases the starting point is a Higher Law, which should serve as the pattern for all human laws.[18] Both of them would be opposed to the absolutism of the legalists.

A very interesting and significant conversation between Confucius and Duke Ting[n] (reigned 509–495 B.C.) is recorded in the *Analects.*[19] The Duke asked if there is a single saying by the adoption of which a country could be made to flourish. With his usual candidness, Confucius replied, "No saying can really be of such potency as that. However, there is the popular saying, 'It is hard to be a prince, and not easy to be a minister.' Now, if the prince realizes how hard it is to be a prince, is it not a good beginning toward the fulfillment of the saying?" The Duke again asked, "Is there a single saying which would ruin a country?" Confucius again pointed out that there really could not be a saying so potent as that. "But," he continued, "there is the common saying, 'I see no pleasure in being a prince except that no one would then dare to disobey my words.' Well, if one's words are always wise, it would be well for them to go

[14] This song of Kao-yao is found in "The Counsels of I and Chi,"[aj] in the *Book of History.*

[15] The *Analects* XV.4.

[16] *Ibid.,* VIII.18.

[17] In ascetic life Lao Tzu advocated extreme renunciation of sensual enjoyment, while Confucius preached only moderation and propriety.

[18] According to Hu Shih,[ak] in China the appeals to the Higher Law or Natural Law have taken five different forms: (1) the authority of the ancient sage-rulers, (2) the Will of Heaven or God, as with Mo Tzu, (3) the Way of Heaven, as with Lao Tzu, (4) the Canon of the Sacred Scriptures, as with the Han Confucians, and (5) Universal Reason or Natural Law, as with the Sung (960–1279) and Ming (1368–1644) Confucians. See Hu Shih, "The Natural Law in the Chinese Tradition," *Natural Law Institute Proceedings,* V (1951), 199–153. If we add to these five Mencius' view of human nature as instituted by Heaven and its fundamental tendencies as the basis of Natural Law, the list would be complete. See Paul K. T. Sih,[al] "The Natural Law Philosophy of Mencius," *New Scholasticism,* XXXI, No. 3 (1957), 317–337.

[19] *Analects* XIII.25.

uncontradicted. But, if they are foolish, and yet carried out without opposition, would that not be almost an instance of a saying that would ruin the country?"

This conversation, casual as it may appear, reveals some of the basic tenets of Confucius' political philosophy. In the first place, what makes it so hard to be a prince is that it is not merely a privilege but a grave responsibility. To realize the difficulty of the task is the beginning of political wisdom. As Lao Tzu says, "He who thinks everything easy will end by finding everything difficult. The sage alone begins by considering everything difficult and ends by having no difficulties."[20] Nothing is easier than to indulge one's self-will, nothing harder than to sacrifice it in favor of justice and the common good. How carefully the monarch should guard against his self-will finds a good illustration in what King Ch'eng[o] said to Chün-ch'en,[p] whom he had appointed magistrate of Hsia-tu,[q] a colony for the people of the superseded Yin Dynasty (1384–1112 B.C.). "When any of the Yin people are under trial for a crime," said the King, "if I should tell you to convict, do not convict; and if I should tell you to release, do not release. Justice is all."[21]

In the second place, the responsibility consists in taking care of the people. All governmental measures and policies must therefore be judged in the light of their effects upon the people's well-being. In answer to a disciple's inquiry as to how to achieve the proper administration of government, Confucius enumerated five good things to be pursued and four evils to be avoided.[22] The five good things are: "That the ruler be beneficent without expending the public revenue, that in exacting service he should take care not to arouse dissatisfaction, that his designs be free from personal greed, that he maintain a dignified ease without being proud, and that where it is necessary to assert his authority he should do it without violence."

Concerning the four evils to be avoided, he said: "Putting men to death without first teaching them their duty is cruelty. Expecting the completion of tasks without giving due warning is called oppression. To be remiss in issuing orders and at the same time demand instant performance is called extreme unreasonableness. Likewise, to show a grudging spirit in giving pay or rewards due to a man is called playing the petty functionary."

It is because Confucius and his followers had a clear view of the true foundations of political authority that they never lost sight of the well-being of the people. They never regarded political authority as an end, but only as a means to an end. The end is the development of the human personality and human civilization. This is why the saying, "I see no pleasure in being a prince except that no one would then dare to oppose my words," was picked out by Confucius as indicating the beginning of all troubles in the State, for this would imply that political authority was taken for an end in itself, and that the arbitrary will of the ruler rather than reason was considered as the essence of law. The

[20] *Tao-te ching* XXXVI.

[21] "The King's Speech to Chün-ch'en," in the *Book of History*. Chün-ch'en was appointed by King Ch'eng (who ascended the throne in 1115 B.C.) to govern Hsia-tu, which was a colony of people of the superseded dynasty.

[22] *Analects* XX.2.

fact is that it is the first duty of the prince to mortify his self-will in order to minister to the actual needs and legitimate desires of the people. In the words of the *Great Learning,* "When a prince loves what the people love, and loathes what the people loathe, then he truly deserves to be called the parent of the people."[23] The Confucians cherish profound respect for the people, who, with few exceptions, can be assumed to be good honest commoners. For, as the *Book of Odes* has it:

> *Heaven gives birth to the teeming people,*
> *Affixing a law to every relationship of man.*
> *Being endowed with a constant norm,*
> *They have a natural love for the beauty of virtue.*[24]

Lao Tzu and Mo Tzu,[25r] each in his own way, shared with the Confucians the same respect for the common people and the Way of Heaven or the Law of Nature. Lao Tzu, for instance, says that the sage has no preconceived intentions, for he takes the heart of the common people for his own heart.[26] Further, he says, "The Way of Heaven is to diminish the superabundant and to supply the needy, while the way of man is to take from the needy to swell the superabundant."[27] Thus, a Higher Law than the positive laws of the State is recognized. The same is true of Mo Tzu, who wrote: "The emperor may not make the standard at will. There is Heaven to give him the standard. The gentlemen of the world all understand that the emperor gives the standard to the world but do not understand that Heaven gives the standard to the emperor."[28]

On the whole, it may be said that Chinese legal and political philosophy has the same starting point as that of Bracton, the Father of the Common Law, who wrote that the king is "under God and the law, for it is the law that makes the king,"[29] and that only the power to do good is derived from God, while the power to do evil is from the devil and not from God. "So long, therefore, as the king administers justice, he is the vicar of the Eternal King, but he would be a servant of the devil if he turned aside to do injustice."[30]

II. LAW AND ETHICS

The outstanding characteristic of the legal system of old China is that it is a system of duties rather than rights. Logically speaking, rights and duties are

[23] Lao Tzu seems to have had the same thing in mind when he declared: "The Sage-Ruler has no heart of his own: he takes the heart of the people for his heart." *Tao-te ching* XLIX.

[24] This stanza is quoted in the *Book of Mencius* VIA.3.

[25] See Y. P. Mei,[am] trans., *The Works of Motse* (London: Arthur Probsthain, 1929). In his *Chinese Political Philosophy* (London: K. Paul, Trench, Trübner & Co., Ltd.; New York: Harcourt-Brace and Company, 1930), p. 105, Liang Ch'i-Ch'ao[an] (1873–1929), while highly critical of Mo Tzu for his condemnation of music, expresses his admiration for him in these terms: "Nevertheless no one can deny the fact that Motse attained spirituality in an extraordinary degree. To do this, he suppressed his material life to the point of zero. For depth of sympathy, for vigour of altruism, and for the richness of the spirit of self-sacrifice there is none like him, save Christ, in the whole world."

[26] *Tao-te ching* XLIX.

[27] *Ibid.*, LXXVII.

[28] Y. P. Mei, trans., *The Works of Motse*, p. 152.

[29] For an English translation of the whole passage, see John C. H. Wu, *Cases and Materials on Jurisprudence* (St. Paul: West Publishing Co., 1958), p. 159.

[30] *Ibid.*, p. 160.

correlatives. If I have a duty, then the one to whom I owe the duty necessarily has the right to demand my performance of the duty. Similarly, if I have a right, then somebody else must owe me a duty corresponding to my right. Thus, rights and duties are inseparable. But here, as elsewhere in the field of moral sciences, emphasis makes the song; and there can be no question that in the Chinese legal system the emphasis is markedly on duties, so much so that the notion of rights was not as fully developed as in the Common Law and Roman Law. The emphasis being on duties, the law has never been freed from its dependence on morality. This forms a contrast to the legal systems of the West in modern times, especially in the heyday of individualism, when the emphasis was decidedly on rights rather than duties, with the result that the science of law tended to be divorced from ethics, and in a number of cases the decision became shocking to the moral sense of man. For the past seventy or eighty years Western jurisprudence has been moving steadily away from the amoral philosophy of law toward a healthy recognition of the social and ethical duties of man. During the same period, the legal thought of China, influenced as it was by its contact with the West in the nineteenth century, experienced at first a violent reaction against the old emphasis on duties, and moved toward a new emphasis on rights. This new vital tendency to Westernization, however, has been moderated by the ironic fact that the West is no longer so "Western" as when the tendency first started. The East wanted to go the whole way in order to meet the West, but the West, without intending it, has met the East halfway. So far as legal thought is concerned, the East and the West have met in the zone of a happy medium.

But it is of more than historical interest to inquire *how* the relation between law and morality came to take the form it did in the old legal system of China after the days of the Han (206 B.C.–A.D. 220). In no other system has there been such a complete identification of law and morality. Whatever is immoral is a penal offence.[31] The underlying philosophy is that morality and law constitute the positive and negative phases of government.

This position was the end-product of a long evolution of ethical and legal philosophy before the Han period. Confucius and his followers advocated as principal methods of government the practice of virtue on the part of the ruler and the inculcation of good manners among the people. For Confucius, to rule is to rectify, and to rectify others presupposes rectitude in oneself.[32] If a ruler does not possess rectitude, he is not worthy of the name, nor can he ever hope to rectify his people, for the simple reason that you cannot impart something to others which you do not have in yourself. On the other hand, if the ruler cultivates the virtues and perfects his own person, the influence of his goodness will permeate the whole population. Once a corrupt officer of Confucius' own State came to ask him how to reduce the prevalence of thieves and robbers.

[31] As Wigmore puts it, the reason for this is that "if a rule has become so settled and obvious that it has arrived at a place in the code, it *ought* morally to be obeyed by all; and the few who may resist must naturally be coerced by a penalty; they merit it." Quoted in John C. H. Wu, *The Art of Law* (Shanghai: Commercial Press, 1936), pp. 47–48.

[32] *Analects* XII.16.

Confucius' answer was: "If you, sir, are not covetous, the people would not steal, even if you should reward them for it."[33]

To Confucians, ethics and government are practically one and the same thing. If you cultivate your virtues so that harmony reigns in your own person, your goodness will radiate its influence around the fireside so that harmony will reign in the family. If one family is perfectly harmonious, it will gradually but surely influence other families. If all families are perfected, the State will enjoy peace and harmony. If all States are what they should be, they will be in peaceful relations with one another, and all under Heaven will enjoy universal peace and harmony.

No two schools of thought could be more completely antithetical to each other than the Confucians and the Legalists. Confucius says: "If you lead the people by political measures and regulate them by penal laws, they will merely avoid transgressing them but will have no sense of honor. If you lead them by the practice of virtue and regulate them by the inculcation of good manners, they will not only keep their sense of honor but will also be thoroughly transformed."[34] But Shang Yang[s] (d. 338 B.C.) says: "If you govern by penal laws, the people will fear; being fearful, they will commit no villainies; there being no villainies, they will find peace and happiness. If, on the other hand, you govern by mere righteousness, they will be lax; and, if they are lax, there will be disorder and the people will suffer great miseries."[35]

Confucians maintain that good government depends upon the employment of good and capable men. But Shang Yang says: "It is the part of good government to set no store by the virtuous and the wise."[36]

Mencius says: "People tend to goodness as water tends downward."[37] But Shang Yang says: "People tend to self-interest, as water tends downward."[38]

Confucius was opposed to the promulgation of penal laws with a fixed and clear-cut tariff of penalties.[39] But Han Fei Tzu[t] (d. 233 B.C.) says: "If a textbook is too summary, pupils will resort to ingenious interpretations. If a law is too general, litigations will multiply. Just as a wise man, when he writes a book, will set forth his arguments fully and clearly, so an enlightened ruler, when he makes his laws, will see to it that every contingency is provided for in detail."[40]

Confucians look to the ancient sage-emperors for models of rulership. But Shang Yang says: "Former generations did not follow the same doctrines, so which antiquity should we imitate? The emperors and kings did not copy one another, so what moral system can one follow?"[41]

33 *Ibid.*, XII.17.
34 *Ibid.*, II.3.
35 The *Book of Lord Shang* VII.
36 *Ibid.*, XXIV.
37 The *Book of Mencius* VIA.2.
38 The *Book of Lord Shang* XXIII.
39 The idea is that to have a tariff of penalties might relativize the notion of right and wrong, and might lead the people to think as though the government were setting forth definite prices for the privilege of committing certain crimes, thus giving rise to a commercial spirit.
40 *Han Fei Tzu* XLIX.
41 The *Book of Lord Shang* I.

Confucians lay greatest emphasis on the study of the *Odes* and the *History* and on the practice of moral virtues. These are all found in Shang Yang's list of "Pests," which includes "ceremony and music, *Odes* and *History,* care for old age, the cultivation of goodness, filial piety and fraternal affection, sincerity and good faith, purity and integrity, humanity and justice."[42]

Confucians have unbounded faith in the persuasive power of moral teachings and example. But Han Fei Tzu says:

> Now take the case of a boy of bad character. His parents are angry with him, but he never changes. The villagers in the neighborhood reprove him, but he is not moved. His masters teach him, but he never reforms. . . . It is not until the district magistrate sends out police forces to search for wicked men in accordance with the law of the State that he becomes afraid and changes his ways and alters his deeds. So the love of parents is not sufficient to educate children. It takes the severe penalties of the district magistrate to accomplish what love cannot. This is because people are naturally spoiled by love and are obedient to authority.[43]

In deciding cases, Confucians would apply the spirit of the law, while the Legalists would adhere strictly to the letter. Han Fei Tzu relates approvingly an anecdote which seems typical of the Legalist position. "Marquis Chao of Han[u] [reigned 509–495 B.C.] was drunk and fell into a nap. The crown-keeper, seeing the ruler exposed to cold, put a coat over him. When the Marquis awoke, he felt pleased. Afterward, however, he inquired of the attendants, 'Who put the coat on me?' 'The crown-keeper,' they answered. Thereupon the Marquis found both the coat-keeper and the crown-keeper guilty; the coat-keeper, because he neglected his duty, the crown-keeper, because he exceeded his office." Han Fei Tzu's comment on the case is interesting: "This was not because the Marquis did not mind catching cold, but because he considered trespassing upon the duties of another's office a more serious evil than his catching cold."[44] Confucians would have condemned this decision as repugnant to the natural dictates of the human heart. In fact, Confucius had said, "If morals and music are not promoted, penal laws will miss the just medium, and . . . the people will not know where to put their hands and feet."[45] The Marquis' decision is a good illustration of this point.

Confucians consider the family as the foundation of society. An unfilial son cannot be expected to become a loyal citizen. For the State to destroy the family is, therefore, suicidal, for it would be undermining its own foundations. That is why Confucius disapproved of the "straightforwardness" or uprightness of that son who stood forth to bear testimony to his father's theft of a sheep.[46] For him, true justice demands that the father and the son should shield each other's guilt. This philosophy is too much for the Legalists. Han Fei Tzu says:

[42] *Ibid.,* XIII.
[43] *Han Fei Tzu* XLIX.
[44] *Ibid.,* VII.
[45] *Analects* XIII.2.
[46] *Ibid.,* XIII.12.

In the State of Ch'u there was a certain upright man who, when his father had stolen a sheep, reported him to the law officer. The authorities said, "The son should be put to death." The reason was that, although the son was upright toward the prince, he was crooked toward the father, and therefore he should be charged with the father's guilt. Thus, a dutiful subject of the prince becomes an unfilial son of his father.[47]

Confucians place the virtues of humanity and justice above all considerations of utility. Legalists base their whole system upon the "calculating minds" of the average people,[48] who would weigh in a sensible manner the pains and pleasures involved in the choice of a course of action and see the overwhelming advantage of obeying the laws. They would not expect even the ruler to be above average in virtue and in intelligence. An average ruler who is willing to let the law rule will accomplish more than a specially gifted ruler trying to do without specific rules of law.

All these antinomies may be reduced to a single issue, namely, whether the business of government depends upon good men or upon effective laws. The Confucian Hsün Tzu[v] (fl. 298–238 B.C.) goes to the extent of saying that only the right men, not the right laws, can produce and maintain a good government.[49] Mencius is much more moderate. He says: "Goodness alone is not capable of governing; laws alone do not enforce themselves."[50] For him, therefore, it takes both the right kind of men and the right kind of laws to produce the right kind of government. His views are similar to those of William Penn, who, in his preface to *The Great Law,* writes: "Though good laws do well, good men do better; for good laws may want good men and be abolished or evaded by ill men; but good men will never want good laws nor suffer ill ones." Legalists, on the other hand, maintain that any government that depends in any way upon the existence of good men cannot be a good government, for the simple reason that it would be precarious, seeing that the existence of good men is a contingency and not a certainty. What they wished to produce was a system of laws built solidly upon the psychology of average rulers and average people, a system under which it would not pay anybody high or low to set the laws at defiance. They had such a narrow and mean conception of human nature that they thought that in order to produce an effective system of law only two motives needed to be reckoned with, namely, fear and profit. They ignored the facts that even terrorism and the inducement of reward have their limits, and that when men are dehumanized nobody is safe and secure. It is no accident that all the leading Legalists, Shang Yang, Han Fei, and Li Ssu[w] (d. 208 B.C.) ended their lives tragically. It is to their credit that they saw the necessity of the Reign of Law; but they did a great disservice to the Reign of Law by conceiving it too narrowly and by attempting to build it upon force alone, and not upon justice, good faith, and the natural dictates of humanity. It was from Hsün Tzu that Han Fei and Li Ssu learned that human nature is evil. But Hsün Tzu's idea was that, since men are by nature evil, they should be made

[47] *Han Fei Tzu* XLIX.

[48] *Ibid.,* XLVI.

[49] *Hsün Tzu* XII.

[50] The *Book of Mencius,* IIIA.1.

good by moral discipline. His Legalist pupils drew different conclusions from the same premise. They held that, since men are by nature evil, they should be taken for what they are and dealt with on that basis. They could see only two sanctions for law, force and profit, force to deter and profit to induce.

Hsün Tzu is at least partly responsible for the blunders of his disciples. In advocating the evil of human nature, he actually dug the grave for Confucian humanism and paved the way for the Legalist uprooting of humanity. He tried to demolish the doctrines of Mencius without understanding them. When Mencius said that human nature is good, he meant the *essential* nature of man is good, that nature which distinguishes man from the other animals. Hsün Tzu, on the other hand, was looking at men as they actually are. But, even then, he should have noted certain good qualities and tendencies along with the evil ones. In saying that men are by nature evil, and that all the good comes only from the teachings of the sages, he actually makes the sages rise above humanity, so that they become superhuman beings. Of all the Confucians, Hsün Tzu is the most superficial, but his influence was great upon the Legalists.

If the Legalists had been more moderate and less intolerant of other schools of thought, they would have succeeded in establishing a stable Rule of Law, comparable to what the Common Law countries have achieved. As it is, they ruined their cause by wedding the Rule of Law to a radically positivistic and materialistic point of view, and by identifying the concept of law exclusively with the positive statutes of the State. Their exclusion of the Natural Law element from the conception of law led to the Han scholars' exaggerated claims for Natural Law.[51]

Taking the tragic failure of the Legalists as a warning, the Han rulers and scholars worked out a penal system in which the polarity of law and morality is embodied, with morality as the positive element and law as the negative element. The result was a *legalization of morality*. They adopted from Confucianism the substance of moral duties, and at the same time adopted from the Legalists the procedure of enforcing them. The Emperor became the Pope and the Monarch combined in one person. If we can imagine a Church with police forces to enforce its precepts and to punish infractions, we can approximate the actual system under which the Chinese people lived for almost two thousand years, until it collapsed in the Revolution of 1911.[52]

But the Revolution was not entirely unprepared for by the revival of the philosophy of Mencius and of some later Confucians such as Huan Tsung-hsi[x] (1610–1695), whose political treatise, *Ming-i tai-fang lu*,[y] [52a] seems to sum up all that is best in the traditional political thought of China. It contains, among other things, essays on the Prince, on Ministership, and on law. The essay on law is particularly valuable as a contribution to Chinese legal philosophy. It starts with a bold statement: "Until the end of the Three Dynasties [Hsia,

[51] Even occasional sayings of Confucius came to be regarded as precepts of Natural Law by the Han (206 B.C.–A.D. 220) scholars.

[52] For a more detailed account of the history of legal thought in China, see John C. H. Wu, "Chinese Legal Philosophy," *Chinese Culture Quarterly*, I, No. 4 (April, 1958), 7–48.

[52a] That is, a treatise on government for use by future rulers.

Shang, and Chou, 2183–256 B.C.] there was law. Since the Three Dynasties there has been no law." The reason for this astonishing statement is that the sage-emperors of old made the laws entirely with the common good in mind; while the later kings made their laws mainly for preserving the Throne. The whole essay is worth serious study, but here I must content myself with one passage:

> The law of the Three Dynasties safeguarded the world for the people. The Prince did not monopolize all the wealth of the land nor did he jealously keep the right to punish and reward out of the people's hands. Position at court was not particularly considered an honor; to live an obscure life in the country was not particularly a disgrace. Later, this kind of Law was criticized for its looseness, but at that time the people were not envious of those in high place, nor did they despise humble status. The looser the law was, the fewer the disturbances which arose. It was what we might call "Law without laws." The laws of later times safeguard the world as if it were something in the [prince's] treasure chest. It is not desired that anything beneficial should be left to the lowly, but rather that all blessings be reserved for the one on high. If the prince employs a man, he is immediately afraid that the man will act in his own interest, and so another man is employed to keep a check on the first one. If one measure is adopted, there are immediate fears of its being abused or evaded, and so another measure must be adopted to guard against abuses or evasions. All men know where the treasure chest lies, and the prince is constantly fretting and fidgeting out of anxiety for the security of the treasure. Consequently, the laws have to be made more comprehensive and detailed, and as they become more detailed, they become the very source of disorder. These are what we might call "unlawful laws."[53]

I should like to point out that, although Huang Tsung-hsi was a Confucian, his was a Confucianism which had been "baptized" by the spirit of Taoism, with its emphasis on the cultivation of non-attachment and selflessness. If the Han scholars had wedded their Confucianism to Taoism instead of placing it in the framework of the Yin Yang[z] philosophy and concentrating their efforts on the institution of court ceremonies, if they had seen eye-to-eye with Ssu-ma T'an[aa] (d. 110 B.C.) in his appraisal of the relative merits of the schools, both ethics and jurisprudence would have found a freer course of development in later generations.[54] As it is, law and morality have been identified with the *yin* and *yang* phases of one and the same process of government, and neither of them has been able to transcend the half-mythical and half-human cosmogony. By moralizing the external universe, this cosmogony has irrationalized the interior world of the spirit. Instead of achieving a true synthesis of the two by transcending both, what the Han and later Confucians have left us is a promiscuous blending of man and Nature. Nature is the macrocosm, while man is the microcosm, and so is everything human. Running through all is the polarity

[53] I am using here a translation in Wm. Theodore de Bary, Wing-tsit Chan, and Burton Watson, eds., *Sources of Chinese Tradition* (New York: Columbia University Press, 1960), pp. 591–592.

[54] For a translation of Ssu-ma T'an's discussion of the essentials of the Six Schools, see Burton Watson, *Ssu-ma Ch'ien:*[ao] *Grand Historian of China* (New York: Columbia University Press, 1958), pp. 43–48.

of *yin* and *yang*. This philosophy underlies the typically Chinese view of the relation between law and morals, as articulated in a commentary on the *Code of T'ang:* "Virtue and morals are the foundation of government and education, while laws and punishments are the operative agencies of government and education. Both the former and the latter are necessary complements to each other, just as it takes morning and evening to form a whole day, and spring and autumn to form a whole year."[55]

III. HARMONY AS THE GOAL OF HUMAN SOCIETY

I do not believe, with the German jurists of the historical school, that each nation has a soul of its own called the "*Volksseele*." But I do believe that every nation has a way of living and thinking which is more or less peculiar to it, constituting, as it were, its distinctive spirit. This spirit permeates all the main channels of its activities, such as law, politics, social economy, literature, social etiquette, and even athletics. For instance, the American way of life is marked by the spirit of democracy and fair play. The spirit may not be fully realized in actual practice, but that makes no difference, so long as it is persistently there, ready to assert itself whenever it can and to the extent it can. Sportsmanship is the spirit of America. It says, "Every dog has his day, and every man his say."

China, too, has her spirit, formed long before the days of Confucius. The most deep-rooted desire of the Chinese people is for harmony. Whether they are speaking of self-cultivation or dealing with the affairs of the world, *harmony* is the keynote of all their thinking. In the practice of virtue, they aim at the harmony of body and soul. In the family, they aim at the harmony of husband and wife and of the brothers and sisters. In the village, they aim at the harmony of neighbors. Even the Golden Rule of Confucius and his principle of reciprocity are little more than an expression of the spirit of harmony. When Confucius says that in a country what is really to be worried about is not the scarcity of goods but the lack of proportion in their distribution, he is aiming at socio-economic harmony. When he says that in hearing litigations he is no better than other people, but that the important thing is to cause litigations to cease, it is very plain that he prefers social harmony, which would prevent any conflicts of interest from arising, to a just resolution of actual conflicts. The *Book of Changes* contains a hexagram called "*sung*,"[ab] [56] meaning litigation, contention, and controversy. The explanation is significant: "*Sung* intimates that, although there is sincerity and justice in one's contention, he will yet meet with opposition and frustration. If he cherish an apprehensive caution, the outcome will be auspicious; but if he prosecutes the ligitation to the end, there will be evil." In summarizing the comments of Confucian scholars on this hexagram, Richard Wilhelm writes: "If a man is entangled in a

[55] *Code of T'ang with Commentaries and Annotations*,[ap] reprinted in Peking in 1890, II, p. 14.

[56] See Carl F. Baynes, trans., *The I ching*,[aq] or *Book of Changes*. The Richard Wilhelm translation rendered into English by Carl F. Baynes. Foreword by C. G. Jung. Bollingen Series No. 19, 2 vols. (New York: Pantheon Books, 1950), Vol. I, pp. 28–32; II, pp. 51–56.

conflict, his only salvation lies in being so clear-headed and inwardly strong that he is always ready to come to terms by meeting the opponent halfway. To carry the conflict to the bitter end has evil effects even when one is in the right, because the enmity is then perpetuated."[57] This represents the typical Chinese attitude toward lawsuits. How different in spirit from Rudolf von Jhering's fiery doctrine of the struggle for law and his advice: "Bring suit, cost what it may!"[58]

For better or for worse, the fact is that practically all the Chinese sages are more or less of the mind of Lao Tzu, who says, "The man of virtue attends to his duties; while a man of no virtue attends to his rights."[59] Real strength of character reveals itself in self-conquest, not in the conquering of another.

In the earliest extant literature of China, we note the Chinese predilection for peace and harmony. I need only to quote the beginning paragraph of the *Book of History*, giving a characterization of Emperor Yao[ac] of antiquity in these terms: "He was reverent, enlightened, refined, and mild. He was most courteous and capable of yielding. . . . By spreading the splendor of his noble virtues, he made affectionate the nine branches of the family. When harmony reigned among the nine branches of the family, he adjusted peacefully the relations of the hundred families. When the hundred families were well regulated, the myriad states were harmonized, and universal order and concord prevailed among all the people."[60] This may have been a myth, but a myth is a very real thing in the life of a nation. It reveals basic evaluations.

It is indeed remarkable that in the very first cabinet recorded in Chinese history there was included a Minister of Music, K'uei,[ad] whom Emperor Shun charged with the duty of teaching music to the eldest sons of the leading families so as to make them "upright and yet mild, big-hearted and yet circumspect, strong without being violent, simple and free in manners without being arrogant."[61]

In other words, the emperor wished the musical master to infuse into the hearts of future leaders the spirit of harmony.

But, although the idea of harmony is richer than the idea of justice, it nevertheless includes justice. At any rate, lack of justice bespeaks lack of harmony. In fact, injustice was considered the surest way of breaking the harmony of the universe and thereby calling down calamities from Heaven. For instance, a poet complained of the injustice of King Yu[ae] (reigned 781–771 B.C.) of Chou (1111–256 B.C.) as follows:

Lands owned by your people
You have occupied by force.
Men that belong to the lords
You have robbed from their hands.

[57] *Ibid.*, I, p. 29.
[58] Rudolf von Jhering, *The Struggle for Law* (Chicago: Callaghan & Company, 1915), p. 26.
[59] *Tao-te ching* LXXVIII.
[60] See "Canon of Yao."
[61] See "Canon of Shun."

This one should be declared innocent,
Yet you have put him in jail.
That one should be found guilty,
Yet you have shown favors to him.[62]

This is one form of injustice that disturbs the harmony of the universe. Another form consists in the lack of proportion in the distribution of burdens and benefits among the people, as is graphically described in the following verses:

Some people live comfortably at home:
Others wear themselves out in public service.
Some lie supinely in bed:
Others are always on the move.

Some never hear a clamorous sound:
Others are never relieved of toil and moil.
Some enjoy the pleasures of leisure:
Others chafe under the load of the King's business.

Some feast and drink in carefree joy:
Others live in constant dread of blame.
Some do nothing but talk and find fault:
Others are doomed to do all things.[63]

Occasionally, a poet would sing the praise of a just man:

Among the people goes the saying:
"Eat the soft, throw out the hard."
It is not so with the Venerable Chung-shan,[af]
Who eats not the soft nor spares the hard.
For he had no fear of the powerful great;
Nor lorded it over the lonely and poor.[64]

The Chinese think of justice and harmony dynamically. The empty is to be filled, and the full is to be diminished. The low is to be exalted, while the high is to be leveled down. In the words of Lao Tzu, "To be great is to go far, and to go far is to return."[65] Many modern thinkers of China are returning to the ancient ideal of the Grand Harmony, as presented in the *Book of Rites:*

When the Great Way prevailed in the world, all mankind worked for the common good. Men of virtue and ability were elected to fill public offices. Good faith was universally observed and friendly relations cultivated. People's love was not confined to their own parents and their own children, so that all the aged ones were enabled to live out the natural span of their lives, all the young ones were brought up in the proper way, all the widows and widowers, the orphans and childless persons, the crippled and the sick, were well taken care of. Each man had a definite work to do, and each woman a home of her own. The people were loath to let the natural resources lie undeveloped in the

[62] The *Book of Odes,* ode no. 264.
[63] *Ibid.,* no. 205.
[64] *Ibid.,* no. 260.
[65] *Tao-te ching* XXV.

earth; but they did not desire to hoard riches in their own houses. They were ashamed to be idle; but they did not labor for their own profit. In this way, the source of all greed was stopped up, and there was no occasion for the rise of theft and banditry, nor was there any need to lock the outer door of one's house. This is called the Age of Grand Harmony.[66]

Neither Confucius nor Mencius was an impractical visionary. They realized very well that, although cultural and spiritual life is of infinitely greater value than physical life, yet the latter must first be taken care of before the people could be expected to devote time and energy to self-cultivation. Confucius once entered a populous city, and uttered a spontaneous exclamation, "Oh, what a population!" A disciple asked him, "Given a multitude of people, what next?" He said, "Enrich them!" "After enriching them, what next?" He said, "Teach them!"[67] This, roughly, represents his program.

Mencius is even more explicit and emphatic on the importance of securing for all the people a regular livelihood. He pointed out that only scholars will be able to adhere unswervingly to the path of virtue even in the absence of economic security. As for the rank and file of the people, their hearts cannot be fixed on goodness as long as their livelihood is not secure. Therefore he proceeds to say,

> . . . an intelligent ruler will regulate the livelihood of the people, so as to make sure that, above, they shall have sufficient wherewithal to serve their parents, and, below, sufficient wherewithal to support their wives and children; that in good years they shall always be abundantly satisfied, and that in bad years they shall not be in danger of perishing. After this he may urge them, and they will proceed to what is good, for in this case the people will follow after that with readiness.[68]

It is only upon this condition that the Confucians set forth their truly thoroughgoing program of the moral reformation of the world with one's own moral transformation as the starting point. Let me quote the opening passage of the *Great Learning*, which seems to me to belong to the perennial philosophy and to contain a message for the modern world:

> The goal of Great Learning consists in the elucidation of Bright Virtue, in renewing the spirit of the people, and in resting in the Supreme Goodness. When a man knows where to rest, his heart is fixed; when the heart is fixed he can really be quiet; when he is quiet, he can enjoy peace; when he enjoys peace he can think for himself; when he thinks for himself he can attain true insights. Things have their root and their branches. Affairs have their end and their beginning. To know what is first and what follows after is to be near to the attainment of Truth.
>
> The ancients who wished to spread the knowledge of Bright Virtue to the world, first ordered well their own States. Wishing to order well their own States, they first regulated their families. Wishing to regulate their families,

[66] See "Evolution of Rites" in the *Book of Rites*. For a modern interpretation, see L. G. Thompson, *Ta Tung Shu:*[ar] *The One-World Philosophy of K'ang Yu-Wei*[as] (London: George Allen & Unwin, Ltd., 1958).
[67] *Analects* XIII.7.
[68] The *Book of Mencius* IA.5.

they first cultivated their persons. Wishing to cultivate their persons, they first rectified their hearts. Wishing to rectify their hearts, they first sought to be sincere in their thoughts. Wishing to be sincere in their thoughts, they sought after true knowledge. The attainment of knowledge depends upon the investigation of the nature of things and relationships.[69]

To put it the other way around, the investigation of the nature of things and relationships leads to true knowledge, which leads to sincerity in thought, which leads to purity of heart, which prepares for the perfection of the whole person, which conduces to an orderly family, which helps to make a well-governed State, which contributes toward the peace of the entire world. In fact, the whole process is a continuous harmonious movement from the innermost harmony to the outermost harmony. For the investigation of things and knowledge represent the harmony of subject and object; sincerity in thought and purity of heart represent the harmony of intellect and will; personal perfection represents the harmony of body and soul; while the orderly family, the well-governed State, and the peaceful world form a progressive series of concentric expansions of transpersonal harmony.

Although in ancient China the "world" designated no more than the whole of the then-known empire, this does not prevent modern Chinese thinkers from extending their mental horizons *pari passu* with the growth of the actual horizons of the world. Thus, the Chinese ideology envisages an open society rather than a closed one. Nor does it consider the authority of the State in terms of absolute sovereignty. The family and the State are but stations, albeit necessary stations, to a harmonious world. When the head of the Chinese delegation to the United Nations Conference in San Francisco said: "If there is any message that my country . . . wishes to give to this Conference, it is that we are prepared... to yield if necessary a part of our sovereignty to the new international organization in the interest of collective security," he was but voicing the traditional spirit of China, the idea of universal harmony.

The Chinese idea of harmony comprehends not only unity but utmost diversity. It is something cosmic. Let me borrow a magnificent description of it from Chuang Tzu[ag] (399–295 B.C.?). "The breath of the universe is called wind. At times, it is inactive. But when active, every aperture resounds to the blast. . . . Caves and dells of hill and forest, hollows in huge trees of many a span in girth; these are like nostrils, like mouths, like ears, like beam-sockets, like goblets, like mortars, like ditches, like bogs. And the wind goes rushing through them, sniffing, snoring, singing, soughing, puffing, purling, whistling, whirring, now shrilly treble, now deeply bass, now soft, now loud; until, with a lull, silence reigns supreme.... The effect of the wind upon these various apertures is not uniform. But what is it that gives to each the individuality, to all the potentiality of sound? Great knowledge embraces the whole: small knowledge, a part only. Great speech is universal: small speech is particular."[70]

[69] For another translation see E. R. Hughes, *The Great Learning and the Mean-in-Action* (New York: E. P. Dutton & Co., 1943), pp. 146 ff.

[70] Herbert Giles, *Chuang Tzu* (Shanghai: Kelly & Walsh, 1926), pp. 12–13.

The interesting point is that it is precisely thanks to the utmost oneness and impartial universality of the breath of the universe that all the diversities of sound are given the fullest expression. It is only when a particular part in the human world claims to be the universal whole that disharmony appears on the scene of history, disfiguring even the cosmic harmony. But cosmic harmony cannot be disturbed for long without avenging itself by disharmonizing the disharmony, until the original harmony is restored.

Chinese historians conceive of the process of history as consisting in an unending series of cycles of ups and downs. They take the moon as a symbol of human affairs with its unceasing successions of waxing and waning. The sages have drawn from this *Weltanschauung* some wisdom of life peculiarly Chinese. We are not to be elated when the winds are with us, nor are we to despair when the winds are against us. But we are tempted to fold our arms and hide our heads during the stormy days, in the confidence that by virtue of the cosmic dialectic the storm will soon blow over. Fatalism is our besetting sin.

I cannot help thinking that the Chinese conception of harmony is not entirely adequate. We are inclined to think of it too exclusively in terms of concord or a succession of concords. Whenever there is a discord, our harmony is disrupted. In other words, we seldom if ever think of a discord as an opportunity for rising to a new concord. The West is more adept in the art of resolution of discord, thus continuing the harmony through the discordant interval. When confronted with such a discordant interval, we Chinese too often feel utterly at a loss as to what to do except to wait patiently for the turning of the tide, and, when our patience is exhausted, to burst out in uncontrollable passion and emotion. We have much to learn from the West in the way of resolution of discord. On the other hand, the West should remember that the discordant intervals are, after all, not the norm and that we cannot rest in restlessness.

The present crisis of the world in general and of China in particular calls for a revival of faith in the super-eminent justice and humanity of God as against the belief in the stars and the blind operations of dialectical materialism. No astral destiny or dialectical process can decide the fate of a nation and of mankind. In Western history, as Mircea Eliade has pointed out in his *Cosmos and History: The Myth of the Eternal Return,* "Christian thought tended to transcend, once and for all, the old themes of eternal repetition, just as it had undertaken to transcend all the other archaic viewpoints by revealing the importance of the religious experience of faith and that of the value of the human personality."[71] It is submitted that Confucian humanism, before it had degenerated into a kind of anthropomorphic cosmogony by being wedded to the philosophy of Yin Yang and the mechanical alternation of the Five Elements (metal, wood, water, fire, earth), comes very near to Christian thought in its rational conception of the mandate of Heaven and in its emphasis on the value of the human person.

[71] Mircea Eliade, *Cosmos and History: The Myth of Eternal Return* (New York: Harper and Brothers, 1959), p. 137.

In conclusion, I should like to call your attention to one more contrast between the East and the West. The East generally puts the Golden Age at the beginning, the West at the end. The East is Epimethean, while the West is Promethean. To my mind, it makes little or no difference whether one looks backward or forward, so long as one looks far enough, for, ultimately, the Alpha and the Omega are absolutely one.

QUESTION: There is some agreement that "mediational law," in which cognizance is taken of the unique factors of a situation, has been paramount in China (through Ch'ing times, 1644–1912). Such "law" seems to contrast with the law of the Ch'ing written penal code, in which comparatively less concern is paid to the unique factors pertaining to the individual's commission of an act even than in many Western codes. For example, the fact that an act was accidentally caused is often of small matter in regard to legal guilt, and there is frequent legal guilt by mere implication. The fact that there was an act, plus its consequences, seems to be more the center of focus.

Do you feel that such a contrast (exceeding the normal one between "mediational law" and determinate written rules) actually existed? If so, how do you reconcile the two interpretations? Is it that the written code embodies the strict focus on commission of the act of the legalist tradition, while the Confucian tradition of applying the spirit of the law is embodied in "mediational law"?

ANSWER: Strictly speaking, so-called "mediational law" is not law, but merely a certain attitude on the part of the Confucian magistrates in the administration of justice, especially in cases involving family relations.

It is not quite true to say that in the old penal system even an accidental act, that is, an act which is neither intentional nor negligent, could constitute the basis of criminal responsibility. In fact, from the earliest classics, it is clear that the greatest emphasis was laid on the presence of intention as the most essential element of a crime. Two basic legal maxims stand out prominently in the *Book of History:* (1) "An intentional act should be punished, however small the injury: but an unintended mishap should be excused, however great the harm." (2) "Better miss the guilty than slay an innocent person."

In all the penal codes of the different dynasties, the distinctions between intentional wrong, negligence, and pure accident are carefully preserved.

Mediation came into play when no grave wrongs were involved and the litigation concerned property rights between members of a family or between neighbors. Only in such cases would a magistrate advise the parties to forget about their rights and wrongs and to reach an amicable settlement.

[a] 吳經熊
[b] 湯
[c] 武
[d] 紂
[e] 桀
[f] 宣
[g] 齊
[h] 楚
[i] 老子
[j] 無爲
[k] 皐陶
[l] 舜
[m] 禹
[n] 定
[o] 成
[p] 君陳
[q] 下都
[r] 墨子
[s] 商鞅
[t] 韓非子
[u] 韓昭侯
[v] 荀子
[w] 李斯
[x] 黃宗羲
[y] 明夷待訪錄
[z] 陰陽
[aa] 司馬談
[ab] 訟
[ac] 堯
[ad] 夔
[ae] 幽
[af] 仲山
[ag] 莊子
[ah] 仲虺
[ai] 道德經
[aj] 益稷
[ak] 胡適
[al] 薛光前
[am] 梅貽寶
[an] 梁啟超
[ao] 司馬遷
[ap] 唐律疏議
[aq] 易經
[ar] 大同書
[as] 康有爲

HAJIME NAKAMURA[a]

Basic Features of the Legal, Political, and Economic Thought of Japan

I. INTRODUCTION

The legal, political, and economic thought of a people cannot be discussed without taking their chief basic philosophical concepts into consideration.

As the main features of the Japanese ways of thinking we must note the following three major characteristics and other subordinate factors:

1. *The acceptance of actuality:* (a) apprehension of the Absolute in the phenomenal world; (b) this-worldliness; (c) acceptance of natural human qualities; (d) the spirit of tolerance; (e) cultural stratification; and (f) weakness of the spirit of direct criticism.
2. *The tendency to emphasize a particular social nexus:* (a) emphasis on human relations; (b) human relationships as of greater importance than the individual; (c) absolute view of limited social organization; (d) reverence for family morality; (e) emphasis upon hierarchical relations of status; (f) the supremacy of the State; (g) absolute obedience to some particular person; (h) emperor worship; (i) closed character of sects and cliques; (j) protection of the particular social nexus by force; (k) emphasis on activity in society; (l) sensitivity to moral introspection; and (m) lack of self-consciousness in religious reverence.
3. *Non-rational tendencies:* (a) non-logical tendencies; (b) weakness in ability to think in terms of logical consequences; (c) intuitional and emotional tendencies; (d) lack of ability to form complex representations; (e) fondness for simple, symbolic representations; (f) weakness in knowledge of objective processes.[1]

[1] These features were discussed in my work, *Tōyōjin no Shii-hōhō*[aq] ("The Ways of Thinking of Eastern Peoples"), 2 vols. (Tokyo: Misuzu-shobo, 1949), Vol. I, pp. 1–378. This has recently been translated under the supervision of the author and published as *The Ways of Thinking of Eastern Peoples,* under the auspices of UNESCO (Tokyo: The Japanese Commission for UNESCO, 1960).

With regard to such legal, political, and economic thought, which is the problem under consideration, the first and the second of these sets of basic attitudes are important, and, with them in mind, we shall proceed with the discussion.

II. ESTEEM OF HUMAN NATURE IN SOCIETY

The Japanese in general are inclined to search for the Absolute within the phenomenal world or in what is actual. Among all the natures that are given and real, the most immediate to man is the nature of man. Hence, the Japanese tend to esteem highly man's natural disposition. So, as one of the most prominent features of traditional Japanese ways of thinking, we may point to an emphasis on the love of human beings. This may be described as the naturalistic view of life.[2] This tendency has been conspicuous among Shintoists. Even Buddhist ideas have been taught with close reference to matters of love, and even sexual love is considered not to be incompatible with religious principles. The tendency to esteem man's nature gave rise to the love of human beings in actual life.

The tendency toward humanitarianism has been traditional among the Japanese, and yet it has generally escaped the attention of scholars. The love of others in its purified form is named "benevolence" or "compassion" (Sanskrit, *maitrī, karuṇā*). This idea was introduced into Japan with the advent of Buddhism, and special emphasis has been put on it in Japanese Buddhism. The attempt to apply universal religions in politics caused rulers to deal with the people with affection and compassion, as in the case of Aśoka. The Constitution of Prince Shōtoku[b] (574–622) esteems the welfare of the people and is sympathetic with them. In this Constitution, the common people came to have a significant place in the consciousness of the ruling class. This role could not be destroyed in later history, and this trend might be regarded as the first step of gradual development toward democracy.

The spirit of benevolence was not preached only by the Buddhists. It made its way into Shintoism, and was associated with one of the three divine symbols of the Japanese Imperial Family, which claimed to rule on the spiritual basis of benevolence. The Tokugawa Shogunate[c] government (1571–1867) inherited this attitude. Benevolence also came to be regarded as one of the principle virtues of the *samurai* (knights), who asserted that it was not sufficient for them to be physically brave and strong, but that they should also be compassionate toward the common people.[3] Japanese Confucian scholars of politics also lay special emphasis upon the love of others. Kumazawa Banzan,[d] a famous Confucian of the Tokugawa period, called Japan "the land of benevolence."[4]

[2] Hajime Nakamura, "Some Features of the Japanese Way of Thinking," *Monumenta Nipponica,* XIV, Nos. 3–4 (1958–1959), 31–72.

[3] The details are set forth in my work *Jihi*[ar] ("Compassion") (Kyoto: Heirakuji Shoten, 1956), pp. 258–271.

[4] Kumazawa Banzan, *Shugi-washo*[as] ("Collection of Discourses"), Vol. X, p. 1a. (An old printed text, with neither date nor publisher mentioned, preserved in the library of the University of Tokyo.)

These facts give ample testimony to the assumption that the ruling class of Japan aimed at benevolence as its principal ideal.

In pre-Buddhist Japan, cruel punishments were not lacking. Emperors killed their subjects arbitrarily.[5] On the occasions of the internment of emperors, their retainers were buried alive around their graves.[6] Such customs were abolished, and after the advent of Buddhism there existed in Japan hardly any punishment that was cruel. In the Heian[e] period (794–1192), capital punishment was not practiced for about three hundred and fifty years. Since crucifixion appeared for the first time in Japanese history during the Age of Civil Wars (1138–1560) it was probably introduced after the advent of Christianity and suggested by it.

The love of human beings seems to be closely connected with the love of the beauties of Nature, which is as old as the Japanese people themselves.

These tendencies give some clues to the basic concepts of the legal, political, and economic thought of the Japanese.

III. THE SPIRIT OF HARMONY OR CONCORD

The unanimous moral solidarity of a community has been sought as the social ideal, on an island scale, of Japan. This was felt intuitively in the spiritual atmosphere of the primitive society of Japan. Later, when the centralized State was established after the conflicts among various tribes had ended, "concord" was stressed as the most important principle of the community. Prince Shōtoku emphasized "harmony" or "concord" in human relations. With deep self-reflection, he advocated such concord in the first Article of his Constitution: "Above all else esteem concord; make it your first duty to avoid discord. People are prone to form partisanships, for few persons are really enlightened. Hence, there are those who do not obey their lords and parents, and who come in conflict with their neighbors. But when those above are harmonious, and those below are friendly, there is concord in the discussion of affairs, and right views of things spontaneously gain acceptance. Then what would there be that could not be accomplished?" Some scholars say that this conception of concord (*wa*[f]) was adopted from Confucianism, for the word *"wa"* was used in the *Analects* of Confucius.[7] But the term *"wa"* was used in connection with propriety or decorum in that work,[8] and concord was not the subject being discussed. Prince Shōtoku, on the other hand, advocated concord as the principle of human behavior.[9] His attitude seems to have been derived from the Buddhist concept of benevolence, or compassion, which should be distinguished from

[5] For example, the stories of *"Mie no Uneme"*[at] and Emperors Kensō[au] and Keitai,[av] in Basil Hall Chamberlain, trans., *Kojiki.*[aw] *Record of Ancient Matters.* Transactions of the Asiatic Society of Japan, Vol. X (Tokyo: The Asiatic Society of Japan, 1906), Supplement, pp. 402, 419, 424, etc.

[6] *Ibid.*, pp. 213, 215.

[7] Confucius, *Analects* I.12: "In practising the rules of propriety a natural ease is to be prized." Here "a natural ease" is the translation of the Chinese word *"wa."* In James Legge's version, edited with notes by Yoshio Ogaeri[ax] (Tokyo: Bunki Shoten, 1950), p. 4.

[8] In the Chinese versions of Buddhist texts such words as *wakyō*[ay] and *wagō*[az] are frequently used.

[9] Prince Shōtoku's Constitution, Article 10.

the Confucian concept. Men are apt to be bigoted and partial. Within a community or between communities conflicts are sure to occur. One should overcome such conflicts, and concord should be realized, so that a harmonious community may be formed in an ideal way. The spirit of concord was stressed throughout all the Articles of the Constitution. Concord between lord and subject, between superior and inferior, among people in general, and among individuals was taught repeatedly. Prince Shōtoku did not teach that the people shall merely follow or obey but that discussion should be carried on in the atmosphere of concord or harmony, so that one might attain right views. Earnest discussion was most desirable. If we discuss affairs with the feeling of harmony, desisting from anger, difficult problems will be settled spontaneously in the right way. In this way alone is it possible that decisions may be reached at conferences.[10]

The democratic way of managing a conference was achieved in the remote past. In the mythology which reflects the primitive society of Japan, deities gathered in a divine assembly in the bed of a river. This tradition was followed and developed by later monarchs. Prince Shōtoku denounced dictatorship and stressed the necessity of discussing things with others: "Decisions on important matters should generally not be made by one person alone. They should be discussed with many others. But small matters are of less importance, and it is unnecessary to consult many persons concerning them. In the case of weighty matters, you must be fearful lest there be faults. You should arrange matters in consultation with many persons, so as to arrive at the right conclusion."[11]

This trend developed into the edict after the Taika[g] Innovation (A.D. 645), which denounced the dictatorship of a sovereign by saying that things should not be instituted by a single ruler. The ancient way of ruling represented in Japanese mythology is not dictatorship by a monarch or by the Lord of All, but a conference of gods in the bed of a river. Where public opinion was not esteemed, a conference could not have been held successfully. So, the spirit of primitive Shintoism must have been inherited and developed by later rulers. This ideal was preserved in the days when the emperors were in power. Japanese monarchy or the Emperor Institution developed as something different from dictatorship.

Professor Northrop holds that when a dispute arises among Asians one does not settle it by recourse to determinate legal principles, but pursues the "middle way" or mediation between the determinate theses of the disputants, by fostering the all-embracing intuitively felt formlessness common to all men and things.[12] Chiang Monlin[h] writes: "Modern legal sense as the West understands it is not developed in China. Avoid the courts if you can. Let us settle our disputes without going to law. Let's compromise. Let's have a cup of tea and sip together with friends and talk things over."[13] This is exactly the situation we find among the Japanese also. There is a well-known Japanese proverb which

[10] Chamberlain, *op. cit.*, p. 112.
[11] Prince Shōtoku's Constitution, Article 17.
[12] F. S. C. Northrop, *The Taming of the Nations* (New York: The Macmillan Co., 1953), p. 62.
[13] Cited by Northrop, *ibid.*, p. 126.

is understood by everybody in practice: "In a quarrel both parties are to blame."

But this is not due to lack of esteem for law on the part of the Japanese people, but due to financial and other considerations. If they should go to court, they would lose much time; sometimes it would take several years to settle even one case. They would have to employ lawyers and spend much money. Even if they should win at court, they would get very little. So, to resort to legal measures very often impairs, taking everything into account, the happiness and welfare of the people concerned and others around them. Barristers-at-law are not always respected, but very often abhorred, by the common people of Japan, who fear that they may take advantage of the people's lack of legal knowledge in order to make money for themselves. The writer personally knows some Japanese intellectuals who claim to be businessmen at home, but to be lawyers when they go abroad. They want to conceal their status as lawyer while they work with the Japanese.

But this does not mean that Japanese laws are applied partially. The Japanese meanings for the expressions of definite laws or codes are the same for all men and occasions. There is no difference at all. Yet, they do not always want to resort to legal measures.

As the objective causes which brought about such a tendency in the Japanese people, we may cite the social life peculiar to their land and climate.

The primitive Indo-Europeans, being nomadic and living chiefly by hunting, were in contact with alien peoples. Here human relations were marked by fierce rivalry. Peoples were in great migration; one race conquered another only to be conquered by still another. In such a situation struggles for existence were based, not on mutual trust, but on rational plan and strategem. This mental feature seems to have been preserved even in modern times in the West.

Japanese society, on the other hand, developed from small localized farming communities. The Japanese did away with nomadic life early, and settled down to cultivate rice fields. People living on rice must inevitably settle permanently in one place. In such a society *families* continue generation after generation. Genealogies and kinships of families through long years become so well known by their members that the society as a whole takes on the appearance of a single family. In such a society, individuals are closely bound to each other, and they form an exclusive human nexus. Here, an individual who asserts himself will hurt the feelings of others and thereby do harm to himself. The Japanese learned to adjust themselves to this type of familial society, and created forms of expression suitable to life in such a society. And here grew the worship of tutelary gods and local deities. Even today, there is a strong tendency in Japanese social structure to settle closely around such tutelary gods and local deities. This tendency is deeply rooted in the people, and it has led to their stressing of human relations, especially the spirit of harmony or concord in society. The Japanese have learned to attach unduly heavy importance to their human nexus in disregard of the individual.

IV. THE CONCEPT OF LAW

Law-giving was not lacking even in the genuinely Shintoist, pre-Buddhist age. To illustrate, it is said that Emperor Seimu[hl] determined the frontiers and civilized the country, and that he issued laws. He held sway, reforming the surnames and selecting the gentle names.[14] The laws of the primitive Japanese, as of all ancient peoples, were those of custom. Though their details have been lost, it is likely that the two fundamental principles—Imperial sovereignty and the family system—were firmly established even in those days. But no positive law of those days is now known to us. It is with Prince Shōtoku that we first come to know something of laws in the modern sense.

Prince Shōtoku, the real founder of the centralized State of Japan, proclaimed the Seventeen-Article Constitution in A.D. 604. This was the first legislation in Japan—the characteristic expression of the original and creative development of the Japanese in those days—adopting the civilizations and thought of China and India sufficiently for their purposes, based chiefly upon the spirit of Buddhism. This is, so to speak, the *Magna Charta* of Japan. The Constitution prescribed the rules of conduct which the officials of the Imperial government should obey, thereby, perchance, revealing how badly needed such rules were. It has been confirmed by scholars that there is a close connection between the spirit of Shōtoku's Constitution and the political regime established at the Taika Innovation, which brought about the unified State of Japan.

In contrast to Prince Shōtoku and his Seventeen-Article Constitution, King Songtsan-Gampo, the founder of the centralized State of Tibet, proclaimed his Sixteen-Article Law of similar purport at nearly the same time, and, looking back to antiquity, we find that King Aśoka published many Rock and Pillar Edicts which proclaimed various precepts whose number was not fixed. The characteristic common to all of these is that they approximate to moral precepts in the form of representation, and that they were different from positive laws in practice.

Positive laws were officially promulgated later. In A.D. 671, a code of laws, said to have consisted of twenty-two volumes, was formed; but the entire code was lost, and its contents are unknown. The work of codification was completed in A.D. 701. This entire code, consisting of eleven volumes of general law concerning government organization, administration, and private relations, and six volumes of criminal laws, was promulgated and enforced; this is known as the *Taihō Code*.[i] This was revised in A.D. 718. These Taihō Laws, with many revisions and supplements, governed the nation for about five hundred years, until 1190. With the establishment of the feudal regime, the individual Shoguns[j] issued laws; and, as the authority of the Shoguns increased, the territory within which the Taihō Laws were enforced decreased. In the Age of Civil Wars, many feudal lords issued their own regulations or family laws. The Tokugawa Shogunate government tried to govern the country according to al-

[14] Chamberlain, *op. cit.*, p. 2.

ready existing customs, and, as far as possible, avoided the making of written laws. Contact with Western nations and a study of their civilization after the Meiji Restoration[k] (1868) showed the necessity of laws in harmony with the modern world. In 1882, the criminal code was promulgated. This was followed in 1889 by the proclamation of the Constitution, and, in 1900, by the civil code. Up to the end of World War II, Japanese laws were characterized by two fundamental principles: the sovereignty of the emperor and the patriarchal family system. In 1946, after the surrender of Japan, the new constitution was promulgated, and these two characteristics were legally abolished, although they are still virtually in effect.

The move to conceptualize human affairs in terms of laws and concepts which are universals has been effected by the Japanese to some extent. The concept of universal law came into existence very early in the time of Prince Shōtoku, when he said: "Sincerely revere the Three Treasures. The Three Treasures, viz., the Buddha, the Law (*Dharma*), and the Congregation (*Saṅgha*), constitute the final ideal of all living beings and the ultimate foundation of all countries. Should any age or any people fail to esteem this truth? There are few men who are really vicious. They will all follow it if adequately instructed. How can the crooked ways of men be made straight unless we take refuge in the Three Treasures?"[15] Here we find the concept of a universal law which is something beyond laws based on the inductively given status of the individual in the joint family and of the family in its respective tribe or caste. According to the Prince, the "Law" is the "norm" of all the living creatures, the "Buddha" is in fact "the Law embodied," which, "being united with reason," becomes the *Saṅgha*. So, according to his teaching, everything converges in the one fundamental principle called the "Law."

It is likely that other Asian kings who adopted Buddhism thought in the same way. Aśoka, however, resorted to *dharma,* which is valid for various religions, and not necessarily Buddhism alone. Things being so, it may seem that there was a fundamental difference between Aśoka and other Asian monarchs, including Prince Shōtoku. Investigating the fundamental ideas which brought these historical facts to reality, however, we find there was not much difference. In the case of Prince Shōtoku, there was only one philosophical system which taught universal laws, Buddhism. It was natural that he termed Buddhism "the final ideal of all living beings and the ultimate foundation of all countries." In the case of Aśoka, however, many religious systems had already become highly developed, and there were many other religions which claimed to be universal philosophical systems. So, he had to consider many religions. When we examine the situation more deeply, we find that the quintessence of Buddhism consists in acknowledging the universal laws taught by all religions and philosophies, as is evidenced in both early and Mahāyāna Buddhism. So, we are led to the conclusion that there is no fundamental difference in ideology between King Aśoka and Prince Shōtoku. In this respect they had this in

[15] Prince Shōtoku's Constitution, Article 2.

common, that they wanted to found their kingdoms on the basis of universal laws or the truth of the universe.

Due to this characteristic of Buddhism, neither Prince Shōtoku nor King Songtsan-Gampo, not to mention Aśoka, suppressed indigenous faiths native to their respective peoples, although they both esteemed and reverenced Buddhism. That is why Shintoism in Japan and the Bon religion in Tibet have been preserved, as their respective religions, up to the present time. In Burma, the faith of Nats is prevalent even now among the common people. Taking this attitude into consideration, we shall be able to understand why such an edict was proclaimed in the reign of Prince Shōtoku as follows: "In my reign, why shall we be negligent of practicing the worship of Shintoist gods. All my officials should worship them sincerely." Both Shintoism and Buddhism have been given protection by the government throughout history.

When we compare these facts with the situation in the West, we find a fundamental difference. Some Western intellectuals say that Eastern peoples hold no distinction between good and bad, right and wrong. But Prince Shōtoku taught that the spirit of esteeming good and hating bad should be cherished: "Punish the vicious and reward the virtuous. This is the excellent rule of antiquity. Do not, therefore, let the good deeds of any person go concealed, nor the bad deeds of any go uncorrected, when you see them. Flatterers and deceivers are like the fatal missile which will overthrow the State, or the sharp sword which will destroy the people."[16] This spirit can be found also in the case of King Aśoka. He deplored the fact that good is difficult to perform, whereas to do bad is easy.[17] Moreover, the Prince wrote: "Light crimes should be embraced by our power of reforming influence, and grave crimes should be surrendered to our power of strong force." He did not avoid resorting to force in order to punish the severely wicked.

In "Bushidō"[1] ("the Way of Knights"), which developed in later times as the peculiarly Japanese "way," and which was regarded as the actual political philosophy of the Japanese, the distinction of good and bad was extremely stressed and strictly observed. *"Bushi"* (Knights) should do nothing mean or despicable even at the cost of their lives.

Considering these historical facts, the assertion made by some scholars that Westerners are keen to the rigid distinction between good and bad, whereas Eastern peoples are not, is untenable.

V. NATIONALISM AND THE PRESTIGE OF THE EMPEROR

It has often been pointed out that the basic social and moral principles of Asian peoples consist essentially of filial piety. With regard to the Japanese, this feature holds true to some extent, but not wholly. In Japan, loyalty to lords in the feudal age and loyalty to the emperor in the days since the Meiji Restoration have been much stronger.

[16] *Ibid.*, Article VI.

[17] Pillar Edict V.

The peculiarly Japanese conception of the prestige of the emperor and the Emperor Institution have close relation to the traditionally fundamental conception of harmony. The atmosphere of "harmony" which has prevailed between the emperor and his subjects has enabled the Emperor Institution to last long as the institution which has been characteristic of the political history of Japan. In other countries dynasties have changed. But in Japan there has been only one ruling dynasty or royal family; it has no specific family name, thus evidencing the remote antiquity of its rulership. This dynasty has never been abolished during a long history of more than two thousand years. In the past, the emperor was looked upon as a child of the Sun Deity,[m] [18] but not with awe. In the olden days, the prestige of a deity was superior to that of an emperor.[19] In the genuinely Shintoist, pre-Buddhist Japan, an emperor who was compassionate with the people was respected with affection as an ideal monarch, as is illustrated in the person of Nintoku.[n] [20] In later days, the prestige of the emperor came to be closely connected with the hierarchical order of Japanese society.

What was stressed by Prince Shōtoku was the relation between lord (emperor), officials, and the common people in the centralized State. The principle of governing the State is propriety, morale or morality in a wider sense. The relationship between the emperor, the officials, and the common people was fashioned after the model of ancient China, which was formulated by State Confucianism, but was implanted in the soil of Japan. It seems that this conception was closely connected with the abolition of ownership of land and people by big clans on the occasion of the Taika Innovation. And this firmly established the basis for the Emperor Institution.

The thought of esteeming the prestige of the emperor is especially conspicuous in the Prince Shōtoku Constitution. "In a country there should not be two lords; the people should not have two masters. The people of the whole country have the sovereign as their sole master. The officials appointed to administer the local affairs are all his subjects."[21] This phase harbingers the absolutism of the later Emperor Institution, which was characteristic of Japan. Such a way of esteeming the prestige of the emperor can hardly be illustrated in the abundant classical literature of India and China. In the West, where Christianity has been the predominant factor, it is also difficult to find a counterpart.

The ultimate form in which the Japanese concept of emphasis upon a specific limited human nexus manifested itself was nationalism, which appeared after the Meiji Restoration. But Japanese nationalism did not suddenly appear in the post-Meiji period. Its beginning can be traced to the very remote past.

The notion of Japanese superiority is most boldly expressed in the concept

[18] Prince Shōtoku, *Shōmangyō-gisho*[ba] ("Exposition of the *Śrīmālā-devīsimhānada Sūtra*"), Shinshō Hanayama,[bb] ed. (Tokyo: Iwanami Shoten, 1948), p. 34.

[19] Chamberlain, *op. cit.*, pp. 161–399.

[20] *Ibid.*, p. 336.

[21] Prince Shōtoku's Constitution, Article 12.

of the Divine Nation. We find the following statement by Kitabatake Chikafusa[o] (1293–1354), a Shintoist writer: "Our Great Nippon is a Divine Nation. Our Divine Ancestors founded it; the Sun Goddess let her descendants reign over it for a long time. This is unique to Our Nation; no other nation has the like of it. This is the reason why Our Nation is called 'Divine Nation!'"[22] This concept of "Divine Nation" was adopted by some Buddhists, such as Nichiren[p] and Zen masters.

Confucianism, however, was the best system to provide a theoretical basis for the theory of nationalism. It will be remembered that Confucianism, which the Chinese had earlier adopted as their official theory of the State, was accepted by the Japanese with hardly any trouble. The only controversial point was the problem of changing unsuitable emperors; even this, however, caused no special friction. When Confucianism was introduced into Japan, the ruling class studied it so that they could "become government officials and Confucians, and serve the country."[23]

This attitude toward Confucianism was to persist among the ruling classes, and, in the Tokugawa period, Confucianism was taught with special reference to the concept of the State (*kokutai*[q]) by almost all the schools and individual scholars of Confucianism including Itō Jinsai,[r] Yamaga Sokō,[s] Yamazaki Ansai,[t] and the Mito[u] school. Japanese Confucianism, associated with the nationalism or the authority-consciousness of the Japanese people, asserted its superiority over foreign systems of thought.

But, since the Confucian concept of the State was formulated in accordance with the needs of Chinese society, it naturally contained a number of principles with which the more thoroughgoing Japanese nationalists could not agree. The State conceived by Chinese philosophers was an idealistic model State; on the other hand, the State that the Japanese nationalists had in mind was the actual Japanese State. This was the reason Japanese nationalism, nurtured, so to speak, by Confucianism, had ultimately to deny the authority of Confucianism. Yoshida Shōin,[v] the most influential leader of the movement to establish the modern State of Japan, declared in his criticism of Confucius and Mencius: "It was wrong of Confucius and Mencius to have left their native States and to have served other countries, for a sovereign and a father are essentially the same. To call one's sovereign unwise and dull, and forsake one's native State in order to find another sovereign in another State, is like calling one's father foolish and moving from one's house to the next house to become the son of a neighbor. That Confucius and Mencius lost sight of this truth can never be justified."[24]

[22] In the introductory manifesto of Kitabatake Chikafusa, *Jinnō Shōtōki*[bc] ("Discourses on the Genealogy of the Imperial Family"). Kōchu Nippon Bungaku Taikei,[bd] Vol. XVIII (Tokyo: Kokumin Tosho Kabushiki Kaisha, 1925), p. 585.

[23] (Ascribed to) Sugahara Michizane,[be] *Kanke Bunsō*[bf] ("Ancient Collection of Works"), Vol. III. Also in *Kitano Bunsō*[bg] ("Collected Works of Kitano Shrine"), Vol. II, p. 24; and in *Kitanoshi*[bh] ("The History of the Kitano Shrine"), edited and published by Kitano Shrine, Kyoto, no date given.

[24] Yoshida Shōin, *Kōmō Tōki*[bi] ("Exposition of the the Teachings of Confucius and Mencius"), Vol. I, in Yoshida Shōin, *Yoshida Shōin Zenshū*[bj] ("Collected Works of Yoshida Shōin"), Vol. II, edited by Yamaguchiken Kyōiku-kai (Educational Committee of Yamaguchi Prefecture) (Tokyo: Iwanami Shoten, 1934), p. 263.

A similar tendency can easily be discerned in the process of the assimilation of Buddhism. Japanese Buddhists carefully picked out such doctrines as would be convenient for, or not inconsistent with, their nationalism.

The *Suvarṇaprabhāsa Sūtra* and some later scriptures of Mahāyāna Buddhism, unlike those of early Buddhism, advance the theory that a monarch is a son of divine beings (*tenshi,*[w] *devaputra*) to whom has been given a mandate of Heaven, and whom Heaven would protect. This theory, which became greatly cherished in Japan, had its origin in the Brāhmaṇistic lawbooks, which regulated the feudal society of medieval India. Later, Indian Buddhists came to mention this theory merely as a prevailing notion of society. It was not characteristic of Buddhism. However, this idea came to be especially stressed by the Japanese.

The attitude which Indian Buddhism assumed toward the State was, from the time of its origination, one of cautiousness. For instance, it placed monarchs in the same category with robbers; both were thought to endanger people's welfare. According to the Buddhist legend, the people in remote antiquity elected a common leader who would see to it that the people were protected, good people rewarded, evil people punished. The sovereign originated from this (social contract). The Buddha Śākyamuni is said to have praised the republic of the Vajjis as the ideal form of the State.

But the Japanese, who accepted Buddhism on a large scale, refused, nevertheless, to adopt its concept of the State, which to them seemed to run counter to the native idea of "State structure" (*kokutai*). One writer named Kitabatake Chikafusa was ready, on the one hand, to accept Buddhism in general but, on the other hand, was eager to emphasize the importance of the Japanese Imperial Family in the following way: "The Buddhist theory (of the State) is merely an Indian theory; Indian monarchs may have been the descendants of a monarch selected for the people's welfare, but Our Imperial Family is the only continuous and unending line of family descending from its Heavenly Ancestors."[25] Hirata Atsutane,[x] a fanatic Shintoist leader, discredits the whole Indian theory of the origin of the State as a mere explanation of the origin of "Indian chieftains."[26]

It is evident from the references in historical documents to the purpose of the adoption of Buddhism that considerations for the protection of the State by means of prayers and religious rites constituted a dominant factor in Japanese Buddhism from the very beginning. Most Japanese monasteries in those early days were State-operated places of worship. The protection of the State, one of the most dominant concerns in the Japanese mind, was thus firmly established in religion. It became the slogan of nearly all the Buddhist schools.

So far we have dealt with the problem from the viewpoint of philosophy and religion. The outstanding features of Japanese nationalism, however, may be summed up as follows:

[25] *Jinnō Shōtōki,* p. 592.

[26] Hirata Atsutane, *Shutsujō-shōgo*[bk] ("Ridicule of the Teachings of the Buddha"), edited by Makoto Nagai (Tokyo: Kōbundō, 1936), p. 41.

The Japanese people of the past dedicated a large and important part of their individual life to their State. In this respect, the Japanese went to an extent to which no other Eastern people has ever gone. The extent of such dedication is itself the first feature of Japanese nationalism.

The second feature is that Japanese nationalism was developed from concern for the particular State of Japan. Now, there are different ways in which nationalism is applied to practice. We know that nationalism has a number of times been expounded by thinkers in India and China, as well as in the West. But their nationalism was theoretically concerned with the State in general, not with their particular State. Now, nationalism tends, from its very nature, to be applied to a State in particular. In India and China, nationalism was theoretical. In Japanese nationalism, on the other hand, the particular State of Japan came to be the sole standard upon which all judgments were based. This, without doubt, has a close relationship with the general tendency in Japanese thinking, especially in the past, to overlook the universal and to lay stress upon an exclusive human nexus. The natural basis for Japan's exclusive concern for herself is, I believe, the insular position of Japan, isolated from the continent by water. The Japanese have only rarely experienced a real fear of alien peoples; they have known the existence of foreign nations only indirectly, except in the case of World War II.

The dominance of the State over individual life was, in a sense, a condition extremely favorable for Japan's making a start as a modern State, if only in form, in the Meiji era. One imagines that it would have been difficult for her to become the modern State that she is today so quickly had it not been for the strong consciousness its people had of the State. As the modern history of the West has shown, the formation of the State is a necessary condition for the active progress of peoples. Japan, in this sense, may be said to have been more favorably conditioned for modernization than other nations of the East which were not so unified.

Certain apprehension may be felt here by some. They may ask: Is not Japanese State-consciousness already a thing of the past? Has not the experience of defeat in World War II brought the Japanese people to consider themselves as individuals who make up their society and who participate in the sovereignty of the State, rather than as "subjects" of the emperor? We are inclined to give only a tentative "yes" to these questions. We must remember that the country is overflowing with people. The network of tightly-formed village communities covers the land. The nation's economy is such that the State must still exercise controls over a large portion of individual life. Above all, from great antiquity the nation's progress has always had its motivation in the Imperial Family, although it is now not so powerful as before. Furthermore, the Japanese sentiment toward the Imperial House has been friendly rather than hostile, as in some foreign countries, and the ruling class was often quite benevolent in their dealings with the people. All in all, an atmosphere of family-like intimacy has always pervaded the country. Such a term as "family State," for instance, would have been rejected by Westerners, and even by Indians, or Chinese, as self-contradictory. The Japanese, however, felt no inconsistency in the term, but found it good and valid. Just as religion was the basis of the ethical thinking of the Indians, family the basis of the practical morals of the Chinese, so the State was the basis of all thought in the Japanese. The Japanese way of thinking is undergoing a change, but their thinking is an inheritance, a tradition. We feel that it is our part to see to it that this tradition never again gives rise to an inhuman ultra-nationalism, but to a world-wide solidarity in the future.

VI. ECONOMIC ACTIVITIES IN THIS-WORLDLY LIFE

It is a problem worthy of study, why several decades ago the Japanese alone among the many Asian countries came to be most advanced in adopting modern civilization. In respect to this, we should like to point out the emphasis upon social activities as one of the features of the Japanese way of thinking.

The phenomenalistic way of thinking that asserts reality itself to be emergent and in flux has been traditionally conspicuous among the Japanese. This emergent and fluid way of thinking is compatible with the inclination of thinking that emphasizes a particular human nexus, which is another way of thinking that is traditionally conspicuous among the Japanese. These two factors are combined to bring about emphasis upon activities within a concrete human nexus.

It is a well-known fact that primitive Shintoism was closely connected with agricultural rituals in agrarian villages, and that Shintoist gods have been symbolized, and still are, as gods of production.

Coming into contact with foreign cultures and becoming acquainted with Chinese philosophies and religions, the Japanese adopted and absorbed Confucianism in particular, which teaches the way of conduct appropriate to a concrete human nexus. The views of Lao Tzu and Chuang Tzu are inclined to a life of seclusion in which one escapes from a particular human nexus and seeks tranquillity for oneself in solitude. Such was not to the taste of the Japanese at large. In contrast, Confucianism, and not Taoism, principally determines the rules of conduct according to a system of human relationships.

In the case of Buddhism, however, certain problems arose. Buddhism declared itself to be a teaching of otherworldliness. The central figures in Buddhist orders were monks and nuns, who were not allowed to be involved in any economic or worldly activities.

Meanwhile, the topographical characteristics of Japan, vastly different from India, required men to serve humanity within a specific human nexus. The doctrine of early Buddhism is not compatible with such requirements. So, it came about that early Buddhism and traditional conservative Buddhism, which inherited the former teachings, were despised and rejected under the name of Hīnayāna (*lit.,* "Lesser Vehicle"), whereas Mahāyāna Buddhism was particularly favored and adopted. Some schools of Mahāyāna Buddhism, if not all, advocated the finding of the absolute truth within secular life. In accepting Buddhism, the Japanese selected in particular that form which had such characteristics. And even in accepting those doctrines which were originally devoid of this nature, they deliberately bestowed such a character upon them.

Such an attitude in accepting Buddhism is clearly shown in the case of Prince Shōtoku. His "Commentaries upon Three Sūtras" are those upon the *Shōman*[y] *(Śrīmālādevīsiṃhānada) Sūtra,"* the *Yuima*[z] *(Vimalakīrtinirdeśa) Sūtra* and the *Hokke*[aa] *(Saddharmapuṇḍarīka) Sūtra.* In the first two *Sūtras,* laymen give sermons to priests and ascetics, reversing the usual order. They commend the idea of grasping the truth in secular life. And, according to the third, all laymen who faithfully follow any of the teachings of the Buddha are expected to be redeemed. The intention of Prince Shōtoku was to put emphasis upon the realization of Buddhist ideals within the concrete human nexus of the people while they remain in secular life. He sought absolute significance within the practical conduct of everyday life. He put special emphasis upon altruistic deeds and considered that *buddhas* and *bodhisattvas* should serve all living beings.

A similar idea underlies the later teachings of Japanese Buddhism. According to Saichō,[ab] both priests and laymen attain the same ideal. According to Kūkai,[ac] the founder of Japanese Vajrayāna (i.e., esoteric Buddhism), absolute reason should be realized through actuality. Pure Land Buddhism also developed along that line. According to the Jōdo-Shin[ad] sect, it is emphasized, not only that all living creatures are saved through their religious faith (the turning toward the Pure Realm), but also that the Great Benevolence saves all those who are lost (those returning from the Pure Realm). During the Tokugawa period, the most famous itinerant merchants of Ōmi,[ae] who peddled assiduously all around the country, were mostly devoted followers of the Jōdo-Shin sect and traveled around in the spirit of service to others.

The emphasis upon the human nexus ran parallel to the stress upon all the productive activities of men.

In a country like India, where the intensity of heat, the abundance of seasonal rainfall, and the fertility of the soil, together, bring forth a rich harvest, without much human labor being exerted on the land, the ethics of distribution rather than that of production is naturally emphasized. That is why almsgiving comes to be considered most important. In a country like Japan, by contrast, production is of vital importance; hence, stress is placed upon the ethics of labor in the various professions. Government and production, therefore, could not be in contradiction with the True Aspect of Reality. Some Japanese Buddhists were thus led to recognize the particularly sacred significance of physical labor. It is a historically well-known fact that Buddhists endeavored to go directly to the people through various welfare activities.

This feature can be noticed even in Japanese Zen literature. Dōgen,[af] the founder of the Sōtō[ag] Zen, thought that Buddhism could be realized within the professional lives of secular society. Suzuki Shōsan,[ah] a Zen master, found absolute significance in the pursuit of one's own profession, be one a warrior, a farmer, a craftsman, a merchant, a doctor, an actor, a hunter, or a priest. Since it is the essence of Buddhism, according to him, to rely upon the original self or upon "the true Buddha of one's own," and because every profession is the function of this "One Buddha," to pursue one's own profession is to obey the Absolute One. So, he teaches farmers: "Farming is nothing but the doings of the Buddha." To merchants he teaches: "Renounce desires and pursue profit single-heartedly. But you should never enjoy profits. You should, instead, work for the good of all the others."[27] Since the afflictions of this world, it is said, are predetermined in former lives, one should torture oneself by working hard in one's own profession, in order to redeem the sins of his past.[28] It is noteworthy that immediately after the death of Calvin, an idea similar to his happened to appear almost contemporaneously in Japan. The fact, however, that it never grew into a capitalistic movement of great consequence ought to be studied in relation to the underdevelopment of the modern bourgeois society in Japan.

Such a theory of religion also lends itself to religious movements outside of Buddhism in Japan. To illustrate, Ninomiya Sontoku's[ai] movement inclines to be practical and activistic. Sectarian Shintoism assumes a similar tendency. The founder of the Tenri religion[aj] teaches: "Keep your heart pure, busy yourself with your profession, and be true to the mind of God."[29] The other newly arisen sects of Shintoism mostly fall into a similar pattern.

Respect for labor in professional life resulted in high esteem for things produced as the fruits of labor. Reverence for foodstuff is especially manifest.

The teaching that we should take good care of economic products, the fruit of human labor, is not necessarily confined to Japanese religions; it seems common to most of the universal religions. In India or South Asian countries, however, where men are not required to labor too hard in order to produce daily necessities, relatively little has been said against waste. The fact that the preservation of economic products is particularly emphasized should be considered in the light of the topological peculiarity of Japan.

The form in which Chinese thought was accepted was also tinged with the activist tendency in interpreting the Way of human beings. Itō Jinsai (1627–1705), in particular, understands what is called the Way as being active and as representing the principle of growth and development. On that basis he rejects the nihilism of Lao Tzu. Ogiu Sorai[ak] (1666–1728), a peculiarly Japanese Confucianist, positively advocated activism, rejecting the static tendency of the Confucians of the Sung period of China (960–1279). Quiet sitting and having reverential love in one's heart are the methods of mental training made most of by the Confucians of the Sung, which was ridiculed by Sorai: "As I look at

[27] Suzuki Shōsan, *Roankyō*[bl] ("Crossing the Bridge on an Ass"), in *Zenmon Hogoshū*,[bm] Vol. III, edited by Kōdō Yamada[bn] and Daikyō Mori[bo] (Tokyo: Kōyūkan, 1921), p. 237.

[28] Suzuki Shōsan, *Banmintokuyō*[bp] ("The Significance of all Vocations"), in *ibid.*, pp. 536 f.

[29] Yasusada Hiyane,[bq] *Nippon Shūkyō-shi*[br] ("History of Japanese Religions") (Tokyo: Sankyo Shuppansha, 1925), p. 825.

them, even gambling appears superior to the quiet sitting and having reverential love in one's heart."[30] A necessary conclusion drawn from such an attitude was the recommendation, made by Sorai, of practical learning, useful in practical life. And such was the mental climate which nurtured the economic theory of Dazai Shundai[al] (1680–1747) and the legal philosophy of Miura Chikkei[am] (1688–1755). Whereas Chinese Confucianism of the Sung period surpassed the Japanese Confucianism which followed it in thinking of metaphysical problems, Japanese Confucianism directed its attention to politics, economics, and law, the practical aspects of human life.

That Japan alone was rapid in the progress of modernization in the years just before World War II, while the other Asian countries were generally slow in this process, may be attributed partly to the emphasis laid by the Japanese upon practical activities within the human nexus.

A great danger lies in the fact that the religious view of the Japanese may easily degenerate into sheer utilitarianism of profit-seeking activities, if it loses sight of the significance of the Absolute, which underlies the productive life of the professions. But, at the same time, credit should be given to the tendency to esteem the human nexus. If the religion of Japan is enhanced to such a height that religious truth may be realized in accordance with the human nexus, which is at once universal and particular, transcending every specific nexus and embracing all of them, then and only then will it achieve universal significance.

QUESTION 1: Dr. Yukawa[an] stressed the irrational character of Japanese thinking. But even in the feudal days of Japan, there appeared some forerunners of modern sciences, although they are little known to the West. How do you evaluate the results of their studies?

QUESTION 2: It seems to me that sciences cannot develop as sciences as such, i.e., in the framework of science alone. Do you find any social hindrances which prevented sciences from developing in Japan?

ANSWER: On the whole I agree with Dr. Yukawa, insofar as the field of my studies is concerned. However, I am not completely disappointed with regard to logical thinking by the Japanese. Studies of Buddhist logic were introduced into Japan in antiquity, approximately thirteen hundred years ago. Buddhist logicians largely occupied themselves only in making glosses on the basic works by Śaṁkarasvāmin and Chinese expounders. But they made slight progress beyond Indian and Chinese Buddhist logic. For example, they came to distinguish between M and P in the syllogism, both of which were occasionally called by the same word (*pakṣadharmatā*) in Indian and Chinese logic. In that context, M was called *shūbō*,[ao] whereas P was called *shūhō*,[ap] in Japanese.

[30] Ogiu Sorai, *Rongochō*[bs] ("Critical Comments on the Analects of Confucius"), cited in Junsei Iwahashi,[bt] *Sorai Kenkyū*[bu] ("Studies on Ogiu Sorai") (Tokyo: Seki-shoin, 1934), p. 300.

[a] 中村元
[b] 聖德太子
[c] 德川幕府
[d] 熊澤蕃山
[e] 平安
[f] 和
[g] 大化改新
[h] 蔣夢麟
[h'] 成務
[i] 大寶律令
[j] 將軍
[k] 明治維新
[l] 武士道
[m] 天照大神
[n] 仁德
[o] 北畠親房
[p] 日蓮
[q] 國體
[r] 伊藤仁齋
[s] 山鹿素行
[t] 山崎闇齋
[u] 水戸學派
[v] 吉田松蔭
[w] 天子
[x] 平田篤胤
[y] 勝鬘經
[z] 維摩經
[aa] 法華經
[ab] 最澄
[ac] 空海
[ad] 淨土眞宗
[ae] 近江商人
[af] 道元
[ag] 曹洞
[ah] 鈴木正三
[ai] 二宮尊德
[aj] 天理教
[ak] 荻生徂徠
[al] 太宰春臺
[am] 三浦竹溪
[an] 湯川秀樹
[ao] 宗法
[ap] 宗法
[aq] 東洋人の思惟方法
[ar] 慈悲
[as] 集義和書
[at] 三重の采女
[au] 顯宗天皇
[av] 繼體天皇
[aw] 古事記
[ax] 魚返善雄
[ay] 和敬
[az] 和合
[ba] 勝鬘經義疏
[bb] 花山信勝
[bc] 神皇正統記
[bd] 校註日本文學大系
[be] 菅原道眞
[bf] 菅家文叢
[bg] 北野文叢
[bh] 北野史
[bi] 講孟劄記
[bj] 吉田松蔭全集
[bk] 出定笑語
[bl] 驢鞍橋
[bm] 禪門法語集
[bn] 山田孝道
[bo] 森大狂
[bp] 萬民德用
[bq] 比屋根安定
[br] 日本宗教史
[bs] 論語徵
[bt] 岩橋遵成
[bu] 徂徠研究

PAUL K. RYU[a]

"Field Theory" in the Study of Cultures: Its Application to Korean Culture

The immediate object of this paper is interpretation of traditional Korean culture in terms of the causes which generated it and the causal consequences it produced, as specifically operative in the field of law. However, the approach to this specific task is determined by a philosophical orientation, which must be discussed first.

I. INTRODUCTION

If this conference is to have practical significance, more than mere description of the various cultures of East and West is needed. Nor would sheer exposition of their detached "meaning" afford a useful basis for their comparison. For "meaning" changes with context, and I might venture to say that meaning apart from context is barren. One can put this differently by saying that the true meaning of a culture is defined by the manner in which it operates in various contexts and situations. This becomes particularly clear when culture is analyzed by lawyers for legal purposes. In law, of course, we are not concerned with culture in itself, for law is a communal norm which serves as a means of social control, and, in the scheme of this norm, cultural meaning serves a specifically legal function. In this area, more than in any other, we can observe that pure identity or disparity of meaning without regard to context is not relevant. An identical meaning may operate differently in different environmental conditions, and disparate meanings may reach substantially identical results, given certain conditions.[1] On an understanding

[1] Myres S. McDougal and Harold D. Lasswell, Mimeographed Materials on Law, Science, and Policy (1956) (Yale Law School).

of this phenomenon is predicated successful social engineering by the lawyer as decision maker. Cultural meaning in a legal framework is thus not meaningful until there is at least a possibility of its connection with a particular legal context.

An example may illustrate the above proposition. We may say, for instance, that there are "rationalistic" elements in both Confucianism[2] and Protestantism.[3] Indeed, we may say further that "rationalism" as such is identical in them. However, the great achievement of Protestant rationalism was to shatter the fetters of the sib,[4] whereas, as will be shown, Confucian rationalism, far from being of any service to the modernization of China, has impeded the adoption of modern ideas. For practical, and specifically legal, purposes, it is thus necessary to study rationalism, Confucian or Protestant, in its operation under varying circumstances.

To carry out my immediate task, I have thus chosen to follow a method which I have called "field theory," since it approximately corresponds to Kurt Lewin's "Psychological field theory."[5] The concept of "field" is necessary in our study of cultures for two reasons: one directed to the nature of the process of linguistic conceptualization, the other oriented to the finding of causal relationships.

1. Of course, language problems arise in science generally, even in natural science.[6] But these problems are far more complex and more frequently confused in social science, for language here must be considered in a dual aspect, since it is both a tool of the science in which we, as observers, are engaged, and a means of communication used in the particular culture that is the subject of our study. An example of historical conflicts due to the fact that the language of the observed culture was not adequately translated into that of the observer may best illustrate the point. Galileo was forced to retract his thesis that the earth is moving around the sun because the contrary view was alleged by the Church to be expressed in the Book of Joshua.[7] However, the words of Joshua in the language which he spoke do not refer to motion at all. Men of Galileo's age imported the views implied in their language into Hebrew thought, because in the language they used the exact meaning conveyed

[2] Hu Shih,[bz] "The Scientific Spirit and Method in Chinese Philosophy," in this volume, pp. 199–221.

[3] Max Weber, *The Religion of China,* Hans H. Gerth, trans. (Glencoe, Ill.: Free Press, 1951), p. 226.

[4] *Ibid.*, p. 237.

[5] Kurt Lewin, *Field Theory in Social Science,* Dorwin Cartwright, ed. (New York: Harper & Brothers, 1951). The concept of "field" originated in modern physics. Einstein stated, "A new concept appears in physics, the most important invention since Newton's time: the field. It needed great scientific imagination to realize that it is not the charges nor the particles but the field in the space between the charges and the particles which is essential for the description of physical phenomena." Albert Einstein and Leopold Infeld, *The Evolution of Physics* (New York: Simon and Schuster, Inc., 1938), p. 259. Later, this concept of "field" was also applied in legal literature. See Henry W. Edgerton, "Legal Cause," 72 U. of Pa. L. Rev. 211, 343 (1924); also F. S. Cohen, "Field Theory and Judicial Logic," 59 Yale L. Journ. 238–259 (1950).

[6] Leonard Bloomfield, "Linguistic Aspects of Science," in Otto Neurath ed., *International Encyclopedia of Unified Science,* Vol. I, No. 4 (Chicago: Chicago University Press, 1939).

[7] Joshua 10:12. According to current translations, Joshua ordered the sun and the moon to "stand still." In the Hebrew version, the word "stand" does not appear. The term used is *"dom,"* which does not occur anywhere in the Bible in the sense of "stand." It suggests "silence." Compare Isaiah 47:5. The passage *"Shemesh b'Gibeon dom"* may as well convey the idea of the sun "appearing as being over Gibeon" (and the corresponding perception of the moon as "appearing over the Valley of Aijalon"). Compare Genesis 1:26.

in Joshua's words could not be expressed. They thus inadvertently disregarded the "field" of Hebrew culture.

Scientific language also must be clarified in order that we may be able to communicate with each other correctly as men of science.

When we speak of "world understanding" between "East and West," what do we mean by "understanding"? Is it enough to find and describe "differences, identities or similarities"[8] of the respective cultures? For instance, are we interested purely in finding that there is present in Confucianism, as in Western thought, an element of "humanism"?[9] Of course, such merely descriptive comparison is needed as a preliminary step. However, "understanding," for any contextual purpose, as e.g., for a legal purpose, must reach beyond description and include exposition of causal connection. In this instance, we must thus inquire: How did Confucian "humanism" operate causally in the various Asian societies, as compared with the manner in which "humanism" operates in the West? "Understanding" must be concurrently understood first.

Second, in this context, we must ask ourselves whether out of this "understanding" there can ever arise "co-operation," if, as many believe, we cannot ever reach common "goals," our values being quite disparate. Can we ever agree on common values, if values are quite subjective and not amenable to scientific determination other than anthropological? This depends on whether it is possible for us to agree on a common initial fundamental ideology, a common institutional goal, e.g., "free society,"[10] a form of society that will enable us to live together peacefully. Such an ultimate goal may be abstracted from our otherwise varying ideologies of lower order. If we agree on such a basic "goal," we can then, by the method of scientific research, compare the different value-systems as related to that goal. This comparison can indeed be quite "scientific," contrary to traditional belief[11] that values are not susceptible of scientific study other than anthropological. According to traditional philosophy, values cannot be compared, because they belong to the realm of quality and cannot be quantified. However, as suggested above, with regard to an initial common "goal," values can very well be quantified and thus subjected to "scientific" study. Indeed, the very concept of "science"[12] is changing in our modern age, so that there is room not only for "the value of science" but also for a "science of value." If we succeed in establishing a common basic institutional goal, we may be able, not merely to compare our different value-patterns, but also to solve ideological conflicts between the different cultures and thus reach true "co-operation" in scientific terms.

[8] See Charles A. Moore, ed., *Essays in East-West Philosophy* (Honolulu: University of Hawaii Press, 1951), p. 5.

[9] See Wing-tsit Chan, "Chinese Theory and Practice, with Special Reference to Humanism," in this volume, pp. 81–95.

[10] It is necessary, of course, to define the term "free society." For a tentative definition, see Paul K. Ryu, "Korean Culture and Criminal Responsibility" (unpublished doctoral dissertation, Library of Yale Law School, 1958), pp. 114 ff.

[11] The traditional belief is represented by Kant's ethical subjectivism. See Richard Kroner, *Kant's Weltanschauung,* John E. Smith, trans. (Chicago: University of Chicago Press, 1956), pp. 66 ff.

[12] John Dewey, "Theory of Valuation," in Neurath ed., *International Encyclopedia of Unified Science,* Vol. II, No. 4 (1939).

Finally, in speaking in terms of "East" as compared with "West," a caveat is in point. We are all too inclined to over-generalize and to disregard the dynamic factor in cultures. Cultures develop and migrate. Perhaps the very generalizations "East" and "West," when used in static terms, tend to be misleading, for the cultures of both East and West have developed and migrated, so that no feature can be attributed as an exclusive permanent characteristic to either. Although the distinction between concepts by postulation and concepts by intuition, drawn by Professor Northrop,[13] is a valid one, there is no ground for exclusively associating the former with the West and the latter with the East. The suggested distinction is said to have a corollary in the area of law in the distinction between mediational and contractual dispute-settling, the former corresponding to intuitional and the latter to postulational concepts. The intuitive, mediational type of dispute-settling is thus said to be characteristic of the "East," whereas the abstract, contractual type is believed to be a feature of the "West."[14] Now, if we look at the classic legal document of the so-called "West," the XII Tables of Rome,[15] and specifically at a provision dealing with the much-discussed *"lex talionis,"* we find the passage, *"Si membrum rupit, ni cum eo pacit, talio esto"* (If anyone breaks another's bodily member, he shall be subject to retribution, unless he negotiates with the victim). According to Jhering,[16] *talio* was hardly ever used. Rather, disputes were settled by mediation. This was, then, the method of Roman law, as it was also the method prevailing among the Germanic tribes, and of early law in England, which then led to the classic formulation of the price lists for various injuries, as later generalized in the "Doomsday Books." At this stage, then, the method of the "West" was not distinguishable from that allegedly obtaining in the "East." Whence came the change of approach? As Northrop shows, concepts by postulation, and with them the contractual type of dispute-settling, were introduced into Roman law under the impact of Stoic philosophy. Perhaps it may be pertinent to note that Stoicism was not a native Greek philosophy but, rather, a philosophy of Eastern origin. In this connection, attention is called to the fact that during the Chou Dynasty (1111–256 B.C.) in China, that is, four centuries before Christ, Mo Tzu developed a logic similar to that used by Zeno. Certainly, "East" and "West" in this regard cannot be treated as rigid categories.[17]

Before proceeding to a discussion of the second issue of the "field" theory, one further problem of linguistic conceptualization must be clarified. Benjamin L. Whorf[18] has pointed to the problem of linguistic relativity in the

[13] In Moore, ed., *Essays in East-West Philosophy*, p. 5; also F. S. C. Northrop, *The Meeting of East and West* (8th printing, New York: The Macmillan Co., 1952).

[14] F. S. C. Northrop, "The Philosophy of Natural Science and Comparative Law," Presidential Address delivered before the Forty-ninth Annual Meeting of the Eastern Division of the American Philosophical Association at the City College of New York, December 29–31, 1952.

[15] Paul K. Ryu, "Causation in Criminal Law, 106" U. of Pa. L. Rev. 773–805, at 800 (1958).

[16] Rudolf von Jhering, *Scherz und Ernst in der Jurisprudenz* (9th ed., Leipzig: Breitkopf und Hartel, 1904), pp. 242–243.

[17] East and West are so interconnected that no strict line of demarcation between them can be drawn. See *Philosophy East and West*, I, No. 1 (April, 1951), 3 ff., 72; also G. P. Conger, "Did India Influence Early Greek Philosophy?" *Philosophy East and West*, II, No. 2 (July, 1952), 102–128.

comparative study of cultures. This relativity has often been misunderstood as constituting an absolute bar to the finding of common elements in different cultures.[19] But Whorf merely suggests that to find the meaning of words used in cultures other than our own we must read them in their appropriate context. We might add that such words should be read in their appropriate field. Language everywhere is a tool in the quest for meaning, and meaning cannot be elucidated without regard to context. Certainly, as Northrop points out, the same symbol "blue" may mean different things, depending on whether it is used postulationally, as "blue" in an electromagnetic wave, or intuitionally, as "blue" in sense-feeling.[20] In such cases, of course, the context determines the meaning. Similarly, the context may indicate the appropriate meaning in less obvious situations. When Dr. Hideki Yukawa[b] speaks of "Japanese irrationalism,"[21] he does not mean, of course, that Japanese culture is devoid of any rational element. Rather, he intends to convey the idea that rationalism has played a relatively less important role in Japanese culture than in other cultures. The term "Japanese irrationalism" is here used in relation to the context of comparative culture.

2. The foregoing discussion was intended to show the need for scientific thinking in establishing correct communication. Lewin's psychological field theory indicates the method in which such thinking may be put into operation in any particular discipline. It proceeds from the observation that "(a)ny behavior or any other change in a psychological field depends only upon the psychological field at that time."[22] As in Lewin's theory, "field" in this paper means that "a given space in a given unit of time"[23] should serve as the frame of reference for the study of the meaning of a culture and of a value-relationship. The dynamic aspects of culture and of human values can be understood only by the use of such a method. Thus, the main theme of this paper will be to explain how Confucianism and other cultural ideas have performed entirely different functions in Korea from those they performed in either Japan or China. This is due to the fact that they were operative in Korea at a different time and in a different environment. A human being is not "a being for death, but a being for value."[24] Thus, he must make for himself some design for living[25] that is adapted to the conditions of his particular life. For this reason, the same cultural value-pattern assumes varying meanings with varying conditions.[26]

[18] B. L. Whorf, *Language, Thought and Reality* (New York: Massachusetts Institute of Technology Press, 1958).
[19] Lewis S. Feuer, "Sociological Aspect of the Relation between Language and Philosophy," *Philosophy of Science*, XX (1953), 94–96.
[20] F. S. C. Northrop, *The Logic of the Sciences and the Humanities* (New York: The Macmillan Co., 1947), pp. 36, 60, 65.
[21] Hideki Yukawa, "Modern Trend of Western Civilization and Cultural Peculiarities in Japan," in this volume, pp. 188–197.
[22] Lewin, *Field Theory in Social Science*, p. 45.
[23] As to the definition of "field," see *ibid.*, pp. 43–59.
[24] *Philosophy East and West*, II, No. 2 (July, 1952), 164.
[25] Ruth Benedict, *The Chrysanthemum and the Sword* (Boston: Houghton Mifflin Company, 1946), p. 12.
[26] W. H. Werkmeister, "Scientism and the Problem of Man," in this volume, pp. 135–155.

II. INTERPRETATION OF KOREAN CULTURE: AS CONTRASTED WITH CHINESE AND JAPANESE CULTURES

Northrop classifies the world's legal procedures into three groups or types of dispute-settling:[27] (1) the intuitive, mediational type; (2) the law-of-status type; and (3) the abstract, contractual type. Until the reception of Western patterns, Korea did not fit into any single one of these, but, rather, presented a mixture of the mediational and law-of-status types. We may proceed from the assumption that human beings share the desire for justice and that justice, in simplest terms, means equality before the law, an ideal best realized in the contractual type of dispute-settling. Our problem is therefore to explain why Korea did not succeed in developing that type, whereas Japan successfully adopted it from the West. The answer lies in the different manner in which Confucianism and other cultural ideas operated in Korea and Japan. In the latter, it was used as a vehicle for adopting a rule of law, whereas in the former it served to stress "man" as a personal being and thus to emphasize personal relationships. This is evident on the very threshold of legal inquiry, beginning with the concept of law, which the Koreans adopted from the Chinese. In China, *"fa"* (法), corresponding to the English term "law," originally meant the release of water (水 means water and 去 means to discard) [what is not just]. As Max Weber pointed out,[28] "(t)he prosperity of the Chinese city did not primarily depend upon the citizens' enterprising spirit in economic and political ventures but rather upon the imperial administration, especially the administration of the rivers.... Chinese public authorities have repeatedly reverted to liturgical controls, but they failed to create a system of guild privileges comparable to that of the West during the Middle Ages. This led to relentless self-help." With the *fa,* Korea adopted from China the Confucian idea that law is secondary, and therefore resorted to self-help. In Japan, on the other hand, Confucianism, as will be shown, operated under different circumstances, leading to different results. It may be instructive to compare the ways in which Confucianism operated in the three cultures, Chinese, Japanese, and Korean.

Confucius[c] was born in China in a feudal age, specifically in a period known as that of the "Spring and Autumn" (772–481 B.C.).[29] There was at that time no sense of national unity among the Chinese, as normally develops in the course of a people's sharing of a common bitter or happy fate. Filial duty was thus a nucleus of social ethics, while loyalty, even between king and subject, was secondary.[30] The basic ethical norm of love, that is, Confucian *jen,*[d] was natural "graded love," based on the maxim of "loving one's relatives more

[27] Northrop, "The Philosophy of Natural Science and Comparative Law," *op. cit.*

[28] Weber, *The Religion of China,* pp. 16–20.

[29] This period was followed by that of the "Warring States" (403–222 B.C.).

[30] Fung Yu-lan,[ca] "The Philosophy at the Basis of Traditional Chinese Society," in F. S. C. Northrop, ed., *Ideological Differences and World Order* (New Haven: Yale University Press, 1949), pp. 24–25. Here, "subject" meant the king's ministers, not the king's citizens. The meaning of "subject" has changed as the sense of national unity has grown.

than others."[31] This was similar to the Old Testament teaching that was not overcome until the advent of the Christian idea of universal love. From this Confucian idea of graded love developed the communal norm that a man owes a duty to another within a certain relationship to him but not to a stranger.[32] Love stemmed from status[33] as a member of *tsu*[e] [34] (meaning a clan) or *hsing*[f] [35] (meaning a surname) or *shih*[g] [36] (meaning a specific surname related to blood) or *chia*[h] [37] (meaning a house). Stress on status and relationship determined by status also brought about emphasis on ethics rather than on any objective value, such as the truth-value of logic, which played such an important role in Stoicism.[38] No objective value-commitment could be made unless the person concerned knew the status of the other party, the group to which the latter belonged. Confucianism had a greater impact upon Chinese society than any philosophy ever had upon Occidental society. No philosophy attained a similarly exclusive prestige in the Western world, and thus none could be used to similar advantage by a worldly ruler.[39] The source of this prestige and of its political utilization lay in a peculiar power-situation at a particular period of Chinese history.

Liu Pang[i] (247–195 B.C.), the founder of the Han Dynasty (206 B.C.–A.D. 220),[40] the first ruler to unify successfully the Kingdom of China, established a great power by use of political wisdom.[41] Thus, after the Han Dynasty, Chinese political leaders learned that human intellect is more valuable than "naked power."[42] This led to the establishment of the basic doctrine of the superiority of civil over military power. When asked what intelligence means, they would resort to Confucianism to the exclusion of any other doctrine. But they would not use force to suppress non-Confucian ideas. The reason for this was that they had learned the power of indoctrination and of government by subtle methods rather than by force. The Ch'in Dynasty (221–207 B.C.) had failed to bring about unification of thought by burning all writings of the "hundred schools" of thought other than those of Ch'in in agriculture, medicine, and divination. Tung Chung-shu[j] (*ca.* 179–104 B.C.) had taught the Han Dynasty how to establish Confucianism as the orthodox belief without resort to force. The Han

[31] *Philosophy East and West,* I, No. 1 (April, 1951), 49–60.

[32] See Northrop, ed., *Ideological Differences and World Order,* p. 443.

[33] The kinship system was also a "classificatory" and not a "descriptive" system. See H. Y. Feng,[cb] "Teknonymy as a Formative Factor in the Chinese Kinship System," *American Anthropologist,* XXXVIII (1936), 59–66. *Wu-fu*[cc] (five ways of mourning) is also a classificatory system.

[34] Hsien-chin Hu,[cd] *The Common Descent Group in China and Its Functions* (New York: Viking Fund Publication, 1948), p. 55. The leaders of the *tsu* were endowed by the government with a good deal of autonomy in dealing with disputes and offences within the *tsu*.

[35] *"Hsing"* means the origin of the clan. Consequently, under no circumstances (for instance, in case of marriage) could it be changed.

[36] Within the feudal system, only persons of the higher class had *shih* to distinguish themselves from commoners. See Hsien-chin Hu, *op cit.,* p. 11. This concept developed differently in Japan than it did in Korea. In Japan it became the name of a family, whereas in Korea it usually means the surname of those who have a common ancestor.

[37] Usually *chia* includes parents, children, and grandchildren. *Ibid.,* pp. 9–11.

[38] *Philosophy East and West,* III, No. 4 (January, 1954), 180.

[39] Weber, *The Religion of China,* p. 176.

[40] The Emperor of Ch'in unified China in 221 B.C., but this unification lasted less than 15 years.

[41] Liu's opponent, Hsiang Yu,[ce] was the strongest general in Oriental history.

[42] Harold D. Lasswell and Abraham Kaplan, *Power and Society: A Framework for Political Inquiry* (New Haven: Yale University Press, 1958), pp. 139–141.

government thus decreed no punishment for the private teaching of ideas other than Confucian, but merely provided that persons who wished to be candidates for official positions must study the Confucian Classics.[43] The practice of selecting government officials on the basis of intellectual merit began in this manner. This practice later developed the refined civil service examination system,[44] which gave a decisive imprint to the Chinese administration of justice and to Chinese culture. As in the case of Indian Brahmanism, the literati became the exponents of the unity of Chinese culture.[45] The characteristic feature of this class is that even in the feudal period the status of the literati was not hereditary or exclusive.[46] Because the literati were highly regarded, education became a most important goal. Throughout the period of the Chinese dynasties after the Han era, a major problem facing the Chinese government was to determine an official version and a "correct meaning" of the Confucian Classics.[47] Such an interpretation was supplied during the Sung Dynasty (960–1279) by Chu Hsi[k] (1131–1200), one of the great Neo-Confucians.[48] His abridgment of Ssu-ma Kuang's[l] (1019–1086) history of China, the *Tzu-chih T'ung-chien*[m] ("A Comprehensive Mirror for the Aid of Government"[49]), is an outstanding work. It was followed until abolition of the State examination system in 1905. Now, Chu Hsi again stressed orthodoxy of thought in rejecting all other schools of thought as heresy. Among these rejected ways of thinking was Mo Tzu's[n] (5th century B.C.) *chien-ai*[o] (universal love). Chu Hsi reitereated that "graded love" is the "correct meaning" of *jen*,[50] thus reaffirming as basic the Chinese value-preference relative to personal value rather than to any universal value.

Such rigid orthodoxy, of course, was an almost insurmountable barrier to progress. This orthodoxy offered certain advantages, however. It reaffirmed the paramount position of intellectual values, grading value-ranks as follows: scholar, farmer, artisan, merchant (*shih, nung, kung, shang*[p]). It eliminated feudal government by installing a civil service examination system two millennia before such a system became known in the West. On the other hand, however, it to some extent blocked free scientific development and brought into the government a fatal nepotistic element by preaching that man is paramount to law. Such anti-democratic elements as the *lou-kuei*[q] [51] (illegal-fees) system and the exclusion of the legal profession,[52] as well as nepotism,[53] were fruits of the orthodox interpretation of Confucian thought. True, there are basically the same elements in the views of Socrates and in those of Confucius. Both recognized the universal existence of moral law. There is, however, one

[43] Fung Yu-lan, *A Short History of Chinese Philosophy* (New York: The Macmillan Co., 1958), pp. 191–216.
[44] This most elaborate civil service examination system has been in practice since A.D. 622. *Ibid.*, p. 266.
[45] Weber, *op. cit.* 107–108.
[46] *Ibid.*, p. 108. See also Fung Yu-lan, *A Short History of Chinese Philosophy*, pp. 191–192.
[47] Fung Yu-lan, *ibid.*, p. 295.
[48] As to Neo-Confucianism, see *ibid.*, pp. 281–318.
[49] Daisetz T. Suzuki,[cf] *Zen and Japanese Culture* (2nd ed., rev. and enlarged, New York: Bollingen Foundation Inc., 1959), p. 53, n. 8.
[50] *Philosophy East and West*, I, No. 1 (April, 1951), 50–54.
[51] Chiang Monlin,[cg] *Tides from the West* (New Haven: Yale University Press, 1947), pp. 16 ff.
[52] Weber, *op. cit.*, p. 102.
[53] *Philosophy East and West*, I, No. 1 (April, 1951), 55.

important difference in their attitudes toward law. Socrates gave his life to preserve the security value of law. Confucius, on the other hand, applied his *jen* doctrine to the theory of government, drawing a sharp distinction between *pa-tao*[r] (way of the despot) and *wang-tao*[s] (kingly way), that is, government by force and government by authority. He further taught that if the emperor, *tien-tzu*[t] (Son of Heaven), loses *jen,* he lacks charisma, leaving room for the "right of rebellion."[54] This, to be sure, is in essence a democratic thought. However, Confucius did not value law for the sheer security it affords. In fact, his approach to law was rather ambivalent. Before becoming a teacher, he was himself a State official, and he recognized that there is a cleft between the magistrate and the subject. He believed in a division of society into common men and noblemen, and in the rule of the former by the latter. He thus denied popular participation in government, advancing the view that ordinary people "may be made to follow a path of action but may not be made to understand."[55] Indeed, he believed the king to be "the Son of Heaven," entitled exclusively to have sacrificial rites to Heaven conducted.[56] These Confucian views resulted in a complete separation of the people from law and government.[57] With this ethos prevailing in China, clearly nothing comparable to a rational entrepreneurial capitalism of the Western style could possibly develop. As stated by Weber, "for twenty centuries social rank in China has been determined more by qualification for office than by wealth. This qualification, in turn, has been determined by education and especially by examination."[58]

Although Japan came into contact with Chinese Confucianism at an early date,[59] the latter's influence in Japan developed in an altogether different direction. There, Confucianism spread along with Zen, for most Zen monks who came to Japan during the Kamakura era (1192–1331) were students of Confucianism as well.[60] This Confucianism was of the Neo-Confucian variety that prevailed at the time of the Chinese Sung Dynasty; it was Confucianism as taught by Chu Hsi.[61] In some respects, Confucianism, on the surface at least, showed tendencies similar to those in China. Thus, it became the nucleus of education during Japan's feudal era. Indeed, the *terakoya* system[u] (*tera*—"Buddhist Temple"; *ko*—"small"; and *ya*—"house") (elementary education in a Buddhist temple) was the only institution of popular education until its replacement by the modern system after the Restoration in 1868.[62] Also, most Japanese legal provisions have been patterned after the Chinese *T'ang-lü*[v] (Code of the T'ang Dynasty, 618–907), or *Ming-lü*[w] (Code of the Ming

[54] Weber, *op. cit.*, p. 39.
[55] Confucian *Analects* VIII. 9 (Chinese Classics, Vol. I, p. 211).
[56] Weber, *op. cit.*, p. 22.
[57] Francis Liu,[ch] "Chinese Legal System," lecture delivered in November, 1945, before the officers and enlisted men of the American Armed Forces in Shanghai.
[58] Weber, *op. cit.*, p. 107.
[59] Confucianism was introduced to Japan via Korea. The first contact was established through the Korean scholar Wani[ci] at the time of Emperor Ojin[cj] (A.D. 285).
[60] Suzuki, *Zen and Japanese Culture*, p. 43.
[61] *Ibid.*, p. 52.
[62] *Ibid.*, p. 45.

Dynasty, 1368–1644). However, with this the parallel ends. The central ethical concepts differ in China and in Japan. In China, filial piety (*hsiao*[x]) is the center of the *san-kang wu-ch'ang*[y] (constant virtues, the Three Bonds and Five Constants), whereas *chū* (*chung*[z] in Chinese, loyalty) is equated with *hsiao* (*kō* in Japanese). *Chūkō-ippon*[aa] (loyalty and filial piety having the same foundation) was the focal concept of Japanese ethics. Thus, Confucianism helped to formulate the family concept of the State in Japan.[63] The emperor was represented as his subjects' father. Shintoism itself incorporated certain Confucian ideas which were exploited in the service of the State. Several Shinto sects,[64] by absorbing Confucian ideas, began to worship the deceased as gods, and such worship was practiced in many Shinto shrines, such as Tōshōgū[ab] (for Tokugawa Ieyasu[ac]), and Toyokuni-jinja[ad] (for Toyotomi Hideyoshi[ae]). This was an incentive to die for causes of which the community approved, and the cause of the State was foremost among these. Confucianism in Japan served State interests in many other ways. Neo-Confucianism in China served to protect Chinese culture against exotic Buddhism. Japanese scholars who learned Neo-Confucianism in China turned its cultural exclusiveness into nationalism and imported it in this form into Japan. It is worth noting that Kitabatake Chikafusa's[af] monumental work on the "Succession of the Imperial Rulers in Japan" (*Jinnō shōtōki*[ag]), which became a cornerstone of ardent Japanese nationalism at the time of the Meiji Restoration,[65] was the product of the author's pursuit of Chu Hsi's philosophy.

Similarly, Confucianism, originally of pacifist origin, has been indirectly used to promote Japanese militarism.[66] Pacifist Confucianism, absorbed by Japanese Buddhism, particularly of the Zen sect, combined with other cultural ideas in advancing the Japanese communal norm of feudal loyalty (*giri*[ah]),[67] based on personal relationship, and this *giri,* in turn, gave rise to *bushidō,*[ai] the knighthood of Japan. The most distinctive Chinese product of Confucianism in law administration, the civil service examination system, was not imitated in Japan, for Japan was steeped in feudal ideology, and its legal system, accordingly, was strictly of the status type. Confucianism in Japan facilitated, indeed, the advance of competing religious trends, Shintoism and Buddhism. As is generally known, Shintoism contributed to the development of a nationalistic spirit in Japan, particularly at the time of the Meiji Restoration. This nationalistic spirit, in turn, promoted a national unity that produced the idea of a strong centralized State. The latter thus encountered no opposition in advancing the adoption of Western civilization, which helped to overthrow feudal bondage—possibly in a manner similar to that of the essentially rationalistic Protestantism of Germany.[68] Thus, Confucianism produced in China and in Japan diametrically opposite results. In the former it retarded, in the latter it promoted, the advance of modern Western ideas.

63 Sokichi Tsuda,[ck] *Tōyōgakuhō*[cl] ("Academic Report on the Orient"), XXV (1937–1938), p. 482.
64 *Ibid.,* pp. 475–483.
65 Suzuki, *op. cit.,* pp. 55 ff.
66 Weber, *op. cit.,* p. 169.
67 Benedict, *op. cit.,* pp. 133–176.
68 F. S. C. Northrop, *The Taming of the Nations* (New York: The Macmillan Co., 1952), p. 177.

Confucianism played a different role in Korea than it did in either China or Japan. From time immemorial, Korea has had contacts with China.[69] It is reported that in 373 B.C. the Kokuryo[aj] Kingdom (37 B.C.–A.D. 668), one of the three Kingdoms in Korea, established a national university, patterned after the Chinese Hanlin Yüan,[ak] the Confucian Academy in China.[70] After Korea's unification (A.D. 668), by Silla[al] (57 B.C.–A.D. 935), one of the three Kingdoms, Chinese influence became dominant in Korea. The Chinese Classics became so overwhelmingly important that Sul Chong[am] of the Silla Dynasty developed the *yidu*[an] [71] (a Korean modification of Chinese characters, similar to the present Japanese *kana*[ao]) in response to a popular demand for the facilitated reading of Chinese. The *yidu* served as an interim written language until, in A.D. 1442, during the Lee Dynasty (1392–1900), the Korean alphabet, "*hangul*"[ap] —the only alphabet known in Far Eastern languages—was invented. Naturally, Confucianism had a strong impact upon the Korean ethical and social system, as well as upon Korea's system of government. It decisively influenced the moral code. The basic Confucian teaching of the five relationships (*wu-lun*[aq])[72] formed the center of Korean ethics. In turn, it produced the patriarchal system, a salient feature in the structure of Korean society. Consistent with Confucian teachings, the value-system was not objective but personal-relative, that is, predicated upon the personal status of the party to the social relation at issue. This system took a more extreme form in Korea than in either China or Japan. Diversification of value in accordance with personal relationship is expressed in Korean language usage. For instance, there are numerous equivalents for the single English term "you," terms of address that vary in accordance with the value attributed to the addressee, depending on the speaker's social relation to him: *zashik*[ar] (contemptuous meaning of "you"), *nuo*[as] (used in addressing an inferior), *tangshin*[at] (used among co-ordinate persons), *kuiha*[au] (usage of esteem), *zonzang*[av] (expression of respect for an older person). The pronoun "you" is never used when addressing a parent or a king. The governmental organization was patterned after that of China, which, as noted above, was the product of Confucian teaching. As early as A.D. 789, during the Koryu[aw] Dynasty (918–1392), Korea introduced the Chinese civil service examination system. As in China, so in Korea, this system constituted the sole democratic element in an otherwise aristocratic social structure. By means of this system, "fresh blood" was absorbed from lower strata.[73] A successful examination was the only manner whereby persons of the lower classes could rise to the status of the elite. This was a strong incentive for ambitious young people to acquire an education. But, as will be shown, this system

[69] According to Chinese records, Prince Kiza[cm] of the State of Yin[cn] came to Korea over three thousand years ago, and Chinese rule over the Korean people lasted for several hundred years. But see Byung-do Lee,[co] *Synopsis of Korean History* (Seoul: Pomun-kak, 1957), p. 28.

[70] Weber states that Hanlin Yüan corresponds to a congregation of the Papal Curia. See Weber, *op. cit.*, p. 102.

[71] H. Hulbert, *The History of Korea* (Seoul: The Methodist Publishing House, 1905), Vol. I, p. 120.

[72] *Wu-lun* means five relationships, that is, (1) moral obligations between prince and minister, (2) father and son, (3) husband and wife, (4) brothers, and (5) friends.

[73] Lang-kuang Hsü,[cp] *Under the Ancestor's Shadow* (New York: Columbia University Press, 1948), pp. 1–6.

ceased to be consistently maintained during the Lee Dynasty, when certain classes of persons were excluded from admission to examinations. As in China, so in Korea, the Chinese "illegal-fees" system (*lou-kuei*) blocked development of anything approaching a contractual type of law.[74] This system applies the "rule of thumb" approach to government.[75] It consists in the king's appointment of local officials for assessment and collection of taxes, which were not determined in advance by law but were imposed at the discretion of the official. In Korea, this system was called the *ajun*[ax] system, the *ajun* being the title of the official. Though his position was low, the *ajun* was "the most important man in the administration of Korean government,[76] for the prefect's efficiency was measured by the *ajun's* skill in gauging the people's patience and in keeping his finger on the public pulse, in order to judge when their suffering had reached a point beyond endurance. If the *ajun* was not sensitive enough to judge popular reactions and if he created excessive resentment, there was danger that the prefect might be driven out by the people. The *ajun* was thus "the scapegoat for everybody's sin, the safety valve which saves the boiler from bursting."[77] Of course, a system that operated in such an arbitrary manner, controlled solely by extreme popular reaction, left the door wide open to corruption.

To sum up, we may say that Confucianism was an asset to the development of Korean intellectual culture but a serious handicap to her political and legal development. It conveyed to Koreans the idea that knowledge constitutes the highest value. Many achievements in the area of science may be products of this value-preference: the invention of the copper printing machine[78] in A.D. 1403, that is, more than half a century before Gutenberg's invention; the invention of the rain gauge in A.D. 1442,[79] that is, about two centuries before this instrument's invention in the West; the founding of the oldest astronomical observatory in Asia[80] (in Kyung Chu, before the unification of Korea by Silla). However, in terms of ethics, government, and politics, Confucianism meant the adoption of a personal-relative value-pattern, estrangement between the people, the law, and law courts, and the adoption of the mediational type of dispute-settling. Since mediation neither recognizes a concept of responsibility proper nor admits any universal doctrines, it represents a primitive approach to law, conducive to arbitrariness. Another product of the personal-relative value-pattern was nepotism in government. An important test of the law's effect upon a people is its own reaction to "law." As a result of the impact of Confucianism upon law and government, "law" to Koreans does not convey the idea of vindication of individual liberty, as it does in England and the United States. Instead, Koreans fear, distrust, and shun the law, as a restriction of their everyday life.[81] A final, fatal by-product

[74] Chiang Monlin, *op. cit.*, p. 16.

[75] *Ibid.*, p. 345.

[76] Homer B. Hulbert, *The Passing of Korea* (London: William Heinemann Co., 1906), p. 52.

[77] *Ibid.*, p. 54.

[78] Byung-do Lee, *op. cit.*, p. 327.

[79] *Ibid.*, pp. 333–334.

[80] *Ibid.*, p. 122.

[81] *Lichō-hōten-kō*[cq] ("Synopsis of the Codes of the Lee Dynasty"), a book published in 1936 by the office of the Advisors to the Japanese Governor in Korea, stated that Korea did not have a civil code in the modern sense until 1907, p. 305.

of Confucianism in Korea is factionalism. Peculiarly enough, this feature developed from the Chinese unification idea, which brought about Chinese Confucian orthodoxy. Korean factionalism was connected with the interpretation of the Chinese Classics in the light of the Chu Hsi school of Neo-Confucianism.[82] Disagreement regarding the interpretation of the teachings of this school among Korean scholars ultimately degenerated into a system of political factionalism and corruption. And factionalism, in turn, became a serious impediment to further scientific development and the major cause of the tragic backwardness of modern Korean society. Combined with the shamanistic value-preference for purity, factionalism also disrupted the civil service examination system for several centuries by barring from admission to examinations the sons of concubines and of women who married a second time.

On superficial observation, it may appear that Confucianism is the dominant philosophy of Korea. However, in Korea as well as in Japan, Confucianism represents an exotic culture. The indigenous belief of Koreans is shamanism. It is the belief of the people, while Confucianism is that of the elite. Korean shamanism, though a more primitive belief than Confucianism, also had an impact beyond the borders of Korea, particularly upon Japan. An understanding of Korean, as of Japanese, culture requires an examination of this native religion in its field operation.

Shamanism is the name given to the native religion of the Ural-Altaic people from the Bering Straits to the borders of Scandinavia.[83] Although variations appear among the different tribes,[84] essentially, shamanism indicates a religious attitude based on an animistic view of Nature, that is, a view that the world is pervaded by spiritual forces—gods and spirits—which beneficially or adversely affect human life, and that certain persons, the shamans, can enter into close relations with these powers and control them, thus functioning as mediators between man and the spirit world. The Buddha, observing the contradiction of human life, consisting in the fact that man kills another living being to maintain his own life, began to meditate about the way of overcoming this contradiction, ultimately finding a solution in total annihilation called *nirvāṇa.* The Korean solution was more optimistic. According to shaman songs, the Korean people found that human beings, coming from Nature, live on Nature, and return to it when they complete their lives.[85] This belief in man's merger with Nature led to an animistic interpretation of the universe.[86]

When shamanism is traced beyond historical memory, its origin may be found to be the same as that of Aryan beliefs. Some scholars have found similarity between the magic ritual of the old Vedas and shamanistic practices.[87] There

[82] Taira Shidehara,[cr] *Korean Factionalism* (Tokyo: Sanseido, 1905). Also see Byung-do Lee, *op. cit.,* pp. 381–391.

[83] *Encyclopaedia of Religion and Ethics,* XI (1921), p. 441.

[84] I. M. Casanowicz, "Shamanism of the Natives of Siberia," in *Annual Report of the Board of Regents of the Smithsonian Institution* (Washington: Smithsonian Institution, 1924), n. 99.

[85] Takashi Akiba[cs] and Chiyo Akamatsu,[ct] *Chosen Buzokunokenkyu* ("A Study of Korean Shaman Custom"), Vol. II (Osaka: Osaka-Ya-go-shoten, 1938), pp. 4–5.

[86] The naturalistic element in Japanese culture has the same root.

[87] James G. Frasier, *The Golden Bough* (3rd ed., New York: The Macmillan Co., 1953), Vol. I, p. 229. See also Hermann Oldenberg, *Die Religion des Veda* (Berlin: W. Hertz, 1894).

may be some connection between Kaltic symbols, a tree and a boar as objects of worship, and Korean symbols, a tree and a bear.[88] Perhaps, also, some relationship exists between the Korean *keopuksun,*[ay] an iron-clad warship constructed by Admiral Lee Soon-sin[az] at the time of the Korean-Japanese war in A.D. 1593, a warship with a dragon at the top, and the Gokstad Viking ship with a serpent on top.[89] While these connections are conjectural, there is firmer evidence that shamanism helped in the formulation of Japanese Shintoism. The very word "Shinto"[ba] (way of gods) is of Korean origin, as is also the term used to denote the Shinto god.[90] *"Kami,"*[bb] meaning "God," is derived from the Korean shamanistic totem,[91] *Kom,*[bc] meaning bear. *Torii,*[bd] the gate of the Shinto shrine, is equated in Korea with *hongsalmoon,*[be] a gate built for the protection of the divine place from uncleanness.[92] There are numerous other identities between Korean shamanism and primitive Shinto beliefs.[93] To mention but a few: Korean shamanism shows a value-preference for "purity," which is symbolized by white clothes—*kannushi*[bf] (a Shinto priest) wears white clothes to purify himself, as Koreans do even today.[94] The present Korean custom of keeping a *kizoong*[bg] period, meaning the period from death to the time of the funeral (*ki*—avoidance; *zoong*—during), is related to the "modern Japanese custom of turning upside down the screen which is placed around a corpse."[95] However, neither Korean shamanism nor Shintoism appears in pure form. Both have been merged with the idea of *yin-yang,*[bh] which is neither a system of ethics nor a religion but was, in the course of time, developed into a naturalistic form of ethics or religion. Also, both have felt the impact of Confucianism, Taoism, and Buddhism, so that the resulting culture in both Korea and Japan is syncretism.[96]

But, beyond these and other similarities, Korean shamanism and Japanese Shintoism have gone separate ways. Their disparity is most conspicuous in an area of greatest importance in the present context of world understanding among nations: the status of religion itself as bearing on political attitudes. Perhaps a historical incident may serve as an illustration of the Japanese attitude. At the time of the Meiji Restoration, Mori Arinori[bi] (1847–1889), one of the most advanced Japanese leaders, then minister of education, had purposely shown disrespect for the shrines of Ise and for this was assassinated by a devout chauvinist. The Japanese people rose in a body to do honor, not to the victim,

[88] D. Chaplin, *Mythological Bonds between East and West* (Copenhagen: E. Munksgaard, 1938), pp. 9–10.

[89] *Ibid.*, pp. 38–39.

[90] In Korea, a shaman priest is called "Shintonim," meaning "Mr. Shinto." Professor Tsuda's view that the word "Shinto" is of Chinese origin is not adequate. See *Tōyōgakuhō*, XXV, No. 1 (1937/1938–), 2–3.

[91] Beasts of prey, such as tigers and bears, have also been referred to in Japanese literature as *"kami."* Antei Hiyane,[cu] *Nihon-Shūkyōshi*[cv] ("History of Japanese Religion") (Tokyo: Sankyo-shuppan, 1924), pp. 41–42.

[92] W. G. Aston, *Shinto* (London: Longmans, Green & Co., 1905), p. 232.

[93] *"Tsurugiwatari"*[cw] is in Korean *"zakdootagi."*[cx] *"Kamioroshi"* is in Korean *"shin-chun,"*[cy] which is, in turn, connected with Taoism. See Percival Lowell, *Occult Japan* (Boston: Houghton Mifflin Company, 1894), pp. 36–96.

[94] The *"oharai"*[cz] (the great purification) in Shintoism is identical with the *"goot"*[da] (purification) process in shamanism. Aston, *op. cit.*, p. 305.

[95] *Ibid.*, p. 252.

[96] Neither shamanism nor Shintoism had a philosophy of its own and therefore incorporated foreign philosophical ideas. See Suzuki, *op. cit.*, p. 57.

but to the murderer.[97] Also, Mori's assassination was the first step on the road to the development of the idea of *shin-koku*[bj] (the country of God), by the use of which Japan contrived to raise her national power to a level equal to that of the other great nations, and at the same time to drive the country into the catastrophe of World War II. Of course, both Confucianism and Buddhism[98] contributed to the integration of Japanese culture and to the strengthening of Japan's nationalism. On the other hand, in Korea shamanism has never played a comparable role in either political or social life. Shamans have been treated by the people, and particularly by the more enlightened members of the community, as superstitious persons. Professional shamans (*zai-in*)[bk] and *kwang-tai*[bl][99] were believed to belong to the lowest classes, with whom no other class would intermarry, although at times, by utilizing superstitious beliefs in the power of magic ceremonies, they were successful even in gaining ascendancy over a king by conducting such ceremonies in court.[100] Contemptuous treatment of shamans in Korea was due to the strength of Confucian influence. This difference in attitude of the Koreans and the Japanese is of great importance and requires a more elaborate analysis.

As stated above, both the Korean and the Japanese cultures are characterized by syncretism. However, as Professor Spicer has pointed out, the process of culture change consists in a recombination of forms and meanings, "giving the modified innovations a culture content quite different from the elements originally offered."[101] Syncretism of identical elements thus led in Japan and in Korea to entirely different constellations. In Japan, it produced two antithetical standards, the militaristic communal norm of *giri*, on the one hand, and *on*[bm] (gratitude), on the other. Though both these standards were opposed to the rule of law, the idea of national unity achieved by means of emperor worship proved to be the stronger force, so that they were indeed utilized in shaping the rule of law promoted by the government. Deification of the ruler, with consequent political totalitarianism, is a sufficient basis for any governmental policy. From this point on, rationalization is secondary, though it typically resorts to ideologies which have already taken root among the people.

In Korea, a militaristic spirit, similar to that found in Japan, was in existence at least a thousand years ago. The Korean *wharangdo*,[bn][102] corresponding to Japanese *bushidō* (the Japanese "samurai,"[bo] equivalent to *"bushi,"* is derived from the Korean *"sammuri,"* meaning fighters), were the groups of warriors who played an important role in bringing about Korea's unification by Silla. But their morale was built on a religious foundation which was destroyed with the

[97] Lowell, *Occult Japan*, p. 19.

[98] It was no mere accident that Buddhism was unusually successful in Japan. The Buddhist principle of *shi-on*[db] satisfied the Japanese ethical inclination, at the same time supplying additional support for emperor worship. See Kawaai Teichi,[dc] *On no Shisō*[dd] ("An Idea of Gratitude") (Tokyo: Tokyo-to, 1942), pp. 26–31.

[99] M. C. Haguenauer, "Sorciers et Sorcières de Corée," *Bulletin de la Maison Franco-Japonaise*, II (1929), 53.

[100] Akiba and Akamatsu, *op. cit.*, chap. II.

[101] E. H. Spicer, "Social Structure and the Acculturation Process," *American Anthropologist*, LX (1958), No. 3, pp. 438–439.

[102] *"Wharang"* literally means "handsome boys"; *"do"* means "way." These young boys were devoted to the Tao-shamanistic belief.

oncoming of Confucian influence, for shamanism in Korea did not display the power of resistance shown by Japanese Shintoism. In fact, shamanism readily yielded ground. For this reason, in the course of time, it was frequently abandoned to women,[103] a factor that contributed to the establishment of a more important position for women in Korea than that possessed by women in Japan.

The fact that Korea did not succeed in developing a nationalistic sense of unity, such as obtains in Japan, serving there as a vehicle for the reception of the Western idea of the "rule of law," does not imply that there was in Korea no sense of co-operation among the people. Rather, the distinctive element of Korean culture lies in the fact that its co-operative movement did not develop beyond a certain stage.[104] There may be found in Korea something similar to the European guild, which was an association of persons having common interests. Whether or not there is any community or parallelism of background is impossible to say, for the origins of the Korean associations are not known. Of the guild, we know that it was originally founded for religious reasons. As suggested before, the rituals of primitive Germanic tribes show some parallel with the magic rituals of shamans. The fact that the literal meaning of the name given to the Korean associations, *"ke,"*[bp] means "swearing" may be also suggestive. The *ke,* of course, is an entirely voluntary association, as the European guild was originally. However, the *ke's* impact on social development is not comparable to that of the European guild, which prepared the way for the growth of capitalistic society. The *ke* in Far Eastern Asia is distinctly Korean.[105] No word corresponding to *ke* can be found either in China or in Japan.[106] The *ke* movement started in the days of the Koryu Dynasty and has continued through the Lee[bq] Dynasty until the present time. The movement grew, so that, according to a 1926 report of the Japanese Governor-General of Korea, there were 677 kinds of *ke* in Korea. Their purposes were religious, moral, charitable, athletic, or economic. It is hard to trace a direct causal connection between the *ke* development and the shamanistic organization. Indeed, it has not been established which of them is the older. At some stage, the shaman organization merged into a separate *ke.* To assess the importance of the *ke* in contemporary Korea, perhaps it should be mentioned that the housewives' *ke* has a strong hold over economic enterprises. In rural communities there are similar associations called *"tule."*[br] The *wharangdo,* the associations of warriors, mentioned above, were such *tules.*[107] The *ke* introduces a decentralizing democratic element into Korean society. It is a spontaneous, autonomous popular organiza-

[103] A characteristic feature of Korean shamanism is the popularity of the female shaman. See Akiba and Akamatsu, *op. cit.*

[104] As the meanings of symbols change, so do human institutions. Thus, potentiality of further development and transformation is itself a cultural feature. It may be instructive to recall in this context that the jury system—now a "palladium of American liberty"—was originally created for the benefit of the king, as an instrument of royal tax collection. Heinrich Brunner, *Die Entstehung der Schwurgerichte* (Berlin: Weidman Verlag, 1872).

[105] E. Zensho,[de] *Chosen ni okeru kei no Fukyu* ("Popularization of *ke* in Korea"), *Chōsen-gakuhō*[df] ("Academic Report on Korea"), VII (March, 1955), 91–116.

[106] *Ibid.,* p. 91. However, the word *"ch'i,"* meaning the same thing, exists in Chinese, although few societies have been so known until recent times.

[107] Byung-do Lee, *op. cit.,* pp. 465–467.

tion for the promotion of various popular interests. At the same time, however, it promotes the people's estrangement from the law, for conflicts may often be resolved through the *ke* without recourse to government courts.[108]

In the area of ethical and social norm proper, shamanism has played a very important role in Korea. To it is referable the Korean value-preference for "purity," symbolized in the wearing of white clothes. This preference, as seen, was also at times abused, as in the case of the exclusion of remarried women's and concubines' sons from civil service examinations. However, as a principle of life, it governs Korean customs to a very great extent. Shamanism has also given an important imprint to the Korean personality structure. The so-called "*ul*"[bs] may, indeed, be said to be an ultimate hypothesis of Korean culture. "*Ul*" is a term of indefinite meaning. Koreans think that he who does not possess *ul* is like an animal. The content of *ul* may be best characterized as a spiritual attitude toward "purity." The shamanistic belief in man's merger with Nature has helped to establish an atmosphere of peace between man, Nature, and religion, the latter becoming close to man. It developed the essentially religious character of Koreans. This character explains the fact that the Nevius method of Protestant Christians, with its stress on a spirit of self-responsibility, was successful in Korea, whereas it failed in China.[109]

While the Buddhist and Taoist influence upon the Koreans has been small as compared with that of Confucianism, we must not underestimate the impact of the former on the ultimate shaping of the Korean cultural pattern. Buddhism has significantly affected two areas of Korean culture. On the one hand, art and architecture,[110] and, on the other, the way of life. Indeed, the Buddhist way of life combined with native shamanism in shaping the Korean personality.

An attempt to offer a general description of Korean culture in terms of a unique hypothesis must fail. Also, any generalized description must be read subject to this important reservation: "The human individual is endlessly simplifying and generalizing his own view of his environment; he constantly imposes on this environment his own constructions and meanings; these constructions and meanings are characteristic of one culture as opposed to another."[111] With this caveat in mind, a summation may be ventured.

The "whole set-up"[112] of Korean society cannot be expressed in terms of either Confucianism or Buddhism or shamanism. No one hypothesis can be offered as either unique or even paramount, for no principle can be said to stand alone or to operate independently. Thus, the Confucian "personal-relative value-pattern," the shamanist ideals of "purity" and of personality endowed with the untranslatable *ul,* and Buddhist ingredients—all combine to form the

[108] *Dai-jun-hyo-tong*[dg] ("Commentary on the Great Code"), edited by the office of the Advisors to the Japanese Governor in Korea, 1939, Appendix, p. 72.

[109] George Paik,[dh] *The History of Protestant Missions in Korea, 1832–1910* (Pyeng Yang: Union Christian College Press, 1929), pp. 151, 282–283.

[110] See Cornelius Osgood, *The Koreans and Their Culture* (New York: The Ronald Press Company, 1951), pp. 260–261.

[111] C. Kluckhohn, "The Philosophy of the Navaho Indians," in Northrop, ed., *Ideological Differences and World Order,* p. 356.

[112] K. N. Llewellyn, *The Bramble Bush* (New York: Columbia University Law School, 1930), p. 109.

total picture of the distinctive culture that is "Korean." Also, each of these elements has operated in Korea in a distinctive manner. The *ke,* when viewed by itself, could have served as a nucleus of Korea's modernization. Perhaps it would have performed an important function in a process of modernization elsewhere, but in Korea this potentiality of the *ke* was in the beginning suppressed by the overwhelming influence of Confucian interpreters with their tendency to monopolize thought and their subtle methods of thought-control. Thus, Korean society has not been an "open society,"[113] in which individuals are confronted with personal decisions, but a "closed society."[114] Confucianism itself, as it developed in China, possessed a rational element; the manner of its propagation in Korea was not rational but, rather, "ideational."[115] Perhaps the best illustration of this method is the *Kyung-kuk tai-chun*[bt] (the great code of administration), a code compiled under Chinese influence by Sung Chong,[bu] the ninth king of the Lee Dynasty. The provisions of this code were special amendments to the *Ming-lü* (code of the Ming Dynasty). The conduct punished there was made criminal, not because there were rational grounds for so doing in the light of Korean standards or conditions, but, rather, simply because Confucian moral teachings seemed to demand it. This may be contrasted with the law of certain American States regarding corruption in baseball, a grave crime.[116] Of course, this code, as well as the autonomous codes of the various organizations, followed the Confucian principle of differentiation according to status. In the area of private law, in conformity with the Confucian aversion to generalization and abstract concepts in the field of human relationships, the mediational type of law prevailed.

With special reference to the legal context, Korean culture may be characterized in terms of "plurality" of legal method. This means that legal authority was not centralized but was plural and that the type of dispute-settling was different, depending on whether the case was criminal or civil. With regard to criminal law, as crystallization of culture, it is important to note that both crime and punishment were based upon status. This means, not only that definitions of crime and the extent of punishment depended on family, social, and public status, but also that in the case of the so-called "elimination of three families"[117] (treason was punishable by execution of three families, those of the offender's father, mother, and wife) the principle followed was collective responsibility.

III. CONCLUSION

The foregoing analysis was concerned with traditional rather than with contemporary Korean culture. The latter can be comprehended only against the

[113] K. R. Popper, *The Open Society and its Enemies* (Princeton: Princeton University Press, 1950), p. 169.
[114] W. E. Griffis, *Korea, the Hermit Nation* (New York: Charles Scribner's Sons, 1882).
[115] P. A. Sorokin, *The Crisis of Our Age* (11th printing, New York: E. P. Dutton & Co., Inc., 1951).
[116] E. Sutherland, *Principles of Criminology* (3rd ed., New York: J. B. Lippincott Company, 1939), p. 76.
[117] This principle was abolished in 1894. See Paul K. Ryu, "The New Korean Criminal Code of October 3, 1953; An Analysis of Ideologies Embedded in It." 48 *Journal of Criminal Law, Criminology and Police Science* 275 (1957).

background of the former. Modern Korean culture is composed of conflicting ideas, the new and the old. But readiness or reluctance to adopt new ideas is part of a given culture itself.

It was Korea's tragedy that the modernization of Korean law was initiated by Japan, the *Hyung-pub tai-chun*[bv] (the great code of penal laws), 1905, being the first modernized code in Korea.[118] But, since her independence, Korea has been increasingly receptive to new ideas. She is beginning to realize the cause of her past inability to direct her own future properly. Accordingly, the Korean government has made a determined effort to eliminate illiteracy and is winning the battle against it, in spite of the fact that Korea has engaged in a war against communist aggression. Christiantiy is growing in strength. In the thirteen years since Korea's liberation, over one hundred colleges and universities have been established. Young people are yearning for education. In accordance with the traditional Korean inclination toward the spiritual *ul,* their interests are more philosophical than practical. As is normal in underdeveloped countries, nationalism is growing. The beneficial effect of such an attitude is its potentiality for breaking through special personal group-patterns. But overcoming the personal-relative value-pattern in Korea is by no means an easy task. It is to be hoped that enlightenment and education, and particularly knowledge of her own culture, will help to democratize Korea, for knowledge makes for freedom—freedom to overcome traditions recognized as undesirable. A change in popular attitudes and social customs is essential, for, to a large extent, political and legal democracy are predicated upon them.

In observing present Korean culture, we must not overlook the importance of realizing what in a changing society is attributable to transformation of a particular traditional concept and what is the result of a change in the institutional framework. In evaluating culture changes, the "field" point of view is essential. This was overlooked, for instance, by Ruth Benedict, when she explained the Japanese people's change from vindictiveness to reconciliation after World War II by reference to the traditional Japanese *giri.*[119] *Giri,* indeed, required a contrary attitude, suicide perhaps if the person concerned was unable to fulfill his duty to the emperor. Inspired by *giri,* numerous Japanese *kamikazes*[bw] devoted their lives to their emperor. The change in attitude had an altogether different source. The Japanese people began to realize that emperor-centered ethics was the product of a deliberate scheme in which chauvinist scholars co-operated with militant groups. Awakening from the illusion of *shin-koku* (the country of God), Japan has adopted a most liberal and progressive Constitution. It is knowledge and not *giri* that has helped to free the Japanese people from the limitations of their past.

The future of Korea depends upon her recognition of both the constructive and the atavistic elements of her culture. As is true of any country, the future depends upon knowledge. Christ said: "Ye shall know the truth, and the truth

[118] *Ibid.*
[119] Benedict, *op. cit.,* pp. 172–176.

shall make you free."[120] Freedom here means the inner freedom to choose and follow a course of action found to be rational.[121]

QUESTION: Your explanation of *"giri"* as referring to the relationship between the Japanese subject and the emperor may be questioned, since use of this concept is limited in Japan to the ethics of the merchant class, while another concept, *"chūgi"*[bx] (loyalty), is used in the ethics applicable to the relation between lord and subject.

ANSWER: This is a purely semantic problem. There is no essential difference between *"giri"* and *"chūgi."* Undoubtedly, *"giri-ninjō"*[by] (justice and humanity) is the basic communal norm in Japan. But it is possible, of course, to subdivide the general concept of *"giri"* into *"giri"* in the narrower sense and *"chūgi."*

QUESTION: Your interpretation of Confucianism in terms of "a personal-relative value-pattern," negating the existence of objective value in Chinese Confucian ethics, is contrary to the belief expressed by many Chinese writers on the objectivity of Confucian ethics.

ANSWER: As clearly stated in my paper, Confucius believed in the "universal existence of moral law." When speaking of "personal-relative value" in Confucianism, I referred, not to the existence of the normative order itself, but to the contents of the norm, which differ, depending on the status of participants and their objective relationship to each other. This contrasts, for instance, with Stoic ethics, which postulates an impersonal logical element. It is noteworthy to mention that the very difference of "field" had the two sages, Confucius and Socrates, taking different approaches to law although both believed in the universal existence of moral law.

QUESTION: Could not the traditional concept of "context" be adequately substituted for that of "field," as used in your paper, and, if so, is the latter concept at all necessary?

ANSWER: The concept of "context" belongs to the science of language. It is true that, to the extent that we use language for the purpose of communicating with each other, "field" often overlaps with "context." But there is an essential difference between the two. "Context" cannot serve as a substitute for "field" in the study of culture any more than it could replace it in physics. To try to understand and correctly describe the meaning of a dynamic culture-change and of value-relationships within it without regard to a concrete field is like trying to catch fish without fishing tools.

QUESTION: When you use the concept of "free society," do you mean to say that "free society" is the only existing objective value?

ANSWER: My remark refers to the general philosophical problem as to whether values can ever be objective. I suggested that, if we assume such a

[120] John 8:32.
[121] Max Planck, *Vom Wesen der Willensfreiheit* (Leipzig: J. A. Barth, 1939), pp. 16–22.

general concept as "free society," we have a basis for an objective quantitative comparison of values. But, of course, this term requires definition. Appropriate dealing with this problem exceeds the scope of this paper. At this time, I should like to suggest only that the meaning of the hypothesis of science is changing and that the view regarding the distinction between fact and value is also changing. Without going more deeply into the comprehensive problem of the definition of "free society," I should like to draw attention to the fact that a minimum hypothesis of "free society" is implied in our present endeavor. In order to compare one culture with another we have to have a common agreement that a free exchange of ideas is to be admitted. Otherwise we cannot compare cultures meaningfully.

[a] 名家劉基天
[b] 湯川秀樹
[c] 孔子
[d] 仁
[e] 族
[f] 姓
[g] 氏
[h] 家
[i] 劉邦
[j] 董仲舒
[k] 朱熹
[l] 司馬光
[m] 資治通鑑
[n] 墨子
[o] 兼愛
[p] 士農工商
[q] 陋規
[r] 霸道
[s] 王道
[t] 天子
[u] 寺小屋式
[v] 唐律

w 明律
x 孝
y 三綱五常
z 忠
aa 忠孝一本
ab 東照宮
ac 德川家康
ad 豊國神社
ae 豊臣秀吉
af 北畠親房
ag 神皇正統紀
ah 義理
ai 武士道
aj 高句麗
ak 翰林院
al 新羅
am 薛聰
an 吏讀
ao 假名
ap 한글
aq 五倫
ar 子息
as 너
at 당신
au 貴下
av 尊長
aw 高麗
ax 衙前
ay 거북선(亀船)
az 李舜臣
ba 神道
bb 神
bc 곰 (熊)
bd 鳥居
be 홍살문
bf 神主
bg 忌中
bh 陰陽
bi 森有禮
bj 神國
bk 才人
bl 광대
bm 恩
bn 花郎道
bo さむらい(侍)
bp 契
bq 季
br 들레
bs 얼
bt 經國大典
bu 成宗
bv 刑法大典
bw 神風
bx 忠義
by 義理人情
bz 胡適
ca 馮友蘭
cb 馮漢驥
cc 五服
cd 胡先進
ce 項羽
cf 鈴木大拙
cg 蔣夢麟
ch 劉
ci 王仁
cj 應神
ck 津田左右吉
cl 東洋學報
cm 箕子
cn 殷
co 李丙燾
cp 許蘭光
cq 李朝法典考
cr 幣原坦
cs 秋葉隆
ct 赤松智城
cu 比屋根安定
cv 日本宗教史
cw ツルギワタリ
cx 작두타기
cy 神遷
cz 大祓
da 天
db 四恩
dc 川合貞一
dd 恩の思想
de 善生永助
df 朝鮮學報
dg 大典會通
dh 白樂濬

VI. Conspectus of Practical Implications for World Understanding and Co-operation

E. A. BURTT

A Basic Problem in the Quest for Understanding Between East and West

I.

As I have listened to the discussions of the preceding five weeks my mind has been asking: Is there a crucial feature in Eastern ways of thinking that is especially hard for Westerners to understand, and is there likewise a crucial assumption typical of the West that is especially hard for Easterners to appreciate? If there is and if these ideas as they have been expressed in the conference papers can be clarified and rendered more intelligible to those who now find them opaque, we shall have found a key to the deeper mutual understanding between East and West that is the goal of this whole series of conferences. Other issues that have proved refractory are, I am sure, so dependent on these crucial features that, once real light falls on the latter, the way to the solution of the former becomes clear.

But a word of warning is needed even before I state what I take these features to be. We have been reminded over and over again in this conference that there is no sharp and simple contrast between "East" and "West." There are important differences within each cultural tradition, whether Eastern or Western. As regards the East, there are important differences between India and China, and between Japan and both these countries; further, Islamic culture is in some sense a bridge between East and West, while revealing distinctive characteristics of its own.[1] I have not forgotten these reminders. Nonetheless, it would be a mistake to allow awareness of these facts to entice us to the other extreme, where we would lose sight of the broad contrast that actually obtains between East and West and would focus attention merely on the similarities

[1] See Bammate's paper, above, pp. 172 ff.

present in all civilized cultures. Such similarities provide a starting-point for comparative philosophy and a common language for communication, but by themselves they throw no light on the profound differences that must be comprehended if a more than superficial mutual understanding is to be achieved. When we consider the major trends of thought in East and West, a significant contrast in approach, in emphasis, and in the central philosophical concepts employed emerges; were this not so, these conferences would never have taken place. It is our basic task to face and to master these differences. My own conviction, ever since I became interested in the philosophies of the East, has been that by a persistent sensitivity to these differences one can achieve rewarding insights about man and the world and his developing experience in it that had been missed before. To explore the worlds in which the philosophers of other cultures live is just as thrilling and instructive as to delve with the scientist into the hitherto unproved energies of the physical realm; and today it is more desperately needed. So, when I use the words "East" and "West" in what follows I mean by them simply a convenient abbreviation for these important and pervasive differences.

What is it that obstructs us in seeking this kind of intercultural understanding? I believe that to this question there is a simple answer, which our papers and discussions confirm. It is our underlying philosophical presuppositions—not the ones that we easily become conscious of but the ones providing the implicit framework of our whole way of thinking. It is vital to remind ourselves that there are presuppositions that we think *with* so naturally and constantly that it requires a severe wrench for us to free ourselves from their clutches sufficiently to think *about* them. Such presuppositions differ between the competing schools in Western thought and those in Eastern thought; that is why the issues between these schools are often hard to resolve. But the most intractable differences arise from the fact that there are more general presuppositions typical of the West as a whole and others typical of the East as a whole; in their case we confront contrasting ways of thinking about everything that philosophers try to interpret. To get past this barrier and achieve mutual comprehension at this level requires a sensitive flexibility that is very difficult to achieve.

The inevitable tendency for a philosopher is to assume that every experience he meets, every philosophical assertion he reads, can be assimilated into the framework of presuppositions with which he now thinks. It is the only framework he has available. And when he finds himself in a situation where this cannot be done, the natural reaction is to explode in impatient frustration: "This is sheer nonsense! How can a philosopher get anywhere if he talks this way?" And his frustration shows that it *is* nonsense in terms of the presuppositional system with which his mind at present operates. But if one has gained the flexibility just mentioned it may prove to be the kind of nonsense which, when taken as a challenge, leads to increased philosophical understanding. I prefer the word "flexibility" here, although I am sure that von Rintelen[2] was not wrong in speaking of a "loving readiness to apprehend the particular perspective . . . proper to each mode of thought and each culture."

In view of this deep-seated obstruction to mutual understanding it would be ridiculous, of course, for me to proceed tonight as though I could translate Eastern presuppositions into terms familiar to the West, and vice versa, so that the difficulties would at once disappear and all become light. What I do hope is that by well-chosen hints and analogies some misunderstandings may begin to fade away and a previously alien set of presuppositions gain some measure of intelligibility.

So, let us return to my central question, namely, is there a crucial feature in the way of thinking characteristic of the East, and similarly in the way typical of the West, that is most difficult for the other half of the world to understand? If so, what is it? I believe there is, and that this feature lies in the fact that Western thinkers trust reason as providing the way to whatever truth and insight man can gain, whereas Eastern thinkers are deeply convinced that ultimate truth can be achieved only by passing beyond reason and the limitations essential to it. Our papers and discussions have revealed many times that the former notion sounds to Easterners very naive, while the latter contention sounds to Westerners like asking them to abandon their hard-won power of logical discrimination for something less trustworthy. Moreover, there is an intrinsic connection between this Eastern insistence and the conviction that we must also in our moral philosophy pass beyond ethics and in religious philosophy beyond the theistic concept of God. The divergence of presuppositions here disclosed is very radical.

Now many of the philosophical concepts that we have found ourselves constantly using in this conference harbor ambiguities that depend on this divergence of conviction. Consider briefly three of them. We have found indispensable the concept of "experience" and its cognate adjective "empirical." Westerners typically give meaning to these words in the setting of inductive science and the quest for truth about the factual realm that naturally employs the methods of inductive science. There are exceptions, of course, but they do not represent the dominant trend. When our Eastern colleagues use these words, however, they obviously mean something different and to the West quite perplexing, namely, the progress of man's mind toward the realization of a deeper selfhood, bringing freedom from worry and an inner tranquillity that had previously been lacking.[3] This realization is an achievement which, as they see it, involves passing beyond reason. For them, the experience of inductive science fills its role within this deepening process and depends for its value on it; whereas the West interprets this "self-realization" as a subjective intuition which, as such, is quite unreliable.

We have also found indispensable the concept of "truth," as constituting the goal of all responsible reflection in philosophy as elsewhere. Western thinkers,

[2] See his paper, above, p. 400.

[3] See Kishimoto's paper, above, pp. 245, 248 f.

almost universally, mean by "truth" a property of propositions or statements, conceived as capable of objective validation by formal or empirical tests. But when Easterners use it they are more likely to have in mind something that may be described as the cognitive aspect of this self-realization, which on the side of the seeker is better indicated by the word "truthfulness" and on the side of the goal by the phrase "reality as a whole." And again, for them, the truth of any particular statement depends on its relation to this more ultimate meaning. If the West objects that there is no way of verifying truth in this sense, the Eastern thinker replies: "Not so; such truth is objective because the saints who have achieved it agree essentially as to its nature and the way to its realization."[4]

Equally indispensable, for the present conference at least, has been the concept of "practice." To the Western thinker this word at once suggests some particular course of action aimed at the satisfaction of an individual or social need; it gains its meaning in such a setting.[5] The Easterner, however, has in mind a much broader meaning, namely, man's search for total fulfillment with all that it may involve. For him, there will be no separation between the practical and the theoretical as there tends to be for the West, because the pursuit of scientific knowledge, and indeed any quest for fuller understanding, will be a part of this search. But he conceives this total fulfillment as requiring a transcendence of reason.[6]

Is it not clear, then, that the ability of East and West to achieve mutual understanding in the presence of these ambiguities, and even to communicate with each other successfully, requires awareness of the presuppositions underlying the use of these philosophical terms by thinkers from each side, and that such an awareness will inevitably lead to the crucial issue between the Western trust in reason and the Eastern conviction that we must pass beyond reason?

II.

We need to begin with a broad base on which these contrasting presuppositions can be clarified and compared. The simplest way to establish it is to ask, first from the perspective of the East and then from that of the West, what is the central idea in the light of which its way of dealing with all problems can be understood.

The answer of the East is: the idea of *liberation*. And what does the East mean by this word? It means man's emancipation from all that obstructs his progress toward self-realization, and toward the apprehension of truth in its wholeness that such realization brings. The major role of philosophy from its point of view is, then, to interpret and guide this process. Now, if we tried to state the characteristic orientation of Western philosophy in terms of this idea,

[4] See above, the papers of Saksena (pp. 55, 63 f.), Chan (pp. 82 ff.), Mahadevan (pp. 492 f.), Nikhilananda (pp. 507 f.).

[5] See Hook's paper, above, pp. 19 f.

[6] For this meaning of "practical" see above, for example, the papers of Hsieh (pp. 411 ff.) and Saksena (p. 64).

a significant difference would at once emerge, and at two points. First, the natural form of the word in the West is not "liberation" but "liberty" or "freedom," by which the West means control by an individual or society over external obstructions to the satisfaction of its desires. Second, and more important, the range of problems with which one is concerned when using these concepts is limited to a narrow area in ethical and social philosophy; the major philosophical problems of the West are dealt with in quite different terms.

The central philosophical concept of the West is not freedom but an idea so universally presupposed that ordinarily no one is conscious of it. I shall refer to it by the phrase *"rational understanding"*—by which I mean intellectual mastery of the world around man, of the social structures in which he lives, and of man himself conceived as a striving individual confronting both world and society. From the Western standpoint the essential role of philosophy is to interpret and guide the progressive enhancement of man's intellectual powers and their successful application to these varied problems. In using the word "rational" here I intend no special interpretation of it, such as that exemplified by the eighteenth-century Enlightenment; I have in mind a common feature of the Western attitude in science, philosophy, and all other intellectual pursuits that has been dominant ever since the Greeks discovered the delights of the exercise of reason. Were we to state the characteristic perspective of the East in terms of this idea it would at once appear that, while its thinkers also prize man's rational powers, the primary purpose which they are expected to fill is that of guiding his quest for the spiritual perfection that is his true destiny and which lies beyond reason. Hence, their inevitable emphasis is on the limits which are intrinsic to reason. The major task of philosophy in their eyes is to transcend these limits through a super-rational insight which builds upon the work of reason but ultimately leaves it behind in a unified apprehension of reality.

Now, even this preliminary sketch of the differences between Eastern and Western presuppositions confronts us with a contrast which threatens to become an irreconcilable conflict. Hence it is important to see before going further that a more hopeful feature is present, too. Both Western and Eastern thinkers share a fundamental common conviction: that of the essential dignity of man and the high worth of his distinctive potentialities in relation to the vast universe that encompasses him. To be sure, differences emerge even in connection with this conviction. It is the faith of the East that all persons will ultimately realize the goal set by man's distinctive promise, however many reincarnations may be needed; whereas the West, skeptical about the doctrine of transmigration, demands that this fulfillment be achieved here and now through the transformation of social institutions which at present fail to foster it. But this core of basic agreement is very significant, and in two ways. On the one hand, it assures us a foundation of common belief as regards fundamental human values, on which our search for fuller mutual understanding can proceed. On the other hand, it makes clearer than ever the central problem calling for clarification. For to the West what is most precious in man, giving him his unique dignity, is precisely his power of reason, while to the East it is his capacity to transcend the limits set by reason. We evidently need to master two contrasting conceptions of man.

III.

Our guiding question takes, then, more definite form: Is it the case that human reason meets a limit beyond which it cannot pass in its search for understanding, and, if so, how are we to conceive this limit and its possible transcendence? Each side confidently gives its own answer, and envisions our main goal as men and our task as philosophers accordingly.

The crucial issue between the two viewpoints thus stands sharp and clear. Is there a flat contradiction between them? Or can we find the key to a solution by drawing a distinction which both West and East will recognize as valid?

I believe there is such a key, in the light of which the two perspectives can appear as complementary instead of contradictory. This is by no means to say that a reconciliation will become easy, but it will become possible. Both sides agree that there is no limit beyond which reason is unable to go *in knowledge of objects and whatever can become an object.* The difference is that the Westerner stops here, seeing nothing beyond or other than this realm of objects to investigate; indeed, his assumed definition of "knowledge" limits it to this realm. He concentrates his energies upon what can thus be known, unaware that he may be seriously restricting himself in doing so. Whereas the Easterner sees something of crucial importance beyond and underlying all objects, namely, the self which apprehends them, the knower which by its very nature is the subject of consciousness and always eludes us when we try to make it an object. In fact, when its true nature is fully realized—and "realization" rather than "knowledge" is the appropriate word in this situation—the separation between subject and object, which is indispensable for all rational knowledge, is transcended, and the self is aware of itself as a unity in which that separation has been overcome.[7]

Our task now is to probe this difference more fully, so as to understand, if we can, how East and West have in each case been led to their characteristic emphasis and belief. A perspective may thus emerge that can include what both of them hold important. The way I shall attempt this task is through an elucidation of the Eastern idea of liberation in terms of more familiar Western concepts, and likewise of the Western faith in rational understanding in terms that may be more intelligible to the East. My aim is to do this in such a way that the crucial issue is kept in focus and that whatever power this key distinction may have to resolve it is fully revealed.

[7] For this last point see especially Suzuki's paper, above, pp. 429 f. For an emphasis on the self as that which is intrinsically subject, see above, papers by Saksena (p. 56 f.), Mahadevan (p. 483), and Werkmeister (pp. 144 ff.).

IV.

Let us begin this part of our enterprise with the rational understanding so eagerly sought by the West. Eastern thinkers often assume that their viewpoint allows for all the positive virtues in this emphasis, but I doubt how many of them really appreciate its deeper significance or have caught the full force of its appeal. Its promise is now coming home to them in the particular form of scientific technology, but this is only one aspect of a challenge that is far more comprehensive and profound. In trying to explain it I shall make much use of Constantin Regamey's paper as presented to the conference three weeks ago.[8]

We may as well concentrate at once on the most provocative point. As his penetrating analysis revealed, there are certain features of the Western conviction that reason fills an exalted role which in the broad sense of the term may be called "spiritual"—a word which the East is accustomed to restrict to the kind of experience that transcends rational understanding. What are these features?

First, the West has discovered that any achievement of reason is by virtue of that fact communicable to all thinkers whoever and wherever they may be. Through reason we are thus able, not only to preserve in stable conceptual form whatever distinctions and relations facilitate comprehension of objects, but also to share them throughout the whole community of human inquirers. Second, through the stable and shared meaning of its concepts reason can secure continuity in the advance of knowledge from generation to generation; no gaps need be left in the systematic evolution of man's cognitive pursuits. Third, this advance can continue without end, because wherever any inadequacy in rational understanding appears, reason is able by its analytic power to locate the source and to remedy the defect by a needed distinction or an improved conceptual system. Now, these features of the work of reason would seem to be unqualifiedly good from any tenable standpoint; they show that in the responsible exercise of this faculty man is growing toward the unique perfection of which he is capable. With our attention on these virtues, we may indeed maintain that the chief significance of modern science does not lie in its conquest of the physical world; it lies, rather, in the universality of the truths it establishes, so that they become a part of the cognitive heritage that will be shared by all human cultures.[9]

One could elaborate on the nature and importance of these features in various directions; for our purpose it will be enough to call attention to the instruments which Western thinkers have developed by which reason can fill its function efficiently. Some of these are quite general instruments; others are specialized. The latter, of course, are many in number and varied in character. On the theoretical side, they consist in the analytic procedures which have

[8] See especially pp. 320 ff., 334 ff.

[9] Many conference papers have emphasized this point; note especially, above, those of Werkmeister (pp. 138 f.), Yukawa (pp. 188 f.), and Bammate (p. 187).

been devised to facilitate systematic penetration of this or that area of the problems the West has attacked, while, on the practical side, they appear in the various inventions by which man's control of the manifold processes of Nature is achieved. The general instruments are two: logic (including mathematics) and the method of empirical science.

Logic is the outstanding achievement of the rational Western mind in ancient times. It embodies the outcome of the search for a methodical pattern of dependable thinking about any reality. Such unquestioned success has crowned this search that many Occidental thinkers believe that their present logical presuppositions provide an absolute and changeless framework which thought must necessarily respect. This notion seems to me mistaken; logic has had its history in the past, sometimes undergoing quite revolutionary changes, and I see no reason to suppose that this history has come to an end. Rather, its ideal should be viewed as one which *deserves to be absolutized* as fully as may prove feasible. I mean by this phrase that it deserves to be freed as completely as possible from the limitations of any particular subject-matter and any particular purpose, so that its structure may express nothing other than the conditions involved in clear understanding itself. New theories of logic will surely appear from time to time, but we may justifiably hope that through their improvement on previous theories this goal will be gradually approached. So far as I can tell, the East never quite conceived logic in this way; any proposed pattern of inference was supposed to derive its validity from some ultimate purpose which, it was believed, thought ought to serve.[10]

The inductive method of the empirical sciences is the outstanding achievement of the modern West. Along with the variations revealed as one passes from one branch of science to another—especially from the physical to the "behavioral" sciences—there are certain common features which express the essential nature of inductive generalization so far as it has achieved clarity to date. The most ambitious ideal here is to develop concepts and procedures that will be self-correcting—that is, will be such that if an error or inadequacy turns up in the outcome of any given inquiry it can be corrected by a further and more systematic application of the same principles. This goal, too, has been realized with high success. And clearly this ideal similarly deserves to be absolutized as fully as possible, so that our quest for reliable explanations of the facts of Nature may proceed with maximum assurance.

Here, too, so far as I can tell, Eastern thinkers have never quite caught the significance of a general inductive method conceived in this way,[11] and therefore missed its promise in a philosophical perspective on man and the world. And this promise, as in the case of logical theory, is not limited from the Western viewpoint to its practical values, nor even to its obvious intellectual virtue. The victories that can be won through these instruments of reason are essential to man's spiritual fulfillment, in any tenable meaning of this phrase,

[10] This assumption is revealed in two passages in Datta's paper, above, pp. 580, 588 f.

[11] The Chinese perhaps came nearest to this idea. See Hu Shih's paper, above, pp. 207 ff., 215 ff.

and for two reasons. One is that man's power of rational explanation of the phenomenal world is a part of his unique potentiality, and its maximum development is part of his total fulfillment. The other is that men cannot progress toward any appealing goal whatever when the majority of them are sunk in the torpor of ignorance, drudgery, and destitution. They are then in bondage to the pressing elementary needs of food and shelter. The East has now become poignantly aware of this bondage and knows that it can be overcome. It realizes more and more that any widespread sharing in spiritual values, however these be defined, is possible only through a rise in the standard of living which depends on mastering the victories achieved by reason in the West. Spiritual freedom for the many can be achieved only through freedom from constant harassment by the material conditions of life.

It is because of all these considerations in their cumulative force that the typical Western thinker views the challenge of today as he confidently does. That challenge is for man to realize, more fully than ever before, the rational potentialities through which such accomplishments as these have been gained. Where, he asks, as he surveys these astonishing victories, is there any limit to what we can expect to achieve by reason in our knowledge of the objects and events that make up our world? Both his aspiration and his successful experience strengthen the conviction that he has no power more trustworthy than reason, and that this faculty can always win new victories wherever they are needed—over physical Nature, over the perplexing problems of society, even over his own self.

But at this point the crucial issue confronts us again, and the boundary of reason's empire insisted upon by the East looms before us. Over his own self also? Is this really a justifiable hope? Assuming that the West is right so far as the mastery of other areas is concerned, how far can our rational powers take us toward this goal? Is something inevitably left out when reason attempts this task, and is that something of vital significance?

The typical Eastern thinker is sure, as we have seen, that the answer to both halves of this question is yes. It is important, he believes, for reason to achieve all that it can achieve in analyzing the nature of human personality. But what is of ultimate value here cannot in the nature of the case be accomplished by reason; it is the realization of a unity of selfhood transcending all rational distinctions. This realization gives meaning to his basic concept of "liberation"; and he is also sure that it is a necessary condition of any dependable achievement of the rational goals sought by the West.

Now this orientation is not so foreign to Western thinkers as might at first appear. They are familiar, of course, with the naturalistic and even behavioristic theories of man which express the conviction that his mind can be rationally understood only in the same basic terms that we take for granted in studying external Nature. This orientation was exemplified at the present conference in Rossow's paper. But they are also aware of theories resting on quite different presuppositions, illustrated by Stace's survey of Western mysticism and by Werkmeister's insistence on the uniqueness of human personality.[12] This approach to the understanding of man, in the West as in the East, has emphasized the distinctive capacity of mind to function not as object but as unifying subject of experience, and also the fact that it is a center of the valuations which not only vary from person to person and from culture to culture but are capable of indefinite growth and of manifold forms of fulfillment. However, the framework of concepts employed by the East for this understanding of man rests on presuppositions which at some points are quite different from those of any Western theory that has achieved historical influence. It is this difference which poses a serious difficulty.

V.

How can this framework be made intelligible to the West? I am not sure that my way of attempting this task will satisfy our Eastern colleagues, or even that my grasp of their viewpoint is wholly accurate, but it seems to me important to make the attempt. I shall keep in mind their own way of expressing their convictions.

The primary questions regarding the philosophical orientation of the East are these: What is the liberated person liberated from, and what is he liberated to? How is the liberation achieved? I believe that the concepts by which its answer to these questions can be best translated into terms familiar to the West are those of the psychoanalytic approach to the nature of man. I do not have in mind here any particular psychoanalytic theory, but simply the general assumptions underlying all such theories with which I am acquainted. Expressed in these terms, the Eastern answer is: The liberated person is liberated from inner conflict and all that goes with it; he is liberated to the realization of an open, alert, and united selfhood from which this conflict has blocked him. To the individual not yet liberated the conflict is largely unconscious, but through the anxiety and tension generated it ever and anon breaks into conscious awareness; the achievement of liberation is essentially a process of hastening and expanding this awareness. In this situation, as elsewhere, it is realization of the truth that makes one free.

What are the main forms in which this conflict is revealed, when we try to describe them in terms which are explicitly stressed in the East and which Western experience might verify?

Well, Eastern thinkers constantly affirm that liberation is both an intellectual and an ethical achievement. In the former respect, it carries to completion man's cognitive quest for systematic understanding—for a unified grasp of reality from which nothing is omitted and in which a purely external relatedness of objects to other objects is transcended.[13] In the latter respect, it carries to completion his search for integrity as a moral being, in which there

[12] For Rossow, see above, pp. 120 ff.; for Stace, pp. 303, 310 f.; for Werkmeister, pp. 144 ff.
[13] Only a whole self can perceive reality as a whole. See below, pp. 687 f.

is no longer any conflict between the intellectual, on the one side, and the emotional and volitional powers of the self, on the other.[14] Thus it brings the inner tranquillity to which our Japanese colleagues have more than once referred. These descriptions imply that the inner conflict itself is in part intellectual and in part moral. Let us pursue this suggestion.

The presence of intellectual conflict reveals itself in the fact—obvious to a Western as well as an Eastern mind—that our power of concentration is more or less weakened and obstructed by what we refer to in general terms as "distractions." A thinker focuses his attention on the subject that he wants to think about, but instead of being able steadily to concentrate on it he finds himself pushed and pulled by irrelevant ideas that seize him and hold his mind captive for a longer or shorter time. He throws one culprit out by an effort of will, but before long another source of distraction has captured him and he has to go through the struggle again. When we take note of this experience, can we avoid admitting that most of us are far from realizing the full capacity of mind-control that might be achieved? We are in unresolved conflict between the self which asserts its right to rule our thinking and another self which is hospitable to these distracting forces. Thus far, Western thinkers have generally viewed this situation as unavoidable; they see nothing to be done about it except to maintain control of attention as long as possible and to give up the effort when the mind is exhausted. Eastern thinkers, however, have discovered that such bondage is not unavoidable. Something can be done to achieve a stable domination of our minds by the self that rightfully claims such a role. This discovery has led to the persistent emphasis in the East on the practice of meditation, which it has found an essential technique in the process of gradually achieving full power of concentration. Through such a discipline, guided by the laws of mental growth that have been mastered in the course of the centuries, some of them have found it possible to bring this intellectual conflict to an end and to win an alert, unhampered control over the mind's activity.

The presence of moral conflict is evidenced by another fact, also verifiable in the West as well as in the East. A person often finds his power to exemplify the ideals approved by his higher self weakened, and at times even hamstrung, by potent urges that drive him to acts inconsistent with those ideals. On the one hand, there is the unified self that he knows he has it in him to be, and feels that he ought to be; on the other hand, there are the blind emotions, self-centered impulses, and narrow loyalties that constitute his connecting link with the screaming, demanding infant that he was at the beginning of his career. Now, it has been a basic conviction of the East that this conflict, too, is not one that we have to live with forever, and that no one can escape the responsibility as a moral being to bring it to an end.[15] Many conference papers by our Eastern colleagues have emphasized this conviction and its bear-

[14] See the passages referred to below, p. 688.
[15] Traditional Western theology has shared this conviction in its concept of "conversion."

ing on various philosophical issues.[16] Among the consequences of this conviction is the important conclusion that the goal of man's ethical life must lie "beyond ethics." By this phrase the East means such a realization of moral integrity that one naturally expresses in conduct his ideal of what is right and good without the conscious effort to follow rules that is characteristic of the ethical stage of his growth. With the end of moral conflict, he no longer needs guidance by such rules; his emotions and volitional urges have been brought into disciplined harmony with his clear vision of the ideal. In Swami Nikhilananda's vivid words, the saint is like a trained and skillful dancer who takes the appropriate steps spontaneously and gracefully but without the conscious effort to avoid mistakes that was needed during the period of his training.[17] This idea has not been absent from Western thought; St. Augustine once said: "Love, and do what you will." His meaning was that any natural expression, in action, of a self motivated by love is a morally good act—better than any he might perform in dutiful obedience to some prescribed rule.

Because of its conviction regarding this form of conflict, the philosophical power of the East has been devoted largely to the discovery of methods facilitating its resolution and the achievement of a trans-ethical unity of selfhood. Such methods are illustrated by many *yoga* practices and by the Buddhist "eightfold path."

VI.

Three questions arise from these considerations which most Western philosophers will wish to have more fully answered. One is: Why is this experience of resolving conflict through deepening self-awareness vitally important? The second is: How, more specifically, does it lead us beyond reason? And the third is: What is its significance for philosophy?

The answer of the East to the first question—if I am right in interpreting its position in the terms I have chosen—is that until a person participates in this experience and commits himself to its goal he has not really achieved either the intellectual or the moral adulthood that he is likely to think he has. As long as this is so, he remains a source of evil to others and to himself instead of becoming an unqualified source of good. In the exercise of his intellectual powers he is subject to enfeebling distraction, and to the confusion which it inevitably generates; when pursuing philosophical discussion with others, instead of exemplifying a single-minded search for truth, he easily falls into argumentative debate in defense of his present presuppositions. In his life as a moral being there is likely to appear a yawning gap, of which he is not aware, between the character-image he has of himself and his actual conduct. And he will use his rational powers to hide the difference from himself instead of honestly facing it.

[16] See, above, the papers by Hsieh (pp. 411 f.), T'ang (pp. 228 ff.), Kishimoto (pp. 247 ff.), Nikhilananda (pp. 511 f., 514 f., 516 f.), and Datta (p. 571).

[17] In the discussion on the evening of July 17, 1959.

Consider as a concrete illustration of these general statements the ethical virtue of love, just mentioned. Each of the high religions and many moral philosophies agree that love is the supreme ideal, and psychotherapy today has provided a remarkable confirmation of this insight; its basic teaching at this point is "Love or perish."[18] But all human experience when frankly surveyed —so the East believes—testifies to the fact that, until a person has deepened his self-awareness, what he is apt to conceive and exemplify as love falls far short of the true ideal for which the word stands, and in some respects is its exact opposite. What he is likely to call "love" is a possessive attachment to those on whom he depends for support, comfort, and security, together with a weak and hesitant good-will toward other people if they have done nothing to arouse his ire. This benevolence, however, will almost surely be drastically qualified by hostility toward those who frustrate the satisfaction of his desires or oppose the program which he zealously identifies with the good of the world. He will use his reason to justify this hatred by calling it "righteous indignation," and by damning as servants of iniquity all who call his virtuous aims into question. But no person of ethical sensitivity believes that it is necessary to remain in this self-deceiving state, and the spiritual leaders of the East have ceaselessly taught that it is every man's obligation as a moral being not to do so. He is challenged to meet the conditions required for growth toward power to exemplify the true meaning of love.

If, before accepting this responsibility for his own moral renewal, man sets himself to reform other people and the institutions of society, his zeal can do much—as the prophetic tradition of the West has shown—to bring crying injustices to an end and to initiate constructive changes. But these positive virtues will be corrupted, and in an age when men are groping for new moral insights may be completely over-balanced, by the vices of dogmatism and self-righteousness. The fanatical moralist is sure that his appealing cause is absolutely right, and that he is serving the will of God in destroying all who perversely stand in his way. Where one fails to see himself as others see him and to face honestly the dark forces in his own soul, the passion for justice that would otherwise be a high moral virtue may be transformed into its very opposite.

It is in this setting, I believe, that we must understand the Eastern thinkers when they tell us that the fundamental truth to be mastered by every man is the truth about his own self, and that this truth provides the needed basis for a stable understanding of all else in his experience and for stable guidance in social action.

We come now to the second question. How, more specifically than has been explained thus far, does acceptance of this orientation carry us "beyond reason"? The general answer to this question from the Eastern standpoint is now clear. Since reason does its work through the analysis of distinctions and relations, grounded in the basic distinction between subject and object, it is inevi-

[18] This is the title of Smiley Blanton's popular book (New York: Simon and Schuster, 1956).

tably left behind when a unity is apprehended which transcends this division and overcomes all sundering distinctions. How can this general answer be made more intelligible and plausible to the West?

Perhaps the realization of such an inclusive unity can be understood by the aid of a helpful analogy. Consider the experience of grasping the meaning of a mural which one confronts for the first time. Let us suppose that it covers an entire wall in a large museum room. At first one cannot apprehend it as a whole. He has to begin by noting parts of it in their separation from each other. He observes a man on horseback in the center of the wall, then a banner held aloft far to the right, then on the left a stream of people winding into the distance. After another partial scene or two has caught his attention he can stand back and survey the whole mural. Suddenly the meaning of the entire panorama is perceived; it is a procession of pilgrims on their way to the celebration of some sacred rite. He could not perceive this meaning before, but once it has been grasped it cannot be lost; it gives unity to the whole scene. Earlier, all that he had been able to see was a collection of distinct parts, each with its own character and form; he could describe their spatial relations to each other but with no reference to any further connection. Such description would be analogous in this situation to the distinguishing work of reason in our experience as a whole, as it clarifies objects in their external relations to each other. And this process is essential, because apprehension of the nature of the whole is possible only when this analytic function of reason has been performed. That apprehension, when it is achieved, exemplifies a super-rational insight into the character of the scene as a whole. Everything in it is now seen in its relation to that unifying form. Nothing that had been perceived before has been lost; but, over and above the relations that separate one part from another, a pattern is grasped that transcends these separations and binds everything into an undivided whole. Now, suppose that someone who has seen the parts but has not yet grasped this unifying pattern were to demand of one who has: "What's your evidence that this unity you talk about is really there? Prove to me that it is there, and that it gives the correct meaning of the picture." What can be the reply? One who has caught the total panorama can only wait until the skeptical questioner has done the same; at most, he might say something that would facilitate the needed apprehension.

If this analogy is valid, our Eastern colleagues are telling us that when one engages in the deepened self-understanding they emphasize he experiences something of this kind; he passes in his view of the world from the indispensable role of reason in drawing distinctions and analyzing relations to the realization of a comprehensive wholeness that leaves nothing out but unites all in a total meaning which, once gained, cannot be lost. His experience, until then in bondage to hampering disunity, has achieved integrity. He has transcended all distinctions so far as they separate one thing from another, and is no longer limited by them. He is beyond reason, not in the sense of succumbing to any irrational caprice, but in that of realizing the unity at which reason aims in its systematizing endeavors but which it is incompetent to achieve.

Raju remarked early in the conference that the chief weakness of Western theories of man is their tendency to fragment the human personality so that all sense of any unifying selfhood is lost.[19] This challenge may well introduce our third question: What is the significance of this trans-rational experience for philosophy? Is not the issue involved here of concern merely to psychologists and moralists? The East's answer to this question, I believe, is twofold.

First, this experience of deepened self-understanding will not only change whatever particular philosophy one holds but will also transform one's whole conception of philosophy, in the direction exemplified by the traditional role of philosophy in the East. The basic change will be this: Instead of concentrating his efforts on rounding off a philosophy in terms of whatever set of presuppositions he now takes for granted, the philosopher will consciously accept as fundamental in experience this dynamic process of self-realization, and will respond to its distinctive needs. Such a radical change will naturally mean that he will use his philosophical powers mainly to clarify and interpret this process—correcting misunderstandings about it, removing obstructions from its path, and offering positive guidance in whatever way he may. This transformation will at once give clear meaning to the concepts of Eastern thought that otherwise remain perplexing to the West—such as liberation, mind-control, concentration, truth and practice in their Eastern setting—for all detailed problems of philosophy will naturally be approached in this perspective.

The second half of the East's answer to this question is more difficult to explain. If a Western philosopher is to consider it seriously, he must place in jeopardy one of his most cherished assumptions. The Eastern thinker has made a very startling discovery, namely, that as one progresses toward the self-realization which is his true goal the whole world of his experience is transformed in ways that cannot be anticipated beforehand, and his whole mode of interpreting it is likewise transformed. He becomes aware that through this process he has left behind as deceptive many of the presuppositions expressed in his earlier perceiving and thinking, although he can understand more clearly than ever how philosophers are led to adopt them. In his growing insight into truth they are analogous to the pattern of external relations first employed by the observer of the mural but which had to be corrected when he caught the true meaning of the scene.

Now the implications of this answer are drastic. One of them is that until this transformation is achieved a philosopher's apprehension of the truth he seeks is undependable, and that reality is truly disclosed only to the insight of the unified self. Several of the Eastern papers at this conference have made statements that become intelligible and plausible in the light of this conclusion. Just as—so Saksena and Mahadevan, for example, have suggested—the

[19] In discussing the papers of Rossow and Werkmeister on the evening of June 29, 1959.

scientist needs perfected instruments in order to observe the world of phenomena aright, so the philosopher needs a perfected instrument to observe reality aright, namely, a purged and disciplined mind. The idea in all these assertions is that as long as one's mind, consciously or unconsciously, is clouded by turbulent emotion he is incapable of seeing the truth; only when this state has been brought to an end and he has achieved inner tranquillity is he in command of the instrument needed for clear cognition. In Saksena's words, a *niṣkama* (non-attached) mind is "a necessary qualification of an ideal philosopher, whose task is to perceive the truth about reality with undefective and clean instruments of reason and heart."[20] One thinks here of the popular Buddhist simile of the mirror or the surface of a lake. When the mirror is tarnished by impurities or the surface of the lake is ruffled by restless forces it cannot reflect truth with clearness or accuracy; this is possible only when it has become free from such disturbances. This searching thought explains the essential connection to the Eastern mind between intellectual and moral conflict, for the distracting influences revealed in the former are found to be the same as appear in the unstable emotions responsible for the latter.

To the Western philosopher, such a contention is a very hard saying. Unless he is an existentialist,[21] he assumes that power of intellectual apprehension, in philosophy as well as science, is quite independent of any moral attainments; and, if he should admit a question on this score, he still takes it for granted that his own approximation to whatever moral perfection may be needed is as satisfactory as that of anyone else. The whole orientation of the East at this point seems quite alien. I hope that I have interpreted our Eastern colleagues in such a way as to render their viewpoint more intelligible. I do not hope, of course, to bridge the gap completely; that will take time, and no single interpreter can accomplish it.

VII.

What can helpfully be said by way of a summarizing conclusion to these remarks? I assumed the task of clarifying a basic contrast that had appeared in this conference between Eastern and Western ways of philosophizing which affects the meaning of many philosophically indispensable terms. I located the heart of this contrast in an issue respecting the capacity of reason: Is it competent to guide us to our philosophical goals, or does it meet a limit which can be passed only by a super-rational insight? The general outcome of my analysis of this issue, and of the viewpoint of each side as it has been revealed in the conference papers, may be briefly indicated as follows:

First, here are two profound and challenging attitudes toward the reality that all of us as human beings confront, and toward the powers with which

[20] See his paper, above, pp. 58, 63. For a similar thought in Mahadevan's paper, see above, p. 476.

[21] Especially in the theological implications of this term.

we are equipped to meet it. These attitudes obviously diverge and are incapable of any easy reconciliation. As I view the situation, however, this is by no means a cause for disappointment or distress. Is it not, rather, a wonderful thing that Western and Eastern cultures have thus far been sufficiently isolated from each other so that these two approaches to philosophy could develop as fully and systematically as they have? The contrasting convictions that have guided them can thus reveal the full force of their challenge to our quest for mutual understanding. As these convictions now interact with increasing vigor, it is possible to see the decisive virtues and defects of each more clearly than would be the case if in the past each had been confused by the provocative presence of the other.

Second, at their heart the two attitudes do not contradict each other; they can be viewed as mutually complementary. Not only do they agree on a high valuation of man in his distinctive potentialities; with regard to the crucial issue I have discussed they also agree that we need assume no limit to what human reason can achieve *in knowledge of objects.* Where they diverge is in what we are called to do as men and philosophers with regard to this final phrase. Here, each can learn from the other much more than it has thus far learned. The East needs to acquire a fuller sympathy with the West's conviction that through man's rational powers he can aspire to become equal to the creative opportunities that reality constantly provides. The West needs a fuller appreciation of the high value found by the East in a super-rational self-understanding, with its promise not only of inner freedom from conflict but also of a more perfect realization of the goals at which reason in its systematizing function aims.

Third, the main philosophical task of the future would appear to be the gradual development of a world philosophy through this process of mutual enrichment. Neither East nor West need lose any part of the heritage it prizes from its philosophical past. What is needed is simply the further clarification and conceptual articulation of whatever insights prove to be involved in this progress toward deeper understanding, with the opportunity for contributions from all parts of the world to take their place in such a setting.

QUESTION: In describing the viewpoint typical of the West by using such terms as "reason" and "rational understanding," are you not describing a kind of rationalism that was indeed influential in the past but which the modern West is leaving behind?

ANSWER: One is handicapped here by words and their associations. If I knew less misleading terms I would have chosen them. What I meant by "reason" was simply our mental power which proceeds by drawing distinctions, analyzing relations, and arranging the results in some conceptual order. Trust in reason in this sense seems to me to be typical of the West throughout its history; it is exemplified in the sciences as well as in philosophy, and in such philosophical schools as pragmatism as well as in the realistic and idealistic schools.

QUESTION: The West believes that man is free because he has reason, whereas the East believes that he can become free by the use of his reason. From its standpoint, reason leads him to a freedom that is beyond reason. Do you not agree?

ANSWER: In general, I do agree. The only difficulty I see in this statement arises from an oversimplification which may be somewhat misleading. The Western conception of man's moral and spiritual freedom does indeed appeal mainly to his faculty of reason. But its usual emphasis is on freedom from external constraints, and the achievement of this freedom depends on many factors of which intelligent skill is only one. As for the Eastern conception of how man's liberation is gained, reason plays a vital role, especially in correcting mistakes and clearing up confusions into which he may have fallen. But other factors play an essential role, too, especially in the *bhakti* and *karma* ways toward liberation. Very likely, you did not mean to deny these qualifications.

QUESTION: Is it not the case that the self as knower is indescribable? In the sentence "I know myself" the word "myself" stands for the object, the self as known, whereas the word "I" stands for the subject, the self as knower. The latter is indispensable to all knowledge, but is always elusive. The attempt to describe it results only in a description of the self as known.

ANSWER: I entirely agree as to the reality and importance of this distinction. When you speak of the self as knower being "indescribable," however, it seems to me that two things can and need to be said. First, certain terms can be truthfully applied to it—such as "undivided unity"—although their descriptive power is certainly very meager. Second, the process which leads to a fuller realization of the self as knower can be described in considerable detail; it involves, for example, such intellectual and moral conditions as I have mentioned. This should be emphasized, since, from the Eastern viewpoint, the vital matter is this realization of one's unified selfhood, not the capacity to describe it in intellectual terms.

QUESTION: Are there not many other common values between East and West, besides the ones which you have mentioned, which provide a basis for agreement and an aid toward mutual understanding? I am thinking of the universal human ideals of justice, wisdom, beauty, power, peace, and fullness of life.

ANSWER: Yes. I did not discuss these common values because they did not seem to be directly involved in the central issue which I felt challenged to clarify. Man's capacity to seek these values and to realize them more fully is indeed a part of his dignity as prized by both East and West. Of course, disagreements arise with regard to their detailed interpretation.

QUESTION: Do you not believe that, in terms of the world as we know it today, we would be more likely to approach the solution of our problems with emphasis not upon "love" but upon *intelligent* love? We have been hearing about love for 2,000 years or more. But would not intelligent love lead us more nearly to those actions which would change social institutions in a desirable way? The means we use are very important. But if by changing institutions intelligently we are much more likely to change human beings, so as to make our world a place of peace and freedom, can this not be done better than by repeating the message of traditional Christianity, traditional Buddhism, traditional Hinduism, or traditional Islam, even if it is dressed up in the metaphor of modern psychotherapy? After all, these doctrines have had their chance and have not succeeded.

COMMENT (Mahadevan): Does not this question really confirm your main point instead of opposing it? You were showing the conditions under which love can become intelligent, in view of the fact that each of us finds it easy to fool himself into thinking that he already exemplifies intelligent love while the other fellow is sadly failing to do so and is thus responsible for the evils of the world.

ANSWER: It is indeed vitally important that love become intelligent, and all the resources of modern thought can play a part in helping it become so. If I am right, however, the basic emphasis of Eastern thought on self-understanding aims precisely to fill the gap left unfilled on the whole by the modern West. It aims, as Mahadevan implies, to guide an individual toward a state in which his own love will be more intelligent, and its conviction is that progress toward this goal is essential if the individual is to contribute dependably toward the reformation of others and the reconstruction of institutions. To become aware through deepened self-understanding of ways in which what one thought to be love is not love, and to grow thus toward a fuller exemplification of genuine love, is surely to make one's love more intelligent and to become better able to reform social institutions wisely.

CORNELIUS KRUSE

Concluding Remarks

It is a great responsibility toward the close of this Third East-West Philosophers' Conference, and after the presentation of such a wealth of material by leading philosophers from so many parts of the world, to try to bring together some concluding remarks and to attempt to guide a general discussion on important issues, presumably still pending. Ten years ago, on returning home after the Second East-West Philosophers' Conference and on being asked what it had meant to me, I replied that I had had an experience that seemed to me somewhat like that of Gertrude Stein when she declared that three times in her life she had met greatness and each time a bell had rung within her to acclaim this fact: once when she had met Einstein for the first time; then again when she had met young Picasso, and, of course, much earlier, when she had met herself. I hasten to add that my experience was also unlike hers, especially since mine referred to cultures rather than to persons. Three times I, too, met greatness: first, when as a young man I encountered French culture for the first time; then, much later, when during a five-month philosophic mission to Latin America I came to appreciate and admire the culture of Latin America; and, finally, I knew I had met greatness when for the first time I was brought face to face with the varied ancient and modern cultures of the East. One can never be the same again after such encounters, after such a widening of horizons and such a deepening of sympathies. I am sure that we all have had this experience here. In fact, these personal experiences may well be the most promising and most productive outcomes of such a conference as this.

I hope it is not out of place—opportunities to say this in public are not numerous—but I feel it incumbent upon me, first, last, and all the time, to call attention to the great debt we all owe to our director, Charles Moore, and to the University of Hawaii. In our early days in Logic we all learned that "that cannot be the cause of a phenomenon in the presence of which it fails to occur, and in the absence of which it nevertheless occurs." From this negative formulation of a great law of induction it is perfectly clear that with Charles Moore and the support he received from his university *absent,* this conference would never have occurred. No one here but our director himself knows the patience, the foresight, the imaginativeness, and the persistence in the face of frustrations which were demanded to make this conference possible. Of course, many others, Charlie would be the first to say, have helped—true—but without Charlie there would have been *nothing to help.**

Now, let us address ourselves to the substance of the meeting. The Steering Committee, or shall we not rebaptize it and call it your "service committee," or, if you like, your "persuading committee," though certainly not composed of hidden persuaders, gathered that it would not advance the interests of this conference to have additional papers from us, especially after we had all heaved a sigh of relief that the sheaves of formal program papers, all duly mimeographed and abstracted, were now all gathered in. Rather, we sensed that it would be more in accord with your wishes and the purposes of this conference, if we planned to provide for what so often had to be curtailed when specific themes were under discussion, namely, ample time for a more cross-topical and general discussion of matters of great interest.

Accordingly, we are presenting such topics, which, rightly or wrongly, we sensed you wished still to discuss. This evening I have selected three or four of these which my notes seemed to indicate would be of interest to you as representing still unfinished business and which, if discussed, might clarify some still outstanding issues.

I shall beg the privilege of presenting these topics together first and shall then invite you to discuss them *seriatim* if you so wish and as fully as you like. Any of these topics not discussed this evening can be held over for the remaining evenings.

First of all, however, let me say that at this conference there did not seem to be a necessity—and this is clearly an advance over previous conferences—to insist that all our cross-cultural comparisons be made, as we said at the previous conference, "on the level." The great temptation for all of us is always to crisscross comparisons in such a way that the *ideals* of our culture are compared with the *practice* of another, to the great disadvantage of the other culture. It is too easy to win at this game since, as T. S. Eliot has reminded us, "between the idea and the act, between the conception and the response there always falls the shadow." This time, fortunately, we successfully avoided this pitfall and almost always compared *ideals* with *ideals* and *practice* with *practice. Our* task will be to persuade our friends at home, especially if they have not had the experience of a face-to-face encounter with representatives of other

* This personal reference is included at the insistence of the author over the editor's protests.—C. K.

cultures, to see the great injustice and lack of sportsmanship in making such unfair crisscrossing comparisons.

But now let us look at an outline of the topics selected for your consideration.

First, I have selected a key term of our conference, namely, "understanding." At various times, conference members have expressed some puzzlement over the meaning of "understanding." Our brochure, announcing the purpose of the conference declared: "The unique significance of the conference lies in the belief that real understanding can be achieved only through a knowledge of the fundamental convictions and values of the peoples of the East and West." Time and again, conference members raised the question as to what is meant by "understanding" and how and why we conceived of it as indispensable for amicable co-operation. Professor Knight, you may remember, strikingly pointed up this perplexity by stating that "the spider and the fly" understand each other only too well, and nevertheless do not achieve amity. Clearly, a very different type of understanding is demanded in order to achieve the ends of this conference, and if, to take an illustration from Lewis Carroll's tales about Alice in Wonderland, the understanding is to go beyond that of the "walrus and the carpenter," who deeply sympathized with the young oysters they ate with such evident relish amid their sobs and tears.

UNESCO is constantly attempting to advance reciprocal understanding among the peoples of the world, but it, too, had to face the question which was placed on the agenda of an earlier meeting: "What kind of understanding is it that the world needs in order to achieve peace through understanding." As is well known, UNESCO has placed at the center of its concern at this time the promotion of better understanding, i.e., mutual appreciation, of Eastern and Western cultural values. One thing is clear: the understanding that we need is not simply "knowledge about," be it ever so extensive or erudite, but, rather, sympathetic "acquaintance with," to use William James's well-known and very useful distinction. Henry Adams, one of our great American philosophical historians of a generation now past, once wrote: "Man had always flattered himself that he knew—or was about to know—something that would make his own energy intelligible to himself, but he invariably found, on further inquiry, that the more he *knew,* the less he understood." Henry Adams here strikingly emphasizes the difference between knowledge about man and the understanding that would reveal the true nature of man. The other day, just when I needed the illustration for these remarks, Charles Moore related to me that the manager of the once exalted but recently defeated World Champion pugilist Patterson ruefully remarked to reporters: "I understand him and respect him, but I don't know him." This manager unwittingly introduced a term of importance for us in our attempt to deepen and clarify the meaning of "understanding": understanding to be of any use to us in our enterprise of establishing world solidarity and world co-operation must include *respect,* respect for the person and respect for the culture he represents. The late Professor E. R. Hughes, a valued participant in the conference held here ten years ago, proposed the hope that in the course of our living and discussing together we might come to agree, as he put it bluntly, "that the other bloke is not as stupid as he looks," in short, that the other person had a point, not only understandable in the context of *his* culture, but which might well be considered as a possible alternative and enrichment of our own way of thinking.

Understanding, then, in the sense which would be of value to us in our work, always involves an *effort at self-transcendence,* at entertaining the possibility of a new perspective, at attempting, at least for a while, to put our received values, as Husserl would say, long enough "in brackets" in order to find out through sympathy and empathy what it would feel like to accept other values as our own. In other words, what is needed is an attempt to judge a culture as much as possible *from within* rather than merely from without. Such an attempt will not be made unless there is the *will to understand.* Fortunately, our very presence here is assurance enough that this prerequisite has been met. The will to understand implies open-mindedness and readiness to listen to what on first hearing may have sounded fantastic. Another prerequisite for achieving the understanding we need is an opportunity to get to know each other on a friendly basis at times and places other than those of formal discussion in this conference room. I am sure we have all discovered that it requires a great deal of informal discussion to discover what a colleague really meant in his formal paper and perhaps, even more importantly, what our colleague really is like. This is the great significance of six weeks of living together and frequenting cafeterias, beaches, and Oriental temples together. I need not add, I am sure, that the understanding here referred to does not at all mean uncritical acceptance of what is understood, if such a kind of acceptance would even be conceivable among philosophers trained and pledged to critical reflection.

The second topic I should like to focus attention upon and propose for discussion is a final general look at the stereotypes or cliches that often hinder understanding. Have we exorcized the most persistent clichés? Ten years ago we agreed to reject a considerable number. Some had enough vitality to linger on and we had to reject them once again. I reminded Wing-tsit Chan, however, that this time he did not have to say: "What's wrong with your arithmetic? You proceed as if all Eastern philosophy were Indian philosophy. Don't you know that every fourth child born into this world is Chinese?" Our Chinese colleagues did have to protest, however, against the still all-too-prevalent view that Chinese are not spiritual and had to remind us that a true understanding of Confucianism and Taoism would show an important spiritual element in both. We also had to be told again that, contrary to accepted clichés, there *is* in India a very serious concern for morality, that, in fact, no philosophy is deemed achievable in India without ethical training and that, as Gandhi contended, moral discipline is a prime necessity for sound politics. Also, we had to reject again the too-simple and too-easy general reference to *the* East and *the* West. Anything one touches, upon closer scrutiny and study, becomes complex. We were told last time that there were twenty different types of Buddhism. This time the number seems to have increased by a factor of ten: we were told the other day in a lecture on Buddhism that actually there were two hundred. I have at home a photograph showing our Indian friends standing before this very blackboard in this room which was covered with a great complex of radiating lines and names designating the great variety of Indian philosophies. But even at this present conference it was again necessary for our Indian friends to remind us that the non-dualistic Śaṁkara type of Vedānta philosophy is not the only Indian philosophy and that practically the whole spectrum of conceivable metaphysical, epistemological, and ethical positions is presented in Indian philosophy. We had to be reminded also that the West, so-called, in being rational and scientific, is so only when it wishes to be so and that the same person, let us say, a Philadelphia lawyer, will appeal to reason before an appellate court in the most decorous fashion conceivable, but that when trying to sway a jury to his will he will make an appeal to everything else but reason. We were also reminded that French peasants and Missouri farmers, all grass-roots Westerners, are as resistant as anyone to any change they cannot understand.

Clichés and stereotypes, as is well known, are always great temptations to all of us because they lull us into the belief that no further inquiry in a given matter is required of us. "We have its number," we say; "it is conveniently classified, and so let's get on with something more interesting." In the sense that stereotypes block further inquiry and hinder or prevent genuine understanding they represent one of the greatest dangers to mankind, one that can scarcely be exaggerated, especially in our day when world understanding and world co-operation are more necessary than ever before.

I may be far too optimistic in thinking that, given free and ample discussion of the topics already proposed, there will be time left for the consideration of further topics. But I should like to propose at least a few more. The third general topic I should like to recommend for discussion is this:

Which "bridge" is best, or would seem most promising, for reaching world understanding, or, if there is no best, but all are of value under certain circumstances, what should be our practical strategy in the use of them? Here are the bridges that at various times during the conference have been mentioned, but which have never been fully discussed:

1. The bridge of *science,* whether natural or social, and its practical companions: technology, modern industry, commerce, and the modern application of psychology, sociology, and political and economic science. This bridge seems to have been used with apparent success in the interchange of visits between scientists and men of affairs in the United States and Russia.

2. The bridge of *art.* Art, we are told, is universal. Music, especially, seems to be a bridge of importance in renewed contacts between the United States

and Russia. Tolstoy's views on art are no doubt narrow, but he seems partially right in recognizing art as a potent factor in fostering the sense of world brotherhood.

3. The bridge of *religion,* especially in its mystical expression, since we are told that, in spite of cultural differences, mystics the world over recognize each other.

4. The bridge of *philosophy*. We have demonstrated in the present conference, as in the earlier ones, that such a bridge is available, and it has been used most effectively to good purpose. In fact, we have had, in spite of our divergent philosophical positions, so much mutual understanding that some of our members have not hesitated to say that toward the end we have achieved a "love-feast." But is philosophy more widely available as a bridge in other contexts? I sincerely believe it is, but in situations of real tensions, in our ideological age, a greater effort may be demanded of philosophers to overcome the initial obstacles to the achievement of mutual understanding.

Of course, if one thinks in terms of strategy, one might well ask, Why not use all available bridges and encourage those most expert in each to use the bridge most convenient for them for bringing together the peoples of this earth in friendship and mutual appreciation? Perhaps all bridges are sound and good, but I have a feeling that the greatest problem confronting us as we return home is to help create in our countries a climate in which scientists, artists, religious persons, and fellow philosophers will all share our *will* to foster understanding.

Finally, and in the fourth place, we have never centrally discussed, though we have often touched upon, the problem as to which value-theory would seem most conducive to world understanding and world co-operation:

1) the theory that stresses the relativity of values, and especially of ethical values, or

2) the theory that value-judgments are, in spite of important differences, essentially like cognitive judgments, subject to confirmation and validation. I take it that this is what Professor Hook meant when he asked: "Is there not a science of values?" It is interesting that many American naturalistic philosophers, such as John Dewey, Roy Wood Sellars, and C. I. Lewis, hold that value-judgments, in their way, are as subject to validation or justification as are judgments of cognition.

Professor Northrop, in the discussion following his public address on "Comparative Philosophy and World Law," stated that the cultural pluralism which he once regarded as the best we could achieve and which he set forth in his *The Taming of the Nations* had been superseded by his *best hope* that a world living-law could be created which, under the inspiration of his multi-cultural audience,[1] much to his own surprise, he declared to be a "Zen-Locke-and-Jeffer-

[1] He was inspired also, undoubtedly, by Dr. Suzuki's statement in an earlier lecture that if Zen were adopted by everybody wars would be unthinkable—and, with a smile on his face, as if to say, "Why, yes, why haven't I thought of this before?" he proposed his new Zen-Locke-Jefferson synthesis, much to the delighted surprise of his audience.

son synthesis" which could be counted upon to give us a valid and universally acceptable world-law. Northrop, I am sure, would give first place, if possible, to a value-theory that made living contact with what was universal in man. It is an interesting fact, I think, which clearly emerges in studying the writings of present-day relativists, positivists, and emotivists that in rejecting the claim that value-judgments are true or false they nevertheless seem more interested in discovering how *discord in value-judgments can be overcome.* If only, as Professor Stevenson holds, by "persuasive definition." Of course, these same relativists admit that there are certain blind alleys in this procedure where further discussion is, they believe, futile. But the question remains whether discussion is ever futile among members of *one* humanity, especially when we believe, as has often been expressed here, that what unites us is far greater and more important than what separates us. And even that which makes each culture distinct may be an enrichment and contribution to world harmony or what I like to regard as the emergence of a magnificent orchestrated unity of all the philosophies and cultures of the world.

I think you will agree that we have here abundant material for an evening's discussion, to which I would now invite you to address yourselves in accordance with your wishes.

CHARLES A. MOORE

Retrospect and Prospects: Achievements and "Unfinished Business"[1]

At this conference we have undertaken a task which has been almost—or, in fact—impossible of fulfillment, and yet we have indeed accomplished much!

Because of the wide range of our concern and because of the complexity of our problem (or problems) we were predestined not to "succeed" in all respects in this vast undertaking. The range of our subject included all the major philosophies of Asia and the West. As for complexity, we have been considering all the philosophies and all the cultures of these two great areas of mankind. In fact, we found narrowness of range and simplicity of interpretation completely out of order—even in dealing with the complexity of the problems relating to "understanding" and in thinking of the nature, function, and social implications of philosophy itself.

Difficult as our over-all problem has been—and this was fully realized in the planning stages—the problem had to be faced because of its vital importance in today's troubled and confused and mutually antagonistic world of the peoples of East and West. The problem of attempting to understand the cultures of each other and to get down to "rock bottom" by attempting to understand, not the superficial "facts" of everyday life, but the underlying and deeper convictions of these several peoples, simply had to be met. Without deep-seated mutual understanding between the peoples of Asia and the peoples of the West significant co-operation, not to mention living at peace with each other, is practically out of the question.

Despite the complexity and near-impossibility of fulfillment of our original task, the significant accomplishments of this conference have been many and

[1] This paper is an elaboration of the very brief statement made at the final session of the conference. It is primarily a recapitulation and an attempt to bring into focus the work of the conference. Personal views are identified as such.

various. There have been immediate and long-range results; technical, professional, and purely academic, as well as general and non-technical, results; in addition, there have been personal and inter-personal results; and, lastly, detailed as well as comprehensive results—all of which attest to the sincerity of those who sit around these tables and to the seriousness and dedication which they have brought to the strenuous work of this conference.

While some of our specific and more professional accomplishments will be noted later, I would like to reiterate, for the record, a point which has been made by many members of this group, namely, that among the greatest and most important results of these six weeks together have been the development of personal (and professional) friendships among the members and, by virtue of the six-week duration of the conference, the breaking down of any sense of "otherness," and its replacement by a sense of cordiality and mutual respect even among the heretofore divergent groups representing the Asian traditions and the West. If no other "result" were forthcoming, these, with all that they imply and promise, would be sufficient to justify all our work we have done here.

However, there has been much more than this. There have been almost innumerable specific "discoveries" made by all of us, on both sides, in the form of new and/or corrected impressions of our fellow philosophers from across the sea and of the cultures and philosophies they represent. Simply by hearing the various traditions described in an atmosphere of cordiality, free —for the most part—of challenges or opposition on provincial bases, we have learned as each person spoke for himself and his culture, and have thus been purified of misinterpretations and have been significantly enlightened.

The uniqueness of this conference and the "makings" of significant achievements lie in many factors. In the first place, to continue with this matter of significant and cordial *listening,* it is, we agreed, the only genuine procedure for learning what the other man believes. There is also the length of the previously mentioned six-week period, which afforded sufficient time and opportunity to pave the way for much greater mutual understanding of other traditions and of each other personally. And, finally, there is the quite unique and fundamental approach embodied in this conference, namely, the attempt to understand each other's culture and each other's people in practice by attempting to probe beneath the surface and to get at the fundamental attitudes, ideas, and ideals which, even though they may not literally and technically provide a basis from which modes of practical action can be logically deduced, do certainly provide the only real basis of genuine and profound understanding. This procedure has been amply justified and demonstrated in the work we have done and in the understanding which we have achieved—a degree of understanding which would have been impossible had we remained on the level of practical activities alone or "culture" without its accompanying or underlying "philosophy." That is to say, the underlying assumption of this conference has been that only—or certainly primarily—through philosophy can we reach deep-seated mutual understanding, but, as we all know, even this assumption has been subjected to thoroughgoing investigation and challenge, as was intended in making it the first topic on the agenda.

Avowedly, the exclusive purpose of this conference has been to understand each other, East and West. We did not gather here to indulge in mutual criticism or in provincial dogmatism. As will be noted later, much remains to be undertaken in the form of mutual *examination* of cultural practices and their underlying philosophies, probably by mutual criticism. But this is another story—though it is clearly one that must be met directly and open-mindedly.

We have learned to overcome the routine and tragic clichés which have in the minds of many isolated East from West—and we started with many: *the* East, *the* West; the East versus the West; the East as monistic and unconcerned about the individual, the West as pluralistic and concerned only about the individual: the East as intuitionistic, the West as rational, in both cases exclusively; the East as spiritual, the West as materialistic; the East as motivated by practical concerns, the West as concerned exclusively with purely intellectualistic or "academic" matters; the West as "scientific," the East as unscientific; the West as strictly logical, the East as non-logical and even illogical; the East as pessimistic and fatalistic, the West as optimistic; the East as concerned with man and his soul exclusively, the West with the universe and especially with external physical Nature; the East as "negative," "escapist," and the like ("world-and-life denying"), the West as positive (world-and-life affirming); the East as characterized by "inwardness," the West by "outwardness"; and, on and on, all designed specifically as establishing sharp contrast, irreconcilable opposition, and mutual inscrutability. We have not merely removed misunderstandings—but, much more positively, we have developed genuine understanding of what the other traditions really believe, what they really value, and, most important of all, why their cultural practices are what they are. This has been no mean task, but the results clearly speak for themselves.

One of the most significant conclusions of this conference—as of the two previous conferences in this series—has been the realization that any simplification is an over-simplification when we are speaking or thinking in terms of entire cultures or philosophical traditions or geographical areas. It has been a battle, but at last we are now convinced that there is no simple or single "East" or "West"—and that even within each of the many cultures and philosophical traditions, East and West, there is wide variety as well as historical variation and that a failure to recognize this genuine diversity is tantamount to no genuine understanding whatsoever. When we discuss the specific topics of our agenda, we will realize that much of the understanding and many of the "discoveries" achieved in these several areas have resulted from the realization of the complexity of all the philosophical and cultural traditions. This complexity makes room for diverse interpretations, values, and practices, and destroys (and certainly proves unjustified) many one-sided and false interpretations which have been so common. Just for example, we now know that India and China are two distinct and quite contrasting traditions, that genuine spirituality characterizes Chinese thought and culture, and that Śaṁkara and his allegedly illusionist Advaita Vedānta are not the sum and substance of Indian—or even of Hindu—philosophy.

It is not the purpose of this summary to list all the specific items under all the many headings of our agenda in attempting to bring into focus the great amount of significant work we have done here. Suffice it to point out two major ways in which our problem was complicated and our work successful.

We have realized, first, that there are unquestionably differences and even disagreements *between* the traditions of East and West in many areas—in terms of basic considerations in practically every "branch" of philosophy, serious as well as superficial facts of cultural practices, philosophical issues, social convention, etc. We have also noted differences—between the various major traditions *within* both East and West, between the various historical periods of East and West, between different schools of thought and of practice within each of the "subdivisions" of East and West, and even among personal representatives of these areas around these tables. Unanimity of view—our old enemy, over-simplification—is not to be expected, and it has not been our purpose here to disregard or overcome such differences of opinion. As we have reminded ourselves many times during this conference, even these differences do not necessitate lack of understanding and the impossibility of co-operation. Nor are these disagreements or differences, genuine as they are, so fundamental as they often appear. This is especially true of "conflicts" between East and West in the large, in terms of basic considerations, where similarities are much more prominent than dissimilarities or conflicts.

A second major over-all observation is that we seem to agree more than we differ. May I develop this point briefly. If we distinguish, as we must, between ideals and practices and between relatively superficial attitudes and fundamental beliefs—the basic perspective of this conference—we will discover, as we have here, that all the peoples of Asia whom we have studied and the over-all tradition of Western philosophy-culture have very much in common. In terms of fundamentals, as we will note later on, there seem to be common ideals, agreement upon fundamental values, and what may be called a common general "idealism" among us all. Of course, such attitudes are not identical in detail or in expression in East and West or even among the various traditions of Asia or the West, but the over-all attitude, composed of basic ideas, ideals, and the reasons for the practices engaged in, have a ring of fundamental similarity that makes for ease of understanding and for significant co-operation. While this point must never militate against a full realization of differences—at least different emphases—or even conflicts that exist between us and among us, our fundamental similarity—what may even be called our philosophical kinship—has eluded serious consideration and widespread comprehension and has led to philosophical neglect or disrespect. Consequently, this is one fundamental point which we must realize in fullness—and a perspective we must adopt—if we would understand and co-operate with each other.

Mutual understanding is made easier and alleged mutual inscrutability proved false by the discovered fact that "we have everything in both." That is, we find in both East and West representatives of and concern with and knowledge of practically all types and colors of philosophy, despite differing emphases. In both, we find: basic concern with the spiritual, fundamental idealism, the primary status of spiritual values, fundamental recognition (with variations) of the importance of morality, the Golden Rule, the ideal of universal love, the use of reason and even science (at least in spirit), a strict conformity with logical principles, a concept of the freedom and dignity of the individual personality, and, though sometimes we in the West do not realize this, the attitudes of non-attachment, *karma-yoga,* and even emancipation. In both, we have (admittedly in different specific forms and emphases at times) metaphysical idealism, materialism, dualism, and vitalism; monism, pluralism, and "harmony" of the one and the many; supernaturalism and naturalism; mysticism and theism—and atheism; skepticism and dogmatism; intuition and intellectualism; metaphysics and positivism; rationalism and empiricism; ethics and "beyond ethics"; positive philosophies of life and the "negative" search for peace, freedom, even salvation; "pure" religion, "pure" philosophy, and philosophy-religion; religion as compatible with philosophy and as incompatible; and, on and on—including the fact that the material side of life as well as the spiritual is duly recognized in both East and West and in all of the major traditions and cultures we have studied here. The serious student of either Eastern or Western philosophies should be thoroughly familiar with all these views in his own tradition and therefore he then will not find any of them in others a barrier to understanding. The fact here alluded to would seem to indicate that the human mind, East *and* West, has concerned itself with much the same problems and has discovered or developed most of the same "answers"—even if, here or there, now or then, one view has seemed more acceptable than another.

Even though these fundamental attitudes or doctrines have received varying or differing emphases in East and West and within both East and West, two points must be noted. First, we must not let these differences of emphases provide the basis for "labels" for these various cultures and traditions, because this falsifies the facts. Second, the fact that all of these, and many other, basic attitudes are represented in all of the areas under study, even though they be of less emphasis in some cultures than in others, means that there is no inscrutability of East or West. We have the basis of significant mutual understanding because, although we do not all equally accept or emphasize all specific attitudes, we know or are directly acquainted with those attitudes and therefore can understand those who do give these attitudes major emphasis. This is a hopeful avenue of approach.

So much, then, for general observations about our work. I hope you agree that these alone are sufficient cause for satisfaction for a job well done. In addition, we have reached a number of specific genuine and significant "discoveries" in the five major subject-areas of our agenda. Let us turn now to each of these five topic-sections to note as specifically as possible the "revelations" that have come to us by virtue of what I have called above "sitting and listening" and through discussion which has attempted to bring about greater clarity.

THE RELATION OF PHILOSOPHICAL THEORIES TO PRACTICAL AFFAIRS

The purpose of this section of the agenda was to engage in some soul-searching, as it were, by examining the significance of philosophy as a factor in explaining cultural practices. (In relation to the over-all significance of the conference in the world today, it may be said that in this aspect of our work we were asking the question whether philosophy could provide leadership in terms of fundamental ideas and ideals.) The very asking of the question—and the devoting of so much time to it, relatively speaking—signifies well the open-minded attitude of the conference.

The discussion in this particular topic-section was perhaps more lively—and controversial—than in any of the other phases of our work. The discussion and the "conclusions" were less clear-cut and precise and less decisive than in any other phase; in fact, there were no general conclusions. Not one single member of the conference, representing any of the traditions under study, defended the view that philosophy has no significant bearing upon practice, social or individual, but a considerable amount of effort was devoted to the questions as to just what we mean by philosophy and just what its function is, as well as its *specific* relation to practice, if any.

All in all, it was pointed out that there were three main views for discussion: first, that philosophy obviously determines and explains practice—or should, although, in its present alleged plight, it fails in this basic and essential mission; second, that principles of conduct, and specifically ethics, cannot be logically derived from metaphysical principles; and, third, that to some extent ideas determine and explain practice and to some extent they do not, since other factors are also involved.

Among the "discoveries" encountered in this section of the agenda may be mentioned the observation, made by several members, that Western philosophy has been much more practically oriented or practically motivated than traditional opinion admits. Ordinarily, it is held that philosophy in Asia is motivated by practical concern, whereas philosophy in the West, originating in intellectual curiosity and wonder or the "love of knowledge," is purely intellectually motivated, without any primary concern with practice. We have heard the view that even "love of knowledge" is not simply a disinterested intellectual pursuit of knowledge, but a very practical matter. We have also heard about outstanding philosophers and their practical concerns with culture. To repeat, no Westerner admitted the general Oriental characterization of Western philosophy as simply an intellectual game, although this interpretation was voiced during the discussion by an Asian.

To be sure, we heard the view, based primarily on the alleged impossibility of logically deriving ethics from metaphysics, that *any* practice is compatible with *any* metaphysical theory. This view was challenged—is hereby challenged—with reference specifically and briefly to two illustrations to the contrary, namely, the basis upon which Indians practice the attitude of *ahiṁsā* (non-injury or non-violence) and the ideal of non-attachment, both of which would seem to require, as their foundation and justification, a specific view of the nature of reality and of man and of the relationship of man to his fellow men and to reality itself. Here, as elsewhere, I contend that it is not true that *any* belief or theory or metaphysics is compatible with *any* practice. What one *really believes* as true and valuable must determine or at least guide a man in his actions—as Socrates said long ago—or in a very significant sense we are wasting our time here. Few, if any, of the great philosophers, in East or West, would consent to a divorce of truth and life.

The customary view that all of Oriental philosophy is practically motivated, to the extent that the clearly intellectual disinterested pursuit of truth is of secondary importance, was thoroughly verified in the papers of Dr. Saksena, Dr. Chan, and Dr. Miyamoto, who strongly defended the practical significance of philosophy throughout the Indian, Chinese, and Japanese-Buddhist traditions.

There was no attempt to argue on this matter, the purpose of the conference being adhered to closely in that the only concern of the conference was the understanding of the respective traditions and their attitudes on the relationship of philosophy to practice and the significance of philosophy on the practical level—in culture generally. Studies of this first week clearly produced understanding as far as the Asian countries are concerned, but did not produce unanimity of opinion on the status of philosophy in the West in its relation to culture and practice. The opposition to the practical significance of philosophy was thoroughly technical, however, and even the most outspoken representative of this point of view admitted, that "It requires considerable intellectual sophistication to deny causal influence to ideas in human affairs," and that [metaphysical] assertions "may express attitudes, commitments, evaluations which have a bearing upon conduct none the less effective for being vague, discontinuous, or episodic. As with so many other things, the influence of ideas on behavior is a matter of more or less, not an affair of either-or or none."[2]

One of the major products of this discussion was the largely, but not totally, accepted point that even fundamental theoretical differences—and conflicts—in terms of ultimates (such as the basis and status of moral distinctions) need not for that reason constitute barriers to mutual understanding

[2] See Dr. Hook's paper, above, p. 20.

and even co-operation on the cultural and practical level, if, as was found to be the case, significant agreement was present on that level.

NATURAL SCIENCE AND TECHNOLOGY IN RELATION TO CULTURAL INSTITUTIONS AND SOCIAL PRACTICE

The starting point of our work here was the usual and widespread interpretation of the comparative character of East and West to the effect that in the matter of science, reason, and strictly intellectual activities East stands over against West and that the best we can hope for would be a supplementary relationship between the intuitive East and the scientific and rationalistic West. If this interpretation should be maintained, it would be rather difficult to think in terms of genuine understanding, much less genuine intellectual co-operation. This basic pre-conference conviction, and its various paraphrases, was found to be, not altogether false, but, at most, a series of half-truths. This conclusion was reached by many avenues of investigation and discussion.

In the first place, evidence was brought out to the effect that genuine scientific activity and the recognition of the significance of such scientific activity have been developed and recognized almost throughout the course of Indian intellectual history and culture. Also, that the spirit and method of science has dominated Chinese intellectual activity to such an extent that in spirit and method Chinese culture may almost be described as scientific. In both of these cases, however, it was pointed out that science has not in the East taken the same turn as it has in the West, being interested primarily in matters other than external physical Nature. Natural science has not developed much in the East, to be sure, except in ancient India—but it was pointed out that this is not of the essence of science in any exclusive sense. In the case of Japan, there was a conflict of interpretations among the Japanese representatives, some maintaining that strictly intellectual activity is incompatible with the Japanese spirit and mentality, others challenging this point of view and this interpretation, pointing to precise evidence, such as in Buddhist studies, as well as in more practical areas, where scientific thinking and intellectual activities predominate and are fundamental.

It was also pointed out that reason is taken very seriously in all of the traditions under study—except for the widespread recognition of the significance of intuition in some instances where scientific and intellectualistic procedure does not meet the needs of the situation—as in the study of the spiritual within and in the attempt to gain knowledge of the Absolute.

It was pointed out, further, that intuition and reason are both used and recognized in both East and West. In this connection, it was indicated that the West is by no means exclusively rationalistic or intellectualistic—or scientific—as is alleged by most Easterners and many Westerners. Attention was called to the fact that Western philosophy and intellectual life are a product of Greek and modern science, to be sure, but also of Judaism and

Christianity, and that it includes significant intuition and mysticism. Considerable discussion was carried on concerning the status of concepts by postulation, as characteristic of the West, and concepts by intuition, as characteristic of the East, without resulting in clear-cut conclusions, a clear indication of the fact that the membership of the conference did not accept in its finality this dichotomous interpretation of East and West.

Another matter of major significance which was considered is the relation of science and values and science and man—again with much argument on both sides and again without unanimous conviction or conclusion.

In this latter connection, science was considered one of the "bridges" between East and West because of the "common language" of science regardless of geographical and other barriers. This interpretation was challenged, however, on the ground that science may be a barrier working against understanding because of its inability, certainly in some interpretations, to handle the problem of man himself and certainly values in human experience, and also because it falsifies the experience of the self or the soul, which is so prominent in Indian thought and in all religion. This problem became extremely complicated—without conclusion.

One final point. The usual interpretation finds the East considering the West scientific, thus interested only in external physical Nature, and therefore embracing materialism. This interpretation was noted and was challenged as being untrue to the facts of Western philosophy, culture, and religion—and it was even hinted that spirituality or non-materialistic points of view are impossible except in an atmosphere of materialistic sufficiency. (More on this point later.)

Be all this as it may, the pre-conference interpretation which was decidedly one pitting the East against the West on the matter of science and reason did not stand up, being subjected to criticism from several angles. However, emphasis upon non-intellectualistic approaches or attitudes, especially in Japan but also in other areas of Asia, was thoroughly recognized as significant.

RELIGION AND SPIRITUAL VALUES

In this area, we studied the nature and status of spiritual values in the various major traditions of East and West. Much was accomplished in the direction of significantly greater mutual understanding and respect.

The pre-conference attitude was largely one of gross misunderstanding of each other and of consequent disrespect or criticism. Although these criticisms were not openly expressed, they were at least implied in the body of some of the papers presented in this section as well as in some of the discussion.

There were three significant results of our work. In the first place, in view of explanations by specialists of their own understanding of the nature and status of the spiritual and of the way in which their particular philosophical traditions and cultures are spiritual, greater understanding on the part of others was brought about—and undoubtedly greater respect within the spiritual area. Where concepts of spirituality had previously been thought to be so extreme (especially in India) as to be practically unrelated to life and the world, we have learned that this was only one side of the story. Where, as in the case of China, many had thought that spirituality was practically non-existent because of China's alleged repudiation or neglect of religion, we have been enlightened on the very high sense of spirituality in that culture, in its philosophical background, and in all of its major philosophies. Similarly, for the West the strong emphasis upon reason in much of Western thought and culture—as well as the strictly religious aspects of Western culture—was shown to represent spirituality to the Western mind, and significantly so. Recall, too, that we were reminded of the significance of mysticism in the West.

The second result of our study here was the realization that in terms of spirituality, in its basic nature, all of the major traditions under study are distinctly spiritual, at least in ultimate outlook. (Also, the significant presence of religion itself was noted in all areas studied.) In this way they present a spirit and the actual fact of a common point of view in this important aspect of life and culture. There is spirituality in all of the cultures studied, even though spirituality does not mean precisely the same thing in any two of the major cultures considered. It may mean (emphasis upon) the religious, intellectual, aesthetic, ethical, or personal values, individually or in any combination—but in all cases they are, to the tradition and culture involved, thoroughly spiritual, and this point, when made, was clear to others as well. (This, if the writer may add a personal comment, is one fine example of the fulfillment of the purpose of this conference, that is, to get down to fundamentals rather than being concerned with surface observations, practices, and interpretations.)

It has been mentioned before that the Eastern criticism of the West on the grounds of its being materialistic was challenged and rejected—and this with the specific "help" in discussion of one of the outstanding representatives from Asia.

The third achievement in this field has been the recognition of the significance of all the spiritual values—the true, the good, and the beautiful—in all the traditions studied. Not all of these receive the same emphasis in all of the cultures and traditions, but there is no question of the fact here noted, and herein lies another rather specific area of a common dimension among us all. Also, not only the significance but also the primacy of the spiritual values was cited by representatives of all the traditions, West and East.

As expressed in some of the papers and as thought rather widely by Asians, the West has been charged with being fundamentally ethical at most—"only ethical"—and worldly at least, not truly spiritual. While this "charge" was not directly examined, the result of our discussion was certainly such as to reject this interpretation as superficial at least.

Another interesting point brought out in the course of our discussion, sometimes in fundamental terms, sometimes casually, was the fact that in all the cultures considered, in spite of emphasis either upon the ultimate spiritual nature and destiny of man or, elsewhere, in spite of the emphasis upon what seemed to be worldly values, both types of values are recognized with due significance in all the cultures under study. Perhaps in the most remarkable case of this, Swami Nikhilananda pointed out the significance which worldly and material values have in the Indian tradition—even within the perspective of what might be called the most extreme spiritual point of view. This, may the writer comment, is the reverse of the situation concerning the West, where, in spite of its apparent emphasis upon material values, the ultimate significance (and primacy) of spiritual values, describe them as one will, is almost universally recognized.

One problem that was not given adequate consideration in this area was that of the status and significance of the individual (and personality?) in the religious sphere—and in ultimate destiny. This variously interpreted point is an important basis of mutual criticism and must be pursued further now or later; it stands therefore as one aspect of the "unfinished business" of this conference.

In sum, then, and in terms of basic considerations, our over-all work in the area of "Religion and Spiritual Values" has successfully overcome almost tragic misunderstandings and animosities. It has pointed out that, although there are significant differences in the particular forms and practices of religion—and of other spiritual values, too—in East and West and in various areas of East and West, spirituality as such is not only basic in all the cultures considered but, with some exceptions in emphasis, is recognized as the supreme value in all the cultures we have been considering.

ETHICS AND SOCIAL PRACTICES

Differences of point of view in the areas of ethics and social practices threatened to make even understanding of each other very difficult to achieve. If pre-conference understandings or interpretations of each other's point of view relative to the origin and status of ethics, not to mention specific ethical principles, were the whole truth, the diversities would almost inevitably be the source of intellectual confusion, moral disrespect, and the near-impossibility of genuine practical co-operation. In this pre-conference interpretation, the major problem concerned the question as to whether or not ethics is really taken seriously in the Hindu and Buddhist traditions—the impression being that ethics is not of ultimate importance in these traditions. By contrast, the pre-conference point of view recognized the almost paramount significance of ethics in China and, to some degree, the ultimacy of ethical distinctions and values in the West. There was also a pre-conference point of view to the effect that throughout Asia, even in China, ethics, as understood in the West, is not in any sense of primary status, especially because of the superior importance attached to personal and family relations. Here were both misunderstanding and confusion.

The results of our discussions were again to the effect that these interpretations were, at most, half-truths. While both Hinduism and Buddhism—*in their more extreme forms*—hold that ethics is fundamental but merely for life in the here-and-now and apparently to be completely transcended (or discarded, like the boat after one has reached the other shore), nevertheless, two at least qualifying points were made with strength: First, that *for this life and in this life* morality is taken with profound seriousness by both Hindus and Buddhists, even being a mandatory prerequisite both for significant accomplishment in philosophy and also for the achievement of emancipation or enlightenment. Second, it was also pointed out, somewhat incidentally, that even Christianity is not unaware of the significance of the point of "beyond ethics"—and that the West thinks in terms of "beyond ethics" in other senses as well. In other words, even on this matter, there is not complete contrast or opposition between East and West, and, most important in view of the insistence of representatives of Hinduism and Buddhism, ethics is taken with genuine seriousness even in their apparently extreme points of view. Recall, too, the important point made above that understanding and co-operation on the practical level are not jeopardized or prevented by such ultimate and theoretical differences. This has special significance or application here.

In the case of India, it was called to our attention quite forcibly that the extreme point of view of Śaṁkara, which is the basis of the "beyond ethics" interpretation, does not constitute the sum and substance of Indian ethics or Indian life or Indian philosophy. It was strongly noted that the Mīmāṁsā and the Dharmaśāstras are much more significant for life and practice and much more widespread in their appeal in Indian culture as a whole.

China, too, according to our discussion, takes ethics to be of primary importance and does not, as alleged, reduce ethics to insignificance in the light of family relations. It will be recalled that when this writer brought up the question of the son's not telling the police that his father had stolen the sheep—or, rather, telling them that he did not—the Chinese response was that I was making a mountain out of a molehill, and also that other classical illustrations could be cited to justify the very opposite point of view as basic. Also, and more important, it was pointed out that I, an outsider, did not really understand the very case I had cited as the Chinese understand it. In fundamental matters, ethics is of supreme importance in Chinese thought and culture or practice.

In Japan, we found that ethics has no theological foundation as is alleged for the West, having been simply adopted from Chinese Confucianism. But, we were advised, this did not in the least minimize the primary significance of ethics in Japanese life and culture.

In sum, then, the point constantly stressed was to the effect that, even if ethics is not ultimately grounded or divinely derived, ethics is, as it were, the foundation or ideal of life (and even of thought in much of the East) throughout East and West—with variations or conflicts in interpretation of its ultimacy and sometimes of its specific forms. In this latter connection, though, it was realized that in terms of basic principles the ethical systems of practically all the traditions and cultures under discussion were very similar—remarkably so, in fact, in such matters as truth, honesty, non-killing, non-lust, unselfishness, non-attachment, self-control, and loyalty to family, friends, and self-transcending causes.

Of course, if it were true that some of the areas under discussion take ethics and ethical conduct with primary significance, whereas others do not, and if it were true that our basic ethical principles were in mutual conflict with each other, area by area, it is obvious that genuine co-operation would be difficult, and that even understanding would require much effort. But, as we have seen, this supposed basis of antagonism was found to be without foundation.

On the matter of general social customs, the result of our work was rather essentially the point that, although social conventions differ widely both between East and West and among the various major traditions within both (perhaps especially in Asia), nevertheless, if representatives of these various conventional traditions are given an opportunity to explain the whys and wherefores of their own points of view, a basis can be established for understanding and even respect, and also for—or certainly not against—genuine co-operation, regardless of differences in detailed practice. Even such seemingly difficult-to-understand and sometimes-to-some-people-objectionable customs as the caste system in India, filial piety in China, and race-relations problems in the West were found to be quite intelligible and understandable in the light of more factual understanding and sympathetic interpretations by representatives of the areas in question. One means of such explanation lies in the direction of pointing out the gross exaggeration and distortion which have been applied to these practices: they are not in themselves or in ideal anything like the obviously unacceptable practices they are alleged to be by those who view them simply from the outside and therefore do not understand them.

A most important point in this connection was the constantly repeated *caveat* that we must not, in comparative philosophy, compare ideals with practices, and vice versa, but must make all comparisons on an even basis, ideals with ideals and practices with practices—this being absolutely essential in any attempt to overcome misunderstandings and mutual disrespect, and yet it seems to be common practice among us all.

POLITICAL, LEGAL, AND ECONOMIC PHILOSOPHY

The problems we faced on the general scene or level of international relations are probably more important in some ways and to some people than any of the others so far recounted. Unfortunately, time for fully adequate consideration of these three comprehensive fields—legal, political, and economic philosophy—was simply unavailable. In all cases, though, pre-conference misinterpretations were examined and more adequate interpretations offered for consideration, though perhaps not as final conclusions.

As in other areas of our work, we were made (especially) conscious of the need for historical perspective in consideration of these aspects of cultures, East and West. We were reminded that throughout the history of the major traditions under discussion significant changes of view and practice had taken place, so that no one set of descriptions could possibly be adequate to represent these cultures or traditions in their entirety or even essentially.

In general, too, we have noted that, for practical purposes, for co-operation, and probably even for significant and genuine understanding, we need not agree with each other in all details in these fields any more than in the others, possibly less. In spite of this lack of a need for precise agreement, we discovered much in common among us in terms of fundamentals—though, of course, not anything like identity of perspective—of thought or practice.

The legal aspect of our problem received more adequate consideration than did the political and economic aspects. To some extent, the core of our work in this area was a consideration of the interpretation that in the scientific and rationalistic West law has been of the corresponding (to-be-expected) type, namely, contractual (definite, impersonal, universal, and absolute), whereas law in the intuitive East lacks these qualities and may be characterized mostly as mediational—or as law of status rather than law of contract, and as rule by man rather than rule by law, in view of the prominence of the family system and personal relations in the Asian cultures.

Our deliberations produced the impression—not a clear-cut conclusion by any means—that any such East-West dichotomy and any such divisive description of the nature and status of law and legal thought—and practices—in all the several areas under discussion, in East and West, was unsound in the sense of being an over-simplified statement of the facts. It was brought out that rule by man is more prominent in some parts of Asia than rule by law, generally speaking, but two other points were also noted: the fact that rule by law is not absolute even in the West, and, second, that rule by law is extremely prominent in Asia, along with rule by man. In an interesting instance, it was pointed out, with special reference to China, that rule by man—and also what has been called mediational law and the avoidance of strictly legal decisions—is applied, generally, to relatively unimportant matters and usually to matters of a strictly family nature. In China, for example, where rule by man and rule of morality are stressed, there is also the point of view of the Legalists—such that China may be described as a composite of these two opposite points of view, with changing relative status during the course of history. (Something like this same conclusion seemed to apply to Japan, too.)

In reference to India, emphasis was placed upon the significance of rule by law, with its universal and mandatory requirements, e.g., in such legal systems as the *Laws of Manu* and all the Dharmaśāstras.

Several Asian representatives indicated that Asians are not especially fond of the law because of its rigidity and its impersonality, but no one denied the significance of universal or absolute law in matters of greatest importance.

Also, the *moral* law, which is basic in this area in India and in China, is fundamental and rigid—even if it seems at times to be at variance with technical legality.

On the Western side, it was pointed out, that, while the West is perhaps fundamentally dominated by rule by law and the rational and universal approach to such matters, there are many qualifying factors as well, including the avoidance of legal entanglements where possible and such personal factors as lenience of the judge, extenuating circumstances, and even emotional appeals of lawyers to juries.

As elsewhere, even when points of view were recognized as substantially different, East versus West, such as in the case of the rule by man in China, personal explanation of the view in question made understanding easy and also provided a sound defence, in spite of contrasts.

There was also the feeling that there was not enough substantial or basic difference in points of view to undermine significant and genuine co-operation. In other words, as before, it was noted that on the practical level there was not too much that was different between East and West, although, as in the case of morality, theoretical differences at the top level, as it were, seemed to be rather substantial.

In the political sphere, it was found that, although specific forms of organization and of political thought varied considerably, all the areas under discussion consider themselves idealistic in political philosophy—in such senses as the fact that force is not accepted as the fundamental method of political action, being replaced by reason and moral principles, that the State exists for the purpose of providing for the welfare of all the people, and that what might be called religion or definite devotion to spiritual values is significant in political thought as well as elsewhere in all the given cultures.

The status of the individual in the political life of the several cultures was a question which was not thoroughly threshed out, so that pre-conference conflicting views on this issue were not clarified too much. One of the "discoveries" of the conference—in the mind of this writer, at least—was the statement by at least one representative of each tradition that his tradition's political philosophy fully recognized the dignity of and respect due to the individual human person. In this connection, it was rather obvious that each of the major areas considered itself decidedly democratic in basic political philosophy, in spite of obvious differences in detail both in theory and in practice in the course of history.

It was emphasized that in China and Japan harmony between the individual and the State is the key idea, rather than exclusive emphasis upon one or the other. Historically, the political life of India, China, and Japan have all been other than strictly democratic in the Western sense of the word, but, here again, we come face to face with the need for historical perspective and with the inadequacy of any dogmatic and restrictive definition of democracy.

The status of economic values and economic thought did not assume major proportions in the discussion at the conference, but the problem was faced squarely in all of the pertinent papers. Here again, historical perspective was shown to be important, not only in Asia but also in the West, and also specifically in the United States. As a matter of fact, the whole concept of freedom, whether it be political or economic, was shown to have changed markedly during the course of even the short span of American history—and the same was found to be the case in the Asian traditions.

In spite of the lack of thoroughgoing treatment of the subject, it was found—contrary to pre-conference impressions—that the economic values are recognized as highly significant aspects of the thought and culture of all the areas under discussion, even in allegedly highly religious India. Also, that economic values are nowhere in Asia considered the ultimate values as compared with spiritual values or human values. The alleged materialism of the West and its domination by economic values did not receive adequate consideration or even explanation except as mentioned previously in connection with our discussion of the spiritual values, where it was noted that spiritual values are primary in all the traditions, East and West. It was pointed out repeatedly that there is no conflict between spiritual values and material values in any of the traditions. It was brought out, though, that, as in the case of India, current materialistic progress is somewhat feared because of possible development of a situation in which spiritual values would become less significant than before.

As was said at the start of this section, the problems in this area were too vast and too changing to be considered adequately, but it was felt that sufficient light was revealed to overcome pre-conference misinterpretations, chiefly in the form of absolute contrasts between the ideas, ideals, and practices of the peoples of Asia and the peoples of the West. Such contrasts, fundamentally based upon over-simplification, were roundly rejected, although differences of both thought and practice as far as details are concerned were duly recognized.

UNFINISHED BUSINESS

It is clear from the foregoing that we have not solved all our problems. We will all agree that we did not expect to solve them all. As noted earlier, the over-all theme of this conference was so vast and complicated that we faced an impossibility if our aim was a clear-cut conclusion in every case. This was not our aim, of course. For this reason, this conference has not formulated any final "conclusions."

On the other hand, it should be obvious from what has been reported here, as well as from the entire set of fine, enlightening papers that have been presented, that we have achieved a remarkable degree of greater mutual understanding in the areas of social thought and action, in the over-all area of culture, both in general and in some detail. We have not examined all of our respective ideas, however, with the thoroughness that the problems require. Practically all the problems with which we have concerned ourselves remain, to some degree or other, "unfinished business." Although we have not reached conclusions, we have decidedly made progress in all the areas of this conference. We were reminded just tonight—although no one at these tables really needed such a reminder—that the problem of mutual understanding is an endless one, and was recognized as such even as long ago as the final words of the *Ṛg Veda!*

Some of the, shall we say, theoretical conflicts which were revealed during the course of our work—but which were relatively ignored here because our concern was with understanding and co-operation and because most of us have felt that understanding and co-operation are possible without complete agreement at the level of metaphysical concern—are still matters of philosophical concern to all of us. Their exhaustive consideration would require many conferences, and so this itself is "unfinished business."

Each of us—and every eventual reader of this volume, which contains all the papers presented here—will find ample "unfinished business" in each section of our agenda. In fact, every paper presented at this conference has opened vast new vistas of understanding and problems for further study. In most cases, our future activities should take the form of more exhaustive comparative studies of particular aspects of our work here, i.e., particular especially important philosophical and social problems which were found to be crucial both for philosophy itself and for East-West understanding.

It is dangerous for anyone to cite *the* problems for the future, but some of the more prominent of these should probably be suggested here—though merely as my personal suggestions. Among the problems which stand out as needing, and almost demanding, thoroughgoing examination are the following:

(1) The matter of the relationship between philosophy and culture or philosophy and practice. The inconclusiveness of our "conclusions" on this matter poses serious problems in relation to the work of these conferences. There is not only the question as to whether or not metaphysical theories provide a logical basis for value-judgments, but also the many relationships which may exist between philosophical theory and practice, ethical, cultural, individual, social, etc.

There is also the related question as to whether philosophy or religion—or what?—provides the basis for understanding by revealing what people "really believe" and the (alleged) explanation for their actions. It may well be that the restriction of our work at these conferences to philosophy proper, as far as that is at all feasible, is open to question.

2. Although this next suggestion may be inappropriate for these conferences which have attempted to concentrate upon matters of philosophy and to avoid, as far as feasible, the field of religion—it has proven impossible (as revealed many times in Section III of our agenda) for us to avoid the matter of comparative religious concepts. It may be advisable for us, sometime, to carry out a thoroughgoing comparative study of the philosophical-religious perspective of the various peoples with whom we have been concerned. To

some, mutual understanding is impossible between East and West because of such diverse views on matters of religion, spirituality, soul, immortality, God, etc., whereas others adopt the view that, despite serious diversities of interpretation and formulation, all the peoples of East and West are fundamentally religious in the sense that they have some type of spirituality which is dominant in their philosophical traditions and cultures. As a "poser," can there be any real understanding between the Hindu, the Buddhist, and the Judaeo-Christian traditions—in terms of their ultimate spiritual attitudes? And, of course, what constitutes their respective ultimate attitudes? Some of these problems have been considered in the papers, but much more thoroughgoing comparative examination and discussion seem advisable.

(3) The comparative philosophy of law—a thoroughgoing examination of law, studied comparatively in the light of full consideration of the philosophical and historical-philosophical views of the several cultures—seems of paramount importance in today's world. There is not only the question as to whether or not peoples can understand and co-operate with each other if their attitudes toward law are seriously different, or in conflict, but also the question as to whether or not world law is possible—theoretically or practically—in the light of seeming, but possibly not actual, serious diversity among the peoples of East and West in this field.

(4) The same sort of problem exists in the field of ethics, a most serious problem in our "business," but one which we could not examine thoroughly at this meeting. Do fundamental attitudes toward ethics—toward its basis, origin, and status—set East and West over against each other to such a degree that even understanding is almost impossible, not to speak of co-operation? Or, on the contrary, are East and West fundamentally in basic agreement at least in terms of major specific ethical principles? Both points of view have been widely defended, but never with thoroughgoing and two-sided examination.

(5) There is also the obvious matter of the relation between traditional theories and values (not values alone), on the one hand, and contemporary changes in both the philosophical and the cultural aspects of life, perhaps especially in Asia. It is a most serious matter in India, for example, as to whether or not current social and political changes are actually compatible with traditional fundamentals of the Indian, and especially the Hindu, point of view. The same may be said of Japan. And, possibly, about some of the West, too. It is of great importance for us to know whether contemporary changes can find a satisfactory foundation in the traditional thought-pattern of a people and therefore have what may be called a firm foundation, or whether current ideas and practices are really revolutionary, in which case the matter of their stability and permanence is of importance, both philosophically and practically. *Or,* is such an effort to find compatibility unnecessary? inadvisable? artificial? dangerous? opposed to progress?

Then there is the related problem of "Westernization" or "Modernization" in Asia, which is a serious one as far as understanding is concerned. The assumption that modernization means Westernization has beclouded many studies in the area of East-West mutual understanding, and it may well be that an exhaustive study of this problem could provide important clues or avenues to clarity, on both sides.

(6) This leads directly to the matter of the possible advisability of a new perspective in studying the problem of East-West philosophy and understanding and the legitimacy of the usual attempt to settle upon the fundamental ideas, ideals, attitudes, and methods of the respective peoples of East and West. Perhaps we would do better if we looked at these peoples, and especially their philosophies, not only in terms of their complexity, but also from a serious historical perspective—and also if we would apply to these studies the attitude or procedure which has been described here as the "field" concept. Perhaps it is impossible to determine the "rock bottom" ideas, values, attitudes, and methods of any people with any finality because of historical and "field" diversity.

(7) As mentioned earlier, one problem which stood out during the course of our deliberations, because it came to light in so many areas and because confusion and some doubt remained to the end, is the matter of the status of the individual, and perhaps the status of the individual *person,* in the various traditions and in the various aspects of our over-all problem. It will be recalled that every tradition represented here was said to pay high respect to, and to accept the high dignity of, the individual human being—but it would seem that this problem, being so fundamental, must be threshed out thoroughly—in the light of allegedly basic and traditional points of view to the contrary, both theoretically and practically, throughout the history of these several traditions. This problem touches the strictly philosophical or metaphysical, the religious, the political, the economic, and the social aspects of our over-all problem. Furthermore, today, when democracy seems to be the fundamental political point of view of all the social traditions represented here, this problem becomes crucial and possibly of genuine urgency.

Some of our "unfinished business," especially in the areas of legal, political, and economic philosophy, are such that it is practically impossible to get at the kernel of the situation because of contemporary cultural changes—accompanied, in some cases, by ideational changes. These areas, it would seem, must await greater stability before any attempt can be made to iron out problems, to correct misinterpretations, and to reach clear understanding. The status, etc., of these changes in the light of traditional attitudes is, of course, one of the major future problems of this area—and a vital one.

What might be considered miscellaneous unfinished business would call for thoroughgoing and mutually critical examination of a number of specific problems relating to social thought and action (or institutions)—not so much in the attempt simply to reach greater mutual understanding, although this was not really achieved in some cases, but in the attempt to work toward improvement in the light of suggestions from "the outside" and in the name of progress and modern perspectives—in East and West.

Let it be repeated at the end of this summary that our theme was understanding and the effort to determine if there is a basis for significant co-operation among the peoples of the West and the peoples of Asia. It seems that we have reached a level of mutual understanding which would make such co-operation genuinely possible. There is not only what might be called a negative basis of genuine co-operation in the sense that some of our extreme (and separating) misinterpretations were recognized as not true. There is also a much more positive basis, in the sense that the peoples of Asia and the peoples of the West, in terms of fundamental values, seem to have so much in common that there exists a kinship of spirit, almost a oneness of purpose, which constitutes substantial philosophical affinity. And this, in the writer's opinion, is the fundamental basis of any genuine understanding and especially of genuine co-operation.

All in all, then, we have accomplished much, but very much still remains to be done. Perhaps in future conferences we can attack major aspects of the unfinished business of this conference—possibly one by one—to see them through to conclusion. We have not answered all our questions or solved all our problems. But we have brought into significant focus many aspects of this fundamental problem of mutual understanding at the cultural level, and we have pioneered in the search for such understanding by seeking our "answers" in terms of basic philosophical beliefs and attitudes—not merely cultural practices—and have thus pointed the way for future and further investigations.

One final word, but an important one. At this conference, our purpose has been understanding and understanding alone. For philosophers, this is not enough. As philosophers, we are seeking the total truth, and we now realize that progress here can come only through cordial and open-minded world-philosophizing, a truly total perspective. We face the future with humility, befitting to philosophers, but also with optimistic hope derived from the enlightening, broadening, deepening, challenging, and chastening, insights of our fellow philosophers, East and West.

Appendix

Public Lectures

N. BAMMATE

The Islamic Cultural Tradition and the West

Being here, in Hawaii, has caused some estrangement to me, so that now the Middle East appears like a foreign land. Seen from East Asia or the Pacific, all Mediterranean civilizations, and this includes essential aspects of Islamic civilization, seem much nearer to each other. But this very nearness of Islam to some classical Western concepts and structures is perhaps the most baffling aspect of Islamic studies. It is true that Islam and Western civilization have common roots. And here, to make things shorter, let me just quote from one of the leaders of these East-West conferences, and one of the outstanding American philosophers, Filmer Northrop. In one of his recent books, *The Taming of the Nations,* Northrop wrote, "There is a realistic, explicitly expressed definiteness and directness about the Quran and its Islam which permits one of the West to breathe more easily and to see things more clearly, as if one were at home in the clime to which one's physiology is adapted." And then further, "Nor is this reaction difficult to understand. The intuition of the inexpressible Brahman, Nirvana, Tao or *jen* is foreign to the general outlook and mentality of the West.... Islam, on the other hand, derives from the same Greek science with its emphasis upon true knowledge as definite lawful knowledge and from the same Hebrew Christian tradition as does the West. In fact, Islam gave to the West through its Arabian universities in Spain much of the source material and the enlightenment which made the West what it now is. Judaism, Christianity and Islam in their historical development derived from common roots even though each adds unique elements.... Thus, for a Westerner to move from the Asian Far East into Islam is, for all the novelty, in a very real and fundamental sense, to be coming home" (pp. 149, 150).

Now, these two basic elements, Greek philosophy and Semitic theology, are certainly the two main elements of Islamic civilization, and this brings us immediately into a land which we believe we know. We meet Aristotle and Plato; we meet Abraham and Moses. We immediately find familiar landmarks, and we readily grasp them. Sometimes these landmarks may be misleading. True, Greek philosophy has been integrated with Islam. The essence of it is the same, practically, as in Western scholastics. But there is a difference in situation. Greek philosophy is somewhat on the brink, on the margin, of Islamic philosophy, and perhaps the traditional lawyers, the *fugaha,* are better exponents, or at least more characteristic exponents, of Islamic thought than the so-called philosophers. On the other hand, the religion is certainly essentially the same. I quote just one paragraph from the Qur'ān: "We believe in God. We believe in what has been revealed to Abraham, Ishmael, Isaac, Jacob, and all the patriarchs. We believe in what has been given to Moses and to Jesus and in what the other prophets have received from their Lord. And we do not make any distinctions among them." This comes from the Qur'ān, the basic, the holy, book of Islam. And, as you know, the Qur'ān and Islam recognize the divine mission of Jesus; call him *"ruh Allah,"* the spirit of God; recognize his miraculous birth from the Virgin Mary; and recognize also the Holy Spirit of Christianity. However, there is one "but" that is essential. It doesn't recognize the Incarnation. And, therefore, all the concepts which seem to be keys, which seem to be clues, suddenly have different connections, imply various connotations. The essential in Islamic theology is the unity and transcendence of God. Therefore, the idea of a Son of God is repelled by Islam, and, therefore, all the other common aspects suddenly take on quite another figure. The keynote in philosophy, as in theology, is the same, but the harmonics are different.

I think this very difficulty is at the same time the most strenuous, but also the most rewarding, aspect of Islamic studies for Westerners. When a Westerner approaches Hinduism, Buddhism, Taoism, he knows that he is going toward foreign lands; his mind is on the alert; he is ready for the unexpected. But the distance between Islam and the West is not a distance made of exoticism, of remoteness. The real distance between Islam and the West is not remoteness, but ambiguity. Since the same values imply various connotations, the real situation is not that of a dialogue but, first of all, that of self-examination, of self-analysis, to be conducted by Muslims as well as by Westerners. As when you look at yourself in a mirror, what is right comes on left, what is left comes on right; this troublesome ambiguity—this is what Islam represents to the West. It is the same, and yet it is not the same. And this is why the very difficulty of a dialogue with Islam is, at the same time, the proof of its necessity and of its fruitfulness. It leads to a critical examination of our own values as reverberated against us from somewhere else. Islam doesn't mean alienation to the Westerner; on the contrary, it means re-integration. The student of Islamic thought meets Aristotle constantly, meets Plato, Abraham, Moses, Jesus, but has to consider them with a new eye after they are passed through the Islamic mirror. So, my first point is to try to express that fundamental ambiguity of Islamic studies among studies of the East.

My second point deals with another ambiguity. What is a Muslim? What does it mean to be a Muslim? When you ask this question of a Bedouin, of an average simple man, and preferably of such an unsophisticated man because a sophisticated one would give you a biased reply—when you ask "Who are you?"—the traditional reply is *"al Lamdou li Allah,"* "Glory be to God." To a Western mind, he doesn't reply to the question; he escapes it. His terms of reference are not "horizontal." He does not define himself essentially with reference to a family, to geography, to an earth, to a blood, to a nation. His terms of reference are "vertical." He does not say "I am"; he says "He is," speaking of God. And, therefore, he himself is only through reverberation, by a reflex. This is the authentic, this is the natural, reply of the Muslim, of the unsophisticated Muslim to the question "Who are you?" Then a Westerner is more than often baffled. Such reference to a spiritual community is not a sufficient reply. He wants a more specific definition of the individual. He wants to know his historical past, his fidelities, what he is true to, what earthly ties, what historical connections, are his. And then, the Westerner usually asks a second, more specific question. Usually, the second question is, "Are you an Arab?" Well, although I am an Oriental and a Muslim, I am not an Arab. So, the second question does not bring the expected identification. But the interesting point is that when my father, for instance, was asked the same second question, the formulation was "Are you a Turk?" because also one generation ago Islam was seen through a specific history which, to Western eyes, was not Arab but Turkish history. And one generation before, my grandfather would certainly have been asked another question, "Are you a Persian?" So, the emphasis shifts.

Islam is the same, but, at each generation, the Westerner has looked at it through different ethnic, historical, territorial eyeglasses, and this has created a misunderstanding. I cannot say through what lenses the next generation of Muslims may be considered. But I may already try to guess, since one of the most important events in Islamic history is happening right now. Islam is no longer the Middle East. The Islamic world is shifting East and West, shifting on one side toward Africa and on another side toward Asia. Cairo has gone to Bandung; and a new era of Islam is starting, an African and Southeast Asian Islam. And this is why Islam is coming to you. And this is why it can't be of indifference to you. It's already an Islam which may seem a little strange to me because I am a Mediterranean, perhaps already an old-fashioned Muslim. But, if the next generation were asked, "Who are you?" and still replied, "Glory be to God," the second question would most probably be, "Are you an Afro-Asian?" This is the concept which is now being born and which is being shaped. So, this is a second ambiguity. This tension between a spiritual assertion of relation to God and, on the other hand, an attempt to specify, to come closer to, historical and national realities—here is one more ambiguity in the dialogue.

There is a third difficulty. Islam and the West have gone along together for a very long time. When you read Thomas Aquinas, you have the same feeling as when reading Averroës. When you are reading Meister Eckhart or St. John of the Cross, you have the same feeling as when you are reading Mūhed-Dīnibn Arabi, for one, or Jalāl al Dīn Rumi, for another. And then you discover that throughout the Middle Ages the values are the same. The Crusades were a civil war, and the very fact that the enemy was branded not as an alien but as an unfaithful is already significant. He is unfaithful to the same values as ours. And, then, after this period in the Middle Ages, when values were shared, suddenly everything changes, and here we are in the midst of the problem we are to discuss tonight. Suddenly something breaks. A new dimension has been brought into the dialogue. And this new dimension is the modern world. After the Renaissance, after the Reformation, but only then, the two communities, Christian and Islamic, are split, and they become foreign to each other. Therefore, the West and the East are not really the borderline between Islam and Western civilization. The borderline is not in geography. It is in time. It is a different tempo which animates our civilizations now. For the Orientals, the problem is complicated by the fact that "modern" means at the same time "Western." The connections of time and geography are bound together. For us, the West is essentially the present modern world. And this is not only Islamic. If you were to ask a Burmese or an Indonesian or an Arab, one of his very first reactions would be to say that the West is a world of movement. This inquisitiveness, this questioning of established values, this creative anxiety we spoke about yesterday, this recklessness—this is the rhythm and the tempo of Western civilization which some of us are afraid of, which others, more and more numerous, are eager to imitate. Anyway, this is the rhythm which, for us, is connected with the West.

This rhythm, this constant quest and re-creation of problems, has become the usual pace of the West. This inquisitiveness is a condition of the life of Western civilization. If this free creation of problems and questionings is taken away from Western civilization, it droops; but let the unexpected come back again as a challenge, and Western civilization is re-animated. Therefore, the West has been modern for five or six hundred years at least—"modern" because of this tendency to ask questions, to create them, and to solve them and move on. Well, this acquiescence to modernism is a completely unique feature in history. And, to Islam, it is an entirely new fact which appeared just fifty or sixty years ago, at the most. And, therefore, the problem is that we have to live immediately, simultaneously, an intellectual and moral crisis comparable to the Reformation, an industrial and social revolution comparable to that of the eighteenth and nineteenth centuries. Furthermore, politically, we are living our nineteenth and our twentieth centuries simultaneously—living the old nineteenth-century idea of nationalism, which comes to us now, but at the same time suddenly thrust into regional or world politics. Therefore, to us, the "West" and the "modern" are not only here and now in 1959. They are all of a sudden and simultaneously in a pack; let's say, Honolulu 1959, but also Florence 1359, Paris 1789, or Moscow 1917. All these simultaneous modernisms are facing us. They don't appear to us in time as a duration. They appear to us like some sort of shop window of formulas. And this is why the Eastern modernist sometimes appears to a Westerner as confused, as too eclectic, as not co-ordinated enough, because he considers these events and these facts in their simultaneity; he does not project them through the pulsation of time. And this is why, sometimes, his mind is driving restlessly, sometimes in a somewhat amateurish way, from one doctrine to another. And he sometimes selects ideas and values which appear antiquated, which appear past. For instance, he does not select in philosophy and in natural science the most modern movements. On the contrary, he selects the nineteenth century. And why the nineteenth century? Because the nineteenth century gives him a reassuring science, a science with causality, a science with forms, with shapes, just at the moment when science baffles reason, when science baffles common sense. Islamic civilization does not need this kind of science, and this is why sometimes some of our modern writers look a little antiquated, a little old-fashioned, to the Western philosopher.

Now I'd like to come to one more point. I tried to define some of the elements of trouble in the problem of a meeting between East and West, Islam and the West. First, there was the foreign element thrust upon Islam. There was the fact that the two cultures were really too near to have a real dialogue. There was also the fact that Western modernism was given suddenly, in all its contradictory aspects, to Islam. But I haven't yet mentioned the essential aspect of the problem. And here I shall try to come to it. The most important part in those relations, and the most dangerous one, is that Islam receives the impact of the West below the floating line, or right in its heart. And, to express this, I'll stop arguing and discussing, and I'll come back to the old method of traditional Islamic demonstration. I promised myself I wouldn't enter into theology here, and I won't. But it is obviously difficult to forget that side in a civilization where culture is merely the external, material face of spiritual reality, where the spiritual and the worldly are apparently united. Moreover, tonight we are speaking mainly of the traditional aspect of Islam. We have another meeting [at the conference] next week where its scientific aspect will be discussed. So, I voluntarily and intentionally leave aside a very important part of Islam, and one has to correct anything I'm saying now, taking this correction into consideration. Tonight we are speaking of the traditional past, of its history, of its ideals.

Therefore, a traditional approach might be in order, and I shall introduce the subject with a parable, an apologue. It can't be better expressed than by turning to the Qur'ān. In the Qur'ān, Abraham's quest for God is vividly presented. Abraham turns first toward the gods of his tribe in Chaldea and worships them. But he concludes, saying, "I cannot attach myself to things that pass by." Then, according to the Qur'ān, he turns toward the stars, then toward the moon, then toward the sun, and each time the same event comes again and again. Night comes, day comes, and the same rhythm comes repeatedly, hauntingly, in the Qur'ān, "I cannot attach myself to anything that passes by." Well, that could be a motto for traditional Islamic civilization. It is opposed to what is just passing by, as being is opposed to becoming, as the sacred is opposed to the analytical, as unity is opposed to plurality. And then Abraham goes on, pushing aside all those idols, and he concludes, "Glory be to God. Everything passes except the face of God." He's found his stability only after having annihilated all that exists, all that has specific shape and color, and he stops at what is beyond as the source of all life, shape, and color. This has been the ideal of traditional Muslim civilization, and this explains its greatness, its stability, its coherence, its integration, but at the same time it is a key to its decay, to the fact that it couldn't easily support the shock of innovation. "I cannot attach myself to anything that passes by." But, tragically enough, there isn't anything which appears more transitory nowadays than the Absolute. And this is the tragedy of Islamic civilization. The fact that the impact is challenging the very core, the very principle, of Islamic civilization—this is the most dramatic aspect of the situation of Islam today. You could say, as many of our fathers and grandfathers said, "Well, our crisis is purely worldly; in the spiritual realm we hold our own." No, because in Islam spiritual and worldly are tightly connected and the worldly is only a sign of the otherworldly, and, therefore, a historical defeat is not only a historical defeat; to Islam it is also a metaphysical scandal. And this is why there are so often bitterness and despair. It is not only a matter of culture, it's a matter of survival.

Now, after having tried to review some general aspects of the problem, let us consider quickly some philosophical notions as interpreted in Islam. I'd like to review with you, first from a traditional outlook and then in their present situation, successively, the notion of man according to Islamic tradition, then the notion of society, then the notion of language, then the notions of time and history.

The notion of man, first. There's one thing which is common to Islam and the West. It's the notion of personality. Man is not an illusion; man is real. And there is something like individual responsibility. Man is a coherent being, and there is a humanism which is common to the West and Islam which is not founded only on Greek philosophy but also on Semitic theology. And, in fact, the first basis of this conception of man, for Islam, is a theological one. There is an idea in Islam that man is the absolute servant of God. And the very word *"muslim"* means "submitted," *"islam"* meaning "submission." But everything, according to Islam, is Muslim, is submitted—the earth, the wind, the grass, the trees. There is only one difference, that the submission of man is free. It's not really submission; it's adhesion, an adhesion through love. And there is a story in the Qur'ān that when the world was created God wanted to grant freedom. And he wanted to grant it first to the most powerful aspect of creation, to the mountains. And the mountains shrank; they were scared, and moved away from freedom, which could lead to rebellion and to punishment from God. And man was the only being which accepted it. Therefore, it is false to say that predestination is the basic notion of man's condition in Islam, as it is false to say that absolute freedom (as some of our apologetics are saying) is the key to the Islamic condition of man. It's a combination; it's free adherence.

But personality, the real self of man, is not to be asserted by the conquest of things, by gripping objects. We saw at the beginning that the same notions have different connotations, have different harmonics, in Islam and in the West. And this is so for the notion of human beings, too. True, man is a person, individually responsible to God. But man is not the measure of the universe for the Muslim, and the self is not the starting point. The self, the real self, on the contrary, is a goal. Islam does not accept the idea of sin, but, at the same time, it believes that man, to fulfill his destiny, has to go beyond natural man. Islam believes that there is an innermost man. And this is asserted as well by philosophers influenced by the Greeks as by the theologians. They consider that there is an inner aspect of man, a part which is beyond reason and feelings, which is beyond passion and opinions, which is even beyond consciousness, and beyond death, which seems to abolish consciousness. It is a point, a virgin point, in the self, which the Arabs through respect call *sirr,* secret, mystery, in order not to name it. And this is the mystery which is tuned to reality, and it is through this mystery that we perceive reality. And this feeling takes even popular forms. For instance, we find a traditional saying even in the *Thousand and One Nights,* "Glory be to those who have abolished their names and surnames to be just a human being, a mirror for the Absolute."

Let us start again with the Qur'ān, to look for a traditional notion of society. The Qur'ān tells us that in order to appreciate a past civilization—and here the examples are taken from the Babylonian, ancient Egyptian, and Hebrew civilizations, and the ancient peoples of Arabia—what we have to do is to look at what kind of ruins it left. It's a kind of spiritual archeology we are invited to undertake. Now, if we apply this criterion to Islam, what do we discover? We discover that Islam has left us, on one side, mosques, and, on the other side, markets. On one side, the mosques—and that is the expression of the City of God, of the absolute community, the fraternity of the brethren. On the other side, the markets—that means the symbol and expression of the intimate community, of the warm, everyday community of the family, of companionship, of trading. But, in between, there is something lacking; there is a gap. And this is the palace. Palaces have disappeared. They have not been built to last, and they have been destroyed. Between the City of God and the city of everyday contacts of man, of simple man, there should have been the field of institutionalized society. It is the very field which has been defined by Roman lawyers, which has been expressed by Greek philosophers, which has been warranted by European cities when they fought for their charters. In Islam it is religion which is institutionalized, and not the city. And, therefore, between the mosque and the market there is a gap which nowadays Muslims are trying in a fever to fill as quickly as they can. Therefore, Islam is either on this side or beyond the institution. Or, we could say that Islam, Islamic society, has been modeled, not according to historical pattern, but according to a sacred law.

And this brings us to the notion of time and history. As psychology is quickly resolved into ontology, and, as social relations are expressed in terms of divine law, in the same way time for Islam is not a historical duration. Islam is either on this side of or beyond history. Historical examples, when they are given by Muslim historians, and first of all by the Qur'ān but also by late historians, are all presented in the form of parables, of ethical examples. There is a short story showing that, for instance, Pharaoh, or Sodom and Gomorrah, having disobeyed divine law, have been destroyed. So, history is a succession of promises given to mankind itself and warnings against temptation. And mankind goes into error, and mankind undergoes the judgment of God. The extent of an event is immediately followed by a consideration of its moral significance. Therefore, history for Islam is, we could say, in suspense between a past which is conceived as prophecy, and a future which is constructed around Judgment Day, as an eschatology. The real time of Islam is not historical tradition; it's either prophecy or eschatology. And we could go even further, saying that the real notion of time in Islam, the most original notion of time, is one which is defined as the renewal of creation at every moment.

And here again it is not a specifically theological notion; it's also to be found in traditional scholastics. Our authors in the Middle Ages, when they tried to assimilate Greek wisdom, found that one of the most difficult points to assimilate was the Greek notion of space and time. To them, the constant tendency of the Greeks to reduce movement to statics and to build up a kind of geometry of essence, of concepts, was extremely foreign to their Semitic language, Arabic, and to their whole temper. And, very often, in the Arabic translations of early Greek texts we find out that space concepts are expressed through words whose roots are really linked with the time concept, time conceived as a moment, as an instant. For the Muslim, time is a vibrating echo of eternity. The traditional Muslim philosopher believes that every second, every moment, is thundering, throbbing, pulsating, from the first day of creation. Every instant, every second, is as fresh as new. And this is the specifically Islamic notion of time. It is expressed by saying that reality appears to our eyes and then is taken away from our eyes, like a colored carpet. The world is a magic world; its pattern can be guessed at sometimes, but it has to be guessed quickly, not through intellectual conceptualization, not through construction, but by an awareness of the fleeting moment, in the sense of the poet who said, "All is always now." Therefore, this a-historical notion of Islam is compensated for by a kind of metaphysical notion of the instant. This is very characteristic, and will have some implications, as I am planning to say in a few days [at a conference meeting], on the Islamic notion of science.

But let us take one more example. Let's take the language. I will not take much of your time with linguistic analysis, but I would like to hint at the structure of the Arabic sentence as opposed to the Indo-European sentence, Sanskrit as well as modern Western languages. The first fact which strikes us when we approach the Arabic language is that the predominance is given, not to the subject, but to the verb. This is the central part of speech. Now, the second impression is that the Arabic language is a disconnected language. It consists mainly of principal prepositions. It has practically no subordinative sentences. There is seldom a "because" or "why"; sentences are simply connected by "and" or "then." It's like beads which are put one after another—simple, immediate facts which are grasped as instantaneously as time. For instance, they wouldn't say in Arabic, "I came here with a light raincoat. It was light because I was afraid it would be too hot, but, on the other hand, I took it because I wondered whether it would rain." A typical Arabic sentence would say, "I came and I took a light coat and I thought it might be hot, and it could rain and it didn't rain." There are practically no "whys" and "becauses" and "therefores." There are few of those subordinative sentences upon which Western thought depends when moving forward. An idea, a thought, a reality, is perceived in its immediacy, in its bluntness. It is not reconstructed by the mind. European languages are conceptual languages. And whenever you are making a sentence you always feel, behind a statement of facts or events, the judgment of the subject, because you have the "I," the "we," the "because," the "author," and so on. A philosopher once said, "There is nothing more momentous than to say of one fact that it is cause or consequence of another." Well, the Arab—and after him the Muslim, because the Arabic language has been the philosophical language of the Muslims—an Arab never says of anything that it is cause or consequence of anything else, because causes and consequences are in the hands of God and God alone. And, therefore, the only thing which man can do is to be open to reality, to accept the shocks of impressions and events, to integrate them, but never to reconstruct them from concepts.

And this leads us to demonstration and proof, according to Islam. According to Islam, proof cannot be given through a real syllogism. Truth cannot be reached through dialectics. Truth is a monolithic block. It can't be picked at. The only thing which can be done (and the word is exactly the same as the Biblical Hebrew word, *"shekina"*) is to offer yourself to contemplation. Truth is not merely reconstructed; it is to a large extent deserved by moral merits, by righteousness. And there is a moral notion of truthfulness which accompanies epistemology. And this again brings us nearer to what our Indian friends were saying yesterday [at the conference] and again leads us somewhat away from the West, or from the modern West at least. The only thing we may do is to open ourselves to this awareness. And then how could it happen? Here for once I won't quote the Qur'ān; I quote a European scholastic, St. Bonaventura, who said that "things can be considered either as objects or as signs." Well, to a traditional Muslim a thing is never an object; it is a sign (*ayāt, dhiuz*). And he lives in a world of signs. The simplest things, drinking a glass of water, looking at a paper, can be revealing of ultimate truth, while the most elaborate construction can be misleading, because truth is not to be trapped. And here again we come nearer to Eastern, Asian methods. And even our scholastics, when they borrowed the Greek, Aristotelian syllogism, constructed it in a somewhat different way. The three elements are present: major, minor, and conclusion. But the emphasis is different.

The main load of the reasoning is put upon the minor and not the major, as with the Greeks. It is "Muhammad is a man," the immediate awareness which has precedence over the universal, the general concept. "Man is mortal."

The major has become somewhat blurred. And then the passing from one proposition to another to come to a conclusion is not, as in Greek thought, on one level, where it gives the impression of a geometry, Euclidean geometry. There's a gap in between. It's not a passage from the particular to the universal, but from the singular, and specific, to the eternal, with a big broad jump over the concept, over dialectics. This is characteristic of Islamic thought. And there is a tendency even in Avicenna to reduce one of the elements of the syllogism. In fact, the Muslim is never happier than when he comes to a situation which Hebrew philosophy also has, and that is the dilemma. It does not stipulate a syllogism. The triangle of dialectics is replaced by the two branches of the dilemma. It's either this or that, and usually it's at the same time this *and* that, depending on the point of view. The purpose is not to come to a third term which would be a synthesis. It is to keep these two alternatives as wide apart as possible, and then to create such a tension, an inner tension, that something should happen, that there should be a flash between the alternatives (between, I was about to say, the *yang* and *yin,* but there are considerable differences). This is just to show how, starting from Greek premises and the syllogism, we come to something which is much nearer to the Far East. This is the ambiguity of Islam. We are in a position which is expressed by the very profession of faith for Islam, "There is no God but God," which is a perfect example of that dilemma. I was speaking of a Jewish philosophy which was expressed by Maimonides when he said that the only definition of reality is that it is the negation of the negation—that *via negativa* is the typical style of a philosophy which is based on the unique and the transcendent, which distrusts concepts and essences, and, even when it deals with them, as do scholastics or modern philosophy, tries to escape from them. And, therefore, there is no fragmentary truth; there is only truth itself. Well, this is the kind of *kōans* we have. We have to split ourselves between two antitheses. And there is no synthesis which is possible on a dialectical level. And it can be reached only by the self-realization of the subject himself. And the most typical example I'll use (and I stop on this) is given by Jesus himself when Pontius asks him, "What is truth?" This is a Greek question. Even more, it is a Roman who has turned Hellene. And what does Jesus say? He replies like Maimonides. He replies like the profession of faith of the Qur'ān. That is, he doesn't start a dialectical discussion. To a discussion on essences, he opposes the evidence of a witness. He replies, "I am the truth." And you find that it's always the same in Islamic philosophy. The personal evidence, the existential evidence, of a truth, is always opposed to the dialectical assertion.

And, to finish, I would like to illustrate what I have been saying by art, where we find exactly the same approaches. It's the arabesque which is the typical art of Islam. The arabesque (I'll say it in two words because it's getting very late) expresses at least two things: First, that there is no reality in the apparent world, that nothing is fixed in the world of sense. And this is why the lines are so capricious that they can't be scrutinized. Second, but behind this game of lines there is a fixed pattern. There are geometrical figures, triangles, pentagons, and all those stable figures which suggest an ideal, transcendent world beyond the appearances. Those two aspects create a tension, a dilemma, which can be solved only in the onlooker's mind. And this idea could be better felt if we compared Islamic art with Renaissance painting, for instance. In Renaissance painting, the unity is an intellectual, personalistic unity, a unity coming from a construction, a pattern which has been imposed by the artist. It is a unity made out of composition. This line responds to that other line. And we take for granted that the man who observes will be in one spot and looking at the picture, just as Greek philosophy postulates that the ego, the thinking self, is outside the flow of events and ideas, in a privileged position to judge the world objectively. In the arabesque, the unity is woven inside, and at the same time it is beyond, has to be grasped by the onlooker, in a meditation which uses the work of art as a starting point. The unity is everywhere, and it is nowhere.

So, we discover also in Muslim art some of the fundamental characteristics we have been considering in Muslim philosophy, or in the classical notions of history or literature. Such cohesion is an essential feature of all Islamic civilization. In spite of the present tensions, it is still a factor that makes for the permanence of its values.

D. T. SUZUKI

Zen and Parapsychology

I.

My subject tonight is "Zen and Parapsychology," but, unfortunately, I do not know very much about parapsychology. In fact, it is better to say that I do not know the subject at all except in a superficial way. My knowledge is very general. I know it treats of such subjects as telepathy, clairvoyance, clairaudience, premonition, levitation, raps, apparitions, or poltergeist. All these subjects are considered to be altogether out of the reach of ordinary sense-experiences; they belong to occultism, whatever that may mean. And these occult phenomena constitute topics of parapsychology, and the scholars naturally apply to them all those scientific techniques used in the study of ordinary psychology. I do not know how far they have succeeded in unraveling the occult phenomena which uniformly defy the application of experimental methods.

Before I left New York last November, there was some commotion on Long Island. I think it was the case of poltergeist, that is to say, some pieces of furniture began to move irregularly, apparently without any ascertainable agent in the vicinity. The professors of Duke University came and investigated the strange phenomena. As far as I know, however, they could not reach any definite conclusion which satisfactorily explains them scientifically. The little boy of the family was a suspect for a while, I remember, but he was proved to be innocent of the whole business. The professors may have given a full report of the case somewhere in their journals, but I am ignorant of it.

Once, when I took part in a "quiet sitters' deep-breathing exercise," I noticed, after the elapsing of some time, some of the sitters hopping about in the fashion of frogs. Though I am afraid that this sort of thing could not be classed under the category of levitation, I heard that sometimes it happens to the sitters that they leap up even as far as to the ceiling almost, though

Japanese houses generally do not have a very high ceiling. I wonder, however, how they felt when they had to come down to the floor.

I think you all know about the ouija board. When you put your hand on it lightly, after a while it begins to move all by itself without your trying consciously to control the movement over the board. You ask a simple question, and the hand will soon spell out either yes or no. This phenomenon can now readily be explained, I think, since we all know something of the working of the unconscious.

Telepathy, clairvoyance, and other "occult" happenings are, however, difficult to understand, I believe, as far as our present knowledge of parapsychology is concerned. When we know all the data about them and can treat them scientifically, and, if possible, test them experimentally, everything, I am sure, will be made clear without resorting to supernaturalism. First, the facts are to be authentically collected and judiciously analyzed.

Historically speaking, one of the most notable cases is that of Swedenborg, the great mystic, who turned away from his scientific studies, when he was pretty old, to Christian theology and established the New Jerusalem Church movement. He is said to have seen a big fire taking place somewhere far away from where he was. Kant makes reference to this incident in one of his writings.

Bankei (1622–1693), the Zen master of the Tokugawa era, seems to have had a telepathic faculty. When he was sojourning at a certain Buddhist temple, he announced one day that his old teacher was not feeling well and that he wished to visit him. One of his friends who were staying there with Bankei ridiculed him, saying, "How can you tell that your teacher is not well when you are so far away from him?" The monk-friend proposed that he accompany Bankei to see if Bankei was not bragging about his unusual sense. They started on their journey. On the way, Bankei told his friend that the wife of Bankei's acquaintance in Osaka was dead and that they had better call on him first, as they had to pass Osaka. When they reached the city, Bankei's acquaintance welcomed them and wondered how Bankei came to know of his wife's death, which had taken place three days ago. Bankei said to his friend, "Don't you see I was right?"

In the old feudal Japan there were many swordsmen who acquired a sense or feeling of an invisible object or person who might do something harmful to them. Yagyu Tajima, who lived about three hundred years ago, was a great swordsman, and the following incident is told of him. One spring day he was out in his garden to see the cherries in full bloom. He looked so absorbed in admiration that his boy-attendant following thought, "My master is a great player of sword, but he is now all carried away with the sight. Is it possible for me to strike him from behind?" The thought quickly passed through the boy's mind and then he was employed again with some other boyish fantasies. The master, however, was in a different mood, for he felt the moving of a "murderous atmosphere" about him. He looked around trying to detect the presence of a possible enemy from whom the atmosphere emanated. However hard he tried, he could not locate any such object in the vicinity, except the attendant boy. Suspicion of the boy was dismissed, because he could not possibly conceive the idea of doing anything harmful to his master. Yagyu was troubled; he could not bring himself to the idea that his sense of the murderous air was wrong. He was confident in his accurate sensitivity, which he had acquired after long training in his profession. The failure displeased him badly and he was not to be consoled until it was finally found out that "the vibration of death" started really from the boy's playful imagination.

Theosophists talk about an "aura" emanating from a person, and Swedenborg also assumes something like this when he ignores spatial proximity as the sign of affective relationship. It is possible that some delicately constructed electric instrument could measure the imperceptible waves accompanying the brain activities.

A friend of mine who was quite sick thought he would not survive the crisis this time and made his mind up for death. He was quietly waiting for the last moment. His friends naturally were consulting as to what to do then. As they were pretty far away from the sick man, they thought he could not hear anything of their talk. In spite of all this, he recovered. Later when I saw him he told me how hypersensitive his auditory sense grew at the critical moment of illness and that he could hear the talk his friends were carrying on in a suppressed tone of voice. As we all know, some animals have far more acute sensitivity than we human beings have. We have lost a great deal of our primitive instincts which were replaced by our thinking powers. It is likely that the world is still full of things of which we have yet no ideas, and for this reason we ought not to be so rash as to deny the reality of all so-called parapsychological phenomena.

Before the invention of the telephone or television, we could not think of being able to hear or see anything going on at a far-away place, especially without any wire connection. Wireless communication was impossible even to imagine, but nowadays it is nothing. If we have a receiver properly adjusted we can hear from other heavenly bodies as readily as we do now from the other side of the earth.

II.

1. Now let me ask, What psychological phenomenon is Zen? Has parapsychology anything to do with it? Some things Zen performs are wonderful; especially what is known as *satori* experience is, psychologically speaking, something revolutionary in the sense that it is the awakening of a certain state of mind which defies intellectualization. The Zen experience is something altogether extraordinary, as recorded in Zen literature, more so in the case of certain personalities. It is partly for this reason that Zen is often thought somewhat or somehow associated with occultism or esoterism. But the fact is that the extraordinariness of the Zen experience has nothing to do with parapsychology. (While I was lecturing in New York, I was often asked questions

which related Zen to parapsychology, and that is the reason this topic was chosen for tonight.)

From another point of view, however, Zen is a parapsychological phenomenon as it is an ordinary psychological event; it is also "super-psychological" if there is such a study. Lately, we hear of depth psychology; perhaps Zen is something to study in this field. But the trouble is that when Zen becomes a special subject to be studied by a special science or by a special branch of philosophical discipline, Zen loses its essential characteristic.

When observation is confined to certain superficial aspects of Zen, or when we are tempted to leave the study of Zen to mere book-reading, we often find scattered here and there in Zen literature (and also in Taoist books) such expressions as the following. For instance, in the *Chuang Tzu:* "The perfect man or true man may go into water, but he is not drowned; he may go into fire, but he may never be burned." Almost identical expressions are also found in Zen books. This kind of description of the perfect man no doubt mystifies us, being quite contrary to our ordinary experience where fire burns and water drowns. But these descriptions are not to be interpreted from the general level of intellection but from (shall I say?) a higher level. In Zen itself there is no higher, no lower; everything is on the same level. But when anything is expressed in language, words showing degrees of relativity come in. Therefore, once on the level of relativity, logic comes along and rules: no contradictions are allowed to take place. When the nature of water is defined to drown anything that falls into it, it cannot be otherwise. So with fire. A fire that does not burn is no fire, nor is it possible for things not to burn when they are in it. The natural laws of necessity are thus to be respected in the world of relativity. Here we cannot experience anything that is contrary to the laws. No freedom is permitted. Therefore, when I say necessity is freedom and vice versa, people will stamp me as insane and utterly irrational. Let me see what freedom is, then.

2. We generally think we are free, but what do we really mean by that? For we are as a matter of fact not at all free: we are restricted on all sides; we are inhibited whenever we try to move to do something "freely." Freedom is an idea born of fantasy, and reality contradicts it. Perhaps we are most free when we are all alone. As soon as we get out of the room, we begin to wear all kinds of masks according to the various situations in which we happen to find ourselves. We try to show the best we have. If we do not actually have it, we pretend as if we had and put on the mask accordingly. We are all mask-wearers in society. We are ourselves when at home, and it is for this reason that the master is not honored by the servant. Confucius says, "The small man does (or thinks) all kinds of bad things when he is all by himself." Because the small man then is really himself and feels no need for a mask. He is a free man, and uninhibited.

Really, how frequently are we truly true to ourselves in our daily living? We are most of the time "actors," mask-wearers, Nō-players, violators of our own nature, that is, untrue to ourselves. This act of violence is what the psychologist means by "inhibition." The inhibited life is just opposite to freedom. We have freedom in its true sense only when we are all alone by ourselves. This is not when we think we are alone in our private room as with the Confucian "small man." We can never be alone as long as we live on the surface of our consciousness. The very moment a man says "I" he is not himself; he has divided himself into two: "I" and "not-I," subject and object. I am really "I" only when I am in the innermost chamber of consciousness, where no bifurcation has yet taken place. This is not exact; it is better to say that "I" can be caught only when I am the act itself, that is, when I am acting, in the midst of action, when "I" does not reflect within itself and say "I." This is the only time when "I" is the man himself, when the actor, the acted, and the act are in perfect unison. Whether in the public or in privacy, this "I" is always free and master of itself. When Buddha is made to have uttered at his birth, "I alone am the most honored one," his "I" is no other than this.

Freedom, however, is to be sharply distinguished from licentiousness, or libertinism, or wantonness. Wantonness is just the opposite of freedom, because it is the assertion of uncontrolled (that is, unenlightened) egoistic impulses. To be free is to be their master and not to be their abject thrall. When the absolute "I" manifests itself, it makes its own rules, obeying no other masters. Those who think wantonness to be freedom are under the greatest illusion we can have of ourselves. Confucius is altogether in the right when he says that we must try to be sincere to our own nature, to our own true self. When we are really sincere to ourselves, that is the time when we are truly free. But we must remember that when we are sincere, that is, when we try to justify ourselves by saying that we are sincere, we are not really so—because we are not "innocent" of ourselves. When this takes place, when we are thoroughly "innocent," we do not know where or what or who we are. We are truly and really sincere when we are not conscious whether we are sincere or insincere. When we are unconscious of ourselves we are like fowls of the air or lilies of the field. But at the same time we must also remember that we are human beings and neither the birds nor the lilies. Which means that to be really sincere and really free is to be unconsciously conscious or consciously unconscious of this fact. Scientists and followers of Aristotelian logic would declare that such a statement is a logically impossible one. But this "logical impossibility" is actually what Zen strives to make us experientially or existentially understand.

3. When a Zen master was asked, "Who is the teacher of all Buddhas and patriarchs?" he answered, "The cat and the dog." How could the dog or the cat be the teacher of all wise men in the world? We generally look at those animals as very much "lower" in every way than ourselves, and what makes the Zen master, above all people, take them for the model of wisdom? What an absurd idea, this! But when we give more time to thinking we will readily find that the greatest spiritual leaders prefer the babes and simple-minded

people to the learned and sophisticated when the issue is concerned with participation in the divine wisdom. The point is that those simple-minded and simple-hearted persons are fresh arrivals from God and hold their being almost completely free from earthly contaminations. They live their whole being just as they did before they left their original homestead. That is to say, their life is thoroughly, sufficiently, and authoritatively their own.

When we observe how the mother cat or dog behaves toward its kitties or puppies, what genuine feeling they exhibit! The mother is really motherly and the little animals are really her children. Each of them in its own way is the whole being, lives its life most genuinely and therefore freely and perfectly. Do we not detect something of absolute significance in their behavior—not necessarily in their outward expressions but in the way they assert themselves from their innermost being? Do not regard them as no more than the "lower" animals; they really make the observer think sincerely of that which moves the whole universe. Nature is not the battlefield for the fittest to survive. The biologist cannot see beyond what appeals to his sense-and-intellect experiences.

What we have to remember in this connection is that we are human beings and not "lower animals." This means that we are endowed with the sense to detect something deeply spiritual in the latter and to reflect on the significance of the thing we have discovered. This sense is really what makes us humans try to be genuinely worthy of our existence.

This applies not only to the dog but to all the so-called lower animals, the lion, deer, cat, bird, cow, snake, and so on. They feel and act, they never reflect, they never dichotomize. Their being is a solid, undivided totality. A Zen master was asked, "When the lion strikes a hare it uses all its power; when it strikes an elephant it uses the same power. What is this totalistic power?" The master answered, "The power of non-deception." Non-deception means sincerity, being true to one's primary nature, not being divided within oneself. It is intellectually an absence of contradiction; morally, sincerity; spiritually, innocence. The Chinese masters are graphic in giving the idea of sincerity or innocence: they would say, "Keep your mind like one solid iron bar ten thousand miles long." This is absolute integrity, with no room for self-deception allowing one tiniest corpuscle of heterogeneous matter or thought. It is knowledge that always gets into the way of totalistic feeling, cutting it into two or three: (1) one who feels, and (2) one that is felt, and (3) then an abstract noun called "feeling." The actual experience is left behind and we talk about it and think that this talk is the real thing.

Thus we see that it is not intellect, not logic, not reason, that governs life. The governing principle comes out of a much deeper source, where neither logic nor intellection can legitimately be sound. The intellect is needed in a certain limited area and not beyond it. When the deeper wisdom is needed, we must seek for it somewhere else than mere ratiocination. The intellect must be controlled by this deeper wisdom.

What is the authentic, directive agency in us? What is that which gives us absolute trust in ourselves and not in others? If the intellect or reason works on the surface of human consciousness within a certain limited area of existence, what is it that works under it, directing its operation to be in harmony with the totality of existence? If it is intellectual discrimination which causes distrust in ourselves by dividing the self into two and making one fight against the other, what is the true and real self? Shakespeare makes Hamlet say, "To be or not to be, that is the question." It is this division that causes Hamlet to be wavering all the time and keeps him from committing an act needed for his ontological integrity. If he could at once "be and not be," the division, and consequently the indecision, would disappear and his self-integrity be preserved.

Self-integrity, or the integration of self in its totalistic phase, in its suchness or emptiness, in its "just-so-ness," is another name for innocence. The integration is the work of the unconscious, which is known as *manas* in Buddhist psychology. *Manas* is self-consciousness, not in its ordinary sense, but as Buddhists have it. Ordinarily, it is the consciousness of self as we grow out of the childish way of thinking and feeling. Buddhists apply the term to our constantly and therefore unconsciously referring all our psychic activities to what I call the cosmic *ālaya-vijñāna*. The *ālaya* is the cosmic psychic storage of infinite potentialities. It is the Godhead psychologically interpreted. I shall not here enter into detailed discussion about this theme. I wish to limit myself to the following points: Zen and the unconscious; conceptualization or abstraction and dynamic concretion, which is act; the animal instinct and innocence and sincerity; knowledge and its transcending; and Zen training.

4. Before I go on, I wish to say a few words about "suchness" (*tathatā*) or isness, or just-so-ness (Japanese, *jinen*)—the term quite frequently greeting students of Far Eastern literature. It not only means "being as it is" spatially but also means dynamically "creative spontaneity." When I state that being is becoming and becoming is being, I mean by being suchness (*tathatā*) or isness, the static or spatial aspect of reality, and by "becoming" spontaneous creative evolution, which is the dynamic or temporal aspect of reality. Reality thus analyzed is the contradiction: "not moving and yet moving," or "to be and not to be," or "A is A and at the same time not-A," "absolute emptiness filled with infinite possibilities." To use Nishida's terminology, Reality or God or Life is "the self-identity of absolute contradiction." Psychologically stated, this is "unconsciously conscious" or "consciously unconscious."

Zen literature is filled with contradictory utterances given by Zen masters of successive generations. To give one or two examples: A master taking out a staff would demand: "Do not call this a staff, nor call it a not-staff: what would you call it?" Another would say: "When you have no staff I will take it away from you; when you have one, I will give you one." Another master would state: "All the mountains are covered white with snow and why is it that there is one solitary peak that is not at all white?" "I am empty-handed and, lo, the spade is in my hands; I am riding horseback and I am walking." The strange thing in all these contradictory statements the Zen masters do not attempt to explain themselves; they just let them alone and make you solve the problem. This is because they know that as soon as they try they will surely involve themselves in absurdities and make a mess of the whole situation. They are on a different level from the one where our ordinary logical mind circulates. Their desire is for us to surmount the limits which the intellect imposes upon us and to discover by our own efforts the domain where the Zen masters enjoy walking. Thus they advise us to give up our precious knowledge, to surrender our logic to which we habitually cling so tenaciously. Life, or Reality, or Emptiness lies very much deeper than the superficial structure of our existence open to intellectual analysis. Life will never yield its secrets to the chemists, or to the biologists, or to the psychologists, or to their combined efforts, however desperately they may attack it with all their ingenuity. Life can be understood only when we live it, only when we are in the midst of it, only when we become Life itself.

5. What Zen proposes to attain in its unique way is to make us dive into the very depths of the Unconscious, which I have called somewhere the cosmic or metaphysical Unconscious, and then rise again into the field of consciousness. This diving, however, is not something distinct from the rising; that is, the diving and rising are not two separate events, but just one act. The diving is the rising. But the very experience of the diving-rising makes the one who actually goes through the event a new personality, for he has now a wider and deeper and richer view of the world and life. He is no more an outsider who stands in the world as a stranger and lives his life as if it were not his own. In a way, he lives like a cow or a lion or a bee. All these creatures live true to their respective natures and have no ambition, no feeling of envy, no greedy, hoarding spirit. The bee gathers honey with no idea of making money; the cow gives milk with no idea of especially making the human baby fat and strong; and the lion roars with no intention of frightening other animals. They do just what their biological necessities demand of them. When this is done, they do not think of doing anything more or less or different in any way. When they are no longer able to adjust themselves to the changing environment, they pass away. They make no complaint, they show no fear, they do not torment themselves by imagining to be other than themselves. They are in this respect quite different from us. But what makes them in a sense superior to us is that they are free in their own way, true to their own nature, content with themselves; above all, they are "innocent." This innocence we lost when we were driven out of the Garden of Eden. And the Zen man strives to recover it with the "knowledge" which we then acquired. To be innocent and yet to be knowing—this is the objective of Zen training, in other words, while retaining and developing the human consciousness in its every phase, at the same time fathoming the depths of the Unconscious or even going beyond it. This is the aim the Zen man is bent upon realizing within himself.

Why does God reveal himself or his truth not to the wise but to the child?

Because the latter's life is simple, whole, and spontaneous, whereas the wise and the learned are conceptual, sophisticated, and always try to see things in some form of dichotomy. They do not see the flowers or fowls simple-mindedly so as not to have any third term between subject and object. To the child, subject and object are one. When it sees the flowers, the latter also see it; it is they and they are it. There is no logical discrepancy between the two terms in one complete, undivided experience. The seeing is not logically or linguistically mediated.

In the world of the child or the animal there is yet no knowledge, no self-consciousness; it is all one where the actor is the act; there is yet no "I" as discriminated from "not-I." One of the modern Western seers tells us that there is in the beginning Act (*Karma*) and not Word (*Logos*). This is a very profound statement, because it is in correspondence with our primary experience. God is reported to have uttered in the beginning of the world, "Let there be light," and this utterance is an act and not a word. There is no conceptualization here but activation—no, the act itself. No discrepancy here of subject and object, but one complete act—God is Light and Light is God.

Let us observe the dog and see how it devours its food. When he is hungry and smells something to eat he goes right to it and finishes it in no time. He asks no question whatever about it. The food was probably meant for somebody else, but this is no concern of his. He takes it for granted that the fact that he is hungry unconditionally entitles him to anything which he knows will satisfy his need at the moment. When finished he goes away. No saying "Thank you." He has asserted his natural rights, no more, no less, and he has nothing further to worry about—not only his being but the entire world around him. He is perfect. The idea of sin is an altogether unnecessary blemish, whether intellectual or moral or spiritual, on his being what he is. He comes directly from God. He might declare as is reported of the Buddha, "I alone am the most honored one on earth." In truth, he does not require any such "ego-centered" statement. It is enough for him just to bark and run away from any sin-conscious human beings who try to do harm to this "innocent" creature still fresh from the Garden of Eden.

Now we shall consider the case of a hungry lion. He is a ferocious wild animal. He has no scruples against attacking a pack of deer peacefully grazing in the field. He will choose a ground of vantage and suddenly rushing into the group pounce upon one which happens to be not quick enough to avoid the enemy. After feeding himself on it, the lion leaves the rest for the jackal to finish. In this he has no vain desire to prove his prowess against the weaker. His biological urge makes him act in the way he naturally displays. He has neither pride nor remorse nor the feeling of anything that he ought not to have done. He is perfectly innocent of all these human feelings. He has absolutely no repentance, as he has no sense of duty and responsibility. He has simply executed what his nature demands. It is too bad for the timid victim which falls as the prey to the ravenous creature. But, from the point of view of the latter, how fortunate he has come across the delicious meat just at the time when his need was absolutely imperative. As long as the world is so constituted and one life subsists on another, it is like a gale passing over a garden, everything in its passage has to give itself to the raging force of Nature. There is here no killer, no killing, no killed. The lion is just as innocent as the atmospheric commotion. If there is anyone who is responsible for all this carnage, the Creator is the one and nobody else. He makes the flowers come to bloom in the spring. How beautiful, and how bountiful! But he is also the one who makes the winds howl over them and rains beat them down mercilessly. Which is the Creator supposed to be, benefactor or destroyer?

6. Now we come to ourselves. How do we behave under the same conditions? The baby is not yet very far from our brother animals such as lions or deer or dogs or cats or frogs or snakes. The baby's clinging to the mother's breast is the same instinctive movement as the lion's pouncing upon the frightened deer, or the dog's not letting go of a piece of bone in his mouth. We may say to the baby, "How touching!" and to the lion, "What savagery!" and to the dog, "Why this clinging?" These are human evaluations, however. As far as the individual creatures concerned go, they have no such ideas; they just feel and act and all is finished, they are ever on the alert to take up what comes next.

The Zen master is asked, "What is Tao (the Way)?" He answers, "Our everyday mind." When he is further asked, "What is that?" he says, "We eat when we are hungry, we drink when we are thirsty." Is this not what the lion and the baby and the dog and other "innocent" beings do? If innocence belongs to Eden, and Eden is the most regrettable place we have ever left behind in our "spiritual progress," the life of the lion or baby–is that not the most enviable state of mind or spirit? Quite logical, reasonable, and justifiable, then, is the Zen master when he informs us that "the cat and the cow are the teacher of Buddhas and patriarchs"?

Christians also may understand where the Zen master is trying to drive us when they recall the saying that God reveals his truth to the babe and not to the wise. For the latter is too sophisticated, too full of "knowledge," too far removed from the state of "innocence." Western people are used to making too sharp a distinction between human beings and the rest of creation–another example of their dualistic way of thinking generally–and for this reason they loathe bringing the biological or, rather, spiritual status of the human baby "down" to the "lower" forms of existence and unreservedly state that the latter has nothing to teach us, the so-called "higher" beings closer to the Creator himself. They forget that the Creator is in every one of us, in every one of his creations, as the artist is in his productions.

7. That "knowledge is sin" is inferable from deeds man practices upon his surrounding objects. Take the case of bird-shooting. The hunter will stealthily approach the game from behind and shoot–the most cowardly behavior a man can imagine. When the old-style shotgun misses the object, he invents shrapnel, so that one of the bursting shells will surely hit it. The lion is hungry

and the deer is sacrificed. But the human hunter is not at all hungry and commits this cowardly deed just for "pleasure." The "lower animals" never kill one another simply because the killing is pleasurable. Their killing is an imperative necessity for self-defense or for some biological impulses which are not calculated, not deliberately planned out. Therefore, when their impulses are fulfilled, they do not dwell on the deed. There is no hate in them, no elation, no showing-off. Momentariness characteristic of innocence is the key to their life. Sin is the outcome of knowledge, which consists in discrimination, and, because of this, time is cut into three: past, present, and future. And then there is memory, recollection, and when this is projected into the future we have eschatology, anticipation, and anxiety.

The biblical saying not to think of the morrow is momentarianism—a philosophical name for innocence. For this reason, the lion as well as the deer and snake are entitled to be residents of Eden, whereas man is decidedly meant for hell. He always sees the reflection of the snake in the cup of knowledge, which has sunk deeply in his Unconscious. He is all the time pursued by its image—the image of guilt—and walks headlong into the opposite side of Paradise.

The Pure Land is the land of innocence, for its residents just act with no purpose projected to the future, with no memory of the past; the present as they live it is all in all. As soon as they feel hungry they find food before them, for desire is action. As soon as they feel hot, a cool breeze is ready to keep them refreshed and utterly comfortable. The feeling waits for no medium, it translates itself straightway to deed. In the *Sūtra of the Pure Land* we read that there are no sufferings of any kind there and therefore that it is known as the land of perfect happiness. "Perfect happiness" is the state of innocence, and sufferings come from knowledge. Where there is the absence of knowledge, there must be the land of perfect happiness and therefore of perfect freedom. Where desire and action are one and there is nothing between them, that must be the state of "non-interference," which is freedom, one of the themes of the Kegon.

In other words, freedom is identification, which means to be itself, to be in the state of as-it-is-ness, of suchness (*tathatā*). To be a pine tree is the truth of the pine tree; when it tries to be a bamboo, it suffers as the desire violates its free nature. The dog barks "bow-wow" and cat cries "miaow," each is in the state of absolute freedom, of innocence. As soon as knowledge enters its mind, the dog desires to cry "miaow" and cat "bow-wow"—which brings all sufferings in its trail—which is hell. Why? Because knowledge breeds the consciousness of the self, and it is this consciousness that breaks up the primary state of identity—innocence—in which we all were in the Garden of Eden. When identity is broken up, discrimination and dichotomization take place in every possible form: A and not-A, yes and no, good and evil, friends and foes, hate and love, past and future, here-now and space-time, etc. The most fundamental form of dichotomy is "I" and not-"I," subject and object. When this gets into one's consciousness, the latter loses its identity and divides itself into two, which means the disappearance of innocence. "I" am no more myself, "I" always stands opposed to "not-I." Deed is separated from its agent, which, reflecting itself on itself, creates a world of opposites. Anything that is done is referred to "I" and "not-I." However much "I" tries to recede to itself and to be all in all by itself, "I" remains opposed to "not-I"—there is always opposition. As long as knowledge asserts itself against innocence as something implying a negation in itself, it is impossible to return to its primary "innocence"; sin can never be wiped off; we, born of "knowledge," are eternally doomed. Goethe's saying that there is in the beginning Act and not Word is a wise one. Act is the paradisiacal innocence.

Engo, great Zen master of the Sung, says: "Even when we refer to 'a beginning' when there was yet no sign of something moving, it is not at all the first—we are already on the second stage. When we say a division has taken place, we are now on the third stage. As to those who cling to words and try thereby to get into the meaning, they are utterly unable to find anything in them." Language is knowledge, knowledge is language, the two are inseparable. When "I" expresses itself as "I"—which is language and is conceptualized—there is no more Eden; a world of innocent acts is forever lost. Inasmuch as we thus face the "expulsion," we are sinners. "I" is the root of all sins, and we human beings have no chance for salvation.

In order to exist, we eat; eating is our primary act. Now, compare our way of eating to the canine way. Our eating is no more eating pure and simple; see how we start and continue: first, we eat not because it is imperative for us—we are not so very hungry—but we sit at the table, and observe what is brought before us, and all kinds of imagination begin to go on in all directions.

It is altogether different from the way our brother animal eats. The dog does not say anything about the food before him. If he likes it, being hungry, he just eats it with no comments whatever. No ambiguities, no equivocations; his eating is simple and straight and clear-cut—its whole being is the act.

Daishu, a disciple of Baso, says: "Most people do not eat, they are given to imagining all kinds of things. The Zen man just eats, drinks, sleeps, works, and so on." Another master would say: "Do not let your mind move from one thing to another, do not let it wander about, but let it go on uniformly undisturbed. Have no 'thoughts,' have no 'mind,' be 'everyday-minded.' " All these remarks point to the state of innocence which we had while still residing in Eden. It was a great mistake on the part of the Creator who kept one particularized object in the Garden and told the inhabitants not to touch it, not to eat it, to have nothing to do with it. This particularization is the root of all evils. Because here lies the origin of knowledge. Knowledge once awakened, the whole scheme of the world goes through transformation, endlessly. "Suchness" is no more, "emptiness" is all gone, there is no "yes" unqualified as before, it now comes along with "no," a world of dichotomies sets in. The sense of sin or guilt grows up among human beings. They have been doing the same things in Eden which after the awakening of "knowledge" turn into sinful deeds destined for hell. Hell is thus really a human creation.

In the age of innocence we live as actors and not as knowers. The actors act in unison with the universe, they are in it, they are it. When knowledge comes in, the actors are separated from the totality of things, and there starts a world of dualities. "I" stands over against "not-I." Thus separated, "I" as knower begins its new life wedging itself in everywhere, in every possible way, and the discrimination so created makes us forget the source we come from. As knowledge succeeds within limits, temporal as well as spatial, it deceives itself and behaves as if it had infinite potentialities within itself. It is this self-deception or self-illusion that leads us to every form of intellectual contradiction, moral tragedy, and spiritual deformity.

8. In Japan, we have a seventeen-syllable form of poem, which, though short indeed, is very expressive of our poetic appreciation of Nature. It significantly contrasts with the Western form. The longer the form, the more intellectual and the less "poetical" grow the contents. The seventeen-syllable style called *haiku* in Japanese is wonderfully communicative of the primary feeling evoked by things beautiful in Nature as well as in human relationship.

The one I wish to quote in order to illustrate the poetic appreciation of the just-so-ness of Nature is a *haiku* by Chiyo (1702–1775), the renowned poetess of Kaga:

Asagao ya,	*Oh, Morning-glory!*
Tsurube torarete	*Bucket being made captive*
Morai mizu.	*I beg for water.*

Living in the countryside, the poetess one morning in June or July got up early to draw water from the well in her yard. She happened to see the morning-glory twining around the bucket. The flowers were in full bloom, probably sprinkled with a few drops of dew. They were so beautiful that there was something of holiness about them. She did not feel like touching them, much less removing the vines and releasing the bucket from their hold. "Oh, Morning-glory!" was all that she could utter. She even failed to add any commentary words. She was so taken by the glorious outburst of Nature that I imagine she must have stood there for a while before she was able to give vent to her emotion. After the utterance, it dawned on her that her morning mission was to get water for her everyday household chores. As she could not think of doing anything to defile the object of beauty, she went to the neighbor and begged for water. Thus the seventeen-syllable poem came into existence.

At the moment of ecstasy, there was no poetess, no morning-glory, just one something which defies any attempt at description. Chiyo and the flowers were one: Chiyo went into the flower and the flower went into the poetess. This mutual participation was possible because of their coming from the same source, which you may call God, or Nature, or the Reason of Heaven and Earth, or Reality, or the Dharmakāya, or Suchness, or Emptiness, or Buddha-nature. There is a multiplicity of names for it. Yes, Chiyo and the morning-glory are identified in this, but we must not forget that, with all this, the poetess is not to lose her individuality, nor is the morning-glory to lose its own being. The feeling of identity is possible only when there is the fact of individuation, and we can speak of participation only when there is the experience of identity. This may sound somewhat self-contradictory, but all such irrationalities are solved in our actually living a life of just-so-ness. The feeling is concrete and synthetic while the thinking is abstract and analytical.

This totalistic primary experience or feeling of identity of contradiction is what Zen masters mean by the sense of just-so-ness or simply of suchness. Somewhere, I have called it the *myō* appreciation of life as we live it in our daily life. This feeling comes out of the innermost depths of our being or nature, which is also the nature or "reason" of heaven and earth or reality itself. It is man, however, who has developed the capacity of becoming conscious of this fact, alone among the ten thousand things making up heaven and earth. Man is thus the most privileged being, but at the same time it is man who would abuse this privilege in a most wanton way. There is no doubt that man is partly an angel and partly a devil.

In the animal and vegetable world, where there is yet no development of consciousness, as soon as they "feel" they act, and there is no time for them to reflect, to deliberate, to calculate; everything is immediate with them. As they have no medium between feeling and acting, they are straightforward, that is, they are sincere in every way. It is different with man. He is conscious of his feeling, and this consciousness gives him time to think about his next movement. He thinks before he acts. It is this thinking that makes him insincere—he is always calculating and this calculation always centers around his ego. Ego-centralism, thus created and nurtured, keeps its author away from his fellow beings. When this separatism is not brought under the control of a wider totalistic view of life, it spells the ruination of the whole universe. The totalistic view, so called, of life arises from the original primary feeling of identity.

Those who are used to the separatist or dualistic view of life or existence generally cling to the idea that what governs the universe is outside it, that there is an agent specifically to be so designated, apart from things particularized. According to them, the *myō* appreciation of Nature in its just-so-ness arises from our capacity to put ourselves in the objective situation and to participate in its working. But we must remember, as I said before, that participation is possible only when the object and the subject are one in possession of the same character which is found in both of them. Otherwise, no participation can take place. When the two are absolutely disparate and there is nothing between them for mutual relationship, we cannot talk of any kind of participation. The *myō* feeling on our side is no other than our discovery of the mutuality or identity that lies hidden in the infinitely diversifying process of individuation. The just-so-ness of my being, when it is truly grasped, is found to coincide with the just-so-ness of the object that lies before us. In the case of Chiyo, the poetess, her being-so-ness went into the being-so-ness of the morning-glory, and, when the encounter took place, the poetess, being endowed with human feeling, was struck with something which she had never had before.

The morning-glory, with no sentiency, remained mute, but when the poetess uttered, "Oh, Morning-glory!" the latter joined her and expressed itself in the utterance. This is not participation but the experience of identity. In other words, it is the revelation of the divine nature which makes each of the so-called participants what it is—the morning-glory as morning-glory and the poetess as poetess. "The participation" is not only on the side of Chiyo with a sensitive heart but also on the side of the morning-glory. This identification is, no doubt, the experience of mutual understanding and appreciation, the one silently and the other vocally. The silent one speaks itself by means of the human voice, especially that of the poet. It is the mission of the latter to give expression to the mystery of being and to make his fellow beings become acquainted with it. In fact, we are all poets when we are simple-hearted and "everyday-minded," for thus we see into the depths of reality as it is and God reveals his secrets unreservedly to our hearts.

9. It was Lao Tzu, the great philosophical seer, who first, before the introduction of Indian culture through Buddhism, made the Far Eastern people informed about Nature in its just-so-ness (*jinen*). Lao Tzu, as we know him in the *Tao-te ching,* might not have been a historical personage, but this does not affect the truth we come across in the book known by his name. We read in Chapter XXV:

There is a something even before the heaven-and-earth came into existence. It is in the state of totalistic unity. How quiet! How lonely! It exists all by itself with no signs of becoming. [Yet] it prevails everywhere and is in no danger of exhausting itself. It is worthy of being known as Mother of all things under the Heaven.

I fail [to know] how to designate it. Provisionally, I may call it the Way (Tao). It defies all forms of qualification. Shall I define it as the Great, meaning thereby its endlessly flowing, its furthest-reaching, and its ever-returning [to its source]?

As the Tao is great, so is Heaven, so is Earth, so is Royalty. [Thus] there are four Greats in the world, including Royalty.

Man is Earth when he models himself thereafter, man is Heaven when he models himself thereafter, man is Tao when he models himself thereafter, and Tao is what is in its just-so-ness.

The following is a more intelligible paraphrase of the text:

Before the world came into existence as it is now with all its multitudinous objects—each in its suchness, in its just-so-ness—there was a something. This something exists all by itself, quietly in its absolute solitariness. It has no equals, it stands all by itself, and shows no signs of becoming. There are no indications whatever for its changing into something else. It is absolutely one, in another word, Emptiness itself. Yet, it contains in itself infinite possibilities, thus becoming Mother of all possible things. It is creativity itself, the source of inexhaustible virtues (*te*).

The Tao is to be called "Great," which means that it knows no magnitudes of any nature. It is the infinite, not just a static totality, but dynamically moving to its furthest ends, which are really no-ends in any direction. As the movement is infinitely far-reaching, it is ever returning to its source. That is to say, it never forgets where it starts. In other words, it never becomes, it never changes, it remains the same. It is dynamic and at the same time static. It can be symbolized: $O = \infty$, $\infty = O$. The zero is the fullness of infinite virtues or potentialities, and, conversely, infinite potentialities are the zero itself. In terms of Buddhist philosophy, form (*rūpa*) is emptiness (*śūnyatā*), and emptiness is form.

When Lao Tzu says that Tao is great, that means infinity, that is, Tao is the infinite. There are four infinites: Tao, Heaven, Earth, and Royalty or Man. And they are all one, each in its holding infinite virtues (*te*) in itself. Thus they are altogether One Great Infinite: Tao = Heaven = Earth = Man; and this Identity is their just-so-ness.

Coming back to Chiyo, the poetess, she encounters the morning-glory in the early morning when the flower is at the height of its glory, somewhat wet with a few drops of dew, and she is at once awakened to its beauty which is no other than the beauty in her own being. Deep calls to deep, one beauty meets another, and the consciousness of this identification makes the poetess utter, "Oh, Morning-glory!" This is not a case of participation but of identification, because here is a perfect unobstructed mutuality between the two. *Myō* is the name I give to this mystical and mysterious state of human consciousness thus brought to light. Chiyo, being an artist, gave the literary touch to her seventeen-syllable poem when she made reference to her rather prosaic business in the morning. Even this daily chore, however, betrays the mystery of just-so-ness as Pang, the Zen Layman of the eighth century, sings:

How divine!
How mysterious!
This, water-drawing,
This, fuel-carrying.

God gave his name to Moses at Mount Sinai as "I am that I am." This is on the part of God no other than confirming the mystery of being. The divine mystery consists in being-just-so, retaining his suchness (*tathatā*) in the midst of all becoming. The multitudinosity of things does not disturb the emptiness of the Godhead; he remains absolutely serene and unmolested by all the hurly-burlies of our daily life, which also include, let me remind you, all the international commotions at present most annoyingly going on around us.

10. The main trouble with intellectualized people—and to this class we all belong—is that they think that thinking comes first and then experience and that thinking must therefore govern experience instead of vice versa. The result is that anything contradicting our ways of thinking has no right to exist—in

fact, whatever contradicts our thinking is non-existent. Strange, they are altogether forgetful of the reality of things as they are. What Zen does is to teach such thinkers or, rather, to remind them of the fact that the reality is just the reverse and that therefore we ought to reform the ways of thinking first so that they will conform to the just-so-ness of our everyday experiences. With us, abstraction comes first and then the concreteness of things, while the just-so-ness of reality is no other than its concreteness.

William James, one of America's great philosophers, tells us about "pure experience," and most of us take it for an experience shorn of all its contents and left to itself, pure and simple, that is, something of abstraction, with its existence in thought only. They fail to recognize the concreteness of pure experience, which lies actually and factually at the basis of all our experiences of whatever kind. I do not know very much about James's own presentation of the concept. From the Zen point of view, pure experience is not a contentless and highly abstracted notion invented to explain our conscious life. It is not the outcome of intellectualization, but the statement of a fact in its just-so-ness or in its suchness or isness. Chiyo's uttering "Oh, Morning-glory!" is such an experience. Buddha's exclamation "I alone am the most honored one in the whole universe!" is another. Such ejaculations run through the philosophy of Zen, and the masters request us to understand them.

From the Zen point of view, there is Zen in Chiyo's absorption in the beauty of the morning-glory, and also there is Zen in her reference to the asking for water because of the entwining plant in bloom. As Pang, the Layman of Zen, declares, there is a mystery or divine glory in conveying the fuel or water into the kitchen for one's daily use; there is also something of this mysterious revelation in Chiyo's "chore." In cleaning the floor, in washing dishes, there is as much display of *myō* as in the blooming vine. Chiyo, however, was a poet of Nature and wished to make ordinary men look away for a while from the humdrum of their daily living, which generally moves on the plane of relativity and limitation. With Zen, the just-so-ness of things is revealed everywhere, not only in Nature but in human affairs. It is unfortunate that we are intellectually tainted so as not to see the divine beauty in things everywhere betraying their "naturalness" or "just-so-ness." It is "knowledge" that veils the paradisiac "innocence" or primitive artlessness which is still everywhere perceptible when the scale drops from our organ of sight.

III.

1. The primary feeling of the just-so-ness or suchness of things as they come to everyday-mindedness or to our ordinary life of experience constitutes the awakening of Zen consciousness. There is nothing abstract in this. Everything presents itself in the most concrete fashion, because it is the living itself; there is no intermediation of anything. As intellection is excluded, there is no problem of the logicalness of things. We live contradictions. What Zen aims at in its training of the human mind is to make it become conscious of this fact.

Whatever ratiocination we feel we must have in our life comes later, operating on what we have already been experiencing. If we think we cannot live contradictions it is our own reasoning that is first to be improved or remodeled so that our experience may not be interfered with. The order must not be reversed. If we make living come after thinking, that is in fact murdering ourselves. When we are rationally arranging our experiences, we are really depriving ourselves of whatever creativity we have within us. This is indeed the source of all the ills we moderns are suffering from. If people say we cannot live contradictions, we must try to do away with "contradictions" first and not with "living." The former is our creation and the latter is "given." Living really goes on serenely undisturbed, undistracted, even when we agitatingly call "halt!" because of intellectual controversies. Philosophers and literary critics and other workers in the outside field of objectivity give all kinds of names to those Zen-men who "live" the just-so-ness of things. It is in fact the philosophers themselves who are thus mentally or psychically upset and assailed by every form of malady.

It is thus important in the study of Zen to know that pure experience is not the outcome of intellectually analyzing the operation of our consciousness, but that it constitutes the very basis of the marvelous structure of "contradictions" or "absurdities" or "nonsensicalness" or "purposely misleading enigmatic paradoxes," which Zen is said to have built up during its long history in China and Japan. It is the very beginning of Zen knowledge and not the end it has reached after elaborate scholarly conceptualization. The utterance of Buddha regarding his absolute dignity, for instance, has nothing to do with his intellectual life. It is an utterance every one of us can give or is giving in every moment of our humble life, to which the Buddha has simply given vent in his individualistic way. This notion of honor is most innerly rooted in every one of us. No amount of sophistry or reasoning can efface the sense of moral dignity or value from our deepest consciousness.

Biologically or karmically speaking, no individual called "I" ever desired to assume his present status of existence. As far as this individual is concerned, as viewed thus, he has no moral responsibility whatever for his being "here and now" and calling himself "John" or "George." He is just as he is in spite of himself. This being an uncontestable matter of fact, his criminality or his anti-sociality or his saintly disposition—if he has any—has nothing to do with his "freedom of will." He is like a piece of rock or a block of wood; he may be kicked around, or he may be prized as something highly precious; he is neither good nor bad, he is entirely devoid of moral or spiritual values. In spite of all this, however, he hates or resents being so regarded and put aside unconcernedly. Why is this so with every one of us?

The feeling of personal dignity or moral responsibility, there is no doubt, comes ahead of logical reasoning or scientific inferences. Whatever one may say about the intellect, it cannot touch our inner feeling lying deep within us; it must take a second seat and await what the feeling will dictate. For this reason, we are far from being merely logical or scientific or impersonal or abstractly conceptual. Some philosophers do not seem to be conscious of this contradiction on their part. They say we must be consistent, logic must be supreme. But we, including those who are persistent advocates of intellectual consistency, refuse to be so treated. For even they loathe to turn into mere bundles of logically tenable propositions. This means that the logicalness of the doctrine of necessity or the impersonal karmic sequence of things or events is in direct opposition to the fact and the truth of the inner sense of absolute freedom. Thus, we are and yet are not. Logically stated, "A" is at once "A" and "not-A." We stand in the midst of the crossroads, and for this very reason we are free to turn in any direction we are innerly inspired to. If we are constituted entirely logically or intellectually, we may not know how to move, and if we at all try to move we may be doomed to be crushed under the wheels of the madly running car.

Zen knows better: in Zen there is no *karma,* no necessity, no objectivity, no contradiction, no abstraction, no scientific or logical necessity. Zen goes its own way, for it has its own Eden to walk about, to live on "innocently" with all its snakes and "forbidden fruits" growing rampantly, and also with multitudes of tempting Eves, wantonly dancing and hopping.

2. To go back, Zen starts with pure experience, concrete and full of content. To Zen, it is not an abstract idea reached after a great deal of analysis and abstraction. The logical process is reversed. What seems to be a logical culmination is Zen's starting point and at the same time the terminus. "I" is Zen's alpha and omega, it is the *Aum* with Zen. Philosophers ask, What is "I"? What is Reality? After much discoursing they come to the conclusion and say, It is "undifferentiated aesthetic continuum," or an "information processing communication system," or the "psychoidal protoself." Each of these definitions may have its own merit. When all is said, however, they amount to this: An apple is a red-colored round fruit. As to the whatness of the actual living apple lying before us, we have not learned anything. The so-called objective description of the fruit, however exactly and minutely analyzed in every possible manner, fails to touch the reality of appleness, that is, the just-so-ness of the fruit.

Let me cite a few examples given by the Zen masters of the T'ang in order to show how ungraspable, how unattainable, how unintelligible, how intellectually baffling they are. And, what is more, they urge you to get into the midst of the thickest fog of unattainability (*anupalabdha*) and find the way to orientation all by yourself. In fact, there is no way to orientation. If there is such a thing it is no longer Zen. The just-so-ness of unattainability is to identify yourself with it, for it is only when this identification is effected that the very truth of the unattainable is attained as such, as just so, and no question is asked, no answer is given; you are simply content with yourself. If the logician approaches you and announces that you have altogether lost your mind, you would never attempt to refute him; you would merely nod and say, "Yes,

yes." The transcendental realm will never be reached by those who have not been able to exhaust all their intellectual resources to come to the ultimate reality of just-so-ness. Because this is the realm of "pure experience" where "I" stands in all nakedness shorn of every possible conceptual wrapping. Let the readers notice that in Zen there is nothing that will lead you to abstract reasoning.

When Bodhidharma came to China from India in the sixth century to propagate the Zen form of Buddhism, as is legendarily recorded, he happened to meet a learned scholar called Shinkō (Shen-kuang), who was versed in Taoism as well as Confucianism. He wished to be instructed in the new teaching of Buddhism. Bodhidharma said, "Buddhism is not to be taught by others, you have to discover it within yourself." Shinkō, however, pleaded, "My mind is not pacified, and will you be gracious enough to pacify it?" Bodhidharma bluntly said, "Bring it out before me and it will be pacified." "I have been in search of it these many long years and find it altogether unattainable." "There!" Bodhidharma declared, "I have your mind pacified!"

However much one may try to take hold of it conceptually, the mind always proves to be elusive, to be utterly ungraspable. That is to say, it cannot be pinned down as this or that. One may give it all kinds of names or definitions with every possible combination of abstract phrases, but it drops off from the finely woven meshes of terminology. For it is something that cannot be made captive by means of conceptualization, that is, by means of language. And this very fact of its being utterly intangible is the very point at which the mind allows itself to be grasped. Its ungraspability is where one can lay one's hands on it. But we must remember that as soon as we say we have it it is no more there—it is "flown away." To have it, therefore, is not to have it, and not to have it is to have it. Or, it may be better to say that we have it by not having it. Logically speaking, if there is something at all to be called logical, we can say that here is the case of identity of absolute contradiction because to have it and not to have it, or its converse, is an absolutely existential experience.

When Bodhidharma was about to die, he had his pupils come together and he asked them to tell him how they understood his teaching. The first one said, "According to my view, not to be bound by language in either way, positive or negative, is the way Tao (*bodhi*) works." Bodhidharma said, "You have my skin." The second one, who happened to be a nun, came up and said, "According to my understanding, it is like Ānanda's seeing the land of Akṣobya: the whole thing presents itself all at once and never for a second time." Bodhidharma said, "You have my flesh." The third one gave this statement, "The four elements are empty from the very first, and the five *skandhas* (groups of elements making up personality) have never been in existence. According to my view, there has not been any *dharma* (object) to be taken as such." "You have my bones," was Bodhidharma's verdict. The last one, Eka (Hui-k'o), alias Shinkō, rose from his seat and folding his hands before his chest stood up before the master without uttering a word. Bodhidharma said, "You have my marrow, and I hand you all the secret treasures there are in my teaching."

If comments are necessary, I give this: There are no secrets whatever here, because everything is exposed in full view. We have here the suchness or just-so-ness of ultimate reality, Jehovah's "I am that I am," Christ's "I am before Abraham was"; it is the biblical God (or rather Godhead) as he is before he gave his fiat, "Let there be light." But let me remind you further that Eka's standing before Bodhidharma is not all there is in Zen, for it has something more as is illustrated in the following transactions:

Hyakujo (Pai-chang), who is the founder of the Zen monastery, was once asked by a monk, "What is the most wonderful event?" The master said, "I sit alone here on the peak of Mount Daiyu (Mahāvīra)." Thereupon the monk bowed, and the master struck him.

The same Hyakujo, while attending his master Baso (Ma-tsu), noticed the latter picking up his *hossu* (a kind of duster). Hyakujo asked, "Is [it] this action itself? or separable from this?" Baso put the *hossu* back where he took it from. After remaining silent for a while, Baso said, "What would you do when you wish to help others by opening your lips?" Hyakujo took the *hossu* and lifted it up. Baso said "Is [it] this action itself, or separable from this?" Hyakujo put it back in its former place. Thereupon Baso uttered a *"Kāts!"* in a most powerful manner. By this it is said that Hyakujo's ears lost their functions for three days.

Some think this striking or uttering a nonsensical cry is something peculiarly Zen. Others go further and declare them to be giving a kind of psychological shock. The only remark I can make in this connection is that most critics of Zen are sadly at fault. I ask them to take the subject here at issue for their quiet study.

After reading this over once more I feel like adding the following remarks on three points:

1. When Eka (that is, Shinkō) confessed that he could not take hold of "the mind," he did not do this searching along the intellectual line of conceptualization. He simply did not know which way to turn, in which direction his groping would be kept up; he was at the end of his wits, as it were. His mental condition was that of Buddha after his six long years' search for the *Ātman,* or something he could not name. They both poured out whatever energy they had in their being; that means that they had to throw away whatever they could take hold of within and without themselves as their own. This is the state of an impasse in which the expurgation reaches its limits and the totality of their being is given up or, rather, gives out due to sheer exhaustion. All traces of intellection are cleared out, all emotional motivation of egocentricity is wiped off. This is the state of "unattainability." As every piece of the crust is fallen off, the kernel alone, which is no kernel, is left behind, and this is called "sincerity," or "suchness," or "just-so-ness," or "the heavenly reason," or "the primary energy." The most favorite name given to it by Buddhist philosophers is "Emptiness," which is filled with infinite potentialities. All this is in the realm of concrete experience, and thus the "unattainability of

the mind" is a matter of existential occurrence. For this reason when Bodhidharma gave his verdict, "I have your mind pacified!" Eka was prepared to understand its meaning fully.

2. In the *mondō* (*wen-ta*) which is recorded to have taken place between Baso and Hyakujo, there is a reference to the "action" first displayed by Baso and later by Hyakujo, in the disposition of the *hossu*. The actual wording is *chi tz'u yung, li tz'u yung,* literally, "Attached to this action, separated from this action." No subject is given. What is attached to and what is separated from in the disposition of the *hossu*? To make the meaning intelligible, the subject "it" is to be supplied, but what does the "it" stand for? The *mondō* is really carried on around the "it." Is "it" no other than the action itself? Or something apart from the action? Conceptually stated, there is one who handles the *hossu,* and there is the object moved from one position to another, and finally there is the action which is enacted between the subject and the object. According to the Buddhist way of thinking generally, all these three are considered to be of Emptiness. If so, where is the "it" to be referred to? It is nonsense to talk about its "being attached to" or "to be separated from," that is, there is no room for logic to enter, no point to make any sort of statement about, positive or negative, confirmative or non-confirmative. This is another form of unattainability. How, then, comes Baso's *"Kāts!"*?

"Emptiness" is not another name for inanity or mere vacuity. It is full of creative potentiality. The spring breeze issues from it, the ocean-tossing hurricane bursts out of it. The explosive atomic galaxies which shake the foundations of the cosmos also have their rest here. Baso's *"Kāts!"*—straight from the bosom of Being—is where nothing is except the primordial urge to express itself. It must then be "the reason of heaven and earth" itself. It is really the sound produced by the *ālayavijñāna* (storehouse of ideas) which goes through its final explosion. In fact, it is not only Hyakujo but the entire universe that was deafened thereby. It is still ringing in our ears even now.

3. The reader by this time will have realized where Zen differs from parapsychology or depth psychology, in fact from any sort of psychology. Zen includes psychology and all other sciences, but none of the latter can subsume Zen. Zen is a unique discipline. When it is understood, all the rest fall in. The reason is that Zen is an experience every one of us will have when he comes to the end of his conceptual search after Reality or the Self. It comes to us in its just-so-ness or in its absolute nakedness. I like to call this kind of experience by another name than intuition or direct perception. It is a kind of feeling in its most primal sense to which self-knowledge is added in such a way that the union is perfect and thoroughgoing, thereby forming the equation:

Śūnyatā = *prajñā* + *karuṇā*

Śūnyatā is Emptiness (O), and out of this O we have *prajñā* ("super-knowledge") and *karuṇā* (compassion or love), which is infinity (∞).

S. RADHAKRISHNAN

The Present Crisis of Faith

Just this afternoon somebody said history is not made by the tumult and uproar but it is made in silence by changes in the minds of men. In this great task of transforming human minds this University has done a great deal. A university's function is to conserve the past and advance into the future. Universities must recognize whatever is valuable in the past and also bring about an adjustment of the human spirit to the changing conditions. Ever so many conditions have altered in our own time.

Today if I speak about the crisis of faith I am not saying that the crisis is something which we will not be able to face. But it is something which we will have to recognize, if the unity of the world is to be established.

I may briefly say that our age is characterized by three important features: the rebirth of Asia, I would say, the eagerness of the oppressed millions of the world to have a better kind of life, and, most important of all, the startling developments in nuclear physics. These characterize the fundamental changes that have taken place. Life cannot remain the same as before. The discovery of fire, of the wheel, of the application of steam to machinery, or electricity to industry, the internal combustion engine—have all brought about changes, but all of them fade into insignificance when we take into account the development of nuclear energy. It gives us the possibility of feeding all the people of the world and of enabling us to live in this world as members of a family of nations. But at the same time it throws on us the great responsibility by which we have to adjust ourselves to the new conditions, if we are not to cease to exist. This adjustment requires an alteration of certain fundamental historical positions we have hitherto adopted.

For one thing, power politics has become outworn, out of date. The military approach to the settlement of problems is no longer feasible if humanity is to survive, if it is not to commit suicide. It is essential, therefore, that in the settlement of international disputes we should try to adopt a non-military approach and not a military one. Again, as the inscription on the Founders' Gate at your University proclaims, "Above all nations is humanity." We have worked with nationalistic ideas. The peoples of the world in the East and in the West have adopted that as a guiding principle for centuries. The Chinese thought they were the elect of the world. We thought our culture was the measuring rod of civilization. The British thought that the two hemispheres revolved around Eton and Harrow, Oxford and Cambridge, and Cheltenham, sometimes. A nineteenth-century visitor to the Middle West, here, was told that Chicago is the "Boss City" of the universe. And, there are people who still think that all roads lead to Rome, except the one from Moscow. There are chosen people, we are the chosen, the Indians, the Chinese, the Jews, the Americans, the British. We have adopted such ideas. Nationalism has distorted our vision, has engendered false pride in us, and given us all sorts of sentimental ideas. But we have come to a time when nationalism is not enough, when we have to adopt a more humane and universal attitude.

The trouble, again, is that these scientific developments have unfortunately bought about a sort of impression that human beings are helpless victims of impersonal forces, that it is not in our hands to mold the future of history, that there is more in the force of events than in the mind of the participants in this great historic struggle. We don't realize, nowadays, under the domination of science, that human beings have also got it in their power to mold the future; between a civilized and an uncivilized society the difference is just here, that a civilized society adopts a creative molding of environment, whereas a static society passively submits to the environment. So, we have to give up this idea that we are at the mercy of history, that we are in the grip of forces much more powerful than our own hopes, fears, and aspirations.

Here are three ideas which we have to give up: the militaristic approach, the nationalist sentiment, and a feeling of helplessness on the part of the human individual. These three things will have to be abandoned if humanity is to make any real progress. But, the tendency to cling to the past is there. The fight today, or the crisis today, is that between the old and the new. It has always been with us, and this fight is full of pain. All growth belongs to the realm of tragedy. We have to give up great ideas which have served us in the past and turn a new leaf. Unless we are able to do it, we will not be able to make any kind of progress. So it is that there is a conflict in the minds of people, between the old and the new, when we talk about St. George killing the dragon. St. George's Christian virtue frightened pagan vicars. When we talk today of the conflict which is raging in men's souls, the hero is the new order, the new international order, which will have the rule of law, which will have the authority to enforce its decisions, while all nations will be able to develop themselves unfettered by other nations. That is the new order; the old order is the order of power politics. While we are engaged in maneuvers, in bargaining, while nationalism itself has assumed an ideological disguise, the fight still continues under other forms. The dragon is in the seat of power. It is the tyrant that we have to overcome. The hero is the new individual, the new man who will be able to fight the enemies within himself: stupidity, folly, clinging to the past, non-recognition of the fact that the world is moving and he who doesn't move will be swept aside. It is that, that is the problem or the crisis which we now face. In all such crises, when we have in our minds a complex about baseness and nobility, patriotism and universalism, these impulses are there.

Till the other day we looked to religion to discipline our passions, to make us integrated individuals, to enable us to overcome the evil by the good in us. That is what we have turned to in all our previous predicaments of a similar situation, though none of the previous situations can compare with the colossal task, with the challenge of destiny, which is today facing us.

Unfortunately, however, religion itself is on the way out. The other day, I read in your *Time* magazine the results of a Gallup poll taken of 2000 young men and women between the years of 18 and 29. The result was that 79% of the people believed in the Bible, but 77% of that number admitted that they had never read the Bible. This is not peculiar to America. This is a feature which we find all over the world today. Everywhere societies are becoming industrialized. Science and technology are becoming universal. New sets of value are springing up and people are asking themselves whether they can cling to the traditional faiths as they came down to them. Science, and the spirit of science, tell them that it is not possible for us to accept incredible dogmas or supernatural miracles or magical rites. We are narrowing the field of the unknown. More and more of it is getting known. Therefore it is not possible for us any longer to believe in that mysterious reality which our ancestors took for granted. Such a faith is becoming unnatural to many people, I don't say to all, to many people in our present world.

Another charge that has been leveled against religion is that it has condoned practices which are repugnant to the conscience of man. Early last year I had the chance of attending a conference at the Mormon Tabernacle in Salt Lake City. From 9:30 to 10 there was a coast-to-coast broadcast there. When it was over, Mr. David O. McKay, President of the Mormon Church, turned and asked me: "Won't you say a few words?" I had heard the last hymn, a Negro spiritual, which asked: "Were you there when they crucified the Lord? Were you there when they laid him in the tomb?" I said, "It is not necessary for us to raise a hypothetical question whether we were there 2000 years ago, but we are here today when we are crucifying the Lord. He is being crucified on the cross of racial discrimination, national bigotry, suppression of nationalities, etc." We are here when we are entombed by our own stupidity and selfishness. Ever so many atrocities are perpetrated in the name of religion in the East and in the West. In both hemispheres, religion has been exploited by people for the perpetuation of inequities and injustices. It's nothing peculiar to this continent or any other continent.

There is a third difficulty which many of us today feel with regard to religion. It has become a dividing force, like the nation-State. In a nation-State we believe, unless we have risen above the battle of nations, we believe that whoever belongs to us is good whatever his character may be; whoever does not belong to us is an alien, a stranger and an enemy. So, also, in religions, whoever belongs to my religion, whether he is good, bad, or indifferent, is good. But whoever belongs to another religion, well, he may be good, but still he has not got the whole virtue about him. We are getting into a world which is becoming universal. In a universal society we would like to have, not a common religion, but a religion which avoids spiritual ambiguity and confusion, but which at the same time respects all traditions which have helped their people to get to their own professed aims.

So you'll see that religion is condemned by people as unscientific, as unethical, as intolerant, exclusive and provincial in character, and not appropriate for the new society which we are attempting to build. I may say immediately that this charge-sheet against religion is not one which we can accept. It only means that we have to re-think some of our postulates. It asks us to make religion grounded in the realities of the new world. It asks us to see that the religion we adopt is something which is commendable to the spirit of reason, which is consistent with the findings of science. It's no use for scientific people to tell us that anything which is not observed empirically is untrue. That very proposition gives you a statement of philosophy for which there is no empirical verification. Again, you will find that it is not possible for you to have empirical verification of even ultimate scientific doctrines like the Quantum Theory. You judge their validity by the empirical consequences which you can calculate and forecast. And, if those consequences verify those theories themselves, you accept them. Similarly, science does not lead us to the conception that matter is everything. Science reveals to us a cosmic process where there has been a progressive unfoldment of ideas and values. While men have developed from their animal minds into human cunning and while a few people have transformed that human cunning into spiritual insight, and science itself reveals to us that the final consummation of the world is the transformation of the whole of humanity into such spiritual beings—when we say we wish to establish the kingdom of spirit all that we mean is man today is a highly equipped scientific intellectual being who has to grow into something higher. But we feel that man's growth has not come to an end. Man himself is an instrument of the evolutionary urge. He can develop from the intellectual to the spiritual level. And there have been cases in the history of humanity where human beings have transformed themselves into a species of spiritual beings. Socrates, Buddha, Jesus, and ever so many more apostles of spirit are there pointing out that what is possible for such individuals is also possible for the whole human race. They are the people who tell us that the end of evolution is not yet. What happened hitherto by instinctive or automatic processes must hereafter be achieved by conscious purpose and by deliberate effort. The scientist does not tell us that man is an automaton, that he is a mere reflex of society, or a set of mass reactions. He tells us that it is possible for the spirit in man to overcome circumstance to penetrate Nature, to get into the heart of it and increase our knowledge. In scientific advance there is the manifestation of the living spirit in the scientist, which is not a mere product of Nature, unless you look upon Nature as something more comprehensive than the mere space-time world of Nature, unless you believe that the spiritual in man is also a part of Nature, unless you affirm that there is a subject in man who cannot be merely reduced to an object, to a mere item in the series of objective happenings that take place. The moment you reduce the subject to an object you reduce him to unthinkingness, mindlessness, rigidity, routine; he ceases to be something beyond the natural processes of which he is also the outcome.

There is in man, besides Nature, what you may call the Super-Nature. Any cosmic survey will have to take into account the reality of this something which goes beyond mere Nature. Otherwise, life would have been mere vegetation and not history. We would have led our lives by pure animal instinct and not by intelligence. The very fact that civilization has made such tremendous progress and that we are now facing the present world-challenge—even that shows that we do have faith in ourselves. If only we adjust our minds to the new world we can reform society and the world. The vision of the prophets and the philosophers that we are one family is no longer a pious hope, is not a mere remote ideal, but is something which is within practical possibilities. Science it is that tells us that the wondrous character of the human subject can penetrate the mysteries of the world of Nature. He is able to do it simply because there is the spirit in him which cannot be equated, so to speak, with a mere natural product. That is why we believe, and all scientists believe, excepting a few here and there—they all believe that, when we look at the cosmic process, its perpetual progression from matter to life, life to mind, mind to intelligence, intelligence to spirit, we all believe that it has an order, a design, a purpose, but, of course, when the ideal is likely to be realized, it depends on you and me, it depends on each one of us. And science again tells us that the spirit of man which can sit in judgment on Nature, which can assert its superiority to mere circumstance, which can throw away its life, which can lacerate its body and torture its mind to find out some secret in this world—that that mind is not merely a product of Nature. It has something akin to the very mystery which is at the heart of the universe. That which is at the back of the universe and that which is working in the mind of man has some fundamental kinship. And, as all the great religious prophets have said, man is made in the image of God. Made in the image because, like the Divine Creator, he can also participate in the creative process. Till now, it is said, my Father worked; hereafter we have to work. In other words, God is the creator of creators. He has made us all to participate in this great creative evolution which is taking place, and he calls upon us to co-operate with him in bringing about a better kind of social order, a more universal order, a civilized society.

If we are to realize this truth, we have to fight the passions, the folly, the beast that is in us. Jeremiah says there is no beast with me except the beast that I ride upon. The essential function of religion is to transform human nature, to make us reborn, so to speak. We are born into the world of Nature and necessity. We have to be born into the world of spirit and freedom. Every great thinker has said that. We say man has to rise from his unregenerate consciousness to a regenerate one. Buddha tells us that from *avidyā,* or ignorance, we have to rise to *bodhi,* or enlightenment. The Jews ask us to change ourselves. When St. Paul says that we should put on a new Man, he means that we must develop the mind that was in Christ. Jesus himself talks to us about metanoia or change of consciousness—they are all asking us to bring about an inward change, to grow from intellectuality to spirituality, from justice to charity, from law to love. If we are able to grow to that kind of stature, there'll be no room in our hearts for judgment. The moment we are able to reach that frame of mind, we become different altogether. A Sufi mystic remarks that when we are born from the womb we are once-born. When we are born from within ourselves we are twice-born. That's our second birth.

Every religious teacher has affirmed that the truth of religion does not consist in the form we adopt or in the object we worship but in the way in which we transmute our personality. The transformation of oneself, the transmutation of one's whole being so as to make it one integrated whole—that is the aim of religion. All the disciplines enjoined on us, all the forms prescribed for us—all these things are different ways by which we are called upon to change our nature. When once we change our nature, we become different.

Religion is not a way out of life; it is a way into life. It is not a way which requires us to withdraw altogether from the world, leave the scene of social agony, retire to our monastery, and there seek our own self-salvation. Religion is something more. As Meister Eckhart said, you have to pour the fruits of your contemplation into the energy of action. It is something in which you are called upon to recollect, to bring your thoughts together, to integrate your whole nature, and with such an integrated personality enter into the world and make the world new by your very presence. Saints have a quality in their blood and bones, in their very existence, which is a challenge to us all. It makes us believe that unless we change there is no possibility of spreading any kind of true enlightenment in the world. Sanctity has different degrees. We happen to be in a world of fallen men, where, though we are taught that we are rational beings, much of our conduct is under unreasoning impulses and passions. That is what it is. If, today, we know where the future lies and still adhere to militarism, to cold-war pacts, to nationalistic gospels, and submit to a sense of despair, a sense of helplessness, it is because we have not changed in our inward life. An eminent theologian recently said that it is not outside the will of Providence that the human race should cease to exist. I find much scriptural evidence for it and nothing against it. That's a counsel of despair. What we need today is not a philosophy of dread, or anxiety, nor a philosophy of despair and nothingness, but a philosophy which will illumine our desperate condition and give us hope, make us believe that we can make a new world. And, more than faith and hope, we need charity—intellectual charity, charity which means understanding of other peoples; breaking down the walls of ignorance, inertia, and incomprehension; building up a better world than the world in which we happen to be. It is that kind of charity that we have to exercise.

When once we realize that science fosters a feeling of a mysterious universe, it encourages the spirit of religion. We can be religious while we are steeped in the spirit of science. When once we also realize that the only way of bringing about a change in our nature is by austere discipline, by self-mastery, by self-conquest, which is emphasized by all religions, we need not claim an exclusive possession of religious truth, the entire truth.

Religion is essentially a transformation of the human being. It is raising the individual from his present intellectual to his spiritual level. That can be done and has been done by many religions. Each one of them has its prophets and saints. They all belong to one indivisible community. The Christian thinkers have affirmed that Socrates and Heraclitus belonged to the Church of Christ. Augustine said the religion called Christianity had been in existence for centuries, but it came to be known as Christianity after Christ arrived. Jacques Maritain, a very eminent Catholic theologian, talking about the saints of India, says they may not belong to the Church of Jesus but they belong to the one indivisible community of God. These people, who come from distant points, with different upbringing and different traditions altogether—they form one family, they recognize one another, they feel that they are one at heart. Their object of worship is the same, whatever name may be given to it. Behind all these forms there is that intrinsic reality which is in all of us. We attempt to describe it by our own ways, by our traditional methods, in the idiom of our age—that is what we attempt to do, but this need not be cause for quarrel, for discussing the definitions of the supreme, I remember when Calvin did away with Servetus, Castellion remarked that the murder of Servetus is not due to difference of faith. It is the murder of a human being. So, also, killing men, women, and children by the atom bomb is not a defense of a faith but is a murder of millions of human beings. Anyone who has risen to that level will feel that his heart will go out for suffering humanity. Gandhi in our own country told us that nationalism should not be interpreted as an exclusive gospel. He remarked: I want my country to be free. A fallen and prostrate India cannot be of any help to herself or to others. A free and enlightened India can be of help to herself and to others. I want my country to be free, that one day she may die that humanity may live.

Remember, all civilizations are mortal. How long they endure is a question of time. And if we adhere to certain fundamental principles of morality we may endure a little longer than others. But, if we do not, we break against that moral law and will be dashed to pieces. All things in this world are subject to change, subject to mutation. Nations are no exception to this law of change. If only we could have such a perspective of the process of events, if we only knew that nothing in this world is stable, if we were able to recognize this, our whole attitude toward the world today, to the problems which face us, would be altogether different. So, it is possible for us to be scientific, to be ethical, to be spiritual, and at the same time not to be dogmatic, and not to support inequities and atrocities, and not to be provincial, intolerant, and exclusive. It is possible for us to develop a religion which is scientific, which is ethical, which is spiritual and universal. What the world needs today, if we are to overcome the crisis which is facing us, is the development of such a religion.

HU SHIH

John Dewey in China

John Dewey was born October 20, 1859, and died in 1952, in his ninety-third year. This coming October there will be a celebration of the Centennial of his birth in many parts of the free world.

Forty years ago, early in 1919, Professor Dewey and his wife, Alice, left the United States for a trip to the Far East. The trip was to be solely for pleasure. But, before their departure from San Francisco, Dewey was invited by cable to give a series of lectures at the Imperial University of Tokyo and later at other centers of higher learning in Japan.

While in Japan, he received a joint invitation from five educational bodies in China to lecture in Peking, Nanking, Shanghai, and other cities. He accepted the invitation, and the Deweys arrived in Shanghai on May 1, 1919—just three days before the outburst of the Student Movement on May 4th in Peking. That was the Student Movement which is often referred to as "The May Fourth Movement."

It was the Student Movement and its successes and failures that so much intrigued the Deweys that they changed their original plan to return to America after the summer months and decided to spend a full year in China. Dewey applied to Columbia University for a year's leave of absence, which was granted, and which was subsequently extended to two years. So, he spent a total of two years and two months in China, from May, 1919, to July, 1921.

When Miss Evelyn Dewey wrote in her Preface to the volume of Dr. and Mrs. Dewey's letters that "the fascination of the struggle going on in China for a unified and independent democracy caused them to alter their plan to return to the United States in the summer of 1919," she was referring to their keen interest in the Student Movement. It is in order, therefore, to give a brief sketch of the May Fourth Movement and its nationwide influence as a background of this talk on John Dewey in China.

World War I had ended only a few months before, and the Peace Conference in Paris was drafting the final terms of the peace treaty. The Chinese people had hoped that, with Woodrow Wilson's idealistic "Fourteen Points" still echoing throughout the world, China might have some of her grievances redressed at the Peace Conference. But in the first days of May, 1919, authentic reports began to reach China that President Wilson had failed to render his moral support to China's demand that the former German possessions and concessions in Shantung be restored to China; and that the Peace Conference had decided to leave the Shantung question to Japan to settle with China. The Chinese delegation was helpless; the Chinese government was powerless. The people were disappointed and disheartened, but helpless.

On Sunday, May 4th, the students in Peking called a mass meeting of all colleges and secondary schools to protest against the Paris decision and to call on the government to instruct the Chinese delegation in Paris to refuse to accept it. The whole thing was a spontaneous and unpremeditated outburst of youthful patriotism. The communists' claim that "the May Fourth Movement" was a part of the World Revolution and was planned and led by Chinese communists is sheerly a big lie. There was no communist in China in 1919.

After the speeches and resolutions, the mass meeting decided on a demonstration parade which ended in forcing the closed gates of the house of the Minister of Foreign Affairs, who had been notorious for his pro-Japanese policies. The marching students went into the house and beat up one of the luncheon guests, who happened to be the Chinese Minister to Tokyo, recalled for consultation. In the turmoil, the house was set on fire—probably to frighten away the demonstrators. A number of students were arrested on their way back to their schools.

That was what happened on the fourth of May, forty years ago.

The Deweys were still in Shanghai when the news of the Peking student movement was first published and was immediately arousing sympathetic responses from students and the general public all over the country.

When the Deweys arrived in Peking, they saw the student movement at its highest moments during the first days of June. Hundreds of students were making speeches in the streets, preaching to the people that China could regain her lost rights by boycotting Japanese goods. On June 5, the Deweys wrote to their daughters at home: "This is Thursday morning, and last night we heard that about a thousand students were arrested the day before. They had filled the building of Law [of the National Peking University, used as a temporary 'prison'], and have begun on the Science building."

Later, on the same day, they reported the most astonishing news: "In the evening, a telephone call came that the tents [of the soldiers] around the university buildings where the students were imprisoned had been struck and the soldiers were leaving. Then the students inside held a meeting and passed a resolution asking the government whether they were guaranteed freedom of speech, because if they were not, they would not leave the building merely to be arrested again, as they planned to go on speaking. So they embarrassed the government by remaining in 'jail' all night."

The Deweys later explained that the government's ignominious surrender was due to the fact that the merchants in Shanghai had called a strike the day before as a protest against the arrest of the thousand students. And they remarked: "This is a strange country. The so-called republic is a joke.... But in some ways there is more democracy than we have. Leaving out the women, there is complete social equality. And while the legislature is a perfect farce, public opinion, when it does express itself, as at the present time, has remarkable influence."

On June 16, the Deweys wrote home that the three pro-Japanese high officials (including the Minister of Foreign Affairs) had resigned from the government, and the students' strike had been called off.

On July 2, they wrote home: "The anxiety here is tense. The report is that the [Chinese] Delegates did not sign [the Peace Treaty]." Two days later, they wrote: "You can't imagine what it means here for China not to have signed [the Peace Treaty]. The entire government had been for it. The President up to ten days before the signing said it was necessary [to sign]. It was a victory for public opinion, and all set going by these little schoolboys and girls."

I have quoted these letters to show a part of the first impressions Dr. and Mrs. Dewey had during their first two or three months in Peking. Somehow, this "strange country" had a strange appeal to them. They decided to stay on, for a year at first, and finally for two years and two months. They visited 11 of the 22 provinces—4 provinces in the North, 5 in Central China, from Shanghai to Changsha, and 2 in the South.

A word may be said about the preparations made for the reception of Dewey's lectures. A month before his arrival in China, I was asked by the sponsoring organizations to give a series of four lectures on the Pragmatic Movement, beginning with Charles S. Peirce and William James, but with special emphasis on Dewey. A series of articles on Dewey's educational philosophy was published in Shanghai under the editorship of Dr. Chiang Monlin, one of his students in Teachers' College at Columbia.

A number of Dewey's students were asked to interpret his lectures in the Chinese language. For example, I was his translator and interpreter for all his lectures in Peking and in the provinces of Shantung and Shansi. For his several major series of lectures, we also selected competent recorders for reporting every lecture in full for the daily newspapers and periodicals. What came to be known as "Dewey's Five Major Series of Lectures" in Peking, totaling 58 lectures, were recorded and reported in full and later published in book form, going through ten large reprintings before Dewey left China in 1921, and continuing to be reprinted for three decades until the communists put a stop to them.

The topics of the Five Series will give some idea of the scope and content of Dewey's lectures:

I. 3 lectures on Modern Tendencies in Education
II. 16 lectures on Social and Political Philosophy
III. 16 lectures on Philosophy of Education
IV. 15 lectures on Ethics
V. 8 lectures on Types of Thinking

His lectures in Peking included two other series:

VI. 3 lectures on Democratic Developments in America
VII. 3 lectures on Three Philosophers of the Modern Period (William James, Henri Bergson, Bertrand Russell—these lectures were given at special request as an introduction to Russell before the latter's arrival in China in 1920 to deliver a number of lectures.)

Dewey's lectures in Nanking included these series:

1) 10 lectures on the Philosophy of Education
2) 10 lectures on the History of Philosophy
3) 3 lectures on Experimental Logic

Typing on his own typewriter, Dewey always wrote out his brief notes for every lecture, a copy of which would be given to his interpreter so that he could study them and think out the suitable Chinese words and phrases before the lecture and its translation. After each lecture in Peking, the Dewey notes were given to the selected recorders, so that they could check their reports before publication. I have recently re-read most of his lectures in Chinese translation after a lapse of 40 years, and I could still feel the freshness and earnestness of the great thinker and teacher who always measured every word and every sentence in the classroom or before a large lecture audience.

After one year of public lectures in many cities, Dewey was persuaded by his Chinese friends to spend another year in China, primarily as a Visiting Professor at the National Peking University, lecturing and discussing with advanced students without the aid of an interpreter, and devoting a part of his time to lectures at the Teachers' College in Peking and in Nanking. He was interested in the few "experimental schools" which had been established by his former students in various educational centers, such as Peking, Nanking, Soochow, and Shanghai. Some of the schools, such as the one at the Teachers' College in Nanking, were named Dewey schools.

The Deweys left China in 1921. In October, 1922, the National Educational Association met in Tsinan to discuss a thorough revision of the national school system and curriculum. Article 4 of the New Educational System of 1922 reads: "The child is the center of education. Special attention should be paid to the individual characteristics and aptitudes of the child in organizing the school system. Henceforth, the elective system should be adopted for secondary and higher education, and the principle of flexibility should be adopted in the arrangement and promotion of classes in all elementary schools." In the new school curriculum of 1923 and the revised curriculum of 1929, the emphasis was placed on the idea that the child was the center of the school. The influence of Dewey's educational philosophy is easily seen in these revisions.

Dewey went to China in May, 1919—forty years ago. Can we now give a rough estimate of his influence in China after the passing of forty years?

Such an estimate has not been easy, because these forty years have been mostly years of great disturbance, of civil wars, revolutions, and foreign wars—including the years of the Nationalist Revolution, the eight years of the Japanese War and the Second World War, the years of the communist wars, and the communist conquest of the Chinese mainland. It is exceedingly difficult to say how much influence any thinker or any school of thought has had on a people that has suffered so much from the tribulations of war, revolution, exile, mass migration, and general insecurity and deprivation.

In our present case, however, the Chinese communist regime has given us unexpected assistance in the form of nationwide critical condemnation and purging of the Pragmatic philosophy of Dewey and of his Chinese followers. This great purge began as early as 1950 in a number of inspired but rather mild articles criticizing Dewey's educational theories, and citing American critics such as Kandel, Bode, Rugg, and Hook in support of their criticism. But the purge became truly violent in 1954 and 1955, when the Chinese communist regime ordered a concerted condemnation and purge of the evil and poisonous thoughts of Hu Shih in many aspects of Chinese intellectual activity—in philosophy, in history, in the history of philosophy, in political thought, in literature, and in histories of Chinese literature. In those two years of 1954 and 1955, more than three million words were published for the purging and exorcising of the "ghost of Hu Shih." And in almost every violent attack on me, Dewey was inevitably dragged in as a source and as the fountainhead of the heinous poison.

And in most of the articles of this vast purge literature, there was a frank recognition of the evil influence of Dewey, Dewey's philosophy and method, and the application of that philosophy and method by that "rotten and smelly" Chinese Deweyan, Hu Shih, and his slavish followers. May we not accept such confessions from the communist-controlled world as fairly reliable, though probably slightly exaggerated, estimates of the "poisonous" influence left by Dewey and his friends in China?

I quote only a few of these confessions from Red China:

1) "If we want to critize the old theories of education, we must begin with Dewey. The educational ideas of Dewey have dominated and controlled Chinese education for thirty years, and his social philosophy and his general philosophy have also influenced a part of the Chinese people" (*The People's Education,* October, 1950).

2) "How was Dewey's poisonous Pragmatic educational philosophy spread over China? It was spread primarily through his lectures in China preaching his Pragmatic philosophy and his reactionary educational ideas, and through that center of Dewey's reactionary thinking, namely, Columbia University, from which thousands of Chinese students, for over thirty years, have brought back all the reactionary, subjective-idealistic, Pragmatic educational ideas of Dewey.... As one who has been most deeply poisoned by his reactionary educational ideas, as one who has worked hardest and longest to help spread his educational ideas, I now publicly accuse that great fraud and deceiver in the modern history of education, John Dewey!" (By Ch'en Ho-ch'in, one of the great educators of the Dewey school, who was responsible for the modernization of the Shanghai schools, who was ordered to make this public accusation in February, 1955. It was published in the *Wenhui Pao,* February 28, 1955.)

3) "The battlefield of the study of Chinese literature has, for over thirty years, been occupied by the representative of bourgeois idealism [that is, Pragmatism], namely, Hu Shih, and his school. Even years after the 'Liberation' when the intellectual circles have supposedly acknowledged the leadership position of Marxism, the evil influence of that school has not yet received the purge it rightly deserves" (*The People's Daily,* the official organ of the Chinese Communist Party and Government, Nov. 5, 1954).

4) "The poison of the philosophical ideas of Pragmatism [as represented by Hu Shih] has not only infiltrated the field of the study of Chinese literature, but has also penetrated deep into the fields of history, education, linguistics, and even the realm of natural science—of course, the greatest evil effect has been in the field of philosophy" (*Kuang-ming Daily,* of Peking, Dec. 15, 1954).

These confessions should be sufficient to give us an idea of the extent of the evil influence of Dewey and his followers and friends in China. According to these confessions, the Pragmatic philosophy and method of Dewey and his Chinese friends have dominated Chinese education for thirty years, and have infiltrated and dominated for over thirty years the fields of the study of Chinese literature, linguistics, history, philosophy, and even the realm of natural science!

What is this Deweyan brand of Pragmatism or Experimentalism that is so much feared in communist China as to deserve three million words of purge and condemnation?

As I examine this vast purge literature, I cannot help laughing heartily at all this fuss and fury. After wading through literally millions of words of abuse, I find that what those Red masters and slaves dread most and want to purge is only a philosophical theory of thinking which Dewey had expounded in many of his logical studies and which he had made popular in his little book, *How We Think.* According to this theory, thinking is not passive and slavish deduction from unquestioned absolute truths, but an effective tool and method for resolving doubt and overcoming difficulties in our daily life, in our active dealings with Nature and man. Thinking, says Dewey, always begins with a situation of doubt and perplexity; it proceeds with a search for facts and for possible suggestions or hypotheses for the resolution of the initial difficulty; and it terminates in proving, testing, or verifying the selected hypothesis by successfully and satisfactorily resolving the perplexing situation which had challenged the mind to think. That's the Deweyan theory of thinking, which I have in the last forty years tried to popularize by pointing out that that was an adequate analysis of the method of science as well as an adequate analysis of the method of "evidential investigation" (*k'ao-chü, k'ao-cheng*), which the great Chinese classical scholars of the last three centuries had been using so efficaciously and fruitfully. That is the method of the disciplined common sense of mankind: it is the essence of the method of science, consisting mainly in a boldness in suggesting hypotheses, coupled with meticulous care in seeking verification by evidence or by experimentation.

Two corollaries from this conception of thinking stand out pre-eminently. First, the progress of man and of society depends upon the patient and successful solution of real and concrete problems by means of the active use of the intelligence of man. "Progress," says Dewey, "is piecemeal. It is always a retail job, never wholesale." That is anathema to all communists, who believe in total and cataclysmic revolution, which will bring about wholesale progress overnight.

The second corollary is equally anathema to the communists, namely, that, in this natural and orderly process of rational thinking, all doctrines and all theories are to be regarded, not as absolute truths, but only as tentative and suggestive hypotheses to be tested in use—only as tools and materials for aiding human intelligence, but never as unquestioned and unquestionable dogmas to stifle or stop thinking. Dewey said in his Peking lecture on moral education: "Always cultivate an open mind. Always cultivate the habit of intellectual honesty. And always learn to be responsible for your own thinking." That was enough to scare the Commies out of their wits, and enough to start years of violent attack and abuse on Dewey and Pragmatism and the "ghost of Hu Shih."

And the most amusing fact was that all those years of violent attack and all those millions of words of condemnation began in 1954 with a communist discussion of a popular Chinese novel of the eighteenth century entitled *The Dream of the Red Chamber*. Why? Because nearly forty years ago I was tempted to apply the method of scientific research to a study of the authorship, the remarkable family background of the author, and the history of the evolution of the text of the novel. In the course of subsequent years, numerous hitherto-unknown materials were discovered and published by me, all of which have verified and strengthened my first researches. That was a conscious application of the Dewey theory of thinking to a subject-matter which was well known to every man and woman who could read at all. I have applied the same theory and method of thinking to several other Chinese novels, as well as to many difficult and forbidding problems of research in the fields of the history of Chinese thought and belief, including the history of Ch'an or Zen Buddhism.

But the best-known example or material with which I illustrated and popularized the Deweyan theory of thinking was the great novel *The Dream of the Red Chamber*. Nearly thirty years ago (November, 1930), at the request of my publisher, I made an anthology of my Essays, in which I included three pieces on *The Dream of the Red Chamber*. I wrote a preface to this anthology intended for younger readers. In my wicked moments, I wrote these words in introducing my three studies of that novel:

> My young friends, do not regard these pieces on *The Dream of the Red Chamber* as my efforts to teach you how to read a novel. These essays are only a few examples or illustrations of a method of how to think and study. Through these simple essays, I want to convey to you a little bit of the scientific spirit, the scientific attitude of mind, and the scientific method. The scientific spirit lies in the search for facts and for truth. The scientific attitude of mind is a willingness to put aside our feelings and prejudices, a willingness to face facts and to follow evidence wherever it may lead us. And the scientific method is only "a boldness to suggest hypotheses coupled with a meticulous care in seeking proof and verification." When evidence is lacking or insufficient, there must be a willingness to suspend judgment. A conclusion is valid only when it is verified. Some Ch'an (Zen) monk of centuries ago said that Bodhidharma came all the way to China in search of a man who would not be deceived by man. In these essays, I, too, wish to present a method of how not to be deceived by men. To be led by the nose by a Confucius or a Chu Hsi is not highly commendable. But to be led by the nose by a Marx, a Lenin, or a Stalin is also not quite becoming a man. I have no desire to lead anybody by the nose: I only wish to convey to my young friends my humble hope that they may learn a little intellectual skill for their own self-protection and endeavor to be men who cannot be deceived by others.

These words, I said then, were penned with infinite love and infinite hope. For these words, I have brought upon my head and the head of my beloved teacher and friend, John Dewey, years of violent attack and millions of words of abuse and condemnation. But, ladies and gentlemen, these same millions of words of abuse and condemnation have given me a feeling of comfort and encouragement—a feeling that Dewey's two years and two months in China were not entirely in vain, that my forty years of humble effort in my own country have not been entirely in vain, and that Dewey and his students have left in China plenty of "poison," plenty of antiseptic and antitoxin, to plague the Marxist-Leninist slaves for many, many years to come.

F. S. C. NORTHROP

Comparative Philosophy and World Law

Since this is the last time that all of us will be together, may I presume to speak for the members of the conference and thank you, our hosts of this community, for what you have done in demonstrating to the world that peoples from the Orient and the Occident can live together amicably under law. You have shown also that the legal and political philosophy, articulated perhaps best by Thomas Jefferson, upon which the United States rests can succeed. This philosophy affirms that all human beings, qua human beings, irrespective of their racial ancestry, their religion, their sex, or their color of skin, are born free and equal with respect to their moral, legal, religious, and political obligations, rights, duties, and privileges before the law. You, by your deeds, have proved that this political philosophy is practical. Hence, you bring, as you come into the United States as an official State, something that makes all Americans and free men everywhere proud. You also add something that the United States of America needs. Some of us on the Mainland have been ashamed of some of the things that have happened in our country with respect to the treatment of people of different colors of skin and ancestries of race. It is, therefore, a great help to us that you are an official member of our nation now.

Another example will underline what you have done. In 1957, a conference was held on the slopes of the Atlas Mountains in the middle of Morocco on the problem of bringing together amicably the Arab Islamic Moors, the Berber Islamic Moors, the medieval Jewish community, and modern contractually democratic legal and political institutions. This conference was the brain child of a Benedictine Prior, Father Martin. This remarkable man developed the idea that it might be possible to bring together these different racial, religious, and social groups in a peaceful political Morocco, the better for the contribution of each, providing the problem was approached by the political and cultural leaders of these different groups at the deepest philosophical and religious level. He also persuaded Sultan Mohammad V, the Crown Prince, the secular leaders of the government, the representatives of all the aforementioned Moroccan racial, religious, and secular communities, and official representatives of every foreign government with either political or military associations with Morocco to be active sponsors of, and participants in, this conference. The foreign governments involved were France, Spain, and, because of her present military bases in Morocco, the United States. With the next generation in mind, Father Martin added as listeners and discussants some two hundred and fifty students of the graduate level of educational maturity of both sexes and of every race from North Africa, Spain, France and the other Western European nations, the Middle East, and even Canada and the United States.

The conference opened with a fifty-minute address, delivered, without even a note before him, in perfect and fluent French by the modern-minded Crown Prince, in which, drawing on the entire scientific and philosophical history of both Islamic and Judaic-Christian Western civilization, he presented both of these civilizations in their respective golden and dark ages as mutually enriching one another. Then, for a week, with official representatives of all the aforementioned governments and cultural groups present, Father Martin had outstanding Jewish, Islamic, and Christian scholars present the concept of the human person and his worth as conceived in Judaism, Islam, and Christianity at their respective bests. During the second week, (a) these same scholars described the kind of education which is required to present Judaism, Islam, the Christian, and the modern secular, West at their best, and (b) the head of the legislative assembly of the Moroccan government and its Minister of Education outlined their practical educational program for creating a modernized free Morocco in which all can live together peacefully under free democratic contractual law in mutual respect, the richer because of the diversity of their racial and religious traditions.

Note what such a deeply philosophical, historical, and religious approach to the problems of practical politics does. First, it removes all sense of inferiority on the part of any group in the nation. Each has a tradition of which at its best it can be proud. Second, it presents the tradition of each, not as an absolutely isolated provincial thing, but as something which in fact has achieved greatness only by drawing on the traditions of the others. Without Judaism, there would have been neither Christianity nor Islam. Without Greek science and philosophy, none of these three religious civilizations would be what it now is. Without Islamic or Jewish scientists and philosophers such as Alhazen, Ibn Raud, and Maimonides, geometrical optics, medieval Christian theology, and the painting of Europe's Renaissance with its foreshortening of images would not have come when and as they did. Thus, a state of mind was created in which the new from the modern French West can be accepted without the feeling that respect for the quality and greatness of the past will be unappreciated and lost.

It is not an accident that you here in Hawaii have succeeded with your somewhat similar political problems of racial and cultural diversity to a greater extent than even Morocco has been able to do. When, moreover, the reason for your remarkable success is completely and correctly described, great, if not major, credit must be given to the University of Hawaii and its curriculum which fostered the comparative study of the literature, art, anthropology, religion, and philosophy of the civilizations of Japan, China, Polynesia, India, and the ancient and modern West at their best. This notable educational experiment in effective practical politics was initiated under President Crawford's regime, given a prodigious acceleration by President and Mrs. Gregg M. Sinclair, and continues today under President Snyder.

But you, the citizens of this new State, also did your part. The Moroccan story helps us all to see what it was and still is. Your public museums, art galleries, beaches, churches, and temples exemplify in the concrete what the courses in the University had described in the abstract. The result was that nobody in this community had any sense of inferiority because he was not of Anglo-Saxon stock or of a parentage not born on the American mainland. Everyone could live here on these islands feeling that his cultural background was that of an ancient and persisting civilization of high quality of which anyone could be proud, knowing that other people here with different cultural backgrounds have respect for the heritage of one's own parents and their ancestors.

Against this background of success, let us now face the grim realities of the present international situation. No less a soldier and statesman than President Eisenhower tells us that man now has it in his power to destroy mankind. Under such circumstances, one might suppose that every political leader throughout the world would be working day and night to settle disputes between nations without recourse to war. Nevertheless, atomic armaments are being made stronger and stronger, and statesmen in both the communist and the free world threaten to use these weapons, unless, or if, other nations do certain things.

There are very good reasons why this is the case. Communist ideals and practice being what they are, such must be the dangerous predicament in which we live until we meet the requirements necessary to settle disputes between nations without recourse to fighting.

What are these requirements? Professor Roscoe Pound, former Dean of the Harvard Law School, reminds us that there is no evidence from history that disputes between people or groups of people are ever settled by peaceful rather than forceful means unless, in interludes of peace, when judgment is more objective and tempers are under control, legal institutions are established. Applied to international relations, this means that we can expect no settlement of disputes without recourse to war, even in this atomic age, until effective international legal institutions are established.

History, and especially legal and political history, shows one other thing. It is that pacificism is impractical even where legal procedures rather than recourse to force works. I know of no domestic community in Confucian, Buddhist, Gandhian Hindu India, or even in the sleepiest village of New Hampshire which does not have, as an essential part of its peace-producing legal system, policemen armed with clubs or revolvers. Even where disputes are settled peacefully by legal processes, physical police power is also necessary.

This consideration raises the question: When is the use of physical force just, when unjust? We have but to look at the prescriptions under which any policeman operates in any peaceful domestic community to find the answer. It is that the use of force is just if it is authorized by the legal processes of the community at large; it is unjust if such is not the case. There is no difference, so far as the biology and physics of the situation are concerned, for the fellow who is killed, whether he is shot by a murderer or by a policeman. But what makes the killing of another by a policeman good, just, and an act of peace, and the killing of another by anyone else an act of murder is that the shot of the murderer is authorized solely by the unilateral decision of the person who pulls the trigger, whereas the shot of the policeman is a duty placed upon him in certain legally specified circumstances by the due processes of the legal system of the community as a whole.

Why haven't we been able to extend this legal method of settling disputes from the domestic to the international field? Three recently developed sciences throw considerable light on this question. They are sociological jurisprudence, cultural anthropology, and the comparative philosophy of the world's cultures. Moreover, they put methods and procedural prescriptions at one's disposal which suggest that, providing certain things are done, an effective international law in this atomic era is not beyond the reach of practical political realism.

Sociological jurisprudence has investigated the relation between law and society with the view, among other things, of determining what requirements must be met if law is to be effective. To point up the two main factors upon which the success or failure of law depend, the Austrian-Hungarian sociological jurist of the last generation, Eugen Ehrlich, coined the words "positive law" and "living law."[1] By the former he meant the normative constitutions, statutes, judicial decisions, and police actions; by the latter he meant the normative customs of the people to whom the positive law is applied.

Ehrlich's living law is equivalent to what the cultural anthropologists call the "pattern of a culture." Like Ehrlich, they have found that this pattern, or what Ehrlich called the "inner order of the associations" of a people, is an essentially and inescapably normative thing.[2] It prescribes an ought-to-be in terms of which deviants are punished; it does not describe merely what is. Like Ehrlich, the cultural anthropologists have found that, since the living

[1] Eugen Ehrlich, *Fundamental Principles of the Sociology of Law,* Walter L. Moll, trans. (Cambridge: Harvard University Press, 1936).

[2] See A. L. Kroeber, Summary in *Anthropology Today,* prepared under the direction of A. L. Kroeber (Chicago: University of Chicago Press, 1953).

customs of a people express a normative "pattern" or "inner order," any culture is an organic normative thing.

The prevalent notion, that some particular non-normative fact in a given society, such as climate, sex, or economic needs or instruments, determines the norms of a culture, is therefore erroneous. Logically, a normative order is not implied by non-normative facts. Furthermore, to be a society with its customs, or a culture with its pattern, is not to be a particular set of facts but a specific normative way of evaluating and ordering the facts in an organic inner order or pattern. Hence, a nation is not merely so much normatively neutral material, economic, or military power. A nation is a normative entity—something that expresses the normative living law or pattern of the customs of its people—or at least it does so when its legal and political institutions are effective.

The latter consideration brings us to the second conclusion of sociological jurisprudence—its criterion of the condition which must be met for positive law to be effective in settling disputes by peaceful means. Put over-briefly, this condition is that the normative content of the positive law must express the high-frequency normative content of the living law, where "high-frequency" means the normative habitual behavior which the majority would exhibit were there little, if any, positive law. The Prohibition Amendment in the case of the United States is a negative example. The high-frequency customs of the living law did not support it, even though, due to peculiar war-time conditions, it was duly passed as positive law. The result, let it be noted, was not merely its flouting and later repeal, but also the corruption of the legal and political officials, as Al Capone's Chicago clearly showed.

The implications internationally of the sociological jurists' criterion of effective positive law should now be obvious. Negatively, it explains why previous attempts at an effective settlement of disputes between nations by legal procedures have been so disheartening. Instead of beginning with an objective culturally anthropological and sociologically jurisprudential determination of the diverse living laws of the many nations and cultures of the world and then framing positive international legal and political institutions so that their normative content will express the high-frequency living normative customs of mankind, thereby winning the living law support, after the manner of the methods of Hawaii and Morocco noted above, international lawyers and politicians have begun at the positive legal end without any regard for the diverse living-law customs of mankind. The marvel, under such circumstances, is not that both the League of Nations and the United Nations have failed to fulfill the initial high hopes of their creators, but that they have been as effective as has been the case. Positively, the practical international implication of the sociological jurisprudential criterion of effective positive law is equally clear. An effective international law may be realistically practical providing we ground it in the world's living law. Note that diversity of living customs is no deterrent, as so many suppose, providing, as Morocco and Hawaii show, we use educational and political methods which take these differences into account, creating a respect upon the part of each living-law group for the different norms of other living-law groups.

Immediately a question arises: What is the method for determining objectively the living law of any particular nation or community? Two recent anthropological publications indicate the answer. The first is Professor E. A. Hoebel's *The Law of Primitive Man: A Study in Comparative Legal Dynamics*.[3] The second is Professor Clyde Kluckhohn's "The Philosophy of the Navaho Indians."[4] Many anthropologists first supposed that an objective determination of any culture required merely that one "live in the field" and describe honestly what one sees and hears and learns from interrogation. This overlooked the fact that science, even when its subject-matter is non-normative, is never mere facts, but facts brought under concepts and a clear and consistent and operationally testable theory of the facts. When one's subject-matter is normative, however, as is the case with the "inner order" of the living law, or the "pattern" of a culture, the interpretation put by the people in question upon the facts which the anthropologist sees and hears becomes all-important. Otherwise, the culture being studied will be distorted in the anthropologist's "description" of it, due to the circumstance that he has interpreted what he sees and hears from the conceptual standpoint of his own culture or of a particular theory of psychology or social science of his own culture, instead of from the standpoint of the way the people in the native culture think about and evaluate what the visiting anthropologist sees and hears them do and say. Thus, Paul Radin, first, and Hoebel and Kluckhohn, later, realized that to describe any culture with objectivity one must do so by finding and using the way of thinking and evaluating what they do which the native people, rather than the visiting anthropologists, employ. Since philosophy is but the name for the elementary concepts and propositions in terms of which people think about, integrate, and evaluate the facts of their experience, we need hardly be surprised, therefore, that when Radin and Kluckhohn sought out the way of thinking of any particular so-called primitive people they found themselves with a unique, and by no means simple-minded, philosophy.

Moreover, this philosophy was both naturalistic and normative. Kluckhohn also found suggestions that there was an essential connection between the evaluative judgments the Navahos made and the non-normative way they thought about natural phenomena. When he also made explicit the normative positive legal rules they used in the peaceful settlement of their disputes, an essential connection between their positive law and their natural and normative philosophy became evident.

Professor Hoebel made similar descriptions of the positive legal norms of seven different primitive societies. So different were these positive laws in their normative content that he had to resort to seven different sets of postu-

[3] Cambridge: Harvard University Press, 1954.

[4] Clyde Kluckhohn, in F. S. C. Northrop, ed., *Ideological Differences and World Order* (New Haven: Yale University Press, 1949), pp. 356–384.

lates to describe them. Moreover, in the case of two American tribes of Indians living in approximately the same climate and geographical terrain, so diverse were their respective living and positive legal norms that those accepted and practiced spontaneously by one tribe would have caused a rebellion if applied to the neighboring tribe. Anyone acquainted with Morocco or with medieval-minded Hindu and Muslim India will not be surprised by these facts. The eating customs, marriage customs, and inheritance laws of Hindus, Muslims, Berber Muslims, Arab Muslims, and Moroccan Jews are similarly different. What is true of these particular, more localized living legal communities is true also of the larger nations and civilizations of Shinto, Confucian, Buddhist, and Hindu Asia and of the Stoic Roman and the modern contractually legal and political West. Each has its particular postulate-set defining a philosophy with its accompanying normative rules for settling disputes.

To approach the creation of an effective international law by way of an objective determination of the world's diverse living laws is to be confronted, therefore, with the world's national and cultural comparative philosophy. It is to be faced also with living-law pluralism and diversity. This is the major reason why one of the two paths to international law specified by the writer in his *The Taming of the Nations*[5] grounded itself in the principle of living-law pluralism, protecting each nation and cultural community in its own living law and philosophy and using international law merely to restrict it to domestic communal or national consumption. Obviously, to make such international law work, the educational methods used by Morocco and Hawaii must be employed. Otherwise, the high-frequency living-law support necessary to make the new positive international law effective will not be forthcoming.

But more than this can be done. Some present nations have a common living-law. Where this is the case, an effective regional international legal, political, economic, and atomic-energy community based on living-law monism can be established where none existed before. An instance is the six nations in Continental European Union. But, it may be said, as did one of my friends in the former Department of International Relations at Yale, "You can't get effective international law by this sociologically jurisprudential method, because, if effective positive international law depends on the living law, you would have it already." Continental European Union proves this contention to be wrong. It overlooks the fact that living-law resources, like crude oil in the ground, may be present but not previously tapped and used legally and politically.

Who would have dared to say in the midst of World War II that French soldiers with the authorization of the French government would be serving beside West German soldiers under a German general in the Brussels Defense Pact European Army and that six nations of Western Europe would cut down their traditional practice of determining their domestic coal, steel, military, and atomic-energy policy unilaterally, by actually transferring part of their

[5] New York: The Macmillan Co., 1952.

domestic sovereignty in these fields to the Continental European Union community? The reason, as the writer has shown elsewhere, is cultural, made possible by the division of Germany at the end of World War II. The high-frequency living-law of West Germany has more in common with that of Luxembourg, Alsace-Lorraine, the remainder of France, Italy, Belgium, and the Netherlands than it ever had with that of East Prussia.

Overlooking this common living-law factor which the Continental European statesmen consciously drew upon in creating Continental European Union,[6] the British initially affirmed that it would not work. Professor Crane Brinton made the same error when, in his factually unsupported review of the writer's *European Union and United States Foreign Policy,* he branded its optimism with respect to the political realism of this internationalism of "the Six" and its pessimism with respect to the effect upon it of the Eisenhower-Dulles "roll-back crusade" language, as a political tract written by an armchair philosopher who was living in fairyland—this notwithstanding the fact that both the optimism and the pessimism were not born in an armchair but were, instead, the findings of four months of interviews in Europe of the political leaders of the major parties in the six Western European nations in Continental European Union. That Professor Brinton, for all his admirable erudition and normal realism of mind, was the one living in fairyland is proved by the quite different review of this book by *The Economist* of London and by Drew Middleton, in the *New York Times,* who was continuously on the spot in Bonn and Luxembourg when the Continental European internationalism of "the Six" was being created and proving its practical effectiveness before his very eyes. That the earlier British governments were equally wrong in their judgment that Continental European Union would not work is proved by recent articles in *The Economist* which show that the main concern of the present British government is (a) lest it has worked too well, and (b) how to frame a British foreign policy which takes its existence and effectiveness into account. Even more important is the demonstration that, providing the new positive law is fitted to previously untapped common normative factors in the living law, effective international law between even modern purportedly absolutely sovereign nations is possible where none existed before.

The triumph of Western contractual legal and political science following its creation by the Stoic Roman lawyers and philosophers confirms this conclusion. Before the discovery of this science there were as many different nations throughout the Western world as there were particular patriarchal families and tribal groupings of such families. The first thing that these Stoic Roman lawyers and politicians did was to give the living law and its corresponding positive law of non-Roman tribal nations the same status under the new Roman legal and political internationalism as the living and cor-

[6] See, for example, the statement of M. Pella, then minister of finance in the De Gasperi government, later Italian prime minister, and still later the head of Luxembourg of the Coal and Steel Community, as reported in F. S. C. Northrop, *European Union and United States Foreign Policy* (New York: The Macmillan Co., 1954).

responding positive law of the tribes of Rome enjoyed. In short, they proceeded to create a new and effective international legal and political community by basing the content of its new international law on living-law pluralism. Any particular tribally national living-law and its corresponding positive law they called the *jus civile.*

Then, as *The Institutes* of Gaius show, the Romans sought out what was common to the otherwise different tribally national instances of the *jus civile.* This common living and positive legal factor they called the *jus gentium.* The subsequent evolution of Western legal and political institutions over the succeeding centuries is the story of the triumph of the living- and postive-law universalism and monism of the *jus gentium* over the living-law diversities and pluralism of the *jus civile.*

Is there such a *jus gentium* in the living-law pluralism of the contemporary world? If so, there is no reason, as the most erudite and mature legal mind of our times, Roscoe Pound, has already suggested,[7] why an effective international legal community cannot be created if we use the methods of the Stoic Roman lawyers and statesmen.

The present occasion permits but the briefest suggestion of what the content of such a world-embracing *jus gentium* may be. Two factors—the one Oriental, the other primarily Western—suggest themselves as possessing the high-frequency living support necessary to provide what is required.

The Oriental factor is the concept of the "true self" or person in all Buddhist and Hindu societies and what Professor Wing-tsit Chan in this 1959 East-West Philosophers' Conference referred to as the "universal" or common man-to-man-ness factor in the somewhat similar Confucian Chinese concept of *jen.* Since the number of Confucian, Buddhist, and Hindu peoples, 90 per cent of whom live in the villages and hence still have this way of thinking in their living-law outlook, constitute a majority of the people on the surface of the earth, this Oriental *jus gentium,* if appealed to as one basis of an effective new positive international law, would have high-frequency living-law support which would have to be reckoned with. The Western living-law belief with similar high-frequency acceptance is the Stoic Roman contractually legal concept that moral and just man is any human being whatever standing equal with any other before a freely assented to, contractually constructed, universal law and its modern equivalent, the Lockean and Jeffersonian Declaration of Independence principle. The evident political fact that Africans, Middle Easterners, and Asians appeal to the latter principle today to make their own Declarations of Independence and set up their popularly and contractually run governments demonstrates that this legal and political philosophy provides, not merely a free Western, but also a world-wide, living-law basis for a new *jus gentium.*

Conversely, as the popularity of Professor Suzuki's lectures and writing on

[7] Roscoe Pound, "Toward a New Jus Gentium," in F. S. C. Northrop, ed., *Ideological Differences and World Order,* pp. 1–17.

Zen Buddhism show, more and more Western psychiatrists and laymen are becoming aware of their need for the intuitive and mediative approach to human nature in which the Oriental is a past master. In short, the *jus gentium* predominant in the West and that predominant in the Orient are increasingly becoming world-embracing in their high-frequency spontaneous acceptance.

Furthermore, these two components are compatible. Both, if given consistent political and social expression, entail a free democratic world society. Has not the time come for the people and their leaders throughout the free world to cease being negative and merely bomb-threatening with respect to the communists' challenge by developing a positive world-embracing program for peace of our own? In short, why not issue our own Confucian-Buddhist-Hindu-Stoic Roman and Jeffersonian Declaration of Independence Manifesto and proceed immediately with this new world-embracing *jus gentium* to construct an international legal and political community for settling disputes between nations in terms of it? Certainly the number of people on the earth's surface today who are vital believers in one or the other or both of the two components of this *jus gentium* is overwhelming as compared with the spontaneous living-law support which any other political and cultural philosophy in the world enjoys.

It appears, therefore, that the methods of sociological jurisprudence indicate three politically realistic ways to an immediately and increasingly effective international law for the peaceful settling of disputes between nations in this atomic age. They are: (1) Living-law pluralism, protecting each national instance of the *jus civile* so long as it restricts itself to home consumption. (2) Regional internationalism, as instanced by Continental European Union, in the case of those nations whose specific as well as generic living-law characteristics have much in common. And (3) moving from (1) via (2) to an international law with increasingly effective content by means of the aforementioned world-embracing *jus gentium*.[8]

[8] For a more detailed description of the implications of Western contractual legal science and its Jeffersonian principle with respect to (3), the interested reader is referred to the last chapter of my *The Complexity of Legal and Ethical Experience* (Boston: Little, Brown, 1959), pp. 273–300. For an indication of the political and cultural methods to use to enable Western free democratic legal and political institutions to combine harmoniously with and take root in the living law of Confucian, Buddhist, and Hindu Asian societies, see the last chapters of my *Philosophical Anthropology and Practical Politics* (New York: The Macmillan Co., 1960).

Biographies and Index

Who's Who

VIRGIL C. ALDRICH

Professor of Philosophy, Kenyon College • B.A., Ohio Wesleyan University; "Diplôme d'Études Supérieures de Philosophie" at the Sorbonne; one year at Oxford; Ph.D., University of California (Berkeley).

Taught philosophy at the Rice Institute, Columbia University, University of Michigan; Ford Foundation Fellow, 1954–1955; Director of Kyoto American Studies Seminar, 1955–1956; Chairman of Publications Committee of the American Philosophical Association since 1953; President of the American Philosophical Association (Western Division), 1957–1958.

Publications: Essays included in two anthologies, and papers in many philosophical periodicals.

VAN METER AMES

Professor of Philosophy, University of Cincinnati • Ph.B., University of Chicago, 1919; Ph.D., 1924.

Department of Philosophy, University of Cincinnati, since 1925; Cornell University, 1931 (Summer); Exchange Professor, University of Texas, 1934–1935; Visiting Professor, University of Hawaii, 1947–1948; Rockefeller Grant to study French philosophy in France, 1948 (Fall); Visiting Professor, University of Aix-Marseille, 1949 (Spring); Columbia University, 1957 (Summer); Fulbright Research Professor, Komazawa University, Tokyo, 1958–1959.

Currently Vice President, American Society for Aesthetics; President, Western Division, American Philosophical Association.

Publications include: *Aesthetics of the Novel; Introduction to Beauty; Proust and Santayana; André Gide;* and *Zen and American Thought.*

N. BAMMATE

Head of the Philosophic and Humanistic Studies Section of UNESCO, Paris, and Professor at the Institute of Diplomatic Studies, Paris • M.A. and Ph.D., University of Lausanne. Studied at the University of Paris, Cambridge University, and al-Azhar Muslim University.

From 1947 to 1949 with the Internation Civil Service in UNESCO as legal adviser. Then in charge of the Middle East area, and later in charge of the Eastern European area. Has lectured throughout Europe on Islam and on comparative philosophy.

Publications: Studies on Islamic culture and on Latin subjects, all in French, among which are included: *Faces of Islam* (a general introduction to Islamic culture) with H. Bammate; *The Concept of Freedom in Islam;* and *Islam Between the Orient and the Occident.*

NIYAZI BERKES

Professor of Islamic Studies, McGill University • Did graduate work in the Department of Philosophy, the Faculty of Letters of the University of Istanbul, and received the Master's degree in Philosophy in 1931; did graduate work in the Department of Sociology at the University of Chicago, 1935–1939; Dozent in Sociology in the Department of Philosophy, University of Ankara, 1940.

Visiting Professor, Institute of Islamic Studies, McGill University, 1952, and member of the staff of that Institute since then; Visiting Professor, Institute of Islamic Studies, Muslim University, Aligarh, India, 1958–1959; participant in numerous conferences and international meetings in Canada, the United States, and Pakistan.

Has translated a number of Western philosophical and sociological works into Turkish. Several of his research works and original articles have been published in Turkish. Has translated into English works of the Turkish social philosopher Ziya Gokalp under the title *Turkish Nationalism and Western Civilization.*

E. A. BURTT

Susan Linn Sage Professor of Philosophy, Cornell University • S.T.M., Union Theological Seminary; Ph.D., Columbia; L.H.D., Chicago.

Taught philosophy: Columbia, 1921–1923; University of Chicago, 1923–

1931; Cornell, since 1932. Visiting Professor: Harvard, 1927–1928; Stanford, 1931–1932; Hawaii, 1941.

Represented the American Philosophical Association in India, Egypt, and China, 1946–1947. Other extensive visits to the East, 1953–1954, 1956. Member, Second East-West Philosophers' Conference, University of Hawaii, 1949.

Author of *Metaphysical Foundations of Modern Physical Science; Right Thinking; English Philosophy from Bacon to Mill; Types of Religious Philosophy; Teachings of the Compassionate Buddha;* and *Man Seeks the Divine.*

WING-TSIT CHAN

Professor of Chinese Culture and Philosophy, Dartmouth College; Chairman, Division of the Humanities • A.B., Lingnan University, Canton, 1924; Ph.D., Harvard, 1929.

Dean, Lingnan University, 1929–1936; Professor of Chinese Philosophy, University of Hawaii, 1936–1942.

Guggenheim Fellow, 1948–1949; Rockefeller Foundation Research Grantee, 1955–1956; American Council of Learned Societies and Social Research Council Research Grantee, 1959.

American Council of Learned Societies Lecturer on Chinese Religion, 1950–1951; Haskell Lecturer, University of Chicago, 1950.

Member, East-West Philosophers' Conferences, Honolulu, 1939 and 1949; Member, Conference on Science, Philosophy and Religion, New York, 1944, 1945; Member, American Council of Learned Societies Committee on Far Eastern Studies, 1950–1953.

Author of *Religious Trends in Modern China; An Outline and an Annotated Bibliography of Chinese Philosophy; Major Works of Wang Yang-ming* (in press); *A Source Book in Chinese Philosophy* (in press), and other books. Contributor, *Encyclopedia Britannica,* other encyclopedias, and symposium volumes.

Member, Board of Editors, *Philosophy East and West;* Consulting Editor, *Tsing-hua Journal.*

GEORGE P. CONGER

Emeritus Professor of Philosophy, University of Minnesota (until his death, August 14, 1960) • A.B., Cornell University, 1907; B.D., Union Theological Seminary, 1910; Fellow of same, Berlin, Jena, Paris, Heidelberg, 1910–1912; Ph.D. Columbia University, 1922.

Ordained, Presbyterian Church, 1913; Y.M.C.A. Secretary, War Prisons, Khabarovsk, Siberia, 1916–1917.

Assistant Professor, Associate Professor, Professor of Philosophy, University of Minnesota, 1920–1952; Chairman, Department of Philosophy, 1940–1952;

Visiting Professor, University of Hawaii; Member, East-West Philosophers' Conferences, 1939 and 1949; Visiting Professor of Philosophy, Ohio Wesleyan University, 1952–1954.

President, Western Division, American Philosophical Association, 1944–1946; Chairman, National Board of Officers, 1946.

Studied in India (visited Gandhi, Tagore, Iqbal, and other leaders), 1933–1934. Delegate to Indian Philosophy Congress, 1950. Ghosh Lecturer, University of Calcutta (walked with Vinoba Bhave; horseback pilgrimage to Lumbini), 1955.

Author of *The Ideologies of Religion; Epitomization; Towards the Unification of the Faiths;* and *Synoptic Naturalism.*

DHIRENDRA MOHAN DATTA

Retired Professor of Philosophy, Patna University, now at Santiniketan, since 1953 • M.A., 1921; Premchand Raychand Scholar, 1927; Ph.D., 1930, Calcutta University.

Received training for social work in Mahatma Gandhi's Ashram at Sabarmati, Bombay, and did social work in Mymensing villages, 1921–1924. Worked as Research Fellow at Indian Institute of Philosophy, Amalner, Bombay, 1924–1925; as Basu Mallik Professor of Indian Philosophy at Bengal National Council of Education, Calcutta, 1925–1928; as Assistant Professor and Professor at Patna College, Patna University, 1928–1953, and, intercurrently, Visiting Professor at the University of Wisconsin and the University of Minnesota, 1951–1952.

Member of Indian Philosophical Congress, since 1925; General President, 1952; Member, East-West Philosophers' Conference, 1949.

Publications: *Six Ways of Knowing; Introduction to Indian Philosophy* (with S. C. Chatterjee); *The Chief Currents of Contemporary Philosophy;* and *The Philosophy of Mahatma Gandhi.*

GRAY L. DORSEY

Professor of Law, Washington University Law School • A.B., University of Kansas, 1941; LL.B., Yale Law School, 1948; J.S.D., Yale Law School, 1950.

Assistant Professor, Associate Professor, and Professor of Law, Washington University School of Law, St. Louis, 1951 to present. Visiting Professor of Constitutional and International Law at National Taiwan University and Soochow University, Taipei, Taiwan, 1952–1953.

Fellow, American Council of Learned Societies, 1948–1950; Member, St. Louis, Mo., and American Bar Associations; Lecturer at Foreign Service Institute, Department of State, 1956–1959; Lecturer, Air War College, 1958–1959.

Has published articles on law and social organization in American and Chinese symposia and journals.

SIDNEY HOOK

Professor of Philosophy, New York University • B.S., College of the City of New York, 1923; M.A., Columbia University, 1926; Ph.D., Columbia University, 1927.

Instructor, New York University, 1927–1932; Instructor, Columbia University, 1930; New York University, Assistant Professor, 1933–1934; Associate Professor, 1934–1939; Chairman, Department of Philosophy, 1934 to present; Professor, 1939 to present. Currently, Head, all-University Department of Philosophy.

Guggenheim Fellow, 1928, 1929, and 1953; Ford Foundation Fellow, 1959; Butler Silver Medal for Distinction in Philosophy and Education, 1943. Organizer: Conference on Methods in Science and Philosophy; Congress for Cultural Freedom. President, Eastern Division, American Philosophical Association, 1959.

Among his most recent publications are: *American Philosophers at Work*, ed.; *Common Sense and the Fifth Amendment;* and *Determinism and Freedom in the Age of Modern Science: A Philosophical Symposium*, ed.

HSIEH YU-WEI

Professor of Philosophy, National Chengchih University, Taipei • B.A., Soochow University, 1926; M.A., Harvard University, 1931.

Editor-in-chief, *Hsin Pao*, Batavia, Java, 1926–1929; Professor, National Kwangtung Law College, Canton, 1932–1937; Professor and Chairman of the Department of Philosophy, National Chekiang University, 1938–1948; Editor-in-chief, *The Free Press*, Djakarta, Indonesia, 1949–1952; Editorial Director, *The Central Daily News*, Taipei, 1953–1954.

HU SHIH

President, Academia Sinica (until his death, February 24, 1962) • B.A., Cornell University; Ph.D., Columbia University. Holder of over thirty honorary degrees from American and European universities.

From 1917, a leading figure in the Literary Revolution of China.

Professor of Philosophy, and later Chairman of the Department of English Literature, at the National Peking University, 1917–1927; President of the China National Institute, 1928–1930; Dean of the College of Arts at the National Peking University, 1930–1937; Ambassador to the U. S., 1942–1945; Chancellor of the National Peking University, 1938–1942.

Major publications include: (in Chinese) *A History of Chinese Philosophy; History of Vernacular Literature; The Philosophy of Tai Chen; Collected Essays; Recent Essays on Learned Subjects; Forty Years—An Autobiography;* (in English) *The Development of the Logical Method in Ancient China; The Chinese Renaissance.*

HIDEO KISHIMOTO

Professor of Religion, Tokyo University • B.A., Tokyo Imperial University, 1926; M.A., Harvard University, 1934; Ph.D., Tokyo University, 1945.

Lecturer at Tokyo University, 1934–1945; Associate Professor, Tokyo University, 1945–1947; Professor, Tokyo University, 1947 to present.

President, Japanese Association for Religious Studies, 1950–1954; Visiting Professor at Stanford University, 1953–1954; Haskell Lecturer, University of Chicago, 1954; participated in UNESCO Conference, San Francisco, 1957; Executive Secretary, The International Congress for the History of Religions, 1958; UNESCO Lecturer for North Europe and U. S. for East-West program, 1958–1959. Has frequently represented his country at international conferences.

FRANK H. KNIGHT

Emeritus Professor of Economics, University of Chicago • Ph.B., Milligan College, Tennessee, 1911; B.S. and M.A., University of Tennessee, 1913; Ph.D., Cornell University, 1916.

Instructor, Cornell University, 1916–1917, and University of Chicago, 1918–1919. Associate Professor, University of Iowa, 1919–1921; Professor, 1921–1928. Professor, University of Chicago, 1928–1951. Professor Emeritus, since 1951, but has continued teaching. In later years, Distinguished Service Professor of Social Sciences and Philosophy, University of Chicago.

Summer Session or Special Lecture Courses at several institutions, including London University, Cambridge and Glasgow universities, and a number of American universities. Occasional lectures at Harvard, Yale, University of California (Berkeley and Los Angeles), University of Oregon, and others.

Fellow at Center for Advanced Study of Behavioral Sciences, Stanford, 1957.

D.Litt., Princeton; LL.D., Northwestern; LL.D., Glasgow; L.H.D., Columbia. Received Walker Medal of American Economics Association, 1957—and was President, 1950. (Note: Dr. Knight was selected early in 1959 by the Chamber of Commerce of the United States as one of seven "great living Americans.")

Among his publications are: *Risk, Uncertainty and Profit; The Ethics of Competition and Other Essays; Freedom and Reform;* and *Intelligence and Democratic Action.*

STELLA KRAMRISCH

Visiting Professor, Departments of Oriental Studies and South Asia Regional Studies, University of Pennsylvania; Curator of Indian Art, Philadelphia Museum of Art • Ph.D., University of Vienna, in History of Art, Philosophy, 1919.

Professor of Indian Art, University of Calcutta, 1922–1952; Lecturer in Indian Art, Courtauld Institute, London University, 1936–1940.

Honorary Member, École Française d'Extrême-Orient, Hanoi; Vice President, Indian Society of Oriental Art, Calcutta; Fellow, Bollingen Foundation.

Publications: *The Hindu Temple; The Art of India; Kerala and Drāvida; Indian Sculpture; The Viṣṇudharmottara; A Survey of Painting in the Deccan; Pāla Sculpture;* and *Principles of Indian Art.*

CORNELIUS KRUSÉ

Professor of Philosophy, Wesleyan University • B.A., Yale University, 1915; M.A., 1917; Ph.D., 1922. L.H.D. (Honorary), Lawrence College, Appleton, Wisconsin, 1952.

Visiting Lecturer in Ethics and Philosophy of Religion, Yale University, 1925, 1942–1943.

Foreign Service Secretary of American Friends Service Committee, 1946–1947; Executive Director, American Council of Learned Societies, 1947–1958, and Chairman of the Board of Directors, 1949–1953; Secretary-Treasurer, Eastern Division, American Philosophical Association, 1937–1939; Acting Secretary-Treasurer, National Association, 1938, and Secretary-Treasurer, 1939–1946; President, Eastern Division, 1947, and Chairman of National Board of Officers, 1947, 1959–1961; Chairman of Committee on International Co-operation.

Member of North American delegation at International Congress of Philosophy, Harvard, 1926; Oxford, 1930; Prague, 1934; Paris, 1937. Secretary-Treasurer, Organizing Committee of First Inter-American Congress of Philosophy, 1941–1943.

On cultural mission to Latin America under auspices of American Philosophical Association and Co-ordinator's Office for Inter-American Affairs, 1943; U. S. Specialist on mission to Latin American, Department of State, Program of International Educational Exchange, 1956 and 1958.

Vice President of Congress International de Philosophie, Port-au-Prince, Haiti, 1944; President, Second Inter-American Congress of Philosophy, 1947;

Chairman of North American Delegation to Third Inter-American Congress of Philosophy, Mexico, 1950; Vice President, Inter-American Congress of Philosophy at Sao Paolo, 1954, Vice President, Congress at Santiago, 1956; President of Inter-American Society of Philosophy, 1957; Member, Second East-West Philosophers' Conference, 1949; Member of Steering Committee, Third East-West Philosophers' Conference, 1959; Member of Executive Board of American Friends Service Committee, 1952–1958; Director of Friends' Program at United Nations, 1954.

Member, Commission on the Occupied Areas, American Council on Education; Member of the Advisory Board of the *Philosophical Review;* of Board of Editors of *Philosophy East and West;* of Editorial Board, *Philosophy and Phenomenological Research;* of Advisory Board of Handbook of Latin American Studies of Hispanic Foundation, Library of Congress; of Sociedad Chilena de Filosofia, also of Uruguay and Costa Rica; of U. S. Advisory Selection Committee of Fellows under Buenos Aires Fellowship Exchange Convention; and of the Pan-American Committee on the History of Ideas, Mexico City.

Co-author, *Essays in East-West Philosophy; The Nature of Man; The Nature of Religious Experience.*

T. M. P. MAHADEVAN

University Professor of Philosophy, University of Madras • B.A., Presidency and Pachaiyappa's colleges, Madras, 1933; University research scholar, 1933–1935; Ph.D., University of Madras, 1937.

Lecturer in Logic, Raja's College, Pudukkottai, 1935–1937; Professor of Philosophy, Pachaiyappa's College, Madras, 1937–1943; Head of the Department of Philosophy, University of Madras, 1943–.

In 1948–1949, lectured on Indian Philosophy at Cornell University and other American universities; gave the Foerster Foundation Lecture at the University of California (Berkeley); participated in the Goethe Bicentennial Convocation at Aspen, Colorado; Program Member, East-West Philosophers' Conference, University of Hawaii, 1949.

General President of the Thirtieth Session of the Indian Philosophical Congress, 1955; Area-Secretary for the Union for the Study of the Great Religions since its inception.

Among his publications are: *The Philosophy of Advaita; Outlines of Hinduism; Guaḍapāda: A Study in Early Advaita; Time and the Timeless; The Idea of God in Śaiva Siddhānta.*

HAROLD E. McCARTHY

Professor of Philosophy, University of Hawaii • B.A., 1937; M.A., 1939; Ph.D., 1947, University of California.

Since 1947, at the University of Hawaii; Professor of Philosophy, 1959–.

Member of the Board of Editors of *Philosophy East and West,* and has published numerous articles in technical journals.

SHOSON MIYAMOTO

Emeritus Professor of Buddhist Philosophy, Tokyo University • M.A., Otani University, 1918; Ph.D., Oxford University, 1929; D. Litt., Imperial University of Tokyo, 1942.

In 1913, turned to Buddhist studies from medical studies at the Chiba Medical College (1911–1913). At Otani University, Kyoto, 1913–1918; and at the Imperial University, Tokyo, 1918–1923; appointed Lecturer at the Imperial University, Tokyo, and sent to Europe as Government Research Scholar. Advanced student at Oxford University, 1924–1928. Doctoral dissertation: "Study of Nāgārjuna."

Assistant Professor, Imperial University of Tokyo, 1928; Professor, 1942–1954; Professor Emeritus, 1954–; Professor at Waseda and Komazawa universities, 1955. Visiting Professor at the University of Chicago, 1958–1959.

Member, Science Council of Japan; Chairman of Directors, Japanese Association of Indian and Buddhist Studies; Member of Executive Board of the International Association for the History of Religions.

Books (in Japanese): *Ultimate Middle and Voidness; Mahāyāna and Hīnayāna; Middle Way Thought and Its Development* (D. Litt. dissertation); Editor, *A Study of the Formative History of Mahāyāna Buddhism;* Editor, *The Fundamental Truth of Buddhism.* Author of many articles in English.

CHARLES A. MOORE

Senior Professor of Philosophy, University of Hawaii • A.B., Yale University, 1926; Ph.D., 1932. Studied at Banaras Hindu University, 1947–1948, and at Oxford University, 1948, with Dr. S. Radhakrishnan.

Instructor in Philosophy at Yale, 1933–1936; Department of Philosophy, University of Hawaii, since 1936; Senior Professor, 1955–. Visiting Professor at Duke, Cornell, and Boston universities, and University of Southern California. Director of East-West Philosophers' Conferences, 1939, 1949.

Guggenheim Fellow and Watumull Foundation Associate, 1947–1948.

Member of the American Philosophical Association, the American Oriental Society, the Indian Philosophical Congress Association, and the Association for Asian Studies.

Editor, *Philosophy—East and West* and *Essays in East-West Philosophy;* Co-editor, with Dr. S. Radhakrishnan, *A Source Book in Indian Philosophy,* and, with Wing-tsit Chan, Junjiro Takakusu's *The Essentials of Buddhist Philosophy;* Editor of the Journal, *Philosophy East and West;* author of numerous articles for philosophical journals and symposium volumes.

PAUL MUS

Professor in Civilizations of the Far East, Collège de France, and Professor of South East Asia Studies, Yale University • Educated at Lycée Albert Sarraut, Hanoi, 1914–1918; Lycée Henri IV, Paris; at the Sorbonne, where he received the Licence de Philosophie; at the École Nationale des Langues Orientales Vivantes, Paris, from which he was graduated in 1925; École Practique des Hautes Études à la Sorbonne, specializing in Sanskrit and Pāli, and graduating in 1926, Collège de France. Docteur ès Lettres, Paris.

Member of the École Française d'Extrême-Orient, 1927–1939; Secretary and Librarian, 1930–1939; Acting Director, 1939; Missions: Java, Siam, 1928; Champa, 1930, 1933–1934. Director-General of Public Education, French West Africa, and Togoland, Dakar, 1941–1943. Director of the National School of Overseas Administration, Paris, 1947–1950. Professor in Civilizations of the Far East, Collège de France, 1946.

Publications include: *Bārābudur Esquisse d'une histoire du bouddhisme fondée sur la critique archéologique des textes; La lumière sur les Six voies, Tableau de la transmigration bouddhique; Viet Nam: Sociologie d'une guerre; Le Destin de l'Union Française;* and numerous articles.

WINFIELD E. NAGLEY

Associate Professor of Philosophy, Chairman, Department of Philosophy, University of Hawaii • B.A., University of Southern California, 1940; B.D., San Francisco Theological Seminary, 1943; Ph.D., University of Southern California, 1947.

Taught philosophy at Lewis and Clark College, 1947–1948, and Washington State College, 1949–1951.

Associate Member of Second East-West Philosophers' Conference, 1949; Member, Board of Editors, *Philosophy East and West.*

Publications: Several articles in *Philosophy East and West* and other periodicals.

HAJIME NAKAMURA

Professor of Indian and Buddhist Philosophy, Tokyo University • Graduated from the Imperial University of Tokyo, 1936; D. Litt., University of Tokyo, 1943.

President, Japan–India Society; Director, Japanese Association for Indian and Buddhist Studies; Director, Japanese Association for Religious Studies; Life Member, Bhandarkar Oriental Research Institute, Poona; Member, American Oriental Society.

Visiting Professor of Philosophy, Stanford University, 1951–1952; Delegate to Congress on Cultural Freedom in Asia, Rangoon, 1955; and Delegate to the Buddhist Symposium sponsored by the Government of India, New Delhi, 1956. Has lectured at University of Michigan, Delhi University, Banaras Hindu University, University of Hawaii, and other universities.

Editor, *Bulletin of the Okurayama Oriental Research Institute;* Editor, *Science of Thought;* Associate Editor, *Monumenta Nipponica;* Contributing Editor, *United Asia.*

Awarded the Imperial Prize by the Japan Academy, 1957, for *A History of Early Vedānta Philosophy* (4 vols.).

Has published in Japanese some twenty-five volumes on Eastern philosophy and many articles in Western languages. His latest book, in Japanese and in English translation, is *Ways of Thinking of Eastern Peoples* (2 vols.).

SWAMI NIKHILANANDA

Founder and Leader, Ramakrishna-Vivekananda Center, New York • Spent four years at University of Calcutta. Joined the Ramakrishna Order in 1921. Came to America in 1931. Founded the Ramakrishna-Vivekananda Center of New York in 1933 and is now its leader.

Delegate to East-West Philosophers' Conference, 1949; taught special course on Indian thought at Columbia University, 1952–1955; Member Seminar on Inter-religious Relations, Columbia University, for past three years. Frequent lecturer at universities, churches, and other cultural organizations. Member, American Philosophical Association.

Among his works are *The Gospel of Sri Ramakrishna; The Bhagavad Gītā; The Upanishads* (4 vols.); *Self-Knowledge; Vedāntasāra;* and, most recently, *Hinduism: Its Meaning for the Liberation of the Spirit.*

F. S. C. NORTHROP

Sterling Professor of Philosophy and Law, Yale University • B.A., Beloit College, 1915; M.A., Yale University, 1919; M.A., 1922, and Ph.D., 1924, Harvard University. Also studied at the University of Freiburg at the Institute of

Science and Technology, London, and at Trinity College, Cambridge. Litt. D. (Honorary), Beloit College; LL.D., University of Hawaii. Professor Extraordinario, La Universidad Nacional Autonoma de Mexico. Order of the Aztec Eagle conferred by Mexican Government (1949).

Visiting Professor, University of Iowa, University of Michigan, University of Virginia, University of Hawaii, National University of Mexico, and Dyasm Lecturer, University of Melbourne.

Fellow of the American Academy of Arts and Sciences, the American Association for the Advancement of Science, and the Connecticut Academy of Arts and Sciences. Member of Phi Beta Kappa, Sigma Xi, the New York Philosophy Club, and the American Academy of Political and Social Science. President of the Society of the History and Philosophy of Science, 1948, and of the American Philosophical Association, Eastern Division, 1952. Member of the Directing or Advisory Board of the Society for the Philosophy of Science, The Wenner-Gren Foundation for Anthropological Research, *Philosophy East and West,* the Natural Law Forum, and the World Association of World Federalists.

Author of *Science and First Principles; The Meeting of East and West; The Logic of the Sciences and the Humanities; The Taming of the Nations; European Union and United States Foreign Policy; The Complexity of Legal and Ethical Experience; Philosophical Anthropology and Practical Politics.* Editor, *Ideological Differences and World Order;* and contributor to many scholarly journals in philosophy, science, and law.

SARVEPALLI RADHAKRISHNAN

Vice President of India and Chancellor, Delhi University • Education: Madras Christian College.

Professor of Philosophy, Presidency College, 1909–1917, and Mysore University, 1918–1921; Professor of Mental and Moral Science, Calcutta University, 1921.

Upton Lecturer, Oxford University; Haskell Lecturer, University of Chicago, 1926; and Hibbert Lecturer, Oxford University, 1929.

Vice Chancellor, Andhra Universtiy, 1931–1936; Spalding Professor of Eastern Religions and Ethics, Oxford University, 1936; Vice Chancellor, Banaras Hindu University, 1938–1948; President, Indian Philosophical Congress, 1927. Chancellor, Delhi University, 1953–.

Member, League of Nations International Committee on Intellectual Cooperation, 1931–1939; Leader of Indian Delegation to UNESCO in 1946, 1947, 1948, 1949, 1950, 1952; Chairman, UNESCO Executive Board, 1948; President, UNESCO, 1952. Ambassador to U.S.S.R., 1949–1952; Vice President of India, 1952 to present.

Major publications include: *Indian Philosophy; Philosophy of Rabindranath Tagore; Hindu View of Life; Reign of Religion in Contemporary Phi-*

losophy; An Idealist View of Life; East and West in Religion; Kalki or the Future of Civilization; Religion and Society; Eastern Religions and Western Thought; India and China; The Bhagavadgītā; The Dhammapada; The Principal Upaniṣads.

P. T. RAJU

University Professor of Philosophy and Psychology, University of Rajasthan • B.A., Allahabad, 1928; Sastri, Sanskrit University, Benares, 1929; M.A., 1931, Ph.D., 1935, Calcutta.

Tata Visiting Professor of Philosophy, The Asia Institute, New York, 1949; Visiting Professor of Philosophy, University of California (Berkeley), 1950; Visiting Professor of Philosophy, University of Illinois, 1952–1953; Sir Hari Singh Gaur Foundation Lecturer, Saugar University, 1956; Visiting Professor, M. S. University, Baroda, 1957; Woodward Lecturer, Yale University, 1950; Century Fund Lecturer, Northwestern University, 1953; lecturer at several other American universities.

General President, All-India Philosophical Conference (Hindi), 1958; Guest Member, New York Philosophy Club, 1949; Member, American Philosophical Association; Member, East-West Philosophers' Conference, 1949.

Dean of the Faculty of Arts, University of Rajasthan, 1950–1953; Member, Committee on Gandhian Studies, Government of India; attended several international conferences and represented the University of Rajasthan at the Commonwealth Universities Congress, 1953.

Awarded the Order of Merit, "Padma Bhushan," by the President of India, 1958, for contributions to East-West understanding at the philosophical level.

Most recent major works are: *Idealistic Thought of India; Thought and Reality;* and *The Concept of Man* (with S. Radhakrishnan).

CONSTANTIN REGAMEY

Professor of Slavic and Oriental Languages, University of Lausanne, and Professor of General Linguistics, University of Fribourg • Educated at University of Warsaw (Indian Philology), Ph.D., 1936, and École des Hautes Études, Paris.

Privatdocent at Warsaw University (Indology), 1937–1939. Also active in the field of music as composer and musicographer.

Major publications: *Bibliographie analytique des travaux concernants les éléments anaryens dans les langues et les civilisations de l'Inde; Three Chapters from the Samādhirājasūtra; Bhadramāyākāravyākarana; Considérations sur le système morphologique du tibétain littéraire; Buddhistische Philosophie Bibliographische Einführung; East and West: Some Aspects of Historic Evolution.*

F. J. VON RINTELEN

Professor of Philosophy, University of Mainz • Doctor of Philosophy, University of Munich, 1924; Dr. Lit. h. c., Dr. en artes h. c.

Assistant Professor, University of Munich, 1928. Professor, University of Bonn, 1934; Munich, 1936. Professor, University of Mainz, 1946, and Director, Philosophical Institute. President, Society for Philosophy in Germany, 1948–1955. Member, Comité Directeur de la Fédération Internationale des Sociétés de Philosophie. Visiting Professor, Universidad de Cordoba, Argentina, 1951–1952. Visiting Professor, University of Southern California, 1957.

Among his recent publications are: *Philosophie der Endlichkeit als Spiegel der Gegenwart; Goethe: Espirito e Vida; Der Rang des Geistes: Goethes Weltverstandnis; Der europäische Mensch; European Man: A Cultural Philosophical Study; Beyond Existentialism.* Co-editor, *Zeitschrift für Philosophische Forschung; Kantstudien; Philosophisches Jahrbuch; Philosophical Bulletin—Visva Tattvajnana Mandira Quarterly.*

ROBERT ROSSOW, JR.

Counselor for Political Affairs, American Embassy, Kabul, Afghanistan • B.S. in Foreign Service, Georgetown University School of Foreign Service, 1939.

University of Pennsylvania, South Asia language and area study, 1948–1949. National War College, 1957–1958.

Commissioned Foreign Service Officer, Secretary in the Diplomatic Service and Vice Consul of Career, 1940. Has served as Vice Consul, American Consulate General, Vancouver, Canada; Third Secretary and Political Officer, American Embassy, Panama, R.P.; Military service, assigned OSS; Vice Consul in Charge, American Consulate, Tabriz, Iran; Third Secretary and Political Officer, American Embassy, Tehran; Second Secretary and Political Officer, American Legation, Sofia, Bulgaria; Area and language study (South Asia), University of Pennsylvania; Consul and Executive Officer and Consul in Charge, American Consulate General, Madras; Officer in Charge, US Information Service, Kathmandu, Nepal; Consul and Public Affairs Officer (in charge USIS), Calcutta; Policy and Programs Officer for South Asia, US Information Agency, Washington; Head, Department of Mid-Career Training, and Chairman, Mid-Career Course on Foreign Affairs, Foreign Service Institute, Washington; and Student, National Air College.

PAUL KICHYUN RYU

Academic Dean, Seoul National University • Graduated Himezi National College in Japan, 1939. LL.B., Tokyo Imperial University Law School, 1943. J.S.D., Yale University, 1958.

Visiting Scholar, Yale University Law School, 1952–1953; Visiting Scholar, Harvard University Law School, 1954–1956.

Assistant Professor of Law, Seoul National University, 1946–1952; Associate Professor, 1953–1954; Professor since 1954. Acting Dean, Law School, 1950–1952. Academic Dean, 1958–.

Has published several articles in American Law Reviews.

S. K. SAKSENA

University Professor and Head of the Department of Philosophy, Saugar University • Educated at the University of Allahabad and at the University of London, where he received his M.A. and Ph.D. degrees in Philosophy.

Has taught philosophy at the University of Agra and Delhi University. Visiting Professor of Indian Philosophy and Culture, University of Hawaii, 1950–1952.

For five years served in the Ministry of Information and Broadcasting of the Government of India as Deputy Director (Editorial) in the Publications Division.

Traveled and lectured widely in Europe, Hawaii, and Japan.

Author of *Nature of Consciousness in Hindu Philosophy,* articles in professional journals, and chapters in many symposium volumes. On Board of Editors, *Philosophy East and West,* and co-editor, *Indian Philosophical Quarterly.*

HERBERT W. SCHNEIDER

Emeritus Professor of Philosophy, Columbia University • Ph.D., Columbia, 1917; L.H.D., Union College, 1947.

Visiting Professor: University of Washington, 1946; Emory University, 1957; Colorado College, 1958–1959; Pomona College, 1959–1960.

On staff of UNESCO in Paris, 1953–1956.

Editor, *Journal of Philosophy.*

Rockefeller Research Fellow in Italy, and Fulbright Fellow in France.

Organized for UNESCO a Symposium on International Obligations, held in Ceylon, 1954. Visited other countries of South East Asia on a UNESCO Mission, 1955.

Organizing Director, Blaisdell Institute for Advanced Study in World Cultures and Religions, 1959–.

M. M. SHARIF

Director, Institute of Islamic Culture, Lahore • Attended Muhammadan Anglo-Oriental College, Aligarh. B.A., Allahabad and Cambridge, 1914 and 1916, respectively.

In 1917, appointed Professor of Philosophy in the Muhammadan Anglo-Oriental College—later University. Chairman of the Department of Philosophy, 1921–1928, 1945–1948. For about three years he was Pro-Vice Chancellor of the University.

General President, Indian Philosophical Congress, 1945.

From 1952 to 1955, Principal of the Islamia College, Lahore, and, in 1956, Dean of the Faculty of Arts at the University of the Panjab. Has since been a member of the governing body of the University, the Chancellor's Committee.

Founder and President, Pakistan Philosophical Congress; Member of the Directorate of the International Federation of Philosophical Societies, Paris; recently appointed Director, Institute of Islamic Culture, Lahore.

Has published four major philosophical works and contributed many articles to philosophical journals. Honorary Editor, *Iqbal;* Editor-Secretary, *History of Muslim Philosophy.* Editor-in-chief, *Pakistan Philosophical Journal.*

W. T. STACE

Emeritus Professor of Philosophy, Princeton University • Educated at Fettes College, Edinburgh, and Dublin University.

In 1910, entered British Civil Service in Ceylon. Worked in Ceylon, as Magistrate, Judge, Private Secretary to the Governor, Mayor of Colombo, and other capacities, 1910–1932.

Lecturer in philosophy, 1932–1935, then Professor, Princeton University, 1935–1955.

Major publications are: *A Critical History of Greek Philosophy; The Philosophy of Hegel; The Theory of Knowledge and Existence; The Concept of Morals; The Nature of the World; The Destiny of Western Man; Religion and the Modern Mind; Time and Eternity; The Gate of Silence.*

ALAN KER STOUT

Professor of Philosophy, University of Sydney; Chairman, Board of Social Work and Fellow of the Senate (University's governing body) • Educated at Fettes College, Edinburgh, and Oriel College, Oxford.

Lecturer in Philosophy, University of Wales, 1924–1934; Independent Lecturer in Social Ethics, University of Edinburgh, 1934–1939.

Original member of Australian National Film Board, 1945–1947; Chairman,

New South Wales Film Council; Patron, Howard Prison Reform Council in New South Wales; Member of Australian Government's UNESCO East-West Philosophy Working-party, Canberra, 1957.

Editor, *Australian Journal of Philosophy;* Editor, *God and Nature* (Gifford Lectures of G. F. Stout); author of articles in *Mind, Proceedings of the Australian Society, The Australian Journal of Philosophy,* etc.

DAISETZ TEITARO SUZUKI

Emeritus Professor of Buddhism, Otani University • Attended Imperial University, Tokyo, but did not officially graduate. Spent his spare time in this period as a novice in a Zen monastery in Kamakura. In 1897, came to the U.S. as translator for the Open Court Publishing Co. Spent eleven years working with Paul Carus, during which time they translated the *Tao-te ching* into English, and wrote his first book in English, *Outline of Mahayana Buddhism.*

Returned to Japan in 1909 to resume studies in Zen.

Starting in 1921, spent twenty years teaching Buddhist philosophy at Otani University, Kyoto.

Attended the World Congress of Faiths in London in 1936. Member, East-West Philosophers' Conference, Honolulu, 1949. Decorated with the Cultural Medal by the Emperor of Japan and elected Member, Japan Academy, 1949.

Lectured at Yale University, 1949. Has been Associate Professor at Columbia University and Professor at Claremont College. Lectured at Columbia University, 1952–1958.

The latest of his many publications is an enlarged and revised edition of his *Zen and Japanese Culture.* Among his numerous publications are: *Outline of Mahayana Buddhism; Essays in Zen Buddhism* (3 "Series"); *The Lankavatara Sutra* (translation); *Studies in the Lankavatara Sutra; Manual of Zen Buddhism; Living by Zen; Zen Buddhism;* and *Mysticism: Christian and Buddhist.*

T'ANG CHÜN-I

Professor of Philosophy, New Asia College, Hong Kong • Educated at Sino-Russian University, Peking University, and National Central University, 1925-1932.

When the Sino-Japanese War broke out in 1937, served in the West China Union University as Lecturer in Philosophy. From 1942–1949, was Associate Professor and later Professor in the National Central University.

After the communist occupation of the Chinese Mainland, went to Hong Kong and joined the work of establishing New Asia College, at which he has served as Dean since its beginning.

His major publications (in Chinese) are: *Comparative Studies in Chinese and Western Philosophies; Reconstruction of the Moral Self; Experience of Human Life; Spiritual Values in Chinese Culture; Reconstruction of the Humanistic Spirit;* and *Cultural Consciousness and Moral Reason.*

THE VENERABLE U THITTILA

Lecturer on Buddhist Philosophy, University of Rangoon • Became a *samanera* (novice) at the age of 15, and then a *bhikkhu* (ordained monk) at 20 under the leadership of the Venerable *Ashin* (Reverend) Adicca Vamsa. For twelve years, teacher and lecturer at the Ashi Adicca Vamsa Monastery, Rangoon.

Went to England in 1938 to undertake studies in education and remained there for fourteen years.

Compiled a Burmese-English Dictionary, wrote *Buddhism and the Personal Life* and many articles on Buddhism for English magazines, and translated the *Dhammapada* into modern Burmese.

Appointed lecturer in Buddhist Philosophy, at the University of Rangoon, 1950.

The title "Agga Maha Pandita" ("the greatest of the wise men"), Burma's highest award for Buddhist learning, was conferred upon him by the Government in 1956.

W. H. WERKMEISTER

Director, School of Philosophy, University of Southern California • Studied at Universities of Muenster and Frankfort, Germany; Ph.D., University of Nebraska, 1927.

University of Nebraska, 1926–1953; Chairman of the Department of Philosophy, 1945–1953; University of Southern California, 1953–. Director, School of Philosophy, 1954–. American Exchange Professor, University of Berlin, 1936–1937; Visiting Lecturer, Harvard University, 1950–1951. Lectured at thirteen German universities. Was Tully Cleon Knoles Lecturer at the College of the Pacific in 1950. Participant in Symposium on "Scientism," sponsored by Emory University, 1958.

Editor, *The Personalist,* a quarterly devoted to philosophy, religion, and literature.

Member: Phi Beta Kappa, American Philosophical Association, International Phenomenological Society, Philosophy of Science Association, and Mind Association.

Author of several books and of many articles in professional journals.

JOHN C. H. WU

Professor of Law, Seton Hall University School of Law, South Orange, New Jersey • LL.B., Comparative Law School of China, Shanghai, 1920. J.D., Michigan University School of Law, 1921. Traveling Fellow of Carnegie Endowment for International Peace, at the Sorbonne and Berlin University.

Research Scholar, Harvard Law School, 1923–1924; Professor of Law, and, later, Principal, of the Comparative Law School of China, 1924–1940; Judge, Chief Justice, and President, successively, of the Provisional Court, later, Special High Court, of the International Settlement of Shanghai, 1927–1929; Rosenthal Lecturer at the Law School of Northwestern University, 1929; Research Fellow, Harvard Law School, 1930; Practiced law in Shanghai, 1930–1932; Member of the Legislative Body of National China, serving successively as Vice Chairman of the Constitution-Drafting Committee, Chairman of the General Committee, and Chairman of the Foreign Relations Committee, 1933–1946; Managing Editor, *T'ien Hsia Monthly,* 1935–1941; Adviser to the Chinese Delegation to the first General Assembly of the United Nations at San Francisco, 1945; Envoy Extraordinary and Minister Plenipotentiary of China to the Holy See, 1946–1949; Visiting Senior Professor of Chinese Philosophy, University of Hawaii, 1949–1951; Professor of Law, Seton Hall University School of Law, 1951; Member of the Permanent Court of Arbitration at the Hague, 1957.

Among his writings are: Chinese versions of *The Psalms* and *The New Testament; Beyond East and West; The Interior Carmel; Fountain of Justice.*

Honorary Degrees: LL.D., University of Oregon, LL.D., Boston College, LL.D., St. John's College. Honorary Membership: American Academy of Arts and Sciences, since 1936; Academy of Living Catholic Authors, since 1956.

*Index**

Abelard, Peter, 330, 331, 465n
Abhinavagupta, 285, 347, 348
Abraham, 722, 725, 726
Absolute, 18, 156, 158, 261, 265, 287, 322, 337n, 347, 374, 430, 436, 507, 575, 606, 607, 631, 632, 646, 726, 727; indeterminate, 158; in phenomenal world, 632
abstract thinking, 246–253; *see also* irrationalism, non-rational tendencies
Abū 'Abdallāh Muhammad ibn Jābir (al-Battāni), 173, 178, 178n
Abū Bakr Muhammad ibn Zakariyyā ar-Rāzī, 175, 177, 177n
Abū Hāmid Muhammad ibn Muhammad al-Ghazzālī, 180, 181n, 294, 468, 469
Abū Naṣr Muhammad ibn Muhammad al-Fārābī, 176, 176n, 180, 465, 466
Abū Yūsuf Ya'qūb ibn Isḥāq ibn al-Sabbāh al-Kindī, 173, 175, 175n
Abūl Waled Muhammad ibn Rushd (Averroës), 181, 181n, 724
"Accents of the World's Philosophies," 60n
achievements, 699–718 *passim*
Ackert, Paul H., 9
activism, 286, 485, 495, 645; disinterested, 485; withdrawal from, 485
"Activism in Indian Thought," 263n, 268n, 270n, 329n
Adams, Henry, 385, 694
Ādiparva, 513n
Adler, Felix, 21
Adler, Mortimer J., 135n
Adolph, E. F., 145n
The Adornment of the Spiritual Marriage, The Sparkling Stone, The Book of Supreme Truth, 307n
adṛṣṭa, 156, 157, 503; *see also* destiny
Advaita, *see* Vedānta
advaitism, 328, 337n, 429–446
Aesthetic Judgment, 345n, 352n
Aesthetic Theories of French Artists, The, 350
"Aesthetic Values in East and West," 342–361
aesthetics, 91, 195, 226, 251, 284–286, 287–291, 289, 342–361, 435, 560, 730–731; Chinese, 238; Japanese, 194–197
Aesthetics, 357
Aesthetik (Hegel), 347n
Aesthetik (Lipps), 349n
Aesthetik und Allegemeine Kunstwissenschaft, 345n, 356, 356n
Africa, 25
agape, 446
Agar, W. E., 145n
aggregates, 274n, 278; *see also skandhas*
Agrarian System in Ancient India, 577n
agreements, 690, 702
Aḥmad ibn Hanbal, 294n
ahamdhī, 276, 277; *see also* I-consciousness
ahaṁkāra (ego, I-consciousness), 272, 277, 282, 323

* Errors in the spelling of names and titles, discovered in the text too late to be corrected there, are corrected here.
The Chinese names and titles which are cited in their Japanese equivalents in the text are listed here in their original forms.
Special thanks are hereby expressed to George T. Artola, Kenneth K. Inada, James J. Y. Liu, Miss Bertha Mueller, Mrs. Floris E. Sakamoto, and Miss Joyce Wright for extraordinary assistance in the preparation of this complicated index.

ahiṁsā, 489, 493, 572, 584, 705; *see also* harmlessness, non-injury, non-violence
Aitareya Āraṇyaka, 488
Aitareya Brāhmaṇa, 159n, 600, 609n
Aitareya Upaniṣad, 267n
Aiyangār, M. V. Varadarāja, 271n
Akamatsu Chiyo, 660n, 662n, 663n
Akamatsu Toshihide, 104n
Akhlāq-i 'Alā'i ('Ali's Ethics), 471n
Akhlāq-i Jalāī (Flashes of Splendor Concerning Excellencies of Dispositions), 471n
Akhlāq-i Muhsinī (Muhsinī's Ethics), 471n
Akhlāq-i Nāṣirī (The Ethics of Nāṣirī), 471n
Akiba Takashi, 660n, 662n, 663n
ālayavijñāna (ideation-store), 240, 265, 738, 753
alchemy, 171, 202
Aldrich, Virgil C., 365–383, 373n, 781
Alexander of Macedon, 70
Alexander, S., 318, 597, 601, 609
Alexandria, 173
algebra, 168, 182, 184–185, 187
'Alī Chelebī, 471n
Alī ibn Hussain Wā'iz al-Kāshifī, 471n
Alī ibn 'Isā al-Asturlābī (Treatise on the Use of the Spherical Astrolabe), 177n
"Alī ibn 'Isā, Das Astrolab und sein Gebrauch," 177n
Alī ibn Yūnis, 177
Allah, 183; *see also* God
Alleged Debt of Islamic to Roman Law, The, 455n
Allen, D. M., 144n
Allport, F. H., 38, 38n
Allport, G. W., 144n, 146n, 147n, 152
Altekar, A. S., 576n, 579n, 583n
Alymer, Maude, 345n
Amano Teiyū, 196n
Amarakośa, 283n
Amaterasu Ōmikami, 104
America, 79, 354, 355, 359, 360, 384–399, 623, 665, 756; international character of, 385–387; *see also* United States
American Anthropologist, 654n, 662n
American Character, The, 386n, 399
American Civilization, 397
American Council of Learned Societies, 10
American Democrat, The, 392, 392n
American Journal of Speculative Philosophy, 19
American Philosophers at Work, 399
American Quarterly, 399
American Society for Aesthetics, 357
American Spirit, The, 399
"American Traits and Principles," 384–399
Ames, Van Meter, 342–361, 352n, 781
Amida Buddha, 105–110, 106, 107, 108, 108n, 109, 110, 112, 196, 232
anābhogacaryā, 440, 443, 444; *see also* no-striving
Analects, 82n, 84n, 85n, 87n, 91n, 93n, 94, 210, 413, 413n, 414, 414n, 420, 423, 423n, 424n, 426, 439n, 614, 614n, 615n, 617n, 619n, 626n, 633, 633n, 656n
Analects of Confucius, The, 84n
analysis, 66, 685–686
Analysis of Beauty, The, 344n
Analysis of Knowledge and Valuation, 368n
ānanda, 106n, 751; *see also* bliss
anātmavāda (theory of no-self), 63
ancestor worship, 113, 420–427
Ancient City, The, 523, 523n, 534, 534n
Ancient Law, The, 521, 525n
ancilla theologiae, 330
anekāntavāda (no-one-truth doctrine), 575
Anesaki Masaharu, 98n, 103n
Angora Reform, The, 457n
Angyal, A., 144n
animism, 660
anitya (impermanence), 257
Annals of the Bhandarkar Oriental Research Institute, 263, 329n
Annual Report of the Board of Regents of the Smithsonian Institution, 660n
Anselm, St., 330
antaḥkaraṇa (inner sense), 277
antarātman (inner self), 587
Anthony, Joseph Garner, 395n
anthropology, 141, 144–145, 155; cultural, 773–779 *passim*
Anthropology Today, 773n
antinomianism, 468
Anuśāsanaparva, 572n
anvīkṣikī (logic), 580
apūrva (extraordinary), 269, 269n, 273
Arabia, 156, 470, 556
Arbman, E., 159n
architecture, 168, 169, 171, 348, 355n, 356n
Aristotle (and Aristotelianism), 33, 39, 49, 69, 70, 80, 173, 174, 176, 179, 181, 232n, 290, 326, 330, 331, 346, 393, 463, 465, 466, 469, 470, 471, 522, 523, 524, 529, 535, 543, 543n, 545, 546, 555, 556, 722, 729, 736
Arjuna, 272, 501, 502, 578, 583, 584, 585, 592
Arnold, E. Vernon, 535, 535n
Art, 351n
"Art and the Public," 358n
art, as bridge, 696–697; *see also* aesthetics
Art as Experience, 345n, 352, 354, 356
Art Education, 357n
Art in America, 356n
Art News Annual, 350n
Art of Law, The, 544n, 617n
artha (material values), 487, 514, 577, 578
Arthaśāstra (Kauṭilya), 496, 501, 502n, 503, 576, 578, 580, 580n, 581, 581n, 583n, 588n, 589, 589n
Arthaśāstras, 578; *see also Arthaśāstra*
arthavāda, 479
Artola, George T., viii
ārya Dharma, 273
Ārya Samāj, 266n, 505
asceticism, 467, 489, 516, 578
"Ascription of Responsibility and Rights, The," 371n
Asia Foundation, The, 10
Asia, rebirth of, 754
Aśoka (and Rock Edicts), 577, 577n, 584, 584n, 585, 588, 592, 632, 636, 637, 638
āśramas, 45, 279, 280, 484; *see also* stages in life
Asrar-i-Khudi (Secrets of the Self), 295n, 296n

Aston, W. C., 661n
astrology, 170
astronomy, 170, 178
al-Asturlabi, 177
ataraxia, 272
Atharva Veda, 497n, 498n, 499n, 507
atheism, 453
Ātmajñānopadeśavidhi, 277n
Ātman (and *ātman*), 57, 63, 170, 265, 267, 268, 269, 270, 273, 274, 274n, 276, 277, 278, 279, 280, 285, 291, 292, 323, 329n, 430, 477, 485, 488, 532, 573, 600, 601, 602, 752
Ātman-Brahman, 321
ātmavāda (doctrine of self), 597
atomism, 157, 170
"Attempt at World Philosophical Synthesis, An," 142n
Aufbau der Persönlichkeit, 146n
Augustine, St., 29, 98, 200, 257, 260, 261, 407, 586, 684, 760
Aum, 750
Aurelius, Marcus, 71
Aurobindo, Sri, 65, 66, 317n, 328, 348, 348n, 493, 573n, 574, 574n, 585
Austin, J. L., 371, 373
Australian Journal of Philosophy, 373n
authority, 619; *see also* testimony
Autobiography (Mill), 28
Autobiography, An (Gandhi), 578n
Avalokiteśvara, 89
Averroës, 181, 181n, 724
Avicenna, 175, 176n, 181, 464, 465, 466, 730
avidyā (ignorance), 231, 443, 573, 759; *see also* ignorance
Ayer, A. J., 369, 369n
āyurveda (medicine, science of longevity), 158, 170, 171

Background of Greek Science, The, 539n
Bacon, Francis, 18, 21, 22, 136, 556
Bacon, Roger, 175, 465n
Baer, Karl Ernst von, 76
Baghdad, 173
Baier, K., 373n
Baillie, J. B., 375n
Bammate, N., 172–187, 673n, 679n, 721–731, 782
Bankei, 444, 733
Bankei Zenji Goroku (Sayings of Bankei), 444n
Banmintokuyō (The Significance of All Vocations), 645n
Banzai attacks, 253
Barabuḍur: Esquisse d'une histoire du Bouddhisme fondée sur la critique archéologique des textes, 605n
Barber, Bernard, 141n
Barth, Karl, 258
"Basic Features of the Legal, Political, and Economic Thought of Japan," 631–647
"Basic Problem in the Quest for Understanding Between East and West, A," 673–691
"Basic Thoughts Underlying Eastern Ethical and Social Practice," 428–447
Basic Writings of Sigmund Freud, The, 144n
Basis and Structure of Knowledge, The, 139n, 141n, 144n, 145n
Basis for the Hindu Act of Truth, The, 163n
Basis of Criticism in the Arts, The, 353n
al-Battānī, 173, 178
al-Battānī sive Albatenii opus astronomicum, 178n
Baudelaire, Charles, 350, 430
Baynes, Carl F., 433n, 623n
Beard, Charles A., 399
Beautiful in Music, The, 351n
Beauvoir, Simone de, 338n, 374, 598, 598n, 599, 606
Becker, C. H., 451n
Becoming: Basic Considerations for a Psychology of Personality, 144n
behaviorism, 142
"Being, Existence, Reality, and Truth," 289n
Beiträge zur Geschichte der Philosophie des Mittelalters, 175n
Beiträge zur Theorie der Rechtsquellen, 535
Belgium, 777
Bell, Clive, 351, 351n, 354
Benardete, José A., 9
Benedict, Ruth, 151n, 652n, 657n, 666, 666n
benevolence, 227, 412, 414, 415, 417, 426, 632, 633, 642
Bentham, Jeremy, 22
Bergaigne, A., 160n, 161n, 163n, 164, 165n, 166n
Bergson, Henri, 80, 247, 338
Berkeley, Bishop George, 21, 335, 523
Berkes, Niyazi, 448–475, 679n, 782
Bernard, C., 146n
Bernard, J. H., 344n
Berolzheimer, Fritz, 586
Bertalanffy, L., von, 145n
Between Man and Man, 151n, 310n
beyond being, 365–366
Beyond Conscience, 393n
"Beyond Ethics" (Aldrich), 365–383
"Beyond Ethics" (Mahadevan), 378, 378n
beyond ethics, 481, 675, 684
Beyond Good and Evil, 374
beyond reason, 308, 675–691 *passim; see also* irrationalism, non-rational tendencies
Bhagavad Gītā, 50, 50n, 54, 54n, 57n, 61n, 93, 264n, 272, 272n, 273–274, 280, 281, 284, 329n, 478, 481, 481n, 485, 486, 486n, 491, 495n, 501, 501n, 502, 509n, 512, 512n, 515, 516n, 517n, 570, 573, 574, 582, 585, 592
Bhāgavatam, 517n
bhakti (devotion), 275, 281, 328, 328n, 690
bhaktimārga (path of devotion), 274
Bharata, 347
Bhāskara, 170
Bhattacharya, K. C., 575n
Bhavabhūti, 285
Bhāve, Vinoba, 493, 574, 575, 592
Bhūdāna-Yajña, 575n
Bible, 510, 555, 756
Bibliothèque de l'École des Hautes Études, 609n
Bigaku (Aesthetics), 357
Bigelow, Julian, 120n
Bigelow, W. S., 195

Bill of Rights, 388, 390
Binswanger, L., 151, 151n
Biochemistry and Morphogenesis, 145n
"Biological Causation," 145n
Biologische Fragmente zu einer Lehre vom Menschen, 144n, 148n
biology, 144–145
Birkeland, H., 452n
Birth-hour of Muslim Law, The, 455n
al-Bīrūnī, 175
Blackney, R. B., 309n
Blake, Max, 371n
Blake, William, 21
Blanshard, Brand, 21
Blanton, Smiley, 685n
Blau, J. L., 399
bliss, 328; *see also ānanda*
Bloomfield, Leonard, 649n
Blue and Brown Books, 371
Boatman, Mrs. Elsie M., 11
Boccaccio, Giovanni, 202
Bodde, Derk, 234n
Bode, Boyd Henry, 766
bodhi (enlightenment), 113, 260, 281, 446, 751, 759
Bodhidharma, 751, 752, 769
bodhisattva (literally, one whose being is knowledge), 107, 240, 253, 281, 443, 446, 644
Bodhisattva Mahāsattva, 103n
Boehme, Jacob, 260
Boethius, Ancius Manlius Severinus, 71, 72
Bogardus, E. S., 36, 36n
Bohr, Niels, 200
Böhtlingk, Otto von, 82n, 85, 603
Bonaventura, St., 729
bondage, 478, 681, 683, 686
Book of Changes, 82n, 85, 209, 212, 216, 217, 623
Book (Classic) of Filial Piety, 415, 415n, 416, 416n, 417, 417n, 419, 419n, 421, 423, 423n
Book of History, 82n, 85, 91, 203, 206, 211, 212, 220, 611, 611n, 612n, 613, 613n, 614n, 615n, 619, 624, 629
Book of Lao Tzu, 204, 205; *see also Lao Tzu, Tao-te ching*
Book of Lord Shang, 618n
Book of Mencius, 82n, 86n, 93n, 231, 233n, 234n, 612n, 618n, 620n, 626n, 413n, 414n, 415n, 416n, 418n, 420n, 423n
Book of Odes (Songs), 82n, 87n, 203, 204, 209, 213, 214, 215, 216, 616, 619, 625n
Book of Propriety (Rites), 82n, 91, 417n, 422n, 424, 424n, 625, 626n; *see also* propriety
Borges, Mrs. Violet, 11
Bosanquet, Bernard, 274, 345
Bose, N. K., 575n, 577n, 581n, 593n
botany, 178
Bousquet, G. H., 469n
Boyle, Robert, 220
Bradley, F. H., 52, 56, 261, 292, 426, 488
Brahma Sūtra, 60n, 62, 169, 171, 256–262, 273, 478, 479, 498, 500, 509, 511, 512
Brahmā, 487
Brahman, 156, 160n, 226, 232, 261, 265, 267, 267n, 268, 270, 271, 283, 287, 323n, 329n, 337, 337n, 380, 430, 492, 499, 500, 507, 508, 509, 510, 516, 517, 532, 573, 574, 575, 576, 581, 587, 606, 608, 721; *Bhauma,* 581; *saguṇa,* 261; *nirguṇa,* 261, 322, 323
Brāhmaṇas, 266, 268, 272n, 273, 587, 589, 600, 608
brahmāṇḍa (cosmic egg), 572
Brahmanism, 232, 597, 600, 602, 606, 655
Brahmāstitvavāda (doctrine of the eternal), 508
brāhmin, 573, 590, 591, 609
Brāhmo Samāj, 341, 505
Brain Mechanisms and Consciousness, 146n
Braisted, Paul J., 9
Bramble Bush, The, 664n
Braque, Georges, 350
Brett, Cecil C., 9
Bṛhadāraṇyaka Upaniṣad, 62n, 157, 271, 272n, 276, 323n, 477, 477n, 481n, 500, 500n, 501n, 507n, 510n, 514, 514n, 600, 600n, 601, 604, 604n
Bṛhat Saṁhitā, 169n
bridge of art, 696–697
bridge of philosophy, 697
bridge of religion, 697
bridge of science, 696
bridges, 155, 696, 697, 707
Brière, O., 382n
Brill, A. A., 144n
Brinton, Crane, 777
British, 359, 588; *see also* England
Broad, C. D., 23
Brogan, D. W., 386n, 399
Brown, B. Warren, 35, 36n
Brown, D. Mackenzie, 9
Brown, F. J., 141n
Brown, W. Norman, 163n
Brownell, Baker, 38, 38n
Browning, Robert, 220
Browning, Robert W., 348n
Bruck, H. W., 128n
Brunner, Heinrich, 663n
Bruno, Giordano, 556
Brunschvicg, Léon, 336n
Brussels Defense Pact, 776
Bryce, Lord James, 562
Buber, Martin, 151n, 153n, 305, 310, 310n
bucchi (the Buddha's wisdom), 106
Buck, Harry M., 9
Buddha, the, 54, 89, 97, 98, 99, 100, 102, 103, 103n, 110, 110n, 111, 195, 232, 239, 240, 249, 257, 260, 261, 265, 273, 274, 281, 285, 381, 444, 487, 493, 570, 584, 585, 593, 641, 644, 660, 736, 740, 741, 744, 748, 749, 757; *see also* Amida Buddha
Buddha and the Christ, The, 107n
Buddhaghoṣa, 597, 598n
Buddhahood, 571
buddhi (individual reason), 271n, 272, 274, 281, 282, 283, 285, 323, 323n, 571
Buddhism, 20, 46, 48, 56, 59, 63, 83, 85, 86, 87, 88, 89, 90, 92, 93, 94, 97–113, 98, 99, 192, 193, 195–197, 227, 231, 239–240, 246, 247, 248, 250, 251, 252, 253, 260, 265, 272, 272n, 273n, 274n, 275, 276, 278, 281, 282, 283n, 286, 286n, 292, 304, 306, 319n, 324, 327, 338n, 349, 357, 378, 421, 422, 428, 429,

432, 433, 440, 441, 445, 478, 479, 505, 507, 524, 525, 532, 571, 575, 589, 597, 598, 632–647 *passim*, 640, 641, 644, 646, 657, 661, 662, 662n, 664, 684, 688, 691, 696, 722, 732–753, 773, 776; as life-affirming, 249; Chinese, 440, 598; Hīnayāna, 379; idealistic, 105, 106, 108, 240; Indian, 111n, 248–249, 440; Japanese, 98n, 103n, 105n, 110n, 111n, 112n, 247–248; Mahāyāna, 92, 99, 110n, 113n, 196, 281, 319, 322, 440, 575
"Buddhist Logic Expounded by Means of Symbolic Logic," 335n
Buitenen, J. A. B. van, 479n
al-Bukhari, 298n, 299n
Bukkoji, 109
Bukkyō Kenkyū (Researches in Buddhism), 97n
Bukkyō no Kompon Shinri (The Fundamental Truth of Buddhism), 108n
Bukkyō Taikei (The Great System of Buddhism—a series), 107n
Bulletin de la Maison Franco-Japonaise, 662n
Bulletin of Mathematical Biophysics, 121n
Bulletin of the School of Oriental and African Studies, 473n
Burke, Edmund, 19, 29, 345, 345n, 376
Burke, Joseph, 344n
Burnet, John, 541n, 542n
Burnier, Raymond, 602n
Burtt, E. A., 11, 523n, 673–691, 782
Bury, John Bagnell, 554
bushidō, 104, 638, 657, 662
Busshin to Bunka (*Buddha*-mind and Culture), 108n
Busshin to sono Hyōgen (*Buddha*-mind and its Revelation), 108n
Butterfield, Herbert, 24n
Byzantine Hesychasm, 328n

Cage, John, 352
Caitanya, 328, 504, 509
Calhoun, John C., 385n
calligraphy, 252, 349
Calvin, John, 645, 760
Campion, C. T., 258n
Cannon, W. B., 146n
Canon of the Sacred Scriptures, 614n
Cantril, H., 144n
Cao-dai, 340
capitalism, 25, 375, 645
Carnap, Rudolph, 369, 524, 529, 529n
Carnegie Corporation of New York, 10
Carritt, E. F., 344n
Cartwright, Dorwin, 649n
Cārvāka, 275, 279, 487, 488, 522
Casanowicz, J. M., 660n
Case for Conservatism, The, 376n
Cases and Materials, 616n
Cassirer, Ernst, 368, 373
caste, 20, 387, 504, 511–513, 517, 523, 532, 590; *see also varṇas*
Castellion (or Castellio or Chateillon) Sebastien, 760
Catálogo de las Ciencias, 176n
Cattel, R. B., 146n
Causation in Criminal Law, 651n
Cauvel, Jane, 9
Cell and Psyche, 146n
Cerebral Mechanisms in Human Behavior, 121n
Chamberlain, Basil Hall, 633n, 634n, 636n, 639n
Ch'an, 99, 240, 429; *see also* Buddhism, Zen
Chan, Wing-tsit, viii, 11, 81–95, 196n, 532, 622n, 650n, 676n, 695, 705, 778, 783
Chāndogya Upaniṣad, 484n, 499n, 500, 500n, 507, 507n, 508n, 600, 604n
Chang Tsai (Chang Heng-ch'ü), 210, 233
Chao-chou Ts'ung-shen, 444
Chapin, I. Stuart, 141n
Chaplin, D., 661n
character, 281, 299, 300
Character of Man, The, 144n, 151n
Charpentier, J., 160n
Chase, D. P., 543n
Chatterjee, M. N., 9
Chatterji, Suniti Kumar, 523, 523n
Chaudhury, Pravas Jivan, 143n, 348n
che (philosophy), 85
chemistry, 182, 184–185
Cheng Ch'iao, 214
Ch'eng-Chu school, 209
Ch'eng Hao (Ch'eng Ming-tao), 83, 86, 209, 233, 241
Cheng Hsüan, 219
Ch'eng I (Ch'eng I-ch'uan), 84, 209, 233
Ch'eng, King, 615
Ch'en Ho-ch'in, 767
Ch'en Ti, 216, 217, 218
Ch'en Tu-hsiu, 228n
"Chess Not Without the Queen," 373n
Chesterton, G. K., 12
ch'i (matter-energy), 85, 86
Chi-i (Tendai Daishi), 104
Chiang Monlin, 634, 655n, 764
Chiang Yee, 539, 539n
Chiang Yu-kao, 217
Chiang Yung, 217
Chiao Hsün, 242
Chiao Hung, 216
Chicago Review, 378n
Chicago School, 355, 356, 356n
Chieh, King, 612
chien-ai, 655; *see also* love
Ch'ien Ta-hsin, 217, 219
Child, C. M., 145n
Chi-lu, 421–423
China (and Chinese), 46, 60, 78, 79, 80, 81–95, 97, 99, 99n, 101, 102, 103n, 136, 156, 199–221, 225–243, 246, 275, 279, 287, 288, 411–427, 428, 429, 437, 484, 539, 540, 540n, 541, 542, 543, 544, 545, 546, 553, 556, 559, 598, 599, 609, 610, 611–629, 634, 639, 642, 643, 645, 652, 653–665, 680n, 699–718 *passim,* 737, 749, 762–769, 778; Republic of, 228n, 248, 413; aesthetics, 345–361 *passim;* Classics, 82, 83, 655, 656n, 660; communists, 766
Chinese Culture Quarterly, 612n, 621n

"Chinese Legal and Political Philosophy," 611–630
"Chinese Legal Philosophy," 621n
"Chinese Legal System," 656n
Chinese Political Philosophy, 616n
Chinese Renaissance, The, 220n
"Chinese Theory and Practice, with Special Reference to Humanism," 81–95, 650n
Ch'ing Dynasty, 228, 240, 242, 629, 654
Ching-i shu-wen (Notes on the Classics as I Have Heard from My Father), 219
Ching-te ch'uan-teng lu (*Keitoku Dentōroku*) (The Record of the Transmission of the Lamp), 439n
Ching-t'u (Jōdo), 429
Chiyo, 744–748
Chōjiya, 107n
Chōsen Buzoku no Kenkyū (A Study of Korean Shaman Custom), 660n
Chōsen Gakuhō (Academic Report on Korea, 663n
"Chosen ni okeru Kei no Fukyū" (Popularization of *ke* in Korea), 663n
Chou, Duke of, 95, 97
Chou Dynasty, 622, 651
Chou, King, 612
Christ, *see* Jesus Christ
"Christian Culture and American Democracy," 399
Christian Ethics and United States Foreign Policy; An Annotated Reading List and Guide to Current Information, 479n
Christianity, 24, 25, 71–73, 93, 151, 174, 200, 229, 231, 232, 238n, 247, 248, 250, 266, 295, 298, 302–315 *passim,* 318, 326, 327, 329, 329n, 330, 331, 334, 337, 340, 341, 374, 375, 391, 465, 484, 505, 552–568 *passim,* 599, 628, 633, 639, 654, 664, 666, 691, 707, 710, 721, 733, 741, 755, 760, 771
Christianity and History, 24n
Chrysanthemum and the Sword, The, 652n
Ch'üan-chou, 215
Ch'uan-hsi lu (Records of Instruction for Practical Living), 84n, 85n, 86n, 233n
Chuang Tzu (and *Chuang Tzu*), 86, 88, 88n, 192, 235, 237, 238, 238n, 239, 433, 437, 437n, 438, 439, 440, 444, 444n, 627, 627n, 643, 735
chūdō-shisō (middle-way thought), 98n
Chūdō-shisō oyobi sono Hattatsu (Middle-Way Thought and Its Development), 97n, 98n
chūgi (loyalty), 667
Chu Hsi, 82, 83, 84, 85, 86, 209, 210, 211, 212, 213, 215, 216, 218, 219, 221, 230, 233, 241, 246, 655, 656, 657, 660, 769
Ch'u-t'zu chi-chu (Prose-Poems of the State of Ch'u), 216
Chu Tzu ch'üan-shu (Complete Works of Chu Hsi), 84n
Chu Tzu yü-lei (Classified Sayings), 211
Chu Yüan-hui, 241
Ch'un-ch'iu (Spring and Autumn Annals), 206, 214
Ch'un-Ts'ew, The, 87n
chün-tzu (superior man), 87; *see also* ideal man
Chung-kuo jen-wen ching-shen chih fa-chan (The Development of the Chinese Humanistic Spirit), 234n
Chung-kuo wen-hua chih ching-shen chia-chih (The Spiritual Worth of Chinese Culture), 423n
Chung-shan, 625
City-States, 534, 540
civil rights, 389
civil service examinations, 82, 92, 655
Civitas Dei, 331
Clark, George A., 9
Classics, Chinese, 82, 83, 655, 656n, 660
Cleugh, James, 153n
clichés, 695–696, 701
Coates, Harper H., 103n
Code of Hammurabi, 536
Code of Manu, 495, 501, 502n, 503; *see also Laws of Manu, Manu, Manu Saṁhitā Manu Smṛti*
Code of T'ang with Commentaries and Annotations, 623n
Cohen, F. S., 649n
Cohen, Morris R., 30
Common Descent Group in China and Its Functions, The, 654n
Common Faith, A, 356, 356n
commonweal, 486
communism, 243, 767, 768, 772; Chinese, 382
Comparative Aesthetics, 348n
"Comparative Philosophy and Science in the Light of Comparative Law," 521–532
"Comparative Philosophy and World Law," 770–779
compassion (*maitrī, karuṇā*), 286, 511, 632, 632n, 633; *see also chien-ai,* love
Compilation of 120 Upaniṣads, A, 570n
"Complementary Emphases of Eastern Intuitive and Western Scientific Philosophy, The," 199n, 522n, 542n
Complete Works of Ralph Waldo Emerson, The, 398n
Complete Works, The (Vivekananda), 506n
Complexity of Legal and Ethical Experience, The, 521n, 525n, 779n
compromise, 393
Comte, Auguste, 76
Conant, James B., 202, 202n, 289, 290, 527
concentration, 683, 687
"Concept of the Spiritual in Indian Thought, The," 263n, 265n, 276n
concepts by intuition, *see* intuition
concepts by postulation, *see* postulation
Concepts of Sociology, The, 36, 36n
conceptualization, 430, 749, 751, 753; *see also* abstract thinking
"Concluding Remarks," 692–698
concord, 497, 634; *see also* harmony
Condit, Carl W., 355, 356n
Confessions (St. Augustine), 258
Confucian Analects, 230n
Confucian Classics, 655
Confucianism, 38, 75, 81, 82, 83, 85, 87, 88, 90, 92, 93, 94, 95, 99, 192, 193, 203, 204, 208–221, 227–235, 228n, 246, 250, 251, 253, 411, 414, 415, 416, 417, 418, 421, 422, 423, 424, 427, 428, 440, 524, 532, 613, 614n, 618, 619, 620, 621, 622, 628, 629, 633, 634, 639,

640, 643, 645, 646, 649, 650, 652, 653, 654, 655, 657, 658, 659, 660, 661, 662, 663, 664, 665, 667, 696, 736, 751, 773, 776, 778; Golden Rule in, 623
Confucius, 45, 49, 82, 85, 86, 87, 88, 90, 93, 97, 193, 203, 204, 205, 208–221, 227, 228, 230, 257, 349, 411, 413, 424, 425, 439, 440, 559, 614, 615, 617, 618, 619, 621n, 623, 626, 633n, 640, 653, 656, 735, 736, 769
Conger, George P., 33–49, 651n, 783–784
conscience, 152, 229, 241, 416, 454; *see also liang chih*
consciousness, 273, 276; pure, 303–304; states of, 158; stream of, 304
conservatism, 82
Conservatism from John Adams to Churchill, 376n
Conservative Mind, The, 376, 376n
Consolations, 71
Constant de Rebecque, Henri-Benjamin, 19
Constitution, Japanese (of 1889), 637
Constitution, Prince Shōtoku's, *see* Shōtoku's Constitution
Constitution, United States, 388, 389, 394, 396
Constitutionalism, 537n
Constitutionalism, Ancient and Modern, 533n
contemplation, 478
Continental European Union, 776, 777, 779
contradiction, 738, 745, 747, 748, 749, 750
contrasts, 689; *see also* differences, disagreements
Contribution to the Theory of the Living Organism, A, 145n
Contributions Toward Medical Psychology, 146n
Cook, T. I., 385n
Cooley, C. H., 40n
Coomaraswamy, A. K., 340, 348n
Cooper, James Fenimore, 392, 392n
co-operation, 663, 666
Cooperation and Competition among Primitive People, 403n
Copernican Revolution, 596
Copernicus, Nicholas, 202, 555
Cornell Law Quarterly, 521n, 532
cosmic egg, 572
cosmic reason, 282n, 283
cosmopolitanism, 71, 80
Cosmos and History: The Myth of the Eternal Return, 628, 628n
Council on Economic and Cultural Affairs, Inc., 10
"Counsels of I and Chi, The," 614n
Courage to Be, The, 374
Course of American Democratic Thought, The, 399
Coyle, G. L., 36, 36n, 47
creation, 328n, 329
Creator, 741, 743, 758
Creed of Mr. Hobbes Examined, 22n
Crisis of Our Age, The, 665n
Critical History of Greek Philosophy, A, 535n
Critique of Jean-Paul Sartre's Ontology, A, 151n
Critique of Judgment, 282n, 349n, 606; *see also Kritik der Urteilskraft*
Critique of Pure Reason, 282n, 526
Croce, Benedetto, 80, 342–361 *passim*
Cromwellians, 29
Cross, J. J., 28n
Cultural Background of Personality, The, 144n, 151n
Cultural Heritage of India, The, 282n
Culture and Personality, 144n, 151n
Cumont, Fr., 554
Cuq, Édouard, 536, 536n
Curti, Merli, 399
Cuttat, Jacques-Albert, 341
Cybernetics, 120n, 123n, 125n, 127n

Dada, 350
Daedalus, 261n
dahr (destiny), 453, 462; *see also adṛṣṭa*
Dai-jun-hyo-tong (Commentary on the Great Code), 664n
Daishu, 743
Daitō Kokushi (Shūhō Myōchō), 431, 442
daṇḍa, 576; *see also* punishment
Danforth Foundation, Inc., 10
Dante, Alighieri, 71–73, 80
dar al-ḥikmat (house of wisdom), 173
Darkness at Noon, 381
darśana (integral vision), 55
Darśanaśāstras, 478
Darwin, Charles, 380, 557
Das Buch der Genesung der Seele, 176n
Das Individuum in der Rolle des Mitmenschen, 151n
Das Kausalitätsprinzip der Biologie, 145n
Das Problem des Menschen, 151n, 153n
Daśabhūmika-sūtra et Bodhisattvabhūmi, 107n
Datta, B. B., 168n
Datta, Dhirendra Mohan, 322, 527, 529, 531, 569–593, 570n, 676n, 680n, 684n, 784
Davenport, Russell W., 143n
Dawn of Philosophy, The, 283n
Dayānanda, Swami Sarasvati, 493, 505
Dazai Shundai, 646
de Bary, William Theodore, 98n, 345n, 622n
De Beer, G. R., 145n
de Boer, T. J., 461n
De Gasperi, Alcide, 777n
De Martino, Richard, 9
De Monarchia, 71n
de Wolf, H., 262
Death and Rebirth of Psychology, The, 150n
Decision-Making as an Approach to the Study of International Politics, 128n
Declaration of Independence, 778
Deledalle, Gérard, 596n
democracy, 24, 25, 27, 30, 31, 155, 200, 205, 267n, 296, 356, 357, 359, 384–389, 390, 392, 394, 397, 512, 524, 542, 561, 562, 566, 585, 592, 632, 634, 663, 762, 779n
Dengyō Daishi (Saichō), 104
dependent origination, 597; *see also pratītyasamutpāda*

Der Aufbau der Person, 144n
Der Historismus und seine Probleme, 403n
Der logische Aufbau der Welt, 529n
Der Rig Veda, 159n, 163n
Der Versuch einer Überwindung des Historismus bei Ernst Troeltsch, 403n
Desan, W., 151n
Descartes, René, 75, 80, 320, 321n, 333, 335, 365
desirelessness, 272
despotism, 287
Dessoir, Max, 345, 345n, 346, 356, 356n, 357
destiny, 503, 727; *see also adṛṣṭa, dahr*
Destiny of Mind: East and West, The, 288n
Deus interior, 336n
Deussen, Paul, 485, 485n
Deutsch, Karl, 122n, 123n
Deutsche Vierteljahrsschrift für Literaturwissenschaft und Geistesgeschichte, 403n
Development and Meaning of Eddington's "Fundamental Theory," The, 140n
"Development of Ideas of Spiritual Value in Chinese Philosophy, The," 225–244
devotion, 273, 281; *see also bhakti*
Dewey, Evelyn, 762, 764
Dewey, John, 19, 21, 27, 28n, 47n, 80, 342–361 *passim,* 368, 369, 376, 396n, 527, 596, 596n, 597, 650n, 697, 762–769
Dhammapada, 273, 273n, 444, 478, 479, 581n
Dhammapada, The, 570n
dharma, 98, 99, 102, 264, 268, 269, 269n, 270, 271, 272, 274, 279, 280, 477, 478, 479, 487, 490, 491, 495, 500, 511, 513, 514, 515, 570, 576, 578, 581, 587, 588, 597, 608, 637, 751; as the law of the state, 586; as man's differentia, 571
"Dharma and Mokṣa," 479n
dharma-dhātu (realm of elements), 113
dharmakāya (*dharma* body), 108, 744
Dharmaśāstras, 269, 279, 477, 478, 490, 492, 569–583 *passim,* 574, 578, 579, 588, 589, 589n, 710, 712
dharmatā (ultimate-reality), 106, 107, 108n, 109, 196, 197
dialectical idealism, 17
dialectical materialism, 17, 25, 143, 337, 342
Dialogues of Plato, 534n
diarchy, 579
Dickey, James, viii, 12
Dickinson, G. Lowes, 539n
"Did India Influence Early Greek Philosophy?," 651n
Die deutsche Ideologie, 18
Die Entstehung der Schwurgerichte, 663n
Die Kosmographie der Inder nach den Quellen dargestellt, 605n
Die Maschinen-theorie des Lebens, 145n
Die philosophischen Abhandlungen des Jaqūb ben Isḥāq al-Kindī, 175n
Die Ṛbhus im Ṛg Veda, 160n, 163n
Die Religion des Veda, 660n
Die Schichten der Persoenlichkeit, 144n
Die Seele des Menschen, 144n
Die Stellung des Menschen im Kosmos, 144n
differences, 674, 702; *see also* contrasts, disagreements
dignitas hominis, 402
dignity, 677, 678
Dignity of Man, The, 143n
Dilthey, Wilhelm, 338, 403, 403n, 550
Dimensions of Society: Quantitative Systematics for the Social Sciences, 141n
dīn (righteousness), 452, 452n, 453, 460, 462
"Dīn and Muruwwa," 456n
Dionne, Roger, 11
Dionysius the Areopagite, 306, 306n, 307
Diplomatic Codification of the Law of Nations, 73
Dirac, P. A. M., 140n, 526
Directive Action and Life, 145n
disagreements, 690, 702; *see also* contrasts, differences
Discipline for Democracy, 393n
divine nation, 640
Doctrine of the Mean, 82n, 83n, 84, 85, 90n, 231, 231n, 412, 412n, 416, 416n
Dodd, Stuart C., 141n
Dodds, E. R., 305n
Dōgen, 103, 104, 195, 196, 196n, 197, 197n, 644
dogmatism, 398, 575
Dokugo Chū Shingyō (Poisonous Comments on the *Prajñā-pāramitā-hṛdaya Sūtra*), 444n
Donaldson, D. M., 470n
Doomsday Books, 651
Dorfles, Gillo, 358, 358n
Dorfman, Joseph, 399
dōri (reason, principle), 106, 109, 196
Dōri no Kankaku (The Sense of Reason), 196n
Dorsey, Gray L., 533–548, 784–785
doubt, 210, 211, 212, 218, 221
Doubt and Certainty in Science, 120n
drama, 353, 361; Chinese, 91; *Noh* (*Nō*), 111n, 343, 352
Dream of the Red Chamber, The, 768, 769
Driesch, H., 145n
dualism, 359, 436, 508; *see also* Sāṁkhya, *yin-yang*
Duff, J. D., 535n
Duke University, 732
Duns Scotus, John, 322
Durgādatta Tripāṭī, 168n
duties, 229, 381, 515–516, 573, 578; obligatory, 480–481; universal, 573; *see also sādharāṇa-dharmas, svadharma*
Dynamic Theory of Personality, A, 144n

E Pluribus Unum, 387
Early Greek Philosophy, 541n
East Prussia, 777
East-West Philosophers' Conferences: First, 528; Second, 316–319, 378, 692; Third, v, viii, 3–11, 692
"East-West Philosophy in Practical Perspective," 3–11
Eastern Religions and Western Thought, 263n, 378n

Eccles, J. C., 146n
Eckhart, Meister, 307, 308, 309, 310, 312, 313, 437, 445, 724, 759
eclecticism, 470, 471
"Economic Activities in This-Worldly Life," 643–646
Economic Mind in American Civilization, The, 399
economic thought, 549–568, 569–583 *passim,* 631–647, 633
Economist, The, 777
Edgerton, Henry W., 649n
education, 141, 397–398, 506
Edward W. Hazen Foundation, 11
Edwards, Richard, 349, 349n
Eggeling, Julius, 605n
Egypt, 321, 539, 540, 600
Ehrlich, Eugen, 535, 535n, 773, 773n
eightfold path, 684; *see also* Noble Eightfold Path
Einstein, Albert, 200, 367, 524, 525, 528, 530, 649n
Eisai, 104
Eisenhower, Dwight David, 772
Ekayāna (One Vehicle), 99
Eken, 108n
electronic computers, 122
Elements of Ethics, 269n
Elements of Experimental Embryology, 145n
Eliade, Mircea, 628, 628n
Eliot, Sir Charles, 98n, 103n, 110, 110n, 111n, 112n
Eliot, T. S., 376, 693
emancipation, 503; *see also* freedom, liberation, *mokṣa*
Emancipation Proclamation, 387, 397
Embryonic Development and Induction, 145n
Emerson, Ralph Waldo, 389, 397
emperor, 634, 637, 638–643, 639, 642, 657; worship of, 631, 662n
empirical reality, 500; *see also* phenomena, *vyāvahārika*
empiricism, 16, 19, 20, 21, 24, 28, 30, 31, 48, 49, 119, 124, 304, 333, 334, 336, 384
emptiness, 429, 430, 432, 432n, 433, 436, 439, 441, 443, 444, 446, 732–753 *passim,* 739, 744, 747, 752, 753; *see also k'ung,* suchness, *śūnya, tathatā,* void
Encyclopaedia of Religion and Ethics, 660n
Encyclopedia of the Social Sciences, 36n
Engels, Friedrich, 18, 26
England, 47, 75, 538, 659; *see also* British
Engo, 743
Enkwan Saian, 444
enjoyment body, 108
enlightenment, 74, 75, 260, 400, 446, 559, 759; *see also bodhi, buddhi*
Enlightenment (the), 677
Enneads, The, 305, 305n
Epictetus, 71
Epicureanism, 192
epistemic correlation, 525
"Epistemological Methods in Chinese Philosophy," 542n
epistemology, 50–66 *passim,* 54, 58, 580, 588
"Epistemology and Politics," 31n
Epistle to the Romans, 258
equality, 512, 562
Erasmus, Desiderius, 73, 202
Erh-ch'eng ch'üan-shu (The Complete Works of the Ch'eng Brothers), 83n, 86n, 241n
Eros and Civilization, 375n
escapism, 314, 516
Escarra, Jean, 544n
Essais (Montaigne), 595n
Essay Concerning Human Understanding, 526n
Essay on the Civilizations of India, China, and Japan, An, 539n
Essays (Montaigne), 595
Essays from Max Weber, 455n
Essays in East-West Philosophy, 142n, 199n, 317n, 318n, 319n, 322n, 323n, 333n, 337n, 378n, 382n, 383n, 542n, 650n, 651n
Essays in Logic and Language, 371n
Essays on the Gita, 573n
essentialism, 374
Ethica Nichomachea, 33n, 543n; *see also Nichomachean Ethics*
Ethical and Religious Classics of East and West, 464n
ethical laws, 500
ethical theory, 521–532
ethical values, 279–282
ethico-aesthetic experience, 432, 433
ethics, 66, 131, 228, 249–251, 279, 279n, 373, 378, 394, 428–446, 440–441, 448–475, 465–472, 476–493, 479n, 510–516, 565, 582, 616–623, 638, 654, 657, 658, 661, 664, 667, 682, 683, 684, 685, 716, 761; American, 393; Chinese, 411–427; Confucian, 95; Hindu, 476–493, 519–516; Islamic, 451–475; Oriental, 413; Western, 365–383, 413
Ethics (Aristotle), 70; *see also Nichomachean Ethics*
Ethics (Nowell-Smith), 373
"Ethics and the Ceremonial Use of Language," 371n
Ethics and Language, 369
"Ethics and Social Practice in Islam," 448–475
Ethics and United States Foreign Policy, 399
Eubank, E. E., 36, 36n, 41n
Euclid, 177, 528, 530
Euclidean geometry, 730
eureka process, 123
Europe, 76, 77, 78, 79, 156, 316–347, 359, 384, 385, 386, 388, 389, 390, 391, 393, 598
European Union and United States Foreign Policy, 777, 777n
everyday-mindedness, 441, 443n, 741
evidential investigation, 199–221, 216, 768
evil, 275, 299, 300; problem of, 275
Evolution and Ethics, 380, 380n
Evolution of Physics, The, 649n
evolution, organic, 550–551
Examination of the Absurdities about the Book of Odes, An, 214
existentialism, 66, 137, 247, 259, 276, 277, 282n, 290, 318, 338, 339n, 350, 373, 374, 379, 409, 688

experience, 675–691 *passim,* 684, 686, 687; pure, 748, 749, 750
Experience and Nature, 44n
Experimental Designs in Social Research, 141n
Explaining the Rhymes in the Ch'u-t'zu, 215

Fa Hsien, 589, 590
faith, 327, 328, 330, 331, 332, 333, 335, 457, 463, 465, 468, 553, 754–761
family, 92, 93, 94, 619, 624, 635, 637, 639; Imperial, 641, 642
family life, 418–420
Fan Ch'ih, 414
fang-pien fa-shen (*hōben-hosshin*), 108; *see also sambhogakāya*
Fang Tung-shu, 219
al-Fārābi, 176, 176n, 180, 465, 466
Farfield Foundation, Inc., 10
al-Farghānī, 178
fatalism, 453, 461, 503
Faulkner, William, 346
Faustian ideal, 136
Fa-yen (Hōgen), 439n
feeling-experience, 431
Feng, H. Y., 654n
Fenollosa, Ernest F., 195
Fen-yang Shan-chao (Funyō Zenshō), 442n
Fessard, A. E., 146n
Feuer, Lewis S., 26n, 652n
Fichte, Johann Gottlieb, 338, 404, 404n, 410
field theory, 648–669
"Field Theory and Judicial Logic," 649n
Field Theory in Social Science, 649n, 652n
" 'Field Theory' in the Study of Cultures: Its Application to Korean Culture," 648–669
Fifty Years of Chinese Philosophy, 382n
Figgis, J. N., 554
filial piety, *see hsiao*
"Filial Piety and Chinese Society," 411–427
Filliozat, Jean, 169n, 603
fine arts, 191, 194
fiqh (science of the *sharī'a*), 457–462, 466, 467, 470
First Principles (Spencer), 40n
Fisch, Max H., 360n
Fitzgerald, S. Vesey, 455n
Five Books, 220
Five Classics, 82
five relationships, 658, 658n; *see also wu-lun*
Fletcher, J. M., 146n
Flew, Anthony G., 371n
Flewelling, R. T., 144n
force, 772, 773
Foreign Elements in Ancient Islamic Law, 455n
Foreign Vocabulary of the Qur'ān, The, 452n
forgiveness, 454, 456n, 503
form in art, 342–361 *passim*
Foulquié, Paul, 596n
Foundation for a Science of Personality, 144n
Foundation for Idealistic Philosophy, 11
Foundations of Sociology, 141n
Four Books, 82, 209
four classes, 578; *see also* caste
four reasonings, 105
four values, 487
fourfold discipline, 61
fourfold division of society, 573; *see also* castes, *varṇas*
Fourth Gospel, 200, 201, 326; *see also* John, St.
France, 73, 75, 350, 358, 777
Francis, St., 330
Franklin, Benjamin, 385
Fraser, Alexander C., 526n, 660n
Frasier, James G., 660n
fraternité, 386
Frear Eleemosynary Trust, 11
free will, 460, 461, 466, 481–483
Free Will and Predestination in Early Islam, 453n
freedom, 19, 376, 390–393, 398, 468, 512, 515, 553, 554–568 *passim,* 677, 681, 690, 735–744, 742, 749, 750; in art, 354–355; of speech, 764; state of, 158; ultimate, 63; *see also* emancipation, liberation, *mokṣa*
"Freedom, Independence, and Peace in Buddhism," 107n, 108n
Freedom versus Organization, 16n
French Encyclopedists, 22
French Enlightenment, 18
French Revolution, 390
Freud, Sigmund, 144n, 350, 375, 380
Freyer, Hans, 77–79
Friends, 585
Fries, Jakob Friedrich, 18
Fromm, Erich, 144n, 147n, 151n, 375
Fu, 211
Fu-chao Te-kuang (Busshō Tokkō), 441n
Fujiwara Yūsetsu, 109n
fulfillment, 677, 681; *see also* realization, self-realization
Fundamental Principles of the Sociology of Law, 535n, 773n
Fundamental Truths in Buddhism: The Middle Way and Nirvāṇa, 108n
Fung Yu-lan, 39n, 88n, 234n, 653n, 655n
Fustel de Coulanges, Numa-Denis, 523, 523n, 534, 534n
Future of the Social Sciences, The, 142n
Future of War, The, 395n
futuwwa (trust in God), 467

Gabriel, R. H., 399
Galen (Galien), 173, 177
Galileo (Galileo Galilei), 21, 202, 219, 220, 365, 523, 525, 555, 649
Gandhi, Mahatma, 65, 283, 493, 502, 512, 524, 574, 575, 577, 578n, 581, 585, 592, 593, 695, 760, 773
Gard, Richard A., 9
Gauḍapāda, 499, 531
Gauss, Charles E., 350
Gautama (not the Buddha), 589
Geden, A. S., 485n
Geldner, K. F., 159n, 163n

Gemeinschaft und Gesellschaft, Grundbegriffe der reinen Soziologie, 39n
General and Logical Theory of Automata, The, 121n
General Biology and Philosophy of Organism, 145n
"General Methodology for the Scientific Study of Aesthetic Appreciation," 358
General Theory of Value, 368n
Genesis, 259n, 649n
genmyō (profound mystery), 434
Genshin, 104
geometry, 172–187 *passim,* 721–731 *passim*
George, St., 755
"German Idealism and American Theories of the Democratic Community," 385n
German philosophy, 18, 192
German Philosophy and Politics, 27n
Germany, 354, 777
Gerth, Hans, 455n, 649n
Gesammelte Schriften (Dilthey), 403n
Geschichte der Kunst des Alterthums (The History of Ancient Art), 344n
Geschichtesphilosophie, 407n
Gestaltist theory, 604
al-Ghazzālī, 180, 181n, 294, 468, 469
Ghoshal, U. N., 577n, 579n
Gibb, H. A. R., 178, 178n, 468
Gibbon, Edward, 554
Gibbs, Josiah Willard, 525
Giddings, F. H., 40n
Gide, André, 350
Gierke, Otto, 533n
Gilbert, Stuart, 257n
Giles, Herbert A., 88n, 613n, 627n
giri (feudal loyalty), 657, 662, 666, 667
gnosticism, 552
God, 17, 18, 19, 20, 23, 24, 31, 32, 72, 73, 87, 88, 136, 180, 181, 183, 185, 200, 201, 204, 206, 207, 225, 226, 228, 232, 232n, 233, 241, 257, 258, 259, 260, 261n, 262, 265, 266, 267, 267n, 268, 269, 271, 273, 274, 275, 277, 278, 279, 280, 281, 283, 285, 287, 293–301, 302–315 *passim,* 326, 327, 327n, 328n, 329, 329n, 330, 335, 336, 337, 339, 340, 341, 374, 376, 379, 383, 391, 407, 409, 430, 431, 432, 436, 445, 451–475 *passim,* 481, 482, 483, 486, 488, 492, 500, 503, 504, 505, 506, 508, 509, 511, 513, 516, 517, 553, 557, 571, 572, 573, 576, 577, 581, 585, 611, 612, 614n, 616, 628, 645, 661, 662, 675, 685, 722, 723, 725, 726, 728, 729, 730, 737, 738, 739, 740, 741, 744, 746, 747, 751, 758, 760; *see also* Allah, Iśvara, *Shang-ti*
Godhead, 243, 308, 310, 327n, 432, 436, 439, 738, 747, 751
Goethe, Johann Wolfgang von, 401, 406, 473
Goitein, S. D., 455n
Golden Bough, The, 660n
golden mean, 573, 584, 592; *see also Doctrine of the Mean*
Golden Rule, 492, 623
Goldstein, K., 144n, 147n
Goldziher, Ignaz, 456n
Gonda, J., 159n
Good (the), 365–367
Good Life, The, 396n
government, 87, 90, 91, 92
Goya y Lucientes, Francisco José de, 346
grace, 229, 327, 328, 330, 440n
Graeco-*gandhāra,* 98
Graeco-Hellenic, 471
Graeco-Roman, 326
Graeco-Roman-Christian, 201
Graeco-Roman world, 324
grammar, Chinese, 594; Islamic, 172–187 *passim,* 721–731 *passim*
Grand Harmony, 625, 626
Granet, Marcel, 540n, 541n, 542n, 543, 543n
Grassmann, Hermann, 163n
gratitude, 111, 662
Graves, E. Boyd, 9
Gray, J. Glenn, 395n
Great Law, The, 620
Great Learning, The, 38, 82n, 209, 411, 411n, 418, 418n, 616, 626
Great Learning and the Mean-in-Action, The, 627n
Great Way, 625
Greek City-States, 534
Greek-Hellenistic heritage, 472
Greek philosophy, 137, 283n, 289, 460, 461n, 462, 463, 722, 731, 771
Greeks, 67, 69–70, 80, 136, 173, 176, 177, 178, 179, 181, 182, 183, 184, 185, 186, 200, 202, 256, 279, 290, 295, 305–315 *passim,* 318, 321, 324, 325, 326, 327, 329, 331, 332, 353, 359, 388, 395, 466, 470, 471, 534 seq., 539, 540, 541, 542, 546, 550, 552, 586, 677, 727, 728, 729, 730
Green, Thomas F., 9
Green, T. H., 21, 526n
Greenidge, A. H. J., 534n
Griffis, W. E., 665n
Grinker, Roy R., 141n
Grose, T. H., 526n
Gross, Llewellyn, 139n, 141n, 142, 142n, 155n
Grosseteste, Robert, 175
Grotius, Hugo, 73, 80
"Group Description," 36, 36n
"Groups," 36n
Growth of American Thought, The, 399
Growth of Political Thought in the West, The, 538n
Grundegung der Allgemeinen Kunstwissenschaft, 356n
Grundformen und Erkenntnis des menschlichen Daseins, 151n
Grundlinien der Philosophie des Rechts, 14n
Grunhill, William Alexander, 177n
Gurney, Edmund, 351, 351n
Gurvitch, G., 35n, 42n
Guyau, Charles, 344, 344n, 345
Gyōnyo, 109

Haas, S. S., 288, 288n
hadīths (reports on Prophet's acts or sayings), 458, 458n, 459, 462, 467
Haguenauer, M. C., 662n
Hahn, Lewis E., 9
haiku, 355, 744

al-Ḥajjāj al-Hāsih, 177
Hakuin, 444
Haldane, J. S., 146n
Halsted, Mrs. Clarissa H., viii
Hamilton, Madison and Jay on the Constitution: Selections from the Federalist Papers, with a Critical Introduction, 399
Hamlet, 259n
Han Fei Tzu, 618, 619, 620
Han Fei Tzu, 618n, 619n, 620n
Han period (and Dynasty), 206, 208, 209, 211, 228, 415, 617, 621, 622, 654
Han scholars, 621n
Hanayama Shinshō, 639n
Handbook of Greek Constitutional History, 534n
Handel, George Frederic, 383
Hanlin Yüan, 658, 658n
Hanslick, Eduard, 351, 351n, 354
happiness, 125, 193–194, 509, 515, 742; ultimate, 468
harakiri (or *seppuku*), 252–253
Hare, R. M., 372, 372n
Hare, William Loftus, 113n
harmlessness, 503; *see also ahiṁsā,* non-injury, non-violence
harmony (and concord), 100, 130, 150, 285, 618, 623, 633–636, 639
Harmony, Grand, *see* Grand Harmony
Harris, William H., 9
Harrison, Philomène, 9, 12
Hart, H. L. A., 371
Hartman, Robert, 23n
Hartmann, Nicholai, 61, 153n, 318, 373, 409
Harvard Oriental Series, 602n
Harvey, William, 220
Hashimoto Gahō, 195n
Hawaii, 386, 721, 770–771, 772, 774, 776
Hawaii Under Army Rule, 395n
Hayek, Friedrich August von, 25
Hayward, Max, 382n
Hayy ibn Yaqaẓān (Hayy, Son of the Valiant), 466
al-Hazan, 771
Heath, Peter, 151n
Heaven (and heaven and heavenly), 88, 92, 204, 206, 207, 230, 231–232, 233, 235, 237, 238, 241, 430, 438, 439, 440, 611, 612, 618, 624, 628, 641; mandate of 87, 611, 612, 628
heavenly reason, 440
Hebrew-Christian religion, 324
Hebrews, 326, 329, 730
hedonism, 480, 488, 578
Hegel, Georg W. F., 17, 18, 26, 53, 61, 75, 77, 80, 255, 256n, 337, 337n, 342, 361 *passim,* 366, 374, 379
Hegelians, 290; Left, 29; Right, 29
Heian period, 345, 633
Heidegger, Martin, 144n, 257, 373
Heiler, Friedrick, 250
Heine-Geldern, Robert von, 605, 605n
Heisenberg, Werner, 140, 140n, 141, 141n, 525, 527
Hellenism, 70–71, 80, 172–173
Henke, Frederick Goodrich, 85n
Henry, Paul, 305n
Heraclitus (and Heraclitean), 43, 283, 321, 760
Herring, Frances, 345, 345n
Hibbert Journal, 282n
Hindú Jurisprudence, 591n
Hindu Philosophy of Law, 586n
Hindu Temple, The, 169n, 602, 602n, 605
Hinduism, 48, 56, 59, 63, 263–292, 319, 327, 338n, 340, 348, 348n, 494–517, 525, 532, 722, 773, 776
Hinduism: Its Meaning for the Liberation of the Spirit, 509n
Hinton, Frank E., 11
Hipparchos, 178
Hippias Major, 355
Hippocrates, 173, 177
Hirata Atsutane, 641, 641n
Hiriyanna, M., 485n
Hisamatsu Hoseki Shin'ichi, 350, 350n
Historical Introduction to the Study of Roman Law, 535n
historicism, 403, 409
History and Human Destiny, 153n
History of American Philosophy, 399
History of the Ancient World, 535n
History of Chinese Literature, 613n
History of Chinese Philosophy, 84n, 234n
History of the Dharmaśāstra, 589n
History of Hindu Law, 588n
History of Hindu Public Life, 579n
History of Japan, 99n
History of Japanese Religion, 98n
History of Korea, The, 658n
History of Nature, The, 140n
History of Philosophy, A, 465n
History of Philosophy in Islam, The, 461n
History of Protestant Misisons in Korea, The, 664n
History of Western Philosophy, A, 51n
Hiyane Antei, 661n
Hiyane Yasusada, 645n
Hobbes, Thomas, 21, 22, 80, 262, 530, 556
Hōbunkan, 107n
Hocking, Richard, 10
Hocking, W. E., 266, 289
Hoebel, E. A., 775
Hogarth, William, 344, 344n
hōjin (enjoyment body), 108; *see also sambhogakāya*
Hōkai, 108n
Homeostasis as an Explanatory Principle in Psychology, 146n
Homeostasis as a Unifying Concept in Personality Theory, 146n
Hōnen, 103, 104, 105, 105n, 108n, 195, 196n
Hōnen, the Buddhist Saint, 103n, 105n
Hongwanji, 109, 110
Hongwanji-Shōnin Shinran Den-e (Illustrated Life of Shinran the Saint), 109n
hōni-dōri (ultimate reality), 106, 108, 196
Honigman, J. J., 151n
Hook, Sidney, 15–32, 399, 524, 676n, 697, 766
hō-on (gratitude to all life), 111
Horioka, C., 194n
Horney, Karen, 144n, 149
Horten, Max Joseph Henrich, 176n
Hossō, 246

householder, 489, 498, 503, 504
How We Know Universals, 121n
How We Think, 767
Hoyer, Harry, 373n
Hoyle, Fred, 140n
Hsia Dynasty, 612, 614, 621
Hsiang-shan ch'üan-chi (The Collected Works of Lu Hsiang-shan), 241n
Hsiang Yü, 654n
hsiao (filial piety), 411–427, 638, 653, 657
Hsiah Yu-wei, 411–427, 676n, 684n, 785
Hsü Lang-kuang, 658n
Hsüan, King, 612
Hsüan Tsang, 583
Hsü-ch'an, 215
Hsün Tzu, 620, 620n, 621
Hu Hsien-chin, 654n
Hu Shih, 8, 82, 199–222, 292, 525, 526, 527, 529, 614n, 649n, 680n, 762–769, 785–786
Huang Tsung-hsi, 235n, 242, 621, 622
Hua-yen, 196, 429
Hughes, E. R., 93n, 421, 627n, 642n, 694
Hui-k'o (Eka), 751, 752
Hulbert, H., 658n
Hull, R. F. C., 283n
Hulyalkar, S. G., 10
Human Career: A Philosophy of Self-Transcendence, 144n
Human Community: Its Philosophy and Practice for a Time of Crisis, The, 38, 38n
human nature: as evil, 620; as good, 231–235
Human Nature in the Light of Psychopathology, 144n
Human Potentialities, 144n
Human Use of Human Beings, The, 121n, 122n, 123n, 127n
humanism, 81–95, 205, 208–221, 264, 329n, 621, 628, 650, 726
humanitarianism, 401, 402, 632
humanity, 227, 667
Humboldt, Alexander von, 176, 176n
Hume, David A., 21, 304, 332, 335, 336, 522, 526, 526n
Hume, R. E., 477, 477n
Humphreys, Christmas, 197n
Hung-ming chi (Essays Elucidating the Doctrine), 89n
Hurd, John C., 385n
Husserl, Edmund, 61, 341, 373, 596, 596n, 597, 598
Huxley, J. S., 145n
Huxley, T. H., 380, 380n
Hyung-pub tai-chun (The Great Code of Penal Laws), 666

'ibādāt (man's relation to God), 460
Ibn al-'Arabī, 724
Ibn al-Haythām (al-Hazen), 175
Ibn Khaldūn, 294
Ibn Miskawaihi, 470, 471
Ibn Raud, 771
Ibn-Rushd, 181, 464, 469
Ibn Sīnā, Abū Alā al-Hussain ibn Abdullah (Avicenna), 175, 176n, 181, 464, 465, 466, 730
Ibn Ṭufail, 466
I ching, 212, 213, 433n
I-Ching, or Book of Changes, The, 433n, 623n
I-consciousness, 276, 277; *see also ahamdhī, ahaṁkāra*
ideal man, 281; *see also chün-tzu*
idealism, 246, 317, 318, 335, 365, 384, 409, 507, 517, 607, 690; Buddhist, 105, 106, 108, 240; dialectical, 375
Ideas of Natural Law and Humanity in World Politics, 533n
identity, 311
Ideological Differences and World Order, 120n, 539n, 653n, 654n, 664n, 775n, 778n
"Ideological Man in His Relation to Scientifically Known Natural Man," 120n, 127n
Ienaga Saburo, 104n
Igishū (Collection of Unorthodox Doctrines), 108n
ignorance, 443; *see also avidyā*
Ihṣā al'ulūm (Classification of Sciences), 176
Ih'ya 'Ouloûm ed-Dīn ou Vivification des Sciences de la foi, 469n
Iḥya' 'ulūm ad-dīn (Revivification of the Sciences), 469
ijmā (consensus), 456, 459
illusionism, 157, 180, 508, 575
'ilm (science), 180, 181
immediacy, 246–252, 320, 321
immortality, 19, 20
Imperial Family, 632
Inada, Kenneth K., viii, 10
Incoherence of the Philosophers, 469
India, 47, 50–66, 78, 79, 89, 136, 156–171, 200, 246, 255–262, 263–292, 302–315 *passim,* 316–341, 319n, 349, 382, 437, 476–493, 494–517, 553, 569–583, 594–610, 642, 643, 644, 646, 696, 699–718, 773, 776; Dark Age, 504–505
Indian Aesthetics, 348n
"Indian Approach to the Religious Problem, The," 255–262
"Indian Ethics and Social Practice," 319n, 476–493
Indian Philosophical Congress Silver Jubilee Volume, The, 378n, 485n
Indian Thought and Its Development, 484n
India's Culture and Her Problems, 266n
individual, 24, 92, 93, 94, 147, 148n, 149, 150, 151, 152, 153, 154, 180, 257, 271, 287, 290, 296, 304, 310, 322, 328, 328n, 331, 332, 338, 339, 375, 376, 382, 406, 448, 469, 494, 500, 501, 511, 514, 515, 552, 553, 557, 558, 560, 561, 566, 570, 571–573, 577, 586, 587, 617, 635, 637, 642, 659, 664, 691, 717, 726, 727, 755
Individual and Society, 572
Individual in East and West, 93n
Individualism Reconsidered, 375n
Individuals, 373n
Individuum und Gemeinschaft: Grundlegung der Kulturphilosophie, 151n
Indra, 605, 606, 609
indriyas (senses), 605, 609
induction, 675, 680
Infeld, Leopold, 649n

infinite, 157, 237, 430, 435, 438, 440, 484, 747, 753; unmanifest, 157
"Influence of Philosophy on Law and Politics in Western Civilization, The," 533–548
inner self, 587
innocence, 737, 738, 740, 741, 742, 743, 744, 750
Inscriptions of Aśoka, 577n
Insight and Outlook: An Inquiry into the Common Foundations of Science, Art and Social Ethics, 126n
Institute for Philosophical Research, 135n
Institutes, The (Gaius), 778
Institutions of the Law of Nature and of Nations, 73
Integrative Action of the Nervous System, The, 44n, 146n
intellect (intellectualism), 72, 188–197, 226, 430, 747, 748
"International Character of the American People," 385–387
International Encyclopedia of Unified Science, 649n, 650n
International Journal of Ethics, 399, 570n
Interpretation of Christian Ethics, 375n
"Interpretation of Surah 107, The," 452n
Introduction to Early Roman Law, 522n, 523, 634n
Introduction to the History of Sciences, 176n
intuition, 29, 54, 55, 56, 57, 64, 196, 197, 247, 260, 262, 289, 297, 325, 326, 338, 339, 377, 414, 431, 435, 552, 559, 675, 706, 707; concepts by, 199–200, 320, 527, 528, 529, 530, 651
investigation, evidential, 199–221, 768
investigation of things, 209, 218, 412, 627
inwardness, 287, 288, 289, 290–291, 560
Iqbal, M., 293n, 294n, 295, 295n, 296, 296n
Iran, 484
irrationalism, 168, 190, 344, 347, 350, 546; Japanese, 188–197 *passim,* 245–254 *passim,* 428–446 *passim,* 631–647 *passim,* 652; *see also* non-rational tendencies
Isaac, 722
Isaiah (Book of), 649n
Īśa Upaniṣad, 57, 62n, 497n, 573, 574, 574n, 592
Ise, 97
Ishizuka Rhūgaku, 103n
Ishmael, 722
I-shu (Preserved Works), 83n, 86n
Isis, 177n
Islam, 172–187, 266, 293–301, 310n, 311, 319n, 340, 448–475, 505, 691, 721–731, 771, 776
"Islam and Spiritual Values," 293–301
"Islamic Cultural Tradition and the West, The," 721–731
Islamic studies, ambiguity of, 723–731
Islamic thought distinguished from the West, 474–475
Islamstudien, 451n
issai shujo shittsu busshō (all sentient beings have *buddha*-nature), 110n
Īśvara, 265, 268, 599; *see also* God
Italy, 777
Itō Jinsai, 645
ius gentium, 73; *see also jus gentium*
Iwahashi Junsei, 646n
Jābir ibn Ḥaiyān, 179
Jabre, F., 181n
Jacob, 722
Jagadananda, Swami, 277n
Jagannātha, 285
Jahrbuch der Schweizerischen Philosophischen Gesellschaft, 144n
Jaimini, 266
"Jaina Theory of *Anekāntavāda,* The," 575n
Jainism, 20, 56, 59, 265, 272, 272n, 278, 279, 281, 282, 286, 478, 487, 571, 575, 585, 589
Jalāl ad-Dīn Dawwānī, 471
Jalāl ad-Dīn Rūmī, 724
Jamāl ad-Dīn al-Afghānī, 474n
James, William, 385
Janaka, 502, 510, 587
Jan van Ruysbroeck, 307, 307n, 308, 309, 312
Japan, 89, 97–113, 188–197, 245–254, 342–361 *passim,* 374, 428–446, 598, 631–647, 652, 653–665, 683, 699–718 *passim,* 732–753
Jaspers, Karl, 270, 374, 400
Jayaswal, K. P., 581n
Jefferson, Thomas, 29, 385, 387, 525, 530, 770, 778, 779n
Jeffery, Arthur, 452n
Jeffress, Lloyd A., 121n
Jehovah, 751; *see also* God, Īśvara, *Ti*
jen (humanity, man to man-ness, etc.), 86, 93, 227, 233, 234, 377, 412, 653, 656, 721, 778
Jen-sheng (Human Life), 230n
"jen-tz'u" (temples of goodness), 89
Jeremiah, 759
Jesus Christ, 227, 234n, 287, 290, 314, 375, 416, 593, 666, 751, 757, 759, 760
Jhering, Rudolf von, 624, 624n, 651, 651n
jihi (compassion), 632
"Jinen Hōni no Kaiken" (Shinran's Concept of "Jinen Hōni), 108n
Jinen hōni no koto (*Jinen hōni shō*), (Essay on *Dharmatā-Yukti*), 106n
Jinnō Shōtōki (The Records of the Legitimate Succession of the Divine Sovereigns *or* Discourse on the Genealogy of the Imperial Family), 196n, 640n, 641, 657
jīva (soul), 278, 282, 570
Jīvānanda Vidyāsāgara, 589n
jñāna (knowledge), 107, 275, 283, 480, 481; *see also vidyā*
jñānamārga (way of knowledge), 274
Jōdo, 104, 109, 429, 435, 644
Johanns, F. Pierre, 328n
"John Dewey in China," 762–769
John, St. (and Book of John), 314, 315, 667n; *see also* Fourth Gospel
John, St., of the Cross, 307–315 *passim,* 437, 724
Johnson, Alvin, 33n
Johnson, Samuel, 21
Jolowicz, Herbert F., 535n
Jones, Charles, 10
Jones, E. R., 461n
Jordon, Elijah, 396n
Joshua, Book of, 649, 650
Journal of Aesthetics and Art Criticism, The, 345n, 348n, 357, 357n, 358n
Journal Asiatique, 159n

Journal of Comparative Legislation and International Law, The, 455n
Journal of Criminal Law, Criminology, and Police Science, 665n
Journal of Indian and Buddhist Studies, 111n, 335n
Journal of the Indian Society of Oriental Art, 168n
Journal Métaphysique (Metaphysical Journal), 277n
Journal of Philosophy and Phenomenological Research, 23n, 289n
Journal of Politics, 385n
Journal of the Royal Asiatic Society of Bengal, 523n
Jowett, B., 365n, 534n
joy, 112, 230n; *see also ānanda,* bliss
Joyce, James, 350
Ju-chia che-hsüeh (The Confucian Philosophy), 412n
Judaeo-Christian mythology, 432
Judaism, 136, 184, 266, 305, 310, 311, 312, 340, 456, 721, 770, 771, 776
Juliette M. Atherton Trust, The, 10
Junaid of Baghdad, 467
Jung, Carl Gustav, 147n, 375n, 380, 433n, 598, 599, 599n, 600, 606, 623n
jus civile, 778, 779
jus gentium, 778, 779; *see also ius gentium*
Just, St., 16
justice, 297, 398, 426, 427, 496, 588–589, 667; distributive, 565–566
Justinian, 173
just-so-ness (*jinen, shizen, tzu-jan*), 438, 439, 441, 738, 746, 748, 749, 750, 752

Kabīr, 504
Kafka, Franz, 350
Kakunyo, 109, 109n, 110
Kakushin-nikō Gyōjitsu no Kenkyū (Life of Kakushin, the Youngest Daughter of Shinran), 109n
kalām (dogmatic side of the *shari'a* tradition), 457–462, 460, 462, 465n, 470
Kālidāsa, 485
kāma (pleasure), 487, 514, 577, 578
Kāma Sūtra, 489
Kamakura Bukkyō no Kenkyū (Studies on Kamakura Buddhism), 104n
Kamakura period, 98, 102, 105, 656
Kamali, S. A., 469n
kāmavilayavāda, 489
kami (spirit), 104, 110, 661, 661n
kamikaze attack, 253, 666
Kandel, Isaac Leon, 766
Kane, P. V., 570n, 580n, 582n, 589n, 590n, 591n
K'ang Yu-wei, 86, 242, 382
Kanke Bunsō (Ancient Collection of Works), 640n
Kano Hōgai, 195n
Kant, Immanuel, 21, 27, 61, 63, 73, 74–75, 80, 146n, 151, 155, 282n, 290, 304, 321, 336, 337, 338, 342–361 *passim,* 366, 369, 381, 382, 407, 445, 482, 526, 571, 650n, 733
Kant und das Problem der Metaphysik, 144n
Kantian schools, 322
Kao-yao, 613, 614n
Kaplan, Abraham, 11, 141n, 654n
Karlgren, Bernard, 215
karma, 20, 62, 113, 231, 232, 240, 267, 268, 272, 275, 278, 282, 483, 503, 508, 522, 570, 573, 591, 601, 610, 690, 740, 750; *niṣkāma,* 62, 63, 272, 485; *nitya* and *naimittika,* 480
karmamārga (path of work or action), 274
karma-yoga, 280, 378, 486, 504n, 515
Karmayogaśāstra, 280
karuṇā, 107, 286, 446, 572, 632, 753; *see also* compassion, love, *maitrī*
Kasahara Kazuo, 103n
Kaṭha Upaniṣad, 61n, 271n, 282n, 476, 495n, 496n, 500n, 508n, 514, 514n, 516n, 571n
Kattsoff, Louis O., 140n
Kātyāyana, 588, 589, 590
Kauṣītakī Upaniṣad, 477 477n, 479
Kauṭilya, 496, 502n, 503, 576, 578, 579, 580, 589, 589n, 592; *see also Arthaśāstra*
Kauṭilya's Arthaśāstra, 496n
ke (swearing, oath), 663, 664, 665
Keene, Donald, 345n
Kegon, 196, 429, 742
Kehrback, Karl, 146n
Keitai, Emperor, 633n
Keith, A. B., 476, 477n, 602, 602n, 603
Keller, W., 144n
Kenchi, 106n
Kenchi Kikigaki (The Record by Kenchi), 106n
Kennyo, 110
Kepler, Johannes, 220
al-Khwārezmī, 177, 178, 184
Kierkegaard, Søren, 327, 379
Kikuya, 107n
Kimmei, Emperor, 97, 98
Kimura, Sueko M., viii
al-Kindī, 173, 175, 175n
king, 579, 589, 592, 612; and his officers, 580–581
Kingrey, Kenneth, viii
Kinshokuji, 109
Kirfel, Willibald, 605, 605n
Kirk, Russell, 376
Kishimoto Hideo, 245–254, 675n, 684n, 786
Kitāb aljadār wal-hasba (A Treatise on the Small-pox and the Measles), 177n
Kitāb Alnoyaj al-sabi (Al-Battānī sive Albatenii opus astronomicum), 178n
Kitāb al-shifā (The Book of Reasoning), 176n
Kitabatake Chikafusa, 196n, 640n, 641, 657
Kitāb fasl al-maqāl, 181n
Kitāb iḥṣā al 'ulum (Classification of Science), 176n
Kitano Bunsō (Collected Works of the Kitano Shrine), 640n
Kitanoshi (The History of the Kitano Shrine), 640n
Kiza, Prince, 658n
Kleinere Schriften, 153n
Kluckhohn, Clyde, 144n, 664n, 775, 775n

Knight, Frank H., 549–568, 694, 786–787
Know thyself, 325
kōans, 730
Koestler, Arthur, 126n, 381
Kojiki. Record of Ancient Matters, 633n
"Kokka-risō to Kojin-jinkaku" ("Taigi to Shiji") (Prince Shōtoku's Ideal of a National State and His Personality), 97n
Kokuryo Kingdom, 658
Kōmō Tōki (Exposition of the Teachings of Confucius and Mencius), 640n
Korea, 97, 98, 101, 648–669
Korea, the Hermit Nation, 665n
Korean Culture and Criminal Responsibility, 650n
Korean Factionalism, 660n
Koreans and Their Culture, The, 664n
Koryu Dynasty, 658, 663
Kosmographie der Inder, 605
Kosmos, 176n
Kramrisch, Stella, 156–171, 602, 602n, 605, 605n, 787
Kritik der Urteilskraft (*Critique of Judgment*), 146n, 344n
Kroeber, A. L., 773n
Kroner, Richard, 650n
Krusé, Cornelius, 11, 692–698, 787–788
kṣatriya (soldier), 169, 498, 502, 511, 583, 608, 610
Ku Yen-wu, 216, 217, 218, 219, 220, 242
Ku-tsun-su Yü-lu (*Kosonshuku Goroku*) (Sayings of the Ancient Worthies), 441n
Kuang-ming Daily, 767
Kuan-yin, 89
Kūkai, 644
Kullūka, 588n
Kulturstaat, 388
Kumārajīva, 433
Kumārila, 269n, 279, 329, 487n
Kumazawa Banzan, 632, 632n
k'ung, 432; *see also* emptiness, nothingness, *śūnya*
Kung-yang school, 242
Kuo Hsi, 90
Kuo Hsiang, 86, 88
Kurtz, Paul, 10, 530, 531
Kuruma Takudō, 112n
Kurzgefasstes Etymologisches Wörterbuch des Altindischen, 159n
Kyōgyōshinshō (Teachings, Practice, Faith, and Attainment), 107, 108, 108n
Kyōgyōshinshō Rokuyōshō Ehon (Collected Text of the Teachings, Practice, Faith, and Attainment), 107n
Kyōgyōshinshō Shōkan Kōdoku (Lectures on the chapter "Attainment" of *Kyōgyō Shinshō*), 108n
Kyung-kuk tai-chun, 665

La Boétie, 595
La Chine antique, 539n
La Doctrine du Sacrifice dans les Brāhmaṇas, 609n
La Lumiere sur les Six Voies, 606n
La Pensée Chinoise, 540n
La pensée religieuse de l'Inde, 328n
La Psychologie Contemporaine, 596n
La Religion Védique, 160n
la Vallée-Poussin, Louis de, 107n
laissez faire, 389, 394, 424
landscape painting, Chinese, 92
language, 182–183, 728–729; Japanese, 245–246; Western, 245–246
Language in Culture, 373n
Language of Morals, The, 372n
Language, Thought and Reality, 652n
Language, Truth and Logic, 369
Laṅkāvatāra Sūtra, The, 440n
Lao Tzu (and *Lao Tzu*), 86, 88, 192, 201n, 204, 205, 207, 209, 235, 237, 239, 243, 428, 433, 434, 435, 439, 440, 444, 613, 614, 614n, 615, 616, 616n, 624, 625, 643, 645, 746, 747
"L'Applaudissement: Une Conduite Sociale," 358n
Lasswell, Harold D., 141n, 648n, 654n
Lavelle, Louis, 597
law, 73–75, 377–390, 398, 467, 468, 521–532, 533–548, 600, 607, 611–629 *passim,* 634, 635, 648–669, 716; and ethics, 616–623; British, 387; Chinese, 529, 533–548 *passim,* 611–629 *passim;* common, 621, 671; concept of, 635–638; constitutional, 395; faith in, in America, 387–390; international, 770–779 *passim;* living, 773–779; mediational, 629; penal, 629, 666; positive, 773–779; Roman, 326, 527, 536, 617, 651; rule of, 620, 621, 663; Western, 533–548 *passim,* 617, 628–629
"Law, The," 455n, 459n
law-abidingness, 398
Law, Higher, 614, 614n, 616
Law of Nations, The, 73
Law of Nature, 616
Law of Primitive Man: A Study in Comparative Legal Dynamics, The, 775
Law of War and Peace, The, 73
Law Quarterly Review, 455n
Lawami' al-ishrāq fī makārim al-akhlaq (Flashes of Splendor Concerning Excellencies of Dispositions), 471n
Laws (Plato), 534n, 601
Laws of Manu, 485, 531, 712; *see also Code of Manu, Manu, Manu Saṁhitā, Manu Smṛti*
Lazarsfeld, Paul F., 141n
Le Droit Chinois, 544n
League of Nations, 774
Leavelle, A. B., 385n
Lecky, P., 144n
Leçons sur les Phénomènes de la Vie, 146n
Lectures in the Philosophy of History, 255, 256n
Ledlie, James C., 535n
Lee Byung-do, 658n, 663n
Lee Dynasty, 658, 659, 663, 665
Lee, Vernon (Violet Paget), 351, 351n
Lefever, Ernest W., 399, 479n
"Legal Cause," 649n
legal philosophy, 631–647
"Legal, Political, and Economic Philosophy in Indian Perspective," 569–593

legal systems, 521–532, 773–779 *passim;* of West, 617
legalism, 455
legalists, 467, 618, 619, 620, 621
Legge, James, 85n, 87n, 91n, 230n, 234n, 633n
Legislative Way of Life, The, 393n
Leibniz, Gottfried Wilhelm, 73, 80, 287, 333, 335, 336, 336n, 385n, 404
Lemaître, Abbé Georges Édouard, 140n
Lenin, Nicolai, 25, 26, 380, 769
Lerner, Max, 399
Les Cathédrales de France, 595n
Les Institutions Juridiques des Romains, 536n
Les Problèmes de l'Esthétique Contemporaine, 344n
L'Esthétique, 345n
Letters from an American Farmer, 390, 390n
Letters on the Aesthetic Education of Mankind, 346n
L'Etre et le Néant: Essai d'ontologie phénomenologique, 144n, 151n, 598n
Lévi, Sylvain, 107n, 609n
Leviathan, 262n
Levy, Marmon J., 141n
Lévy-Bruhl, Lucien, 604
Lewin, Kurt, 144n, 649, 649n, 652, 652n
Lewis, Bernard, 473n
Lewis, C. I., 368, 369, 372, 697
Leys, Wayne A. R., 396n
li (principle), 85, 196n, 209, 230, 234n, 319n
Li Kung, 242
Li Ssu, 620
Liang ch'i-ch'ao, 412, 412n, 616n
liang-chih (conscience), 230, 241
liberalism, 16, 21, 27, 30, 31, 48, 497, 549–568 *passim*
liberation, 59, 60, 270, 271, 478, 496, 497, 501, 510, 511, 513, 515, 577, 585, 679–691; *see also* emancipation, freedom, *mokṣa*
liberty, 659, 677
Lieh Tzu, 234n
Life and Times of Po Chü-i, The, 348, 348n
Life Divine, The, 348n
"Life Stress and Bodily Disease," 146n
Li-huo lun (The Disposition of Error), 89
Lillie, R. S., 145n
Lin Yutang, 83n
Lin-chi I-hsüan (Rinzai Gigen), 104, 432, 432n, 444
Lin-chi lu (*Rinzai Roku*) (Sayings of Rinzai), 432n, 444n
Lincoln, Abraham, 387, 397
L'Inde Classique, 169n
Lindley, Samuel E., 10
Linguistic Aspects of Science, 649n
Linton, R., 144n, 151n
Lippmann, Walter, 376, 376n, 396n
Lipps, Theodor, 349, 349n
litigation, 623, 624
Litt, Th., 151n
Little Rock, 548
Liu, Ch'i-shan, 235n
Liu, Francis, 656n
Liu, James J. Y., viii
Liu Pang, 654, 654n
living as creativity, 439
Llewellyn, K. N., 664n
Lo Chin-ch'i, 235n
Lo Nien-an, 235n
Locke, John, 80, 365, 526, 526n, 530, 778
logic, 106, 183–184, 359, 360, 377, 429, 430, 575, 580, 588–589, 646, 680, 729–730, 732-753 *passim;* Buddhist, 196; Greek 462; Islamic, 172–187 *passim,* 721–731 *passim*
Logic of the Sciences and the Humanities, The, 124n, 522n, 528, 652n
logical empiricism, 370
logical positivism, 66
logically true, never satisfactory, 433
Logos, 69, 80, 201n, 271, 272, 282n, 283, 283n, 284, 286, 286n, 325, 326, 328, 435, 740
lokasaṁgraha (commonweal), 486
longevity, 158–171 *passim,* 498; *see also āyurveda,* medicine
Lotus of the True Law, The, 103n
love, 227, 234, 285, 297, 299, 315, 374, 383, 420, 426, 427, 446, 468, 469, 515, 516, 581, 619, 632, 633, 645, 654, 684, 685, 691, 753; of God, 467, 468; Platonic, 68; universal, 234, 414, 416–417, 655; *see also chien-ai,* compassion, *karuṇa, maitrī*
Lowell, Percival, 661n, 662n
Löwith, K., 151n
loyalty, 417, 657, 667
Lu Chiu-yüan (Lu Hsiang-shan), 210, 233, 234n, 241
Lü Tsu-ch'ien, 214
Luke, Book of, 326n
Lundberg, George A., 141n, 142, 142n
Lung-t'an Ch'ung-hsin (Ryūtan Sōshin), 443n
Lun-heng (Essays in Criticism), 205, 206n
Lysenko, T. D., 26

McCarthy, Harold E., 9, 789
McCulloch, Warren Sturgis, 121n, 122
Macdonald, Margaret, 371
Macdonell, A. A., 159n, 163n
Macdonell, Sir John, 586n
McDougal, Myres S., 648n
Mach, Ernst, 530
Machiavelli, Niccolò, 202
McIlwain, C. H., 533, 533n, 535, 537n, 538n
McInerny Foundation, 11
MacIver, R. M., 36, 36n, 37, 39n, 41, 41n
Mackenzie, J. S., 482n
macrocosm, 156, 622
Madhva, 328n
Mādhyamika, 106, 108, 196, 265, 239, 240
Madhyandina, 605
magic, 169, 170
Mahā Upaniṣad, 261
Mahābhārata, 490, 491, 495, 501, 502n, 503n, 513n, 570n, 571, 572n, 574, 577, 577n, 578, 580, 580n, 581n, 582, 583, 587, 589, 590, 590n, 610
Mahadevan, T. M. P., 319n, 378, 378n, 476–493, 483n, 485n, 489n, 527, 529, 676n, 678n, 687, 688n, 691, 788
Mahān Ātmā (Cosmic Reason), 282n; *see also mahat*
Mahānirvāṇa Tantra, 503

Mahānārāyaṇa Upaniṣad, 570n
mahat (cosmic reason), 271, 271n, 282n, 286n
Mahāvīra, 265, 273, 493, 593
Mahāyāna, see Buddhism
Mahāyāna-abhidharma-samuccaya-vyākhyā, 105n
Mahāyāna-sūtrālaṁkāra, 105n, 107, 107n
Mahmud Shabistari, 309
Maimonides, 730, 771
"Main Contrasts Between Eastern and Western Philosophy," 199n
Maine, Sir Henry S., 521, 522, 522n, 523, 525n, 531, 560
Maistre, Joseph-Marie de, 19
Maitreyī, 514
maitrī, 572, 632; *see also chien-ai,* compassion, *karuṇā,* love
Majjhima Nikāya, 54n
Malaya, 594
Malinowski, Bronislaw, 371
Mallarmi, Stéphane, 350
Mallas, Licchavi, 579
Malraux, André, 357, 357n
Man and Society in an Age of Reconstruction, 142n
Man for Himself—An Inquiry into the Psychology of Ethics, 144n, 147n
manana (reflection), 262
manas (mind), 170, 274, 282, 323, 571, 738
Manchester, Frederick, 303n
maṇḍala (symbolic diagram), 101, 339n, 594–610, esp. 598, 599
Mandarins, The, 374, 381
Māṇḍūkya Upaniṣad, 302, 303, 305, 308, 310
Mann, Thomas, 350
Mannheim, Karl, 142, 142n
Manu (and *Manu*), 485, 512, 570, 573, 573n, 576, 576n, 577, 577n, 578, 579, 579n, 580n, 581n, 582, 582n, 584, 587, 587n, 588, 588n, 589, 590, 592, 601, 609; *see also Code of Manu, Laws of Manu, Manu Saṁhitā, Manu Smṛti*
Manu Saṁhitā, 497n
Manu Smṛti, 485n, 570n
Manual of Buddhism, 432n
Manual of Ethics, A, 482n
Manya Harari, 382n
Mao school, 213, 214
Mao-shih ku-yin (An Inquiry into the Ancient Pronunciation of the *Book of Odes*), 216
Marcel, Gabriel, 270, 278
Marcuse, Herbert, 375n
Margenau, Henry, 140n, 524
Maritain, Jacques, 760
Martin, Father, 770, 771
Martin, R. M., 524n
Marx (and Marxism), 17, 18, 24, 25, 26, 28, 75, 242, 380, 382, 564, 769
Marx-Engels Gesamtausgabe, 18n
Maslow, A. H., 144n
Mason, A. T., 399
Maspero, Henri, 539, 539n
Massenpsychologie, 375
Massenpsychologie und Ich-Analyse, 375n
materialism, 21, 29, 333, 384, 487, 607; French, 29
Mathematical Biology of Social Behavior, 141n
mathematical physics, 523, 524, 528, 530
Mathematical Thinking in the Social Sciences, 141n
mathematical zero, 157
mathematics, 156, 172–187 *passim,* 680, 721–731 *passim*
Ma-tsu (Baso), 443, 743, 752, 753
Matsuno Junko, 103n, 104n, 109n
Mattōshō (The Light of the Latter Days), 106n
Mattōshō Jinshinki (Notes of Mattōshō in the Year of North Monkey), 108n
Mattōshō Kankiroku (Mattōshō Collection), 107n
Mattōshō Setsugi (The Gist of Mattōshō), 107n
Mauryan Empire, 579
Maxwell, James Clark, 525
May Fourth Movement, The, 762, 763
māyā (illusion, mysterious power, appearance), 60, 61, 157, 506, 508, 516
Mayerhofer, M., 159n
Máynez, Eduardo García, 405, 405n
Mead, G. H., 151n, 399
Mead, Margaret, 403, 403n
Meaning and Being of Values Within the Framework of an Empirically Oriented Value Theory, The, 143n
"Meaning and Significance of Spirituality in Europe and in India, The," 316–341
Meaning of Meaning, 369
Mechanisms of Nervous Integration and Conscious Experience, 146n
mediation, 243, 546
Mediational Approval Theory of Law in American Legal Realism, The, 524n
medicine (science of longevity), 157–158, 170, 171; *see also āyurveda*
Medicus, Fritz, 404n
meditation, 241, 276, 506, 509, 521
Meditation schools, 89, 90
Meditations (Marcus Aurelius), 71n
Méditations Cartésiennes, 596n
Meeting of East and West, The, 56n, 200n, 377, 524n, 574n, 651n
Megasthenes, 583, 589
Mei Tsu, 212
Mei, Y. P., 349n, 616n
Meiji Restoration (and era), 102, 110, 192, 195, 637, 638, 639, 656, 657, 661
Meister Eckhart: A Modern Translation, 309n
Men and Movements in American Philosophy, 399
Mencius, 93, 203, 205, 228, 230, 233, 234n, 413, 414, 415, 416, 418, 423, 612, 613, 618, 620, 621, 626, 640; *see also Book of Mencius,* Confucianism
Mencius' Philosophy of Human Nature and Natural Law, 612n
Mensching, Gustav, 250
mental training, 247–248, 252
"Mentorgarten Dialogue," 378n
Merleau-Ponty, Maurice, 598, 598n, 608

Merton, R. K., 37, 38n
Messiah, 383
meta-ethics, 367
Metaphysical Foundations of Modern Physical Science, The, 523n
Metaphysical Journal (Journal Métaphysique), 277n
metaphysics, 12, 16, 22, 52, 53, 57, 256–260, 358
meteorology, 170
Methode der Geisteswissenschaften, 403
miao (*myō*) (mystery), 432–438, 439, 441, 444, 445, 745, 747, 748
microcosm, 156, 622
microcosm-macrocosm, 156, 602
Middle Ages, 201, 202, 330, 331, 332, 334, 549–568 *passim,* 559, 653, 724, 728
Middle Way, 197
Middleton, Drew, 777
militarism, 662, 755, 759
military force, 129
Mill, John Stuart, 28, 80, 381
Miller, R., 146n
Mills, C. W., 455n
Mīmāṁsā, 157, 262, 263n, 265, 266, 267, 268, 269, 269n, 270, 271, 272n, 273, 274, 275, 276, 279n, 280, 281, 286, 288, 291, 319n, 329n, 476, 525, 531, 532, 710
Mīmāṁsā Sūtra, 262n
mind 120–131, 170, 571; universal, 232, *see also manas*
Mind, 483n
Mind and Matter, 141n
Mind, Self, and Society, 151n
Ming Dynasty, 201n, 234n, 235, 242, 243, 429, 440, 614n
Ming-i tai-fang lu (book on government for rulers), 621
Ming-jü hsüeh-an (Writings of Ming Confucians), 235n
Ming-lü (Code of the Ming Dynasty), 656, 665
Minor Anthologies of the Pāli Canon, The, 261n
Mirza Hairat Dehlvi, 295n
Miscellaneous Writings of Francis Lieber, The, 385n
Miscellanies (Emerson), 398n
Misch, George, 283n
Mishkat, 295n
Mito school, 640
Miura Chikkie, 646
Miyamoto Shōson, 97–116, 98n, 107n, 108n, 113n, 194–197, 705, 789
Models of Man: Social and Rational, 141n
Models: Their Uses and Limitations, 122n
Modern Theme, The, 153n
"Modern Trend of Western Civilization and Cultural Peculiarities in Japan," 188–197, 652n
Modern Trends in Islam, 178n, 468n
modernization, 253, 665, 666
mokṣa, 59, 171, 270, 271, 478, 479, 481, 484, 485, 486, 487, 489, 514, 516–517, 577; *see also* emancipation, freedom, liberation
Moll, Walter L., 535n, 773n
monarchy, 579, 634, 637, 641
Mongol (Yüan) Dynasty, 212
monism, 107n, 265, 267, 324, 467, 575
Monophysites, 173
Montague, W. P., 56
Montaigne, Michel Eyquem de, 202, 595 595n
Montesquieu, Charles Louis-de, 387, 389
Monumenta Nipponica, 632n
Moore, Charles A., 3–12, 50n, 142, 142n, 199n, 317n, 319, 319n, 378, 378n, 383, 478n, 497n, 501n, 522n, 542n, 572n, 589n, 650n, 651n, 699–718, 789–790
Moore, G. E., 292, 366, 366n, 367, 368, 369, 370, 370n, 371
Moore, W. E., 35n, 42n
"Moral Conception of Nature in Indian Philosophy, The," 570n
moral excellence, 478
moral introspection, 631
moral law, 655
moral requirements, 478
moral values, 440, 494
morality, 61–64, 65, 66, 74–75, 83, 95, 226, 229, 231, 398, 433, 571, 576, 577, 580, 583, 584, 585, 586, 588, 592, 639, 643, 695, 756, 757, 760, 761; in art, 355–356, 359, 361
Morgan, Conwy Lloyd, 267n
Morgan, J. P., 385
Morgan, Morris J., 10
Morgan, T. H., 145n
Mori Arinori, 661, 662
Mori Daikyō, 645n
Morocco, 770, 771, 772, 774, 776
Morris, Aldyth V., vii
Morris, Charles, 54, 151n, 370, 370n, 403, 403n
Moses, 722, 747
Mo Tzu, 416, 614n, 616, 616n, 651, 655
Motivation and Personality, 144n
Motonobu, 194n, 195
Motse the Neglected Rival of Confucius, 349n
Mou Tzu, 89
Mounier, Emmanuel, 144n, 151, 151n
Mueller, Bertha, viii
Muhammad, 98, 448–475 *passim*
Muhammad V, Ottoman Sultan, 771
Muhammad ibn Aḥmad al-Khwārezmī, 177, 178, 184
Muhammedanische Studien, 456n
Muirhead, John Henry, 269
Mujintō (Unlimited Light), 109n
Müller, F. Max, 266
Müller, Marcus Joseph, 181n
multiplicity, 303, 309, 500; *see also* individual, pluralism
Mumford, Lewis, 65
Munakata Shikō, 350
Muṇḍaka Upaniṣad, 496, 497n, 509n, 510, 510n, 516n
Munk, Arthur W., 10
Munqidh min ad-dalāl (Escape from Error), 181, 181n
Munro, Donald, 10
Munro, Thomas, 357, 357n
Murakami Senshō, 109n
Murasaki Shikibu (Lady), 345, 345n
Muromachi-Sengoku period, 111n
Murphy, G., 144n, 146n, 147n

Murray, H. A., 144n
muruwwa (manliness), 456
Mus, Paul, 323n, 338n, 339n, 594–610, 605n, 790
music, 696; Chinese, 91
Music and Its Lovers, 351n
Muslim Creed, The, 462n
Muslim Discovery of Europe, The, 473n
Musnad, 294n
Mu'tazila, 460, 461, 461n, 462
mutual understanding, 409
Myers, Gerald E., 13
Myres, J. L., 539n
myō; see miao
mystery, 433; *see also miao*
"Mystical Form of Western Spirituality, The," 302–315
mysticism, 57, 192, 236, 248, 292, 302–315, 321, 335, 379, 380, 429, 434, 435, 465–472, 469, 472, 473, 503, 552, 707; Christian, 327, 328; Islamic 467; practical aspect of, 312–315; Western, 302–315 *passim*, 681–682
Mysticism, Christian and Buddhist, 108n
Mysticism East and West; A Comparative Study of the Nature of Mysticism, 313n
Mythological Bonds between East and West, 661n

Naciketas, 496, 514
nādabrahman, 285, 286n
Nagai Makoto, 641n
Nāgārjuna, 104
Nagley, Winfield E., 9, 790
Nagy, Albino, 175n
Nairuktas, 270, 329n
Naiyāyikas, 270
Nakamura Hajime, 335n, 631–647, 791
Nakazawa Kenmyō, 109n
Nallino, C. A., 178n
Nameless, infinite, 435
Nānamoli, Bhikkhu, 598n
Nan-Ch'üan Pu-yüan, 441n
Nanjō Bunyū, 440n
Nan-kuo Tzu-chi, 438
Nan-yüeh Huijang (Nangaku Ejo), 441n
Napoleon, 73
Nārada, 507
Nārada-purāṇa, 476n
Naritasanshi (History of Naritasan Temple), 112n
Nāṣir-i Khusraw, 471
Naṣr ed-Dine Thūsī (Nasīr ad-Dīn aṭ-Ṭūsī), 177, 471
Natanson, M., 151n
National Education Association, 765
nationalism, 104, 130, 614n, 638, 639, 640, 646, 657, 662, 663, 666, 774
Natural Law, 82, 83, 586, 612, 614n, 621
Natural Law and the Theory of Society, 533n
"Natural Law in the Chinese Tradition, The," 82n, 614n
Natural Law Institute Procedings, 82n, 614n
"Natural Law Philosophy of Mencius, The," 614n
"Natural Man, Philosophy, Behavior," 117–131
"Natural Science and Technology in Relation to Cultural Patterns and Social Practices in India," 156–171
naturalism, 205, 304, 317, 333, 365, 367, 369, 661, 697
naturalness, 428–446 *passim*, 732–753 *passim*
Nature, 65, 67, 68, 69, 72, 93, 136, 209, 225, 226, 228, 233, 259, 573, 583, 586, 660, 744, 745, 748, 758; as source of joy, 440; harmony with, 190–197; hostility toward, 190–197; knowledge of, 135, 136, 137, 138, 139, 140, 141, 142, 143, 144, 145, 146, 147, 148, 149, 150, 151, 152, 153, 154, 155; love of, 354–355; moral concept of, 570
Nature of Metaphysics, The, 57n
"Nature of Mind and Its Activities, The," 282n
Nature of Personality, The, 144n, 146n
Nature of Physical Reality, The, 140n
Nature of Sympathy, 151n
"Naturphilosophie und Anthropologie," 153n
Neanderthal man, 153
Needham, Joseph, 145n, 196n, 523, 527, 529, 542n, 543n
negation, Indian, 485, 486
"Neglected Ideal of Life, A," 485n
Negroes, 345, 386
Nehru, Jawaharlal, 493
nembutsu, 103, 105, 106, 109
Neo-Confucianism, 82, 83, 94, 95, 208, 209, 210, 228, 232, 240, 241, 242, 243, 319n, 382, 413, 655, 655n, 656, 657, 660
neo-idealism, 317
Neo-Kantians, 409
Neo-Platonism, 174, 261, 463, 465, 466, 468; *see also* Plotinus
Neo-Taoism, 85, 86
Neo-Thomism, 318
Nestorians, 173
Netherlands, 777
neti, neti, 306, 366
Neumann, John von, 121, 121n, 122, 122n
Neurath, Otto, 649n, 650n
Neurophysiological Basis of Mind, The, 146n
Neurosis and Human Growth: The Struggle Toward Self-Realization, 144n
New Christianity, The, 75
"New Korean Criminal Code of October 1953, The," 665n
New Scholasticism, 614n
New Ways in Psychoanalysis, 147n
New York Times, 376, 777
Newell, Allen, 122n
Newton, Isaac, 75, 77, 220, 333, 335, 525, 526, 528, 556
Nichiren, 103, 104, 105, 195, 196n, 640
Nicholson, R. A., 295n
Nichomachean Ethics, 33, 543n; *see also Ethica Nichomachea*
Nickerson, Thomas, viii, 11
Nielson, Niels, 10
Nietzsche, Friedrich, 80, 374, 380, 402, 553
nihilism, 507; *see also* non-being

Nihon Bukkyō no Kenkyū (Studies on Japanese Buddhism), 97n
Nihon Bukkyō-shi (History of Japanese Buddhism), 103n
Nihon Dōtoku Shisōshi (History of Japanese Moral Thought), 104n
Nihongi (*Nihonshoki*) (Chronicles of Japan), 97
Nihon-Shūkyōshi (*Nippon Shukyō-shi*) (History of Japanese Religions), 645n, 661n
Nikhilananda, Swami, 319, 323n, 494–517, 509n, 510n, 676n, 684, 684n, 791
Nilsson, Martin P., 534n
Nimbārka, 328n
Ninomiya Sontoku, 645
Nintoku, 639
nirmāṇakāya, 108, 327
nirvāṇa (and *Nirvāṇa*), 89, 92, 106, 107, 276, 278, 377, 437, 446, 478, 525, 660, 721; of non-abode, 105, 107
Nishida Kitarō, 192, 196n, 374, 738
Nishitani Keiji, 374
Nītiśāstras, 589
no-striving, 440, 443, 444; *see also anābhoga-caryā*
Noble Eightfold Path, 281; *see also* eightfold path
Noguchi Hideo, 195
Noh (*Nō*) dramas, 111n, 343, 352, 354–355
non-action, 509; *see also wu-wei*
non-attachment, 478, 513, 514, 622, 688
non-being, 236n, 366, 373, 374, 377, 379, 434, 468; *see also* nihilism
non-dualism, 108, 197, 265, 494, 499–500, 507, 508, 510, 516, 524, 531; *see also* Vedānta, Advaita
non-injury, 511, 572, 591; *see also ahiṁsā*, harmlessness, non-violence
non-naturalism, 367, 369, 370
non-rational tendencies, 631; *see also* irrationalism
non-violence, 16, 491, 493, 584; *see also ahiṁsā*, harmlessness, non-injury
Northrop, F. S. C., 8, 11, 56, 120n, 121n, 124n, 127n, 128n, 131, 199, 200, 201n, 289, 319n, 320, 325, 326n, 332n, 377, 378, 521–532, 524n, 525n, 538, 539n, 542, 542n, 543, 546, 574n, 634, 634n, 638n, 651, 651n, 652, 652n, 653, 653n, 654n, 657n, 664n, 697, 721, 770–779, 775n, 777n, 778n, 791–792
Notes on Brahman, 159n
nothing (and nothingness), 236, 236n, 237, 239, 243, 430, 432, 434; *see also śūnya*
Nowell-Smith, P. H., 373, 373n
nuclear physics, 754
Nyāya, 276, 279, 480, 481, 588, 589
Nyāya-Vaiśeṣika, 59
Nyogen Senzaki, 378n

objectivism, 432, 436
Occult Japan, 661n, 662n
Ogaeri Yoshio, 633n
Ogburn, W. F., 35n, 40n, 47n
Ogden, C. R., 369, 369n
oharai (purification ceremony), 661n
Okakura Kakuzō, 195n
Old Testament, 326, 328, 654
Oldenberg, Hermann, 660n
Olsen, Jennings J., 10
Omar Khayyam, 184
Omaston, F. P. B., 347n
On Describing a World, 144n
On the Athenian Constitution, 393
On the Divine Names and the Mystical Theology, 306, 306n
On the Knowledge of Good and Evil, 373n
On the Law of Nature and Nations, 73
"On Nationalism and Internationalism," 385n
On no Shisō (An Idea of Gratitude), 662
On Perpetual Peace, 73
"On Semantical Rules and Definable Predicates," 524n
On Understanding Science, 202, 202n
On World Government, 71n
Open Self, The, 54n
Open Society and Its Enemies, The, 665n
Order and Life, 145n
orchestrated unity, 698
Organ, Troy, 10
Organism, The, 147n
Organization Man, The, 138n
Original Pronunciation of the Book of Odes, The, 216
Origins of Muhammadan Jurisprudence, The, 458n
Ortega y Gasset, José, 153n
Osgood, Cornelius, 664n
Oshima Yasumasa, 10
Ostroróg, L., 457n
Ōtani, 109
"Other Minds," 371n
otherworldliness, 20, 574
Otto, Rudolph, 313n
Our Inner Conflicts, 147n
Our Knowledge of the External World, 52n
Out of My Life and Thought, 258, 258n
"Outline of a Decision Procedure for Ethics," 373n
Outline of History, The, 584n
Outline of Psychoanalysis, An, 144n
Oxford philosophers, 371, 373, 379

pacifism, 773
Page, C. H., 36n
Pai-chang (Hyakujo), 752, 753
Paik, George, 664n
painting, Chinese, 91
pairs of opposites, 108, 197
Palencia, A. Gonzáley, 176n
pañcaśīla (five moral principles), 493, 575
Pandey, K. C., 348n
Pang, 747, 748
Pang, C. L., 10
pantheism, 468, 469
paramārtha (and *pāramārthika*) (ultimate reality), 507, 575
parapsychology, 732–753
Parker, De Witt H., 346, 346n
Parmenides, 324

Parson, Talcott, 37, 37n, 141n
Partmann, A., 148n
Pascal, Blaise, 257, 332
Pasternak, Boris, 382
Patañjali, 60, 264n, 510n
paternalism, State, 562
Paths of Life, The, 370, 370n
Patterns and Problems of Development, 145n
Patterns of Culture, 151n
Paul, R. B., 586n, 588n
Paul, St., 200, 306, 313, 326n, 327n, 759
Pauly, Herta, 10
Payne, Richenda A., 313n
Pax Romana, 71, 80
peace, 73, 74, 75, 285, 398, 415, 418, 426, 437, 502, 618; universal, 72
peaceful state of mind, 445
Peano, Giuseppe, 530
Pearce, D. F., 57n
Peirce, Charles S., 764
Pella, M., 777n
P'eng Tsu, 438
Penn, William, 620
People's Daily, The, 767
People's Educaion, The, 766
Pepper, Stephen C., 353, 353n
Perry, Charner M., 396n
Perry, R. B., 368, 399
Persia, 256, 470, 540
person, 322, 326, 328, 328n, 727; Supreme Person, 572; *see also* individual, *puruṣa*
Person, The, 144n
personalism, 318, 339
Personalist, The, 153n
personality, 146n, 147n, 681, 682, 687, 727
Personality: A Biosocial Approach to Origins and Structure, 144n, 146n, 147n
Personality in Nature, Society, and Culture, 144n
Persönlichkeit: Eine dynamische Interpretation, 146n, 147n
Persons, Stow, 399
pessimism, 553
Petrarch, 202
Pfänder, A., 144n
Pfuetze, P. E., 151n
Phänomenologie und Begegnung der Religionen, 341
Phaedrus, 347
pharmacology, 156
phenomena 508, 509, 575, 631, 632; *see also* empirical reality, *vyāvahārika*
Phénoménologie de la Perception, 598n
phenomenology, 317, 602, 605, 643
Phenomenology of Mind, The, 375
Philebus, 344, 344n, 351
Phillips, Bernard, 10
"philosophers" (Islamic), 467, 448–475 *passim*
philosophic man, 126–128
philosophic State, 128–130
Philosophical Analysis, 371n
philosophical anthropology, 144, 154
Philosophical Anthropology and Practical Politics, 521n, 779n
Philosophical Basis of Chinese Painting, The, 539n
Philosophical Investigations, 371, 373n
Philosophical Review, 373n
Philosophical Studies, 524n
Philosophie der Griechen, 586n
Philosophie und Theologie von Averroës, 181n
Philosophies of Beauty, 344n
Philosophies of India, 380n
"Philosophies of Royce, James, and Dewey in Their American Setting, The," 399
philosophy, as bridge, 697
"Philosophy and Human Conduct," 15–32
Philosophy and Phenomenological Research, 144n
Philosophy and Politics, 16n, 27n
philosophy and religion, 462–465
"Philosophy and Social Institutions in the West," 549–568
Philosophy and the Public Interest, 396n
"Philosophy at the Basis of Traditional Chinese Society, The," 653n
Philosophy East and West, 60n, 107n, 196n, 199n, 200, 263n, 319n, 323n, 479n, 522n, 542n, 651n, 652n, 654n, 655n
Philosophy of G. E. Moore, The, 370n
Philosophy of John Dewey, The, 347n
Philosophy of Law, 17
"Philosophy of Natural Science and Comparative Law, The," 651n, 653n
Philosophy of Sarvepalli Radhakrishnan, The, 348n
philosophy of science, 135–155, 140n, 145n
Philosophy of Science, 120n, 140n, 145n, 529n
Philosophy of Science, A, 141n, 145n
Philosophy of Science, The, 143n
"Philosophy of the Navaho Indians, The," 664n, 775
Philosophy of the Upanishads, The, 485n
Philosophy of Wang Yang-Ming, The, 85n
phonetics, Chinese, 208–218
Physical Science and Physical Reality, 140n
Physicist's Conception of Nature, The, 140n, 141n
physics, 157, 170
Physics and Philosophy, 141n
Physiological Regulations, 145n
Pi-ch'eng (Notes), 216
Picasso, Pablo, 346
Pitts, Walter, 121n, 122
Place of Reason in Ethics, The, 372n
Planck, Max, 525, 527, 667n
Plato, 61, 67, 68, 69, 70, 173, 226, 228, 264, 276, 289, 290, 294, 295, 325, 342–361 *passim,* 365, 366, 367, 437, 465, 466, 470, 471, 524, 534n, 535, 542, 550, 722
Plattard, Jean, 595n
pleasure, 230n, 487, 490, 578; *see also kāma*
Plotinus, 305–315 *passim,* 437, 468, 476n; *see also* Neo-Platonism
pluralism, 48, 266, 278, 387, 395, 396, 396n, 398, 550, 575; *see also* individual, multiplicity
Poe, Edgar Allan, 350
Poetical Works of Percy Bysshe Shelley, The, 261n

poetry, 344; Chinese, 91, 348, 361
"Point of View of Morality, The," 373n
Politbureau, 26
political philosophy, 521–532 *passim*, 533–548 *passim*, 569–583 *passim*, 611–629 *passim*, 631–647 *passim*, 773–779 *passim*
polytheism, 248, 267
Popper, K. R., 665n
Portmann, A., 144n
positivism, 119, 124, 318, 384
post-Kantian idealism, 322, 336, 337, 337n
post-Kantian schools, 322
postulation, 707; concepts by, 200, 320, 522, 528, 529, 530, 651
Potter, Karl H., 10
Pound, Roscoe, 772, 778, 778n
Power and Society: A Framework for Political Inquiry, 141n, 654n
power politics, 755, 756
Prabhākara, 269n, 279
Prābhākara Mīmāṁsakas, 480
Prabhavananada, Swami, 303n
Practical Philosophy of Muhammadan People, The, 471n
pragmatism, 48, 49, 375, 384, 690, 764, 767, 768
Prajāpati, 602, 606, 607, 608, 690
prajñā (wisdom), 63, 322, 323, 323n, 446, 753
Prajñā-pāramitā texts, 432n, 444
Prakaraṇāryavācā Sāstra, 105n, 107
prakṛti (Nature), 573
Prall, D. W., 344, 345n, 351, 352n
prāṇa (life movement), 171, 602, 603, 604, 605
pratītyasamutpāda, 597; *see also* dependent origination
pravṛtti (activity), 485
pre-Ch'in period, 240
predestination, 461, 462, 467
"Present Crisis of Faith, The," 754–761
Present State of the Ottoman Empire, The, 471n
pre-Socratics, 324
presuppositions (or assumptions), 673–691
pre-Upaniṣadic traditions, 329n
Price, H. H., 282n
Principia (Newton), 220
Principia Ethica, 366, 366n
Principia Mathematica, 122
Principles of Aesthetics, The, 346
Principles of Criminology, 665n
Principles of Sociology, 40n
Principles of Quantum Mechanics, 140
Problem of Physical Reality, The, 140n
"Problematic of the Self, West and East, and the Maṇḍala Pattern, The," 323n, 594–610
Problems of Life: An Evaluation of Modern Biological Thought, 145n
Proceedings of the American Philosophical Association (1958), 373n
Proceedings of the Aristotelian Society, 31n
Proceedings of the Third International Congress of Aesthetics, 352n
Proceedings of the Twenty-Second Congress of Orientalists, 455n
"Professor Margenau and the Problem of Physical Reality," 140n
Progoff, I., 150n
progress, 75–76, 515, 554–568 *passim*
Progress, Its Law and Cause, 76
Prohibition Amendment, 774
Promethean philosophy, 186
Pronunciation of the Book of Changes, The, 217
Prophecy in Islam, 464n
propriety, 417; *see also Book of Propriety (Rites)*
prosperity, 415, 418, 490, 498, 510
Protestantism, 20, 48, 649, 657, 664
Proust, Marcel, 350
provincialism, 3–11
Psalms, 430n
psychoanalysis, 29, 375, 682
Psychological Review, 146n
Psychologie und Philosophie des Wallens, 144n
psychology, 141, 142, 144–145, 312–313, 594–610; in India, 170; Japanese, 433
Psychology and the Social Order, 141n
Psychology and the Soul, 150n
Psychology of Art (Psychologie de l'art), 357n
psychotherapy, 685, 691
Ptolemy, 178
Public and its Problems, The, 396n
Public Opinion—A Democratic Dilemma, 399
Public Philosophy, The, 396n
Pufendorf, Samuel von, 73
punishment, 576, 582, 589–590, 591–592; capital, 590, 591; *see also daṇḍa*
Purāṇas, 501, 510, 572, 589
Pure Land, 89, 437, 890
Puritan Mind, The, 382
Puritanism and Democracy, 399
puruṣa, 63, 572, 599, 602, 604; *see also* person, self
Puruṣa Sūkta, 572n
puruṣārthas (basic human values), 487
Pyrrhus et Cinéas, 598, 598n
Pythagoras (Pythagoreans and Pythagoreanism), 168, 271, 283, 283n, 314

Quashairī, 467
Queen Mab, 261n
Quest for Certainty: A Study of the Relation of Knowledge and Action, The, 368n, 596n
quiescence, 236, 237
Qur'ān, 172–187 *passim*, 293–301 *passim*, 451–475 *passim*, 721–731 *passim*

Rabelais, François, 202
Radhakrishnan, S., 8, 66, 255–262, 263, 282n, 288, 320, 348, 378, 378n, 380n, 478n, 497n, 501n, 507n, 754–761, 792–793

Radhakrishnan, S., and C. A. Moore, 50n, 572n, 589n; *see also A Source Book in Indian Philosophy*
radical empiricism, 247
radicalism, 21
Radin, Paul, 775
Raffé, W. G., 348n
"Ragas and Raginis: A Key to Hindu Aesthetics," 348n
Rahder, Johannes, 107n
Rahman, F., 464n
Rājanīti-ratnākara, 581n, 589n
Raju, P. T., 263–292, 318, 320, 322n, 323n, 329n, 333, 337n, 383n, 527, 529, 531, 687, 793
Ramakrishna, 66, 328, 340, 341, 484, 505, 506
Ramakrishna Mission, 505–507
Ramaṇa Maharshi and His Philosophy of Existence, 483n
Ramaṇa, Maharshi Sri, 317n, 483, 493
Rāmāṇuja, 268, 270, 270n, 271, 271n, 274, 275, 276, 276n, 277, 277n, 278, 280, 281, 286, 328n, 504, 513
Rāmāyana, 495, 501, 502, 502n
Rangāchārya, M., 271n
Rank, O., 150n
Rasa 'il al-falsafa (Epistles on Philosophy), 175, 175n
Rasheosky, Nicholas, 141n
rational understanding, 677–691 *passim*
rationalism, 48, 49, 64, 188–197, 336, 469, 546, 559, 649, 676–691 *passim;* Kantian, 480; *see also* logic, reason
Rawls, J., 373n
al-Rāzī, 175, 177
Ṛbhus, 159–167
Reader's Digest, 483
Readings from the Mystics of Islām, 309n
realism, 246, 321, 384, 507, 517, 583–584, 690
"Realistic Aspect of Indian Spirituality, The," 494–517
realistic relativism, 575
realization, 276, 690; *see also* fulfillment, self-realization
Realm of Personality, The, 144n
reason, 54, 55, 58, 106, 282, 283, 285, 290, 318–347 *passim,* 430, 461, 462, 463, 464, 465, 571, 675–693, 677–693, 737; and faith, 258–262; and law, 27n; *see also* logic, rationalism
"Reason and Intuition in Buddhism," 323n
"Reason and Types of Intuition in Radhakrishnan's Philosophy," 348n
rebellion, right of, 656
recluse, 485
Reconstruction in Philosophy, 28n
Reconstruction of Religious Thought in Islam, 293, 296n
Recontre des Religions, 341
rectification of names, 84
rectitude, 412, 617, 627
reductionism, 130-131, 142, 143
Reflections on the French Revolution, 29
Reflections on the Revolution in France, 376
Reformation, 332, 334, 553, 724
Regamey, Constantin, 316–341, 408, 679, 793–794
Reichel, Oswald, J., 586n
reincarnation, 17, 553
Reinhardt, Kurt F., 311n
Reissig, John, 10
"Relation of Indian Philosophical Theories to Practical Affairs," 59–66
"Relation of Philosophical Theories to Practical Affairs, The," 704–706
"Relation of Philosophical Theories to the Practical Affairs of Men," 50–66
"Relation of Philosophical Theory to Practical Affairs in Japan, The," 97–116
relativism, 128, 462
release, 487; universal, 486; *see also* emancipation, freedom, liberation, *mokṣa*
religion, 50–51, 53, 64, 92, 228, 245–254, 260, 263–292, 302–315, 342–361 *passim,* 420, 448–475, 534, seq., 552, 601, 607, 632, 637, 645, 646, 661, 662, 722–731, 754–761; and philosophy, 450–475; and science, 180–182; and spiritual values, 263–292, 707–709; as bridge, 697
Religion and Philosophy of the Vedas and Upanishads, The, 477n, 602, 602n
Religion of China, The, 649n, 653n, 654n
Religions of the Empire, a Conference on Some Living Religions within the Empire, 113n
religious persecutions, 234
"Religious Rejections of the World and Their Directions," 455n
Religious Revolt Against Reason, The, 262n
Renaissance, 53, 202, 332, 334, 724, 771; Italian, 333, 345; painting of, 731
Rennyo, 104, 106n, 109, 110
Renou, Louis, 159n, 163n, 169n
renunciation, 366, 495, 510, 511, 512
Republic, The, 344n, 347, 347n, 352n, 355, 365n, 533, 535
res cogitantes, 335
res extensae, 335
resignation, 462
Respiration, 146n
Retrospect and Prospects: Achievements and Unfinished Business," 699–718
revelation, 85, 330, 452, 457, 458, 461, 462, 463, 464, 553, 559
Revelations (Book of), 454
Review of Religion, 163n
Revista de Ideas Estéticus, 357
Revival of Learning, 219, 221
revolution, 18, 29, 621
Revolution of 1911, 621
Revue d' Esthétique, 357
Ṛg Veda, 157, 158, 159–167, 159n, 291, 487, 497n, 498n, 499n, 507, 517n, 570, 570n, 572, 586, 600, 715
Rhyming Groups of the T'ang Period, 217
Ricci, Matteo, 234n
Rice, P. B., 373n
Richards, J. A., 369, 369n
Riesman, David, 375, 380
righteousness, 426, 448–475 *passim,* 452, 453, 487
rights, 229; and duties, 616–617; legal, 591–592
Rimbaud (John Nicholas) Arthur, 350

Rintelen, Fritz-Joachin von, 400–410, 403n, 794
Rinzai Roku (*Lin-chi lu*) (Sayings of Rinzai), 432n, 444n
Risshun Zenwa (New Spring Talk of Zen), 112n
rites, 91; *see also* propriety
Ritter, W. E., 145n
Rivista di Estetica, 357
Roankyō (Crossing the Bridge on an Ass), 645n
Rock and Pillar Edicts, 636, 638n
Rodin, Auguste, 595, 595n
Rokuyōshō (Essentials of Six Volumes), 107n
Romans (and Rome), 25, 70–71, 202, 256, 257n, 326, 326n, 327, 327n, 395, 525, 531, 533, 535, 586, 651, 776, 777, 778
Romantic era, 75
romanticism, 340
Rongochō (Critical Comments on the *Analects* of Confucius), 646n
rope and snake, 508
Rose, Herbert J., 534n
Rosenblueth, Arture, 120n
Ross, Sir E. Denison, 113n
Ross, W. D., 33n
Rossiter, Clinton, 376n
Rossow, Robert, Jr., 117–131, 681, 682n, 687n, 794
Rostovtzeff, Michael Ivanovich, 534, 535n
Rothacker, Erich, 144n, 407, 407n
Rousseau, Jean Jacques, 73, 560
Rowland, Cynthia, 144n
Roy, Ram Mohan, 493, 505
Royce, Josiah, 151
Ṛta, 570, 586, 587
Rugg, Harold Ordway, 766
Ruskin, John, 355, 355n, 585
"Ruskin and the Moral Imagination in Architecture," 355n
Russell, Bertrand, 16, 21, 22, 27, 51, 52, 122, 289, 604
Russia, 697; *see also* Soviet Union
Russian October Revolution, 25
Rutherford, Ernest, 200
Rycaut, Sir Paul, 471n
Ryder, A. W., 160n, 163n
Ryōshō, 108
Ryu, Paul K., 648–669, 650n, 651n, 665n, 795

Sa'ādatnāma (The Book of Happiness), 470n
Sabhā (king's court), 588
saccidānanda, 507, 516
Sacred Books of the East, 103n
sacredization, 458
sacredizing the world, 457
sacrifice, 496
saddharma (true law), 433
Saddharma-puṇḍarīka Sūtra, 101, 103n, 104
sādhārana-dharmas (universal duties), 573; *see also* duties
sage, 64, 67
sagehood, universal attainability of, 231–235
Sahih (Correct Ones), 298n, 299n
Saichō (Dengyō Daishi), 644
Saint-Simon, Claude-Henri de Rouvroy de, 75, 76, 77
Saito, Shiro, viii
Śaivism, 274
Sakamaki, Shunzo, 11
Saksena, S. K., 50-66, 676n, 678, 687, 705, 795
Śaktism, 274
Śākyamuni, *see* Buddha, the
salvation, 90, 274, 275, 278, 283, 552, 553
Śalyaparva, 570n
Sāma Veda, 507
samādhi, 280, 341, 509, 517
samanvayā (reconciliation), 260–262
Sambandha-vārttika of Sureśvarācārya, The, 489n
sambhogakāya (enjoyment body), 108; *see also hōjin*
Saṁdhinirmocana Sūtra, 105n, 107
Śaṁkara, 261, 265, 268, 270, 270n, 271, 275, 276, 277, 277n, 278, 280, 281, 286, 287, 310, 337n, 478, 485, 487, 487n, 495n, 499, 502, 507n, 509, 510, 512, 512n, 517, 531, 571, 574, 597, 646, 696, 702
Sāṁkhya, 60, 157, 265, 271, 271n, 272, 276, 279, 282, 282n, 285, 286n, 323, 580
Sāṁkhya-Yoga, 59
saṁsāra, 20, 107, 437, 550; *cakra*, 64
saṁskāras (inborn tendencies), 278
Samuel N. and Mary Castle Foundation, 10
samurai, 104
Sanatkumāra, 507
sanbō (Three Treasures), 113
san-chiao (three teachings), 227
Sanderson, D., 36, 36n,
Sane Society, The, 151n
sang-wo (losing the self), 437
Sanjō Wasan (Hymns in Three Volumes), 106n
sannyāsin, 63, 485, 517, 613
Sansom, Sir George, 99n
Santayana, George, 21, 344n, 345, 347, 351
śānti (peace), 285
Śāntiparva, 18, 490, 503n 571, 571n, 577, 577n, 578, 581n, 582, 583, 589n, 590n
Sapin, Burton, 128n
Sapir, E., 33, 36n
Sargent, S. S., 144n
Sarton, George, A. L., 176, 176n
Sartre, Jean-Paul, 144n, 151, 151n, 338n, 346, 374, 444, 598, 598n
Sarva-darśana-saṁgraha, 282n
Sasaki Genchi, 108n, 109n
Sasaki Gesshō Zenshū (The Complete Works of Sasaki Gesshō), 108n
Śatapatha Brāhmaṇa, 159n, 168, 600, 604, 605, 605n
satori, 195, 197, 315, 734
Scaevola, Q. M., 535, 536
Sceptre, 576, 577, 579, 589
Schacht, J., 455n, 458n, 459n
Schandler, Herbert Y., 10
Scheicho, L., 177n
Scheler, M., 144n, 151n, 328n, 373, 407, 409
Schelling, F. W. J., 338
Scherz und Ernst in der Jurisprudenz, 651n
Schiller, Friedrich, 346, 346n

Schilpp, P. A., 348n, 370n
Schneider, Herbert W., 67–80, 153n, 382n, 384–399, 676, 795
Schoeck, Helmut, 155n
Schopenhauer, Arthur, 228
Schoy, C., 177n
Schrödinger, Erwin, 123n, 127n, 141, 141n, 527
Schultz, J., 145n
Schweitzer, Albert, 258, 258n, 290, 484, 484n, 485, 486n
science, 7, 12, 19, 22, 23, 26, 28, 30, 50–51, 53, 56, 61, 75, 117–131, 156–171, 172–187, 199–221, 292, 318, 333, 333n, 357, 359, 360, 365, 367, 401, 430, 507, 521–532, 650, 651, 675, 676, 679, 680, 688, 754–761 *passim:* in art, 356–361; Asian, 529; Chinese, 523, 529; developments in, 755; Greek, 538, 539, 545, 721, 771; Japanese, 188–197; Western, 156, 319; as bridge, 696; of value, 135–155 *passim,* 650
Science and Civilization in China, 543n
Science and Common Sense, 202n
Science and Philosophy of the Organism, The, 145n
Science and the Social Order, 141n
Science and Society in Ancient China, 542n
Science of the Śulba, The, 168n
Sciences and Philosophy, The, 146n
Scientific Monthly, 142n
"Scientific Spirit and Method in Chinese Philosophy, The," 199–221, 649n, 525n
scientism, 131, 135–155, 155n, 318
"Scientism and the Problem of Man," 135–155, 652n
Scudder, Delton, L., 10
Secret of the Golden Flower: A Chinese Book of Life, The, 599, 599n
Secrets of the Self, 295n
Seimu, Emperor, 636
Sein und Zeit, 144n
Selections (Bose), 577n, 581n, 593n
Selections from Gandhi, 575n
self (and Self), 92, 265, 303, 304, 348, 430, 481, 486, 489, 492, 574, 594–610; universal, cosmic, 304, 311; Supreme, 573
self-control, 571
self-cultivation, 626
selfhood, 673–691 *passim*
self-interest, 391
self-purification, 485
self-realization, 325, 328n, 489, 493, 675, 687; *see also* fulfillment, realization
self-rule, 579
Seligman, E. R. A., 36n
Sellars, Roy Wood, 697
Selye, H., 146n
semanticists, 601
Sen, P. N., 591n
Sénart, Émile, 600n, 603, 604, 604n
Seneca, 71
"Sengai: Zen and Art," 350n
Seng-yu, 89n
Senmyō, 107n
Sense of Beauty, The, 344n
Sermon on the Mount, 585
Servetus, Michael, 760
Seth, James, 482n
Seven Lamps of Architecture, The, 355n
Seventeen-Article Constitution, 99, 101
Shakespeare, 738
Shakunyo, 109
shamanism, 660, 661, 661n, 662, 663, 663n, 664
"Shamanism of the Natives of Siberia," 660n
Shamasastry, R., 496n, 580n, 588n, 589n
Shang Dynasty, 612, 612n, 622
Shang Yang, 618, 619, 620
Shang-ti, 421; *see also* God
Shan-tao, 104
sharī'a (holy law of Islam, or a systematization of worldly practices), 457–462, 463, 466, 467, 469, 471, 472
Sharif, M. M., 293–301, 531, 796
Sheldon, Wilmon Henry, 199
Shelley, Percy Bysshe, 261n
shen (spirit), 238
Shen-kuang (Shinkō), 751
Sherrington, C. S., 44, 44n, 146n
Shih ching, 203; *see also Book of Odes*
Shijō no Shinran (Historical Life of Shinran), 109n
Shimaji Daitō, 108n
Shimomura Kwanzan, 195n
Shin, 99, 108, 196
Shingon, 102, 103n, 195, 196
Shinran, 99, 103, 103n, 104, 104n, 105, 106, 106n, 107, 107n, 108, 108n, 109, 110, 195, 196, 196n, 197, 250
Shinran, sono Shōgai to Shisō no Tenkai Kwatei (Shinran: Historical Studies of His Life and Thought), 103n
Shinran Shōnin-den-e no Kenkyū (Studies of the Illustrated Life of Shinran-shōnin), 109n
Shinran Shōnin Zenshū (Collected Works of Saint Shinran), 106n, 109n
Shinran to Tōgaku Nōmin (Shinran and Farmers of East Japan), 103n
Shinshū, 104, 109, 110, 112
Shinshū Seiten (Holy Scriptures of the Shinshū Sect), 108n
Shinshū Shōgyō Zensho (Collected Works of Shinshū), 106n
Shinshū Taikei (A Great System of Shinshū Books), 107n, 108n
Shinshū Zenshi (The Complete History of Shinshū), 109n
Shinshū Zensho (Complete Collection of Shinshū Books), 107n
Shinshūshi no Kenkyū (Studies on Shinshū History), 109n
Shinto and Shintoism, 97, 98, 104, 110, 247, 248, 249, 250, 251, 253, 632, 638, 639, 640, 641, 643, 645, 657, 661, 661n, 663, 776
Shintoism-Buddhism, 112n
Shisō to Shinkō (Thought and Faith), 108n
Shōgunate, 102
Shokanshū (Collected Letters), 108n
Shōman (*Śrīmālādevīsiṁhanāda Sūtra*), 644
Shomangyō-gisho (Exposition of the *Śrīmālādevīsiṁhanāda Sūtra*), 639n

Shōnin no Gohonbyō-Hongwanji (Shinran's Mausoleum-Hongwanji), 109n
Shoo King, The, 85n, 91n
Short History of Chinese Philosophy, A, 39n, 655n
Shōtoku, Prince (Shōtoku Taishi), 97, 98, 98n, 99, 99n, 100, 100n, 101, 101n, 104, 113, 113n, 632–647, 639n
Shōtoku's Constitution, Prince, 632, 633, 633n, 634n, 636, 637n, 639, 639n; *see also* Seventeen-Article Constitution
Shou-chih, 442n
Shōzōmatsu Wasan Kankiroku (Views on Shōzōmatsu-Wasan), 108n
Shōzōmatsu Wasan Kōgi (Lectures on Shōzōmatsu-Wasan), 108n
Shugi Washo (Collection of Discourses), 632n
shugyō (mental training), 252
Shun, Emperor, 614, 624
Shute, Clarence, 10
Shutsujō shogo (Ridicule of the Teachings of the Buddha), 641n
Sibree, J., 256n
Signs, Language, and Behavior, 370n
Sih, Paul K. T., 614n
Silla, 658, 662
similarities, 673–674
Simmel, J., 41, 41n
Simon, Herbert A., 122n, 141n
sin, 727, 740, 741, 742, 743
sincerity, 737, 752
Sinclair, Gregg M., 772
Sinn und Sein: Ein Philosophisches Symposium, 143n, 450n
Sinngebung und Sinnerfüllung, 153n
Sinnot, E. W., 146n
Sirca, D. C., 577n
situation ethics, 374
skandhas, 274n, 751; *see also* aggregates
skepticism, 51–52, 54–59, 336
Skorpen, Joseph M., 11
Slater, Noel B., 140n
slaves, 385, 386, 387, 397
Small, Willard, 534n
Smith, Huston, 60
Smith, John E., 650n
Smith, M. Campbell, 74n
Smith, M. W., 144n
Smith, Margaret, 309n
Smith, Ronald Gregor, 310n
Smith, T. V., 393, 393n
Snell, Reginald, 346n
Snyder, Laurence H., 11, 772
Snyder, Richard C., 128n
Social Change, 35n
Social Forces, 36n
Social Groups, 36n
social justice, 229
social life in China, 423–426
Social Mobility, 35n
social organicism, 572
Social Organization, 37n
Social Process in Organized Groups, 36, 36n
social psychology, 34–49
Social Research, 143n
"Social Science and the Problem of Value," 155n
Social Self, The, 151n
"Social Structure and the Acculturation Process," 662n
Social System, The, 141n
Social Teaching of the Christian Churches, The, 240n
Social Theory and Social Structure, 37, 38n
social values, 227, 497–504, 505, 507, 509
social welfare, 496, 645
Sociers et Socières de Corée, 662n
"Societal Structures and Processes," 33–49
Society: An Introductory Analysis, 36n
Society: A Textbook of Sociology, 36n
Society: Its Structure and Changes, 36, 36n
"Sociography of Groups, The," 37
"Sociological Aspect of the Relation between Language and Philosophy," 652n
sociological jurisprudence, 773–779 *passim*
Sociology, 36n
sociology, 33–49, 141
"Sociology of Groups, The," 35n
"Sociology of Philosophic Ideas, The," 29n
Sociology of Religion, 288n
Socrates, 67, 70, 203, 264, 276, 289, 325, 326n, 331, 655, 656, 667, 705, 757, 760
Socratic tradition, 68, 202, 203, 204, 209
Sohm, Rudolf, 535n, 536, 536n
solipsism, 321
Solon, 393
"Some Features of the Japanese Way of Thinking," 632n
"Some Japanese Cultural Traits and Religions in Japan," 245–254
"Some Notes on Research on the Role of Models in the Natural and Social Sciences," 122n
Somerwell, D. C., 265n
"Sōmoku Kokudo Shikkai Jōbutsu no Busshōron-teki Igi to sono Sakusha" (On the Cultural Meaning of the Buddhist Motto "Earth, Herbs, and Trees, All Attain Buddhahood"), 111n
Song of Songs, 344
Songtsan-Gampo, King, 636, 638
sophia, 85
Sorai Kenkyū (Studies on Sorai Ogiu), 646n
Sorai Ogiu, 645, 646, 646n
Sorokin, P. A., 35n, 665n
Soshi Shinran denjyu-sōjō (The Founder Shinran's Transmitted Orthodoxy), 109n
Sōtō, 104, 644
soul, 54, 57, 58, 93, 170, 274n, 280, 508, 510, 550, 553; *see also jīva,* self
Source Book in Indian Philosophy, A, 50–66n *passim,* 380n, 478n, 497n, 502n, 572n, 589n
Sources of Chinese Tradition, 622n
Sources of Japanese Tradition, 98n, 345n
Souriau, Etienne, 358, 358n
Southern Sung Dynasty, 98
Soviet Union, 25, 28, 345; *see also* Russia
Sōyō, 107n
Soziologie, 41n
space, 170, 182–183
Spemann, H, 145n
Spencer, Herbert, 36, 40, 41n, 76, 77, 380
Spengler, Oswald, 75, 200

Spicer, E. H., 662, 662n
Spinoza, Baruch, 21, 80, 267n, 335, 383
spirit (and spirits), 87, 237; Absolute, 337; Supreme, 336, 339
Spirit and Nature: Papers from the Eranos Yearbooks, 147n
Spirit of Psychology, The, 147n
spiritual freedom, 681
spiritual fulfillment, 680
spiritual values, 225–244, 263–292, 293, 301
spirituality, 225–243, 316–347, 494–517, 679; French, 318; Indian, 169; in West, 302–315, 316–347
spontaneity, 439
sportsmanship, 557, 623, 694
Spring and Autumn Annals, 87n, 91
Śrī-Bhāṣya, 271, 276n, 277n
Śrīkaṇtha, 268
Śrīmatā, 101
Śrīmadbhāgavatam, 570n
Śrīmālādevīsiṁhānanda Sūtra, 644
Ssu-ma Ch'ien: Grand Historian of China, 622n
Ssu-ma Kuang, 655
Ssu-ma T'an, 622
Stace, Walter T., 302–315, 524, 535n, 681, 682n, 796
stages in life, 279, 280, 484, 513, 578; *see also āśramas*
Stagner, R., 146n
Stalin, Joseph, 769
Stannard, Jerry, 10
State, 102, 103, 128, 129, 418, 425, 451, 463, 471, 569–583 *passim,* 584, 586, 587, 641; kinds of, 579; centralized, 639; ethical, 580; origin of, 576
State and Government in Ancient India, 576n
State Department, 117–119
State religion, 101, 206, 207
State of the Social Sciences, The, 122n
"Status of Science and Technique in Islamic Civilization, The," 172–187
Stcherbatsky, Th., 107n
Stevenson, C. L., 369, 370, 370n, 698
Stoicism (and Stoics), 70–71, 326, 327, 525, 527, 530, 535, 546, 586, 667, 776, 777; Roman, 535, 535n
Stone, Wendell C., 10
Stout, A. K., 9, 796–797
Strachey, J., 144n
Strange Finale, The: An Essay on the Philosophy of Jean-Paul Sartre, 151n
Strawson, P. F., 373n
Strecker, F., 145n
Streeter, B. H., 107n
Stress: The Physiology and Pathology of Exposure to Stress, 146n
Structure of Social Action, The, 37, 37n
Structure of Society, The, 141n
Struggle for Law, The, 624n
Studia Islamica, 452n
Studia Philosophica, 341
Studies in the History of Ideas, 22n
Studies in the Middle Way, 197n
Studies in Muslim Ethics, 470n
Studies in Philosophy, 575n
Study of Ethical Principles, A, 482n
Study of History, A, 265n, 539n
Sturges, Wesley, 524
Sturm und Drang, 344
Sublime and the Beautiful, The, 345n
submission, 454, 726
suchness, 443, 444, 738, 742, 744, 745, 747, 748, 752; *see also* emptiness, *śūnya, tathatā,* void
śūdra (laborer), 171, 512
suffering, 63, 90, 514
Sufism, 57, 341, 467, 468, 759
Sugahara Michizane, 640n
suicide, 252–253
Suiko, Empress, 98
Śukra (and Śukra), 578, 579, 580, 582, 583, 583n, 588n, 590, 592
Śukranītisāra, The, 576, 589, 589n
Sul Chong, 658
Sullivan, H. S., 147n
Sullivan, Louis, 355
Sun Yat-sen, 413
"sung" (hexagram for litigation), 623
Sung Dynasty, 228, 429, 439n, 614n, 655, 656
Sung-Ming period, 228, 232, 240, 413
Sung-t'an Chung-hsin (Ryūtan Sōshin), 443, 443n
sunna (custom or tradition), 452, 458, 459
śūnya (and *śūnyatā* and *Śūnyatā*), 157, 197, 239–240, 265, 273, 278, 306, 432, 432n, 446, 747, 753; *see also* emptiness, suchness, *tathatā*
superior man, 416, 424; *see also chün tzu*
supernaturalism, 85, 365, 367, 758
Supplement on the Rhymes of the Book of Odes, A, 215
Supplement to the Standard Rhyme Book, A, 215
Supreme Court from Taft to Warren, The, 399
Supreme Court of the United States, 22, 387, 388, 548
"Sur la notion de Brahman," 159n
surrealism, 350
Suso, Henry, 304
Sutherland, E., 665n
Sūtra of the Pure Land, 743
Sūtra of Wei Lang, 197
Sūtrālaṁkāra (Mahāyāna Sūtrālaṁkāra), 109
Suvarṇaprabhāsa Sūtra, 641
Suzuki, D. T., 8, 108n, 197, 315, 315n, 323n, 350, 428–447, 444n, 655n, 656n, 657n, 661n, 678n, 732–753, 778, 797
Suzuki Shōsan, 644, 645n
svadharma (one's own duty), 573
Swedenborg, Emanuel, 734
syādvāda ("maybe" doctrine), 573
Sylvester, Robert P., 10
sympathy, 403
Symposium (Plato), 347
Symposium on Sociological Theory, 130n
syncretism, 662
Synopsis of Korean History, 658n
Synthèse, 122n
Syria, 470

Ta Hsüeh (Great Learning), 39n
Ta T'ung Shu: The One-World Philosophy of K'ang Yu-Wei, 626n
Tagore, Rabindranath, 65, 493, 570, 574
Tahāfut al-Falāsifa (Refutation of Philosophy), 181
Tahāfut al-Tahāfut (Refutation of the Refutation), 181
al-Tahdhīb al-akhlāq wa taṭhīr al-'araq (Doctrine of Dispositions and the Cleansing of Veins), 470n
Tai Chen, 217, 219, 228, 242
Taihō Code, 636
Taika Innovation, 634, 636, 639
Taira Masakado, 112n
Taira Shidehara, 660n
Taishi-kō (Shōtoku Taishi Union), 100
Taittirīya Āraṇyaka, 570n
Taittirīya Saṁhitā, 159, 159n
Taittirīya Upaniṣad, 477, 477n, 481n, 487, 487n, 500n, 501n, 507n
Tajima Yagyū, 733–734
Takada Senjuji, 109
Takagi Kiyoko, 10
Takakusu Junjirō, 439n
Takei, Franklin, 10
Takhallaqu bi akhlaq-Allah-Ḥadīth, 295n
Tale of Genji, The, 345, 345n
Tales of Genji, 108n
Taming of the Nations, The, 128n, 319, 325n, 326n, 332n, 377, 377n, 538n, 634, 657n, 697, 721, 776
T'an-lüan (Donran), 104, 106, 108
T'ang Chün-i, 225–244, 423, 423n, 427, 684n, 797–798
T'ang-lü (Code of the T'ang Dynasty), 656
T'ang period, 102, 349, 429, 434, 440,. 612n, 750
Tanishita Ichimu, 109n
Tannishō Seiritsu-kō (On the Formation of Tannishō), 109n
Tantra-vārttika, 487n
Tao (and *tao*), 80, 196n, 201n, 204, 205, 207, 234, 235–238, 377, 430, 433, 435, 436, 438, 441, 443, 446, 543, 721, 741, 746, 747, 751
Tao-ch'o, 104
Tao-te ching, 88, 201n, 428, 433, 433n, 434n, 444n, 613n, 615n, 616n, 624n, 625n, 746; *see also Book of Lao Tzu, Lao Tzu*
Tao-wu Yüan-chi (Dōgo Enchi), 442, 443
Tao-yüan, 439n
Taoism, 83, 87, 88, 89, 90, 93, 94, 99, 205, 207, 209, 227, 235–238, 240, 241, 243, 319, 319n, 379, 421, 422, 428, 433, 434, 440, 599, 600, 622, 661, 661n, 664, 695, 722, 751
Taoist religion, 92; *see also* Taoism
tathatā, 738, 742, 747; *see also* emptiness, suchness, *śūnya*
Ta-yü Shou-chih (Daigu Shushi), 442
te (virtue), 746
Teachers' College at Columbia, 764
technology, 135–155, 156–171, 188–197
Teishi-ikkō-senju-ki (Suspension of the Practice of *Nembutsu*-absolutism), 103n
Teknonymy as a Formative Factor in the Chinese Kinship System, 654n
temple, Hindu, 169; *see also The Hindu Temple*
Tendai, 102, 103n, 111n, 195, 196n, 246, 429; *see also* T'ien-t'ai
Tendai Daishi (Chi-i), 104
Tenison, Thomas, 22n
Tenmu, 112
Tenri, 645
Teresa, St., 313
"Testability and Meaning," 529, 529n
testimony, 58
theism, 274, 453, 571, 675
theology, 56, 722
Theoretische Biologie, 145n
Theorie des Gegenwärtigen Zeitalters, 77n
Theories of Perception and the Concept of Structure, 35, 35n
Theory Construction and the Problem of Objectivity, 139n, 141n, 155n
Theory Construction in Sociology, 142n
Theory of our National Existence, The, 385n
"Theory of Rasa, The," 348n
Theory of Resonance, The, 140n
Theory of Valuation, 650n
"Theory of the Present Epoch, The," 77–79
Theosophists, 734
Thirteen Principal Upanishads, The, 477n
"32 Sciences and 64 Arts, The," 168n
Thittila, U, 8, 798
Thomae, H., 146n, 147n
Thomas Aquinas, 71, 200, 330, 342, 525, 530,, 556, 723
Thomism, 232, 337; *see also* Neo-Thomism
Thompson, L. G., 382n, 626n
Thompson, W. F., 471n
Thoreau, Henry David, 585
Thousand and One Nights, A, 727
Three Dimensions of Public Morality, 153n
Three Dynasties (Hsia, Shang, Chou), 621, 622
three steps to wisdom, 262
Three Treasures, 113
Thuc, Nguyen Dang, 10
Thurber, James, 389
thusness, *see śūnya*
Ti (Supreme God), 204; *see also* God, *Shang-ti*
Tibet, 594
Tibetan Book of the Dead, The, 304
Tides from the West, 655n
t'ien (Heaven), 204, 206
T'ien-chu shih-i (The True Meaning of the Heavenly Lord), 234n
t'ien-chun (heavenly equity), 438, 438n
t'ien-fu (*tenfu*) (heavenly storehouse), 439
T'ien-huang Tao-wu (Tennō Dōgo), 443n
t'ien-i (heavenly unity), 438
t'ien-li (heavenly equity), 438n
T'ien-t'ai, 429; *see also* Tendai
Tilak, B. G., 574, 585
Tillich, Paul, 261n, 374, 375, 379
time (and *kāla*), 103, 156, 170, 182–183, 728
Time, 757
Ting, Duke, 614
Tirukkuṛal, 478
Tokugawa Ieyasu, 105, 657
Tokugawa period, 104, 111, 733
Tokuryū, 108n

tolerance, 21, 237, 610, 631
Tolstoy, Leo, 345, 345n, 585, 697
Tomita, K., 194n
Tönnies, F., 39n
Torricelli, Evangelista, 220
Tōshōgū, 657
totalitarianism, 31
"Touch: The Neglected Sense," 345n
Toulmin, Stephen, 372, 373n
"Toward a New Jus Gentium," 778n
Toward a Philosophy of History, 153n
Toward a Science of Aesthetics, 375n
Toward a Unified Theory of Human Behavior, 141n
Toynbee, Arnold Joseph, 75, 265n, 290, 376, 539, 539n
Tōyōgakuhō (Academic Report on the Orient), 657n, 661n
Tōyōjin no Shui-hōhō (The Ways of Thinking of Eastern Peoples), 631n
Traité de Métaphysique, 596n
tranquillity, 236, 237, 251, 252, 643, 675, 683, 688
Transactions of the Asiatic Society of Japan, 633n
transcendentalism, 19, 20, 468, 750
"Transformation of Buddhism in China," 90n
Transformation of Man, The, 65n
Transformation of Nature in Art, The, 348n
transmigration, 113, 677
"Transmission of the Lamp," 441n, 443n, 444n; *see also Ching-te ch'uan-teng lu*
trapped universals, 121, 129
Treatise of Human Nature, 526, 526n
Treatise on the Small-pox and the Measles, A, 177n
"Trend Away from Formalism in the Arts, The," 352n
Trinity, 308, 312
trivarga (threefold value), 577
Troelsch, Ernst, 24, 403, 403n, 404, 533n
truth (and truthfulness), 81–84, 94, 511, 572, 581, 676, 729
Tsai ching-shen sheng-huo fa-chan chung chih hui-yü i-shih (A Phenomenological Study of the Consciousness of Praise and Defamation in the Development of Spiritual Life), 230n
Tseng Tzu, 411, 417, 424
Tso, 91
Tso chuan (Tso's Commentary on the *Spring and Autumn Annals*), 87n, 214
Tsuda Sokichi, 657n, 661n
Ts'ui-yen (Pure Words), 83n, 84n
Tsukiyama, S., viii
Tsunoda Ryusaku, 345n
Tuan Yü-ts'ai, 217
Tufts, J. H., 465n
T'ung-chih (General Record), 214
Tung Chung-shu, 86, 206
Twentieth Century Sociology, 35n
Tyāgarāja, 285
Tzu-chih T'ung-chien (A Comprehensive Mirror for the Aid of Government), 655
Tzu-hsia, 214

Udāna, 261n
ul (spiritual attitude toward purity), 664, 666
Ulich, Robert, 144n
Uḷḷadu Nārpadu (Forty Verses on Existence), 483n
unconscious, 739, 742
Under the Ancestor's Shadow, 658n
Underhill, Evelyn, 307n
undifferentiated continuum, 302–315 *passim,* 377
UNESCO, 11, 610, 694
unfinished business, 699–718
Union-State, The, 385n
United Nations, 47, 627, 774
United Nations' Universal Declaration of Human Rights, 390
United States, 47, 73, 74, 359, 538, 659, 696, 770; *see also* America
unity (union), 302–315 *passim*
Unity and Variety in Muslim Civilization, 455n
unity in diversity, 574–575, 685, 688
unity, mystical, 302–315 *passim*
Unity of the Organism, The, 145n
Unity of Science Congress, 528
unity, undifferentiated, 302–315 *passim*
universal attainability of sagehood, 231–235; *see also* sage
University of California Chronicle, 539n
University of Hawaii, v, viii, 772
untouchability, 513
untruth, 584, 585
Upaniṣads, 57, 59, 62, 266, 273, 283, 291, 302–315 *passim,* 321, 324, 380, 477, 481, 484, 489, 495, 499, 501, 505–507, 508, 510, 510n, 531, 574, 587, 589, 599
Upanishads, The, 303n
utilitarianism, 29
Utitz, Emil, 356
Uttara Gītā, 479n
Uyehara, Yukuo, viii

Vaiśeṣika, 157, 170, 276, 279
Vaiśeṣika Sūtra, 477
Vaiṣṇavism, 274
vaiśya (merchant), 512
Vajjis, 641
Vajracchedikā-prajñāpāramitā Sūtra, 103n
Vajrayāna (esoteric Buddhism), 644; *see also* Shingon
Vākyavṛttim, 277n
value, 225–243; intellectual, 231, 282–286; intrinsic, 408
value-judgments, 697–698
value-possibility, 406
value-realism, 403, 408
value-theory, 365–366, 367, 368, 369, 370, 371, 372, 373, 383, 697
"Values as a Foundation for Encounter," 401–410
Vanaparva, 490
Varieties of Human Values, 403n

varṇas, 42; *see also* caste
varṇāśrama dharma (duties of castes and stages of life), 517
Varuṇa, 496, 570, 589
Vasiṣṭha, 589
Vasubandhu, 104, 106, 106n, 108, 321n
Vatsyāyana, 489
Vattel, Emmerich de, 73
Vedānta, 59, 60, 266, 267, 267n, 268, 270, 271, 271n, 273, 274, 276, 277, 279n, 280, 281, 282, 282n, 285, 286, 286n, 287, 291, 323n, 338n, 341, 478, 481, 486, 489, 493, 524, 531, 532, 574, 580, 598, 696, 702; Advaita, 270, 328, 337n, 571, 574, 575 (*see also* non-dualism); theistic, 574, 575
Vedānta-Sūtras with the Śrī-Bhāṣya of Rā mānujāchārya, 271n
Vedas, 266, 269, 273, 279, 286, 495, 496, 497, 500, 501, 505, 509, 512, 515, 516, 531, 574, 584, 587, 589, 602, 660
Vedic India, 163n
Vedic Mythology, 159n, 163n
Véron, Eugène, 345, 345n
Vesalius, Andreas, 202, 556
via contemplativa, 330
via negativa, 730
Victoroff, David, 358, 358n
Vidura, 491, 492
vidyā (knowledge), 156, 573; *see also jñāna*
Viereck, Peter R. E., 376n
vijñāna (intellectual knowledge), 273, 276, 283, 283n, 323, 323n
Vijñānavāda, 196, 265, 270, 270n, 276, 337n
Vijñaptimātratā-siddhi, 107n
Vimalakīrtinirdeśa Sūtra, 101, 644
Viṁśatika, 321n
violence, 360, 584, 585, 593
Virginia Law Review, 524n
Viṣṇu, 581
Viṣṇu Saṁhitā, 158
Visuddhimagga, 598n
Vivekacūḍāmaṇi, 270n
Vivekananda, Swami, 493, 504n, 505, 506, 506n, 585
Voegelin, Eric, 143n
Voices of Silence, The, 357, 357n
void, 157, 197, 237, 238, 265, 273, 278; *see also* emptiness, nothingness, suchness, *śūnya, tathatā*
Volksseele, 623
volonté générale, 388
voluntarism, 469
Vom Wesen der Willensfreiheit, 667n
"Vom Wesen des Menschen," 144n
Vom Wesenssinn des Rechtes, 405n
Von Grunebaum, Gustave Edmund, 455n
Von Mises, Ludwig, 25
vows, 325; great, 489; lesser, 489
Vyākhyā, 107
Vyāsa, Krishna Dvaipāyana, 523
"Vyāsa, Krishna Dvaipāyana and Krishna Vāsudeva," 523
vyāvahārika, 507, 575; *see also* empirical reality, phenomena
Wach, Joachim, 288n
"Waga-hō Tōryū" (Eastern Flow of Our Teachings), 98n
Wahl, Jean, 596, 596n, 598
Waley, Arthur, 84n, 87n, 345n, 348, 348n
Wall, Bernard, 277n
Wallace, Alfred Russel, 557
Wang Ch'ung, 205, 206, 207, 208
Wang Fu-chih, 242
Wang Lung-ch'i, 235n
Wang Nien-sun, 217, 219
Wang Yang-ming (Wang Shou-jen), 82, 84, 85, 86, 230, 233, 235, 241, 246, 413
Wang Yin-chih, 219
war, 502, 582, 583, 592, 772
Ward, L. F., 36
Warriors, The, 395n, 499
Watanabe, K., 439n
Watkins, J. W. N., 31n
Watson, Burton, 622n
Watt, W. Montgomery, 453n, 458n, 462, 462n
Watumull Foundation, 11
Way of Heaven, 614, 614n, 616
Way of Nature, 614
Ways of Knowing, The, 56n
Ways of Thinking of Eastern Peoples, The, 631n
wealth, 487, 503, 504, 577, 578, 592
Weber, Max, 454, 461, 649n, 653, 653n, 654n, 655n, 656, 656n, 657n, 658n
Weedon, William S., 10
Weider, A., 146n
Wei-i, 441n
Weil, Simone, 440
Weizsäcker, Carl Friedrich von, 140, 140n
Welbon, Guy R., 10
Wells, H. G., 584n
"Weltbild und Bauform in Südostasien," 605, 605n
Weltgeschichte Europas, 77n
Wen-chi (Literary Works), 86n
Wen-hui Pao, 767
Wensinck, A. J., 462n
Werke (Fichte), 404n
Werkmeister, W. H., 131, 135–155, 139n, 140n, 143n, 144n, 145n, 153n, 155n, 291n, 652n, 678n, 679n, 682, 682n, 687n, 798
"Western Philosophy and Practical Affairs," 67–80
westernization, 253
Westrup, C. W., 522n, 523, 523n, 534n, 539n, 540n
wharangdo (way of warriors), 662, 662n, 663
What Is Art?, 345n
What Is Life?, 123n
Wheland, George Willard, 140n
White, Bruce E., 12
White, Leonard D., 122n
Whitehead, A. N., 83, 122, 289, 318
Whorf, Benjamin L., 373, 651, 652n
Why of Man's Experience, The, 144n
Whyte, William H., 138n, 143n
Wiener Bieträge zur-Kunst-und Kulturgeschichte Asiens, 605n
Wiener, Norbert, 120n, 121, 121n, 122n, 123n, 125n, 126n, 127n
Wiggins, James W., 155n

Wigmore, John Henry, 617n
Wilhelm, Richard, 599, 599n, 623, 623n
Will of Heaven, 614, 614n
Will to Believe and Other Essays, The, 482n
Wilson, Francis, 376n
Wilson, Logan, 35n, 37
Wilson, Willard, 11
Wilson, Woodrow, 763
Windelband, Wilhelm, 465, 465n
Winkelmann, J. J., 344, 344n, 358
Wisdom of the Body, The, 146n
Wisdom of Confucius, The, 83n
Wisser, Richard, 143n, 405n
Wittgenstein, Ludwig, 371, 373, 373n, 524, 529
Wolff, H. G., 146n
Wolffs, Christian, 73, 75
Woodward, F. L., 261n
women, in Korea, 663
Works (Edmund Burke), 345
Works of Aristotle Translated into English, The, 30n
Works of Chuang Tzu, The, 416n
Works of Motse, The, 616n
world-and-life affirmation, 484
world-and-life negation, 484–486
world government, 72
World War II, 642, 662, 666
worldliness, 448, 574, 631
worldly welfare in Indian philosophy, 485, 494–517
World's Legal Philosophies, The, 586n
Wörterbuch zum Rig-Veda, 163n
Wright, Joyce, viii
wu (non-being in phenomena), 236n
Wu-ch'eng (section of *Book of History*), 203, 212
Wu, John C. H., 544, 544n, 546, 611–630, 612n, 616n, 617n, 621n, 799
Wu, King, 612n
wu-kung-yung hsing, 440; *see also anābhogacaryā,* no-striving
wu-lun (five relationships), 658, 658n
wu-ming (ignorance), 443; *see also avidyā,* ignorance
wu-wei (non-action), 88, 204, 205, 444, 614
wu-wei erh wu-pu-wei (action in non-action), 444
Wu Yü, 215, 216, 218
wu-yung chih yung (the usefulness of the useless), 444
Wynschenk, Dom C. A., 307n

Yahveh, 265
Yaḥyā ibn abu Manṣur, 177
Yājñavalkya, 501, 514, 587, 589, 590
Yājñavalkya Smṛti, 581n
Yajur Veda, 498n, 499n, 507, 517n
Yama, 496
Yamada Bunshō, 109n
Yamada Kōdō, 645
Yamaguchiken Kyōiku-kai, 640n
Yamamoto Kōsho, 108n
Yamasaki, Beatrice, 10
Yao, Emperor, 624
Yao and Shun, 82
Yaudheyas, 579
Yen-ch'eng Tzu-yu, 437
Yen Hui, 203
Yen Jo-ch'ü, 212, 219, 220
Yen Yüan, 242
Yin Dynasty, 615
Yin-hsüeh wu-shu (Five Books of Phonology), 216
yin-yang, 80, 85, 86, 99, 208, 599, 622, 623, 628, 661
Yoga (and *yoga*), 56, 58, 60, 66, 158, 170, 171, 264, 276, 286n, 319, 328n, 502, 509–510, 580, 684
Yoga-Bhāṣya, 578
Yoga Sūtra, 56n, 510n
Yogācāra school, 240
Yogācārabhūmi Śāstra, 105, 107
Yokoyama Taikwan, 195n
Yoshida Shōin, 640, 640n
Yoshida Shōin Zenshū (Collected Works of Yoshida Shōin), 640n
Young India, 575n
Young, J. Z., 120n, 123n, 125n
Yu, King, 624
Yü-lei (Classified Conversations), 83n
Yu Tzu, 413
Yudhiṣṭhira, 592
Yüeh-shan Wei-yen (Yakusan), 441, 441n, 442
yūgen, 347
Yuima, 644
Yukawa Hideki, 188–197, 646, 652, 652n, 679n, 799
Yün-pu (A Supplement to the Standard Rhyme Book), 215
Yün-yen T'an-ch'eng (Ungan), 442
Yung-chia school, 228
Yung-k'ang school, 228

Zeller, Eduard, 586, 586n
Zen, 98, 99, 104, 193, 240, 252, 260, 288n, 341, 342–361 *passim,* 378, 429, 431, 439n, 440, 441, 442, 443, 444, 445, 446, 640, 644, 656, 657, 732–753, 769, 779; Rinzai, 196, 197; Sōtō, 196, 197n, 644
Zen and Fine Arts, 350n, 354
Zen and Japanese Culture, 655n, 656n
"Zen and Parapsychology," 732–753
Zen Buddhism, Selected Writings, 315n
Zenmon Hōgōshū (Collection of Zen Teachings), 645n
Zennyo, 109
Zeno, 542, 651
Zeno, Emperor, 173
Zensho, E., 663n
Zhivago, Dr., 382
Zimmer, Heinrich, 380, 380n
Zimmern, Helen, 374n
Znaniecki, F., 27, 37n
Zonkaku, 106, 107, 107n, 109, 109n, 110
Zonkaku Ichigoki no Kenkyū narabini Kaisetsu (Study and Explanation of the Life of Zonkaku), 109n
Zonnyo, 109
zoology, 170, 178